People Places & Things

People Places & Things

A List of Popular Library of Congress Subject Headings with Dewey Numbers

Forest Press
A Division of OCLC Online Computer Library Center, Inc.
Dublin, Ohio

DDC, Dewey, Dewey Decimal Classification, Forest Press, NetFirst, and WorldCat are registered trademarks of OCLC Online Computer Library Center, Inc. CORC and WebDewey are trademarks of OCLC Online Computer Library Center, Inc.

Some of the subject headings contained herein list products and services, some of which are identified by trademarks that are proprietary to their owners.

Cover Photography/Art Credits:
· Orlando, Florida (flamingos) by Sharon Adams, OCLC
· Taj Mahal by Catherine Bonser, OCLC Europe, the Middle East & Africa
· Delaware, Ohio (sunrise/sunset) by Christy Carpenter, OCLC
· Hilton Head, South Carolina (boats) by Janet Maples, OCLC
· Clematis by Jeff May, OCLC
· Dexter (cat) by Donna Schleich, OCLC
· Abe, an Eastern Box Turtle by Larry Wolkan, OCLC
· Photo images of Mother Teresa and Nelson Mandela by Corel Corporation

Library of Congress Cataloging-in-Publication Data

People places & things : a list of popular Library of Congress subject headings with Dewey numbers.
    p. cm.
   ISBN 0-910608-69-5 (alk. paper)
    1. Classification, Dewey decimal. 2. Subject headings, Library of Congress. I. Title: People, places & things. II. Forest Press.

Z696.D7P46 2001
025.4'31–dc21

                                           2001094027

∞

The paper used in this publication meets the requirements of
ANSI/NISO Z39.48-1992 (Permanence of Paper).
ISBN: 0-910608-69-5
Recycled paper

CONTENTS

ACKNOWLEDGMENTS

People, Places & Things is the result of close cooperation between the OCLC Office of Research and Dewey editorial staff. Peter J. Paulson, retired executive director of OCLC Forest Press, first conceived of a companion to *Subject Headings for Children* that would serve a general audience. Diane Vizine-Goetz, research scientist in the OCLC Office of Research, built on her previous experience working on *Subject Headings for Children* and subsequent research with Lois Mai Chan, professor at the University of Kentucky, to extract Dewey number-Library of Congress Subject Headings (LCSH) pairs from WorldCat. Winton Matthews, assistant editor of the Dewey Decimal Classification and the chief editorial collaborator on *Subject Headings for Children*, provided invaluable advice to Diane and her group on the development of an editorial tool to permit review of the headings. Jean Godby, senior research scientist in the Office of Research, provided programming support for implementation of the statistical association measure. Roger Thompson, consulting systems analyst in the OCLC Office of Research, provided programming support for the data extraction and statistical correlations of Dewey number-LCSH pairs. Andy Houghton, senior consulting systems analyst in the OCLC Office of Research, provided programming support for the tool development, validation, and production of the final list. The Dewey assistant editors—Julianne Beall, Giles Martin, Winton Matthews, and Gregory New—reviewed Dewey number-LCSH pairs, and made numerous updates and additions. Giles Martin also provided the editorial team with numerous data extracts and handled data mergers and delivery to the OCLC Office of Research. Two Library of Congress Decimal Classification Division staff members, Ruth S. Freitag, classification specialist, and Virginia A. Schoepf, team leader, provided comments on selected Dewey numbers. Carol Hickey, research associate in the OCLC Office of Research, assisted in final heading validation. Libbie Crawford, Brad Gauder, and Linda Shepard of OCLC designed the cover art using photographs from public sources and those contributed by OCLC staff. Consultants Lisa Hanifan and Judith Kramer-Greene furnished assistance with graphic design, proofreading, and final production.

People, Places & Things could not have come into existence without the vision of Peter J. Paulson and Diane Vizine-Goetz, and the hard work of colleagues mentioned above.

Joan S. Mitchell
Executive Director & Editor in Chief
OCLC Forest Press

INTRODUCTION

People, Places & Things provides a list of over 50,000 Library of Congress Subject Headings (LCSH) paired with corresponding Dewey Decimal Classification (DDC) numbers. This list will help library patrons find the right places to browse for information on topics of interest. The list of headings includes personal, corporate-body, and geographic names; and topical and title headings.

HOW THIS BOOK WAS PREPARED. *People, Places & Things* is based on previous experience using records from WorldCat (the OCLC Online Union Catalog) in developing the two editions of *Subject Headings for Children*. An additional source is the research done by Chan and Vizine-Goetz[1] on the correlation between frequency of subject use and validity.

In developing *People, Places & Things*, we identified WorldCat records with DDC numbers (MARC tag 082) and subject headings (MARC tags 600-651) assigned by the Library of Congress (LC). The DDC number and the first LCSH were extracted from each record. We then applied a term co-occurrence measure to identify candidate pairs. Frequency counts were used to restrict the candidate pairs to those with headings that had been used at least five times.

Data files were prepared with the LCSH, the Dewey number, the DDC Relative Index entry closest to the LCSH, and the caption associated with the DDC number. In addition to the heading-number pairs derived from WorldCat records, heading-number pairs were added from other sources. These included editorially mapped headings from WebDewey, headings from *Subject Headings for Children*, and headings used in the NetFirst database, all accompanied by Dewey numbers. The resulting list contained over 50,000 headings and the DDC number or numbers most frequently associated with them.

The heading-number pairs were then labeled to indicate which ones needed further review. If the heading and its corresponding number were exactly the same as the heading and corresponding number in the DDC Relative Index or the editorially mapped heading and its corresponding number in the WebDewey database, the entry was labeled as approved. Heading-number pairs from *Subject Headings for Children* and NetFirst headings were labeled as provisionally approved. Headings paired with invalid numbers from old editions of the DDC were flagged.

The list was sorted in DDC number order and divided by subject area, and then given to the editor with expertise in each area. The subject headings and classification numbers were edited for accuracy and currency. When forms, time periods, places, or other

---

[1]Lois Mai Chan and Diane Vizine-Goetz. 1998. Toward a Computer-Generated Subject Validation File: Feasibility and Usefulness. *Library Resources & Technical Services* 42: 45-60.

subdivisions were included in the subject headings, either the Dewey numbers were adjusted to reflect those subdivisions or additional Dewey numbers were added. Consistent policies were followed in determining which numbers would be assigned to certain kinds of headings, e.g., a social group received a number both in 305 and in 930-990. When an LCSH with a subheading was in the list but the LCSH without the subheading was not, the missing LCSH was usually added. Any questions were resolved by consultation with the other editors.

The combined list was then checked from A to Z for consistency. Two additional sources of headings were added to the list during the final stage. First, nearly 2,500 selected headings with high frequency of use in WorldCat in popular areas such as history, literature, and music were added to the file with Dewey numbers assigned by the editors. Second, headings selected by the editors from the *LC Subject Headings Weekly Lists* and added to WebDewey since the original merge were added to the file. Because the preferred version of a subject heading can change over time (e.g., the form "Afro-American" was changed to "African American" during the editing stage), all headings were verified for currency. The Dewey numbers associated with any changed headings were reviewed. *People, Places & Things* reflects current LC and Dewey practice through April 2001. Catalogers should verify the use of the DDC numbers and subject headings in the latest versions of the Dewey Decimal Classification system and LC name and subject authority files before using the information in cataloging.

ROLES OF *PEOPLE, PLACES & THINGS.* *People, Places & Things* acts as a tool for information seekers in guiding users to Dewey numbers that are often assigned in conjunction with certain subject headings. Additionally, *People, Places & Things* can assist classifiers in application of the DDC. It also is a source of vocabulary enhancement to the DDC database. We expect to include many of these subject heading mappings in a future release of WebDewey.

COMMENTS AND SUGGESTIONS. Comments and suggestions for improving *People, Places & Things* may be sent to OCLC Forest Press:

OCLC Forest Press
6565 Frantz Road
Dublin, Ohio 43017-3395

E-mail: dewey@oclc.org

HOW TO USE *PEOPLE, PLACES & THINGS*

ONE DEWEY NUMBER. Many headings in *People, Places & Things* have only one number, which is often the number for comprehensive works on the topic, e.g., **Acupuncture** 615.892; **Fossils** 560.

MORE THAN ONE DEWEY NUMBER. Some headings have two or more numbers. Sometimes, these can be numbers in different areas, e.g., **Meat inspection** 363.1929 [product safety aspects], and 664.907 [food technology aspects]; **Dogs** 599.772 [biological aspects], and 636.7 [agricultural aspects].

In other instances, two or more numbers in the same general subject area are provided. One is often the comprehensive number, and the other usually represents a subtopic of the heading, e.g., **Missionaries** 266.0092 [the number for Christian missionaries], and 291.72092 [the comprehensive works number for missionaries regardless of religion].

Catalogers using *People, Places & Things* as an aid to assignment should consult with the latest version of the Dewey Decimal Classification system to determine the meaning of each number.

FILING ORDER. Following ALA filing rules, entries are alphabetized word by word, and letter by letter within words. Punctuation marks, such as periods and apostrophes, are ignored; dashes and hyphens are treated as spaces. Time subdivisions are filed in chronological order. Numbers file before letters.

FICTION, POETRY, AND DRAMA. Topical headings with subheadings of **"–Fiction,"** **"–Poetry,"** and **"–Drama"** are not included in this publication.

1-2-3 for Windows 005.369
35mm cameras 771.32
87th Precinct (Imaginary place) 813.54
87th Precinct (Imaginary place)—Fiction 813.54
360–degree feedback (Rating of employees) 658.3125
401(a) plans 332.02401
401(k) plans 332.02401; 658.325
401(k) plans—Law and legislation 344.73012164
401(k) plans—Management 658.325
401(k) plans—Taxation—Law and legislation
  343.7305233
A-10 (Jet attack plane) 623.746
Aalto, Alvar, 1898–1976 720.92
Aaron, Hank, 1934– 796.357092
Abacus 513.0284
Abandoned children 305.906945
ABAP/4 (Computer program language) 005.133
Abbey, Edward, 1927– 813.54
Abbey, Edward, 1927– —Criticism and interpretation
  813.54
Abbey Theatre 792.0941835
Abbott, Jim, 1967– 796.357092
Abbreviations 411
Abbreviations, English 421.1
Abbreviations, French 441.1
Abbreviations, German 431.1
Abbreviations, Russian 491.711
Abby (Fictitious character : Wiebe) 813.6
'Abd al-Laṭīf, Shah, ca. 1689–ca. 1752 891.4113
'Abd al-Laṭīf, Shah, ca. 1689–ca. 1752—Criticism and
  interpretation 891.4113
Abdomen—Diseases 617.55
Abdomen—Diseases—Diagnosis 617.55075; 617.550754
Abdomen—Endoscopic surgery 617.55059
Abdomen—Radiography 617.5507572
Abdomen—Surgery 617.55059
Abdomen—Ultrasonic imaging 617.5507543
Abduction 364.154
Abdul-Jabbar, Kareem, 1947– 796.323092
Abelard, Peter, 1079–1142 189.4
Abelian groups 512.2
Abelian varieties 516.353
Abenaki Indians—Folklore 398.2089973
Aberdeen (Scotland) 941.23
Aberdeen (Scotland)—Guidebooks 914.12304;
  914.12304859; 914.1230486
Aberdeen (Scotland)—History 941.23
Aberdeen (Scotland)—Maps 912.4123
Aberdeenshire (Scotland) 941.232
Abhidharma 294.3824
Ability 153.9
Ability grouping in education 371.254
Ability—Testing 371.262
Abnormalities, Human 599.949; 616.043
Abnormalities, Human—Etiology 616.043
Abolitionists 326.8092
Abolitionists—United States 973.7114
Abortion 363.46
Abortion—Law and legislation 342.084; 344.04192
Abortion—Law and legislation—United States
  342.73084; 344.7304192; 344.73048; 344.730546
Abortion—Law and legislation—United States—Cases
  344.7304192; 344.73041920264
Abortion—Moral and ethical aspects 179.76
Abortion—Moral and ethical aspects—United States
  179.760973
Abortion—Political aspects 363.46
Abortion—Political aspects—United States 363.460973

Abortion—Psychological aspects 363.46019
Abortion—Religious aspects 291.56976
Abortion—Religious aspects—Catholic Church 241.6976
Abortion—Religious aspects—Christianity 241.6976
Abortion—United States 363.460973
Abortion—United States—History 363.460973
Abortion—United States—Psychological aspects 155.93
Abraham (Biblical patriarch) 222.11092
Abrasives 553.65
Abrasives industry 338.47666
Absentee voting 324.65
Absentee voting—United States 324.65
Absenteeism (Labor) 331.2598
Absolute music 784.1
Absolute, The 111.6
Absorption spectra 535.84
Abstract data types (Computer science) 005.73
Abstract expressionism 709.04052
Abstract expressionism—United States 759.1309045
Abstracting 808.062
Abstracting and indexing services 025.3
Abstracting and indexing services industry 338.470253
Abstraction 153.24
Absurd (Philosophy) in literature 808.80384; 809.93384
Abuse of administrative power 353.46
Abused children 305.906945; 362.76
Abused children—Mental health 362.2086945
Abused children—Rehabilitation 618.9285822303
Abused children—Services for 362.76
Abused children—Services for—Great Britain
  362.760941
Abused children—Services for—United States
  362.760973
Abused children—United States 362.760973
Abused women 362.8292
Abused women in literature 808.803520694;
  809.933520694
Abused women—Pastoral counseling of 248.86
Abused women—United States 362.82920973
Abused women—United States—Psychology
  362.8292019
Abusive adult children 362.8292
Abyssinian cat 636.826
Acacia 583.748
Academic achievement 371.262
Academic achievement—Testing 371.262
Academic art—19th century 709.4409034
Academic costume 378.28
Academic freedom 371.104; 378.121
Academic freedom—United States 378.121
Academic libraries 027.7
Academic libraries—Administration 025.1977
Academic libraries—Australia 027.70994
Academic libraries—Collection development 025.21877
Academic libraries—Collection development—United
  States 025.218770973
Academic libraries—Departmental libraries 027.7
Academic libraries—Food and beverage policies 025.1
Academic libraries—Great Britain 027.70941
Academic libraries—India 027.70954
Academic libraries—Reference services 025.52777
Academic libraries—Services to the handicapped
  027.663
Academic libraries—United States 027.70973
Academic libraries—United States—Administration
  025.19770973
Academic libraries—United States—History 027.70973
Academic libraries—United States—Statistics
  027.70973021

Academic library directors 025.1977092
Academic medical centers 362.12
Academic spin-outs 338.926
Academic writing 808.02; 808.066
Academic writing—Handbooks, manuals, etc. 808.02
Academy Awards (Motion pictures) 791.43079
Acadia National Park (Me.) 974.145
Acadia National Park (Me.)—Guidebooks 917.414504;
  917.41450443; 917.41450444
Acadians 971.601
Acapulco (Mexico) 972.73
Acapulco (Mexico)—Guidebooks 917.273
Acarology 595.42
Accelerated life testing 620.0044
Accelerometers 681.2
Acceptance sampling 658.562
Access to the sea (International law) 341.45
Accident investigation 363.1065
Accidents 363.1
Accidents in literature 808.80355; 809.93355
Accidents—Prevention 613.6
Accomack County (Va.) 975.516
Accomack County (Va.)—Genealogy 929.375516
Accordion 788.86; 788.8619
Accordion music 788.86
Accordion orchestras 784.4
Accountants 657.092
Accountants—Malpractice 346.0631
Accountants—Malpractice—United States 346.730631
Accountants—Professional ethics 174.9657
Accountants—Professional ethics—United States
  174.9657
Accounting 657; 657.044; 657.046
Accounting—Australia 657.0994
Accounting—Australia—History 657.0994
Accounting—Bibliography 016.657
Accounting—Computer-assisted instruction 657.0785
Accounting—Computer programs 657.0285536;
  657.0440285536
Accounting—Data processing 657.0285
Accounting—Decision making 657.0684
Accounting—Dictionaries 657.03
Accounting—Examinations, questions, etc. 657.076
Accounting—Examinations, questions, etc.—Periodicals
  657.076
Accounting firms 338.7657
Accounting firms—Management 657.068
Accounting—Handbooks, manuals, etc. 657
Accounting—History 657.09
Accounting—Law and legislation 346.063
Accounting—Law and legislation—United States
  346.73063
Accounting—Law and legislation—United States—Cases
  346.730630264
Accounting—Marketing 657.0688
Accounting—Periodicals 657.05
Accounting—Periodicals—Bibliography 016.65705
Accounting—Problems, exercises, etc. 657.076
Accounting—Research 657.072
Accounting—Research—Methodology 657.072
Accounting—Social aspects 657
Accounting—Standards 657.0218
Accounting—Standards—Great Britain 657.021841
Accounting—Standards—United States 657.021873
Accounting—Standards—United States—Periodicals
  657.021873
Accounting—Study and teaching 657.071
Accounting—Study and teaching—United States
  657.071073

Accounting—United States 657.0973
Accounting—United States—History 657.0973
Accounting—United States—Quality control 657.0685
Accounting—Vocational guidance 657.023
Accounts receivable 657.72
Accounts receivable loans 332.742
Accreditation (Education) 379.158
Acculturation 303.482
Aceraceae 583.78
Acetylene 547.413
Acetylene compounds 547.413
Achebe, Chinua 823.914
Achebe, Chinua—Criticism and interpretation 823.914
Achebe, Chinua. Things fall apart 823.914
Achievement motivation 158.1
Achievement tests 371.262
Achilles (Greek mythology) in literature 808.80351;
  809.93351
Achromatism 535.4
Acid-base imbalances 616.3992
Acid deposition—Environmental aspects 363.7386
Acid mine drainage 628.16832
Acid rain 363.7386
Acid rain—Environmental aspects 363.7386
Acids 546.24
Ackerley, J. R. (Joe Randolph), 1896–1967
  306.7662092; 828.91209
Ackroyd, Laura (Fictitious character) 823.914
Ackroyd, Laura (Fictitious character)—Fiction 823.914
Acne 616.53
Acolytes 253
Acorna (Fictitious character) 813.54
Acoustic emission testing 620.1127
Acoustic neuroma 616.99285
Acoustic surface waves 530.416
Acoustical engineering 620.2
Acoustooptical devices 621.3828
Acquaintance rape 362.883
Acquaintance rape—Religious aspects 291.178331532
Acquaintance rape—United States 362.883
Acquaintance rape victims 362.883
Acquisition of computer software 025.284
Acquisition of databases 025.284
Acquisition of developing country publications
  025.291724
Acquisition of electronic journals 025.2832
Acquisition of Latin American publications 025.298
Acquisition of Russian publications 025.2947
Acquisition of serial publications 025.2832
Acquisitions (Libraries) 025.2
Acquisitions (Libraries)—Costs 025.2
Acquisitions (Libraries)—United States 025.20973
Acquisitiveness 155.232; 178
Acrasiomycetes 579.52
Acrobatics 796.47
Acronyms 411; 421.1
Acrylic painting 751.426
Acrylic painting—Technique 751.426
ACT Assessment 378.1662
Act! (Computer file) 005.369
Act (Philosophy) 128.4
Acting 792.028
Acting—Auditions 792.028
Acting—Psychological aspects 792.028019
Acting—Study and teaching 792.028071
Acting—Vocational guidance 792.028023
Acting—Vocational guidance—United States
  792.02802373
Actinide elements 546.42; 669.292

Actinomycetales 579.37
Action potentials (Electrophysiology) 573.854437
Action research 303.4072
Action research in education 370.72
Action research in education—United States 370.72073
Action research in public health 362.1072
Action theory 301.01
Actions and defenses 347.05
Active galactic nuclei 523.112
Active galaxies 523.112
Active imagination 150.1954
Active learning 370.1523; 371.3; 371.39
Active learning—United States 371.39
Active oxygen—Pathophysiology 616.071
Active server pages 005.276
ActiveX 005.2762
Activity-based costing 657.42
Activity programs in education 371.3
Actors 792.028092
Actors—Biography 792.028092
Actors—United States 792.028092273
Actors—United States—Interviews 792.028092273
Actresses 792.028092
Actualities (Motion pictures) 791.433
Actuaries 368.01092
Acupressure 615.822
Acupuncture 615.892
Acupuncture points 615.892
Acute abdomen 617.55
Acute abdomen—Diagnosis 617.55075
Acute renal failure 616.614
Ada 95 (Computer program language) 005.133
Ada (Computer program language) 005.133
Adair County (Iowa) 977.773
Adair County (Iowa)—Maps 912.77773
Adair County (Ky.)—Genealogy 929.3769675
Adam (Biblical figure) 222.1109505
Adams, Abigail, 1744–1818 973.44092
Adams, Ansel, 1902– 770.92
Adams County (Ill.) 977.344
Adams County (Ill.)—Maps 912.77344
Adams County (Iowa) 977.776
Adams County (Iowa)—Maps 912.77776
Adams County (Neb.) 978.2397
Adams County (Neb.)—Maps 912.782397
Adams County (Pa.)—Genealogy 929.374842
Adams County (Wis.) 977.556
Adams County (Wis.)—Maps 912.77556
Adams, Doc (Fictitious character) 813.54
Adams, Doc (Fictitious character)—Fiction 813.54
Adams family 929.20973
Adams, Gillian (Fictitious character) 813.54
Adams, Gillian (Fictitious character)—Fiction 813.54
Adams, Henry, 1838–1918 973.07202
Adams, John, 1735–1826 973.44092
Adams, John Quincy, 1767–1848 973.55092
Adams, Nick (Fictitious character) 813.52
Adams, Nick (Fictitious character)—Fiction 813.52
Adams, Samantha (Fictitious character) 813.54
Adams, Samantha (Fictitious character)—Fiction 813.54
Adaptability (Psychology) 155.24
Adaptability (Psychology) in old age 155.672
Adaptation (Biology) 578.4; 591.4
Adaptive antennas 621.3824
Adaptive control systems 629.836
Adaptive filters 621.3815324
Adaptive signal processing 621.3822
Addams, Jane, 1860–1935 361.3092; 361.92
Addicts 362.29092

Addington family 929.20973
Addition 513.211
Addition polymerization 547.28
Adelaide Metropolitan Area (S. Aust.) 994.231
Adelaide Metropolitan Area (S. Aust.)—Maps 912.94231
Adenosine—Physiological effect 615.7
Adenosine triphosphate 572.475
Adhesion 668.3
Adhesive bindings (Bookbinding) 686.35
Adhesives 620.199; 668.3
Ādi-Granth 294.682
Ādi-Granth—Criticism, interpretation, etc. 294.682
Adirondack Mountains (N.Y.) 974.75
Adirondack Mountains (N.Y.)—Description and travel
917.47504; 917.4750443; 917.4750444
Adirondack Mountains (N.Y.)—Guidebooks 917.47504
Adirondack Mountains (N.Y.)—History 974.75
Adirondack Park (N.Y.) 974.75
Adirondack Park (N.Y.)—Guidebooks 917.47504
Adjoining landowners 346.0432
Adjoining landowners—United States 346.730432
Adjustable rate mortgages 332.72
Adjustable rate mortgages—Law and legislation
346.04364
Adjustable rate mortgages—Law and legislation—
United States 346.7304364
Adjustable rate mortgages—United States 332.7220973
Adjustment (Psychology) 155.24
Adjustment (Psychology) in children 155.41824
Adler, Alfred, 1870–1937 150.1953
Adlerian psychology 150.1953
Administrative agencies 351
Administrative agencies—Connecticut—Management
351.746
Administrative agencies—Discipline 353.46
Administrative agencies—Evaluation 352.35
Administrative agencies—Great Britain 351.41
Administrative agencies—Great Britain—Management
352.30941
Administrative agencies—United States 351.73
Administrative agencies—United States—Auditing
352.4390973
Administrative agencies—United States—Directories
351.73025
Administrative agencies—United States—Management
352.30973
Administrative agencies—United States—
Reorganization 352.280973
Administrative and political divisions 352.14
Administrative assistants 651.3
Administrative law 342.06
Administrative law—Great Britain 342.4106
Administrative law—United States 342.7306
Administrative law—United States—Cases 342.73060264
Administrative law—United States—Outlines, syllabi,
etc. 342.7306
Administrative procedure 342.066
Administrative procedure—Canada 342.71066
Administrative procedure—Florida 342.759066
Administrative procedure—United States 342.73066
Admiralty 343.096
Admiralty—Great Britain 343.41096
Adnexa oculi—Surgery 617.71
Adobe FrameMaker 686.225445369
Adobe Illustrator (Computer file) 006.6869
Adobe PageMaker 686.225445369
Adobe PageMill 005.72
Adolescence 305.235; 649.125
Adolescence in literature 808.80354; 809.93354

Adolescence—Religious aspects 291.17834235
Adolescent medicine 616.00835
Adolescent psychiatry 616.8900835
Adolescent psychology 155.5
Adolescent psychopathology 616.8900835
Adolescent psychotherapy 616.89140835
Adopted children 306.874
Adopted children—United States 362.7340973
Adoptees 306.874
Adoption 362.734
Adoption agencies 362.734
Adoption—Great Britain 362.7340941
Adoption—Law and legislation 346.0178
Adoption—Law and legislation—United States 346.730178
Adoption—Religious aspects 291.17835874
Adoption—United States 362.7340973
Adoption—United States—Handbooks, manuals, etc. 362.7340973
Adoption—United States—Psychological aspects 362.734019
Adorno, Theodor W., 1903–1969 193
Adrenomedullin 573.464; 612.45
Adsorption 541.33
Adult child abuse victims 362.764; 616.8582239
Adult child abuse victims—Psychology 616.8582239
Adult child abuse victims—United States 362.7640973
Adult child sexual abuse victims 616.858369
Adult child sexual abuse victims—Counseling of 362.764
Adult child sexual abuse victims—Mental health 616.858369
Adult child sexual abuse victims—Pastoral counseling of 261.83272
Adult child sexual abuse victims—Prayer-books and devotions 242.66
Adult child sexual abuse victims—Psychology 362.764019
Adult child sexual abuse victims—Rehabilitation 616.85836903
Adult child sexual abuse victims—Religious life 248.86
Adult child sexual abuse victims—United States 362.7640973
Adult child sexual abuse victims—United States—Psychology 362.764019
Adult children of aging parents 306.874; 362.60854
Adult children of alcoholics 616.8619
Adult children of alcoholics—Mental health 616.8619
Adult children of alcoholics—Psychology 362.2924019
Adult children of alcoholics—United States 362.29240973
Adult children of divorced parents 306.89
Adult children of divorced parents—Mental health 155.924; 616.89
Adult children of dysfunctional families 616.89
Adult children of dysfunctional families—Religious life 248.86
Adult college students 378.1982
Adult education 374
Adult education—Administration 374.12
Adult education—Africa 374.96
Adult education and state 379
Adult education—Australia 374.994
Adult education—Great Britain 374.941
Adult education—India 374.954
Adult education—Nigeria 374.9669
Adult education—Philosophy 374.001
Adult education—Social aspects 306.43
Adult education—United States 374.973

Adult learning 374.0019
Adult learning—United States 374.0019
Adultery 306.736
Adultery in literature 808.80353; 809.93353
Adultery—Russia 306.7360947
Adultery—United States 306.7360973
Adultery—United States—Psychological aspects 306.7360973
Adulthood 155.6; 305.24
Adulthood—Psychological aspects 155.6
Advaita 181.482
Advance directives (Medical care) 362.1
Advance directives (Medical care)—Religious aspects 291.5697
Advanced placement programs (Education) 371.264
Advanced supplementary examinations 378.1662
Advent 263.912
Advent—Meditations 242.332
Advent music 781.722
Advent—Prayer-books and devotions 242.332
Advent sermons 252.612
Advent services 263.912
Adventure and adventurers 904; 910.4
Adventure education 371.384
Adventure films 791.43655; 791.43658
Adventure games 793.93
Adventure racing 796.5
Adventure stories 808.8387
Adventure stories, American 813.087
Adventure stories, English 823.087
Adventure therapy 616.0014
Advertisers 659.1092
Advertising 659.1
Advertising—Accountants 659.19657
Advertising agencies 659.1125
Advertising—Airlines 659.193877
Advertising—Airplanes 659.1962913334
Advertising—Alcoholic beverages 659.196631
Advertising—Audio-visual equipment 659.196213897
Advertising—Automobiles 659.19629222
Advertising—Banks and banking 659.193321
Advertising—Beer 659.1964123
Advertising—Bicycle industry 659.193883472
Advertising—Books 659.19002
Advertising—Brand name products 659.13
Advertising—Brewing industry 659.196633
Advertising—Business 659.1965
Advertising campaigns 659.113
Advertising—Cheese 659.19641373
Advertising, Classified 659.132
Advertising—Clothing and dress 659.19687
Advertising—Collectibles—United States—Catalogs 659.133; 741.670973075
Advertising—Computers 659.19004
Advertising—Condoms 659.1936396
Advertising copy 659.132
Advertising—Cosmetics 659.1964672
Advertising—Cut flower industry 659.19635966
Advertising, Direct-mail 659.133
Advertising, Direct-mail—United States 659.133
Advertising, Direct-mail—United States—Directories 659.133
Advertising drinking glasses—Collectors and collecting—United States—Catalogs 748.830973075
Advertising—Florists 659.196359
Advertising—Food 659.196413; 659.19664
Advertising—Handbooks, manuals, etc. 659.1
Advertising—Hospitality industry 659.1964794
Advertising—Hotels 659.1964794

Advertising, Industrial 659.1315
Advertising—Jewelry 659.1973927
Advertising laws 343.082
Advertising laws—United States 343.73082
Advertising layout and typography 741.67
Advertising, Magazine 659.132
Advertising, Magazine—United States 659.132
Advertising, Magazine—United States—Statistics—
   Periodicals 659.132
Advertising—Management 659.1068
Advertising media planning 659.111
Advertising—Motion pictures 659.1979143
Advertising, Newspaper 659.132
Advertising openers (Implements) 683.8
Advertising—Periodicals 659.105
Advertising photography 659.133; 778
Advertising, Political 324.73; 659.1932
Advertising, Political—United States 324.730973;
   659.19320973
Advertising postcards 659.133; 741.683
Advertising—Psychological aspects 659.1019
Advertising—Radios 659.1962138418
Advertising—Real estate business 659.1933333
Advertising—Research 659.1072
Advertising—Sex oriented businesses 659.193067
Advertising—Social aspects 659.1042
Advertising—Social aspects—United States
   659.10420973
Advertising specialties 659.13
Advertising t-shirts 659.13
Advertising—Telecommunication 659.19384
Advertising—Telephone companies 659.193846
Advertising—Television programs 659.1979145
Advertising-to-sales ratio 659.1
Advertising—Tourism 659.1991
Advertising—United States 659.10973
Advertising—United States—History 659.10973
Advertising—Vocational guidance 659.1023
Advertising—West (U.S.) 659.10978
Advertising—West (U.S.)—Periodicals 659.1097805
Advertising—Wine 659.1964122
Advice columnists 070.444
Advice columns 070.444
Advisory boards 352.743
Advisory opinions 348.05
Advocacy advertising 659.13
Aegean Islands (Greece and Turkey) 949.58
Aegean Islands (Greece and Turkey)—Description and
   travel 914.95804; 914.9580476
Aegean Islands (Greece and Turkey)—Guidebooks
   914.95804; 914.9580476
Aegean Sea Region 949.58
Aegean Sea Region—Antiquities 939.1
Aegithalidae 598.8
Aeneas (Legendary character) 398.22
Aerial observation (Military science) 358.454
Aerial photogrammetry 526.982
Aerial photography 778.35
Aerial photography in agriculture 631
Aerial photography in geology 778.35
Aerial reconnaissance 358.454; 623.71
Aerial reconnaissance—Equipment and supplies 623.71
Aerobic dancing 613.715
Aerobic exercises 613.71
Aerodynamics 533.62; 629.1323
Aerodynamics, Hypersonic 629.132306
Aerodynamics—Mathematics 629.13230151
Aerodynamics, Supersonic 629.132305
Aerodynamics, Transonic 629.132304

Aeroelasticity 629.132362
Aerofoils 629.13432
Aeronautical charts 629.13254
Aeronautical engineers 629.13092
Aeronautical instruments 629.135
Aeronautical instruments—Display systems 629.135
Aeronautical laboratories 629.130072
Aeronautical libraries 026.62913
Aeronautical museums 629.130075
Aeronautics 629.13
Aeronautics and state 629.13
Aeronautics, Commercial 387.7
Aeronautics, Commercial—Chartering 387.7428
Aeronautics, Commercial—Deregulation—United States
   387.71
Aeronautics, Commercial—Freight 387.744
Aeronautics, Commercial—Law and legislation 343.0978
Aeronautics, Commercial—Law and legislation—
   European Economic Community countries 343.40978
Aeronautics, Commercial—Law and legislation—United
   States 343.730978
Aeronautics, Commercial—Management 387.7068
Aeronautics, Commercial—Passenger traffic 387.742
Aeronautics, Commercial—Security measures 363.2876
Aeronautics, Commercial—United States 387.70973
Aeronautics, Commercial—United States—Passenger
   traffic 387.7420973
Aeronautics—Dictionaries 629.13003
Aeronautics—Examinations, questions, etc. 629.130076;
   629.13252076; 629.1325216076
Aeronautics—Flights 629.1309
Aeronautics—History 629.13009
Aeronautics in agriculture 631
Aeronautics in art 704.94962913
Aeronautics in education 629.130071
Aeronautics in meteorology 629.1324
Aeronautics—Law and legislation 341.7567
Aeronautics—Law and legislation—United States
   343.73097
Aeronautics, Military 358.4; 623.66
Aeronautics, Military—Research 358.407
Aeronautics, Military—Research—United States—History
   358.4070973
Aeronautics, Military—United States 358.400973
Aeronautics—Periodicals 629.13005
Aeronautics—Safety measures 629.1300289;
   629.132520289
Aeronautics—Soviet Union 629.1300947
Aeronautics—Soviet Union—History 629.1300947
Aeronautics—United States 629.1300973
Aeronautics—United States—History 629.1300973
Aeronautics—Vocational guidance 629.130023;
   629.13252023
Aerosols 541.34515
Aerosols—Charts, diagrams, etc. 551.5113
Aerospace engineering 629.1
Aerospace engineers 629.1092
Aerospace industries 338.346291
Aerospace telemetry 621.3678
Aerostar van 629.2234
Aerostar van—Maintenance and repair 629.28734
Aerostar van—Maintenance and repair—Handbooks,
   manuals, etc. 629.28734
Aeschylus 882.01
Aeschylus—Criticism and interpretation 882.01
Aeschylus—Translations into English 882.01
Aesop's fables—Adaptations 398.2452
Aesop's fables—Translations into English 398.2452
Aesthetic movement (Art) 709.4109034; 709.7309034

Aesthetics 111.85; 701.17
Aesthetics, American 111.840973
Aesthetics, Ancient 111.84093
Aesthetics, British 111.840941
Aesthetics, British—18th century 111.84094109033
Aesthetics, British—19th century 111.84094109034
Aesthetics, Chinese 111.840951
Aesthetics, French 111.840944
Aesthetics, French—18th century 111.84094409033
Aesthetics, German—18th century 111.84094309033
Aesthetics, German—19th century 111.84094309034
Aesthetics—History 111.8509
Aesthetics, Indic 111.850954; 700.1
Aesthetics, Japanese 111.840952
Aesthetics, Korean 111.8409519
Aesthetics, Medieval 111.840902
Aesthetics, Modern 111.85
Aesthetics, Modern—17th century 111.8509032
Aesthetics, Modern—18th century 111.8509033
Aesthetics, Modern—19th century 111.8509034
Aesthetics, Modern—20th century 111.850904
Aesthetics—Psychological aspects 111.85019
Aesthetics—Religious aspects 210
Aesthetics—Religious aspects—Christianity 230.01
Aesthetics, Slovak 111.85094373
Affect (Psychology) 152.4
Affective disorders 616.8527
Affective disorders—Chemotherapy 616.8527061
Affective education 370.153
Affiliate programs (World Wide Web) 380.1; 658.8
Affiliation (Philosophy) 128
Affinity chromatography 543.089
Affirmations 158.12
Affirmative action programs 331.133
Affirmative action programs—United States 331.1330973
Afghan hound 636.7533
Afghan Wars 958.103
Afghanistan 958.1
Afghanistan—Description and travel 915.8104; 915.810446
Afghanistan—Foreign relations 327.581
Afghanistan—Foreign relations—Soviet Union 327.581047
Afghanistan—History 958.1
Afghanistan—History—Soviet occupation, 1979–1989 958.1045
Afghanistan—History—Soviet occupation, 1979–1989—Personal narratives 958.1045
Afghanistan—Politics and government 958.1
Afghanistan—Politics and government—1973– 320.9581; 320.958109047; 958.104
Afghans (Coverlets) 746.4340437
Africa 960
Africa—Bibliography 016.96
Africa—Civilization 960
Africa—Civilization—Western influences 960
Africa—Colonization 325.6
Africa—Description and travel 916.04; 916.04329; 916.044
Africa—Discovery and exploration 960.2
Africa, East 967.6
Africa, East—Geography 916.76
Africa, East—Guidebooks 916.7604; 916.76044
Africa, East—History 967.6
Africa, Eastern 967.6
Africa, Eastern—Guidebooks 916.7604; 916.76044
Africa, Eastern—History 967.6
Africa—Economic conditions 330.96

Africa—Economic conditions—1960– 330.96032
Africa—Economic conditions—1960– —Periodicals 330.96032
Africa—Economic policy 338.96
Africa—Foreign relations 327.096
Africa—Foreign relations—1960– 327.096
Africa—Foreign relations—Soviet Union 327.4706
Africa—Foreign relations—United States 327.7306
Africa—Geography 916
Africa—Guidebooks 916.04; 916.04329; 916.044
Africa—Historical geography 911.6
Africa—Historical geography—Maps 911.6
Africa—Historiography 960.072
Africa—History 960
Africa—History—To 1498 960.21
Africa—History—To 1884 960.2
Africa—History—19th century 960.23
Africa—History—1884–1960 960.31
Africa—Library resources 016.916
Africa—Maps 912.6
Africa, North 961
Africa, North—History 961
Africa, North—History—To 647 939.7
Africa, Northeast 963
Africa, Northeast—Politics and government 320.963
Africa, Northeast—Politics and government—1974– 320.963
Africa—Periodicals 960.05
Africa—Politics and government 960
Africa—Politics and government—1945–1960 320.9609045; 960.32
Africa—Politics and government—1960– 320.9609045; 320.9609046; 960.326; 960.328; 960.329
Africa—Population 304.6096
Africa—Religion 299.6
Africa—Religion—Periodicals 200.96
Africa—Social conditions 960
Africa—Social conditions—1960– 960.32
Africa—Social life and customs 960
Africa, Southern 968
Africa, Southern—Commerce 382.0968
Africa, Southern—Commerce—Directories 380.102568
Africa, Southern—Economic conditions 330.968
Africa, Southern—Economic conditions—1975–1994 330.9680009047
Africa, Southern—Economic integration 337.168
Africa, Southern—Economic policy 338.968
Africa, Southern—Foreign relations 327.0968
Africa, Southern—Foreign relations—1975–1994 327.0968
Africa, Southern—Foreign relations—United States 327.73068
Africa, Southern—Guidebooks 916.804; 916.80465
Africa, Southern—History 968
Africa, Southern—Maps 912.68
Africa, Southern—Politics and government 320.968
Africa, Southern—Politics and government—1975–1994 320.96809048
Africa, Southern—Relations 327.0968
Africa, Southern—Relations—United States 327.73068
Africa, Southern—Road maps 912.68
Africa, Sub-Saharan 967
Africa, Sub-Saharan—Bibliography 016.967
Africa, Sub-Saharan—Civilization 967
Africa, Sub-Saharan—Description and travel 916.704; 916.704329; 916.70433
Africa, Sub-Saharan—Economic conditions 330.967
Africa, Sub-Saharan—Economic conditions—1960– 330.967032

Africa, Sub-Saharan—Economic policy 338.967
Africa, Sub-Saharan—Foreign relations 327.0967
Africa, Sub-Saharan—Foreign relations—United States
 327.73067
Africa, Sub-Saharan—History 967
Africa, Sub-Saharan—Politics and government 967
Africa, Sub-Saharan—Politics and government—1960–
 320.96709045; 320.96709046; 967.032
Africa, Sub-Saharan—Religion 299.6
Africa, Sub-Saharan—Social conditions 967
Africa, West 966
Africa, West—Description and travel 916.604;
 916.604329
Africa, West—Geography 916.6
Africa, West—History 966
Africa, West—History—To 1884 966.02
Africa, West—Politics and government 320.966
Africa, West—Politics and government—1960–
 320.96609045
African American abolitionists—Biography
 920.009296073
African American art 704.0396073
African American artists 704.0396073
African American artists—Biography 700.8996073
African American arts 700.8996073
African American arts—New York (State)—New York
 700.899607307471
African American athletes 796.08996703
African American athletes—Biography 796.08996703
African American authors 810.9896073
African American baseball players 796.35708996073
African American baseball players—Biography
 796.35708996073
African American businesspeople 650.08996073
African American Catholics 282.7308996073
African American children 305.2308996073;
 362.708996073
African American children—Education 371.82996073
African American consumers 658.83408996073
African American cookery 641.59296073
African American criminals 364.3496073
African American dance—History 793.308996073
African American engineers 620.008996073
African American entertainers 791.08996073
African American families 306.8508996073
African American families—Michigan
 306.85089960730774
African American families—Michigan—Detroit
 306.8508996073077434
African American families—New York (State)
 306.85089960730747
African American gays 305.896073
African American History Month 973.0496073
African American homeless persons 305.569
African American inventors—Biography 604.8996073
African American lesbians 305.48896073
African American librarians 020.08996073
African American men 305.38896073
African American men—Conduct of life 305.38896073
African American men—New York (State)
 305.388960730747
African American men—New York (State)—New York
 305.3889607307471
African American men—Psychology 155.8496073;
 305.38896073
African American models 746.92092
African American musicians 708.8996073
African American neighborhoods 307.336208996073
African American newspapers 070.484

African American oral tradition 398.208996073
African American police 363.208996073
African American preaching 251.008996073
African American scientists—Biography 509.2;
 509.2396073
African American students 371.82996073
African American theological seminaries 230.071173
African American universities and colleges
 378.1982996073
African American universities and colleges—Directories
 378.1982996073025
African American wit and humor 817.0080896
African American women 305.48896073
African American women—Biography 920.7208996073
African American women—History 305.48896073
African American women—Life skills guides
 646.7008996073
African American women—Literary collections
 810.80352042
African American women—New York (State)
 305.488960730747
African American women—New York (State)—New York
 305.4889607307471
African American women poets 811.009928708996073
African American women—Psychology 155.63308996073
African American women—Social conditions
 305.48896073
African American women—Southern States
 305.48896073075
African Americans 305.896; 305.896073; 973.0496073
African Americans and libraries 027.63
African Americans—Bibliography 016.305896073;
 016.9730496073
African Americans—Biography 920.009296073
African Americans—Biography—Dictionaries
 920.009296073
African Americans—Civil rights 323.1196073
African Americans—Civil rights—History 323.1196073
African Americans—Civil rights—History—20th century
 323.1196073
African Americans—Civil rights—Mississippi
 305.8960730762
African Americans—Color 305.896073
African Americans—Color—Social aspects 305.896073
African Americans—Conduct of life 305.896073
African Americans—Economic conditions
 330.973008996073
African Americans—Education 371.82996073
African Americans—Education (Higher) 378.1982996073
African Americans—Employment 331.6396073
African Americans—Encyclopedias 973.0496073003
African Americans—Finance, Personal 332.0240396073
African Americans—Florida—History 975.900496073
African Americans—Folklore 398.208996073
African Americans—Genealogy 929.308996073
African Americans—Genealogy—Handbooks, manuals,
 etc. 929.108996073
African Americans—Health and hygiene 362.108996073;
 610.8996073; 613.08996073
African Americans—Health and hygiene—Periodicals
 613.08996073
African Americans—Historiography 973.04960730072
African Americans—History 973.0496073
African Americans—History—To 1863 973.049607300903
African Americans—History—19th century 973.0496073
African Americans—History—1863–1877
 973.0496073009034
African Americans—History—1863–1877—Sources
 973.0496073009034

African Americans—History—1877–1964
973.049607300904
African Americans—History—20th century 973.0496073
African Americans—History—1964– 973.049607300904
African Americans—History—Chronology
973.049607300202
African Americans—History—Sources 973.04960730072
African Americans in art 704.942
African Americans in motion pictures 791.436520396073
African Americans in radio broadcasting
384.5408996073
African Americans—Intellectual life 305.896073
African Americans—Legal status, laws, etc. 342.730873
African Americans—Legal status, laws, etc.—History
342.730873
African Americans—Life skills guides 646.7008996073
African Americans—Louisiana 305.8960730763
African Americans—Migrations—History—20th century
973.0496073
African Americans—Music 780.8996073; 781.6296073;
781.6408996073
African Americans—Music—History and criticism
780.8996073; 781.6408996073
African Americans—Music—History and criticism—
Periodicals 780.8996073
African Americans—New York (State) 305.8960730747
African Americans—New York (State)—New York
305.89607307471
African Americans—New York (State)—New York—
History 974.7100496073
African Americans—North Carolina 305.8960730756
African Americans—Ohio 305.8960730771
African Americans—Ohio—History 977.100496073
African Americans—Ohio—History—19th century
977.100496073
African Americans—Periodicals 973.0496073005
African Americans—Politics and government
323.1196073
African Americans—Psychology 155.8496073
African Americans—Race identity 305.896073
African Americans—Relations with Jews 305.896073
African Americans—Religion 200.8996073;
277.3008996073
African Americans—Social conditions 305.896073
African Americans—Social conditions—To 1964
305.896073
African Americans—Social conditions—1964–1975
305.896073
African Americans—Social conditions—1975–
305.896073
African Americans—Social life and customs 305.896073;
973.0496073
African Americans—Southern States 305.896073075
African Americans—Southern States—Social life and
customs 305.896073075
African Americans—Study and teaching 305.896073
African Americans—Suffrage 342.73072
African Americans—West (U.S.) 305.896073078
African Americans—West (U.S.)—History 978.00496073
African Americans—West (U.S.)—History—19th century
978.00496073
African buffalo 599.642
African bullfrog 597.892
African cooperation 327.17096; 337.16
African diaspora 304.8096; 909.0496
African drama (English) 822; 822.008096
African elephant 599.674
African elephant—Africa 599.674
African fiction (English) 823; 823.008096

African fiction (English)—History and criticism
823.00996
African fiction (French) 843.008096
African fiction (French)—History and criticism
843.00996
African languages 496
African languages—Periodicals 496.05
African literature 809.8896; 809.896
African literature (English) 820; 820.8096
African literature (English)—History and criticism
820.9896; 820.996
African literature (French) 840.80896; 840.8096
African literature (French)—History and criticism
840.9896; 840.996
African literature—History and criticism 809.8896;
809.896
African literature—History and criticism—Periodicals
809.8896005
African National Congress 324.268083
African National Congress—History 324.268083
African philology 496
African philology—Periodicals 496.05
African poetry 896
African poetry (English) 821; 821.008096
African poetry—Translations into English 896
African Synod (1994 : Rome, Italy). Instrumentum
laboris 282.609049
African violets 635.93395
Africanized honeybee 595.799
Afrikaners 305.83936
Afrikaners—Ethnic identity 305.83936
Afroasiatic languages 492
Afrobeat 781.64
Afrocentrism 960
Afternoon teas 641.53
Agaricaceae 579.6
Agaricales 579.6
Agassi, Andre, 1970– 796.342092
Agaves 584.352
Age and employment 331.3
Age and employment—United States 331.30973
Age discrimination in employment 331.3
Age discrimination in employment—Law and legislation
344.01398
Age discrimination in employment—Law and
legislation—United States 344.7301398
Age discrimination in employment—United States
331.30973
Age groups 305.2
Aged 305.26
Aged—Abuse of 362.6
Aged—Abuse of—Canada 362.6
Aged—Abuse of—United States 362.6
Aged—Bibliography 016.30526
Aged—Canada 305.260971
Aged—Canada—Statistics 305.260971021
Aged—Care 362.6
Aged—Care—United States 362.60973
Aged consumers—United States 658.8340846
Aged—Counseling of 362.66
Aged—Crimes against—United States 362.8808460973;
364.108460973
Aged—Crimes against—United States—Prevention
362.8808460973
Aged—Diseases 362.19897; 618.97
Aged—Dwellings 363.5946
Aged—Dwellings—United States 363.59460973
Aged—Employment 331.398
Aged—Employment—Law and legislation 344.01398

Aged—Employment—Law and legislation—United States
344.7301398
Aged—Employment—United States 331.3980973
Aged—Family relationships 306.870846
Aged—Finance, Personal 332.0240565
Aged—Government policy 362.6
Aged—Government policy—United States 362.60973
Aged—Great Britain 362.60941
Aged—Health and hygiene 613.0438
Aged—Health and hygiene—United States
362.1989700973
Aged—Home care 362.63
Aged—Home care—United States 362.63
Aged—Housing 363.5946
Aged—Housing—Great Britain 363.59460941
Aged—Housing—United States 363.59460973
Aged—Legal status, laws, etc. 346.013
Aged—Legal status, laws, etc.—New York (State)
346.7470135
Aged—Legal status, laws, etc.—United States
344.730326; 346.73013
Aged—Legal status, laws, etc.—United States—
Periodicals 346.73013
Aged—Life skills guides 646.79
Aged—Long-term care 362.16
Aged—Medical care 362.19897
Aged—Medical care—Moral and ethical aspects
362.19897
Aged—Medical care—United States 362.1989700973
Aged—Mental health 362.20846
Aged—Mental health services 362.20846
Aged—Nutrition 613.20846
Aged—Periodicals 305.2605
Aged—Psychological testing 155.670287
Aged—Psychology 155.67; 305.26
Aged—Recreation 790.1926
Aged—Recreation—United States 790.19260973
Aged—Religious life 248.85
Aged—Services for 362.6
Aged—Services for—United States 362.60973
Aged—Services for—United States—Directories
362.602573; 362.6302573
Aged—Sexual behavior 306.70846
Aged—Social conditions 305.26
Aged—Social networks 305.26
Aged—Suicidal behavior 362.280846
Aged—Suicidal behavior—United States 362.2808460973
Aged—Taxation—Law and legislation—United States
343.730526
Aged—Transportation—United States 362.63
Aged—United States 305.260973
Aged—United States—Economic conditions 305.260973
Aged—United States—Finance, Personal 332.0240565
Aged—United States—Life skills guides 646.790973
Aged—United States—Psychology 155.670973
Aged—United States—Social conditions 305.260973
Aged—United States—Statistics 305.260973021
Aged veterans—Medical care—United States 362.108697
Aged women 305.26
Aged women—Social conditions 305.26
Aged women—United States 305.26
Aged women—United States—Bibliography 016.30526
Aged women—United States—Psychology 155.67082;
305.26
Aged, Writings of the, American 810.809285
Agency (Law) 346.029
Agency (Law)—United States 346.73029
Agency (Law)—United States—Cases 346.730290264
Agenda (Computer file) 650.028557565

Agent (Philosophy) 126
Aggada 296.19
Aggada—Commentaries 296.19
Aggregate industry 338.2762
Aggregates (Building materials) 553.62
Aggression (International law) 341.58; 341.62
Aggressive behavior in animals 591.566
Aggressiveness 155.232
Aggressiveness in children 155.418232
Aging 305.26; 571.878; 612.67
Aging—Genetic aspects 612.67
Aging in literature 808.80354; 809.93354
Aging—Literary collections 808.80354
Aging—Molecular aspects 571.878
Aging parents 306.8740846
Aging parents—Care 306.8740846
Aging parents—Care—United States 306.8740846
Aging parents—Home care 362.63
Aging parents—Home care—United States 362.63
Aging parents—United States 306.8740846
Aging parents—United States—Family relationships
306.8740846
Aging parents—United States—Psychology 306.8740846
Aging—Physiological aspects 571.878; 612.67
Aging—Psychological aspects 155.67
Aging—Religious aspects 291.1783426; 291.440846
Aging—Religious aspects—Christianity 248.85;
261.83426
Aging—Social aspects 305.26
Agitation (Psychology) 152.4
Agnon, Shmuel Yosef, 1888–1970 892.435
Agnon, Shmuel Yosef, 1888–1970—Criticism and
interpretation 892.435
Agnosticism 149.72; 211.7
Agora (Athens, Greece) 938.5
Agoraphobia 616.85225
Agricultural administration 630.68
Agricultural administrators 354.5092
Agricultural assistance 341.7592
Agricultural biotechnology 664.024
Agricultural chemicals 631.8
Agricultural chemicals—Environmental aspects
363.7384
Agricultural chemicals—Environmental aspects—United
States 363.7384
Agricultural chemicals industry 338.476686
Agricultural chemistry 630.24
Agricultural colleges 630.711
Agricultural colleges—United States 630.71173
Agricultural conservation 333.7616
Agricultural consultants 630.68
Agricultural credit 332.71
Agricultural credit—Developing countries 332.71091724
Agricultural credit—India 332.710954
Agricultural credit—Law and legislation 346.073
Agricultural credit—Law and legislation—United States
346.73073
Agricultural credit—United States 332.710973
Agricultural ecology 577.55; 630.277
Agricultural economists 338.1092
Agricultural education 630.71
Agricultural engineering 630
Agricultural engineers 630.92
Agricultural exhibitions 630.74
Agricultural experiment stations 630.724
Agricultural extension work 630.715
Agricultural extension work—Africa 630.715
Agricultural genome mapping 631.5233
Agricultural geography 630.9

Agricultural industries 338.1
Agricultural information networks 630.28553
Agricultural innovations 338.16; 630.7
Agricultural innovations—India 338.160954
Agricultural intensification 338.162; 631.58
Agricultural laboratories 630.72
Agricultural laborers 305.563; 331.763
Agricultural laborers—Health and hygiene 363.11963
Agricultural laborers—India 331.7630954
Agricultural laborers—United States 331.7630973
Agricultural laws and legislation 343.076
Agricultural laws and legislation—United States
 343.73076
Agricultural libraries 026.63
Agricultural machinery 631.3; 631.37
Agricultural mechanics 631.3
Agricultural pests 632.6
Agricultural pests—Biological control 632.96
Agricultural pests—Integrated control 632.9
Agricultural pollution 628.1684
Agricultural price supports—United States 338.180973
Agricultural productivity 338.16
Agricultural services 630
Agricultural systems 338.1; 630
Agricultural systems—Research 630.72
Agricultural wastes 363.7288
Agriculture 630
Agriculture—Accounting 630.681
Agriculture—Africa 630.96
Agriculture and politics 338.18
Agriculture and state 338.18
Agriculture and state—Africa, Sub-Saharan 338.1867
Agriculture and state—Brazil 338.1881
Agriculture and state—Canada 338.1871
Agriculture and state—China 338.1851
Agriculture and state—Developing countries
 338.18091724
Agriculture and state—Europe 338.184
Agriculture and state—European Economic Community
 countries 338.184
Agriculture and state—European Union countries
 338.184
Agriculture and state—Great Britain 338.1841
Agriculture and state—India 338.1854
Agriculture and state—Mexico 338.1872
Agriculture and state—Pakistan 338.5491
Agriculture and state—Soviet Union 338.1847
Agriculture and state—United States 338.1873
Agriculture and state—Zambia 338.186894
Agriculture—Bibliography 016.63
Agriculture—Brazil 630.981
Agriculture—China 630.951
Agriculture, Cooperative 334.683
Agriculture—Data processing 630.285
Agriculture—Developing countries 630.91724
Agriculture—Dictionaries 630.3
Agriculture—Economic aspects 338.1
Agriculture—Economic aspects—Africa 338.1096
Agriculture—Economic aspects—Africa, Sub-Saharan
 338.10967
Agriculture—Economic aspects—Australia 338.10994
Agriculture—Economic aspects—Canada 338.10971
Agriculture—Economic aspects—China 338.10951
Agriculture—Economic aspects—Developing countries
 338.1091724
Agriculture—Economic aspects—Great Britain
 338.10941
Agriculture—Economic aspects—Great Britain—History
 338.10941

Agriculture—Economic aspects—India 338.10954
Agriculture—Economic aspects—Japan 338.10952
Agriculture—Economic aspects—Mathematical models
 338.1015118
Agriculture—Economic aspects—Nigeria 338.109669
Agriculture—Economic aspects—Periodicals 338.105
Agriculture—Economic aspects—Philippines 338.109599
Agriculture—Economic aspects—Soviet Union
 338.10947
Agriculture—Economic aspects—Statistics 338.1021
Agriculture—Economic aspects—Statistics—Periodicals
 338.1021
Agriculture—Economic aspects—United States
 338.10973
Agriculture—Economic aspects—United States—
 Periodicals 338.10973
Agriculture—Economic aspects—United States—
 Statistics 338.10973021
Agriculture—England 630.942
Agriculture—Great Britain 630.941
Agriculture—Handbooks, manuals, etc. 630
Agriculture—History 630.9
Agriculture—India 630.954
Agriculture—Moral and ethical aspects 174.963
Agriculture—Oceania 630.99
Agriculture—Origin 630.901
Agriculture—Periodicals 630.5
Agriculture, Prehistoric 630.901
Agriculture publishing 070.57
Agriculture—Research 630.72
Agriculture—Research—Developing countries
 630.7201724
Agriculture—Research—Management 630.72
Agriculture—Research—On-farm 630.72
Agriculture—Research—Philippines 630.720599
Agriculture—Soviet Union 630.947
Agriculture—Statistical methods 630.727
Agriculture—Statistics 630.2011
Agriculture—Terminology 630.14
Agriculture—Tropics 630.913
Agriculture—United States 630.973
Agriculture—United States—History 630.973
Agriculture—United States—Periodicals 630.97305
Agriculture—Vocational guidance 630.203
Agrobiodiversity 333.95; 631.58
Agrobiodiversity conservation 333.9516; 639.9
Agroforestry 634.99
Agromyzidae 595.774
Agronomy 630
Ahab, Captain (Fictitious character) 813.3
Ahab, Captain (Fictitious character)—Fiction 813.3
Ahiṃsā 179.1
Aid to families with dependent children programs—
 United States 362.7130973
AIDS (Disease) 362.1969792; 616.9792
AIDS (Disease)—Africa 362.19697920096; 616.97920096
AIDS (Disease)—Alternative treatment 616.979206
AIDS (Disease) and mass media 362.1969792
AIDS (Disease)—Atlases 616.979200222
AIDS (Disease)—Bibliography 016.3621969792;
 016.6169792
AIDS (Disease)—Chemotherapy 616.9792061
AIDS (Disease)—Developing countries
 362.19697920091724
AIDS (Disease)—Diagnosis 616.9792075
AIDS (Disease)—Diet therapy 616.97920654
AIDS (Disease)—Epidemiology 614.599392
AIDS (Disease)—Etiology 616.9792071
AIDS (Disease)—Government policy 362.1969792

AIDS (Disease)—Government policy—United States 362.196979200973
AIDS (Disease)—Great Britain 362.196979200941
AIDS (Disease)—Handbooks, manuals, etc. 616.9792
AIDS (Disease)—History 616.9792009
AIDS (Disease) in children 618.929792
AIDS (Disease) in women 362.19697920082
AIDS (Disease) in women—Social aspects 362.19697920082
AIDS (Disease)—Law and legislation 344.04369792
AIDS (Disease)—Law and legislation—United States 344.7304369792
AIDS (Disease)—Molecular aspects 616.979207
AIDS (Disease)—Moral and ethical aspects 179
AIDS (Disease)—Nursing 610.73699
AIDS (Disease)—Nutritional aspects 616.97920654
AIDS (Disease)—Palliative treatment 362.196979205
AIDS (Disease)—Patients 362.1969792
AIDS (Disease)—Patients—Care 362.1969792
AIDS (Disease)—Patients—Counseling of 362.1969792
AIDS (Disease)—Patients—Employment—Law and legislation—United States 344.7301159; 344.730465
AIDS (Disease)—Patients—Hospital care 362.1969792
AIDS (Disease)—Patients—Mental health 616.97920019
AIDS (Disease)—Patients—Pastoral counseling of 259.41969792
AIDS (Disease)—Patients—Services for 362.1969792
AIDS (Disease)—Patients—Services for—United States 362.196979200973
AIDS (Disease)—Patients—United States 362.196979200973
AIDS (Disease)—Periodicals 362.1969792005; 616.9792005
AIDS (Disease)—Political aspects—United States 362.1969792
AIDS (Disease)—Prevention 616.979205
AIDS (Disease)—Psychological aspects 362.19697920019; 616.97920019
AIDS (Disease)—Religious aspects 291.178321969792
AIDS (Disease)—Religious aspects—Christianity 261.8321969792
AIDS (Disease)—Social aspects 362.1969792
AIDS (Disease)—Social aspects—United States 362.196979200973
AIDS (Disease)—Study and teaching (Elementary) 372.37
AIDS (Disease)—Transmission 362.1969792; 616.9792071
AIDS (Disease)—Treatment 616.979206
AIDS (Disease)—Uganda—Prevention 362.19697920096761
AIDS (Disease)—United States 362.196979200973
AIDS (Disease)—United States—Directories 362.1969792002573
AIDS (Disease)—United States—Prevention 362.196979200973
AIDS (Disease)—Zimbabwe 362.19697920096891
AIDS (Disease)—Zimbabwe—Prevention 362.19697920096891
Aids to air navigation 629.1351
Aids to navigation 387.155
AIDS vaccines 615.372
Aikido 796.8154
Aikido in art 704.9497968154
Aikman, Troy, 1966– 796.332092
Ailey, Alvin 792.82092
Ainu 305.8946
Air 533.6; 551.5
Air bag restraint systems 629.276

Air bag restraint systems—Maintenance and repair—Handbooks, manuals, etc. 629.276
Air bases 358.417
Air conditioning 697.93
Air conditioning—Control 697.9322
Air conditioning—Electric equipment 697.932
Air conditioning—Equipment and supplies 697.932
Air conditioning industry 338.4769793
Air cooled engines 621.434
Air cooled engines—Maintenance and repair 621.434
Air courier service 387.744
Air defenses 358.4145
Air defenses—United States 358.41450973
Air ducts 697.92
Air—Experiments 533.60724; 533.6078
Air filters 660.284245
Air flow 621.6
Air forces 358.4
Air—Microbiology 579.17; 628.536
Air pilots 629.13092
Air pilots—United States—Biography 629.13092273
Air—Pollution 363.7392; 628.53
Air—Pollution—California 363.739209794
Air—Pollution—Economic aspects 363.7392
Air—Pollution—Environmental aspects 577.276
Air—Pollution—Law and legislation 344.046342
Air—Pollution—Law and legislation—California 344.794046342
Air—Pollution—Law and legislation—United States 344.73046342
Air—Pollution—Mathematical models 628.53015118
Air—Pollution—Measurement 628.530287
Air—Pollution—Periodicals 628.5305
Air—Pollution—Physiological effect 571.956; 615.902; 616.20047
Air power 358.403; 623.746
Air power—Great Britain—History 358.4030941
Air power—United States—History 358.4030973
Air—Purification 628.53
Air—Purification—Equipment and supplies 628.53
Air quality 363.7392
Air quality indexes 363.7392
Air quality management 363.7392
Air quality management—United States 363.73920973
Air shows 797.54
Air-to-surface missiles 358.4282
Air traffic control 387.740426; 629.1366
Air traffic control clearances 629.1366
Air traffic control—United States—Handbooks, manuals, etc. 629.13660973
Air traffic controllers 629.1366092
Air travel 387.7; 387.742
Air warfare 358.4
Airborne operations (Military science) 358.414
Airborne troops 356.166
Airbrush art 751.494
Airbrush art—Technique 751.494
Aircraft accidents 363.124; 629.132520289
Aircraft accidents—Human factors 363.12414; 629.132520289
Aircraft accidents—Investigation 363.12465
Aircraft carriers 359.9435; 359.94835
Aircraft carriers—United States 359.94350973
Aircraft carriers—United States—History 359.94350973
Aircraft engine industry 338.4762913435
Aircraft industry 338.4762913334
Aircraft industry—United States 338.47629133340973
Aircraft partnership 387.73
Aircraft supplies industry 387.730688

American drama 812; 812.008
American drama—20th century 812.5; 812.508; 812.52; 812.5208; 812.54; 812.5408
American drama—20th century—History and criticism 812.509; 812.5209; 812.5409
American drama—20th century—History and criticism—Theory, etc. 812.5409
American drama—African American authors 812.0080896073; 812.54080896073
American drama—Asian American authors 812.080895
American drama (Comedy) 812.0523
American drama—History and criticism 812.009
American drama—Women authors 812.540809287
American essays 814; 814.008
American essays—20th century 814.52; 814.5208; 814.54; 814.5408
American farces 812.05232
American fiction 813; 813.008
American fiction—19th century 813.3; 813.308; 813.4; 813.408
American fiction—19th century—History and criticism 813.309; 813.409
American fiction—19th century—History and criticism—Theory, etc. 813.309
American fiction—20th century 813.5; 813.508; 813.52; 813.5208; 813.54; 813.5408
American fiction—20th century—History and criticism 813.509; 813.5209; 813.5409
American fiction—20th century—History and criticism—Theory, etc. 813.509
American fiction—African American authors 813.0080896073
American fiction—African American authors—History and criticism 813.009896073; 813.509896073; 813.5409896073
American fiction—Bibliography 016.813008
American fiction—History and criticism 813.009
American fiction—Southern States 813.0080975
American fiction—Southern States—History and criticism 813.009975
American fiction—Women authors 813.00809287
American fiction—Women authors—History and criticism 813.0099287; 813.3099287; 813.4099287; 813.5099287
American ginseng industry 338.17388384
American League of Professional Baseball Clubs—History 796.357640973
American literature 810; 810.8
American literature—Colonial period, ca. 1600–1775 810.8001
American literature—Colonial period, ca. 1600–1775—History and criticism 810.9001
American literature—1783–1850 810.8002
American literature—1783–1850—History and criticism 810.9002
American literature—19th century 810.8003; 810.8004
American literature—19th century—History and criticism 810.9003; 810.9004
American literature—19th century—History and criticism—Theory, etc. 810.9003
American literature—20th century 810.8005; 810.80052; 810.80054
American literature—20th century—History and criticism 810.9005; 810.90052; 810.90054
American literature—20th century—Periodicals 810.800505; 810.8005205; 810.8005405
American literature—African American authors 810.80896073; 810.80928708996073; 810.9896073

American literature—African American authors—Bio-bibliography 810.9896073
American literature—African American authors—Bio-bibliography—Dictionaries 810.989607303
American literature—African American authors—Dictionaries 810.989607303
American literature—African American authors—History and criticism 810.9896073; 810.9928708996073
American literature—African American authors—History and criticism—Theory, etc. 810.9896073
American literature—Asian American authors 810.80895
American literature—Asian American authors—History and criticism 810.9895
American literature—Bibliography 016.81
American literature—Bibliography of bibliographies 016.01681
American literature—Bio-bibliography 016.81
American literature—Bio-bibliography—Dictionaries 016.81; 810.90003
American literature—California 810.809794
American literature—Dictionaries 810.3; 810.90003
American literature—English influences 810.9
American literature—Hispanic American authors 810.80868
American literature—Hispanic American authors—History and criticism 810.9868
American literature—History and criticism 810.9
American literature—History and criticism—Periodicals 810.90005
American literature—History and criticism—Theory, etc. 810.9
American literature—Illinois 810.809773
American literature—Illinois—Skokie 810.8097731
American literature—Indian authors 810.80897
American literature—Indian authors—History and criticism 810.9897
American literature—Indian authors—History and criticism—Theory, etc. 810.9897
American literature—Indiana 810.809772
American literature—Italian American authors 810.80851
American literature—Italian American authors—History and criticism 810.9851
American literature—Jewish authors 810.808924
American literature—Jewish authors—History and criticism 810.98924
American literature—Mexican American authors 810.8086872
American literature—Minority authors 810.80920693
American literature—Minority authors—History and criticism 810.9920693
American literature—New England 810.80974
American literature—New England—History and criticism 810.9974
American literature—Scottish American authors 810.8089163
American literature—Southern States 810.80975
American literature—Southern States—History and criticism 810.9975
American literature—Southern States—History and criticism—Theory, etc. 810.9975
American literature—Southwestern States 810.80979
American literature—Southwestern States—History and criticism 810.9979
American literature—Study and teaching (Higher) 810.711
American literature—West (U.S.) 810.80978

American literature—West (U.S.)—History and criticism 810.9978

American literature—Women authors 810.809287

American literature—Women authors—History and criticism 810.99287

American literature—Women authors—History and criticism—Theory, etc. 810.99287

American lobster 595.384

American loyalists 973.314

American Medical Association. Auxiliary 362.120973

American newspapers 071.3

American newspapers—Directories 071.3

American newspapers—History 071.3

American paint horse 636.13

American periodicals 051

American periodicals—Directories 051

American pit bull terrier 636.7559

American poetry 811; 811.008

American poetry—Colonial period, ca. 1600–1775 811.1; 811.108

American poetry—Colonial period, ca. 1600–1775—History and criticism 811.109

American poetry—19th century 811.3; 811.308

American poetry—19th century—History and criticism 811.309

American poetry—20th century 811.5; 811.508; 811.52; 811.5208; 811.54; 811.5408

American poetry—20th century—Dictionaries 811.503; 811.5403

American poetry—20th century—History and criticism 811.509; 811.5209; 811.5409

American poetry—20th century—Periodicals 811.505

American poetry—African American authors 811.0080896073; 811.5080896073; 811.54080896073

American poetry—African American authors—History and criticism 811.009896073

American poetry—California 811.00809794

American poetry—California—Los Angeles 811.0080979494

American poetry—History and criticism 811.009

American poetry—Indian authors 811.0080897

American poetry—Mexican American authors 811.008086872

American poetry—Women authors 811.00809287; 811.540809287

American poetry—Women authors—History and criticism 811.0099287; 811.5099287; 811.54099287

American prose literature 818.08

American prose literature—Colonial period, ca. 1600–1775—History and criticism 818.108

American prose literature—20th century 818.508; 818.50808; 818.5208; 818.520808; 818.5408; 818.540808

American prose literature—20th century—History and criticism 818.50809

American prose literature—History and criticism 818.0809

American prose literature—Women authors 818.08

American Red Cross—Periodicals 361.7634097305

American Revolution Bicentennial, 1776–1976 973.36

American Sign Language 419

American Sign Language—Dictionaries 419

American Sign Language—Handbooks, manuals, etc. 419

American wit and humor 817; 817.008; 818.02

American wit and humor—Dictionaries 817.003

American wit and humor—History and criticism 817.009

American wit and humor, Pictorial 741.5973

Americanisms—Dictionaries 427.973

Americans—Employment—Europe 650.14094

Americans—Employment—Foreign countries 331.12791; 650.14

Americans—Employment—Foreign countries—Handbooks, manuals, etc. 650.14

Americans—Foreign countries 305.813

Americans—Foreign countries—Handbooks, manuals, etc. 303.48273

Americans—France 305.813044

Americans—France—Paris 305.81304436

Americans—Travel—Caribbean Area 917.29008913

Americans—Travel—England 914.2008913

Americans—Travel—England—London 914.21008913

Americans—Travel—Europe 914.008913

Americans—Travel—France 914.4008913

Americans—Travel—France—Paris 914.4361008913

Americans—Travel—Himalaya Mountains 915.496008913

Americans—Travel—Israel 915.694008913

Americans—Travel—Mexico 917.2008913

America's Cup 797.14

America's Cup—History 797.14

Ames, Aldrich Hazen, 1941– 327.12092

Amherst Region (Mass.) 974.423

Ami pro 686.22544536

Amichai, Yehuda 892.416

Amichai, Yehuda—Translations into English 892.416

Amiga (Computer) 004.165

Amiga (Computer)—Periodicals 004.165

Amiga (Computer)—Programming 005.265

Aminos 547.042

Amino acid sequence 547.75; 572.633

Amino acids 572.65

Amino acids—Metabolism 612.398

Amino acids—Synthesis 547.750459

Amino acids—Therapeutic use 615.3

Amis, Kingsley 828.91409

Amis, Kingsley—Criticism and interpretation 828.91409

Amish 289.73; 305.687

Amish—United States 289.773

Amish—United States—Social life and customs 973.088287

Amiss, Robert (Fictitious character) 823.914

Amiss, Robert (Fictitious character)—Fiction 823.914

Amistad (Schooner) 326

Ammonia 546.7112

Ammonoidea 564.53

Ammonoidea, Fossil 564.53

Ammons, A. R., 1926– 811.54

Ammons, A. R., 1926– —Criticism and interpretation 811.54

Ammunition 623.45

Amnesia 616.85232

Amnesia in literature 808.80356; 809.93356

Amniotes 596

Amniotes, Fossil 566

Amoebida 579.432

Amorphous semiconductors 621.38152

Amorphous substances 530.413

Amory, Cleveland 818.5403

Amphetamines 362.299

Amphibians 597.8

Amphibians as pets 639.378

Amphibians—Larvae 597.8139

Amphibious warfare 355.46

Amphipoda 595.378

Amphoras 666.68

Amplifiers (Electronics) 621.381535

Amputation 617.58059

Amputees 362.43; 617.58
Amritsar (India) 954.552
Amsterdam (Netherlands) 949.2352
Amsterdam (Netherlands)—Description and travel 914.9235204; 914.923520473
Amsterdam (Netherlands)—Guidebooks 914.9235204; 914.923520473
Amtrak—Appropriations and expenditures 343.730958
Amulets 133.44
Amusement parks 791.068
Amusement parks—United States 791.06873
Amusement parks—United States—Directories 791.06873
Amusement rides 791.068
Amusements 790
Amylin 573.3774; 612.34
Amyloidosis 616.3995
Amyotrophic lateral sclerosis 616.83
Anabaptists 284.3
Anabaptists—Doctrines 230.43
Anaerobic bacteria 579.3149
Anaerobic infections 571.993
Anaerobiosis 572.478
Analgesics 615.783
Analog electronic systems 621.3815
Analog-to-digital converters 621.3815322; 621.39814
Analog-to-digital converters—Design and construction 621.39814
Analogy 169
Analysis of variance 519.538
Analysis (Philosophy) 146.4; 149.94
Analytic functions 515.73
Analytic spaces 515.94
Analytical biochemistry 572.36
Analytical geochemistry 551.90287
Analytical toxicology 615.907
Analytical toxicology—Laboratory manuals 615.907
Anand, Mulk Raj, 1905– 823.912
Anand, Mulk Raj, 1905– —Criticism and interpretation 823.912
Anandamayi, 1896– 294.5092
Anansi (Legendary character)—Legends 398.2452544
Anaphora (Linguistics) 415
Anaphylaxis 614.5993; 616.97025
Anarchism 320.57; 335.83
Anarchism—History 335.8309
Anarchism—United States 335.830973
Anarchism—United States—History 335.830973
Anarchists 335.83092
Anarky (Fictitious character) 741.5973
Anastasia, Grand Duchess, daughter of Nicholas II, Emperor of Russia, 1901–1918 947.083092
Anatidae 598.41
Anatomical museums 571.31074
Anatomy 571.3; 571.31
Anatomy, Artistic 743.49
Anatomy, Comparative 571.31; 571.316
Anatomy, Comparative—Laboratory manuals 571.31078
Anatomy, Pathological 571.933
Anatomy, Surgical and topographical 611
Anatomy, Surgical and topographical—Atlases 611.00222
Anatosaurus 567.914
Ancestor worship 291.213
Ancestral shrines 291.35; 726.1
Anchorage (Alaska) 979.835
Anchorage (Alaska)—Maps 912.79835
Andersen, H. C. (Hans Christian), 1805–1875 839.8136

Andersen, H. C. (Hans Christian), 1805–1875—Translations into English 839.8136
Anderson family 929.20973
Anderson, John (Fictitious character) 823.914
Anderson, Mali (Fictitious character) 813.54
Anderson, Marian, 1897–1993 782.1092
Anderson, Maxwell, 1888–1959 812.52
Anderson, Maxwell, 1888–1959—Bibliography 016.81252
Anderson, Sherwood, 1876–1941 813.52
Anderson, Sherwood, 1876–1941—Criticism and interpretation 813.52
Anderson, Shifty Lou (Fictitious character) 813.54
Anderson, Shifty Lou (Fictitious character)—Fiction 813.54
Andersonville Prison 973.771
Andes 980
Andes—Description and travel 918.04; 918.0439; 918.044
Andes Region 980
Andes Region—Description and travel 918.04; 918.0439; 918.044
Andhra Pradesh (India) 954.84
Andhra Pradesh (India)—Economic conditions 330.95484
Andhra Pradesh (India)—History 954.84
Andhra Pradesh (India)—Politics and government 954.84
Andrade, Carlos Drummond de, 1902– 869.141
Andrade, Carlos Drummond de, 1902– —Translations into English 869.141
Andrews family 929.20973
Andrews, Julie 791.43028092
Andrews, Lynn V. 299.93
Androgenesis 571.887
Androgyny (Psychology) in literature 808.80353; 809.93353
Andrology 612.61
Andy Griffith show (Television program) 791.4572
Anencephaly 614.5983; 616.83
Anesthesia 617.96
Anesthesia—Complications 617.96041
Anesthesia—Examinations, questions, etc. 617.96076
Anesthesia—Handbooks, manuals, etc. 617.96
Anesthesia—History 617.9609
Anesthesia in cardiology 617.967412
Anesthesia in dentistry 617.9676
Anesthesia in neurology 617.96748
Anesthesia in neurology—Handbooks, manuals, etc. 617.96748
Anesthesia in obstetrics 617.9682
Anesthesiologists 617.96092
Anesthesiology 617.96
Anesthesiology—Apparatus and instruments 617.960284
Anesthesiology—Examinations, questions, etc. 617.96076
Anesthesiology—Handbooks, manuals, etc. 617.96
Anesthetics 615.781
Anesthetics—Physiological effect 615.781
Aneuploidy 572.877; 616.042
Aneurysms 616.133
Angel Academy (Imaginary organization : Tym) 823.914
Angel, Fitzroy Maclean (Fictitious character) 823.914
Angelou, Maya 818.5409
Angelou, Maya—Criticism and interpretation 818.5409
Angels 235.3; 291.215
Angels—Biblical teaching 235.3

Angels F.C. (Imaginary organization) 823.914
Angels in art 704.94864
Angels (Investors) 332.67253; 658.15224
Angels—Literary collections 808.8382353
Angels—Prayer-books and devotions 235.3; 291.215
Anger 152.47
Anger in children 155.41247
Anger—Religious aspects 291.5698
Anger—Religious aspects—Christianity 241.3
Angina pectoris 616.122
Angiocardiography 616.1207572
Angiography 616.1307548; 616.1307572
Angiosperms 580
Angiosperms, Fossil 561
Angkor (Extinct city) 959.6
Anglican Communion 283
Anglican Communion—Doctrines 230.3
Anglican Communion—Liturgy 264.03
Anglo-American cataloging rules (British text) 025.32
Anglo-American cataloguing rules 025.32
Anglo-Norman dialect 447.941
Anglo-Saxons 942.01
Anglo-Saxons—Kings and rulers 942.010922
Angola 967.3
Angola—History 967.3
Angola—History—Revolution, 1961–1975 967.303
Angola—History—Civil War, 1975– 967.304
Angola—Politics and government 320.9673; 967.3
Angola—Politics and government 1975–
 320.967309047; 967.304
Angstrom, Harry (Fictitious character) 813.54
Angstrom, Harry (Fictitious character)—Fiction 813.54
Anguilla 972.973021
Anguilla—Appropriations and expenditures
 352.460972973
Anguilla—Appropriations and expenditures—Statistics
 352.460972973021
Anguilla—Appropriations and expenditures—Statistics—
 Periodicals 352.460972973021
Angular momentum (Nuclear physics) 539.725
Anhalt, Mici (Fictitious character) 813.54
Anhalt, Mici (Fictitious character)—Fiction 813.54
Animal behavior 591.5
Animal behavior—Evolution 591.5
Animal behavior—Miscellanea 591.5
Animal behavior—Periodicals 591.505
Animal behavior—Simulation methods 591.5011
Animal biotechnology 660.6
Animal breeding 636.082
Animal cages 636.0831
Animal cell biotechnology 660.6
Animal cemeteries 636.08946
Animal communication 591.59
Animal culture 636
Animal defenses 591.47
Animal diversity 333.954; 591.7
Animal diversity conservation 333.95416
Animal ecology 591.7
Animal experimentation 590.724; 619
Animal experimentation—Moral and ethical aspects
 179.4
Animal experimentation—United States 179.40973
Animal genetics 591.35
Animal genome mapping 572.86331
Animal ghosts 133.14
Animal health 636.0893
Animal homing 591.568
Animal industry 338.176
Animal intelligence 591.513

Animal introduction 591.6
Animal locomotion 573.79; 591.479
Animal massage therapists 636.0895822092
Animal mechanics 573.79343
Animal migration 591.568
Animal navigation 573.87; 591.568
Animal nutrition 572.41; 636.0852
Animal pedigrees 636.0822
Animal-plant relationships 577.8
Animal populations 591.788
Animal psychology 591.5
Animal remains (Archaeology) 930.1
Animal rescue 179.3
Animal rights 179.3
Animal rights—Philosophy 179.3
Animal rights—United States 179.30973
Animal sanctuaries 333.95416
Animal shelters 636.0832
Animal societies 591.56; 591.782
Animal sounds 591.594
Animal specialists 590.92
Animal specialists—Vocational guidance 636.0023
Animal Stars (Imaginary organization) 823.914
Animal swimming 591.5
Animal tracks 591.479
Animal trainers 636.0835092
Animal training 636.0835
Animal traps 639.10284
Animal-water relationships 591.76
Animal weapons 591.47
Animal welfare 179.3
Animal welfare—Great Britain 179.30941
Animal welfare—Moral and ethical aspects 179.3
Animal welfare—United States 179.30973
Animals 590; 599
Animals as aids for the handicapped 362.40483;
 636.0886
Animals—Folklore 398.369
Animals—Food 591.53
Animals, Fossil 560
Animals—Habitations 591.564
Animals—Identification 590
Animals in art 704.9432; 743.6
Animals in literature 808.80362; 809.93362
Animals in logging 634.98
Animals in motion pictures 791.43662
Animals in the Bible 220.859
Animals in the Hadith 297.1240859
Animals—Infancy 591.39; 599.139
Animals—Miscellanea 590
Animals, Mythical 398.2454
Animals, Mythical, in art 704.947
Animals, Mythical, in heraldry 745.66; 929.6
Animals—Pictorial works 590.222
Animals—Religious aspects 291.212
Animals—Religious aspects—Christianity 241.693
Animals—Wintering 591.5
Animated film music 781.542
Animated films 741.58; 791.433
Animated films—History and criticism 791.433
Animated films—Technique 741.58
Animated films—United States 791.433
Animated films—United States—History and criticism
 791.433
Animated television programs 791.453
Animation cels 741.58
Animation (Cinematography) 778.5347
Animators 791.433
Ankle 612.98

Ankylosaurus 567.915
Annapolis (Md.) 975.256
Annapolis (Md.)—Pictorial works 975.25600222
Anne Arundel County (Md.) 975.255
Anne Arundel County (Md.)—Genealogy 929.375255
Anne Arundel County (Md.)—Maps 912.75255
Anne Boleyn, Queen, consort of Henry VIII, King of England, 1507–1536 942.052092
Anne, Queen, consort of Richard III, King of England, 1456–1485 942.046092
Annie (Fictitious character : Stevenson) 813.54
Anning, Mary, 1799–1847 560.92
Anniversaries 394.2
Annotations and citations (Law) 348.027
Annotations and citations (Law)—California 348.794047
Annotations and citations (Law)—Connecticut 348.746047
Annotations and citations (Law)—Idaho 348.796047
Annotations and citations (Law)—Montana 348.786047
Annotations and citations (Law)—Nebraska 348.782047
Annotations and citations (Law)—New York (State) 348.747047
Annotations and citations (Law)—Ohio 348.771047
Annotations and citations (Law)—Papua New Guinea 348.953027
Annotations and citations (Law)—Tennessee 348.768047
Annotations and citations (Law)—Texas 348.764047
Annotations and citations (Law)—United States 348.7327; 348.7347
Annotations and citations (Law)—Washington (State) 348.797047
Annuals (Plants) 635.9312
Annuities 368.37
Annuities—Taxation—Law and legislation 343.0524
Annuities—Taxation—Law and legislation—United States 343.730524
Anointing of the Holy Spirit 234.13
Anomia 616.8552
Anomochilidae 597.969
Anonymous stockholders 346.0666
Anonyms and pseudonyms 929.4
Anorexia nervosa 616.85262
Anorexia nervosa—Social aspects 362.25
Anorexia nervosa—Treatment 616.85262
Anouilh, Jean, 1910– 842.914
Anouilh, Jean, 1910– —Criticism and interpretation 842.914
Anoxemia 616.2
Anselm, Saint, Archbishop of Canterbury, 1033–1109 189.4; 282.092
ANSYS (Computer system) 620.0028553
Ant lions 595.747
Antagonists (Game) 794.82
Antarctic Ocean 551.469
Antarctica 919.89; 998.9
Antarctica—Description and travel 919.8904
Antarctica—Discovery and exploration 919.8904
Antarctica—Discovery and exploration—History 919.8904
Antarctica—Handbooks, manuals, etc. 998.9
Antarctica—History 998.9
Antarctica—International status 341.29
Antelope hunting 799.2764
Antelopes 599.64
Antennas (Electronics) 621.3824
Antennas (Electronics)—Design and construction 621.3824
Antenuptial contracts 346.016

Antenuptial contracts—United States 346.73016
Anterior cruciate ligament—Surgery 617.47
Anthems 782.265
Anthologies 808.8
Anthony, of Padua, Saint, 1195–1231 282.092
Anthony, Susan B. (Susan Brownell), 1820–1906 305.42092; 324.623092
Anthropic principle 113.8
Anthropogenic soils 577.57
Anthropological linguistics 306.44089
Anthropological museums and collections 301.074
Anthropologists 301.092
Anthropology 301; 599.9
Anthropology—Field work 301.0723
Anthropology in popular culture 301
Anthropology—Methodology 301.01
Anthropology—Periodicals 301.05
Anthropology—Philosophy 301.01
Anthropology, Prehistoric 569.9
Anthropometry 599.94
Anthroposophical therapy 610; 615.53
Anthroposophy 299.935
Anti-apartheid movements—South Africa 323.168
Anti-communist movements 324.13
Anti-communist movements—United States—History 973.91
Anti-environmentalism 323.46; 333.7; 363.7
Anti-feminism 305.42
Anti-feminism—United States 305.420973
Anti-imperialist movements 325.32
Anti-infective agents 615.1; 616.90461
Anti-infective agents—Handbooks, manuals, etc. 615.1
Anti-infective agents industry 338.476151
Anti-Nazi movement 943.086
Anti-Nazi movement—Germany 943.086
Anti-rape movement 362.883
Anti-submarine warfare 359.93
Anti-submarine warfare—United States 359.93
Antibiotics 615.329
Antibody-directed enzyme prodrug therapy 616.994061
Antibody-enzyme conjugates 615.36
Anticensorship activists 363.31
Antichrist 236
Antichrist—History of doctrines 236
Antichrist in art 704.9482
Anticoagulants (Medicine) 615.718
Anticonvulsants 616.853061
Antidepressants 616.8527061
Antidumping duties—Law and legislation 343.087
Antidumping duties—Law and legislation—United States 343.73087
Antietam, Battle of, Md., 1862 973.7336
Antifertility vaccines 615.766
Antifoaming agents industry 338.4766
Antifungal agents 615.1; 616.969061
Antigone (Greek mythology) in literature 808.80351; 809.93351
Antineoplastic agents 616.994061
Antinuclear movement 327.1747
Antinuclear movement—United States 327.17470973; 333.79240973
Antiochian school 281.5
Antioncogenes 616.992042
Antioxidants 613.28; 661.8
Antioxidants—Health aspects 613.28
Antipatterns (Software engineering) 005.1
Antiprotons 539.72123
Antipsychiatry 616.89
Antipsychotic drugs industry 338.476157882

Antiquarian booksellers 381.4509
Antiquarian booksellers—United States—Directories 381.450902573
Antique and classic aircraft 629.13334309041
Antique and classic cars 629.222
Antique and classic cars—Conservation and restoration 629.28722
Antique and classic cars—United States 629.2220973
Antique and classic motorcycles 629.2275
Antique and classic motorcycles—History 629.227509
Antique auctions 381.457451
Antique dealers 380.1457451
Antiques 745.1
Antiques—Catalogs 745.1075
Antiques—Conservation and restoration 745.10288
Antiques—Dictionaries 745.103
Antiques—Handbooks, manuals, etc. 745.1
Antiques, Oriental 745.1095
Antiques—Periodicals 745.105
Antiques—United States 745.10973
Antiquities 930.1
Antiquities—Collection and preservation 363.69
Antiquities, Prehistoric 930.1
Antiquities, Prehistoric—Europe 936
Antiquities, Prehistoric—Great Britain 936.1
Antiquities, Prehistoric—India 934
Antisemitism 305.8924; 323.11924
Antisemitism—History 261.2609; 305.8924
Antisemitism in literature 808.80355; 809.93355
Antisemitism—Soviet Union 305.8924047
Antisemitism—United States 305.8924073
Antisense nucleic acids 572.8
Antisense nucleic acids—Therapeutic use 615.31
Antislavery movements 326.8
Antislavery movements—Great Britain 326.80941
Antislavery movements—United States 973.7114
Antislavery movements—United States—History—19th century 973.7114
Antisocial personality disorders 616.8582
Antitrust investigations 363.25968
Antitrust law 343.0721
Antitrust law—Economic aspects 338.8
Antitrust law—Economic aspects—United States 338.80973; 343.730721
Antitrust law—European Economic Community countries 343.40721
Antitrust law—United States 343.730721
Antitrust law—United States—Cases 343.7307210264
Antitrust law—United States—History 343.73072109
Antitrust law—United States—Periodicals 343.73072105
Antiviral agents 615.1; 616.925061
Antler industry 338.372965
Antonius, Marcus, 83?-30 B.C. 937.05092
Antrim County (Mich.) 977.485
Antrim County (Mich.)—Maps 912.77485
Ants 595.796
Anus—Surgery 617.555
Anxiety 616.85223
Anxiety in children 155.41246; 618.9285223
Anxiety—Physiological aspects 612.8; 616.8522307
Anxiety sensitivity 616.85223
Anxiety—Treatment 616.8522306
Apache Indians 305.8972; 979.004972
Apache Indians—History 979.004972
Apache Indians—Wars 973.8
Apache Indians—Wars, 1883-1886 973.84
Apalone 597.926
Apartheid 305.800968
Apartheid—South Africa 305.800968; 342.680873

Apartheid—South Africa—History 305.800968
Apartheid—South Africa—Periodicals 305.800968
Apartment houses 647.92
Apartment houses—Management 647.92
Apartment houses—United States—Finance 363.582
Apartments 643.2
Apatosaurus 567.9138
Aperitifs 641.21; 641.874; 663.1
Apes 599.88
Aphasia 371.9142; 616.8552
Aphasia—Treatment 616.855206
Aphasic children 618.928552
Aphasic children—Education 371.9142
Aphasic persons—Rehabilitation 616.855203
Aphididae 595.752
Aphorisms and apothegms 398.9
Aphrodisiac cookery 641.563
Aphrodisiacs 615.766
Aphrodisiacs—Dictionaries 615.766
APL (Computer program language) 005.133
Aplastic anemia 616.152
Apocalypse in literature 808.8038228; 808.80382369; 809.9338228; 809.93382369
Apocalyptic literature 220.046
Apocalyptic literature—History and criticism 220.046
Apocryphal Acts of the Apostles 229.8
Apocryphal books (New Testament) 229
Apollinaire, Guillaume, 1880-1918 841.912
Apollinaire, Guillaume, 1880-1918—Criticism and interpretation 841.912
Apollo (Computer system) 387.74220285
Apollo Soyuz Test Project 629.454
Apollonius, Rhodius 883.01
Apollonius, Rhodius. Argonautica 883.01
Apologetics 239
Apologetics—History 239.09
Apologetics—History—Early church, ca. 30-600 239.1
Apologetics—History—20th century 239.0904
Apoptosis 571.936
Apostles 225.92; 225.922
Apostles—Biography 225.922
Apostles' Creed 238.11
Apostolic Fathers 270.1
Appalachian Region 974
Appalachian Region—Social conditions 974
Appalachian Region, Southern 975
Appalachian Region, Southern—Social life and customs 975
Appalachian Trail 974
Appalachian Trail—Guidebooks 917.4
Appaloosa horse 636.13
Appanoose County (Iowa) 977.789
Appanoose County (Iowa)—Genealogy 929.377789
Appanoose County (Iowa)—Maps 912.77789
Apparitions 133.1
Appeal to popular opinion (Logical fallacy) 165
Appellate courts 347.03
Appellate courts—United States 347.7324
Appellate procedure 347.08
Appellate procedure—Alaska 347.79808
Appellate procedure—Massachusetts 347.74408
Appellate procedure—Pennsylvania 347.74808
Appellate procedure—United States 347.738
Appendix (Anatomy) 611.345
Apperception 153.73
Appetite depressants 615.78
Appetizers 641.812
Apple II (Computer) 004.165
Apple II (Computer)—Programming 005.265

Apple IIGS (Computer) 004.165
Apple IIGS (Computer)—Programming 005.265
Apple computer 004.165
Apple computer—Periodicals 004.165
Apple computer—Programming 005.265
Apple Writer 652.55369
Applebroog, Ida 759.13
Applebroog, Ida—Exhibitions 759.13
Appleby, John, Sir (Fictitious character) 823.912
Appleby, John, Sir (Fictitious character)—Fiction 823.912
Apples 583.73; 634.11; 641.3411
AppleScript (Computer program language) 005.43
Appleseed, Johnny, 1774–1845 634.11092
AppleTalk 004.68
Appleton, Susanna, Lady (Fictitious character) 813.54
AppleWorks 005.369
Appleyard family (Fictitious characters) 823.914
Application program interfaces (Computer software) 005.3
Application service providers 384.33; 658.84
Application software 005.3
Application software porting 005.1
Application specific integrated circuits 621.3815; 621.395
Application specific integrated circuits—Computer-aided design 621.3815; 621.395
Application specific integrated circuits—Design and construction 621.395
Application specific integrated circuits—Design—Data processing 621.395
Applications for positions 650.14
Applied anthropology 301
Applied ecology 333.95; 639.9
Applied ethics 170
Applied linguistics 418
Applied sociology 301
Appliqué 746.445
Appliqué—Patterns 746.445041
Appointment books 651.29
Appomattox Campaign, 1865 973.738
Apportionment (Election law) 328.3345
Apportionment (Election law)—California 328.79407345; 342.794053
Apportionment (Election law)—United States 342.73053
Appraisers 333.332092
Apprenticeship programs 331.25922
Apprenticeship programs—United States 331.259220973
Appropriate technology 338.927
Appropriate technology—Developing countries 338.927091724
Approximation theory 511.4
APRS (Telecommunication) 621.38416
Apuleius 873.01
Apuleius. Metamorphoses 873.01
Aquacultural engineering 639.8
Aquaculture 639.8
Aquaculture industry 338.371
Aquaculture—Periodicals 639.805
Aquaculture stations 639.8
Aquaculture surveys 338.371; 639.8072
Aquarium animals 639.8
Aquarium fishes 639.34
Aquariums 597.073; 639.34
Aquariums, Public 597.073
Aquatic animals 591.76
Aquatic biology 578.76
Aquatic ecology 577.6
Aquatic exercises 613.716

Aquatic habitats 577.6
Aquatic insects 595.7176
Aquatic organisms 578.76
Aquatic parks and reserves 333.784
Aquatic plants 581.76
Aquatic resources conservation 333.952816; 639.9
Aquatic sports 797
Aquatic sports—Safety measures 797.0289
Aquatic weeds—Control 628.97
Aquifers 551.49
Aquifers—Colorado 551.4909788
Aquifers—Southern States 551.490975
Aquino, Corazon Cojuangco 959.9047092
Aquitaine, House of 944.6014
Arab Americans 305.8927073
Arab countries 909.0974927
Arab countries—Economic conditions 330.9174927
Arab countries—Foreign relations 327.09174927
Arab countries—Foreign relations—United States 327.730174927
Arab countries—History 909.0974927
Arab countries—Politics and government 320.9174927; 909.0974927
Arab countries—Politics and government—1945– 320.917492709045
Arab countries—Social conditions 909.0974927
Arab countries—Social life and customs 909.0974927
Arab-Israeli conflict 956.04
Arab-Israeli conflict—1967–1973 956.04
Arab-Israeli conflict—1973–1993 956.05
Arab-Israeli conflict—1993– 956.053
Arab-Israeli conflict—1993– —Peace 956.053
Arab-Israeli conflict—Maps 956.04
Arab students 371.829927
Arabian English pleasure horses 636.112
Arabian horse 636.112
Arabian horse—Pedigrees 636.11222
Arabian nights 398.2
Arabian Peninsula 953
Arabian Peninsula—Description and travel 915.304; 915.30453
Arabian Peninsula—Discovery and exploration 953
Arabian Peninsula—History 953
Arabic language 492.7
Arabic language—Dialects 492.77
Arabic language—Dialects—Egypt 492.770962
Arabic language—Dictionaries 492.73
Arabic language—Dictionaries—English 492.7321
Arabic language—Grammar 492.75; 492.782; 492.782421
Arabic language—Textbooks for foreign speakers—English 492.782421; 492.783421
Arabic language—Verb 492.75; 492.782; 492.782421
Arabic literature 892.7; 892.708
Arabic literature—1801– 892.708005
Arabic literature—1801– —History and criticism 892.709005
Arabic literature—History and criticism 892.709
Arabic poetry 892.71; 892.71008
Arabic poetry—20th century 892.716; 892.71608
Arabic poetry—20th century—Translations into English 892.71608
Arabic poetry—Translations into English 892.71008
Arabidopsis 583.64
Arabs—Folklore 398.2089927
Araceae 584.64
Arachnida 595.4
Arafat, Yasir, 1929– 956.94054092
Aragon (Spain) 946.55
Aragon (Spain)—History 946.02

Arakelov theory 516.35
Aran Islands (Ireland) 941.748
Arapaho philosophy 191.089973
Araucaria 585.3
Arbitrage 332.645
Arbitration (Administrative law) 347.09
Arbitration and award 341.522; 347.09
Arbitration and award—Great Britain 347.4109
Arbitration and award—India 347.5409
Arbitration and award, International 341.522
Arbitration and award, International—Periodicals
 341.52205
Arbitration and award—United States 347.739
Arbitration and award—United States—Bibliography
 016.347739
Arbitration, Industrial 331.89143
Arbitration, Industrial—United States 331.891430973;
 344.730189143
Arbitration, International 341.522
Arboretums 582.16073
Arboriculture 635.977
Arbors 635.91546; 717
Arboviruses 579.2562
Arbutus 583.66; 635.977366
Arcadia in literature 808.80321734; 809.93321734
Archaebacteria 579.321
Archaeocyathidae 563.47
Archaeological dating 930.10285
Archaeological expeditions 930.10283
Archaeological geology 930.1
Archaeological museums and collections 930.1074
Archaeological parks 930.1074
Archaeologists 930.1092
Archaeology 930.1
Archaeology and history 930.1
Archaeology and history—United States 973
Archaeology and religion 200.9; 291.175
Archaeology—Bibliography 016.9301
Archaeology—Data processing 930.1028
Archaeology—Dictionaries 930.103
Archaeology—Field work 930.1028
Archaeology—History 930.1
Archaeology in motion pictures 791.43658
Archaeology—Maps 912
Archaeology, Medieval 909.07
Archaeology—Methodology 930.1028
Archaeology—Periodicals 930.105
Archaeology—Philosophy 930.101
Archaeometry 930.1028
Archaeopteryx 568.22
Archchess 794.18
Archer, Carolyn (Fictitious character) 813.54
Archer, Isabel (Fictitious character) 813.4
Archer, Isabel (Fictitious character)—Fiction 813.4
Archer, Lew (Fictitious character) 813.52
Archer, Lew (Fictitious character)—Fiction 813.52
Archer, Owen (Fictitious character) 813.54
Archer, Owen (Fictitious character)—Fiction 813.54
Archery 799.32
Archetype (Psychology) in literature 808.80353;
 809.93353
Architects 720.92
Architects—Legal status, laws, etc. 343.07872
Architects—Legal status, laws, etc.—Great Britain
 343.4107872
Architects—Malpractice 344.097
Architects—Malpractice—United States 344.73097
Architectural acoustics 690.2; 729.29

Architectural and Transportation Barriers Compliance
 Board—Periodicals 353.539
Architectural design 721; 729
Architectural design—Data processing 721.0285;
 729.028
Architectural drawing 720.284
Architectural drawing—Detailing 720.284
Architectural drawing—Technique 720.284
Architectural firms 720.6
Architectural firms—United States—Management
 720.68
Architectural historians 720.92
Architectural ironwork 739.47
Architectural libraries 026.72
Architectural models 720.22
Architectural photography 778.94; 779.4
Architectural photography—Exhibitions 779.4074
Architectural photography—United States 779.40973
Architectural practice—Management 720.68
Architectural practice—United States 720.6
Architectural practice—United States—Management
 720.68
Architectural rendering 720.284
Architectural services marketing—United States
 720.688
Architecture 720
Architecture—Aesthetics 720.1
Architecture, Ancient 722
Architecture and climate 720.47
Architecture and energy conservation 720.472
Architecture and science 720
Architecture and society 720.103
Architecture and solar radiation 720.472
Architecture and the handicapped 720.87
Architecture and the handicapped—United States
 720.87
Architecture and the physically handicapped 720.87
Architecture and the physically handicapped—Law and
 legislation 342.087
Architecture and the physically handicapped—Law and
 legislation—United States 342.73087
Architecture and the physically handicapped—United
 States 720.87
Architecture, Baroque 724.16
Architecture—Bibliography 016.72
Architecture—Brazil 720.981
Architecture, Byzantine 723.2
Architecture—California—Los Angeles 720.979494
Architecture—California—San Francisco—Guidebooks
 720.979461
Architecture—China 720.951
Architecture, Classical 722.8
Architecture, Colonial 724.19
Architecture—Competitions 720.79
Architecture—Composition, proportion, etc. 720.1
Architecture—Conservation and restoration 363.69;
 720.288
Architecture—Data processing 720.285
Architecture—Denmark 720.9489
Architecture—Designs and plans 720.222
Architecture—Details 721
Architecture—Dictionaries 720.3
Architecture, Domestic 728; 728.37
Architecture, Domestic—China 728.0951
Architecture, Domestic—Designs and plans 728.0222
Architecture, Domestic—Designs and plans—Periodicals
 728.0222
Architecture, Domestic—England 728.0942
Architecture, Domestic—France 728.0944

Architecture, Domestic—Great Britain 728.0941
Architecture, Domestic—Italy 728.0945
Architecture, Domestic—Japan 728.0952
Architecture, Domestic—United States 728.0973; 728.370973
Architecture, Domestic—United States—Designs and plans 728.0222; 728.370222
Architecture, Domestic—United States—Designs and plans—Periodicals 728.370222
Architecture—England 720.942
Architecture—England—London 720.9421
Architecture—Environmental aspects 720.47
Architecture—Environmental aspects—United States 720.470973
Architecture—Europe 720.94
Architecture—France 720.944
Architecture—Germany 720.943
Architecture, Gothic 723.5
Architecture—Great Britain 720.941
Architecture—Greece 720.9495
Architecture, Hindu 720.954
Architecture—History 720.9
Architecture—Human factors 720.108
Architecture—Illinois 720.9773
Architecture—Illinois—Chicago—Guidebooks 720.977311
Architecture in art 704.944
Architecture in literature 808.80357; 809.93357
Architecture—India 720.954
Architecture, Islamic 720.917671
Architecture—Italy 720.945
Architecture—Italy—20th century 720.9450904
Architecture—Japan 720.952
Architecture—Japan—To 1868 720.952
Architecture—Japan—Edo period, 1600–1868 720.9520903
Architecture—Japan—1868– 720.95209034; 720.9520904
Architecture—Japan—20th century 720.9520904
Architecture, Japanese 720.952
Architecture, Medieval 723
Architecture—Mexico 720.972
Architecture, Modern 724
Architecture, Modern—19th century 724.5
Architecture, Modern—20th century 724.6
Architecture, Modern—20th century—Philosophy 724.601
Architecture, Modern—20th century—Themes, motives 724.6
Architecture, Modern—20th century—United States 720.9730904
Architecture, Mogul 720.954
Architecture—Netherlands 720.9492
Architecture—New York (State) 720.9747
Architecture—New York (State)—New York 720.97471
Architecture—New York (State)—New York—Guidebooks 720.97471
Architecture on postage stamps 769.5644
Architecture—Orders 721
Architecture, Ottoman 720.956
Architecture—Periodicals 720.5
Architecture—Philosophy 720.1
Architecture, Postmodern 724.6
Architecture—Psychological aspects 720.19
Architecture, Renaissance 724.12
Architecture, Renaissance—Italy 720.94509024
Architecture—Research 720.72
Architecture, Roman 722.7
Architecture, Romanesque 723.4
Architecture—Rome 720.945632

Architecture—Soviet Union 720.947
Architecture—Spain 720.946
Architecture—Study and teaching 720.71
Architecture—Study and teaching—United States 720.71073
Architecture—Technological innovations 720.105
Architecture—Turkey 720.9561
Architecture—United States 720.973
Architecture—United States—19th century 720.97309034
Architecture—United States—20th century 720.9730904
Architecture—United States—Examinations 720.76
Architecture—United States—Guidebooks 720.973
Architecture, Victorian—United States 720.97309034
Architecture—Vocational guidance 720.23
Architecture—Working drawings 720.284
Archival materials 025.1714
Archival materials—Digitization 025.7; 025.84; 651.59
Archival resources 027
Archives 027
Archives—Administration 025.1714
Archives, Technical 026.6
Archivists 027.0092
Arctic fox 599.7764
Arctic Ocean 551.468
Arctic peoples 998.00992
Arctic regions 909.0913; 971.9; 998
Arctic regions—Discovery and exploration 919.804
Arctic regions—International status 341.29
Arcticidae 594.4
Ardennes, Battle of the, 1944–1945 940.54219348
Ardennes horse 636.15
Area studies 909
Area vocational-technical centers 374.8
Arenac County (Mich.) 977.473
Arenac County (Mich.)—Maps 912.77473
Arenas 725.8
Arendt, Hannah 320.092
Arendt, Hannah—Contributions in political science 320.092
Argentina 982
Argentina—Description and travel 918.204; 918.20464
Argentina—Economic conditions 330.982
Argentina—Economic conditions—1983– 330.982064
Argentina—Economic conditions—1983– —Periodicals 330.982064
Argentina—Economic policy 338.982
Argentina—Politics and government 320.982; 982
Argentina—Politics and government—1955–1983 320.98209046; 982.064
Argentina—Politics and government—1983– 320.98209048; 982.064
Argentina—Social life and customs 982
Argentine fiction 863.0080982
Argentine fiction—20th century 863.00809820904
Argentine fiction—20th century—History and criticism 863.0099820904
Argentine wit and humor 867.0080982
Argentine wit and humor, Pictorial 741.5982
Argyll, Jonathan (Fictitious character) 823.914
Arianism 273.4
Arid regions 551.415
Arid regions agriculture 630.9154
Arid regions climate 551.69154
Ariel (Fictitious character : Disney) 791.4375; 791.4572
Ariosto, Lodovico, 1474–1533 851.3
Ariosto, Lodovico, 1474–1533. Orlando furioso 851.3
Arisaema 584.64
Aristocracy (Social class) 305.52

Aristocracy (Social class)—France 305.520944
Aristophanes 882.01
Aristophanes—Criticism and interpretation 882.01
Aristophanes—Political and social views 882.01
Aristophanes—Translations into English 882.01
Aristotle 185
Aristotle. Categoriae 160
Aristotle—Contributions in metaphysics 110.92
Aristotle—Contributions in political science 320.092
Aristotle. De anima 128
Aristotle—Ethics 171.3
Aristotle—Influence 185
Aristotle. Nicomachean ethics 171.3
Aristotle. Physics 530
Aristotle. Poetics 808.2
Aristotle. Politics 320.101
Aristotle. Rhetoric 808.5
Arithmetic 513
Arithmetic—Early works to 1900 513
Arithmetic—Study and teaching 513.071
Arithmetic—Study and teaching (Elementary) 372.72;
   372.72044
Arithmetic—Study and teaching (Primary) 372.72
Arithmetical algebraic geometry 516.35
Arizona 979.1
Arizona—Guidebooks 917.9104; 917.910453; 917.910454
Arizona—History 979.1
Arizona—Maps 912.791
Arizona—Politics and government 320.9791
Arizona—Tours 917.9104; 917.910453; 917.910454
Arkansas 976.7
Arkansas—Economic conditions 330.9767
Arkansas—Economic conditions—Statistics
   330.97670021
Arkansas—Genealogy 929.3767
Arkansas. General Assembly 328.767
Arkansas. General Assembly. House of Representatives
   328.767072
Arkansas. General Assembly. House of
   Representatives—Rules and practice 328.76705
Arkansas—Guidebooks 917.6704; 917.670453;
   917.670454
Arkansas—History 976.7
Arkansas—Maps 912.767
Arkansas—Road maps 912.767
Arlington County (Va.) 975.5295
Arlington County (Va.)—Maps 912.755295
Arlington National Cemetery (Arlington, Va.) 975.5295
Arm—Wounds and injuries 617.574044
Armada, 1588 942.055
Armadillos 599.312
Armah, Ayi Kwei, 1939- 823.914
Armah, Ayi Kwei, 1939- —Criticism and interpretation
   823.914
Armed Forces 355; 355.033
Armed Forces—Appropriations and expenditures
   355.6226
Armed Forces—Officers 355.0092
Armed Forces—Periodicals 355.005
Armed Forces—Political activity 322.5
Armed Services Vocational Aptitude Battery 355.0076
Armenia 956.62
Armenia—History 956.62
Armenia—History—To 428 939.55
Armenia (Republic) 947.56
Armenia (Republic)—History 947.56
Armenian Americans 973.0491992
Armenian language 491.992
Armenian massacres, 1915–1923 956.62015

Armenian question 956.62
Armenians 909.0491992; 956.62
Armies 355.3
Armillaria 579.6
Armor, Ancient 739.75093
Armored vehicles, Military 358.1883
Armories 355.75
Arms control 327.174
Arms control—Europe 327.174094
Arms control—History 327.17409
Arms control—Middle East 327.1740956
Arms control—Periodicals 327.17405
Arms control—United States 327.1740973
Arms control—Verification 327.174
Arms race 327.174
Arms transfers 382.453558; 382.456234
Arms transfers—Government policy—United States
   382.4562340973
Arms transfers—United States 382.4562340973
Armstrong family 929.20973
Armstrong, Louis, 1901–1971 781.65092
Armstrong, Neil, 1930- 629.450092
Army ants 595.796
Arnhem, Battle of, 1944 940.54219218
Arnold, Benedict, 1741–1801 973.382092
Arnold-Chiari deformity 614.5983; 616.83
Arnold, Lucy Richards (Fictitious character) 813.54
Arnold, Lucy Richards (Fictitious character)—Fiction
   813.54
Arnold, Matthew, 1822–1888 821.8
Arnold, Matthew, 1822–1888—Correspondence 821.8;
   826.8
Arnold, Matthew, 1822–1888—Criticism and
   interpretation 821.8
Arnold, Matthew, 1822–1888—Knowledge—France
   821.8
Arnold, Matthew, 1822–1888—Knowledge—Literature
   821.8
Arnold, Rain (Fictitious character) 813.54
Aromatherapy 615.321
Aromatherapy for children 615.321
Aromatic compounds 547.6
Aromatic plants 635.968
Aromaticity (Chemistry) 547.6
Arranged marriage 392.5
Arrangement (Music) 781.37
Arrangers (Musicians) 781.37092
Arrest 345.0527
Arrest (Police methods) 363.232
Arrest—United States 345.730527
Arrhythmia 616.128
Arrhythmia—Diagnosis 616.128075
Arrhythmia—Pathophysiology 616.128
Arrhythmia—Treatment 616.12806
Arsenite Schism, 1261–1310 273.6
Arson investigation 363.25964
Art 700
Art, Abstract 709.04052
Art—Addresses, essays, lectures 700
Art, African 709.6
Art, American 709.73
Art, American—20th century 709.730904
Art, American—Catalogs 709.73074
Art, American—Exhibitions 709.73074
Art, American—Exhibitions—Periodicals 709.73074
Art, American—Periodicals 709.7305
Art, American—Themes, motives 709.73
Art, Ancient 709.01; 709.3
Art, Ancient—Catalogs 709.01

Art and anthropology 701.03; 709.011
Art and history 709
Art and holography 774
Art and literature 700
Art and photography 770.11
Art and religion 701.04
Art and science 701.05
Art and society 701.03
Art and state 701.03
Art and state—United States 701.03
Art and technology 701.05
Art, Anglo-Saxon 709.42
Art appreciation 701.1
Art, Arab 709.53
Art, Argentine 709.82
Art, Armenian 709.4756; 709.5662
Art, Asian 709.5
Art auctions 702.94
Art, Australian 709.94
Art, Australian aboriginal 709.011
Art, Australian aboriginal—Exhibitions 709.011
Art, Austrian 709.436
Art, Baroque 709.032
Art, Belgian 709.493
Art, Belgian—20th century 709.4930904
Art—Bibliography 016.7
Art—Bibliography—Catalogs 016.7
Art, Black 704.0396
Art, Black—Africa, Sub-Saharan 709.67
Art, Brazilian 709.81
Art, British 709.41
Art, Buddhist 704.2943
Art, Bulgarian 709.499
Art, Byzantine 709.0214
Art calendars 700
Art, Canadian 709.71
Art, Canadian—Exhibitions 709.71074
Art, Carolingian 709.021; 709.4
Art—Catalogs 707.4; 708
Art, Celtic 709.354
Art centers 708
Art, Central American 709.728
Art, Chinese 709.51
Art, Chinese—20th century 709.510904
Art, Classical 709.38
Art—Collectors and collecting 707.5
Art, Colombian 709.861
Art commissions 353.77
Art—Conservation and restoration 702.88
Art, Costa Rican 709.7286
Art criticism 701.18
Art criticism—Authorship 808.0667
Art, Czech 709.437; 709.4371
Art, Danish 709.489
Art dealers 380.1457
Art deco 709.04012
Art—Dictionaries 703
Art, Dutch 709.492
Art, Dutch—20th century 709.4920904
Art, Early Christian 709.0212
Art, East Asian 709.5
Art, East Asian—Catalogs 709.5
Art, Egyptian 709.32
Art, English 709.42
Art, English—19th century 709.4209034
Art, Etruscan 704.039994
Art, European 709.4
Art—Exhibition techniques 707.53
Art—Exhibitions 707.4; 708

Art—Expertising 702.88
Art festivals 700.79
Art festivals—Pacific Area 700.799
Art, Finnish 709.4897
Art, Flemish 709.4931
Art for art's sake (Movement) 111.85
Art—Forgeries 702.874
Art, French 709.44
Art, French—19th century 709.4409034
Art, French—20th century 709.440904
Art galleries, Commercial 708
Art, German 709.43
Art, German—20th century 709.430904
Art, Gothic 709.022
Art, Greco-Roman 709.38
Art, Greek 709.38
Art, Greek—History 709.38
Art, Greek—Themes, motives 709.38
Art, Hawaiian 709.969
Art, Hindu 704.2945
Art historians 709.2
Art—Historiography 707.2
Art—History 709
Art—History—Outlines, syllabi, etc. 709
Art, Hungarian 709.439
Art in education 707.1
Art in hospitals 615.85156
Art in literature 808.80357; 809.93357
Art in universities and colleges 707.11
Art—India 709.54
Art, Indic 709.54
Art, Indic—20th century 709.540904
Art informel 709.04052
Art, Iraqi 709.567
Art, Irish 709.567; 759.2915
Art, Islamic 704.94897; 709.17671
Art, Israeli 709.5694
Art, Italian 709.45
Art, Italian—Catalogs 709.45074
Art—Italy 709.45
Art—Italy—Florence 709.4551
Art, Jamaican 709.7292
Art—Japan 709.52
Art, Japanese 709.52
Art, Japanese—To 1868 709.52
Art, Japanese—Edo period, 1600–1868 709.520903
Art, Japanese—1868- 709.5209034; 709.520904
Art, Jewish 704.03924
Art, Jordanian 709.5695
Art, Korean 709.519
Art, Korean—To 1900 709.519
Art, Korean—20th century 709.5190904
Art, Kuwaiti 709.5367
Art, Late Renaissance 709.031
Art, Latin American 709.8
Art, Lebanese 709.5692
Art libraries 026.7
Art—Marketing 706.88
Art—Mathematics 701.51
Art, Medieval 709.02
Art, Medieval—Themes, motives 704.90902
Art metal-work 739
Art, Mexican 709.72
Art—Middle East 709.56
Art, Modern 709.04
Art, Modern—17th century 709.032
Art, Modern—19th century 709.034
Art, Modern—20th century 709.04
Art, Modern—20th century—Europe 709.04

Artistic collaboration 700.92
Artists 700.92; 709.2
Artists and community 700.103
Artists—Biography 709.2
Artists—Biography—Dictionaries 709.2
Artists' books 700
Artists' books—United States 700
Artists—Italy—Biography 709.2245
Artists' materials 702.8
Artists' materials industry 751.2
Artists' models 702.8
Artists—Portraits 704.942; 779.2
Artists—Psychology 701.15
Artists' studios 700.284; 702.84
Artists' tools 702.84
Artists—United States 709.73
Artists—United States—Biography 709.2273
Artists—United States—Biography—Dictionaries 709.2273
Artists—United States—Interviews 700.92273; 709.2273
Arts 700
Arts, African 700.96
Arts, American 700.973
Arts, American—New York (State)—New York 700.97471
Arts, American—Periodicals 700.97305
Arts and crafts gardens 635.9; 712
Arts and crafts movement 709.034
Arts and crafts movement—United States 745.0973
Arts and religion 291.175
Arts and society 700.103
Arts and society—History 700.10309
Arts and society—History—20th century 700.1030904
Arts and society—United States 700.1030973
Arts and youth 704.055
Arts audiences—United States 700.1030973
Arts, Australian 700.994
Arts, Austrian 700.9436
Arts, Brazilian 700.981
Arts, British 700.941
Arts, Canadian 700.971
Arts, Chinese 700.951
Arts, Chinese—20th century 700.9510904
Arts, Dutch 700.9492
Arts—Economic aspects 338.477
Arts, English 700.942
Arts, European 700.94
Arts—Experimental methods 702.8
Arts facilities 725.8042
Arts, French 700.944
Arts, German 700.943
Arts—History 700.9
Arts, Hungarian 700.9439
Arts in literature 808.80357; 809.93357
Arts, Indic 700.954
Arts, Italian 700.945
Arts, Japanese 700.952
Arts, Korean 700.9519
Arts, Medieval 700.902
Arts, Modern 700.903; 700.904
Arts, Modern—19th century 700.9034
Arts, Modern—20th century 700.904
Arts, Modern—20th century—Brazil 700.9810904
Arts, Modern—20th century—Exhibitions 700.904074
Arts, Modern—20th century—Periodicals 700.90405
Arts, Modern—20th century—United States 700.9730904
Arts—Periodicals 700.5
Arts—Philosophy 700.1
Arts—Psychological aspects 700.19

Arts publicity 659.197
Arts, Renaissance 700.94
Arts, Russian 700.947
Arts—Scholarships, fellowships, etc. 700.79
Arts—Scholarships, fellowships, etc.—United States 700.7973
Arts—Scholarships, fellowships, etc.—United States—Directories 700.7973
Arts, Soviet 700.947
Arts, Spanish 700.946
Arts—Study and teaching 700.71
Arts—Study and teaching (Elementary) 372.5
Arts—Study and teaching (Elementary)—United States 372.50973
Arts—Study and teaching—United States 700.71073
Arts—United States 700.973
Arts—United States—Management 700.68
Arya-Samaj 294.5563
Asbestos 553.672
Asbestos cement houses 693.1
Asbestos in building—Safety measures 363.1791
Asceticism 291.447
Asch, Jacob (Fictitious character) 813.54
Asch, Jacob (Fictitious character)—Fiction 813.54
ASCII (Character set) 005.72
Asclepiadaceae 583.93
Asclepiads 583.93
Ascomycetes 579.56
ASEAN 341.2473
Ashanti (African people)—History 966.7018
Ashe, Arthur 796.342092
Ashe County (N.C.)—Genealogy 929.3756835
Ashtabula County (Ohio) 977.134
Ashtabula County (Ohio)—Maps 912.77134
Ashton, Carol (Fictitious character) 813.54
Ashton, Carol (Fictitious character)—Fiction 813.54
Ashton under Hill (England) 942.449
Ashton under Hill (England)—Social life and customs 942.449
Asia 950
Asia—Bibliography 016.95
Asia, Central 958
Asia, Central—Description and travel 915.804; 915.804429; 915.80443
Asia, Central—Economic conditions 330.958
Asia, Central—Economic conditions—Periodicals 330.958005
Asia, Central—Foreign relations 327.0958
Asia, Central—Foreign relations—1991– 327.0958
Asia, Central—History 958
Asia, Central—History—1991– 958.0429
Asia, Central—Politics and government 958
Asia—Civilization 950
Asia—Commerce 382.095
Asia—Commercial policy 380.13095
Asia—Description and travel 915.04; 915.04429; 915.0443
Asia—Description and travel—Early works to 1800 915.04
Asia—Economic conditions 330.95
Asia—Economic conditions—1945– 330.95042
Asia—Economic conditions—1945– —Periodicals 330.95042
Asia—Economic integration 337.15
Asia—Economic policy 338.95
Asia—Foreign economic relations 337.5
Asia—Foreign relations 327.095
Asia—Foreign relations—United States 327.7305
Asia—Geography 915

Astronautics and civilization 303.483
Astronautics and state 629.4
Astronautics and state—United States 333.940973
Astronautics—Communication systems 629.4743
Astronautics—Data processing 629.40285
Astronautics—Dictionaries 629.403
Astronautics—Europe—History 387.8094
Astronautics—History 629.409
Astronautics in earth sciences 550
Astronautics in geodesy 526.1
Astronautics in meteorology 551.5
Astronautics in oceanography 551.46
Astronautics, Military 358.8
Astronautics, Military—United States 358.80973
Astronautics—Periodicals 629.405
Astronautics—Soviet Union 629.40947
Astronautics—Technology transfer 338.926
Astronautics—United States 629.40973
Astronautics—United States—History 629.40973
Astronauts 629.450092; 629.4507
Astronomers 520.92
Astronomical instruments 522.2
Astronomical observatories 522.1
Astronomical photography 522.63
Astronomical photometry 522.62
Astronomical spectroscopy 522.67
Astronomy 520
Astronomy, Ancient 520.93
Astronomy, Arab 520.9174927
Astronomy, Assyro-Babylonian 520.935
Astronomy—Charts, diagrams, etc. 520.223
Astronomy, Chinese 520.51
Astronomy—Data processing 520.285
Astronomy—Dictionaries 520.3
Astronomy—Encyclopedias 520.3
Astronomy—Experiments 520.724; 520.78
Astronomy, Greek 520.938
Astronomy—Handbooks, manuals, etc. 522
Astronomy—History 520.9
Astronomy in the Bible 220.68
Astronomy, Medieval 520.902
Astronomy—Miscellanea 520
Astronomy—Observations 522
Astronomy—Observers' manuals 522; 523.80223
Astronomy—Periodicals 520.5
Astronomy—Philosophy 520.1
Astronomy—Pictorial works 520.222
Astronomy projects 520.78
Astronomy—Study and teaching 520.71
Astronomy—Study and teaching—Activity programs 520.78
Astronotus 597.74; 639.3774
Astrophysical jets 522.682; 523
Astrophysics 523.01
Astrophysics—Data processing 523.010285
Astrophysics—Periodicals 523.0105
Astrophysics—Technique 523.01072
Aśvamedha 294.534
Asylum, Right of 341.488
Asylum, Right of—Europe 342.4083
Asylum, Right of—United States 342.73083
Asymmetric synthesis 547.2
Asymmetric warfare 355.42
Asymptotic expansions 511.4
Asynchronous circuits 621.395
Asynchronous transfer mode 004.66
Atari computer 004.165
Atari computer—Programming 005.265
Atari ST computers 004.165

Atatürk, Kemal, 1881–1938 956.1024092
Atchison, Topeka, and Santa Fe Railway Company 385.0978
Aterien culture 930.12
Athanasius, Saint, Patriarch of Alexandria, d. 373 270.2092
Athapascan Indians—Folklore 398.2089972
Atheism 211.8
Atheists 211.8092
Athelstan, Brother (Fictitious character) 823.914
Athens (Greece) 938.5; 949.512
Athens (Greece)—Civilization 938.5
Athens (Greece)—Guidebooks 914.951204; 914.95120476
Athens (Greece)—History 938.5; 949.512
Athens (Greece)—Politics and government 320.9385
Atherosclerosis 616.136
Atherosclerosis—Etiology 616.136071
Atherosclerosis—Pathogenesis 616.136071
Atherosclerosis—Pathophysiology 616.13607
Athletes 796.092
Athletes—Biography 796.092
Athletes in art 704.942
Athletes in mass media 302.23088796
Athletes—Nutrition 613.2088796
Athletes—Prayer-books and devotions 242.68
Athletes—United States—Biography 796.092273
Athletes—United States—Biography—Dictionaries 796.092273
Athletic clubs 796.06
Athletic shoes 685.36
Athletic trainers 796.092
Athletics 796
Athos (Greece) 949.565
Atkins family 929.20973
Atlanta Braves (Baseball team) 796.3576409758231
Atlanta Braves (Baseball team)—History 796.3576409758231
Atlanta Campaign, 1864 973.7371
Atlanta (Ga.) 975.8231
Atlanta (Ga.)—Guidebooks 917.5823104; 917.582310443; 917.582310444
Atlanta (Ga.)—History 975.8231
Atlanta (Ga.)—Maps 912.758231
Atlanta Metropolitan Area (Ga.) 975.8231
Atlanta Metropolitan Area (Ga.)—Maps 912.758231
Atlanta Region (Ga.) 975.8231
Atlanta Region (Ga.)—Maps 912.758231
Atlantic Coast (N.J.) 974.9
Atlantic Coast (N.J.)—Guidebooks 917.4904; 917.490443; 917.490444
Atlantic Coast (U.S.) 974; 975
Atlantic Coast (U.S.)—Description and travel 917.404; 917.40443; 917.40444; 917.504; 917.50443; 917.50444
Atlantic Ocean 551.461
Atlantic Provinces 971.5
Atlantic Provinces—History 971.5
Atlantic salmon 597.56
Atlantic salmon fishing 799.1756
Atlantic States 974
Atlantic States—Description and travel 917.404
Atlantic States—Guidebooks 917.404; 917.40443; 917.40444
Atlantis 398.234; 398.42
Atlases 912
Atlases, Australian 912
Atlases, British 912
Atlases, Canadian 912
Atlases, Chinese 912

Austen, Jane, 1775–1817—Political and social views 823.7

Austen, Jane, 1775–1817. Pride and prejudice 823.7

Austen, Jane, 1775–1817—Technique 823.7

Austen, Kate (Fictitious character) 813.54

Austin, Kurt (Fictitious character) 813.54

Austin, Mary Hunter, 1868–1934 818.5209

Austin Metropolitan Area (Tex.) 976.431

Austin Metropolitan Area (Tex.)—Maps 912.76431

Austin (Tex.) 976.431

Austin (Tex.)—Guidebooks 917.643104; 917.64310463; 917.64310464

Austin (Tex.)—Pictorial works 976.43100222

Australia 994

Australia—Bibliography 016.994

Australia—Biography 920.094

Australia—Biography—Dictionaries 920.09403

Australia—Civilization 994

Australia—Commerce 382.0994

Australia—Commerce—Statistics 382.09940021

Australia—Commerce—Statistics—Periodicals 382.09940021

Australia—Defenses 355.033094

Australia—Description and travel 919.404; 919.40466; 919.4047

Australia—Discovery and exploration 994.02

Australia—Economic conditions 330.994

Australia—Economic conditions—1945- 330.99405

Australia—Economic conditions—1945- —Periodicals 330.99405

Australia—Economic policy 338.994

Australia—Emigration and immigration 325.94

Australia—Emigration and immigration—Government policy 304.894; 325.94

Australia—Encyclopedias 919.4003; 994.003

Australia—Environmental conditions 363.700994

Australia—Foreign relations 327.94

Australia—Foreign relations—1900-1945 327.94

Australia—Foreign relations—1945- 327.94

Australia—Genealogy 929.1072094; 929.394

Australia—Genealogy—Handbooks, manuals, etc. 929.1072094

Australia—Geography 919.4

Australia—Guidebooks 919.404; 919.40466; 919.4047

Australia—Historiography 994.0072

Australia—History 994

Australia—History—To 1788 994.01

Australia—History—1788-1851 994.02

Australia—History—1788-1900 994.02; 994.03

Australia—History—20th century 994.04

Australia—History—Chronology 994.00202

Australia—Literary collections 820.803294

Australia—Maps 912.94

Australia—Military policy 355.033594

Australia—Pictorial works 919.400222

Australia—Politics and government 320.994; 994

Australia—Politics and government—1945- 320.99409045; 994.05

Australia—Religion 306.60994

Australia—Road maps 912.94

Australia. Royal Australian Air Force—History 358.400994

Australia—Social conditions 994

Australia—Social life and customs 994

Australia—Social life and customs—19th century 994.02

Australia—Social policy 361.610994

Australian aborigines 305.89915; 599.989915

Australian aborigines—Antiquities 994.01

Australian aborigines—Civil rights 323.119915

Australian aborigines—Folklore 398.20899915

Australian aborigines—Government relations 305.89915; 323.119915

Australian aborigines—Health and hygiene 362.10899915

Australian aborigines—History 994.0049915

Australian aborigines—Legal status, laws, etc. 346.94013

Australian aborigines—Poetry 821.008089915

Australian aborigines—Politics and government 323.119915

Australian aborigines—Social conditions 305.89915

Australian aborigines—Social life and customs 305.89915

Australian drama 822.0080994

Australian drama—20th century 822.91080994

Australian drama—20th century—History and criticism 822.9109994

Australian fiction 823.0080994

Australian fiction—20th century—History and criticism 823.9109

Australian fiction—Women authors 823.008092870994

Australian Labor Party 324.29407

Australian Labor Party—History 324.29407

Australian languages 499.15

Australian literature 820; 820.80994

Australian literature—20th century 820.809940904

Australian literature—20th century—History and criticism 820.99940904

Australian literature—History and criticism 820.9994

Australian literature—Women authors 820.909287

Australian literature—Women authors—History and criticism 820.992870994

Australian poetry 821; 821.0080994

Australian poetry—20th century 821.91; 821.91080994

Australian poetry—20th century—History and criticism 821.9109994

Australian robins 598.84

Australian shepherd dog 636.737

Australian Sign Language 419.94

Australian studies 994.0072

Australian wit and humor 827.0080994

Australian wit and humor, Pictorial 741.5994

Australians 305.824

Australopithecines 569.9

Austria 943.6

Austria—Guidebooks 914.3604; 914.360453

Austria—History 943.6

Austria—History—1867-1918 943.6044

Austria—Pictorial works 914.3600222

Austrian literature 830.809436

Austrian literature—19th century 830.809436

Austrian literature—19th century—History and criticism 830.99436

Austrian literature—20th century 830.809436

Austrian literature—20th century—History and criticism 830.99436

Austrian school of economics 330.157

Austrian wit and humor, Pictorial 741.59436

Austronesian languages 499.2

Auteur theory (Motion pictures) 791.43023301

Authentic movement (Dance therapy) 615.85155

Authigenesis 552.03

Authoritarianism 303.36

Authority 303.36

Authority files (Information retrieval) 025.3222

Authority—Religious aspects 291.61

Authority—Religious aspects—Christianity 262.8

Authority—Religious aspects—Christianity—History of doctrines 262.809
Authors 809
Authors, American 810.9
Authors, American—20th century 810.9005
Authors, American—20th century—Interviews 810.9005; 810.90052; 810.90054
Authors, American—Maine 810.99741
Authors and publishers 070.52
Authors and publishers—United States 343.730998; 346.730482
Authors and the theater 808.2
Authors, Australian 820.9994
Authors, Australian—20th century 820.999404
Authors, Australian—20th century—Interviews 820.99940904
Authors—Biography 809
Authors, Canadian 809.811
Authors, English 820.9
Authors, English—20th century 820.90091
Authors—Interviews 809
Authors, Irish 820.9415
Authorship 808.02
Authorship—Collaboration 808.02
Authorship—Data processing 808.020285
Authorship—Handbooks, manuals, etc. 808.02
Authorship—Marketing 070.52
Authorship—Marketing—Directories 070.52
Authorship—Marketing—Handbooks, manuals, etc. 070.52
Authorship—Psychological aspects 808.02019
Authorship—Style manuals 808.027
Authorship—Vocational guidance 808.02023
Autism 616.8982
Autism in children 618.928982; 649.154
Autism in children—Treatment 618.92898206
Autistic children 618.928982; 649.154
Autistic children—Education 371.94
Autistic children—Education—United States 371.94
Autistic children—Rehabilitation 618.92898203
Autobiographical memory 153.13
Autobiography 809.93592
Autobiography—Authorship 808.06692
AutoCAD 620.004202855369
Autocross 796.72
Autogenic training 615.8512
Autographs 929.88
Autographs—Catalogs 928.88075
Autoimmune diseases 616.978
Autoimmunity 616.978
AutoLISP (Computer program language) 620.004202855369
Automated tellers 332.17
Automatic checkout equipment 629.89
Automatic control 629.8
Automatic control—Data processing 629.80285; 629.89
Automatic control equipment industry 338.47670427
Automatic control—Mathematical models 629.8015118
Automatic control—Periodicals 629.805
Automatic control—Reliability 629.8
Automatic control—Study and teaching 629.8071
Automatic data collection systems 006
Automatic machinery 670.427
Automatic pistols 683.432
Automatic speech recognition 006.454
Automatic theorem proving 006.333; 511.30285
Automation 303.4834; 670.427
Automobile auctions 629.2220294
Automobile dealers 338.47629222

Automobile detailing 629.26
Automobile drivers 629.283092
Automobile driving 629.283
Automobile driving—Automation 388.312; 629.283
Automobile engineers 629.222092
Automobile industry and trade 338.47629222
Automobile industry and trade—Europe 338.47629222094
Automobile industry and trade—Great Britain 338.476292220941
Automobile industry and trade—Great Britain—History 338.476292220941
Automobile industry and trade—Quality control—Standards—United States 338.476292220973
Automobile industry and trade—United States 338.476292220973
Automobile industry and trade—United States—History 338.476292220973
Automobile leasing and renting 388.342
Automobile leasing and renting—United States 388.32
Automobile parking 388.474
Automobile parking for the physically handicapped 388.4740873
Automobile racing 796.72
Automobile racing—Biography 796.72092
Automobile racing drivers 796.72092
Automobile racing drivers—Biography 796.72092
Automobile racing drivers—United States—Biography 796.72092273
Automobile racing—History 796.7209
Automobile racing—United States 796.720973
Automobile racing—United States—History 796.720973
Automobile rallies 796.73
Automobile repair shops 629.2872
Automobile showrooms 725.21
Automobile supplies industry 338.4752922
Automobile supplies industry—United States 381.4562920973
Automobile theft 364.162
Automobile trailers 629.226
Automobile travel 796.7
Automobile travel—Europe—Guidebooks 914.04; 914.04559; 914.0456
Automobile travel—Great Britain—Guidebooks 914.204; 914.204859; 914.20486
Automobile travel—Ireland—Guidebooks 914.1504; 914.1504824
Automobile travel—Pacific States—Guidebooks 917.904; 917.90433; 917.90434
Automobile travel—Scotland—Guidebooks 914.1104; 914.1104859; 914.110486
Automobile travel—United States—Guidebooks 917.304; 917.304929
Automobiles 388.342; 629.222
Automobiles—Aerodynamics 629.231
Automobiles—Air conditioning 629.2772
Automobiles—Air conditioning—Maintenance and repair 629.2772
Automobiles—Air conditioning—Maintenance and repair—Handbooks, manuals, etc. 629.2772
Automobiles—Air suspension 629.243
Automobiles—Antilock brake systems 629.246
Automobiles—Antilock brake systems—Maintenance and repair 629.246
Automobiles—Antilock brake systems—Maintenance and repair—Handbooks, manuals, etc. 629.246
Automobiles—Bodies 629.26
Automobiles—Bodies—Maintenance and repair 629.260288

Autonomic nervous system 612.89; 616.88
Autonomic nervous system—Diseases 616.88
Autonomic nervous system—Physiology 612.89
Autonomous robots 629.892
Autonomy 320.15
Autonomy and independence movements 320.15
Autopsy 616.0759
AutoSketch (Computer file) 604.202855369
Autumn 508.2; 578.43
Auxiliary police 363.2
Available light photography 778.76
Avant-garde (Aesthetics) 111.85
Avarice 178
Averroës, 1126–1198 181.9
Aversion 152.4
Avestan language 491.52
Aviaries 598.073
Aviation medicine 616.980213
Aviation psychology 629.13252019
Avicenna, 980–1037 181.5
Avionics 629.11; 629.135
Avocado 641.34653
Award presentations 394.2
Awards 929.81
Awareness 152.1; 153; 153.7
Awolowo, Obafemi, 1909– 966.905092
Axiomatic set theory 511.3
Ayer, A. J (Alfred Jules), 1910– 192
Ayers family 929.20973
Ayodhya (Faizabad, India) 954.2
Ayodhya (Faizabad, India)—History 954.2
Ayodhya (Faizabad, India)—Politics and government 954.2
Ayres 782.42168
Āzād, Abūlkalām, 1888–1958 954.035092
Azaleas 635.93366
Azikiwe, Nnamdi, 1904– 966.9051092
Azospirillum 579.323
Aztec art 704.0397452
Aztec calendar 529.32978452
Aztec cosmology 523.108997452
Aztec Ruins National Monument (N.M.) 978.982
Aztecs 305.897452; 972; 972.00497452; 972.018
Aztecs—Folklore 398.208997452
Aztecs—History 305.89745209; 972; 972.018
B-1 bomber 358.4283
B-2 bomber 358.4283
B-17 bomber 358.4283; 623.7463
B-17 bomber—History 358.4283
B-24 bomber 623.7463
B-29 bomber 623.7463
B-52 bomber 358.4283; 623.7463
B films—United States—History and criticism 791.433
B method (Computer science) 005.1
Babbitt, Irving, 1865–1933 191
Babel', I. (Isaak), 1894–1941 891.7342
Babel', I. (Isaak), 1894–1941—Translations into English 891.7342
Baboons 599.865
Baby boom generation 305.2
Baby boom generation—United States 305.2
Baby foods 641.300832
Baby rattles 688.72; 745.592
Babylon (Extinct city) in the Bible 220.9; 228.064
Babylonia 935.02
Babylonia—History 935.02
Babysitters 649.1; 649.10248
Babysitting 649.10248
Babysitting—Handbooks, manuals, etc. 649.10248

Baca, Sonny (Fictitious character) 813.54
Baccarat 795.42
Bach, Johann Sebastian, 1685–1750 780.92
Bach, Johann Sebastian, 1685–1750—Criticism and interpretation 780.92
Bachelor of liberal studies 378.2
Bachelorette parties 392.5; 793.2
Bachelors in literature 808.803520652; 809.933520652
Bacillus (Bacteria) 579.362
Bacillus subtilis 579.362
Back exercises 613.71
Backache 617.564
Backache—Alternative treatment 617.56406
Backache—Chiropractic treatment 617.56406
Backache—Exercise therapy 617.564062
Backache—Physical therapy 617.564062
Backache—Prevention 617.564052
Backache—Treatment 617.56406
Backgammon 795.15
Backpacking 796.51
Backpacking—Handbooks, manuals, etc. 796.51
Backpacking injuries 617.1027
Backpacking—Peru 796.510984
Backpacking—Peru—Guidebooks 918.504; 918.50464
Backpacking—Sierra Nevada (Calif. and Nev.) 796.51097944
Backpacking—Sierra Nevada (Calif. and Nev.)— Guidebooks 917.94404; 917.9440453; 917.9440454
Backpacks 685.51; 796.510284
Backward masking 621.38932
Backyard camping 796.54
Bacon, Francis, 1561–1626 192
Bacon, Francis, 1561–1626—Contributions in philosophy of science 192
Bacon, Francis, 1909– 759.2
Bacon, Francis, 1909– —Exhibitions 759.2
Bacteria 579.3
Bacterial cell surfaces 571.64293
Bacterial diseases 614.57; 616.92
Bacterial genetics 579.3135
Bacterial leaching 669.0283
Bacterial toxins 615.95293
Bacterial wilt diseases 632.32
Bacteriology 579.3
Bacteriophages 579.26
Bactrosaurus 567.914
Baculitidae 564.53
Baculoviruses 579.2436
Bad breath 616.31
Bādarāyaṇa. Brahmasūtra 181.48
Badgers 599.767
Badges 769.5
Badlands 551.415; 910.9154
Badminton (Game) 796.345
Baffin Island (Nunavut) 971.95
Baggins, Frodo (Fictitious character) 823.912
Baggins, Frodo (Fictitious character)—Fiction 823.912
Bagpipe 788.49; 788.4919
Bagpipe music 788.49
Bagthorpe family (Fictitious characters) 823.914
Bahai ethics 297.935
Bahai Faith 297.93
Bahai Faith—Doctrines 297.932
Bahai literature 808.803829793
Bahamas 972.96
Bahamas—Guidebooks 917.29604
Bahamas—History 972.96
Bahá'u'lláh, 1817–1892 297.93092

Bahrain 953.65
Bahrain—Pictorial works 953.6500222
Bai, Juyi, 772–846 895.113
Bai, Juyi, 772–846—Translations into English 895.113
Bail 345.072
Bail—Canada 345.71072
Bailey, Beetle (Fictitious character) 741.5973
Bailey family 929.20973
Bait fishing 799.122
Bait industry 338.371
Baitworm industry 338.37175
Baitworms 639.75
Baja California (Mexico : Peninsula) 972.2
Baja California (Mexico : Peninsula)—Description and travel 917.2204; 917.2204836
Baja California (Mexico : Peninsula)—Guidebooks 917.2204; 917.2204836
Baked products 664.752
Baked products industry 338.47664752
Baker family 929.20973
Baker, Josephine, 1906–1975 792.7092; 792.8092
Bakers and bakeries 664.752; 664.752092
Bakhtin, M. M. (Mikhail Mikhaĭlovich), 1895–1975 801.95092
Baking 641.71
Bakker, Jim, 1940– 269.2092
Bakunin, Mikhail Aleksandrovich, 1814–1876 335.83092
Balaklava (Ukraine), Battle of, 1854 947.073
Balalaika ensembles 785.7875
Balalaika orchestras 784.7
Balance of payments 332.152; 382.17
Balance of payments—Developing countries 332.152091724; 382.17091724
Balance of power 327.112
Balance of trade 382.17
Balance of trade—United States 382.170973
Balanchine, George 792.82092
Bald eagle 598.943
Baldness 616.546
Baldridge, Masey (Fictitious character) 813.54
Baldridge, Masey (Fictitious character)—Fiction 813.54
Baldwin family 929.20973
Baldwin, James, 1924– 818.5409
Baldwin, James, 1924– —Criticism and interpretation 818.5409
Balfour Declaration 956.9404
Bali Island (Indonesia) 959.86
Bali Island (Indonesia)—Civilization 959.86
Bali Island (Indonesia)—Guidebooks 915.986
Bali Island (Indonesia)—Pictorial works 915.986; 959.86
Balkan Peninsula 949.6
Balkan Peninsula—Description and travel 914.9604; 914.96044
Balkan Peninsula—History 949.6
Balkan Peninsula—Politics and government 320.9496; 949.6
Balkan Peninsula—Politics and government—20th century 320.94960904
Balkan Peninsula—Politics and government—1989– 320.949609049; 949.6
Ball-bearings 621.822
Ball family 929.20973
Ball games 796.3
Ball, Hollis (Fictitious character) 813.54
Ball, Lucille, 1911– 791.45028092
Ballades (Instrumental music) 784.1896
Ballads 808.8144

Ballads, English 821.04408
Ballads, English—England 821.04408942
Ballads, English—England—History and criticism 821.04409942
Ballads, English—England—Texts 821.04408942
Ballads, English—Texts 821.04408
Ballads, English—United States 811.04408
Ballads, Scots 821.044089411
Ballads, Scots—Scotland 821.044089411
Ballads, Scots—Scotland—History and criticism 821.044099411
Ballads, Scots—Scotland—Texts 821.044089411
Ballasts (Electricity) 621.3815
Ballet 792.8
Ballet companies 792.809
Ballet dancers 792.8028092
Ballet dancing 792.8
Ballet—Dictionaries 792.803
Ballet—Great Britain 792.80941
Ballet—History 792.809
Ballet programs 792.84
Ballet—Soviet Union 792.80947
Ballet—Soviet Union—History 792.80947
Ballet—Stage-setting and scenery 792.8025
Ballets 792.84
Ballets—Excerpts 781.556
Ballets—Excerpts—Scores 781.556
Ballets—Piano scores 781.556
Ballets russes 792.80947
Ballets russes—History 792.80947
Ballets—Scores 781.556
Ballets—Stories, plots, etc. 792.84
Ballistic missile defenses 358.174
Ballistic missile defenses—United States 358.1740973
Ballistic missiles 358.175482
Ballistics 623.51
Balloon ascensions 629.1332209
Balloon music 786.88
Balloon sculpture 745.594
Ballooning 629.13322; 797.51
Balloons 629.13322
Balloons as musical instruments 786.88
Balloons in astronomy 522
Ballroom dancing 793.33
Ballroom dancing—Study and teaching 793.33071
Balsamic vinegar 641.62; 664.55
Balthasar, Hans Urs von, 1905– 230.2092
Baltic States 947.9
Baltic States—Economic conditions 330.9479
Baltic States—Economic conditions—Periodicals 330.9479005
Baltic States—Foreign relations 327.09479
Baltic States—Guidebooks 914.47904; 914.4790486
Baltic States—History 947.9
Baltic States—History—Autonomy and independence movements 947.9085
Baltimore County (Md.)—Genealogy 929.375271
Baltimore County (Md.)—Maps 912.75271
Baltimore (Md.) 975.26
Baltimore (Md.)—Genealogy 929.37526
Baltimore (Md.)—Guidebooks 917.52604; 917.5260443; 917.5260444
Baltimore (Md.)—History 975.26
Baltimore (Md.)—Maps 912.7526
Baltimore Orioles (Baseball team) 796.35764097526
Baltimore Orioles (Baseball team)—History 796.35764097526
Balzac, Honoré de, 1799–1850 843.7

Balzac, Honoré de, 1799–1850—Criticism and interpretation 843.7
Balzic, Mario (Fictitious character) 813.54
Balzic, Mario (Fictitious character)—Fiction 813.54
Bamboo 584.9
Bamboo in art 704.9434
Banach algebras 512.55
Banach spaces 515.732
Bananas 634.772; 641.34772
Band music 784
Band music, Arranged 784
Band saws 684.083
Bandini, Arturo (Fictitious character) 813.52
Bands (Music) 784.8
Bandura 787.75
Bangkok (Thailand) 959.3
Bangkok (Thailand)—Description and travel 915.93
Bangkok (Thailand)—Guidebooks 915.93
Bangladesh 954.92
Bangladesh—Economic conditions 330.95492
Bangladesh—Economic policy 338.95492
Bangladesh—Foreign relations 327.5492
Bangladesh—History 954.92
Bangladesh—History—Revolution, 1971 954.92051
Bangladesh—Politics and government 954.92
Bangladesh—Politics and government—1971– 320.9549209047; 954.9205
Bangladesh—Social conditions 954.92
Banjo music 787.88
Bank accounts 332.1752
Bank accounts—Law and legislation 346.0821752
Bank consortia 332.1
Bank credit cards 332.178
Bank directors—Legal status, laws, etc. 346.0821092
Bank directors—Legal status, laws, etc.—United States 346.730821092
Bank examination 657.8333045
Bank examination—United States 657.83330450973
Bank examination—United States—Periodicals 332.1097305; 657.8333045097305
Bank failures 332.1
Bank failures—Law and legislation 346.082
Bank failures—Law and legislation—United States 344.73082; 346.73082
Bank failures—United States 332.10973
Bank holding companies 332.16
Bank investments 332.1754
Bank loans 332.1753
Bank loans—Law and legislation 346.0821753
Bank loans—Law and legislation—United States 346.730821753
Bank loans—United States 332.17530973
Bank management 332.1068; 332.12068
Bank management—Employee participation 331.7613321; 332.1068
Bank management—United States 332.1068
Bank management—United States—Handbooks, manuals, etc. 332.1068
Bank marketing 332.10688
Bank mergers 332.16
Bank mergers—United States 332.16; 346.7308216
Bank of Credit and Commerce International—Corrupt practices 364.168
Bank robberies 364.1552
Banking law 346.082
Banking law—Australia 346.94082
Banking law—Canada 346.71082
Banking law—Great Britain 346.41082
Banking law—India 346.54082

Banking law—Nigeria 346.669082
Banking law—Pakistan 346.5491082
Banking law—Philippines 346.599082
Banking law—Texas 346.764082
Banking law—United States 346.73082
Banking law—United States—Periodicals 346.7308205
Bankruptcy 332.75; 346.078
Bankruptcy—Australia 346.94078
Bankruptcy—Canada 346.71078
Bankruptcy—Great Britain 346.41078
Bankruptcy—Massachusetts 346.744078
Bankruptcy—Pennsylvania 346.748078
Bankruptcy—Scotland 346.411078
Bankruptcy—South Africa 346.68078
Bankruptcy—Taxation—United States 343.7305236
Bankruptcy—United States 332.750973; 346.73078
Bankruptcy—United States—Cases 346.730780264
Bankruptcy—United States—Digests 346.7307802648
Bankruptcy—United States—Forms 346.730780269
Bankruptcy—United States—Periodicals 346.7307805
Banks, Alan (Fictitious character) 823.914
Banks, Alan (Fictitious character)—Fiction 823.914
Banks and banking 332.1
Banks and banking—Accounting 657.8333
Banks and banking, Central 332.11
Banks and banking—Corrupt practices—Switzerland—History—20th century 364.168
Banks and banking—Customer services 332.10688
Banks and banking—Customer services—United States 332.170973
Banks and banking—Data processing 332.10285
Banks and banking—Deregulation 332.1
Banks and banking—Deregulation—United States 332.10973
Banks and banking—Developing countries 332.1091724
Banks and banking—Dictionaries 332.103
Banks and banking—Directories 332.1025
Banks and banking—Encyclopedias 332.103
Banks and banking—Europe 332.1094
Banks and banking—Europe, Eastern 332.10947
Banks and banking—Europe—History 332.1094
Banks and banking—European Economic Community countries 332.1094
Banks and banking, Foreign 332.15
Banks and banking, Foreign—Law and legislation 346.08215
Banks and banking, Foreign—Law and legislation—United States 346.7308215
Banks and banking—Great Britain 332.10941
Banks and banking—India 332.10954
Banks and banking—Insurance business 332.178
Banks and banking—Insurance business—United States 332.178
Banks and banking, International 332.15
Banks and banking, International—Law and legislation 341.7511
Banks and banking, International—Law and legislation—Periodicals 341.751105
Banks and banking—Islamic countries 332.10917671
Banks and banking—Nigeria 332.109669
Banks and banking—Periodicals 332.105
Banks and banking—Ratings 332.1
Banks and banking—Ratings—United States 332.10973
Banks and banking—Ratings—United States—Periodicals 332.10973021
Banks and banking—Records and correspondence—Law and legislation 346.082
Banks and banking—Records and correspondence—Law and legislation—United States 346.73082

Banks and banking—Russia (Federation) 332.10947
Banks and banking—Securities processing 332.178
Banks and banking—Securities processing—United States 332.178
Banks and banking—Switzerland 332.109494
Banks and banking—United States 332.10973
Banks and banking—United States—Accounting 657.83330973
Banks and banking—United States—Data processing 332.10285
Banks and banking—United States—Directories 332.102573
Banks and banking—United States—History 332.10973
Banks and banking—United States—Periodicals 332.1097305
Banks and banking—United States—State supervision 332.10973
Banks and banking—United States—Statistics 332.10973021
Banks and banking—United States—Statistics— Periodicals 332.10973021
Banned Books Week 025.213; 098.1; 363.31
Banneker, Benjamin, 1731–1806 520.92
Banners 929.92
Bantu-speaking peoples—Folklore 398.20899639
Baptism 234.161; 265.1
Baptism—Biblical teaching 234.161
Baptism—History 286.09
Baptism in the Holy Spirit 234.13
Baptist associations 286.06
Baptist church buildings 726.586
Baptist theological seminaries 230.0736
Baptist universities and colleges 378.0716
Baptists 286
Baptists—Doctrines 230.6
Baptists—History 286.09
Baptists—Missions 266.6
Baptists—Sermons 252.06
Baptists—United States—History 286.0973
Bar associations 340.06
Bar associations—United States 340.06073
Bar coding 006.42; 658.780285642
Bar coding equipment industry 338.4700642
Bar examinations—California 349.794076
Bar examinations—United States 349.73076
Bar mitzvah 296.4424
Baraga County (Mich.) 977.4973
Baraga County (Mich.)—Maps 912.774973
Baraka, Imamu Amiri, 1934– 818.5409
Baraka, Imamu Amiri, 1934– —Criticism and interpretation 818.5409
Barbados 972.981
Barbados—Guidebooks 917.298104
Barbecue cookery 641.5784; 641.76
Barber family 929.20973
Barbershop quartets 783.140922
Barbershop singing 783.14
Barbie dolls 688.7221; 688.72210979493
Barbie dolls—Collectibles—Catalogs 688.72210979493
Barbie dolls—Collectors and collecting—Catalogs 688.72210979493
Barcelona (Spain) 946.72
Barcelona (Spain)—Guidebooks 914.67204; 914.6720483
Barcelona (Spain)—Tours 914.67204; 914.6720483
Bard, Lily (Fictitious character) 813.54
Bards and bardism 808.814
Barefoot water skiing 797.35
Barges 386.229
Bark beetles 595.768

Barker family 929.20973
Barkley, Charles, 1963– 796.323092
Barlow, Charlie (Fictitious character) 823.914
Barlow, Charlie (Fictitious character)—Fiction 823.914
Barn owl 598.97
Barnaby, Chief Inspector (Fictitious character) 823.914
Barnaby, Chief Inspector (Fictitious character)—Fiction 823.914
Barnacles 595.35
Barnes County (N.D.) 978.432
Barnes County (N.D.)—Maps 912.78432
Barnes family 929.20973
Barns—United States 728.9220973
Barnum, P. T. (Phineas Taylor), 1810–1891 338.7617913092
Barometers 681.753
Barometers—History 681.753
Baron family (Fictitious characters) 813.54
Barotse cattle 636.28
Barrel piano 786.66
Barren County (Ky.)—Genealogy 929.376972
Barrett family 929.20973
Barrie, J. M. (James Matthew), 1860–1937 828.91209
Barrington, Stone (Fictitious character) 813.54
Barrington, Stone (Fictitious character)—Fiction 813.54
Barron County (Wis.) 977.518
Barron County (Wis.)—Maps 912.77518
Barry County (Mich.) 977.416
Barry County (Mich.)—Maps 912.77416
Bars (Desserts) 641.8654
Bars (Drinking establishments) 647.95
Bars (Drinking establishments)—England 647.9542
Bars (Drinking establishments) in literature 808.80355; 809.93355
Bars (Drinking establishments)—Management 647.95068
Bars (Drinking establishments)—New York (State)— New York 647.957471
Bars (Drinking establishments)—New York (State)— New York—Guidebooks 647.957471
Bars (Drinking establishments)—United States 647.9573
Bars (Drinking establishments)—United States— Guidebooks 647.9573
Bars (Engineering) 624.1774
Barsetshire (England : Imaginary place) 823.912
Barsetshire (England : Imaginary place)—Fiction 823.912
Bartending 641.874
Bartending—Handbooks, manuals, etc. 641.874
Barter 332.5
Barth, John 813.54
Barth, John—Criticism and interpretation 813.54
Barth, Karl, 1886–1968 230.044092
Barthelme, Donald 813.54
Barthelme, Donald—Criticism and interpretation 813.54
Barthes, Roland 410.92
Bartlett (Fictitious character : Hirsch) 823.914
Bartók, Béla, 1881–1945 780.92
Bartók, Béla, 1881–1945—Criticism and interpretation 780.92
Barton, Clara, 1821–1912 361.7634092
Baryons 539.72164
Baryonyx 567.912
Basal ganglia 573.86
Basal ganglia—Physiology 573.86; 612.825
Basal reading instruction 372.4
Basalt 552.26
Baseball 796.357

Baseball—Anecdotes 796.357
Baseball—Biography 796.357092
Baseball caps 391.43; 796.3570284
Baseball cards—Collectors and collecting—United States
  769.497963570973075; 796.357075
Baseball cards—Prices—United States—Catalogs
  769.497963570973075
Baseball cards—United States—Catalogs
  769.497963570973075
Baseball—Coaching 796.357077
Baseball—Collectibles 796.357075
Baseball—Collectibles—United States 796.3570973075
Baseball fields 796.357068
Baseball for children 796.357083; 796.35762
Baseball for children—Coaching 796.357083
Baseball—History 796.35709
Baseball insignia 796.357
Baseball—Law and legislation—United States 344.73099
Baseball—Literary collections 810.80355
Baseball managers 796.357092
Baseball managers—United States—Biography
  796.357092273
Baseball—Miscellanea 796.357
Baseball—New York (State)—New York—History
  796.357097471; 796.35764097471
Baseball players 796.357092
Baseball players—Rating of—United States 796.357
Baseball players—United States—Biography
  796.357092273
Baseball players—United States—Biography—
  Dictionaries 796.357092273
Baseball players—United States—Interviews
  796.357092273
Baseball—Records—United States 796.3570973
Baseball—Rules 796.35702022
Baseball—Scouting—United States 796.357
Baseball stories, American 813.0108355
Baseball teams 796.35764
Baseball teams—United States 796.357640973
Baseball teams—United States—History 796.357640973
Baseball—Training 796.357071
Baseball—United States 796.3570973
Baseball—United States—Anecdotes 796.3570973
Baseball—United States—History 796.3570973
Baseball—United States—History—19th century
  796.357097309034
Baseball—United States—History—20th century
  796.35709730904
Baseball—United States—Humor 796.3570973
Baseball—United States—Miscellanea 796.3570973
Baseball—United States—Periodicals 796.357097305
Baseball—United States—Statistics 796.3570973021
Baseball—United States—Statistics—Periodicals
  796.3570973021
Basenji 636.7536
Bashfulness 155.232
Basic Christian communities 250; 262.26
Basic education 370
Basic education—United States 370.973
Basic needs 306
BASIC Stamp computers 004.165
Basic training (Military education)—United States
  355.540973
Basic writing (Remedial education) 808.0420711
Basidiomycetes 579.59
Basins (Geology) 551.44; 551.8
BASIS-E (Information retrieval system) 025.04
BASIS (Information retrieval system) 025.0655146134
Basket making 746.412

Basketball 796.323
Basketball—Coaching 796.323077
Basketball—Defense 796.3232
Basketball fans 796.323
Basketball for children—Coaching 796.323083
Basketball for women 796.323082; 796.3238
Basketball—Offense 796.3232
Basketball players 796.323092
Basketball players—Biography 796.323092
Basketball players—United States—Biography
  796.323092273
Basketball—Rules 796.32302022
Basketball—Rules—Periodicals 796.3230202205
Basketball—Shooting 796.3232
Basketball teams 796.323092
Basketball—Training 796.323071
Basketball—United States 796.3230973
Basketball—United States—History 796.3230973
Basketball—United States—Periodicals 796.323097305
Baskets 746.412
Basnett, Andrew (Fictitious character) 823.912
Basnett, Andrew (Fictitious character)—Fiction 823.912
Basque language 499.92
Basques 305.89992
Bass-baritones 782.88
Bass fishing 799.1773
Basset hound 636.7536
Bast (Fictitious character) 813.54
Bast (Fictitious character)—Fiction 813.54
Bat mitzvah 296.4434
Bat watching 599.40723
Batá 786.94
Bataan (Philippines : Province), Battle of, 1942
  940.5425
Bates family 929.20973
Bates, Joshua T. (Fictitious character) 813.54
Bath (England) 942.398
Bath (England)—Antiquities, Roman 936.2398
Bath (England)—History 942.398
Bathing customs in literature 808.80355; 809.93355
Bathrooms 643.52; 747.78
Bathrooms—Design and construction 643.52
Bathrooms—Remodeling 643.520288
Baths, Roman 725.730937
Bathtub toys 688.72
Batik 746.662
Batman (Comic strip) 741.5973
Batman (Fictitious character) 741.5973
Batman (Fictitious character)—Comic books, strips, etc.
  741.5973
Batman (Fictitious character)—Fiction 813.54
Batman (Fictitious character) in mass media 700.451
Bats 599.4
Battered woman syndrome 616.85822
Battery chargers 621.312424
Battery industry 338.4762131242
Batting (Baseball) 796.35726
Battle-axes 623.441; 739.72
Battles 355.4; 904.7
Battles—Dictionaries 904.7
Battles in art 704.9493554
Battleships 359.8352; 623.8252
Baudelaire, Charles, 1821–1867 841.8
Baudelaire, Charles, 1821–1867—Criticism and
  interpretation 841.8
Baudelaire, Charles, 1821–1867—Translations into
  English 841.8
Baudrillard, Jean 194
Bauer, Tory (Fictitious character) 813.54

Bauer, Vicky (Fictitious character) 813.54
Bauhaus 709.04
Baum, L. Frank (Lyman Frank), 1856–1919 813.4
Baum, L. Frank (Lyman Frank), 1856–1919. Wizard of Oz 813.4
Bauxite 553.4926
Bavaria (Germany) 943.3
Bavaria (Germany)—Guidebooks 914.3304; 914.3304879; 914.330488
Bay County (Mich.) 977.447
Bay County (Mich.)—Maps 912.77447
Bayesian statistical decision theory 519.542
Bayeux tapestry 746.3942; 746.39442
Bayfield County (Wis.) 977.513
Bayfield County (Wis.)—Maps 912.77513
Bayles, China (Fictitious character) 813.54
Bayles, China (Fictitious character)—Fiction 813.54
Baylor, Breanna (Fictitious character) 813.54
Baynes family (Fictitious characters) 813.54
Baynes family (Fictitious characters)—Fiction 813.54
Bayreuther Festspiele 782.107943315
BBC Microcomputer 004.165
BBC Microcomputer—Programming 005.265
Be stars 523.87
Beach balls 688.7653; 796.53
Beach erosion—Monitoring 333.917; 551.36; 627.58
Beach party films 791.43653
Beach volleyball 796.325
Beaches 551.457
Beachy family 929.20973
Beadwork 745.582; 746.5
Beadwork—Patterns 745.582; 764.5041
Beagle (Dog breed) 636.7537
Beal family 929.20973
Beam dynamics 539.73
Beam optics 535.5
Bean family 929.20973
Bean (Fictitious character : Card) 813.54
Beanbag toys 688.724; 745.5924
Beanie Babies (Trademark) 688.724; 745.5924
Beanie Babies (Trademark)—Collectors and collecting 688.724
Beanie Babies (Trademark)—Collectors and collecting—United States—Catalogs 688.724
Beanie Buddies (Trademark) 688.724; 745.5924
Beans 641.3565
Bear (Fictitious character : Blackstone) 823.914
Bear, Goldy (Fictitious character) 813.54
Bear, Goldy (Fictitious character)—Fiction 813.54
Bear watching 599.780723
Bearded collie 636.7374
Bearded dragons (Reptiles) 597.955
Bearded dragons (Reptiles) as pets 639.3955
Bearden, Romare, 1911–1988 709.2; 759.13
Beardsley, Aubrey, 1872–1898 760.092
Beardsley, Aubrey, 1872–1898—Criticism and interpretation 741.092; 741.6092; 760.092
Bearings (Machinery) 621.822
Bearpaw, Molly (Fictitious character) 813.54
Bearpaw, Molly (Fictitious character)—Fiction 813.54
Bears 599.78
Beast of Exmoor 001.944
Beat generation 810.80054
Beatitudes 241.53
Beatitudes—Criticism, interpretation, etc. 241.53
Beatitudes—Devotional literature 241.53
Beatles 782.421660922
Beatles—Collectibles—Prices—United States 782.421660922

Beatles—Discography 016.782421660922; 782.421660922
Beatles—History—Chronology 782.421660922
Beatles—Pictorial works 782.421660922
Beaumont, Francis, 1584–1616 822.3
Beaumont, Francis, 1584–1616—Criticism and interpretation 822.3
Beaumont, J. P. (Fictitious character) 813.54
Beaumont, J. P. (Fictitious character)—Fiction 813.54
Beauty contests 791.6
Beauty culture 646.72
Beauty culture—Vocational guidance 646.72023
Beauty, Personal 646.7; 646.72; 646.726
Beauty shop supplies industry 338.4764672
Beauty shops 646.72
Beauty shops—Management 646.72068
Beauvoir, Simone de, 1908– 848.91409
Beauvoir, Simone de, 1908– —Criticism and interpretation 848.91409
Beaver County (Pa.)—Genealogy 929.374892
Beaverbrook, Max Aitken, Baron, 1879–1964 941.084092
Beavers 599.37
Bebb, Leo (Fictitious character) 813.54
Bech, Henry (Fictitious character) 813.54
Beck, Martin (Fictitious character) 839.7374
Beck, Martin (Fictitious character)—Fiction 839.7374
Becker County (Minn.) 977.684
Becker County (Minn.)—Maps 912.77684
Beckett, Samuel, 1906– 842.914; 848.91409
Beckett, Samuel, 1906– —Criticism and interpretation 848.91409
Beckett, Samuel, 1906– —Dramatic production 792.95
Beckett, Samuel, 1906– —Dramatic works 842.914
Beckett, Samuel, 1906– . En attendant Godot 842.914
Beckett, Samuel, 1906– —Fictional works 843.914
Beckwourth, James Pierson, 1798–1866 978.02092
Bed and breakfast accommodations 647.94
Bed and breakfast accommodations—California 647.9479403
Bed and breakfast accommodations—California—Guidebooks 647.9479403
Bed and breakfast accommodations—Canada 647.947103
Bed and breakfast accommodations—England 647.944203
Bed and breakfast accommodations—England—Guidebooks 647.944203
Bed and breakfast accommodations—France 647.944403
Bed and breakfast accommodations—France—Guidebooks 647.944403
Bed and breakfast accommodations—Italy 647.944503
Bed and breakfast accommodations—Italy—Guidebooks 647.944503
Bed and breakfast accommodations—Middle Atlantic States 647.947403
Bed and breakfast accommodations—Middle Atlantic States—Guidebooks 647.947403
Bed and breakfast accommodations—New England 647.947403
Bed and breakfast accommodations—New England—Guidebooks 647.947403
Bed and breakfast accommodations—Southern States 647.947503
Bed and breakfast accommodations—Southern States—Guidebooks 647.947503
Bed and breakfast accommodations—Texas 647.9476403

Bed and breakfast accommodations—Texas—
  Guidebooks 647.9476403
Bed and breakfast accommodations—United States
  647.947303
Bed and breakfast accommodations—United States—
  Directories 647.947303
Bed and breakfast accommodations—United States—
  Guidebooks 647.947303
Bedding 643.53
Bede, the Venerable, Saint, 673–735 878.0209
Bedford County (Pa.)—Genealogy 929.374871
Bedford County (Tenn.)—Genealogy 929.3768583
Bedouins—Saudi Arabia 305.89272
Bedroom furniture industry 338.476841
Bedrooms 747.77
Bedrooms—Religious aspects 291.44
Beds 645.4
Beds (Gardens) 635.962
Bedsores 616.545
Bedsores—Prevention 616.545
Bedtime 649.6
Bedtime prayers 242.2; 291.43
Bee attacks 595.79915
Bee culture 638.1
Bee, Jane (Fictitious character) 813.54
Bee products industry 338.17816
Beef 641.362
Beef cattle 636.213
Beef cattle—Feeding and feeds 636.213
Beef industry 338.176213
Beef, William (Fictitious character) 823.912
Beef, William (Fictitious character)—Fiction 823.912
Beepers (Pagers) 621.3892
Beer 641.23
Beer bottles 666.192
Beer industry 338.4766342
Bees 595.799
Beethoven, Ludwig van, 1770–1827 780.92
Beethoven, Ludwig van, 1770–1827—Criticism and
  interpretation 780.92
Beethoven, Ludwig van, 1770–1827. Sonatas, piano
  786.2183092
Beetles 595.76
Begonias 583.627
Behan, Brendan 822.914
Behavior disorders in children 305.90824; 618.9289
Behavior disorders in children—Treatment 618.928914
Behavior genetics 155.7; 591.5
Behavior modification 153.85; 370.153; 371.393
Behavior modification—United States 370.153
Behavior therapists 616.89142092
Behavior therapy 616.89142
Behavior therapy for children 618.9289142
Behavior therapy—Periodicals 616.8914205
Behavioral assessment 371.264
Behavioral optometry 617.75
Behavioral scientists 300.92
Behavioral toxicology 616.89071
Behaviorism (Political science) 320.019
Behaviorism (Psychology) 150.1943
Behn, Aphra, 1640–1689 822.4; 828.409
Behn, Aphra, 1640–1689—Criticism and interpretation
  828.409
Beidao, 1949– 895.1152
Beidao, 1949– —Translations into English 895.1152
Beijing (China) 951.156
Beijing (China)—Guidebooks 915.115604; 915.11560459;
  915.1156046
Beijing (China)—Pictorial works 951.15600222

Beijing (China)—Social life and customs 951.156
Bektashi 297.48
Belacqua, Lyra (Fictitious character) 823.914
Belarus 947.8
Belarus—History 947.8
Belarusian poetry 891.7991; 891.7991008
Belching 612.32
Beleriand (Imaginary place) 823.912
Belfast (Northern Ireland) 941.67
Belfast (Northern Ireland)—History 941.67
Belfast (Northern Ireland)—Politics and government
  941.67
Belgium 949.3
Belgium—Description and travel 914.9304; 914.930444
Belgium—Guidebooks 914.9304; 914.930444
Belgium—Social life and customs 949.3
Belgium—Social life and customs—19th century
  949.303
Belief and doubt 121.6
Belief and doubt in literature 808.80384
Belize 972.82
Belize—Guidebooks 917.28204; 917.282045
Belize—History 972.82
Belize—Maps for children 912.7282
Bell, Alexander Graham, 1847–1922 621.385092
Bell family 929.20973
Bellow, Saul 813.52
Bellow, Saul—Criticism and interpretation 813.52
Bells 786.8848
Belly dance 793.3
Belmont County (Ohio) 977.193
Belmont County (Ohio)—Genealogy 929.377193
Belt drives 621.852
Beltane 133.43; 299; 299.16; 394.262
Beltrami County (Minn.) 977.682
Beltrami County (Minn.)—Maps 912.77682
Belzec (Concentration camp) 940.5318
Ben-Gurion, David, 1886–1973 956.9405092
Benbow, Angela (Fictitious character) 813.54
Benbow, Angela (Fictitious character)—Fiction 813.54
Bench vises 621.992
Benchmarking (Management) 658.4013
Bender-Gestalt Test 155.284
Benedetti, Niccolo (Fictitious character) 813.54
Benedetti, Niccolo (Fictitious character)—Fiction
  813.54
Benedict, Saint, Abbot of Monte Cassino 271.1092
Benedict, Saint, Abbot of Monte Cassino. Regula
  255.106
Benedictines 271.1
Benedictines—Rules 255.106
Benedictines—Spiritual life 255.1
Benedictions 296.45
Beneficial insects 595.7163
Benefit performances 790.2
Benelux countries 949.2
Benelux countries—Guidebooks 914.9204; 914.920473
Beneš, Edvard, 1884–1948 943.703092
Bengal (India) 954.14
Bengal (India)—Civilization 954.14
Bengal (India)—History 954.14
Bengal (India)—Politics and government 954.14
Bengali poetry 891.441; 891.441008
Bengali poetry—Bangladesh 891.441008095492
Bengali poetry—Bangladesh—Translations into English
  891.441008095492
Bengali poetry—Translations into English 891.441008
Bengali (South Asian people)—Folklore 398.20899144
Benign prostatic hyperplasia 616.65

Benjamin, Walter, 1892–1940 838.91209
Benjamin, Walter, 1892–1940—Criticism and
    interpretation 838.91209
Benji (Dog) 791.430280929
Benji (Fictitious character : Camp) 791.4375
Benn, Tony, 1925– 941.085092
Benn, Tony, 1925– —Diaries 941.085092
Bennett, Arnold, 1867–1931 823.912
Bennett, Arnold, 1867–1931—Criticism and
    interpretation 823.912
Bennett family 929.20973
Bennett, Lilly (Fictitious character) 813.54
Bennett, Lilly (Fictitious character)—Fiction 813.54
Bennett, Reid (Fictitious character) 813.54
Bennett, Reid (Fictitious character)—Fiction 813.54
Benny the Breakdown Truck (Fictitious character)
    823.914
Benson County (N.D.) 978.439
Benson County (N.D.)—Maps 912.78439
Bentham, Jeremy, 1748–1832 192
Benthos 551.46
Bento cookery 641.5952
Benton County (Iowa) 977.761
Benton County (Iowa)—Maps 912.77761
Benton County (Mo.) 977.8493
Benton County (Mo.)—Maps 912.778493
Benton, Thomas Hart, 1889–1975 759.13
Benzodiazepines 615.7882
Beothuk Indians 971.800497
Beowulf 829.3
Beowulf clusters (Computer systems) 004.35
Beowulf—Concordances 829.3
Beowulf—Versification 829.3
Berber poetry 893.3
Berberova, Nina Nikolaevna 891.7342
Berberova, Nina Nikolaevna—Translations into English
    891.7342
Berbers in literature 808.8035203933; 809.9335203933
Bereavement 155.937
Bereavement in children 155.937083
Bereavement—Psychological aspects 155.937
Bereavement—Religious aspects 291.442
Bereavement—Religious aspects—Christianity 248.866
Beresford, Tommy (Fictitious character) 823.912
Beresford, Tommy (Fictitious character)—Fiction
    823.912
Berg, Alban, 1885–1935 780.92
Berg, Alban, 1885–1935—Criticism and interpretation
    780.92
Bergen County (N.J.)—Maps 912.74921
Bergerettes (Songs) 782.43
Bergman, Ingmar, 1918– 791.430233092
Bergman, Ingmar, 1918– —Criticism and interpretation
    791.430233092
Bergson, Henri, 1859–1941 194
Berit milah 296.4422
Berkeley, George, 1685–1753 192
Berks County (Pa.)—Genealogy 929.374816
Berkshire Hills (Mass.) 974.41
Berlin, Battle of, 1945 940.54213155
Berlin (Germany) 943.155
Berlin (Germany)—Guidebooks 914.315504;
    914.315504879; 914.31550488
Berlin (Germany)—History 943.155
Berlin (Germany)—History—Bombardment, 1943–1944
    940.54213155
Berlin (Germany)—History—1945–1990 943.155087
Berlin (Germany)—History—Blockade, 1948–1949
    943.1550874

Berlin (Germany)—Social life and customs 943.155
Berlin, Irving, 1888– 782.14092; 782.42164092
Berlin Wall, Berlin, Germany, 1961–1989 943.155087
Berlioz, Hector, 1803–1869 780.92
Bermuda Islands 972.99
Bermuda Islands—Guidebooks 917.29904
Bermuda Triangle 001.94
Bernard family 929.20973
Bernard, of Clairvaux, Saint, 1090 or 91–1153 271.1202
Bernardin, Joseph Louis, 1928– 282.092
Bernese mountain dog 636.73
Bernhardt, Sarah, 1844–1923 792.028092
Bernstein, Leonard, 1918– 780.92
Berries 634.7
Berry family 929.20973
Bert (Fictitious character : Henson) 791.4375; 791.4575
Best books 011.73
Best books—United States—Bibliography 015.73
Best friends 302.34
Best sellers 381.45002
Beta decay 539.7523
Bethany, Tom (Fictitious character) 813.54
Bethany, Tom (Fictitious character)—Fiction 813.54
Bethune, Mary McLeod, 1875–1955 370.92
Better business bureaus 381.34
Betweenness relations (Mathematics) 511.33
Beverage industry 380.1456412; 381.456412
Beverages 641.2; 641.87
Bewley family 929.20973
Bewley family—Periodicals 929.20973
Bhagavadgītā 294.5924
Bhagavadgītā—Commentaries 294.5924047
Bhagavadgītā—Criticism, interpretation, etc.
    294.5924046
Bharata natyam 793.31954
Bhattacharya, Bhabani 823.914
Bhattacharya, Bhabani—Criticism and interpretation
    823.914
Bhopal Union Carbide Plant Disaster, Bhopal, India,
    1984 363.179
Bhutto, Benazir 954.9105092
Bhutto, Zulfikar Ali 342.5491062; 954.9105092
Bias-free language 306.44; 418; 808.027
Bible 220
Bible and evolution 231.7652
Bible—Antiquities 220.9; 220.93
Bible as literature 220.66; 809.93522
Bible—Bibliography 016.22
Bible—Biography 220.92
Bible—Biography—Dictionaries 220.92
Bible—Biography—Meditations 220.92
Bible—Biography—Sermons 220.92
Bible—Biography—Textbooks 220.92
Bible—Canon 220.12
Bible colleges 220.0711
Bible—Commentaries 220.7; 220.77
Bible—Concordances, English 220.52033
Bible—Concordances, English—New International
    220.520813
Bible—Concordances, English—New King James
    220.5208
Bible crafts 268.432
Bible—Criticism, interpretation, etc. 220.6
Bible—Criticism, interpretation, etc.—History 220.609
Bible—Criticism, interpretation, etc.—History—Early
    church, ca. 30–600 220.609015
Bible—Devotional literature 242.5
Bible—Dictionaries 220.3
Bible. English 220.52

Bible. N.T. Peter, 1st—Commentaries 227.9207; 227.92077

Bible. N.T. Peter, 1st—Criticism, interpretation, etc. 227.9206

Bible. N.T. Peter, 2nd 227.93

Bible. N.T. Peter, 2nd—Commentaries 227.93077

Bible. N.T. Peter—Commentaries 227.92077

Bible. N.T. Philippians 227.6

Bible. N.T. Philippians—Commentaries 227.607; 227.6077

Bible. N.T. Philippians—Criticism, interpretation, etc. 227.606

Bible. N.T. Philippians—Meditations 227.606

Bible. N.T. Revelation 228

Bible. N.T. Revelation—Commentaries 228.07; 228.077

Bible. N.T. Revelation—Criticism, interpretation, etc. 228.06

Bible. N.T. Revelation—Prophecies 228.015

Bible. N.T. Romans 227.1

Bible. N.T. Romans—Commentaries 227.107; 227.1077

Bible. N.T. Romans—Criticism, interpretation, etc. 227.106

Bible. N.T.—Study and teaching 225.071

Bible. N.T.—Textbooks 225.61

Bible. N.T.—Theology 230

Bible. N.T. Thessalonians 227.81

Bible. N.T. Thessalonians—Commentaries 227.8107; 227.81077

Bible. O.T. 221

Bible. O.T. Amos 224.8

Bible. O.T. Amos—Commentaries 224.8077

Bible. O.T.—Antiquities 221.93

Bible. O.T.—Biography 221.922

Bible. O.T.—Canon 221.12

Bible. O.T. Chronicles 222.6

Bible. O.T. Chronicles—Commentaries 222.6077

Bible. O.T. Chronicles—Criticism, interpretation, etc. 222.606

Bible. O.T.—Chronology 221.95

Bible. O.T.—Commentaries 221.7; 221.77

Bible. O.T.—Criticism, interpretation, etc. 221.6; 221.66

Bible. O.T.—Criticism, interpretation, etc.—History 221.609

Bible. O.T.—Criticism, interpretation, etc.—History— 20th century 221.60904

Bible. O.T.—Criticism, Textual 221.4046

Bible. O.T. Daniel 224.5

Bible. O.T. Daniel—Commentaries 224.507; 224.5077

Bible. O.T. Daniel—Criticism, interpretation, etc. 224.506

Bible. O.T. Daniel—Prophecies 224.5015

Bible. O.T. Deuteronomy 222.15

Bible. O.T. Deuteronomy—Commentaries 222.1507; 222.15077

Bible. O.T. Deuteronomy—Criticism, interpretation, etc. 222.1506

Bible. O.T. Ecclesiastes 223.8

Bible. O.T. Ecclesiastes—Commentaries 223.807; 223.8077

Bible. O.T. Ecclesiastes—Criticism, interpretation, etc. 223.806

Bible. O.T. Ecclesiastes—Meditations 223.806

Bible. O.T. Esther 222.9

Bible. O.T. Esther—Commentaries 222.9077

Bible. O.T. Esther—Criticism, interpretation, etc. 222.906

Bible. O.T. Exodus 222.12

Bible. O.T. Exodus—Commentaries 222.1207; 222.12077

Bible. O.T. Exodus—Criticism, interpretation, etc. 222.1206

Bible. O.T. Ezekiel 224.4

Bible. O.T. Ezekiel—Commentaries 224.407; 224.4077

Bible. O.T. Ezekiel—Criticism, interpretation, etc. 224.406

Bible. O.T. Ezra 222.7

Bible. O.T. Ezra—Commentaries 222.707

Bible. O.T. Genesis 222.11

Bible. O.T. Genesis I-XI 222.11

Bible. O.T. Genesis I-XI—Criticism, interpretation, etc. 222.1106

Bible. O.T. Genesis—Commentaries 222.1107; 222.11077

Bible. O.T. Genesis—Criticism, interpretation, etc. 222.1106

Bible. O.T. Genesis—History of Biblical events 222.11095

Bible. O.T. Genesis—Study and teaching 222.110071

Bible. O.T. Greek—Versions 221.48

Bible. O.T. Greek—Versions—Septuagint 221.48

Bible. O.T.—Hermeneutics 221.601

Bible. O.T.—History of Biblical events 221.95

Bible. O.T.—History of contemporary events 221.95

Bible. O.T.—Homiletical use 251

Bible. O.T. Hosea 224.6

Bible. O.T. Hosea—Commentaries 224.607

Bible. O.T. Hosea—Criticism, interpretation, etc. 224.606

Bible. O.T.—Introductions 221.61

Bible. O.T. Isaiah I-XXXIX—Commentaries 224.107; 224.1077

Bible. O.T. Isaiah XL-LV—Criticism, interpretation, etc. 224.106

Bible. O.T. Isaiah XL-LXVI 224.1

Bible. O.T. Isaiah XL-LXVI—Commentaries 224.107; 224.1077

Bible. O.T. Isaiah—Commentaries 224.107; 224.1077

Bible. O.T. Isaiah—Criticism, interpretation, etc. 224.106

Bible. O.T. Jeremiah 224.2

Bible. O.T. Jeremiah—Commentaries 224.207; 224.2077

Bible. O.T. Jeremiah—Criticism, interpretation, etc. 224.206

Bible. O.T. Job 223.1

Bible. O.T. Job—Commentaries 223.107; 223.1077

Bible. O.T. Job—Criticism, interpretation, etc. 223.106

Bible. O.T. Job—Meditations 223.106

Bible. O.T. Jonah 224.92

Bible. O.T. Jonah—Commentaries 224.9207; 224.92077

Bible. O.T. Jonah—Criticism, interpretation, etc. 224.9206

Bible. O.T. Joshua 222.2

Bible. O.T. Joshua—Commentaries 222.207; 222.2077

Bible. O.T. Joshua—Criticism, interpretation, etc. 222.206

Bible. O.T. Judges 222.32

Bible. O.T. Judges—Commentaries 222.3207

Bible. O.T. Kings 222.5

Bible. O.T. Kings—Commentaries 222.507; 222.5077

Bible. O.T.—Language, style 221.66

Bible. O.T. Leviticus 222.13

Bible. O.T. Leviticus—Commentaries 222.1307; 222.13077

Bible. O.T.—Meditations 242.5

Bible. O.T. Minor Prophets 224.9

Bible. O.T. Minor Prophets—Commentaries 224.907; 224.9077

Bible. O.T. Minor Prophets—Criticism, interpretation, etc. 224.906

Bible. O.T. Numbers 222.14
Bible. O.T. Numbers—Commentaries 222.1407; 222.14077
Bible. O.T. Pentateuch 222.1
Bible. O.T. Pentateuch—Commentaries 222.107; 222.1077
Bible. O.T. Pentateuch—Criticism, interpretation, etc. 222.106
Bible. O.T. Pentateuch—Meditations 222.106
Bible. O.T. Pentateuch—Sermons 296.47
Bible. O.T. Prophets 224
Bible. O.T. Prophets—Criticism, interpretation, etc. 224.06
Bible. O.T. Prophets—Introductions 224.061
Bible. O.T. Proverbs 223.7
Bible. O.T. Proverbs—Commentaries 223.707; 223.7077
Bible. O.T. Proverbs—Criticism, interpretation, etc. 223.706
Bible. O.T. Psalms 223.2
Bible. O.T. Psalms XXIII 223.2
Bible. O.T. Psalms XXIII—Meditations 223.206
Bible. O.T. Psalms—Commentaries 223.207; 223.2077
Bible. O.T. Psalms—Criticism, interpretation, etc. 223.206
Bible. O.T. Psalms—Devotional literature 223.206
Bible. O.T. Psalms—Devotional use 242.2
Bible. O.T. Psalms—Liturgical use 264.15
Bible. O.T. Psalms—Paraphrases, English 223.205209
Bible. O.T. Psalms—Sermons 223.206
Bible. O.T. Ruth 222.35
Bible. O.T. Ruth—Commentaries 222.3507; 222.35077
Bible. O.T. Ruth—Criticism, interpretation, etc. 222.3506
Bible. O.T. Samuel 222.4
Bible. O.T. Samuel—Commentaries 222.4077
Bible. O.T. Samuel—Criticism, interpretation, etc. 222.406
Bible. O.T.—Sermons 252
Bible. O.T. Song of Solomon 223.9
Bible. O.T. Song of Solomon—Commentaries 223.907; 223.9077
Bible. O.T. Song of Solomon—Criticism, interpretation, etc. 223.906
Bible. O.T. Song of Solomon—Sermons 223.906
Bible. O.T.—Study and teaching 221.071
Bible. O.T.—Textbooks 221.61
Bible. O.T.—Theology 230.0411
Bible—Outlines, syllabi, etc. 220.0202
Bible—Paraphrases, English 220.9505
Bible plays, American 812.54
Bible—Prophecies 220.15
Bible—Prophecies—End of the world 220.15; 236.9
Bible—Prophecies—International organization 220.15; 236.9
Bible—Prophecies—Middle East 220.15; 236.9
Bible—Reference editions 220.5
Bible stories 220.9505
Bible stories, English 220.9505
Bible stories, English—N.T. 225.9505
Bible stories, English—O.T. 221.9505
Bible stories, English—O.T. Genesis 222.1109505
Bible—Structuralist criticism 220.6
Bible—Study and teaching 220.071
Bible—Study and teaching—Catholic Church 220.071
Bible—Theology 230.041
Bible—Versions 220.4; 220.5
Bibliographers 010.92
Bibliographical citations 025.324
Bibliographical services 025.52

Bibliography 010
Bibliography, Critical 010.42
Bibliography—Dictionaries 010.3
Bibliography—Methodology 010.44
Bibliography, National 015
Bibliography, National—Bibliography of bibliographies 016.015
Bibliography of bibliographies 016.01; 016.016
Bibliometrics 010.727
Bibliotherapy 615.8516
Bibliotherapy for children 618.9289166
Biculturalism—Canada 306.4460971
Bicycle commuting 388.3472; 388.4132
Bicycle helmets 629.2272028
Bicycle industry 388.3472
Bicycle messengers 384
Bicycle motocross 796.62
Bicycle police 363.232
Bicycle racing 796.62
Bicycle stores 381.456292272
Bicycle touring 796.64
Bicycle touring—California—San Francisco Bay Area—Guidebooks 917.94604; 917.9460453; 917.9460454
Bicycle touring—Connecticut—Guidebooks 917.4604; 917.460443; 917.460444
Bicycle touring—Europe—Guidebooks 914.04; 914.04559; 914.0456
Bicycle touring—Massachusetts 796.6409744
Bicycle touring—Massachusetts—Cape Cod—Guidebooks 917.449204; 917.44920443; 917.44920444
Bicycle touring—Massachusetts—Guidebooks 917.4404; 917.440443; 917.440444
Bicycle touring—New England 796.640974
Bicycle touring—New England—Guidebooks 917.404; 917.40443; 917.40444
Bicycle touring—New Jersey—Guidebooks 917.4904; 917.490443; 917.490444
Bicycle touring—New York Metropolitan Area—Guidebooks 917.47104; 917.4710443; 917.4710444
Bicycle touring—New York (State)—Long Island—Guidebooks 917.4704; 917.470444; 917.472104; 917.47210443; 917.47210444
Bicycle touring—Pennsylvania—Guidebooks 917.4804; 917.480443; 917.480444
Bicycle touring—Rhode Island—Guidebooks 917.4504; 917.450443; 917.450444
Bicycle touring—United States 796.640973
Bicycle touring—United States—Guidebooks 917.304; 917.304929; 917.304931
Bicycle touring—Vermont—Guidebooks 917.4304; 917.430443; 917.430444
Bicycle touring—Washington Metropolitan Area—Guidebooks 917.5304; 917.530441; 917.530442
Bicycle touring—Washington Region—Guidebooks 917.5304; 917.530441; 917.530442
Bicycle touring—Washington (State) 796.6409797
Bicycle touring—Washington (State)—Guidebooks 917.9704; 917.970443; 917.970444
Bicycle trails 388.12
Bicycle Woman (Fictitious character) 741.5973
Bicycles 388.3472; 629.2272; 796.6
Bicycles—Maintenance and repair 629.28772
Bicycles—Maintenance and repair—Handbooks, manuals, etc. 629.28772
Bifurcation theory 515.35
Big band music 784.48
Big band music—History and criticism 784.4809
Big bang theory 523.18
Big Bend National Park (Tex.) 976.4932

Big Bend National Park (Tex.)—Guidebooks 917.64932
Big Bird (Fictitious character) 791.4375; 791.4575
Big business 338.644
Big business—Great Britain 338.6440941
Big business—United States 338.6440973
Big business—United States—History 338.6440973
Big game fishing 799.16
Big game hunting 799.26
Big game hunting—North America 799.26097
Big Mike (Fictitious character) 813.54
Big Mike (Fictitious character)—Fiction 813.54
Bighorn sheep 599.6497
Bilayer lipid membranes 572.57
Bildungsroman 833.009
Bile ducts—Surgery 617.5567
Biliary tract—Surgery 617.556
Bilingual authors 809.89
Bilingual communication in organizations 306.449;
    658.45
Bilingualism 306.446; 404.2
Bilingualism in children 404.2083
Bill drafting 328.373
Bill drafting—United States 328.730773
Billiard parlors 725.84; 794.73
Billiards 794.72
Billionaires 305.5234
Bills, Legislative 328.37
Bills, Legislative—Maryland 348.75201
Bills, Legislative—Oklahoma—Digests 348.76601
Bills of exchange 332.77
Bills of lading 341.75668
Billy, the Kid 364.1552092
Bilo 786.8843
Bindery records 025.7
Bingham family 929.20973
Binks, Jar Jar (Fictitious character) 791.4375
Binoculars 681.4125
Binton, Margaret (Fictitious character) 813.54
Binton, Margaret (Fictitious character)—Fiction 813.54
Biochemical engineering 660.63
Biochemical genetics 572.8
Biochemistry 572; 612.015
Biochemistry—Examinations, questions, etc. 572.076;
    612.015076
Biochemistry—Handbooks, manuals, etc. 572
Biochemistry—Outlines, syllabi, etc. 572
Biochemistry—Periodicals 572.05
Biochemistry—Technique 572.36
Biochips 572.36; 610.28
Bioclimatology 577.22
Biodegradation 571.9448
Biodiesel fuels 662.669
Bioelectrochemistry 572.437
Bioelectronics 572.437
Bioenergetics 572.43; 577.13
Bioengineering 660.6
Bioethics 174.957
Biofeedback training 615.851
Biofilms 579.17
Biogas 665.776
Biogeochemical cycles 577.14
Biogeochemistry 577.14
Biogeography 578.09
Biographical films 791.43651; 920
Biographical television programs 791.45651; 920
Biography 920
Biography—Middle Ages, 500–1500 920.00902
Biography—19th century 920.009034
Biography—20th century 920.00904

Biography—20th century—Dictionaries 920.0090403
Biography as a literary form 808.06692
Biography—Dictionaries 920.003
Bioinorganic chemistry 572.51
Biointensive gardening 635.0484
Biolinguistics 401; 612.78
Biological control systems 571.7
Biological diversity 333.95; 577; 578.7; 591.7
Biological diversity conservation 333.9516
Biological diversity conservation—Awards 333.9516079
Biological diversity conservation—India 333.95160954
Biological diversity conservation—Law and legislation
    341.762
Biological diversity conservation—Law and legislation—
    United States 346.730469516
Biological diversity conservation—United States
    333.95160973
Biological diversity—Periodicals 333.9505
Biological invasions 577.18
Biological laboratories 570.72
Biological models 570.228
Biological monitoring 615.902
Biological psychiatry 616.89
Biological response modifiers 615.7; 616.994061
Biological response modifiers—Therapeutic use
    616.994061
Biological rhythms 571.77; 612.022
Biological specimens 570.74
Biological specimens—Collection and preservation
    570.75; 570.752
Biological stations 333.95
Biological systems 571; 577
Biological systems—Computer simulation 571.0133
Biological systems—Mathematical models 571.011;
    571.015118
Biological transport 571.64
Biological transport, Active 571.64
Biological warfare 358.38
Biological weapons 623.4594
Biologicals 615.3
Biologists 570.92
Biology 570
Biology—Classification 570.12; 578.012
Biology—Data processing 570.285
Biology—Dictionaries 570.3
Biology, Economic 578.6
Biology—Examinations 570.76
Biology—Examinations, questions, etc. 570.76
Biology, Experimental 570.724; 571.538
Biology—Experiments 570.724; 570.78
Biology—History 570.9
Biology in motion pictures 791.4366
Biology—Laboratory manuals 570.78
Biology—Mathematical models 570.15118
Biology—Outlines, syllabi, etc. 570
Biology—Periodicals 570.5
Biology—Philosophy 570.1
Biology—Research 570.72
Biology—Study and teaching 570.71
Biology—Study and teaching (Secondary) 570.712
Biology—Technique 570.28
Bioluminescence 572.4358
Bioluminescence assay 572.36
Biomagnetism 612.01442
Biomass chemicals 661.8
Biomass—Combustion 662.88
Biomass conversion 333.7938
Biomass energy 333.9539; 662.88
Biomass gasification 665.776

Biomathematics 570.151
Biomechanics 571.43; 612.76
Biomedical engineering 610.28
Biomedical engineering—Periodicals 610.28
Biomedical materials 610.284
Biomedical materials—Periodicals 610.284
Biometry 570.15195
Biomimetics 572.011
Biomineralization 572.51; 573.76451
Biomolecules 572
Biomolecules—Analysis 572.36
Biomolecules—Separation 660.6
Biomolecules—Structure 572.33
Bionics 003.5
Biopharmaceutics 615.1; 615.7
Biophysicists 571.4092
Biophysics 571.4
Biopolymers 572; 572.33
Bioreactors 660.6
Bioremediation 628.5
Biosensors 610.284
Biospeleology 578.7584
Biosphere 333.95
Biosphere reserves 333.9516
Biosynthesis 572.45
Biotechnological microorganisms 660.62
Biotechnology 660.6
Biotechnology—Abstracts—Periodicals 660.605
Biotechnology—Dictionaries 660.603
Biotechnology industries 338.470606
Biotechnology industries—Law and legislation
    343.0786606; 346.038
Biotechnology industries—Law and legislation—United
    States 343.730786606; 346.73038
Biotechnology laboratories 341.76754
Biotechnology—Moral and ethical aspects 174.25
Biotechnology—Periodicals 660.605
Biotechnology projects 660.6078
Biotechnology—Technique 660.6
Biotechnology—Technology transfer 338.476606
Biotechnology—United States—Patents 346.730486
Biotelemetry 639.0284
Bioterrorism 303.625; 364.1
Biotic communities 577.82
Bipedidae 597.948
Biphenyl compounds 547.613
Bipolar outflows (Astrophysics) 523.88
Bipolar transistors 621.3815282
Birbynė 788.62
Birbynė ensembles 785.862
Birbynė music 788.62
Birch 583.48
Birch, Jefferson (Fictitious character) 813.54
Birch, Jefferson (Fictitious character)—Fiction 813.54
Bird attracting 598.07234
Bird banding 598.07232
Bird breeders 636.6092
Bird feeders 639.978
Bird feeders—Design and construction 690.892
Bird, Larry, 1956– 796.323092
Bird refuges 333.958
Bird watching 598.07234
Bird watching—United States 598.0723473
Birdhouses 636.50831; 690.8927; 728.927
Birdhouses—Design and construction 690.8927
Birding sites 598.07234
Birds 598
Birds—Africa, Southern 598.0968
Birds—Africa, Southern—Identification 598.0968

Birds—Anatomy 571.318
Birds—Australia 598.0994
Birds—Behavior 598.15
Birds—Ecology 598.17
Birds—Embryology 571.8618
Birds—Europe 598.094
Birds—Europe—Identification 598.094
Birds—Evolution 598.138
Birds—Feeding and feeds 598.07234
Birds—Flight 598.15
Birds—Folklore 398.24528
Birds—Food 598.153
Birds, Fossil 568
Birds—Great Britain 598.0941
Birds in art 704.94328
Birds in art—Exhibitions 704.94328
Birds in literature 808.803628; 809.933628
Birds—India 598.0954
Birds—Latin America 598.098
Birds—Migration 598.1568
Birds—Miscellanea 598
Birds—Nests 598.1564
Birds—New Zealand 598.0993
Birds—New Zealand—Identification 598.0993
Birds—North America 598.097
Birds—North America—Identification 598.097
Birds of prey 598.9
Birds of prey—North America 598.9097
Birds—Parasites 571.99918
Birds—Physiology 571.18
Birds—Pictorial works 598.0222
Birds, Protection of 333.95816; 639.978
Birds—Sri Lanka 598.095493
Birds—West (U.S.) 598.0978
Birds—West (U.S.)—Identification 598.0978
Birdsongs 598.1594
Birkenau (Concentration camp) 940.5318
Birman cat 636.824
Birmingham (England) 942.496
Birmingham family (Fictitious characters) 813.54
Birth charts 133.54
Birth control 304.666; 363.96
Birth control—Africa 363.96096
Birth control—Africa, Sub-Saharan 363.960967
Birth control—Bangladesh 363.96095492
Birth control—Botswana 363.96096883
Birth control clinics 363.96
Birth control—Developing countries 363.96091724
Birth control—Great Britain 363.960941
Birth control—India 363.960954
Birth control—Kenya 363.96096762
Birth control—Law and legislation 344.048
Birth control—Moral and ethical aspects 176
Birth control—Pakistan 363.96095491
Birth control—Religious aspects 291.566
Birth control—Religious aspects—Catholic Church
    241.66
Birth control—Tanzania 363.9609678
Birth control—Thailand 363.9609593
Birth control—Zimbabwe 363.96096891
Birth customs 392.12
Birth order 155.924
Birth order—Psychological aspects 155.924
Birthday books 133.54042
Birthdays 394.2
Birthfathers 306.8742
Birthmarks in literature 808.80353; 809.93353
Birthmothers 306.8743
Birthparents 306.874

Biscotti 641.8654
Biscuits 641.815
Bisexual men 305.389663
Bisexual students 371.82663
Bisexual women 305.489663
Bisexuality 306.765
Bisexuality in motion pictures 791.43653
Bisexuality—United States 306.7650973
Bisexuals 305.90663
Bisexuals' writings 808.89920663; 809.8920663
Bishop, Elizabeth, 1911–1979 811.54
Bishop, Elizabeth, 1911–1979—Criticism and
    interpretation 811.54
Bishop family 929.20973
Bishops 262.12
Bismarck (Battleship) 940.545943
Bismarck, Otto, Fürst von, 1815–1898 943.08092
Bison 599.643
Bison farming 636.292
Bison industry 338.176292
Bit-mapped graphics 006.6
Bites and stings 617.1
BITNET (Computer network) 004.67
Bituminous materials 553.2; 620.196
Bivalvia 594.4
Bivalvia, Fossil 564.4
Black-and-white photography 778.3
Black bass fishing 799.1738
Black bear 599.785
Black Beauty (Fictitious character) 823.8
Black business enterprises 338.6420896
Black Carib Indians 305.8984; 972.83004979
Black death 614.5732; 616.9232; 940.192
Black Elk, 1863–1950 978.004975
Black English 427.973
Black English—United States 427.973
Black family 929.20973
Black-footed ferret 599.76629
Black Hawk County (Iowa) 977.737
Black Hawk County (Iowa)—Maps 912.77737
Black Hawk, Sauk chief, 1767–1838 973.56
Black, Helen (Fictitious character) 813.54
Black, Helen (Fictitious character)—Fiction 813.54
Black holes (Astronomy) 523.8875
Black, Hugo LaFayette, 1886–1971 347.732634
Black metal (Music) 781.66
Black Muslims 297.87
Black nationalism 305.896
Black nationalism—United States 305.896073
Black newspapers 070.484
Black Panther Party 322.420973
Black power 323.1196
Black power—United States 323.1196073
Black race 305.8036; 305.896
Black rhinoceros 599.668
Black theology 230.08996; 230.08996073
Black, Thomas (Fictitious character) 813.54
Black, Thomas (Fictitious character)—Fiction 813.54
Black widow spider 595.44
Blackberry industry 338.174713
Blackbirding 306.363
Blackbirds 598.874
Blackboard systems (Computer programs) 006.338
Blackboards 371.335
Blackburn family 929.20973
Blackhouses 643.2; 728.92
Blackjack (Game) 795.423
Blacks 305.896; 909.0496
Blacks and mass media 302.2308996

Blacks—Biography 920.009296
Blacks—Brazil 305.896081
Blacks—Education—South Africa 371.829968
Blacks—Great Britain 305.896041
Blacks—History 909.0496
Blacks in art 704.942
Blacks in the Bible 220.8305896
Blacks—Race identity 305.8036; 305.896
Blacks—South Africa 305.896068
Blacks—South Africa—Social conditions 305.896068
Blacksmithing 682
Blackwell, Elizabeth, 1821–1910 610.92
Bladder 612.467
Bladder—Cancer 616.99462
Bladder—Diseases 616.62
Bladderworts 583.95
Blair, Bonnie, 1964– 796.914092
Blair, Elizabeth (Fictitious character) 823.914
Blair family 929.20973
Blair, Tony, 1953– 941.0859092
Blaise, Modesty (Fictitious character) 823.914
Blaise, Modesty (Fictitious character)—Fiction 823.914
Blake, Lucy (Fictitious character) 823.914
Blake, William, 1757–1827 821.7
Blake, William, 1757–1827—Aesthetics 821.7
Blake, William, 1757–1827—Catalogs 760.092
Blake, William, 1757–1827—Criticism and
    interpretation 821.7
Blake, William, 1757–1827—Exhibitions 760.092;
    769.92
Blake, William, 1757–1827—Knowledge—Psychology
    821.7
Blake, William, 1757–1827—Manuscripts 821.7
Blake, William, 1757–1827. Milton 821.7
Blake, William, 1757–1827—Philosophy 821.7
Blake, William, 1757–1827—Political and social views
    821.7
Blake, William, 1757–1827—Religion 760.092; 821.7
Blake, William, 1757–1827. Songs of innocence and of
    experience 821.7
Blakeney, Percy, Sir (Fictitious character) 823.912
Blakeney, Percy, Sir (Fictitious character)—Fiction
    823.912
Blame—Religious aspects 291.5
Blanc-Sec, Adèle (Fictitious character) 741.5944
Blanchard, Ursula (Fictitious character) 823.914
Blanchot, Maurice 843.912
Blanchot, Maurice—Philosophy 843.912
Blandings Castle (England : Imaginary place) 823.912
Blas, Gil (Fictitious character) 843.5
Blasket Islands (Ireland) 941.96
Blasket Islands (Ireland)—Social life and customs
    941.96
Blast effect 624.176
Blast furnaces 669.1413
Blasting 624.152
Blaue Reiter (Group of artists) 759.3
Blavatsky, H. P. (Helena Petrovna), 1831–1891
    299.934092
Blavatsky, H. P. (Helena Petrovna), 1831–1891. Secret
    doctrine 299.934092
Blended fabrics 677.02864
Blenders (Cookery) 641.589
Blenniidae 597.77
Blepharoplasty 617.7710592
Blind 362.41
Blind, Apparatus for the 362.4183
Blind—Books and reading—Bibliography 011.63
Blind-deaf 362.41

Blind dogs 636.70897712
Blind—Education 371.911
Blind—Employment—Law and legislation 344.01591
Blind—Employment—Law and legislation—United States 344.7301591
Blind—Printing and writing systems 411
Blind—Rehabilitation 362.418
Blindfold chess 794.17
Blindness 362.41; 617.712
Blindness in animals 636.0897712
Blintzes 641.815
Blishen, Edward, 1920– 828.91409
Bliss, Vicky (Fictitious character) 813.54
Bliss, Vicky (Fictitious character)—Fiction 813.54
Blizzards 551.555
Bloch, Ernst, 1885–1977 193
Block building (Children's activity) 372.5
Block printing 761
Blok, Aleksandr Aleksandrovich, 1880–1921 891.713
Blok, Aleksandr Aleksandrovich, 1880–1921—
    Translations into English 891.713
Blonde d'Aquitaine cattle 636.242
Blood 612.11
Blood alcohol 615.7828
Blood—Analysis 616.07561
Blood banks 362.1784
Blood banks—Quality control 362.17840685
Blood-brain barrier 612.824
Blood cells 612.11
Blood chits (Military science) 358.4154
Blood—Circulation 612.13
Blood—Circulation, Artificial 617.41
Blood—Coagulation 612.115
Blood coagulation disorders 616.157
Blood coagulation disorders—Diagnosis 616.157075
Blood coagulation disorders in pregnancy 618.3
Blood—Diseases 616.15
Blood—Diseases—Handbooks, manuals, etc. 616.15
Blood—Examination 616.15075
Blood flow 612.1181
Blood gases 612.11
Blood gases—Analysis 616.07561
Blood group antigens 616.0792
Blood groups 612.11825
Blood platelets 612.117
Blood pressure 612.14
Blood proteins 612.12
Blood substitutes 615.39
Blood sugar monitoring 616.46207561
Blood—Transfusion 362.1784; 615.39
Blood—Transfusion—Complications 615.39
Blood vessel prosthesis 617.4130592
Blood-vessels 573.18
Blood-vessels—Diseases 616.13
Blood-vessels—Diseases—Diagnosis 616.13075
Blood-vessels—Endoscopic surgery 617.413059
Blood-vessels—Surgery 617.413
Blood-vessels—Surgery—Atlases 617.41300222
Blood-vessels—Surgery—Complications 617.41301
Blood-vessels—Surgery—Handbooks, manuals, etc. 617.413
Blood-vessels—Ultrasonic imaging 616.1307543
Bloodborne infections—Prevention 614.44
Bloodborne infections—Prevention—Standards—United States 614.44
Bloodsucking animals 591.53
Bloom, Leopold (Fictitious character) 823.912
Bloom, Leopold (Fictitious character)—Fiction 823.912
Bloomsbury group 700.942

Bloomsbury (London, England) 942.142
Bloomsbury (London, England)—Intellectual life 942.142
Bloomsbury (London, England)—Intellectual life—20th century 942.142
Blount County (Tenn.)—Genealogy 929.3768885
Blouses 646.435
Blowflies 595.774
Blue and white transfer ware—Collectors and collecting 738.27
Blue-chip stocks 332.6322
Blue Earth County (Minn.) 977.621
Blue Earth County (Minn.)—Maps 912.77621
Blue Mountains (N.S.W. : Mountains) 994.45
Blue Ridge Mountains 975.5
Blue Ridge Mountains—Guidebooks 917.5504; 917.550443; 917.550444
Blue stragglers (Stars) 523.88
Blue whale 599.5248
Bluebirds 598.842
Bluefin tuna 629.27783
Bluegrass music—1981–1990 781.64209048
Blueprinting 604.25
Blueprints 604.25
Blues festivals 781.643079
Blues (Music) 781.643
Blues (Music)—To 1931 781.6430904
Blues (Music)—1931–1940 781.64309043
Blues (Music)—1941–1950 781.64309044
Blues (Music)—1951–1960 781.64309045
Blues (Music)—1961–1970 781.64309046
Blues (Music)—1971–1980 781.64309047
Blues (Music)—1981–1990 781.64309048
Blues (Music)—Discography 016.781643078766
Blues (Music)—History and criticism 781.64309
Blues (Music)—Texts 782.4216430268
Blues musicians 781.643092
Bluetooth technology 004.62
Bly, Nellie, 1864–1922 070.92
BMW automobiles 629.2222
BMW automobiles—History 629.2222
BMW automobiles—Maintenance and repair 629.28722
BMW automobiles—Maintenance and repair—Handbooks, manuals, etc. 629.28722
BMW motorcycle—Maintenance and repair 629.28775
BMW motorcycle—Maintenance and repair—Handbooks, manuals, etc. 629.28775
BMX bikes 629.2272; 796.62
Boa constrictors as pets 639.3967
Board games 794
Board of Governors of the Federal Reserve System (U.S.) 332.110973
Board of Governors of the Federal Reserve System (U.S.)—History 332.110973
Boarding school students 373.18
Boarding schools 373.222
Boardinghouses 647.94
Boards of trade 380.106; 381.06
Boat living 643.2
Boatbuilders 623.8202092; 623.82092
Boatbuilding 623.82; 623.8202
Boathouses 725.87
Boating industry 338.47623.82
Boats and boating 797.1
Boats and boating—Chartering 386.24; 387.54
Boats and boating—Design and construction 623.82; 623.8202
Boats and boating—Electric equipment 623.8503
Boats and boating—Electronic equipment 623.8504

Boats and boating—Equipment and supplies 623.880284
Boats and boating—Florida—Florida Keys 797.10975941
Boats and boating—Florida—Florida Keys—Guidebooks
  917.594104; 917.59410463; 917.59410464
Boats and boating—Law and legislation 343.096
Boats and boating—Law and legislation—United States
  343.73096
Boats and boating—Maine 797.109741
Boats and boating—Maine—Guidebooks 917.404;
  917.40444; 917.410443
Boats and boating—Maintenance and repair
  623.8200288; 623.82020288; 623.83
Boats and boating—Michigan, Lake—Maps
  623.89229774
Boats and boating—Periodicals 797.105
Boats and boating—Safety measures 623.888;
  797.10289
Boaz family 929.20973
Bob the Builder (Fictitious character) 823.914
Bobbin lace 746.222
Bobbin lace—Patterns 746.222041
Bobcat 599.7536
Boccaccio, Giovanni, 1313–1375 853.1; 858.109
Boccaccio, Giovanni, 1313–1375. Decamerone 853.1
Body composition 612
Body covering (Anatomy) 573.5; 591.47
Body fluid disorders 616.3992
Body fluids 612.01522
Body, Human 612
Body, Human (Philosophy) 128.6
Body, Human—Religious aspects 291.22
Body, Human—Religious aspects—Christianity 233.5
Body, Human—Social aspects 306.4
Body image disturbance 616.852
Body image in men 155.332; 306.4
Body language 153.69; 302.222
Body marking 391.65
Body odor 612.7921
Body painting 391.6
Body size 591.41
Body temperature 612.01426
Body temperature—Measurement 612.014260287;
  616.0754
Body temperature—Regulation 571.7637; 612.01426
Body weight 591.41
Bodybuilders 646.75092
Bodybuilders—Nutrition 646.75
Bodybuilding 646.75
Bodybuilding for women 646.75082
Bodybuilding industry 338.4764675
Bodyguards 363.289
Boeing 747 (Jet transports)—History 629.133349
Boerboel 636.73
Boethius, d. 524 189
Bog ecology 577.68
Bogart, Humphrey, 1899–1957 791.43028092
Bognor, Simon (Fictitious character) 823.914
Bognor, Simon (Fictitious character)—Fiction 823.914
Bohemia (Czech Republic) 943.71
Bohemia (Czech Republic)—History 943.71
Boiling water reactors 621.4834
Boldt, Lou (Fictitious character) 813.54
Boldt, Lou (Fictitious character)—Fiction 813.54
Bolen family 929.20973
Bolero (Dance) 793.33
Boletaceae 579.6
Boletus 579.6
Bolívar, Simón, 1783–1830 980.02092
Bolivia 984

Bolivia—Description and travel 918.404; 918.40452
Bolivia—Guidebooks 918.404
Bolivia—History 984
Bolivia—History—1938–1982 984.051
Böll, Heinrich, 1917– 833.914
Böll, Heinrich, 1917– —Criticism and interpretation
  833.914
Böll, Heinrich, 1917– —Translations into English
  833.914
Bolted joints 621.882
Bombay (India) 954.7923
Bombay (India)—Description and travel 915.4792304;
  915.479230452
Bombay (India)—History 954.7923
Bombers 358.4283; 623.7463
Bombers—Germany 623.74630943
Bombing investigation 363.25
Bombings 358.4283
Bombyliidae 595.773
Bonaparte, Napoleon, Inspector (Fictitious character)
  823
Bonaparte, Napoleon, Inspector (Fictitious character)—
  Fiction 823.912
Bonaventure, Saint, Cardinal, ca. 1217–1274 189.4
Bond insurance 368.853
Bond, James (Fictitious character) 823.914
Bond, James (Fictitious character)—Fiction 823.914
Bond lawyers 346.0922
Bond market 332.6323
Bondage (Sexual behavior) 306.775
Bonds 332.6323
Bonds, Barry, 1964– 796.357092
Bonds—Europe 332.6323094
Bonds—Handbooks, manuals, etc. 332.6323
Bonds—Prices 332.6323
Bonds—Ratings 332.6323
Bonds—Ratings—Periodicals 332.632305
Bonds—United States 332.63230973
Bone-grafting 617.4710592
Bone marrow 573.1556
Bone marrow purging 617.44
Bone marrow—Transplantation 617.44
Bone, Robert (Fictitious character) 823.914
Bone, Robert (Fictitious character)—Fiction 823.914
Bones 573.76; 612.75
Bones—Diseases 616.71
Bones—Diseases—Diagnosis 616.71075
Bones—Growth 612.75
Bones—Metabolism 612.75
Bones—Metabolism—Disorders 616.716
Bones—Tumors 616.99271
Bonfires 394.2
Bonhoeffer, Dietrich, 1906–1945 230.044092
Boniface VIII, Pope, d. 1303 282.092
Bonkei 712.0228
Bonnefoy, Yves 841.914
Bonnefoy, Yves—Translations into English 841.914
Bonsai 635.9772
Bonus Expeditionary Forces 973.916
Bonus system 658.3225
Boobies (Birds) 598.43
Booch method 005.117
Book auctions 381.45002
Book brands (Owners' marks) 002.0277
Book clubs 070.5
Book collecting 002.075; 020.75; 027.1
Book collecting—United States 002.075
Book coupons 002.0688
Book design 686

Brain damage—Diagnosis 616.80475
Brain damage—Patients 362.197481
Brain damage—Patients—Rehabilitation 616.8043;
617.4810443
Brain-damaged children 617.481044083; 618.928
Brain-damaged children—Education 371.91
Brain-damaged children—Education—United States
371.91
Brain—Diseases 616.8
Brain—Diseases—Diagnosis 616.80475
Brain drain 331.12791
Brain—Evolution 612.82
Brain—Growth 612.82
Brain—Imaging 616.804754
Brain—Localization of functions 612.82
Brain—Magnetic resonance imaging 616.8047548
Brain mapping 612.82
Brain—Physiology 612.82
Brain stem 612.826
Brain—Surgery 617.481
Brain—Surgery—Complications 617.48101
Brain—Tomography 616.804757
Brain—Tomography—Atlases 616.8047570222
Brain—Tumors 614.5999; 616.99281; 616.99481
Brain—Tumors—Diagnosis 616.99281075
Brain—Wounds and injuries 617.481044
Brain—Wounds and injuries—Complications 617.481044
Brain—Wounds and injuries—Patients 362.197481
Brain—Wounds and injuries—Patients—Rehabilitation
617.4810443
Brainerd, David, 1718–1747 266.51092
Brainwashing 153.853
Brambly Hedge (Imaginary place) 823.912
Branch County (Mich.) 977.421
Branch County (Mich.)—Maps 912.77421
Branch libraries 027.4
Branching processes 519.234
Branchiopoda 595.32
Brand family (Fictitious characters) 823.914
Brand, Jason (Fictitious character) 823.914
Brand loyalty 658.8343
Brand name products 658.827
Brand name products—Management 658.827; 658.8343
Brand name products—Marketing 658.827
Brand name products—Marketing—Management
658.827
Brandeis, Louis Dembitz, 1856–1941 347.732634
Brando, Marlon 791.43028092
Brandon, Smokey (Fictitious character) 813.54
Brandstetter, Dave (Fictitious character) 813.54
Brandstetter, Dave (Fictitious character)—Fiction
813.54
Brandt family 929.20973
Brannigan, Kate (Fictitious character) 823.914
Brannigan, Kate (Fictitious character)—Fiction 823.914
Brannon, Stuart (Fictitious character) 813.54
Brannon, Stuart (Fictitious character)—Fiction 813.54
Brass band music 784.9
Brass ensembles 785.9
Brass instruments 788.9; 788.919
Brass quintets (Horn, trombone, trumpets (2), tuba)
785.9
Bray, Nell (Fictitious character) 823.914
Bray, Nell (Fictitious character)—Fiction 823.914
Brazil 981
Brazil—Civilization 981
Brazil—Description and travel 918.104; 918.10464
Brazil—Economic conditions 330.981
Brazil—Economic conditions—1964–1985 330.981063

Brazil—Economic conditions—1985– 330.981064
Brazil—Economic conditions—1985– —Periodicals
330.981064
Brazil—Economic policy 338.981
Brazil—Guidebooks 918.104; 918.10464
Brazil—History 981
Brazil—History—To 1822 981.01; 981.03
Brazil—Politics and government 320.981
Brazil—Politics and government—1964–1985
320.98109047
Brazil—Race relations 305.800981
Brazil—Social life and customs 981
Brazilian wit and humor 869.70080981
Brazilian wit and humor, Pictorial 741.5981
Brazing 671.56; 731.41; 739.14
Bre-X (Firm) 364.16309598
Breach of contract 346.022
Bread 641.815; 664.7523
Bread dough craft 745.5
Break dancing 793.3
Breakfasts 641.52
Breast 612.664
Breast—Cancer 616.99449
Breast—Cancer—Diagnosis 616.99449075
Breast—Cancer—Endocrine aspects 616.99449;
616.99449061; 616.99449071
Breast—Cancer—Molecular aspects 616.9944907
Breast—Cancer—Patients 362.19699449;
362.196994490092
Breast—Cancer—Patients—United States—Biography
362.196994490092273
Breast—Cancer—Prevention 616.99449052
Breast—Cancer—Psychological aspects
362.196994490019; 616.994490019
Breast—Cancer—Risk factors 616.99449071
Breast—Cancer—Surgery 616.99449059
Breast—Cancer—Treatment 616.9944906
Breast—Care and hygiene 618.1906
Breast—Diseases 618.19
Breast feeding 613.269; 649.33
Breast feeding promotion 613.269; 649.33
Breast—Imaging 618.190754
Breast implants 618.190592
Breast implants—Complications 618.190592
Breast milk 612.664; 613.269
Breast milk—Collection and preservation 613.269;
649.33
Breast milk—Composition 612.664; 613.269
Breast—Needle biopsy 618.190758
Breast prosthesis 618.19
Breast—Radiography 616.9944907572; 618.1907572
Breast—Surgery 618.19059
Breast—Ultrasonic imaging 618.1907543
Breathing apparatus 620.86
Breathing exercises 613.192
Brecht, Bertolt, 1898–1956 832.912
Brecht, Bertolt, 1898–1956—Criticism and
interpretation 832.912
Brecht, Bertolt, 1898–1956—Translations into English
832.912
Breeches parts 792.028; 792.5028
Breeder reactors 621.4834
Bremer County (Iowa) 977.734
Bremer County (Iowa)—Maps 912.77734
Brennan, William J. (William Joseph), 1906–
347.732634
Brew-on-premises facilities 663.42
Brewer family 929.20973
Breweries 663.3; 663.42

Broom, Andrew (Fictitious character)—Fiction 813.54
Broomball 796.96
Brothers 306.875
Brothers and sisters 155.443; 306.875
Brothers and sisters—England 306.8750942
Brothers and sisters in literature 808.80352045;
    809.93352045
Brothers—Scotland 306.87509411
Broussard, Andy (Fictitious character) 813.54
Broussard, Andy (Fictitious character)—Fiction 813.54
Broward County (Fla.)—Maps 912.75935
Brown bear 599.784; 639.979784
Brown bear—Alaska 599.78409798; 639.97978409798
Brown, Charles Brockden, 1771–1810 813.2
Brown, Charles Brockden, 1771–1810—Criticism and
    interpretation 813.2
Brown, Charlie (Fictitious character) 741.5973
Brown County (Ill.) 977.3473
Brown County (Ill.)—Maps 912.773473
Brown County (Ind.) 977.2253
Brown County (Ind.)—Genealogy 929.3772253
Brown County (S.D.) 978.3144
Brown County (S.D.)—Maps 912.783144
Brown County (Wis.) 977.561
Brown County (Wis.)—Maps 912.77561
Brown family 929.20973
Brown, Father (Fictitious character) 823.912
Brown, Father (Fictitious character)—Fiction 823.912
Brown, John, 1800–1859 973.7116092
Brown Willie (Fictitious character) 027.914
Browne, Thomas, Sir, 1605–1682 828.409
Browne, Thomas, Sir, 1605–1682—Criticism and
    interpretation 828.409
Brownfields 333.77137
Brownian motion processes 519.233; 530.475
Brownie Girl Scouts 369.463
Brownies (Cookery) 641.8653
Browning, Elizabeth Barrett, 1806–1861 821.8
Browning, Elizabeth Barrett, 1806–1861—Criticism and
    interpretation 821.8
Browning, Robert, 1812–1889 821.8
Browning, Robert, 1812–1889—Correspondence 821.8
Browning, Robert, 1812–1889—Criticism and
    interpretation 821.8
Browning, Robert, 1812–1889—Influence 821.8
Browning, Robert, 1812–1889—Religion 821.8
Browning, Robert, 1812–1889. Ring and the book
    821.8
Brownists 285.8
Browsers (Computer programs) 005.71376; 025.04
Bruce, Lenny 792.7028092
Bruegel, Pieter, ca. 1525–1569 759.9493; 760.092
Brunches 641.53
Brunei 959.55
Bruno, Giordano, 1548–1600 195
Brunswick County (N.C.)—Genealogy 929.375629
Brunswick County (Va.)—Genealogy 929.3755575
Brunt, Tom (Fictitious character) 823.914
Brussels (Belgium) 949.332
Brussels (Belgium)—Guidebooks 914.933204;
    914.93320444
Bryant family 929.20973
Bryant, Paul W. 796.332092
Bryology 588
Bryophytes 588
Bryophytes, Fossil 561.8
Bryozoa 594.67
Bryozoa, Fossil 564.67
BSA motorcycle 629.2275

Bubble wrap 668.49
Bubbles 530.4275
Buber, Martin, 1878–1965 296.3092
Buchanan County (Iowa) 977.7382
Buchanan County (Iowa)—Maps 912.777382
Buchanan family 929.20973
Buchanan, James, 1791–1868 973.68092
Buchenwald (Concentration camp) 940.5318
Büchner, Georg, 1813–1837 832.7
Büchner, Georg, 1813–1837—Criticism and
    interpretation 832.7
Büchner, Georg, 1813–1837—Translations into English
    832.7
Buck, Pearl S. (Pearl Sydenstricker), 1892–1973
    813.52
Buck, Pearl S. (Pearl Sydenstricker), 1892–1973—
    Criticism and interpretation 813.52
Buckingham County (Va.)—Genealogy 929.3755623
Buckingham Palace (London, England) 942.132
Buckley, William F. (William Frank), 1925– 070.92
Buckling (Mechanics) 620.11233; 624.176
Bucks County (Pa.)—Genealogy 929.374821
Bucks County (Pa.)—Maps 912.74821
Budapest (Hungary) 943.912
Budapest (Hungary)—Guidebooks 914.391204;
    914.39120454
Budapest (Hungary)—Pictorial works 914.391200222
Buddha 294.363
Buddha—Relics 294.363
Buddha (The concept) 294.363
Buddhism 294.3
Buddhism and science 294.3375
Buddhism—China 294.30951
Buddhism—China—History 294.30951
Buddhism—China—Tibet 294.3923
Buddhism—China—Tibet—Doctrines 294.340423
Buddhism—China—Tibet—Rituals 294.3438
Buddhism—Dictionaries 294.303
Buddhism—Doctrines 294.342
Buddhism—History 294.309
Buddhism—History—To ca. 100 A.D. 294.30901
Buddhism—India 294.30954
Buddhism—India—History 294.30954
Buddhism—Japan 294.30952
Buddhism—Japan—History 294.30952
Buddhism—Japan—History—To 794 294.3095209021
Buddhism—Japan—History—To 1185 294.309520902
Buddhism—Japan—History—1185–1600 294.309520902
Buddhism—Korea 294.309519
Buddhism—Korea—History 294.309519
Buddhism—Periodicals 294.305
Buddhism—Prayer-books and devotions—Tibetan
    294.3438
Buddhism—Relations—Christianity 261.243; 294.3372
Buddhism—Relations—Hinduism 294.3372; 294.5172
Buddhism—Rituals—Texts 294.3438
Buddhism—Sacred books 294.382
Buddhism—Social aspects 294.337
Buddhism—Sri Lanka 294.3095493
Buddhism—Sri Lanka—History 294.3095493
Buddhist cosmology 294.3424
Buddhist education 294.37
Buddhist ethics 294.35
Buddhist fundamentalism 294.309
Buddhist meditations 294.34432
Buddhist monks 294.3657
Buddhist poetry, American 811.0080382943
Budding (Zoology) 571.89; 571.891
Budgerigar 636.6864

Budget 352.48
Budget analysts 352.48092; 658.154092
Budget—California 336.794
Budget—California—Periodicals 336.79405
Budget—Colorado—Periodicals 352.49788005
Budget deficits 339.523
Budget deficits—United States 339.5230973
Budget—Great Britain 336.41
Budget—Idaho—Statistics—Periodicals 352.497960021
Budget in business 658.154
Budget—Law and legislation 343.034
Budget—Law and legislation—Maryland 343.752034
Budget—Law and legislation—United States 343.73034
Budget—Nigeria—Niger State—Periodicals
  352.4966965005
Budget—North Dakota—Statistics—Periodicals
  352.497840021
Budget—United States 352.4973
Budget—United States—Periodicals 352.4973005
Budget—United States—States 352.42130973
Budgets, Personal 640.42
Buena Vista County (Iowa) 977.718
Buena Vista County (Iowa)—Maps 912.77718
Buffalo Bill, 1846–1917 978.02092
Buffalo County (Neb.) 978.245
Buffalo County (Neb.)—Maps 912.78245
Buffalo County (Wis.) 977.548
Buffalo County (Wis.)—Maps 912.77548
Buffalo meat 641.36292
Buffalo Metropolitan Area (N.Y.)—Maps 912.74797
Buffer zones (Ecosystem management) 333.72; 639.95
Buffets (Cookery) 642.4
Buffett, Jimmy 782.42164092
Buffett, Warren 332.6092
Bug fishing 799.12
Bugs (Fishing lures) 688.7912; 799.120284
Buick automobile 629.2222
Buick automobile—History 629.2222
Buick automobile—Maintenance and repair 629.28722
Buick automobile—Maintenance and repair—
  Handbooks, manuals, etc. 629.28722
Buick Century automobile 629.2222
Buick Century automobile—Maintenance and repair
  629.28722
Buick Century automobile—Maintenance and repair—
  Handbooks, manuals, etc. 629.28722
Buick Electra automobile 629.2222
Buick Electra automobile—Maintenance and repair
  629.28722
Buick Electra automobile—Maintenance and repair—
  Handbooks, manuals, etc. 629.28722
Building 624; 690
Building, Brick 691.4
Building cleaning industry 338.476485
Building—Details 721
Building—Details—Drawings 692.2; 721.0222
Building—Dictionaries 624.03; 690.03
Building—Economic aspects 690.0681
Building—Estimates 692.5
Building—Estimates—Great Britain 692.50941
Building—Estimates—Handbooks, manuals, etc. 692.5
Building—Estimates—Periodicals 692.505
Building—Estimates—United States 692.50973
Building—Estimates—United States—Periodicals
  692.5097305
Building, Fireproof 693.82
Building—Handbooks, manuals, etc. 690
Building—History 624.09
Building inspection 690.21

Building inspectors 690.21
Building-integrated photovoltaic systems 621.31244
Building, Iron and steel 624.1821; 691.7; 693.71
Building, Iron and steel—Handbooks, manuals, etc.
  624.1821
Building laws 343.07869
Building laws—Ohio 343.77107869
Building laws—United States 343.7307869
Building management 658.2
Building materials 691
Building materials—Catalogs—Periodicals 691.0294
Building materials industry 338.47691
Building materials—Standards 691.0218
Building materials—Standards—United States
  691.021873
Building materials—Testing 691.0287
Building—Periodicals 690.05
Building permits 343.07869
Building—Quality control 690.0685
Building—Research 690.072
Building—Safety measures 690.22
Building sites 690
Building sites—Planning 720.28
Building, Stone 693.1
Building stones 691.2; 691.3
Building, Stormproof 693.8
Building—Superintendence 690.068
Building trades 690
Building, Wooden 624.184; 721.0448
Buildings 690; 720
Buildings—Aerodynamics 690.153362
Buildings—Earthquake effects 693.852
Buildings—Effect of nearby construction on 690.21
Buildings—Electric equipment 621.31924
Buildings—Energy conservation 333.796216
Buildings—Environmental engineering 696
Buildings in art 704.944; 751.42244
Buildings—Maintenance 690.24
Buildings—Mechanical equipment 696
Buildings—Mechanical equipment—Estimates 696.0299
Buildings—Performance 690.22
Buildings, Portable 721.04
Buildings, Prefabricated 691.97
Buildings—Remodeling for other use 720.286
Buildings—Repair and construction 690.24
Buildings—Repair and reconstruction 690.24
Buildings—Specifications 692.3
Buildings—Specifications—Great Britain 692.30941
Built-in furniture 684.16
Bukowski, Charles 811.54
Bulbs 635.94
Bulgakov, Mikhail Afanas'evich, 1891–1940 891.7242;
  891.7342; 891.784209
Bulgakov, Mikhail Afanas'evich, 1891–1940. Master i
  Margarita 891.7342
Bulgakov, Mikhail Afanas'evich, 1891–1940—
  Translations into English 891.7242; 891.7342
Bulgaria 949.9
Bulgaria—Economic conditions 330.9499
Bulgaria—Economic conditions—1944–1989
  330.9499031
Bulgaria—Economic policy 338.9499
Bulgaria—Economic policy—1944–1989 338.9499
Bulgaria—Foreign relations 327.499
Bulgaria—Foreign relations—1944–1990 327.499
Bulgaria—Guidebooks 914.904; 914.90432
Bulgaria—History 949.9
Bulgaria—History—1944–1990 949.903; 949.9031
Bulgaria—Intellectual life 949.9

Business enterprises—Computer networks—Security measures 658.478
Business enterprises—Finance 658.15
Business enterprises—Finance—Data processing 658.150285
Business enterprises, Foreign 658.049; 658.1599
Business enterprises—Law and legislation 346.065
Business enterprises—Law and legislation—Florida 346.759065
Business enterprises—Law and legislation—Hungary 346.439065
Business enterprises—Law and legislation—Maryland 346.752065
Business enterprises—Law and legislation—North Carolina 346.756065
Business enterprises—Law and legislation—United States 346.73065
Business enterprises—Law and legislation—United States—Cases 346.730650264
Business enterprises—Purchasing 658.72
Business enterprises—Soviet Union 338.70947
Business enterprises—Taxation—Law and legislation 343.068
Business enterprises—Taxation—Law and legislation—United States 343.73068
Business enterprises—Taxation—Law and legislation—United States—Cases 343.730680264
Business enterprises—Taxation—United States 343.73068
Business enterprises—United States 338.70973
Business enterprises—Valuation 658.15
Business ethics 174.4; 241.644
Business ethics—United States 174.40973
Business etiquette 395.52
Business etiquette—Japan 395.520952
Business failures 332.75
Business forecasting 338.544; 658.40355
Business—Forms 651.29
Business—Handbooks, manuals, etc. 658
Business incubators 658.11
Business information services 658.4038
Business information services—Computer network resources 025.0665
Business information services—Computer network resources—Directories 025.0665
Business information services—Directories 016.65
Business information services—United States 027.690973
Business information services—United States—Directories 016.65
Business intelligence 658.47
Business intelligence—United States 658.470973
Business law 346.07
Business law—United States 346.7307
Business law—United States—Cases 346.73070264
Business libraries 027.69
Business life insurance—Law and legislation 346.086
Business life insurance—Law and legislation—United States 346.73086; 346.7308632
Business literature 650
Business logistics 658.5; 658.7
Business logistics—Cost effectiveness 658.5
Business losses 336.2417
Business mathematics 650.01513
Business mathematics—Problems, exercises, etc. 650.01513
Business meetings 658.456
Business meetings—Handbooks, manuals, etc. 658.456
Business names 929.97

Business networks 650.13
Business—Periodicals 650.05
Business—Periodicals—Bibliography 016.65005
Business planning 658.4012
Business planning—Handbooks, manuals, etc. 658.4012
Business planning—Mathematical models 658.4012015118
Business planning—United States 658.40120973
Business presentations 658.452
Business presentations—Graphic methods 658.45
Business presentations—Graphic methods—Computer programs 005.369
Business records 651.5
Business records—Law and legislation 346.065; 346.0664
Business records—Law and legislation—United States 346.73065; 346.730664
Business records—Management 651.5
Business records—Management—Data processing 651.50285
Business records—Management—Data processing—Periodicals 651.50285
Business referrals 658.8
Business relocation 658.383
Business report writing 808.066651
Business—Research—Methodology 650.072
Business schools 650.0711
Business schools—United States 650.071173
Business schools—United States—Evaluation 650.071173
Business schools—United States—Handbooks, manuals, etc. 650.071173
Business—Software—Catalogs 650.028553
Business students 650.0711
Business tax 336.207
Business teachers 650.092
Business travel 658.383; 910.2
Business travel consultants 910.2
Business travel—Guidebooks 910.202
Business travel—United States—Guidebooks 647.947301; 917.304; 917.304929
Business—United States 650.0973
Business—Vocational guidance 650.023; 658.0023
Business writing 651.74; 808.06665
Business writing—Handbooks, manuals, etc. 808.06665
Businessmen 305.33338; 338.092
Businesspeople 338.092
Businesspeople—Biography 338.040922
Businesspeople—Prayer-books and devotions 242.68
Businesspeople—Religious life 248.88
Businesspeople—United States 338.04092273
Businesspeople—United States—Biography 338.04092273
Businesspeople—United States—Biography—Dictionaries 338.04092273
Businesswomen 305.43338; 338.7082
Businesswomen—United States 338.092
Butler County (Iowa) 977.729
Butler County (Iowa)—Maps 912.77729
Butler County (Mo.) 977.893
Butler County (Mo.)—Genealogy 929.377893
Butler County (Neb.) 978.2322
Butler County (Neb.)—Maps 912.782322
Butler family 929.20973
Butte County (Calif.) 979.432
Butte County (Calif.)—Genealogy 929.30979432; 929.379432
Butter pats (Tableware) 642.7; 666.3
Butter sculpture 736.9

Butterflies 595.789
Butterflies—Life cycles 595.789156
Butterfly gardens 635.96
Butterfly valves 621.84
Button craft 745.584
Buttons 391.45
Byfield family (Fictitious characters) 823.914
Byrd Antarctic Expedition (1st : 1928–1930) 919.8904
Byrd Antarctic Expedition (2nd : 1933–1935) 919.8904
Byrd family 929.20973
Byrd, Richard Evelyn, 1888–1957 919.8
Byron, George Gordon Byron, Baron, 1788–1824 821.7
Byron, George Gordon Byron, Baron, 1788–1824. Childe
     Harold's pilgrimage 821.7
Byron, George Gordon Byron, Baron, 1788–1824—
     Correspondence 821.7
Byron, George Gordon Byron, Baron, 1788–1824—
     Criticism and interpretation 821.7
Byron, George Gordon Byron, Baron, 1788–1824. Don
     Juan 821.7
Byron, George Gordon Byron, Baron, 1788–1824—
     Dramatic works 822.7
Byron, George Gordon Byron, Baron, 1788–1824—
     Friends and associates 821.7
Byron, George Gordon Byron, Baron, 1788–1824—
     Knowledge—Literature 821.7
Byron, George Gordon Byron, Baron, 1788–1824—
     Manuscripts 821.7
Byron, George Gordon Byron, Baron, 1788–1824—
     Political and social views 821.7
Byron, George Gordon Byron, Baron, 1788–1824—
     Religion 821.7
Byzantine chants 782.32219
Byzantine Empire 949.502
Byzantine Empire—Civilization 949.502
Byzantine Empire—Civilization—527–1081 949.502
Byzantine Empire—History 949.502
Byzantine Empire—History—527–1081 949.502
Byzantine Empire—History—1081–1453 949.503;
     949.504
C-3PO (Fictitious character) 791.4375
C*-algebras 512.55
C (Computer program language) 005.133
C++ (Computer program language) 005.133
CA-Clipper 005.7565
Cabala 135.47; 296.16
Cabala—History 296.16
Cabbage palmetto 584.5
Cabell, James Branch, 1879–1958 813.52
Cabell, James Branch, 1879–1958—Bibliography
     016.81352
Cabell, James Branch, 1879–1958—Criticism and
     interpretation 813.52
Cabeza de Vaca, Alvar Núñez, 16th cent. 970.016092
Cabinet officers 352.293
Cabinet officers—United States 352.24092
Cabinet system 321.8043
Cabinetmakers 684.10092
Cabinetwork 684.16
Cable structures 624.1774
Cable television 384.555; 621.38857
Cable television—Access 384.555
Cable television advertising 659.143
Cable television—Law and legislation 343.09946
Cable television—Law and legislation—United States
     343.7309946
Cable television—Periodicals 621.3885705
Cable television—United States 384.5550973

Cable television—United States—Periodicals
     384.555097305
Cable television—United States—Statistics—Periodicals
     384.5550973021
Cables 621.31934
Cabooses (Railroads) 625.22
Cache memory 005.435
Cactus 583.56; 635.93356
CAD/CAM systems 670.285
CADCore (Computer file) 620.004202855369
Caddisflies 595.745
Caddo art 704.03979
Cadette Girl Scouts—United States—Handbooks,
     manuals, etc. 369.463
Cadfael, Brother (Fictitious character) 823.912
Cadfael, Brother (Fictitious character)—Fiction 823.912
Cadillac automobile 629.2222
Cadillac automobile—Maintenance and repair 629.28722
Cadillac automobile—Maintenance and repair—
     Handbooks, manuals, etc. 629.28722
CADKey 620.004202855369
Cadmium 546.662
Cadmium—Toxicology 615.925662
Caesar, Julius 937.05092
Cafeteria benefit plans 331.255
Caffeine 613.84
Cage birds 636.68
Cage, John 780.92
Cage, John—Criticism and interpretation 780.92
Cahokia Mounds State Historic Park (Ill.) 977.389
Cain family 929.20973
Cain, Jenny (Fictitious character) 813.54
Cain, Jenny (Fictitious character)—Fiction 813.54
Cairn terrier 636.755
Cairo (Egypt) 962.16
Cajuns 976.300441
Cake 641.8653
Cake decorating 641.8653
Cake pans 641.86530284; 683.82
Calamity Jane, 1852–1903 978.02092
Calanoida 595.34
Calcification 572.516
Calcium 546.393
Calcium—Antagonists 616.12061
Calcium-binding proteins 572.69
Calcium—Metabolism 612.3924
Calcium—Physiological effect 572.516
Calcium regulating hormones 612.44
Calculators 681.145
Calculators—Problems, exercises, etc. 510.284
Calculus 515
Calculus—Data processing 515.0285
Calculus—Examinations, questions, etc. 515.076
Calculus—Graphic methods—Data processing 515.0285
Calculus of tensors 515.63
Calculus of variations 515.64
Calculus, Operational 515.72
Calculus—Outlines, syllabi, etc. 515.0202
Calculus—Problems, exercises, etc. 515.076
Calcutta (India) 954.147
Calcutta (India)—Description and travel 915.414704;
     915.41470452
Calcutta (India)—History 954.147
Calcutta (India)—Pictorial works 954.14700222
Calder, Alexander, 1898–1976 709.2; 730.92
Calder, Alexander, 1898–1976—Exhibitions 709.2;
     730.92
Calder family (Fictitious characters) 813.54
Calder family (Fictitious characters)—Fiction 813.54

Calder, Keith (Fictitious character) 823.914
Calder, Keith (Fictitious character)—Fiction 823.914
Caldwell County (Ky.)—Genealogy 929.3769815
Caldwell, Erskine, 1903– 813.52
Caldwell family 929.20973
Caleb, Jack (Fictitious character) 813.54
Calendar 529.3
Calendar, Chinese 529.30951
Calendar, Gregorian 529.36
Calendar—History 529.309
Calendar, Jewish 529.326
Calendars 529.3
Calgary (Alta.) 971.233
Calgary (Alta.)—Maps 912.71233
Calhoun County (Ill.) 977.3853
Calhoun County (Ill.)—Maps 912.773853
Calhoun County (Iowa) 977.743
Calhoun County (Iowa)—Maps 912.77743
Calhoun County (Mich.) 977.422
Calhoun County (Mich.)—Maps 912.77422
Calhoun family 929.20973
Calhoun, John C. (John Caldwell), 1782–1850 973.5092
Calhoun, Mackenzie (Fictitious character) 813.54
California 979.4
California Basic Educational Skills Test 371.262
California—Civilization 979.4
California condor 598.92
California—Constitutional history 342.794029
California Current 551.4763
California—Description and travel 917.9404;
917.940453; 917.940454
California—Encyclopedias 979.4003
California—Genealogy 929.3794
California—Gold discoveries 979.404
California—Guidebooks 917.9404; 917.940453;
917.940454
California High School Proficiency Examination
373.1262
California—History 979.4
California—History—To 1846 979.4
California—History—1846–1850 979.404
California—History—1850–1950 979.404
California—Maps 912.794
California, Northern 979.4
California, Northern—Guidebooks 917.9404;
917.940453; 917.940454
California, Northern—Tours 917.94; 917.940453;
917.940454
California—Pictorial works 917.9400222
California—Politics and government 320.9794
California—Politics and government—1951–
320.979409045
California Psychological Inventory 155.283
California—Road maps 912.794
California—Social life and customs 979.4
California, Southern 979.49
California, Southern—Guidebooks 917.94904;
917.9490453; 917.9490454
California, Southern—History 979.49
California, Southern—Tours 917.94904; 917.9490453;
917.9490454
California—Tours 917.9404; 917.940453; 917.940454
Caliphate 297.61
Call centers 658.812; 658.84
Call of Cthulhu (Game) 793.9325369
Callaghan, Morley, 1903– 813.52
Callaghan, Morley, 1903– —Criticism and interpretation
813.52
Callas, Maria, 1923–1977 782.1092

Callaway County (Mo.) 977.8335
Callaway County (Mo.)—Maps 912.778335
Caller ID telephone service 384.64
Calligraphy 745.61
Calligraphy, Chinese 745.619951
Calligraphy, Chinese—History—Qin-Han dynasties, 221
B.C.–220 A.D. 745.6199510915; 745.6199510921
Calligraphy, Chinese—History—Three kingdoms-Sui
dynasty, 220–618 745.6199510921
Calligraphy, Chinese—History—Tang-Five dynasties,
618–960 745.6199510921
Calligraphy, Chinese—History—Song-Yuan dynasties,
960–1368 745.6199510902
Calligraphy, Chinese—History—Ming-Qing dynasties,
1368–1912 745.6199510903
Calligraphy, Chinese—History—20th century
745.6199510904
Calligraphy, Hebrew 745.619924
Calligraphy, Islamic 745.619927
Calligraphy, Japanese 745.619956
Calligraphy, Korean 745.619957
Calligraphy—Periodicals 745.6105
Calligraphy—Technique 745.61
Calloway County (Ky.) 976.992
Calloway County (Ky.)—Genealogy 929.376992
Calorimetry 536.6
Calumet County (Wis.) 977.566
Calumet County (Wis.)—Maps 912.77566
Calvert County (Md.)—Genealogy 929.375244
Calvert County (Md.)—Maps 912.75244
Calvin (Fictitious character : Watterson) 741.5973
Calvin, Jean, 1509–1564 284.2092
Calvin, Jean, 1509–1564. Institutio Christianae
religionis 230.42
Calvinism 230.42
Camaro automobile 629.2222
Camaro automobile—History 629.2222
Camaro automobile—Maintenance and repair 629.28722
Camaro automobile—Maintenance and repair—
Handbooks, manuals, etc. 629.28722
Cambodia 959.6
Cambodia—Description and travel 915.9604; 915.960442
Cambodia—History 959.6
Cambodia—History—1953–1975 959.6041
Cambodia—History—1975–1979 959.6042
Cambodia—Politics and government 959.6
Cambodia—Politics and government—1975–1979
320.956909047; 959.6042
Cambodia—Politics and government—1979–
320.956909048; 320.959609048; 959.6042
Cambodian-Vietnamese Conflict, 1977–1991 959.6042
Cambridge (England) 942.659
Cambridge (England)—Guidebooks 914.265904;
914.265904859; 914.26590486
Cambridge (Mass.) 974.44
Cambridge University Press 070.50942659
Cambridge University Press—History 070.50942659
Camcorders 778.5993
Camellias 583.624; 635.933624
Camelot (Legendary place) 398.20942034; 398.42;
808.80372
Camels 599.6362; 636.295
Camera industry 338.47681418
Cameras 681.418; 771.3
Cameron, Donald (Fictitious character) 823.914
Cameron, Donald (Fictitious character)—Fiction
823.914
Cameron family 929.20973
Cameroon 967.11

Canada—Social life and customs—19th century 971.03
Canada—Social life and customs—20th century 971.06
Canada—Social policy 361.610971
Canada—Study and teaching 971.0071
Canada—Tours 917.104; 917.104648
Canada. Treaties, etc. 1992 Oct. 7 382.917
Canada. Treaties, etc. United States, 1988 Jan. 2
  382.971073
Canada, Western 971.2
Canada, Western—Guidebooks 917.1204; 917.12043
Canadian horse 636.15
Canadian literature 810; 810.80971
Canadian literature—20th century 810.8005; 810.80052;
  810.80054
Canadian literature—History and criticism 810.9971
Canadian literature—History and criticism—Theory, etc.
  810.9971
Canadian literature—Indian authors 810.80897
Canadian literature—Women authors 810.809287
Canadian literature—Women authors—History and
  criticism 810.992870971
Canadian poetry 811; 811.0080971
Canadian poetry—20th century 811.54080971
Canadian poetry—20th century—History and criticism
  855.5409971
Canadian poetry—History and criticism 811.009971
Canadian poetry—Women authors 811.5408092870971
Canadian prose literature 818.08
Canadian Rockies (B.C. and Alta.) 971.1
Canadian Rockies (B.C. and Alta.)—Guidebooks
  917.1104; 917.11044
Canadian wit and humor 817.0080971
Canadian wit and humor, Pictorial 741.5971
Canadians 305.811
Canals 386.4; 627.13
Canaries 636.68625
Canberra (A.C.T.) 994.71
Canberra (A.C.T.)—Guidebooks 919.47104;
  919.4710466; 919.471047
Canberra (A.C.T.)—History 994.71
Canberra (A.C.T.)—Pictorial works 919.47100222
Cancer 616.994
Cancer—Alternative treatment 616.99406
Cancer cells 616.99407
Cancer cells—Growth 616.99407
Cancer cells—Growth—Regulation 616.99407
Cancer—Chemoprevention 616.994052
Cancer—Chemotherapy 616.994061
Cancer—Chemotherapy—Complications 616.994061
Cancer—Chemotherapy—Handbooks, manuals, etc.
  616.994061
Cancer—Complications 616.994
Cancer—Cytodiagnosis 616.99407582
Cancer—Diagnosis 616.994075
Cancer—Diet therapy 616.9940654
Cancer—Diet therapy—Recipes 641.5631
Cancer—Environmental aspects 616.994071
Cancer—Epidemiology 614.59994
Cancer—Etiology 616.994071
Cancer—Gene therapy 616.994042
Cancer—Genetic aspects 616.994042
Cancer—Handbooks, manuals, etc. 616.994
Cancer—Immunological aspects 616.994079
Cancer—Immunotherapy 616.994061
Cancer in children 618.92994
Cancer—Intraoperative radiotherapy 616.9940642
Cancer—Molecular aspects 616.99407
Cancer—Nursing 610.73698
Cancer—Nursing—Handbooks, manuals, etc. 610.73698

Cancer—Nutritional aspects 616.994071
Cancer pain 616.994
Cancer—Palliative treatment 616.99406
Cancer—Patients 362.1969940092
Cancer—Patients—Biography 362.1969940092
Cancer—Patients—United States 362.19699400973
Cancer—Periodicals 616.994005
Cancer—Photochemotherapy 616.994061
Cancer—Prevention 616.994052
Cancer—Psychological aspects 616.9940019
Cancer—Psychosomatic aspects 616.99408
Cancer—Radioimmunoimaging 616.99407575
Cancer—Radiotherapy 616.9940642
Cancer—Reporting 614.59994
Cancer—Research 616.9940072
Cancer—Research—United States 616.9940072073
Cancer—Social aspects 362.196994
Cancer—Surgery 616.994059
Cancer—Thermotherapy 616.9940632
Cancer—Treatment 616.99406
Cancer—Treatment—Complications 616.99406
Candidiasis 616.969
Candidiasis—Diet therapy 616.969
Candlemaking 745.59332
Candles 747.92
Candy 641.853
Canidae 599.77
Canine sports medicine 636.708971027
Cannabis 633.79
Canned meat 641.66
Canned salmon 641.692
Canneries 664.0282
Cannibalism 394.9
Cannibalism in animals 591.53
Canning and preserving 641.4; 641.42; 664.028;
  664.0282
Canoe camping 796.54
Canoe racing 797.14
Canoes and canoeing 797.122
Canoes and canoeing—Alaska 797.12209798
Canoes and canoeing—Alaska—Guidebooks 917.9804;
  917.980451; 917.980452
Canoes and canoeing—Maine 797.12209741
Canoes and canoeing—Maine—Guidebooks 917.404;
  917.40444; 917.410443
Canoes and canoeing—Minnesota—Boundary Waters
  Canoe Area 797.1220977675
Canoes and canoeing—Minnesota—Boundary Waters
  Canoe Area—Guidebooks 917.7675
Canoes and canoeing—New Jersey—Pine Barrens
  797.12209749
Canoes and canoeing—New Jersey—Pine Barrens—
  Guidebooks 917.4904; 917.490443; 917.490444
Canoes and canoeing—New York (State) 917.470444
Canoes and canoeing—New York (State)—Guidebooks
  797.12209747; 917.4704; 917.470443
Canoes and canoeing—Oregon 797.12209795
Canoes and canoeing—Oregon—Guidebooks 917.9504;
  917.950443; 917.950444
Canoes and canoeing—United States—Guidebooks
  797.1220973; 917.304; 917.304929
Canon camera 771.31
Canon law 262.9
Canon law—History 262.909
Canon (Literature) 809
Canons, fugues, etc. (Harpsichord) 786.4187
Canons, fugues, etc. (Organ) 786.5187
Canons, fugues, etc. (Piano) 786.2187
Cant 417.2

Cantar de mío Cid 861.1
Cantatas 782.24
Cantatas, Sacred 782.24
Cantatas, Sacred (Children's voices) 782.24; 782.724
Cantatas, Sacred—Vocal scores with piano 782.24
Cantatas, Secular 782.48
Cantatas, Secular (Children's voices) 782.48; 782.748
Canterbury (England) 942.234
Canterbury (England)—Description and travel
  914.223404; 914.223404859; 914.22340486
Canton (Ohio) 977.162
Canton (Ohio)—Maps 912.77161
Cantonese dialects 495.17
Canvas embroidery 746.442
Canvas embroidery—Patterns 746.442041
Canyoneering 796.52
Capability maturity model (Computer software)
  005.10685
Capacitors 621.315
Capacity theory (Mathematics) 515.94
Cape Archives Depot—Catalogs 016.9687
Cape Breton Island (N.S.) 971.69
Cape Breton Island (N.S.)—History 971.69
Cape Breton Island (N.S.)—Social life and customs
  971.69
Cape Cod (Mass.) 974.492
Cape Cod (Mass.)—Description and travel 917.449204;
  917.44920443; 917.44920444
Cape Cod (Mass.)—Guidebooks 917.449204;
  917.44920443; 917.44920444
Cape Cod (Mass.)—History 974.492
Cape Girardeau County (Mo.) 977.896
Cape Girardeau County (Mo.)—Maps 912.77896
Cape of Good Hope (South Africa) 968.7
Cape of Good Hope (South Africa)—History 968.7
Cape Town Metropolitan Area (South Africa)—Maps
  912.687355
Cape Town (South Africa) 968.7355
Cape Town (South Africa)—Description and travel
  916.8735504; 916.873550465
Cape Town (South Africa)—Guidebooks 916.8735504;
  916.873550465
Caper Court (London, England : Imaginary place)
  823.914
Caper films 791.43655
Capillarity 541.33
Capillary electrophoresis 541.372
Capital 332.041
Capital budget 658.154
Capital budget—New York (State)—New York
  352.49747105
Capital gains tax 336.2424
Capital gains tax—Law and legislation 343.05245
Capital gains tax—Law and legislation—Great Britain
  343.4105245
Capital gains tax—Law and legislation—United States
  343.7305245
Capital gains tax—United States 336.24240973
Capital investments 332.63; 658.152
Capital investments—Decision making 658.152;
  658.1522
Capital investments—Evaluation 332.63; 658.152
Capital investments—United States 332.630973
Capital investments—United States—Periodicals
  332.63097305
Capital market 332.0415
Capital market—Europe, Eastern 332.04150947
Capital market—Mathematical models 332.0415015118
Capital market—United States 332.04150973

Capital movements 332.042
Capital movements—Developing countries 332.042
Capital movements—Law and legislation 341.751
Capital punishment 345.0773; 364.66
Capital punishment—United States 345.730773;
  364.660973
Capital punishment—United States—History 364.660973
Capital—United States 332.0410973
Capitalism 330.122
Capitalism—History 330.12209
Capitalism—Moral and ethical aspects 174.4
Capitalism—Religious aspects 291.1785
Capitalism—Religious aspects—Christianity 261.85
Capitalists and financiers 332.092
Capitalists and financiers—United States 332.092273
Capitalists and financiers—United States—History
  332.0973
Capitation fees (Medical care) 338.433621; 362.10681
Capone, Al, 1899–1947 364.1092
Capriati, Jennifer 796.342092
Caprice automobile 629.2222
Caprice automobile—Maintenance and repair 629.28722
Caprice automobile—Maintenance and repair—
  Handbooks, manuals, etc. 629.28722
Caps (Headgear) 391.43
Captive reptiles 639.39
Captive reptiles—Diseases 639.39
Captive snakes 639.396
Captive turtles 639.392
Captivity narratives 808.80355
Capybara 599.359
Car wash industry 338.47629287
Caravan van 629.2234
Caravan van—Maintenance and repair 629.28734
Caravan van—Maintenance and repair—Handbooks,
  manuals, etc. 629.28734
Carbenes (Methylene compounds) 547.1224
Carbide cutting tools 621.93
Carbocations 547.1372
Carbohydrates 547.78; 572.56
Carbohydrates—Metabolism 572.564
Carbon 546.681; 620.193
Carbon composites 620.193
Carbon cycle (Biogeochemistry) 577.144
Carbon dioxide 546.6812
Carbon dioxide—Environmental aspects 363.7387
Carbon dioxide lasers 621.3663
Carbon dioxide mitigation 363.738746
Carbon—Isotopes 546.681588
Carbon monoxide 546.6812
Carbonate reservoirs 552.58; 622.3382
Carbonated beverages 641.875; 663.62
Carcharhinidae 597.34
Carcinogenesis 616.994071
Carcinogenicity testing 616.994071
Carcinogens 616.994071
Card games 795.4
Card tricks 793.85
Cardano, Girolamo, 1501–1576 610.92
Cardiac arrest 616.123025
Cardiac catheterization 616.120754
Cardiac catheterization—Handbooks, manuals, etc.
  616.120754
Cardiac intensive care 616.12028
Cardiac pacemakers 616.1280645; 617.4120645
Cardiac pacing 617.4120645
Cardigan, Jake (Fictitious character) 813.54
Cardigan, Jake (Fictitious character)—Fiction 813.54
Cardigan Welsh corgi 636.737

Cardinals (Birds) 598.883
Cardiologists 616.120092
Cardiology 616.12
Cardiology—Terminology 616.120014
Cardiomyoplasty 617.4120592
Cardiopulmonary system 573.1; 612.1
Cardiopulmonary system—Diseases 616.1
Cardiopulmonary system—Diseases—Physical therapy 616.1062
Cardiopulmonary system—Physiology 612.1
Cardiovascular agents 615.71
Cardiovascular agents—Handbooks, manuals, etc. 615.71
Cardiovascular emergencies 616.1025
Cardiovascular equipment industry 338.47681761
Cardiovascular fitness 616.105
Cardiovascular pharmacology 615.71
Cardiovascular system 611.1; 612.1
Cardiovascular system—Diseases 616.1
Cardiovascular system—Diseases—Diagnosis 616.1075
Cardiovascular system—Diseases—Examinations, questions, etc. 616.10076
Cardiovascular system—Diseases—Nursing 610.73691
Cardiovascular system—Diseases—Nutritional aspects 616.10654
Cardiovascular system—Diseases—Prevention 616.105
Cardiovascular system—Diseases—Risk factors 616.1071
Cardiovascular system—Diseases—Treatment 616.106
Cardiovascular system—Pathophysiology 616.107
Cardiovascular system—Physiology 612.1
Cardiovascular system—Surgery 617.41
Cardozo, Benjamin N. (Benjamin Nathan), 1870–1938 347.732634
Cardsharping 794.4; 795.4
Career changes 331.702; 650.14
Career changes—United States 650.14
Career development 650.14
Career development—United States 650.140973
Career education 370.113
Career education—United States 370.1130973
Career education—United States—Curricula 370.113
Caregivers 362.0425
Carey, Neal (Fictitious character) 813.54
Carey, Neal (Fictitious character)—Fiction 813.54
Carey, William, 1761–1834 266.61092
Cargo cults 299.9
Cargo handling 623.8881
Cargo ships 387.245; 623.8245
Caribbean Americans 970.004729
Caribbean Area 972.9
Caribbean Area—Civilization 972.9
Caribbean Area—Description and travel 917.2904; 917.290452
Caribbean Area—Economic conditions 330.9729
Caribbean Area—Economic conditions—1945– 330.9729052
Caribbean Area—Economic integration 337.1729
Caribbean Area—Economic policy 338.9729
Caribbean Area—Foreign relations 327.09729
Caribbean Area—Foreign relations—United States 327.729073
Caribbean Area—Guidebooks 917.2904; 917.290452
Caribbean Area—History 972.9
Caribbean Area—Periodicals 972.9005
Caribbean Area—Politics and government 320.9729
Caribbean Area—Politics and government—1945– 320.972909045
Caribbean Area—Social life and customs 972.9

Caribbean literature 809.89729
Caribbean literature (English) 810.809729
Caribbean literature (English)—History and criticism 810.99729
Caribbean literature (English)—Women authors 810.80928709729
Caribbean literature (English)—Women authors— History and criticism 810.9928709729
Caribbean literature—History and criticism 809.89729
Caribbean poetry (English) 811.00809729
Caribbean studies 972.90072
Caribou 599.658
Caribou Eskimos 971.270049712
Caricatures and cartoons 741.59
Caricatures and cartoons—United States 741.5973
Carillons 786.64
Caring 177.7
Caring—Religious aspects 291.61
Caring—Religious aspects—Christianity 253
Carlos, the Jackal 364.1092
Carlton County (Minn.) 977.673
Carlton County (Minn.)—Maps 912.77673
Carlucci, Rugs (Fictitious character) 813.54
Carlyle, Carlotta (Fictitious character) 813.54
Carlyle, Carlotta (Fictitious character)—Fiction 813.54
Carlyle, Thomas, 1795–1881 824.8
Carlyle, Thomas, 1795–1881—Correspondence 824.8
Carlyle, Thomas, 1795–1881—Criticism and interpretation 824.8
Carlyle, Thomas, 1795–1881—Political and social views 824.8
Carmen Sandiego (Game) 793.932
Carnatic music 780.9548
Carnatic music—History and criticism 780.9548
Carnegie, Andrew, 1835–1919 338.7672092
Carnegie libraries 027.4
Carnival 394.25
Carnival glass—Collectors and collecting— Encyclopedias 748.290491075
Carnival—Louisiana—New Orleans—History 394.250976335
Carnival masks 394.25
Carnivals in literature 808.80357
Carnivora 599.7
Carnivorous plants 583.75; 635.93375
Caroline County (Md.)—Maps 912.75231
Caroline County (Va.)—Genealogy 929.3755362
Caroline, Queen, consort of George IV, King of Great Britain, 1768–1821 941.074092; 942.074092
Carolingians 944.014
Carols 782.28
Carols, German—Texts 782.280268
Carols—Texts 782.280268
Carotid artery—Surgery 617.413
Carpal tunnel syndrome 616.87
Carpathia, Nicolae (Fictitious character) 813.54
Carpatho-Rusyn literature 891.7
Carpenter, Edward, 1844–1929 335.0092; 828.809
Carpenter, Liz 070.92
Carpenter, Scott (Fictitious character) 813.54
Carpenter, Scott (Fictitious character)—Fiction 813.54
Carpentry 694
Carpets 645.1
Carpo, Michael (Fictitious character) 813.54
Carrey, Jim, 1962– 791.43028092
Carriages and carts 388.341
Carrick, Webb (Fictitious character) 823.914
Carriers 388.041
Carriers—Law and legislation 343.093

Catalogs 017
Catalogs, Booksellers' 017
Catalogs, Classified 017
Catalogs, College 378.00216
Catalogs, Publishers' 017
Catalogs, Subject 017
Catalogs, Union 021.642
Catalysis 541.395
Catalysts 541.395; 660.2995
Catalytic cracking 665.533
Catalytic RNA 572.88
Catamarans 797.124
Cataract 617.742
Cataract—Surgery 617.742059
Catasetums 584.4; 635.9344
Catastrophes (Geology) 576.84
Catastrophes (Mathematics) 514.74
Catechetics 268
Catechetics—Catholic Church 268.82
Catechisms 238
Categorial grammar 415
Categories (Mathematics) 511.3
Categorization (Linguistics) 401.43
Caterers and catering 642.4; 642.4092
Caterers and catering—Management 642.4068
Caterpillars 595.78139
Catfishes 597.49; 597.492
Catharine Howard, Queen, consort of Henry VIII, King
    of England, d. 1542 942.052092
Catharine, of Aragon, Queen, consort of Henry VIII,
    King of England, 1485–1536 942.052092
Cathédrale de Chartres 726.609445124
Cathedrals 726.6
Cathedrals—France 726.60944
Cather, Willa, 1873–1947 813.52
Cather, Willa, 1873–1947—Criticism and interpretation
    813.52
Cather, Willa, 1873–1947. My Ántonia 813.52
Catherine de Médicis, Queen, consort of Henry II, King
    of France, 1519–1589 944.028092
Catherine, of Siena, Saint, 1347–1380 282.092
Catherine, of Valois, Queen, consort of Henry V, King of
    England, 1401–1437 942.042092
Catholic action 266.2
Catholic Church 282
Catholic Church—Africa 282.6; 282.609049
Catholic Church—Apologetic works 230.2; 282
Catholic church buildings 246.9582
Catholic Church—Byzantine rite 281.5
Catholic Church—California 282.794
Catholic Church—California—History 282.794
Catholic Church—Caribbean Area 282.729
Catholic Church—Caribbean Area—Clergy 282.092
Catholic Church—Caribbean Area—Clergy—Political
    activity 322.109729
Catholic Church—Catechisms 238.2
Catholic Church. Catechismus Ecclesiae Catholicae
    238.2
Catholic Church—Clergy 262.142
Catholic Church—Clergy—Training of 282.0711
Catholic Church—Controversial literature 282
Catholic Church—Customs and practices 264.02
Catholic Church—Doctrines 230.2
Catholic Church—Doctrines—History 230.2
Catholic Church—Education 371.0712; 378.0712
Catholic Church—Education—United States 371.071273
Catholic Church—Encyclopedias 282.03
Catholic Church—England 282.42
Catholic Church—England—History 282.42

Catholic Church—Government 262.02
Catholic Church—Handbooks, manuals, etc. 282
Catholic Church—History 282.09
Catholic Church—History—20th century 282.0904
Catholic Church—History—1965– 282.09045
Catholic Church—Ireland 282.415
Catholic Church—Ireland—Clergy 282.092
Catholic Church—Latin America 282.8
Catholic Church—Latin America—History 282.8
Catholic Church—Latin America—History—20th century
    282.8
Catholic Church—Liturgy 264.02
Catholic Church—Liturgy—History 264.02
Catholic Church—Maronite rite—Liturgy 264.015
Catholic Church—Missions 266.2
Catholic Church. National Conference of Catholic
    Bishops 282.73
Catholic Church. National Conference of Catholic
    Bishops. Challenge of peace 261.87308822
Catholic Church. Ordo initiationis Christianae adultorum
    264.020813
Catholic Church—Oriental rites 281.5
Catholic Church—Pastoral letters and charges 282.73
Catholic Church—Periodicals 282.05
Catholic Church—Philippines 282.599
Catholic Church. Pope (1963-1978 : Paul VI) 282.092
Catholic Church. Pope (1963-1978 : Paul VI). Humanae
    vitae 241.66
Catholic Church. Pope (1978- : John Paul II) 282.092
Catholic Church. Pope (1978- : John Paul II). Veritatis
    splendor 241.042
Catholic Church—Prayer-books and devotions 242.802;
    264.7
Catholic Church—Reception of baptized Christians
    264.02099
Catholic Church—Relations 261.2
Catholic Church—Relations—Judaism 261.26
Catholic Church—Sermons 252.02
Catholic Church—Teaching office 262.8
Catholic Church—United States 282.73
Catholic Church—United States—Clergy 282.092
Catholic Church—United States—History 282.73
Catholic Church—United States—History—20th century
    282.7309049
Catholic Church—United States—History—1965–
    282.7309045
Catholic ex-priests 262.142
Catholic high schools 373.21712
Catholic high schools—United States 373.2171273
Catholic high schools—United States—Entrance
    examinations—Study guides 373.1262
Catholic schools 371.0712
Catholic schools—United States 371.07120973
Catholic schools—United States—Administration 371.2
Catholic schools—United States—Finance 371.206
Catholic universities and colleges 378.0712
Catholic women 305.41
Catholic women—Religious life 248.843
Catholic Worker Movement 261.8
Catholics 305.62
Catholics—Biography 282.0922
Catholics—England 282.42
Catholics—United States 282.73
Catholics—United States—Biography 282.092273
Catholics—United States—History 282.73
Catholics—United States—History—20th century
    282.730904
Catlin, George, 1796–1872 759.13
Cats 599.752; 636.8

Cats—Anatomy 571.319752
Cats—Anecdotes 636.8
Cats—Behavior 636.8
Cats—Behavior therapy 636.8089689142
Cats—Caricatures and cartoons 741.5973
Cats—Diseases 636.80896
Cats—Encyclopedias 636.8003
Cats—England—Yorkshire—Anecdotes 636.8094281
Cats—Folklore 398.2452974428; 398.369974428
Cats—Food 636.8085
Cats—Food—Recipes 636.8085
Cats—Health 636.8083
Cats—Humor 636.800207
Cats in art 704.9432975
Cats—Literary collections 808.803629752
Cats—Names 636.80887; 929.97
Cats—Physiology 571.1975
Cats—Pictorial works 636.800222
Cats—Training 636.80887
Cattle 636.2
Cattle—Diseases 636.20896
Cattle herding 636.20845
Cattle trade 380.14162
Catullus, Gaius Valerius 874.01
Catullus, Gaius Valerius—Criticism and interpretation 874.01
Catullus, Gaius Valerius—Translations into English 874.01
Caucasus 947.5
Cauchy problem 515.35
Caucus 328.36
Causality (Physics) 530.01
Causation 122
Cavafy, Constantine, 1863–1933 889.132
Cavafy, Constantine, 1863–1933—Translations into English 889.132
Cavalier County (N.D.) 978.437
Cavalier County (N.D.)—Maps 912.78437
Cavalier King Charles spaniel 636.7524
Cavaquinho 787.85
Cave animals 591.564
Cave conservation 333.73
Cave divers 796.525
Cave paintings 709.011
Caves 551.447
Caves—Religious aspects 291.212; 291.35
Caviidae 599.3592
Caving 796.525
Cavitation 620.1064
Cavity-ringdown spectroscopy 543.0858
Caxton, William, ca. 1422–1491 686.2092
Cayapo philosophy 199.81089984
Cayce, Edgar, 1877–1945 133.8092
Cayley graphs 511.5
cc:Mail 005.71369
CCD cameras 522.63
CD-I technology 004.565
CD-ROM books 070.5797
CD-ROM industry 338.47004565
CD-ROM publishing 070.5797
CD-ROMs 004.565
CD-ROMs—Handbooks, manuals, etc. 004.565
CD-ROMs—Periodicals 004.565
CD-Rs 004.565; 384; 621.38932; 621.39767
Cebrionidae 595.765
Cecil County (Md.)—Genealogy 929.375238
Cecil County (Md.)—Maps 912.75238
Cecile, Sister (Fictitious character) 813.54
Cedar County (Iowa) 977.766

Cedar County (Iowa)—Maps 912.77766
Ceilings 721.7
Celan, Paul 831.914
Celan, Paul—Criticism and interpretation 831.914
Celan, Paul—Translations into English 831.914
Celebrities 920.02
Celebrities—Biography 920.02
Celebrities—Biography—Dictionaries 920.0203
Celebrities—Caricatures and cartoons 741.5973
Celebrities—Directories 920.0025
Celebrities in mass media 302.2308621
Celebrities—Portraits 704.942; 779.2
Celebrities—Portraits—Exhibitions 704.942; 779.2
Celebrities—United States—Biography 920.073
Celebrity automobile 629.2222
Celebrity automobile—Maintenance and repair 629.28722
Celebrity automobile—Maintenance and repair—Handbooks, manuals, etc. 629.28722
Celebrity weddings 392.508621
Celestial mechanics 521
Celiac disease 616.399
Celibacy 306.732
Celibacy—Catholic Church 253.25
Céline, Louis-Ferdinand, 1894–1961 843.912
Céline, Louis-Ferdinand, 1894–1961—Criticism and interpretation 843.912
Cell culture 571.638
Cell cycle 571.84
Cell death 571.936
Cell determination 571.8636
Cell differentiation 571.835
Cell membranes 571.64
Cell metabolism 572.4
Cell nuclei 571.66
Cell organelles 571.65
Cell physiology 571.6
Cell proliferation 571.84; 616.994071
Cell receptors 572.69
Cells 571.6
Cells—Growth 571.849
Cells—Growth—Regulation 571.84937
Cells—Morphology 571.633
Cells—Motility 571.67
Cellular automata 511.3
Cellular immunity 616.0797
Cellular signal transduction 571.74
Cellular telephone equipment industry 384.53
Cellular telephone equipment industry—United States 384.53
Cellular telephone services industry 384.534
Cellular telephone systems 384.535; 621.38456
Cellular telephone systems—United States—Directories 384.53502573
Cellular telephones 384.53
Cellular telephones—Law and legislation 343.09943
Cellulose 547.782; 572.56682; 661.802
Celtic antiquities 936.1
Celtic Church 274.102
Celtic harp music 787.95
Celtic languages 491.6
Celtic literature 891.6
Celtic literature—History and criticism 891.609
Celtic music 781.62916
Celtic philology 491.6
Celts 305.8916; 940.04916
Celts—Folklore 398.2089916
Celts—Religion 299.16
Cement 620.135

Cement composites 620.135
Cemeteries 363.75
Cenci, Beatrice, 1577–1599 945.07092
Cendrars, Blaise, 1887–1961 841.912
Cendrars, Blaise, 1887–1961—Translations into English 841.912
Censorship 363.31
Censorship—United States 363.310973
Census 310
Census districts 310
Census districts—California—Alameda County—Maps 912.79465
Census districts—California—Los Angeles County—Maps 912.79493
Census districts—California—San Bernardino County—Maps 912.79495
Census districts—California—San Diego County—Maps 912.79498
Census districts—California—San Francisco—Maps 912.79461
Census districts—California—Santa Barbara County—Maps 912.79491
Census districts—California—Santa Clara County—Maps 912.79473
Census districts—Washington (State)—King County—Maps 912.79777
Cent 737.4973
Centaurs in literature 808.80375; 809.93375
Centenaries 394.2
Centennial Olympic Park Bombing, Atlanta, Ga., 1996 364.1523
Centers for the performing arts 725.83
Central America 972.8
Central America—Description and travel 917.2804; 917.280453; 917.280454
Central America—Economic conditions 330.9728
Central America—Economic conditions—1979– 330.9728053
Central America—Economic policy 338.9728
Central America—Foreign relations 327.09728
Central America—Foreign relations—1979– 327.0972809048
Central America—Foreign relations—United States 327.730728
Central America—Guidebooks 917.2804; 917.280453; 917.280454
Central America—Politics and government 972.8
Central America—Politics and government—1979– 320.972809048; 972.8053
Central America—Relations 303.482728
Central America—Relations—United States 303.482728073
Central labor councils 331.872
Central-local government relations 320.8
Central nervous system 573.86
Central nervous system—Imaging 616.804754
Central nervous system—Infections 616.8
Central nervous system—Magnetic resonance imaging 616.8047548
Central-plan buildings 720.48
Central planning 338.9
Central planning—Soviet Union 338.947
Central Railroad of New Jersey 385.09749
Central Valley (Calif.) 979.45
Central Valley (Calif.)—Maps 912.7945
Centrifugal pumps 621.67
Centrifuges 542; 681.754
Centrosomes 571.65
Cephalopoda 594.5

Cephalopoda, Fossil 564.5
Cerambycidae 595.7648
Ceramic engineering 666
Ceramic materials 620.14; 666
Ceramic materials—Corrosion 620.1404223
Ceramic materials—Surfaces 620.14
Ceramic materials—Testing 620.140287
Ceramic-matrix composites 620.14
Ceramic powders 666
Ceramic to metal bonding 666.042
Ceramics 666; 738
Ceramics in medicine 610.284
Cercopithecidae 599.86
Cereal products industry 338.476647; 664.7
Cerebral arteriovenous malformations 573.86213976; 616.81
Cerebral circulation 612.824
Cerebral cortex 573.86; 612.825
Cerebral dominance 612.825
Cerebral edema 616.8
Cerebral ischemia 616.81
Cerebral ischemia—Pathophysiology 616.81
Cerebral malaria 616.83
Cerebral palsied children 618.92836
Cerebral palsied children—Rehabilitation 618.9283603
Cerebral palsy 616.836
Cerebrovascular disease 616.81
Cerebrovascular disease—Diagnosis 616.81075
Cerebrovascular disease—Patients 362.19681
Cerebrovascular disease—Patients—Rehabilitation 616.8103
Cerebrovascular disease—Surgery 617.481
Cerebrovascular disease—Ultrasonic imaging 616.8107543
Ceremonial objects 291.38
Cerro Gordo County (Iowa) 977.725
Cerro Gordo County (Iowa)—Genealogy 929.30977725
Cerro Gordo County (Iowa)—Maps 912.77725
Certainty 121.63
Certificates of deposit 332.1752
Cervantes Saavedra, Miguel de, 1547–1616 863.3
Cervantes Saavedra, Miguel de, 1547–1616—Criticism and interpretation 863.3
Cervantes Saavedra, Miguel de, 1547–1616. Don Quixote 863.3
Cervantes Saavedra, Miguel de, 1547–1616. Novelas ejemplares 863.3
Cervical vertebrae—Diseases 616.73
Cervical vertebrae—Surgery 617.471
Cervidae 599.65
Cervix uteri—Cancer 616.99466
Cesarean section 618.86
Cetacea 599.5
Cetacea, Fossil 569.5
Cézanne, Paul, 1839–1906 759.4
Cézanne, Paul, 1839–1906—Criticism and interpretation 759.4
CGI (Computer network protocol) 004.62
Chaco War, 1932–1935 989.20716
Chaco War, 1932–1935—Campaigns 989.2071642
Chadwick, Geoffry (Fictitious character) 813.54
Chaetognatha 592.38
Chaetomium 579.567
Chafing dish cookery 641.585
Chagall, Marc, 1887– 709.2; 759.7
Chagall, Marc, 1887– —Criticism and interpretation 709.2
Chain restaurants 647.95
Chain stores 381.12

Chair caning 684.13
Chairs 684.13; 749.32
Chaitanya, 1486–1534 294.5512092
Chaka, Zulu Chief, 1787?–1828 968.041092
Chakra (Hinduism) 294.543
Chakras 131
Chalcid wasps 595.79
Challenged books 098.1
Challenger, Professor (Fictitious character) 823.8
Challenger, Professor (Fictitious character)—Fiction
  823.8
Challenger (Spacecraft)—Accidents 363.124
Chamaemelum 583.99
Chamber music 785
Chamber music groups 784.3
Chamber music—History and criticism 785.009
Chamber orchestra music 784.3
Chamberlain, Joshua Lawrence, 1828–1914 973.7441;
  974.1041092
Chamberlain, Lindsay (Fictitious character) 813.54
Chambers, Oswald, 1874–1917 269.2092
Chambrun, Pierre (Fictitious character) 813.52
Chambrun, Pierre (Fictitious character)—Fiction 813.52
Chameleons 597.956
Chameleons as pets 639.3956
Champagne (Wine) 641.2224
Champaign County (Ill.) 977.366
Champaign County (Ill.)—Maps 912.77366
Chancellorsville (Va.), Battle of, 1863 973.733
Chandler family 929.20973
Chanel, Coco, 1883–1971 746.92092
Change 116
Change (Psychology) 158.1
Changelings 398.22
Changgo music 786.94
Channel Islands 942.34
Channel Islands—Guidebooks 914.23404; 914.23404859;
  914.2340486
Channeling (Spiritualism) 133.91
Channels (Hydraulic engineering) 627.23
Chanson de Roland 841.1
Chants royaux 841.04
Chaotic behavior in systems 003.857
Chapbooks 398.5
Chaplains 291.61
Chaplin, Charlie, 1889–1977 791.43028092
Chapman family 929.20973
Character 155.2
Character actors and actresses 792.028092
Character cake pans 641.86530284; 683.82
Character sets (Data processing) 005.72
Character tests 155.28
Characters and characteristics in literature 808.8027;
  809.927
Characters and characteristics in literature—
  Dictionaries 809.92703
Charadriiformes 598.33
Charanga 784.4
Chardonnay (Wine) 641.2222
Charge coupled devices 621.38152
Charitable uses, trusts, and foundations 346.064
Charitable uses, trusts, and foundations—Great Britain
  346.41064
Charitable uses, trusts, and foundations—Taxation
  343.0668
Charitable uses, trusts, and foundations—Taxation—
  Canada 343.710668
Charitable uses, trusts, and foundations—Taxation—
  United States 343.73052668; 343.730668

Charitable uses, trusts, and foundations—United States
  346.73064
Charities 361.7
Charities—Great Britain 361.70941
Charities—United States 361.70973
Charities—United States—Finance 361.70681
Charities—United States—Handbooks, manuals, etc.
  361.760973
Charity 177.7
Charity golf tournaments 796.3526
Charity organization 361.706
Charity sports events 796.04
Charlemagne, Emperor, 742–814 944.014092
Charles I, King of England, 1600–1649 941.062092
Charles II, King of England, 1630–1685 941.066092
Charles County (Md.)—Genealogy 929.375247
Charles County (Md.)—Maps 912.75247
Charles Edward, Prince, grandson of James II, King of
  England, 1720–1788 941.072092
Charles, Prince of Wales, 1948– 941.085092
Charles, Prince of Wales, 1948– —Marriage 941.085092
Charles, Ray, 1930– 782.42164092
Charleston (S.C.) 975.7915
Charleston (S.C.)—Guidebooks 917.5791504;
  917.579150443; 917.579150444
Charleston (S.C.)—History 975.7915
Charleston (S.C.)—Pictorial works 975.791500222
Charlottes (Desserts) 641.865
Charms 133.44
Charophyta, Fossil 561.93
Charter schools 371; 379.1
Charter schools—Law and legislation 344.071
Charter schools—United States 371
Charters 352.84
Chartism 322.20941
Chase, Elizabeth (Fictitious character) 813.54
Chase, Salmon P. (Salmon Portland), 1808–1873
  973.7092
Chastity 241.66
Chastity—Law and legislation 346.0253
Chattanooga (Tenn.), Battle of, 1863 973.7359
Chatterton, Thomas, 1752–1770 821.6
Chaucer, Geoffrey, d. 1400 821.1
Chaucer, Geoffrey, d. 1400—Bibliography 016.8211
Chaucer, Geoffrey, d. 1400. Canterbury tales 821.1
Chaucer, Geoffrey, d. 1400. Canterbury tales—Criticism,
  Textual 821.1
Chaucer, Geoffrey, d. 1400—Characters 821.1
Chaucer, Geoffrey, d. 1400—Characters—Women 821.1
Chaucer, Geoffrey, d. 1400—Criticism and
  interpretation 821.1
Chaucer, Geoffrey, d. 1400—Criticism, Textual 821.1
Chaucer, Geoffrey, d. 1400—Ethics 821.1
Chaucer, Geoffrey, d. 1400. Hous of fame 821.1
Chaucer, Geoffrey, d. 1400. Knight's tale 821.1
Chaucer, Geoffrey, d. 1400—Knowledge 821.1
Chaucer, Geoffrey, d. 1400—Knowledge—Literature
  821.1
Chaucer, Geoffrey, d. 1400—Language 821.1
Chaucer, Geoffrey, d. 1400—Language—Glossaries, etc.
  821.1
Chaucer, Geoffrey, d. 1400. Legend of good women
  821.1
Chaucer, Geoffrey, d. 1400—Literary style 821.1
Chaucer, Geoffrey, d. 1400—Manuscripts 821.1
Chaucer, Geoffrey, d. 1400—Philosophy 821.1
Chaucer, Geoffrey, d. 1400—Political and social views
  821.1
Chaucer, Geoffrey, d. 1400—Religion 821.1

Chaucer, Geoffrey, d. 1400—Technique 821.1
Chaucer, Geoffrey, d. 1400. Troilus and Criseyde 821.1
Chaucer, Geoffrey, d. 1400—Versification 821.1
Chaucer, Geoffrey, d. 1400. Wife of Bath's tale 821.1
Chauffeurs 388.321
Chavez, Cesar, 1927– 331.8813092
Chechni͡a (Russia) 947.52
Chechni͡a (Russia)—History—Civil War, 1994– 947.52
Checkers 794.2
Checking accounts 332.1752
Checks 346.096
Checks—United States 346.73096
Cheddar Man 569.9
Chee, Jim (Fictitious character) 813.54
Chee, Jim (Fictitious character)—Fiction 813.54
Cheerleading 791.64
Cheese 637.3; 641.373
Cheese shops 381.4173
Cheese—Varieties 637.35; 641.3735
Cheesecake (Cookery) 641.8653
Cheesemaking 637.3
Cheeseman family 929.20973
Cheetah 599.759
Chekhov, Anton Pavlovich, 1860–1904 891.723;
891.733
Chekhov, Anton Pavlovich, 1860–1904—Criticism and
interpretation 891.723
Chekhov, Anton Pavlovich, 1860–1904—Dramatic
works 891.723
Chekhov, Anton Pavlovich, 1860–1904—Translations
into English 891.723; 891.733
Chelates industry 338.4754759044242
Chemical arms control 341.735
Chemical arms control—Verification 327.1745
Chemical bonds 541.224
Chemical carcinogenesis 616.994071
Chemical detectors 681.2
Chemical ecology 577.14
Chemical elements 546; 660; 661.1; 669
Chemical engineering 660
Chemical engineering—Equipment and supplies 660.283
Chemical engineering—Handbooks, manuals, etc. 660
Chemical engineering—Periodicals 660.05
Chemical engineering—Safety measures 660.2804
Chemical engineers 660.092
Chemical equilibrium 541.392
Chemical industry 338.4766; 660
Chemical industry—Accidents 660.2804
Chemical industry—Safety measures 660.2804
Chemical industry—United States 338.476600973
Chemical industry—Waste disposal 660.0286
Chemical kinetics 541.394
Chemical laboratories 542.1
Chemical laboratories—Safety measures 542.89
Chemical lasers 621.3664
Chemical literature 540
Chemical models 540.228
Chemical mutagenesis 572.838
Chemical oceanography 551.4601
Chemical peel 617.4770592
Chemical plants 660
Chemical plants—Design and construction 660
Chemical plants—Equipment and supplies 660.283
Chemical plants—Equipment and supplies—Corrosion
660.283
Chemical plants—Piping—Drawings 660.283
Chemical plants—Risk assessment 660.2804
Chemical plants—Safety measures 660.2804

Chemical process control 660.2815
Chemical process control—Data processing 660.2815
Chemical process control—Instruments 660.2815
Chemical processes 660.28
Chemical reaction, Conditions and laws of 541.394
Chemical reactions 541.39
Chemical reactors 660.2832
Chemical senses 573.877
Chemical structure 541.22
Chemical templates 547.2
Chemical tests and reagents 543.01
Chemical warfare 358.34
Chemical warfare (International law) 341.735
Chemical weapons 358.3482; 623.445
Chemical weapons disposal 623.445
Chemical weapons—United States 623.4450973
Chemicals 540; 660
Chemicals—Dictionaries 660.03
Chemicals—Law and legislation 344.30424
Chemicals—Law and legislation—United States
344.730424
Chemicals—Safety measures 660.2804
Chemiluminescence 572.4358
Chemistry 540
Chemistry, Analytic 543
Chemistry, Analytic—Periodicals 543.005
Chemistry, Analytic—Qualitative 544
Chemistry, Analytic—Quantitative 545
Chemistry, Analytic—Statistical methods 543.00727
Chemistry—Bibliography 016.54
Chemistry—Bio-bibliography 540.92
Chemistry—Data processing 542.85
Chemistry—Dictionaries 540.3
Chemistry—Encyclopedias 540.3
Chemistry—Examinations 540.76
Chemistry—Examinations, questions, etc. 540.76
Chemistry—Experiments 540.724; 540.78
Chemistry, Forensic 363.25
Chemistry—History 540.9
Chemistry, Inorganic 546
Chemistry—Laboratory manuals 540.78; 542
Chemistry—Mathematics 540.151
Chemistry—Nomenclature 540.14
Chemistry, Organic 547
Chemistry, Organic—Laboratory manuals 547.0078
Chemistry, Organic—Nomenclature 547.0014
Chemistry, Organic—Problems, exercises, etc. 547.0076
Chemistry, Organic—Tables 547.0021
Chemistry—Outlines, syllabi, etc. 540
Chemistry—Periodicals 540.5
Chemistry, Physical and theoretical 541; 541.3; 547.1
Chemistry, Physical and theoretical—Mathematics
541.0151
Chemistry, Physical organic 547.13
Chemistry—Problems, exercises, etc. 540.76
Chemistry—Study and teaching 540.71
Chemistry, Technical 660
Chemistry, Technical—Encyclopedias 660.03
Chemistry, Technical—Periodicals 660.05
Chemists 540.92
Chemists—Biography 540.92
Chemokines 616.079
Chemoreceptors 573.87728
Chemotherapy 615.58
Chemotherapy—Handbooks, manuals, etc. 615.58
Chenier plains 578.7683
Chernobyl Nuclear Accident, Chornobyl', Ukraine, 1986
363.17990947714

Child abuse—Great Britain 362.760941
Child abuse—Law and legislation 345.025554
Child abuse—Law and legislation—United States
   345.73025554
Child abuse—United States 362.760973
Child analysis 618.928917
Child artists 704.054
Child authors 809.89282
Child care 649.1
Child care—Costs 338.43362712
Child care services 362.7
Child care services—Government policy 362.7
Child care services—Government policy—United States
   362.70973
Child caregivers 362.0425; 649.083
Child development 305.231
Child development deviations 618.92
Child development—Periodicals 305.23105
Child development—Testing 618.920075
Child development—United States 305.2310973
Child health services 362.19892
Child health services—United States 362.19892000973
Child labor 331.31
Child labor—Developing countries 331.31091724
Child labor—India 331.310954
Child labor—Law and legislation 344.0131
Child labor—Law and legislation—United States
   344.730131
Child labor—United States 331.310973
Child labor—United States—History 331.310973
Child mental health 362.2083
Child mental health services 362.2083
Child mental health services—United States
   362.20830973
Child migrant agricultural laborers 331.31
Child prostitutes 306.745
Child prostitution 306.745
Child prostitution—United States 306.7450973
Child psychiatry 618.9289
Child psychiatry—Handbooks, manuals, etc. 618.9289
Child psychiatry—Periodicals 618.9289005
Child psychology 155.4
Child psychopathology 618.9289
Child psychopathology—Prevention 618.928905
Child psychotherapy 618.928914
Child psychotherapy—Residential treatment 362.21083
Child rearing 649.1
Child rearing—Moral and ethical aspects 649.7
Child rearing—Religious aspects 291.441
Child rearing—Religious aspects—Christianity 248.845
Child rearing—Religious aspects—Judaism 296.74
Child rearing—United States 649.10973
Child rearing—United States—Handbooks, manuals, etc.
   649.10973
Child rearing—United States—Problems, exercises, etc.
   649.10973
Child restraint systems in automobiles 363.12572
Child restraint systems in automobiles—Florida—
   Statistics—Periodicals 363.12572
Child sexual abuse 362.76; 616.85836
Child sexual abuse by teachers 364.153; 371.786
Child sexual abuse—Canada 362.760971
Child sexual abuse—Investigation 363.259536
Child sexual abuse—Prevention 362.767
Child sexual abuse—Prevention—Study and teaching—
   United States 362.767071073
Child sexual abuse—United States 344.7303276;
   362.760973; 616.8583600973

Child sexual abuse—United States—Prevention
   362.7670973; 362.88; 616.85836050973
Child support 346.0172; 362.71
Child support—Government policy—United States
   362.71
Child support—Law and legislation 346.0172
Child support—Law and legislation—California
   346.7940172
Child support—Law and legislation—Michigan
   346.7740172
Child support—Law and legislation—United States
   346.730172
Child support—United States 362.710973
Child volunteers—United States 361.37083
Child welfare 362.7
Child welfare—Australia 362.70994
Child welfare—Developing countries 362.7091724
Child welfare—Government policy 362.7
Child welfare—Government policy—United States
   362.70973
Child welfare—Great Britain 362.70941
Child welfare—New York (State)—New York
   353.536097471; 362.7097471
Child welfare—United States 362.70973
Child welfare—United States—History 362.70973
Child welfare—United States—Periodicals 362.7097305
Childbirth 612.63; 618.4
Childbirth at home 792.028083
Childhood disintegrative disorder 618.9289
Childhood in art 704.9425
Childlessness 306.87
Childlessness—United States 306.87
Childlessness—United States—Psychological aspects
   306.87
Children 305.23
Children—Alcohol use—United States 649.4
Children and death 155.937083
Children and genocide 304.663083; 364.151083
Children and politics 306.2083
Children and strangers 613.6
Children and violence 303.6083; 362.88083
Children and violence—United States 303.6083
Children and war 303.66083
Children—Bibliography 016.30523
Children, Blind—Education 371.911
Children, Blind—Orientation and mobility 362.41083
Children—Books and reading 028.55
Children—Books and reading—United States
   028.550973
Children—Conduct of life 170.83
Children—Conversion to Christianity 248.246083
Children—Costume 646.478083
Children—Death 306.9083
Children—Death—Religious aspects 291.442
Children—Death—Religious aspects—Christianity
   248.866
Children—Diseases 618.92
Children—Diseases—Diagnosis 618.920075
Children—Diseases—Homeopathic treatment
   615.532083
Children—Diseases—Treatment 615.542
Children—Drug use 649.4
Children—Drug use—United States 649.4
Children—Finance, Personal 332.024054
Children—Folklore 398.2083; 398.22
Children—Great Britain 305.230941
Children—Great Britain—Social conditions 305.230941
Children—History 305.2309
Children—Hospital care 362.19892

Children in art 704.9425
Children in literature 808.80352054; 809.93352054
Children in popular culture 305.23
Children in public worship 264.0083
Children—Institutional care 362.732
Children—Institutional care—Great Britain 362.7320941
Children—Institutional care—United States 362.7320973
Children—Intelligence levels 155.4139
Children—Intelligence testing 155.41393
Children (International law) 341.481
Children—Language 408.3
Children—Legal status, laws, etc. 346.0135
Children—Legal status, laws, etc.—Great Britain 346.410135
Children—Legal status, laws, etc.—United States 346.730135
Children—Medical examinations 618.920075
Children—Nigeria 305.2309669
Children—Nigeria—Social conditions 305.2309669
Children—Nutrition 613.2083; 649.3
Children—Nutrition—Handbooks, manuals, etc. 613.2083
Children of alcoholics—United States 362.29230973
Children of divorced parents 306.89
Children of divorced parents—Mental health 362.2
Children of divorced parents—Psychology 306.89
Children of divorced parents—United States 306.89
Children of divorced parents—United States—Psychology 306.89
Children of ex-Jews 305.8924
Children of Holocaust survivors 940.5318
Children of Holocaust survivors—United States 940.5318
Children of immigrants 305.23
Children of immigrants—Education 371.8269; 371.82691
Children of migrant laborers 362.85083
Children of migrant laborers—Education 371.82691
Children of migrant laborers—Education—United States 371.82691
Children of minorities—Education 371.829
Children of minorities—Education—United States 371.82900973
Children of minorities—Mental health—United States 362.2
Children of murder victims 362.88
Children of presidents—United States 973.099
Children of presidents—United States—Biography 973.099
Children of single parents 306.874
Children of single parents—United States 306.874
Children—Pacific Area 305.23099
Children—Pacific Area—Books and reading 028.55099
Children—Portraits 704.9425
Children—Prayer-books and devotions 242.62; 242.82
Children—Psychic ability 133.8083
Children—Religious life 248.82
Children—Services for 362.7
Children—Services for—Great Britain 362.70941
Children—Services for—United States 362.70973
Children—Sexual behavior 306.7083
Children—Sleep 154.6083; 649.4
Children—Social conditions 305.23
Children—Surgery 617.98
Children—Travel 910.83
Children—Travel—California, Northern 917.940083
Children—Travel—California, Northern—Guidebooks 917.9404; 917.940453; 917.940454
Children—Travel—California, Southern 917.9490083

Children—Travel—California, Southern—Guidebooks 917.94904; 917.9490453; 917.9490454
Children—Travel—Europe 914.0083
Children—Travel—Europe—Guidebooks 914.045082
Children—Travel—New York (State) 917.470083
Children—Travel—New York (State)—New York 917.4710083
Children—Travel—New York (State)—New York—Guidebooks 917.47104; 917.4710443; 917.4710444
Children—Travel—Washington (D.C.) 917.530083
Children—Travel—Washington (D.C.)—Guidebooks 917.5304; 917.530441; 917.530442
Children—United States 305.230973
Children—United States—Books and reading 028.50973
Children—United States—History 305.230973
Children—United States—Social conditions 305.230973
Children—United States—Statistics 305.230973021; 362.70973021
Children—Wounds and injuries 617.10083
Children—Writing 808.0083
Children's accidents—Prevention 613.6; 649.10289
Children's art 704.054
Children's atlases 912.083
Children's clothing 646.36; 646.406
Children's drawings 741.083
Children's drawings—Psychological aspects 741.019
Children's electronic reference sources 025.04
Children's encyclopedias and dictionaries 030
Children's films 791.43083
Children's furniture 684.1083
Children's gardens 635.003
Children's librarians 027.625092
Children's libraries 027.625
Children's libraries—Activity programs 027.625
Children's libraries—Activity programs—United States 027.625
Children's literature 808.899282
Children's literature, American 810.809282
Children's literature, American—Bibliography 001.62
Children's literature, American—History and criticism 810.99282
Children's literature, Australian 820.809282
Children's literature, Australian—History and criticism 820.992820994
Children's literature—Authorship 808.068
Children's literature—Authorship—Vocational guidance 808.068023
Children's literature—Bibliography 011.62; 016.808899282
Children's literature—Bibliography—Catalogs 011.62
Children's literature—Bibliography of bibliographies 016.01162
Children's literature—Bio-bibliography 809.89282
Children's literature, Canadian 810.8092820971
Children's literature, Canadian—History and criticism 810.992820971
Children's literature, English 820.809282
Children's literature, English—Bibliography 011.62
Children's literature, English—History and criticism 820.99282
Children's literature—History and criticism 809.89282
Children's literature—History and criticism—Bibliography 011.62; 016.80989282
Children's literature—Illustrations 741.642
Children's literature—Illustrations—Themes, motives 028.5; 741.642
Children's literature—Publishing 070.5
Children's literature—Publishing—United States 070.5

Children's literature—Publishing—United States—
  Directories 070.5; 070.573
Children's literature—Stories, plots, etc. 809.89282
Children's literature—Study and teaching (Elementary)
  372.64; 372.64044
Children's literature—Study and teaching
  (Elementary)—United States 372.640440973;
  372.640973
Children's museums 069.083
Children's parties 793.21
Children's periodicals 050.83
Children's plays, American 812.00809282;
  812.540809282
Children's plays, Canadian 812.008092820971
Children's plays, English 822.00809282
Children's plays—Presentation, etc. 792.0226
Children's plays—Presentations, etc. 372.66
Children's poetry 808.810083
Children's poetry, American 811.00809282
Children's poetry, Australian 821.008092820994
Children's poetry, Canadian 811.008092820971
Children's poetry, English 821.00809282
Children's poetry, French 841.00809282
Children's poetry, German 831.00809282
Children's poetry, German—Translations into English
  831.00809282
Children's poetry, Scottish 821.008092809411
Children's poetry, Spanish 861.00809282
Children's questions and answers 031.02
Children's reference books 028.52
Children's reference books—Bibliography 001.62
Children's reference books—United States 028.52
Children's reference books—United States—
  Bibliography 011.02
Children's rights 323.352
Children's rooms 747.77083
Children's secrets 155.418
Children's sermons 252.53
Children's songs 782.42083
Children's songs—Texts 782.420268; 782.421640268
Children's songs—United States—Texts 782.420268
Children's stories 808.830083
Children's stories, American 813.00809282
Children's stories, American—Bibliography
  016.81300809282
Children's stories, English 823.00808282
Children's stories, English—History and criticism
  823.0099282
Children's Web sites 025.04
Children's writings 808.899282
Chile 983
Chile—Economic conditions 330.983
Chile—Economic conditions—1970-1973 330.9830646
Chile—Economic conditions—1973-1988 330.983065
Chile—Economic policy 338.983
Chile—History 983
Chile—History—Coup d'état, 1973 983.064
Chile—Politics and government 320.983; 983
Chile—Politics and government—1920-1970
  320.9830904
Chile—Politics and government—1970-1973
  320.98309047
Chile—Politics and government—1973-1988
  320.98309047; 983.065
Chili con carne 641.823
Chilkat Indians 305.8972
Chimney cleaning industry 338.476978
Chimpanzees 599.885
Chimpanzees as laboratory animals 619.98

Chimpanzees—Behavior 599.88515
Chin, Lydia (Fictitious character) 813.54
China 951
China—Antiquities 931
China—Armed Forces 355.00951
China—Bibliography 016.951
China—Biography 920.051
China—Civilization 951
China—Civilization—1644-1912 951.03
China—Civilization—1949- 951.05
China—Civilization—Western influences 951
China—Commerce 382.0951
China—Commerce—Handbooks, manuals, etc. 382.0951
China—Commercial policy 381.30951; 382.30951
China—Defenses 355.033051
China—Description and travel 915.1; 915.104;
  915.10459; 915.1046
China—Economic conditions 330.951
China—Economic conditions—1949-1976 330.95105
China—Economic conditions—1976- —Periodicals
  330.951058
China—Economic conditions—1976-2000 330.951058
China—Economic policy 338.951
China—Economic policy—1949- 338.951
China—Economic policy—1976-2000 338.951
China—Encyclopedias 951.003
China—Foreign relations 327.51
China—Foreign relations—1949- 327.51
China—Foreign relations—1949-1976 327.51
China—Foreign relations—1976- 327.51
China—Foreign relations—Great Britain 327.41051
China—Foreign relations—Japan 327.51052
China—Foreign relations—Soviet Union 327.51047
China—Geography 915.1
China—Guidebooks 915.104; 915.10459; 915.1046
China—Historiography 951.0072
China—History 951
China—History—Song dynasty, 960-1279 951.024
China—History—Qing dynasty, 1644-1912 951.03
China—History—19th century 951.033
China—History—Opium War, 1840-1842 951.033
China—History—Boxer Rebellion, 1899-1901 951.035
China—History—20th century 951.05
China—History—Revolution, 1911-1912 951.036
China—History—Republic, 1912-1949 951.04
China—History—1937-1945 951.042
China—History—Civil War, 1945-1949 951.042
China—History—1949- 951.05
China—History—1949-1976 951.05
China—History—Cultural Revolution, 1966-1976
  951.056
China—History—Cultural Revolution, 1966-1976—
  Bibliography 016.95105
China—History—Cultural Revolution, 1966-1976—
  Personal narratives 951.056
China—History—1976- 951.05
China—History—Tiananmen Square Incident, 1989
  951.058
China—Intellectual life 951
China—Intellectual life—1976- 951.05
China—Maps 912.51
China—Military policy 355.033551
China painting 738.15
China painting—Technique 738.15
China painting—Themes, motives 738.15
China—Periodicals 951.005
China—Politics and government 320.951; 951
China—Politics and government—20th century
  320.9510904

Choral societies 782.506
Choral speaking 808.55
Choral speaking—Study and teaching (Elementary) 372.676
Chorale preludes 784.18992
Chorales 784.189925
Choreographers 792.82092
Choreography 792.82
Choros 784.1888
Chorti mythology 299.7208997415
Choruses 782.5
Choruses (Mixed voices), Unaccompanied 782.5
Choruses, Sacred 782.522
Choruses, Sacred (Men's voices) 782.822
Choruses, Sacred (Mixed voices) 782.522
Choruses, Secular 782.54
Choruses, Secular (Men's voices) 782.854
Choruses, Secular (Mixed voices) 782.54
Choruses, Secular (Women's voices) 782.654
Chow chow (Dog breed) 636.72
Chrétien, de Troyes, 12th cent. 841.1
Chrétien, de Troyes, 12th cent. Chevalier au lyon 841.1
Chrétien, de Troyes, 12th cent.—Criticism and interpretation 841.1
Chrétien, de Troyes, 12th cent. Perceval le Gallois 841.1
Chrétien, de Troyes, 12th cent.—Translations into English 841.1
Chrétien, Jean, 1934- 971.0648092
Christian aged 305.26
Christian aged—Prayer-books and devotions 242.65
Christian aged—Religious life 248.85
Christian antiquities 270.09
Christian art and symbolism 246; 704.9482
Christian art and symbolism—To 500 704.94820901
Christian art and symbolism—Medieval, 500-1500 704.94820902
Christian art and symbolism—Modern period, 1500- 704.94820903
Christian biography 270.092; 270.0922
Christian biography—United States 277.300922
Christian Church (Disciples of Christ) 286.63
Christian college students 378.19828204
Christian college students—Religious life 248.834
Christian communities 262.26
Christian communities—Catholic Church 262.26
Christian converts 248.246
Christian converts—Biography 248.240922
Christian converts from Judaism 248.246
Christian County (Ill.) 977.381
Christian County (Ill.)—Maps 912.77381
Christian County (Ky.)—Genealogy 929.376978
Christian drama 808.82516
Christian drama, American 812.051608
Christian education 230.071; 268; 371.071
Christian education—Activity programs 268.6
Christian education—Home training 248.845
Christian education of adults 268.434
Christian education of children 268.432
Christian education of preschool children 268.432
Christian education of preteens 268.432
Christian education of teenagers 268.433
Christian education of young people 268.433
Christian education—Philosophy 268.01
Christian education—Teacher training 268.3071
Christian education—Teaching methods 268.6
Christian education—United States 268.0973
Christian ethics 241
Christian ethics—Anglican authors 241.043

Christian ethics—Catholic authors 241.042
Christian ethics—Methodist authors 241.047
Christian family 929.20973
Christian fiction 808.8393823
Christian fiction, American 813.00803823
Christian, Fletcher, 1764-1793 996.18
Christian gays 305.6
Christian giving 248.6
Christian leadership 253; 262.1
Christian leadership—Biblical teaching 262.1
Christian leadership—Catholic Church 253
Christian life 248.4
Christian life—Anecdotes 248.4
Christian life—Anglican authors 248.483
Christian life—Baptist authors 248.486
Christian life—Biblical teaching 248.4
Christian life—Caricatures and cartoons 741.5973
Christian life—Catholic authors 248.482
Christian life—History 270
Christian life—History—Early church, ca. 30-600 270.1
Christian life—Humor 248.40207
Christian life—Lutheran authors 248.4841
Christian life—Meditations 242
Christian life—Mennonite authors 248.4897
Christian life—Methodist authors 248.487
Christian life—Mormon authors 248.4893
Christian life—Orthodox Eastern authors 248.4819
Christian life—Presbyterian authors 248.485
Christian life—Quaker authors 248.4896
Christian life—Reformed authors 248.4
Christian life—Seventh-Day Adventist authors 248.486732
Christian life—Study and teaching 248.4071
Christian life—Unity School of Christianity authors 248.48997
Christian literature 261.58
Christian literature—Authorship 808.06623
Christian literature, Early 270.1; 281.1
Christian literature, Early—History and criticism 270.1
Christian literature, English 820.803823
Christian literature, Latin (Medieval and modern) 870.8003; 870.8004
Christian literature, Latin (Medieval and modern)—Translations into English 870.8003; 870.8004
Christian martyrs 272
Christian martyrs—Biography 272.0922
Christian martyrs—England 272
Christian martyrs—England—Biography 272.092242
Christian men 305.31
Christian men—Religious life 248.842
Christian patron saints 270.092
Christian philosophers 108.8204
Christian pilgrims and pilgrimages 263.041
Christian pilgrims and pilgrimages—England 263.04242
Christian pilgrims and pilgrimages—England—Canterbury 263.04242234
Christian pilgrims and pilgrimages—England—Canterbury—Poetry 821.1
Christian pilgrims and pilgrimages in literature 808.8038263041; 809.9338263041
Christian pilgrims and pilgrimages—Spain 263.04246
Christian pilgrims and pilgrimages—Spain—Santiago de Compostela 263.0424611
Christian poetry 808.803823
Christian poetry, American 811.00803823
Christian poetry, English 821.00803823
Christian poetry, English—History and criticism 821.0093823
Christian poetry, English (Middle) 821.10803823

Chrysler automobile—Maintenance and repair—Handbooks, manuals, etc. 629.28722
Chrysomelidae 595.7648
Chrysophyceae 579.86
Chumash art 704.039757
Chumash Indians 305.89757; 979.40049757
Chumash Indians—Antiquities 979.401
Chupacabras 001.944
Church 262; 262.7
Church and education 261.8; 379.28
Church and social problems 261.83
Church and social problems—Catholic Church 261.83
Church and state 291.177
Church and state—England 322.10941
Church and state—France 322.10944
Church and state—France—History 322.10944
Church and state—Germany 322.10943
Church and state—Germany—History 322.10943
Church and state—Germany—History—1933–1945 322.1094309043
Church and state—Italy 322.10945
Church and state—Mexico 322.10972
Church and state—Mexico—History—20th century 322.109720904
Church and state—Soviet Union 261.70947; 322.10947
Church and state—United States 322.10973; 342.730852
Church and state—United States—Cases 342.7308520264
Church and state—United States—History 322.10973
Church and substance abuse 261.83229
Church and the world 261.87
Church architecture 726.5
Church architecture—England 726.50942
Church architecture—France 726.50944
Church archives 027.67
Church—Authority 262.8
Church—Biblical teaching 262
Church buildings 726.5
Church buildings—England 726.50942
Church buildings—United States 726.50973
Church bulletins 254.3
Church camps 796.5422
Church—Catholicity 262.72
Church charities 361.75
Church college students 378.1982
Church colleges 378.071
Church colleges—United States 378.0710973
Church controversies 250
Church decoration and ornament 247
Church development, New 254.1
Church discipline 262.9
Church facilities 254.7
Church facilities—Planning 254.7
Church finance 254.8
Church fund raising 254.8
Church group work 253.7
Church group work with teenagers 259.23
Church group work with youth 259.23
Church growth 254.5
Church history 270
Church history—Primitive and early church, ca. 30–600 270.1
Church history—Middle Ages, 600–1500 270.3; 270.4
Church history—Historiography 270.0722
Church—History of doctrines 262
Church libraries 027.67
Church libraries—Administration 025.19767
Church management 254
Church management—Handbooks, manuals, etc. 254

Church meetings 254.6
Church music 781.71
Church music—Catholic Church 781.712
Church music—Church of England 781.713
Church music—England 781.7100942
Church music—Instruction and study 781.710071
Church music—Periodicals 781.71005
Church music—Protestant churches 781.71
Church of England 283.42
Church of England—Doctrines 230.342
Church of England—England 283.42
Church of England—England—Clergy 283.092
Church of England—History 283.42
Church of England—Liturgy 264.03
Church of England—Liturgy—Texts 264.03
Church of England—Sermons 252.03
Church of God 286.73
Church of Jesus Christ of Latter-day Saints 289.332
Church of Jesus Christ of Latter-day Saints—Apologetic works 289.332
Church of Jesus Christ of Latter-day Saints—Controversial literature 289.332
Church of Jesus Christ of Latter-Day Saints—Doctrines 230.9332
Church of Jesus Christ of Latter-day Saints—History 289.33209
Church of Jesus Christ of Latter-day Saints—Missions 266.9332
Church of Jesus Christ of Latter-Day Saints—Presidents 289.3320922
Church of Jesus Christ of Latter-Day Saints—Presidents—Biography 289.30922
Church of Scotland 285.233
Church of the Brethren 286.5
Church of the Brethren—History 286.5
Church officers 254
Church pennants 246.55
Church polity 262
Church public relations 254.4
Church publicity 254.4
Church renewal 262.0017
Church renewal—United States 262.0017
Church schools 371.071
Church schools—Law and legislation 342.0852
Church schools—Law and legislation—United States 342.730852
Church schools—United States 371.0710973
Church signs 254.3; 659.1342
Church Slavic type 686.2191817
Church work 253; 259
Church work—Catholic Church 253
Church work with abused women 259.086949
Church work with adopted children 259.22
Church work with adoptive parents 259.085
Church work with children 259.22
Church work with children—United States 259.220973
Church work with executives 259.088658
Church work with families 259.1
Church work with Hispanic Americans 282.7308968
Church work with leprosy patients 259.4196998
Church work with minorities 259.089
Church work with minorities—United States 259.08900973
Church work with poor children 259.22
Church work with preteens 259.22
Church work with prisoners 259.5
Church work with single people 259.08652
Church work with stepfamilies 259.1
Church work with teenagers 259.23

City and town life—France 307.760944
City and town life—France—Paris 307.760944361
City and town life—Georgia 307.7609758
City and town life—Illinois 307.7609773
City and town life—Illinois—Chicago 307.760977311
City and town life in literature 809.93321732
City and town life—Ireland 307.7609415
City and town life—Ireland—Dublin 307.760941835
City and town life—Louisiana 307.7609763
City and town life—Louisiana—New Orleans
    307.760976335
City and town life—Middle West 307.760977
City and town life—New England 307.760974
City and town life—New Hampshire 307.7609742
City and town life—New Mexico 307.7609789
City and town life—New York (State) 307.7609747
City and town life—New York (State)—New York
    307.76097471
City and town life—New York (State)—New York—
    History 307.76097471
City and town life—New York (State)—New York—
    History—19th century 307.7609747109034
City and town life—New York (State)—New York—
    Literary collections 808.80327471; 810.80327471
City and town life—North Carolina 307.7609756
City and town life—Pennsylvania 307.7609748
City and town life—Scotland 307.7609411
City and town life—Scotland—Glasgow 307.760941443
City and town life—Southern States 307.760975
City and town life—Texas 307.7609764
City and town life—United States 307.760973
City and town life—Virginia 307.7609755
City and town life—Virginia—Richmond 307.7609755451
City and town life—Washington (D.C.) 307.7609753
City churches 250.91732; 253.091732
City councils 320.854
City dwellers 307.76092
City Hospital (Imaginary organization) 823.914
City missions 266.022
City planners 307.1216092
City planning 307.1216; 711.4
City planning and redevelopment law 346.045
City planning and redevelopment law—California
    346.794045
City planning and redevelopment law—Great Britain
    346.41045
City planning and redevelopment law—United States
    346.73045
City planning—Canada 307.12160971
City planning—Citizen participation 307.1216
City planning districts 711.4
City planning—Great Britain 307.12160941
City planning—Periodicals 711.405
City planning—United States 307.12160941;
    307.12160973; 711.40973
City planning—United States—History 307.12160941;
    307.12160973
City planning—Washington (D.C.) 711.409753
City promotion 659.2930776
City traffic 388.41
Civic centers 711.551
Civic improvement 307.34
Civics 320.4
Civics—Study and teaching 320.4071; 370.115
Civics—Study and teaching (Elementary) 372.832
Civics—Study and teaching—United States 320.4071073
Civil defense 363.35
Civil defense—New Zealand 363.3509931
Civil defense—Soviet Union 363.350947

Civil defense—United States 353.950973; 363.350973
Civil disobedience 303.61; 322.4
Civil engineering 624
Civil engineering—Cold weather conditions 620.411
Civil engineering contracts 343.078624
Civil engineering contracts—Great Britain 343.41078624
Civil engineering—Data processing 624.0285
Civil engineering—Dictionaries 624.03
Civil engineering—Handbooks, manuals, etc. 624
Civil engineering—History 624.09
Civil engineering—Periodicals 624.05
Civil engineers 624.092
Civil law 340.56
Civil law—Philippines 349.599
Civil-military relations 322.5
Civil-military relations—Latin America 322.5098
Civil-military relations—United States 322.50973
Civil procedure 347.05
Civil procedure—California 347.79405
Civil procedure—Florida 347.75905
Civil procedure—Florida—Forms 347.759055
Civil procedure—Great Britain 347.4105
Civil procedure—Illinois 347.77305
Civil procedure (International law) 341.55
Civil procedure—Massachusetts 347.74405
Civil procedure—New York (State) 347.74705
Civil procedure—North Carolina 347.75605
Civil procedure—Pakistan 347.549105
Civil procedure—Pennsylvania 347.74805
Civil procedure—Philippines 347.59905
Civil procedure—South Africa 347.6805
Civil procedure—Texas 347.76405
Civil procedure—United States 347.735
Civil procedure—United States—Cases 347.7350264
Civil procedure—United States—Forms 347.7355
Civil procedure—United States—Outlines, syllabi, etc.
    347.735
Civil procedure—Virginia 347.75505
Civil procedure—Wisconsin 347.77505
Civil reserve air fleet 358.44
Civil RICO actions 345.7302; 347.7353
Civil rights 323; 342.085
Civil rights—Africa 323.096; 342.6085
Civil rights—Australia 323.0994; 342.94085
Civil rights—Canada 323.0971; 342.71085
Civil rights—China 323.0951; 342.51085
Civil rights—El Salvador 323.097284; 342.7284085
Civil rights—Europe 323.094; 341.481094
Civil rights—Europe—Periodicals 323.09405;
    341.48109405
Civil rights—Great Britain 323.0941; 342.41085
Civil rights—History 323.09
Civil rights—India 323.0954; 342.54085
Civil rights—Kenya 323.096762; 342.6762085
Civil rights—Korea (South) 323.095195; 342.5195085
Civil rights movements 323
Civil rights movements—United States 323.0973
Civil rights movements—United States—History
    323.0973
Civil rights movements—United States—History—20th
    century 323.09730904
Civil rights—Nicaragua 323.097285; 342.7285085
Civil rights—Nigeria 323.09669; 342.669085
Civil rights—Northern Ireland 323.09416; 342.416085
Civil rights—Periodicals 323.05
Civil rights—Philippines 323.09599; 342.599085
Civil rights—Religious aspects 291.177
Civil rights—Religious aspects—Christianity 261.7
Civil rights—Romania 323.09498; 342.498085

Civil rights—South Africa 323.0968; 342.68085
Civil rights—Sri Lanka 323.095493; 342.5493085
Civil rights—Turkey 323.09561; 342.561085
Civil rights—Uganda 323.096761; 342.6751085
Civil rights—United States 323.0973; 342.73085
Civil rights—United States—Cases 342.730850264
Civil rights—United States—History 323.0973;
 342.7308509
Civil rights workers 323.092
Civil service 342.068; 352.63
Civil service—California 342.794068
Civil service ethics 172.2
Civil service ethics—United States 172.2
Civil service—Great Britain 352.630941
Civil service—India 342.54068; 352.630954
Civil service—India—Digests 342.5406802638
Civil service—New York (State)—New York—
 Examinations 351.7471076
Civil service—Nigeria 352.6309669
Civil service—Pakistan 342.5491068
Civil service—Pensions 353.549
Civil service—Personnel management 352.6
Civil service positions 352.64
Civil service positions—United States 352.640973
Civil service positions—United States—Handbooks,
 manuals, etc. 352.640973
Civil service reform 352.63
Civil service reform—United States 352.63
Civil service—United States 352.630973
Civil service—United States—Examinations 351.73076
Civil service—United States—History 342.73068
Civil service—United States—Personnel management
 352.60973
Civil society 306.2
Civil society—China 320.951
Civil war 341.68; 355.0218
Civilian review boards (Police administration)
 353.36288
Civilization 909
Civilization, Aegean 939.1
Civilization, Ancient 930
Civilization, Ancient—Extraterrestrial influences
 001.942
Civilization, Ancient—History 930
Civilization, Ancient, in literature 808.80358; 809.93358
Civilization, Anglo-Saxon 942.01
Civilization, Arab 909.0974927
Civilization, Arab—20th century 909.0974927082
Civilization, Assyro-Babylonian 935.02; 935.03; 935.04
Civilization, Baroque 940.252
Civilization, Celtic 909.04916
Civilization, Christian 261
Civilization, Classical 938
Civilization, Greco-Roman 937; 938
Civilization, Hindu 954
Civilization, Hispanic 946
Civilization—History 909
Civilization—History—Sources 909
Civilization, Homeric 938
Civilization, Islamic 909.097671
Civilization, Medieval 909.07; 940.1
Civilization, Medieval—12th century 909.1
Civilization, Medieval, in literature 808.80358;
 809.93358
Civilization, Medieval—Periodicals 909.0705
Civilization, Medieval—Sources 909.07
Civilization, Modern 909; 909.8
Civilization, Modern—17th century 909.6
Civilization, Modern—18th century 909.7

Civilization, Modern—19th century 909.81
Civilization, Modern—20th century 909.82
Civilization, Modern—1950- 909.825
Civilization, Modern—History 909; 909.8
Civilization, Mycenaean 938; 938.01
Civilization, Oriental 950
Civilization—Philosophy 901
Civilization, Slavic 947
Civilization, Western 909.09821
Civilization, Western—History 909.09821
Civilization, Western—History—Sources 909.09821
Civilization, Western—Outlines, syllabi, etc. 909.09821
Civilization, Western—Philosophy 909.09821001
Cixous, Hélène, 1937- 848.91409
Cixous, Hélène, 1937- —Criticism and interpretation
 848.91409
Cladistic analysis 578.012
Cladocera 595.32
Claiborne, Claire (Fictitious character) 813.54
Claiborne County (Tenn.)—Genealogy 929.3768944
Claiborne, Dan (Fictitious character) 813.54
Clairvoyance 133.84
Clallam Indians 979.7004979
Clans 929.6
Clans—Scotland 929.209411
Clapton, Eric 787.87166092
Clare County (Mich.) 977.471
Clare County (Mich.)—Maps 912.77471
Clare, John, 1793-1864 821.7
Clare, John, 1793-1864—Criticism and interpretation
 821.7
Clare, of Assisi, Saint, 1194-1253 271.97302
Clarinet and piano music 788.62
Clarinet music 788.62
Clarion County (Pa.)—Maps 912.74869
ClarisWorks 005.369
Clark, C. M. H. (Charles Manning Hope), 1915-
 994.007202
Clark County (Ark.)—Genealogy 929.376749
Clark County (Mo.) 977.8343
Clark County (Mo.)—Maps 912.778343
Clark County (Wash.) 979.786
Clark County (Wash.)—Genealogy 929.379786
Clark County (Wis.) 977.528
Clark County (Wis.)—Maps 912.77528
Clark family 929.20973
Clarke, Arthur Charles, 1917- 823.914
Clarke, Arthur Charles, 1917- —Criticism and
 interpretation 823.914
Clarke County (Iowa) 977.7856
Clarke County (Iowa)—Maps 912.777856
Class actions (Civil procedure) 347.053
Class actions (Civil procedure)—United States 347.7353
Class field theory 512.74
Class periods 371.242
Class reunions 371.8
Class size 371.251
Classical antiquities 930; 938
Classical dictionaries 938.003
Classical drama (Comedy) 882.0108
Classical drama (Comedy)—History and criticism
 882.0109
Classical drama (Tragedy) 882
Classical education 480.071
Classical geography 913.8
Classical languages 480
Classical literature 880; 880.08
Classical literature—Bibliography 016.88
Classical literature—Criticism, Textual 880.09

Classical literature—History and criticism 880.09; 880.9001
Classical literature—History and criticism—Theory, etc. 880.09
Classical literature—Translations into English 880.08
Classical philology 480
Classical poetry 881; 881.008; 881.01; 881.0108
Classical poetry—History and criticism 881.009; 881.0109
Classical school of economics 330.153
Classicism 700.414
Classicism in art 709.033
Classicism in music 780.9033
Classification 001.012
Classification, BBK 025.43
Classification—Books 025.4
Classification—Books—Law 025.4634
Classification—Books—Political science 025.4632
Classification—Books—Social sciences 025.463
Classification, Dewey decimal 025.431
Classification, Library of Congress 025.433
Classification—Music 780.12
Classification, Universal decimal 025.432
Classism 305.5
Classroom environment 371.02; 371.1024
Classroom management 371.1024
Classroom management—Handbooks, manuals, etc. 371.1024
Classroom management—United States 371.10240973
Classroom simulators 370.711
Classrooms 371.621
Clathrate compounds 541.22
Clatsop County (Or.) 979.546
Clatsop County (Or.)—Genealogy 929.30979546
Claudel, Paul, 1868–1955 848.91209
Claudel, Paul, 1868–1955—Criticism and interpretation 848.91209
Claudius, Emperor of Rome, 10 B.C.–54 A.D. 937.07092
Claudius (Fictitious character : Updike) 813.54
Clavicytherium music 786.4
Clay 552.5
Clay—Analysis 552.5
Clay County (Iowa) 977.7153
Clay County (Iowa)—Maps 912.777153
Clay County (Minn.) 977.692
Clay County (Minn.)—Maps 912.77692
Clay minerals 549.6
Clay pot cookery 641.589
Clayton County (Iowa) 977.736
Clayton County (Iowa)—Maps 912.77736
Clayton family 929.20973
Clean rooms 620.86
Cleaning 667.1
Cleaning compounds 668.1
Cleaning compounds industry 338.476681
Cleaning machinery and appliances 621.54
Cleaning machinery and appliances industry 338.4768383
Clearinghouses 025.52
Clearinghouses (Banking) 332.12
Clearinghouses (Banking)—United States 332.178
Cleft lip 617.522
Cleft lip—Surgery 617.522
Cleft palate 617.5225
Cleft palate—Complications 616.855; 617.5225
Clematis 635.93334
Clemency 364.65
Clement, Jules (Fictitious character) 813.54
Clemente, Roberto, 1934–1972 796.357092

Clements family 929.20973
Clemons, Frank (Fictitious character) 813.54
Cleopatra, Queen of Egypt, d. 30 B.C. 932.021092
Clergy 248.892
Clergy—Appointment, call, and election 253.2
Clergy—Office 253
Clergy—Professional ethics 241.641
Clergy—Psychology 253.2
Clergy—Religious life 248.892
Clergy—Relocation 253.2
Clergy—Sexual behavior 253.2
Clermont County (Ohio) 977.1794
Clermont County (Ohio)—Genealogy 929.3771794
Cleveland Browns (Football team) 796.332640977132
Cleveland Browns (Football team)—History 796.332640977132
Cleveland Indians (Baseball team) 796.357640977132
Cleveland Indians (Baseball team)—History 796.357640977132
Cleveland (Ohio) 977.132
Cleveland (Ohio)—Guidebooks 917.7132044; 917.71320443; 917.71320444
Cleveland (Ohio)—History 977.132
Cleveland (Ohio)—Maps 912.77132
Clichés 418; 428; 808
Clichés—Dictionaries 423.1
Clicker training (Animal training) 636.0887
Client-centered psychotherapy 616.8914
Client/server computing 004.36
Cliff-dwellings 978.901
Cliff ecology 577
Clifford algebras 512.57
Climate 551.6
Climatic changes 551.6; 577.22; 632.1
Climatic changes—Government policy—United States 363.7387405610973
Climatic changes—International cooperation 363.73874056
Climatic changes—Social aspects 304.25
Climatology 551.6
Climatology—Handbooks, manuals, etc. 551.6
Climbing gyms 796.5224
Climbing plants 582.18
Cline, Patsy, 1932–1963 782.421642092
Clinical biochemistry 612.015; 616.07
Clinical chemistry 616.0756
Clinical chemistry—Examinations, questions, etc. 616.0756076
Clinical chemistry—Handbooks, manuals, etc. 616.0756
Clinical chemistry—Laboratory manuals 616.0756
Clinical chemistry—Quality control 616.07560685
Clinical chemistry—Technique 616.0756
Clinical child psychology 618.9289
Clinical chronobiology 616.07
Clinical clerkship 610.711
Clinical enzymology 616.0756
Clinical health psychology 613.019; 616.0019; 616.89
Clinical health psychology—Periodicals 616.0019
Clinical immunology 616.079
Clinical medicine 616
Clinical medicine—Examinations, questions, etc. 616.0076
Clinical medicine—Handbooks, manuals, etc. 616
Clinical medicine—Outlines, syllabi, etc. 616
Clinical neuropsychology 616.8
Clinical pharmacologists 615.1092
Clinical pharmacology 615.1
Clinical pharmacology—Handbooks, manuals, etc. 615.1
Clinical psychologists 616.890092

Clinical psychologists—Prescription privileges
362.19689082
Clinical psychology 616.89
Clinical psychology—Practice 616.890068
Clinical psychology—Practice—United States
616.890068
Clinical psychology—Research 616.890072
Clinical psychology—Research—Methodology
616.890072
Clinical trials 610.724; 615.50724
Clinical trials—Statistical methods 610.727; 615.50727
Clinics 362.12
Clinton, Bill, 1946– 973.929092
Clinton, Bill, 1946– —Friends and associates
973.929092; 973.9290922
Clinton, Bill, 1946– —Humor 973.929092
Clinton, Bill, 1946– —Impeachment 342.73062;
973.929092
Clinton, Bill, 1946– —Sexual behavior 973.929092
Clinton County (Ill.) 977.3875
Clinton County (Ill.)—Maps 912.773875
Clinton County (Iowa) 977.767
Clinton County (Iowa)—Maps 912.77767
Clinton County (Mich.) 977.424
Clinton County (Mich.)—Maps 912.77424
Clinton, Hillary Rodham 973.929092
Clip art 741.6
Clipper ships 387.224
Clitoridectomy 392.1
Clock and watch makers 681.113092; 681.111092
Clock and watch making 681.113; 681.114
Clock chimes 681.113; 739.3
Clocks and watches 681.113; 681.114
Clocks and watches—Repairing 681.1130288;
681.1140288
Clones (Plants) 631.5233
Cloning 660.65
Close corporations 346.0668
Close corporations—California 346.7940668
Close corporations—Taxation 343.067
Close corporations—Taxation—United States 343.73067
Close corporations—United States 346.730668
Close corporations—Valuation 346.0668
Close corporations—Valuation—United States
346.730668
Closed-circuit television 384.556
Closed ecological systems 333.95
Closed ecological systems (Space environment) 577
Closed-end funds 332.6327
Closed-end funds—United States 332.6327
Closed-end funds—United States—Directories 332.6327
Clothes trees 645.4; 684.1
Clothing and dress 646.3; 646.404; 687
Clothing and dress—Catalogs 687.075
Clothing and dress—Psychological aspects 646.3019
Clothing care labels 646.6
Clothing trade 338.47687; 380.145687; 687
Clothing trade—United States—Statistics—Periodicals
382.456870973021
Cloud forest conservation 333.7516
Cloud forest ecology 577.3
Cloud forest plants 581.73
Cloud of unknowing 248.22
Cloud physics 551.576
Clouds 551.576
Clouds—Mythology 291.212
Clouds—Remote sensing 551.5760287
Clough, Arthur Hugh, 1819–1861 821.8

Clough, Arthur Hugh, 1819–1861—Criticism and
interpretation 821.8
Clouseau, Inspector (Fictitious character) 791.4375
Clowning 791.33
Clowns 791.33
Clowns—Religious aspects 291.37
Clowns—Religious aspects—Christianity 246.7
Cloze procedure 372.472
Clubs 367
Cluster analysis 519.53
Cluster theory (Nuclear physics) 539.7
Cnidaria 593.5
Cnidian school of medicine 610.938
Coaches (Athletics) 796.077
Coaching (Athletics) 796.077
Coaching (Athletics)—Religious aspects 291.175
Coal 553.24; 662.62
Coal—Analysis 662.622
Coal-cutting bits—Testing 622.334
Coal gasification 665.772
Coal—Geology 553.24
Coal leases 333.822
Coal leases—United States 333.8220973; 346.73046822
Coal liquefaction 662.6622
Coal mine waste 363.7288; 622.3340286
Coal miners—United States 622.334092273
Coal mines and mining 622.334
Coal mines and mining—China 622.3340951
Coal mines and mining—Dust control 622.83
Coal mines and mining—England 622.3340942
Coal mines and mining—England—Midlands
622.33409424
Coal mines and mining—Safety measures 622.3340289
Coal mines and mining—Scotland 622.33409411
Coal mines and mining—Scotland—History
622.33409411
Coal-mining machinery 622.3340284; 681.76
Coal preparation 662.623
Coal slurry pipelines—Law and legislation 343.093
Coal slurry pipelines—Law and legislation—United
States 343.73093
Coal Strike, Great Britain, 1984–1985
331.8928223340941
Coal—Sulphur content 662.622
Coal trade 333.822; 338.2724
Coal trade—Great Britain 338.27240941
Coal trade—Great Britain—History 338.27240941
Coal trade—United States 338.27240973
Coal trade—United States—Statistics 338.27240973021
Coal trade—United States—Statistics—Periodicals
338.27240973021
Coal—Transportation—United States 387.164
Coalition governments 324
Coarse fishes 597.176
Coarse fishing 799.11
Coast changes 551.457
Coast defenses—United States 355.45097309146
Coastal ecology 577.51
Coastal engineering 627.58
Coastal forest ecology 577.3
Coastal forests 333.7509146; 577.3; 578.73
Coastal surveillance 363.286
Coastal zone management 333.917
Coastal zone management—Law and legislation
346.046917
Coastal zone management—Law and legislation—United
States 346.73046917
Coastal zone management—United States 333.9170973
Coasts 551.457

Coastwise navigation 623.8922
Coastwise shipping 387.524
Coatings 667.9
Coatings industry 338.476679
Coatracks 645.4; 684.1
Coaxial cables 621.31934
Cobb County (Ga.)—Maps 912.758245
Cobb, Matt (Fictitious character) 813.54
Cobb, Matt (Fictitious character)—Fiction 813.54
Cobb, Ty, 1886–1961 796.357092
Cobbett, William, 1763–1835 941.073092; 942.073092
COBOL (Computer program language) 005.133
Coca-Cola Company 338.766362
Coca-Cola Company—Collectibles 338.766362
Coca-Cola Company—Collectibles—Catalogs
  338.766362; 663.62
Coca-Cola Company—History 338.766362
Cocaine habit 616.8647
Cocaine habit—United States 616.8647
Cocaine—Physiological effect 615.785
Cocaine—Toxicology 615.952379
Coccidae 595.752
Cochlear implants 617.882
Cockatiel 636.68656
Cocker spaniels 636.7524
Cockpit voice recorders 629.135
Cockroaches 595.728
Cocktails 641.874
Cocktails in motion pictures 791.43655
Cockthrowing 791.8
Cocoa 641.3374
Cocoa trade 338.17374
Cocoa trade—Ghana 338.1737409667
Cocteau, Jean, 1889–1963 841.912; 848.91209
Code division multiple access 621.38456
Code switching (Linguistics) 306.446
Codependency 616.869
Codependency—Religious aspects 291.1783229; 291.442
Codependency—Religious aspects—Christianity
  248.8629; 261.83229
Codependents—Rehabilitation 616.86903
Codependents—Religious life 248.86
Codicology 091
Coding theory 003.54
Codlets 597.63
Coeducation 371.822
Coelacanth 597.39
Coelomycetes 579.55
Coelophysis 567.912
Coetzee, J. M., 1940– 823.914
Coetzee, J. M., 1940– —Criticism and interpretation
  823.914
Coevolution 576.87
Coffee 641.3373; 641.877
Coffee brewing 641.877
Coffee industry 338.17373; 381.45641373; 382.41373
Coffee roasting industry 338.4766393
Coffeehouses 647.95
Coffeehouses—Management 647.95068
Coffin, John (Fictitious character) 823.914
Coffin, John (Fictitious character)—Fiction 823.914
Cogeneration of electric power and heat 333.793;
  621.199
Cogenerators 621.199
Cognition 153
Cognition—Age factors 153
Cognition and culture 153
Cognition disorders 362.2; 616.8
Cognition—Effect of drugs on 153; 615.78

Cognition—Effect of exercise on 153; 612.82
Cognition in animals 591.513
Cognition in children 155.413
Cognition in old age 155.6713
Cognition—Physiological aspects 612.82
Cognitive grammar 415
Cognitive learning 370.1523
Cognitive learning—United States 370.1523
Cognitive neuroscience 153; 612.82
Cognitive psychology 153
Cognitive science 153
Cognitive therapy 616.89142
Cognitive therapy for children 618.9289142
Cohen, Avram (Fictitious character) 813.54
Coherence (Optics) 535.2
Cohesion (Linguistics) 401.41; 415
Coin dealers 380.1457374
Coin tricks 793.8
Coincidence 123.3
Coincidence—Psychic aspects 133.8
Coins 737.4
Coins, American 737.4973
Coins, American—Catalogs 737.4973075
Coins, Ancient 737.4093
Coins, Anglo-Saxon 737.4942
Coins as an investment 332.63
Coins, British 332.40420941; 737.4942
Coins—Catalogs 737.4075
Coins, Chinese 737.4951
Coins—Collectors and collecting 737.4075
Coins—Collectors and collecting—Handbooks, manuals,
  etc. 737.4075
Coins, Foreign 737.4
Coins, Greek 737.4938
Coins, Indic 737.4954
Coins, Indic—Catalogs 737.4954075
Coins, Roman 737.4937
Coke 662.72
Cola drinks 641.875
Cold adaptation 578.42
Cold (Disease) 616.205
Cold fusion 539.764
Cold—Physiological effect 612.014465
Cold storage 664.02852
Cold-tolerant plants 571.4642; 635.952
Cold War 909.825; 940.55
Cold War in motion pictures 791.43658
Cold War—Sources 909.825
Cold weather clothing 391
Cole, Elvis (Fictitious character) 813.54
Cole, Elvis (Fictitious character)—Fiction 813.54
Cole family 929.20973
Cole, Larry (Fictitious character) 813.54
Cole, Larry (Fictitious character)—Fiction 813.54
Cole, Lewis (Fictitious character) 813.54
Cole, Nat King, 1917–1965 782.42164092
Coleman, Bessie, 1896–1926 629.13092
Coleridge, Samuel Taylor, 1772–1834 821.7
Coleridge, Samuel Taylor, 1772–1834—Aesthetics
  821.7
Coleridge, Samuel Taylor, 1772–1834—Criticism and
  interpretation 821.7
Coleridge, Samuel Taylor, 1772–1834—Knowledge—
  Literature 821.7
Coleridge, Samuel Taylor, 1772–1834—Philosophy
  821.7
Coleridge, Samuel Taylor, 1772–1834—Religion 821.7
Coleridge, Samuel Taylor, 1772–1834. Rime of the
  ancient mariner 821.7

Coles County (Ill.) 977.372
Coles County (Ill.)—Maps 912.77372
Colette, 1873–1954 848.91209
Colette, 1873–1954—Criticism and interpretation 848.91209
Colette, 1873–1954—Translations into English 848.91209
Coll, Matthew (Fictitious character) 823.914
Collage 702.812
Collage—Technique 702.812
Collagen 572.67
Collectibles 708
Collecting of accounts 658.88
Collecting of accounts—United States 658.88
Collection development (Libraries) 025.21
Collection development (Libraries)—United States 025.210973
Collection laws 346.077
Collection laws—United States 346.73077
Collection level cataloging 025.3
Collection management (Libraries) 025.21
Collective bargaining 331.89; 658.3154
Collective bargaining—Canada 331.890971
Collective bargaining—Education 331.8904137
Collective bargaining—Education—United States 331.89041370973
Collective bargaining—Government employees 331.89041351
Collective bargaining Government employees—United States 331.8904135173
Collective bargaining—Great Britain 331.890941
Collective bargaining—Teachers 331.890413711
Collective bargaining—Teachers—United States 331.89041371100973
Collective bargaining—United States 331.890973
Collective behavior 302.35
Collective labor agreements 344.01891
Collective labor agreements—Blue collar workers 331.89
Collective labor agreements—Government employees—United States 344.730189041353
Collective labor agreements—United States 344.7301891
Collective labor agreements—United States—Cases 344.73018910264
Collective settlements 335.9
Collective settlements—United States 335.973
Collective settlements—United States—History 335.973
Collectivism 320.53
Collectors and collecting 790.132
Collectors and collecting in literature 808.8035; 809.9335
College administrators 378.0092; 378.111
College admission officers 378.1616
College and school drama 792.0222
College applications 378.1616
College applications—United States 378.1616
College applications—United States—Handbooks, manuals, etc. 378.1616
College art museums 708
College athletes 796.043092
College attendance 378.1619
College attendance—California 378.1619794
College attendance—California—Statistics—Periodicals 378.1619794021
College attendance—United States—Statistics 378.161973; 378.161973021
College buildings 378.196
College chaplains 259.24

College choice 378.161; 378.198
College costs 378.38
College costs—United States 378.380973
College discipline 378.195
College entrance achievement tests 378.1662
College environment 306.43
College facilities 378.196
College graduates 305.55
College graduates—Employment 331.11423
College graduates—Employment—Great Britain 331.11423
College graduates—Religious life 248.84
College Level Academic Skills Test 378.1662
College-level examinations 378.1662
College librarians 027.7092
College majors 378.241
College majors—United States—Handbooks, manuals, etc. 378.241
College museums 069
College personnel management 378.11
College placement services 331.128
College presidents 378.0092; 378.111
College presidents—United States 378.0092
College publications 070.594
College publicity 659.29378
College radio stations 384.5453
College readers 808.0427
College reading improvement programs 418.4
College registrars 378.161
College-school cooperation 378.1
College-school cooperation United States 378.1
College science museums 507.4
College sports 796.043
College sports—United States 796.0430973
College sports—United States—Directories 796.04302573
College stores 381.1; 381.45002
College student development programs 378.194; 378.198
College student development programs—United States 378.1940973
College student government 378.1959
College student newspapers and periodicals 378.19805; 378.198974
College student orientation 378.198
College student orientation—Handbooks, manuals, etc. 378.198
College student orientation—United States 378.1980973
College student orientation—United States—Handbooks, manuals, etc. 378.1980973
College student records 378.16; 378.161; 378.198
College students 378.198
College students—Health and hygiene 613.0434
College students—Legal status, laws, etc. 344.0793
College students—Legal status, laws, etc.—United States 344.730793
College students—Recruiting 378.161
College students—Recruiting—United States 378.161
College students—United States 378.1980973
College students—United States—Political activity 378.19810973
College students—United States—Psychology 378.198019
College teachers 378.12
College teachers—Employment—United States 331.125137812
College teachers—England 378.120942
College teachers—Legal status, laws, etc. 344.3078

College teachers—Legal status, laws, etc.—United States 344.73078
College teachers—Massachusetts 378.1209744
College teachers—Massachusetts—Cambridge 378.12097444
College teachers—Professional ethics 174.9372
College teachers—Professional ethics—United States 174.9372
College teachers—Rating of 378.1224
College teachers—Rating of—United States 378.12240973
College teachers—Salaries, etc. 331.28137812
College teachers—Salaries, etc.—Great Britain 331.281378120941
College teachers—Salaries, etc.—United States 331.281378120973
College teachers—Selection and appointment—United States 378.12
College teachers—Tenure—United States 378.121
College teachers—United States 378.120973
College teachers—United States—Retirement 331.2529137873
College teaching 378.125
College teaching—Great Britain 378.1250941
College teaching—Handbooks, manuals, etc. 378.125
College teaching—United States 378.120973; 378.1250973
College teaching—Vocational guidance—United States 378.12023
College theater 792.0222
College trustees 378.1011
Colliders (Nuclear physics) 539.73
Collie 636.7374
Collier family 929.20973
Collier, Jeremy, 1650–1726. Short view of the immorality and profaneness of the English stage 792.013
Collins family 929.20973
Collins, Michael, 1890–1922 941.50821092
Collins, Wilkie, 1824–1889 823.8
Collins, Wilkie, 1824–1889—Criticism and interpretation 823.8
Collins, William, 1721–1759 821.5
Collins, William, 1721–1759—Criticism and interpretation 821.5
Collisions at sea 341.75666
Collisions at sea—Prevention 623.8884
Collisions (Nuclear physics) 539.757
Colloids 541.345
Colobine monkeys 599.86
Colombia 986.1
Colombia—Economic policy 338.9861
Colombian American literature (Spanish) 860.809861
Colon (Anatomy) 611.347; 612.36
Colon (Anatomy)—Cancer 616.994347
Colon (Anatomy)—Diseases 616.34
Colon (Anatomy)—Endoscopic surgery 617.5547059
Colon (Anatomy)—Surgery 617.5547
Colonies 325.3
Colonies—Africa 325.6
Color 155.91145; 535.6
Color blindness 617.759
Color computer graphics 006.6
Color computer printers 004.77
Color confinement (Nuclear physics) 539.7548
Color in art 701.85; 752
Color in design 701.85; 745.4
Color in gardening 635.968
Color in interior decoration 747.94

Color of animals 591.472
Color photography 778.6
Color photography—Printing processes 778.66
Color—Pictorial works 535.60222
Color printer industry 338.476862
Color printing 686.23042
Color printing—Data processing 686.230420285
Color—Psychic aspects 133
Color—Psychological aspects 155.91145
Color television 621.38804
Color—Therapeutic use 615.831
Color-variation (Biology) 578.47
Color vision 152.145; 612.84
Colorado 978.8
Colorado—Economic conditions 330.9788
Colorado—Economic conditions—Periodicals 330.9788005
Colorado. General Assembly 328.788
Colorado. General Assembly—Rules and practice 328.78805
Colorado—Guidebooks 917.88; 917.8804; 917.880433; 917.880434
Colorado—History 978.8
Colorado, Kat (Fictitious character) 813.54
Colorado, Kat (Fictitious character)—Fiction 813.54
Colorado—Maps 912.788
Colorado Plateau 979.13
Colorado Plateau—Pictorial works 979.1300222
Colorado River (Colo.-Mexico) 979.13
Colorado River (Colo.-Mexico)—Description and travel 917.91304; 917.9130453; 917.9130454
Colorado River Watershed (Colo.-Mexico) 979.13
Colorado—Road maps 912.788
Colorado Rockies (Baseball team) 796.357640978883
Colorado—Tours 917.8804; 917.880433; 917.880434
Colorado Trail (Colo.) 978.8
Colorado Trail (Colo.)—Guidebooks 917.88
Colored pencil drawing 741.24
Colored pencil drawing—Technique 741.24
Colorimetry 535.60287
Coloring books 741.2
Coloring matter in food 664.062
Colors 535.6
Colt revolver 683.436
Coltrane, John, 1926–1967 788.7165092
Columba, Saint, 521–597 270.2092
Columbia County (Wis.)—Maps 912.77581
Columbia Records, Inc.—Catalogs 016.780266
Columbia River 979.7
Columbia River—History 979.7
Columbia University—Students 378.198097471
Columbo, Lieutenant (Fictitious character) 813.54
Columbo, Lieutenant (Fictitious character)—Fiction 813.54
Columbus, Christopher 970.015092
Columbus, Christopher—Diaries 970.015092
Columbus, Christopher—Influence 970.015092
Columbus, Christopher—Journeys 970.015
Columbus, Christopher—Journeys—America 970.015
Columbus Day 970.015
Columbus Quincentenary, 1992–1993 970.015
Columns 624.1772
COM (Computer architecture) 004.22
Coma 616.849
Coma—Patients 362.196849
Comanche Indians 305.89745; 978.0049745
Comanche Indians—History 978.0049745
Combat 355.4
Combat—Mathematical models 355.48

Common law—Great Britain—History 340.570941
Common lectionary (1992) 264.13
COMMON LISP (Computer program language) 005.133
Common loon 598.442
Commonplace-books 080
Commons 333.2
Commonwealth countries 909.0971241
Commonwealth countries—History 909.0971241
Commonwealth Games 796
Commonwealth literature (English) 820.809171241
Commonwealth literature (English)—History and criticism 820.99171241
Commonwealth literature (English)—History and criticism—Periodicals 820.9917124105
Commonwealth of Independent States 947.086
Commonwealth of Nations 909.0971241
Commonwealth of Nations—Bibliography 016.9090971242; 016.91002171242
Commonwealth of Nations—History 909.0971241
Commonwealth (Organization) 320.9171241; 909.0971241
Communalism 302.14
Communicable diseases 614.5; 616.9
Communicable diseases—Atlases 616.90222
Communicable diseases—Diagnosis 616.90475
Communicable diseases—Handbooks, manuals, etc. 616.9
Communicable diseases in children 618.929
Communicable diseases in pregnancy 618.3
Communication 302.2
Communication and culture 302.2
Communication and technology 302.2
Communication and traffic 380; 388.041
Communication devices for the disabled 362.40483; 616.85503
Communication—Handbooks, manuals, etc. 302.2
Communication—History 302.209
Communication in agriculture 630.14
Communication in chemistry 540.14
Communication in community development 307.14014
Communication in conservation of natural resources 333.72014
Communication in dentistry 617.60014; 617.6023
Communication in design 741.6; 761.4
Communication in education 370.14; 371.1022
Communication in education—United States 371.10220973
Communication in engineering 620.0014
Communication in foreign language education 418.0071
Communication in industrial safety 363.11
Communication in information science 020.14
Communication in international trade 381.014
Communication in law 347.0504
Communication in law enforcement 363.24
Communication in law—United States 347.73504; 347.737
Communication in management 658.45
Communication in management—United States 658.450973
Communication in marketing 658.80014
Communication in marriage 646.78
Communication in marriage—United States 646.78
Communication in medicine 610.14; 610.696
Communication in nursing 610.73014; 610.730699
Communication in organizations 658.45
Communication in personnel management 658.30014
Communication in politics 320.014
Communication in politics—United States 320.973014
Communication in public administration 352.384

Communication in rural development—India 307.14120954
Communication in science 501.4; 808.0665
Communication in small groups 302.34
Communication in the family 306.87
Communication in the family—United States 306.87
Communication, International 302.2
Communication—International cooperation 302.2
Communication of technical information 601.4; 620.0014; 808.066; 808.0666
Communication—Periodicals 302.205
Communication—Philosophy 302.201
Communication policy 302.2; 384
Communication—Political aspects 302.2
Communication—Religious aspects 291.175
Communication—Religious aspects—Christianity 261.52
Communication—Research 302.2072
Communication—Research—Methodology 302.2072
Communication—Sex differences 305.3014
Communication—Social aspects 302.2
Communication—Technological innovations 302.234
Communications, Military 355.24; 358.24
Communications software 005.713
Communicative disorders 362.196855; 371.914; 616.855
Communicative disorders in children 371.914; 618.92855
Communicative disorders in old age 618.976855
Communicative disorders—Patients 362.196855
Communicative disorders—Patients—Counseling of 616.85506
Communicative disorders—Research—Methodology 616.8550072
Communicative disorders—Treatment 616.85506
Communism 320.532; 335.43
Communism and Christianity 261.21
Communism and ecology 306.345
Communism and Islam 297.273
Communism and religion 291.1785
Communism—Brazil 335.430981
Communism—Bulgaria 335.4309499
Communism—China 320.53230951; 335.4345
Communism—Cuba 335.4347
Communism—Europe 335.43094
Communism—Europe, Eastern 335.430947
Communism—Europe, Eastern—History 335.430947
Communism—Europe, Eastern—History—20th century 335.430947
Communism—Germany 335.430943
Communism—History 335.4309
Communism—History—20th century 335.430904
Communism—India 335.430954
Communism—Italy 335.430945
Communism—Latin America 335.43098
Communism—Periodicals 335.4305
Communism—Soviet Union 335.430947
Communism—Soviet Union—History 320.5320947; 335.430947
Communism—United States 320.5320973; 335.430973
Communism—United States—Bibliography 016.335430973
Communist countries 909.09717
Communist countries—Economic conditions 330.91717
Communist countries—Economic policy 338.90091717
Communist countries—Politics and government 320.91717
Communist ethics 171.7
Communist International 324.175
Communist parties 324.2175

Computer programming—Ability testing
658.31125028551
Computer programming—Management 005.1068;
658.0551
Computer programming—Problems, exercises, etc.
005.1076
Computer programming—Programmed instruction
371.33451
Computer programming—Vocational guidance 005.1023
Computer programs 005.3
Computer programs—Testing 005.14
Computer programs—Validation 005.14
Computer science 004
Computer science—Bibliography 016.004
Computer science—Dictionaries 004.03
Computer science—Encyclopedias 004.03
Computer science—Examinations, questions, etc.
004.076
Computer science literature 016.004
Computer science—Mathematics 004.0151
Computer science—Periodicals 004.05
Computer science—Research 004.072
Computer science—Study and teaching (Higher)
004.0711
Computer science—Study and teaching (Higher)—
United States 004.071173
Computer science—Vocational guidance 004.023
Computer scientists 004.092
Computer security 005.8; 658.478
Computer security equipment industry 338.4762139
Computer security—Management 658.0558; 658.478
Computer security—Management—Handbooks,
manuals, etc. 658.0558; 658.478
Computer security—Periodicals 005.805
Computer service industry 338.47004
Computer sex 025.063067; 306.70285
Computer simulation 003.3
Computer software 005.3
Computer software—Catalogs 005.30216
Computer software—Catalogs—Periodicals 016.005305
Computer software developers 005.1092
Computer software—Development 005.1
Computer software—Development—Management
005.1068
Computer software—Development—Periodicals 005.105
Computer software—Evaluation 005.30287
Computer software—Human factors 005.3019
Computer software industry 338.470053
Computer software industry—United States
338.4700530973
Computer software industry—United States—
Directories 005.302573
Computer software industry—United States—
Periodicals 338.470053097305
Computer software—Law and legislation 343.0999
Computer software—Law and legislation—United States
343.730999
Computer software—Periodicals 005.305
Computer software—Quality control 005.10685
Computer software—Reliability 005
Computer software—Reusability 005.1
Computer software—Testing 005.14
Computer software—Validation 005.14
Computer software—Verification 005.14
Computer sound processing 006.5
Computer storage device industry 338.470045
Computer storage devices 004.5; 621.397
Computer stores 381.45004
Computer system conversion 005.1

Computer system failures 004
Computer technical support 004.0688
Computer technicians 621.39092
Computer technicians—Certification 621.39
Computer terminals 004.75
Computer terminals—Interactive terminals 004.75
Computer theft 364.162
Computer users 004.092
Computer value-added resellers 381.45004
Computer viruses 005.84
Computer vision 006.37
Computer vision equipment industry 338.4700637;
338.47621399
Computer vision—Industrial applications 670.0285637
Computer war games 793.920285
Computer word games 793.7340285
Computerized self-help devices for the handicapped
617.03
Computerized typesetting 686.22544
Computers 004
Computers—Access control 005.8
Computers—Access control—Passwords 005.8
Computers and children 004.083
Computers and civilization 303.4834
Computers and the handicapped 004.087; 362.40483
Computers and the handicapped—United States
362.40483
Computers and the visually handicapped 004.0871
Computers and women 004.082
Computers—Caricatures and cartoons 741.5973
Computers—Dictionaries 004.03
Computers—History 004.09
Computers—Law and legislation 343.0999
Computers—Law and legislation—Great Britain
343.410999
Computers—Law and legislation—Periodicals
343.099905
Computers—Law and legislation—United States
343.730999
Computers, Optical 621.391
Computers—Optical equipment 004.7; 621.39
Computers—Periodicals 004.05
Computers—Social aspects 303.4834
Computers—Study and teaching 004.071
Comstock Lode (Nev.) 979.3
Conan (Fictitious character) 813.52
Conan (Fictitious character)—Fiction 813.52; 813.54
Concentration camp inmates as artists 704.069
Concentration camps 365.45
Concentration camps—Germany 940.531743
Conceptual art 709.04075
Conceptual structures (Information theory) 003.54
Concert programs 780.78
Concert tours 780.78
Concerti grossi 784.24
Concertos 784.23
Concertos (Bassoon) 784.2858
Concertos (Clarinet) 784.2862
Concertos (Flute) 784.2832
Concertos (Flute with string orchestra) 784.72832
Concertos (Guitar) 784.2787
Concertos (Harp) 784.279
Concertos (Harpsichord with string orchestra)
784.7264
Concertos (Horn) 784.2894
Concertos (Horn with string orchestra) 784.72894
Concertos (Oboe) 784.2852
Concertos (Oboe with string orchestra) 784.72852
Concertos (Orchestra) 784.2186

Congo (Democratic Republic)—Politics and government 967.51
Congo (Democratic Republic)—Politics and government—1960–1997 320.9675109046; 967.51031; 967.51033
Congregational churches 285.8
Congregational churches—Sermons 252.058
Congregational universities and colleges 378.07158
Congresses and conventions 060
Congresses and conventions—Handbooks, manuals, etc. 658.456
Congreve, William, 1670–1729 822.4
Congreve, William, 1670–1729—Criticism and interpretation 822.4
Conifers 585
Connecticut 974.6
Connecticut—Genealogy 929.3746
Connecticut—Guidebooks 917.4604; 917.460443; 917.460444
Connecticut—History 974.6
Connecticut—History—Colonial period, ca. 1600–1775 974.602
Connecticut—Maps 912.746
Connection machines 004.11
Connectionism 153
Connections (Mathematics) 516.35
Connective tissues 571.56
Connective tissues—Diseases 616.77
Connolly, Cyril, 1903–1974 820.9
Connor, Gail (Fictitious character) 813.54
Connor, Gail (Fictitious character)—Fiction 813.54
Connors, Liz (Fictitious character) 813.54
Connors, Liz (Fictitious character)—Fiction 813.54
Conrad, Joseph, 1857–1924 823.912
Conrad, Joseph, 1857–1924—Criticism and interpretation 823.912
Conrad, Joseph, 1857–1924—Ethics 823.912
Conrad, Joseph, 1857–1924. Heart of darkness 823.912
Conrad, Joseph, 1857–1924. Lord Jim 823.912
Conrad, Joseph, 1857–1924. Nostromo 823.912
Conrad, Joseph, 1857–1924—Political and social views 823.912
ConRail 385.0974
Conscience 170; 171.6
Conscience—Religious aspects 291.5
Conscience—Religious aspects—Catholic Church 241.108822
Conscience—Religious aspects—Christianity 241.1
Conscientious objectors 355.224
Conscious automata 006.3
Conscious sedation 617.96; 617.9676
Consciousness 153
Consciousness in literature 808.80353; 809.93353
Consciousness—Physiological aspects 153; 612.82
Consequentialism (Ethics) 171.5
CONSER Program 025.3432
CONSER Program—Handbooks, manuals, etc. 025.3432
Conservation biology 333.9516
Conservation leadership 346.044
Conservation of natural resources 333.72
Conservation of natural resources—United States 333.720973
Conservation of natural resources—United States—History 333.720973
Conservation plants 581.63
Conservation Reserve Program (U.S.) 333.76160973
Conservationists 333.72092
Conservatism 320.52
Conservatism—Great Britain 320.520941

Conservatism—History 320.52
Conservatism—Religious aspects 291.177
Conservatism—Religious aspects—Christianity 261.7
Conservatism—United States 320.520973
Conservatism—United States—History 320.520973
Conservatism—United States—History—20th century 320.5209730904
Conservative Judaism 296.8342
Conservative Party (Great Britain) 324.24104
Conservative Party (Great Britain)—History 324.24104
Conservatories 631.583
Conservatories of music 725.81
Conservatorships 346.018
Conservatorships—California 346.794018
Consignment sale shops 381.19
Consolation 248.86
Consolation—Prayer-books and devotions 242.4
Consolidation and merger of corporations 338.83; 658.16
Consolidation and merger of corporations—Great Britain 338.830941
Consolidation and merger of corporations—Law and legislation 346.06626
Consolidation and merger of corporations—Law and legislation—European Economic Community countries 346.406626
Consolidation and merger of corporations—Law and legislation—Great Britain 346.4106626
Consolidation and merger of corporations—Law and legislation—United States 346.7306626
Consolidation and merger of corporations—Management 658.16
Consolidation and merger of corporations—Periodicals 338.8305
Consolidation and merger of corporations—Taxation—Law and legislation 343.067
Consolidation and merger of corporations—Taxation—Law and legislation—United States 343.73067
Consolidation and merger of corporations—United States 338.830973
Consolidation and merger of corporations—United States—Finance 338.830973
Consolidation and merger of corporations—United States—Handbooks, manuals, etc. 658.16
Consolidation and merger of corporations—United States—Periodicals 338.830973
Consortia 338.8
Conspiracies 364.1
Conspiracies—England 364.10942
Conspiracies—England—London 364.109421
Conspiracies—United States 364.10973
Constable, John, 1776–1837 759.2; 760.092
Constable, John, 1776–1837—Exhibitions 759.2
Constantine I, Emperor of Rome, d. 337 937.08092
Constellations 523.8
Constellations—Observers' manuals 523.80223
Constipation in old age 618.9763428
Constitution (Frigate) 359.3220973
Constitutional amendments 342.03
Constitutional amendments—India 342.5403
Constitutional amendments—Texas 342.76403
Constitutional amendments—United States 342.7303
Constitutional amendments—United States—History 342.73039
Constitutional conventions 342.0292
Constitutional conventions—United States 342.730292
Constitutional conventions—United States—States 342.73024

Constitutional conventions—United States—States—
  Bibliography 016.34273024
Constitutional courts 347.035
Constitutional history 342.029
Constitutional history—Australia 342.94029
Constitutional history—Canada 342.71029
Constitutional history—Germany 342.43029
Constitutional history—Germany (West) 342.43029
Constitutional history—Great Britain 342.41029
Constitutional history—Greece 342.495029
Constitutional history—Greece—Athens 342.385029
Constitutional history—Greece—Athens—To 146 B.C.
  342.385029
Constitutional history—India 342.54029
Constitutional history, Medieval 342.029; 342.40290902
Constitutional history—New York (State) 342.747029
Constitutional history—Nigeria 342.669029
Constitutional history—Pakistan 342.5491029
Constitutional history—Philippines 342.599029
Constitutional history—South Africa 342.68029
Constitutional history—Soviet Union 342.47029
Constitutional history—United States 342.73029
Constitutional history—United States—Bibliography
  016.34273029
Constitutional law 342
Constitutional law—Australia 342.94
Constitutional law—Australia—Cases 342.9400264
Constitutional law—California 342.794
Constitutional law—Canada 342.71
Constitutional law—Canada—Cases 342.6800264
Constitutional law—China 342.51
Constitutional law—France 342.44
Constitutional law—Georgia 342.758
Constitutional law—Germany (West) 342.43
Constitutional law—Great Britain 342.41
Constitutional law—Great Britain—Cases 342.4100264
Constitutional law—Illinois 342.773
Constitutional law—India 342.54
Constitutional law—India—Cases 342.5400264
Constitutional law—Kansas 342.781
Constitutional law—Louisiana 342.763
Constitutional law—New Jersey 342.749
Constitutional law—Pakistan 342.5491
Constitutional law—Philippines 342.599
Constitutional law—South Africa 342.68
Constitutional law—Soviet Union 342.47
Constitutional law—Texas 342.764
Constitutional law—United States 342.73
Constitutional law—United States—Bibliography
  016.34273
Constitutional law—United States—Cases 342.7300264
Constitutional law—United States—Compends 342.73
Constitutional law—United States—Digests
  342.73002638
Constitutional law—United States—Encyclopedias
  342.73003
Constitutional law—United States—Interpretation and
  construction 342.73
Constitutional law—United States—Moral and ethical
  aspects 174.3
Constitutional law—United States—Outlines, syllabi,
  etc. 342.73
Constitutional law—United States—Philosophy
  342.73001
Constitutions 342.023
Constitutions—Alaska 342.798023
Constitutions—Arizona 342.791023
Constitutions—Canada 342.71023
Constitutions—China 342.51023

Constitutions—Florida 342.759023
Constitutions—Idaho 342.796023
Constitutions—India 342.54023
Constitutions—Maryland 342.752023
Constitutions—Missouri 342.778023
Constitutions—Nebraska 342.782023
Constitutions—Nevada 342.793023
Constitutions—New Jersey 342.749023
Constitutions—New Mexico 342.789023
Constitutions—New York (State) 342.747023
Constitutions—Pakistan 342.5491023
Constitutions—Philippines 342.599023
Constitutions—South Africa 342.68023
Constitutions—South Dakota 342.783023
Constitutions—Texas 342.764023
Constitutions—United States 342.73023
Constitutions—United States—States 342.73023
Constitutions—Wyoming 342.787023
Constraint databases 005.75
Constraint programming (Computer science) 005.11
Constraints (Linguistics) 415
Constructed wetlands 628.35
Construction contracts 343.078624; 343.07869; 692.8
Construction contracts—California 343.79407869
Construction contracts—Canada 343.7107869
Construction contracts—Florida 343.75907869
Construction contracts—Great Britain 343.41078624;
  343.4107869
Construction contracts—Massachusetts 343.74407869
Construction contracts—South Africa 343.6807869
Construction contracts—United States 343.73078624;
  343.7307869
Construction contracts—United States—Forms
  343.730786900269
Construction contracts—United States—States
  343.7307869
Construction contracts—United States—Trial practice
  343.730786240269
Construction equipment 681.76; 690.0284
Construction equipment industry 338.4768176
Construction industry 338.47624
Construction industry—Accounting 657.869
Construction industry—Law and legislation 343.07869
Construction industry—Law and legislation—California
  343.79407869
Construction industry—Law and legislation—United
  States 343.73078624
Construction industry—Management 624.068; 690.068;
  690.8068
Construction industry—Safety regulations 344.30465
Construction industry—Safety regulations—United
  States 344.730465
Construction on contaminated sites 363.11969; 690.22
Constructive mathematics 511.3
Constructivism (Education) 370.152
Constructivism (Philosophy) 149
Consular law 342.0412
Consultants 658.46
Consultants—Marketing 001.0688
Consultation-liaison psychiatry 616.89
Consulting engineers 620.0023; 620.0092
Consulting firms 658.46
Consumer affairs departments 381.34
Consumer behavior 658.8342
Consumer behavior—United States 658.83420973
Consumer complaints 381.3
Consumer cooperatives 334.5
Consumer credit 332.743
Consumer credit—Great Britain 332.743

Cookery, African 641.596
Cookery, American 641.5973
Cookery, American—California style 641.59794
Cookery, American—History 641.5973
Cookery, American—Louisiana style 641.59763
Cookery, American—Midwestern style 641.5977
Cookery, American—New England style 641.5974
Cookery, American—Pacific Northwest style 641.59795
Cookery, American—Southern style 641.5975
Cookery, American—Southwestern style 641.5976;
  641.5979
Cookery, American—Western style 641.5978
Cookery, Amish 641.566
Cookery (Apples) 641.6411
Cookery, Armenian 641.59291992
Cookery, Asian 641.595
Cookery, Australian 641.5994
Cookery, Austrian 641.59436
Cookery (Baby foods) 641.5622
Cookery, Basque 641.5929992
Cookery (Beans) 641.6565
Cookery (Beef) 641.662
Cookery (Beer) 641.623
Cookery, Belgian 641.59493
Cookery (Berries) 641.647
Cookery—Bibliography 016.6415
Cookery, Brazilian 641.5981
Cookery (Bread) 641.815
Cookery, British 641.5941
Cookery (Buffalo meat) 641.66292
Cookery, Cajun 641.59763
Cookery—California 641.509794; 641.59794
Cookery—California—San Francisco 641.50979461;
  641.5979461
Cookery, Canadian 641.5971
Cookery (Canola oil) 641.63853
Cookery, Caribbean 641.59729
Cookery (Cereals) 641.631
Cookery (Cheese) 641.673
Cookery (Chicken) 641.665
Cookery, Chinese 641.5951
Cookery, Chinese—Beijing style 641.59511
Cookery (Chocolate) 641.6374
Cookery (Coffee) 641.6373
Cookery (Cold dishes) 641.79
Cookery (Corn) 641.6567
Cookery (Crabs) 641.695
Cookery, Creole 641.59763
Cookery, Cuban 641.597291
Cookery, Czech 641.59437
Cookery (Dairy products) 641.67
Cookery—Dictionaries 641.503
Cookery (Dill) 641.6382
Cookery (Dried foods) 641.614
Cookery (Duck) 641.691
Cookery, Dutch 641.59492
Cookery (Eggs) 641.675
Cookery (Emu) 641.6669
Cookery—Encyclopedias 641.503
Cookery, English 641.5941; 641.5942
Cookery—Equipment and supplies 641.50284; 683.8
Cookery, European 641.594
Cookery, Finnish 641.594897
Cookery (Fish) 641.692
Cookery—Florida 641.509759; 641.59759
Cookery (Flowers) 641.659
Cookery for one 641.561
Cookery for the physically handicapped 641.5631
Cookery for the sick 641.5631

Cookery for two 641.561
Cookery, French 641.5944
Cookery, French-Canadian 641.592114
Cookery, French—Provençal style 641.59449
Cookery (Frozen foods) 641.6153
Cookery (Fruit) 641.64
Cookery (Game) 641.691
Cookery (Garlic) 641.6526
Cookery (Gelatin) 641.864
Cookery, German 641.5943
Cookery, Greek 641.59495
Cookery (Greens) 641.654
Cookery (Hashish) 641.6379
Cookery, Hawaiian 641.59969
Cookery (Herbs) 641.657
Cookery (Honey) 641.68
Cookery (Hot pepper sauces) 641.6384
Cookery (Hot peppers) 641.6384
Cookery—Humor 641.50207
Cookery, Hungarian 641.59439
Cookery—Indiana 641.509772; 641.59772
Cookery, Indic 641.5954
Cookery, Indonesian 641.59598
Cookery, International 641.59
Cookery, Iranian 641.5955
Cookery, Irish 641.59415
Cookery, Israeli 641.595694
Cookery, Italian 641.5945
Cookery, Italian—Northern style 641.59451
Cookery, Italian—Sicilian style 641.59458
Cookery, Italian—Southern style 641.59457
Cookery, Italian—Tuscan style 641.59455
Cookery, Jamaican 641.597292
Cookery, Japanese 641.5952
Cookery, Jewish 641.5676
Cookery (Kefir) 641.67146
Cookery, Korean 641.59519
Cookery, Latin American 641.598
Cookery, Lebanese 641.595692
Cookery (Leftovers) 641.552
Cookery (Lemons) 641.64334
Cookery, Liberian 641.596662
Cookery (Liquors) 641.625
Cookery (Lobsters) 641.695
Cookery, Malayan 641.59595
Cookery, Marine 641.57; 641.5753
Cookery (Marshmallow) 641.853
Cookery (Meat) 641.66
Cookery, Medieval 641.50902
Cookery, Mediterranean 641.591822
Cookery, Mennonite 641.566
Cookery, Mexican 641.5972
Cookery, Middle Eastern 641.5956
Cookery (Moose) 641.691
Cookery, Moroccan 641.5964
Cookery (Mozzarella cheese) 641.67356
Cookery (Mushrooms) 641.658
Cookery (Mustard) 641.6384
Cookery (Natural foods) 641.563; 641.5637; 641.6
Cookery, Nigerian 641.59669
Cookery—North Carolina 641.509756; 641.59756
Cookery, Norwegian 641.59481
Cookery (Nuts) 641.645
Cookery (Oat bran) 641.6313
Cookery (Olive oil) 641.6463
Cookery (Onions) 641.6525
Cookery, Oriental 641.595
Cookery (Ostrich) 641.66694
Cookery (Pasta) 641.822

Cookery (Peanut butter) 641.656596
Cookery—Pennsylvania 641.509748; 641.59748
Cookery (Peppers) 641.6384
Cookery—Periodicals 641.505
Cookery, Philippine 641.59599
Cookery, Polish 641.59438
Cookery (Pork) 641.664
Cookery, Portuguese 641.59469
Cookery (Potatoes) 641.6521
Cookery (Poultry) 641.665
Cookery, Puerto Rican 641.597295
Cookery (Pumpkin) 641.6562
Cookery (Relishes) 641.812
Cookery (Rice) 641.6318
Cookery, Russian 641.5947
Cookery (Salmon) 641.692
Cookery (Sausages) 641.66
Cookery, Scandinavian 641.5948
Cookery, Scottish 641.59411
Cookery (Seafood) 641.692
Cookery, Sephardic 641.5676
Cookery (Shad) 641.692
Cookery, Shaker 641.566
Cookery (Shellfish) 641.694
Cookery (Shrimp) 641.695
Cookery (Sourdough) 641.815
Cookery, South African 641.5968
Cookery, Southeast Asian 641.5959
Cookery (Soybeans) 641.65655
Cookery, Spanish 641.5946
Cookery, Spanish—Catalonian style 641.59467
Cookery (Spices) 641.6383
Cookery (Squash) 641.6562
Cookery (Strawberries) 641.6475
Cookery (Sunflower seeds) 641.656
Cookery, Swedish 641.59485
Cookery, Swiss 641.59494
Cookery (Tarragon) 641.657
Cookery—Texas 641.509764; 641.59764
Cookery—Texas—Houston 641.5097641411;
   641.597641411
Cookery, Thai 641.59593
Cookery (Tofu) 641.65655
Cookery (Tomatoes) 641.65642
Cookery (Turkey) 641.66592
Cookery, Turkish 641.59561
Cookery, Ukrainian 641.59477
Cookery (Vegetables) 641.65
Cookery (Venison) 641.691
Cookery, Vietnamese 641.59597
Cookery (Vinegar) 641.62
Cookery, Welsh 641.59429
Cookery, West Indian 641.59729
Cookery (Wild foods) 641.6
Cookery (Wine) 641.622
Cookery (Yogurt) 641.671476
Cookery (Zucchini) 641.6562
Cookie Monster (Fictitious character) 791.4375;
   791.4575
Cookies 641.8654
Cookies (Computer science) 005.276
Cooks 641.5092
Cookware 641.50284
Cool stars 523.88
Coolidge, Calvin, 1872–1933 973.915092
Cooling towers 621.197
Cooper, Alexandra (Fictitious character) 813.54
Cooper family 929.20973
Cooper, James Fenimore, 1789–1851 813.2

Cooper, James Fenimore, 1789–1851—Criticism and
   interpretation 813.2
Cooper, James Fenimore, 1789–1851—Political and
   social views 813.2
Cooper, Lila (Fictitious character) 813.54
Cooperation 334
Cooperation—India 334.0954
Cooperative industrial research 341.7675
Cooperative societies 334
Cooperman, Benny (Fictitious character) 813.54
Cooperman, Benny (Fictitious character)—Fiction
   813.54
Coordination compounds 541.2242
Cop shows 791.45655
Copenhagen (Denmark) 948.913
Copenhagen (Denmark)—Guidebooks 914.891304;
   914.89130459; 914.8913046
Copepoda 595.34
Copernicus, Nicolaus, 1473–1543 520.92
Copland, Aaron, 1900– 780.92
Copp, Joseph (Fictitious character) 813.54
Copp, Joseph (Fictitious character)—Fiction 813.54
Copper 669.3
Copper alloys 669.3
Copper industry and trade 338.2743
Copper—Metallurgy 622.343; 669.3
Copper mines and mining 622.343
Copper ores 669.3
Copper oxide superconductors 537.623
Copper—Religious aspects 291.37
Copperplates 767.20284
Coppola, Francis Ford, 1939– 791.430233092
Coptic chants 782.32215
Coptic Church 281.72
Coptic Church—Liturgy 264.0172
Copulas (Mathematical statistics) 519.535
Copy-reading 808.06607
Copy writers 659.1
Copying machine equipment industry 338.4768165
Copying machines 681.6
Copying processes 686.4
Copying services 025.12
Copyright 346.0482
Copyright—Australia 346.940482
Copyright—Australia—Periodicals 346.940482
Copyright—Canada 346.710482
Copyright clearinghouses 338.473460482
Copyright—Computer programs 346.0482
Copyright—Computer programs—United States
   346.730482
Copyright—Databases 346.0482
Copyright—Databases—United States 346.730482
Copyright—Great Britain 346.410482
Copyright infringement 346.0482
Copyright infringement—United States 346.730482
Copyright, International 341.7582
Copyright—Motion pictures 346.0482
Copyright—Motion pictures—United States 346.730482
Copyright—Music 346.0482
Copyright—Music—United States 346.730482
Copyright—Performing rights 346.0482
Copyright—United States 346.730482
Copyright—United States—Cases 346.7304820264
Coral reef animals 591.7789
Coral reef biology 578.7789
Coral reef ecology 577.789
Coral reefs and islands 578.7789
Corals 593.6
Corals, Fossil 563.6

CORBA (Computer architecture) 005.276
Corbett, Hugh (Fictitious character) 823.914
Corbett, Hugh (Fictitious character)—Fiction 823.914
Core competencies 331.1142; 370.113; 658.4012
Core drilling 622.24
Core-mantle boundary 551.11
Corey family 929.20973
Coriolanus, Cnaeus Marcius 937.03092
Cork (Ireland) 941.956
Cork (Ireland : County) 941.95
Cork (Ireland : County)—Social life and customs 941.95
Cork (Ireland)—Social life and customs 941.956
Corleone family (Fictitious characters) 791.4375;
   813.54
Cormorants 598.43
Corn 584.92; 633.15; 641.3315
Corn chips 664.75
Cornea—Diseases 617.719
Cornea—Laser surgery 617.719059
Cornea—Surgery 617.719059
Corneille, Pierre, 1606–1684 842.4
Corneille, Pierre, 1606–1684—Criticism and
   interpretation 842.4
Corneille, Pierre, 1606–1684—Tragedies 842.4
Corneille, Pierre, 1606–1684—Translations into English
   842.4
Cornwall (England : County) 942.37
Cornwall (England : County)—Description and travel
   914.23704; 914.23704859; 914.2370486
Cornwall (England : County)—Guidebooks 914.23704;
   914.23704859; 914.2370486
Cornwall (England : County)—History 942.37
Cornwall (England : County)—History—Sources 942.37
Cornwall (England : County)—Social life and customs
   942.37
Coronado, Francisco Vásquez de, 1510–1554 979.01092
Coronal holes (Astronomy) 523.75
Coronary artery bypass 617.412
Coronary care units 362.1961204
Coronary heart disease 616.123
Coronary heart disease—Etiology 616.123071
Coronary heart disease—Pathophysiology 616.12307
Coronary heart disease—Prevention 616.12305
Coronary heart disease—Psychological aspects
   616.1230019
Coronary heart disease—Risk factors 616.123071
Coronary heart disease—Surgery 617.412
Coronation music 781.57
Coronaviruses 579.256; 616.0194
Corotating interaction regions 523.58
Corporate culture 302.35
Corporate culture—Japan 302.350952
Corporate culture—United States 302.350973
Corporate governance 658.4
Corporate governance—Law and legislation 346.0664
Corporate governance—Law and legislation—United
   States 346.730664
Corporate governance—United States 658.400973
Corporate image 659.285
Corporate lawyers 346.066023
Corporate legal departments 658.12
Corporate legal departments—United States 346.73066;
   658.120973
Corporate legal departments—United States—
   Periodicals 346.73066
Corporate libraries 027.69
Corporate power 306.34; 322.3; 338.8
Corporate reorganizations 346.06626
Corporate reorganizations—United States 346.7306626

Corporate sponsorship 659.285
Corporate treasurers 658.15
Corporate turnarounds 658.4063
Corporate turnarounds—Management 658.4063
Corporation law 346.066
Corporation law—Australia 346.94066
Corporation law—British Columbia 346.711066
Corporation law—California 346.794066
Corporation law—Canada 346.71066
Corporation law—Delaware 346.751066
Corporation law—European Economic Community
   countries 346.4066
Corporation law—Florida 346.759066
Corporation law—Georgia 346.758066
Corporation law—Great Britain 346.41066
Corporation law—India 346.54066
Corporation law—Ireland 346.417066
Corporation law—Kentucky 346.769066
Corporation law—Massachusetts 346.744066
Corporation law—New Jersey 346.749066
Corporation law—Nigeria 346.669066
Corporation law—North Carolina 346.756066
Corporation law—Ohio 346.771066
Corporation law—Pakistan 346.5491066
Corporation law—Pennsylvania 346.748066
Corporation law—Philippines 346.599066
Corporation law—South Africa 346.68066
Corporation law—Texas 346.764066
Corporation law—United States 346.73066
Corporation law—United States—Cases 346.7306602
Corporation law—United States—Criminal provisions
   345.730268
Corporation law—United States—Forms 346.730660269
Corporation law—United States—Outlines, syllabi, etc.
   346.73066
Corporation law—United States—Periodicals
   346.7306605
Corporation law—Virginia 346.755066
Corporation reports 658.1512
Corporations 338.74
Corporations—Accounting 657.95
Corporations—Accounting—Law and legislation
   346.06648
Corporations—Accounting—Law and legislation—United
   States 346.7306648
Corporations, American 338.88973
Corporations, Canadian 338.88971
Corporations—Charitable contributions—United States
   361.7650973
Corporations—Charitable contributions—United States—
   Directories 361.76502573
Corporations—Europe 338.74094
Corporations, European 338.8894
Corporations—Finance 658.15
Corporations—Finance—Computer programs
   658.1502855369
Corporations—Finance—Data processing 658.150285
Corporations—Finance—Law and legislation—United
   States 346.730666
Corporations—Finance—Periodicals 658.1505
Corporations, Foreign 338.88
Corporations, Foreign—Canada 338.88871
Corporations, Foreign—Taxation 336.243
Corporations, Foreign—Taxation—United States
   336.243
Corporations, Government 352.266
Corporations—Great Britain 338.740941
Corporations—Great Britain—Finance 658.150941
Corporations—Growth 658.406

Corporations—Handbooks, manuals, etc. 658.045
Corporations—Investor relations 659.285
Corporations—Investor relations—United States 659.285
Corporations, Japanese 338.88952
Corporations, Japanese—United States 338.88952073
Corporations, Japanese—United States—Management 338.88952073
Corporations—Philippines 338.7409599
Corporations—Philippines—Finance—Statistics—Periodicals 338.7409599
Corporations—Public relations 659.285
Corporations—Taxation 336.243
Corporations—Taxation—Consolidated returns—Law and legislation 343.05267
Corporations—Taxation—Consolidated returns—Law and legislation—United States 343.7305267; 343.73067
Corporations—Taxation—Law and legislation 343.067
Corporations—Taxation—Law and legislation—European Economic Community countries 343.4067
Corporations—Taxation—Law and legislation—Great Britain 343.41067
Corporations—Taxation—Law and legislation—United States 343.73067
Corporations—Taxation—Law and legislation—United States—Cases 343.730670264
Corporations—Taxation—Law and legislation—United States—Outlines, syllabi, etc. 343.73067
Corporations—Taxation—Law and legislation—United States—States 343.73067
Corporations—Taxation—United States 336.2430973
Corporations—United States 338.740973
Corporations—United States—Accounting 657.950973
Corporations—United States—Auditing 657.45
Corporations—United States—Directories 338.7402573
Corporations—United States—Finance 658.150973
Corporations—United States—Finance—Directories 338.7402573
Corporations—United States—Finance—Periodicals 658.15097305
Corporations—United States—History 338.740973
Corporations—United States—Rankings 338.740973
Corporations—United States—Rankings—Directories 338.7402573
Corporations—Valuation 658.15
Corporations—Valuation—Mathematical models 658.15
Correctional institutions 365.5
Correctional law 345.077
Correctional law—United States 345.73077
Correctional law—United States—Cases 345.730770264
Correctional personnel—United States—Examinations 365.64076
Correctional psychology 365.66
Corrections 364.6
Corrections—United States 364.60973
Corrections—United States—History 364.60973
Correlation (Statistics) 519.537
Correspondence analysis (Statistics) 519.535
Correspondence schools and courses 371.356; 374.4
Correspondence schools and courses—United States 374.40973
Correspondence schools and courses—United States—Directories 374.402573
Corrosion and anti-corrosives 620.11223
Corrosion and anti-corrosives—Testing 620.112230287
Corrosive wastes 363.179029
Corrugated paperboard 676.288; 676.32
Corsica automobile 629.2222

Corsica automobile—Maintenance and repair 629.28722
Corsica automobile—Maintenance and repair—Handbooks, manuals, etc. 629.28722
Cortázar, Julio 863.64
Cortázar, Julio—Criticism and interpretation 863.64
Cortés, Hernando, 1485–1547 972.02092
Corvette automobile 629.2222
Corvette automobile—History 629.2222
Corvette automobile—Maintenance and repair 629.28722
Corvette automobile—Maintenance and repair—Handbooks, manuals, etc. 629.28722
Corvidae 598.864
Corythosaurus 567.914
Cosby, Bill, 1937– 792.7028092
Cosmetic delivery systems 668.55
Cosmetics 646.72; 668.55
Cosmetics—Analysis 668.55
Cosmetics—Dictionaries 668.5503
Cosmetics industry 338.4764672
Cosmic background radiation 523.1
Cosmic dust 523.1125
Cosmic magnetic fields 523.0188
Cosmic noise—Antarctica—Charts, diagrams, etc. 551.5276
Cosmic physics 523.01
Cosmic rays 523.0197223; 539.7223
Cosmochemistry 523.02
Cosmochronology 523.1
Cosmogony 523.12
Cosmography 570; 523.1
Cosmology 215.2; 523.1
Cosmology, Ancient 523.10901
Cosmology, Medieval 523.10902
Cost accounting 657.42
Cost and standard of living 339.42; 339.47
Cost control 658.1552
Cost effectiveness 658.1554
Costa Rica 972.86
Costa Rica—Guidebooks 917.28604; 917.286045
Costs, Industrial 338.51; 658.1552
Costs (Law) 347.077
Costs (Law)—United States 347.7377
Costume 391; 646.478; 792.026
Costume—China 391.00951
Costume—China—History 391.00951
Costume design 746.92; 792.026
Costume design—England 746.920942
Costume design—England—London 746.9209421
Costume design—England—London—History 746.9209421
Costume design—England—London—History—20th century 746.92094210904
Costume design—France—History—20th century 746.9209440904
Costume—England—History 391.00942
Costume—Erotic aspects 391.0019
Costume—Great Britain—History 391.00941
Costume—History 391.009
Costume—History—Medieval, 500–1500 391.00902
Costume—History—19th century 391.009034
Costume—History—20th century 391.00904
Costume in art 704.949391
Costume jewelry 391.7
Costume—Social aspects 391
Costume—United States—History 391.00973
Costume—United States—History—19th century 391.0097309034
Côte d'Ivoire 966.68

Côte d'Ivoire—Economic conditions 330.96668
Côte d'Ivoire—Economic conditions—1960–
330.9666805
Côte d'Ivoire—Economic conditions—1960– —
Periodicals 330.9666805
Cottage gardening 635; 712.6
Cottage gardens 635; 712.6
Cotton 633.51
Cotton fabrics 677.2164
Cotton growing 633.51
Cotton plantation workers 331.763351
Cotton thread 677.2162
Cottontails 599.324
Cottonwood County (Minn.) 977.628
Cottonwood County (Minn.)—Maps 912.77628
Council for Mutual Economic Assistance 337.147
Councils and synods, Ecumenical 262.52
Councils and synods, Episcopal (Catholic) 262.52
Counseling 158.3; 158.3023; 361.06
Counseling in adult education 374.14
Counseling in elementary education 372.14; 372.1422
Counseling in elementary education—United States
372.140973
Counseling in higher education 378.194
Counseling in higher education—United States
378.1940973
Counseling in middle school education 373.14
Counseling in middle school education—United States
373.140973
Counseling in secondary education 373.14; 373.1422
Counseling in secondary education—Great Britain
373.140941
Counseling in secondary education—United States
373.140973
Counseling—Religious aspects 291.61
Counseling—Religious aspects—Christianity 253.5
Counseling—Vocational guidance 361.06023
Counselor and client 158.3
Counselors 361.06092
Counselors—Professional ethics 174.915
Counter-Reformation 270.6
Counterfeits and counterfeiting 364.133
Counterpoint 781.286
Counterpoint—18th century 781.28609033
Countertrade 382.1
Countertransference (Psychology) 616.8914; 616.8917
Counting 513.211
Counting-out rhymes 398.84
Country clubs 367
Country-dance 793.31
Country-dance—United States 793.31973
Country-dances 784.1882
Country homes 643.2
Country homes—England 728.80942
Country homes—United States—Purchasing 643.2
Country life 307.72
Country life—England 307.720942; 942
Country life in art 704.949909
Country life in literature 808.80321734; 809.93321734
Country life—Ireland 307.7209415
Country life—United States 973.09734
Country life—Vermont 974.3
Country music 781.642; 782.421642
Country music—1931–1940 781.64209043
Country music—1951–1960 781.64209045
Country music—1981–1990 781.64209048
Country music—Dictionaries 781.64203
Country music—Discography 016.7816420266
Country music—Encyclopedias 781.64203

Country music festivals 781.642079; 782.421642079
Country music—History and criticism 781.64209;
782.42164209
Country music—History and criticism—Periodicals
781.64209005
Country music—Religious aspects 291.175
Country music—Texts 782.4216420268
Country musicians 781.642092; 782.421642092
Country musicians—United States—Biography
781.642092273; 782.421642092273
Country rock music 781.642
County courts 347.02
County government 352.15
County government—Great Britain 352.150941
County school systems 379.153
County services 352.15
Couple-owned business enterprises 338.642
Couples 306.7
Coupons (Retail trade) 658.82
Coups d'état 321.09
Courage 179.6
Courage in literature 808.80353; 809.93353
Course in miracles 299.93
Court administration 347.013
Court administration—United States 347.7313
Court congestion and delay 347.013
Court congestion and delay—United States 347.7313
Court marshals 347.016
Court of Justice of the European Communities 341.55
Court rules 347.051
Court rules—Michigan 347.774051
Court rules—New Jersey 347.749051
Court rules—Philippines 347.599051
Court rules—Texas 347.764051
Court rules—United States 347.7351
Court rules—Washington (State) 347.797051
Courtesy 177.1; 395
Courtesy in literature 808.80353; 809.93353
Courtney family (Fictitious characters) 823
Courtney family (Fictitious characters)—Fiction 823
Courts 347.01
Courts and courtiers 395
Courts—Great Britain 347.4101
Courts-martial and courts of inquiry 343.0143
Courts-martial and courts of inquiry—United States
343.730143
Courts—Maryland 347.75201
Courts—Michigan 347.77401
Courts—Minnesota 347.77601
Courts—New York (State) 347.74701
Courts—Nigeria 347.66901
Courts of last resort 347.035
Courts—Philippines 347.59901
Courts—United States 347.731
Courts—United States—Cases 347.732
Courts—United States—History 347.73109
Courts—United States—States 347.733
Courts—Utah—Periodicals 347.7920105
Courtship 646.77
Courtship in literature 808.803543; 809.933543
Courtship of animals 591.562
Courtship—United States 306.7340973
Cousins 306.87
Cousteau, Jacques Yves 551.460092
Covenant theology 231.76
Covenant theology—Biblical teaching 231.76
Covenanters 285.2411
Covenants 346.02
Covenants—Biblical teaching 231.76

Covenants—Religious aspects 291.2117
Covenants—Religious aspects—Christianity 231.76
Covenants—Religious aspects—Judaism 296.31172
Covens 133.43; 299
Cover letters 650.14
Coveralls 646.47; 687.16
Coward, Noel, 1899–1973 822.912
Cowardice 152.46; 179.6
Cowardly Lion (Fictitious character) 791.4372; 813.4
Cowboys 636.213092
Cowboys in art 704.9426
Cowboys in literature 808.80352636; 809.93352636
Cowboys—West (U.S.) 636.213092278
Cowboys—West (U.S.)—History 636.213092278
Cowboys—West (U.S.)—Humor 636.213092278
Cowboys—West (U.S.)—Pictorial works 636.213092278
Cowgirls—West (U.S.) 636.213092278
Cowper, William, 1731–1800 821.6
Cowper, William, 1731–1800—Criticism and
    interpretation 821.6
Cowrie (Fictitious character : Dunsford) 823.914
Cows 636.2
Cox family 929.20973
Coxswaining 797.14
Coyne, Brady (Fictitious character) 813.54
Coyne, Brady (Fictitious character)—Fiction 813.54
Coyote 599.7725
Coyote (Legendary character) 398.245297725
Coyotes in art 704.943297725
CP/M 005.4469
CP violation (Nuclear physics) 539.725
CPR (First aid) 616.1025
CPR (First aid) for children 618.921025
CPR (First aid)—Handbooks, manuals, etc. 616.1025
CR submanifolds 516.36
Crab pots 639.560284; 681.7636
Crabbe, George, 1754–1832 821.7
Crabbe, George, 1754–1832—Criticism and
    interpretation 821.7
Crabs 595.386
Crack (Drug) 362.298
Craft malls 381.4568
Craft shops 680.68
Cram schools 373.2
Cramer family 929.20973
Crampton Gap (Md.), Battle of, 1862 973.733
Cranberry sauce 641.81; 664.58
Crane, Hart, 1899–1932 811.52
Crane, Hart, 1899–1932. Bridge 811.52
Crane, Hart, 1899–1932—Criticism and interpretation
    811.52
Crane, Stephen, 1871–1900 813.4
Crane, Stephen, 1871–1900—Criticism and
    interpretation 813.4
Cranes (Birds) 598.32
Craniology 599.948
Craniosacral therapy 615.82
Craniosynostoses 618.92097514
Cranmer, Thomas, 1489–1556 283.092
Craps (Game) 795.12
Crash injuries 617.1028
Crash sensors 629.276
Crashaw, Richard, 1613?–1649 821.4
Crashaw, Richard, 1613?–1649—Criticism and
    interpretation 821.4
Crawford County (Iowa) 977.745
Crawford County (Iowa)—Maps 912.77745
Crawford County (Mich.) 977.477
Crawford County (Mich.)—Maps 912.77477

Crawford County (Wis.) 977.574
Crawford County (Wis.)—Maps 912.77574
Crawford family 929.20973
Crawford, Francis (Fictitious character) 823.914
Crawford, Francis (Fictitious character)—Fiction
    823.914
Cray computers 004.11
Crayfish 595.384
Creation 213; 231.765; 233.11; 291.24
Creation—Biblical teaching 231.765
Creation in rabbinical literature 296.34
Creation (Literary, artistic, etc.) 153.35
Creationism 231.7652; 576.8
Creative ability 153.35
Creative ability in business 658.0019; 658.40019
Creative ability—Problems, exercises, etc. 153.35
Creative ability—Religious aspects 291.44
Creative ability—Religious aspects—Christianity 248.4
Creative activities and seat work 371.3; 372.13; 372.5;
    649.51
Creative activities and seat work—Handbooks, manuals,
    etc. 371.3
Creative thinking 370.157
Creative thinking—Study and teaching 370.157
Creative writing 808.02
Creative writing (Elementary education) 372.623
Creative writing (Higher education) 808.020711
Creative writing—Therapeutic use 615.8515; 616.89165
Credibility theory (Insurance) 368.01; 368.012
Credit 332.7
Credit bureaus 332.706
Credit cards 332.765
Credit cards—Forgeries 364.163
Credit cards—United States 332.7650973
Credit derivatives 332.632
Credit—Management 658.88
Credit managers 658.88
Credit titles (Motion pictures, television, etc.) 778.535;
    778.593
Credit unions 334.22
Credit unions—Law and legislation 346.0668
Credit unions—Law and legislation—United States
    346.730668
Credit unions—Management 334.22068
Credit unions—United States 334.220973
Credit unions—United States—Directories 334.2202573
Credit unions—United States—Management 334.22068
Credit unions—United States—Statistics 334.220973021
Credit unions—United States—Statistics—Periodicals
    334.220973021
Cree Indians 305.8973; 971.2004973
Cree Indians—Folklore 398.2089973
Creeds 238
Creeds in the Bible 238
Creek law 340.52089973
Creek philosophy 191.089973
Creel boats 623.82026; 639.20284
Creels (Fishing) 639.20284; 681.763; 799.10284
Creole dialects 417.22
Crete (Greece) 939.18; 949.59
Crete (Greece)—Antiquities 939.18
Crete (Greece)—Guidebooks 914.95904; 914.9590476
Cribb, Sergeant (Fictitious character) 823.914
Cribb, Sergeant (Fictitious character)—Fiction 823.914
Cribrilinidae 594.676
Cribs (Children's furniture) 684.150832
Crichton, Tessa (Fictitious character) 823.914
Cricket 796.358
Cricket bats 688.76358; 796.35826

Cricket—England 796.3580942
Cricket—England—History 796.3580942
Cricket—Humor 796.3580207
Cricket matches 796.35865
Cricket players 796.358092
Crickets 595.726
Crime 364; 364.1
Crime analysis 363.25
Crime and race 364.256
Crime—Australia 364.994
Crime—Bibliography 016.364
Crime—Canada 364.971
Crime—Case studies 364.0722
Crime—Economic aspects 364; 364.042
Crime—Economic aspects—United States 364.973
Crime—Encyclopedias 364.03
Crime—England 364.942
Crime—England—History 364.942
Crime—England—History—18th century 364.94209033
Crime—England—London 364.9421
Crime—Europe 364.94
Crime—Great Britain 364.10941; 364.941
Crime—History 364.109; 364.9
Crime in literature 808.80355; 809.93355
Crime in mass media 364
Crime—India 364.954
Crime—India—History 364.954
Crime laboratories 363.25
Crime—New York (State) 364.9747
Crime—New York (State)—New York 364.97471
Crime prevention 362.88; 364.4
Crime prevention and architectural design 364.49
Crime prevention—Great Britain 364.40941
Crime prevention—United States 364.40973
Crime prevention—United States—Citizen participation 364.430973
Crime scene searches 363.252
Crime scenes 363.25
Crime—South Africa 364.968
Crime stoppers programs 364.43
Crime—Sweden 364.9485
Crime—United States 364.973
Crime—United States—Bibliography 016.364973
Crime—United States—Public opinion 364.973
Crime—Washington (D.C.) 364.9753
Crimean War, 1853–1856 947.0738
Crimes against humanity 341.481; 364.135
Criminal anthropology 364.2
Criminal behavior 364.3
Criminal courts 345.01
Criminal courts—United States 345.7301
Criminal intent 345.04
Criminal investigation 363.25
Criminal investigation—Handbooks, manuals, etc. 363.25
Criminal investigation—United States 363.250973
Criminal jurisdiction 341.488; 345.01
Criminal justice, Administration of 345.05; 364
Criminal justice, Administration of—Australia 364.994
Criminal justice, Administration of—Canada 364.971
Criminal justice, Administration of—Dictionaries 364.03
Criminal justice, Administration of—Great Britain 345.4105; 364.941
Criminal justice, Administration of—Louisiana 364.9763
Criminal justice, Administration of—Moral and ethical aspects 174.9364
Criminal justice, Administration of—New York (State) 364.9747
Criminal justice, Administration of—Periodicals 364.05

Criminal justice, Administration of—Research 364.072
Criminal justice, Administration of—Research—Methodology 364.072
Criminal justice, Administration of—Research—United States 364.072073
Criminal justice, Administration of—Texas 364.9764
Criminal justice, Administration of—United States 364.973
Criminal justice, Administration of—United States—Cases 345.7305
Criminal justice, Administration of—United States—Periodicals 345.730505; 364.97305
Criminal justice personnel 364.092
Criminal law 345
Criminal law—Australia 345.94
Criminal law—California 345.794
Criminal law—California—Outlines, syllabi, etc. 345.794
Criminal law—Canada 345.71
Criminal law—China 345.51
Criminal law—China—Hong Kong 345.5125
Criminal law—China—Hong Kong—Digests 345.5125002648
Criminal law—Great Britain 345.41
Criminal law—India 345.54
Criminal law—India—Digests 345.54002648
Criminal law—Louisiana 345.763
Criminal law—Massachusetts 345.744
Criminal law—Michigan 345.774
Criminal law—New York (State) 345.747
Criminal law—Nigeria 345.669
Criminal law—North Carolina 345.756
Criminal law—Pakistan 345.5491
Criminal law—Pennsylvania 345.748
Criminal law—Philippines 345.599
Criminal law—Philosophy 345.001
Criminal law—South Africa 345.68
Criminal law—South Carolina 345.757
Criminal law—Texas 345.764
Criminal law—United States 345.73
Criminal law—United States—Cases 345.7300264
Criminal law—United States—Outlines, syllabi, etc. 345.73
Criminal liability 345.04
Criminal liability of juristic persons 345.0268
Criminal liability of juristic persons—United States 345.730268
Criminal procedure 345.05
Criminal procedure—California 345.79405
Criminal procedure—Canada 345.7105
Criminal procedure—Florida 345.75905
Criminal procedure—Great Britain 345.4105
Criminal procedure—India 345.5405
Criminal procedure (International law) 341.77
Criminal procedure—Massachusetts 345.74405
Criminal procedure—Missouri 345.77805
Criminal procedure—New York (State) 345.74705
Criminal procedure—North Carolina 345.75605
Criminal procedure—Pakistan 345.549105
Criminal procedure—Philippines 345.59905
Criminal procedure—South Africa 345.6805
Criminal procedure—Texas 345.76405
Criminal procedure—United States 345.7305
Criminal procedure—United States—Cases 345.73050264
Criminal procedure—United States—Digests 345.730502648
Criminal procedure—United States—Outlines, syllabi, etc. 345.7305

Criminal procedure—United States—Periodicals
345.730505
Criminal psychology 364.3
Criminal statistics 364.021; 364.1021
Criminal statistics—Minnesota—Periodicals
364.09776021; 364.9776021
Criminals 364.3
Criminals—Biography 364.10922; 364.3092
Criminals—Identification 364.41
Criminals—Rehabilitation 364.8
Criminals—Rehabilitation—Great Britain 364.80942
Criminals—Rehabilitation—United States 344.7303566;
364.80973
Criminals—United States 364.3092273
Criminals—United States—Biography 364.1092273
Criminology 364
Criminology—Bibliography 016.364
Criminology—History 364.09
Criminology—Methodology 364.01
Criminology—Philosophy 364.019
Criminology—Research 364.072
Criminology—Research—Europe 364.07204
Criminology—Research—Methodology 364.072
Criminology—United States 364.973
Crinoidea, Fossil 563.92
Crioulo literature 869
Crisis intervention (Mental health services)
362.204251; 616.89025
Crisis intervention (Mental health services)—
Handbooks, manuals, etc. 616.89025
Crisis management 658.4056
Crisis management—Religious aspects 291.442
Critical care medicine 616.028
Critical care medicine—Examinations, questions, etc.
616.028076
Critical care medicine—Handbooks, manuals, etc.
616.028
Critical criminology 364
Critical discourse analysis 401.41
Critical discourse analysis—Religious aspects 210.14
Critical legal studies 340.1
Critical path analysis 658.4032
Critical pedagogy 370.115
Critical pedagogy—United States 370.115
Critical phenomena (Physics) 530.424; 530.474
Critical point theory (Mathematical analysis) 514.74
Critical psychology 150.198
Critical theory 142
Critical thinking 160; 370.152
Critical thinking—Study and teaching 370.152
Critically ill children 618.920028
Criticism 801.95; 809
Criticism—Great Britain 801.950941
Criticism—Great Britain—History 801.950941
Criticism—Great Britain—History—18th century
801.950941033
Criticism—History 801.9509
Criticism—History—20th century 801.950904
Criticism—Periodicals 801.9505; 809.005
Criticism, Personal 158.1; 158.2
Criticism—Terminology 801.95014
Criticism, Textual 801.959
Criticism—United States 801.950973
Criticism—United States—History 801.950973
Criticism—United States—History—20th century
801.9509730904
Crittenden County (Ky.)—Genealogy 929.3769893
Cro-Magnon man 569.9
Croatia 949.72

Croatia—History 949.72
Croatian language 491.82
Croatian language—Dictionaries 491.823
Croatian language—Dictionaries—English 491.82321
Croatian periodicals 059.9182
Croatian philology 491.82
Croce, Benedetto, 1866–1952 195
Croce, Benedetto, 1866–1952—Aesthetics 111.85; 195
Crocheting 746.434
Crocheting—Patterns 746.434041
Crockett, Davy, 1786–1836 976.804092
Crocodiles 597.982
Crocodilians 597.98; 597.982
Crocodylidae 597.98
Croft, Joshua (Fictitious character) 813.54
Croft, Joshua (Fictitious character)—Fiction 813.54
Croft, Lara (Fictitious character) 793.932
Croft, Mike (Fictitious character) 823.914
Crofts 333.33553
Crohn's disease 616.344
Cromwell, Oliver, 1599–1658 941.064092
Crook, Arthur (Fictitious character) 823.912
Crook, Arthur (Fictitious character)—Fiction 823.912
Crop art 709.04076
Crop diversification 338.162; 631.58
Crop insurance 368.121
Crop insurance—Law and legislation 346.086121
Crop insurance—Law and legislation—United States
346.73086121
Crop insurance—United States 368.12100973
Crop science 630.2
Crop yields 338.1; 631.550
Crops 630
Crops and climate 338.14
Crops—Drought tolerance 632.12
Crops—Ecophysiology 571.2
Crops—Effect of drought on 632.12
Crops—Effect of stress on 632.1
Crops—Effect of sulphur on 631.8
Crops—Effect of temperature on 571.462; 632.1
Crops—Genetic engineering 631.5233
Crops—Genetics 631.5233
Crops—Growth 571.82
Crops—Nutrition 572.42
Crops—Physiology 571.2
Crosby, Detective Constable W. (Fictitious character)
823.914
Cross, Alex (Fictitious character) 813.54
Cross, Alex (Fictitious character)—Fiction 813.54
Cross-country ski trails 796.932
Cross-country skiing 796.932
Cross-cultural counseling 158.3
Cross-cultural counseling—United States 158.3
Cross-cultural orientation 303.482
Cross-cultural studies 306; 370.117
Cross-examination 347.075
Cross-examination—United States 347.7375
Cross family 929.20973
Cross-language information retrieval 025.04
Cross-platform software development 005.1
Cross references (Information retrieval) 025.322
Cross-stitch 746.443
Cross-stitch—Patterns 746.443041
Crossopterygii, Fossil 567.39
Crossword puzzles 793.732
Crossword puzzles—Glossaries, vocabularies, etc.
793.73203
Crow Indians 305.89752; 978.60049752
Crow Indians—Folklore 398.2089975

Crow Indians—History 978.60049752
Crow, Titus (Fictitious character) 823.914
Crow, Titus (Fictitious character)—Fiction 823.914
Crow Wing County (Minn.) 977.671
Crow Wing County (Minn.)—Maps 912.77671
Crowds 302.33
Crowley, Aleister, 1875–1947 133.092; 828.91209
Crown ethers 547.035
Crown jewels—Great Britain 739.270941
Crown lands—Leasing 333.16
Crown of God 296.3112
Crown-of-thorns starfish 593.93
Crown-of-thorns starfish—Australia—Great Barrier Reef (Qld.) 593.93
Crows 598.864
Cruciferae 583.64
Crucifixion in art 704.94853
Cruise lines 387.542
Cruise missile defenses 358.174; 623.45194
Cruise missiles 358.17182; 358.175482; 623.4519
Cruise ships 387.542
Cruise ships—Vocational guidance 387.542023
Cruise ships—Vocational guidance—United States 387.54202373
Crumhorn 788.5
Crusades 909.07; 940.18
Crusades—First, 1096–1099 940.18; 956.014
Crusades—First, 1096–1099—Sources 940.18; 956.014
Crusades—Third, 1189–1192 940.18
Crusades—Fourth, 1202–1204 949.618013
Crush syndrome 617.21
Crusoe, Edwina (Fictitious character) 813.54
Crusoe, Edwina (Fictitious character)—Fiction 813.54
Crustacea 595.3
Crying 152.4
Cryobiology 571.4645
Cryoelectronics 621.38104
Cryonics 614.6
Cryopreservation of organs, tissues, etc. 570.752
Crypto-Muslims 297
Cryptogams 586
Cryptograms 793.73
Cryptographers 652.8092
Cryptography 652.8
Cryptography—History 652.809
Cryptozoology 001.944
Crystal gazing 133.322
Crystal growth 548.5
Crystal lattices 548.81
Crystal optics 548.9
Crystallization 548.5; 660.284298
Crystallization—Industrial applications 660.284298
Crystallographers 548.092
Crystallography 548
Crystallography, Mathematical 548.7
Crystallography—Periodicals 548.05
Crystals 548
Crystals—Defects 548.8
Crystals—Magnetic properties 548.85
Crystals—Psychic aspects 133
Crystals—Therapeutic use 615.852
Ctenidae 595.44
Ctenophora 593.5
Cuarteto (Music) 784.1888
Cuba 972.91
Cuba—Description and travel 917.29104; 917.2910464
Cuba—Economic conditions 330.97291
Cuba—Economic conditions—1959–1990 330.97291064
Cuba—Economic policy 338.97291

Cuba—Foreign relations 327.7291
Cuba—Foreign relations—1959– 327.7291
Cuba—Guidebooks 917.29104; 917.2910464
Cuba—History 972.91
Cuba—History—1810–1899 972.9105
Cuba—History—Revolution, 1895–1898 972.9105
Cuba—History—1933–1959 972.91063
Cuba—History—Revolution, 1959 972.91064
Cuba—History—1959– 972.91064
Cuba—Pictorial works 972.9100222
Cuba—Politics and government 320.97291; 972.91
Cuba—Politics and government—1959– 320.9729109045; 972.91064
Cuban Americans 305.8687291073; 973.04687291
Cuban Americans—Florida 305.86872910759
Cuban Americans—Florida—Miami 305.86872910759381
Cuban Missile Crisis, 1962 972.91064; 973.922
Cuban Missile Crisis, 1962—Sources 972.91064; 973.922
Cubism 709.04032
Cucurbita 583.63
Cucurbitaceae 583.63
Cuddy, John Francis (Fictitious character) 813.54
Cuddy, John Francis (Fictitious character)—Fiction 813.54
Cues (Billiards) 688.7472; 794.720284
Cult members 291.9; 305.6
Cults 291
Cults—Japan 291.90952
Cults—Rome 292.07
Cults—United States 200.973
Cultural industries 338.470705; 384
Cultural parks 341.7625
Cultural policy 306
Cultural property—Protection 363.69
Cultural property—Protection (International law) 341.7677
Cultural property—Protection—Law and legislation 344.094
Cultural property—Repatriation 341.767
Cultural psychiatry 362.2
Cultural relations 303.482
Culture 306
Culture and law 340.115
Culture conflict 303.6
Culture—Philosophy 306.01
Culture—Semiotic models 306.014
Culture—Study and teaching 306.071
Culverts 625.7342
Cumberland County (Ky.)—Genealogy 929.3769683
Cumberland County (Pa.)—Genealogy 929.374843
Cumberland River (Ky. and Tenn.) 976.85
Cumbia (Music) 781.64
Cuming County (Neb.) 978.2232
Cuming County (Neb.)—Maps 912.782232
Cummings, E. E. (Edward Estlin), 1894–1962 811.52
Cummings, E. E. (Edward Estlin), 1894–1962— Bibliography 016.81152
Cummings, E. E. (Edward Estlin), 1894–1962—Criticism and interpretation 811.52
Cumulative effects assessment (Environmental assessment) 333.714
Cuneiform inscriptions, Akkadian 492.1
Cunningham family 929.20973
Cunningham, John (Fictitious character) 823.914
Cunningham, John (Fictitious character)—Fiction 823.914
Cup rosinweed 583.99; 633.39
Cupola furnaces 672.24
Curculionidae 595.768

Curie, Marie, 1867–1934 540.92
Curiosities and wonders 030; 031.02
Curiosities and wonders in literature 808.803; 809.933
Curlers (Athletes) 796.964092
Curling 796.964
Currency convertibility 332.45
Current awareness services 025.525
Current events 909.83
Curriculum-based assessment—United States 371.264
Curriculum change 375.006
Curriculum enrichment 375.001
Curriculum evaluation 375.006
Curriculum planning 375.001
Curriculum planning—Great Britain 375.0010941
Curriculum planning—United States 375.0010973
Curves 516.15
Curves, Algebraic 516.352
Curves, Algebraic—Data processing 516.3520285
Curves, Elliptic 516.352
Curves on surfaces 516.362
Curves on surfaces—Mathematical models 516.352
Cushions 746.95
Custer family 929.20973
Custer, George Armstrong, 1839–1876 973.82092
Custody of children 346.0173
Custody of children—Massachusetts 346.7440173
Custody of children—United States 346.730173
Customary law 340.5
Customary law, International 341
Customer clubs 658.87
Customer loyalty 658.812; 658.8343
Customer loyalty programs 658.812
Customer relations 658.812
Customer services 658.812
Customer services—Handbooks, manuals, etc. 658.812
Customer services—Management 658.812
Customer services—Quality control 658.812
Customer services—United States 658.812
Customs administration 352.448
Customs administration—Law and legislation 343.087
Customs administration—Law and legislation—Canada 343.71087
Customs administration—Law and legislation—Pakistan 343.5491087
Customs administration—Law and legislation—United States 343.73087
Customs unions 382.91
Cut flowers 635.9666; 745.92
Cut steel jewelry 391.7; 688.2; 745.5942
Cutaneous manifestations of general diseases 616.5
Cutlass Ciera automobile 629.28722
Cutlass Ciera automobile—Maintenance and repair 629.28722
Cutlass Ciera automobile—Maintenance and repair—Handbooks, manuals, etc. 629.28722
Cutler family (Fictitious characters) 813.54
Cutler family (Fictitious characters)—Fiction 813.54
Cyanobacteria 579.39
Cyanobacterial blooms 579.39
Cyanobacterial blooms—Monitoring 363.7394; 579.39
Cybercafes 384.33; 647.95
Cybernetics 003.5
Cyberspace 303.4834
Cyberterrorism 303.625; 364.147
Cycads 585.9
Cyclamen 583.675
Cycling 796.6
Cycling for women 796.6082
Cycling—Safety measures 796.60289

Cycling—Training 796.6071
Cyclists 796.6092
Cyclone forecasting 551.5520112
Cyclones 551.5513
Cyclones—Tropics 551.55130913
Cyclopoida 595.34
Cyclotrons 539.733
Cylindrophiidae 597.967
Cynewulf 829.4
Cynewulf—Criticism and interpretation 829.4
Cyprinidae 597.482
Cyprinodontidae 597.665
Cyprus 956.93
Cyprus—Antiquities 939.37
Cyprus—Economic conditions 330.95693
Cyprus—Economic conditions—Periodicals 330.95693005
Cyprus—Guidebooks 915.69304; 915.693044
Cyprus—History 956.93
Cyprus—History—Cyprus Crisis, 1963 956.9304
Cyprus—History—Cyprus Crisis, 1974- 956.9304
Cyprus—International status 341.29
Cyprus—Politics and government 320.95693; 956.93
Cyprus—Politics and government—1960- 956.9304
Cyrano de Bergerac, 1619–1655 848.409
Cyrillic alphabet 686.21918
Cystic fibrosis 616.37
Cystic fibrosis in children 618.9237
Cystitis 616.623
Cysts (Zoology) 571.876
Cytochemistry 572
Cytodiagnosis 616.07582
Cytodiagnosis—Atlases 616.075820222
Cytodiagnosis—Handbooks, manuals, etc. 616.07582
Cytogenetics 572.8
Cytokines 616.079
Cytokines—Physiological effect 616.079
Cytology 571.6
Cytology—Laboratory manuals 571.6078
Cytology—Periodicals 571.605
Cytology—Technique 571.6072
Cytoplasm 571.65
Cytoskeleton 571.654
Czech Republic 943.71
Czech Republic—Commerce 382.094371
Czech Republic—Commerce—Periodicals 382.09437105
Czech Republic—Economic conditions 330.94371
Czech Republic—Economic conditions—Periodicals 330.94371005
Czech Republic—Guidebooks 914.37104; 914.371045
Czechoslovakia 943.7
Czechoslovakia—Economic conditions 330.943703
Czechoslovakia—Economic conditions—1945–1992 330.943704
Czechoslovakia—Economic conditions—1945–1992—Periodicals 330.943704
Czechoslovakia—Economic policy 338.9437
Czechoslovakia—Economic policy—1945–1992 338.9437
Czechoslovakia—Guidebooks 914.3704; 914.37045
Czechoslovakia—History 943.7
Czechoslovakia—History—1945–1992 943.704
Czechoslovakia—History—Intervention, 1968 943.7042
Czechoslovakia—Politics and government 320.9437; 943.7
Czechoslovakia—Politics and government—1945–1992 320.943709045
Czechoslovakia—Politics and government—1968–1989 320.943709047; 943.7043

Czechoslovakia—Politics and government—1989–1992 320.943709049; 943.7043
Da Free John, 1939– 299.93092
Da Silva, Jane (Fictitious character) 813.54
Da Silva, Jane (Fictitious character)—Fiction 813.54
Dac Easy accounting 657.02855369
Dachau (Concentration camp) 940.5318
Dachshunds 636.7538
Dadaism 709.04062
Daffodils 584.34
Dafydd ap Gwilym, 14th cent. 891.6611
Dafydd ap Gwilym, 14th cent.—Translations into English 891.6611
Daguerreotype 772.12; 779
Dahl, Roald 823.914
Dahlias 583.99
Daimyo in literature 808.80358
Dairy cattle 636.2142
Dairy cattle—Feeding and feeds 636.2142
Dairy farming 636.2142
Dairy farms 636.2142
Dairy processing 637
Dairy products 641.37
Dairy products industry—United States—Statistics—Periodicals 382.4170973021
Dairy scientists 637.092
Dairy substitutes 641.3; 664.6
Dairying 637
Daisy (Fictitious character : Theobalds) 823.914
Dakota County (Minn.) 977.656
Dakota County (Minn.)—Maps 912.77656
Dakota Indians 305.89752; 978.0049752
Dakota Indians—Folklore 398.2089975
Dakota Indians—Religion 299.7852
Dakota Indians—Wars 973.7
Dakota Indians—Wars, 1862–1865 973.7
Dakota Indians—Wars, 1876 973.82
Dalceridae 595.78
Dalgliesh, Adam (Fictitious character) 823.914
Dalgliesh, Adam (Fictitious character)—Fiction 823.914
Dalí, Salvador, 1904– 709.2; 759.6
Dalí, Salvador, 1904– —Criticism and interpretation 709.2; 759.6
Dalits 305.568
Dalits—India 305.568
Dallas County (Iowa) 977.757
Dallas County (Iowa)—Maps 912.77757
Dallas Cowboys (Football team) 796.33264097642812
Dallas Cowboys (Football team)—History 796.33264097642812
Dallas Metropolitan Area (Tex.)—Maps 912.7642812
Dallas (Tex.) 976.42812
Dallas (Tex.)—Guidebooks 917.64281204; 917.6428120463; 917.6428120464
Dallas (Tex.)—History 976.42812
Dalmatian dog 636.72
Dalrymple, Daisy (Fictitious character) 823.914
Dalrymple, Daisy (Fictitious character)—Fiction 823.914
Dalton family 364.155
Dalziel, Andrew (Fictitious character) 823.914
Dalziel, Andrew (Fictitious character)—Fiction 823.914
Dam retirement 627.8
Dam safety 363.3493; 627.80289
Damages 347.077
Damages—Australia 347.94077
Damages—Taxation 343.0523
Damages—Taxation—United States 343.730523
Damages—United States 347.7377
Dame schools 372.1042209033

Damien, Father, 1840–1889 266.2092
Damon, Matt 791.43028092
Damping (Mechanics) 620.37
Dampness in buildings 693.893
Dams 627.8
Dams—India 627.80954
Damselflies 595.733
Dance 792.8; 793.3
Dance—Asia 792.8095; 793.3195
Dance—Bibliography 016.7928; 016.7933
Dance—Bibliography—Catalogs 016.7933
Dance companies 792.806
Dance—Dictionaries 793.303
Dance—England 793.31942
Dance—Film catalogs 016.7928
Dance for children 792.8083
Dance for children—Study and teaching (Elementary) 372.868
Dance—Greece 793.319495
Dance—History 792.809; 793.309; 793.319
Dance in art 709.497928; 709.497933
Dance—India 792.80954; 793.31954
Dance—Japan 793.31952
Dance—Latin America 793.33
Dance—Law and legislation 344.099
Dance music 781.554
Dance—New York (State)—New York 792.8097471
Dance notation 792.82
Dance of death 700.4548
Dance orchestra music 784.48
Dance—Philosophy 792.801; 793.301
Dance photography 779.97928
Dance—Pictorial works 792.802922; 793.30222
Dance—Production and direction 792.8023
Dance schools 792.807I
Dance—Social aspects 306.484
Dance—Sociological aspects 306.484
Dance—Spain 792.80946; 793.31946
Dance—Study and teaching 792.807I; 793.3071
Dance therapy 615.85155; 616.891655
Dance—United States 792.80973; 793.30973
Dance—United States—History 792.80973; 793.30973; 793.31973
Dance—Vocational guidance 792.8093
Dancers 792.8028092; 793.3092
Dancers—Biography 792.8028092; 792.8092; 793.3092
Dancing injuries 617.1
Dandelions 583.99
Dane County (Wis.) 977.583
Dane County (Wis.)—Maps 912.77583
Dangerous animals 591.65
Dangerously mentally ill 364.38; 616.8582
Daniel (Biblical character) 224.5092
Daniel Kearny Associates (Imaginary organization) 813.54
Daniel Kearny Associates (Imaginary organization)—Fiction 813.54
Daniels, Charmian (Fictitious character) 823.914
Daniels, Charmian (Fictitious character)—Fiction 823.914
Danish language 439.81
Danish wit and humor, Pictorial 741.59489
Dante Alighieri, 1265–1321 851.1
Dante Alighieri, 1265–1321—Criticism and interpretation 851.1
Dante Alighieri, 1265–1321. Divine comedy 851.1
Dante Alighieri, 1265–1321. Inferno 851.1
Dante Alighieri, 1265–1321—Translations into English 851.1

Danwei 306.360951
Dark matter (Astronomy) 523.1126
Dark shadows (Television program : 1966–1971)
  791.4572
Darling, Annie Laurance (Fictitious character) 813.54
Darling, Annie Laurance (Fictitious character)—Fiction
  813.54
Darling, Wendy (Fictitious character : Barrie) 791.4372;
  822.912
Darts (Game) 794.3
Darwin, Charles, 1809–1882 576.82092
Darwin, Charles, 1809–1882. On the origin of species
  576.82
Darwīsh, Maḥmūd 892.716
Darwīsh, Maḥmūd—Translations into English 892.716
Data compression (Computer science) 005.746
Data compression (Telecommunication) 005.746
Data dictionaries 005.742
Data disk drives industry 380.145004563
Data encryption (Computer science) 005.82
Data flow computing 004.35
Data libraries 025.04
Data marts 658.40380285574
Data mining 006.3
Data processing service centers 004.068
Data protection 005.8
Data protection—Law and legislation 342.0858
Data protection—Law and legislation—Europe
  342.40058
Data protection—Law and legislation—Great Britain
  342.410858
Data recovery (Computer science) 005.86
Data structures (Computer science) 005.73
Data tape drives 621.3976
Data tapes 004.56
Data transmission equipment industry 338.476213981
Data transmission systems 004.6; 621.3981
Data transmission systems—Handbooks, manuals, etc.
  004.6
Data transmission systems—Standards 004.62
Data warehousing 658.40380285574
Database design 005.74
Database industry 338.4700574
Database management 005.74; 005.74068; 650.0285574
Database management—Bibliography 016.00574
Database management—Computer programs 005.75
Database management—Periodicals 005.7405
Database marketing 005.740688; 658.84
Database searching 025.524
Database security 005.8
Databases 005.74; 025.04
Databases—Australia 025.040994
Databases—Australia—Directories 025.0402594
Databases—Directories 025.04025
Dating (Social customs) 306.73; 646.77
Dating (Social customs)—Computer network resources
  306.730285
Dating (Social customs)—United States 646.770973
Dating violence—United States 362.88
Datsun automobile 629.2222
Daughters 306.874
Dauphin County (Pa.)—Genealogy 929.374818
Davenport, Lucas (Fictitious character) 813.54
Davenport, Lucas (Fictitious character)—Fiction 813.54
David, King of Israel 222.4092
Davidson County (Tenn.)—Genealogy 929.376855
Davidson, Donald, 1917– 191
Davis, Bette, 1908– 791.43028092
Davis County (Iowa) 977.797

Davis County (Iowa)—Maps 912.77797
Davis Cup 796.342
Davis family 929.20973
Davis, Jefferson, 1808–1889 973.713092
Davis, Miles 788.92165092
Davis, Terrell, 1972– 796.332092
Da'wah (Islam) 297.74
Day 529.1
Day camps 796.5423
Day care centers 362.712
Day care centers—Finance—Law and legislation
  343.078362712
Day care centers for the aged 362.63
Day care centers—United States 362.7120973
Day care centers—United States—Administration
  362.712068
Day care centers—United States—Handbooks, manuals,
  etc. 362.7120973
Day, Dorothy, 1897–1980 267.182092
Day family 929.20973
Day fines 364.68
Day, Jane (Fictitious character) 813.54
Day laborers 331.544
Day reporting centers (Corrections) 365.34
Day trading (Securities) 332.6420285
Daylight saving 389.17
Daylilies 635.93432
dBASE III 005.7565
dBASE III plus (Computer file) 005.7565
dBASE IV (Computer file) 005.7565
dBASE for Windows 005.7565
De Kalb County (Ill.) 977.328
De Kalb County (Ill.)—Genealogy 929.377328
De Kalb County (Ill.)—Maps 912.77328
De Kooning, Willem, 1904– 759.13
De Kooning, Willem, 1904– —Exhibitions 759.13
De la Hoya, Oscar, 1973– 796.83092
De la Mare, Walter, 1873–1956 821.912
De la Mare, Walter, 1873–1956—Criticism and
  interpretation 821.912
De Man, Paul 801.95092
De Man, Paul—Contributions in criticism 801.95092
De Mille, Agnes 792.82092
De Quincey, Thomas, 1785–1859 828.809
De Quincey, Thomas, 1785–1859—Criticism and
  interpretation 828.809
De Quincey, Thomas, 1785–1859—Knowledge—
  Literature 820.9
De Soto, Hernando, ca. 1500–1542 970.016092
De Valera, Eamonn, 1882–1975 941.70822092
De Witt County (Ill.) 977.3585
De Witt County (Ill.)—Maps 912.773585
De Wolfe, John, Sir (Fictitious character) 823.914
Deacons 270.092
Dead animals 591.6
Dead Sea scrolls 221.44; 296.155
Dead Sea scrolls—Criticism, interpretation, etc. 296.155
Dead Sea scrolls—Relation to the New Testament
  296.155
Deadheads (Music fans) 782.421660922
Deadly sins 241.3
Deaf 362.42
Deaf children 155.4512; 362.42083
Deaf children—Education 371.912
Deaf children—Education—United States 371.9120973
Deaf children—Family relationships 362.423083
Deaf dogs 636.708978
Deaf—Education 371.912

Deaf—Education—Law and legislation 344.079112
Deaf—Education—Law and legislation—United States 344.73079112
Deaf—Education—United States 371.9120973
Deaf—Legal status, laws, etc. 346.013
Deaf—Legal status, laws, etc.—United States 346.73013
Deaf—Means of communication 419
Deaf—Nazi persecution 940.53180872
Deaf—Rehabilitation 362.428
Deaf—United States 362.420973
Deaf—United States—Social conditions 305.9081620973
Deafness 617.8
Deafness in children 618.920978
Deafness in children—Education 371.912
Deafness—Psychological aspects 362.42019
Dealers (Retail trade) 658.870092
Dean, Forest of (England) 942.413
Dean, Forest of (England)—Social life and customs 942.413
Dean, James, 1931–1955 791.43028092
Deane, Sarah (Fictitious character) 813.54
Deane, Sarah (Fictitious character)—Fiction 813.54
Deans (Education) 378.111
Deans (Education)—Illinois 378.111
Deans (Education)—United States 378.111
Death 128.5; 306.9; 616.078
Death (Biology) 571.939
Death—Causes 614.1
Death—Causes—Statistics 614.42
Death—Causes—Statistics—Periodicals 614.42
Death Gate Universe (Imaginary place) 813.54
Death Gate Universe (Imaginary place)—Fiction 813.54
Death in art 700.4548; 704.9493069
Death in dreams 154.632; 155.937
Death in literature 808.803548; 809.933548
Death—Literary collections 808.803548
Death—Moral and ethical aspects 179.7
Death—Psychological aspects 155.937
Death—Religious aspects 291.23
Death—Religious aspects—Christianity 236.1
Death—Religious aspects—Hinduism 294.523
Death—Religious aspects—Judaism 296.33
Death row inmates—United States 364.66092273
Death—Social aspects 306.9
Death—Social aspects—United States 306.90973
Death—Symbolic aspects 306.9; 700.4548
Death Valley (Calif. and Nev.) 979.487
Death Valley National Park (Calif. and Nev.) 979.487
Death Valley National Park (Calif. and Nev.)—Guidebooks 917.948704; 917.94870453; 917.94870454
Debate poetry, English (Middle) 821.1
Debates and debating 808.53
Debit cards 332.76
Debt 332
Debt equity conversion 336.363
Debt equity conversion—Developing countries 336.363091724
Debt relief 336.36
Debt relief—Developing countries 336.36
Debt relief (Islamic law) 346.1671077
Debtor and creditor 346.077
Debtor and creditor—United States 346.73077
Debtor and creditor—United States—Cases 346.730770264
Debts, External 336.3435
Debts, External—Africa 336.3435096
Debts, External—Africa, Sub-Saharan 336.34350967
Debts, External—Developing countries 336.3435091724

Debts, External—Developing countries—Statistics 336.3435091724021
Debts, External—Latin America 336.3435098
Debts, External—Law and legislation 341.751
Debts, External—Law and legislation—Developing countries 341.75115
Debts, External—Philippines 336.3409599
Debts, Public 336.34
Debts, Public—Law and legislation 343.037
Debts, Public—Law and legislation—United States 343.73037
Debts, Public—United States 336.340973
Debugging in computer science 005.14
Debussy, Claude, 1862–1918 780.92
DEC computers 004.145
Decapoda (Crustacea) 595.38
Decathletes 796.42092
Decca Records (Firm)—Catalogs 016.780266
Deccan traps 552.26
Decedents' estates 346.052
Decedents' estates—New York (State) 346.747052
Decedents' estates—Taxation 343.053
Decedents' estates—Taxation—Massachusetts 343.744053
Decedents' estates—Taxation—United States 343.73053
Decedents' estates—United States 346.73052
Decedents' estates—United States—Cases 346.730520264
Decembrists 947.073
Decentralization in government 352.283
Decentralization in government—Great Britain 352.2830941
Deception 001.95
Deceptive advertising 364.163
Deceptive advertising—United States 364.163
Decimal system 332.4048; 389.15
Decision making 003.56; 153.83; 658.403
Decision making—Addresses, essays, lectures 658.403
Decision making—Computer simulation 658.40352
Decision making—Data processing 658.4030285
Decision making—Mathematical models 658.4033
Decision making—Moral and ethical aspects 170
Decision making—Religious aspects 291.44
Decision making—Religious aspects—Christianity 248.4
Decision support systems 658.403
Decker, Peter (Fictitious character) 813.54
Decker, Peter (Fictitious character)—Fiction 813.54
Decks (Architecture, Domestic) 690.184
Decks (Architecture, Domestic)—Design and construction 690.184; 690.893; 721.84
Decomposition method 519.4
Deconstruction 801.95
Decoration and ornament 745.4
Decoration and ornament—Animal forms 745.4
Decoration and ornament, Architectural 729
Decoration and ornament, Architectural—New York (State)—New York 729.097471
Decoration and ornament—Art deco 745.4442
Decoration and ornament—Art nouveau 745.4441
Decoration and ornament, Celtic 745.449364; 745.44944
Decoration and ornament—China 745.44951
Decoration and ornament—Japan 745.44952
Decoration and ornament—Plant forms 745.4
Decoration and ornament, Rustic 747
Decoration and ornament, Rustic—United States 747.213
Decoration and ornament—Themes, motives 745.4
Decoration and ornament—Victorian style 745.4441
Decorations of honor 929.81

Democracy—Developing countries 321.8091724
Democracy—Germany 320.443
Democracy—Greece 320.4495
Democracy—Greece—Athens 320.4385
Democracy—Greece—Athens—History 320.4385
Democracy—History 321.809
Democracy—History—20th century 321.80904
Democracy—Latin America 321.8098
Democracy—Nigeria 320.4669
Democracy—South Africa 320.468
Democracy—United States 320.473
Democratic centralism 335.43
Democratic Party (U.S.) 324.2736
Democratic Party (U.S.)—History 324.273609
Democratization 321.8
Demographic anthropology 304.6
Demographic surveys 304.6
Demographic transition 304.62
Demography 304.6
Demography—Methodology 304.6072
Demoniac possession 133.426
Demonology 133.42; 235.4
Demonology in motion pictures 791.43675
Demonstration forests 333.7507
Demonstrations 303.484; 322.44
Demospongiae 593.46
Dendrimers 620.192; 668.9
Dendritic cells 616.079
Dendrochronology 582.16; 930.10285
Deng, Xiaoping, 1904– 951.058092
Denmark 948.9
Denmark—Guidebooks 914.8904; 914.890459; 914.89046
Denmark—History 948.9
Denmark—History—To 1241 948.901
Dennison family 929.20973
Denny, Louisa Boren 792.092
Density functionals 541.28
Denson, John (Fictitious character) 813.54
Denson, John (Fictitious character)—Fiction 813.54
Dental anthropology 599.943
Dental assistants 617.60233
Dental care 617.6
Dental caries 617.67
Dental ceramics 617.695
Dental emergencies 617.6026
Dental hygiene 617.601
Dental implants 617.692
Dental libraries 026.6176
Dental materials 617.695
Dental offices—Management 617.60068
Dental pharmacology 615.10246176
Dental public health 362.1976
Dental schools 617.600711
Dental technology 617.69
Dental therapeutics—Planning 617.606
Dentistry 617.6
Dentistry—Data processing 617.600285
Dentistry—Dictionaries 617.6003
Dentistry—Handbooks, manuals, etc. 617.6
Dentistry—History 617.6009
Dentistry—Practice 617.60068
Dentistry—Psychological aspects 617.60019
Dentists 617.60092
Dentures 617.692
Denver and Rio Grande Western Railroad Company—
    History 385.09788
Denver Broncos (Football team) 796.332640978883
Denver Broncos (Football team)—History
    796.332640978883

Denver (Colo.) 978.883
Denver (Colo.)—Guidebooks 917.888304; 917.88830433;
    917.88830434
Denver (Colo.)—History 978.883
Denver Metropolitan Area (Colo.) 978.883
Denver Metropolitan Area (Colo.)—Maps 912.78883
Deontic logic 160
Department store Santas 394.2663; 658.82
Department stores 658.871
Departmental chairmen (Universities) 378.111
Departmental chairmen (Universities)—United States
    378.111
Dependence (Statistics) 519.53
Dependency grammar 415
Deposit banking 332.1752
Deposit insurance 368.854
Deposit insurance—Law and legislation 346.086854
Deposit insurance—Law and legislation—United States
    346.73086854
Deposit insurance—United States 368.85400973
Depositions 347.072
Depositions—United States 347.7372
Depository libraries 025.25
Depository libraries—Reference services 025.52
Depreciation 657.73
Depreciation allowances—Law and legislation
    343.05234
Depreciation allowances—Law and legislation—United
    States 343.7305234
Depression glass—Collectors and collecting—Catalogs
    748.29130904075
Depression in adolescence 616.852700835
Depression in children 618.928527
Depression in old age 618.9768527
Depression, Mental 362.25; 616.8527
Depression, Mental—Alternative treatment 616.852706
Depression, Mental—Chemotherapy 616.8527061
Depression, Mental—Physiological aspects 616.852707
Depression, Mental—Religious aspects 291.1783225;
    291.442
Depression, Mental—Religious aspects—Christianity
    248.8625; 261.83225
Depression, Mental—Treatment 616.852706
Depressions 338.542
Depressions—1929 973.916
Depressions—1929—United States 338.542097309043
Depressions—United States 338.5420973
Derbyshire (England) 942.51
Derbyshire (England)—History 942.51
Deregulation 338.92; 352.8
Deregulation—United States 338.973
Derivative securities 332.632; 332.645
Derivative securities—Law and legislation 346.0922
Derivative securities—Law and legislation—United
    States 346.730922
Derivative securities—Taxation 336.24
Derivative securities—Taxation—Law and legislation
    343.05246
Derivative securities—United States 332.645
Dermaptera 595.739
Dermatoglyphics 599.945
Dermatologic agents 616.5061
Dermatologic agents—Handbooks, manuals, etc.
    615.778
Dermatology 616.5
Dermatology—Atlases 616.500222
Dermatology—Handbooks, manuals, etc. 616.5
Dermatopharmacology 615.778
Dermatotoxicology 616.507!

Derocheilocarididae 595.36
Derrida, Jacques 194
Des Moines County (Iowa) 977.796
Des Moines County (Iowa)—Genealogy 929.377796
Desai, Anita, 1937– 823.914
Desai, Anita, 1937– —Criticism and interpretation
  823.914
DeSales, Frank (Fictitious character) 813.54
DeSales, Frank (Fictitious character)—Fiction 813.54
Descartes, René, 1596–1650 194
Descartes, René, 1596–1650. Meditationes de prima
  philosophia 194
Descriptive cataloging 025.32
Descriptive cataloging—Great Britain 025.320941
Descriptive cataloging—Great Britain—Rules
  025.320941
Descriptive cataloging—Rules 025.32
Deseret alphabet 421.1
Desert animals 591.754
Desert biology 578.754
Desert biology—Southwestern States 578.754
Desert ecology 577.54
Desert landscape architecture 712.09154
Desert people 306.0809154
Desert plants 581.754
Desert survival 613.69
Desertification 333.736
Desertification—Control—Law and legislation
  346.04673616
Desertion and non-support 346.0172
Deserts 508.3154; 551.415; 910.02154
Design 745.4
Design—History 745.44
Design—History—20th century 745.4442
Design, Industrial 745.2
Design, Industrial—Data processing 620.00420285;
  745.20285
Design, Industrial—Environmental aspects 745.2
Design, Industrial—Management 658.5752
Design protection 341.7584; 346.0484
Design protection—United States 346.730484
Design services 745.2
Design—Study and teaching (Elementary) 372.52
Designers 745.4492
Desire for God 248.4
Desk pads 651.2
Desktop publishing 686.22544416; 686.22544536
Desktop publishing industry 338.4768622544
Desktop publishing—Periodicals 686.22544416
Desmidiaceae 579.837
DeSoto automobile 629.2222
Despotism 321.9
Desserts 641.86
Desserts—Italy 641.860945
Destination weddings 392.5
Detective and mystery films 791.43655
Detective and mystery films—History and criticism
  791.43655
Detective and mystery radio programs 791.44655
Detective and mystery stories 808.83872
Detective and mystery stories, American 813.0872;
  813.087208
Detective and mystery stories, American—History and
  criticism 813.087209
Detective and mystery stories, American—Stories,
  plots, etc. 813.087209
Detective and mystery stories—Authorship 808.3872
Detective and mystery stories—Bibliography
  016.80883872

Detective and mystery stories, Canadian 813.087208971
Detective and mystery stories, English 823.0872;
  823.087208
Detective and mystery stories, English—Bibliography
  016.823087208
Detective and mystery stories, English—Dictionaries
  823.087209
Detective and mystery stories, English—History and
  criticism 823.087209
Detective and mystery stories, English—Stories, plots,
  etc. 823.087209
Detective and mystery stories, French 843.0872
Detective and mystery stories, French—Translations
  into English 843.087208
Detective and mystery stories—History and criticism
  809.3872
Detective and mystery television programs 791.45655
Detectives 363.2
Detectives—England 363.2
Detectors 621.381536; 681.2
Detergent industry 338.4766814
Detergents 668.14
Determinantal varieties 516.353
Deterrence (Strategy) 355.0217
Detoxification (Health) 613
Detoxification (Substance abuse treatment) 362.2918;
  616.8606
Detroit Metropolitan Area (Mich.) 977.434
Detroit Metropolitan Area (Mich.)—Maps 912.77434
Detroit (Mich.) 977.434
Detroit (Mich.)—Pictorial works 977.43400222
Detroit Pistons (Basketball team) 796.323640977434
Detroit Pistons (Basketball team)—History
  796.323640977434
Detroit Red Wings (Hockey team) 796.962640977434
Detroit Red Wings (Hockey team)—History
  796.962640977434
Detroit Tigers (Baseball team) 796.357640977434
Detroit Tigers (Baseball team)—History
  796.357640977434
Deutsche Nationalbibliographie classification system
  025.43
Developing countries 330.91724; 909.09724
Developing countries—Commercial policy 381.3091724;
  382.3091724
Developing countries—Dependency on foreign countries
  337.091724
Developing countries—Economic conditions 330.91724
Developing countries—Economic conditions—
  Periodicals 330.91724005
Developing countries—Economic integration 337.11724
Developing countries—Economic policy 338.90091724
Developing countries—Foreign economic relations
  337.091724
Developing countries—Foreign relations 327.091724
Developing countries—Foreign relations—Soviet Union
  327.4701724
Developing countries—Foreign relations—United States
  327.7301724
Developing countries—Periodicals 909.09724005
Developing countries—Politics and government
  320.91724
Developing countries—Population 304.6091724
Developing countries—Population—Economic aspects
  304.6091724
Developing countries—Social conditions 909.09724
Development banks 332.153
Development economics 338.9
Developmental biology 571.8

Dickens, Charles, 1812–1870. Great expectations—Examinations 823.8
Dickens, Charles, 1812–1870. Hard times 823.8
Dickens, Charles, 1812–1870. Hard times—Examinations 823.8
Dickens, Charles, 1812–1870—Homes and haunts—England—London 823.8
Dickens, Charles, 1812–1870—Knowledge—London (England) 823.8
Dickens, Charles, 1812–1870—Knowledge—Performing arts 823.8
Dickens, Charles, 1812–1870—Literary style 823.8
Dickens, Charles, 1812–1870—Political and social views 823.8
Dickens, Charles, 1812–1870. Tale of two cities 823.8
Dickens, Charles, 1812–1870. Tale of two cities—Examinations 823.8
Dickens, Charles, 1812–1870—Technique 823.8
Dickey County (N.D.) 978.454
Dickey County (N.D.)—Maps 912.78454
Dickey family 929.20973
Dickinson County (Iowa) 977.7123
Dickinson County (Iowa)—Maps 912.777123
Dickinson County (Mich.) 977.4955
Dickinson County (Mich.)—Maps 912.774955
Dickinson, Emily, 1830–1886 811.4
Dickinson, Emily, 1830–1886—Bibliography 016.8114
Dickinson, Emily, 1830–1886—Correspondence 811.4
Dickinson, Emily, 1830–1886—Criticism and interpretation 811.4
Dickinson, Emily, 1830–1886—Literary style 811.4
Dickinson family 929.20973
Dicotyledons 583
Dicotyledons—Illinois—Identification 583.09773
Dictating machines industry 338.47621389324
Dictation (Office practice) 651.74
Dictators 321.9
Dictators—Africa 321.9096
Dictatorship 321.9
Dictionaries, Polyglot 413
Didactic fiction, Canadian 813.54
Didactic poetry, Latin 871; 871.01
Didactic poetry, Latin—Translations into English 871.008; 871.0108
Diderot, Denis, 1713–1784 194; 848.509
Diderot, Denis, 1713–1784—Criticism and interpretation 848.509
Diderot, Denis, 1713–1784—Translations into English 848.509
Didion, Joan 813.54
Didion, Joan—Criticism and interpretation 813.54
Die-casting 671.253
Dielectrics 537.24
Điện Biên Phủ (Vietnam), Battle of, 1954 959.704142
Dies (Metal-working) 621.984; 671.253
Diesel locomotives 625.266
Diesel locomotives—Great Britain 625.2660941
Diesel locomotives—United States 625.2660973
Diesel motor 621.436
Diesel motor—Alternate fuels 621.436; 629.2538
Diesel motor—Combustion 621.4361
Diesel motor industry 338.47621436
Diesel motor industry—North America 338.47621436097
Diesel motor industry—North America—Periodicals 338.4762143609705
Diesel motor—Maintenance and repair 621.4368
Diesel motor—Maintenance and repair—Handbooks, manuals, etc. 621.4368
Diet 613.2

Diet in disease 615.854
Diet therapy 615.854
Diet therapy—Handbooks, manuals, etc. 615.854
Dietary supplements 613.2; 615.1
Dietary supplements industry 338.476132
Dietetics 613.2
Dietetics—Practice 613.2068
Dietetics—Vocational guidance 613.2023
Diethylstilbestrol 615.366
Dietitians 613.2092
Dietrich, Marlene 791.43028092
Difference equations 515.625
Difference operators 515.7246
Difference (Philosophy) 111
Difference (Psychology) in literature 808.80353; 809.93353
Differentiable dynamical systems 514.74
Differentiable manifolds 516.36
Differentiable mappings 515.352
Differential algebra 512.56
Differential calculus 515.33
Differential equations 515.35
Differential equations—Asymptotic theory 515.35
Differential equations, Elliptic 515.353
Differential equations, Elliptic—Numerical solutions 515.353
Differential equations, Hyperbolic 515.353
Differential equations, Hyperbolic—Numerical solutions 515.353
Differential equations, Linear 515.354
Differential equations, Nonlinear 515.355
Differential equations, Nonlinear—Numerical solutions 515.355
Differential equations—Numerical solutions 515.35
Differential equations—Numerical solutions—Data processing 515.350285
Differential equations, Parabolic 515.353
Differential equations, Parabolic—Numerical solutions 515.353
Differential equations, Partial 515.353
Differential equations, Partial—Numerical solutions 515.353
Differential equations, Partial—Numerical solutions—Data processing 515.3530285
Differential equations—Periodicals 515.3505
Differential equations—Problems, exercises, etc. 515.35076
Differential forms 515.37
Differential games 519.3
Differential operators 515.7242
Differential topology 514.72
Differentiated teaching staffs 371.14123
Diffraction 535.42
Diffusion processes 519.233
Digenea 592.48
Digestion 612.3
Digestive organs 573.3; 612.3
Digestive organs—Cancer 616.9943
Digestive organs—Diseases 616.3
Digital art 700.285
Digital audio broadcasting 621.384
Digital avionics 629.135
Digital communications 621.382
Digital computer simulation 003.35133
Digital control systems 629.8; 629.8312
Digital divide 303.4833; 384.3
Digital electronics 621.395
Digital filters (Mathematics) 621.3815324
Digital integrated circuits 621.3815; 621.395

Digital integrated circuits—Computer-aided design 621.395

Digital integrated circuits—Design and construction 621.3815

Digital integrated circuits—Design and construction— Data processing 621.3815

Digital integrated circuits—Testing 621.38150287

Digital libraries 025.00285

Digital libraries—Access control 005.8; 025.04

Digital mapping 526

Digital media 302.234; 384

Digital multimeters 621.37

Digital preservation 651.59

Digital printing presses 686.23

Digital signatures 005.82; 346.022

Digital telephone systems 621.385

Digital television 621.388

Digital video 621.38833

Digital video tape recorders 621.38833

Digitalis (Drug) 615.711

DiGriz, James Bolivar (Fictitious character) 813.54

DiGriz, James Bolivar (Fictitious character)—Fiction 813.54

Dilatation and extraction abortion 618.88

Dilatation and extraction abortion—Law and legislation 344.04192

Dillard family 929.20973

Dillinger, John, 1903–1934 364.1523092

Diluted magnetic semiconductors 537.6223

Dime novels 808.83

Dimensional analysis 530.8

Dimitrov, Georgi, 1882–1949 949.9031092

Dimity, Aunt (Fictitious character) 813.54

Dimity, Aunt (Fictitious character)—Fiction 813.54

Dinah (Fictitious character : Carroll) 823.914

Dinamoebales 579.87

Dinesen, Isak, 1885–1962 839.81372

Dingo 599.772

Dinner theater 792.022

Dinners and dining 641.54; 642.4

Dinners and dining in literature 808.80355; 809.93355

Dinoflagellate cysts 561.93; 571.8472987

Dinoflagellates 579.87

Dinoflagellates, Fossil 561.93

Dinosaur tracks 567.9

Dinosaurs 567.9

Dinosaurs—Encyclopedias 567.903

Dinosaurs in art 704.9432; 743.6

Dinosaurs—Infancy 567.9

Dinosaurs—Miscellanea 567.9

Dinosaurs—Pictorial works 567.90222

Dioceses 262.3

Diodes, Semiconductor 621.381522

Dionysus (Greek deity) 292.2113

Diophantine analysis 512.74

Diophantine approximation 512.73

Diophantine equations 512.72

Dioxins 615.9512

Dioxins—Toxicology 615.9512

Diplodocus 567.913

Diplomacy 327.2

Diplomacy—History 327.209

Diplomatic and consular service 341.33

Diplomatic and consular service—Australia 353.132630994

Diplomatic and consular service—California 327.2025794

Diplomatic and consular service, Sri Lankan 341.33095493

Diplomatic and consular service, Venezuelan 341.330987

Diplomatic privileges and immunities 341.33

Dips (Appetizers) 641.812

Diptera 595.77

Dipterocarpaceae 583.624

Direct broadcast satellite television 384.552; 621.38853

Direct delivery of books 002.0688

Direct energy conversion 621.042; 621.3124

Direct-mail fund raising—United States 658.15224

Direct marketing 381.1; 658.84

Direct marketing—Data processing 658.84

Direct marketing—Handbooks, manuals, etc. 658.84

Direct marketing—Periodicals 658.84

Direct selling 658.84

Director (Computer file) 006.7869

Directories 011.7

Directories—Bibliography 011.7

Directories—Bibliography—Periodicals 011.7

Directors of corporations 658.422

Directors of corporations—Great Britain 658.4220941

Directors of corporations—Legal status, laws, etc. 346.06642

Directors of corporations—Legal status, laws, etc.— United States 346.7306642

Directory services (Computer network technology) 005.71376

Dirichlet forms 519.233

Disability studies 305.90816; 362.4

Disabled passenger lifts 362.40483; 621.877

Disappeared persons' spouses 362.87

Disappointment 152.47

Disappointment in children 155.4124

Disarmament 327.174

Disarmament—Economic aspects 327.174

Disarmament—Economic aspects—United States 338.473550973

Disarmament—Periodicals 327.17405

Disaster relief 363.348

Disaster relief—United States 363.3480973

Disasters 363.34

Disasters—Press coverage—United States 303.4850973

Disasters—Psychological aspects 155.935

Disc jockeys 791.443

Discernment of spirits 235

Disciples of Christ 286.6

Discipline of children 649.64

Discipline of children—United States 649.64

Disclosure of information—Law and legislation 346.0666

Disclosure of information—Law and legislation—United States 346.730666

Discomycetes 579.57

Discount houses (Retail trade) 381.149

Discount houses (Retail trade)—United States— Directories 381.14902573

Discourse analysis 401.41

Discourse analysis—Data processing 401.410285

Discourse analysis, Literary 808.0014

Discourse analysis, Narrative 401.41

Discourse analysis—Psychological aspects 401.41019

Discourse analysis—Social aspects 306.44

Discourse markers 401.41

Discoveries in geography 910.9

Discoveries in geography—History 910.9

Discoveries in geography—Portuguese 910.9469

Discoveries in science 500; 509

Discovery (Law) 347.072

Discovery (Law)—California 347.794072

Discovery (Law)—Florida 347.759072
Discovery (Law)—United States 347.7372
Discrete groups 512.2
Discrete-time systems 003.83
Discriminant analysis 519.535
Discrimination 305
Discrimination against the handicapped 305.90816;
   344.07911; 346.013
Discrimination against the handicapped—Law and
   legislation 344.0324; 346.013
Discrimination against the handicapped—Law and
   legislation—United States 344.730324; 346.73013
Discrimination against the homeless 305.569
Discrimination against the mentally ill 305.90824
Discrimination against the mentally ill—Law and
   legislation 346.013
Discrimination in capital punishment—United States
   364.660973
Discrimination in commercial loans 332.742
Discrimination in criminal justice administration—
   United States 364.08
Discrimination in education 379.26
Discrimination in education—Law and legislation
   344.0798
Discrimination in education—Law and legislation—
   United States 344.730798
Discrimination in employment 331.133
Discrimination in employment—Law and legislation
   344.01133
Discrimination in employment—Law and legislation—
   Great Britain 344.4101133
Discrimination in employment—Law and legislation—
   Massachusetts 344.74401133
Discrimination in employment—Law and legislation—
   Oregon 344.79501133
Discrimination in employment—Law and legislation—
   United States 344.7301133
Discrimination in employment—Law and legislation—
   United States—Cases 344.73011330264
Discrimination in employment—Law and legislation—
   United States—History 344.730113309
Discrimination in employment—United States
   331.1330973
Discrimination in financial services 332.1
Discrimination in housing 363.51
Discrimination in housing—Law and legislation
   344.0636351
Discrimination in housing—Law and legislation—United
   States 344.730636351
Discrimination in housing—United States 363.51
Discrimination in juvenile justice administration 364.36
Discrimination in public accommodations 344.063635
Discrimination in restaurants 647.95
Discrimination in sports—South Africa 306.4830968
Discrimination in sports—United States 306.4830973
Discrimination—Law and legislation 341.481; 342.085
Discrimination—Law and legislation—Canada 342.71085
Discrimination—Law and legislation—Ontario
   342.713085
Discrimination—Law and legislation—United States
   342.73085
Discus (Fish) 639.3774
Discussion 808.53
Discussion—Study and teaching 371.37
Discworld (Imaginary place) 823.914
Discworld (Imaginary place)—Fiction 823.914
Disease management 362.1
Diseases 362.1
Diseases—Handbooks, manuals, etc. 616

Diseases—Relapse 616.07
Diseases—Religious aspects—Christianity 261.8321
Diseases—Religious aspects—Christianity—Meditations
   242.4
Dishwashing 648.5
Dishwashing—Equipment and supplies 648.5; 683.88
Disinfection and disinfectants 614.48
Disk access (Computer science) 004.56
Dislocations in crystals 548.842
Disney characters 741.50979493
Disney, Walt, 1901–1966 741.58092; 791.43092
Dispatch cases 685.51
Dispensationalism 231.76
Dispensatories 615.13
Display of merchandise 659.157
Display type 686.224
Displays in education 371.335
DisplayWrite 3 (Computer file) 652.55369
DisplayWrite 4 (Computer file) 652.55369
Disposable cameras 681.418; 771.32
Disposable medical devices 610.284; 681.761
Dispositors 133.53
Dispute resolution (Law) 347.09
Dispute resolution (Law)—Australia 347.9409
Dispute resolution (Law)—Great Britain 347.4109
Dispute resolution (Law)—Texas 347.76409
Dispute resolution (Law)—United States 347.739
Dispute resolution (Law)—United States—Bibliography
   016.347739
Dispute resolution (Law)—United States—Cases
   347.7390264
Dispute resolution (Law)—United States—Periodicals
   347.73905
Disqualification of public prosecutors 345.01
Disraeli, Benjamin, Earl of Beaconsfield, 1804–1881
   823.8; 941.081092
Disraeli, Benjamin, Earl of Beaconsfield, 1804–1881—
   Criticism and interpretation 823.8
Dissection 571.31072
Dissenters, Religious 280.4
Dissenters, Religious—England 274.2
Dissertations, Academic 378.242; 808.02
Dissertations, Academic—Authorship 808.02
Dissertations, Academic—Authorship—Handbooks,
   manuals, etc. 808.02
Dissertations, Academic—Bibliography 011.75
Dissertations, Academic—Handbooks, manuals, etc.
   808.02
Dissertations, Academic—United States 378.2420973
Dissociative disorders 616.8523
Dissociative disorders in children 618.928523
Distance education 371.35; 374.4; 378.03
Distance education—India 371.350954
Distance education—United States 371.350973
Distances—Measurement 530.8
Distillation 660.28425
Distilleries 338.476635
Distilling industries 338.476635
Distributed artificial intelligence 006.3
Distributed databases 005.758
Distributed operating systems (Computers) 005.4476
Distributed resources (Electric utilities) 333.7932
Distribution (Economic theory) 330.1
Distribution (Probability theory) 519.24
Distributive justice 172.2; 340.115
Distributors (Commerce) 658.81
District courts 347.02
District courts—United States 347.7322
Ditidaht Indians 305.8979; 971.1004979

Diuretics 615.761
Dive computers 627.72028541
Diversification in industry 658.16
Diversity in the workplace 658.3008
Divided government 324
Dividend reinvestment 332.63221
Dividers (Mathematical instruments) 516.200284; 681.2
Divination 133.3
Divination cards 133.3242
Divination—China 133.330951
Divine commands (Ethics) 171.1; 291.5
Diving 627.72
Divorce 306.89
Divorce—Economic aspects 306.89
Divorce—England—History 306.890942
Divorce—Humor 306.890207
Divorce—Law and legislation 346.0166
Divorce—Law and legislation—California 346.7940166
Divorce—Law and legislation—Florida 346.7590166
Divorce—Law and legislation—Georgia 346.7580166
Divorce—Law and legislation—Great Britain 346.410166
Divorce—Law and legislation—India 346.540166
Divorce—Law and legislation—Massachusetts
 346.7440166
Divorce—Law and legislation—Michigan 346.7740166
Divorce—Law and legislation—New Jersey 346.7490166
Divorce—Law and legislation—New York (State)
 346.7470166
Divorce—Law and legislation—Pennsylvania
 346.7480166
Divorce—Law and legislation—Texas 346.7640166
Divorce—Law and legislation—United States
 346.730166
Divorce mediation 306.89
Divorce mediation—United States 306.89
Divorce—Psychological aspects 306.89
Divorce—Religious aspects 291.1783589
Divorce—Religious aspects—Christianity 241.63
Divorce settlements 346.0166
Divorce settlements—United States 346.730166
Divorce suits 346.01660269
Divorce suits—Florida 346.75901660269
Divorce suits—Massachusetts 346.74401660269
Divorce suits—United States 346.7301660269
Divorce—United States 306.890973
Divorce—United States—Handbooks, manuals, etc.
 306.890973
Divorce—United States—Psychological aspects
 306.890973
Divorced fathers 306.8742
Divorced fathers—United States 306.8742
Divorced people 305.90653
Divorced people—Religious life 248.846
Divorced women 305.489653
Divorced women—United States—Psychology
 305.4890653
Dix, Dorothea Lynde, 1802–1887 361.92
Dixon County (Neb.) 978.2223
Dixon County (Neb.)—Maps 912.782223
Dixon family 929.20973
Dizziness 616.841
DNA 572.86
DNA fingerprinting 614.1
DNA—Methylation 572.8645
DNA microarrays 572.8636
DNA-protein interactions 572.864
DNA repair 572.86459
DNA replication 572.8645
DNA—Structure 572.8633

DNA topoisomerases 572.786
Do-it-yourself products industry 338.476437
Do-it-yourself work 643.7
Doberman pinscher 636.736
Doctor of arts degree 378.2
Doctor Who (Television program) 791.4572
Doctorow, E. L., 1931– 813.54
Doctorow, E. L., 1931– —Criticism and interpretation
 813.54
Doctrinal preaching 251
Doctrine and Covenants 289.32
Document delivery 025.6
Document imaging systems 006.42; 651.59
Documentary films 070.18
Documentary films—History and criticism 070.18
Documentary films—Production and direction 070.18
Documentary photography 070.49; 778.9907
Documentary photography—United States 779.9973
Documentary-style films 791.436
Documentary television programs 791.453
Dodd family 929.20973
Dodge County (Minn.) 977.6153
Dodge County (Minn.)—Maps 912.776153
Dodge County (Neb.) 978.2235
Dodge County (Neb.)—Maps 912.782235
Dodge County (Wis.) 977.582
Dodge County (Wis.)—Maps 912.77582
Dodge family 929.20973
Dodge, Lark (Fictitious character) 813.54
Dodge, Lark (Fictitious character)—Fiction 813.54
Dodge Omni automobile 629.2222
Dodge Omni automobile—Maintenance and repair
 629.28722
Dodge Omni automobile—Maintenance and repair—
 Handbooks, manuals, etc. 629.28722
Dodge trucks 629.2232
Dodge trucks—History 629.2232
Dodge trucks—Maintenance and repair 629.28732
Dodge trucks—Maintenance and repair—Handbooks,
 manuals, etc. 629.28732
Dodge vans 629.2234
Dodge vans—Maintenance and repair 629.28734
Dodge vans—Maintenance and repair—Handbooks,
 manuals, etc. 629.28734
Dog adoption 636.70887
Dog breeders 636.70092
Dog breeds 636.71
Dog industry 338.1767
Dog licenses 354.56
Dog rescue 636.0832
Dog shows 636.0811
Dog trainers 636.035092
Dōgen, 1200–1253 294.3927092
Doghouses 636.70831; 690.892; 728.92
Dogs 599.772; 636.7
Dogs—Anatomy 636.70891
Dogs—Anecdotes 636.7
Dogs as laboratory animals 636.70885
Dogs—Behavior 636.7
Dogs—Behavior therapy 636.7089689142
Dogs—Breeding 636.7082
Dogs—Caricatures and cartoons 741.5973
Dogs—Diseases 636.70896
Dogs—Diseases—Alternative treatment 636.70895
Dogs—Diseases—Diagnosis 636.70896075
Dogs—England—Yorkshire—Anecdotes 636.7094281
Dogs—Food 636.70855
Dogs—Food—Recipes 636.70855

Dogs—Humor 636.700207
Dogs in art 704.9432977
Dogs in motion pictures 636.70888
Dogs—Law and legislation 346.047
Dogs—Law and legislation—United States 346.73047
Dogs—Literary collections 808.803629772
Dogs—Names 929.97
Dogs—Nutrition 636.70852
Dogs—Obedience trials 636.70886079
Dogs on television 636.70888
Dogs—Physiology 571.1977
Dogs—Showing 636.70811
Dogs—Surgery 636.70897
Dogs—Therapeutic use 636.7088
Dogs—Training 636.70835; 636.70886; 636.70887
Dogs—Wounds and injuries 636.708971
Dogs—Wounds and injuries—Treatment 636.708971
Dogue de Bordeaux 636.73
Dolan, Trixie (Fictitious character) 813.54
Dolan, Trixie (Fictitious character)—Fiction 813.54
Dole, Robert J., 1923- 328.73092
Dolichosauridae 567.95
Doll clothes 688.7221; 745.59221
Doll clothes—Patterns 745.59221
Doll furniture 745.5923
Doll hospitals 688.72210288
Dollar, American 332.40973
Dollhouses 745.5923
Dollmaking 745.59221
Dollmaking—Periodicals 745.5922105
Dolls 688.7221
Dolls—Collectors and collecting 688.7221075
Dolls—Collectors and collecting—Catalogs 688.7221075
Dolly (Sheep) 636.30821
Dolphinfishes 597.72
Dolphins 599.53
Domesday book 333.3220942
Domestic animals 636
Domestic animals—Behavior 636
Domestic animals—History 636.009
Domestic animals—Infancy 636.07
Domestic education 371.39; 649.68
Domestic education—United States 649.680973
Domestic fiction, English 820.80355
Domestic fiction, English—History and criticism 820.9355
Domestic partner benefits 362.82
Domestic partner benefits—Law and legislation 346.015
Domestic relations 346.015
Domestic relations—Alberta 346.7123015
Domestic relations—Australia 346.94015
Domestic relations—British Columbia 346.711015
Domestic relations—California 346.794015
Domestic relations courts 346.0150269
Domestic relations courts—California 346.7940150269
Domestic relations—Florida 346.759015
Domestic relations—Great Britain 346.41015
Domestic relations (Islamic law) 346.17671014
Domestic relations—Kentucky 346.769015
Domestic relations—Massachusetts 346.744015
Domestic relations—Minnesota 346.776015
Domestic relations—New Jersey 346.749015
Domestic relations—New York (State) 346.747015
Domestic relations—North Carolina 346.756015
Domestic relations—Ohio 346.771015
Domestic relations—Ontario 346.713015
Domestic relations—Pennsylvania 346.748015
Domestic relations—Texas 346.764015
Domestic relations—United States 346.73015

Domestic relations—United States—Cases 346.730150264
Domestic relations—United States—Outlines, syllabi, etc. 346.73015
Domestic relations—Virginia 346.755015
Domingo, Plácido, 1941- 782.1092
Dominican monasteries 271.2
Dominican Republic 972.93
Dominican Republic—Guidebooks 917.29304; 917.2930454
Dominion theology 230.046
Dominoes 795.32
Don Juan (Legendary character) in literature 808.80351; 809.93351
Donation of organs, tissues, etc. 617.95
Donkeys 636.182
Donne, John, 1572-1631 821.3
Donne, John, 1572-1631—Criticism and interpretation 821.3
Donne, John, 1572-1631—Literary style 821.3
Donne, John, 1572-1631—Religion 821.3
Donovan family (Fictitious characters) 813.54
Doom (Computer file) 793.92
Doonesbury (Comic strip) 741.5973
Door County (Wis.) 977.563
Door County (Wis.)—Maps 912.77563
Door-to-door selling 658.85
Doors 694.6
Doors (Musical group) 782.421660922
Doping in sports 362.29088796
Doppler echocardiography 616.1207543
Doppler effect 534.3
Doppler radar 629.1324
Doppler ultrasonography 616.07543
Dorchester County (Md.) 975.227
Dorchester County (Md.)—Genealogy 929.375227
Dorchester County (Md.)—Maps 912.75227
Doré, Gustave, 1832-1883 769.92
Dormitories 371.871
Dormitory life 371.871; 378.19871
Dorsai (Imaginary place) 813.54
Dorsai (Imaginary place)—Fiction 813.54
Dorset (England) 942.33
Dorset (England)—Pictorial works 942.330222
Dorsey, Carroll (Fictitious character) 813.54
Dortmunder (Fictitious character) 813.54
Dortmunder (Fictitious character)—Fiction 813.54
DOS 4.0 005.4469
DOS device drivers (Computer programs) 005.713582
Dos Passos, John, 1896-1970 813.52
Dos Passos, John, 1896-1970—Criticism and interpretation 813.52
DOS/VSE 005.4429
Dostoyevsky, Fyodor, 1821-1881 891.733
Dostoyevsky, Fyodor, 1821-1881. Bratʹia Karamazovy 891.733
Dostoyevsky, Fyodor, 1821-1881. Crime and punishment 891.733
Dostoyevsky, Fyodor, 1821-1881—Criticism and interpretation 891.733
Dostoyevsky, Fyodor, 1821-1881—Knowledge—Literature 891.733
Dostoyevsky, Fyodor, 1821-1881—Translations into English 891.733
Double effect (Ethics) 170
Double monasteries 255; 271
Double stars 523.841
Double taxation 341.4844
Double taxation—Great Britain 343.410526

Double taxation—Great Britain—Treaties 341.4844026441

Double taxation—Treaties 341.4844026

Double taxation—United States 343.730526

Double taxation—United States—Treaties 341.4844026473

Doubles in literature 808.8027; 809.927

Dougal, William (Fictitious character) 823.914

Dougal, William (Fictitious character)—Fiction 823.914

Douglas County (Ga.)—Maps 912.758243

Douglas County (Minn.) 977.645

Douglas County (Minn.)—Maps 912.77645

Douglas County (Mo.) 977.8832

Douglas County (Mo.)—Genealogy 929.3778832

Douglas DC-3 (Transport plane) 629.133340423

Douglas DC-3 (Transport plane)—History 629.133340423

Douglas family 929.20973

Douglass, Frederick, 1817?–1895 973.7114092; 973.8092

Doulas 618.45

Dover, Wilfred (Fictitious character) 823.914

Dover, Wilfred (Fictitious character)—Fiction 823.914

Dow Jones averages 332.632220973

Dow Jones averages—History 332.632220973

Dow Jones transportation average 332.632220973

Dow Jones utility average 332.632220973

Dowling, Father (Fictitious character) 813.54

Dowling, Father (Fictitious character)—Fiction 813.54

Down syndrome 362.3; 616.858842; 618.92858842

Downhill ski racing 796.935

Downsizing of organizations 658.3134

Downward mobility (Social sciences) 305.513

Dowsing 133.323

Doxazosin 615.71

Doyle, Arthur Conan, Sir, 1859–1930 823.8

Doyle, Arthur Conan, Sir, 1859–1930—Characters 823.8

Doyle, Arthur Conan, Sir, 1859–1930—Characters—Sherlock Holmes 823.8

Doyle family 929.20973

Drabble, Margaret, 1939– 823.914

Drabble, Margaret, 1939– —Criticism and interpretation 823.914

Dracula, Count (Fictitious character) 812.54; 823.8

Draft 355.22363

Draft—Australia 355.223630994

Draft—Law and legislation 343.0122

Draft—Law and legislation—United States 343.730122

Draft registration 355.22363

Draft registration—United States 343.730122; 355.223630973

Draft—United States 355.223630973

Drafters 604.2092

Drag (Aerodynamics) 533.62; 629.13234

Drag racing 796.72

Dragonflies 595.733

Dragons 398.2454

Dragons in art 704.947

Drainage 627.54

Drainage—California—San Joaquin Valley 631.62097948

Drake, Francis, Sir, 1540?–1596 359.0092; 942.055092

Drake, Jessie (Fictitious character) 813.54

Drama 808.2; 808.82

Drama—20th century 808.8204

Drama—20th century—History and criticism 809.204

Drama—Collections 808.82

Drama—Explication 808.2

Drama—History and criticism 809.2

Drama in Christian education 246.72

Drama in education 371.399; 372.66

Drama in public worship 246.72

Drama, Medieval 808.8202

Drama, Medieval—History and criticism 809.202

Drama—Study and teaching 808.2071

Drama—Technique 808.2

Drama—Therapeutic use 616.891523

Dramatists 792.092

Dramatists, American 792.092273

Draperies 646.21; 746.94

Draperies in interior decoration 645.3; 747.5

Dravidian languages 494.8

Drawing 741

Drawing, American 741.973

Drawing books 741.2

Drawing, European 741.94

Drawing, European—Exhibitions 741.94

Drawing, French 741.944

Drawing, Italian 741.945

Drawing, Psychology of 741.019

Drawing—Study and teaching 741.071

Drawing—Study and teaching (Elementary) 372.52

Drawing—Technique 741.2

DrawPerfect 006.6869

Dream interpretation 135.3; 154.63

Dream interpretation—Dictionaries 154.6303

Dreamcatchers 398.208997; 745.59

Dreams 135.3; 154.63

Dreams—Dictionaries 154.6303

Dreams in literature 808.80353; 809.93353

Dreams—Religious aspects 291.42

Dreams—Religious aspects—Christianity 248.29

Dreams—Therapeutic use 616.8914

Dreamtime (Australian aboriginal mythology) 299.9215; 398.27

Dredges 627.73

Dredging 627.73

Dreiser, Theodore, 1871–1945 813.52

Dreiser, Theodore, 1871–1945—Bibliography 016.81352

Dreiser, Theodore, 1871–1945—Criticism and interpretation 813.52

Dreiser, Theodore, 1871–1945. Sister Carrie 813.52

Dress accessories 646.3; 646.48

Dress codes in the workplace 331.2; 658.312

Dressage 798.23

Dressage—Competitions 798.24

Dressmaking 646.404

Dressmaking—Pattern design 646.4072

Dressmaking—Patterns 646.4072

Drew, Charles Richard, 1904–1950 617.092

Drexel Burnham Lambert Incorporated 332.660973

Dreyfus, Alfred, 1859–1935 944.0812092

Dried flower arrangement 745.92

Dried flower industry 338.4774592

Drift boats 623.828; 639.20284

Drilling and boring machinery 621.952

Drilling platforms 627.98

Drinking and traffic accidents 363.12514

Drinking and traffic accidents—United States 363.125140973

Drinking cups 748.83

Drinking customs 394.12

Drinking games 793.2

Drinking games—United States 793.2

Drinking in popular music 781.64159; 782.42164159

Drinking of alcoholic beverages 394.13

Drinking of alcoholic beverages—United States—Statistics 381.4564121

Drinking water 363.61; 628.1

Drinking water—Health aspects 613.287
Drinking water—Law and legislation 346.0469122
Drinking water—Law and legislation—United States 346.730469122
Drinking water—Microbiology 628.16
Drinking water—Purification 628.162
Drinkwater, Nathaniel (Fictitious character) 823.914
Drinkwater, Nathaniel (Fictitious character)—Fiction 823.914
Drive-by shootings 364.1555
Driving ranges 796.352068
Dropouts 371.2913
Dropouts—United States 371.29130973
Drosophila 595.774
Drosophilidae 595.774
Droughts 363.34929; 551.5773
Droughts—California 363.3492909794
Drowning—Resuscitation 617.18
Drucker, Peter Ferdinand, 1909– 300.92
Drug abuse 362.29
Drug abuse and crime 364.177
Drug abuse and crime—United States 364.24
Drug abuse counseling 362.29186
Drug abuse—Government policy—United States 363.450973
Drug abuse in pregnancy 618.3; 618.3268
Drug abuse—Physiological aspects 616.8607
Drug abuse—Prevention 362.2917
Drug abuse—Prevention—Study and teaching (Elementary)—United States 372.37
Drug abuse—Psychological aspects 616.060019
Drug abuse—Social aspects 362.29
Drug abuse—Study and teaching 362.29071
Drug abuse—Study and teaching—United States 362.29071073
Drug abuse surveys—United States 362.29120723
Drug abuse—United States 362.290973
Drug abuse—United States—Prevention 362.290973
Drug abuse—United States—Statistics—Periodicals 362.290973021
Drug carriers (Pharmacy) 615.7
Drug couriers 363.45; 364.177
Drug delivery systems 615.6
Drug development 615.19
Drug-herb interactions 615.7045
Drug interactions 615.7045
Drug interactions—Handbooks, manuals, etc. 615.7045
Drug legalization 364.177
Drug legalization—United States 363.450973
Drug monitoring 615.7
Drug receptors 615.7
Drug resistance 616.01
Drug resistance in cancer cells 616.994061
Drug resistance in microorganisms 616.01
Drug targeting 615.7
Drug testing 331.2598
Drug traffic 363.45
Drug traffic—Investigation 363.25977
Drug traffic—Investigation—United States 363.259770973
Drug traffic—United States 363.450973
Drugged driving 363.12514; 364.147
Drugs 615.1
Drugs—Administration 615.58
Drugs—Administration—Handbooks, manuals, etc. 615.58
Drugs—Administration—Law and legislation 344.04233
Drugs—Analysis 615.1901
Drugs and employment 658.3822

Drugs and employment—United States 658.3822
Drugs—Controlled release 615.6
Drugs—Design 615.19
Drugs—Dictionaries 615.103
Drugs—Dosage forms 615.4
Drugs—Granulation 615.4
Drugs—Handbooks, manuals, etc. 615.1
Drugs in popular music 781.64159; 782.42164159
Drugs—Law and legislation 344.304233
Drugs—Law and legislation—United States 344.7304233
Drugs—Marketing 615.10688
Drugs—Metabolism 615.7
Drugs, Nonprescription 615.1
Drugs, Nonprescription—Handbooks, manuals, etc. 615.1
Drugs of abuse 362.29; 615.78
Drugs—Outlines, syllabi, etc. 615.1
Drugs—Physiological effect 615.7
Drugs—Prescribing 615.14
Drugs—Prices 338.436151
Drugs—Prices—United States 338.4361510973
Drugs—Religious aspects 291.1783229; 291.42
Drugs—Research 615.19
Drugs—Research—Methodology 615.1072; 615.19
Drugs—Side effects 615.7042
Drugs—Structure-activity relationships 615.1; 615.7
Drugs—Testing 615.1901; 615.70287
Drugs—Toxicity testing 615.7040287
Drugstores 381.456151
Druids and Druidism 299.16
Drum 786.9; 786.919
Drum and bugle Corps 785.57
Drummers (Musicians) 786.9092
Drummond, Bulldog (Fictitious character) 791.4375; 791.4472; 823.912
Drunk driving 363.12514; 364.147
Drunk driving—New York (State) 345.7470247
Drunk driving—Prevention 363.1257
Drunk driving—Texas 345.7640247
Drunk driving—United States 345.730247
Druzes 297.85
Dry-bodied stoneware 738.37
Dry marker drawing 741.26
Dry marker drawing—Technique 741.26
Dry stone walls 693.1
Dryden, John, 1631–1700 821.4
Dryden, John, 1631–1700. Absalom and Achitophel 821.4
Dryden, John, 1631–1700—Criticism and interpretation 821.4
Dryden, John, 1631–1700—Dramatic works 822.4
Dryden, John, 1631–1700—Political and social views 821.4
Drying 660.28426
Drywall construction 690.12
Du Bois, W. E. B. (William Edward Burghardt), 1868–1963 323.1196073092
Du Page County (Ill.) 977.324
Du Page County (Ill.)—Maps 912.77324
Du Pré, Gabriel (Fictitious character) 813.54
Du Pré, Gabriel (Fictitious character)—Fiction 813.54
Dual-brain psychology 153; 616.89
Dual-brain therapy 616.8914
Dual-career families 306.85
Dual-career families—Finance, Personal 332.0240655
Dual-career families—United States 306.872
Dual diagnosis 362.29; 616.86
Dublin Core 025.344
Dublin (Ireland) 941.835

Dublin (Ireland)—Antiquities 936.1835
Dublin (Ireland)—Description and travel 914.183504;
914.183504824
Dublin (Ireland)—Guidebooks 914.183504;
914.183504824
Dublin (Ireland)—History 941.835
Dublin (Ireland)—History—Pictorial works
941.83500222
Dublin (Ireland)—Social life and customs 941.835
Dublin (Ireland)—Social life and customs—20th century
941.835082
Dubuque County (Iowa) 977.739
Dubuque County (Iowa)—Maps 912.77739
Duchamp, Marcel, 1887–1968 709.2
Duchamp, Marcel, 1887–1968—Criticism and
interpretation 709.2
Duchenne muscular dystrophy 616.748
Ducklings 598.41139; 636.597
Ducks 598.41
Dude ranches 796.56
Due process of law 347.05
Due process of law—United States 347.7305
Duets (Unspecified instrument and computer) 786.76
Duikers 599.64
Duke, David Ernest 976.3063092
Duke Nukem 3D 793.932
Dulcie (Fictitious character) 813.54
Duluoz (Fictitious character) 813.54
Dump trucks 629.225
Dumping (International trade) 382.63
Dumping (International trade)—Law and legislation
341.754
Dunaliella 579.832
Dunbar family 929.20973
Dunbar, Paul Laurence, 1872–1906 811.4
Dunbaria 583.74
Duncan family 929.20973
Dune (Imaginary place) 813.54
Dune (Imaginary place)—Fiction 813.54
Dung beetles 595.7649
Dungeons and dragons (Game) 793.93
Dunham, Katherine 792.82092
Dunkerque (France), Battle of, 1940 940.5421428
Dunn County (Wis.) 977.543
Dunn County (Wis.)—Maps 912.77543
Dunne, Finley Peter, 1867–1936 814.52
Dunne, Finley Peter, 1867–1936—Criticism and
interpretation 814.52
Duns Scotus, John, ca. 1266–1308 189.4
Duplicating fluids 686.40284
Duplin County (N.C.)—Genealogy 929.3756382
Dura-Europos (Extinct city) 935
Durango & Silverton Narrow Gauge Railroad
385.5209788
Duras, Marguerite 843.912
Duras, Marguerite—Criticism and interpretation
843.912
Duras, Marguerite—Translations into English 843.912
Durban Metropolitan Area (South Africa)—Maps
912.68455
Dürer, Albrecht, 1471–1528 769.92
Durham Metropolitan Area (N.C.)—Maps 912.756563
Durian 634.6
Durrell, Lawrence 828.91209
Durrell, Lawrence—Correspondence 828.91209
Durrell, Lawrence—Criticism and interpretation
828.91209
Dust explosions 604.7
Dust storms 551.559

Dusty plasmas 530.44
Dutch language 439.31
Dutch language—Grammar 439.315; 439.3182;
439.3182421
Dutch oven cookery 641.589
Dutch poetry 839.311; 839.31108
Dutch poetry—20th century 839.3116; 839.311608;
839.31164; 839.3116408
Dutch poetry—20th century—Translations into English
839.3116408
Dutch students 371.8293931
Dutch wit and humor, Pictorial 741.59492
Dutchess County (N.Y.)—Genealogy 929.374733
Duval, Justine (Fictitious character) 823.914
Duvall, Cheney (Fictitious character) 813.54
Duvall, Cheney (Fictitious character)—Fiction 813.54
Dvaita (Vedanta) 181.4841
DVD-ROMs 004.565; 621.39767
DVD videodiscs 384.558; 621.388332
DVDs 004.565; 621.388332
Dvořák, Antonín, 1841–1904 780.92
Dwarf rabbits 636.9322
Dwarfs 599.949
Dwellings 643.7
Dwellings—Energy conservation 644; 696
Dwellings—Heating and ventilation 697
Dwellings—History 392.36009
Dwellings—Inspection 643.12
Dwellings—Inspection—Handbooks, manuals, etc.
643.12
Dwellings—Insulation 693.83
Dwellings—Lighting 747.92
Dwellings—Maintenance and repair 643.7
Dwellings—Remodeling 643.7
Dwellings—Remodeling—Costs 643.70299
Dwellings—Remodeling—Great Britain 643.70941
Dwellings—Remodeling—Periodicals 643.705
Dwellings—Security measures 643.16
Dworkin, R. M. 340.1092
Dye lasers 621.3664
Dye plants 581.636
Dyes and dyeing 667.2; 667.3
Dyes and dyeing—Chemistry 667.20154
Dyes and dyeing, Domestic 648.1; 667.26
Dyes and dyeing—Textile fibers 746.6
Dylan, Bob, 1941– 782.421620092
Dylan, Bob, 1941– —Criticism and interpretation
782.421620092
Dynamic programming 519.703
Dynamics 531.11; 620.104; 620.1054
Dyslexia 371.9144; 616.8553; 618.928553
Dyslexic children—Education 371.9144
Dyslexic children—Education—United States
371.91440973
Dystopias in literature 808.80372; 809.93372
Dytiscidae 595.762
Dzibilchaltún Site (Mexico) 972.65
E-zines 050
Eagles 598.942
Ear 573.89; 611.85; 612.85
Ear—Diseases 617.8
Ear piercing 391.7
Ear—Surgery 617.8059
Ear training 781.424
Earhart, Amelia, 1897–1937 629.13092
Early childhood education 372.21
Early childhood education—Activity programs 372.13
Early childhood education—Activity programs—United
States—Handbooks, manuals, etc. 372.130973

Early childhood education—Curricula 372.19
Early childhood education—Great Britain 372.210941
Early childhood education—Parent participation 372.1192; 649.68
Early childhood education—Parent participation—United States 372.11920973
Early childhood education—United States 372.210973
Early childhood education—United States—Curricula 372.190973
Early maps 912
Early maps—Collectors and collecting 912.075
Early-music groups 780.922
Early printed books 094.2
Early printed books—Bibliography 011.42
Early printed books—Bibliography—Catalogs 011.42
Early stars 523.88
Earp, Wyatt, 1848–1929 978.02092
Earth 525; 550; 551
Earth—Core 551.112
Earth—Crust 551.13
Earth Day 333.72
Earth—Figure 525.1
Earth—Internal structure 551.1; 551.11
Earth—Mantle 551.116
Earth—Miscellanea 550
Earth—Origin 525
Earth resources technology satellites 778.35
Earth—Rotation 525.35
Earth sciences 550
Earth sciences—Antarctica 559.89
Earth sciences—Dictionaries 550.3
Earth sciences—Experiments 550.724; 550.78
Earth sciences libraries 026.55
Earth sciences—Miscellanea 550
Earth sciences—Periodicals 550.5
Earth sciences—Remote sensing 550.287
Earth stations (Satellite telecommunication) 629.461
Earth temperature 551.14
Earth temperature—Effect of volcanic eruptions on 551.21
Earthmoving machinery 629.225
Earthquake engineering 624.1762
Earthquake engineering laboratories 624.1762072
Earthquake hazard analysis 363.349563
Earthquake hazard analysis—California—San Francisco Bay Area 363.34956309794
Earthquake hazard analysis—United States 363.3495630973
Earthquake magnitude 551.220287
Earthquake prediction 551.220112
Earthquake resistant design 624.1762; 693.852
Earthquakes 551.22
Earthquakes—California 551.2209794
Earthquakes in literature 808.8036; 809.9336
Earthquakes—Missouri—New Madrid region 551.2209778985
Earthquakes—Safety measures 363.34957
Earthwork 624.152
Earthworks (Art) 709.04076
Earthworm culture 639.75
Earthworms 592.64
East Asia 950
East Asia—Civilization 950
East Asia—Economic conditions 330.95
East Asia—Economic policy 338.95
East Asia—Foreign relations 327.095
East Asia—Foreign relations—United States 327.7305
East Asia—History 950
East Asia—Library resources 016.95

East Asia—Periodicals 950.05
East Asia—Relations 303.4825
East Asia—Relations—United States 303.4825073; 327.7305
East Asian business enterprises 338.708995
East European drama 808.8200947
East India Company—History 954.031
East Indian Americans 305.891411073; 973.04914
East Indian business enterprises 338.7089914
East Indians 305.891411
East Indians—Trinidad and Tobago 305.891411072983
East (U.S.) 974
East (U.S.)—Guidebooks 917.404
East-West trade 382.09171301717
Easter 263.93; 394.2667
Easter decorations 745.5941
Easter egg hunts 394.2667
Easter eggs (Computer programs) 005.3
Easter Island 996.18
Easter Island—Antiquities 996.18
Easter music 781.727
Easter—Sermons 252.63
Eastern Air Lines, Inc. 387.706573
Eastern question (Balkan) 949.6
Eastwood, Clint, 1930– 791.43028092
Eastwood, Clint, 1930– —Criticism and interpretation 791.430233092; 791.43028092
Eating disorders 616.8526
Eating disorders in adolescence 616.852600835
Eating disorders in children 618.928526
Eating disorders—Patients 362.27
Eating disorders—Patients—Prayer-books and devotions 242.6625
Eating disorders—Psychological aspects 616.8526
Eating disorders—Treatment 616.852606
Eaton County (Mich.) 977.423
Eaton County (Mich.)—Maps 912.77423
Eaton, Jake (Fictitious character) 813.54
Eau Claire County (Wis.) 977.545
Eau Claire County (Wis.)—Maps 912.77545
Ebla (Extinct city) 939.4
Ebola virus disease 614.575; 616.925
Eccentrics and eccentricities 920.02
Eccentrics and eccentricities—New York (State) 920.0747
Eccentrics and eccentricities—New York (State)—New York 920.07471
Eccentrics and eccentricities—United States 920.073
Ecclesiastical law 262.9
Ecclesiastical law—Great Britain 262.90941
Ecclesiastical law—Great Britain—History 262.90941
Echinacea (Plants)—Therapeutic use 615.32399
Echinidae 593.95
Echinodermata, Fossil 563.9
Echo suppression (Telecommunication) 621.3828
Echocardiography 616.1207543; 618.921207543
Eckankar (Organization) 299.93
Eckert, James (Fictitious character) 813.54
Eckert, James (Fictitious character)—Fiction 813.54
Eclectic psychotherapy 616.8914
Eclecticism in architecture 724.5
Eclecticism in architecture—United States 720.973
Eclipses 523.99
Eclipsing binaries—Light curves 523.8444
Ecofeminism 305.4201
Ecohydrology 577.6
Ecolinguistics 306.44
Ecological disturbances 577.2
Ecological engineering 628

Economics—Mathematical models 330.015118
Economics—Methodology 330.01
Economics—Periodicals 330.05
Economics—Philosophy 330.01
Economics—Political aspects 338.9
Economics—Problems, exercises, etc. 330.076
Economics—Psychological aspects 330.019
Economics—Religious aspects 291.1785
Economics—Religious aspects—Catholic Church 261.85
Economics—Religious aspects—Christianity 261.85
Economics—Religious aspects—Islam 291.1785
Economics—Religious aspects—Judaism 296.383
Economics—Sociological aspects 306.3
Economics—Statistical methods 330.015195
Economics—Study and teaching 330.071
Economics—United States 330.0973
Economics—United States—History 330.0973
Economies of scale 338.5144
Economists 330.092
Economists—Biography 330.0922
Ecosystem health 333.95; 577
Ecosystem management 333.95
Ecosystem management—United States 333.950973
Ecoterrorism 303.625; 364.1
Ecotones 577
Ecotourism 338.4791
Ecstasy 152.42
Ecstasy (Drug) 362.299; 615.7883
Ecstatic dance 291.43
Ectopic pregnancy 618.31
Ecuador 986.6
Ecuador—Description and travel 918.6604; 918.660474; 918.660475
Ecuador—Economic conditions 330.9866
Ecuador—Economic conditions—1972- 330.9866074
Ecuador—Economic conditions—1972- —Periodicals 330.9866074
Ecuador—Guidebooks 918.6604; 918.660474; 918.660475
Ecumenical movement 280.042
Eddy currents (Electric) 621.31042
Eddy, Mary Baker, 1821–1910 289.5092
Edelman, Marian Wright 362.7092
Eden 222.1109505
Eden, Anthony, Earl of Avon, 1897- 941.0855092
Edgar County (Ill.) 977.369
Edgar County (Ill.)—Maps 912.77369
EDGAR (Information retrieval system) 332.64273
Edgecombe County (N.C.)—Genealogy 929.375646
Edgefield County (S.C.)—Genealogy 929.375737
Edible frog 597.892
Edinburgh (Scotland) 941.44
Edinburgh (Scotland)—Guidebooks 914.14404; 914.14404859; 914.1440486
Edinburgh (Scotland)—Maps 912.4134
Edison, Thomas A. (Thomas Alva), 1847–1931 621.3092
Editing 808.027
Editing—Handbooks, manuals, etc. 808.027
Editorials 070.442
Editors 808.027092
Edmond (Fictitious character : Duchesne) 843.914
Edmund (Fictitious character : Jackson) 813.54
Education 370
Education—Africa 370.96
Education—Aims and objectives 370.11
Education—Aims and objectives—Great Britain 370.941
Education—Aims and objectives—United States 370.973
Education—Alaska 370.9798
Education, Ancient 370.901; 370.93

Education and state 379
Education and state—Australia 379.94
Education and state—Germany 379.43
Education and state—Great Britain 379.41
Education and state—India 379.54
Education and state—South Africa 379.68
Education and state—United States 379.73
Education and training services industry 338.47374013; 374.013
Education—Asia 370.95
Education—Australia 370.994
Education—Bibliography 016.37
Education, Bilingual 370.1175
Education, Bilingual—Great Britain 370.11750941
Education, Bilingual—United States 370.11750973
Education—Botswana 370.96883
Education—Botswana—Periodicals 370.9688305
Education—Canada 370.971
Education—China 370.951
Education—China—History 370.951
Education—China—History—To 1912 370.951
Education—China—History—1912–1949 370.95109041
Education—China—History—1949–1976 370.95109045
Education—China—History—1976- 370.95109048
Education—Computer network resources 025.0637
Education—Computer network resources—Directories 025.0637
Education, Cooperative 371.227
Education, Cooperative—United States 371.2270973
Education—Costs 371.206
Education—Curricula 375
Education—Data processing 370.285; 371.334
Education—Denmark 370.9489
Education—Developing countries 370.91724
Education—Dictionaries 370.3
Education—Economic aspects 338.4737
Education—Egypt 370.962
Education, Elementary 372
Education, Elementary—Activity programs 372.13
Education, Elementary—Curricula 372.19
Education, Elementary—Great Britain 372.941
Education, Elementary—Great Britain—Curricula 372.190941
Education, Elementary—History 372.9
Education, Elementary—India 372.954
Education, Elementary—Parent participation 372.1192
Education, Elementary—United States 372.973
Education—England 370.942
Education—England—History 370.942
Education—Europe 370.94
Education—Evaluation 379.158
Education—Experimental methods 370.724; 371.30724
Education—Finance 371.206
Education—France 370.944
Education—Germany 370.943
Education—Germany (East) 370.9431
Education—Germany (West) 370.943
Education—Great Britain 370.941
Education—Great Britain—Curricula 375.000941
Education—Great Britain—History 370.941
Education—Greece 370.9495
Education, Greek 370.938
Education, Higher 378
Education, Higher—Africa 378.6
Education, Higher—Aims and objectives 378
Education, Higher—Aims and objectives—Great Britain 378.41
Education, Higher—Aims and objectives—United States 378.73

Education, Higher—Australia 378.94
Education, Higher—Australia—Western Australia 378.941
Education, Higher—Economic aspects 338.47378
Education, Higher—Economic aspects—United States 338.4737873
Education, Higher—Europe 378.4
Education, Higher—Evaluation 379.158
Education, Higher—Finland 378.4897
Education, Higher—Great Britain 378.41
Education, Higher—Great Britain—Administration 378.1010941
Education, Higher—Great Britain—Evaluation 379.158
Education, Higher—India 378.54
Education, Higher—Japan 378.52
Education, Higher—Moral and ethical aspects 174.937
Education, Higher—Moral and ethical aspects—United States 174.937
Education, Higher—Nigeria 378.669
Education, Higher—Parent participation 378.103
Education, Higher—Philosophy 378.001
Education, Higher—Political aspects—United States 378.73
Education, Higher—Research 378.0072
Education, Higher—South Africa 378.68
Education, Higher—Texas 378.764
Education, Higher—United States 378.73
Education, Higher—United States—Administration 378.1010973
Education, Higher—United States—Curricula 378.1990973
Education, Higher—United States—Data processing 378.730285
Education, Higher—United States—Data processing—Periodicals 378.730285
Education, Higher—United States—Finance 378.1060973; 379.1190973
Education, Higher—United States—History 378.73
Education, Higher—United States—Philosophy 378.7301
Education—History 370.9
Education, Humanistic 370.112
Education, Humanistic—United States 370.1120973
Education in literature 808.80355; 809.93355
Education—India 370.954
Education—India—History 370.954
Education—India—Periodicals 370.95405
Education—Indonesia 370.9598
Education—Israel 370.95694
Education—Italy 370.945
Education—Japan 370.952
Education—Japan—History 370.952
Education—Japan—History—1868- 370.95209034; 370.9520904
Education—Japan—History—1945- 370.95209045
Education—Kenya 370.96762
Education—Latin America 370.98
Education—Malawi 370.96897
Education—Malaysia 370.9595
Education, Medieval 370.902
Education—Minnesota 370.9776
Education—Minnesota—Finance 379.1109776; 379.12209776
Education—New York (State) 370.9747
Education—New York (State)—Finance 379.1109747; 379.12209747
Education—New York (State)—New York 370.97471
Education—New York (State)—New York—Finance 379.11097471; 379.123097471
Education—New Zealand 370.9931

Education—Nigeria 370.9669
Education—Nigeria—History 370.9669
Education—Nigeria—Periodicals 370.966905
Education of princes 371.82621
Education—Ontario 370.9713
Education—Pakistan 370.9549; 370.95491
Education—Parent participation 371.192
Education—Parent participation—United States 371.1920973
Education—Parent participation—United States—Handbooks, manuals, etc. 371.1920973
Education parks 711.57
Education—Periodicals 370.5
Education—Philippines 370.9599
Education—Philosophy 370.1; 370.12
Education—Philosophy—History 370.1
Education, Preschool 372.21
Education, Preschool—Activity programs 372.13
Education, Preschool—Activity programs—United States 372.130973
Education, Preschool—Curricula 372.19
Education, Preschool—Great Britain 372.210941
Education, Preschool—Parent participation 372.1192
Education, Preschool—Parent participation—United States 372.11920973
Education, Preschool—United States 372.210973
Education, Preschool—United States—Curricula 372.19
Education, Primary 372.241
Education, Primary—Activity programs 372.13; 372.5
Education, Primary—Activity programs—United States 372.130973
Education, Primary—Curricula 372.19
Education, Primary—Great Britain 372.2410941
Education—Research 370.72
Education—Research—Great Britain 370.72041
Education—Research—Methodology 370.72
Education—Research—Philosophy 370.72
Education—Research—United States 370.72073
Education, Rural 370.91734
Education, Rural—United States 370.0973091734
Education savings accounts 336.24216
Education, Secondary 373
Education, Secondary—Aims and objectives 373
Education, Secondary—Great Britain 373.41
Education, Secondary—Great Britain—Curricula 373.190941
Education, Secondary—Parent participation 373.1192
Education, Secondary—United States 373.73
Education, Secondary—United States—Curricula 373.190973
Education, Secondary—United States—History 373.73
Education—Simulation methods 371.397
Education—Social aspects 306.43
Education—Social aspects—South Africa 306.430968
Education—Social aspects—United States 306.430973
Education—South Africa 370.968
Education—South Africa—Aims and objectives 370.968
Education—Soviet Union 370.947
Education—Soviet Union—History 370.947
Education—Spain 370.946
Education—Standards—United States 379.1580973
Education—Study and teaching 370.71; 370.711
Education—Study and teaching—United States 370.71173
Education—Sweden 370.9485
Education—Taiwan 370.951249
Education—Taiwan—History—1945- 370.94124909045
Education—Tanzania 370.9678
Education—Texas 370.9764

Egill Skallagrímsson, ca. 910–ca. 990—Romances 839.61
Ego (Psychology) 154.22
Egoism 171.9
Egypt 962
Egypt—Antiquities 932
Egypt—Antiquities—Exhibitions 932.0074
Egypt—Antiquities—Guidebooks 916.204; 916.20455
Egypt—Civilization 962
Egypt—Civilization—To 332 B.C. 932
Egypt—Civilization—To 332 B.C.—Dictionaries 932
Egypt—Description and travel 916.204; 916.20455
Egypt—Economic conditions 330.962
Egypt—Economic conditions—1952- 330.96205
Egypt—Economic conditions—1952- —Periodicals 330.96205
Egypt—Economic policy 338.962
Egypt—Foreign relations 327.62
Egypt—Foreign relations—Israel 327.6205694
Egypt—Guidebooks 916.204; 916.20455
Egypt—History 962
Egypt—History—To 332 B.C. 932
Egypt—History—To 640 A.D. 932
Egypt—History—Eighteenth dynasty, ca. 1570–1320 B.C. 932.014
Egypt—History—640–1250 962.02
Egypt—History—1250–1517 962.02
Egypt—History—1517–1882 962.03
Egypt—History—Intervention, 1956 962.053
Egypt—Politics and government 962
Egypt—Politics and government—1952–1970 320.96209045; 962.05
Egypt—Religion 299.31
Egypt—Social conditions 962
Egypt—Social life and customs 932; 962
Egypt—Social life and customs—To 332 B.C. 932
Egyptian language 493.1
Egyptian language—Writing, Hieroglyphic 493.1
Egyptian literature 893.1; 893.108
Egyptian literature—Translations into English 893.108
Egyptian poetry 893.11; 893.11008
Egyptian poetry—Translations into English 893.11008
Egyptologists 932.0092
Egyptology 962.0072
Eichmann, Adolf, 1906–1962 364.151092
Eiffel (Computer program language) 005.133
Eigenvalues 512.9434
Eighteenth century 909.7
Einstein, Albert, 1879–1955 530.092
Eisenhower, Dwight D. (Dwight David), 1890–1969 973.921092
Ekelöf, Gunnar, 1907–1968 839.7174
Ekelöf, Gunnar, 1907–1968—Translations into English 839.7174
Ekue 786.98
El Alamein, Battle of, Egypt, 1942 940.5423
El Niño Current 551.4761
El Salvador 972.84
El Salvador—History 972.84
El Salvador—History—1979–1992 972.84053
El Salvador—Politics and government 320.97284; 972.84
El Salvador—Politics and government—1979–1992 320.9728409048; 972.84053
Elastic analysis (Engineering) 624.171
Elastic plates and shells 624.1176
Elasticity 531.382; 620.11232
Elastomers 678
Elbow—Surgery 617.574
Elder family 929.20973

Elderhostels 647.94
Eldridge family 929.20973
Eldridge, Louise (Fictitious character) 813.54
Eleanor, of Aquitaine, Queen, consort of Henry II, King of England, 1122?–1204 942.031092
Election districts 328.3345
Election districts—California 328.79407345
Election law 342.07
Election law—California 342.79407
Election law—Florida 342.75907
Election law—India 342.5407
Election law—New Jersey 342.74907
Election law—North Carolina 342.75607
Election law—Philippines 342.59907
Election law—United States 342.7307
Election monitoring 324.65
Election sermons 252.68
Election sermons—Connecticut 252.68
Election sermons—Massachusetts 252.68
Election sermons—New Hampshire 252.68
Elections 324; 324.9
Elections—Great Britain 324.941
Elections—India 324.954
Elections—Kenya 324.96762
Elections—Nicaragua 324.97285053
Elections—Pakistan 324.95491
Elections—South Africa 324.968
Elections—Taiwan 324.95124905
Elections—United States 324.973
Elections—United States—History 324.973
Elections—Zambia 324.96894
Electoral college 324.63
Electoral college—United States 324.630973
Electric apparatus and appliances 621.3; 621.31042
Electric batteries 621.31242
Electric cables 621.31934
Electric circuit analysis 621.3192
Electric circuit analysis—Data processing 621.31920285
Electric circuit-breakers 621.317
Electric circuits 621.3192
Electric circuits, Linear 621.3192
Electric circuits—Problems, exercises, etc. 621.3192076
Electric conductivity 537.62
Electric conductors 537.62
Electric contacts 621.38152
Electric controllers 621.46; 629.8043
Electric cookery, Slow 641.5884
Electric current converters 621.317; 621.3815322
Electric currents, Alternating 621.31913
Electric currents—Grounding 621.317
Electric discharges through gases 537.53
Electric driving 621.46
Electric driving—Automatic control 621.46
Electric engineering 621.3
Electric engineering—Dictionaries 621.303
Electric engineering—Estimates 621.30299; 621.319240299
Electric engineering—Examinations, questions, etc. 621.31924076
Electric engineering—Handbooks, manuals, etc. 621.3
Electric engineering—Insurance requirements 621.319240218
Electric engineering—Insurance requirements—United States 621.31924021873
Electric engineering—Law and legislation 343.0786213
Electric engineering—Law and legislation—United States 343.730786213
Electric engineering—Mathematics 621.30151; 621.3015195

Electric engineering—Periodicals 621.305
Electric engineering—Problems, exercises, etc. 621.3076
Electric engineering—Safety measures 621.30289; 621.319240289
Electric engineering—Safety measures—Standards—United States 621.30289
Electric engineering—United States—Examinations, questions, etc. 621.3076; 621.31924076
Electric engineers 621.3092
Electric filters 621.3815324
Electric filters—Design and construction 621.3815324
Electric filters, Digital 621.3815324
Electric generators 621.313
Electric guitar 787.87
Electric guitar—Methods (Heavy metal) 787.87193
Electric heating 621.4028; 697.045
Electric household appliances industry 338.4768383
Electric industries 338.476213
Electric insulators and insulation 621.31937
Electric lamps 621.326
Electric lighting 621.32
Electric lighting—Equipment and supplies—Catalogs 621.3260216
Electric lines 621.31922
Electric lines—Health aspects 363.189
Electric lines—Poles and towers 621.31922
Electric lines—Poles and towers—Design and construction 621.31922
Electric locomotives 625.263
Electric machinery 621.31042
Electric measurements 621.37
Electric metal-cutting 671.53
Electric meters 621.373
Electric motors 621.46
Electric motors—Handbooks, manuals, etc. 621.46
Electric network analysis 621.3192
Electric networks 621.3192
Electric power 333.7932; 631.31
Electric power distribution 621.319
Electric power distribution—High tension 621.31913
Electric power failures 333.7932
Electric power-plants 333.7932; 621.3121
Electric power-plants—Environmental aspects 333.793214
Electric power-plants—Equipment and supplies 621.31210284
Electric power production 621.3121
Electric power supplies to apparatus 621.381044
Electric power system stability 621.31; 621.319
Electric power systems 621.31; 621.3191
Electric power systems—Control 621.31
Electric power systems—Protection 621.317
Electric power transmission 621.319
Electric power transmission—Direct current 621.31912
Electric prospecting 622.154
Electric railroads—Cars 625.2
Electric railroads—Power supply 621.33
Electric signs 659.136
Electric standards 621.372
Electric switchgear 621.317
Electric transformers 621.314
Electric utilities 333.7932
Electric utilities—Law and legislation 343.0929
Electric utilities—Law and legislation—United States 343.730929
Electric utilities—United States 333.79320973
Electric utilities—United States—Costs 333.79320973

Electric utilities—United States—Directories 333.793202573
Electric utilities—United States—Finance 333.7932310973
Electric utilities—United States—Finance—Statistics—Periodicals 333.7932310973021
Electric utilities—United States—Management 333.7932068
Electric utilities—United States—Periodicals 333.7932097305
Electric utilities—United States—Rates 333.7932310973
Electric utilities—United States—Statistics 333.79320973021
Electric utilities—United States—Statistics—Periodicals 333.79320973021
Electric vehicles 629.2293
Electric welding 671.521
Electric wheelchairs 617.03; 681.761
Electric wiring 621.31924
Electric wiring—Handbooks, manuals, etc. 621.31924
Electric wiring—Insurance requirements 621.30218
Electric wiring, Interior 621.31924
Electric wiring, Interior—Handbooks, manuals, etc. 621.31924
Electricity 537
Electricity—Experiments 537.0724; 537.078; 621.3078
Electricity in agriculture 631.371
Electricity in mining 622.48
Electricity in transportation 629.04
Electro-acoustics 621.3828
Electrocardiography 616.1207547
Electrocardiography—Handbooks, manuals, etc. 616.1207547
Electrocardiography—Interpretation 616.1207547
Electrocatalysis 541.395
Electrochemical analysis 543.0871
Electrochemistry 541.37
Electrochemistry, Industrial 660.297
Electroconvulsive therapy 616.89122
Electrodes 541.3724
Electrodynamics 537.6
Electroencephalography 616.8047547
Electroencephalography—Atlases 616.80475470222
Electrolyte solutions 541.372
Electrolytes 541.372
Electromagnetic compatibility 621.38224
Electromagnetic devices 621.316
Electromagnetic fields 530.141
Electromagnetic fields—Health aspects 363.189; 612.01442
Electromagnetic fields—Mathematics 530.141
Electromagnetic interference 621.38224
Electromagnetic theory 530.141
Electromagnetic theory—Mathematics 530.141
Electromagnetic waves 539.2
Electromagnetic waves—Scattering 539.2
Electromagnetic waves—Transmission 539.2
Electromagnetism 537
Electromagnetism—Physiological effect 571.47; 612.01442
Electromechanical devices 621.31042
Electrometallurgy 669.0284
Electromyography 616.7407547
Electron accelerators 539.73712
Electron microscopy 502.825; 570.2825
Electron microscopy—Technique 570.2825
Electron optics 537.56
Electron paramagnetic resonance 538.364

Electron paramagnetic resonance spectroscopy 543.0877

Electron-positron interactions 539.75

Electron spectroscopy 543.0858

Electronic alarm systems industry 338.4762138928

Electronic apparatus and appliances 621.381

Electronic apparatus and appliances—Design and construction 621.381

Electronic apparatus and appliances—Effect of radiation on 621.381

Electronic apparatus and appliances—Maintenance and repair—Handbooks, manuals, etc. 621.381

Electronic apparatus and appliances—Power supply 621.381044

Electronic apparatus and appliances—Protection 621.381

Electronic apparatus and appliances—Reliability 621.381

Electronic apparatus and appliances—Temperature control 621.381; 621.381044

Electronic apparatus and appliances—Testing 621.381548

Electronic apparatus and appliances—Thermal properties 621.381

Electronic behavior control 621.38928

Electronic benefits transfers—Law and legislation 344.03105

Electronic books 070.5797

Electronic calendars 529.30285

Electronic ceramics 621.381

Electronic circuit design 621.3815

Electronic circuit design—Data processing 621.3815

Electronic circuits 621.3815

Electronic circuits—Handbooks, manuals, etc. 621.3815

Electronic circuits—Noise 621.38224

Electronic circuits—Testing 621.381548

Electronic commerce 658.84

Electronic commerce—Periodicals 658.84

Electronic commerce—Security measures 380.1

Electronic control 629.8043

Electronic controllers 621.317; 621.381044

Electronic data interchange 004.6; 005.71

Electronic data processing 004

Electronic data processing—Auditing—Standards 658.478

Electronic data processing—Backup processing alternatives 005.86

Electronic data processing—Batch processing 004.3

Electronic data processing consultants 004.092

Electronic data processing—Data entry 005.72

Electronic data processing departments 004.068

Electronic data processing departments—Auditing 658.478

Electronic data processing departments—Contracting out 658.05

Electronic data processing departments—Management 658.05

Electronic data processing departments—Security measures 658.478

Electronic data processing—Dictionaries 004.03

Electronic data processing—Distributed processing 004.36

Electronic data processing documentation 808.066004; 808.066005

Electronic data processing—Examinations, questions, etc. 004.076

Electronic data processing—Humor 004.0207

Electronic data processing—Moral and ethical aspects 174.90904

Electronic data processing—Periodicals 004.05

Electronic data processing personnel 004.092

Electronic data processing personnel—Certification 004.076

Electronic data processing—Structured techniques 005.113

Electronic data processing—Vocational guidance 004.023

Electronic digital computers 004

Electronic digital computers—Circuits—Computer-aided design 621.3950285

Electronic digital computers—Circuits—Design 621.395

Electronic digital computers—Circuits—Design and construction 621.395

Electronic digital computers—Evaluation 004.0297; 004.24

Electronic digital computers—Reliability 004.24

Electronic dissertations 378.242

Electronic dog training collars 636.708870284

Electronic encyclopedias 030

Electronic equipment enclosures 621.381

Electronic filing of tax returns 343.04; 343.052044

Electronic flash photography 778.37; 778.72

Electronic fund raising 361.70681; 658.15224

Electronic funds transfers 332.10285

Electronic funds transfers—Law and legislation 346.08210285

Electronic funds transfers—Law and legislation—United States 346.7308210285

Electronic funds transfers—Law and legislation—United States—States 346.7308210285

Electronic funds transfers—Security measures 332.1028558

Electronic funds transfers—United States 332.10285

Electronic games 794.8

Electronic government information 025.04; 352.74

Electronic government information—United States 025.040973

Electronic government information—United States—Directories 025.0402573

Electronic industries 338.47621381; 381.4562138

Electronic industries—Management 621.381068

Electronic industries—United States 338.476213810973

Electronic information resource literacy 338.4702504

Electronic information resource searching 025.04

Electronic information resources 025.04

Electronic information resources—Access control 005.8; 025.04

Electronic instruments—Design and construction 621.381

Electronic instruments, Digital 786.7

Electronic journals 070.5797

Electronic keyboard (Synthesizer) 786.74

Electronic locking devices 683.32

Electronic mail art 760

Electronic mail equipment industry 384.34

Electronic mail messages 004.692

Electronic mail systems 004.692; 384.34

Electronic mail systems—Handbooks, manuals, etc. 004.692

Electronic measurements 621.381548; 681.2

Electronic monitoring in the workplace 331.2598; 658.314

Electronic monitoring of parolees and probationers 364.63

Electronic monitoring of parolees and probationers—Law and legislation 345.077

Electronic music 786.74

Electronic news gathering 070.43

Electronic newsletters 070.1
Electronic newspapers 070.1
Electronic noise 621.38224
Electronic office machine industry 338.476816
Electronic office machines—Periodicals 651.805
Electronic packaging 621.381046
Electronic packaging—Handbooks, manuals, etc.
 621.381046
Electronic packaging—Materials 621.3810460284
Electronic public records 352.387
Electronic public records—Law and legislation 342.0662
Electronic publications 070.5797
Electronic publishing 070.5797
Electronic publishing equipment industry
 338.4768622544
Electronic publishing—Periodicals 070.579705
Electronic publishing—United States 070.57970973
Electronic records 070.5797
Electronic reference sources 025.04
Electronic security systems 363.252; 621.38928
Electronic spreadsheets 005.3
Electronic structure 623.8504
Electronic surveillance 621.38928
Electronic systems 623.8504
Electronic technicians 621.381092
Electronic toys 790.133
Electronic trading of securities 332.6420285
Electronic traffic controls 625.794
Electronic villages (Computer networks) 004.67
Electronic Warfare aircraft 358.4183
Electronics 621.381
Electronics—Dictionaries 621.38103
Electronics engineers 621.381092
Electronics—Examinations, questions, etc. 621.381076
Electronics—Handbooks, manuals, etc. 621.381
Electronics in military engineering 623.043
Electronics in military engineering—Periodicals
 623.04305
Electronics in navigation 623.893
Electronics in printing 686.2
Electronics in transportation 388.312
Electronics—Materials 621.3810284
Electronics—Materials—Corrosion 621.3810284
Electronics—Mathematics 621.3810151; 621.381015195
Electronics—Periodicals 621.38105
Electronics—Problems, exercises, etc. 621.381076
Electrons 539.72112
Electrons—Scattering 539.758
Electrooptical devices 621.381045
Electrooptics 537.56; 621.381045
Electrooptics—Materials 621.3810450284
Electrophoresis 541.372
Electrophotography 686.233; 771.44
Electrophysiology 612.813
Electroplating 671.732
Electroplating industry 338.47671732
Electrostatic accelerators 539.73
Electrostatics 537.2
Electrotherapeutics 615.845
Electroweak interactions 539.7544
Elegiac poetry, English 821.04
Elegiac poetry, English—History and criticism 821.04
Elegiac poetry, Latin 874; 874.01
Elegiac poetry, Latin—Translations into English
 874.008; 874.0108
Elementary school libraries 027.8222
Elementary school libraries—Activity programs
 027.8222

Elementary school libraries—Book selection
 025.21878222
Elementary school principals 372.12012; 372.92
Elementary school principals—United States
 372.120120973
Elementary school teachers 372.11; 372.92
Elementary school teaching 372.1102
Elementary school teaching—Great Britain
 372.11020941
Elementary school teaching—Handbooks, manuals, etc.
 372.1102
Elementary school teaching—United States
 372.11020973
Elementary schools 372
Elephant seals 599.794
Elephants 599.67
Elephants, Fossil 569.67
Eleusinian mysteries 292.9
Elevators 621.877
Elevators—Design and construction 621.877
Elgar, Edward, 1857–1934 780.92
Elgin marbles 733.309385
Eliade, Mircea, 1907– 200.92
Elijah (Biblical prophet) 222.5092
Eliot family (Fictitious characters) 823.912
Eliot, George, 1819–1880 823.8
Eliot, George, 1819–1880—Criticism and interpretation
 823.8
Eliot, George, 1819–1880—Ethics 823.8
Eliot, George, 1819–1880. Middlemarch 823.8
Eliot, George, 1819–1880—Political and social views
 823.8
Eliot, T. S. (Thomas Stearns), 1888–1965 821.912
Eliot, T. S. (Thomas Stearns), 1888–1965—Aesthetics
 821.912
Eliot, T. S. (Thomas Stearns), 1888–1965—Criticism
 and interpretation 821.912
Eliot, T. S. (Thomas Stearns), 1888–1965—Dramatic
 works 822.912
Eliot, T. S. (Thomas Stearns), 1888–1965. Four
 quartets 821.912
Eliot, T. S. (Thomas Stearns), 1888–1965—Knowledge—
 Literature 821.912
Eliot, T. S. (Thomas Stearns), 1888–1965—Philosophy
 821.912
Eliot, T. S. (Thomas Stearns), 1888–1965—Political and
 social views 821.912
Eliot, T. S. (Thomas Stearns), 1888–1965. Waste land
 821.912
Elisabeth, Empress, consort of Franz Joseph I, Emperor
 of Austria, 1837–1898 943.6044092
Elisha (Biblical prophet) 222.54092
Elite (Social sciences) 305.52
Elite (Social sciences)—Soviet Union 305.520947
Elite (Social sciences)—United States 305.520973
Elizabeth I, Queen of England, 1533–1603 942.055092
Elizabeth II, Queen of Great Britain, 1926– 941.085092
Elizabeth II, Queen of Great Britain, 1926– —Family
 941.0850922
Elizabeth, Queen, consort of George VI, King of Great
 Britain, 1900– 941.084092
Elk 599.6542
Ellington, Duke, 1899–1974 781.65092
Elliott family 929.20973
Elliott, Maggie (Fictitious character) 813.54
Elliott, Maggie (Fictitious character)—Fiction 813.54
Elliott, Scott (Fictitious character) 813.54
Elliptic functions 515.983
Ellis family 929.20973

Ellis Island Immigration Station (N.Y. and N.J.) 325.73; 725.1

Ellis Island Immigration Station (N.Y. and N.J.)— History 325.73

Ellis, Trade (Fictitious character) 813.54

Ellison, Ralph 813.54; 818.5409

Ellison, Ralph—Criticism and interpretation 818.5409

Ellison, Ralph. Invisible man 813.54

Elminster (Fictitious character) 813.54

Elmo (Fictitious character : Henson) 791.4375; 791.4575

Elocution 808.5

Elsa (Lion) 599.757

Elvis Presley impersonators 782.42166; 792.028

Elway, John, 1960– 796.332092

Elytēs, Odysseas, 1911– 889.132

Elytēs, Odysseas, 1911– —Translations into English 889.132

Emancipation Proclamation 973.714

Emanuel, Cedric 741.994

Embankments 624.162

Embargo 341.582; 382.53

Embarrassment in adolescence 155.5124

Embassy buildings 725.17

Embassy buildings—Security measures 342.0412

Embassy buildings—Security measures—United States 342.730412

Embedded computer systems 004.16

Embedded computer systems—Design and construction 004.256

Embedded computer systems—Programming 005.26

Embellishment (Music) 781.247

Emblems 929.9

Emblems—Early works to 1800 929.9

Emblems, National 929.9

Emblems, State 929.9

Embroidery 746.44

Embroidery, Machine 677.77; 746.44028

Embroidery, Medieval 746.4420902

Embroidery—Patterns 746.44041

Embroidery—Themes, motives 746.44

Embryology 571.86

Embryology, Experimental 571.860724

Embryology, Human 612.64

Embryology, Human—Atlases 611.0130222

Embryology—Mammals 571.8619

Embryology—Vertebrates 571.8616

Emergency communication systems 384.5

Emergency management 363.348; 658.477

Emergency management—United States 363.3480973

Emergency medical personnel 362.18092

Emergency medical services 362.18

Emergency medical services—Law and legislation 344.041

Emergency medical services—Law and legislation— United States 344.73041

Emergency medicine 616.025

Emergency medicine—Diagnosis 616.025; 616.075

Emergency medicine—Examinations, questions, etc. 616.025076

Emergency medicine—Handbooks, manuals, etc. 616.025

Emergency nursing 610.7361

Emergency nursing—Examinations, questions, etc. 610.7361

Emergency nursing—Handbooks, manuals, etc. 610.7361

Emergency physicians 616.025092

Emerson, Ralph Waldo, 1803–1882 814.3

Emerson, Ralph Waldo, 1803–1882—Criticism and interpretation 814.3

Emerson, Ralph Waldo, 1803–1882—Knowledge— Literature 814.3

Emerson, Ralph Waldo, 1803–1882—Literary style 814.3

Emerson, Ralph Waldo, 1803–1882—Philosophy 814.3

Emerson, Ralph Waldo, 1803–1882—Poetic works 811.3

Emerson, Ralph Waldo, 1803–1882—Political and social views 814.3

Emerson, Ralph Waldo, 1803–1882—Religion 814.3

Emery, Ralph 781.642092

Emigration and immigration 304.82; 325

Emigration and immigration—Economic aspects 304.82

Emigration and immigration—Government policy 325

Emigration and immigration law 341.4842; 342.082

Emigration and immigration law—Canada 342.71082

Emigration and immigration law—Great Britain 342.41082

Emigration and immigration law—United States 342.73082

Emigration and immigration law—United States—Cases 342.730820264

Emigration and immigration law—United States— Periodicals 342.7308205

Emigration and immigration—Periodicals 325.05

Emigration and immigration—Psychological aspects 304.82

Emigration and immigration—Social aspects 304.82

Eminent domain 343.0252

Eminent domain—Great Britain 343.410252

Eminent domain (International law) 341.4846

Eminent domain—United States 343.730252

Emmet County (Mich.) 977.488

Emmet County (Mich.)—Maps 912.77488

Emmons County (N.D.) 978.478

Emmons County (N.D.)—Maps 912.78478

Emmy Awards 384.553207973

Emotional Freedom Techniques 616.891

Emotional intelligence 152.4

Emotional intelligence tests 152.40287

Emotional maturity—Religious aspects 291.44

Emotional maturity—Religious aspects—Christianity 248.4

Emotional problems of children 155.4124; 618.926

Emotions 152.4

Emotions—Health aspects 616.08; 616.89

Emotions in animals 591.5

Emotions in children 155.4124

Emotions in literature 808.80353; 809.93353

Emotions (Philosophy) 128.37

Emotions—Physiological aspects 152.4

Emotions—Religious aspects 291.44

Emotions—Religious aspects—Christianity 248.4

Emotive (Linguistics) 401.43

Empathy 152.41

Emperor worship—Japan 299.561213

Emperors 321.03

Emperors—Japan 952.0099

Emperors—Japan—Succession 342.52062

Emperors—Rome 937.060922

Emperors—Rome—Biography 937.060922

Empiricism 146.44

Empiricism—History 146.4409

Employee assistance programs 658.382

Employee assistance programs—United States 658.3820973

Employee crimes 658.38

End of the world 236.9
End of the world—Biblical teaching 236.9
End of the world—History of doctrines 291.23
End-user computing 004.019
Endangered fungi 333.953; 579.516
Endangered plants 581.68
Endangered species 333.9522; 333.9542; 578.68; 591.68
Endangered species—Law and legislation 346.0469522
Endangered species—Law and legislation—United
    States 346.730469522
Endangered species—Maine—Maps 578.6809741
Endocrine glands 573.4; 616.4
Endocrine glands—Diseases 616.4
Endocrine glands—Diseases—Diagnosis 616.4075
Endocrine glands—Physiology 612.4
Endocrine glands—Tumors 616.9944
Endocrine gynecology 618.1
Endocrine toxicology 616.4071
Endocrinologists 616.4092
Endocrinology 616.4
Endodontics 617.6342
Endogenous growth (Economics) 338.9
Endometriosis 618.1
Endoscopic surgery 617.05
Endoscopic ultrasonography 616.07543
Endoscopy 616.07545
Endosseous dental implants 617.692
Endosymbiosis 577.85
Endourology 617.461059
Endowed public schools (Great Britain) 371.020941
Endowed public schools (Great Britain)—History—19th
    century 373.222094109034
Endowment of research 001.44
Endowments 001.44; 361.7632
Endowments—United States 361.76320973
Endowments—United States—Directories
    361.763202573
Energy auditing 333.7914; 696
Energy auditing—Handbooks, manuals, etc. 658.26; 696
Energy-band theory of solids 530.41
Energy conservation 333.7916; 621.042
Energy conservation—Handbooks, manuals, etc.
    621.042
Energy conservation—Law and legislation 346.0467916
Energy conservation—Law and legislation—United
    States 346.730467916
Energy conservation—United States 333.79160973
Energy consumption 333.7913
Energy consumption—United States 333.79130973
Energy development 333.7915; 621.042
Energy development—Environmental aspects 333.7915
Energy industries 333.79; 338.473379
Energy industries—Periodicals 333.7905
Energy industries—United States 333.790973
Energy labeling 381.34; 658.823
Energy levels (Quantum mechanics) 539.725
Energy metabolism 572.43
Energy policy 333.79
Energy policy—Canada 333.790971
Energy policy—Developing countries 333.79091724
Energy policy—European Economic Community
    countries 333.79094
Energy policy—Great Britain 333.790941
Energy policy—United States 333.790973
Energy policy—United States—Periodicals 333.79097305
Energy storage 621.3126
Engels, Friedrich, 1820–1895 335.4092
Engineered wood 674.83
Engineered wood industry 338.4767483

Engineering 620
Engineering—Computer programs 620.002855369
Engineering contracts 346.024; 620.0068; 624.068
Engineering—Data processing 620.00285
Engineering—Data processing—Periodicals 620.00285
Engineering—Databases 620.00285574
Engineering design 620.0042; 620.00425
Engineering design—Data processing 620.00420285
Engineering design—Mathematical models
    620.0042015118
Engineering drawings 604.2; 604.25
Engineering drawings—Dimensioning 604.243
Engineering economy 658.15
Engineering—Estimates 620.00299
Engineering ethics 174.962
Engineering—Examinations, questions, etc. 620.0076
Engineering—Experiments 620.0078
Engineering firms 620.006
Engineering geology 624.151
Engineering graphics 604.2
Engineering—Handbooks, manuals, etc. 620
Engineering—History 620.009
Engineering inspection 658.568; 670.425
Engineering inspection—Automation 670.425
Engineering instruments 620.0028; 681.2
Engineering instruments—Periodicals 681.205
Engineering laboratories 620.0044
Engineering libraries 026.62
Engineering—Management 620.0068
Engineering—Mathematical models 620.0015118
Engineering mathematics 620.00151
Engineering mathematics—Data processing
    620.001510285
Engineering models 620.00228; 624.0228
Engineering—Periodicals 620.005
Engineering schools 620.00711
Engineering—Software 620.0028553
Engineering—Software—Catalogs 620.0028553
Engineering—Statistical methods 620.0015195;
    620.0072
Engineering students 620.00711
Engineering—Study and teaching 620.00711
Engineering—Study and teaching—United States
    620.0071173
Engineering—Tables 620.00212
Engineering—United States 620.00973
Engineering—United States—Examinations 620.0076
Engineering—Vocational guidance 620.0023
Engineers 620.0092
Engineers—Employment 620.0023
Engineers—Employment—United States 620.002373
Engineers—United States 620.0092273
Engineers' writings 808.899262
Engines 621.4
England 942
England—Biography 920.042
England—Church history 274.2
England—Church history—449–1066 274.202; 274.203
England—Church history—1066–1485 274.204; 274.205
England—Church history—16th century 274.206
England—Church history—17th century 274.206;
    274.207
England—Civilization 942
England—Civilization—1066–1485 942
England—Civilization—16th century 942.05
England—Civilization—17th century 942.06
England—Civilization—18th century 942.07
England—Civilization—19th century 942.081
England—Civilization—20th century 942.082

England—Description and travel 914.204; 914.204859; 914.20486

England—Genealogy 929.1072041

England—Genealogy—Handbooks, manuals, etc. 929.1072042

England—Guidebooks 914.204

England—Historical geography 911.42

England—Historiography 942.0072

England—Maps 912.42

England, Northern 942.7

England, Northern—History 942.7

England—Pictorial works 914.200222

England—Religious life and customs 274.2

England—Road maps 912.42

England—Rural conditions 307.720942

England—Social conditions 942

England—Social conditions—18th century 942.07

England—Social conditions—19th century 942.081

England—Social life and customs 390.0942; 942

England—Social life and customs—1066–1485 942.02

England—Social life and customs—16th century 942.05

England—Social life and customs—17th century 942.06

England—Social life and customs—18th century 942.07

England—Social life and customs—19th century 942.081

England—Social life and customs—19th century—Literary collections 820.803242

England—Social life and customs—20th century 942.002

England—Social life and customs 1915 942.085

England—Tours 914.204; 914.204859; 914.20486

English composition test 808.042076

English drama 822; 822.008

English drama—To 1500 822.1; 822.108

English drama—To 1500—History and criticism 822.109

English drama—Early modern and Elizabethan, 1500–1600 822.2; 822.208; 822.3; 822.308

English drama—Early modern and Elizabethan, 1500–1600—History and criticism 822.209; 822.309

English drama—Early modern and Elizabethan, 1500–1600—History and criticism—Bibliography 016.822309

English drama—17th century 822.4; 822.408

English drama—17th century—History and criticism 822.409

English drama—Restoration, 1660–1700 822.4; 822.408

English drama—Restoration, 1660–1700—History and criticism 822.409

English drama—18th century 822.5; 822.508

English drama—18th century—History and criticism 822.509

English drama—19th century 822.7; 822.708; 822.8; 822.808

English drama—19th century—History and criticism 822.709; 822.809

English drama—20th century 822.91; 822.9108; 822.912; 822.91208; 822.914; 822.91408

English drama—20th century—History and criticism 822.9109; 822.91209; 822.91409

English drama—Bibliography 016.822

English drama (Comedy) 822.0523

English drama (Comedy)—History and criticism 822.052309

English drama—History and criticism 822.009

English drama—Irish authors 822.00809415

English drama—Irish authors—History and criticism 822.0099415

English drama (Tragedy) 822.0512

English drama (Tragedy)—History and criticism 822.051209

English essays 824; 824.008

English essays—Early modern, 1500–1700 824.3

English essays—18th century 824.5; 824.508

English essays—18th century—History and criticism 824.509

English essays—20th century 824.91; 824.9108

English essays—History and criticism 824.009

English fiction 823.08

English fiction—Early modern, 1500–1700 823.308

English fiction—Early modern, 1500–1700—History and criticism 823.309

English fiction—18th century 823.508

English fiction—18th century—History and criticism 823.509; 823.609

English fiction—19th century 823.808

English fiction—19th century—Bibliography 016.8238

English fiction—19th century—Dictionaries 823.809

English fiction—19th century—History and criticism 823.709; 823.809

English fiction—19th century—History and criticism—Theory, etc. 823.809

English fiction—20th century 823.9108

English fiction—20th century—Dictionaries 823.910903

English fiction—20th century—Handbooks, manuals, etc. 823.9109

English fiction—20th century—History and criticism 823.9109; 823.91209; 823.91409

English fiction—Bibliography 016.823

English fiction—History and criticism 823.009

English fiction—History and criticism—Theory, etc. 823.009

English fiction—Irish authors 823.0089415

English fiction—Irish authors—20th century 823.910809415

English fiction—Women authors 823.0089287

English fiction—Women authors—History and criticism 823.0099287

English language 420

English language—Old English, ca. 450–1100 429

English language—Old English, ca. 450–1100—Glossaries, vocabularies, etc. 429.3

English language—Old English, ca. 450–1100—Grammar 429.5

English language—Old English, ca. 450–1100—Versification 829.1

English language—Middle English, 1100–1500 427.02

English language—Middle English, 1100–1500—Dictionaries 427.0203

English language—Middle English, 1100–1500—Grammar 427.02

English language—Middle English, 1100–1500—Style 820.9002

English language—18th century—Dictionaries 423

English language—20th century—Dictionaries 423

English language—Adjective 425; 428.2

English language—Alphabet 421.1; 428.1

English language—Australia 427.994

English language—Australia—Dictionaries 423; 427.994

English language—Australia—Slang 427.994

English language—Australia—Slang—Dictionaries 427.994

English language—Business English 428.002465; 428.2402465; 808.06665; 808.06665021

English language—Business English—Handbooks, manuals, etc. 808.06665

English language—Business English—Problems, exercises, etc. 428.2402465; 808.06665; 808.06665021

English language—Clauses 425
English language—Composition and exercises 808.042
English language—Composition and exercises—Data processing 808.0420285
English language—Composition and exercises—Examinations 808.042076
English language—Composition and exercises—Handbooks, manuals, etc. 808.042
English language—Composition and exercises—Study and teaching 428.0071
English language—Composition and exercises—Study and teaching (Elementary) 372.623; 372.623044
English language—Composition and exercises—Study and teaching (Elementary)—United States 372.6230440973; 372.6230973
English language—Composition and exercises—Study and teaching (Secondary) 808.0420712
English language—Composition and exercises—Study and teaching (Secondary)—United States 808.042071273
English language—Conversation and phrase books 428.34
English language—Conversation and phrase books (for tourism industry employees) 428.34
English language—Conversation and phrase books—Russian 428.349171
English language—Data processing 420.285
English language—Dialects 427
English language—Dialects—Conversation and phrase books 427
English language—Dialects—England—London 427.1
English language—Dialects—Great Britain 427.941
English language—Dialects—Southern States—Glossaries, vocabularies, etc. 427.975
English language—Dialects—Ulster (Northern Ireland and Ireland)—Glossaries, vocabularies, etc. 427.9416
English language—Dialects—United States 427.973
English language—Dictionaries 423
English language—Discourse analysis 420.141
English language—Eponyms—Dictionaries 423.1
English language—Errors of usage 428
English language—Errors of usage—Dictionaries 428.003
English language—Errors of usage—Humor 428
English language—Etymology 422
English language—Etymology—Dictionaries 422.03
English language—Euphemism—Dictionaries 423.1
English language—Examinations 428.0076
English language—Examinations, questions, etc. 428.0076
English language—Foreign words and phrases—Dictionaries 422.403
English language—Glossaries, vocabularies, etc. 423.1; 428.1
English language—Grammar 425; 428; 428.2
English language—Grammar, Generative 425
English language—Grammar, Generative—Problems, exercises, etc. 425
English language—Grammar—Handbooks, manuals, etc. 428.2
English language—Grammar, Historical 425.09
English language—Grammar—Problems, exercises, etc. 428.2
English language—Grammar—Programmed instruction 428.2077
English language—Grammar—Study and teaching 428.2071
English language—Great Britain—Dictionaries 423.1
English language—History 420.9

English language—Homonyms 428.1
English language—Homonyms—Dictionaries 423.1
English language—Idioms 428.1
English language—Idioms—Dictionaries 423.1
English language—India 427.954
English language—India—Etymology—Dictionaries 422.4911; 427.954
English language—Intonation 421.6
English language—Lexicography 423.028
English language—Modality 425
English language—New words 428.1
English language—New words—Dictionaries 423; 423.1
English language—New words—Humor 428.1
English language—Obsolete words—Dictionaries 427
English language—Orthography and spelling 421.52; 428.1
English language—Orthography and spelling—Dictionaries 423.1
English language—Orthography and spelling—Problems, exercises, etc. 428.1
English language—Orthography and spelling—Study and teaching 428.1071
English language—Orthography and spelling—Study and teaching (Elementary) 372.632
English language—Paragraphs 808.042
English language—Paragraphs—Problems, exercises, etc. 808.042
English language—Phonetics 421.58
English language—Phonology 421.5
English language—Prepositions 425
English language—Programmed instruction 428.2077
English language—Pronoun 425
English language—Pronunciation 421.52
English language—Pronunciation by foreign speakers 428.34
English language—Pronunciation—Dictionaries 423.1
English language—Punctuation 428.2
English language—Punctuation—Handbooks, manuals, etc. 428.2
English language—Research—Data processing 420.285
English language—Reverse indexes 423.1
English language—Rhetoric 808.042
English language—Rhetoric—Computer network resources 025.06808042
English language—Rhetoric—Data processing 808.0420285
English language—Rhetoric—Examinations 808.042076
English language—Rhetoric—Handbooks, manuals, etc. 808.042
English language—Rhetoric—Problems, exercises, etc. 808.042076
English language—Rhetoric—Programmed instruction 808.042077
English language—Rhetoric—Study and teaching 808.042071
English language—Rhetoric—Study and teaching—Bibliography 016.80804207
English language—Rhetoric—Study and teaching—Data processing 808.0420785
English language—Rhetoric—Study and teaching—Evaluation 808.042071
English language—Rhetoric—Study and teaching—Foreign speakers 808.042071
English language—Rhetoric—Study and teaching—Psychological aspects 808.042071
English language—Rhetoric—Study and teaching—Research 808.042071; 808.042072
English language—Rhetoric—Study and teaching—United States 808.042071073

English language—Rhetoric—Study and teaching—
  United States—History 808.042071073
English language—Rhyme 811; 821.009
English language—Rhyme—Dictionaries 423.1
English language—Roots 422
English language—Roots—Dictionaries 422.03
English language—Self-instruction 428.2; 428.24
English language—Semantics 420.143
English language—Sentences 428.2
English language—Sentences—Problems, exercises, etc.
  428.2; 808.042
English language—Slang 427.09
English language—Slang—Dictionaries 427.09
English language—Study and teaching (Elementary)
  372.6
English language—Study and teaching (Elementary)—
  Foreign speakers 372.6521
English language—Study and teaching (Elementary)—
  Great Britain 372.60941
English language—Study and teaching (Elementary)—
  United States 372.60973
English language—Study and teaching—Foreign
  speakers 372.6521; 428.0071; 428.24071; 428.34071
English language—Study and teaching—Foreign
  speakers—Aids and devices 428.0071
English language—Study and teaching—Foreign
  speakers—Handbooks, manuals, etc. 428.0071
English language—Study and teaching—Foreign
  speakers—Periodicals 428.0071
English language—Study and teaching (Higher) 420.711
English language—Study and teaching—Japanese
  speakers 428.0071052
English language—Study and teaching (Primary)
  372.6521
English language—Study and teaching (Primary)—
  Kenya 372.6521044096762
English language—Study and teaching (Secondary)
  420.712; 428.00712
English language—Study and teaching (Secondary)—
  Great Britain 428.0071241
English language—Study and teaching (Secondary)—
  United States 428.0071273
English language—Style 808.042
English language—Synonyms and antonyms 420.143
English language—Synonyms and antonyms—
  Dictionaries 423.1
English language—Syntax 425
English language—Technical English 808.0666
English language—Tense 425
English language—Textbooks for foreign speakers
  428.24; 428.34
English language—Textbooks for foreign speakers—
  African 428.2496; 428.3496
English language—Textbooks for foreign speakers—
  French 428.2441; 428.3441
English language—Textbooks for foreign speakers—
  Japanese 428.24956; 428.34956
English language—Textbooks for foreign speakers—
  Russian 428.249171; 428.349171
English language—Textbooks for foreign speakers—
  Spanish 428.2461; 428.3461
English language—United States 427.973
English language—United States—Dictionaries 423
English language—United States—History 420.973
English language—United States—Idioms—Dictionaries
  423.1
English language—United States—Pronunciation 421.54
English language—United States—Slang 427.973

English language—United States—Slang—Dictionaries
  427.973
English language—United States—Terms and phrases
  427.973
English language—United States—Usage—Dictionaries
  423.1; 428.00973
English language—Usage 428
English language—Usage—Dictionaries 428.003
English language—Usage—Handbooks, manuals, etc.
  428
English language—Variation 427
English language—Variation—Foreign countries 427
English language—Variation—United States 427.973
English language—Verb 425; 428.2
English language—Versification 821.009
English language—Vowels 428.1
English letters 826; 826.008
English literature 820; 820.8
English literature—Old English, ca. 450–1100 829.08
English literature—Old English, ca. 450–1100—History
  and criticism 829.09
English literature—Old English, ca. 450–1100—
  Modernized versions 829; 829.08
English literature—Middle English, 1100–1500 820.8001
English literature—Middle English, 1100–1500—
  Bibliography 016.8208001
English literature—Middle English, 1100–1500—
  Criticism, Textual 820.9001
English literature—Middle English, 1100–1500—History
  and criticism 820.9001
English literature—Early modern, 1500–1700 820.8003
English literature—Early modern, 1500–1700—
  Bibliography 016.82
English literature—Early modern, 1500–1700—
  Criticism, Textual 820.9003
English literature—Early modern, 1500–1700—History
  and criticism 820.9003; 820.9004
English literature—Early modern, 1500–1700—History
  and criticism—Bibliography 016.8209
English literature—Early modern, 1500–1700—History
  and criticism—Theory, etc. 820.9003
English literature—18th century 820.8005
English literature—18th century—History and criticism
  820.9005; 820.9006
English literature—18th century—History and
  criticism—Theory, etc. 820.9005
English literature—19th century 820.8007; 820.8008
English literature—19th century—Criticism, Textual
  820.9008
English literature—19th century—History and criticism
  820.9007; 820.9008
English literature—19th century—History and
  criticism—Bibliography 016.8209008
English literature—20th century 820.800912;
  820.800914
English literature—20th century—History and criticism
  820.90091; 820.900912; 820.900914
English literature—Bibliography 016.82
English literature—Bibliography of bibliographies
  016.01682
English literature—Bio-bibliography 820.9
English literature—Bio-bibliography—Dictionaries 820.9
English literature—Dictionaries 820.3; 820.90003
English literature—Examinations 820.76
English literature—First editions 016.82
English literature—Foreign countries 820.8
English literature—Foreign countries—History and
  criticism 820.9
English literature—French influences 820.9

English literature—History and criticism 820.9
English literature—History and criticism—Bibliography 016.82
English literature—History and criticism—Periodicals 820.90005
English literature—History and criticism—Theory, etc. 820.9
English literature—Irish authors 820.8089162; 820.809415; 820.809417
English literature—Irish authors—History and criticism 820.99415; 820.99417
English literature—Italian influences 820.9
English literature—Medieval influences 820.9
English literature—Outlines, syllabi, etc. 820.9
English literature—Research 820.72
English literature—Research—Methodology 820.72
English literature—Study and teaching 820.71
English literature—Women authors 820.809287
English literature—Women authors—History and criticism 820.99287
English newspapers 072
English philology 420
English philology—Old English, ca. 450–1100 429
English philology—Examinations 420.76
English philology—Periodicals 420.5
English philology—Study and teaching (Higher) 420.711
English philology—Study and teaching (Higher)—United States 420.71173
English poetry 821; 821.008
English poetry—Old English, ca. 450–1100 829.1
English poetry—Old English, ca. 450–1100—History and criticism 829.109
English poetry—Old English, ca. 450–1100—Modernized versions 829.1; 829.108
English poetry—Middle English, 1100–1500 821.1; 821.108
English poetry—Middle English, 1100–1500—History and criticism 821.109
English poetry—Middle English, 1100–1500—Modernized versions 821.108
English poetry—Early modern, 1500–1700 821.3; 821.308; 821.4; 821.408
English poetry—Early modern, 1500–1700—History and criticism 821.209; 821.309; 821.409
English poetry—Early modern, 1500–1700—History and criticism—Theory, etc. 821.309
English poetry—18th century 821.5; 821.508; 821.6; 821.608
English poetry—18th century—History and criticism 821.509; 821.609
English poetry—19th century 821.7; 821.708; 821.8; 821.808
English poetry—19th century—Dictionaries 821.803
English poetry—19th century—History and criticism 016.821809; 821.709; 821.809
English poetry—19th century—History and criticism—Theory, etc. 821.809
English poetry—20th century 821.91; 821.9108; 821.912; 821.91208; 821.914; 821.91408
English poetry—20th century—History and criticism 821.9109; 821.91209
English poetry—20th century—History and criticism—Theory, etc. 821.9109
English poetry—History and criticism 821.009
English poetry—History and criticism—Theory, etc. 821.009
English poetry—Irish authors 821.00809415
English poetry—Irish authors—20th century 821.910809415

English poetry—Welsh authors 821.00809429
English poetry—Women authors 821.00809287
English poetry—Women authors—History and criticism 821.0099287
English prose literature 828.08
English prose literature—Old English, ca. 450–1100 829.8
English prose literature—Old English, ca. 450–1100—Modernized versions 829.8
English prose literature—Early modern, 1500–1700 828.40808
English prose literature—Early modern, 1500–1700—History and criticism 828.40809
English prose literature—19th century 828.80808
English prose literature—19th century—History and criticism 828.80809
English prose literature—20th century 828.910808
English prose literature—20th century—History and criticism 823.91209
English prose literature—History and criticism 828.0809
English sparrow 598.887
English springer spaniels 636.7524
English teachers 420.92
English wit and humor 827; 828.02
English wit and humor, Pictorial 741.5942
Engraving 686.2314
Enhanced oil recovery 622.3382
Enigma cipher system 358.24; 940.548743
Enlightenment 190.9033; 940.25
Enlightenment—Europe 940.25
Enneagram 155.26
Enochian magic 133.43
Ensemble theater 792.6
Enteral feeding 615.854
Enterococcal infections 573.37399355; 616.3401455
Enteroscopy 616.3407545
Enterprise (Aircraft carrier : CVA(N) 65) 359.94350973
Enterprise zones 338.92
Entertainers 790.2092; 791.092
Entertainers—Biography 790.2092; 791.092
Entertainers in literature 808.80352791
Entertainers—Legal status, laws, etc. 344.099
Entertainers—Legal status, laws, etc.—United States 344.73099
Entertaining 642.4; 793.22
Entertainment centers (Cabinetwork) 684.16
Entertainment events 790.2
Entitlement spending 336.39
Entitlement spending—United States 336.39; 353.52460973
Entity-relationship modeling 005.756
Entomology 595.7
Entomology—Periodicals 595.705
Entrapment neuropathies 616.87
Entrées (Cookery) 641.82
Entrepreneurship 338.04; 658.421
Entrepreneurship—Periodicals 338.0405
Entrepreneurship—United States 338.040973; 658.4210973
Entropy 536.73
Entropy (Information theory) 003.54
Enuresis 618.92849
Environment (Aesthetics) 111.85
Environment and children 333.7083
Environment (Art) 709.04074
Environmental archaeology 930.1
Environmental auditing 363.706
Environmental chemistry 577.14; 628.50154
Environmental chemistry—Industrial applications 660

Environmental risk assessment—United States 363.700973

Environmental sciences 304.2; 363.7

Environmental sciences—Bibliography 016.3337

Environmental sciences—Dictionaries 363.7003

Environmental sciences—Encyclopedias 363.7003

Environmental sciences—Handbooks, manuals, etc. 363.7

Environmental sciences—Information services 025.063337

Environmental sciences—Mathematical models 304.20151

Environmental sciences—Periodicals 304.205; 363.7005

Environmental sciences—Statistical methods 363.700727

Environmental sciences—Study and teaching (Elementary) 372.357

Environmental sciences—Study and teaching (Elementary)—Activity programs 372.357044

Environmental sciences—Vocational guidance 363.70023

Environmental testing 363.70076

Environmental toxicology 615.902

Environmentalism 363.7

Environmentalism—Social aspects 304.2

Environmentalists 363.70092

Environmentally induced diseases 616.98

Enzymatic browning 664.00154723; 664.800154723

Enzyme inhibitors industry 338.476153

Enzyme kinetics 572.744

Enzymes 572.7; 612.0151

Enzymes—Biotechnology 660.634

Enzymes—Industrial applications 660.634

Enzymes—Therapeutic use 615.35

Enzymology 572.7; 612.0151

Ephemerides 528

Ephydridae 595.774

Epic films 791.436

EPIC (Information retrieval system) 025.04

Epic literature 808.8132

Epic literature—History and criticism 809

Epic literature, Irish 891.62103208

Epic literature, Irish—History and criticism 891.62103209

Epic literature, Irish—Translations into English 891.62103208

Epic poetry 808.8132

Epic poetry, Assyro-Babylonian 892.1

Epic poetry, Assyro-Babylonian—Translations into English 892.1

Epic poetry, Classical 883; 883.008; 883.01; 883.0108

Epic poetry, Classical—History and criticism 883.009; 883.0109

Epic poetry, English 821.032; 821.03208

Epic poetry, English—History and criticism 821.03209

Epic poetry, English (Old) 829.3

Epic poetry, English (Old)—History and criticism 829.109

Epic poetry, German 831.1032

Epic poetry, German—Translations into English 831.103208

Epic poetry, Greek 883; 883.008; 883.01; 883.0108

Epic poetry, Greek—History and criticism 883.009; 883.0109

Epic poetry, Greek—Translations into English 883.008; 883.0108

Epic poetry—History and criticism 809.132

Epic poetry, Latin 873; 873.01

Epic poetry, Latin—History and criticism 873.009; 873.0109

Epic poetry, Latin—Translations into English 873.008; 873.0108

Epicurus 187

Epidemics 614.4

Epidemics—History 614.49

Epidemiology 614.4

Epidemiology—Periodicals 614.405

Epidemiology—Research—Methodology 614.4072

Epidemiology—Statistical methods 614.40727

Epigrams 808.882

Epigrams, American 818.02

Epigrams, English 828.02

Epigrams, Latin 878.0102

Epigrams, Latin—Translations into English 878.010208

Epilepsy 362.196853; 616.853

Epilepsy—Chemotherapy 616.853061

Epilepsy in children 618.92853

Epilepsy in old age 618.976853

Epilepsy—Pathophysiology 616.85307

Epilepsy—Psychological aspects 616.8530019

Epilepsy—Surgery 617.481

Epiphytic lichens 579.7

Episcopacy 262.12

Episcopal Church 283.73

Episcopal Church—Doctrines 230.373

Episcopal Church—History 283.73

Episcopal Church—Liturgy 264.03

Episcopal Church—Liturgy—Texts 264.03

Episcopal Church—Relations—Evangelical Lutheran Church in America 280.042

Episcopal Church—Sermons 252.0373

Epistasis (Genetics) 572.865

Epistolary poetry, Latin 871; 871.01

Epistolary poetry, Latin—Translations into English 871.008; 871.0108

Epitaphs 929.5

Epithalamia 808.8193543; 821.00803543

Epithelium 571.55

Epoxy resins 668.374

Epton, Rosa (Fictitious character) 823.914

Epton, Rosa (Fictitious character)—Fiction 823.914

Equal rights amendments—United States 342.73085; 342.730878

Equality 305; 323.42

Equality before the law 342.085

Equality before the law—Canada 342.71085

Equality before the law—India 342.54085

Equality before the law—United States 342.73085

Equality—United States 305.0973

Equations 515.25

Equations—Numerical solutions 519.4

Equestrian centers 725.89

Equiano, Olaudah, b. 1745 305.567092

Equidae 599.665

Equilibration (Cognition) 155.413

Equilibrium (Economics) 339.5

Equilibrium (Economics)—Mathematical models 339.5015118

Equine dentistry 636.108976

Equine sports medicine 636.108971027

Equitable distribution of marital property 346.0166

Equitable distribution of marital property—United States 346.730166

Erasers 681.6

Erasmus, Desiderius, d. 1536 199.492

Ergodic theory 515.42

Ericaceae 583.66

Erie Canal (N.Y.)—History 386.4809747
Erie, Lake 977.12
Erie, Lake, Battle of, 1813 973.5254
Erigena, Johannes Scotus, ca. 810–ca. 877 189
Erikson, Erik H. (Erik Homburger), 1902– 150.195092
Erinaceidae 599.332
Eritrea 963.5
Eritrea—Guidebooks 916.3504; 916.350472
Eritrea—History 963.5
Eritrea—History—Revolution, 1962–1993 963.5071
Eritrea—Politics and government 963.5
Eritrea—Politics and government—1962–1993
    320.963509046; 963.5071
Eritrean-Ethiopian War, 1998– 963.5072
Ernie (Fictitious character : Henson) 791.4375;
    791.4575
Erosion 551.302
Erotic art 704.9428
Erotic drama 808.8293538
Erotic films 791.436538
Erotic films—Catalogs 016.791436538
Erotic films—History and criticism 791.43653809
Erotic literature 808.803538
Erotic literature, American 810.803538
Erotic literature—History and criticism 809.933538
Erotic poetry 808.8193538
Erotic poetry, American 811.00803538
Erotic stories 808.8393538
Erotic stories, American 013.00803538
Erotic stories, English 823.00803538
Erotica 700.4538; 808.803538
Erotomania 616.858
Error analysis (Mathematics) 511.43
Error-correcting codes (Information theory) 005.72
Error messages (Computer science) 005.3
Errors 001.96
Errors, Popular 001.96
Erythrocyte membranes 612.111
Erythrocytes 612.111
Escape artists 793.8
Escapes 365.641
Eschatology 236
Eschatology—Biblical teaching 236
Eschatology in rabbinical literature 296.33
Escher, M. C. (Maurits Cornelis), 1898–1972 769.92
Escherichia coli 579.342
Escort automobile 629.2222
Escort automobile—Maintenance and repair 629.28722
Escort automobile—Maintenance and repair—
    Handbooks, manuals, etc. 629.28722
Eskimo arts 704.039712
Eskimo sculpture 732.209701
Eskimos 305.8971; 979.8004971
Eskimos—Alaska 979.8004971
Eskimos—Folklore 398.2089971
Esophagus—Diseases 616.32
Esoteric astrology 133.5
Esperanto 499.992
Espionage 327.12
Espionage—Encyclopedias 327.1203
Espionage, Soviet 327.1247
Espionage, Soviet—United States 327.1247073
Espresso 641.877
Essay 809.4
Essay—Authorship 808.4
Essay—Authorship—Problems, exercises, etc. 808.02
Essays 808.84
Essence (Philosophy) 111.1
Essences and essential oils 661.806

Essenes 296.814
Essex County (Va.)—Genealogy 929.375534
Essiac 616.994061
Estate planning 346.052
Estate planning—Florida 346.759052
Estate planning—Massachusetts 346.744052
Estate planning—New Jersey 346.749052
Estate planning—Ohio 346.771052
Estate planning—Pennsylvania 346.748052
Estate planning—United States 346.73052
Estate planning—Virginia 346.755052
Estate sales 381.19
Estate settlement costs 657.47
Estefan, Gloria 782.42164092
Esther, Queen of Persia 220.9092
Estimation theory 519.544
Estonia 947.98
Estonia—Guidebooks 914.79804; 914.7980486
Estonia—History 947.98
Estonian language 494.545
Estrogen—Therapeutic use 618.175061
Estuaries 551.4609
Estuaries—Mathematical models 551.4609
Estuarine ecology 577.786
Estuarine oceanography 551.4609
Etching 767.2
Ether (Space) 530.1
Ether (Space)—History 530.1
Ethernet (Local area network system) 004.68
Ethical problems 170
Ethical relativism 171.7
Ethics 170
Ethics, Ancient 170.938
Ethics—China 170.951
Ethics—Encyclopedias 170.3
Ethics, Evolutionary 171.7
Ethics—History 170.9
Ethics in literature 808.80353; 809.93353
Ethics in the Bible 241
Ethics—India 170.954
Ethics—Japan 170.952
Ethics, Jewish 296.36
Ethics—Korea 170.9519
Ethics, Medieval 170.902
Ethics, Medieval, in literature 808.80353; 809.93353
Ethics, Modern 170
Ethics, Modern—17th century 170.9032
Ethics, Modern—18th century 170.9033
Ethics, Modern—19th century 170.9034
Ethics, Modern—20th century 170.904
Ethiopia 963
Ethiopia—Bibliography 016.963
Ethiopia—Civilization 963
Ethiopia—Description and travel 916.304; 916.30472
Ethiopia—Economic conditions 330.963
Ethiopia—Economic conditions—1974– 330.96307
Ethiopia—Economic policy 338.963
Ethiopia—Guidebooks 916.304; 916.30472
Ethiopia—History 963
Ethiopia—Periodicals 963.005
Ethiopia—Politics and government 963
Ethiopia—Politics and government—1974–1991
    320.96309048; 963.07
Ethiopia—Politics and government—1991–
    320.96309049; 963.07
Ethiopic book of Enoch 229.913
Ethiopic book of Enoch—Commentaries 229.913
Ethnic art 306.47089
Ethnic attitudes 303.387

Ethnic conflict 305.8
Ethnic groups 305.8
Ethnic relations 305.8
Ethnic relations—Political aspects 323.11
Ethnic restaurants 647.95089
Ethnicity 305.8
Ethnicity—Africa 305.80096
Ethnicity—Europe 305.80094
Ethnicity—India 305.800954
Ethnicity—United States 305.800973
Ethnoarchaeology 930.1089
Ethnoastronomy 520.89
Ethnobiology 306.45; 578.63
Ethnobotany 581.63
Ethnocentrism 305.8
Ethnographic informants 305.800723
Ethnohistory 909.04
Ethnological expeditions 305.8
Ethnological museums and collections 305.80074
Ethnology 305.8
Ethnology—Africa 305.80096; 599.97096
Ethnology—Africa, East 305.8009676
Ethnology—Africa, Southern 305.800968
Ethnology—Africa, Sub-Saharan 305.800967
Ethnology—Africa, West 305.800966
Ethnology—Asia 305.80095
Ethnology—Asia, Central 305.800958
Ethnology—Asia, Southeastern 305.800959
Ethnology—Australia 305.800994
Ethnology—Authorship 808.066305
Ethnology—Balkan Peninsula 305.8009496
Ethnology—Brazil 305.800981
Ethnology—Bulgaria 305.8009499
Ethnology—China 305.800951
Ethnology—Congo (Democratic Republic) 305.80096751
Ethnology—Ethiopia 305.800963
Ethnology—Europe 599.97094
Ethnology—Europe, Eastern 305.800947
Ethnology—Field work 305.800723
Ethnology—French Polynesia—Tahiti 305.800996211
Ethnology—Great Britain 305.800941
Ethnology—Hungary 305.8009439
Ethnology—India 305.800954
Ethnology—Indonesia 305.8009598
Ethnology—Japan 305.800952
Ethnology—Kenya 305.80096762
Ethnology—Madagascar 305.8009691
Ethnology—Melanesia 305.800995
Ethnology—Methodology 305.8001
Ethnology—Middle East 305.800956
Ethnology—Nepal 305.80095496
Ethnology—Nigeria 305.8009669
Ethnology—Oceania 305.800995
Ethnology—Papua New Guinea 305.8009953
Ethnology—Periodicals 305.8005
Ethnology—Philippines 305.8009599
Ethnology—Philosophy 305.8001
Ethnology—Poland 305.8009438
Ethnology—Polynesia 305.800996
Ethnology—Religious aspects 291.175
Ethnology—Research 305.80072
Ethnology—South Africa 305.800968
Ethnology—Soviet Union 305.800947
Ethnology—Spain 305.800946
Ethnology—Taiwan 305.800941249
Ethnology—Thailand 305.8009593
Ethnology—Ukraine 305.8009477
Ethnology—United States 305.800973
Ethnology—Vietnam 305.8009597

Ethnomathematics 510.89
Ethnomathematics—Africa, Sub-Saharan 510.967
Ethnomethodology 305.8001
Ethnomusicology 780.89
Ethnophilosophy 305.8001
Ethnopsychology 155.82
Ethnopsychology—Africa 155.82096
Ethnoscience 001.089; 500.89
Etiquette 395
Etiquette for children and teenagers 395.122; 395.123
Etiquette in literature 808.80355; 809.93355
Etiquette—United States 395.0973
Etruscan language 499.94
Etruscans 937.501
Euastacus 595.384
Eucalyptus 583.766
Eugenics 363.92
Eugenics in literature 808.80355; 809.93355
Eukaryotic cells 571.6
Eulogies 808.51
Euphausiacea 595.389
Euphonium 788.975; 788.97519
Eurasian red squirrel 599.362
Euripides 882.01
Euripides—Criticism and interpretation 882.01
Euripides. Hippolytus 882.01
Euripides—Translations into English 882.01
Euro 332.4566094; 332.494
Euro-bond market 336.31
Euro-dollar market 332.45
Eurocentrism in literature 808.80355; 809.93355
Europe 940
Europe—Antiquities 936
Europe, Central 943
Europe, Central—Economic conditions 330.943
Europe, Central—Economic policy 338.943
Europe, Central—History 943
Europe—Civilization 940
Europe—Civilization—1945- 940.55
Europe—Civilization—American influences 940; 940.55
Europe—Cultural policy 306.094
Europe—Defenses 355.03304
Europe—Description and travel 914.04; 914.04559; 914.0456
Europe, Eastern 947
Europe, Eastern—Commerce 382.0947
Europe, Eastern—Economic conditions 330.947
Europe, Eastern—Economic conditions—1945–1989 330.9470009045
Europe, Eastern—Economic conditions—1989- 330.9470009049
Europe, Eastern—Economic conditions—1989- —Periodicals 330.9470009049
Europe, Eastern—Economic policy 338.947
Europe, Eastern—Economic policy—1989- 338.947
Europe, Eastern—Ethnic relations 305.800947
Europe, Eastern—Foreign relations 327.0947
Europe, Eastern—Foreign relations—1945–1989 327.0947
Europe, Eastern—Foreign relations—Soviet Union 327.47047
Europe, Eastern—Foreign relations—United States 327.73047
Europe, Eastern—Guidebooks 914.704
Europe, Eastern—History 947
Europe, Eastern—History—1945- 947.0009045
Europe, Eastern—History—1945–1989 947.0009045
Europe, Eastern—History—1989- 947.0009049
Europe, Eastern—Politics and government 947

European Union countries—Politics and government 320.94
European Union countries—Social policy 361.61094
European Union—Great Britain 337.4041
Europeans 305.8034
Europeans—Africa 305.803406
Europeans—Islands of the Pacific 305.803409
Eurythmics 372.868; 780.71
Euthanasia 179.7
Euthanasia—Moral and ethical aspects 179.7
Eutrophication 577.63158
Evaluation 001.4
Evaluation research (Social action programs) 361.61072
Evangelicalism 230.04624; 270.82
Evangelicalism—Relations—Catholic Church 280.042
Evangelicalism—United States 280.40973
Evangelicalism—United States—History 277.3082
Evangelicalism—United States—History—20th century 277.3082
Evangelistic sermons 252.3
Evangelistic work 269.2
Evangelistic work—Philosophy 269.201
Evangelistic work—United States 269.20973
Evangelists 269.2092
Evans, Evan (Fictitious character) 823.914
Evans family 929.20973
Evaporation 536.44
Evaporation—Physiological effect 572.539
Evaporative cooling 697.93
Evaporites 552.5
Evening and continuation schools 374.8
Event history analysis 300.722
Eventing (Horsemanship) 798.24
Events (Philosophy) 111
Everard, Nick (Fictitious character) 823.914
Everglades (Fla.) 975.939
Everson, William, 1912– 811.52
Everworld (Imaginary place) 813.54
Evidence-based dentistry 617.6
Evidence-based medicine 616
Evidence, Criminal 345.06
Evidence, Criminal—Canada 345.7106
Evidence, Criminal—Great Britain 345.4106
Evidence, Criminal—United States 345.7306
Evidence, Expert 347.067
Evidence, Expert—United States 345.73067; 347.7367
Evidence (Law) 347.06; 347.736
Evidence (Law)—Australia 347.9406
Evidence (Law)—California 347.79406
Evidence (Law)—Florida 347.75906
Evidence (Law)—Great Britain 347.4106
Evidence (Law)—Indiana 347.77206
Evidence (Law)—Louisiana 347.76306
Evidence (Law)—Massachusetts 347.74406
Evidence (Law)—Michigan 347.77406
Evidence (Law)—Missouri 347.77806
Evidence (Law)—New York (State) 347.74706
Evidence (Law)—North Carolina 347.75606
Evidence (Law)—Ohio 347.77106
Evidence (Law)—Oklahoma 347.76606
Evidence (Law)—Pennsylvania 347.74806
Evidence (Law)—Philippines 347.59906
Evidence (Law)—Texas 347.76406
Evidence (Law)—United States 347.736
Evidence (Law)—United States—Cases 347.736; 347.7360264
Evidence (Law)—United States—Outlines, syllabi, etc. 347.736

Evidence (Law)—Virginia 347.75506
Evidence preservation 363.24
Evidence, Prima facie 347.06
Evidence, Prima facie—United States 347.736
Evolution 116; 213; 576.8
Evolution (Biology) 576.8; 576.82; 591.38
Evolution (Biology)—History 576.809
Evolution (Biology)—Mathematical models 576.8015118
Evolution (Biology)—Philosophy 576.801
Evolution equations 515.353
Evolution equations, Nonlinear 515.353
Evolution—Religious aspects 213
Evolution—Religious aspects—Christianity 231.7652
Evolutionary computation 006.32
Evolutionary economics 330.1
Evolutionary genetics 572.838
Evolutionary paleobiology 560; 576.8
Evolutionary paleoecology 560.45
Evolutionary programming (Computer science) 005.1
Evolutionary robotics 629.892
Ewing family 929.20973
Ewing, Patrick Aloysius, 1962– 796.323092
eWorld (Online service) 025.04
Ex-church members 248.24
Ex-church members—Catholic Church 248.24
Ex-concentration camp inmates 365.45; 940.5317; 940.5318
Ex-concentration camp inmates—Return visits to concentration camp sites 365.45; 940.5317; 940.5318
Ex-convicts 364.8
Ex-Jews 305.8924
Ex-police officers 363.2
Ex-prime ministers 321
Ex-smokers 613.85
Examination of witnesses 347.075
Examination of witnesses—United States 347.7375
Examinations 371.26
Examinations—Design and construction 371.261
Examinations—Study guides 371.26076
Examinations—Validity 371.26013
Exarchates 281.9
Excavating machinery 624.1520284
Excavations (Archaeology) 930.1
Excavations (Archaeology)—Cyprus 939.37; 956.93
Excavations (Archaeology)—Egypt 932; 962
Excavations (Archaeology)—England 936.2; 942
Excavations (Archaeology)—Great Britain 936.1
Excavations (Archaeology)—Greece 938; 949.5
Excavations (Archaeology)—India 934; 954
Excavations (Archaeology)—Interpretive programs 930.1
Excavations (Archaeology)—Iraq 935; 956.7
Excavations (Archaeology)—Israel 933; 956.94
Excavations (Archaeology)—Italy 937; 945
Excavations (Archaeology)—Middle East 939.4
Excavations (Archaeology)—Spain 936.6; 946
Excavations (Archaeology)—Syria 939.43; 956.91
Excavations (Archaeology)—Turkey 939.2; 939.4; 956
Excavations (Archaeology)—Ukraine 947.7
Exceptional children 362.7
Exceptional children—Psychology 155.45
Exchange of oceanographic information 551.460072
Exchange of persons programs 303.482
Exchanges, Literary and scientific 370.116
Excimer lasers 621.3663
Excise tax 336.271
Excise tax—Law and legislation 343.0553
Excise tax—Law and legislation—United States 343.730553

Excited state chemistry 541.22
Exciton theory 530.416
Exclosures 333.9516; 639.95
Excommunication 262.935
Executions and executioners 364.66
Executions and executioners—United States 364.660973
Executions (Law) 347.077
Executions (Law)—Alaska 347.798077
Executions (Law)—United States 346.73077
Executive ability 658.409
Executive advisory bodies 352.743
Executive departments 351
Executive departments—Alabama 351.761
Executive departments—Alabama—Handbooks, manuals, etc. 351.761
Executive departments—California 351.794
Executive departments—Great Britain 351.41
Executive departments—India 351.54
Executive departments—Reorganization 352.29
Executive departments—United States 351.73
Executive departments—United States—Directories 351.73025
Executive departments—United States—Management 351.73
Executive departments—United States—Management— Data processing 351.7302854
Executive power 352.235
Executive power—United States 352.2350973
Executive privilege (Government information) 342.06
Executive search firms 331.120; 650.407111
Executives 658.4
Executives—Health programs 362.1088658; 658.40782
Executives—Protection 362.88; 658.473
Executives—Psychology 658.40019; 658.409
Executives—Recruiting 658.407111
Executives—Salaries, etc. 331.2816584; 658.4072; 658.40722
Executives—Salaries, etc.—Law and legislation—United States 344.73012816584
Executives—Salaries, etc.—United States 331.281658400973; 658.40720973; 658.407220973
Executives—Salaries, etc.—United States—Periodicals 658.4072097305
Executives—Salaries, etc.—United States—Statistics 331.281658400973021
Executives—Salaries, etc.—United States—Statistics— Periodicals 331.281658400973021
Executives' spouses 306.876
Executives—Time management 658.4093
Executives—Training of 658.407124
Executives—United States 658.4
Executives—United States—Recruiting—Directories 658.40711102573
Executors and administrators 346.052
Executors and administrators—Massachusetts 346.744056
Executors and administrators—United States 346.73056
Exemplary damages 346.03
Exemplary damages—United States 346.7303
Exercise 613.71
Exercise for middle aged persons 613.710844
Exercise for pregnant women 618.24
Exercise for the aged 613.710846
Exercise for women 613.71082
Exercise—Health aspects 613.7; 613.71
Exercise—Immunological aspects 616.079
Exercise—Physiological aspects 612.044
Exercise—Psychological aspects 613.71; 613.71019
Exercise therapy 615.82

Exhibition catalogs 069.52; 907.4
Exhibition equipment and supplies industry 338.47659152
Exhibitions 659.152; 907.4
Exiles' writings 808.89920691
Exiles' writings—History and criticism 809.8920694
Existential psychology 150.192
Existential psychotherapy 616.8914
Existentialism 142.78
Existentialism in literature 808.80384; 809.93384
Exogeneity (Econometrics) 330.015195
Exotic animals 591.6; 599.16
Exotic birds 636.6
Exotic options (Finance) 332.645
Exotic plants 581.6
Exotic shorthair cat 636.82
Expanding universe 523.18
Expansion boards (Microcomputers) 004.53
Expatriate sculptors 730.92
Expectation-maximization algorithms 519.54
Expenditures, Public 336.39; 352.46
Experience 128.4
Experience (Religion) 291.42
Experiential learning 370.1523
Experimental design 001.434
Experimental fiction, American 813.008011
Experimental films 791.4375
Experimental films—United States—History and criticism 791.43750973
Experimental forests 634.9072
Experimental theater 792.022
Expert systems (Computer science) 006.33
Expert systems (Computer science)—Periodicals 006.3305
Expertise 153.4
Explicit memory 153.13
Exploitation 179.8
Exploitation films 791.43655
Explorers 910.92; 910.922
Explorers—Biography 910.922
Explorers—Biography—Dictionaries 910.922
Explosive ordnance disposal 604.7
Explosives 662.2
Explosives, Military 623.452
Export controls 343.0878; 354.7328; 382.64
Export controls—United States 343.730878; 354.73280973; 382.640973
Export credit 332.742; 382.63
Export credit—Periodicals 332.742
Export marketing 658.848
Export marketing—Handbooks, manuals, etc. 658.848
Export marketing—Management 658.848
Export marketing—Social aspects 658.848
Export marketing—United States 658.8480973
Export marketing—United States—Handbooks, manuals, etc. 658.8480973
Export marketing—United States—Management 658.8480973
Export sales contracts 341.754
Export sales contracts—Great Britain 343.410878
Export sales contracts—Taxation 336.263
Export sales contracts—United States 343.730878
Export trading companies 382.6065
Exports 382.6
Exports—Developing countries 382.6091724
Exports—United States 382.60973
Exports—United States—Finance 332.742
Exports—United States—Statistics 382.60973021
Exposition (Rhetoric) 808.066

Express highway interchanges 388.13; 625.7
Express highways 388.122
Express service 388.044
Express trains 385.22
Express trains—United States 385.220973
Expressionism (Art) 709.04042
Expressionism in literature 808.80115; 809.9115
Exterior insulation and finish systems 693.832
Exterior walls 690.12
Externalities (Economics) 330.1
Exterritoriality 341.4
Extinct animals 560; 591.68
Extinct birds 568; 598.168
Extinct insects 565.7
Extinct languages 417.7
Extinction (Biology) 333.95137; 576.84; 591.38
Extortion investigation 363.25965
Extracellular matrix 571.5; 611.0182
Extracellular matrix proteins 572.6
Extrachromosomal DNA 572.869
Extraction (Chemistry) 543.0892
Extraction (Linguistics) 415
Extradition 341.488
Extradition—United States 341.4880973
Extranets (Computer networks) 004.6; 650.028546
Extrapyramidal disorders 616.83
Extrasensory perception 133.8
Extrasensory perception in animals 133.89
Extrasolar planets 523
Extreme environments—Microbiology 579.1758
Extreme sports 796.046
Exxon Valdez (Ship) 363.7382097983
Eye 573.88; 591.4; 611.84; 612.84
Eye—Accommodation and refraction 612.84; 617.755
Eye—Anatomy 611.84
Eye—Care and hygiene 617.706
Eye—Diseases 617.7
Eye—Diseases—Atlases 617.700222
Eye—Diseases—Diagnosis 617.715
Eye—Diseases—Genetic aspects 617.7042
Eye—Diseases—Handbooks, manuals, etc. 617.7
Eye—Diseases—Immunological aspects 617.71
Eye—Examination 617.715
Eye—Examination—Handbooks, manuals, etc. 617.715
Eye—Laser surgery 617.71
Eye movement desensitization and reprocessing 616.85210651
Eye—Movements 573.88; 612.846
Eye—Physiology 612.84
Eye—Surgery 617.71
Eye—Surgery—Atlases 617.71
Eye—Surgery—Complications 617.701
Eye—Wounds and injuries 617.713
Eyeglass frames 617.7522
Eyeglasses 617.7522
Eyelids—Surgery 617.771059
Eyespot (Plant disease) 633.10494
Eyewitness identification 345.066
Eyewitness identification—United States 345.73066
Ezekiel, Nissim, 1924– 821.914
Ezekiel, Nissim, 1924– —Criticism and interpretation 821.914
F-16 (Jet fighter plane) 358.4383
F-100 (Jet fighter plane) 358.4383
F-111 (Jet fighter plane) 358.4383; 623.7464
F-117 (Jet fighter plane) 358.4383
F (Computer program language) 005.133
Fabergé eggs 739.2
Fabergé (Firm) 729.206

Fabergé, Peter Carl, 1846–1920 739.2092
Fabergé, Peter Carl, 1846–1920—Catalogs 739.2092
Fables 398.24
Fables, African 398.209604
Fables, American 398.2097304
Fables, English 398.20421
Fables, French 398.2094404
Fables, French—Translations into English 398.2094404
Fables, Greek 398.20949504
Fables, Greek—Translations into English 398.20949504
Fables, Latin 398.20471
Fables, Latin—Translations into English 398.20471
Fables, Nahuatl 398.208997452
Fables—Translations into English 398.24
Fabulous Four (Fictitious characters) 823.914
Face 611.92
Face—Care and hygiene 646.726
Face in art 704.942
Face painting 745.5
Face perception 153.75
Face—Surgery 617.520592
Face—Wounds and injuries 617.52044
Facelift 617.520592
Facial expression 153.69
Facial nerve 612.81
Facial paralysis 616.842
Facility management 658.2
Facsimile transmission 384.14
Facsimile transmission—United States—Directories 384.14
Factor analysis 519.5354
Factories—Design and construction 690.54; 725.4
Factories—Power supply 621.31
Factoring (Finance) 332.84
Factoring services industry 332.84
Factorization (Mathematics) 512.74
Factory and trade waste 363.7288; 628.4
Factory and trade waste—Incineration 628.4457
Factory and trade waste—Management 628.4068
Factory and trade waste—Purification 628.4; 628.445
Factory management 658.5
Facts (Philosophy) 111
Faculty advisors 378.194; 378.194046
Fads 306
Faeroes pony 636.16
Failure (Psychology) 158.1
Failure (Psychology)—Religious aspects 291.442
Failure (Psychology)—Religious aspects—Christianity 248.4
Failure time data analysis 519.5
Fair use (Copyright) 346.0482
Fair use (Copyright)—United States 346.730482
Fairacre (England : Imaginary place) 823.914
Fairacre (England : Imaginary place)—Fiction 823.914
Fairchild, Faith Sibley (Fictitious character) 813.54
Fairchild, Faith Sibley (Fictitious character)—Fiction 813.54
Fairfax County (Va.)—Genealogy 929.3755291
Fairfax County (Va.)—Maps 912.755291
Fairfield County (Conn.)—Maps 912.7469
Fairfield County (Ohio) 977.158
Fairfield County (Ohio)—Genealogy 929.377158
Fairies 398.21
Fairies in literature 808.80375; 809.93375
Fairness 179.9
Fairweather, Doran (Fictitious character) 823.914
Fairweather, Doran (Fictitious character)—Fiction 823.914
Fairy poetry, English 821.0080375

Fairy tales 398.2
Fairy tales—Arab countries 398.22
Fairy tales—Denmark 398.209489
Fairy tales—France 398.20944
Fairy tales—France—Translations into English
398.20944
Fairy tales—Germany 398.20943
Fairy tales—History and criticism 398.209
Fairy tales—Indexes 016.3982
Fairy tales—Ireland 398.209415
Fairy tales—Japan 398.20952
Fairy tales—Norway 398.209481
Fairy tales—Russia 398.20947
Faith 234.23
Faith and reason 210
Faith—Biblical teaching 234.23
Faith movement (Hagin) 289.94
Faiz, Faiz Ahmad, 1911– 891.43917
Faiz, Faiz Ahmad, 1911– —Translations into English
891.43917
Falco, Marcus Didius (Fictitious character) 823.914
Falco, Marcus Didius (Fictitious character)—Fiction
823.914
Falconiformes 598.9
Falconry 799.232
Falkland Islands 997.11
Falkland Islands—History 997.11
Falkland Islands War, 1982 997.11024
Fall of man in literature 808.803823314; 809.933823314
Fallacies (Logic) 165
Falls (Accidents) in old age—Prevention 613.6;
617.100846
False memory syndrome 616.85822390651
Falstaff, John, Sir (Fictitious character) 822.33
Familial behavior in animals 591.563
Families of clergy 253.22; 270
Families of military personnel 355.12
Families of prisoners of war 362.829
Families of the mentally ill 362.2
Family 306.85
Family—Africa 306.85096
Family—Anecdotes 306.85
Family—Arkansas 306.8509767
Family assessment 616.89156
Family—Australia 306.850994
Family—California 306.8509794
Family—Canada 306.850971
Family—Canada—Statistics 306.850971021
Family—Caricatures and cartoons 741.5973
Family corporations—Management 658.045
Family corporations—United States 346.730668
Family counseling 362.8286
Family day care 362.712
Family day care—United States 362.7120973
Family demography 306.85
Family—Economic aspects—United States 306.850973
Family—England 306.850942
Family—England—History 306.850942
Family—England—London 306.8509421
Family—England—Midlands 306.8509424
Family—England, Northern 306.8509427
Family—Europe 306.85094
Family farms 636.01
Family farms—United States 338.16
Family festivals—United States 394.2
Family—Georgia 306.8509758
Family—Great Britain 306.850941
Family—Great Britain—History 306.850941
Family—Health and hygiene 613

Family—History 306.8509
Family—Illinois 306.8509773
Family—India 306.850954
Family—Indiana 306.8509771
Family—Ireland 306.8509415
Family life 306.85
Family life education 372.82; 646.7
Family—Massachusetts 306.8509744
Family medicine 610
Family medicine—Examinations, questions, etc. 610.76
Family medicine—Handbooks, manuals, etc. 610
Family medicine—Outlines, syllabi, etc. 610
Family—Mental health 616.89156
Family—Mississippi 306.8509762
Family—Montana 306.8509786
Family—New England 306.850974
Family—New York (State) 306.8509747
Family—New York (State)—New York 306.85097471
Family—North Carolina 306.8509756
Family nursing 610.73
Family-owned business enterprises 338.7
Family-owned business enterprises—Management
658.04
Family policy 362.82561
Family policy—United States 306.850973
Family—Prayer-books and devotions 249
Family—Psychological aspects 306.85
Family psychotherapy 616.89156
Family psychotherapy—Periodicals 616.8915605
Family recreation 790.191; 796
Family recreation—United States 649.50973
Family—Religious life 248.4
Family—Research 306.85072
Family reunions 394.2
Family reunions—United States—Planning 394.2
Family services 362.82
Family services—United States 362.8280973
Family social work 362.8253
Family—Southern States 306.850975
Family staging 616.8914
Family—Texas 306.8509764
Family therapists 616.89156092
Family—United States 306.850973
Family—United States—History 306.850973
Family—United States—Psychological aspects
306.850973
Family—United States—Religious life 248.4
Family violence 362.8292
Family violence—United States 362.82920973
Family violence—United States—Prevention
362.829270973
Family—Virginia 306.8509755
Family—Wales 306.8509429
Famines 363.8
Famines—Ethiopia 363.80963
Famines—Ireland—History—19th century
363.80941509034
Fancy work 746.4
Fanfares 784.18924
Fangs 591.47
Fans (Machinery) 621.61
Fans (Persons) 306.487
Fansler, Kate (Fictitious character) 813.54
Fansler, Kate (Fictitious character)—Fiction 813.54
Fantastic architecture 720
Fantasy 154.3
Fantasy comedies (Motion pictures) 791.43675
Fantasy drama 808.82915; 809.2915
Fantasy fiction 808.838766

Fantasy fiction, American 813.08766; 813.0876608
Fantasy fiction, American—Bibliography 016.81308766
Fantasy fiction, Canadian 808.83876608971;
    813.08766080971
Fantasy fiction, English 823.08766; 823.0876608
Fantasy fiction, English—History and criticism
    823.0876609
Fantasy fiction, English—Irish authors 823.08766089415
Fantasy fiction, French 843.08766
Fantasy fiction, French—Translations into English
    843.0876608
Fantasy fiction—History and criticism 809.38766
Fantasy fiction, Scottish 823.08766089411
Fantasy films 791.43615
Fantasy films—History and criticism 791.4361509
Fantasy films—Plots, themes, etc. 791.43615
Fantasy football (Game) 796.332
Fantasy football (Game)—Periodicals 796.332
Fantasy games 793.93
Fantasy in advertising 659.1
Fantasy in art 700.415
Fantasy in literature 808.8015; 809.915
Fantasy literature 808.8015
Fantasy literature, American 810.8015
Fantasy literature, English 820.8015
Fantasy literature, English—History and criticism
    820.915
Fantasy literature—History and criticism 809.38766;
    809.915
Fantasy poetry, American 811.008015
Fantasy poetry, English 821.008015
Fanzines 070.48
Faraday, Michael, 1791–1867 530.092
Faribault County (Minn.) 977.622
Faribault County (Minn.)—Maps 912.77622
Farm equipment 631.3
Farm life 630
Farm life—Africa, Southern 630.968
Farm life—Australia 630.994
Farm life—England 630.942; 914.2
Farm life—United States 630.973; 917.3
Farm life—Wales 630.9429; 914.29
Farm management 630.68
Farm produce 338.1
Farm produce—Marketing 630.688; 635.0688
Farm produce—United States—Marketing 630.688;
    635.0688
Farm tractors 629.2252
Farm tractors—United States—History 629.2252
Farmers 305.555; 630.92
Farmers' markets 381.41
Farms 630
Faro, Jeremy (Fictitious character) 823.914
Faro, Jeremy (Fictitious character)—Fiction 823.914
Farragut, David Glasgow, 1801–1870 973.75092
Farrakhan, Louis 297.87
Farrell, John Sebastian (Fictitious character) 813.54
Farrow, Mia, 1945– 791.43028092
Fasciola 592.48
Fascioliasis 616.362; 636.0896362
Fascism 320.533
Fascism—Germany 335.60943
Fascism—Italy 320.5330945
Fascism—Italy—1945– 335.60945
Fascism—Italy—History 320.5330945
Fashion 391
Fashion designers 746.92092
Fashion designers—Biography 746.92092
Fashion drawing 741.672

Fashion—History 391.009
Fashion merchandising 687.0688
Fashion merchandising—United States 687.0688
Fashion—Periodicals 391.005
Fashion photography 778.99391
Fassbinder, Rainer Werner, 1946– 791.430233092
Fassbinder, Rainer Werner, 1946– —Criticism and
    interpretation 791.430233092
Fast food restaurants 647.95
Fasteners 621.88
Fasting 248.47
Fasts and feasts 263.9
Fasts and feasts—Hinduism 294.536
Fasts and feasts—Judaism 296.43
Fasts and feasts—Judaism—Meditations 296.43
Father and child 306.8742
Fatherhood 306.8742
Fatherhood—Religious aspects 291.44
Fatherhood—Religious aspects—Christianity 248.8421
Fatherhood—United States 306.87420973
Fathers 306.8742
Fathers and daughters 306.8742
Fathers and daughters—England 306.8742
Fathers and daughters—Québec (Province) 306.8742
Fathers and daughters—Religious aspects 291.441
Fathers and daughters—Southern States 306.8742
Fathers and daughters—United States 306.8742
Fathers and sons 306.8742
Fathers and sons—California 306.8742
Fathers and sons—England 306.8742
Fathers and sons—England—London 306.8742
Fathers and sons—Montana 306.8742
Fathers and sons—Scotland 306.8742
Fathers and sons—United States 306.8742
Fathers of Confederation (Canada) 971.0490922
Fathers of the church 270.1; 281.3
Fathers—Prayer-books and devotions 242.6421
Fathers—Psychology 306.8742
Fathers—Religious life 248.8421
Fathers—United States 306.87420973
Fatigue 152.1886
Fatigue—Prevention 613
Fatou theorems 515.9
Fatty acids 547.77
Fatty acids—Metabolism 572.574; 612.397
Faucets 621.84
Faulkner family 929.20973
Faulkner, William, 1897–1962 813.52
Faulkner, William, 1897–1962. Absalom, Absalom!
    813.52
Faulkner, William, 1897–1962. As I lay dying 813.52
Faulkner, William, 1897–1962—Criticism and
    interpretation 813.52
Faulkner, William, 1897–1962. Go down, Moses 813.52
Faulkner, William, 1897–1962—Knowledge—History
    813.52
Faulkner, William, 1897–1962—Knowledge—
    Psychology 813.52
Faulkner, William, 1897–1962—Manuscripts 813.52
Faulkner, William, 1897–1962—Political and social
    views 813.52
Faulkner, William, 1897–1962. Sound and the fury
    813.52
Faulkner, William, 1897–1962—Technique 813.52
Fault location (Engineering) 620.0044
Fault tolerance (Engineering) 620.00452
Fault-tolerant computing 004.2
Fault zones 551.22; 551.872
Faults (Geology) 551.872

Fauquier County (Va.)—Genealogy 929.3755275
Fauquier County (Va.)—Maps 912.755275
Faux pas 395
Favored nation clause 382.9
Favored nation clause—United States 382.973
Favre, Brett 796.332092
Favre family 929.20973
Fax machines 621.38235
Fayette County (Ill.) 977.3797
Fayette County (Ill.)—Maps 912.773797
Fayette County (Iowa) 977.735
Fayette County (Iowa)—Maps 912.77735
Fayette County (W. Va.)—Genealogy 929.375471
Fear 152.46
Fear in children 155.41246
Fear in literature 808.80353; 809.93353
Fear of flying 616.85225
Feature writing 070.44
Fecal incontinence 616.35
Federal aid to child welfare 362.7
Federal aid to early childhood education 379.112;
    379.1212; 379.322
Federal aid to education 379.121
Federal aid to higher education 379.1214
Federal aid to higher education—United States
    379.12140973
Federal aid to housing 353.55273; 363.582
Federal aid to Indians—United States 353.53497
Federal aid to medical research 610.79
Federal aid to minority business enterprises—United
    States 354.279908
Federal aid to research 352.74
Federal aid to research—United States 338.97306
Federal aid to services for the homeless 362.58
Federal Crop Insurance Corporation 368.12100973
Federal government 321.02
Federal government—Australia 320.494
Federal government—Canada 320.471; 342.71042
Federal government—Canada—History 320.471
Federal government—India 320.454; 342.54042
Federal government—Soviet Union 320.447
Federal government—United States 320.473; 342.73042
Federal Reserve banks 332.110973
Federalist 342.73029
Federations, Financial (Social service) 361.7
Feed-water purification 628.162
Feed-water purification—Handbooks, manuals, etc.
    628.162
Feedback control systems 629.83
Feeding of the five thousand (Miracle) 226.7
Feeds 636.085; 664.66; 664.76
Feeds—Biotechnology 664.76
Feeds—Composition 636.0852
Feeds—Enzyme content 636.08522
Feeds—Vitamin content 636.08528
Feiffer, Harry (Fictitious character) 823.914
Feiffer, Harry (Fictitious character)—Fiction 823.914
Feldenkrais method 613.71; 615.82
Felidae 599.75
Felis 599.752
Fell, Gideon (Fictitious character) 813.52
Fell, Gideon (Fictitious character)—Fiction 813.52
Fellini, Federico 791.430233092
Fellini, Federico—Criticism and interpretation
    791.430233092
Felse, George (Fictitious character) 823.912
Felse, George (Fictitious character)—Fiction 823.912
Felt work 746.0463
Female circumcision 392.1

Female friendship 302.34082
Female friendship—England 302.340820942
Female friendship—Religious aspects 291.56762
Female juvenile delinquents 364.36082
Female juvenile delinquents—United States
    364.360820973
Female nude in art 704.9424
Female offenders 364.374
Female offenders—United States 364.3740973
Female sex offenders 364.153082
Femininity 155.333
Femininity of God 231.4; 291.2114
Femininity—Religious aspects 291.44
Feminism 305.42
Feminism and art 701.03; 704.042
Feminism and art—United States 701.03; 704.0420973
Feminism and education 370.822
Feminism and motion pictures 791.43082
Feminism and music 780.82
Feminism and the arts 700.103
Feminism and theater 792.082
Feminism—Australia 305.420994
Feminism—Bibliography 016.30542
Feminism—Canada 305.420971
Feminism—Great Britain 305.420941
Feminism—Great Britain—History 305.420941
Feminism—History 305.4209
Feminism—India 305.420954
Feminism—Literary collections 808.80355
Feminism—Periodicals 305.4205
Feminism—Political aspects 305.42
Feminism—Religious aspects 291.1783442
Feminism—Religious aspects—Christianity 261.83442
Feminism—Religious aspects—Judaism 296.38
Feminism—United States 305.420973
Feminism—United States—History 305.420973
Feminism—United States—History—19th century
    305.42097309034
Feminism—United States—History—20th century
    305.4209730904
Feminist criminology 364.082
Feminist criticism 305.4201
Feminist economics 330.082
Feminist ethics 170.82
Feminist jurisprudence 340.082
Feminist literary criticism 801.95082; 809.89287
Feminist music—History and criticism 780.82
Feminist psychology 150.82
Feminist television criticism 791.45082
Feminist theology 230.082
Feminist theory 305.4201
Feminist theory—United States 305.420973
Feminists 305.42092
Fen, Gervase (Fictitious character) 823.912
Fen, Gervase (Fictitious character)—Fiction 823.912
Fences 631.27
Fences—Design and construction 631.27; 717
Fencing 796.86
Fenestellidae 564.67
Feng shui 133.3337
Feng shui gardens 635; 712.2
Feng shui in interior decoration 747
Fenians 941.7081; 971.048
Fenn family 929.20973; 929.20994
Fens, The (England) 942.6
Fens, The (England)—Antiquities 936.26
Fens, The (England)—History 942.6
Ferguson family 929.20973
Fermat's last theorem 512.74

Fermentation 660.28449; 664.024
Fermi surfaces 530.417
Ferns 587.3
Ferns, Ornamental 635.9373
Ferrari automobile 629.2222
Ferrari automobile—History 629.2222
Ferret 599.76628
Ferrets as pets 636.976628
Ferries 386.2234
Ferroelectric crystals 548.85
Ferroelectric devices 621.31042
Ferroelectric thin films 621.38152
Ferroelectricity 537.2448
Ferromagnetism 538.45
Fertility clinics 362.19692
Fertility, Human 612.6
Fertility, Human—Developing countries 304.632091724
Fertilization (Biology) 571.864
Fertilization in vitro, Human 618.178059
Fertilization in vitro, Human—Moral and ethical aspects 176
Fertilizer requirements 631.811
Fertilizers 631.8
Fescue 584.9
Festivals 394.26
Festivals—China 394.26951
Festivals—Europe 394.2694
Festivals—India 394.26954
Festivals—Japan 394.26952
Festivals—Mexico 394.26972
Festivals—United States 394.26973
Fetal alcohol syndrome 618.3268
Fetal growth retardation 618.32
Fetal monitoring 618.32075
Fetishism (Sexual behavior) 306.77
Fetoscopy 618.3207545
Fett, Boba (Fictitious character) 741.5973; 791.4375
Fetterman Fight, Wyo., 1866 973.81
Fetus 612.647
Fetus—Abnormalities 618.32
Fetus—Diseases 618.32
Fetus—Effect of drugs on 618.32
Fetus—Effect of tobacco on 614.599232; 618.32
Fetus—Growth 612.647
Fetus—Physiology 612.64; 612.647
Fetus—Ultrasonic imaging 618.3207543
Feudal law 340.55
Feudalism 321.3
Feudalism—Japan 320.452
Fever 616.047
Few-body problem 530.14
Feyerabend, Paul K., 1924– 193
Feynman diagrams 539.750223
Feynman, Richard Phillips 530.092
Fezzes 391.43
Fiat 128 automobile 629.2222
Fiber bundles (Mathematics) 514.224
Fiber deficiency diseases 616.396
Fiber in human nutrition 612.3; 613.28
Fiber optic cables 621.3692
Fiber optics 621.3692
Fiber optics industry 338.476213692
Fiber optics—Periodicals 621.369205
Fiber optics—Reliability 621.3692
Fibers 620.197; 677.02832
Fiberwork 620.197
Fibonacci numbers 512.72
Fibrinogen 612.115
Fibrinolysis 612.115

Fibromyalgia 616.74
Fibrous composites 620.118
Fiction 808.3
Fiction—19th century 808.83034
Fiction—19th century—History and criticism 809.3034
Fiction—20th century 808.8304
Fiction—20th century—History and criticism 809.304
Fiction—Authorship 808.3
Fiction—Authorship—Vocational guidance 808.3023
Fiction—Bibliography 016.80883
Fiction—Collections 808.83
Fiction—History and criticism 809.3
Fiction—History and criticism—Theory, etc. 809.3
Fiction—Indexes 016.80883
Fiction—Technique 808.3
Fiddle tunes 787.2162; 787.21642
Fiddler (Fictitious character) 813.54
Fiddler (Fictitious character)—Fiction 813.54
Field crops 633
Field-effect transistors 621.3815284
Field extensions (Mathematics) 512.74
Field hockey 796.355
Field programmable gate arrays 621.395
Field recordings 384
Field sparrow 598.883
Field theory (Physics) 530.14
Fielding, Henry, 1707–1754 823.5
Fielding, Henry, 1707–1754—Criticism and interpretation 823.5
Fielding, Henry, 1707–1754. History of Tom Jones 823.5
Fielding, John, Sir, 1721–1780 364.92
Fiesta San Antonio, San Antonio, Tex. 394.262
Fifteen Years' War, 1591–1606 943.9041
Fifteenth century 909.4
Fifth Avenue (New York, N.Y.) 974.71
Fighter pilots 358.43092
Fighter planes 358.4383
Fighter planes—United States 358.43830973
Figural bottle openers 683.8
Figural novelties 688.726
Figurative drawing 741.0904
Figure drawing 743.4
Figure drawing—Technique 743.4
Fiji 996.11
Fiji—Guidebooks 919.61104
Fiji—History 996.11
Fiji—Politics and government 320.99611
Filamentous fungi 579.5
File organization (Computer science) 005.741
File processing (Computer science) 005.74
File Transfer Protocol (Computer network protocol) 004.62
FileMaker pro 005.7565
Filing systems 651.53
Filipinos 959.9
Fillmore County (Minn.) 977.616
Fillmore County (Minn.)—Maps 912.77616
Film adaptations 791.436
Film archives 025.1773
Film criticism 791.43015; 809.23
Film festivals 791.43079
Film festivals—Directories 791.43079
Film genres 791.436
Film makeup 791.43027
Film noir 791.43655
Film noir—United States—History and criticism 791.43655
Film novelizations 808.83

Finnish Americans 973.0494541
Finnish baseball 796.3578
Finnish language 494.541
Finnish periodicals 059.94541
Finnish poetry 894.5411; 894.5411008
Finnish poetry—Translations into English 894.5411008
Finsler spaces 516.375
Fionavar (Imaginary place) 813.54
Fire 541.361
Fire alarms 628.9225
Fire chiefs 363.37092
Fire departments 363.37
Fire departments—Equipment and supplies
  628.9250284
Fire departments—Management 363.37068
Fire drills 363.377
Fire ecology 577.2
Fire engines 628.9259; 629.225
Fire engines—Pictorial works 628.92590222
Fire engines—United States—History 628.92590973;
  629.225
Fire extinction 628.925
Fire extinction—Examinations, questions, etc.
  628.925076
Fire extinction—Handbooks, manuals, etc. 628.925
Fire extinction—United States—Examinations,
  questions, etc. 628.925076
Fire extinction—Vocational guidance 363.37023
Fire extinction—Water-supply 628.9252
Fire fighters 363.37092; 628.925092
Fire fighting equipment industry 629.225
Fire investigation 363.3765
Fire management 333.76152; 363.379; 632.18
Fire prevention 363.377; 628.922
Fire prevention—Handbooks, manuals, etc. 628.922
Fire prevention—Law and legislation 344.05377
Fire prevention—Law and legislation—United States
  344.7305377
Fire protection engineering 628.922
Fire pumps 628.9252
Fire sprinklers 628.9252
Fire sprinklers—Handbooks, manuals, etc. 628.9252
Fire stations 363.37; 628.925
Fire—Symbolic aspects 302.2223
Fire warfare 355.422
Firearms 363.33; 623.4; 623.442; 683.4
Firearms and crime 364.2
Firearms—Catalogs 683.40075
Firearms—Collectors and collecting 623.4075;
  623.442075; 683.40075
Firearms industry and trade 363.33
Firearms—Law and legislation 344.0533
Firearms—Law and legislation—California 344.7940533
Firearms—Law and legislation—Great Britain
  344.410533
Firearms—Law and legislation—United States
  344.730533
Firearms—Law and legislation—United States—States
  344.730533
Firearms owners 363.33092
Firearms ownership 363.33
Firearms—United States—History 683.400973
Firebird automobile 629.2222
Firebird automobile—History 629.2222
Firebird automobile—Maintenance and repair 629.28722
Firebird automobile—Maintenance and repair—
  Handbooks, manuals, etc. 629.28722
Fireflies 595.7644
Fireplace industry 338.476971

Fireplaces 697.1; 721.8
Fireproofing agents 628.9223
Fires 363.37; 628.92
Fires—Demographic aspects 363.372
Fires—Safety measures 628.922
Firewalls (Computer security) 005.8
Fireworks 662.1
Fireworks in the theater 792.024
Fireworks industry 338.476621
Firing (Ceramics) 666.443; 738.143
First aid for animals 636.08960252
First aid in illness and injury 362.18; 616.0252
First aid in illness and injury—Handbooks, manuals, etc.
  616.0252
First aid in illness and injury—Law and legislation
  344.03218
First-order logic 160; 511.3
First philosophy 194
First year teachers 371.144
First year teachers—United States 371.1440973
FirstSearch (Online information service) 025.04
Fiscal policy 336.3; 339.52
Fiscal policy—Developing countries 339.52091724
Fiscal policy—United States 336.30973; 339.520973
Fischer, Bobby, 1943– 794.1092; 794.159
Fischman, Nina (Fictitious character) 813.54
Fischman, Nina (Fictitious character)—Fiction 813.54
Fish as food 641.392
Fish-culture 639.3
Fish hatcheries 639.311
Fish management areas 333.956
Fish ponds 639.31
Fish populations 639.3
Fish surveys 333.95611; 597
Fish trapping 639.2
Fisher family 929.20973
Fisher, M. F. K. (Mary Frances Kennedy), 1908–
  641.092
Fisher (Mammal) 599.7665
Fisheries 338.3727
Fisheries—Economic aspects 338.3727
Fisheries—Equipment and supplies 639.20284
Fisheries—Washington (State)—Statistics
  338.372709797
Fisheries—Washington (State)—Statistics—Periodicals
  338.372709797021
Fishers 639.2092
Fishery conservation 333.95616
Fishery discards 333.956; 639.2
Fishery law and legislation 341.7622; 343.07692
Fishery law and legislation—United States
  343.7307692; 343.7807692; 346.73046956
Fishery management 338.3727
Fishery policy 338.3727
Fishes 597; 639.3
Fishes—Anatomy 571.317
Fishes—Behavior 597.15
Fishes—Boning 641.692; 664.94
Fishes—Breeding 639.3
Fishes—Classification 597.012
Fishes—Diseases 639.3
Fishes—Effect of water pollution on 597.17
Fishes—Eggs 597.1468
Fishes—Eggs—Geographical distribution 597.146809
Fishes—Evolution 576.817
Fishes—Feeding and feeds 639.3
Fishes—Food 597.153
Fishes, Fossil 567
Fishes—Genetics 576.517

Floor paint 667.69; 698.146
Floor polishes 667.72; 698.33
Flooring 690.16
Floors 690.16
Floors, Wooden 694.2
Floral decorations 745.92
Florence County (Wis.) 977.532
Florence County (Wis.)—Maps 912.77532
Florence (Italy) 945.51
Florence (Italy)—Description and travel 914.55104;
914.55104929; 914.5510493
Florence (Italy)—Guidebooks 914.55104; 914.55104929;
914.5510493
Florence (Italy)—History 945.51
Florence (Italy)—History—1421–1737 945.5105
Florence (Italy)—Pictorial works 914.55100222
Floriculture 635.9
Florida 975.9
Florida—Appropriations and expenditures—Periodicals
352.460975905
Florida—Genealogy 929.3759
Florida—Guidebooks 917.5904; 917.590463; 917.590464
Florida—History 975.9
Florida Keys (Fla.) 975.941
Florida Keys (Fla.)—Guidebooks 917.5941
Florida—Maps 912.759
Florida panther 599.752409759
Florida—Road maps 912.759
Florida—Social life and customs 975.9
Florida—Tours 917.5904; 917.590463; 917.590464
Florist suppliers 381.4159
Floristry 745.92
Florists 381.4159
Florivores 591.54
Florivorous insects 595.7154
Flotation 622.752
Flow cytometry 571.60287; 616.07582
Flow cytometry—Diagnostic use 616.07582
Flow meters 681.28
Flow visualization 681.28
Flower arrangement 745.92
Flower arrangement—Handbooks, manuals, etc. 745.92
Flower arrangement in interior decoration 747.9
Flower arrangement, Japanese 745.92252
Flower gardening 635.9; 635.966
Flower language 398.368213
Flowering shrubs 635.976
Flowers 575.6; 582.13; 635.9
Flowers—Drying 745.92
Flowers—Folklore 398.242
Flowers in art 704.9434; 743.7; 751.422434; 751.45434;
758.42
Flowers—Therapeutic use 615.321
Flows (Differentiable dynamical systems) 514.74
Floyd County (Iowa) 977.726
Floyd County (Iowa)—Maps 912.77726
Fluency (Language learning) 407.1; 418.0071
Fluid dynamic measurements 620.10640287; 681.28
Fluid dynamics 532.05; 620.1064
Fluid dynamics—Data processing 532.050285
Fluid mechanics 532; 620.106
Fluid mechanics—Industrial applications 620.106
Fluid mechanics—Periodicals 620.10605
Fluid power technology 620.106; 621.2
Fluid power technology—Handbooks, manuals, etc.
620.106
Fluid-structure interaction 624.171
Fluidization 660.284292
Fluidized-bed combustion 621.4023

Fluids 530.42; 532
Fluorescence 535.352
Fluorescence angiography 617.71572; 617.73507572
Fluorescence in situ hybridization 502.82; 616.0758
Fluorescence spectroscopy 543.08584
Fluorescent lighting 621.3273
Fluoropolymers 547.84; 668.4238
Flute 788.32; 788.3219
Flute and guitar music 785.44
Flute and harp music 785.44
Flute and piano music 788.32
Flute—Instruction and study 788.32071
Flute—Methods 788.32193
Flute music 788.32
Flute music (Flutes (2)) 785.832192
Flute with orchestra 784.2832
Fly casting 799.124
Fly fishing 799.124
Fly tying 688.79124
Fly tying—Equipment and supplies 688.79124
Flyball (Dog sport) 798.8
Flying foxes 599.49
Flying helmets 629.13443
Flying squirrels 599.369
FMS (Information retrieval system) 025.0665815
Focke-Wulf 190 (Fighter planes) 358.4383
Fodder trees 636.0855
Folding cycles 388.3472; 629.2272
Folding tables 645.4; 684.13
Folds (Geology) 551.875
Foley, Malachy (Fictitious character) 813.54
Foliage plants 635.975
Foliations (Mathematics) 514.72
Folic acid in human nutrition 613.286
Folk art 745
Folk art—India 745.0954
Folk art—United States 745.0973
Folk dance music 781.620554
Folk dance music—Mexico 781.6205540972
Folk dancing 793.31
Folk dancing in art 700.455; 704.94979331
Folk dancing—India 793.31954
Folk dancing, Scottish 793.319411
Folk festivals 782.42162079
Folk literature 398.2
Folk literature, African—History and criticism 398.2096
Folk literature—History and criticism 398.209
Folk literature, Indian 398.20897
Folk music 781.62
Folk music groups 781.6200922
Folk music—Ireland 781.629162
Folk music—Ireland—History and criticism 781.629162
Folk music—Scotland—History and criticism
782.42162009411
Folk music—United States 781.6213
Folk music—United States—History and criticism
781.6213
Folk singers 781.620092
Folk songs 782.42162
Folk songs, English 782.421622
Folk songs, English—Australia 782.4216224
Folk songs, English—Australia—Indexes 782.4216224
Folk songs, English—England 782.4216221
Folk songs, English—England—History and criticism
782.4216221
Folk songs, English—England—Texts 782.421622100268
Folk songs, English—Texts 782.42162200268;
782.421622100268
Folk songs, English—United States 782.4216213

Folk songs, English—United States—History and criticism 782.4216213
Folk songs, English—United States—Texts 782.421621300268
Folklore 398; 398.2
Folklore—Australia 398.20994
Folklore—Brazil 398.20981
Folklore—China 398.20951
Folklore—England—Cornwall (County) 398.2094237
Folklore—Europe 398.2094
Folklore—France 398.20944
Folklore—Germany 398.20943
Folklore—Great Britain 398.20941
Folklore—Great Smoky Mountains (N.C. and Tenn.) 398.20976889
Folklore—Greece 398.209495
Folklore—India 398.20954
Folklore—Ireland 398.209415
Folklore—Italy 398.20945
Folklore—Japan 398.20952
Folklore—Methodology 398.01
Folklore—Periodicals 398.05
Folklore—Poland 398.209438
Folklore—Romania 398.209498
Folklore—Russia (Federation) 398.20947
Folklore—Scandinavia 398.20948
Folklore—Soviet Union 398.20947
Folklore—Spain 398.20946
Folklore—Texas 390.09764
Folklore—Turkey 398.209561
Folklore—United States 398.20973
Folklore—Venezuela 398.20987
Follain, Jean, 1903–1971 841.912
Follain, Jean, 1903–1971—Translations into English 841.912
Fond du Lac County (Wis.) 977.568
Fond du Lac County (Wis.)—Maps 912.77568
Fonda, Jane, 1937– 791.43028092
Fondue 641.81
Fontana, Mac (Fictitious character) 813.54
Fontana, Mac (Fictitious character)—Fiction 813.54
Fonteyn, Margot, Dame, 1919– 792.8092
Fonts 247.1
Food 641.3; 664
Food additives 641.3; 664.06
Food additives—Dictionaries 664.0603
Food additives—Specifications 664.060212
Food additives—Standards 664.060218
Food additives—Standards—United States 664.06021873
Food additives—Toxicology 664.06
Food adulteration and inspection 363.19264
Food—Aeration 664.024
Food allergy 616.975
Food allergy—Diet therapy 616.9750654
Food allergy—Diet therapy—Recipes 641.5631
Food allergy in children 618.92975
Food—Analysis 664.07
Food and Agriculture Organization of the United Nations 341.762
Food animals 636.0883
Food banks 363.883
Food—Biotechnology 664; 664.024
Food brokers 641.30092
Food—Caloric content—Tables 613.23021
Food—Carbohydrate content 613.283
Food—Catalogs 641.300294
Food chains (Ecology) 577.16
Food—Cholesterol content—Tables 613.284

Food combining 613.2
Food—Composition 664
Food—Composition—Tables 613.2
Food contamination 363.192
Food crops 630; 633
Food—Dictionaries 641.3003
Food—Drying 641.44
Food—Encyclopedias 641.3003
Food—Experiments 641.30078
Food—Fat content—Tables 613.284021
Food—Gluten content 641.331
Food habits—United States 394.120973
Food handling 363.192; 664.00289
Food handling—Law and legislation 344.04232
Food—History 641.3009
Food in literature 808.80355; 809.93355
Food industry and trade 338.47664; 664
Food industry and trade—Automation 664.02
Food industry and trade—Handbooks, manuals, etc. 664
Food industry and trade—Periodicals 664.005
Food industry and trade—Quality control 664.07
Food industry and trade—Sanitation 664.00286
Food—Labeling 363.192
Food—Labeling—Law and legislation 344.04232
Food—Labeling—Law and legislation—United States 344.7304232
Food law and legislation 344.04232
Food law and legislation—United States 344.7304232
Food—Microbiology 664.001579
Food mixes 641.55
Food of animal origin 641.306
Food—Packaging 664.09
Food—Pictorial works 641.300222
Food poisoning 615.954
Food—Preservation 641.4; 664.028
Food relief 363.883
Food relief, American 363.8830973
Food relief—Law and legislation 344.033
Food relief—Law and legislation—United States 344.73033
Food relief—United States 363.8830973
Food riots 303.623; 322.4
Food—Sensory evaluation 664.07
Food service 642.5; 647.95
Food service—Cost control 647.950681
Food service—Equipment and supplies 647.950284
Food service management 647.95068
Food service purchasing 647.950687
Food service—Sanitation 363.7296
Food service—Vocational guidance 647.95023
Food service—Vocational guidance—United States 647.9502373
Food—Sodium content—Tables 613.28
Food stamps 363.882
Food stamps—Law and legislation 344.033
Food stamps—Law and legislation—United States 344.73033
Food stamps—United States 363.8820973
Food steamers 641.587; 683.82
Food—Storage 641.48
Food supply 338.19; 363.8
Food supply—Africa 363.8096
Food supply—Developing countries 363.8091724
Food supply—Government policy 338.19
Food supply—Government policy—Developing countries 338.191724
Food supply—India 363.80954
Food—Testing 664.07

Food testing reagents 664.070284
Food—Toxicology 615.954
Food waste as feed 636.08556
Food—Water activity 664
Food writing 808.066641
Foodborne diseases 615.954
Foot 612.98
Foot—Abnormalities 617.585
Foot—Abnormalities—Treatment 617.585
Foot—Care and hygiene 617.58506
Foot care products 617.58506; 646.72
Foot—Diseases 617.585
Foot—Surgery 617.585059
Footbag 796.33
Football 796.33; 796.332
Football—Betting—United States 796.332
Football coaches 796.332092
Football coaches—United States—Biography 796.332092
Football—Coaching 796.33077; 796.332077
Football—Coaching—Philosophy 796.3307701;
  796.33207701
Football—Defense 796.3322
Football films 791.43655
Football—History 796.3309; 796.33209
Football—Humor 796.330207; 796.3320207
Football—Offense 796.3322
Football players 796.33092; 796.332092
Football players—United States—Biography 796.332092
Football—Records—United States 796.332
Football stadiums 725.827; 796.332068
Football teams 796.33264
Football—Training 796.33071; 796.332071
Football—United States 796.332
Football—United States—History 796.33209
Football—United States—Humor 796.3320207
Football—United States—Periodicals 796.33205
Football—United States—Statistics 796.332021
Footprints, Fossil 560; 566
Footwear 685.3
Footwear industry 336.476853
For better or for worse (Comic strip) 741.5971
Forage plants 633.2
Foraminifera 579.44
Foraminifera, Fossil 561.994
Forbs 582.12
Force and energy 333.79; 531.6
Force and energy—Experiments 531.60724; 531.6078
Forced labor 331.1173
Forced labor—Soviet Union 331.11730947
Forced migration 325
Ford automobile 629.2222
Ford automobile—History 629.2222
Ford automobile—Maintenance and repair 629.28722
Ford automobile—Maintenance and repair—Handbooks,
  manuals, etc. 629.28722
Ford County (Ill.) 977.362
Ford County (Ill.)—Maps 912.77362
Ford, Doc (Fictitious character) 813.54
Ford, Doc (Fictitious character)—Fiction 813.54
Ford family 929.20973
Ford, Ford Madox, 1873–1939 823.912
Ford, Ford Madox, 1873–1939—Criticism and
  interpretation 823.912
Ford, Gerald R., 1913– 973.925092
Ford, Henry, 1863–1947 338.76292092
Ford, John, 1894–1973 791.430233092; 791.4302330922
Ford Probe automobile 629.2222
Ford Probe automobile—Maintenance and repair
  629.28722

Ford Probe automobile—Maintenance and repair—
  Handbooks, manuals, etc. 629.28722
Ford Ranger truck 629.2232
Ford Ranger truck—Maintenance and repair 629.28732
Ford Ranger truck—Maintenance and repair—
  Handbooks, manuals, etc. 629.28732
Ford Tempo automobile 629.2222
Ford Tempo automobile—Maintenance and repair
  629.28722
Ford Tempo automobile—Maintenance and repair—
  Handbooks, manuals, etc. 629.28722
Ford tractors 629.2252
Ford tractors—History 629.2252
Ford trucks 629.2232
Ford trucks—History 629.2232
Ford trucks—Maintenance and repair 629.28732
Ford trucks—Maintenance and repair—Handbooks,
  manuals, etc. 629.28732
Ford trucks—Periodicals 629.224
Ford vans 629.2234
Ford vans—Maintenance and repair 629.28734
Ford vans—Maintenance and repair—Handbooks,
  manuals, etc. 629.28734
Forecasting 003.2; 303.49
Foreclosure 346.04364
Foreclosure—Massachusetts 346.74404364
Foreclosure—United States 346.7304364
Foreign exchange 332.45
Foreign exchange administration 332.456
Foreign exchange administration—United States
  332.450973
Foreign exchange futures 332.45
Foreign exchange—Law and legislation 343.032
Foreign exchange—Law and legislation—India
  343.54032
Foreign exchange market 332.45
Foreign exchange—Mathematical models 332.45015118
Foreign exchange rates 332.456
Foreign exchange rates—Canada 332.4560971
Foreign exchange rates—Developing countries
  332.456091724
Foreign exchange rates—Econometric models 332.456
Foreign exchange rates—Mathematical models
  332.456015118
Foreign exchange—United States 332.4560973
Foreign language films 791.43
Foreign language publications 070.57
Foreign news 070.4332
Foreign study 370.116
Foreign study—Directories 370.116025
Foreign study—Handbooks, manuals, etc. 370.116
Foreign trade and employment 331.12
Foreign trade promotion 382.63
Foreign trade promotion—Developing countries
  382.63091724
Foreign trade promotion—United States 382.630973
Foreign trade regulation 341.754; 343.087
Foreign trade regulation—Canada 343.71087
Foreign trade regulation—Periodicals 341.75405
Foreign trade regulation—United States 343.73087
Forensic accounting 347.067
Forensic accounting—United States 347.7367
Forensic anthropologists 363.25; 599.9; 614.1
Forensic anthropology 599.9
Forensic economics 363.25
Forensic epidemiology 614.1
Forensic neuropsychology 614.1
Forensic nursing 614.1
Forensic orations 347.075

Forensic pathology 614.1
Forensic pathology—Atlases 614.10222
Forensic psychiatric nursing 614.1
Forensic psychiatry 614.1
Forensic psychiatry—Religious aspects 291.175
Forensic psychiatry—United States 347.7367; 614.1
Forensic sciences 363.25
Forensic toxicology 614.1
Forensics (Public speaking) 808.51
Foreplay 306.77; 613.96
Forest animals 591.73
Forest canopy ecology 577.3
Forest conservation 333.7516
Forest ecology 577.3
Forest entomologists 634.967092
Forest fire fighters 634.9618092
Forest fires 634.9618
Forest fires—Australia 634.96180994
Forest fires—Prevention and control 634.9618
Forest fires—United States 634.96180973
Forest fires—Yellowstone National Park
  634.96180978752
Forest fungi 579.5173
Forest genetics 634.956
Forest insects 595.7173
Forest management 634.92
Forest pathologists 634.96092
Forest plants 581.73
Forest policy 333.75
Forest policy—United States 333.750973
Forest products industry 338.17498
Forest products industry—United States—Directories
  338.1749802573
Forest reserves 719.33
Forest soils—Fertilization 634.95
Forest surveys 634.90723
Forest type groups 333.75012; 577.3012
Forested wetlands 333.95288
Forestry engineering 634.98
Forestry investment 338.1349
Forestry law and legislation 346.04675
Forestry law and legislation—United States
  346.7304675
Forestry schools and education 634.9071
Forests and forestry 634.9
Forests and forestry—Bibliography 016.6349
Forests and forestry—British Columbia 333.7509711
Forests and forestry—China 333.750951; 634.90951
Forests and forestry—Economic aspects 338.1749
Forests and forestry—India 333.750954; 634.90954
Forests and forestry—Mensuration 634.9285
Forests and forestry—Periodicals 634.905
Forests and forestry—Remote sensing 634.9
Forests and forestry—Southern States 634.90975
Forests and forestry—Tropics 333.750913
Forests and forestry—United States 635.90973
Forfaiting 332.742
Forfaiting—Law and legislation 346.073
Forfeiture 345.0773
Forfeiture—United States 345.730522
Forgery 364.163
Forging 671.332
Forging industry 338.47671332
Forgiveness 179.9
Forgiveness of sin 234.5
Forgiveness—Religious aspects 291.22
Forgiveness—Religious aspects—Christianity 234.5
Forgotten realms (Imaginary place) 813.54
Forgotten realms (Imaginary place)—Fiction 813.54

Form headings 025.49
Form perception 152.1423; 153.752
Formal gardens 712
Formal gardens—Design 712
Formal languages 511.3
Formal methods (Computer science) 004.0151
Format radio broadcasting 384.544
Formations (Geology) 551.7
Former Soviet republics 947; 947.086
Former Soviet republics—Commerce 382.0947
Former Soviet republics—Economic conditions
  330.947086
Former Soviet republics—Economic conditions—
  Periodicals 330.947086
Former Soviet republics—Ethnic relations 305.800947
Former Soviet republics—Foreign relations 327.0947
Former Soviet republics—History 947
Former Soviet republics—Maps 912.47
Formes frustes (Psychiatry) 616.89
Forms (Law) 347.055
Forms (Law)—Great Britain 347.41055
Forms (Law)—New York (State) 347.747055
Forms (Law)—Philippines 347.599055
Forms (Law)—United States 347.7355
Forms (Mathematics) 512.944
Forms, Quadratic 512.74
Formylation 547.2
Forrest, Nathan Bedford, 1821–1877 973.73092
Forster, E. M. (Edward Morgan), 1879–1970 823.912
Forster, E. M. (Edward Morgan), 1879–1970—Criticism
  and interpretation 823.912
Forster, E. M. (Edward Morgan), 1879–1970. Howards
  End 823.912
Forster, E. M. (Edward Morgan), 1879–1970. Passage
  to India 823.912
Forster, E. M. (Edward Morgan), 1879–1970. Passage
  to India—Examinations 823.912
Forsyte family (Fictitious characters) 823.912
Forsyte family (Fictitious characters)—Fiction 823.912
Forsythe, Robert (Fictitious character) 813.54
Forsythe, Robert (Fictitious character)—Fiction 813.54
Fort Bend County (Tex.)—Maps 912.764135
Fort Michilimackinac (Mackinac City, Mich.) 977.4923
Fort Point National Historic Site (San Francisco, Calif.)
  979.461
Fort Wayne (Ind.) 977.274
Fort Wayne (Ind.)—History 977.274
Fort Worth Metropolitan Area (Tex.) 976.45315
Fort Worth Metropolitan Area (Tex.)—Maps
  912.7645315
Fort Worth (Tex.) 976.45315
Fort Worth (Tex.)—History 976.45315
FORTH (Computer program language) 005.133
Fortification 623.1
Fortification—History 623.109
Fortification—Texas—Guidebooks 623.19764
FORTRAN IV (Computer program language) 005.133
FORTRAN IV (Computer program language)—
  Programmed instruction 005.133
FORTRAN 77 (Computer program language) 005.133
FORTRAN 90 (Computer program language) 005.133
FORTRAN (Computer program language) 005.133
Fortress-churches 726.5
Fortune cookies 641.8654
Fortune, Dan (Fictitious character) 813.54
Fortune, Dan (Fictitious character)—Fiction 813.54
Fortune-tellers 133.3092
Fortune-telling 133.3
Fortune-telling by cards 133.3242

Fortune-telling by runes 133.33
Fortune-telling by scarabs 133.322
Forty-Eighters (American immigrants) 973.0431
Forty-two (Game) 795.32
Forums (Discussion and debate) 371.37; 808.53
Fosse, Bob, 1927–1987 792.82092
Fossil fuels 553.2; 662.6
Fossil hominids 569.9
Fossilization 560
Fossils 560
Fossils—Collection and preservation 560.75
Foster children 362.733
Foster children—United States 362.7330973
Foster family 929.20973
Foster home care 362.733
Foster home care—Great Britain 362.7330941
Foster home care—Law and legislation 344.3032733
Foster home care—Law and legislation—United States 344.73032733
Foster home care—New York (State)—New York 362.733097471
Foster home care—United States 362.7330973
Foster, Jodie 791.43028092
Foster mothers 306.8743; 362.733
Fostoria Glass Company—Catalogs 748.2915416
Foucault, Michel 194
Foucault's pendulum 525.36
Foundations 624.15; 690.11
Foundations—Design and construction 624.15
Founding 671.2
Founding—Periodicals 671.205
Foundries 671.2
Fountain of youth (Legendary place) 398.234
Fountain pens 681.6
Fountain pens—History 681.6
Four-manifolds (Topology) 514.3
Four Noble Truths 294.342
Four temperaments 155.262
Fourier analysis 515.2433
Fourier series 515.2433
Fourier transform spectroscopy 543.0858
Fourier transformations 515.723
Fourth dimension 530.11
Fourth of July 394.2634
Fourth of July orations 973.36
Fowles, John, 1926– 823.914
Fowles, John, 1926– —Criticism and interpretation 823.914
Fowling 799.24
Fox family 929.20973
Fox, George, 1624–1691 289.6092
Fox hunting 799.259775
Fox squirrel 599.362
Fox trot (Comic strip) 741.5973
Foxes 599.775
FoxPro (Computer file) 005.7565
Fractals 514.742
Fractals—Data processing 514.7420285
Fractals in art 704.949514742
Fractional calculus 515
Fractions 513.26
Fractography 620.1126
Fracture fixation 617.15
Fracture mechanics 620.1126
Fracture mechanics—Mathematical models 620.1126015118
Fractures 617.15
Fractures in children 617.15083
Fractures—Treatment 617.15

Fragile X syndrome 616.85884
Fragmented landscapes 333.95; 577
Fragrant gardens 635.968
Frame, Janet 823.914
Frame, Janet—Criticism and interpretation 823.914
Frame relay (Data transmission) 004.66; 621.3981
Framework (Computer file) 005.369
Framing (Building) 694.2
France 944
France. Armée. Légion étrangère 355.3590944
France—Civilization 944
France—Civilization—1000–1328 944.02
France—Civilization—18th century 944.034
France—Civilization—20th century 944.08
France—Civilization—1945– 944.082; 944.083
France—Description and travel 914.404; 914.404839; 914.40484
France—Description and travel—Early works to 1800 914.404
France—Economic conditions 330.944
France—Economic policy 338.944
France—Economic policy—1945– 338.944
France—Foreign relations 327.44
France—Foreign relations—1945– 327.44009045
France—Geography 914.4
France—Guidebooks 914.404; 914.404839; 914.40484
France—History 944
France—History—To 987 944.01
France—History—Capetians, 987–1328 944.021
France—History—Louis XI, 1461–1483 944.027
France—History—Wars of the Huguenots, 1562–1598 944.029
France—History—Louis XIV, 1643–1715 944.033
France—History—Revolution, 1789–1799 944.04
France—History—Revolution, 1789–1799—Biography 944.040922
France—History—Revolution, 1789–1799—Causes 944.035; 944.04
France—History—Revolution, 1789–1799—Historiography 944.04072
France—History—Revolution, 1789–1799—Influence 944.04
France—History—Revolution, 1789–1799—Literature and the revolution 820.9006
France—History—Revolution, 1789–1799—Sources 944.04072
France—History—Revolution, 1789–1799—Women 944.04082
France—History—Consulate and First Empire, 1799–1815 944.046; 944.05
France—History—19th century 944.06
France—History—Third Republic, 1870–1940 944.081
France—History—1914–1940 944.0814
France—History, Military 355.00944
France—History, Military—1789–1815 355.0094409033
France—Maps 912.44
France—Military policy 355.033544
France—Pictorial works 914.400222
France—Politics and government 320.944; 944
France—Politics and government—17th century 320.94409032; 944.032
France—Politics and government—1789–1799 320.94409033; 944.04
France—Politics and government—20th century 320.9440904; 944.081
France—Politics and government—1945– 320.94409045; 944.082
France—Politics and government—1958– 320.94409045; 944.083

France—Politics and government—1981–1995
320.944090458; 944.0838; 944.0839
France—Road maps 912.44
France—Social life and customs 944
France—Social life and customs—18th century 944.034
France—Social life and customs—19th century 944.06
France, Southern 944.8
France, Southern—Guidebooks 914.4804; 914.4804839;
914.480484
France—Tours 914.404; 914.404839; 914.40484
Franchises (Retail trade) 381.13; 658.8708
Franchises (Retail trade)—Law and legislation 343.0887
Franchises (Retail trade)—Law and legislation—United
States 343.730887
Franchises (Retail trade)—Self-regulation 658.8708
Franchises (Retail trade)—United States 381.130973;
658.87080973
Franchises (Retail trade)—United States—Directories
381.1302573
Francis, of Assisi, Saint, 1182–1226 271.302
Franciscan monasteries 271.3
Franciscans 255.3
Franciscans—History 271.3
Franciscans—Spiritual life 255.3
Franco-Prussian War, 1870–1871 943.082
Frank, Anne, 1929–1945 940.5318092
Frank, Anne, 1929–1945. Achterhuis 940.5318092
Frank, Anne, 1929–1945—Diaries 940.5318092
Frankenstein (Fictitious character) 823.7
Frankenstein (Fictitious character)—Drama 791.4372
Frankenstein (Fictitious character)—Fiction 823.7
Frankfurt school of sociology 301.01
Frankia 579.37
Franklin, Benjamin, 1706–1790 973.3092
Franklin County (Ga.)—Genealogy 929.3758135
Franklin County (Iowa) 977.728
Franklin County (Iowa)—Maps 912.77728
Franklin County (Mo.) 977.863
Franklin County (Mo.)—Maps 912.77863
Franklin County (N.C.)—Genealogy 929.375654
Franklin County (Ohio) 977.156
Franklin County (Ohio)—Genealogy 929.377156
Franklin Delano Roosevelt Memorial (Washington, D.C.)
973.917092
Franky (Fictitious character : Rayner) 823.914
Fraser family 929.20973
Fraser, Jamie (Fictitious character) 813.54
Fraud 364.163
Fraud in science 344.095
Fraud investigation 345.0263
Freckles 612.7927
Frederick II, King of Prussia, 1712–1786 943.053092
Frederick County (Md.)—Genealogy 929.375287
Frederick County (Md.)—Maps 912.75287
Frederick County (Va.)—Genealogy 929.375495;
929.3755992
Frederick County (Va.)—Maps 912.755992
Fredericksburg (Va.), Battle of, 1862 973.733
Free banking 332.1
Free climbing 796.5223
Free computer software 005.3
Free electron lasers 621.366
Free electron theory of metals 530.41
Free enterprise 330.122
Free logic 160
Free material 011.03; 658.82
Free material—Catalogs 011.03
Free ports and zones 387.13
Free ports and zones—China 387.130951

Free press and fair trial 345.056
Free press and fair trial—United States 345.73056
Free probability theory 512.55
Free radical reactions 547.139
Free radicals (Chemistry) 541.224
Free radicals (Chemistry)—Pathophysiology 616.071
Free radicals (Chemistry)—Periodicals 541.224
Free radicals (Chemistry)—Physiological effect
612.01524
Free schools 371.04
Free thought 211.4
Free trade 382.71
Free trade—Canada 382.710971
Free trade—North America 382.71097; 382.917
Free will and determinism 123.5
Free will and determinism in literature 808.80384;
809.93384
Freeborn County (Minn.) 977.618
Freeborn County (Minn.)—Maps 912.77618
Freedmen 973.714
Freedom of association 323.47
Freedom of information 323.445
Freedom of movement 323.44
Freedom of movement—European Economic Community
countries 341.763
Freedom of religion 261.72; 323.442
Freedom of religion—United States 323.4420973;
342.730852
Freedom of religion—United States—Cases
342.7308520264
Freedom of religion—United States—History
342.73085209
Freedom of speech 323.443
Freedom of speech—United States 323.4430973;
342.730853
Freedom of speech—United States—History 342.730853
Freedom of the press 323.445
Freedom of the press—Great Britain 342.410853
Freedom of the press—India 342.540853
Freedom of the press—United States 342.730853
Freedom of the press—United States—History
342.730853
Freedom of the seas 341.45
Freedom Trail (Boston, Mass.)—Guidebooks
917.446104; 917.44610443; 917.44610444
FreeHand (Computer file) 006.6869
Freehand technical sketching 741.2
Freelance journalism 070.4
Freelance photography 770.68
Freemasonry 366.1
Freemasonry—History 366.109
Freemasonry—Religious aspects—Christianity 366.12
Freemasonry—Rituals 366.12
Freemasonry—Symbolism 366.1
Freemasons 366.1092
Freemasons—History 366.1092
Freestyle skiing 796.937
Freethinkers 211.4092
Freeze-drying 621.56
Freezes (Meteorology) 551.5253
Frege, Gottlob, 1848–1925 193
Freight and freightage 388.044
Freight and freightage—United States 388.0440973
Freight forwarders 388.044
Freire, Paulo, 1921– 370.92
Fremont County (Iowa) 977.777
Fremont County (Iowa)—Maps 912.77777
Frémont, John Charles, 1813–1890 973.6092
French-Canadian poetry 841.0080971

French-Canadian poetry—Translations into English 841.0080971

French-Canadians 305.8114

French departments (Political divisions of France) 320.830944; 352.150944

French drama 842; 842.008

French drama—17th century 842.4; 842.408

French drama—17th century—History and criticism 842.409

French drama—18th century 842.5; 842.508

French drama—18th century—History and criticism 842.509

French drama—20th century 842.91; 842.9108; 842.914; 842.91408

French drama—20th century—History and criticism 842.9109; 842.91409

French drama (Tragedy) 842.0512

French drama (Tragedy)—History and criticism 842.051209

French fiction 843; 843.008

French fiction—18th century 843.5; 843.508

French fiction—18th century—History and criticism 843.509

French fiction—19th century 843.7; 843.708

French fiction—19th century—History and criticism 843.709

French fiction—20th century 843.91; 843.9108; 843.912; 843.91208

French fiction—20th century—History and criticism 843.9109; 843.91209; 843.91409

French fiction—History and criticism 843.009

French fiction—Women authors 843.00809287

French fiction—Women authors—History and criticism 843.0099287

French language 440

French language—Canada 447.971

French language—Conversation and phrase books 448.34

French language—Conversation and phrase books— English 448.3421

French language—Dictionaries 443

French language—Dictionaries—English 443.21

French language—Examinations 448.0076

French language—Glossaries, vocabularies, etc. 443

French language—Grammar 445; 448.2; 448.2421

French language—History 440.9

French language—Idioms 448.1

French language—Idioms—Dictionaries 443.1

French language—Paronyms—Dictionaries 443.1

French language—Pronunciation 441.52; 448.1; 448.3421

French language—Readers 448.6; 448.6421

French language—Readers—France 448.6421

French language—Rhetoric 808.0441

French language—Syntax 445

French language—Textbooks for foreign speakers— English 448.2421; 448.3421

French language—Verb 445; 448.2; 448.2421

French language—Versification 841.009

French language—Vocabulary 448.1; 448.2421

French literature 840; 840.8

French literature—To 1500 840.8001

French literature—To 1500—History and criticism 840.9001

French literature—16th century 840.8003

French literature—16th century—History and criticism 840.9003

French literature—17th century 840.8004

French literature—17th century—History and criticism 840.9004

French literature—18th century 840.8005

French literature—18th century—History and criticism 840.9005

French literature—19th century 840.8007; 840.8008

French literature—19th century—History and criticism 840.9007; 840.9008

French literature—20th century 840.80091; 840.800912; 840.800914

French literature—20th century—History and criticism 840.90091; 840.900912; 840.900914

French literature—History and criticism 840.9

French literature—Women authors 840.809287

French literature—Women authors—History and criticism 840.99287

French philology 440

French poetry 841; 841.008

French poetry—To 1500 841.1; 841.108

French poetry—To 1500—History and criticism 841.209

French poetry—To 1500—Translations into English 841.108

French poetry—16th century 841.3; 841.308

French poetry—16th century—History and criticism 841.309

French poetry—19th century 841.7; 841.708; 841.8; 841.808

French poetry—19th century—History and criticism 841.709; 841.809

French poetry—20th century 841.91; 841.9108; 841.914; 841.91408

French poetry—20th century—History and criticism 841.91209

French poetry—20th century—Translations into English 841.9108

French poetry—History and criticism 841.009

French poetry—Translations into English 841.008

French Polynesia 996.2

French regions 320.444049; 352.130944

French toast 641.815

French wit and humor 847.008; 848.02

French wit and humor, Pictorial 741.5944

Freneau, Philip Morin, 1752–1832 811.2

Frente Sandinista de Liberación Nacional 324.27285075; 972.85053; 972.85054

Frequency (Linguistics) 410.151

Frequency synthesizers 621.3815486

Frequent flyer programs 387.742

Freshwater animals 591.76

Freshwater biology 578.76

Freshwater ecology 577.6

Freshwater fishes 597.176; 799.11

Freshwater fishes—North America 597.176097; 799.11097

Freshwater microbiology 579.176

Freshwater phytoplankton 579.8176

Freshwater plants 581.76

Freshwater zooplankton 592.176

Freud, Sigmund, 1856–1939 150.1952092

Freud, Sigmund, 1856–1939—Correspondence 150.1952092

Freud, Sigmund, 1856–1939—Friends and associates 150.19520922

Freud, Sigmund, 1856–1939—Religion 150.1952092

Freud, Sigmund, 1856–1939. Traumdeutung 154.634

Friar Tuck (Legendary character) 398.2094202

Friction 621.89

Friday the thirteenth 001.96

Friedan, Betty 305.42092

Fundamental education 370.111
Fundamentalism 270.82
Fundamentalist churches 270.82
Fundus oculi—Diseases—Atlases 617.74
Funeral consultants 393.9
Funeral music 781.588
Funeral rites and ceremonies 393.9
Funeral rites and ceremonies, Early Christian
  265.85090015
Funeral rites and ceremonies—Egypt 393.90962
Funeral rites and ceremonies, Jewish 296.445
Funeral rites and ceremonies—United States 393.90973
Funeral sermons 252.1
Funeral service 265.85
Funeral service—Catholic Church 264.020985
Fungal colonies 579.51782
Fungal diseases of plants 632.4
Fungal populations 579.51788
Fungal viruses 579.27
Fungi 579.5
Fungi as biological pest control agents 632.96
Fungi-bacteria relationships 579.51785
Fungi—Biotechnology 660.62
Fungi, Fossil 561.92
Fungi—India 579.50954
Fungi—Physiology 571.295
Funk musicians 781.64
Funny bone 612.97
Fur 573.58; 599.7147
Fur trade 380.145685
Furnaces 621.4025
Furniture 645.4
Furniture, Colonial—United States 749.214
Furniture design 749
Furniture designers 749.22
Furniture finishing 684.1; 684.1043
Furniture industry and trade 338.476841
Furniture industry and trade—Canada 338.47684100971
Furniture industry and trade—United States
  338.47684100973
Furniture making 684.1; 684.1042; 749
Furniture painting 749
Furniture polishes 667.72
Furniture—Repairing 684.1044; 749.10288
Furniture—Styles 749.2
Furniture—United States 749.213
Furniture—United States—Catalogs 749.213075
Furniture—United States—History 749.213
Furniture—United States—History—18th century
  749.214
Furniture—United States—Styles 749.213
Furtwängler, Wilhelm, 1886–1954 784.2092
Fusarium diseases of plants 632.4677
Fused salts 546.34
Fusion 536.42
Fusion reactors 621.484
Fusion reactors—Design and construction 621.484
Future in popular culture 303.49
Future life 291.23
Future life—Christianity 236.2
Futures 332.645
Futures market 332.645
Futures market—United States 332.645
Futures—Periodicals 332.645
Futures—United States 332.645
Futurism (Art) 709.04033
Fuzzy graphs 511.5
Fuzzy hypergraphs 511.5
Fuzzy integrals 515.42

Fuzzy logic 511.3
Fuzzy mathematics 511
Fuzzy measure theory 515.42
Fuzzy sets 511.322
Fuzzy systems 003.7
Fuzzy topology 514.322
Fyfe, David (Fictitious character) 823.914
GABA—Physiological effect 612.82; 615.78
GABA—Receptors 573.8528; 615.78
Gadamer, Hans Georg, 1900– 193
Gaelic games 796.09415
Gaia hypothesis 550
Gain sharing 658.3225
Gait in humans 612.76
Gaita (Flute) 788.35
Galactans 572.566
Galagos 599.83
Galapagos Islands 986.65
Galaxies 523.112
Galaxies—Clusters 523.112
Galaxies—Evolution 523.112
Galaxies—Formation 523.112
Gale, Dorothy (Fictitious character) 791.4372; 813.4
Galilee (Israel) 956.945
Galilee (Israel)—History 933; 956.945
Galileo, 1564–1642 520.92
Galileo Project 523.45; 629.43545
Gallium arsenide industry 338.4766106752
Gallium arsenide semiconductors 621.38152
Galloway, Tiller (Fictitious character) 813.54
Galloway, Tiller (Fictitious character)—Fiction 813.54
Galois theory 512.3
Galsworthy, John, 1867–1933 823.912
Galsworthy, John, 1867–1933—Criticism and
  interpretation 823.912
Galveston (Tex.) 976.4139
Galveston (Tex.)—History 976.4139
Gama, Vasco da, 1469–1524 910.92
Gamadge, Clara (Fictitious character) 813.54
Gamadge, Clara (Fictitious character)—Fiction 813.54
Gamadge, Henry (Fictitious character) 813.52
Gamadge, Henry (Fictitious character)—Fiction 813.52
Gambits (Chess) 794.122
Gamblers 795.092
Gambling 795
Gambling and crime 364.25
Gambling in art 704.949795
Gambling industry 338.47795
Gambling—Law and legislation 344.0542
Gambling—Law and legislation—Great Britain
  344.410542
Gambling—Law and legislation—Nevada 344.7930542
Gambling—Law and legislation—New Jersey
  344.7490542
Gambling on Indian reservations—Law and legislation—
  United States 344.73099
Gambling on Indian reservations—United States
  344.73054208997
Gambling on river boats 795
Gambling systems 795.01
Gambling—United States 363.420973
Game and game-birds 591.63; 598.163; 636.0888;
  636.63; 799.2; 799.24
Game calling (Hunting) 799.2028
Game laws 346.0469549
Game laws—Alaska 346.7980469549
Game protection 333.954916
Game theory 519.3
Gamelan 784.209598

Gamelan music 784.209598
Games 790.1; 793; 796.1; 796.14
Games for dogs 636.7
Games for girls 790.194; 793.08352
Games for one 790.13
Games for travelers 793.08891; 794.08891
Games—History 306.48709
Games in Christian education 268.6
Games on horseback 798
Games—Religious aspects 291.175
Games—Rules 790.1
Gamma ray astronomy 522.6862
Gamma ray bursts 522.6862
Gamma ray detectors 539.77
Gammasphere 539.77
Gandhi, Indira, 1917–1984 954.045092
Gandhi, Mahatma, 1869–1948 954.035092
Gandhi, Mahatma, 1869–1948—Philosophy 954.035092
Gandhi, Mahatma, 1869–1948—Political and social
  views 954.035092
Gandhi, Rajiv, 1944– 954.052092
Gaṇeśa (Hindu deity) 294.52113
Gang prevention 302.34; 364.4
Gangs 302.34; 364.1066
Gangs—United States 364.10660973
Gangster films 791.43655
Gangster films—History and criticism 791.43655
Gangsters in literature 808.8035206927;
  809.9335206927
Ganymede (Satellite) 523.985
Gap analysis (Conservation biology) 333.9516
Gap junctions (Cell biology) 571.5
Garage sales 381.195; 658.87
Garand rifle 683.422
Garbo, Greta, 1905– 791.43028092
Garcia, Jerry, 1942– 782.42166092
García Lorca, Federico, 1898–1936 861.62; 862.62;
  868.6209
García Lorca, Federico, 1898–1936—Criticism and
  interpretation 868.6209
García Lorca, Federico, 1898–1936—Translations into
  English 861.62; 862.62
García Márquez, Gabriel, 1928– 863.64
García Márquez, Gabriel, 1928– —Criticism and
  interpretation 863.64
García Márquez, Gabriel, 1928– —Translations into
  English 863.64
Garden animals 591.7554
Garden borders 635.963
Garden ecology 577.554
Garden ornaments and furniture 717
Garden pests 635.0496
Garden pests—Control 635.0499
Garden pests—Control—Handbooks, manuals, etc.
  635.0499
Garden soils 635.0489
Garden structures 690.89
Garden structures—Design and construction 690.89
Garden tools 681.7631
Garden walks—Design and construction 717
Gardening 635; 635.96
Gardening—Anecdotes 635
Gardening—Dictionaries 635.03; 635.903
Gardening—Encyclopedias 635.03; 635.903
Gardening—Handbooks, manuals, etc. 635
Gardening—Humor 635.0207
Gardening in the shade 635.9543
Gardening—Middle West 635.0977
Gardening—Periodicals 635.05; 635.905

Gardening—Southern States 635.0975
Gardening—Therapeutic use 615.8515
Gardening to attract wildlife 635.96; 639.92
Gardening—United States 635.0973; 635.90973
Gardens 635; 712
Gardens, Chinese 712.0951
Gardens—Design 712; 712.6
Gardens—Designs and plans 712; 712.6
Gardens—England 712.0942; 712.60942
Gardens—Great Britain 712.0941; 712.60941
Gardens—Great Britain—Guidebooks 635.90941;
  712.0941
Gardens—History 712.09
Gardens—Japan 635.90952; 712.0952
Gardens, Japanese 712.0952; 712.60952
Gardens—Pictorial works 779.3
Gardner family 929.20973
Gardner, John, 1933– 813.54
Gardner, John, 1933– —Criticism and interpretation
  813.54
Garfield (Comic strip) 741.5973
Garfield (Fictitious character) 741.5973
Garfield (Fictitious character)—Comic books, strips, etc.
  741.5973
Garibaldi (Fish) 597.72
Garibaldi, Giuseppe, 1807–1882 945.083092
Garland, Hamlin, 1860–1940 813.52
Garland, Judy 782.42164092; 791.43028092
Garlic 641.3526
Garlic—Therapeutic use 615.32433
Garnishes (Cookery) 641.81
Garrard County (Ky.)—Genealogy 929.3769525
Garrett, Amanda Lee (Fictitious character) 813.54
Garrett, Dave (Fictitious character) 813.54
Garrett, Dave (Fictitious character)—Fiction 813.54
Garrett family 929.20973
Garrity, Callahan (Fictitious character) 813.54
Garrity, Callahan (Fictitious character)—Fiction 813.54
Garter snakes 597.962
Gas as fuel 665.7
Gas chromatography 543.0896; 544.926
Gas companies 363.63
Gas-detectors 681.2
Gas dynamics 533.2; 620.1074
Gas engineering 622.3385
Gas furnaces 697.043
Gas industry 338.476657
Gas industry—Government policy 338.476657
Gas industry—Government policy—United States
  338.4766570973; 388.560973
Gas industry—United States 338.4766570973;
  388.560973
Gas lasers 621.3663
Gas producers 665.77092
Gas-turbines 621.433
Gas well drilling 622.3381
Gas wells 622.3385
Gasdynamic lasers 621.3663
Gases 665.7
Gases—Absorption and adsorption 660.28423;
  660.284235
Gases from plants 575.8
Gases, Rare 546.75; 553.97
Gases—Separation 660.2842
Gaskell, Elizabeth Cleghorn, 1810–1865 823.8
Gaskell, Elizabeth Cleghorn, 1810–1865—Criticism and
  interpretation 823.8
Gaskell, Elizabeth Cleghorn, 1810–1865—Political and
  social views 823.8

Gasoline 665.53827
Gasoline supply—United States 381.45665538270973
Gasteria 584.32
Gasteromycetes 579.599
Gastner, Bill (Fictitious character) 813.54
Gastner, Bill (Fictitious character)—Fiction 813.54
Gastroenterology 616.33
Gastroesophageal reflux in children 618.9232
Gastrointestinal hormones 612.32
Gastrointestinal system 612.32
Gastrointestinal system—Cancer 616.99433
Gastrointestinal system—Diseases 616.33
Gastrointestinal system—Diseases—Handbooks, manuals, etc. 616.33
Gastrointestinal system—Endoscopic surgery 617.43059
Gastrointestinal system—Infections 616.33
Gastrointestinal system—Innervation 612.32
Gastrointestinal system—Motility—Disorders 616.33
Gastrointestinal system—Pathophysiology 616.3307
Gastrointestinal system—Physiology 612.32
Gastrointestinal system—Radiography 616.3307572
Gastrointestinal system—Surgery 617.43
Gastronomy 641.013
Gastropoda 594.3
Gastropoda, Fossil 564.3
Gastrulation 571.865
Gated communities 307.77
Gatehouses (Hydraulic structures) 627.882
Gates, Bill, 1955- 338.7610053092
Gates family 929.20973
Gateways (Computer networks) 004.6
Gaudion family (Fictitious characters) 823.914
Gauge fields (Physics) 530.1435
Gauguin, Paul, 1848-1903 759.4
Gauguin, Paul, 1848-1903—Correspondence 759.4
Gaul 936.4
Gaul—History 936.4
Gaul—History—Gallic Wars, 58-51 B.C. 936.402
Gaul—History—58 B.C.–511 A.D. 936.4
Gaulle, Charles de, 1890-1970 944.0836092
Gaunt, Jonathan (Fictitious character) 823.914
Gaunt, Jonathan (Fictitious character)—Fiction 823.914
Gaussian distribution 519.24
Gaussian processes 519.23
Gautama Buddha—Christian interpretations 294.363
Gautama Buddha—Teachings 294.363
Gautier, Jean-Paul (Fictitious character) 823.914
Gautier, Jean-Paul (Fictitious character)—Fiction 823.914
Gawain and the Grene Knight 821.1
Gay activists 305.90664092
Gay and lesbian studies 305.9066407
Gay business enterprises 338.708664
Gay clubs 367
Gay college students 305.9375
Gay communities 305.90664
Gay couples 306.848
Gay couples—Legal status, laws, etc. 346.016
Gay couples—Legal status, laws, etc.—United States 346.73016
Gay couples—United States 306.8480973
Gay erotic drama 808.829353808664
Gay erotic literature 808.80353808664; 809.93353808664
Gay erotic videos 791.45653808664
Gay erotica 700.453808664
Gay, John, 1685-1732 822.5
Gay, John, 1685-1732. Beggar's opera 822.5
Gay liberation movement 305.90664
Gay liberation movement—History 305.90664

Gay liberation movement—United States 305.906640973
Gay liberation movement—United States—History 305.906640973
Gay libraries 026.306766
Gay male couples 306.848
Gay male couples—United States 305.389664
Gay men 305.389664
Gay men—Alcohol use—United States 362.2920866420973
Gay men—California 305.38966409794
Gay men—California—Los Angeles 305.3896640979494
Gay men—California—San Francisco 305.3896640979461
Gay men—England 305.3896640942
Gay men—Legal status, laws, etc. 346.013
Gay men—New York (State) 305.38966409747
Gay men—New York (State)—New York 305.389664097471
Gay men—Relations with heterosexual women 306.7662
Gay men—Relations with heterosexuals 305.389664
Gay men—Religion 200.86642
Gay men—Religious life 291.44086642
Gay men—Sexual behavior 306.7662
Gay men—Sexual behavior—Literary collections 808.803538
Gay men—Social life and customs 305.389664
Gay men—United States 305.3896640973
Gay men—United States—Family relationships 305.389664
Gay men—United States—Psychology 305.389664
Gay men—United States—Social life and customs 305.3896640973
Gay motorcycle clubs 629.227506
Gay musicians 305.389664
Gay parents—United States 306.87408664
Gay press publications 070.59
Gay rights 323.3264
Gay rights—United States 305.906640973
Gay skinheads 305.389664
Gay teenagers—United States 305.235
Gay theater 792.022
Gay travelers 910.8664
Gay youth 305.235
Gays 305.90664
Gays—Biography 306.7660922
Gays—Employment—Law and legislation 344.0153
Gays—Identity 305.90664
Gays in popular culture 305.90664
Gays—Psychology 305.90664
Gays—Religious life 291.4408664
Gays—United States 305.90664
Gays' writings, American 810.80920664
Gays' writings, American—History and criticism 810.9920664
Gazebos 690.89; 728.9
Gazetteers 910.3
Gearing 621.833
Geeks (Computer enthusiasts) 004.092
Geese 598.417
Gehrig, Lou, 1903-1941 796.357092
Gem cutting 736.2028
Gems 133.322
Gems—Folklore 398.26
Gender identity 305.3
Gene expression 572.865
Gene libraries 026.57286
Gene mapping 572.8633; 611.01816
Gene silencing 572.865; 616.042
Gene targeting 572.877

Gene therapy 616.042
Genealogical libraries 026.9291
Genealogical literature 929.1
Genealogists 929.1092
Genealogists—Directories 929.1025
Genealogy 929.1
Genealogy—Authorship 808.066929; 929.1
Genealogy—Bibliography 016.9291
Genealogy—Bibliography—Catalogs 016.9291
Genealogy—Computer programs 929.10285
Genealogy—Data processing 929.10285
Genealogy—Dictionaries 929.103
Genealogy—Periodicals 929.105
General Agreement on Tariffs and Trade (Organization) 382.92
General certificate of education examination (Great Britain) 371.262
General education 370.11; 378.01
General education—United States 378.01
General educational development tests 373.1262
General Motors Corporation 338.762920973
General Motors J-cars 629.2222
General Motors J-cars—Maintenance and repair 629.28722
General Motors J-cars—Maintenance and repair—Handbooks, manuals, etc. 629.28722
General Motors N-cars 629.2222
General Motors N-cars—Maintenance and repair 629.28722
General Motors N-cars—Maintenance and repair—Handbooks, manuals, etc. 629.28722
General National Vocational Qualifications (Great Britain) 373.1262
General relativity (Physics) 530.11
General semantics 149.94
General stores 381.14
General stores—Collectibles—United States—Catalogs 745.10973075
Generalized spaces 514.3
Generals 355.0092
Generals in art 704.942
Generals in literature 808.80352355; 809.93352355
Generation-skipping transfer tax—Law and legislation 343.053
Generation-skipping transfer tax—Law and legislation—United States 343.73053
Generation X 305.2
Generational accounting 339.5
Generative grammar 415
Generative organs 573.6; 612.6
Generative organs—Diseases 616.65
Generative organs, Female 573.66
Generative organs, Female—Cancer 616.99465
Generative organs, Female—Diseases 618.1
Generative organs, Female—Endoscopic surgery 618.1059
Generative organs, Female—Infections 618.1
Generative organs, Female—Laser surgery 618.1059
Generative organs, Female—Surgery 618.0459; 618.1059
Generative organs, Female—Surgery—Complications 618.1059
Generative organs, Female—Ultrasonic imaging 618.107543
Generative organs, Male 573.65
Generative organs, Male—Diseases 616.65
Generative programming (Computer science) 005.11
Generic programming (Computer science) 005.11
Generosity 179.9

Genes 572.86
Genesee County (Mich.) 977.437
Genesee County (Mich.)—Maps 912.77437
Genet, Jean, 1910- 842.912
Genet, Jean, 1910- —Criticism and interpretation 842.912
Genetic algorithms 511.8
Genetic counseling 362.196042
Genetic disorders 571.948; 616.042
Genetic disorders—Diagnosis 616.042
Genetic disorders in animals 571.9481; 636.0896042
Genetic disorders in children 618.920042
Genetic engineering 660.65
Genetic engineering industry 338.476605
Genetic engineering—Law and legislation 344.0957
Genetic engineering—Moral and ethical aspects 174.25
Genetic markers 572.86
Genetic programming (Computer science) 006.31
Genetic psychology 155.7
Genetic recombination 572.877
Genetic regulation 572.865
Genetic screening 362.19604207; 616.042
Genetic toxicology 616.042
Genetic transcription 572.8845
Genetic transcription—Regulation 572.8845
Genetic transformation 571.9648
Genetic translation 572.645
Genetic vectors 660.65
Genetically modified foods 641.3; 664
Genetics 576.5
Genetics—History 576.509
Genetics—Periodicals 576.505
Genetics—Research 576.5072
Genghis Khan, 1162-1227 950.2092
Genie Awards 791.4307971
Genitourinary organs 573.6; 612.46
Genitourinary organs—Cancer 616.9946
Genitourinary organs—Diseases 616.6
Genitourinary organs—Imaging 616.60754
Genitourinary organs—Radiography 616.607572
Genitourinary organs—Surgery 617.46
Genitourinary organs—Surgery—Atlases 617.4600222
Genitourinary organs—Surgery—Complications 617.4601
Genitourinary organs—Ultrasonic imaging 616.607543
Genius 153.98
Genocide 304.663
Genocide—History—20th century 304.6630904
Genocide in art 700.455; 704.949364151
Genomes 572.86
Genomic imprinting 572.865
Genotype-environment interaction 576.85
Gently, George (Fictitious character) 823.914
Gently, George (Fictitious character)—Fiction 823.914
Geochemical prospecting 622.13
Geochemistry 551.9
Geochronometry 551.701
Geodesic domes 721.042
Geodesy 526.1
Geodetic astronomy 526.6
Geodynamics 550; 551
Geoffrey, of Monmouth, Bishop of St. Asaph, 1100?-1154. Historia regum Britanniae 941.01
Geographers 910.92
Geographic information systems 025.0691
Geographic information systems—Periodicals 025.069105
Geographic information systems—Standards 025.06910218

Geographical myths 398.234
Geographical perception 304.23; 910.019
Geographical positions 526.64
Geography 910
Geography, Ancient 913
Geography, Ancient—Maps 911; 911.3; 912.3
Geography, Arab 910.89927
Geography—Bibliography 016.91
Geography—Data processing 910.285
Geography—Dictionaries 910.3
Geography—Early works to 1800 910
Geography—Encyclopedias 910.3
Geography—History 910.9
Geography—Mathematics 910.0151
Geography, Medieval 910.902
Geography—Methodology 910.01
Geography—Miscellanea 910
Geography—Periodicals 910.5
Geography—Philosophy 910.01
Geography—Research 910.72
Geography—Statistical methods 910.72
Geography—Study and teaching 910.71
Geography—Study and teaching (Elementary) 372.891
Geography—Study and teaching (Secondary) 910.712
Geography—Terminology 910.014
Geography—Textbooks—1945- 910
Geological libraries 026.551
Geological mapping 550.223
Geological modeling 550.15118; 551.0228
Geological museums 551.074
Geological surveys 551
Geological time 551.701
Geologists 551.092
Geology 550; 551
Geology—Alaska 557.98
Geology—Alberta 557.123
Geology—Antarctica 559.89
Geology—Australia 559.4
Geology—Australia—New South Wales 559.44
Geology—Australia—Queensland 559.43
Geology—Australia—Sydney Basin (N.S.W.) 559.44
Geology—Australia—Western Australia 559.41
Geology—Bibliography 016.55
Geology—Botswana 556.883
Geology—Brazil 558.1
Geology—British Columbia 557.11
Geology—California 557.94
Geology—China 555.1
Geology—Colorado 557.88
Geology—Data processing 550.285
Geology—Dictionaries 550.3
Geology, Economic 553
Geology—Experiments 550.724; 550.78; 551.0724; 551.078
Geology—Florida 557.59
Geology—France 554.4
Geology—Himalaya Mountains 555.496
Geology—History 550.9
Geology in art 704.94955
Geology—India 555.4
Geology—Kenya—Marsabit District 556.7627
Geology—Maps 550.223
Geology—Mathematics 550.151
Geology—Montana 557.86
Geology—Nevada 557.93
Geology—New Mexico 557.89
Geology—North America 557
Geology—Ontario 557.13
Geology—Ontario—Algoma (District) 557.13132

Geology—Ontario—Kenora (District) 557.13112
Geology—Ontario—Sudbury (District) 557.13133
Geology—Ontario—Thunder Bay (District) 557.1312
Geology—Periodicals 550.5
Geology—Poland 554.38
Geology—Saskatchewan 557.124
Geology—South Africa 556.8
Geology—Statistical methods 550.727
Geology, Stratigraphic 551.7
Geology, Stratigraphic—Archaean 551.712
Geology, Stratigraphic—Cambrian 551.723
Geology, Stratigraphic—Carboniferous 551.75
Geology, Stratigraphic—Cenozoic 551.78
Geology, Stratigraphic—Cretaceous 551.77
Geology, Stratigraphic—Devonian 551.74
Geology, Stratigraphic—Eocene 551.784
Geology, Stratigraphic—Holocene 551.793
Geology, Stratigraphic—Jurassic 551.766
Geology, Stratigraphic—Mesozoic 551.76
Geology, Stratigraphic—Miocene 551.787
Geology, Stratigraphic—Mississippian 551.751
Geology, Stratigraphic—Neogene 551.786
Geology, Stratigraphic—Oligocene 551.785
Geology, Stratigraphic—Ordovician 551.731
Geology, Stratigraphic—Paleocene 551.783
Geology, Stratigraphic—Paleogene 551.782
Geology, Stratigraphic—Paleozoic 551.72
Geology, Stratigraphic—Pennsylvanian 551.752
Geology, Stratigraphic—Permian 551.756
Geology, Stratigraphic—Pleistocene 551.792
Geology, Stratigraphic—Pliocene 551.788
Geology, Stratigraphic—Precambrian 551.71
Geology, Stratigraphic—Proterozoic 551.715
Geology, Stratigraphic—Quaternary 551.79
Geology, Stratigraphic—Silurian 551.732
Geology, Stratigraphic—Tertiary 551.78
Geology, Stratigraphic—Triassic 551.762
Geology, Structural 551.8
Geology, Structural—North America 551.8097
Geology—Texas 557.64
Geology—Ukraine 554.77
Geology—United States 557.3
Geology—United States—Guidebooks 557.3
Geology—Utah 557.92
Geology—Virginia 557.55
Geology—Virginia—Bibliography 016.55755
Geology—Wyoming 557.87
Geomagnetism 538.7; 538.72
Geomagnetism—Secular variations 538.72
Geomancy 133.333
Geomatic files 025.06526; 526
Geomatics 526
Geometric dissections 516; 793.74
Geometric function theory 515.9
Geometric group theory 512.2
Geometric measure theory 515.42
Geometric probabilities 519.2
Geometrical constructions 516.2
Geometrical models 516.00228
Geometrical optics 535.32
Geometry 516; 530.156
Geometry, Affine 516.4
Geometry, Algebraic 516.35
Geometry, Algebraic—Data processing 516.350285
Geometry, Analytic 516.3
Geometry—Data processing 516.00285
Geometry, Descriptive 516.6
Geometry, Differential 516.36; 530.15636
Geometry—Foundations 516

Geometry—History 516.009
Geometry, Hyperbolic 516.9
Geometry, Non-Euclidean 516.9
Geometry, Plane 516.22
Geometry—Problems, exercises, etc. 516.0076
Geometry, Projective 516.5
Geometry, Riemannian 516.373
Geomorphological tracers 551.410284
Geomorphology 551.41
Geomorphology—History 551.4109
Geomorphology—Tropics 551.410913
Geophysical observatories 550.723
Geophysical well logging 622.1828
Geophysicists 550.92
Geophysics 550
Geophysics—Periodicals 550.5
Geophysics—Remote sensing 550.287
Geopolitics 320.12
George III, King of Great Britain, 1738–1820
  941.073092
George IV, King of Great Britain, 1762–1830
  941.074092; 942.074092
George family 929.20973
George, Saint, d. 303—Legends 398.22
George Washington National Forest (Va. and W. Va.)
  975.5922
George Washington National Forest (Va. and W. Va.)—
  Guidebooks 917.55922
Georgia 975.8
Georgia—Description and travel 917.5804; 917.500443;
  917.580444
Georgia—Genealogy 929.10720758; 929.3758
Georgia—Guidebooks 917.5804; 917.580443; 917.580444
Georgia—History 975.8
Georgia—History—Colonial period, ca. 1600–1775
  975.802
Georgia—History—1775–1865 975.803
Georgia—History—Civil War, 1861–1865 973.7458
Georgia—Maps 912.758
Georgia—Politics and government 320.4758; 975.8
Georgia—Politics and government—1951–
  320.975809045; 975.8043
Georgia (Republic) 947.59
Georgia (Republic)—History 947.59
Georgia (Republic)—History—To 1801 947.59
Georgia—Social life and customs 975.8
Georgia—Tours 917.5804; 917.580443; 917.580444
Geostationary satellites 629.4642
Geotextiles 620.1923; 624.18923
Geothermal engineering 621.44
Geothermal power plants 333.88
Geothermal resources 333.88
Geraldi, James (Fictitious character) 813.52
Geraniums 583.79
Gerbils 599.3583; 639.9583
Gerbils as pets 639.9583
Geriatric cardiology 618.97612
Geriatric neurology 618.9768
Geriatric neuropsychiatry 618.9768
Geriatric nursing 610.7365
Geriatric nursing—Handbooks, manuals, etc. 610.7365
Geriatric nursing—Outlines, syllabi, etc. 610.7365
Geriatric oncology 618.976994
Geriatric pharmacology 615.580846
Geriatric pharmacology—Handbooks, manuals, etc.
  615.580846
Geriatric psychiatry 362.20846; 618.97689
Geriatric psychiatry—Handbooks, manuals, etc.
  618.97689

Geriatric psychopharmacology 618.9768918
Geriatrics 618.97
Geriatrics—Handbooks, manuals, etc. 618.97
Geriatrics—Immunological aspects 618.97079
Germ cells 571.845
German Americans 973.0431
German Americans—Genealogy 929.108931073
German Americans—Genealogy—Handbooks, manuals,
  etc. 929.108931073
German Americans—Genealogy—Periodicals
  929.108931073
German Americans—History 973.0431
German Americans—History—19th century
  973.043109034
German Americans—Pennsylvania—Genealogy
  929.1089310748
German drama 832; 832.008
German drama—20th century 832.914; 832.91408
German drama—20th century—Translations into English
  832.91408
German drama—History and criticism 832.009
German drama—Translations into English 832.008
German fiction 833; 833.008
German fiction—20th century 833.91; 833.9108;
  833.912; 833.91208; 833.914; 833.91408
German fiction—20th century—History and criticism
  833.9109; 833.91409
German fiction—20th century—Translations into English
  833.91208
German fiction—History and criticism 833.009
German language 430
German language—Conversation and phrase books
  438.34
German language—Conversation and phrase books—
  English 438.3421
German language—Dictionaries 433
German language—Dictionaries—English 433.21
German language—Grammar 435; 438.2; 438.2421
German language—Grammar—1950– 438.2
German language—Readers 438.6; 438.6421
German language—Readers—Germany 438.6421
German language—Textbooks for foreign speakers—
  English 438.2421; 438.3421
German language—Verb 435; 438.2; 438.2421
German language—Verb—Tables 438.2421
German literature 830; 830.8
German literature—Middle High German, 1050–1500
  830.8002
German literature—Middle High German, 1050–1500—
  History and criticism 830.9002
German literature—Early modern, 1500–1700 830.8004
German literature—Early modern, 1500–1700—History
  and criticism 830.9004
German literature—18th century 830.8006
German literature—18th century—History and criticism
  830.9006
German literature—19th century 830.8007
German literature—19th century—History and criticism
  830.9007
German literature—20th century 830.80091;
  830.800912; 830.800914
German literature—20th century—History and criticism
  830.90091; 830.900912; 830.900914
German literature—Germany (East) 830.80909431
German literature—History and criticism 830.9
German literature—Jewish authors 830.808924
German literature—Jewish authors—History and
  criticism 830.98924
German literature—Translations into English 830.8

German philology 430
German poetry 831; 831.008
German poetry—Middle High German, 1050–1500
  831.2; 831.208
German poetry—Middle High German, 1050–1500—
  History and criticism 831.209
German poetry—20th century 831.91; 831.9108;
  831.914; 831.91408
German poetry—20th century—Translations into
  English 831.9108; 831.91408
German poetry—Translations into English 831.008
German reunification question (1949-1990) 943.087
German shepherd dog 636.7376
German shorthaired pointer 636.7525
German wit and humor 837.008; 838.02
German wit and humor, Pictorial 741.5943
Germanic languages 430
Germanic peoples 943
Germanic philology 430
Germans—Foreign countries 305.831
Germans—Soviet Union 305.831047
Germans—Soviet Union—History 947.00431
Germany 943
Germany—Armed Forces 355.00943
Germany—Armed Forces—Uniforms 355.140943
Germany—Armed Forces—Uniforms—History
  355.140943
Germany—Armed Forces—Uniforms—History—20th
  century 355.1409430904
Germany—Church history 274.3
Germany—Church history—1933–1945 322.1094309043
Germany—Civilization 943
Germany—Description and travel 914.304; 914.304879;
  914.30488
Germany (East) 943.1087
Germany (East)—Economic conditions 330.9431
Germany (East)—Economic policy 338.9431
Germany (East)—Foreign relations 327.431009045
Germany (East)—Foreign relations—Germany (West)
  327.430431
Germany (East)—Politics and government
  320.943109045; 943.1087
Germany (East)—Politics and government—1989–1990
  320.943109049; 943.10879
Germany—Economic conditions 330.943
Germany—Economic conditions—1918–1945
  330.943085
Germany—Economic conditions—1990– 330.9430879
Germany—Economic policy 338.943
Germany—Economic policy—1990– 338.943
Germany—Foreign relations 327.43
Germany—Foreign relations—1990– 327.43009049
Germany—Genealogy 929.1072043
Germany—Genealogy—Handbooks, manuals, etc.
  929.1072043
Germany—Guidebooks 914.304; 914.304879; 914.30488
Germany. Heer—History 355.00943; 940.541343
Germany—History 943
Germany—History—To 1517 943.01; 943.02
Germany—History—843–1273 943.02
Germany—History—1789–1900 943.06; 943.07
Germany—History—Revolution, 1848–1849 943.076
Germany—History—1871–1918 943.08
Germany—History—1918–1933 943.085
Germany—History—1933–1945 943.086
Germany—History—1945–1955 943.0874
Germany—History—Unification, 1990 943.0879
Germany—Intellectual life 943
Germany. Luftwaffe—History 358.400943

Germany. Luftwaffe—History—World War, 1939–1945
  940.544943
Germany—Military policy 355.033543
Germany—Politics and government 320.943; 943
Germany—Politics and government—1789–1900
  320.94309034
Germany—Politics and government—1918–1933
  320.94309041; 320.94309042; 943.085
Germany—Politics and government—1933–1945
  320.94309043; 943.086
Germany—Politics and government—1945–1990
  320.94309045; 943.087
Germany—Politics and government—1990–
  320.94309049; 943.0879
Germany—Social conditions 943
Germany—Social life and customs 943
Germany (West) 943.087
Germany (West)—Economic conditions 330.943087
Germany (West)—Economic conditions—1974–1990
  330.9430877
Germany (West)—Economic policy 338.943
Germany (West)—Economic policy—1974–1990
  338.943
Germany (West)—Foreign relations 327.43009045
Germany (West)—Guidebooks 914.304; 914.304879;
  914.330488
Germany (West)—Politics and government
  320.94309034
Germany (West)—Social conditions 943.087
Germfree animals 619; 636.0885
Germinal centers 612.42
Germination 571.862
Germplasm resources 333.9534
Germplasm resources—Law and legislation
  346.0469534
Germplasm resources, Plant 333.9534; 631.523
Gerontology 305.26
Gerontology and the humanities 305.26
Gerontology—Bibliography 016.30526; 016.3626
Gerontology—United States 305.260973
Gershwin, George, 1898–1937 780.92
Gertrude (Fictitious character : Updike) 813.54
Gestalt psychology 150.1982
Gestalt therapy 616.89143
Getty, J. Paul (Jean Paul), 1892–1976 332.092
Gettysburg Campaign, 1863 973.7349
Gettysburg (Pa.), Battle of, 1863 973.7349
Gettysburg (Pa.), Battle of, 1863—Personal narratives
  973.7349092
Gettysburg (Pa.), Battle of, 1863—Pictorial works
  973.73490222
Geysers 551.23
Ghana 966.7
Ghana—Description and travel 916.6704; 916.67045
Ghana—Economic policy 338.9667
Ghana—Geography 916.67
Ghana—Guidebooks 916.6704; 916.67045
Ghana—History 966.7
Ghana—Periodicals 966.7005
Ghana—Politics and government 320.9667; 966.7
Ghana—Politics and government—1957–1979
  320.9667046; 320.966709045; 966.705
Ghana—Politics and government—1979– 320.9667048;
  320.966709048; 966.705
Ghana—Social life and customs 966.7
Ghanaian literature (English) 820; 820.809667
Ghose, Aurobindo, 1872–1950 821.912
Ghose, Aurobindo, 1872–1950. Savitri 821.912
Ghost dance 299.74

Ghost stories 398.25; 808.838733
Ghost stories, American 813.08733; 813.0873308
Ghost stories, Chinese 398.2095105; 895.1308733
Ghost stories, English 823.08733; 823.0873308
Ghost towns—Arizona 979.1
Ghost towns—Colorado 978.8
Ghost towns—Nevada 979.3
Ghost towns—West (U.S.) 978
Ghost towns—West (U.S.)—Pictorial works
   779.9917800222; 978
Ghosts 133.1
Ghosts—Southern States 133.10975
Ghosts—United States 133.10973
Ghote, Ganesh (Fictitious character) 823.914
Ghote, Ganesh (Fictitious character)—Fiction 823.914
Ghouls and ogres in literature 808.80375
Giant panda 599.789
Giant sequoia 585.5
Gibbon, Edward, 1737–1794 937.06092
Gibbons 599.882
Gibbons, Cuthbert (Fictitious character) 813.54
Gibbons, Cuthbert (Fictitious character)—Fiction 813.54
Gibbs phenomenon 515.2433
Gibran, Kahlil, 1883–1931 811.52; 892.715
Gibran, Kahlil, 1883–1931—Criticism and interpretation
   811.52
Gibran, Kahlil, 1883–1931—Translations into English
   892.715
Gibson, Carole Ann (Fictitious character) 813.54
Gibson family 929.20973
Gibson, Mel 791.43028092
Gide, André, 1869–1951 848.91209
Gide, André, 1869–1951—Criticism and interpretation
   848.91209
Gideon, George (Fictitious character) 823.912
Gideon, George (Fictitious character)—Fiction 823.912
Gielgud, John, Sir, 1904– 792.028092
Gift baskets 745.59
Gift of the Holy Ghost (Mormon theology) 234.13
Gift shops 658.8704
Gift wrapping 745.54
Gifted children 155.455; 649.155
Gifted children—Education 371.95
Gifted children—Education—Curricula 371.953
Gifted children—Education—United States 371.950973
Gifted children—Identification 371.952
Gifted children—United States 649.1550973
Gifted persons 305.90829
Gifts 394; 658.82
Gifts, Spiritual 234.13
Gifts, Spiritual—Biblical teaching 234.13
Gifts—Taxation—Law and legislation 343.053
Gifts—Taxation—Law and legislation—United States
   343.730535
Gifts to politicians 172.2
Giftware 680
Giftware industry 338.4768
Gigantopithecus 569.88
Gilbert family 929.20973
Gilbert, W. S. (William Schwenck), 1836–1911
   782.12092; 822.8
Gilbert, W. S. (William Schwenck), 1836–1911—
   Criticism and interpretation 822.8
Gilbert, W. S. (William Schwenck), 1836–1911—
   Dictionaries 782.12092
Gilding 745.75
Giles County (Tenn.)—Genealogy 929.376861
Gilgamesh 892.1
Gill, Eric, 1882–1940 700.92

Gillard, Patrick (Fictitious character) 823.914
Gillard, Patrick (Fictitious character)—Fiction 823.914
Gilman, Charlotte Perkins, 1860–1935 818.409
Gilt glass 748.6
Gingerbread 641.8653
Gingerbread houses 745.5
Ginglymostoma 597.3
Gingrich, Newt 328.73092
Ginkgo—Therapeutic use 615.3257
Ginsberg, Allen, 1926– 811.54
Ginsburg, Ruth Bader 347.732634
Ginseng 583.84; 633.88384
Ginseng industry 338.17388384
Ginseng—Therapeutic use 615.32384
Ginzburg, Natalia 853.912
Giotto, 1266?–1337 759.5
Giotto, 1266?–1337—Criticism and interpretation 759.5
Giovani cannibali (Literary movement) 853.91409
Giraffe 599.638
Girders 624.17723
Girl Scout cookies 664.7525
Girlie magazines 363.47
Girls 305.23
Girls' bedrooms 643.53083; 747.77083
Girls' computer network resources 025.04
Girls—Education 371.823
Girls in popular culture 305.23
Girls' pants 646.43306; 687.113
Girls—Prayer-books and devotions 242.62
Girls—Psychology 305.23
Girls—United States 305.23
Girls—United States—Social conditions 305.23
Giselle (Choreographic work) 792.842
Gissing, George, 1857–1903 823.8
Gissing, George, 1857–1903—Criticism and
   interpretation 823.8
Glacial epoch 551.792
Glacial isostasy 551.313
Glacial landforms 551.315
Glacier National Park (Mont.) 978.652
Glaciers 551.312
Glaciology 551.31
Gladstone, W. E. (William Ewart), 1809–1898
   941.081092
Gladwin County (Mich.) 977.472
Gladwin County (Mich.)—Maps 912.77472
Gladys the Dragon (Fictitious character) 823.914
Glamour photography 778.924
Glasgow, Ellen Anderson Gholson, 1873–1945 813.52
Glasgow, Ellen Anderson Gholson, 1873–1945—
   Criticism and interpretation 813.52
Glasgow (Scotland) 941.443
Glasnost 947.0854
Glass 620.144; 666.1
Glass art 748
Glass blowing and working 666.122; 748.20282
Glass construction 693.96; 721.04496
Glass craft 748.5
Glass craft—Patterns 748.5
Glass fiber industry 338.47666157
Glass fibers 666.157
Glass—Fracture 620.1446
Glass holiday decorations 666.19; 748.8
Glass manufacture 666.1
Glass mugs 666.19; 748.83
Glass painting and staining 748.50282
Glass painting and staining—Patterns 748.50282
Glassware 748.2
Glassware—Collectors and collecting 748.2075

Glassware—History 748.29
Glassware industry 338.4766619; 666.19
Glassware—United States 748.2913
Glaucoma 617.741
Glaucoma—Surgery 617.741059
Glaucomys volans 599.369
Glazes 666.427; 738.127
Glencannon, Mr. (Fictitious character) 813.52
Glenning, Paula (Fictitious character) 823.914
Glenning, Paula (Fictitious character)—Fiction 823.914
Gliders (Aeronautics) 629.14
Gliders (Mammals) 599.232
Gliding and soaring 797.55
GLIM 519.502855369
Global analysis (Mathematics) 514.74
Global capitation (Medical care) 338.433621; 362.10681
Global Climate Observing System 551.6072
Global differential geometry 516.362
Global environmental change 551.6
Global method of teaching 372.0116
Global Positioning System 526.64; 623.893
Global system for mobile communications 384.535; 621.38456
Global temperature changes 551.5253
Global warming 363.73874; 577.276
Globalization 303.482; 327.1
Globalization—Religious aspects 291.1787
Globe Theatre (Southwark, London, England) 792.0942164
Globes 912
Glomerulonephritis 616.612
Gloria in excelsis Deo (Music) 782.3232
Glosa (Artificial language) 499.99
Glossolalia 234.132
Glossopteris 561.597
Gloucester County (Va.)—Genealogy 929.375532
Gloucestershire (England) 942.41
Gloucestershire (England)—Guidebooks 914.24104; 914.24104859; 914.2410486
Gloucestershire (England)—History 942.41
Glow-in-the-dark books 741.64
Gluskap (Legendary character) 398.2089973
Glutamic acid—Receptors 573.8528
Gluten-free diet—Recipes 641.5638
Glycemic index 613.283
Glycoconjugates 572.567
Glycoprotein hormones 571.7468
Glycoproteins 572.68
Glycosides 572.567
GMC trucks 629.2232
GMC trucks—Fuel systems—Maintenance and repair—Handbooks, manuals, etc. 629.253
GMC trucks—Maintenance and repair 629.28732
GMC trucks—Maintenance and repair—Handbooks, manuals, etc. 629.28732
GMC vans 629.2234
GMC vans—Maintenance and repair 629.28734
GMC vans—Maintenance and repair—Handbooks, manuals, etc. 629.28734
Gnats 595.772
Gnostic literature 299.932
Gnosticism 273.1; 299.932
Go-betweens in literature 808.8035239; 809.9335239
Go (Game) 794.4
Go (Game)—Collections of games 794.4
Go (Game)—Handicap games 794.4
Go (Game)—Jōseki 794.4
Go (Game)—Openings 794.4
Go (Game) problems 794.4

Go (Game)—Tesuji 794.4
Goa, Daman and Diu (India) 954.799
Goa, Daman and Diu (India)—History 954.799
Goa (India : State) 954.799
Goa (India : State)—History 954.799
Goajiro literature 898.39
Goal (Psychology) 158.1
Goal setting in personnel management 658.301; 658.314
Goat milk industry 338.17717
Goats 599.648; 636.39
God 211; 231
God—Attributes 231.4
God—Biblical teaching 231
God—Fatherhood 231.1
God (Hinduism) 294.5211
God—History of doctrines 231
God (Judaism) 296.311
God (Judaism)—History of doctrines 296.311
God—Love 231.6
God—Name 231.4
God—Name—Biblical teaching 231.4
God—Omniscience 212.7
God—Promises 231.7
God—Proof 212.1
God—Proof, Cosmological 212.1
God—Study and teaching 231.071
God—Will 231.4
Goddess religion 291.14
Goddesses 291.2114
Goddesses, Hindu 294.52114
Goddesses, Phoenician 299.26
Godhead (Mormon theology) 231
Gods 291.211
Gods, Buddhist 294.3211
Gods, Buddhist, in art 704.94843211
Gods, Chinese 299.51
Gods, Egyptian 299.31
Gods, Greek 292.211
Gods, Greek, in literature 808.8038292211; 809.9338292211
Gods, Hindu 294.5211
Gods, Hindu, in art 704.94845211
Gods in art 704.948
Gods, Roman 292.211
Gods, Shinto 299.561211
Godwin, William, 1756–1836 823.6
Godwin, William, 1756–1836—Criticism and interpretation 828.609
Goebbels, Joseph, 1897–1945 943.086092
Goethe, Johann Wolfgang von, 1749–1832 831.6
Goethe, Johann Wolfgang von, 1749–1832—Criticism and interpretation 831.6
Goethe, Johann Wolfgang von, 1749–1832. Faust 832.6
Goethe, Johann Wolfgang von, 1749–1832—Knowledge—Art 701.17; 831.6
Goethe, Johann Wolfgang von, 1749–1832—Translations into English 831.6
Goff family 929.20973
Goffman, Erving 301.092
Gofrette (Fictitious character : Brasset) 843.914
Goge 787.6
Gogebic County (Mich.) 977.4983
Gogebic County (Mich.)—Maps 912.774983
Gogh, Vincent van, 1853–1890 759.9492
Gogh, Vincent van, 1853–1890—Catalogs 759.9492
Gogh, Vincent van, 1853–1890—Correspondence 759.9492

Government accountants 657.835
Government advertising 659.19351
Government aid to education 379.11
Government aid to education—New York (State) 379.1109747; 379.12209747
Government aid to education—United States 379.110973
Government aid to higher education 379.118
Government aid to higher education—United States 379.1180973
Government aid to publishing 070.5079; 353.77
Government aid to the arts 353.77
Government aid to the motion picture industry 353.77; 791.43079
Government aid to the theater 353.77; 792.079
Government and the press 352.748
Government and the press—United States 071.3
Government attorneys 351.088344
Government attorneys—United States 340.02373
Government auctions 352.554
Government-binding theory (Linguistics) 415
Government business enterprises 338.62; 352.266
Government business enterprises—Developing countries 338.62091724
Government business enterprises—Great Britain 338.620941
Government business enterprises—India 338.620954; 352.2660954
Government business enterprises—India—Auditing 352.2662430954
Government business enterprises—India—Management 352.2660954
Government communication systems 352.383
Government consultants—United States 352.3730973
Government contractors 352.53
Government employees 352.63
Government employees' long-term care insurance 368.42
Government employees' long-term care insurance—Law and legislation 346.08642
Government executives 352.3
Government executives—United States 352.30973
Government information 341.0662
Government information agencies 352.74
Government investigators 352.8; 363.1065; 363.25
Government liability 342.088
Government liability (International law) 341.26
Government liability—United States 342.73088
Government libraries 027.5
Government libraries—United States 027.50973
Government libraries—United States—Directories 027.502573
Government ownership 335; 338.924
Government ownership—Great Britain 338.94104
Government paperwork 352.387
Government productivity 352.375; 352.66
Government property 333.1
Government property—United States 333.10973
Government publications 011.53
Government publications—Great Britain 015.41053
Government publications—Great Britain—Bibliography 015.41053
Government publications—Great Britain—Bibliography—Periodicals 015.41053
Government publications—United States 015.73053
Government publications—United States—Bibliography 015.73053
Government publicity 352.748
Government purchasing 352.53

Government purchasing—Law and legislation 346.023
Government purchasing—Law and legislation—European Economic Community countries 346.4023
Government purchasing—Law and legislation—United States 346.73023
Government purchasing—United States 352.530973
Government purchasing—United States—Data processing 352.530285
Government relations with ethnic groups 323.11
Government risks insurance claims 368.8
Government securities—Law and legislation 346.0922
Government securities—Law and legislation—United States 346.730922; 353.008258
Government securities—United States 332.632320973
Government spending policy 336.39
Government spending policy—United States 336.390973
Government travel 352.67
Government travel—Law and legislation 342.0686
Government travel—Law and legislation—United States 342.730686
Governmental investigations 353.463
Governmental investigations—United States 353.4530973
Governors 352.23213
Governors general 352.23
Governors—India 352.2320954; 954.0099
Governors—United States 352.232130973; 973.0099
Gower, John, 1325?–1408 821.1
Gower, John, 1325?–1408. Confessio amantis 821.1
Goya, Francisco, 1746–1828 760.092
Goya, Francisco, 1746–1828—Exhibitions 760.092
Grace at meals 242.2; 291.43
Grace (Fictitious character : Hoffman) 823.914
Grace, Princess of Monaco, 1929–1982 944.949
Grace (Theology) 234
Grace (Theology)—Biblical teaching 234
Grade repetition 371.285
Grading and marking (Students) 371.272
Grading and marking (Students)—United States 371.2720973
Grading (Earthwork) 624.152; 625.733
Graduate Management Admission Test 650.076; 658.0076
Graduate Management Admission Test—Study guides—Periodicals 650.076
Graduate Record Examination 378.1662
Graduate students 378.1982
Graduate students in science 507.11
Graduate students—Supervision of 378.1794; 378.194046
Graf, Stephanie, 1969– 796.342092
Graffiti 080
Graft rejection 617.95
Grafton, Jake (Fictitious character) 813.54
Grafton, Jake (Fictitious character)—Fiction 813.54
Graham, Billy, 1918– 269.2092
Graham, Charlotte (Fictitious character) 813.54
Graham, Charlotte (Fictitious character)—Fiction 813.54
Graham family 929.20973
Graham, Katharine, 1917– 070.5092
Graham, Martha 792.82092
Grail 398.4
Grain 633.1; 664.7
Grain amaranths 583.53
Grain boundaries 620.11299; 669.95
Grain—Storage 633.10468
Grain trade 380.14131; 381.4131; 382.4131

Grain trade—Government policy—United States 382.41310973
Grain trade—United States 338.17310973; 380.141310973; 381.41310973; 382.41310973
Grain—Transportation 388.044
Grameen Bank 332.1095492
Grammar, Comparative and general 415
Grammar, Comparative and general—Adjuncts 415
Grammar, Comparative and general—Aspect 415
Grammar, Comparative and general—Case 415
Grammar, Comparative and general—Clauses 415
Grammar, Comparative and general—Clitics 415
Grammar, Comparative and general—Deixis 415
Grammar, Comparative and general—Demonstratives 415
Grammar, Comparative and general—Diminutives 415
Grammar, Comparative and general—Grammatical categories 415
Grammar, Comparative and general—Grammaticalization 415
Grammar, Comparative and general—History 415.09
Grammar, Comparative and general—Infinitival constructions 415
Grammar, Comparative and general—Morphology 415
Grammar, Comparative and general—Morphosyntax 415
Grammar, Comparative and general—Negatives 415
Grammar, Comparative and general—Noun phrase 415
Grammar, Comparative and general—Number 415
Grammar, Comparative and general—Phonology 414
Grammar, Comparative and general—Pronoun 415
Grammar, Comparative and general—Quantifiers 415
Grammar, Comparative and general—Reciprocals 415
Grammar, Comparative and general—Sentences 415
Grammar, Comparative and general—Syntax 415
Grammar, Comparative and general—Tense 415
Grammar, Comparative and general—Topic and comment 415
Grammar, Comparative and general—Verb 415
Grammar, Comparative and general—Verb phrase 415
Grammar, Comparative and general—Word order 415
Gramsci, Antonio, 1891–1937 335.43092
Grand Canyon (Ariz.) 551.442; 979.132
Grand Canyon (Ariz.)—Description and travel 917.913204; 917.91320453; 917.91320454
Grand Canyon (Ariz.)—Pictorial works 917.913200222
Grand Canyon National Park (Ariz.) 979.132
Grand Canyon National Park (Ariz.)—Guidebooks 917.9132
Grand Forks County (N.D.) 978.416
Grand Forks County (N.D.)—Maps 912.78416
Grand jury 345.072
Grand jury—United States 345.73072
Grand Prix racing 796.72
Grand Prix racing—History 796.7209
Grand Teton National Park (Wyo.) 978.755
Grand Teton National Park (Wyo.)—Guidebooks 917.8755
Grand tours (Education) 914.04
Grand Traverse County (Mich.) 977.464
Grand Traverse County (Mich.)—Maps 912.77464
Grand unified theories (Nuclear physics) 530.142
Grand Western Canal (England) 386.480942354
Granddaughters 306.8745
Grandfathers 306.8745
Grandmothers 306.8745
Grandparent and child 306.8745
Grandparent and child—Religious aspects 291.178358745

Grandparenting 306.8745
Grandparenting—United States 306.87450973
Grandparents 306.8745
Granite 552.3
Granite industry and trade 622.352
Grant, Alan (Fictitious character) 823.912
Grant, Alan (Fictitious character)—Fiction 823.912
Grant, Cary, 1904– 791.43028092
Grant, Celia (Fictitious character) 823.914
Grant, Celia (Fictitious character)—Fiction 823.914
Grant County (S.D.) 978.324
Grant County (S.D.)—Maps 912.78324
Grant family 929.20973
Grant family (Fictitious characters) 813.54
Grant-maintained schools 371; 379.1
Grant, Ulysses S. (Ulysses Simpson), 1822–1885 973.73092; 973.82092
Grant, Ulysses S. (Ulysses Simpson), 1822–1885—Military leadership 355.331092
Grants-in-aid 336.185
Grants-in-aid—Monitoring 352.73243
Grants-in-aid—United States 336.185
Granular materials 620.43
Granville County (N.C.)—Genealogy 929.3756535
Grapes 634.8; 641.348
Graph theory 511.5
Graph theory—Data processing 511.50285
Graphic arts 760
Graphic arts—Study and teaching 746.071
Graphic arts—Technique 741.6
Graphic arts—United States—Marketing 741.60688
Graphic design (Typography) 686.22; 006.224
Graphic design (Typography)—Data processing 686.2240285
Graphic methods 001.4226
Graphic notation (Music) 780.148
Graphic novels 741.5973
Graphical user interfaces (Computer systems) 005.437
Graphite 553.26
Graphology 155.282
Graphotherapy 616.891
Graptolites 563.55
Grasses 584.9
Grasshoppers 595.726
Grassland animals 591.74; 599.173; 599.6
Grassland ecology 577.4
Grassland people 306.09153
Grasslands 333.74
Grateful Dead (Musical group) 782.421660922
Gratiot County (Mich.) 977.449
Gratiot County (Mich.)—Maps 912.77449
Gratitude 179.9
Grave robbing 364.162
Graves County (Ky.) 976.993
Graves County (Ky.)—Genealogy 929.376993
Graves family 929.20973
Graves, Robert, 1895– 821.912
Graves, Robert, 1895– —Criticism and interpretation 821.912
Gravimeters (Geophysical instruments) 526.70284
Gravitation 531.14
Gravitational fields 521.1; 531.14
Gravitational lenses 523.112
Gravity 531.14
Gravity—Measurement 526.7
Gray family 929.20973
Gray, George (Fictitious character) 813.54
Gray, Jennifer (Fictitious character) 813.54
Gray, Thomas, 1716–1771 821.6

Gray, Thomas, 1716–1771—Criticism and interpretation
821.6
Gray whale 599.522
Grayson, David, 1870–1946 818.5203
Grayson, David, 1870–1946—Homes and haunts—
Massachusetts—Amherst Region 818.5203
Grazing 633.202
Grazing—Management 633.202
Grazing (Television) 302.2345
Grazing—United States 333.740973
Great Awakening 277.307
Great Barrier Reef (Qld.) 578.7789476
Great Basin 979
Great Britain 941
Great Britain—Antiquities 936.1
Great Britain—Antiquities, Celtic 936.1
Great Britain—Antiquities, Celtic—Guidebooks 936.1
Great Britain—Antiquities—Guidebooks 936.1
Great Britain—Appropriations and expenditures
352.460941
Great Britain. Army—Biography 940.548141
Great Britain. Army—History 355.00941
Great Britain—Bibliography 016.941
Great Britain—Biography 920.041
Great Britain—Biography—Dictionaries 920.04103
Great Britain—Church history 274.1
Great Britain—Church history—To 449 274.101
Great Britain—Church history—19th century 274.109
Great Britain—Civilization 941
Great Britain—Civilization—1066–1485 941
Great Britain—Civilization—16th century 941.05;
942.052
Great Britain—Civilization—18th century 941.07
Great Britain—Civilization—19th century 941.081
Great Britain—Civilization—1945– 941.085; 942.085
Great Britain—Civilization—European influences 941
Great Britain—Colonies 325.341
Great Britain—Colonies—Administration 353.150941
Great Britain—Colonies—History 325.341; 325.41
Great Britain—Defenses 355.033041
Great Britain—Description and travel 914.104;
914.104859; 914.10486
Great Britain—Description and travel—Early works to
1800 914.104
Great Britain—Economic conditions 330.941
Great Britain—Economic conditions—16th century
330.94105
Great Britain—Economic conditions—1760–1860
330.94107
Great Britain—Economic conditions—19th century
330.941081
Great Britain—Economic conditions—1918–1945
330.941083
Great Britain—Economic conditions—1945– —
Periodicals 330.941085
Great Britain—Economic conditions—1945–1964
330.941085
Great Britain—Economic conditions—1964–1979
330.9410856
Great Britain—Economic conditions—1964–1979—
Regional disparities 330.9410856
Great Britain—Economic conditions—1979–1997
330.9410858
Great Britain—Economic policy 338.941
Great Britain—Economic policy—1945–1964 338.941
Great Britain—Economic policy—1964–1979 338.941
Great Britain—Economic policy—1979–1997 338.941
Great Britain—Emigration and immigration 325.41
Great Britain—Foreign relations 327.41

Great Britain—Foreign relations—1485–1603
327.42009031
Great Britain—Foreign relations—1837–1901 327.41
Great Britain—Foreign relations—1910–1936 327.41
Great Britain—Foreign relations—1945– 327.41
Great Britain—Foreign relations—China 327.41051
Great Britain—Foreign relations—France 327.41044
Great Britain—Foreign relations—Germany 327.41043
Great Britain—Foreign relations—Japan 327.41052
Great Britain—Foreign relations—Middle East 327.41056
Great Britain—Foreign relations—Soviet Union
327.41047
Great Britain—Genealogy 929.1072041
Great Britain—Genealogy—Bibliography—Catalogs
929.1072041
Great Britain—Genealogy—Directories 929.102541
Great Britain—Genealogy—Handbooks, manuals, etc.
929.1072041
Great Britain—Genealogy—Manuscripts—Union lists
929.341
Great Britain—Geography 914.2
Great Britain—Guidebooks 914.104; 914.104859;
914.10486
Great Britain—Historical geography 911.41
Great Britain—Historical geography—Maps 911.41
Great Britain—Historiography 941.0072
Great Britain—History 941; 942
Great Britain—History—To 1066 942.01
Great Britain—History—To 1485 942
Great Britain—History—Roman period, 55 B.C.–449 A.D.
936.104
Great Britain—History—Anglo-Saxon period, 449–1066
942.01
Great Britain—History—William I, 1066–1087 942.021
Great Britain—History—Norman period, 1066–1154
941.02; 942.02
Great Britain—History—Medieval period, 1066–1485
941.03; 942.03
Great Britain—History—Medieval period, 1066–1485—
Historiography 942.03072
Great Britain—History—Medieval period, 1066–1485—
Sources 942.03072
Great Britain—History—Stephen, 1135–1154 942.024
Great Britain—History—Angevin period, 1154–1216
942.031
Great Britain—History—Plantagenets, 1154–1399
942.03
Great Britain—History—Richard I, 1189–1199 941.032;
942.032
Great Britain—History—John, 1199–1216 941.033;
942.033
Great Britain—History—13th century 942.034
Great Britain—History—Henry III, 1216–1272 941.034;
942.034
Great Britain—History—14th century 941.037; 942.037
Great Britain—History—Edward III, 1327–1377
941.037; 942.037
Great Britain—History—Richard II, 1377–1399 942.038
Great Britain—History—Richard II, 1377–1399—
Sources 942.038072
Great Britain—History—Lancaster and York, 1399–1485
942.04
Great Britain—History—Wars of the Roses, 1455–1485
942.04
Great Britain—History—Tudors, 1485–1603 942.05
Great Britain—History—Henry VIII, 1509–1547 942.052
Great Britain—History—Edward VI, 1547–1553 942.053
Great Britain—History—Elizabeth, 1558–1603 942.055

Great Britain—History—Elizabeth, 1558–1603—Sources 942.055072

Great Britain—History—Early Stuarts, 1603–1649 941.061

Great Britain—History—Stuarts, 1603–1714 941.06; 942.06

Great Britain—History—Civil War, 1642–1649 942.062

Great Britain—History—Civil War, 1642–1649—Causes 942.0621

Great Britain—History—Civil War, 1642–1649—Sources 942.062072

Great Britain—History—Puritan Revolution, 1642–1660 941.063

Great Britain—History—Puritan Revolution, 1642–1660—Historiography 941.063072

Great Britain—History—Commonwealth and Protectorate, 1649–1660 941.063

Great Britain—History—Charles II, 1660–1685 941.066

Great Britain—History—Revolution of 1688 941.067

Great Britain—History—18th century 941.07

Great Britain—History—Anne, 1702–1714 941.069

Great Britain—History—1714–1837 942.07

Great Britain—History—George II, 1727–1760 941.072

Great Britain—History—1800–1837 942.07

Great Britain—History—19th century 941.081

Great Britain—History—Victoria, 1837–1901 941.081

Great Britain—History—Victoria, 1837–1901—Biography 941.081092; 941.0810922

Great Britain—History—George VI, 1936–1952 941.084

Great Britain—History—Elizabeth II, 1952– 941.085

Great Britain—History—Bibliography 016.941

Great Britain—History—Chronology 941.00202

Great Britain—History—Invasions 941

Great Britain—History, Military 355.00941

Great Britain—History, Military—18th century 355.0094109033

Great Britain—History, Military—19th century 355.0094109034

Great Britain—History, Naval 359.00941

Great Britain—History, Naval—Tudors, 1485–1603 359.0094209031

Great Britain—History, Naval—18th century 359.0094109033

Great Britain—History, Naval—19th century 359.0094109034

Great Britain—History—Outlines, syllabi, etc. 942.00202

Great Britain—Intellectual life 942

Great Britain—Intellectual life—16th century 942.05

Great Britain—Intellectual life—18th century 941.07

Great Britain—Kings and rulers 941.0099

Great Britain—Kings and rulers—Biography 941.0099

Great Britain—Maps 912.41; 912.42

Great Britain—Military policy 355.033541

Great Britain. Parliament 328.41

Great Britain. Parliament—History 328.4109

Great Britain. Parliament. House of Commons 328.41072

Great Britain. Parliament. House of Lords 328.41071

Great Britain—Politics and government 941

Great Britain—Politics and government—449–1066 320.94209021; 942.01

Great Britain—Politics and government—1154–1399 320.94209022; 942.03

Great Britain—Politics and government—1485–1603 320.94209031; 942.05

Great Britain—Politics and government—1509–1547 320.94209031; 942.052

Great Britain—Politics and government—1558–1603 320.94209031; 942.055

Great Britain—Politics and government—1603–1649 320.941; 320.94109032; 941.061

Great Britain—Politics and government—1603–1714 320.94109032; 941.06

Great Britain—Politics and government—1660–1688 320.94109032; 941.066

Great Britain—Politics and government—18th century 320.94109033; 941.07

Great Britain—Politics and government—1702–1714 320.94109033; 941.069

Great Britain—Politics and government—1727–1760 320.94109033; 941.072

Great Britain—Politics and government—1760–1789 320.94209033; 942.073

Great Britain—Politics and government—1789–1820 320.94109034; 941.073

Great Britain—Politics and government—1837–1901 320.94109034

Great Britain—Politics and government—1936–1945 320.94109043; 941.084

Great Britain—Politics and government—1945– 320.941; 320.94109045

Great Britain—Politics and government—1945–1964 320.94109045; 941.085

Great Britain—Politics and government—1964–1979 320.94109046

Great Britain—Politics and government—1979–1997 320.94109048; 320.94109049; 941.0858; 941.0859

Great Britain—Population 304.60941

Great Britain—Population—History 304.60941

Great Britain—Race relations 305.000941

Great Britain—Race relations—Political aspects 305.800941

Great Britain—Road maps 912.41

Great Britain. Royal Air Force 358.400941

Great Britain. Royal Air Force—History 358.400941

Great Britain. Royal Navy—History 359.00941; 359.30941

Great Britain—Social conditions 941

Great Britain—Social conditions—20th century 941.082

Great Britain—Social conditions—1945– 941.085

Great Britain—Social life and customs 941

Great Britain—Social life and customs—18th century 941.07

Great Britain—Social life and customs—19th century 941.081

Great Britain—Social life and customs—20th century 941.082

Great Britain—Social policy 361.610941

Great Britain—Social policy—1979– 361.61094109048

Great Commission (Bible) 226.206; 266.001

Great Dane 636.73

Great Fire, Chicago, Ill., 1871 977.311041

Great Lakes 551.4820977

Great Lakes—History 977

Great Lakes Region 977

Great Lakes Region—Description and travel 917.704; 917.70433; 917.70434

Great Northern Railway Company (U.S.) 385.0978

Great Plains 978

Great Plains—History 978

Great Pyramid (Egypt) 932

Great Pyrenees 636.73

Great Smoky Mountains (N.C. and Tenn.) 976.889

Great White Brotherhood 299.93

Great Zimbabwe (Extinct city) 968.91

Greece 949.5

Greece—Antiquities 938

Greece—Antiquities—Guidebooks 914.9504; 914.950476

Greece—Biography 920.038
Greece—Civilization 949.5
Greece—Civilization—To 146 B.C. 938
Greece—Description and travel 914.9504; 914.950476
Greece—Economic conditions 330.9495
Greece—Economic conditions—1974- 330.9495076
Greece—Foreign relations 327.495
Greece—Foreign relations—Turkey 327.4950561
Greece—Guidebooks 914.9504; 914.950476
Greece—Historiography 938.0072
Greece—History 938
Greece—History—To 146 B.C. 938
Greece—History—Persian Wars, 500–449 B.C. 938.03
Greece—History—Peloponnesian War, 431–404 B.C. 938.05
Greece—History—War of Independence, 1821–1829 949.506
Greece—History—Civil War, 1944–1949 949.5074
Greece—Politics and government 320.938; 949.5
Greece—Politics and government—1935–1967 320.949509045; 949.5074
Greece—Religion 292.08
Greece—Social life and customs 938; 949.5
Greek Americans 305.8893073
Greek drama 882; 882.008; 882.01; 882.0108
Greek drama (Comedy) 882; 882.008; 882.01; 882.0108
Greek drama (Comedy)—History and criticism 882.0109
Greek drama (Comedy)—Translations into English 822.008; 822.0108
Greek drama—History and criticism 882.0109
Greek drama (Tragedy) 882; 882.008; 882.01; 882.0108
Greek drama (Tragedy)—History and criticism 882.009; 882.0109
Greek drama (Tragedy)—History and criticism—Theory, etc. 882.0109
Greek drama (Tragedy)—Translations into English 882.0108
Greek drama—Translations into English 882.0108
Greek fiction 883; 883.008; 883.01; 883.0108
Greek fiction—History and criticism 883.009; 883.0109
Greek language 480
Greek language, Biblical 487.4
Greek language, Biblical—Dictionaries 487.4
Greek language, Biblical—Glossaries, vocabularies, etc. 487.4
Greek language, Biblical—Grammar 487.4
Greek language, Biblical—Grammar—Outlines, syllabi, etc. 487.4
Greek language, Biblical—Grammar—Problems, exercises, etc. 487.4
Greek language, Biblical—Syntax 487.4
Greek language, Biblical—Vocabulary 487.4
Greek language—Grammar 485; 488.24; 488.2421
Greek language—Metrics and rhythmics 881.009
Greek language, Modern 489.3
Greek language, Modern—Dictionaries 489.33
Greek language, Modern—Dictionaries—English 489.3321
Greek language, Modern—Grammar 489.35; 489.382; 489.382421
Greek language, Modern—Textbooks for foreign speakers—English 489.382421; 489.383421
Greek letter societies 371.85
Greek literature 880; 880.8; 880.8001
Greek literature—History and criticism 880.9; 880.9001
Greek literature—History and criticism—Theory, etc. 880.9001
Greek literature—Translations into English 880.8; 880.8001

Greek philology 480
Greek poetry 881; 881.008; 881.01; 881.0108
Greek poetry, Hellenistic 881; 881.008; 881.01; 881.0108
Greek poetry, Hellenistic—History and criticism 881.009; 881.0109
Greek poetry—History and criticism 881.009; 881.0109
Greek poetry—Translations into English 881.008; 881.0108
Greeks 949.5
Green Bay Packers (Football team) 796.332640977561
Green Bay Packers (Football team)—History 796.332640977561
Green cards 342.73082
Green County (Wis.) 977.586
Green County (Wis.)—Maps 912.77586
Green family 929.20973
Green iguanas as pets 639.39542
Green Lake County (Wis.) 977.559
Green Lake County (Wis.)—Maps 912.77559
Green marketing 658.8; 658.802
Green movement 363.7
Green products 333.72
Green technology 363.7
Greenbrier County (W. Va.)—Genealogy 929.375488
Greene & Greene 720.922
Greene, Charlie (Fictitious character) 813.54
Greene, Charlie (Fictitious character)—Fiction 813.54
Greene County (Ill.) 977.384
Greene County (Ill.)—Maps 912.77384
Greene County (Iowa) 977.7466
Greene County (Iowa)—Maps 912.777466
Greene County (Mo.) 977.878
Greene County (Mo.)—Genealogy 929.377878
Greene County (Mo.)—Maps 912.77878
Greene County (Tenn.)—Genealogy 929.376891
Greene, Graham, 1904- 823.912
Greene, Graham, 1904- —Criticism and interpretation 823.912
Greenhouse effect, Atmospheric 363.73874; 577.276
Greenhouse gardening 635.0483; 635.9823
Greenhouse gas mitigation 363.738746
Greenhouse gases—Environmental aspects 363.73874
Greenhouse gases—Environmental aspects—United States 363.738740973
Greenhouse gases—Physiological effect 571.956
Greenhouse management 635.9823068
Greenhouse plants 635.0483
Greenhouses 631.583; 635.0483; 635.9823
Greenhouses—Design and construction 690.892
Greenland 998.2
Green's functions 515.35
Greenup County (Ky.)—Genealogy 929.3769293
Greenwich (London, England) 942.162
Greenwich (London, England)—Guidebooks 914.216
Greenwich Village (New York, N.Y.) 974.71
Greer family 929.20973
Greeting cards 741.684; 745.5941
Greeting cards industry 338.477955941
Gregorian chants 782.292; 782.3222
Gregorian chants—History and criticism 782.29209; 782.3222
Gregory, Alan (Fictitious character) 813.54
Gregory, Alan (Fictitious character)—Fiction 813.54
Gregory family 929.20973
Grenada 972.9845
Grenada—History 972.9845
Grenada—History—American Invasion, 1983 972.9845
Grenada—Politics and government 972.9845

Grenada—Politics and government—1974–1983 320.972984509047; 972.9845
Gretzky, Wayne, 1961– 796.962092
Grevillea 583.89
Grey, Joe (Fictitious character) 813.54
Greyhounds 636.7534
Greylag goose 598.4173
Grief 152.4; 155.937
Grief in adolescence 152.40835; 155.9370835
Grief in children 152.4083
Grief in literature 808.80353; 809.93353
Grief—Religious aspects 291.442
Grief—Religious aspects—Christianity 248.86
Grief therapy 155.937
Grievance procedures 331.8896
Grievance procedures—United States 331.8896; 658.31550973
Griffith family 929.20973
Griggs County (N.D.) 978.434
Griggs County (N.D.)—Maps 912.78434
Grijpstra, Henk (Fictitious character) 813.54
Grijpstra, Henk (Fictitious character)—Fiction 813.54
Grimes family 929.20973
Grinding and polishing 621.92
Grist, Simeon (Fictitious character) 813.54
Grist, Simeon (Fictitious character)—Fiction 813.54
Gristmills 725.4
Grizzard, Lewis, 1946– 814.54
Grizzly bear 599.784
Grizzly bear hunting 799.77784
Gröbner bases 512.24
Grocers 381.456413
Grocery shopping 641.31
Grocery shopping—United States 641.31
Grocery trade 381.456413
Grolier Club—Periodicals 070.5097471
Grooming behavior in animals 591.563
Grooming for boys 646.7046
Grooming for men 646.7044
Gross domestic product 339.31
Gross family 929.20973
Gross national product 339.31
Gross national product—Maps 339.310223
Grotesque in art 700.415
Grotesque in literature 808.8015; 809.915
Ground beetles 595.762
Ground control (Mining) 622.28
Ground cover plants 635.964
Ground source heat pump systems 621.4025
Ground support systems (Astronautics) 629.478
Groundhog Day 394.261
Grounds maintenance 658.2
Groundwater 551.49; 553.79; 622.379
Groundwater—California—San Joaquin Valley 553.79097948
Groundwater ecology 577.6
Groundwater flow 551.49
Groundwater flow—Mathematical models 551.49015118
Groundwater flow—Measurement 551.490287; 553.790287
Groundwater—Georgia 551.4909758; 553.7909758
Groundwater—Idaho—Quality 363.7394
Groundwater—Illinois 553.7909773
Groundwater—Management 333.910415; 628.114
Groundwater—Mathematical models 551.49015118
Groundwater—Middle West 551.490977
Groundwater mounding 551.492
Groundwater—North Dakota 363.7394
Groundwater—Pennsylvania 553.7909748

Groundwater—Pollution 363.7394; 628.168
Groundwater—Pollution—Handbooks, manuals, etc. 363.7394; 628.168
Groundwater—Pollution—Law and legislation 344.3046343
Groundwater—Pollution—Law and legislation—United States 344.73046343
Groundwater—Pollution—Mathematical models 628.168015118
Groundwater—Pollution—United States 363.7394
Groundwater—Purification 628.164
Groundwater—Sampling 628.161
Groundwater—Texas 551.4909764; 553.7909764
Groundwater—United States 553.790973
Groundwater—United States—Quality 363.7394
Groundwater—Virginia 551.4909755
Group counseling 158.35
Group decision making 658.4036
Group games 790.15
Group guidance in education 371.4047
Group homes for the handicapped 362.40485
Group identity 302.4
Group medical practice 610.65
Group medical practice—United States 610.650973
Group ministry 253
Group of Seven (Group of artists) 759.11
Group play therapy 616.891653; 618.9289153; 618.92891653
Group problem solving 658.4036
Group psychoanalysis 616.8917
Group psychotherapy 616.89152
Group psychotherapy for teenagers 616.891520835
Group psychotherapy—Problems, exercises, etc. 616.89152076
Group-randomized trials 610.724; 619
Group reading 028
Group reading—United States 374.22
Group relations training 302.14
Group relations training—Problems, exercises, etc. 302.14
Group speech therapy 616.85506
Group technology 658.5; 670.42
Group theory 512.2; 530.1522
Group theory—Data processing 512.20285
Group work in education 371.36; 371.395
Group work in education—Handbooks, manuals, etc. 371.36
Group work in education—United States 371.360973
Groupers 597.736
Grove, Frederick Philip, 1879–1948 813.52
Grove, Frederick Philip, 1879–1948—Criticism and interpretation 813.52
Growth 571.8
Growth disorders 616.4; 618.924
Growth factors industry 338.476157
Growth (Plants) 571.82
Gruber, Franz Xaver, 1787–1863. Silent night, holy night 782.281723
Grundy County (Ill.)—Maps 912.773265
Grundy County (Iowa)—Maps 912.777537
Grundy County (Tenn.)—Genealogy 929.376878
Grünen (Political party) 324.243087
Grunge groups 781.66; 782.42166
Gryllus 595.726
Guabinas 782.4216268861
Guacamole 641.812
Guadalcanal (Solomon Islands) 995.933
Guadalcanal (Solomon Islands), Battle of, 1942–1943 940.5426

Guadalupe, Our Lady of 232.917097253
Guam 996.7
Guam—History 996.7
Guanaco 599.6367
Guardian and ward 346.018
Guardian and ward—United States 346.73018
Guardian angels 235.3; 291.215
Guarnaccia, Marshal (Fictitious character) 823.914
Guarnaccia, Marshal (Fictitious character)—Fiction
   823.914
Guatemala 972.81
Guatemala—Description and travel 917.28104;
   917.2810453
Guatemala—Guidebooks 917.28104; 917.2810453
Guatemala—Politics and government 972.81
Guatemala—Politics and government—1945–1985
   320.9728109045; 972.81052
Guatemala—Politics and government—1985–
   320.9728109049; 972.81053
Guerrilla warfare 355.0218; 355.425
Guidance systems (Flight) 629.135
Guide dogs 362.4183; 636.70886
Guided missiles 358.17182
Guided missiles—Aerodynamics 623.4519
Guided missiles—United States 358.171820973
Guides (Spiritualism) 133.91
Guilds 338.632
Guilford County (N.C.)—Genealogy 929.375662
Guillain-Barré syndrome 616.87
Guillaume, de Lorris, fl. 1230 841.1
Guillaume, de Lorris, fl. 1230. Roman de la Rose 841.1
Guilt 152.4
Guilt in adolescence 155.5124
Guilt in children 155.4124
Guilt in literature 808.80353; 809.93353
Guilt (Law) 345.04
Guilt—Religious aspects 291.22
Guilt—Religious aspects—Christianity 233.4
Guinea pigs 599.3592; 636.93592
Guinea pigs as pets 636.93592
Guitar 787.87; 787.8719
Guitar—Construction 787.871923
Guitar—Electronic equipment 787.87
Guitar—History 787.871909
Guitar—Instruction and study 787.87071
Guitar—Methods 787.87193
Guitar—Methods—Self-instruction 787.87193076
Guitar music 787.87
Guitar music (Country) 787.871642
Guitar music (Flamenco) 787.87162610468
Guitar music (Guitars (2)) 785.787192
Guitar music (Jazz) 787.87165
Guitar orchestra music 784
Guitarists 787.87092
Gumbo (Soup) 641.813
Gun control 363.33
Gun control—United States 363.330973
Gunite 624.1834
Gunner, Aaron (Fictitious character) 813.54
Gunner, Aaron (Fictitious character)—Fiction 813.54
Guns n' Roses (Musical group) 782.421660922
Gunships (Military aircraft) 358.4183
Gunsmithing 683.4
Gunther, Bernhard (Fictitious character) 823.914
Gunther, Bernhard (Fictitious character)—Fiction
   823.914
Gunther, Joe (Fictitious character) 813.54
Gunther, Joe (Fictitious character)—Fiction 813.54
Gupta dynasty 934.06

Gurdjieff, Georges Ivanovitch, 1872–1949 197
Gurus 294.561
Gusli music 787.75
Gutenberg, Johann, 1397?–1468 686.1092; 686.2092
Guthrie County (Iowa) 977.749
Guthrie County (Iowa)—Genealogy 929.377749
Guthrie, Woody, 1912–1967 782.42162130092;
   782.4262130092
Guy Fawkes Day 394.264
Guyana 988.1
Guyana—History 988.1
Guyana—Politics and government 320.9881; 988.1
Guyana—Politics and government—1966–
   320.988109046; 988.1032
Guyana—Social life and customs 988.1
GW-BASIC (Computer program language) 005.133
Gwich'in Indians 971.910049722; 979.8004972
Gwinnett County (Ga.)—Maps 912.758223
Gymnasiums 796.4068
Gymnastics 796.44
Gymnastics for children 796.44083
Gymnastics for girls 796.4408352
Gymnastics for women 796.44082
Gymnoascaceae 579.565
Gymnosperms 585
Gynecologic nursing 610.73678
Gynecologic pathology 618.107
Gynecologic pathology—Atlases 618.1070222
Gynecology 618.1
Gynecology—Atlases 618.100222
Gynecology—Examinations, questions, etc. 618.10076
Gynecology—Handbooks, manuals, etc. 618.1
Gynecology—Outlines, syllabi, etc. 618.1
Gypsies 305.891497; 909.0491497
Gypsies—Folklore 398.208991497
Gypsies in popular culture 305.891497
Gyroscopes 681.753
H. D. (Hilda Doolittle), 1886–1961 811.52
H. D. (Hilda Doolittle), 1886–1961—Criticism and
   interpretation 811.52
H [infinity symbol] control 629.8312
H.L. Hunley (Submarine) 973.757
Habad 296.83322
Habaneras 781.554
Habeas corpus 345.056
Habeas corpus—United States 345.73056
Habermas, Jürgen 193
Habitat conservation 639.9; 639.92
Habitat conservation—Law and legislation 346.0469516
Habitat (Ecology) 577
Habitat suitability index models 333.954
Habitat surveys 333.95; 577
Hadith 297.124
Hadith (Shiites) 297.1248
Hadith (Shiites)—Texts 297.1248
Hadith—Texts 297.124
Hadlee (Fictitious character : Dean) 823.914
Hadrian's Wall (England) 936.2881
Hadrian's Wall (England)—Guidebooks 914.2881
Hadron colliders 539.7376
Hadron interactions 539.75
Hadron spectroscopy 539.7216
Hadrons 539.7216
Haggadah 296.437
Haggadot 296.437
Haggadot—Texts 296.437
Haggard, H. Rider (Henry Rider), 1856–1925 823.8
Haggerty, Leo (Fictitious character) 813.54
Haggerty, Leo (Fictitious character)—Fiction 813.54

Hagiography 200.92
Haida art 704.03972
Haida Indians—Folklore 398.2089972
Haiku 808.8141; 895.61041
Haiku, American 811.041
Haiku—History and criticism 809.141
Haiku—Translations into English 895.6104108
Hair 611.78
Hair—Care and hygiene 646.724
Hair—Dyeing and bleaching 647.724
Hair preparations 646.7240284
Hair—Removal 617.4779; 646.724
Hair—Transplantation 617.47790592
Haircutting 647.724
Hairdressing 646.724
Hairdressing of African Americans 646.72408996073
Hairstyles 647.724
Haiti 972.94
Haiti—Politics and government 320.97294; 972.94
Haiti—Politics and government—1986–
 320.9729409049; 972.94073
Hakka (Chinese people) 305.8951; 951.7
Hakka dialects 495.17
Hale-Bopp comet 523.64
Hale family 929.20973
Half-Moon Ranch (Imaginary place) 823.914
Halfhyde, St. Vincent (Fictitious character) 823.914
Halfhyde, St. Vincent (Fictitious character)—Fiction
 823.914
Halfway houses 362.223
Halifax County (N.C.)—Genealogy 929.375648
Halifax County (Va.)—Genealogy 929.3755661
Halifax (N.S.) 971.622
Halifax (N.S.)—History 971.622
Hall churches 726.5
Hall County (Neb.) 978.241
Hall County (Neb.)—Maps 912.78241
Hall family 929.20973
Halley, Sid (Fictitious character) 823.914
Halley, Sid (Fictitious character)—Fiction 823.914
Halley's comet 523.642
Halloween 394.2646
Halloween decorations 745.5941
Hallucinogenic drugs 362.294; 615.7883
Hallucinogenic drugs and religious experience
 291.42019
Halobacterium 579.321
Halogens 546.73
Halogens—Physiological effect 572.556
Halophilic animals 591.758
Halophilic microorganisms 579.321
Halophilic organisms 578.758
Ham industry 338.47641364
Hamburgers 641.84
Hamel, Neil (Fictitious character) 813.54
Hamel, Neil (Fictitious character)—Fiction 813.54
Hamer, Fannie Lou 973.04960730092
Hamilton, Alexander, 1757–1804 973.4092
Hamilton County (Ill.) 977.395
Hamilton County (Ill.)—Maps 912.77395
Hamilton County (Iowa) 977.752
Hamilton County (Iowa)—Maps 912.77752
Hamilton County (Neb.) 978.2354
Hamilton County (Neb.)—Maps 912.782354
Hamilton County (Ohio) 977.177
Hamilton County (Ohio)—Genealogy 929.377177
Hamilton family 929.20973
Hamilton spaces 516.36
Hamiltonian systems 514.74

Hamlin family 929.20973
Hamm, Mia, 1972– 796.334092
Hammer, Mike (Fictitious character) 813.54
Hammer, Mike (Fictitious character)—Fiction 813.54
Hammett, Dashiell, 1894–1961 813.52
Hammett, Dashiell, 1894–1961—Criticism and
 interpretation 813.52
Hampshire County (W. Va.)—Genealogy 929.375495
Hampton Roads (Va.), Battle of, 1862 973.752
Hampton (Va.)—Maps 912.755412
Hamptons (N.Y.) 974.725
Hamptons (N.Y.)—Guidebooks 917.4725
Hamsters 599.356; 636.9356
Hamsters as pets 636.9356
Hancock County (Ill.) 977.343
Hancock County (Ill.)—Maps 912.77343
Hancock family 929.20973
Hand 612.97
Hand—Anatomy 611.97
Hand—Movements 612.97
Hand spinning 746.14
Hand—Surgery 617.575059
Hand-to-hand fighting 796.8
Hand-to-hand fighting, Oriental 796.815
Hand weaving 746.14
Hand weaving—Patterns 746.14041
Hand—Wounds and injuries 617.575044
Handbooks, vade-mecums, etc. 031.02
Handel, George Frideric, 1685–1759 780.92
Handel, George Frideric, 1685–1759. Messiah 782.23
Handfishes 597.62
Handicapped 305.90816; 362.4
Handicapped children 362.4083
Handicapped children—Education 371.9
Handicapped children—Education (Early childhood)
 371.90472
Handicapped children—Education (Early childhood)—
 United States 371.90472; 371.904720973
Handicapped children—Education (Elementary)
 371.90472
Handicapped children—Education—Great Britain
 371.910941
Handicapped children—Education—Language arts
 371.90446
Handicapped children—Education—Law and legislation
 344.307911
Handicapped children—Education—Law and
 legislation—United States 344.7307911
Handicapped children—Education (Preschool)
 371.90472
Handicapped children—Education (Preschool)—United
 States 371.90472
Handicapped children—Education (Secondary)
 371.90473
Handicapped children—Education—United States
 371.910973
Handicapped children—Family relationships
 362.4043083
Handicapped children—Rehabilitation 618.92003
Handicapped children—Services for 362.4083
Handicapped children—Services for—United States
 362.40480830973
Handicapped children—United States—Family
 relationships 362.40430830973
Handicapped—Civil rights 323.3
Handicapped—Civil rights—United States 323.3
Handicapped college students 362.40842
Handicapped—Education 371.9
Handicapped—Education (Higher) 371.90474

Handicapped—Education (Higher)—United States 371.904740973

Handicapped—Education (Higher)—United States—Directories 371.9047402573

Handicapped—Education—United States 371.90973

Handicapped—Employment 331.59

Handicapped—Employment—Law and legislation 344.0159

Handicapped—Employment—Law and legislation—United States 344.730159

Handicapped—Employment—United States 331.590973

Handicapped—Government policy—United States 362.404560973

Handicapped—Great Britain 362.40941

Handicapped in the civil service 351.6087

Handicapped—Legal status, laws, etc. 346.013

Handicapped—Legal status, laws, etc.—United States 346.73013

Handicapped—Legal status, laws, etc.—United States—Digests 346.73013

Handicapped—Periodicals 362.405

Handicapped—Recreation 790.196

Handicapped—Recreation—United States 790.1960973

Handicapped—Services for 362.4

Handicapped—Services for—United States 362.40480973

Handicapped—Services for—United States—Directories 362.404802573

Handicapped students 371.91

Handicapped students—Education 371.91

Handicapped students—Education—United States 371.90973; 371.91

Handicapped teachers 371.11

Handicapped teenagers—Education (Secondary) 371.90473

Handicapped—United States 305.90816

Handicapped—United States—Psychology 155.916; 362.40973

Handicapped youth—Vocational education—United States 371.9

Handicraft 745.5

Handicraft industries 745.5

Handicraft industries—Management 745.5068

Handicraft—Mexico 745.50972

Handicraft—Study and teaching (Elementary) 372.55

Handicraft—United States 745.50973

Handkerchief codes 306.77

Handloading of ammunition 683.406

Hang gliders 629.14

Hang gliding 797.55

Hank the Cowdog (Fictitious character) 813.54

Hanks, Arly (Fictitious character) 813.54

Hanks, Arly (Fictitious character)—Fiction 813.54

Hannasyde, Inspector (Fictitious character) 823.912

Hannasyde, Inspector (Fictitious character)—Fiction 823.912

Hannay, Richard (Fictitious character) 823.912

Hannay, Richard (Fictitious character)—Fiction 823.912

Hannibal, 247–182 B.C. 937.04092

Hannibal, 247–182 B.C.—Military leadership 355.0092

Hansberry, Lorraine, 1930–1965 812.54

Hansen, Em (Fictitious character) 813.54

Hansen, Em (Fictitious character)—Fiction 813.54

Hansen family 929.20973

Hantavirus infections 616.925

Hanukkah 296.435; 394.267

Hapkido 796.815

Haplosclerida 593.46

Happiness 170

Happiness in literature 808.80353; 809.93353

Happiness—Religious aspects 291.44

Happiness—Religious aspects—Christianity 248.4

Harald, Sigrid (Fictitious character) 813.54

Harald, Sigrid (Fictitious character)—Fiction 813.54

Harare (Zimbabwe)—Maps 912.6891

Harassment 345.025; 364.15

Harbor porpoise 599.539

Harbors 387.1; 627.2

Harbors—China 387.10951

Harbors—Design and construction 627.2

Harbors—New York (State)—New York 387.1097471

Harbors—United States 387.10973

Hard disk management 004.563

Hard disks (Computer science) 004.563

Hardanger needlework 746.44

Hardanger needlework—Patterns 746.44

Hardaway, Anfernee 796.323092

Hardin County (Iowa) 977.7535

Hardin County (Iowa)—Maps 912.777535

Harding, Warren G. (Warren Gamaliel), 1865–1923 973.914092

Hardware 683

Hardware industry 338.47683

Hardwoods 634.972

Hardy, Cliff (Fictitious character) 823.914

Hardy, Cliff (Fictitious character)—Fiction 823.914

Hardy, Dismas (Fictitious character) 813.54

Hardy, Dismas (Fictitious character)—Fiction 813.54

Hardy family 929.20973

Hardy spaces 515.94

Hardy, Thomas, 1840–1928 823.8

Hardy, Thomas, 1840–1928—Criticism and interpretation 823.8

Hardy, Thomas, 1840–1928. Dynasts 821.8; 822.8

Hardy, Thomas, 1840–1928—Fictional works 823.8

Hardy, Thomas, 1840–1928—Knowledge—Wessex (England) 823.8

Hardy, Thomas, 1840–1928. Mayor of Casterbridge 823.8

Hardy, Thomas, 1840–1928—Philosophy 823.8

Hardy, Thomas, 1840–1928—Poetic works 821.8

Hardy, Thomas, 1840–1928—Settings 823.8

Hardy, Thomas, 1840–1928—Technique 823.8

Hardy, Thomas, 1840–1928. Tess of the d'Urbervilles 823.8

Hare Krishnas 294.5092

Harford County (Md.) 975.274

Harford County (Md.)—Genealogy 929.375274

Harford County (Md.)—Maps 912.75274

Haristeen, Harry (Fictitious character) 813.54

Haristeen, Harry (Fictitious character)—Fiction 813.54

Harlem (New York, N.Y.) 974.71

Harlem (New York, N.Y.)—History 974.71

Harlem Renaissance 810.9896073

Harley-Davidson Motor Company 338.762922750973

Harley-Davidson Motor Company—History 338.762922750973

Harley-Davidson motorcycle 629.2275

Harley-Davidson motorcycle—Customizing 629.2275; 629.28775

Harley-Davidson motorcycle—History 338.762922750973; 629.2275

Harley-Davidson motorcycle—Maintenance and repair 629.28775

Harley-Davidson motorcycle—Maintenance and repair—Handbooks, manuals, etc. 629.28775

Harley-Davidson motorcycle—Performance 629.2275

Harmonic analysis 515.2433; 515.785

Harmonic canon (Musical instrument) 787.75
Harmonic functions 515.53
Harmonic maps 514.74
Harmony 781.25
Harp 787.9; 787.919
Harp music 787.9
Harp seal 599.7929
Harpacticoida 595.34
Harper, Benni (Fictitious character) 813.54
Harper, Benni (Fictitious character)—Fiction 813.54
Harpers Ferry (W. Va.)—History—John Brown's Raid, 1859 973.7116
Harpsichord music 786.4
Harpur, Colin (Fictitious character) 823.914
Harpur, Colin (Fictitious character)—Fiction 823.914
Harrell family 929.20973
Harrington family 929.20973
Harrington, Honor (Fictitious character) 813.54
Harrington, Honor (Fictitious character)—Fiction 813.54
Harris family 929.20973
Harrison County (Iowa) 977.747
Harrison County (Iowa)—Maps 912.77747
Harrison family 929.20973
Harrison, George, 1943- 782.42166092
HART field communications protocol (Computer network protocol) 004.62
Hartshorne, Charles, 1897- 191
Harvard graphics (Computer file) 006.6869
Harvest festivals 394.264
Harwood, Gwen 821.914
Harwood, Gwen—Criticism and interpretation 821.914
Hasidic parables 296.19
Hasidism 296.8332
Hasidism—History 296.833209
Haskell, Ellie (Fictitious character) 813.54
Haskell, Ellie (Fictitious character)—Fiction 813.54
Hastings, Alcee L.—Impeachment 347.732234
Hastings, Battle of, 1066 942.021
Hastings, Frank (Fictitious character) 813.54
Hastings, Frank (Fictitious character)—Fiction 813.54
Hastings, Stanley (Fictitious character) 813.54
Hastings, Stanley (Fictitious character)—Fiction 813.54
Hate 152.4
Hate crimes 364.15
Hate crimes—United States 345.73025; 364.150973
Hate groups 305.568
Hate speech 364.156
Hate speech—United States 342.730853
Hats 391.43; 646.5
Hats—History 391.43
Hattic cults 299.92
Haughey, Charles J. 941.70824092
Haunted house films 791.43675
Haunted house television programs 791.45675
Haunted houses 133.122
Haunted houses in literature 808.80375; 809.93375
Haunted houses—United States 133.122
Havoc, Johnny (Fictitious character) 813.54
Havoc, Johnny (Fictitious character)—Fiction 813.54
Hawaii 996.9
Hawaii—Description and travel 919.6904; 919.690441; 919.690442
Hawaii—Guidebooks 919.6904; 919.690441; 919.690442
Hawaii—History 996.9
Hawaii—History—To 1893 996.902
Hawaii Island (Hawaii) 996.91
Hawaii Island (Hawaii)—Guidebooks 919.69104; 919.6910441; 919.6910442

Hawaii—Maps 912.969
Hawaii—Pictorial works 919.6900222
Hawaii—Social life and customs 996.9
Hawaiians 996.9
Hawaiians—Antiquities 996.902
Hawkes, John, 1925- 813.54
Hawkes, John, 1925- —Criticism and interpretation 813.54
Hawking, S. W. (Stephen W.) 530.092
Hawkins family 929.20973
Hawks 598.944
Hawks—North America 598.944097
Hawthorne, Nathaniel, 1804-1864 813.3
Hawthorne, Nathaniel, 1804-1864—Criticism and interpretation 813.3
Hawthorne, Nathaniel, 1804-1864—Knowledge—Psychology 813.3
Hawthorne, Nathaniel, 1804-1864—Religion 813.3
Hawthorne, Nathaniel, 1804-1864. Scarlet letter 813.3
Hawthorne, Nathaniel, 1804-1864. Scarlet letter—Examinations 813.3
Hawthorne, Nathaniel, 1804-1864—Technique 813.3
Hawthorns 583.73
Hay-fever plants 581.657
Haydn, Joseph, 1732-1809 780.92
Haydn, Joseph, 1732-1809—Criticism and interpretation 780.02; 780.92
Hayek, Friedrich A. von (Friedrich August), 1899- 330.092; 330.15
Hayes family 929.20973
Hayes, Helen, 1900- 792.028092
Hayle, Tamara (Fictitious character) 813.54
Hayle, Tamara (Fictitious character)—Fiction 813.54
Haymarket Square Riot, Chicago, Ill., 1886 977.311041
Haynes family 929.20973
Hayrides 798.6
Hazardous substances 363.17; 604.7
Hazardous substances—Accidents—Handbooks, manuals, etc. 604.7
Hazardous substances—Environmental aspects 628.42
Hazardous substances—Handbooks, manuals, etc. 604.7
Hazardous substances—Law and legislation 344.304622
Hazardous substances—Law and legislation—United States 344.7304622
Hazardous substances—Transportation 604.7
Hazardous substances—Transportation—Law and legislation 343.09322
Hazardous substances—Transportation—Law and legislation—United States 343.7309322
Hazardous substances—Transportation—United States 363.170973
Hazardous substances—Transportation—United States—Safety measures 363.170973
Hazardous substances—United States—Safety measures 363.1760973
Hazardous waste management industry 338.473637287
Hazardous waste site remediation 628.5
Hazardous waste sites 363.7287
Hazardous waste sites—Law and legislation 344.304622
Hazardous waste sites—Law and legislation—United States 344.7304622
Hazardous waste sites—United States 363.72870973
Hazardous wastes 363.7287; 628.42
Hazardous wastes—Biodegradation 628.42
Hazardous wastes—Environmental aspects—United States 363.72870973
Hazardous wastes—Government policy—United States 363.728705610973

Hazardous wastes—Incineration 628.4457
Hazardous wastes—Incineration—United States 363.7287
Hazardous wastes—Law and legislation 344.304622
Hazardous wastes—Law and legislation—United States 344.7304622
Hazardous wastes—Management 363.7287
Hazardous wastes—Purification 628.42
Hazardous wastes—Risk assessment 363.72876
Hazardous wastes—Stabilization 628.42
Hazardous wastes—Transportation—Law and legislation 341.75692
Hazardous wastes—United States—Management 363.72870973
Hazing 371.58
Hazlitt, William, 1778-1830 824.7
Head 611.91
Head—Anatomy 611.91
Head—Cancer 616.99491
Head halters 636.0837
Head—Imaging 617.510754
Head Start Program (U.S.) 372.210973
Head Start programs 371.82694; 372.21
Head Start programs—United States 372.210973
Head—Surgery 617.51059
Head—Wounds and injuries 617.51044
Head—Wounds and injuries—Complications 617.510441
Headache 616.8491
Headache—Alternative treatment 616.849106
Headache—Handbooks, manuals, etc. 616.8491
Heads of state 352.23
Heads of state—Biography 321.00922
Healing 615.5
Healing circles 615.852
Healing—Psychological aspects 616.0019
Healing—Religious aspects 234.131; 291.31
Health 613
Health behavior 613
Health behavior in adolescence 613.0433
Health—Biblical teaching 261.8321
Health—Bibliography 016.613
Health boards 353.6225
Health care rationing 362.1042
Health care rationing—Religious aspects 291.178321
Health care rationing—United States 362.1042
Health care reform 362.10425
Health care reform—Economic aspects 338.433621
Health care reform—Economic aspects—United States 338.4336210973; 362.10425
Health care reform—North Carolina 362.10425
Health care reform—United States 362.10425
Health care reform—United States—States 362.10425
Health care teams 362.1068; 610.69
Health counseling 362.104256
Health education 613.071
Health education—Developing countries 613.07101724
Health education (Elementary) 372.37
Health education (Elementary)—United States 372.370973
Health education—Evaluation 613.071
Health education (Middle school) 613.0712
Health facilities 362.1
Health facilities—Administration 362.1068; 362.11068
Health facilities—Business management 362.1068
Health facilities—Costs—Accounting 657.8322042
Health facilities—Design and construction 725.51
Health facilities—Employees—Legal status, laws, etc. 344.041

Health facilities—Employees—Legal status, laws, etc.—United States 344.73041
Health facilities—Finance 362.10681; 362.110681
Health facilities—Food service—Management 362.176068
Health facilities—Law and legislation 344.03211
Health facilities—Law and legislation—United States 344.7303211
Health facilities—Personnel management 362.10683; 362.110683
Health facilities, Proprietary 362.11
Health—Handbooks, manuals, etc. 613
Health insurance agents 368.3820092
Health maintenance organizations 362.104258
Health maintenance organizations—United States 362.104258
Health maintenance organizations—United States—Statistics—Periodicals 362.104258
Health occupations schools 610.711
Health—Periodicals 613.05
Health planning 362.1042
Health planning—United States 362.10425
Health products 610.284
Health promotion 613
Health promotion—United States 613.0973
Health—Religious aspects 291.178321
Health—Religious aspects—Christianity 261.8321
Health risk assessment 614.4; 615.902
Health services accessibility 362.1
Health services accessibility—Law and legislation 344.04
Health services administration 353.6; 362.1068
Health services administration—Moral and ethical aspects 174.2
Health services administration—Periodicals 362.1068
Health services administration—United States 362.1068
Health status indicators 614.42
Health status indicators—Great Britain 614.4241
Health status indicators—Utah 614.42792
Health surveys 614.42
Health surveys—United States 614.4273
Heaney, Seamus 821.914
Heaney, Seamus—Criticism and interpretation 821.914
Hearing 573.89; 612.85
Hearing aids 617.89
Hearing aids—Fitting 617.89
Hearing disorders 617.8
Hearing disorders in children 618.920978
Hearing impaired 305.908162
Hearing impaired children 305.23
Hearing impaired children—Education 371.912
Hearing impaired—Education 371.912
Hearing impaired—Rehabilitation 362.428; 617.89
Hearn, Lafcadio, 1850-1904 813.4
Hearst-San Simeon State Historical Monument (Calif.) 917.9478
Hearst, William Randolph, 1863-1951 070.5092
Heart 573.17; 612.17
Heart, Artificial 617.4120592
Heart cells 612.17
Heart—Diseases 616.12
Heart—Diseases—Alternative treatment 616.1206
Heart—Diseases—Atlases 616.1200222
Heart—Diseases—Diet therapy 616.120654
Heart—Diseases—Diet therapy—Recipes 641.56311
Heart—Diseases—Exercise therapy 616.12062
Heart—Diseases—Handbooks, manuals, etc. 616.12
Heart diseases in women 616.120082
Heart—Diseases—Nursing 610.73691

Heller, Joseph—Criticism and interpretation 813.54
Heller, Nathan (Fictitious character) 813.54
Heller, Nathan (Fictitious character)—Fiction 813.54
Hellman, Lillian, 1906– 812.52
Hellman, Lillian, 1906– —Criticism and interpretation 812.52
Hello Kitty (Fictitious character) 741.6
Hell's Angels 364.10660973
Helmet-mounted displays 623.46
Helophytes 581.768
Help-wanted advertising 650.14; 658.3111; 659.19331124
Helping behavior 158.3
Helping behavior in children 158.3083
Helplessness (Psychology) 155.232
Helvite 549.68
Hemapheresis 615.39
Hematology 616.15
Hematopoiesis 573.155
Hematopoietic stem cells—Transplantation 617.44
Hemingway, Ernest, 1899–1961 813.52
Hemingway, Ernest, 1899–1961—Criticism and interpretation 813.52
Hemingway, Ernest, 1899–1961. Farewell to arms 813.52
Hemingway, Ernest, 1899–1961—Homes and haunts—Florida—Key West 813.52
Hemingway, Ernest, 1899–1961—Homes and haunts—France—Paris 813.52
Hemingway, Ernest, 1899–1961—Literary style 813.52
Hemingway, Ernest, 1899–1961. Old man and the sea 813.52
Hemingway, Ernest, 1899–1961. Sun also rises 813.52
Hemingway, Ernest, 1899–1961—Technique 813.52
Hemiptera 595.754
Hemizonia 583.99
Hemodialysis 617.461059
Hemodialysis—Complications 617.461059
Hemodynamic monitoring 616.10754
Hemoglobin 612.1111
Hemophilia 616.1572
Hemp industry 338.17353
Henderson County (Ill.) 977.3413
Henderson County (Ill.)—Maps 912.773413
Henderson family 929.20973
Hendrix, Jimi 787.87166092
Henrie O (Fictitious character) 813.54
Henrie O (Fictitious character)—Fiction 813.54
Henry IV, King of England, 1367–1413 942.041092
Henry IV, King of France, 1553–1610 944.031092
Henry V, King of England, 1387–1422 942.042092
Henry VI, King of England, 1421–1471 942.043092
Henry VII, King of England, 1457–1509 942.051092
Henry VIII, King of England, 1491–1547 942.052092
Henry VIII, King of England, 1491–1547—Marriage 942.052092
Henry County (Ga.)—Genealogy 929.3758435
Henry County (Ill.)—Maps 912.77338
Henry County (Iowa)—Maps 912.77795
Henry County (Va.)—Genealogy 929.3755692
Henry family 929.20973
Henry, Katherine (Fictitious character) 813.54
Henry, Katherine (Fictitious character)—Fiction 813.54
Henry, Patrick, 1736–1799 973.3092
Henson, Jim 791.53092
Heparin 612.115
Hepatic encephalopathy 616.83
Hepatitis A 616.3623
Hepatitis B 616.3623

Hepatitis C 616.3623
Hepatitis, Viral 616.3623
Hepatotoxicology 616.362071
Hepburn, Audrey, 1929– 791.43028092
Hepburn, Katharine, 1909– 791.43028092
Heptathlon 796.42
Heracles (Greek mythology) 398.2093802
Heraclitus, of Ephesus 182.4
Heraldry 929.6
Heraldry—Great Britain 929.60941
Herb gardening 635.7
Herbal cosmetics 646.72; 668.55
Herbal teas 641.357
Herbals 615.321
Herbaria 580.74
Herbert, George, 1593–1633 821.3
Herbert, George, 1593–1633—Concordances 821.3
Herbert, George, 1593–1633—Criticism and interpretation 821.3
Herbicides 632.954; 668.654
Herbig Ae/Be stars 523.88
Herbivores 591.54
Herbs 581.63; 635.7
Herbs—Folklore 398.242
Herbs—Therapeutic use 615.321
Herbs—Therapeutic use—Encyclopedias 615.32103
Herbs—Therapeutic use—Handbooks, manuals, etc. 615.321
Hercules (Turboprop transports) 358.4483
Heredity 576.5
Heredity, Human 599.935
Hereford cattle 636.222
Heresies, Christian 273
Heresies, Christian—History 273
Heresies, Christian—History—Early church, ca. 30–600 273
Heresies, Christian—History—Middle Ages, 600–1500 273.6
Heresy 262.8
Heritage tourism 910
Herman Miller, Inc.—Catalogs 749.213075
Herman, Woody, 1913–1987 781.65092
Hermanos Penitentes 267.242789
Hermeneutics 121.686
Hermeneutics—History 121.68609
Hermes (Greek deity) 292.2113
Hermetic Order of the Golden Dawn 135.45
Hermetic Order of the Golden Dawn—Rituals 135.45
Hermetism 135.45
Hermit crabs 595.387
Hermitian operators 515.7246
Hermits 305.568
Herodotus 938.007202
Herodotus. History 938.03
Heroes 291.213
Heroes—Biography 920.02
Heroes in literature 808.80352; 809.93352
Heroes in motion pictures 791.43653
Heroes—Scandinavia—Poetry 829.3
Heroes—United States—Biography 920.073
Heroin 362.293; 363.45; 615.32335
Heroin habit 362.293; 616.8632
Heroin habit—United States 362.2930973
Herpes genitalis 616.9518
Herpesviruses 616.925
Herpetologists 597.9092
Herpetology 597.9
Herrick, Robert, 1591–1674 821.4

Highway research—United States 625.7072073
Highway research—United States—Periodicals 625.7072073
Hijacking of aircraft 363.2876
Hiking 796.51
Hiking—Alaska 796.5109798
Hiking—Alaska—Guidebooks 917.9804; 917.980451; 917.980452
Hiking—Appalachian Trail 796.510974
Hiking—Appalachian Trail—Guidebooks 917.404; 917.40443; 917.40444
Hiking—Appalachian Trail—Planning 796.510974
Hiking—Arizona 796.5109791
Hiking—Arizona—Grand Canyon National Park 796.510979132
Hiking—Arizona—Grand Canyon National Park—Guidebooks 917.913204; 917.91320453; 917.91320454
Hiking—Arizona—Guidebooks 917.9104; 917.910433; 917.910454
Hiking—California 796.5109794
Hiking—California—Guidebooks 917.9404; 917.940453; 917.940454
Hiking—California—Los Padres National Forest 796.510979476
Hiking—California—Los Padres National Forest—Guidebooks 917.9476
Hiking—California, Northern 796.5109794
Hiking—California, Northern—Guidebooks 917.9404; 917.940453; 917.940454
Hiking—California—San Diego County 796.51097498
Hiking—California—San Diego County—Guidebooks 917.949804; 917.94980453; 917.94980454
Hiking—California—San Francisco Bay Area 796.51097946
Hiking—California—San Francisco Bay Area—Guidebooks 917.94604; 917.9460453; 917.9460454
Hiking—California—San Gabriel Mountains 796.510979493
Hiking—California—San Gabriel Mountains—Guidebooks 917.9493
Hiking—California—Sequoia National Park 796.510979486
Hiking—California—Sequoia National Park—Guidebooks 917.9486
Hiking—California, Southern 796.51097949
Hiking—California, Southern—Guidebooks 917.94904; 917.9490453; 917.9490454
Hiking—California—Yosemite National Park 796.510979447
Hiking—California—Yosemite National Park—Guidebooks 917.944704; 917.94470453; 917.94470454
Hiking—Cascade Range 796.5109795
Hiking—Cascade Range—Guidebooks 917.9504; 917.950443; 917.950444
Hiking—Colorado 796.5109788
Hiking—Colorado—Boulder Region 796.510978863
Hiking—Colorado—Boulder Region—Guidebooks 917.886304; 917.88630433; 917.88630434
Hiking—Colorado—Colorado Trail 796.5109788
Hiking—Colorado—Colorado Trail—Guidebooks 917.8804; 917.880434
Hiking—Colorado—Guidebooks 917.8804; 917.880434
Hiking—Colorado—Rocky Mountain National Park 796.510978869
Hiking—Colorado—Rocky Mountain National Park—Guidebooks 917.886904; 917.88690433; 917.88690434
Hiking—Connecticut 796.5109746
Hiking—Connecticut—Guidebooks 917.4604; 917.460443; 917.460444

Hiking—George Washington National Forest (Va. and W. Va.) 796.510975591
Hiking—George Washington National Forest (Va. and W. Va.)—Guidebooks 917.559104; 917.55910443; 917.55910444
Hiking—Georgia—Guidebooks 796.5109758; 917.5804; 917.580443; 917.580444
Hiking—Great Britain—Guidebooks 914.104859; 914.10486
Hiking—Great Smoky Mountains National Park (N.C. and Tenn.) 796.510976889
Hiking—Great Smoky Mountains National Park (N.C. and Tenn.)—Guidebooks 917.688904; 917.68890453; 917.68890454
Hiking—Hawaii 796.5109969
Hiking—Hawaii—Guidebooks 919.6904; 919.690441; 919.690442
Hiking—Hawaii—Hawaii Island 796.51099691
Hiking—Hawaii—Hawaii Island—Guidebooks 919.69104; 919.6910441; 919.6910442
Hiking—Hawaii—Kauai 796.510996941
Hiking—Hawaii—Kauai—Guidebooks 919.694104; 919.69410441; 919.69410442
Hiking—Hawaii—Maui 796.51099692
Hiking—Hawaii—Maui—Guidebooks 919.69204; 919.6920441; 919.6920442
Hiking—Hawaii—Oahu 796.51099693
Hiking—Hawaii—Oahu—Guidebooks 919.69304; 919.6930441; 919.6930442
Hiking—Idaho 796.5109796
Hiking—Idaho—Guidebooks 917.9604; 917.960433; 917.960434
Hiking—Ireland 796.5109417
Hiking—Ireland—Guidebooks 914.1704; 914.1704824
Hiking—Maine 796.5109741
Hiking—Maine—Guidebooks 917.4104; 917.410443; 917.410444
Hiking—Massachusetts—Cape Cod 796.5109744
Hiking—Massachusetts—Cape Cod—Guidebooks 917.449204; 917.44920443; 917.44920444
Hiking—Montana 796.5109786
Hiking—Montana—Guidebooks 917.8604; 917.860433; 917.860434
Hiking—Nepal 796.510954
Hiking—Nepal—Guidebooks 915.49604
Hiking—New England 796.510974
Hiking—New England—Guidebooks 917.404; 917.40443; 917.40444
Hiking—New Hampshire 796.5109742
Hiking—New Hampshire—Guidebooks 917.4204; 917.420443; 917.420444
Hiking—New Jersey 796.5109749
Hiking—New Jersey—Guidebooks 917.4904; 917.490443; 917.490444
Hiking—New Mexico 796.5109789
Hiking—New Mexico—Guidebooks 917.8904; 917.890453; 917.890454
Hiking—New York (State) 796.51097475
Hiking—New York (State)—Adirondack Mountains 796.51097475
Hiking—New York (State)—Adirondack Mountains—Guidebooks 796.51097475; 917.47504; 917.4750443
Hiking—New York (State)—Adirondack Park 796.51097475
Hiking—New York (State)—Adirondack Park—Guidebooks 917.47504; 917.4750444
Hiking—New York (State)—Long Island 796.51097472
Hiking—New York (State)—Long Island—Guidebooks 917.472104; 917.47210443; 917.47210444

Hiking—North Carolina 796.5109756
Hiking—North Carolina—Guidebooks 917.5604;
917.560443; 917.560444
Hiking—Northwest, Pacific 796.5109795
Hiking—Northwest, Pacific—Guidebooks 917.9504;
917.950443; 917.950444
Hiking—Ohio 796.5109771
Hiking—Ohio—Guidebooks 917.71044; 917.710443;
917.710444
Hiking—Oregon 796.5109795
Hiking—Oregon—Guidebooks 917.9504; 917.950443;
917.950444
Hiking—Pennsylvania 796.5109748
Hiking—Pennsylvania—Guidebooks 917.4804;
917.480443; 917.480444
Hiking—Sierra Nevada (Calif. and Nev.) 796.51097944
Hiking—Sierra Nevada (Calif. and Nev.)—Guidebooks
917.94404; 917.9440453; 917.9440454
Hiking—South Carolina 796.5109757
Hiking—South Carolina—Guidebooks 917.5704;
917.570443; 917.570444
Hiking—Switzerland—Alps, Swiss 796.510947
Hiking—Switzerland—Alps, Swiss—Guidebooks
914.94704; 914.9470473; 914.9470474
Hiking—Tennessee 796.5109768
Hiking—Tennessee—Guidebooks 917.6804; 917.680453;
917.680454
Hiking—Texas—Guidebooks 796.5109764; 917.6404;
917.640463; 917.640464
Hiking—United States 796.510973
Hiking—United States—Guidebooks 917.304;
917.304929
Hiking—Utah 796.5109792
Hiking—Utah—Guidebooks 917.9204; 917.920433;
917.920434
Hiking—Vermont 796.5109743
Hiking—Vermont—Guidebooks 917.4304; 917.430443;
917.430444
Hiking—Virginia 796.5109755
Hiking—Virginia—Guidebooks 917.5504; 917.550443;
917.550444
Hiking—Virginia—Shenandoah National Park
796.51097559
Hiking—Virginia—Shenandoah National Park—
Guidebooks 917.55904; 917.5590443; 917.5590444
Hiking—Washington (State)—Puget Sound Region
796.51097977
Hiking—Washington (State)—Puget Sound Region—
Guidebooks 917.97704; 917.9770443; 917.9770444
Hiking—White Mountains (N.H. and Me.) 796.51097422
Hiking—White Mountains (N.H. and Me.)—Guidebooks
917.42204; 917.4220443; 917.4220444
Hiking with dogs 796.51
Hiking—Wyoming 796.5109787
Hiking—Wyoming—Grand Teton National Park
796.510978755
Hiking—Wyoming—Grand Teton National Park—
Guidebooks 917.8755
Hiking—Wyoming—Guidebooks 917.8704; 917.870433;
917.870434
Hiking—Yellowstone National Park 796.510978752
Hiking—Yellowstone National Park—Guidebooks
917.875204; 917.87520433; 917.87520434
Hilbert space 515.733
Hildegard, Saint, 1098–1179 282.092
Hill family 929.20973
Hill, Grant 796.323092
Hill, Hank (Fictitious character) 791.4572
Hillary, Edmund, Sir 796.522092

Hillsborough County (Fla.)—Maps 912.75965
Hillsdale County (Mich.) 977.429
Hillsdale County (Mich.)—Maps 912.77429
Himalaya Mountains—Pictorial works 915.49600222;
954.9600222
Himalaya Mountains Region 954.96
Himalaya Mountains Region—Description and travel
915.49604
Himes, Chester B., 1909– 813.54
Himes, Chester B., 1909– —Criticism and interpretation
813.54
Himmler, Heinrich, 1900–1945 943.086092
Hindi language 491.43
Hindi language—Grammar 491.435; 491.4382;
491.4382421
Hindsight bias (Psychology) 153
Hindu astrology 133.59445
Hindu astronomy 520.954
Hindu converts from Christianity 294.542
Hindu demonology 294.5216
Hindu diaspora 908.82945
Hindu ethics 294.548
Hindu law 294.594
Hindu literature 891.43; 891.4308
Hindu meditations 294.5435
Hindu symbolism 294.537
Hinduism 294.5
Hinduism and culture 294.5175
Hinduism and science 294.5175
Hinduism—Doctrines 294.52
Hinduism—Relations—Christianity 294.5172
Hinduism—Rituals 294.538
Hinduism—Sacred books 294.592
Hindustani music 780.954
Hines family 929.20973
Hip joint 612.98
Hippies 305.568
Hippocampus (Brain) 573.86; 612.825
Hippolyta (Greek mythology) 292.13; 398.2093802
Hippopotamidae 599.635
Hippopotamus 599.635
Hirohito, Emperor of Japan, 1901– 952.033092
Hiroshima-shi (Japan)—History—Bombardment, 1945
940.5425
Hiroshima-shi (Japan)—History—Bombardment, 1945—
Personal narratives 940.5425
Hiroshima-shi (Japan)—History—Bombardment, 1945—
Pictorial works 940.5425
Hispanic American art 704.0368
Hispanic American businesspeople 650.08968
Hispanic American Catholics 282.7308968
Hispanic American children 305.23
Hispanic American consumers 658.83408968
Hispanic American engineers 620.008968
Hispanic American homeless persons 305.569
Hispanic Americans 973.0468
Hispanic Americans—Biography 920.009268
Hispanic Americans—Education 371.82968073
Hispanic Americans—Employment 331.6368073
Hispanic Americans—Ethnic identity 305.868073
Hispanic Americans—History 973.0468
Hispanic Americans—Politics and government
323.1168073
Hiss, Alger 364.131
Histochemistry 572
Histocompatibility testing 616.07987
Histology 571.5; 611.018
Histology—Atlases 611.0180222
Histology—Examinations, questions, etc. 611.018076

Histology—Outlines, syllabi, etc. 611.018
Histology, Pathological 616.07583
Histology, Pathological—Technique 616.07583
Historians 907.202
Historians—United States 907.202273
Historiated initials 745.67
Historic agricultural landscapes 363.69; 630.9
Historic buildings 720.9
Historic buildings—Conservation and restoration
  363.69; 720.288
Historic buildings—England—Guidebooks 914.2
Historic buildings—England—London 942.1
Historic buildings—Great Britain 941
Historic buildings—Law and legislation 344.094
Historic buildings—Law and legislation—United States
  344.73094
Historic buildings—Maintenance and repair 690.24
Historic buildings—New York (State)—New York 974.71
Historic buildings—Scotland—Guidebooks 914.11
Historic buildings—United States 973
Historic districts 363.69
Historic farms 363.69
Historic preservation 363.69
Historic preservation—Law and legislation 344.094
Historic preservation—Law and legislation—United
  States 344.73094
Historic preservation—United States 363.690973
Historic ships 387.2
Historic sites 910
Historic sites—Colorado 978.8
Historic sites—Conservation and restoration 363.69
Historic sites—Korea (South) 951.95
Historic sites—Law and legislation 344.094
Historic sites—Law and legislation—United States
  344.73094
Historic sites—Texas—Guidebooks 917.6404;
  917.640463; 917.640464
Historic sites—United States 973
Historic sites—United States—Directories 973.025
Historical fiction 808.83081
Historical fiction, American 813.081; 813.08108
Historical fiction, American—History and criticism
  813.08109
Historical fiction, English 823.081
Historical films 791.43658
Historical films—History and criticism 791.43658
Historical films—United States—History and criticism
  791.43658
Historical geography 911
Historical geography—Maps 911
Historical geology 551.7
Historical libraries 026.9
Historical linguistics 417.7
Historical markers—Texas—Guidebooks 917.6404;
  917.640463; 917.640464
Historical materialism 335.4119
Historical museums 907.4
Historical museums—United States 973.07473
Historical prints 769.9
Historical reenactments 900
Historicism 901
Historiography 907.2
Historiography—Handbooks, manuals, etc. 907.2
Historiography—History—20th century 909.82072
History 900
History, Ancient 930
History, Ancient—Historiography 930.072
History—Bibliography 016.9
History—Data processing 902.85

History—Dictionaries 903
History—Examinations, questions, etc. 907.6
History in art 704.9499
History in literature 808.80358; 809.93358
History materials 016.9
History—Methodology 901; 907.2
History, Modern 909.08
History, Modern—17th century 909.6
History, Modern—18th century 909.7
History, Modern—19th century 909.81
History, Modern—19th century—Sources 909.81
History, Modern—20th century 909.82
History, Modern—20th century—Chronology 909.820202
History, Modern—20th century—Dictionaries 909.8203
History, Modern—20th century—Sources 909.82
History, Modern—1945– 909.825
History—Outlines, syllabi, etc. 902.02
History—Periodicals 905
History—Philosophy 901
History—Religious aspects 291.175
History—Research 907.2
History—Statistical methods 907.2
History—Study and teaching 907.1
History—Study and teaching (Elementary) 372.89
History—Study and teaching (Elementary)—United
  States 372.890973
History—Study and teaching (Higher) 907.11
History—Study and teaching (Higher)—United States
  907.1173
History—Study and teaching—United States 907.1073
Hitchcock, Alfred, 1899– 791.430233092
Hitchcock, Alfred, 1899– —Criticism and interpretation
  791.430233092
Hitchhiking—Europe 796.51094
Hitchhiking—Europe—Guidebooks 914.04; 914.04559;
  914.0456
Hitler, Adolf, 1889–1945 943.086092
Hitler, Adolf, 1889–1945—Death and burial 943.086092
Hitler, Adolf, 1889–1945—Psychology 943.086092
HIV infections 362.1969792; 616.9792
HIV infections—Handbooks, manuals, etc. 616.9792
HIV infections—Psychological aspects 616.97920019
HIV-positive men 362.19697920081
HIV (Viruses) 616.979201
Hồ, Chí Minh, 1890–1969 959.704092
Hoabinhian culture 959.01
Hoag, Stewart (Fictitious character) 813.54
Hoag, Stewart (Fictitious character)—Fiction 813.54
Hoare, Bartholomew (Fictitious character) 813.54
Hoare, Dido (Fictitious character) 823.914
Hob (Fictitious character : Horn) 823.914
Hobbes (Fictitious character) 741.5973
Hobbes, Thomas, 1588–1679 192
Hobbes, Thomas, 1588–1679. Leviathan 320.1
Hobbies 790.13
Hobby equipment industry 790.13
Hockaday, Neil (Fictitious character) 813.54
Hockaday, Neil (Fictitious character)—Fiction 813.54
Hockey 796.355; 796.962
Hockey—Biography 796.962092
Hockey—Coaching 796.962077
Hockey goalkeepers 796.962092
Hockey goalkeepers—Biography 796.962092
Hockey—History 796.96209
Hockey players 796.962092
Hockey players—Biography 796.962092
Hockey—Rules 796.96202022
Hockey teams 796.96264
Hockey—Training 796.962071

Hocking County (Ohio) 977.1835
Hocking County (Ohio)—Genealogy 929.3771835
Hockney, David 759.2
Hockney, David—Exhibitions 759.2
Hodges family 929.20973
Hodgkin's disease 616.99446
Hoffman family 929.20973
Hoffman, Nick (Fictitious character) 813.54
Hoffmann, E. T. A. (Ernst Theodor Amadeus), 1776–1822 833.6
Hoffmann, E. T. A. (Ernst Theodor Amadeus), 1776–1822—Translations into English 833.6
Hogans 392.360089972; 728.373089972
Hogarth, William, 1697–1764 760.092
Hogle family 929.20973
Hogwarts School of Witchcraft and Wizardry (Imaginary place) 823.914
Hoisting machinery 621.862
Hokan languages 497.57
Holcroft family 929.20973
Holden, Vicky (Fictitious character) 813.54
Hölderlin, Friedrich, 1770–1843 831.6
Hölderlin, Friedrich, 1770–1843—Translations into English 831.6
Holding companies 338.86
Holdings (Bibliographic data) 025.3
Holiday, Billie, 1915–1959 782.42165092
Holiday cookery 641.568
Holiday decorations 745.5941
Holiday stress 155.9?
Holidays 394.26
Holidays—Literary collections 808.8033
Holidays—United States 394.26973
Holiness 234.8
Holiness—Biblical teaching 234.8
Holiness churches 289.94
Holism 111.82
Holistic medicine 610; 613
Holistic nursing 610.73
Holland family 929.20973
Holland ware 738.27
Holley carburetors 629.2533
Holliday, John Henry, 1851–1887 364.1523092
Hollister, Corrie Belle (Fictitious character) 813.54
Holloway family 929.20973
Holly, Buddy, 1936–1959 781.66092; 782.42166092
Hollywood (Los Angeles, Calif.) 979.494
Holmes family 929.20973
Holmes, Mycroft (Fictitious character) 813.54
Holmes, Oliver Wendell, 1841–1935 347.732634
Holmes, Sherlock (Fictitious character) 823.8
Holmes, Sherlock (Fictitious character)—Fiction 813.54
Holocaust (Christian theology) 231.76
Holocaust denial 940.5318
Holocaust denial literature 940.5318
Holocaust, Jewish (1939-1945) 940.5318
Holocaust, Jewish (1939-1945)—Bibliography 016.9405318
Holocaust, Jewish (1939-1945)—Causes 940.5318
Holocaust, Jewish (1939-1945)—Historiography 940.5318072
Holocaust, Jewish (1939-1945), in art 704.9499405318
Holocaust, Jewish (1939-1945), in literature 808.80358; 809.93358
Holocaust, Jewish (1939-1945), in motion pictures 791.43658
Holocaust, Jewish (1939-1945)—Influence 940.5318
Holocaust, Jewish (1939-1945)—Moral and ethical aspects 179.7

Holocaust, Jewish (1939-1945)—Personal narratives 940.5318092
Holocaust, Jewish (1939-1945)—Personal narratives—History and criticism 940.5318092
Holocaust, Jewish (1939-1945)—Poland 940.531809438
Holocaust, Jewish (1939-1945)—Press coverage 070.4499405318
Holocaust, Jewish (1939-1945)—Psychological aspects 940.5318019
Holocaust, Jewish (1939-1945)—Public opinion 940.5318
Holocaust, Jewish (1939-1945)—Sources 940.5318
Holocaust (Jewish theology) 296.31174
Holocaust memorials 940.5318
Holocaust survivors 940.5318092
Holocaust survivors—United States 940.5318092273
Holocaust victims 940.5318092
Holographic interferometry 621.3675
Holography 621.3675; 774
Holography—Equipment and supplies 621.36750284
Holography industry 338.47774
Holography—Materials 621.36750284
Holomorphic functions 515.94
Holothurians 593.96
Holt family (Fictitious characters) 813.54
Holt family (Fictitious characters)—Fiction 813.54
Holub, Miroslav, 1923– 891.8615
Holub, Miroslav, 1923– —Translations into English 891.8615
Holy Shroud 232.966
Holy Spirit 231.3
Holy Spirit—Biblical teaching 231.3
Holy Spirit—Meditations 231.3
Holy Spirit—Prayer-books and devotions 242.72
Holy Spirit—Sermons 231.3
Holy, The 211
Holy water fonts 726.5291
Holy Week 263.925
Holy Week music 781.726
Holy-Week sermons 252.625
Home accidents 363.13
Home accidents—Prevention 613.6; 643.0289
Home and school 306.432; 371.192
Home and school—United States 371.1920973
Home automation 643.6; 696
Home banking services 332.178
Home-based businesses 658.041
Home-based businesses—Management 658.041
Home-based businesses—United States 658.041
Home-based businesses—Vocational guidance 658.041
Home-based mental health services 362.24
Home care services 362.14
Home care services—Administration 362.14068
Home care services—Law and legislation 344.03214
Home care services—Law and legislation—United States 344.7303214
Home care services—Prospective payment 368.382
Home care services—United States 362.140973
Home children (Canadian immigrants) 304.871041083
Home computer networks 004.68
Home drug infusion therapy 362.178; 615.6
Home economics 640
Home economics—Accounting 640.42
Home economics extension work 640.715
Home economics—Periodicals 640.5
Home economics—Study and teaching 640.71
Home economics—United States 640.973
Home economics—United States—History 640.973
Home economics—Vocational guidance 640.23

Home entertainment industry 381.453845; 381.45621388; 381.456213893
Home entertainment systems 621.388
Home equity loans 332.722
Home exchanging 643.12
Home health aides 362.14; 610.7343
Home improvement loans 332.722
Home improvement loans—United States 332.722
Home in literature 808.80355; 809.93355
Home in motion pictures 791.43655
Home labor 331.25
Home nursing 362.14; 649.8
Home nursing—Handbooks, manuals, etc. 610.7343
Home ownership 643.12
Home ownership—United States 643.120973
Home rule 342.042
Home rule—Ireland 320.1509415
Home rule—Washington (D.C.) 342.753042
Home runs (Baseball)—United States—History 796.35726
Home safety equipment industry 363.13
Home schooling 371.042
Home schooling—Handbooks, manuals, etc. 371.042
Home schooling—United States 371.0420973
Home schooling—United States—Curricula 375
Home schooling—United States—Handbooks, manuals, etc. 371.0420973
Home video systems 621.38833
Homeless boys 305.23; 362.7086942
Homeless children 305.23
Homeless children—United States 362.7086942
Homeless families 306.85; 362.53
Homeless girls 305.23; 362.7086942
Homeless persons 305.569; 362.5
Homeless persons as artists 704.06942
Homeless persons—New York (State)—New York 305.569097471; 362.5097471
Homeless persons—Services for 362.58
Homeless persons—Services for—United States 362.580973
Homeless persons—United States 362.50973
Homeless teenagers 305.235; 362.7086942
Homeless youth 362.7086942
Homeless youth—United States 362.7086942
Homelessness 305.569; 362.5
Homelessness—United States 362.50973
Homeopathy 615.532
Homeopathy—Materia medica and therapeutics 615.532
Homeostasis 571.75
Homeowners' associations 346.043
Homeowners' associations—United States 643.106073
Homeowner's insurance 368.096
Homeowner's insurance—United States 368.0960973
Homer 883.01
Homer—Adaptations 883.01
Homer—Criticism and interpretation 883.01
Homer. Iliad 883.01
Homer—Language 883.01
Homer—Literary style 883.01
Homer. Odyssey 883.01
Homer—Technique 883.01
Homer—Translations into English 883.01
Homer—Versification 883.01
Homer, Winslow, 1836–1910 759.13
Homer, Winslow, 1836–1910—Criticism and interpretation 759.13
Homer, Winslow, 1836–1910—Exhibitions 759.13
Homework 371.30281
Homework centers in libraries 025.5

Homicide 364.1523
Homicide—United States 364.15230973
Homiletical illustrations 251.08
Homiliaries 252; 291.43
Homo erectus 569.9
Homology theory 514.23
Homonyms 401.43
Homoousian controversy 273.4
Homophobia 306.766
Homophobia in higher education 378.008664
Homophobia in psychoanalysis 150.19508664; 616.891708664
Homophobia in schools 370.8664
Homophobia in sports 796.08664
Homoplasy 576.8
Homosexuality 306.766
Homosexuality and dance 792.808664
Homosexuality and education—United States 370.8664
Homosexuality and literature 809.93353
Homosexuality and motion pictures 306.766; 791.4308664
Homosexuality—History 306.76609
Homosexuality in dance 792.8
Homosexuality in literature 808.80353; 809.93353
Homosexuality in motion pictures 791.43653
Homosexuality—Law and legislation 342.087; 346.013
Homosexuality—Law and legislation—United States 342.73087; 346.73013
Homosexuality—Law and legislation—United States—Periodicals 346.73013
Homosexuality—Literary collections 808.80353
Homosexuality, Male 306.7662
Homosexuality, Male—Psychological aspects 306.7662
Homosexuality, Male—Religious aspects 291.178357662
Homosexuality, Male—United States 306.76620973
Homosexuality—Philosophy 306.76601
Homosexuality—Political aspects—United States 323.3264
Homosexuality—Psychological aspects 306.766; 306.766?
Homosexuality—Religious aspects 291.17835766
Homosexuality—Religious aspects—Catholic Church 261.835766
Homosexuality—Religious aspects—Christianity 230.08664; 261.835766
Homosexuality—United States 306.7660973
Homotopy theory 514.24
Honda Accord automobile 629.2222
Honda Accord automobile—Maintenance and repair 629.28722
Honda Accord automobile—Maintenance and repair—Handbooks, manuals, etc. 629.28722
Honda Civic automobile 629.2222
Honda Civic automobile—Maintenance and repair 629.28722
Honda Civic automobile—Maintenance and repair—Handbooks, manuals, etc. 629.28722
Honda motorcycle 629.2275
Honda motorcycle—Maintenance and repair 629.28775
Honda motorcycle—Maintenance and repair—Handbooks, manuals, etc. 629.28775
Honduras 972.83
Honesty 179.9
Honey 638.16; 641.38
Honey as food 641.38
Honey-Bear Farm (Imaginary place) 823.914
Honeybee 595.799; 638.12
Honeybee—Behavior 595.799
Honeyguides 598.72

Honeymooners (Television program) 791.4572
Hong Kong (China) 951.25
Hong Kong (China)—Census, 1981 315.125
Hong Kong (China)—Commerce 382.095125
Hong Kong (China)—Commerce—Handbooks, manuals, etc. 382.095125
Hong Kong (China)—Description and travel 915.12504; 915.125046
Hong Kong (China)—Economic conditions 330.95125
Hong Kong (China)—Guidebooks 915.12504; 915.125046
Hong Kong (China)—History 951.25
Hong Kong (China)—History—Transfer of Sovereignty from Great Britain, 1997 951.2506
Hong Kong (China)—Maps 912.5125
Hong Kong (China)—Officials and employees 352.63095125
Hong Kong (China)—Officials and employees—Salaries, etc. 352.67095125
Hong Kong (China)—Politics and government 320.95125; 951.25
Hong Kong (China)—Social conditions 951.25
Hong Kong (China)—Social life and customs 951.25
Honolulu (Hawaii) 996.931
Honolulu (Hawaii)—Guidebooks 919.693104; 919.69310441; 919.69310442
Honor in literature 808.80353; 809.93353
Honor system (Higher education) 378.195
Hoodoos (Geomorphology) 551.43
Hook, Bert (Fictitious character) 823.914
Hooke, Robert, 1635–1703 509.2
Hooking 746.74
Hoover, Herbert, 1874–1964 973.916092
Hoover, J. Edgar (John Edgar), 1895–1972 363.25092
Hope 152.4
Hope—Biblical teaching 234.25
Hope, Bob, 1903– 792.7028092
Hope diamond 736.23
Hope, Matthew (Fictitious character) 813.54
Hope, Matthew (Fictitious character)—Fiction 813.54
Hope—Religious aspects 291.22
Hope—Religious aspects—Christianity 234.25
Hopi Indians 305.89745; 979.10049745
Hopi Indians—History 979.10049745
Hopi Indians—Religion 299.7845
Hopi magic 299.74; 398.20899745
Hopi pottery 738.37
Hopkins County (Ky.)—Genealogy 929.3769823
Hopkins, Gerard Manley, 1844–1889 821.8
Hopkins, Gerard Manley, 1844–1889—Criticism and interpretation 821.8
Hopper, Edward, 1882–1967 759.13
Horace 874.01
Horace. Carmina 874.01
Horace—Criticism and interpretation 874.01
Horace—Translations into English 874.01
Horary astrology 133.56
Horizontal oil well drilling 622.3381; 622.3382
Hormones 612.405
Hormones, Sex 571.8374; 612.6
Horn and piano music 788.94
Horn family 929.20973
Horn music 788.94
Hornbills 598.78
Hornblower, Horatio (Fictitious character) 823.912
Hornblower, Horatio (Fictitious character)—Fiction 823.912
Horned frogs 597.875
Horned toads as pets 639.3954
Hornet (Jet fighter plane) 358.4383; 623.7464

Horology 529.7
Horoscopes 133.54
Horror comic books, strips, etc. 741.5973
Horror films 791.436164
Horror films—Encyclopedias 791.43616403
Horror films—History and criticism 791.43616409
Horror films—History and criticism—Periodicals 791.43616409005
Horror films—United States—History and criticism 791.4361640973
Horror in literature 808.80164; 809.9164
Horror tales 808.38738; 808.838738
Horror tales, American 808.838738; 813.08738; 813.0873808
Horror tales, American—History and criticism 813.0873809
Horror tales, English 823.08738; 823.0873808
Horror tales, English—History and criticism 823.0873809
Horror tales—History and criticism 809.38738
Horror television programs 791.45616
Horse arenas 636.10811; 725.82; 798.24
Horse breeders 636.1082092
Horse breeds 636.1
Horse collars 636.10837; 685.1
Horse farms 636.101
Horse owners 798.092
Horse racing 798.4
Horse racing—Betting 798.401
Horse racing—Betting—United States 798.4010973
Horse racing—Great Britain 798.400941
Horse racing—Law and legislation 344.099
Horse racing—Law and legislation—California 344.794099
Horse racing—Law and legislation—Kentucky 344.769099
Horse racing—Law and legislation—Oklahoma 344.766099
Horse shows 798.24
Horse sports 798
Horse trading 380.14161
Horse trainers 798.2092
Horse whisperers 636.10835
Horseflies 595.773
Horsemanship 798.2
Horsemanship—Psychological aspects 798.2019
Horsemanship—Study and teaching 798.2071
Horsemanship—Therapeutic use 615.8515
Horses 636.1
Horses—Anecdotes 636.1
Horses—Behavior 636.1
Horses—Breeding 636.1082
Horses—Dictionaries 636.1003
Horses—Diseases 636.10896
Horses—Diseases—Handbooks, manuals, etc. 636.10896
Horses—Encyclopedias 636.1003
Horses—Feeding and feeds 636.1085
Horses—Health 636.1083
Horses in art 704.943296655; 743.696655
Horses—Reproduction 636.1082
Horses—Showing 798.24
Horses—Surgery 636.10897
Horses—Training 636.10835; 636.10886
Horseshoeing 636.10833; 682.1
Horticultural crops 635
Horticultural literature 635
Horticultural machinery 635.0284
Horticulture 635
Horton family 929.20973

Hospice care 362.1756
Hospice nurses 610.7361
Hospices (Terminal care) 362.1756
Hospital architecture 725.51
Hospital care 362.11
Hospital care—Quality control 362.110685
Hospital consultants 362.11
Hospital films 362.11; 791.43656
Hospital management companies 362.11068
Hospital patients 362.11
Hospital pharmacies 362.1782
Hospital-physician joint ventures 362.11068
Hospital-physician relations 362.11068
Hospital purchasing 362.110687
Hospital television programs 362.11; 791.45656
Hospital utilization 362.11
Hospital utilization—California—Statistics—Periodicals
  362.1109794021
Hospital utilization—Length of stay—United States—
  Statistics 362.110973021
Hospital utilization—United States—Statistics
  362.110973021
Hospital ward clerks 362.11068; 651.504261
Hospitality 177.1
Hospitality industry 647.94
Hospitality industry—Accounting 647.94; 657.837
Hospitality industry—Data processing 647.940285
Hospitality industry—Management 647.94068
Hospitality industry—Marketing 647.940688
Hospitality industry—Personnel management
  647.940683
Hospitality industry—Vocational guidance 647.94023
Hospitality—Religious aspects 291.5671
Hospitality—Religious aspects—Christianity 241.671
Hospitals 362.11
Hospitals—Accounting 657.8322
Hospitals—Accreditation—United States 362.11021873
Hospitals—Administration 362.11068
Hospitals—Administration—Data processing
  362.110285; 362.11068
Hospitals—Admission and discharge 362.11
Hospitals—Business management 362.11068
Hospitals—Case management services 362.11068
Hospitals—Cost control 338.4336211
Hospitals—Design and construction 725.51
Hospitals—Emergency service 362.18
Hospitals—Finance 362.110681
Hospitals in literature 808.80355; 809.93355
Hospitals—Law and legislation 344.03211
Hospitals—Law and legislation—United States
  344.7303211
Hospitals—Materials management 362.110687
Hospitals—Maternity services 362.1982
Hospitals—Medical staff 362.110683
Hospitals—Outpatient services 362.12
Hospitals—Personnel management 362.110683
Hospitals—Planning 362.11068
Hospitals, Proprietary 362.11
Hospitals—Public relations 659.2936211
Hospitals—Safety measures 362.110684; 363.15
Hospitals—Sanitation 363.7297
Hospitals—United States 362.110973
Hospitals—United States—Administration 362.11068
Hospitals—United States—Directories 362.1102573
Host desecration accusation 261.26; 305.8924
Host desecration accusation in literature
  808.803826126; 809.933826126
Host-fungus relationships 579.517857
Host-parasite relationships 577.857

Hosta 635.93432
Hostages 303.625
Hot air balloons 629.13322
Hot carriers 537.6226
Hot food tables 642.50284
Hot pants 646.433; 687.113
Hot pepper sauces 641.3384
Hot peppers 641.3384
Hot rods 629.2286
Hot rods—History 629.228609
Hot-water heating 697.4
Hot weather clothing 646.3
Hotel chains 338.76164794
Hotel housekeeping 648
Hotel management 647.94
Hotel management schools 647.94
Hotelkeepers 647.94092
Hotels 338.4764794; 647.94; 728.5
Hotels—Accounting 657.837
Hotels—Austria 647.9443601
Hotels—Austria—Guidebooks 647.9443601
Hotels—California 647.9479401
Hotels—California—Directories 647.9479401
Hotels—California—Guidebooks 647.9479401
Hotels—California, Northern—Guidebooks 647.94794101
Hotels—Caribbean Area—Guidebooks 647.9472901
Hotels—Directories 647.94
Hotels—Employees 647.94
Hotels—England 647.944201
Hotels—England—Guidebooks 647.944201
Hotels—England—London 647.9442101
Hotels—England—London—Guidebooks 647.9442101
Hotels—Europe 647.94401
Hotels—Europe—Directories 647.94401
Hotels—Europe—Guidebooks 647.94401
Hotels—Finance 647.94
Hotels—Florida 647.9475901
Hotels—Florida—Guidebooks 647.9475901
Hotels—France 647.944401
Hotels—France—Guidebooks 647.944401
Hotels—Germany 647.944301
Hotels—Germany—Guidebooks 647.944301
Hotels—Great Britain 338.476479441; 647.944101
Hotels—Great Britain—Directories 647.944101
Hotels—Great Britain—Guidebooks 647.944101
Hotels—Great Britain—History 647.94410109
Hotels—Guidebooks 647.94
Hotels—Ireland 647.9441501
Hotels—Ireland—Guidebooks 647.9441501
Hotels—Italy 647.944501
Hotels—Italy—Guidebooks 647.944501
Hotels—Law and legislation 343.07864794
Hotels—Law and legislation—Great Britain
  343.4107864794
Hotels—Law and legislation—United States
  343.7307864794
Hotels—Maintenance and repair 647.94
Hotels—Marketing 647.94
Hotels—Middle Atlantic States 647.947401
Hotels—Middle Atlantic States—Directories 647.947401
Hotels—Middle Atlantic States—Guidebooks 647.947401
Hotels—Middle West 647.947701
Hotels—Middle West—Directories 647.947701
Hotels—New England 647.947401
Hotels—New England—Directories 647.947401
Hotels—New England—Guidebooks 647.947401
Hotels—Northwest, Pacific 647.9479501
Hotels—Northwest, Pacific—Guidebooks 647.9479501
Hotels—Periodicals 647.94

Hotels—Personnel management 647.94
Hotels—Pet accommodations—United States—
  Guidebooks 647.947301
Hotels—Planning 647.94
Hotels—Portugal 647.9446901
Hotels—Portugal—Guidebooks 647.9446901
Hotels—Rocky Mountains Region 647.947801
Hotels—Rocky Mountains Region—Guidebooks
  647.947801
Hotels—Southern States 647.947501
Hotels—Southern States—Directories 647.947501
Hotels—Southern States—Guidebooks 647.947501
Hotels—Spain 647.944601
Hotels—Spain—Guidebooks 647.944601
Hotels—Switzerland 647.9449401
Hotels—Switzerland—Guidebooks 647.9449401
Hotels—United States 647.947301
Hotels—United States—Directories 647.947301
Hotels—United States—Guidebooks 647.947301
Hotels—Vocational guidance 647.94
Hotels—West (U.S.) 647.947801
Hotels—West (U.S.)—Directories 647.947801
Hotlines (Counseling) 361.06
Houdini, Harry, 1874–1926 793.8092
Houghton County (Mich.) 977.4993
Houghton County (Mich.)—Maps 912.774993
Hours of labor 331.2572
Hours of labor, Flexible 331.2572
Hours of labor—United States 331.25720973
House buying 333.338; 643.12
House buying—California 643.1209794
House buying—United States 643.120973
House buying—United States—Handbooks, manuals,
  etc. 643.120973
House cleaning 648.5
House construction 690.8; 690.837
House construction—Handbooks, manuals, etc. 690.837
House construction—Specifications 690.80212; 690.837
House family 929.20973
House framing 694.2
House furnishings 645
House music 781.64
House organs 658.455
House painting 698.1
House plants 635.965
House plants—Encyclopedias 635.96503
House plants in interior decoration 747.98
House selling 333.3383
House selling—Handbooks, manuals, etc. 333.3383
House selling—United States 333.33830973
Housefly 595.774
Household appliances 643.6
Household appliances, Electric 643.6; 683.83
Household appliances, Electric—Maintenance and repair
  683.830288
Household appliances—Maintenance and repair
  643.60288
Household ecology 577.554
Household electronics 621.38154; 621.382; 643.6
Household electronics industry 338.4768383
Household linens 646.21
Household pests—Control 648.7
Household surveys 001.433
Households 306.85
Houseman, Carl (Fictitious character) 813.54
Houses (Astrology) 133.53042
Housewives 640.92
Housing 363.5
Housing and health 613.5

Housing—Bibliography 016.3635
Housing, Cooperative 334.1
Housing development 333.337
Housing—England—London 307.33609421
Housing—Finance 363.582
Housing—Great Britain 307.3360941
Housing—Great Britain—History 307.3360941
Housing—Law and legislation 344.063635
Housing—Law and legislation—United States
  344.73063635
Housing—New York (State)—New York 363.5097471
Housing policy 363.5561
Housing policy—Developing countries 363.5561091724
Housing policy—Europe 363.5561094
Housing policy—Great Britain 363.55610941
Housing policy—New York (State)—New York
  363.5097471
Housing policy—United States 363.55610973
Housing, Rural 307.33612
Housing, Rural—United States 307.336120973
Housing starts 333.338
Housing starts—Arizona—Phoenix Metropolitan Area—
  Remote-sensing maps 333.3380979173
Housing subsidies 363.582
Housing—United States 307.3360973; 363.50973
Housing—United States—Bibliography 016.36350973
Housing—United States—Bibliography—Microform
  catalogs 016.36350973
Housing—United States—Statistics 363.5109730021
Housing—United States—Statistics—Periodicals
  363.510973002
Housman, A. E. (Alfred Edward), 1859–1936 021.012
Housman, A. E. (Alfred Edward), 1859–1936—Criticism
  and interpretation 821.912
Houston family 929.20973
Houston Metropolitan Area (Tex.)—Maps 912.7641411
Houston Region (Tex.) 976.41411
Houston Region (Tex.)—Guidebooks 917.64141104;
  917.6414110463; 917.6414110464
Houston Rockets (Basketball team)
  796.32364097641411
Houston Rockets (Basketball team)—History
  796.32364097641411
Houston, Sam, 1793–1863 976.404092
Houston (Tex.) 976.41411
Houston (Tex.)—Guidebooks 917.64141104;
  917.6414110463; 917.6414110464
Houston (Tex.)—Maps 912.7641411
Houston, Whitney 782.42164092
Howard County (Iowa)—Maps 912.777312
Howard County (Md.)—Maps 912.75281
Howard, J. W. (John Winston), 1939– 994.066092
Howard, Jeri (Fictitious character) 813.54
Howard, Jeri (Fictitious character)—Fiction 813.54
Howard, Robert Ervin, 1906–1936 813.52
Howard, Robert Ervin, 1906–1936—Criticism and
  interpretation 813.52
Howard, Roz (Fictitious character) 813.54
Howard, Roz (Fictitious character)—Fiction 813.54
Howe, Julia Ward, 1819–1910 818.409
Howell family 929.20973
Howells, William Dean, 1837–1920 813.4; 818.409
Howells, William Dean, 1837–1920—Criticism and
  interpretation 813.4
Howells, William Dean, 1837–1920—Knowledge—
  America 813.4
HP LaserJet printers 004.77; 681.62
HP LaserJet printers—Handbooks, manuals, etc.
  004.77; 681.62

Hrotsvitha, ca. 935–ca. 975 872.03
Hrotsvitha, ca. 935–ca. 975—Translations into English
    872.03
HTML (Document markup language) 005.72
HTML editors (Computer programs) 005.72
HTTP (Computer network protocol) 004.678; 005.71376
Hua, Mulan (Legendary character)—Legends
    398.2095102
Hubbard family 929.20973
Hubbard, L. Ron (La Fayette Ron), 1911– 299.936092
Hubbard model 530.41
Hubble, Edwin Powell, 1889–1953 520.92
Hubble Space Telescope (Spacecraft) 522.2919
Hudson family 929.20973
Hudson, Henry, d. 1611 910.92
Hudson River (N.Y. and N.J.) 974.73
Hudson River (N.Y. and N.J.)—Description and travel
    917.47304; 917.4730443; 917.4730444
Hudson River Valley (N.Y. and N.J.) 974.73
Hudson River Valley (N.Y. and N.J.)—Guidebooks
    917.47304; 917.4730443; 917.4730444
Hudson River Valley (N.Y. and N.J.)—History 974.73
Hudson's Bay Company 971.201
Huế (Vietnam), Battle of, 1968 959.704342
Hughes family 929.20973
Hughes, Howard, 1905–1976 338.76092
Hughes, Langston, 1902–1967 818.5209
Hughes, Langston, 1902–1967—Criticism and
    interpretation 818.5209
Hughes, Ted, 1930– 821.914
Hughes, Ted, 1930– —Criticism and interpretation
    821.914
Hugo Award 823.08762079
Hugo, Victor, 1802–1885 848.709
Hull, Brett, 1964– 796.962092
Hull House (Chicago, Ill.)—History 361.92
Hulls (Naval architecture) 623.84
Human-alien encounters 001.942
Human anatomy 611
Human anatomy—Atlases 611.0022; 611.00222
Human anatomy—Examinations, questions, etc.
    611.0076
Human anatomy—Laboratory manuals 611.0078
Human anatomy—Outlines, syllabi, etc. 611
Human-animal relationships in literature 808.80362;
    809.93362
Human-animal relationships—Religious aspects
    291.5693
Human behavior 150
Human behavior—Humor 150.207
Human beings 128; 901
Human beings—Animal nature 599.9
Human beings—Effect of Saturn on 133.537
Human beings in art 704.942
Human beings in literature 808.80353; 809.93353
Human beings—Migrations 304.8
Human beings—Origin 569.9
Human biology 599.9; 612
Human biology—Social aspects 306.45
Human capital 331.125
Human chromosome abnormalities 616.042
Human chromosome abnormalities—Catalogs and
    collections 616.042
Human chromosomes 611.01816
Human cloning 612.6
Human cloning—Moral and ethical aspects 174.25
Human-computer interaction 004.019
Human-computer interaction—Periodicals 004.019
Human dissection 611

Human dissection—Laboratory manuals 611.0078
Human ecology 304.2
Human ecology—History 304.209
Human ecology—Periodicals 304.205
Human ecology—Philosophy 304.201
Human ecology—Religious aspects 291.178362
Human ecology—Religious aspects—Christianity
    241.691; 261.8362
Human ecology—Religious aspects—Judaism 296.38
Human ecology—Study and teaching 304.2071
Human embryo 612.646
Human engineering 620.82
Human engineering—Handbooks, manuals, etc. 620.82
Human engineering—Periodicals 620.8205
Human evolution 599.938
Human experimentation in medicine 619.98
Human experimentation in medicine—Moral and ethical
    aspects 174.28
Human experimentation in medicine—United States
    174.280973
Human face recognition (Computer science) 006.37
Human figure in art 704.942; 743.4; 757
Human gene mapping 611.01816
Human genetics 599.935; 611.01816
Human genetics—Law and legislation 344.04196
Human genetics—Moral and ethical aspects 174.25
Human genome 611.01816
Human Genome Project 611.01816
Human geography 304.2; 910
Human geography—Africa 916
Human geography—Dictionaries 304.203
Human geography—Philosophy 304.201
Human geography—United States 917.3
Human geography—United States—History 304.20973
Human growth 612.6
Human information processing 153
Human locomotion 612.76
Human-machine systems 620.82
Human mechanics 612.76
Human molecular genetics 611.01816
Human physiology 612; 612.0024613
Human physiology—Examinations, questions, etc.
    612.0076
Human physiology—Laboratory manuals 612.0078
Human physiology—Outlines, syllabi, etc. 612
Human physiology—Problems, exercises, etc. 612.0076
Human powered aircraft 629.13334
Human remains (Archaeology) 930.1
Human remains (Archaeology)—Repatriation 930.1
Human reproduction 612.6
Human reproduction—Endocrine aspects 612.6
Human reproduction—Immunological aspects
    616.65079
Human reproduction in art 704.9496126
Human reproduction (Jewish law) 296.366; 296.38
Human reproduction—Study and teaching (Elementary)
    372.372
Human reproductive technology 616.69206
Human reproductive technology—Moral and ethical
    aspects 176
Human reproductive technology—Social aspects
    306.461; 362.198178
Human rights 323; 341.481; 342.085
Human rights advocacy 323
Human rights—Africa 323.096; 341.481096; 342.6085
Human rights—Africa—Periodicals 323.09605
Human rights—Bibliography 016.323
Human rights—Burma 323.09591
Human rights—Chile 323.0983

Human rights—China 323.0951
Human rights—Developing countries 323.091724
Human rights—El Salvador 323.097284
Human rights—Europe 341.481094; 342.4085
Human rights—Great Britain 342.41085
Human rights—Guatemala 323.097281
Human rights—History 323.09; 341.48109
Human rights—India 323.0954
Human rights movements 323
Human rights—Nicaragua 323.097285
Human rights—Periodicals 323.05; 341.48105
Human rights—Peru 323.0985
Human rights—Philippines 323.09599
Human rights—Philosophy 323.01
Human rights—Religious aspects 291.177
Human rights—Romania 323.09498
Human rights—South Africa 323.0968
Human rights—Soviet Union 323.0947
Human rights—Study and teaching 323.071
Human rights—Sudan 323.09624
Human rights—United States 323.0973
Human rights workers 323.092
Human sacrifice in art 704.948
Human services 361
Human services—Data processing 361.00285
Human services—Evaluation 361.0068
Human services—Great Britain 361.941
Human services—Management 361.0068
Human services—Research 361.0072
Human services—United States 361.973
Human services—United States—Management 361.0068
Human services—Vocational guidance—United States 361.002373
Human settlements 307
Human skeleton 599.947; 611.71
Human skin color 612.7927
Humane education 370.114
Humanism 144; 171.2
Humanism—20th century 144
Humanism in art 704.949144
Humanism in literature 808.80384; 809.93384
Humanistic ethics 171.2
Humanistic Judaism 296.834
Humanistic psychology 150.198
Humanists 211.6092
Humanitarian assistance 361.26
Humanitarian intervention 327.117; 341.584
Humanitarian law 341.67
Humanitarianism 361.74
Humanities 001.3
Humanities—Data processing 001.30285
Humanities—Digital libraries 025.060013
Humanities literature 016.0013
Humanities—Methodology 001.301
Humanities—Periodicals 001.305
Humanities—Study and teaching (Higher) 001.30711
Humanities—Study and teaching (Higher)—United States 001.3071173
Humber keels 387.224; 623.8224
Humboldt County (Iowa) 977.7272
Humboldt County (Iowa)—Maps 912.777272
Hume, David, 1711-1776 192
Hume, David, 1711-1776. Treatise of human nature 128
Humidors 688.4
Humility 179.9
Humility—Christianity 241.4
Hummel figurines 738.82094331

Hummel figurines—Collectors and collecting—United States—Catalogs 738.82094331
Hummingbirds 598.764
Humor in literature 808.87; 809.7
Humor in music 780.0152
Humorous poetry 808.817
Humorous poetry, American 811.07
Humorous poetry, English 821.0708
Humorous stories, English 823.008017
Humpback whale 599.525
Humus 631.417
Huna 222.9242
Hundred Years' War, 1339-1453 944.025
Hungarian language 494.511
Hungarian poetry 894.5111; 894.5111008
Hungarian poetry—Translations into English 894.5111008
Hungarian wit and humor 894.5117008
Hungary 943.9
Hungary—Commerce 382.09439
Hungary—Commerce—Periodicals 382.0943905
Hungary—Economic conditions 330.9439
Hungary—Economic conditions—1968-1989 330.9439053
Hungary—Economic conditions—1989- 330.9439054
Hungary—Economic policy 338.9439
Hungary—Economic policy—1968-1989 338.9439
Hungary—Economic policy—1989- 338.9439
Hungary—Guidebooks 914.3904; 914.390454
Hungary—History 943.9
Hungary—History—To 896 939.8
Hungary—History—1945-1989 943.9053
Hungary—History—Revolution, 1956 943.9052
Hungary—Pictorial works 943.900222
Hungary—Politics and government 943.9
Hungary—Politics and government—1989- 320.943909049; 943.9054
Hungary—Social conditions 943.9
Hungary—Social conditions—1945-1989 943.905
Hunger 363.8
Hunger—Religious aspects 291.178326
Hunger—Religious aspects—Christianity 261.8326
Hunt family 929.20973
Hunter family 929.20973
Hunter, John, 1728-1793 610.92; 617.092
Hunting 799.2
Hunting dogs 636.752
Hunting dogs—Training 636.752
Hunting guides 639.1092
Hunting guns 799.20283
Hunting in art 704.9432
Hunting lodges 728.7
Hunting—Moral and ethical aspects 179.3
Hunting—North America 799.297
Hunting rifles 799.202832
Hunting stories, American 813.54
Hunting—Texas 799.29764
Hunting—Texas—Maps 799.29764022
Huntington (N.Y.)—Genealogy 929.374725
Huntington's chorea 616.851
Hurd family 929.20973
Hurley family 929.20973
Huron County (Mich.) 977.444
Huron County (Mich.)—Maps 912.77444
Hurricane Andrew, 1992 363.34922
Hurricane Hugo, 1989 363.34922
Hurricanes 551.552
Hurston, Zora Neale 813.52

Hurston, Zora Neale—Criticism and interpretation 813.52
Husband abuse 362.8292
Husband and wife 306.872
Husbands 646.7808655
Husbands—Religious life 248.8425
Hussars 357.1094
Hussein, Saddam, 1937- 956.7044092
Husserl, Edmund, 1859–1938 193
Hussites 284.3
Hutchins family 929.20973
Hutchinson family 929.20973
Hutchinson, Thomas, 1711–1780 974.402092
Huts—Design and construction 690.837
Huxley, Aldous, 1894–1963 823.912
Huxley, Aldous, 1894–1963. Brave new world 823.912
Huxley, Aldous, 1894–1963—Criticism and interpretation 823.912
Hybrid computers 004.19; 629.89
Hybrid electric cars 629.2293
Hybrid power 333.7932; 621.3121
Hybridity (Social sciences) 306
Hydration rind dating 930.10285
Hydraulic accumulators 621.254
Hydraulic control 629.8042
Hydraulic conveying 621.8672
Hydraulic engineering 627
Hydraulic engineering—Data processing 627.0285
Hydraulic machinery 621.2
Hydraulic mining 622.2927
Hydraulic structures 627
Hydraulic structures—Design and construction 627
Hydraulics 627
Hydrocarbon reservoirs 553.28; 622.338
Hydrocarbons 547.01
Hydrocarbons—Tables 547.01021
Hydrocephalus 616.858843
Hydrochloric acid 546.73222; 661.23
Hydrodynamics 532.5
Hydroelectric power plants 621.312134
Hydroformylation 547.2
Hydrogen 546.2
Hydrogen as fuel 665.81
Hydrogen bonding 541.226; 572.33
Hydrogen buses 388.34; 629.229
Hydrogen ions 541.3728
Hydrogen ions—Physiological transport 572.475
Hydrogen mitigation 363.7387
Hydrogen/potassium ATPase 572.475
Hydrogenation 547.23
Hydrogeology 551.35; 551.48; 551.49
Hydrologic cycle 551.48
Hydrologic models 551.48011; 551.480228
Hydrological forecasting 551.480112
Hydrology 551.48
Hydrology—Data processing 551.480285
Hydrology—Dictionaries 551.4803
Hydrology—Mathematical models 551.48011; 551.48015118
Hydrology—Statistical methods 551.480727
Hydrology—United States 551.480973; 553.70973
Hydrolysis 551.393; 660.284425
Hydrometallurgy 669.0283
Hydrometeorology 551.57
Hydromys 599.35
Hydrophyllaceae 583.94
Hydroponics 631.585; 635.0485
Hydrosaurus 597.955
Hydrotherapy 615.853

Hydrothermal deposits 333.88; 551.23
Hydrothermal vent ecology 577.79
Hydrothermal vents 551.23; 551.4608
Hydroxy acids 547.037
Hydrozoa 593.55
Hyenas 599.743
Hygiene 613
Hygiene products 613.4
Hygiene, Sexual 613.95
Hygiene, Taoist 613
Hylidae 597.878
Hymenoptera 595.79
Hymns 782.27
Hymns—Devotional use 264.23
Hymns, English 264.23; 782.270942
Hymns, English—History and criticism 264.23
Hymns, English—United States 782.270973
Hymns, German 782.27
Hymns, Greek 782.27
Hymns, Greek (Classical)—Translations into English 292.38
Hymns—History and criticism 264.2309
Hymns, Latin 782.27
Hyperactive children—Education 371.93
Hyperandrogenism 618.1
Hyperbaric chambers 615.836
Hyperbaric oxygenation 615.836
Hypercholesteremia 616.3997
Hyperfine interactions 539.754
Hypergeometric functions 515.55
Hypergroups 512.55
Hyperlipidemia 616.3997
Hypersonic planes 629.132306
HyperTalk (Computer program language) 005.265
Hypertension 616.132
Hypertension—Atlases 616.13200222
Hypertension—Chemotherapy 616.132061
Hypertension in children 618.92132
Hypertension—Pathophysiology 616.13207
Hypertension—Treatment 616.13206
Hypertext systems 005.72
Hypervalence (Theoretical chemistry) 547.1224
Hyphomycetes 579.55
Hypnotism 154.7
Hypnotism—Therapeutic use 615.8512; 616.89162
Hypocausts 697.3
Hypogeous fungi 579.57
Hypoglycemia 616.466
Hypothalamus 573.459
Hypsilophodon 567.914
Hyraxes 599.68
Hysterectomy 618.1453
Hysteria 616.8524
Hysteroscopy 618.1407545
Hyundai Excel automobile 629.2222
Hyundai Excel automobile—Maintenance and repair 629.28722
Hyundai Excel automobile—Maintenance and repair—Handbooks, manuals, etc. 629.28722
I AM Religious Activity 299.93
Iacocca, Lee A. 338.76292092
Iatrogenic diseases 362.1; 615.5
Ibex 599.648
Ibis 598.34
Ibiza Island (Spain)—Guidebooks 914.6756
IBM 370 (Computer) 004.125
IBM 370 (Computer)—Programming 005.225
IBM AS/400 (Computer) 004.145
IBM AS/400 (Computer)—Programming 005.245

IBM-compatible computers 004.165
IBM-compatible computers—Upgrading 004.165;
   621.3916
IBM computers 004.2525
IBM computers—Programming 004.2525
IBM Database 2 005.7585
IBM microcomputers 004.165
IBM microcomputers—Programming 005.265
IBM MVS 005.4429
IBM PCjr (Computer) 004.165
IBM Personal System/2 (Computer system) 004.165
IBM RISC System/6000 computers 004.165
IBM Systems Application Architecture 004.22
IBM Token-Ring Network (Local area network system)
   004.68
Ibn Khaldūn, 1332–1406 907.202
Ibsen, Henrik, 1828–1906 839.8226
Ibsen, Henrik, 1828–1906—Criticism and interpretation
   839.8226
Ibsen, Henrik, 1828–1906—Translations into English
   839.8226
Ice 551.31
Ice booms 627.9
Ice cream, ices, etc. 637.4; 641.862; 641.863
Ice cream industry 338.476374
Ice cream pies 641.862
Ice crystals 548
Ice fields 551.31
Ice mummies 599.9
Ice on rivers, lakes, etc. 551.345
Icebergs 551.342
Iced tea 641.877
Iceland 949.12
Iceland—Description and travel 914.91204; 914.912045
Iceland—Guidebooks 914.91204; 914.912045
Icelandic literature 839.69; 839.6908
Ichnology 560; 566
Ichthyoliths 567
Ichthyologists 597.092
Ichthyology 597
Icon covers 749.7
Iconicity (Linguistics) 401.41; 415
Icons 704.948
Icons (Computer graphics) 005.3; 005.437
Icons—Cult 246.53
Icons, Greek 704.9482
Icons, Russian—Catalogs 755.2
Ictaluridae 597.492
Icterus (Birds) 598.874
Idaho 979.6
Idaho—Description and travel 917.9604; 917.960433;
   917.960434
Idaho—Genealogy 929.3796
Idaho—Guidebooks 917.9604; 917.960433; 917.960434
Idaho—History 979.6
Idaho—History, Local 979.6
Idaho—Pictorial works 917.9600222
Iddq testing 621.3950287
Idea (Philosophy) 121.4
Ideal spaces 515.73
Idealism 141
Idealism in literature 808.8013; 809.913
Ideals (Algebra) 512.4
Identification cards 929.9
Identity (Philosophical concept) 126
Identity (Psychology) 155.2
Identity (Psychology) in adolescence 155.5182
Identity (Psychology) in literature 808.80353;
   809.93353

Ideology 140
Ideology—History 140
Ideology in literature 808.80384; 809.93384
Iditarod Trail Sled Dog Race, Alaska 798.83097984
Ido 499.99
Idols and images in art 700.48291218; 704.948
Ifa (Religion) 299.68333
Igbo (African people) 966.900496332
Igbo (African people)—History 966.900496332
Igbo (African people)—Religion 299.68332
Ignatius, of Loyola, Saint, 1491–1556 271.5302
Ignatius, of Loyola, Saint, 1491–1556. Exercitia
   spiritualia 248.3
Iguanas 597.9542
Iguanas as pets 639.39542
Iguanodon 567.914
IHC tractors 629.2252
IHC tractors—History 629.2252
Iktomi (Legendary character)—Legends 398.208997
Illegal aliens 342.083
Illegal aliens—United States 323.6310973
Illegitimate children 362.7086945
Illegitimate children of royalty 929.7
Illinois 977.3
Illinois—Economic policy 338.9773
Illinois—Genealogy 929.3773
Illinois—Guidebooks 917.73044; 917.730443; 917.730444
Illinois—History 977.3
Illinois—Maps 912.773
Illinois—Pictorial works 917.7300222
Illumination of books and manuscripts 745.67
Illumination of books and manuscripts, Byzantine
   754.67487
Illumination of books and manuscripts, English
   754.67421
Illumination of books and manuscripts, French
   745.670944
Illumination of books and manuscripts, German
   754.67431
Illumination of books and manuscripts, Gothic
   754.6709409032
Illumination of books and manuscripts, Iranian
   745.670955
Illumination of books and manuscripts, Italian
   754.67451
Illumination of books and manuscripts, Jewish
   754.674924
Illumination of books and manuscripts, Medieval
   754.670902
Illustrated books 096.1; 741.64
Illustrated books—History 096.109; 741.6409
Illustrated books—History—19th century—Bibliography
   016.7416409034
Illustrated children's books 741.642
Illustrated children's books—Awards 741.642079
Illustration of books 741.64
Illustration of books—20th century 754.670904
Illustration of books—Exhibitions 754.67074
Illustrators 741.6092
iMac (Computer) 004.165
Image analysis 621.367
Image compression 005.746
Image intensifiers 621.381542
Image of God in rabbinical literature 296.311
Image processing 006.42; 621.367
Image processing—Digital techniques 006.42; 621.367
Image processing—Digital techniques—Mathematics
   621.3670151
Image processing equipment industry 338.47621367

Image processing—Mathematics 621.3670151
Image processing—Periodicals 621.36705
Image reconstruction 621.367
Image transmission 621.3827
Imagery (Psychology) 153.32
Imagery (Psychology)—Therapeutic use 616.8914
Images, Photographic 770.1
Imaginary biography 808.83935
Imaginary letters 813.54
Imagination 153.3
Imagination (Philosophy) 128.3
Imaging systems 006.42; 621.367
Imaging systems in astronomy 522
Imaging systems in biology 570.72
Imaging systems in medicine 616.0754
Imago relationship therapy 616.89156
Imitation in literature 808
Immersion method (Language teaching) 418.0071
Immigrant children 305.23
Immigrants 305.90691
Immigrants—Cultural assimilation 305.90691
Immigrants—Education 371.82691
Immigrants—Great Britain 325.41
Immigrants—United States 305.90691
Immigrants—United States—Biography 325.73
Immigrants—United States—History 304.873
Immigration advocates 325.1092
Immigration opponents 325.1092
Immobilized cells 660.62
Immobilized nucleic acids 572.8
Immortality 236.22
Immortality (Philosophy) 129
Immune response 616.0795
Immune response—Regulation 616.0795
Immune system 616.079
Immunities of foreign states 341.26
Immunity 616.079
Immunity—Nutritional aspects 616.079
Immunization 614.47
Immunization of children 614.47083
Immunization of infants 614.470832
Immunization of the aged 614.470846
Immunoassay 616.0756
Immunochemistry 571.964; 616.079
Immunocytochemistry 571.964; 616.0756
Immunodeficiency 616.979
Immunodiagnosis 616.0756
Immunogenetics 616.0796
Immunoglobulins 571.967; 616.0798
Immunoglobulins—Therapeutic use 615.37
Immunohematology 615.39
Immunologic diseases 616.97
Immunological adjuvants 571.9645
Immunological deficiency syndromes 616.979
Immunological tolerance 616.079
Immunologists 616.079092
Immunology 571.96; 616.079
Immunology—Outlines, syllabi, etc. 616.079
Immunology—Periodicals 571.9605
Immunopathology 616.079
Immunosuppressive agents 615.7; 617.95
Immunotechnology 615.37; 660.6
Immunotherapy 615.37
Immunotoxicology 616.97; 616.97071
Impact 620.1125
Impasse (Psychotherapy) 616.8914
Impeachments 342.068
Imperialism 325.32
Imperialism in literature 808.80358; 809.93358

Implant-supported dentures 617.692
Implantable cardioverter-defibrillators 617.4120645
Implants, Artificial 617.95
Implants, Artificial—Materials 617.95
Implicit memory 153.13
Imports 382.5
Impostors and imposture 364.163
Impotence 616.692
Impressionism (Art) 709.0344; 759.054
Impressionism (Art)—France 709.4409034; 759.409034
Impressionism (Art)—United States 759.1309034
Imprisonment 365
Imprisonment—United States 365.973
Improv for Windows 005.369
Improvisation (Acting) 792.028
Improvisation (Music) 781.65136
In-line skating 796.21
Inboard-outboard engines 623.87234
Inboard-outboard engines—Maintenance and repair—Handbooks, manuals, etc. 623.872340288
Inca architecture 720.898323
Incantations 133.44
Incantations, Egyptian 299.31
Incarnation 232.1
Incas 984.01; 985.019
Incas—Antiquities 985.019
Incas—History 985.019
Incas—Politics and government 984.01; 985.019
Incendiary weapons (International law) 341.735
Incentives in industry 658.3142
Incentives in industry—United States 658.31420973
Incest 306.877
Incest (Canon law) 262.9
Incest—United States 306.8770973
Incest victims—Rehabilitation 616.85836903
Incident command systems 363.348068
Incidental music 781.552
Incineration 628.4457
Incinerators 628.4457
Inclosures 333.2
Inclusive education 371.9046
Inclusive education—United States 371.90460973
Income 339.22
Income distribution 339.2
Income distribution—China 339.20951
Income distribution—Mathematical models 339.2015118
Income distribution—United States 339.20973; 339.220973
Income maintenance programs 362.582
Income maintenance programs—Canada 362.582
Income maintenance programs—United States 362.582
Income tax 336.24
Income tax—Accounting—Law and legislation 343.0523
Income tax—Accounting—Law and legislation—United States 343.73052042
Income tax—Canada 336.240971
Income tax deductions 343.0523
Income tax deductions for charitable contributions 343.05232
Income tax deductions for charitable contributions—United States 343.7305232
Income tax deductions for child care expenses 336.24216; 343.0523
Income tax deductions for educational expenses 343.0523
Income tax deductions for educational expenses—United States 343.730523
Income tax deductions for expenses 343.0523

India—History—Partition, 1947 954.042
India—History—1947- 954.04
India—Intellectual life 954
India—Languages 409.54
India—Maps 912.54
India—Military policy 355.033554
India, Northeastern 954.1
India, Northeastern—Politics and government 320.9541
India—Officials and employees 352.630954
India—Officials and employees—Selection and appointment 352.650954
India-Pakistan Conflict, 1965 954.9045
India-Pakistan Conflict, 1971 954.9205
India. Parliament. Lok Sabha 328.54072
India. Parliament. Lok Sabha—Elections 324.954
India—Periodicals 954.005
India—Pictorial works 915.400222
India—Politics and government 954
India—Politics and government—To 997 320.934
India—Politics and government—1857–1919 320.95409033; 954.035
India—Politics and government—1919–1947 320.95409041; 320.95409042; 954.035
India—Politics and government—1947- 320.95409045; 954.04
India—Politics and government—1975–1977 320.95409047; 954.051
India—Politics and government—1977- 320.95409048; 954.052
India—Politics and government--1977- —Periodicals 954.052
India—Population 304.60954
India—Relations 303.48254
India—Relations—Nepal 303.4825405496
India—Religion 200.954; 294
India—Road maps 912.54
India—Rural conditions 307.720954
India—Scheduled tribes 305.5680954
India—Scheduled tribes—Government policy 305.5680954
India—Social conditions 954
India—Social conditions—To 1200 934
India—Social conditions—1947- 954.04
India—Social life and customs 954
India—Social policy 361.610954
India, South 954.8
India, South—Civilization 934; 954.8
India, South—History 954.8
India. Supreme Court 347.54035
Indian architecture 720.897
Indian architecture—Mexico 720.897072
Indian art 704.0397
Indian art—Mexico 704.0397072
Indian art—North America 704.0397
Indian art—North America—Exhibitions 704.03970074
Indian art—Peru 704.0398085
Indian art—Southwest, New 704.0397078; 745.08997078
Indian astronomy—North America 520.897
Indian authors 013.0397
Indian baskets 746.41208997
Indian baskets—North America 746.41208997
Indian business enterprises 338.642208997
Indian captivities 970.00497
Indian captivities—United States 973.0497
Indian children 305.23
Indian children—North America—Legal status, laws, etc. 344.73032708997
Indian cookery 641.59297
Indian courts—United States 347.7328

Indian craft 745.08997
Indian dance 299.74; 394.3
Indian dance—North America 394.3; 399
Indian dance—United States 394.3; 399
Indian handicraft industries 338.47745508997
Indian ledger drawings 741.08997078
Indian literature 897
Indian literature—Translations into English 897
Indian literature—United States—History and criticism 810.9897; 897.09
Indian literature—United States—Translations into English 897
Indian masks 731.75
Indian motorcycle 629.2275
Indian motorcycle—History 629.2275
Indian mythology 299.72
Indian mythology—Mexico 299.72
Indian mythology—North America 299.72
Indian National Congress 324.254083
Indian National Congress—History 324.25408309
Indian Ocean Region 909.09824
Indian Ocean Region—History 909.09824
Indian Ocean Region—Politics and government 320.91824
Indian philosophy 191.08997
Indian philosophy—North America 191.08997
Indian poetry—North America—Translations into English 897
Indian poetry—Translations into English 897
Indian prisoners 970.00497
Indian reservations 333.208997
Indian sign language 419
Indian theater 792.08997
Indian women 305.48897
Indiana 977.2
Indiana—Genealogy 929.3772
Indiana—Guidebooks 917.72044; 917.720443; 917.720444
Indiana—History 977.2
Indiana—Maps 912.772
Indianapolis Colts (Football team) 796.332640977252
Indianapolis Colts (Football team)—History 796.332640977252
Indianapolis Speedway Race 796.7206877252
Indians 305.897; 970.00497
Indians—Antiquities 970.01
Indians as mascots 305.897
Indians—Bibliography 016.97000497
Indians—Bibliography—Catalogs 016.97000497
Indians—First contact with Europeans 970.01
Indians—Folklore 398.208997
Indians—History 970.00497
Indians in literature 808.803520397; 809.933520397
Indians in popular culture 305.897
Indians of Central America 972.800497
Indians of Central America—Antiquities 972.801
Indians of Central America—Guatemala—Antiquities 972.8101
Indians of Mexico 972.00497
Indians of Mexico—Antiquities 972.01
Indians of Mexico—Folklore 398.2089072
Indians of Mexico—Religion 299.792
Indians of Mexico—Social life and customs 305.897072
Indians of North America 970.00497
Indians of North America—Alaska—Claims 346.7980432
Indians of North America—Alberta 971.2300497
Indians of North America—Alberta—Antiquities 971.2301
Indians of North America—Antiquities 970.01

Indians of North America—Wars—West (U.S.) 978.00497
Indians of North America—Washington (State) 979.700497
Indians of North America—West (U.S.) 978.00497
Indians of North America—West (U.S.)—Antiquities 978.01
Indians of North America—Wyoming 978.700497
Indians of North America—Wyoming—Antiquities 978.701
Indians of South America 980.00498
Indians of South America—Antiquities 980.01
Indians of South America—Bolivia 984.00497
Indians of South America—Brazil 981.00497
Indians of South America—Colombia 986.100497
Indians of South America—Colombia—Antiquities 986.101
Indians of South America—Ecuador 986.600497
Indians of South America—Ecuador—Antiquities 986.601
Indians of South America—Folklore 398.208998
Indians of South America—Missions 266.0098
Indians of South America—Missions—Paraguay 266.009892
Indians of South America—Peru 985.00498
Indians of South America—Peru—Antiquities 985.01
Indians of South America—Religion 299.8
Indians—Origin 599.9897; 970.01
Indians—Religion 299.7
Indians—Social life and customs 970.00497
Indians, Treatment of 323.1197; 970.00497
Indians, Treatment of—Latin America 323.1198; 980.00498
Indians, Treatment of—United States 323.1197073; 973.0497
Indic fiction (English)—20th century—History and criticism 823.910954
Indic fiction (English)—History and criticism 823.00909954; 823.009954
Indic fiction (English)—Women authors—History and criticism 823.0092870954
Indic literature 809.8954; 891.1; 891.4
Indic literature (English)—20th century—History and criticism 820.99540904
Indic literature (English)—History and criticism 820.9954
Indic literature—History and criticism 809.8954
Indic literature—Translations into English 891.1; 891.4
Indic philology 491.1
Indic poetry 891.1; 891.4
Indic poetry (English) 821; 821.0080954
Indic poetry (English)—20th century 821.91; 821.91080954
Indic poetry (English)—20th century—History and criticism 821.9109954
Indic poetry (English)—History and criticism 821.009954
Indic poetry—Translations into English 891.1; 891.4
Indic wit and humor, Pictorial 741.5954
Indigenous crops 630
Indigenous peoples 306.08
Indigenous peoples—Africa 599.97096
Indigenous peoples and mass media 302.23089
Indigenous peoples—Government relations 323.11
Indigenous peoples in popular culture 305.8
Indigenous peoples—India 306.080954
Indigenous peoples—Legal status, laws, etc. 341.481; 346.013

Indigenous peoples—Legal status, laws, etc.—Canada 342.710872; 346.71013
Indigenous peoples—Legal status, laws, etc.—United States 342.730872; 346.73013
Indigenous peoples—South Africa 305.800968
Indigenous women 305.488
Individual development accounts 362.582
Individual differences 155.22
Individual retirement accounts 332.02401
Individual retirement accounts—Law and legislation 343.05233
Individual retirement accounts—Law and legislation—United States 343.7305233
Individual retirement accounts—Taxation—Law and legislation 343.05233
Individual retirement accounts—Taxation—Law and legislation—United States 343.7305233
Individual retirement accounts—United States 332.02401
Individualism 141.4; 302.54
Individuality 155.2
Individualized education programs 371.904394
Individualized instruction 371.394; 372.1394
Individualized reading instruction 372.417
Indo-Aryans 934
Indo-European languages 410
Indo-Europeans 599.98034
Indochina 959
Indochina—Description and travel 915.904; 915.90453; 915.90454
Indochina—Politics and government 959
Indochina—Politics and government—1945– 320.95909045; 959.053
Indochinese War, 1946–1954 959.7041
Indochinese War, 1946–1954—Campaigns 959.70414
Indonesia 959.8
Indonesia—Civilization 959.8
Indonesia—Commerce 382.09598
Indonesia—Commerce—Periodicals 382.0959805
Indonesia—Description and travel 915.9804; 915.980439; 915.98044
Indonesia—Economic conditions 330.9598
Indonesia—Economic conditions—1945– 330.959803
Indonesia—Economic conditions—1945– —Periodicals 330.959803
Indonesia—Economic policy 338.9598
Indonesia—Foreign relations 327.598
Indonesia—Guidebooks 915.9804; 915.980439; 915.98044
Indonesia—History 959.8
Indonesia—History—Revolution, 1945–1949 959.8035
Indonesia—Politics and government 320.9598; 959.8
Indonesia—Politics and government—20th century 320.95980904; 959.803
Indonesia—Politics and government—1966–1998 320.959809045; 320.959809046; 959.803
Indonesia—Social conditions 959.8
Indonesian Sign Language 419.598
Indoor air pollution 628.53
Indoor air pollution—Health aspects 613.5
Indoor air pollution—Law and legislation 344.3046342
Indoor air pollution—Law and legislation—United States 344.73046342
Indoor air pollution—Measurement 628.530287
Indoor bonsai 635.9772
Indoor electric grills 641.586; 683.83
Indoor games 793
Indoor gardening 635.965
Indoor hockey 796.355

Indoor rock climbing 796.5224
Indopakistan Sign Language 419.54
Indra (Hindu deity) in literature 808.803829452113;
    809.933829452113
Induced seismicity 551.22
Induction heating 621.402
Induction (Logic) 161
Inductively coupled plasma mass spectrometry
    543.0873
Indus civilization 934
Indus script 490
Industrial accidents 363.11
Industrial accidents—Law and legislation 344.0465
Industrial accidents—Ohio—Statistics—Periodicals
    363.11209771021
Industrial archaeology 609
Industrial arts 670; 745.2
Industrial arts—Study and teaching 670.71; 745.2071
Industrial arts—Study and teaching (Elementary)
    372.358
Industrial buildings 725.4
Industrial buildings—Design and construction 690.54;
    725.4
Industrial buildings—Fires and fire prevention 628.922
Industrial concentration 338.8
Industrial design coordination 745.2
Industrial development projects 338.9
Industrial districts 338.9
Industrial ecology 658.408
Industrial electronics 621.381
Industrial engineering 670
Industrial equipment 670
Industrial equipment industry 338.476218
Industrial equipment leases 658.15242
Industrial equipment leases—United States 346.73047
Industrial hygiene 613.62
Industrial hygiene—Law and legislation 344.0465
Industrial hygiene—Law and legislation—Great Britain
    344.410465
Industrial hygiene—Law and legislation—United States
    344.730465
Industrial hygiene—Management 658.382
Industrial laws and legislation 343.07
Industrial laws and legislation—United States 343.7307
Industrial location 338.6042; 658.21
Industrial location—Bibliography 016.3386042
Industrial location—Great Britain 338.60420941
Industrial location—India 338.60420954
Industrial location—United States 338.0973
Industrial management 658; 658.4
Industrial management—Bibliography 016.658
Industrial management—China 658.00951; 658.400951
Industrial management—Decision making 658.403
Industrial management—Developing countries
    658.0091724; 658.40091724
Industrial management—Effect of deflation on 658
Industrial management—Employee participation
    331.0112; 338.6
Industrial management—Employee participation—Great
    Britain 331.0112
Industrial management—Employee participation—Law
    and legislation 344.0188
Industrial management—Employee participation—Law
    and legislation—United States 344.730188
Industrial management—Employee participation—
    United States 338.6
Industrial management—Environmental aspects
    658.408; 658.567

Industrial management—Environmental aspects—
    United States 658.4080973
Industrial management—Europe 658.0094; 658.40094
Industrial management—Great Britain 658.00941;
    658.400941
Industrial management—Handbooks, manuals, etc. 658
Industrial management—India 658.00954; 658.400954
Industrial management—Japan 658.00952; 658.400952
Industrial management—Mathematical models
    658.4033
Industrial management—Periodicals 658.005
Industrial management—Research 658.0072; 658.40072
Industrial management—Soviet Union 658.00947;
    658.400947
Industrial management—Statistical methods
    650.015195; 650.0727; 658.4033
Industrial management—United States 658.00973;
    658.400973
Industrial management—United States—History
    658.00973
Industrial marketing 658.8
Industrial marketing—Management 658.8
Industrial marketing—Periodicals 658.8005
Industrial microbiology 660.62
Industrial microorganisms 579.163
Industrial microorganisms—Genetics 579.163; 660.62
Industrial minerals 553.6; 622.36
Industrial museums 607.34
Industrial music 781.64
Industrial noise 363.741
Industrial nursing 610.7346
Industrial organization 338.6
Industrial organization (Economic theory) 338
Industrial policy 322.3; 338.9
Industrial policy—Asia 338.95
Industrial policy—Australia 338.994
Industrial policy—Bibliography 016.3389
Industrial policy—Brazil 338.981
Industrial policy—Canada 338.971
Industrial policy—China 338.951
Industrial policy—Developing countries 338.90091724
Industrial policy—East Asia 338.95
Industrial policy—Europe 338.94
Industrial policy—European Economic Community
    countries 338.94
Industrial policy—European Union countries 338.94
Industrial policy—France 338.944
Industrial policy—Germany (West) 338.943
Industrial policy—Great Britain 322.30941; 338.941
Industrial policy—Great Britain—History 338.941
Industrial policy—Great Britain—History—20th century
    338.94100904
Industrial policy—India 338.954
Industrial policy—Ireland 338.9417
Industrial policy—Japan 338.952
Industrial policy—Korea (South) 338.95195
Industrial policy—Latin America 338.98
Industrial policy—Mexico 338.972
Industrial policy—Pakistan 338.95491
Industrial policy—South Africa 338.968
Industrial policy—United States 338.973
Industrial policy—United States—Bibliography
    016.338973
Industrial policy—United States—History 338.973
Industrial policy—United States—States 338.973
Industrial priorities—Law and legislation 343.07
Industrial priorities—Law and legislation—India
    343.5407
Industrial priorities—United States 355.260973

Industrial procurement 658.72
Industrial procurement—Management 658.72
Industrial procurement—United States 658.720973
Industrial procurement—United States—Management
658.720973
Industrial productivity 658.515
Industrial productivity—United States 338.060973
Industrial project management 658.404
Industrial project management—Data processing
658.4040285
Industrial promotion 338.9
Industrial promotion—United States 338.973
Industrial promotion—United States—States 338.973
Industrial property 341.758; 346.048
Industrial property (International law) 341.758
Industrial psychiatry 616.89
Industrial publicity 659
Industrial real estate 346.043
Industrial relations 331; 658.315
Industrial relations—Australia 331.0994
Industrial relations—Canada 331.0971
Industrial relations—Europe 331.094
Industrial relations—European Economic Community
countries 331.094
Industrial relations—Great Britain 331.0941
Industrial relations—Great Britain—History 331.0941
Industrial relations—India 331.0954
Industrial relations—Ireland 331.09415
Industrial relations—Japan 331.0952
Industrial relations libraries 026.331
Industrial relations—Nigeria 331.09669
Industrial relations—Russia (Federation) 331.0947
Industrial relations—South Africa 331.0968
Industrial relations—United States 331.0973
Industrial relations—United States—History 331.0973
Industrial revolution 330.9034
Industrial revolution—Europe 330.94028
Industrial revolution—Great Britain 330.94107
Industrial safety 363.11; 620.86
Industrial safety—Handbooks, manuals, etc. 363.11;
658.382
Industrial safety—Law and legislation 344.0465
Industrial safety—Law and legislation—California
344.7940465
Industrial safety—Law and legislation—United States
344.730465
Industrial safety—Management 658.382; 658.408
Industrial safety—Psychological aspects 658.382
Industrial safety—Standards—United States 363.110218
Industrial safety—United States 363.110973
Industrial sites—Gulf Coast (U.S.)—Maps
338.60420976022
Industrial sociology 306.36
Industrial statistics 338.0021
Industrial statistics—India 338.0954021
Industrial statistics—Philippines 338.09599021
Industrial statistics—United States 338.0973021
Industrial supply houses 381.4565
Industrial technicians 609.2
Industrial technicians—Vocational guidance 602.3
Industrial toxicology 615.902
Industrial toxicology—Handbooks, manuals, etc.
615.902
Industrial welfare 362.85; 658.382
Industrial Workers of the World 331.886
Industrial Workers of the World—History 331.886
Industrialists 338.092
Industrialization 338
Industrialization—Africa 338.096

Industrialization—Asia 338.095
Industrialization—Developing countries 338.091724
Industrialization—Europe 338.094
Industrialization—Europe—History 338.094
Industrialization—India 338.0954
Industrialization—Japan 338.0952
Industrialization—Latin America 338.098
Industrialization—Nigeria 338.09669
Industrialization—Tanzania 338.09678
Industries 338
Industries—Africa 338.096
Industries—Asia, Southeastern 338.0959
Industries—Australia 338.0994
Industries—Brazil 338.0981
Industries—Bulgaria 338.09499
Industries—Canada 338.0971
Industries—China 338.0951
Industries—Classification 338.0012
Industries—Developing countries 338.091724
Industries—Energy conservation 333.796516
Industries—England—Birmingham 339.0942496
Industries—Environmental aspects 658.408
Industries—Environmental aspects—United States
363.731
Industries—Europe 338.094
Industries—Europe—History 338.094
Industries—European Economic Community countries
338.094
Industries—Germany (West) 338.0943
Industries—Great Britain 338.0941
Industries—History 338.09
Industries—India 338.0954
Industries—India—Andhra Pradesh 338.095484
Industries—India—Rajasthan 338.09544
Industries—India—Uttar Pradesh 338.09542
Industries—Indonesia 338.09598
Industries—Information services—Management
658.4038
Industries—Iran 338.0955
Industries—Ireland 338.09415
Industries—Japan 338.0952
Industries—Korea 338.09519
Industries—Korea (South) 338.095195
Industries—New York (State) 338.09747
Industries—Norway 338.09481
Industries—Pakistan 338.095491
Industries—Pennsylvania 338.09748
Industries—Philippines 338.09599
Industries—Scotland 338.09411
Industries—Scotland—History 338.09411
Industries—Security measures 658.47
Industries—Security measures—Great Britain 658.47
Industries—Security measures—Management 658.47
Industries—Singapore 338.095952
Industries—Size 338.64
Industries—Social aspects 658.408
Industries—Social aspects—United States 306.360973;
658.4080973
Industries—South Africa 338.0968
Industries—Soviet Union 338.0947
Industries—Sweden 338.09485
Industries—Taiwan 338.0951249
Industries—United States 338.0973
Industries—United States—History 338.0973
Industries—United States—History—20th century
338.09730904
Industry and education 371.195
Industry and education—United States 371.1950973
Indy cars 629.228

Inequalities (Mathematics) 515.26
Infancy narratives (Gospels) 226.08305232
Infant baptism 234.1612
Infant psychiatry 618.9289
Infant psychology 155.422
Infantry drill and tactics 356.1154
Infants 305.232; 649.122
Infants—Care 649.122
Infants—Care—Handbooks, manuals, etc. 649.122
Infants—Care—United States 649.1220973
Infants' clothing 646.36; 646.406
Infants—Health and hygiene 613.0432; 649.4
Infants (Newborn) 649.122
Infants (Newborn)—Care 649.122
Infants (Newborn)—Diseases 618.9201
Infants (Newborn)—Diseases—Diagnosis—Atlases 618.9201
Infants (Newborn)—Medical examinations 618.9201
Infants (Newborn)—Nutrition 613.20832
Infants (Newborn)—Physiology 612.652
Infants (Newborn)—Surgery 617.98
Infants (Premature) 618.92011
Infants' supplies 649.1220284
Infants—United States—Mortality—Statistics 305.232
Infection 616.9
Infective endocarditis 616.11
Inference 160
Infertility 616.692
Infertility, Female 618.178
Infertility, Female, in literature 808.80353; 809.93353
Infertility, Male 616.692
Infertility—Psychological aspects 616.6920019
Infertility—Treatment 616.69206
Infinite 111.6
Infinite dimensional Lie algebras 512.55
Inflammation 616.0473; 617.22
Inflammation—Mediators 616.0473
Inflammation—Pathophysiology 616.0473
Inflammatory bowel diseases 616.344
Inflation (Finance) 332.41
Inflation (Finance)—France 332.410944
Inflation (Finance)—Great Britain 332.410941
Inflation (Finance)—Mathematical models 332.41015118
Inflation (Finance)—United States 332.410973
Inflation-indexed bonds 332.6323
Inflationary universe 523.18
Influence (Psychology) 153.852
Influenza 614.518; 616.203
Infomediaries 658.834
Informal sector (Economics) 330.122
Informal sector (Economics)—Developing countries 330; 330.122
Information consultants 023.2
Information display systems 621.045; 621.3815422
Information display systems industry 338.47621381542
Information literacy 028.7
Information measurement 003.54
Information modeling 005.74
Information networks 025.04
Information organization 025
Information policy 338.926
Information resources 020
Information resources management 658.4038
Information resources management—Periodicals 658.403805
Information retrieval 025.524
Information science 020
Information science literature 016.02

Information science—Periodicals 020.5
Information scientists 020.92
Information services 025.52
Information services—India 027.054
Information services industry 338.4702504
Information services industry—Management 025.52068; 658.4038
Information services—United States 027.073
Information services—United States—Directories 027.073
Information society 303.4833
Information storage and retrieval systems 025.04
Information storage and retrieval systems—Aeronautics 025.0662913
Information storage and retrieval systems—Architecture 025.0672
Information storage and retrieval systems—Archival material 025.06027
Information storage and retrieval systems—Astronomy 025.0652
Information storage and retrieval systems—Biology 025.0657
Information storage and retrieval systems—Chemistry 025.0654
Information storage and retrieval systems—Court administration 025.06347013
Information storage and retrieval systems—Ecology 025.06577
Information storage and retrieval systems—Engineering 025.0662
Information storage and retrieval systems—Environmental protection 025.063637
Information storage and retrieval systems—Geography 025.0691
Information storage and retrieval systems—Government publications 025.04
Information storage and retrieval systems—Housing 025.063635
Information storage and retrieval systems—Humanities 025.060013
Information storage and retrieval systems—Law 343.0999
Information storage and retrieval systems—Law—United States 025.0634973; 343.730999
Information storage and retrieval systems—Medicine 025.0661
Information storage and retrieval systems—Nucleotide sequence 025.065728633
Information storage and retrieval systems—Oncology 025.06616992
Information storage and retrieval systems—Public health 025.063621
Information storage and retrieval systems—Science 025.065
Information storage and retrieval systems—Securities 025.06332632
Information storage and retrieval systems—Seismology 025.0655122
Information storage and retrieval systems—Serial publications 025.04
Information storage and retrieval systems—Social sciences 025.063
Information storage and retrieval systems—Telecommunication 025.06384
Information storage and retrieval systems—Water quality 025.066281
Information superhighway 004.678
Information superhighway—United States 004.6780973
Information technology 004

Information technology—Dictionaries 004.03
Information technology—Management 658.4038
Information technology—Moral and ethical aspects 174.90904
Information technology—Periodicals 004.05
Information technology—Religious aspects 291.175
Information technology—Social aspects 303.4833
Information theory 003.54
Information theory—Religious aspects 291.175
Information warfare 355.343
Informed consent (Medical law) 344.0412
Informed consent (Medical law)—United States 344.730412
Infrared astronomy 522.683
Infrared cirrus (Astronomy) 523.1135
Infrared detectors 621.362
Infrared detectors—Materials 621.362
Infrared imaging 621.3672
Infrared radiation 535.012
Infrared spectra 535.842
Infrared spectroscopy 543.08583
Infrared technology 621.3612; 621.362
Infrared technology—Materials 621.362
Infrared telescopes 522.2
Infrastructure (Economics) 363; 388
Infrastructure (Economics)—United States 363.0973; 388.0973
Infrastructure (Economics)—United States—Finance 338.433630973
Ingalik Indians 979.8004972
Ingham County (Mich.) 977.426
Ingham County (Mich.)—Maps 912.77426
Ingres, Jean-Auguste-Dominique, 1780–1867 759.4
Ingres, Jean-Auguste-Dominique, 1780–1867—Criticism and interpretation 759.4
Inhalers 615.8360284; 681.761
Inheritance and succession 346.052
Inheritance and succession—England 346.42052
Inheritance and succession—India 346.54052
Inheritance and succession—United States 346.7305
Inheritance and succession—United States—Cases 346.730520264
Inheritance and succession—United States—Outlines, syllabi, etc. 346.73052
Inheritance and transfer tax 336.276
Inheritance and transfer tax—Law and legislation 343.053
Inheritance and transfer tax—Law and legislation—Massachusetts 343.744053
Inheritance and transfer tax—Law and legislation—Philippines 343.599053
Inheritance and transfer tax—Law and legislation—United States 343.73053
Inheritance and transfer tax—Law and legislation—United States—Cases 343.730530264
Iniopterygiformes 567.3
INIS (Information retrieval system) 025.063337924
Inism (Art movement) 709.04
Initial teaching alphabet 372.465
Initial value problems 515.353
Initiation rites 291.38
Initiation rites—Religious aspects 291.38
Initiation rites—Religious aspects—Catholic Church 265.13
Injection metallurgy 669.0282
Injection molding of plastics 668.412
Injections 615.6
Injections—Handbooks, manuals, etc. 615.6
Ink industry 338.476674

Inland navigation 386
Inland navigation—Ohio River—Maps 623.8922977
Inn signs 659.1342
Inner child 158.1
Inner cities 307.76
Innocent III, Pope, 1160 or 61–1216 282.092
Innovation relay centers 338.926
Inorganic compounds 546
Inorganic polymers 541.2254
Input-output analysis 339.23
Inquiry (Theory of knowledge) 121.6
Inquisition 272.2
Inquisition—Spain 272.20946
Insanity—Jurisprudence 346.0138
Insanity—Jurisprudence—United States 345.7304
Inscriptions 411.7
Inscriptions, Ancient 411.7
Inscriptions, Greek 938
Inscriptions, Linear B 487.1
Insect allergy 616.97
Insect pests 632.7
Insect pests—Biological control 632.7
Insect pests—Control 632.7
Insect-plant relationships 595.7178
Insect pollinators 571.8642; 595.715
Insect populations 595.71788
Insect societies 595.71782
Insect zoos 595.7073
Insecticides 632.9517
Insecticides—Physiological effect 632.9517
Insects 595.7
Insects—Anatomy 571.3157
Insects as carriers of disease 614.432
Insects as pets 638
Insects—Behavior 595.715
Insects—Collection and preservation 595.7075
Insects—Development 571.8157
Insects—Evolution 576.8157
Insects, Fossil 565.7
Insects—Geographical distribution 595.709
Insects in art 704.943257; 743.657
Insects—Larvae 595.7139
Insects—Miscellanea 595.7
Insects—Parasites 571.999157
Insects—Physiology 571.157
Insider trading in securities 364.168
Insider trading in securities—Law and legislation 346.092
Insider trading in securities—Law and legislation—United States 345.730268
Insight 153.4
Insomnia 616.8498
Insomnia—Treatment 616.8498
Installation of equipment 620
Installment plan 332.743
Instinct 155.7
Institutional care 362.0425
Institutional care—Great Britain 362.0425
Institutional economics 330
Institutional investments 332.67154
Institutional linens 680
Institutional missions 266
Instructional materials centers 027.7
Instructional materials industry 338.4737133
Instructional materials personnel 371.33
Instructional systems 370; 371.3
Instructional systems—Design 370; 371.3
Instructions to juries 347.0758
Instructions to juries—United States 347.73758

Insurance, Property—United States 368.100973
Insurance—Statistical methods 368.01
Insurance, Surety and fidelity 346.08683
Insurance, Surety and fidelity—United States
346.7308683; 346.7308684
Insurance, Title 368.88
Insurance, Title—Texas 346.76408688
Insurance, Title—United States 346.7308688
Insurance, Travelers' 368.24
Insurance, Unemployment 368.44
Insurance, Unemployment—Law and legislation
344.024
Insurance, Unemployment—Law and legislation—Maine
344.741024
Insurance, Unemployment—Law and legislation—United
States 346.7308644
Insurance, Unemployment—Law and legislation—
Virginia 344.755024
Insurance, Unemployment—United States 368.4400973
Insurance, Uninsured motorist—Law and legislation
346.086
Insurance, Uninsured motorist—Law and legislation—
California 346.794086572
Insurance—United States 368.973
Insurance—United States—Handbooks, manuals, etc.
368.973
Insurance—United States—State supervision
354.852130973; 368.973
Insurgency 355.0218
Integer programming 519.77
Integral equations 515.45
Integral equations—Numerical solutions 515.45
Integral geometry 516.362
Integral operators 515.723
Integral transforms 515.723
Integrals 515.43
Integrals, Generalized 515.42
Integrated circuits 621.3815
Integrated circuits—Catalogs—Periodicals
621.38150216
Integrated circuits—Computer-aided design 621.3815
Integrated circuits—Design and construction 621.3815
Integrated circuits—Design and construction—Data
processing 621.3815; 621.38150285
Integrated circuits—Handbooks, manuals, etc.
621.3815
Integrated circuits industry 338.476213815
Integrated circuits—Inspection 621.3815; 621.38150287
Integrated circuits—Large scale integration 621.3815;
621.395
Integrated circuits—Masks 621.3815
Integrated circuits—Reliability 621.3815
Integrated circuits—Testing 621.38150287
Integrated circuits—Ultra large scale integration
621.395
Integrated circuits—Ultra large scale integration—
Design and construction 621.395
Integrated circuits—Very large scale integration
621.395
Integrated circuits—Very large scale integration—
Computer-aided design 621.3950285
Integrated circuits—Very large scale integration—
Design and construction 621.395
Integrated circuits—Very large scale integration—
Design and construction—Data processing
621.3950285
Integrated circuits—Very large scale integration—
Testing 621.3950287
Integrated delivery of health care 362.1; 362.1068

Integrated logistic support 355.411
Integrated optics 621.3693
Integrated services digital networks 384; 621.382
Integrated software 005.3
Integrated solid waste management 363.728
Integrity 179.9
Intel 80x86 series microprocessors 004.165
Intel 80x86 series microprocessors—Programming
005.265
INTEL 8051 (Computer) 004.165
Intel 8086 (Microprocessor) 004.165
Intel 8088 (Microprocessor) 004.165
Intel 80386 (Microprocessor) 004.165
Intel 80386 (Microprocessor)—Programming 005.265
Intellect 153.9
Intellect—Genetic aspects 155.7
Intellect—Problems, exercises, etc. 153
Intellect—Social aspects 153
Intellectual capital 658.4038
Intellectual cooperation 370.116
Intellectual life 001.1
Intellectual life—History 001.109
Intellectual property 346.048
Intellectual property—Australia 346.94048
Intellectual property—Canada 346.71048
Intellectual property—Great Britain 346.41048
Intellectual property (International law) 341.758
Intellectual property—United States 346.73048
Intellectual property—United States—Cases
346.730480264
Intellectual property—United States—Periodicals
346.7304805
Intellectuals 305.552
Intellectuals—Political activity 306.208631
Intellectuals—United States 305.5520973
Intelligence levels 153.9
Intelligence service 327.12
Intelligence service—Great Britain 327.1241
Intelligence service—History 327.1209
Intelligence service—History—20th century 327.120904
Intelligence service—United States 327.1273
Intelligence service—United States—History 327.1273
Intelligence service—United States—History—20th
century 327.127300904
Intelligence tests 153.93
Intelligent agents (Computer software) 006.3
Intelligent buildings 696
Intelligent control systems 629.8; 629.89563
Intelligent tutoring systems 371.33463
Intelligent Vehicle Highway Systems 388.312
Intelligent Vehicle Highway Systems—United States
388.312
Intensive care nursing 610.7361
Intensive care nursing—Examinations, questions, etc.
610.7361
Intensive care nursing—Handbooks, manuals, etc.
610.7361
Intensive care nursing—Outlines, syllabi, etc. 610.7361
Intentionality (Philosophy) 128.2
Inter-American conferences 068.7
Inter-parliamentary Union 328.0601
Inter-school cooperation 371.2
Interactive art 702.81
Interactive computer systems 004
Interactive multimedia 006.7; 371.33467; 384
Interactive television 384.55
Interactive video 371.33467
Intercession 303.342
Intercessory prayer 291.43

International cooperation 327.17
International Court of Justice 341.552
International courts 341.55; 341.552
International Covenant on Civil and Political Rights (1966) 341.481
International economic integration 337.1
International economic relations 337
International economic relations—History 337.09
International economic relations—History—20th century 337.0904
International economic relations—Periodicals 337.05
International education 370.116
International education—United States 370.1160973
International finance 332.042
International Finance Corporation 332.153
International finance—History 332.04209
International finance—History—20th century 332.0420904
International finance—Law and legislation 341.751
International finance—Periodicals 332.04205
International labor activities 331.8
International Labour Organisation 331.0601; 341.763
International law 341
International law—Cases 341.0268
International law (Greek law) 341.0938
International law—Periodicals 341.05
International law—Philosophy 341.01
International law (Roman law) 341.0937
International librarianship 020.621
International liquidity 332.45
International Monetary Fund 332.152
International Museum Day 394.2
International museums 069
International offenses 341.77
International organization 060; 341.2
International Personality Disorder Examination 616.858
International police 341.766
International relations 303.482; 327; 353.13
International relations and culture 303.482
International relations—History 327.09
International relations in literature 808.80358; 809.93358
International relations—Methodology 327.101
International relations—Moral and ethical aspects 172.4
International relations—Periodicals 327.05
International relations—Philosophy 327.101
International relations—Political aspects 327.101
International relations—Psychological aspects 327.1019
International relations—Research 327.072
International relations—Risk assessment 327.1
International relations specialists 303.482092
International relief 361.26
International rivers 341.442
International Society for Krishna Consciousness 294.5512
International Society for Krishna Consciousness—Doctrines 294.5512
International Standard Bibliographic Description 025.324
International Standard Bibliographic Description for Electronic Resources 025.344
International Standard Music Numbers 025.3488
International Standard Serial Numbers 025.3432
International trade 382
International trade agencies 382.06
International trade—Dictionaries 382.03

International trade—Econometric models 382.015195
International trade—Handbooks, manuals, etc. 658.848
International trade—Mathematical models 382.015118
International trade—Periodicals 382.05
International travel regulations 341.756
International Tribunal for the Prosecution of Persons Responsible for Serious Violations of International Humanitarian Law Committed in the Territory of the Former Yugoslavia since 1991 341.7709497
International Union for Conservation of Nature and Natural Resources 333.720601
International Women's Day 394.2
International Year of Older Persons, 1999 305.26
Internationalism 327.17
Internationalized territories 341.29
Internet 004.678; 395.5
Internet abduction 364.154
Internet access for library users 025.04
Internet access for library users—Law and legislation 343.0999
Internet addiction 616.8584
Internet addresses 004.678
Internet addresses—Directories 025.04
Internet advertising 659.13
Internet and children 004.678083; 025.04083
Internet and teenagers 004.6780835; 025.04
Internet auctions 381.1702854678
Internet banking 332.102854678; 332.1702854678
Internet bookstores 380.145002028454678
Internet—Computer programs 005.713
Internet consultants 004.678
Internet—Dictionaries 004.67803
Internet—Directories 025.04025
Internet domain names 004.678; 346.048
Internet entertainment 790.2
Internet fraud 364.163
Internet gambling 795.02854678
Internet gambling—Law and legislation 344.099
Internet games 794.814678
Internet—Handbooks, manuals, etc. 004.678
Internet in education 025.0637
Internet in political campaigns 324.73
Internet in public administration 351.02854678
Internet in public relations 659.202854678
Internet in publicity 659.02854678
Internet industry 338.47004678; 384.33
Internet—Law and legislation 343.09944
Internet literacy 004.678; 025.04
Internet marketing 658.84
Internet—Periodicals 004.67805
Internet pornography 363.4702854678
Internet programming 005.276
Internet publishing 070.5797
Internet radio broadcasting 006.5
Internet Relay Chat 004.693
Internet searching 025.04
Internet—Security measures 005.8
Internet service providers 004.678; 384.33
Internet—Social aspects 303.4833
Internet software industry 338.47005376; 384.33
Internet television 006.7876; 384.5502854678
Internet—United States 004.6780973
Internet videoconferencing 004.6; 006.7
Internetworking (Telecommunication) 004.6
Interns (Clinical psychology) 616.891407155
Interns (Medicine) 610.7155; 610.92
Internship programs 331.2592; 658.31243
Internship programs—United States 331.2592

Investments, Foreign—Law and legislation—Yugoslavia 346.49707
Investments, Foreign—Mexico 332.6730972
Investments, Foreign—Periodicals 332.67305
Investments, Foreign—South Africa 332.6730968
Investments, Foreign—Taxation—Law and legislation 343.05248
Investments, Foreign—Taxation—Law and legislation— United States 343.7305248
Investments, Foreign—United States 332.6730973
Investments—Great Britain 332.60941
Investments—Handbooks, manuals, etc. 332.6
Investments, Hong Kong 332.67395125
Investments—Information services 025.063326
Investments, Japanese 332.67352
Investments, Japanese—United States 332.67352073
Investments—Mathematical models 332.6015118
Investments—Mathematics 332.60151
Investments—Periodicals 332.605
Investments—Psychological aspects 332.6019
Investments—Religious aspects 291.1785
Investments—Religious aspects—Christianity 261.85
Investments—Social aspects 306.3
Investments—Social aspects—United States 306.3
Investments—Taxation 336.207
Investments—Taxation—Canada 336.207
Investments—Taxation—Law and legislation 343.0523
Investments—Taxation—Law and legislation—United States 343.7305246
Investments—United States 332.60973
Investments—United States—Handbooks, manuals, etc. 332.60973
Investments—United States—Periodicals 332.6097305
Investors in People 331.2592; 658.3124
Invoices 657.72
Ion bombardment 530.416
Ion channels 571.64
Ion exchange 541.3723
Ion exchange chromatography 543.0893
Ion implantation 621.38152
Ion-permeable membranes 571.64
Ion sources 539.73
Ionesco, Eugène 842.914; 848.91403
Ionesco, Eugène—Criticism and interpretation 842.914
Ionesco, Eugène—Translations into English 842.914
Ionia County (Mich.) 977.454
Ionia County (Mich.)—Maps 912.77454
Ionization 530.444
Ionization of gases 530.444; 537.532
Ionized gases 530.44; 537.532
Ionizing radiation 539.722; 571.459
Ionizing radiation—Measurement 539.77
Ionizing radiation—Physiological effect 612.01448
Ionizing radiation—Toxicology 616.9897
Ionosphere 538.767; 551.5145
Ionospheric radio wave propagation 621.38411
Ions 541.372
Ions—Migration and velocity 541.372
Ions—Physiological transport 571.64
Iosco County (Mich.) 977.474
Iosco County (Mich.)—Maps 912.77474
Iowa 977.7
Iowa County (Wis.) 977.578
Iowa County (Wis.)—Maps 912.77578
Iowa—Genealogy 929.3777
Iowa—Guidebooks 917.7704; 917.770433; 917.770434
Iowa—History 977.7
Iowa—Maps 912.777
Iowa—Road maps 912.777

Iqbal, Muhammad, Sir, 1877–1938 891.43915
Iqbal, Muhammad, Sir, 1877–1938—Criticism and interpretation 891.43915
Iran 955
Iran—Antiquities 935
Iran—Civilization 955
Iran-Contra Affair, 1985–1990 355.032550973; 973.927
Iran—Foreign relations 327.55
Iran—Foreign relations—1979–1997 327.55
Iran—Guidebooks 915.504; 915.504543
Iran—History 955
Iran—History—To 640 935
Iran—History—Mohammed Reza Pahlavi, 1941–1979 955.053
Iran—History—1979–1997 955.054
Iran Hostage Crisis, 1979–1981 955.054
Iran-Iraq War, 1980–1988 955.0542
Iran—Pictorial works 955.00222
Iran—Politics and government 320.955; 955
Iran—Politics and government—20th century 320.9550904; 955.05
Iran—Politics and government—1941–1979 320.95509045; 955.053
Iran—Politics and government—1979–1997 320.95509048; 955.054
Iran—Social life and customs 955
Iran-United States Claims Tribunal 341.522
Iranian literature 891.5
Iranian philology 491.5
Iranians 305.89155
Iraq 956.7
Iraq—Antiquities 935
Iraq—Civilization 956.7
Iraq—Civilization—To 634 935
Iraq—Foreign relations 327.567
Iraq—History 956.7
Iraq—History—To 634 935
Iraq-Kuwait Crisis, 1990–1991 956.70442
Iraq—Politics and government 956.7
Iraq—Politics and government—1991- 320.956709049; 956.7043
Ireland 941.5
Ireland—Antiquities 936.15; 941.5
Ireland—Antiquities—Pictorial works 936.1500222; 941.500222
Ireland—Biography 920.0415
Ireland—Biography—Dictionaries 920.041503
Ireland—Church history 274.15
Ireland—Church history—To 1172 274.15
Ireland—Church history—600–1500 274.15; 274.1506
Ireland—Civilization 941.5
Ireland—Civilization—To 1172 941.501; 941.502
Ireland—Civilization—20th century 941.5082
Ireland—Description and travel 914.1504; 914.1504824; 914.1704; 914.1704824
Ireland—Economic conditions 330.9415
Ireland—Economic policy 338.9415; 338.9417
Ireland—Genealogy 929.10720415
Ireland—Genealogy—Handbooks, manuals, etc. 929.10720415
Ireland—Guidebooks 914.1504; 914.1504824; 914.1704824
Ireland—Historical geography 911.415
Ireland—Historiography 941.50072
Ireland—History 941.5
Ireland—History—To 1172 941.501; 941.502
Ireland—History—To 1603 941.5
Ireland—History—1172–1603 941.5
Ireland—History—16th century 941.505

Islam—United States 297.0973
Islamic countries 909.097671
Islamic countries—Economic policy 338.900917671
Islamic countries—History 909.097671
Islamic education 297.77; 371.077
Islamic education—Philosophy 371.07701
Islamic Empire 909.097671
Islamic Empire—History 909.097671
Islamic Empire—History—622–661 909.09767101; 953.02
Islamic Empire—History—661–750 909.09767101
Islamic Empire—History—750–1258 909.09767101
Islamic ethics 297.5
Islamic fundamentalism 320.55
Islamic fundamentalism in literature 808.80358; 808.803829709; 809.93358; 809.933829709
Islamic law 340.59
Islamic law—History 340.5909
Islamic law—India 340.590954
Islamic law—Interpretation and construction 340.5901
Islamic law—Pakistan 340.59095491
Islamic law—Periodicals 340.5905
Islamic leadership 297.61
Islamic literature 016.297
Islamic parables 297.18
Islamic religious education 297.77
Islamic religious education—Textbooks for children 297.77
Islamic sects 297.8
Islamic sermons, English 297.37
Island ecology 577.52
Island people 306.0809142
Islands 551.42
Islands of the Pacific 990
Islands of the Pacific—Guidebooks 919.04
Islands of the Pacific—Social life and customs 990
Ismailites 297.822
ISO 9000 Series Standards 658.5620218
ISO 9000 Series Standards—Handbooks, manuals, etc. 658.5620218
ISO 14000 Series Standards 658.408
Isoenzymes 572.7
Isoflavones 615.32
Isolationism 327.1
Isomerism 547.12252
Isopoda 595.372
Isostatic pressing 671.37
Isotope geology 551.9
Isotopes 541.388
Israel 956.94
Israel—Antiquities 933
Israel-Arab War, 1948–1949 956.042
Israel-Arab War, 1948–1949—Diplomatic history 956.042
Israel-Arab War, 1967 955.046; 956.046
Israel-Arab War, 1967—Causes 955.046
Israel-Arab War, 1967—Diplomatic history 955.046
Israel-Arab War, 1967—Occupied territories 956.046
Israel-Arab War, 1967—Personal narratives 955.046
Israel-Arab War, 1973 956.048
Israel-Arab War, 1973—Peace 956.048
Israel—Defenses 355.03305694
Israel—Description and travel 915.69404; 915.6940454
Israel—Economic conditions 330.95694
Israel—Economic conditions—Periodicals 330.95694005
Israel—Emigration and immigration 325.5694
Israel—Ethnic relations 305.80095694
Israel—Foreign public opinion, American 956.94
Israel—Foreign relations 327.5694

Israel—Foreign relations—Jordan 327.569405695
Israel—Guidebooks 915.69404; 915.6940454
Israel. Ḥel ha-aṿir—History 358.40095694
Israel—History 956.94
Israel—History, Military 255.0095694
Israel—Maps 912.5694
Israel—Pictorial works 915.69400222
Israel—Poetry 821.008095694
Israel—Politics and government 320.95694; 956.94
Israel—Road maps 912.5694
Israel—Social conditions 956.94
Israel—Social life and customs 956.94
Israel. Treaties, etc. Munaẓẓamat al-Taḥrīr al-Filasṭīnīyah, 1993 Sept. 13 956.94054
Israeli poetry 808.81995694; 892.41008095694
Israeli poetry—Translations into English 892.41008095694
Israeli students 371.829924
Israeli wit and humor 892.47008095694
Israeli wit and humor, Pictorial 741.595694
Istanbul (Turkey) 949.618
Istanbul (Turkey)—Description and travel 914.961804; 914.96180439; 914.9618044
Istanbul (Turkey)—Guidebooks 914.961804; 914.96180439; 914.9618044
Istanbul (Turkey)—History 949.618
Italian Americans 305.851073; 973.0451
Italian Americans—History 973.0451
Italian Americans—New York (State)—New York 305.85107471; 974.7100451
Italian Americans—New York (State)—New York—Social conditions 305.85107471
Italian language 450
Italian language—Conversation and phrase books 458.34
Italian language—Conversation and phrase books—English 458.3421
Italian language—Dictionaries 453
Italian language—Dictionaries—English 453.21
Italian language—Grammar 455; 458.2; 458.2421
Italian language—Readers 458.6
Italian language—Self-instruction 458.2421
Italian language—Textbooks for foreign speakers—English 458.2421; 458.3421
Italian language—Verb 455; 458.2; 458.2421
Italian literature 850; 850.8
Italian literature—To 1400 850.8002
Italian literature—To 1400—History and criticism 850.9002
Italian literature—History and criticism 850.9
Italian poetry 851; 851.008
Italian poetry—20th century 851.91; 851.9108
Italian poetry—History and criticism 851.009
Italian poetry—Translations into English 851.008
Italian provinces 320.830945; 352.150945
Italian Sign Language 419.45
Italian wit and humor 857.008; 858.02
Italian wit and humor, Pictorial 741.5945
Italo-Ethiopian War, 1935–1936 963.056
Italy 945
Italy—Civilization 945
Italy—Civilization—1268–1559 945.05
Italy—Description and travel 914.504; 914.504929; 914.50493
Italy—Economic conditions 330.945
Italy—Economic conditions—1945–1976 330.945092
Italy—Economic policy 338.945
Italy—Guidebooks 914.504; 914.504929; 914.50493
Italy—History 945

Jazz record clubs 381.45781650266
Jazz vocals 782.42165
Jealousy 152.48
Jealousy in children 155.41248
Jealousy in the Bible 220.815248
Jeep automobile 623.74722
Jeep automobile—History 623.7472209; 629.2222
Jeep automobile—Maintenance and repair 629.28722
Jeep automobile—Maintenance and repair—Handbooks, manuals, etc. 629.28722
Jeeves (Fictitious character) 823.912
Jeeves (Fictitious character)—Fiction 823.912
Jeffers, Robinson, 1887–1962 811.52
Jeffers, Robinson, 1887–1962—Criticism and interpretation 811.52
Jefferson County (Ill.)—Maps 912.773793
Jefferson County (Ohio)—Genealogy 929.377169
Jefferson County (Tenn.)—Genealogy 929.3768924
Jefferson County (Wash.)—Genealogy 929.379798
Jefferson County (Wis.)—Maps 912.77585
Jefferson, Thomas, 1743–1826 973.46092
Jefferson, Thomas, 1743–1826—Correspondence 973.46092
Jefferson, Thomas, 1743–1826—Influence 973.46092
Jefferson, Thomas, 1743–1826—Political and social views 973.46092
Jeffries family 929.20973
Jeffry, Jane (Fictitious character) 813.54
Jeffry, Jane (Fictitious character)—Fiction 813.54
Jehovah's Witnesses 289.92
Jehovah's Witnesses—Controversial literature 230.992; 289.92
Jehovah's Witnesses—Doctrines 230.992
Jellikins (Fictitious characters) 791.4572
Jelly 641.852; 664.152
Jellybeans 641.853
Jellyfishes 593.53
Jemima Puddle-Duck (Fictitious character) 823.912
Jemison, Mary, 1743–1833 974.7004975
Jenkins family 929.20973
Jenner, Edward, 1749–1823 614.521092
Jensen, Margaret T. (Margaret Tweten), 1916– 286.1092
Jeremiah (Fictitious character : Smith) 813.54
Jersey County (Ill.) 977.3855
Jersey County (Ill.)—Maps 912.773855
Jerusalem 956.9442
Jerusalem—Description and travel 915.6944204; 915.694420454
Jerusalem—Guidebooks 915.6944204; 915.694420454
Jerusalem—History 956.9442; 956.944203
Jerusalem—History—Latin Kingdom, 1099–1244 956.9403
Jerusalem—International status 956.9442
Jerusalem—Maps 912.569442
Jerusalem—Pictorial works 956.944200222
Jerusalem—Politics and government 956.9442
Jerusalem—Tours 915.6944204; 915.694420454
Jess (Fictitious character : Daniels) 823.914
Jessamine County (Ky.)—Genealogy 929.3769483
Jesse windows 246.9528; 748.5
Jesuits 255.53; 271.53
Jesuits—History 271.53
Jesuits—Spiritual life 255.53
Jesus Christ 232
Jesus Christ—Apparitions and miracles 232.97
Jesus Christ—Biography 232.901
Jesus Christ—Biography—Apocryphal and legendary literature 232.9

Jesus Christ—Biography—Devotional literature 232.901
Jesus Christ—Biography—History and criticism 232.901
Jesus Christ—Biography—Meditations 232.901
Jesus Christ—Biography—Passion Week 232.96
Jesus Christ—Biography—Sources, Biblical 232.901
Jesus Christ—Biography—Study and teaching 232.901071
Jesus Christ—Childhood 232.92
Jesus Christ—Crucifixion 232.963
Jesus Christ—Crucifixion—Meditations 232.963
Jesus Christ—Crucifixion—Sermons 232.963
Jesus Christ—Devotional literature 232
Jesus Christ—Divinity 232.8
Jesus Christ—Ethics 232.954
Jesus Christ—Example 232.904
Jesus Christ—Historicity 232.908
Jesus Christ—History of doctrines 232.09
Jesus Christ—History of doctrines—Early church, ca. 30–600 232.09015
Jesus Christ—History of doctrines—20th century 232.0904
Jesus Christ—Humanity 232.8
Jesus Christ in the Book of Mormon 232
Jesus Christ—Islamic interpretations 297.2465
Jesus Christ—Jewish interpretations 296.396
Jesus Christ—Meditations 232
Jesus Christ—Messiahship 232.1
Jesus Christ—Miracles 226.706; 232.955
Jesus Christ—Mormon interpretations 232.088283
Jesus Christ—Name 232
Jesus Christ—Nativity 232.92
Jesus Christ—Nativity—Songs and music—Texts 782.2817230268
Jesus Christ—New Age movement interpretations 232.0882999
Jesus Christ—Parables 226.8; 226.806
Jesus Christ—Parables—Homiletical use 251
Jesus Christ—Parables—Sermons 226.806
Jesus Christ—Passion 232.96
Jesus Christ—Passion—Meditations 232.96
Jesus Christ—Passion—Sermons 232.96
Jesus Christ—Person and offices 232; 232.8
Jesus Christ—Person and offices—Biblical teaching 232.8
Jesus Christ—Person and offices—Study and teaching 232.8071
Jesus Christ—Political and social views 232.954
Jesus Christ—Prayers 248.32
Jesus Christ—Psychology 232.903
Jesus Christ—Rationalistic interpretations 232
Jesus Christ—Resurrection 232.5; 232.97
Jesus Christ—Resurrection—Biblical teaching 232.97
Jesus Christ—Seven last words 232.9635
Jesus Christ—Seven last words—Meditations 232.9635
Jesus Christ—Spiritual life 232.901
Jesus Christ—Teaching methods 232.904
Jesus Christ—Teachings 232.954
Jesus Christ—Temptation 232.95
Jesus Christ—Trial 232.962
Jesus Christ—Washing of the apostles' feet 232.95
Jesus prayer 242.7
Jet boats 623.8231
Jet boats—Maintenance and repair—Handbooks, manuals, etc. 623.82310288
Jet transports 629.133349
Jewelers 739.27092
Jewelry 739.27
Jewelry—History 739.2709
Jewelry making 739.274; 745.5942

Jewelry stores 381.4573927
Jewelry trade 338.4773927; 381.4573927
Jewelry trade—Periodicals 338.477392705
Jewett, Sarah Orne, 1849–1909 813.4
Jewett, Sarah Orne, 1849–1909—Criticism and
    interpretation 813.4
Jewish-Arab relations 327.56940174927; 956.94004927
Jewish archives 027.67
Jewish camps 796.5422089924
Jewish chants 782.36
Jewish children 305.2
Jewish children in the Holocaust—Biography
    940.5318083
Jewish children—Religious life 296.7083
Jewish Christians 289.9
Jewish college students 378.19829924
Jewish converts 296.714
Jewish crafts 680.089924
Jewish day schools 298.68083; 371.076
Jewish diaspora 909.04924
Jewish educators 296.68092
Jewish families 306.85089924
Jewish families—Religious life 296.74
Jewish folk literature 398.2089924
Jewish gays 305.8924
Jewish ghettos 909.04924
Jewish law 296.18
Jewish law—History 296.18
Jewish law—Interpretation and construction 296.18
Jewish law—Palestine 296.18095694
Jewish law—Philosophy 296.1801
Jewish leadership 305.8924
Jewish libraries 027.67
Jewish literature 809.88924
Jewish literature—History and criticism 809.88924
Jewish meditations 296.72
Jewish men 305.388924
Jewish men—United States 305.388924073
Jewish mourning customs 296.445
Jewish musicians 780.92089924
Jewish needlework 746.44089924
Jewish newspapers 070.482
Jewish question 305.8924
Jewish religious education 296.68
Jewish religious education of children 296.68083
Jewish religious education—United States 296.680973
Jewish religious poetry, American 811.008038296
Jewish religious schools 298.68083
Jewish renewal 296.834
Jewish sermons, American 296.47
Jewish sermons, English 296.47
Jewish students 371.829924
Jewish way of life 296.7
Jewish way of life—Anecdotes 296.7
Jewish wit and humor 808.870089924; 808.882089924
Jewish women 305.488924
Jewish women—Bibliography 016.305488924
Jewish women—Biography 920.72089924
Jewish women—England 305.488924042
Jewish women—England—Poetry 821.00809287
Jewish women—New York (State)—New York
    305.48892407471
Jewish women—Religious life 296.443
Jewish women—United States 305.488924073
Jewish youth 305.235
Jews 305.8924
Jews—Australia 994.004924
Jews—Australia—Periodicals 994.00492405
Jews—Bibliography 016.3058924; 016.90904924

Jews—Bibliography—Catalogs 016.3058924;
    016.90904924
Jews—Biography 920.0092924
Jews—Canada 305.8924071
Jews—Canada—Politics and government 323.11924071
Jews—China 951.004924
Jews—China—History 951.004924
Jews—Civilization 909.04924
Jews—Cultural assimilation 305.8924
Jews—Cultural assimilation—United States 305.8924073
Jews—Dietary laws 296.73
Jews, East European 305.8924047
Jews, East European—New York (State)—New York
    305.892407471
Jews—Emancipation 323.11924
Jews—Encyclopedias 909.04924003
Jews—Ethiopia 963.004924
Jews—Ethiopia—History 963.004924
Jews—Europe 940.04924
Jews—Europe, Eastern 947.004924
Jews—Europe, Eastern—History 947.004924
Jews—Europe—History 940.04924
Jews—Folklore 398.2089924
Jews—France 944.004924
Jews—France—History 944.004924
Jews—Genealogy 929.1089924
Jews—Genealogy—Periodicals 929.1089924
Jews—Germany 305.8924043; 943.004924
Jews—Germany—History 943.004924
Jews—Germany—History—1800–1933 943.004924
Jews—Germany—History—1933–1945 943.004924
Jews—Germany—History—1945– 943.004924
Jews—Germany—Intellectual life 943.004924
Jews—Great Britain 305.8924041; 941.004924
Jews—Great Britain—History 941.004924
Jews—Historiography 909.049240072
Jews—History 909.04924
Jews—History—To 1200 B.C. 933.01
Jews—History—To 586 B.C. 933
Jews—History—To 70 A.D. 933
Jews—History—1200–953 B.C. 933.02
Jews—History—953–586 B.C. 933.03
Jews—History—586 B.C.–70 A.D. 933
Jews—History—168 B.C.–135 A.D. 933.04; 933.05;
    956.9402
Jews—History—Rebellion, 66–73 933.05
Jews—History—70– 909.04924
Jews—History—70–638 909.04924; 956.9402
Jews—History—70–1789 909.04924
Jews—History—1789–1945 909.0492408
Jews—History—Philosophy 909.049240019
Jews—History—Sources 909.04924
Jews—Hungary 943.9004924
Jews—Hungary—History 943.9004924
Jews—Identity 305.8924
Jews in art 704.942
Jews in motion pictures 791.4365203924
Jews in the New Testament 225.9; 261.2609014
Jews—India 954.004924
Jews—India—History 954.004924
Jews—Indiana 977.2004924
Jews—Indiana—History 977.2004924
Jews—Intellectual life 909.04924082
Jews—Israel—Identity 305.892405694
Jews—Legal status, laws, etc. 342.0873
Jews—Legal status, laws, etc.—Great Britain
    342.410873
Jews—Music 780.89924; 781.62924
Jews—Music—History and criticism 780.89924

Jews—New York (State)—New York 974.71004924
Jews—New York (State)—New York—History
974.71004924
Jews—New York (State)—New York—Intellectual life
974.71004924
Jews—New York (State)—New York—Social life and
customs 974.71004924
Jews—Palestine 956.94004924
Jews—Periodicals 909.04924005
Jews—Persecutions 940.5318
Jews—Persecutions—France 940.53180944
Jews—Persecutions—Germany 940.53180943;
943.004924
Jews—Persecutions—Hungary 940.531809439
Jews—Persecutions—Lithuania 940.5318094793
Jews—Persecutions—Lithuania—Kaunas
940.5318094793
Jews—Persecutions—Poland—Kraków 940.5318094386
Jews—Persecutions—Poland—Łódź 940.531809438;
940.5318094384
Jews—Persecutions—Poland—Warsaw 940.5318094384
Jews—Persecutions—Romania 940.531809498
Jews—Persecutions—Soviet Union 323.11924047
Jews—Persecutions—Ukraine 940.531809477
Jews—Persecutions—Ukraine—L'viv 940.5318094779
Jews—Poland 943.8004924
Jews—Poland—History 943.8004924
Jews—Poland—History—20th century 943.8004924
Jews—Politics and government 323.11924
Jews—Politics and government—1948- 323.1192409045
Jews—Restoration 296.38
Jews—Russia 947.004924
Jews—Russia—Politics and government 323.11924047;
947.004924
Jews—Social conditions 305.8924
Jews—Social life and customs 296.7; 305.8924; 956.94
Jews—Social life and customs—To 70 A.D. 305.8924
Jews—Soviet Union 305.8924047; 947.004924
Jews—Soviet Union—Economic conditions
330.9470089924
Jews—Soviet Union—History 305.8924047; 947.004924
Jews—Soviet Union—Intellectual life 947.004924
Jews—Soviet Union—Politics and government
323.11924047
Jews—Spain 946.004924
Jews—Spain—History 946.004924
Jews—Spain—History—Expulsion, 1492 946.004924
Jews—Turkey 956.1004924
Jews—Turkey—History 956.1004924
Jews—United States 973.04924
Jews—United States—Biography 920.0092924073;
973.04924022
Jews—United States—History 973.04924
Jews—United States—Identity 305.8924073
Jews—United States—Intellectual life 305.8924073
Jews—United States—Politics and government
323.11924073
Jews—United States—Social conditions 305.8924073
Jews—United States—Social life and customs
305.8924073
Jhabvala, Ruth Prawer, 1927- 823.914
Jhabvala, Ruth Prawer, 1927- —Criticism and
interpretation 823.914
Jíbaro (Puerto Rican identity) 305.8687295
Jig saws 745.513
Jigs and fixtures 621.992
Jigs and fixtures—Design and construction 621.992
Jigsaw puzzle art 741.6
Jigsaw puzzles 793.73

Jihad 297.72
Jinnah, Mahomed Ali, 1876-1948 954.9042092
Jiu-jitsu 796.8152
Jo Daviess County (Ill.) 977.3343
Jo Daviess County (Ill.)—Genealogy 929.3773343
Jo Daviess County (Ill.)—Maps 912.773343
Joachim, of Fiore, ca. 1132-1202 230.2092
Joan, of Arc, Saint, 1412-1431 944.026092
Joan, Sister (Fictitious character) 823.914
Joan, Sister (Fictitious character)—Fiction 823.914
Job analysis 658.306
Job Control Language (Computer program language)
005.434
Job creation 331.12042; 331.1377
Job creation—United States 331.120420973
Job descriptions 658.306
Job evaluation 658.306
Job hotlines 331.128
Job hotlines—United States 331.1280973
Job hotlines—United States—Directories 331.12802573
Job hunting 650.14
Job hunting—California, Southern 650.14097949
Job hunting—California, Southern—Directories
331.1280257949
Job hunting—Computer network resources 025.0665014
Job hunting—Handbooks, manuals, etc. 650.14
Job hunting—Texas—Dallas 650.14097642812
Job hunting—United States 650.140973
Job hunting—United States—Directories 650.14
Job hunting—United States—Handbooks, manuals, etc.
650.140973
Job hunting—Washington (State)—Seattle
650.1409797772
Job hunting—Washington (State)—Seattle—Directories
331.128025797772
Job postings 331.124
Job security 331.2596
Job security—United States 331.25960973
Job shadowing 331.2592; 371.227
Job stress 158.72; 650.019
Job vacancies 331.124
Joe Camel (Trademarked symbol) 679.730275
Jogging 613.7172
Johan (Fictitious character : Peyo) 741.59493
Johannesburg Metropolitan Area (South Africa)
968.221
Johannesburg Metropolitan Area (South Africa)—Maps
912.68221
Johannesburg (South Africa) 968.221
Johannesburg (South Africa)—Maps 912.68221
Johannesburg (South Africa)—Pictorial works
968.22100222
Johansson, Hilda (Fictitious character) 813.54
John Chrysostom, Saint, d. 407 270.2092
John Day Fossil Beds National Monument (Or.)
560.979581
John Deere tractors 629.2252
John Deere tractors—History 629.2252
John Henry (Legendary character)—Legends
398.2097302
John, King of England, 1167-1216 942.033092
John of the Cross, Saint, 1542-1591 271.7302; 861.3
John of the Cross, Saint, 1542-1591—Translations into
English 861.3
John Paul II, Pope, 1920- 282.092; 891.85173
John Paul II, Pope, 1920- —Assassination attempt,
1981 364.1524092
John Paul II, Pope, 1920- —Translations into English
891.85173

Joyce, James, 1882–1941—Technique 823.912
Joyce, James, 1882–1941. Ulysses 823.912
Joyce, James, 1882–1941. Ulysses—Criticism, Textual 823.912
Joyner-Kersee, Jacqueline, 1962– 796.42092
Juan, Don, 1891– 299.7845
Juana Inés de la Cruz, Sister, 1651–1695 861.3
Juárez, Benito, 1806–1872 972.07092
Judaism 296
Judaism—20th century 296.0904
Judaism and science 296.375
Judaism and social problems 296.38
Judaism—Apologetic works 296.35
Judaism—Ari rite—Liturgy—Texts 296.4504
Judaism (Christian theology) 231.76; 261.26
Judaism—Controversial literature 239.2; 239.9; 296
Judaism—Customs and practices 296.4
Judaism—Dictionaries 296.03
Judaism—Doctrines 296.3
Judaism—Essence, genius, nature 296
Judaism—Germany 296.0943
Judaism—History 296.09
Judaism—History—To 70 A.D. 296.0901
Judaism—History—Post-exilic period, 586 B.C.–210 A.D. 296.09014
Judaism—History—Talmudic period, 10–425 296.09015
Judaism—History—Talmudic period, 10–425—Historiography 296.09015
Judaism—History—Medieval and early modern period, 425–1789 296.0902
Judaism—History—Modern period, 1750– 296.0903
Judaism in literature 808.8038296; 809.9338296
Judaism—Liturgy 296.45
Judaism—Liturgy—History 296.45
Judaism—Liturgy—Texts 296.45
Judaism—Periodicals 296.05
Judaism—Prayer-books and devotions 296.45
Judaism—Relations 296.39
Judaism—Relations—Catholic Church 261.26
Judaism—Relations—Christianity 261.26; 296.396
Judaism—Relations—Christianity—1945– 261.26
Judaism—Relations—Islam 296.397; 297.282
Judaism—Study and teaching 296.071
Judaism—United States 296.0973
Judaism—United States—History 296.0973
Judaism—Works to 1900 296
Judas burning (Social custom) 394.2667
Judas Iscariot 226.092
Judges 347.014
Judges—Canada 347.71014
Judges—Great Britain 347.41014
Judges—Selection and appointment 347.014
Judges—Selection and appointment—United States 347.7314
Judges—Selection and appointment—United States—History 347.7314
Judges—Selection and appointment—United States—States 347.7314
Judges—United States 347.7314
Judges—United States—Biography 347.7314092
Judges—United States—Discipline 347.7314
Judgment 153.46
Judgment Day 236.9; 291.23
Judgment (Ethics) 170
Judgments 347.077; 348.044
Judgments—United States 347.7377
Judicial assistance 341.78
Judicial assistance—Europe 341.78
Judicial corruption 364.1323

Judicial councils 347.01306
Judicial ethics 347.014
Judicial ethics—United States 347.7314
Judicial opinions 348.044
Judicial opinions—Philippines 348.599044
Judicial power 347
Judicial power—United States 347.7312
Judicial process 347.05
Judicial process (Canon law) 262.9
Judicial review 347.012
Judicial review of administrative acts 342.06
Judicial review of administrative acts—Great Britain 342.4106; 347.41012
Judicial review—United States 347.7312
Judicial review—United States—History 347.7312
Judicial statistics 347.013
Judicial statistics—Washington (State)—Periodicals 347.797013
Judith (Jewish heroine) 229.24092
Judo 796.8152
Jug bands 784.4
Juggling 793.87
Juicers 641.875
Julian, of Norwich, b. 1343 248.22092
Julian, of Norwich, b. 1343. Revelations of divine love 248.22
Jumpsuits 391; 646.4; 687.1
Juneau County (Wis.) 977.555
Juneau County (Wis.)—Maps 912.77555
Jung, C. G. (Carl Gustav), 1875–1961 150.1954092
Jungian psychology 150.1954; 616.8917
Jungle ecology 577.34
Jungle films 791.4362152
Jungle (Music) 781.64
Jungle television programs 791.4562152
Junior college libraries 027.7
Junior colleges 378.1543
Junior colleges—United States 378.15430973
Junior high school students 373.18
Junior high school students—Prayer-books and devotions 242.63
Junior high schools 373.236
Junior high schools—United States 373.2360973
Junk bonds 332.63234
Junk bonds—United States 332.63234
Jupiter (Planet) 523.45
Jurisdiction 347.012
Jurisdiction (International law) 341.4
Jurisdiction—United States 347.7312
Jurisprudence 340
Jurisprudence—History 340.09
Jurisprudence—United States 349.73
Jurnet, Benjamin (Fictitious character) 823.914
Jurnet, Benjamin (Fictitious character)—Fiction 823.914
Jury 347.0752
Jury in literature 808.80355; 809.93355
Jury nullification 347.075
Jury, Richard (Fictitious character) 813.54
Jury, Richard (Fictitious character)—Fiction 813.54
Jury selection 347.0752
Jury selection—United States 347.73752
Jury—United States 347.73752
Just-in-time systems 658.51
Just war doctrine 241.6242
Justice 320.011; 340.11
Justice, Administration of 347
Justice, Administration of—Australia 347.94
Justice, Administration of—France 347.44

Justice, Administration of—Great Britain 347.41
Justice, Administration of—India 347.54
Justice, Administration of—Philippines 347.599
Justice, Administration of—United States 347.73
Justice, Administration of—United States—Periodicals 347.73005
Justice, Benjamin (Fictitious character) 813.54
Justice in literature 808.80353; 809.93353
Justice League of America (Fictitious characters) 741.5973
Justice (Philosophy) 172.2
Justices of the peace 347.016
Justices of the peace—Great Britain 347.41016
Justification 234.7
Justification (Theory of knowledge) 121.6
Juvenal 871.01
Juvenal—Criticism and interpretation 871.01
Juvenal—Translations into English 871.01
Juvenile corrections 364.60835
Juvenile corrections—Massachusetts 364.6083509744
Juvenile corrections—United States 364.608350973
Juvenile courts 345.081
Juvenile courts—Great Britain 345.41081
Juvenile courts—United States 345.73081
Juvenile delinquency 364.36
Juvenile delinquency—Great Britain 364.360941
Juvenile delinquency—New York (State)—New York 364.36097471
Juvenile delinquency—Prevention 364.36
Juvenile delinquency—United States 364.360973
Juvenile delinquency—United States—Prevention 364.360973
Juvenile delinquents 364.36
Juvenile delinquents—Education 371.93
Juvenile delinquents—Education—United States 365.66
Juvenile delinquents—Rehabilitation 364.36
Juvenile delinquents—Rehabilitation—California 364.3609794
Juvenile delinquents—Rehabilitation—Great Britain 364.360941
Juvenile delinquents—Rehabilitation—Minnesota 364.3609776
Juvenile delinquents—Rehabilitation—United States 364.360973
Juvenile delinquents—United States 364.360973
Juvenile detention homes 365.42
Juvenile detention homes—Great Britain 365.42
Juvenile justice, Administration of 364.36
Juvenile justice, Administration of—California 364.3609794
Juvenile justice, Administration of—New York (State) 364.3609747
Juvenile justice, Administration of—United States 345.7308; 353.408350973; 364.360973
Juvenile wood 575.46; 674.1
K-theory 512.55; 514.23
Kabir, 15th cent. 891.4312
Kabir, 15th cent.—Translations into English 891.4312
Kabuki 792.0952
Kac-Moody algebras 512.55
Kachina dolls 299.74
Kafa (Armenian poetry) 891.992104
Kafka, Franz, 1883–1924 833.912
Kafka, Franz, 1883–1924—Criticism and interpretation 833.912
Kafka, Franz, 1883–1924—Translations into English 833.912
Kahlo, Frida 759.972
Kahn, Louis I., 1901–1974 720.92

Kahn, Louis I., 1901–1974—Criticism and interpretation 720.92
Kaine, Daniel (Fictitious character) 813.54
Kaine, Jennifer (Fictitious character) 813.54
Kaiser family 929.20973
Kakapo 598.71
Kālacakra (Tantric rite) 294.3438
Kālacakra (Tantric rite)—China—Tibet 294.3438
Kalamazoo County (Mich.) 977.417
Kalamazoo County (Mich.)—Maps 912.77417
Kaldor, Nicholas, 1908–1986 330.092
Kaleidoscopes 688.72
Kalevala 894.54111
Kalkaska County (Mich.) 977.465
Kalkaska County (Mich.)—Maps 912.77465
Kalman filtering 629.8312
Kanawha County (W. Va.)—Genealogy 929.375437
Kandinsky, Wassily, 1866–1944 759.7
Kandiyohi County (Minn.) 977.648
Kandiyohi County (Minn.)—Maps 912.77648
Kane, Alex (Fictitious character) 813.54
Kane County (Ill.) 977.323
Kane County (Ill.)—Genealogy 929.377323
Kane County (Ill.)—Maps 912.77323
Kangaroo rats 599.35987
Kangaroos 599.222
Kankakee County (Ill.) 977.363
Kankakee County (Ill.)—Maps 912.77363
Kansas 978.1
Kansas City (Mo.) 977.8411
Kansas City (Mo.)—Guidebooks 917.7841104; 917.784110443; 917.784110444
Kansas—Genealogy 929.3781
Kansas—Guidebooks 917.8104; 917.810433; 917.810434
Kansas—History 978.1
Kansas—History—1854–1861 978.102
Kant, Immanuel, 1724–1804 193
Kant, Immanuel, 1724–1804—Aesthetics 111.85092
Kant, Immanuel, 1724–1804—Contributions in ethics 170.92
Kant, Immanuel, 1724–1804—Ethics 170.92
Kant, Immanuel, 1724–1804. Kritik der reinen Vernunft 121
Kant, Immanuel, 1724–1804. Kritik der Urteilskraft 121
Kaplan, Hyman (Fictitious character) 813.52
Karachi (Pakistan) 954.9183
Karachi (Pakistan)—History 954.9183
Karajan, Herbert von 784.2092
Karate 796.8153
Karate for children 796.8153083
Karate—History 796.815309
Karma 294.522
Karnataka (India) 954.87
Karnataka (India)—Civilization 954.87
Karnataka (India)—Pictorial works 954.8700222
Karp, Butch (Fictitious character) 813.54
Karp, Butch (Fictitious character)—Fiction 813.54
Karren 551.447
Karsavina, Tamara 792.82092
Karst 551.447
Karst conservation 333.73
Kasparov, G. K. (Garri Kimovich) 794.1092; 794.159
Katahdin, Mount (Me.) 974.125
Katyn Forest Massacre, 1940 940.5405094762
Kauai (Hawaii) 996.941
Kauai (Hawaii)—Guidebooks 919.694104; 919.69410441; 919.69410442
Kauṭalya. Arthaśāstra 320.101

Kavanagh, Patrick, 1904–1967 821.912
Kavanagh, Patrick, 1904–1967—Criticism and
  interpretation 821.912
Kavanaugh, Timothy (Fictitious character) 813.54
Kawasaki motorcycle 629.2275
Kawasaki motorcycle—Maintenance and repair
  629.28775
Kawasaki motorcycle—Maintenance and repair—
  Handbooks, manuals, etc. 629.28775
Kayak touring 797.1224
Kayaking 797.1224
Kayaks 623.829; 797.12240092
Kayaks—Design and construction 623.829
Kazakhstan 958.45
Keane, Owen (Fictitious character) 813.54
Keane, Owen (Fictitious character)—Fiction 813.54
Keaton, Buster, 1895–1966 791.43028092
Keaton, Sam (Fictitious character) 813.54
Keats, John, 1795–1821 821.7
Keats, John, 1795–1821—Correspondence 821.7
Keats, John, 1795–1821—Criticism and interpretation
  821.7
Keats, John, 1795–1821. Endymion 821.7
Keats, John, 1795–1821—Knowledge—Literature 821.7
Keats, John, 1795–1821—Manuscripts 821.7
Keats, John, 1795–1821—Periodicals 821.7
Keller family 929.20973
Keller, Helen, 1880–1968 362.41092
Kelley family 929.20973
Kelling, Sarah (Fictitious character) 813.54
Kelling, Sarah (Fictitious character)—Fiction 813.54
Kellogg-Briand Pact (1928) 341.52
Kelly, Homer (Fictitious character) 813.54
Kelly, Homer (Fictitious character)—Fiction 813.54
Kelly, Irene (Fictitious character) 813.54
Kelly, Irene (Fictitious character)—Fiction 813.54
Kelly, Ned, 1855–1880 364.155092
Kelp bed ecology 577.78
Keltner, Jason (Fictitious character) 813.54
Kemp, Lennox (Fictitious character) 823.914
Kemp, Lennox (Fictitious character)—Fiction 823.914
Kendall County (Ill.) 977.3263
Kendall County (Ill.)—Maps 912.773263
Kendo 796.86
Kennan, George Frost, 1904– 327.730092
Kennedy, Christy (Fictitious character) 823.914
Kennedy, Edward Moore, 1932– 973.92092
Kennedy family 929.20973
Kennedy, Jerry (Fictitious character) 813.54
Kennedy, Jerry (Fictitious character)—Fiction 813.54
Kennedy, John F. (John Fitzgerald), 1917–1963
  973.922092
Kennedy, John F. (John Fitzgerald), 1917–1963—
  Assassination 364.1524092
Kennedy, Joseph P. (Joseph Patrick), 1888–1969
  973.9092
Kennedy, Robert F., 1925–1968 973.922092
Kennedy, Rose Fitzgerald, 1890– 973.9092
Kennedy Round (1964-1967 : Geneva, Switzerland)
  382.92
Kennels 636.70831
Kennewick Man 979.701
Kenobi, Obi-Wan (Fictitious character) 791.4375
Kent County (Del.)—Maps 912.7514
Kent County (Md.)—Maps 912.75236
Kent County (Mich.)—Maps 912.77455
Kent (England) 942.23
Kent (England)—Guidebooks 914.22304; 914.22304859;
  914.2230486

Kent (England)—Maps 912.4223
Kent family (Fictitious characters) 813.54
Kent family (Fictitious characters)—Fiction 813.54
Kent State University—Riot, 1970 (May 4) 378.77137;
  972.924
Kentucky 976.9
Kentucky Derby, Louisville, Ky. 798.400976944
Kentucky Derby, Louisville, Ky.—Anecdotes
  798.400976944
Kentucky—Description and travel 917.6904; 917.69044;
  917.690443
Kentucky—Genealogy 929.3769
Kentucky—Guidebooks 917.6904; 917.69044; 917.690443
Kentucky—History 976.9
Kentucky—History—To 1792 976.901; 976.902
Kentucky—History—Civil War, 1861–1865 976.903
Kentucky—Road maps 912.769
Kentucky—Social life and customs 976.9
Kenwood House (Hampstead, London, England)
  707.442142; 942.142
Kenworthy, Simon (Fictitious character) 823.914
Kenworthy, Simon (Fictitious character)—Fiction
  823.914
Kenya 967.62
Kenya—Economic conditions 330.96762
Kenya—Economic conditions—1963– 330.9676204
Kenya—Economic conditions—1963– —Periodicals
  330.9676204
Kenya—Economic policy 338.96762
Kenya—Guidebooks 916.76204; 916.7620442
Kenya—History 967.62
Kenya—History—Mau Mau Emergency, 1952–1960
  967.6203
Kenya—Maps 912.6762
Kenya—Politics and government 320.96762; 967.62
Kenya—Politics and government—To 1963 967.62
Kenya—Politics and government—1978–
  320.9676209048
Kenya—Road maps 912.6762
Kenya—Social life and customs 967.62
Kenya—Social life and customs—1895–1963 967.6203
Kenzie, Patrick (Fictitious character) 813.54
Kenzie, Patrick (Fictitious character)—Fiction 813.54
Kepesh, David (Fictitious character) 813.54
Kepler, Johannes, 1571–1630 520.92
Kerala (India) 954.83
Keratoconus 617.719
Keratotomy, Radial 617.719059
Kermode bear 599.785
Kerney, Kevin (Fictitious character) 813.54
Kerouac, Jack, 1922–1969 813.54
Kerouac, Jack, 1922–1969—Criticism and interpretation
  813.54
Kerr family 929.20973
Kerr, Margaret (Fictitious character) 813.54
Kerrigan, Nancy, 1969– 796.912092
Kerry (Ireland) 941.96
Kerry (Ireland)—Social life and customs 941.96
Kestrel, Julian (Fictitious character) 813.54
Kestrel, Julian (Fictitious character)—Fiction 813.54
Kettle hole plants 581.768
Kettle holes 551.315
Key, Francis Scott, 1779–1843 811.2
Key West (Fla.) 975.941
Key West (Fla.)—Pictorial works 917.5941; 975.941
Keyboard harmony 786.125
Keyboard instrument music 786
Keyboard instruments 786
Keyboarding 652.3

Keyboarding—Problems, exercises, etc. 652.307
Keyboards (Electronics) 786.19
Keynes, John Maynard, 1883–1946 330.156092
Keynes, John Maynard, 1883–1946. General theory of employment, interest and money 330.156
Keynesian economics 330.156
Keyword searching 025.04
Khmer language 495.932
Khmer language—Conversation and phrase books 495.932834
Khmer language—Conversation and phrase books—English 495.93283421
Khmer language—Dictionaries 495.9323
Khmer language—Dictionaries—English 495.932321
Khrushchev, Nikita Sergeevich, 1894–1971 947.0852092
Kibbutzim 307.776; 307.776095694
Kid pix (Computer file) 372.1334
Kidd (Fictitious character : Camp) 813.54
Kidnapping 364.154
Kidnapping victims 362.88; 364.154092
Kidney cortex 573.496; 612.463
Kidneys 612.463
Kidneys—Cancer 616.99461
Kidneys—Diseases 616.61
Kidneys—Diseases—Diagnosis 616.61075
Kidneys—Diseases—Treatment 616.6106
Kidneys—Pathophysiology 616.6107
Kidneys—Physiology 612.463
Kidneys—Radionuclide imaging 616.6107575
Kidneys—Transplantation 617.4610592
Kierkegaard, Søren, 1813–1855 198.9
Kiho school 181.119
Kildare, Doctor (Fictitious character) 813.52
Kildare, Doctor (Fictitious character)—Fiction 813.52
Killer cells 616.0799
Killer whale 599.536
Kilns 666.436; 731.2; 738.136
Kilvert, Robert Francis, 1840–1879 283.092
Kilvert, Robert Francis, 1840–1879—Diaries 283.092
Kim, Il-sŏng, 1912– 951.93043092
Kimonos 391.00952
Kin recognition in animals 591.563
Kincaid, Ben (Fictitious character) 813.54
Kincaid, Ben (Fictitious character)—Fiction 813.54
Kincaid, Duncan (Fictitious character) 813.54
Kincaid, Duncan (Fictitious character)—Fiction 813.54
Kincaid, Libby (Fictitious character) 813.54
Kincaid, Libby (Fictitious character)—Fiction 813.54
Kinder- und Hausmärchen 398.20943
Kindergarten 372.218
Kindergarten—Curricula 372.19
Kindergarten—Parent participation 372.1192
Kindergarten teachers 372.11
Kindergarten—United States 372.2180973
Kindertransports (Rescue operations) 940.5318
Kindness 177.7
Kinematics 531.112
Kinesiology 612.76; 613.7
Kinetic theory of gases 533.7
Kinetic theory of matter 530.136
King, Coretta Scott, 1927– 323.092
King County (Wash.) 979.777
King County (Wash.)—Maps 912.79777
King family 929.20973
King George County (Va.)—Genealogy 929.375525
King, Martin Luther, Jr., 1929–1968 323.092
King, Martin Luther, Jr., 1929–1968—Assassination 364.1524092

King, Martin Luther, Jr., 1929–1968—Philosophy 323.092
King Philip's War, 1675–1676 973.24
King, Stephen, 1947– 813.54
King, Stephen, 1947– —Criticism and interpretation 813.54
King, Willow (Fictitious character) 823.914
King, Willow (Fictitious character)—Fiction 823.914
Kingdom of God 231.72
Kingdom of God—Biblical teaching 231.72
Kingfishers 598.78
Kings and rulers 352.23
Kings and rulers—Biblical teaching 220.8321
Kings and rulers—Biography 321.00922
Kings and rulers in art 704.949321
Kinorhyncha 592.55
Kinsella, Thomas 821.914
Kinsella, Thomas—Criticism and interpretation 821.914
Kinship 306.83
Kinship—Religious aspects 291.1783583
Kipling, Rudyard, 1865–1936 828.809
Kipling, Rudyard, 1865–1936—Criticism and interpretation 828.809
Kipling, Rudyard, 1865–1936—Knowledge—India 828.809
Kirby family 929.20973
Kirby, Jacqueline (Fictitious character) 813.54
Kirk, Devlin (Fictitious character) 813.54
Kirk, Devlin (Fictitious character)—Fiction 813.54
Kirkendall effect 530.415
Kissing 394
Kissinger, Henry, 1923– 327.730092
Kitchen appliances 641.50284; 683.88
Kitchen cabinets 684.16
Kitchen gardens 635
Kitchen utensils 683.82
Kitchens 643.3; 747.797
Kitchens—Design and construction 643.3
Kitchens—Planning 643.3
Kitchens—Remodeling 643.30288
Kite surfing 797.3
Kites 629.13332; 796.158
Kitsap County (Wash.) 979.776
Kitsap County (Wash.)—Maps 912.79776
Kitsch 709.0348
Kittens 636.807
Kiwis 598.54
Klee, Paul, 1879–1940 759.9494; 760.092
Klee, Paul, 1879–1940—Criticism and interpretation 759.9494; 760.092
Klee, Paul, 1879–1940—Exhibitions 759.9494
Klein, A. M. (Abraham Moses), 1909–1972 811.52
Klein, A. M. (Abraham Moses), 1909–1972—Criticism and interpretation 811.52
Klein, Dylan (Fictitious character) 813.54
Klein family 929.20973
Klein, Melanie 150.195092; 616.8917
Kleist, Heinrich von, 1777–1811 832.6; 833.6; 838.609
Kleist, Heinrich von, 1777–1811—Criticism and interpretation 838.609
Kleist, Heinrich von, 1777–1811—Translations into English 832.6; 833.6
Klezmer music 784.089924
Klimt, Gustav, 1862–1918 709.2
Klingon (Artificial language) 499.99
Klondike River Valley (Yukon)—Gold discoveries 971.91
Knee 612.98
Knee—Surgery 617.582059
Knee—Wounds and injuries 617.582044

Knife fighting 355.548; 613.66; 796.8
Knight family 929.20973
Knight, Jerry (Fictitious character) 813.54
Knight, Micky (Fictitious character) 813.54
Knights and knighthood 940.1088355
Knights and knighthood—History 940.1088355
Knitting 746.432
Knitting—Maine—Patterns 746.432041
Knitting—Patterns 746.432041
Knives 621.932
Knives—Collectors and collecting 621.932075
Knock-knock jokes 818.02
Knot theory 514.224
Knots and splices 623.8882
Knott, Deborah (Fictitious character) 813.54
Knott, Deborah (Fictitious character)—Fiction 813.54
Knott family 929.20973
Knotwork, Celtic 745.67; 746.44
Knowledge acquisition (Expert systems) 006.33
Knowledge management 658.4038
Knowledge representation (Information theory) 006.332
Knowledge, Sociology of 306.42
Knowledge, Theory of 121
Knowledge, Theory of (Hinduism) 294.501
Knowledge workers 331.7
Knox County (Ill.) 977.349
Knox County (Ill.)—Genealogy 929.377349
Knox County (Ill.)—Maps 912.77349
Knox, John, ca. 1514-1572 205.2092
Knoxville (Tenn.) 976.885
Knoxville (Tenn.)—History 976.885
Koala 599.25
Koan 294.3443; 294.3927
Kodiak bear 599.784
Koesler, Robert (Fictitious character) 813.54
Koesler, Robert (Fictitious character)—Fiction 813.54
Koestler, Arthur, 1905- 828.91209
Koi 639.37483
Kolla, Kathy (Fictitious character) 823.914
Kommunisticheskaia partiia Sovetskogo Soiuza 324.247075
Kommunisticheskaia partiia Sovetskogo Soiuza—History 324.24707509
Kommunisticheskaia partiia Sovetskogo Soiuza—Party work 324.247075
Komodo dragon 597.95968
Kook, Abraham Isaac, 1865-1935 296.3092
Koontz, Dean R. (Dean Ray), 1945- 813.54
Koontz, Dean R. (Dean Ray), 1945- —Criticism and interpretation 813.54
Kootenai County (Idaho) 979.694
Kootenai County (Idaho)—Genealogy 929.379694
Koran 297.122
Koran and science 297.12285
Koran—Commentaries 297.1227
Koran—Criticism, interpretation, etc. 297.1226
Koran—Theology 297.2
Korczak, Janusz, 1878-1942 891.858709
Korea 951.9
Korea—Civilization 951.9
Korea—Description and travel 915.1904; 915.190443
Korea—Economic conditions 330.9519
Korea—Economic policy 338.9519
Korea—History 951.9
Korea (North) 951.93
Korea (North)—Economic policy 338.95193
Korea (North)—Politics and government 320.95193
Korea—Politics and government 320.9519; 951.9

Korea—Politics and government—1945-1948 320.951909045; 951.9041
Korea—Social life and customs 951.9
Korea (South) 951.95
Korea (South)—Economic conditions 330.95195
Korea (South)—Economic conditions—1960- 330.95195043
Korea (South)—Economic conditions—1960- —Periodicals 330.95195043
Korea (South)—Economic policy 338.95195
Korea (South)—Economic policy—1960- 338.95195
Korea (South)—Guidebooks 915.19504; 915.1950443
Korea (South)—Pictorial works 951.9500222
Korea (South)—Politics and government 320.95195; 951.95
Korea (South)—Politics and government—1960-1988 320.951909046; 320.9519509046; 951.95043
Korea (South)—Politics and government—1988- 320.951909049; 951.95043
Korean Air Lines Incident, 1983 909.096454
Korean Americans 973.04957
Korean Demilitarized Zone (Korea) 951.9043
Korean fiction 895.73; 895.73008
Korean fiction—20th century 895.734; 895.73408
Korean fiction—20th century—Translations into English 895.73408
Korean language 495.7
Korean language—Conversation and phrase books 495.7834
Korean language—Conversation and phrase books—English 495.783471
Korean literature 895.7; 895.708
Korean literature—History and criticism 895.709
Korean poetry 895.71; 895.71008
Korean poetry—20th century 895.714; 895.71408
Korean poetry—20th century—Translations into English 895.71408
Korean poetry—Translations into English 895.71008
Korean resistance movements, 1905-1945 951.903
Korean reunification question (1945-) 320.951909045; 951.904; 951.9043
Korean War, 1950-1953 951.9042
Korean War, 1950-1953—Aerial operations 951.904248
Korean War, 1950-1953—Aerial operations, American 951.904248
Korean War, 1950-1953—Armistices 951.90422
Korean War, 1950-1953—Campaigns 951.90424
Korean War, 1950-1953—Campaigns—Korea (North)—Changjin Reservoir 951.904242
Korean War, 1950-1953—China 951.9042
Korean War, 1950-1953—Personal narratives, American 951.9042092
Korean War, 1950-1953—Personal narratives, Korean 951.9042092
Korean War, 1950-1953—Prisoners and prisons 951.90427
Korean War, 1950-1953—Regimental histories—United States 951.90424
Korean wit and humor 895.77008
KornShell (Computer program language) 005.133
Koro (Disease) 616.8522
Kosciusko County (Ind.) 977.282
Kosciusko County (Ind.)—Genealogy 929.377282
Kosher restaurants 641.5676
Kosovo (Serbia) 949.71
Kosovo (Serbia)—History 949.71
Kosovo (Serbia)—History—1980- 949.71
Kosovo (Serbia)—History—Civil War, 1998- 949.71
Kovak, Milton (Fictitious character) 813.54

Kovak, Milton (Fictitious character)—Fiction 813.54
Koyukon Indians—Folklore 398.2089972
Kozak, Thea (Fictitious character) 813.54
Kozak, Thea (Fictitious character)—Fiction 813.54
Kramer, Trompie (Fictitious character) 823.914
Kramer, Trompie (Fictitious character)—Fiction 823.914
Krautrock (Music) 781.64
Kraychik, Stan (Fictitious character) 813.54
Kraychik, Stan (Fictitious character)—Fiction 813.54
Kreident, Craig (Fictitious character) 813.54
Kremlin (Moscow, Russia) 708.731
Krishna (Hindu deity) 294.52113
Krishna (Hindu deity) in literature 808.80382912113;
    809.93382912113
Krishnamurti, J. (Jiddu), 1895– 181.4
Kristallnacht, 1938 940.5318
Kristeva, Julia, 1941– 801.95092
Krone, Julie 798.40092
Kronshtadt (Russia)—History—1917–1921 947.0841
Kropotkin, Petr Alekseevich, kníaz', 1842–1921
    335.83092
Kruger, Herbie (Fictitious character) 823.914
Kruger, Herbie (Fictitious character)—Fiction 823.914
Krynn (Imaginary place) 813.54
Krynn (Imaginary place)—Fiction 813.54
Ku-Klux Klan (1866-1869) 322.420973
Ku Klux Klan (1915-) 322.420973
Ku Klux Klan (1915-)—History 322.420973
Kuhn family 929.20973
Kuiper Belt 523.48
Kuṇḍalinī 294.5436
Kundera, Milan 891.86354; 891.8685409
Kundera, Milan—Criticism and interpretation
    891.8685409
Kung fu 796.8159
Kuprin, A. I. (Aleksandr Ivanovich), 1870–1938
    891.733
Kuprin, A. I. (Aleksandr Ivanovich), 1870–1938—
    Translations into English 891.733
Kura-Araxes culture 939.5
Kurds 956.0049159
Kuril Islands (Russia) 957.7
Kurosawa, Akira, 1910– 791.430233092
Kurosawa, Akira, 1910– —Criticism and interpretation
    791.430233092
Kuwait 953.67
Kuwait—Economic conditions 330.95367
Kuwait—Economic conditions—Periodicals
    330.95367005
Kwakiutl Indians 305.8979; 971.1100497
Kwakiutl Indians—Religion 299.789
Kwan, Michelle, 1980– 796.912092
Kwanzaa 394.261
KwaZulu-Natal (South Africa) 968.4
KwaZulu-Natal (South Africa)—Politics and government
    968.4
KwaZulu-Natal (South Africa)—Politics and
    government—1910– 320.96840904; 968.405
Kyrie eleison (Music) 782.3232
L-functions 512.73
La Crosse County (Wis.) 977.571
La Crosse County (Wis.)—Maps 912.77571
La Fayette, Madame de (Marie-Madeleine Pioche de La
    Vergne), 1634–1693. Princesse de Clèves 843.4
La Guardia, Fiorello H. (Fiorello Henry), 1882–1947
    974.71042092
La Guma, Alex 823.914
La Guma, Alex—Criticism and interpretation 823.914
La Moure County (N.D.) 978.453

La Moure County (N.D.)—Maps 912.78453
La Niña Current 551.4761; 551.6
La Salle County (Ill.) 977.327
La Salle County (Ill.)—Maps 912.77327
La Salle, Jean Baptiste de, Saint, 1651–1719 271.7802
Labanotation 792.82
Labels 686.28
Labor 331
Labor—Canada 306.360971
Labor contract 344.01891
Labor contract—Great Britain 344.4101891
Labor contract—United States 344.7301891
Labor discipline—Law and legislation 344.012598
Labor discipline—Law and legislation—United States
    344.73012598
Labor economics 331
Labor economics—Bibliography 016.331
Labor economics—Bibliography—Catalogs 016.331
Labor—History 306.3609
Labor inspection 354.9283
Labor laws and legislation 344.01
Labor laws and legislation—Australia 344.9401
Labor laws and legislation—British Columbia 344.71101
Labor laws and legislation—California 344.79401
Labor laws and legislation—Canada 344.7101
Labor laws and legislation—Europe 344.401
Labor laws and legislation—European Economic
    Community countries 344.401
Labor laws and legislation—European Union countries
    341.763094
Labor laws and legislation—Florida 344.75901
Labor laws and legislation—Georgia 344.75801
Labor laws and legislation—Great Britain 344.4101
Labor laws and legislation—India 344.5401
Labor laws and legislation, International 341.763
Labor laws and legislation—Massachusetts 344.74401
Labor laws and legislation—Michigan 344.77401
Labor laws and legislation—Minnesota 344.77601
Labor laws and legislation—New Jersey 344.74901
Labor laws and legislation—New York (State)
    344.74701
Labor laws and legislation—North Carolina 344.75601
Labor laws and legislation—Ohio 344.77101
Labor laws and legislation—Ontario 344.71301
Labor laws and legislation—Oregon 344.79501
Labor laws and legislation—Pakistan 344.549101
Labor laws and legislation—Pennsylvania 344.74801
Labor laws and legislation—Philippines 344.59901
Labor laws and legislation—South Africa 344.6801
Labor laws and legislation—Texas 344.76401
Labor laws and legislation—United States 344.7301
Labor laws and legislation—United States—Cases
    344.73010264
Labor laws and legislation—United States—Digests
    344.730102648
Labor laws and legislation—United States—Outlines,
    syllabi, etc. 344.7301
Labor laws and legislation—United States—Periodicals
    344.730105
Labor laws and legislation—Wisconsin 344.77501
Labor leaders 322.2092
Labor literature 331
Labor-management committees 331.89
Labor market 331.12
Labor market—Australia 331.120994
Labor market—Canada 331.120971
Labor market—Developing countries 331.12091724
Labor market—Great Britain 331.120941
Labor market—Japan 331.120952

Labor market—United States 331.120973
Labor mobility 331.127
Labor movement 331.8
Labor movement—Great Britain 331.880941
Labor movement—Great Britain—History 331.80941
Labor movement—United States 331.80973
Labor movement—United States—History 331.80973
Labor (Obstetrics) 618.4
Labor (Obstetrics)—Complications 618.5
Labor policy 331.12042
Labor, Premature 618.397
Labor productivity 658.314
Labor productivity—United States 331.1180973
Labor supply 331.11
Labor supply—Arkansas 331.1109767
Labor supply—Arkansas—Statistics 331.1109767021
Labor supply—Colorado 331.1109788
Labor supply—Colorado—Statistics 331.1109788021
Labor supply—Colorado—Statistics—Periodicals
331.1109788021
Labor supply—Developing countries 331.11091724
Labor supply—Effect of technological innovations on
331.11
Labor supply—Effect of technological innovations on—
Great Britain 331.120941
Labor supply—Effect of technological innovations on—
United States 331.120973
Labor supply—Hawaii 331.1109969
Labor supply—Hawaii—Statistics 331.1109969021
Labor supply—Iowa 331.1109777
Labor supply—Iowa—Statistics 331.1109777021
Labor supply—Maine 331.1109741
Labor supply—Maine—Statistics 331.1109741021
Labor supply—Maine—Statistics—Periodicals
331.1109741021
Labor supply—Maryland 331.1109752
Labor supply—Maryland—Statistics 331.1109752021
Labor supply—Massachusetts 331.1109744
Labor supply—Massachusetts—Statistics
331.1109744021
Labor supply—Michigan 331.1109774
Labor supply—Michigan—Statistics 331.1109774021
Labor supply—Minnesota 331.1109776
Labor supply—Minnesota—Statistics 331.1109776021
Labor supply—Nevada 331.1109793
Labor supply—New Hampshire 331.1109742
Labor supply—New Hampshire—Statistics
331.1109742021
Labor supply—New Hampshire—Statistics—Periodicals
331.1109742021
Labor supply—New Mexico 331.1109789
Labor supply—New Mexico—Statistics 331.1109789021
Labor supply—North Carolina 331.1109756
Labor supply—North Carolina—Statistics
331.1109756021
Labor supply—North Carolina—Statistics—Periodicals
331.1109756021
Labor supply—Oklahoma 331.1109766
Labor supply—Oklahoma—Statistics 331.1109766021
Labor supply—South Carolina 331.1109757
Labor supply—South Carolina—Statistics
331.1109757021
Labor supply—South Carolina—Statistics—Periodicals
331.1109757021
Labor supply—United States 331.110973
Labor supply—United States—Statistics 331.110973021
Labor supply—Virginia 331.1109755
Labor supply—Virginia—Statistics 331.1109755021
Labor theory of value 335.412

Labor turnover 331.126
Labor unions 331.88
Labor unions and international relations 322.2
Labor unions and international relations—United States
322.20973
Labor unions—Australia 331.880994
Labor unions—Australia—History 331.880994
Labor unions—Canada 331.880971
Labor unions—Canada—History 331.880971
Labor unions—Government employees—United States
352.68
Labor unions—Great Britain 331.880941
Labor unions—Great Britain—History 331.880941
Labor unions—Great Britain—Political activity
322.20941
Labor unions—Great Britain—Political activity—History
322.20941
Labor unions—Law and legislation 344.0188
Labor unions—Law and legislation—United States
344.730188
Labor unions—Organizing 331.8912
Labor unions—Organizing—United States 331.8912
Labor unions—South Africa 331.880968
Labor unions—Soviet Union 331.880947
Labor unions—United States 331.880973
Labor unions—United States—History 331.880973
Labor unions—United States—History—20th century
331.880973
Labor—United States 331.0973
Labor—United States—History 331.0973
Laboratories 001.4; 371.623
Laboratories—Design and construction 727.5
Laboratory animals 619; 636.0885
Laboratory schools 370.724; 371.04
Laboratory schools—United States 370.724
Laboratory technicians 001.4092
Laborers in the vineyard (Parable) 226.8
Laboulbeniales 579.567
Labour Party (Great Britain) 324.24107
Labour Party (Great Britain)—History 324.24107
Labour Party (Great Britain)—History—20th century
324.24107
Labrador retriever 636.7527
LabVIEW 006
Labyrinths 793.73
Lac qui Parle County (Minn. : 1871–) 977.638
Lac qui Parle County (Minn. : 1871–)—Maps 912.77638
Lacan, Jacques, 1901– 150.195092
Lace and lace making 746.22
Lace and lace making—Patterns 746.22041
Lacrimal apparatus—Diseases 617.764
Lactation 573.679; 612.664; 618.71
Lactic acid bacteria 579.35
Lactose-free foods 641.3
Lactose intolerance 616.3998
Lacy family 929.20973
Ladybugs 595.769
Laennec, R. T. H. (René Théophile Hyacinthe), 1781–
1826 610.92
Lafayette County (Wis.) 977.579
Lafayette County (Wis.)—Maps 912.77579
Lafayette, Marie Joseph Paul Yves Roch Gilbert Du
Motier, marquis de, 1757–1834 944.04092
Lagomorpha 599.32
Lagoon ecology 577.63
Lagos (Nigeria)—Maps 912.6691
Lahore (Pakistan) 954.9143
Lahore (Pakistan)—Description and travel 915.4914304
Laidlaw, Jack (Fictitious character) 823.914

Laidlaw, Jack (Fictitious character)—Fiction 823.914
Laird, Andrew (Fictitious character) 823.914
Laity 262.15
Laity—Catholic Church 262.15
Lake County (Fla.)—Maps 912.75922
Lake County (Ill.) 977.321
Lake County (Ill.)—Maps 912.77321
Lake County (Ohio) 977.1334
Lake County (Ohio)—Maps 912.771334
Lake District (England) 942.78
Lake District (England)—Guidebooks 914.27804;
    914.27804859; 914.2780486
Lake District (England)—Pictorial works 914.27800222
Lake ecology 577.63
Lake renewal 333.9163153
Lake renewal—Law and legislation 346.0469163
Lake Wobegon (Minn. : Imaginary place) 813.54
Lake Wobegon (Minn. : Imaginary place)—Fiction
    813.54
Lakes 551.482
Lakes—California—Recreational use—Guidebooks
    333.784409794
Lāladāsī (Sect) 294.55
Lam-rim 294.34435
Lama (Genus) 599.6367
Lamarck, Jean Baptiste Pierre Antoine de Monet de,
    1744–1829 570.92
Lamb, Charles, 1775–1834 824.7
Lamb (Meat) 641.363
Lambda calculus 511.3
Lambert, John (Fictitious character) 823.914
Lambert, Lucy (Fictitious character) 823.914
Lamborghini automobile 629.2222
Lambros, Julia (Fictitious character) 813.54
Lambros, Nick (Fictitious character) 813.54
Lameness in horses 636.1089758
Lamerino, Gloria (Fictitious character) 813.54
Laminar flow 629.13232
Laminated materials 620.118
Lammas 133.43; 299
Lamps 621.32
Lancashire (England) 942.76
Lancashire (England)—History 942.76
Lancaster County (Pa.)—Genealogy 929.374815
Lancaster County (Pa.)—Maps 912.74815
Land capability for wildlife 333.954
Land grants 343.0253
Land mine victims 362.19719
Land mines 355.825115
Land mines (International law) 341.73
Land reform 333.31
Land reform—Developing countries 333.31091724
Land reform—India 333.3154
Land reform—Latin America 333.318
Land reform—Law and legislation 346.044
Land reform—Law and legislation—Philippines
    346.599044
Land reform—Philippines 333.31599
Land tenure 333.3
Land tenure—Law and legislation 346.0432
Land tenure—Law and legislation—Great Britain
    346.410432
Land tenure—Law and legislation—Philippines
    346.5990432
Land titles 346.0438
Land titles—Registration and transfer 346.0438
Land titles—Registration and transfer—Philippines
    346.5990438

Land titles—Registration and transfer—United States
    346.730438
Land trusts 333.3234
Land trusts—Florida 346.759068
Land use 333.73
Land use—Government policy 333.73
Land use—Government policy—United States
    333.730973
Land use—Law and legislation 346.045
Land use—Law and legislation—California 346.794045
Land use—Law and legislation—Maine 346.741045
Land use—Law and legislation—Massachusetts
    346.744045
Land use—Law and legislation—Nigeria 346.669045
Land use—Law and legislation—United States
    346.73045
Land use, Rural 333.76
Land use, Rural—United States 333.760973
Land use—United States 333.730973
Land use—United States—Planning 333.730973
Land use—Wisconsin 333.7309775
Land use—Wisconsin—Data processing 333.730285
Landforms 551.41
Landlord and tenant 333.54
Landlord and tenant—California 346.7940434
Landlord and tenant—Great Britain 346.410434
Landlord and tenant—Massachusetts 346.7440434
Landlord and tenant—New York (State) 346.7470434
Landlord and tenant—Ontario 346.7130434
Landlord and tenant—Pennsylvania 346.7480434
Landlord and tenant—United States 346.730434
Landlord and tenant—Virginia 346.7550434
Landon, Arnold (Fictitious character) 823.914
Landon, Arnold (Fictitious character)—Fiction 823.914
Landon, Michael, 1936–1991 791.45028092
Landry, Tom 796.332092
Landsat satellites 526.982
Landscape 700.42
Landscape architects 712.092
Landscape architectural firms 712.06
Landscape architecture 712
Landscape architecture—History 712.09
Landscape architecture—United States 712.0973
Landscape assessment 304.2
Landscape assessment—United States 304.2
Landscape construction 624; 712
Landscape design 712
Landscape drawing—Technique 743.836
Landscape gardening 712
Landscape gardening—Handbooks, manuals, etc. 712
Landscape in art 704.9436; 760.04436
Landscape in literature 808.8032; 809.9332
Landscape painting 758.1
Landscape painting, American 758.10973
Landscape painting, American—19th century
    758.1097309034
Landscape painting, American—Exhibitions
    758.10973074
Landscape painting, Chinese 758.10951
Landscape painting, Chinese—20th century
    758.109510904
Landscape painting—Technique 751.422436; 751.45436
Landscape photography 778.936; 779.36
Landscape photography—Southwest, New 779.3679
Landscape plants 715
Landscape plants—Florida 716.09759
Landscape plants—United States 716.0973
Landscaping industry—Management 712.068
Landslides 551.307

Laser printers 686.233
Laser printing 686.233
Laser pulses, Ultrashort 621.366
Laser spectroscopy 621.366
Lasers 621.366
Lasers in chemistry 542
Lasers in dentistry 617.60028; 617.605
Lasers in medicine 610.28
Lasers in ophthalmology 617.70028
Lasers in surgery 617.05
Lasers—Industrial applications 621.366
Lasers—Periodicals 621.36605
Lasers—Physiological effect 571.455
Lasers—Resonators 621.366
Lasers—Therapeutic use 615.83
LASIK (Eye surgery) 617.719059
Lassiter (Fictitious character) 813.54
Lassiter (Fictitious character)—Fiction 813.54
Lassiter, Jake (Fictitious character) 813.54
Lassiter, Jake (Fictitious character)—Fiction 813.54
Last in, first out (Accounting) 657.72
Latchkey children 306.874; 649.1
Latchkey children—United States 306.874; 649.1
Latent structure analysis 519.535
Latent variables 519.535
Laterality 152.335
Latex 547.8425
LaTeX (Computer file) 686.225445369
Latex garments 687
Lathes 621.942
Latin America 980
Latin America—Bibliography 016.918; 016.98
Latin America—Bibliography of bibliographies
    016.01698
Latin America—Civilization 980
Latin America—Civilization—20th century 980.033
Latin America—Commerce 382.098
Latin America—Commercial policy 382.3098
Latin America—Description and travel 918.04;
    918.0439; 918.044
Latin America—Economic conditions 330.98
Latin America—Economic conditions—1945–
    330.980033
Latin America—Economic conditions—1982–
    330.980038
Latin America—Economic conditions—1982– —
    Periodicals 330.980038
Latin America—Economic conditions—1982– —Statistics
    330.980038
Latin America—Economic conditions—1982– —
    Statistics—Periodicals 330.980038
Latin America—Economic integration 337.18
Latin America—Economic policy 338.98
Latin America—Foreign relations 327.098
Latin America—Foreign relations—1980– 327.098
Latin America—Foreign relations—Soviet Union
    327.4708
Latin America—Foreign relations—United States
    327.7308
Latin America—Geography 918
Latin America—Guidebooks 918.04; 918.0439; 918.044
Latin America—History 980
Latin America—History—To 1830 980.01; 980.02
Latin America—History—Wars of Independence, 1806–
    1830 980.02
Latin America—History—1830– 980.03
Latin America—History—20th century 980.033
Latin America—Library resources 016.98
Latin America—Periodicals 980.005

Latin America—Politics and government 320.98; 980
Latin America—Politics and government—20th century
    320.980904; 980.033
Latin America—Politics and government—1948–
    320.9809045
Latin America—Politics and government—1980–
    320.9809048
Latin America—Population 304.6098
Latin America—Relations 303.4828
Latin America—Relations—United States 303.4827308
Latin America—Social conditions 980
Latin America—Social conditions—1945–1982 980.033
Latin America—Study and teaching 918.0071
Latin American fiction 863.008098
Latin American fiction—20th century 863.0080980904
Latin American fiction—20th century—History and
    criticism 863.009980904
Latin American literature 860.8098
Latin American literature—20th century 860.80980904
Latin American literature—20th century—History and
    criticism 860.9980904
Latin American literature—History and criticism
    860.998
Latin American poetry 808.1998
Latin Americanists 980.0072
Latin Americans 980
Latin drama (Comedy) 872; 872.01
Latin drama (Comedy)—Translations into English
    872.008; 872.0108
Latin language 470
Latin language—Composition and exercises 478.24;
    478.2421; 808.0471
Latin language—Dictionaries 473
Latin language—Dictionaries—English 473.21
Latin language—Grammar 475; 478.24; 478.2421
Latin language—Grammar—Problems, exercises, etc.
    478.2421
Latin language—Readers 478.64; 478.6421
Latin literature 870; 870.8; 870.8001
Latin literature—History and criticism 870.9; 870.9001
Latin literature, Medieval and modern 870.8003;
    870.8004
Latin literature, Medieval and modern—History and
    criticism 870.9003; 870.9004
Latin literature—Translations into English 870.8;
    870.8001
Latin poetry 871; 871.008
Latin poetry—History and criticism 871.009; 871.0109
Latin poetry—History and criticism—Theory, etc.
    871.0109
Latin poetry, Medieval and modern 871.0308; 871.0408
Latin poetry, Medieval and modern—History and
    criticism 871.0309; 871.0409
Latin poetry, Medieval and modern—Translations into
    English 871.0308; 871.0408
Latin poetry—Translations into English 871.0108
Lattice dynamics 530.411
Lattice theory 511.33
Latvia 947.96
Laudatory poetry, Latin 871.0108
Laudatory poetry, Latin—Translations into English
    871.0108
Laughter 152.4
Laughter in literature 808.80353; 809.93353
Launch vehicles (Astronautics) 387.8; 629.457
Laundry 648.1
Launeddas 788.62
Laurano, Lauren (Fictitious character) 813.54
Laurano, Lauren (Fictitious character)—Fiction 813.54

Laurence, Margaret 813.54
Laurence, Margaret—Criticism and interpretation 813.54
Laurentia (Geology) 551.715
Lavender, Jimmie (Fictitious character) 813.52
Lavoisier, Antoine Laurent, 1743–1794 540.92
Law 340
Law—Africa 349.6
Law, Ancient 340.53
Law and anthropology 340.115
Law and art 344.097
Law and art—United States 344.73097
Law and economics 343.07
Law and ethics 340.112
Law and geography 340
Law and gospel 241.2
Law and literature 809.93355
Law and politics 340.115
Law and socialism 340.115
Law, Anglo-Saxon 340.550942
Law—Australia 349.94
Law—Australia—History 349.9409
Law—Australia—Periodicals 349.9405
Law—Bibliography 016.34
Law—Bibliography—Catalogs 016.34
Law—Brazil 349.81
Law—California 349.794
Law—Canada 349.71
Law—Canada—History 349.7109
Law—China 349.51
Law—China—History 349.5109
Law—Dictionaries 340.03
Law enforcement 363.2
Law enforcement—United States 363.20973
Law enforcement—Vocational guidance—United States 363.202373
Law—England 349.42
Law—England—History 349.4209
Law—Europe 349.4
Law—Europe—History 349.409
Law—European Economic Community countries 349.4
Law—European Union countries 341.2422
Law—Finland 349.4897
Law firms 346.06
Law firms—United States 340.068
Law—Florida 349.759
Law—France 349.44
Law—Georgia 349.758
Law—Germany 349.43
Law—Great Britain 349.41; 349.42
Law—Great Britain—Dictionaries 349.4103
Law—Great Britain—History 349.4109; 349.4209
Law—Great Britain—Interpretation and construction 349.41
Law—Great Britain—Periodicals 349.4105
Law—Great Britain—Terminology 340.014
Law, Greek 340.538
Law—History 340.09
Law—Humor 340.0207
Law—Hungary 349.439
Law—Illinois 349.773
Law in literature 808.80355; 809.93355
Law—India 349.54
Law—India—History 349.5409
Law—India—Periodicals 349.5405
Law—Indiana 349.772
Law—International unification 340.9
Law—Interpretation and construction 340; 340.1
Law—Ireland 349.417

Law—Israel 349.5694
Law—Israel—Jewish influences 349.5694
Law—Italy 349.45
Law—Japan 349.52
Law—Japan—History 349.5209
Law, John, 1671–1729 332.092
Law—Language 340.014
Law librarians 026.340092
Law libraries 026.34
Law libraries—Handbooks, manuals, etc. 026.34
Law libraries—United States 026.3400973
Law—Maine 349.741
Law—Malaysia 349.595
Law—Malta 349.4585
Law—Massachusetts 349.744
Law—Massachusetts—History 349.74409
Law, Medieval 340.55
Law—Methodology 340.1
Law—Methodology—Data processing 340.02854
Law—Michigan 349.774
Law—Netherlands 349.492
Law—New Jersey 349.749
Law—New Jersey—Compends 349.749
Law—New Jersey—Outlines, syllabi, etc. 349.749
Law—New York (State) 349.747
Law—New York (State)—Periodicals 349.74705
Law—Nigeria 349.669
Law—Nigeria—Periodicals 349.66905
Law of large numbers 519
Law of the sea 341.45
Law of the sea—Bibliography 016.34145
Law offices 340.068
Law offices—United States 340.068; 340.0681
Law offices—United States—Automation 340.0285; 651.8024344
Law offices—United States—Automation—Periodicals 340.0285; 651.8024344
Law offices—United States—Periodicals 340.068
Law—Pakistan 340.59095491; 349.5491
Law partnership 346.0682
Law partnership—United States 346.730682
Law—Pennsylvania 349.748
Law—Pennsylvania—Periodicals 349.74805
Law—Periodicals 340.05
Law—Philippines 349.599
Law—Philippines—Interpretation and construction 349.599
Law—Philosophy 340.1
Law—Poland 349.438
Law—Portugal 349.469
Law, Primitive 340.52
Law—Psychological aspects 340.019; 340.19
Law reform 340.3
Law reporting 347.016
Law reporting—United States 347.7316
Law reports, digests, etc. 348.026
Law reports, digests, etc.—Florida 348.759046
Law reports, digests, etc.—Nigeria 348.669046
Law reports, digests, etc.—Pakistan 348.5491046
Law reports, digests, etc.—Pennsylvania 348.748046
Law reports, digests, etc.—Philippines 348.599044
Law reports, digests, etc.—United States 348.7326; 348.734; 348.7346
Law reviews 340.05
Law, Romani 340.5208991497
Law School Admission Test 340.076
Law schools 370.0711
Law schools—Accreditation—United States 340.071173
Law schools—United States 340.071173

Law schools—United States—Admission 340.071173
Law schools—United States—Directories 340.071173
Law schools—United States—Entrance examinations 340.076
Law schools—United States—Periodicals 340.071173
Law—Scotland 349.411
Law—Scotland—History 349.41109
Law—South Africa 349.68
Law—Soviet Union 349.47
Law—Soviet Union—History 349.4709
Law—Spain 349.46
Law—Spain—Autonomous communities 349.46
Law students 340.092
Law students—United States 340.092273
Law—Study and teaching 340.071
Law—Study and teaching (Elementary) 372.83
Law—Study and teaching (Elementary)—United States 372.83
Law—Study and teaching—Great Britain 340.071141
Law—Study and teaching (Secondary) 340.0712
Law—Study and teaching (Secondary)—United States 340.071273
Law—Study and teaching—United States 340.071173
Law—Study and teaching—United States—Periodicals 340.071173
Law—Switzerland 349.494
Law—Terminology 340.14
Law—Texas 349.764
Law—Texas—Indexes 348.764028
Law—United States 349.73
Law—United States—Abbreviations 349.730148
Law—United States—Anecdotes 349.73
Law—United States—Bibliography 016.3400973; 016.34973
Law—United States—Bibliography—Catalogs 016.34973
Law—United States—Cases 349.73
Law—United States—Dictionaries 349.7303
Law—United States—Examinations, questions, etc. 349.73076
Law—United States—History 349.7309
Law—United States—Humor 349.730207
Law—United States—Methodology 349.7301
Law—United States—Outlines, syllabi, etc. 349.73
Law—United States—Periodicals 349.7305
Law—United States—Philosophy 349.7301
Law—United States—States 349.73
Law—United States—States—Bibliography 016.34973
Law—United States—Terminology 340.14; 349.73014
Law—Vocational guidance 340.023
Law—Vocational guidance—United States 340.02373
Law—Wisconsin 349.775
Lawless, Brett (Fictitious character) 823.914
Lawless, Jane (Fictitious character) 813.54
Lawless, Jane (Fictitious character)—Fiction 813.54
Lawn care industry 338.175647
Lawn mowers 635.96470284
Lawns 635.9647
Lawrence, D. H. (David Herbert), 1885–1930 823.912
Lawrence, D. H. (David Herbert), 1885–1930—Characters—Women 823.912
Lawrence, D. H. (David Herbert), 1885–1930—Correspondence 823.912
Lawrence, D. H. (David Herbert), 1885–1930—Criticism and interpretation 823.912
Lawrence, D. H. (David Herbert), 1885–1930—Knowledge—Psychology 823.912
Lawrence, D. H. (David Herbert), 1885–1930. Lady Chatterley's lover 823.912

Lawrence, D. H. (David Herbert), 1885–1930—Poetic works 821.912
Lawrence, D. H. (David Herbert), 1885–1930—Political and social views 823.912
Lawrence, D. H. (David Herbert), 1885–1930. Rainbow 823.912
Lawrence, D. H. (David Herbert), 1885–1930—Religion 823.912
Lawrence, D. H. (David Herbert), 1885–1930. Sons and lovers 823.912
Lawrence family 929.20973
Lawrence, Jacob, 1917– 759.13
Lawrence, T. E. (Thomas Edward), 1888–1935 940.415092
Lawson, Henry, 1867–1922 821.8; 823.8
Lawson, Henry, 1867–1922—Criticism and interpretation 823.8
Lawson, Loretta (Fictitious character) 823.914
Lawson, Loretta (Fictitious character)—Fiction 823.914
Lawyers 340.023; 340.092
Lawyers—Fees 344.0128134
Lawyers—Fees—United States 344.730128134
Lawyers—Malpractice 347.05041
Lawyers—Malpractice—United States 347.7305041
Lawyers on television 791.45652344
Lawyers—Salaries, etc. 331.28134
Lawyers—Salaries, etc.—United States 331.28134973
Lawyers—Salaries, etc.—United States—Statistics 331.28134973; 344.730128134021
Lawyers—Specialties and specialists 340.023
Lawyers—United States 340.092273
Lawyers—United States—Accounting 657.024344
Lawyers—United States—Biography 340.092273; 349.730922
Lawyers—United States—Directories 349.73025
Lawyers—United States—Discipline 174.30973
Lawyers—United States—Humor 349.730207
Lawyers—United States—Marketing 340.0688; 349.730688
Lay ministry 253; 262.15
Lay ministry—Catholic Church 253
Lay preaching 251
Layer structure (Solids) 530.411
Layout (Printing) 686.2252
Layton family 929.20973
Le Carré, John, 1931– 823.914
Le Carré, John, 1931– —Criticism and interpretation 823.914
Le Corbusier, 1887–1965 720.92
Le Corbusier, 1887–1965—Criticism and interpretation 720.92
Le Guin, Ursula K., 1929– 813.54
Le Guin, Ursula K., 1929– —Criticism and interpretation 813.54
Le Page, Tim (Fictitious character) 823.914
Le Sueur County (Minn.) 977.6553
Le Sueur County (Minn.)—Maps 912.776553
Lead 669.4
Lead abatement 363.7384; 628.52
Lead-acid batteries 621.312424
Lead based paint 363.1791
Lead industry and trade 338.476694
Lead poisoning 615.925688
Lead poisoning in children 615.925688083
Lead—Toxicology 615.925688
Lead—Toxicology—United States 363.1791
Leaders (Fishing) 688.7912; 799.120284
Leadership 158.4; 303.34; 352.39; 359.33041; 658.4092
Leadership—Moral and ethical aspects 174.4

Leadership—Psychological aspects 158.4
Leadership—Religious aspects 291.61
Leadership—Religious aspects—Christianity 253
Leading ladies (Actresses) 792.028082
Leading men (Actors) 792.028081
Leafhoppers 595.752
League of Nations 341.22
Leaphorn, Joe, Lt. (Fictitious character) 813.54
Leaphorn, Joe, Lt. (Fictitious character)—Fiction 813.54
Lear, Edward, 1812–1888 821.8
Learned institutions and societies 060
Learning 370.1523
Learning ability 370.1523
Learning and scholarship 001.2
Learning contracts 371.39
Learning disabilities 371.9; 618.9285889
Learning disabilities—United States 371.90973
Learning disabled 616.85889
Learning disabled children—Education 371.9
Learning disabled children—Education (Elementary)
    371.90472
Learning disabled children—Education (Elementary)—
    United States 371.904720973
Learning disabled children—Education—Great Britain—
    Curricula 371.90941
Learning disabled children—Education—Handbooks,
    manuals, etc. 371.9
Learning disabled children—Education—Language arts
    371.90446
Learning disabled children—Education—United States
    371.90973
Learning disabled children—United States 371.90973
Learning disabled—Education 371.9; 371.926
Learning disabled—Education (Higher) 371.90474
Learning disabled—Education (Higher)—United States
    371.904740973
Learning disabled—Education—United States 371.90973
Learning disabled teenagers 371.90835
Learning disabled teenagers—Education 371.90835
Learning disabled teenagers—Education—United States
    371.908350973
Learning disabled women 305.90824
Learning in animals 591.514
Learning, Psychology of 153.15; 370.1523
Lease and rental services 333.5
Leases 346.04346
Leases—United States 346.7304346
Least squares 511.42
Leather 675; 675.2
Leather bars 647.95086642
Leather chemicals 675.20284
Leather goods 685
Leather industry and trade 338.47675; 338.47685
Leather industry and trade—Canada 338.476850971
Leather industry and trade—Canada—Statistics—
    Periodicals 338.476850971021
Leather life style (Sexuality) 306.775
Leather life style (Sexuality)—United States 306.775
Leatherwork 745.531
Leaves 575.57; 581.48
Leaves, Fossil 561
Leavis, F. R. (Frank Raymond), 1895– 801.95092
Lebanon 956.92
Lebanon County (Pa.)—Genealogy 929.374819
Lebanon—Economic conditions 330.95692
Lebanon—Economic conditions—Periodicals
    330.95692005
Lebanon—Guidebooks 915.69204; 915.692044
Lebanon—History 956.92

Lebanon—History—Civil War, 1975–1990 956.92044
Lebanon—History—Israeli intervention, 1982–1984
    956.052
Lebanon—Politics and government 956.92
Lebanon—Politics and government—1975–1990
    320.9569209047; 956.92044
Lebesgue integral 515.43
Lecter, Hannibal (Fictitious character) 813.54
Lectins 572.69
Lectionaries 264.029; 264.34
Lectionaries—Texts 264.029; 264.34
Lectionary preaching 251
Lecture method in teaching 371.396
Lecturers 371.10092
Lectures and lecturing 808.51
Lecythidaceae 583.76
Led Zeppelin (Musical group) 782.421660922
Led Zeppelin (Musical group)—Pictorial works
    782.421660922
Lee, Anna (Fictitious character) 823.914
Lee, Anna (Fictitious character)—Fiction 823.914
Lee, Bruce, 1940–1973 791.43028092
Lee County (Ill.) 977.336
Lee County (Ill.)—Maps 912.77336
Lee County (Iowa) 977.799
Lee County (Iowa)—Maps 912.77799
Lee family 929.20973
Lee, Robert E. (Robert Edward), 1807–1870 973.73092
Lee, Robert E. (Robert Edward), 1807–1870—Military
    leadership 355.331092
Lee, Spike 791.430233092
Lee, Will (Fictitious character) 813.54
Leeches 592.66
Leelanau County (Mich.) 977.4635
Leelanau County (Mich.)—Maps 912.774635
Left- and right-handedness 152.335; 370.155
Left and right (Psychology) 152.335
Leg 573.79; 591.479; 612.98
Leg—Amputation 617.584
Leg—Blood-vessels—Surgery 617.413
Leg exercises 613.71
Leg—Wounds and injuries 617.584
Legal advertising 659.1934
Legal aid 362.58
Legal aid—United States 347.7317
Legal aid—United States—Directories 347.7317025
Legal assistance to gays 362.8
Legal assistance to the aged 362.66
Legal assistance to the poor 344.03258
Legal assistance to the poor—United States
    344.7303258; 347.7317
Legal assistants 340.023
Legal assistants—United States 340.02373
Legal assistants—United States—Handbooks, manuals,
    etc. 340.02373
Legal assistants—Vocational guidance—United States
    340.02373
Legal composition 808.06634
Legal consultants 340.092
Legal documents 348
Legal ethics 174.3
Legal ethics—California 174.309794
Legal ethics—Massachusetts 174.309744
Legal ethics—Pennsylvania 174.309748
Legal ethics—Philippines 174.309599
Legal ethics—United States 174.30973
Legal ethics—United States—Cases 174.30973
Legal literature 348
Legal opinions 348.05

Legal photography 363.25
Legal polycentricity 340.9
Legal positivism 340.112
Legal research 340.072
Legal research—Australia 340.072094
Legal research—Canada 340.072071
Legal research—Florida 340.0720759
Legal research—United States 340.072073; 349.73072
Legal secretaries 651.3741
Legal service corporations 362.58
Legal services 347
Legal Services Corporation—Appropriations and
    expenditures 347.730681
Legends 398.2
Legends—China 398.20951
Legends—Germany 398.20943
Legends—Ireland 398.209415
Legends, Jewish 296.19
Legends—Romania 398.209498
Legends—Vietnam 398.209597
Legionnaires' disease 616.241
Legislation 328
Legislation—United States 328.73077
Legislation—United States—Cases 328.73077
Legislative bodies 328
Legislative bodies—Committees 328.365
Legislative bodies—Language 328.014
Legislative bodies—United States 328.73
Legislative bodies—United States—States 328.73
Legislative calendars 328.05
Legislative hearings 328.345
Legislative histories 348.01
Legislative oversight 328.3456
Legislative oversight—United States 328.7307456
Legislative power 328.34; 342.052
Legislative power—United States 328.73076; 342.73052
Legislative reference bureaus 027.65
Legislative reporting 328.1
Legislators 328.092
Legislators—Farewell addresses 328.33
Legislators—Taxation—Law and legislation—United
    States 343.73052
Legislators—United States 328.73073
Legitimacy of governments 320.011
LEGO toys 688.725
Legume industry 338.1733
Legumes 583.74; 633.3
Lehigh Valley Railroad Company 385.09747
Leia, Princess (Fictitious character) 791.437
Leia, Princess (Fictitious character)—Fiction 813.54
Leibniz, Gottfried Wilhelm, Freiherr von, 1646–1716
    193
Leiris, Michel, 1901- 848.91203; 848.91209
Leisure 306.4812; 790.0135
Leisure class 305.52
Leisure—Philosophy 790.013501
Leisure—Social aspects 306.4812
Leisure—Sociological aspects 306.4812
Leisure—Study and teaching 370.119
Leisure suit Larry 793.9325369
Leisure—United States 790.01350973
Lemieux, Mario, 1965- 796.962092
Lemurs 599.83
Lenawee County (Mich.) 977.431
Lenawee County (Mich.)—Maps 912.77431
Lender liability 346.0823
Lender liability—United States 346.73073
L'Engle, Madeleine 813.54
L'Engle, Madeleine—Criticism and interpretation 813.54

Lenin, Vladimir Il'ich, 1870–1924 947.0841092
Lennon, John, 1940–1980 781.66092
Lenong 792.095982
Lenong plays 899.2212
Lenses—Design and construction 681.423
Lenson, Dan (Fictitious character) 813.54
Lent 263.92
Lent—Meditations 242.34
Lent—Prayer-books and devotions 242.34
Lenten sermons 252.62
Leonard family 929.20973
Leonardo, da Vinci, 1452–1519 709.2
Leonardo, da Vinci, 1452–1519—Criticism and
    interpretation 709.2
Leonardo, da Vinci, 1452–1519—Exhibitions 709.2;
    741.945
Leopard 599.7554
Leopardi, Giacomo, 1798–1837 851.7
Leopardi, Giacomo, 1798–1837—Translations into
    English 851.7
Lepidoptera 595.78
Leprosy 616.998
Leptodactylus 597.875
Leptons (Nuclear physics) 539.7211
Leroy, Peter (Fictitious character) 813.54
Leroy, Peter (Fictitious character)—Fiction 813.54
Lesbian activists 305.489664
Lesbian authors 808.899206643; 809.89206643
Lesbian couples 305.489664
Lesbian couples—United States 305.489664
Lesbian erotica 700.4538086643
Lesbian feminist theory 306.7663
Lesbianism 306.7663
Lesbianism in motion pictures 791.43653
Lesbianism—Psychological aspects 306.7663
Lesbianism—United States 306.76630973
Lesbians 305.489664
Lesbians—Caricatures and cartoons 741.5973
Lesbians—Identity 305.489664
Lesbians—Legal status, laws, etc. 346.013
Lesbians—Literary collections 808.80353
Lesbians—Relations with heterosexuals 305.489664
Lesbians—Social life and customs 305.489664
Lesbians—United States 305.4896640973
Lesbians—United States—Literary collections 810.80353
Lesbians—United States—Sexual behavior 306.7663
Lesbians' writings, American 810.809206643
Lesbians' writings, American—History and criticism
    810.99206643
Leskov, N. S. (Nikolaĭ Semenovich), 1831–1895
    891.733
Leskov, N. S. (Nikolaĭ Semenovich), 1831–1895—
    Translations into English 891.733
Lessing, Doris May, 1919- 823.914
Lessing, Doris May, 1919- —Criticism and
    interpretation 823.914
Lesson planning 371.3028
Lestrade, Inspector (Fictitious character) 823.914
Lethal injection (Execution) 364.66
Letocetum Site (England) 936.2468
Letter carriers 383.492
Letter writing 395.4; 808.6
Letter writing—Handbooks, manuals, etc. 808.6
Lettering 745.61
Letters 383.122
Letters of credit 346.096
Letters of credit—United States 346.73096
Letting of contracts 346.023; 658.723

Letting of contracts—United States 346.73023; 658.7230973
Leucocytes 612.112
Leukemia 616.99419
Leukemia in children 618.9299419
Leveraged buyouts—Law and legislation 346.06626
Leveraged buyouts—Law and legislation—United States 346.7306626
Levers 621.8
Levi, Primo 853.914
Lévinas, Emmanuel 194
LeVine, Jack (Fictitious character) 813.54
Lewis and Clark Expedition (1804-1806) 917.8042
Lewis, C. S. (Clive Staples), 1898–1963 823.912
Lewis, C. S. (Clive Staples), 1898–1963. Chronicles of Narnia 823.912
Lewis, C. S. (Clive Staples), 1898–1963—Criticism and interpretation 823.912
Lewis, C. S. (Clive Staples), 1898–1963—Fictional works 823.912
Lewis, C. S. (Clive Staples), 1898–1963—Religion 230.092
Lewis, Carl, 1961– 796.42092
Lewis County (Mo.) 977.8345
Lewis County (Mo.)—Maps 912.778345
Lewis family 929.20973
Lewis, Meriwether, 1774–1809 917.8042092
Lewis, Sinclair, 1885–1951 813.52
Lewis, Sinclair, 1885–1951—Criticism and interpretation 813.52
Lewis, Wyndham, 1882–1957 828.91209
Lewis, Wyndham, 1882–1957—Criticism and interpretation 828.91209
Lewrie, Alan (Fictitious character) 813.54
Lewrie, Alan (Fictitious character)—Fiction 813.54
Lexicography 413.028
Lexicography—Data processing 413.0285
Lexicology 401.4; 420.14
Lexicology—Data processing 401.4
Leys 936.101
Lhasa apso 636.72
Lhasa (China) 951.5
Lhasa (China)—Description and travel 915.15
Li, Bo, 701–762 895.113
Li, Bo, 701–762—Translations into English 895.113
Liability for aircraft accidents 346.0322
Liability for aircraft accidents—United States 346.730322
Liability for elevator accidents 346.0322
Liability for environmental damages 341.762; 344.046
Liability for environmental damages—United States 344.73046
Liability for hazardous substances pollution damages 344.04633
Liability for hazardous substances pollution damages—United States 344.7304633
Liability for nuclear damages 344.0472
Liability for oil pollution damages 344.046332
Liability for sports accidents 346.0322
Liability for sports accidents—United States 346.730322
Liability for traffic accidents 346.0322
Liability for traffic accidents—United States 346.730322
Liability for traffic accidents—United States—Trial practice 346.730322
Liability (Law) 346.02
Libel and slander 346.034
Libel and slander—United States 346.73034
Liberal Party (Great Britain) 324.24106

Liberal Party of Australia 324.29405
Liberalism 148; 320.51; 320.513
Liberalism—History 320.5109
Liberalism (Religion) 230.046
Liberalism—Religious aspects 291.177
Liberalism—United States 320.510973
Liberalism—United States—History 320.510973
Liberalism—United States—History—20th century 320.510973
Liberation theology 230.0464; 261.7
Liberia 966.6
Liberia—History 966.6
Liberia—History—Civil War, 1989– 966.6203
Liberia—History—Civil War, 1989– —Peace 966.6203
Liberia—Social life and customs 966.6
Libertarianism 320.512
Libertarianism—United States 320.512
Libertarians 320.512
Liberty 320.011; 323.44
Liberty—History 323.4409
Liberty in literature 808.80358; 809.93358
Liberty of conscience 323.442
Librarians 020.92
Librarians' unions 331.881102
Libraries 027
Libraries and booksellers 025.23
Libraries and booksellers—Great Britain 025.23
Libraries and community 021.2
Libraries and distance education 025.5; 371.35
Libraries and electronic publishing 025.174
Libraries and Indians 027.63
Libraries and museums 020
Libraries and new literates 027.6
Libraries and new literates—United States 027.6
Libraries and poor children 027.625
Libraries and readers 025.5
Libraries and readers—United States 025.5
Libraries and scholars 025.5
Libraries and society 021.2
Libraries and state 021.8
Libraries and the handicapped 027.663
Libraries and the handicapped—United States 027.6630973
Libraries and the socially handicapped 027.6
Libraries and the visually handicapped 027.663
Libraries and the visually handicapped—United States 027.663
Libraries—Automation 025.00285
Libraries—Automation—Management 025.00285
Libraries—Censorship 025.213
Libraries—Censorship—United States 025.2130973
Libraries—Censorship—United States—Handbooks, manuals, etc. 025.2130973
Libraries—Data processing 025.00285536
Libraries—Evaluation 027.00296
Libraries—Great Britain 027.041
Libraries—Great Britain—History 027.041
Libraries—Great Britain—History—Bibliography 016.027041
Libraries—History 027.009
Libraries—India 027.054
Libraries—India—History 027.054
Libraries—Public relations 021.7
Libraries—Public relations—Handbooks, manuals, etc. 021.7
Libraries—Public relations—United States 021.0973
Libraries—Reorganization 025.1
Libraries—Services to caregivers 027.6
Libraries—Space utilization 022.3

Lipids—Metabolism 612.397
Lipids—Metabolism—Disorders 616.3997
Lipinski, Tara, 1982- 796.912092
Lipoproteins 572.68
Liposomes 571.655
Liposomes—Therapeutic use 615.6; 615.7
Liposuction 617.95
Lipoxygenases 572.791
Lipreading 418
Lipreading—Study and teaching 418
Lipstick 391.63; 646.72; 668.55
Liqueurs 641.255; 663.55
Liquid chromatography 543.0894
Liquid crystal devices 621.38; 621.3815422
Liquid crystal displays 621.3815422
Liquid crystal displays—Materials 621.3815422
Liquid crystal films 530.429
Liquid crystals 530.429
Liquid dielectrics 537.24
Liquid helium 665.822
Liquid-liquid interfaces 541.33
Liquid nitrogen as fuel 665.824
Liquid scintillation counting 539.775
Liquids 530.42; 541.0422
Liquids—Effect of reduced gravity on 620.106
Liquor industry 338.4764125
Liquor laws 344.0541
Liquor laws—New Jersey 344.7490541
Liquors 641.25
Lisbon (Portugal)—Guidebooks 914.6942504;
914.694250444; 946.9425
Lisle, Darina (Fictitious character) 823.914
Lisle, Darina (Fictitious character)—Fiction 823.914
LISP (Computer program language) 005.133
LISREL 519.53502855369
Lissencephaly 616.83
Listening 153.68
Listening—Study and teaching (Elementary) 372.69
Listeriosis 616.92
Liszt, Franz, 1811–1886 780.92
Litanies 264.13
Litanies (Music) 782.292
Literacy 302.2244; 379.24
Literacy programs 374.0124; 379.24
Literacy programs—Nigeria 374.012409669;
379.2409669
Literacy programs—United States 374.01240973;
379.240973
Literacy—Social aspects 302.2244
Literacy—United States 302.22440973
Literary agents 070.52
Literary cookbooks 641.5
Literary forgeries and mystifications 821.6
Literary landmarks—Great Britain 820.9; 820.9941
Literary landmarks—Great Britain—Guidebooks 820.9
Literary landmarks—United States 810.9973
Literary landmarks—United States—Guidebooks
810.9973
Literary museums 807.4
Literary prizes 807.9
Literary recreations 793.73
Literature 800
Literature—Aesthetics 801.93
Literature and history 809.93358
Literature and morals 801.3
Literature and science 809.93356
Literature—Black authors—History and criticism
809.8896
Literature—Collections 808.8

Literature, Comparative 809
Literature, Comparative—Oriental and Western 809
Literature, Comparative—Periodicals 809.005
Literature, Comparative—Themes, motives 809
Literature—Dictionaries 803
Literature—Examinations 807.6
Literature—Examinations, questions, etc. 807.6
Literature—History and criticism 809
Literature—History and criticism—Periodicals 809.005
Literature—History and criticism—Theory, etc. 801.95
Literature, Medieval 808.8002
Literature, Medieval—Criticism, Textual 809.02
Literature, Medieval—History and criticism 809.02
Literature, Modern 808.8003
Literature, Modern—18th century 808.80033
Literature, Modern—18th century—History and criticism
809.033
Literature, Modern—19th century 808.80034
Literature, Modern—19th century—History and criticism
809.034
Literature, Modern—20th century 808.8004
Literature, Modern—20th century—Bio-bibliography
809
Literature, Modern—20th century—History and criticism
809.04
Literature, Modern—20th century—History and
criticism—Theory, etc. 809.04
Literature, Modern—20th century—Periodicals
808.800405
Literature, Modern—20th century—Translations into
English 808.8004
Literature, Modern—History and criticism 809.03
Literature, Modern—History and criticism—Theory, etc.
809.03
Literature—Periodicals 805
Literature—Philosophy 801
Literature rejected for publication 809
Literature—Stories, plots, etc. 808.803548
Literature—Study and teaching 807.1
Literature—Study and teaching (Elementary) 372.64;
372.64044
Literature—Study and teaching (Elementary)—United
States 372.640973
Literature—Study and teaching (Higher) 807.11
Literature—Study and teaching (Higher)—United States
807.1173
Literature—Study and teaching (Secondary) 807.12
Literature—Terminology 801.4
Literature—Translations into English 808.8
Literature—Women authors 808.899287
Literature—Women authors—History and criticism
809.89287
Lithium 553.499
Lithium cells 621.312423
Lithium compounds 546.3812
Lithium—Therapeutic use 616.8918; 616.895061
Lithography 763
Lithography, Electron beam 621.38152; 621.381531
Lithuania 947.93
Lithuania—History 947.93
Lithuania—Periodicals 947.93005
Lithuanian Americans 305.89192073
Little Bear (Fictitious character : Banks) 823.914
Little Bighorn, Battle of the, Mont., 1876 973.82
Little Bighorn, Battle of the, Mont., 1876—Personal
narratives 973.82
Little Bighorn Battlefield National Monument (Mont.)
973.82
Little family 929.20973

Lockhouses 386.48; 728.37
Locks and keys 683.32
Locksmithing 683.3
Locomotive engineers 625.26092
Locomotives 385.36; 625.26
Locomotives—Germany 625.260943
Locomotives—Great Britain 625.260941
Locomotives—Great Britain—History 625.260941
Locomotives—History 625.2609
Locomotives—United States 625.260973
Locus of control 153.8
Łódź (Poland) 943.84
Log cabins 728.73
Log cabins—Design and construction 690.873
Log domain filters 621.3815324
Log-linear models 519.535
Logan County (Ill.)—Maps 912.77357
Logan County (Ky.)—Genealogy 929.376976
Logan County (W. Va.)—Genealogy 929.375444
Logan family (Fictitious characters) 813.54
Logging 634.98
Logic 160
Logic circuits 621.395
Logic circuits—Design and construction 621.395
Logic circuits—Testing 621.3950288
Logic design 621.395
Logic design—Data processing 621.3950285
Logic—History 160.9
Logic, Medieval 160.902
Logic programming 005.115
Logic puzzles 793.73
Logic, Symbolic and mathematical 511.3
Logical positivism 146.42
Logistics 355.411
LOGO (Computer program language) 005.133
Logography 302.2; 658.827
Logotherapy 616.8914
Loire River Valley (France) 944.5
Loire River Valley (France)—Guidebooks 914.4504;
  914.4504839; 914.450484
Lollards 284.3
Lomax, Jacob (Fictitious character) 813.54
Lomax, Jacob (Fictitious character)—Fiction 813.54
Lombardi, Vince 796.332092
Lomé Convention (1975) 341.754302664; 382.9142
Lonchaeidae 595.774
London (England) 942.1
London (England)—Antiquities 942.1
London (England)—Buildings, structures, etc. 720.9421
London (England)—Description and travel 914.2104;
  914.2104859; 914.210486
London (England)—Guidebooks 914.2104; 914.2104859;
  914.210486
London (England)—History 942.1
London (England)—History—17th century 942.106
London (England)—History—18th century 942.107
London (England)—History—Bombardment, 1940–1941
  940.542121
London (England)—Maps 912.421
London (England)—Pictorial works 914.2100222
London (England)—Social life and customs 942.1
London (England)—Social life and customs—19th
  century 942.1081
London, Jack, 1876–1916 813.52
London, Jack, 1876–1916. Call of the wild 813.52
London, Jack, 1876–1916—Criticism and interpretation
  813.52
London Metropolitan Area (England) 942.1
London Metropolitan Area (England)—Maps 912.421

Lone Scouts 369.430973091734
Loneliness 158.2
Loneliness in literature 808.80353; 809.93353
Loneliness—Religious aspects 291.442
Loneliness—Religious aspects—Christianity 248.86
Long distance telephone service 384.64
Long distance telephone service—United States 384.64
Long family 929.20973
Long, Huey Pierce, 1893–1935 976.3062092
Long Island (N.Y.) 974.721
Long Island (N.Y.)—Guidebooks 917.4721
Long-range weather forecasting 551.6365
Long-term care facilities 362.16
Long-term care facilities—Administration 362.16068
Long-term care facilities—Recreational activities
  362.16
Long-term care facilities—Standards—United States
  362.16021873
Long-term care of the sick 362.16; 610.7361
Long-term care of the sick—Government policy—United
  States 362.160973
Long-term care of the sick—Handbooks, manuals, etc.
  610.7361
Long-term care of the sick—United States 362.160973
Long-term care of the sick—United States—Finance
  338.43362160973; 362.160973
Long waves (Economics) 338.542
Longevity 571.879; 612.68
Longevity—Nutritional aspects 613.2
Longfellow, Henry Wadsworth, 1807–1882 811.3
Looms 677.02854
Loons 598.442
Loop tiling (Computer science) 005.453
Loose-leaf binders 651.2
Loose-leaf paper 676.28
Lõõtspill 788.863
Lorain County (Ohio) 977.123
Lorain County (Ohio)—Maps 912.77123
Loran 623.8932
Loran—Atlantic Coast (U.S.)—Tables 623.8932
Lord's prayer 226.9606
Lord's prayer—Meditations 226.9606; 242.722
Lord's prayer—Sermons 226.9606
Lord's Supper 234.163
Lord's Supper—Catholic Church 234.163
Lord's Supper—History 234.16309
Lord's Supper—History—Early church, ca. 30–600
  234.16309015
Lord's Supper (Liturgy) 264.36
Lord's Supper (Liturgy)—Texts 264.36
Los Alamos (N.M.) 978.958
Los Alamos (N.M.)—History 978.958
Los Angeles (Calif.) 979.494
Los Angeles (Calif.)—Civilization 979.494
Los Angeles (Calif.)—Description and travel
  917.949404; 917.94940453; 917.94940454
Los Angeles (Calif.)—Guidebooks 917.949404;
  917.94940453; 917.94940454
Los Angeles (Calif.)—History 979.494
Los Angeles (Calif.)—Maps 912.79494
Los Angeles (Calif.)—Social conditions 979.494
Los Angeles County (Calif.) 979.493
Los Angeles County (Calif.)—Maps 912.79493
Los Angeles Dodgers (Baseball team)
  796.357640979494
Los Angeles Dodgers (Baseball team)—History
  796.357640979494
Los Angeles Lakers (Basketball team)
  796.323640979494

Los Angeles—Lucas

Los Angeles Lakers (Basketball team)—History 796.323640979494
Los Padres National Forest (Calif.) 979.49
Los Padres National Forest (Calif.)—Guidebooks 917.949
Loss control 620.86; 658.408
Loss (Psychology) 155.93
Loss (Psychology) in children 155.93; 155.937083
Loss (Psychology) in literature 808.80353; 809.93353
Loss (Psychology)—Religious aspects 291.442
Loss (Psychology)—Religious aspects—Christianity 248.86
Lost architecture 720
Lost architecture—Illinois—Chicago 720.977311
Lost articles 346.047
Lost continents 001.94
Lost films 791.43
Lost in space (Television program) 791.4572
Lost sheep (Parable) 226.8
Lost tribes of Israel 909.04924
Lotteries 795.38
Lotteries—United States 795.380973
Lottery proceeds 336.17
Lotto 795.38
Lotus 1-2-3 (Computer file) 005.369
Lotus automobiles 629.2222; 629.228
Lotus automobiles—History 629.228; 796.72
Lotus Domino 005.713769
Lotus Freelance plus (Computer file) 006.6869
Lotus HAL 005.369
Lotus Manuscript (Computer file) 652.55369
Lotus Notes 005.369; 650.028553769
Lotus Symphony (Computer file) 005.369; 650.02855369
Loudoun County (Va.)—Genealogy 929.375528
Loudoun County (Va.)—Maps 912.75528
Loudspeakers 621.38284
Loudspeakers—Design and construction 621.38284; 621.38933
Louis XIV, King of France, 1638-1715 944.033092
Louis, Joe, 1914- 796.83092
Louisbourg (N.S.) 971.6955
Louisbourg (N.S.)—History 971.6955
Louisiana 976.3
Louisiana—Description and travel 917.6304; 917.630463; 917.630464
Louisiana—Genealogy 929.3763
Louisiana—Guidebooks 917.6304; 917.630463; 917.630464
Louisiana—History 976.3
Louisiana—History—To 1803 976.3
Louisiana—History—Civil War, 1861-1865 973.7463
Louisiana—Maps 912.763
Louisiana Purchase 973.46
Louisiana—Social life and customs 976.3
Lourdes, Our Lady of 232.917094478
Love 128.46; 152.41
Love—Biblical teaching 241.4
Love in art 700.4543
Love in literature 808.803543; 809.933543
Love in motion pictures 791.436543
Love-letters 808.8693543
Love—Literary collections 808.803543
Love, Pharoah (Fictitious character) 813.54
Love poetry 808.8193543
Love poetry, American 811.00803543
Love poetry, Canadian 811.00803543
Love poetry, Egyptian 893.1100803543
Love poetry, Egyptian—Translations into English 893.1100803543
Love poetry, English 821.00803543
Love poetry, English—Irish authors 821.00803543
Love poetry, Latin 871.0080353; 871.01080353
Love—Religious aspects 291.5677
Love—Religious aspects—Catholic Church 248.482
Love—Religious aspects—Christianity 241.4
Love—Religious aspects—Christianity—Meditations 241.4
Love songs 782.42158
Love stories 808.8385
Love stories, American 813.085; 813.08508
Love stories—Authorship 808.385
Love stories, English 823.085; 823.08508
Love stories, English—History and criticism 823.08509
Lovebirds 636.6864
Lovecraft, H. P. (Howard Phillips), 1890-1937 813.52
Lovecraft, H. P. (Howard Phillips), 1890-1937—Criticism and interpretation 813.52
Lovejoy (Fictitious character) 823.914
Lovejoy (Fictitious character)—Fiction 823.914
Lovelace, Clarisse (Fictitious character) 813.54
Low-allergen gardens 635.9
Low-allergen plants 581.63
Low altitude aeronautics 629.13
Low budget cookery 641.552
Low budget motion pictures 791.4361
Low budget television programs 384.5532
Low-calorie diet 613.25
Low-calorie diet—Recipes 641.5635
Low-carbohydrate diet 613.283
Low-cholesterol diet 613.284
Low-cholesterol diet—Recipes 641.5638
Low-dimensional topology 514.2
Low-fat diet 613.284
Low-fat diet—Recipes 641.5638
Low-impact trail riding 333.78; 798.23
Low-income housing 363.596942
Low-income housing—United States 363.5969420973
Low-intensity conflicts (Military science) 355.0218
Low mass stars 523.8
Low-oxalate diet 613.26
Low power radio 384.5453; 621.384152
Low temperature engineering 621.59
Low temperatures 536.56
Low vision 617.712
Lowell, Robert, 1917-1977 811.52
Lowell, Robert, 1917-1977—Criticism and interpretation 811.52
Lower East Side (New York, N.Y.) 974.71
Lowry family 929.20973
Lowry, Malcolm, 1909-1957 813.54
Lowry, Malcolm, 1909-1957—Criticism and interpretation 813.54
Loxocemidae 597.967
Loyalty 179.9
LSD (Drug) 615.7883
LSD (Drug)—Therapeutic use 616.8918
Lu, Xun, 1881-1936 895.1351; 895.185109
Lu, Xun, 1881-1936—Translations into English 895.185109
Luaus 641.59969
Lubricating oils 665.5385
Lubrication and lubricants 621.89; 665.5385
Lucan, 39-65 873.01
Lucan, 39-65. Pharsalia 873.01
Lucas County (Iowa) 977.7863
Lucas County (Iowa)—Maps 912.777863
Lucas, George 791.430233092
Lucas numbers 512.72

Luce County (Mich.) 977.4925
Luce County (Mich.)—Maps 912.774925
Lucia (Fictitious character) 823.912
Lucia (Fictitious character)—Fiction 823.912
Lucid dreams 154.63
Lucknow (India) 954.2
Lucknow (India)—Civilization 954.2
Lucretius Carus, Titus. De rerum natura 187
Lucy (Prehistoric hominid) 569.9
Ludwig II, King of Bavaria, 1845–1886 943.308092
Luges 796.95
Luggage 685.51
Luggage—Packing 646.6
Lukács, György, 1885–1971 199.439
Lullabies 782.421582
Lullabies—Texts 782.4215820268
Lumbar vertebrae—Surgery 617.471
Lumber 674
Lumber—Drying 674.38
Lumber trade 338.47674
Lumber trade—Canada 338.4767420971
Lumber trade—Canada—Statistics—Periodicals
  338.4767420971021
Lumber trade—United States 338.4767420973
Lumbricidae 592.64
Lumina automobile 629.2222
Lumina automobile—Maintenance and repair 629.28722
Lumina automobile—Maintenance and repair—
  Handbooks, manuals, etc. 629.28722
Lumina van 629.2234
Lumina van—Maintenance and repair 629.28734
Lumina van—Maintenance and repair—Handbooks,
  manuals, etc. 629.28734
Luminescence 535.35
Lunar bases 919.9104
Lunar geology 559.91
Lunar mining 622.09991
Lunar petrology 552.09991
Lunar terminator 523.32
Lunchbox cookery 641.53
Luncheons 641.53
Lunenburg County (Va.)—Genealogy 929.3755643
Lungs 573.25
Lungs—Biopsy 616.240758
Lungs—Cancer 616.99424
Lungs—Diseases 616.24
Lungs—Diseases—Diagnosis 616.24075
Lungs—Diseases, Obstructive 616.24
Lungs—Dust diseases 616.244
Lungs—Pathophysiology 616.2407
Lungs—Physiology 612.2
Lupin, Arsène (Fictitious character) 843.912
Lusitania (Steamship) 940.4514
Lute 787.319; 787.83
Lute ensembles 785.783
Lute music 787.3
Luteoviruses 579.28
Luthéal 786.2
Luther, Martin, 1483–1546 284.1092
Lutheran Church 284.1
Lutheran Church—Catechisms 238.41
Lutheran Church—Doctrines 230.41
Lutheran Church—History 284.109
Lutheran Church—Liturgy 264.041
Lutheran Church—Missions 266.41
Lutheran Church—Sermons 252.041
Lutheran universities and colleges 371.07141
Lutheran women 284.1082
Lutra 599.7692

Luxemburg, Rosa, 1871–1919 335.43092
L'viv (Ukraine) 947.79
Lycopsida, Fossil 561.79
Lydgate, John, 1370?–1451? 821.2
Lydgate, John, 1370?–1451?—Criticism and
  interpretation 821.2
Lyme disease 616.92
Lymph 612.42
Lymph nodes—Biopsy 616.420758
Lymphangiomyomatosis 616.99373
Lymphocytes 616.079
Lymphomas 362.196994; 616.99446
Lynching—United States 364.134
Lynley, Thomas (Fictitious character) 813.54
Lynley, Thomas (Fictitious character)—Fiction 813.54
Lynn family 929.20973
Lynx 599.753
Lyon County (Iowa)—Maps 912.777114
Lyon County (Ky.)—Genealogy 929.3769813
Lyon County (Minn.) 977.6363
Lyon County (Minn.)—Maps 912.776363
Lyotard, Jean François 194
Lyric poetry 808.814
Lyric poetry—History and criticism 809.14
Lyricists 782.0092
Lysosomes 571.655
M.G. automobile 629.2222
Mabinogion 891.6631
Mac OS 005.4469
Macadamia nut 641.345
MacAlister, Marti (Fictitious character) 813.54
MacAlister, Marti (Fictitious character)—Fiction 813.54
Macaques 599.864
Macaronic literature 808.81
MacArthur, Douglas, 1880–1964 355.0092
Macau (China : Special Administrative Region)—
  History—Transfer of Sovereignty from Portugal, 1999
  951.2606
MacBeth, Hamish (Fictitious character) 791.4572;
  823.914
MacBeth, Hamish (Fictitious character)—Fiction
  823.914
Maccabees 933.04
MacDiarmid, Hugh, 1892– 821.912
MacDiarmid, Hugh, 1892– —Criticism and interpretation
  821.912
MacDonald, George, 1824–1905 823.8
MacDonald, George, 1824–1905—Criticism and
  interpretation 823.8
Macdonald, Ross, 1915– 813.52
Macedonia 938.1
Macedonia—History 938.1
Macedonia—History—To 168 B.C. 938.1
MacGowen, Maggie (Fictitious character) 813.54
MacGowen, Maggie (Fictitious character)—Fiction
  813.54
Machado, Antonio, 1875–1939 861.62
Machado, Antonio, 1875–1939—Translations into
  English 861.62
Machiavelli, Niccolò, 1469–1527 320.092
Machiavelli, Niccolò, 1469–1527—Contributions in
  political science 320.092
Machiavelli, Niccolò, 1469–1527. Principe 320.1
Machine appliqué 746.455028
Machine appliqué—Patterns 746.455028
Machine design 621.815
Machine design—Handbooks, manuals, etc. 621.815
Machine guns 623.4424
Machine guns—History 355.82424; 623.4424

Magnetohydrodynamic generators 621.31245
Magnetohydrodynamics 538.6
Magnetosphere 538.766
Magnetotherapy 615.845
Magnets 538.4
Magnets—Experiments 538.078
Magnificat (Music) 782.326
Magritte, René, 1898–1967 759.9493
Magritte, René, 1898–1967—Criticism and
  interpretation 759.9493
Mahābhārata 294.5923
Mahābhārata—Criticism, interpretation, etc.
  294.5923046
Maharashtra (India) 954.792
Maharashtra (India)—Economic policy 338.954792
Mahaska County (Iowa) 977.784
Mahaska County (Iowa)—Maps 912.77784
Mahāwitthayālai Kasētsāt 630.711593
Mahayana Buddhism 294.392
Mahayana Buddhism—Doctrines 294.342042
Maḥfūẓ, Najīb, 1912– 892.736
Maḥfūẓ, Najīb, 1912– —Criticism and interpretation
  892.736
Mahler, Gustav, 1860–1911 780.92
Maḥzor 296.453
Maḥzor. High Holidays 296.431
Maiasaura 567.914
Maigret, Jules (Fictitious character) 843.912
Maigret, Jules (Fictitious character)—Fiction 843.912
Mail order brides 306.82
Mail-order business 381.142; 658.872
Mail-order business—Handbooks, manuals, etc. 658.872
Mail-order business—United States 658.8720973
Mail-order business—United States—Directories
  381.14202573
Mail-order sound recording industry 381.45780266
Mail receiving and forwarding services 383.1
Mailer, Norman 813.54
Mailer, Norman—Criticism and interpretation 813.54
Mailing lists 383
Maimonides, Moses, 1135–1204 296.181
Maine 974.1
Maine (Battleship) 973.895
Maine coon cat 636.83
Maine—Economic policy 338.9741
Maine—Genealogy 929.3741
Maine—Guidebooks 917.4104; 917.410443; 917.410444
Maine—History 974.1
Maine—Maps 912.741
Maine—Politics and government 320.9741; 974.1
Maine—Politics and government—1951– 320.974109045
Maine—Road maps 912.741
Maine—Social life and customs 974.1
Mainstreaming in education 371.252; 371.9046
Mainstreaming in education—United States
  371.90460973
Maintainability (Engineering) 620.0045
Mairs, Nancy, 1943– 818.5409
Maitland, Antony (Fictitious character) 823.914
Maitland, Antony (Fictitious character)—Fiction 823.914
Majolica, Italian—Catalogs 738.372075
Major, John Roy, 1943– 941.0859092
Majorca (Spain) 946.754
Majorca (Spain)—Guidebooks 914.675404;
  914.67540483
Make-ahead cookery 641.555
Maker, Alvin (Fictitious character) 813.54
Maker, Alvin (Fictitious character)—Fiction 813.54
Makeup (Printing) 686.225

Maktab Tarighe Oveyssi Shahmaghsoudi 297.4
Malaboch War, South Africa, 1894 968.2047
Malamud, Bernard 813.54
Malamud, Bernard—Criticism and interpretation 813.54
Malaria 614.532; 616.9362
Malaria—Prevention 614.532
Malaussène, Benjamin (Fictitious character) 843.914
Malawi 968.97
Malawi Congress Party 324.26897083
Malawi—Guidebooks 916.89704; 916.8970442
Malawi—Maps 912.6897
Malaya 959.51
Malaya—Politics and government 959.51
Malaysia 959.5
Malaysia—Civilization 959.5
Malaysia—Constitutional law 342.595
Malaysia—Economic conditions 330.9595; 330.95951
Malaysia—Economic conditions—Periodicals
  330.9595005
Malaysia—Economic policy 338.9595
Malaysia—Guidebooks 915.9504; 915.950454
Malaysia—History 959.5
Malaysia—Politics and government 320.9595; 959.5
Malaysia—Road maps 912.595
Malaysian literature 899.2
Malaysian newspapers 079.595
Malaysian wit and humor, Pictorial 899.2
Malaysians 305.89928
Malcolm Baldrige National Quality Award 658.56207973
Male child care workers 331.7616491081
Male feminists 305.42081
Male friendship 302.34081
Male nude in art 704.9423
Male primary school teachers 372.110081
Malgudi (India : Imaginary place) 823.912
Malgudi (India : Imaginary place)—Fiction 823.912
Malicious accusation 364.156
Mallard 598.4134
Mallarmé, Stéphane, 1842–1898 841.8
Mallarmé, Stéphane, 1842–1898—Criticism and
  interpretation 841.8
Mallarmé, Stéphane, 1842–1898—Translations into
  English 841.8
Malliavin calculus 519.2
Mallory (Fictitious character) 813.54
Mallory (Fictitious character)—Fiction 813.54
Mallory, Kathleen (Fictitious character) 813.54
Mallory, Kathleen (Fictitious character)—Fiction 813.54
Malloy, Claire (Fictitious character) 813.54
Malloy, Claire (Fictitious character)—Fiction 813.54
Malnutrition 363.8
Malocclusion 617.643
Malone, Karl 796.323092
Malone, Scobie (Fictitious character) 823.914
Malone, Scobie (Fictitious character)—Fiction 823.914
Malory, Sheila (Fictitious character) 823.914
Malory, Sheila (Fictitious character)—Fiction 823.914
Malory, Thomas, Sir, 15th cent. 823.2
Malory, Thomas, Sir, 15th cent. Morte d'Arthur 823.2
Malouf, David, 1934– 823.914
Malouf, David, 1934– —Criticism and interpretation
  823.914
Malpractice 344.0411
Malraux, André, 1901–1976 843.912
Malraux, André, 1901–1976—Criticism and
  interpretation 843.912
Malt 572.56
Malt liquors 663.3
Malta 945.85

Malta—Guidebooks 914.58504
Malta—History 945.85
Malta—Pictorial works 945.8500222
Maltese dog 636.76
Maltese fiction 892.793
Malthus, T. R. (Thomas Robert), 1766–1834
 330.153092
Malthusianism 330.153
Mambos (Music) 784.1888
Mamet, David 812.54
Mamet, David—Criticism and interpretation 812.54
Mammal populations 599.1788
Mammalogy 599
Mammals 599
Mammals—Africa 599.096
Mammals—Africa, Southern—Identification 599.0968
Mammals—Anatomy 571.319
Mammals—Behavior 599.15
Mammals—Evolution 576.819
Mammals, Fossil 569
Mammals—Miscellanea 599
Mammals—North America 599.097
Mammals—North America—Identification 599.097
Mammals—Physiology 571.19
Mammals—Reproduction 573.619
Mammaplasty 618.190592
Mammary glands 573.679
Mammoths 567.67; 569.67
Man (Christian theology) 233
Man (Christian theology)—Biblical teaching 233
Man (Theology) 291.22
Man-woman relationships 306.7; 392.6
Man-woman relationships in the Bible 220.83067
Man-woman relationships—United States 306.70973
Managed care plans (Medical care) 362.104258
Managed care plans (Medical care)—Finance
 338.43362104258; 362.1042580681
Managed care plans (Medical care)—Law and
 legislation 344.032104258
Managed care plans (Medical care)—Law and
 legislation—United States 344.73032104258
Managed care plans (Medical care)—Management
 362.104258; 362.104258068
Managed care plans (Medical care)—Moral and ethical
 aspects 174.2
Managed care plans (Medical care)—United States
 362.1042580973
Managed care plans (Medical care)—United States—
 Periodicals 362.104258
Managed mental health care 362.20425
Managed mental health care—United States 362.20425
Managed mental health care—United States—
 Periodicals 362.2905
Management 658; 658.4
Management audit 658.4013
Management—Bibliography 016.658
Management by objectives 658.4012
Management—Data processing 658.05; 658.40285
Management—Developing countries 658.0091724
Management—Dictionaries 658.003
Management—Employee participation 658.3152
Management—Employee participation—Europe
 658.3152094
Management—Employee participation—Great Britain
 331.0112; 658.31520941
Management—Employee participation—India
 658.31520954
Management—Employee participation—Sweden
 658.315209485

Management—Employee participation—United States
 658.31520973
Management—Employee participation—Yugoslavia
 658.315209497
Management—Europe 658.0094
Management games 658.40353
Management—Handbooks, manuals, etc. 658
Management—History 658.009
Management—Humor 658.00207
Management information systems 658.4038;
 658.4038011
Management information systems—Handbooks,
 manuals, etc. 658.4038
Management information systems—Periodicals
 658.403805
Management—Japan 658.00952
Management—Mathematical models 658.4033
Management—Periodicals 658.005
Management—Philosophy 658.001
Management—Psychological aspects 658.0019
Management—Research 658.40072
Management science 658; 658.4
Management—Simulation methods 658.40352
Management—Social aspects 658.408
Management—Statistical methods 658.00727; 658.4033
Management—Study and teaching 658.00711;
 658.400711
Managerial accounting 658.1511
Managerial accounting—Examinations, questions, etc.
 658.1511076
Managerial economics 330.5; 330.5021658
Managing your boss 650.13
Manatee County (Fla.)—Maps 912.75962
Manatees 599.55
Manchester United (Soccer team) 796.334630942733
Manchester United (Soccer team)—History
 796.334630942733
Manchuria (China) 951.8
Mandala 291.37
Mandala (Buddhism) 294.3437
Mandates—Namibia 341.27
Mandela, Nelson, 1918– 968.065092
Mandela, Winnie 968.06092
Mandelbrot sets 514.742
Mandel'shtam, Osip, 1891–1938 891.713
Mandel'shtam, Osip, 1891–1938—Translations into
 English 891.713
Mandó 782.42162914
Mandolin ensembles 785.784
Manet, Edouard, 1832–1883 759.4
Manet, Edouard, 1832–1883—Criticism and
 interpretation 759.4
Maneuvering boards 623.892
Manganese 669.732
Manganese group compounds 546.54
Manganese—Metallurgy 669.732
Manganite 553.4629
Mangifera 583.77
Mangrove ecology 577.698
Mangrove forests 333.75; 577.698
Mangrove plants 583.763
Manhattan (New York, N.Y.) 974.71
Manhattan (New York, N.Y.)—Guidebooks 917.47104;
 917.4710443; 917.4710444
Manhattan (New York, N.Y.)—History 974.71
Manhattan (New York, N.Y.)—Maps 912.7471
Manhattan (New York, N.Y.)—Pictorial works
 779.997471; 917.47100222; 974.7100222

Manhattan Project (U.S.)—History
355.825119097309044
Mania 616.895
Manic-depressive illness 616.895
Manic-depressive illness—Treatment 616.89506
Manichaeism 299.932
Manidae 599.31
Manifolds (Mathematics) 516.07
Manila (Philippines) 959.916
Manila (Philippines)—History 959.916
Manipulation (Therapeutics) 615.82
Manipulative behavior 303.3
Manipulators (Mechanism) 620.46; 629.892
Manipur (India) 954.17
Manipur (India)—Civilization 954.17
Manipur (India)—History 954.17
Manistee County (Mich.) 977.462
Manistee County (Mich.)—Maps 912.77462
Manitoba 971.27
Manitoba—Economic conditions 330.97127
Manitoba—Population—Statistics—Periodicals
304.6097127021
Manitowoc County (Wis.) 977.567
Manitowoc County (Wis.)—Maps 912.77567
Mankiller, Wilma Pearl, 1945– 975.0049755
Mann, Thomas, 1875–1955 833.912
Mann, Thomas, 1875–1955—Criticism and
interpretation 833.912
Mann, Thomas, 1875–1955. Doktor Faustus 833.912
Mann, Thomas, 1875–1955. Magic mountain 833.912
Mann, Thomas, 1875–1955—Translations into English
833.912
Manned space flight 629.45
Manned undersea research stations 551.460072
Mannering, John (Fictitious character) 823.912
Mannering, John (Fictitious character)—Fiction 823.912
Mannerism (Art) 709.031
Manners and customs 390
Manners and customs in literature 808.80355;
809.93355
Manning, Mark (Fictitious character) 813.54
Manors 728.8
Manors—England 728.80942
Manpower planning 658.301
Manpower policy 331.11
Manpower policy—Canada 331.110971
Manpower policy—Developing countries 331.11091724
Manpower policy—Europe 331.11094
Manpower policy—India 331.110954
Manpower policy—United States 331.110973
Mansfield, Katherine, 1888–1923 823.912
Mansfield, Katherine, 1888–1923—Correspondence
823.912
Mansfield, Katherine, 1888–1923—Criticism and
interpretation 823.912
Mansions 728.8
Manson, Charles, 1934– 364.1523092
Mantellidae 597.89
Mantillas 391.43
Mantle, Mickey, 1931– 796.357092
Mantras 294.537
Mantrell, Matthew (Fictitious character) 813.54
Manual training 607.1
Manufacturers' agents 381.4500092
Manufactures 338.4767; 670
Manufactures—Technological innovations 658.514
Manufacturing industries 338.4767
Manufacturing industries—Canada 338.47670971

Manufacturing industries—Canada—Statistics
338.40971021
Manufacturing industries—Canada—Statistics—
Periodicals 338.47670971021
Manufacturing industries—Great Britain 338.47670941
Manufacturing industries—Management 658.5; 670.68
Manufacturing industries—Technological innovations
338.064
Manufacturing industries—Technological innovations—
United States 338.0640973
Manufacturing industries—United States 338.47670973
Manufacturing industries—United States—History
338.47670973
Manufacturing industries—United States—Management
658.50973
Manufacturing industries—United States—Statistics
338.47670973
Manufacturing processes 670
Manufacturing processes—Automation 670.427
Manufacturing processes—Mathematical models
670.15118
Manufacturing resource planning 658.503
Manuscript preparation (Authorship) 808.02; 808.027
Manuscripts 091
Manuscripts, American 091
Manuscripts, English 091
Manuscripts, English—England—London—Catalogs
016.091
Manuscripts, Greek (Papyri) 480
Manuscripts in literature 808.80357
Manuscripts, Medieval 091
Manuscripts—New York (State)—New York 091.097471
Manuscripts—New York (State)—New York—Catalogs
011.31097471
Manuscripts on microfilm 011.36
Manuscripts on microfilm—Catalogs 016.091
Manuscripts (Papyri) 091
Manuscripts, Slovenian 091.094973
Many-body problem 530.144
Many-body problem—Approximation methods
530.144015114
Many-valued logic 511.3
Mao, Zedong, 1893–1976 895.115; 951.050924
Mao, Zedong, 1893–1976—Translations into English
895.115
Maori language 499.442
Maori language—Dictionaries 499.4423
Maori (New Zealand people) 305.899442; 993.004994;
993.00499442; 993.01
Maori (New Zealand people)—Boats 623.820089994
Maori (New Zealand people)—Education 371.82999442
Maori (New Zealand people)—Folklore 398.20899442
Maori (New Zealand people)—Government relations
305.899442; 353.5349944209931
Maori (New Zealand people)—History 993.01
Maori (New Zealand people)—Politics and government
323.1199442
Maori (New Zealand people)—Population
304.608999442
Maori (New Zealand people)—Religion 222.92442
Map collections 912.075
Map-coloring problem 514.22
Map dealers 380.145912
Map drawing 526.0221
Map projection 526.8
Map reading 912.014
Map thefts 025.82
Maple 583.78
Maple (Computer file) 510.2855369

Maple syrup 641.3364
Maple syrup industry 338.476413364
Mappings (Mathematics) 511.33
Mapplethorpe, Robert 770.92
Maps 912
Maps—Bibliography 016.912
Maps—Bibliography—Catalogs 016.912
Maps for the blind 912.0871
Maps, Military 355.00223
Maps, Pictorial 912.0222
Maps—Symbols 912.0148
Maratha (Indic people) 954.792
Maratha (Indic people)—History 954.792
Maratha (Indic people)—History—Sources 954.792
Marathon County (Wis.) 977.529
Marathon County (Wis.)—Maps 912.77529
Marathon running 796.4252
Marathon running—Training 796.4252071
Marble sculpture, Greek 733.3
Marbling 676.234; 745.7
Marbling (Bookbinding) 686.36
MARC formats 025.316
MARC formats—Canada 025.3160971
MARC formats—United States 025.3160973
MARC formats—United States—Handbooks, manuals, etc. 025.3160973
March family (Fictitious characters) 813.4
March family (Fictitious characters)—Fiction 813.4
Marchantia 588.3
Marches (Band) 784.01097
Marches (Orchestra) 784.21897
Marches (Piano) 786.21897
Marching bands 784.83
Marching drills 791.6
Marconi, Guglielmo, marchese, 1874–1937 621.384092
Marcos, Ferdinand E. (Ferdinand Edralin), 1917– 959.9046092
Marcos, Imelda Romualdez, 1929– 959.9046092
Marginal gardening 635.0481
Marginality, Social 305.568
Marginality, Social—United States 305.5680973
Marguerite, Queen, consort of Henry II, King of Navarre, 1492–1549. Heptaméron 843.3
Mari (Extinct city) 939.43
Mariachi 784.4
Mariana Islands 996.7
Mariana Islands—History 996.7
Maricopa County (Ariz.) 979.173
Maricopa County (Ariz.)—Road maps 912.79173
Maricopa Indians 305.89757; 979.10049757
Mariculture 639.8
Marie Antoinette, Queen, consort of Louis XVI, King of France, 1755–1793 944.035092
Marie, de France, 12th cent. 841.1
Marie, de France, 12th cent. Lais 841.1
Marijuana 362.29; 362.295; 613.83; 633.79
Marijuana in popular culture 306.1; 394.14
Marijuana—Law and legislation 344.0545
Marijuana—Law and legislation—United States 344.730545
Marijuana—Therapeutic use 615.32345; 615.7827
Marijuana—Toxicology 615.952345
Marimba music 786.843
Marin County (Calif.) 979.462
Marin County (Calif.)—Guidebooks 917.946204; 917.94620453; 917.94620454
Marin County (Calif.)—Maps 912.79462
Marin, John, 1870–1953 759.13
Marin, John, 1870–1953—Exhibitions 759.13

Marinas 387.15; 627.38
Marinas—Design and construction 627.38
Marine algae 579.8; 639.89
Marine animals 591.77; 599.5
Marine animals—Effect of water pollution on 591.77
Marine animals—Miscellanea 591.77
Marine animals—Pictorial works 591.770222
Marine aquarium animals 639.8
Marine aquarium fishes 639.34
Marine aquariums 597.177073; 639.342
Marine aquariums, Public 597.177073
Marine biological diversity 333.956; 578.77
Marine biological diversity conservation 333.95616
Marine biological diversity conservation—Law and legislation 346.04695616
Marine biology 578.77
Marine biology—Periodicals 578.7705
Marine bioremediation 628.1683
Marine biotechnology 660.609162
Marine chemical ecology 577.714
Marine ecology 577.7
Marine engineering 623.87
Marine engines 623.87
Marine fishes 597.177
Marine geophysics 551.46
Marine invertebrates 592.177
Marine laboratories 578.77072
Marine mammalogy 599.5
Marine mammals 599.5
Marine meteorology 551.509162; 551.5246; 551.69162
Marine meteorology—Charts, diagrams, etc. 551.509162022; 551.52460223
Marine mineral resources 333.8509162; 553.09162
Marine organisms 578.77
Marine paint 623.80284; 667.69
Marine parks and reserves 363.6809162
Marine photography 778.937
Marine phytoplankton 579.81776
Marine plants 579.8177
Marine pollution 363.7394
Marine pollution—Environmental aspects 577.727
Marine pollution—Law and legislation 341.76253
Marine reptiles, Fossil 567.937
Marine resources 333.9164
Marine resources conservation 333.916416; 333.95616
Marine resources conservation—Law and legislation 341.762
Marine resources—Government policy 333.9164
Marine resources—Government policy—United States 333.91640973
Marine science libraries 026.55146
Marine sciences 551.46
Marine sediments 551.46083
Marine zooplankton 592.1776
Marines 359.96
Marinette County (Wis.) 977.533
Marinette County (Wis.)—Maps 912.77533
Marino, Dan, 1961– 796.332092
Marion County (Fla.)—Maps 912.75975
Marion County (Iowa) 977.783
Marion County (Iowa)—Maps 912.77783
Marion County (Mo.) 977.8353
Marion County (Mo.)—Maps 912.778353
Marion County (S.C.)—Genealogy 929.375786
Marion County (Tenn.)—Genealogy 929.376879
Marionettes 745.59224
Maritain, Jacques, 1882–1973 194
Marital conflict 306.872
Marital deduction—Law and legislation 343.0523

Marital deduction—Law and legislation—United States 343.730523

Marital property 346.0166

Marital property—Valuation 346.0166

Marital property—Valuation—United States 346.730166

Marital psychotherapy 616.89156

Marital status 305.906

Mariticide 364.1523

Maritime law 341.7566; 343.096

Maritime law—Great Britain 343.41096

Maritime law—United States 343.73096

Maritime law—United States—Periodicals 343.7309605

Maritime Provinces 971.5

Maritime Provinces—Guidebooks 917.1504; 917.15044

Market segmentation 658.802; 658.835

Market surveys 658.83

Market surveys—United States—Maps 380.10973022

Marketing 380.1; 381; 382; 658.8

Marketing—Bibliography 016.3801

Marketing channels 658.84

Marketing consultants 658.83

Marketing—Data processing 658.800285

Marketing—Decision making 658.802

Marketing—Dictionaries 380.103; 658.8003

Marketing—Handbooks, manuals, etc. 658.8

Marketing—History 380.109; 658.8009

Marketing—Law and legislation 343.084

Marketing—Law and legislation—United States 343.73084

Marketing literature 380.1

Marketing—Management 658.8

Marketing—Management—Data processing 658.800285

Marketing—Management—Handbooks, manuals, etc. 658.8

Marketing—Mathematical models 658.80015118

Marketing—Periodicals 658.8005

Marketing—Planning 658.802

Marketing research 658.83

Marketing research companies 338.76165883

Marketing—United States 658.800973

Marketing—United States—Management 658.00973

Marketing—Vocational guidance 658.80023

Markets 380.1; 381; 382

Markham, Beryl 629.13092

Markham, George (Fictitious character) 823.914

Marklin, Peter (Fictitious character) 823.914

Marklin, Peter (Fictitious character)—Fiction 823.914

Markov processes 519.233

Marlborough, John Churchill, Duke of, 1650–1722 941.069092

Marley, Bob 782.421646092

Marley, Cal (Fictitious character) 813.54

Marley, Plato (Fictitious character) 813.54

Marlins 597.78

Marlowe, Christopher, 1564–1593 822.3

Marlowe, Christopher, 1564–1593—Criticism and interpretation 822.3

Marlowe, Christopher, 1564–1593. Doctor Faustus 822.3

Marlowe, Philip (Fictitious character) 813.52

Marlowe, Philip (Fictitious character)—Fiction 813.52

Marmosets 599.84

Maronite chants 782.32215

Marple, Jane (Fictitious character) 823.912

Marple, Jane (Fictitious character)—Fiction 823.912

Marquetry 745.512

Marquette County (Mich.) 977.496

Marquette County (Mich.)—Maps 912.77496

Marrakech (Morocco) 964.6

Marrakech (Morocco)—Description and travel 916.46

Marriage 306.81; 646.78

Marriage—Biblical teaching 261.83581

Marriage brokerage 392.5

Marriage counseling 362.8286

Marriage counseling—United States 362.8286; 362.82860973

Marriage customs and rites 392.5

Marriage customs and rites, Jewish 296.444

Marriage customs and rites, Medieval 392.50902

Marriage in literature 808.803543; 809.933543

Marriage in popular culture 306.81

Marriage law 346.016

Marriage law—India 346.54016

Marriage law—United States 346.73016

Marriage—Literary collections 808.803543

Marriage—Problems, exercises, etc. 646.78076

Marriage—Psychological aspects 155.645

Marriage—Religious aspects 291.441

Marriage—Religious aspects—Catholic Church 261.83581

Marriage—Religious aspects—Christianity 261.83581

Marriage—Religious aspects—Judaism 296.444

Marriage service 265.5; 392.5

Marriage—United States 306.810973

Marriage—United States—Psychological aspects 306810973

Marriages of celebrities 392.508621

Married people 306.872

Married people—Finance, Personal 332.0240655

Married people—Religious life 248.844

Married people—United States—Psychology 155.6450973

Married women 306.872

Married women—Employment 331.43

Married women—Employment—United States 331.430973

Married women—Legal status, laws, etc. 346.0163

Married women—Legal status, laws, etc.—Great Britain—History 346.410163

Mars landing sites 629.43543

Mars (Planet) 523.43

Mars (Planet)—Exploration 523.430723; 919.92304

Mars probes 629.43543

Marsala, Cat (Fictitious character) 813.54

Marsala, Cat (Fictitious character)—Fiction 813.54

Marsalis, Wynton, 1961– 788.92092

Marsh ecology 577.68

Marsh family 929.20973

Marsh, Ngaio, 1895–1982 823.912

Marshall, Alfred, 1842–1924 330.157092

Marshall County (Ala.)—Genealogy 929.376194

Marshall County (Ky.) 976.991

Marshall County (Ky.)—Genealogy 929.376991

Marshall, George C. (George Catlett), 1880–1959 973.918092

Marshall, John, 1755–1835 347.732634

Marshall Plan 338.917304

Marshall, Thurgood, 1908–1993 347.732634

Marshmallow 641.853

Marston, John, 1575?–1634 822.3

Marston, John, 1575?–1634—Criticism and interpretation 822.3

Marsupials 599.2

Martel family (Fictitious characters) 823.914

Martes 599.7665

Martha's Vineyard (Mass.) 974.494

Martha's Vineyard (Mass.)—Guidebooks 917.4494

Martí, José, 1853–1895 972.9105092

Martial artists 796.8092; 796.815092
Martial arts 796.8; 796.81
Martial arts—China 796.80951
Martial arts injuries 617.1027
Martial arts—Psychological aspects 796.8019
Martial arts schools 796.8071
Martial arts—Study and teaching 796.8071
Martial arts—Training 796.8071
Martial law 342.0628
Martial law—Philippines 342.5990628
Martin County (Minn.) 977.6232
Martin County (Minn.)—Maps 912.776232
Martin, Dorothy (Fictitious character) 813.54
Martin, Dorothy (Fictitious character)—Fiction 813.54
Martin family 929.20973
Martin Luther King, Jr., Day 394.261
Martineau, Harriet, 1802–1876 823.8
Martínez, María Montoya 738.092
Martingales (Mathematics) 519.287
Martinis 641.874
Marvel Comics Group 741.5973
Marvell, Andrew, 1621–1678 821.4
Marvell, Andrew, 1621–1678—Criticism and
  interpretation 821.4
Marx, Groucho, 1891–1977 792.7028092
Marx, Karl, 1818–1883 335.4092
Marx, Karl, 1818–1883. Kapital 335.41
Marxian economics 335.4
Marxian school of sociology 301.01
Marxist criticism 801.95
Mary I, Queen of England, 1516–1558 942.054092
Mary, Blessed Virgin, Saint 232.91
Mary, Blessed Virgin, Saint—Apparitions and miracles
  232.917
Mary, Blessed Virgin, Saint—Apparitions and miracles—
  Bosnia and Hercegovina—Medugorje 232.9170949742
Mary, Blessed Virgin, Saint—Art 704.94855; 755.55
Mary, Blessed Virgin, Saint—Biblical teaching 232.91
Mary, Blessed Virgin, Saint—Biography 232.91
Mary, Blessed Virgin, Saint—Cult 232.91
Mary, Blessed Virgin, Saint—History of doctrines 232.91
Mary, Blessed Virgin, Saint—Meditations 232.91
Mary, Blessed Virgin, Saint—Prayer-books and
  devotions 242.74
Mary, Blessed Virgin, Saint—Sermons 232.91
Mary, Blessed Virgin, Saint—Theology 232.91
Mary, Blessed Virgin, Saint—Visitation 232.91
Mary Helen, Sister (Fictitious character) 813.54
Mary Helen, Sister (Fictitious character)—Fiction
  813.54
Mary Magdalene, Saint 226.092
Mary, of Bethany, Saint 226.4092
Mary, Queen of Scots, 1542–1587 941.105092
Mary Teresa, Sister (Fictitious character) 813.54
Mary Teresa, Sister (Fictitious character)—Fiction
  813.54
Maryland 975.2
Maryland Campaign, 1862 973.7336
Maryland—Census, 1990 304.60975209049
Maryland—Economic conditions 330.9752
Maryland—Genealogy 929.3752
Maryland—Guidebooks 917.5204; 917.520443;
  917.520444
Maryland—History 975.2
Maryland—History—Colonial period, ca. 1600–1775
  975.202
Maryland—Maps 912.752
Maryland—Politics and government 975.2

Maryland—Politics and government—To 1775
  320.975209033; 975.202
Masada Site (Israel) 933
Masai (African people) 967.62004965
Mascarene literature (French) 840
Mascots 302.2223
Masculinity 155.332
Masers 621.381336
Mask making 731.75
Masking tape 668.38
Masks 391.434
Masks—Social aspects 391.434
Masochism 616.85835
Mason County (Ill.)—Maps 912.773553
Mason County (Ky.)—Genealogy 929.3769323
Mason County (Mich.)—Maps 912.77461
Mason family 929.20973
Mason, Perry (Fictitious character) 791.4575; 813.52
Mason, Perry (Fictitious character)—Fiction 813.52
Masonry 624.183; 693.1
Masonry—Standards 693.10218
Masonry—Standards—United States 693.1021873
Masorah 221.44
Masques 782.15
Mass 264.02036; 264.36
Mass burials 363.75
Mass—Celebration 264.02036
Mass media 302.23
Mass media and children 302.23083
Mass media and culture 302.23
Mass media and culture—United States 302.230973
Mass media and education 306.43
Mass media and immigrants 302.2308691
Mass media and judicial power 347.012
Mass media and language 302.23014
Mass media and minorities 302.2308
Mass media and minorities—United States 302.2308
Mass media and public opinion 302.23
Mass media and publicity 302.23; 659
Mass media and technology 302.23
Mass media and women 302.23082
Mass media and youth 384.5443
Mass media—Audiences 302.23
Mass media—Australia 302.230994
Mass media—Authorship 808.066302
Mass media—Canada 302.230971
Mass media criticism 302.23
Mass media—Dictionaries 302.2303
Mass media—Directories 302.23025
Mass media—Economic aspects 338.4730223
Mass media in education 371.358
Mass media in health education 613.071
Mass media—India 302.230954
Mass media—Influence 302.23
Mass media—Law and legislation 343.099
Mass media—Law and legislation—United States
  343.73099
Mass media—Law and legislation—United States—Cases
  343.73099
Mass media—Methodology 302.2301
Mass media—Objectivity 302.23
Mass media—Periodicals 302.2305
Mass media—Philosophy 302.2301
Mass media—Political aspects 302.23
Mass media—Political aspects—Canada 302.230971
Mass media—Political aspects—United States
  302.230973
Mass media—Psychological aspects 302.23019
Mass media—Ratings 302.23

Mass media—Religious aspects 291.175
Mass media—Religious aspects—Christianity 261.52
Mass media—Research 302.23072
Mass media—Research—Methodology 302.23072
Mass media—Social aspects 302.23
Mass media—Social aspects—United States 302.230973
Mass media—Soviet Union 302.230947
Mass media—Study and teaching 302.23071
Mass media—Technological innovations 302.23
Mass media—United States 302.230973
Mass media—United States—Directories 302.2302573
Mass media—United States—History 302.230973
Mass media—United States—Periodicals 302.23097305
Mass murder 364.1523
Mass murder investigation 363.259523
Mass murder—United States 364.15230973
Mass murderers 364.1523
Mass (Music) 782.323
Mass spectrometry 539.60287; 572.36
Mass transfer 660.28423
Massac County (Ill.) 977.3997
Massac County (Ill.)—Genealogy 929.3773997
Massachusetts 974.4
Massachusetts—Economic conditions 330.9744
Massachusetts—Economic policy 338.9744
Massachusetts—Genealogy 929.3744
Massachusetts—Guidebooks 917.4404; 917.440443;
   917.440444
Massachusetts—History 974.4
Massachusetts—History—Colonial period, ca. 1600–
   1775 974.402
Massachusetts—History—Colonial period, ca. 1600–
   1775—Sources 974.402
Massachusetts—Maps 912.744
Massachusetts—Road maps 912.744
Massacres—India—Amritsar 954.0357
Massage 615.822
Massage for infants 649.4
Massage schools 615.8220715
Massage therapy 615.822
Mast cell disease 616.77
Master of business administration degree 650.0711;
   658.00711
Master of business administration degree—United
   States 658.U8740071173
Master of business administration degree—United
   States—Directories 658.0071173
Master teachers 371.1; 371.1412
Masters Golf Tournament 796.3527
Masters, Molly (Fictitious character) 813.54
Masts and rigging 623.862
Masturbation 306.772
Masuto, Masao (Fictitious character) 813.52
Masuto, Masao (Fictitious character)—Fiction 813.52
Matarenga (Africa : Imaginary place) 813.54
Matchbox toys 688.72
Matchbox toys—Collectors and collecting 629.221075;
   688.72075
Mate selection 306.82; 646.77
Mate selection—United States 646.770973
Materia medica 615.1
Materia medica, Vegetable 615.32; 615.321
Materia medica, Vegetable—China 615.3210951
Materia medica, Vegetable—India 615.320954;
   615.3210954
Material culture 306; 930.1
Material culture—United States 973
Materialism 146.3
Materialized views (Computer science) 005.74

Materials 620.11
Materials at high pressures 620.1123; 620.11242
Materials at high temperatures 620.11217
Materials at low temperatures 620.11216
Materials—Biodeterioration 620.11223
Materials—Creep 620.11233
Materials—Dictionaries 620.1103
Materials—Dynamic testing 620.1125
Materials—Effect of radiation on 620.11228
Materials—Effect of space environment on 620.112;
   620.419
Materials—Encyclopedias 620.1103
Materials—Fatigue 620.1126
Materials—Fatigue—Testing 620.1126
Materials—Handbooks, manuals, etc. 620.11
Materials handling 658.781
Materials management 658.7
Materials—Mathematical models 620.11015118
Materials—Mechanical properties 620.11292
Materials—Microscopy 620.11299
Materials—Periodicals 620.1105
Materials—Research 620.11072
Materials science 620.11
Materials—Testing 620.110287
Materials testing laboratories 620.110287
Materials—Thermal properties 620.11296
Maternal health services 362.1982
Maternal health services—United States 362.198200973
Maternity clothes 646.47
Maternity leave 331.44
Maternity leave—Law and legislation 344.0144
Maternity leave—Law and legislation—United States
   344.730144
Maternity nursing 610.73678
Maternity nursing—Handbooks, manuals, etc.
   610.73678
Mateship (Australia) 177.62; 302.34
Math anxiety 510.71
Mathematica (Computer file) 510.2855369
Mathematica (Computer program language)
   510.2855133
Mathematical ability 153.9
Mathematical ability—Sex differences 155.3
Mathematical analysis 515
Mathematical analysis—Foundations 515
Mathematical analysis—Periodicals 515.05
Mathematical analysis—Problems, exercises, etc.
   515.076
Mathematical constants 513
Mathematical instruments 510.284
Mathematical linguistics 410.151
Mathematical literature 016.510
Mathematical models 511.8
Mathematical models—Periodicals 511.805
Mathematical notation 510.148
Mathematical optimization 519.3
Mathematical physics 530.15
Mathematical physics—Periodicals 530.1505
Mathematical recreations 793.74
Mathematical statistics 519.5
Mathematical statistics—Asymptotic theory 519.5
Mathematical statistics—Data processing 519.50285
Mathematical statistics—History 519.509
Mathematical statistics—Periodicals 519.505
Mathematicians 510.92
Mathematicians—Biography 510.922
Mathematics 510
Mathematics, Ancient 510.901
Mathematics, Arab 510.89927

Mazda trucks—Maintenance and repair—Handbooks, manuals, etc. 629.28732
Maze puzzles 793.738
Mazurkas 784.1884
McAuliffe, Christa, 1948–1986 629.450092
McCadden, Carl (Fictitious character) 823.914
McCain family 929.20973
McCandler, Doan (Fictitious character) 813.54
McCarthy, Cormac, 1933– 813.54
McCarthy, Cormac, 1933– —Criticism and interpretation 813.54
McCarthy, Mary, 1912– 818.5209
McCartney, Paul 782.42166092
McCaskill family (Fictitious characters) 813.54
McChesney, Emma (Fictitious character) 813.52
McCleet, Adam (Fictitious character) 813.54
McCleet, Adam (Fictitious character)—Fiction 813.54
McClellan family 929.20973
McClintoch, Lara (Fictitious character) 813.54
McCone, Sharon (Fictitious character) 813.54
McCone, Sharon (Fictitious character)—Fiction 813.54
McCullers, Carson, 1917–1967 813.52
McCullers, Carson, 1917–1967—Criticism and interpretation 813.52
McCunn, Dickson (Fictitious character) 823.912
McCunn, Dickson (Fictitious character)—Fiction 823.912
McCurdy family 929.20973
McDaniel family 929.20973
McDonald family 929.20973
McDonald's Corporation 338.7616479573
McDonald's Corporation—Collectibles—Catalogs 688.72075
McDonough County (Ill.) 977.342
McDonough County (Ill.)—Maps 912.77342
McDoodle, Polly (Fictitious character) 813.54
McEntire, Reba 782.421642092
McFarland family 929.20973
McGarr, Peter (Fictitious character) 813.54
McGarr, Peter (Fictitious character)—Fiction 813.54
McGarvey, Kirk (Fictitious character) 813.54
McGee, Travis (Fictitious character) 813.54
McGee, Travis (Fictitious character)—Fiction 813.54
McGrail, Nuala Anne (Fictitious character) 813.54
McGrail, Nuala Anne (Fictitious character)—Fiction 813.54
McGwire, Mark, 1963– 796.357092
McHenry County (Ill.) 977.322
McHenry County (Ill.)—Maps 912.77322
McHenry County (N.D.) 978.462
McHenry County (N.D.)—Maps 912.78462
McKay family 929.20973
McKee family 929.20973
McKenna, Brian (Fictitious character) 813.54
McKinley, William, 1843–1901 973.88092
McLanahan, Patrick (Fictitious character) 813.54
McLean County (Ill.) 977.359
McLean County (Ill.)—Maps 912.77359
McLean County (N.D.) 978.475
McLean County (N.D.)—Maps 912.78475
McLean family 929.20973
McLeish, John (Fictitious character) 823.914
McLeish, John (Fictitious character)—Fiction 823.914
McLeod family 929.20973
McLuhan, Marshall, 1911– 302.23092
McMillan family 929.20973
McMurtry, Larry 813.54
McMurtry, Larry—Criticism and interpretation 813.54
McNair, Hattie (Fictitious character) 813.54
McNally, Archy (Fictitious character) 813.54

McNally, Archy (Fictitious character)—Fiction 813.54
McRae family 929.20973
McTavish, Stoner (Fictitious character) 813.54
McTavish, Stoner (Fictitious character)—Fiction 813.54
McWhinny, Tish (Fictitious character) 813.54
McWhinny, Tish (Fictitious character)—Fiction 813.54
Mead 641.229
Mead, George Herbert, 1863–1931 191
Mead, Margaret, 1901–1978 306.092
Meadow ecology 577.46
Meadowlarks 598.874
Mealybugs 595.752
Mean field theory 530.144
Meaning (Philosophy) 121.68
Means tests 361.3
Measure theory 515.42
Measuring instruments 681.2
Meat 641.36
Meat industry and trade 338.176
Meat industry and trade—United States—Statistics 338.17600973021
Meat industry and trade—United States—Statistics—Periodicals 338.17600973021
Meat inspection 363.1929; 664.907
Meat inspection—United States 363.1929
Meat loaf 641.824
Meat slicing machines 681.7664
Mecca (Saudi Arabia) 953.8
Mechanical alloying 671.37
Mechanical drawing 604.2
Mechanical engineering 621
Mechanical engineering—Dictionaries 621.03
Mechanical engineering—Handbooks, manuals, etc. 621
Mechanical engineering laboratories 621.07
Mechanical engineering—Periodicals 621.05
Mechanical engineering—Problems, exercises, etc. 621.076
Mechanical horses (Commercial vehicles) 388.344; 629.224
Mechanical movements 621.811
Mechanical musical instruments 786.6
Mechanical toys 745.592
Mechanical wear 620.11292
Mechanics 531
Mechanics, Analytic 530
Mechanics, Analytic—Periodicals 530.05
Mechanics, Applied 620.1
Mechanics, Applied—Mathematics 620.100151
Mechanics, Applied—Periodicals 620.1005
Mechanics' liens 346.024
Mechanics' liens—California 346.794024
Mechanics' liens—Florida 346.759024
Mechanics' liens—Texas 346.764024
Mechatronics 621; 621.3
Mecklenburg County (Va.)—Genealogy 929.3755645
Mecosta County (Mich.)—Maps 912.77452
Medal of Honor 355.1342
Medals 737.22
Medea (Greek mythology) in literature 808.80351; 809.93351
Media consultants 659.2
Media literacy 302.23
Media programs (Education) 371.33; 371.335; 372.672
Media programs (Education)—Administration 371.33
Mediation 303.69; 347.09
Mediation, International 341.52
Mediation—United States 347.739
Medicaid 368.4200973
Medicaid—California 368.42009794

Medical microbiology—Examinations, questions, etc. 616.01076
Medical microbiology—Handbooks, manuals, etc. 616.01
Medical microbiology—Laboratory manuals 616.01078
Medical microbiology—Outlines, syllabi, etc. 616.01
Medical mycology 616.015
Medical offices 610.682
Medical offices—Management 651.961
Medical parasitology 616.96
Medical personnel 610.69
Medical personnel and patient 610.696
Medical personnel-caregiver relationships 610.696
Medical personnel—Malpractice 344.0411
Medical personnel—Malpractice—United States 344.730411
Medical personnel—United States 610.69
Medical personnel, Writings of 808.899261
Medical physics 610.153
Medical policy 362.1
Medical policy—Australia 362.10994
Medical policy—Europe 362.1094
Medical policy—Great Britain 362.10941
Medical policy—India 362.10954
Medical policy—Oregon 362.109795
Medical policy—United States 362.10973
Medical policy—United States—Periodicals 362.1097305
Medical policy—United States—States 362.10425; 362.10973
Medical protocols 362.1068
Medical publishing 070.57
Medical records 651.504261
Medical records—Access control 651.504261
Medical records—Data processing 651.5042610285
Medical records—Law and legislation 344.041
Medical records—Law and legislation—United States 344.73041
Medical records—Management 651.504261
Medical rehabilitation 617.03
Medical savings accounts 338.433621
Medical sciences 610
Medical sciences—Examinations, questions, etc. 610.76
Medical screening 362.177
Medical social work 362.10425
Medical social work—United States 362.10425
Medical statistics 610.21; 610.727
Medical students 610.88375
Medical supplies 610.284
Medical technology 610.28
Medical technology—United States 610.28
Medical telematics 025.0661
Medical transcription 653.18
Medical transcription—Handbooks, manuals, etc. 653.18
Medical virology 616.0194
Medical writing 808.06661
Medical writing—Handbooks, manuals, etc. 808.06661
Medically uninsured persons 362.10425; 368.382
Medically uninsured persons—Medical care—United States 362.108
Medically uninsured persons—United States 368.38200973
Medicare 368.42600973
Medicare—Claims administration 368.42600973
Medicare—Costs 368.42600973
Medicare—Finance 368.42600973
Medicare fraud 345.730263
Medicare—Handbooks, manuals, etc. 344.730226
Medicare—Law and legislation 344.730226

Medication abusers 362.299
Medicinal plants 581.634; 633.88
Medicinal plants in literature 808.80356; 809.93356
Medicinal plants—India 615.3210954
Medicine 610
Medicine—Abbreviations 610.148
Medicine, Ancient 610.93
Medicine and psychology 610.19
Medicine and psychology—Periodicals 610.19
Medicine—Anecdotes 610
Medicine, Arab 610.9174927
Medicine, Arab—History 610.9174927
Medicine, Ayurvedic 615.53
Medicine, Ayurvedic—India 615.530954
Medicine—Bibliography 016.61
Medicine—Bibliography—Catalogs 016.61
Medicine—Caricatures and cartoons 741.5973
Medicine, Chinese 610.951
Medicine—Computer network resources 025.0661
Medicine—Computer simulation 610.113
Medicine—Data processing 610.285
Medicine—Decision making 610
Medicine—Dictionaries 610.3; 610.321
Medicine—Early works to 1800 610
Medicine—Early works to 1800—Bibliography 016.61
Medicine—Early works to 1800—Bibliography—Catalogs 016.61
Medicine, Egyptian 610.932
Medicine—Encyclopedias 610.3
Medicine—Examinations 610.76
Medicine—Examinations, questions, etc. 610.76
Medicine, Experimental 619
Medicine—Formulae, receipts, prescriptions 615.13
Medicine, Greek and Roman 610.938
Medicine—Handbooks, manuals, etc. 610
Medicine—History 610.9
Medicine—Humor 610.207
Medicine in literature 808.80356; 809.93356
Medicine in the Bible 220.861
Medicine, Industrial 616.9803
Medicine—Mathematical models 610.15118
Medicine, Medieval 610.902
Medicine, Military 616.98023
Medicine, Oriental 610.95
Medicine—Periodicals 610.5
Medicine—Philosophy 610.1
Medicine, Physical 615.82
Medicine, Popular 610
Medicine, Popular—Encyclopedias 610.3
Medicine, Popular—Handbooks, manuals, etc. 610
Medicine, Popular—Periodicals 610.5
Medicine—Practice 610.68
Medicine—Practice—Accounting 657.834
Medicine—Practice—Economic aspects 610.681
Medicine, Preventive 613
Medicine, Psychosomatic 616.08
Medicine—Religious aspects 291.175
Medicine—Religious aspects—Christianity 261.561
Medicine—Religious aspects—Judaism 296.376
Medicine—Research 610.72
Medicine—Research—Methodology 610.72
Medicine—Research—Statistical methods 610.727
Medicine—Research—United States 610.72073
Medicine, State 362.1
Medicine, State—United States 362.10973
Medicine—Study and teaching 610.711
Medicine—Study and teaching (Continuing education) 610.715
Medicine—Terminology 610.14

Men's choral societies 782.806
Men's clothing 646.32; 646.402
Men's clothing—Periodicals 391.105
Men's movement 305.32
Men's movement—United States 305.320973
Menstrual cycle 612.662
Menstruation 612.662
Menstruation disorders 618.172
Mensuration 530.8
Mental discipline 153.42
Mental healing 615.852
Mental health 362.2
Mental health boards 353.64225
Mental health—Canada—Statistics 362.20971021
Mental health consultation 362.204256
Mental health counseling 362.204256
Mental health courts 344.0440269
Mental health education 362.2072
Mental health facilities 362.21
Mental health laws 344.044
Mental health laws—United States 344.73044;
346.730138
Mental health policy 362.2
Mental health policy—United States 362.20425
Mental health—Religious aspects 291.178322
Mental health—Religious aspects—Christianity 248.862
Mental health services 362.2
Mental health services—Administration 362.2068
Mental health services—United States 362.20973
Mental health services—Virginia 362.209755
Mental illness 362.2; 616.89
Mental illness—Chemotherapy 616.8918
Mental illness—Chemotherapy—Handbooks, manuals,
etc. 616.8918
Mental illness—Classification 616.890012; 616.89075
Mental illness—Diagnosis 616.89075
Mental illness—Diagnosis—Handbooks, manuals, etc.
616.89075
Mental illness—Etiology 616.89071
Mental illness—Examinations, questions, etc.
616.890076
Mental illness—Genetic aspects 616.89042
Mental illness in literature 808.80353; 809.93353
Mental illness—Nutritional aspects 616.89071; 616.891
Mental illness—Pathophysiology 616.8907
Mental illness—Prevention 362.20425; 616.8905
Mental illness—Treatment 616.891
Mental representation 153
Mental retardation 362.3; 616.8588
Mentally handicapped 362.3
Mentally handicapped—Care 362.38
Mentally handicapped—Care—Great Britain 362.380941
Mentally handicapped children 305.90824; 371.928;
649.1528
Mentally handicapped children—Education 371.92;
371.928
Mentally handicapped children—Life skills guides
649.1528
Mentally handicapped—Education 371.92; 371.928
Mentally handicapped—Services for 362.38
Mentally handicapped—Services for—Great Britain
362.380941
Mentally handicapped—Services for—United States
362.380973
Mentally handicapped—United States 362.380973
Mentally ill 362.2
Mentally ill children 305.90824
Mentally ill children—Education 371.94
Mentally ill—Family relationships 616.89

Mentally ill—Home care 362.24
Mentally ill offenders 364.38
Mentally ill prisoners 365.60874
Mentally ill—Rehabilitation 616.8903
Mentoring in business 650.13; 658.3124
Mentoring in education 371.102
Mentoring in education—Great Britain 371.1020941
Mentoring in social service 361.06
Mentoring of authors 808.02
Menus 642
Menzies, Robert Gordon, Sir, 1894–1978 994.05092
Mercantile system 330.1513
Mercedes automobile 629.2222
Mercedes automobile—History 629.2222
Mercenary troops 355.354
Mercer County (Ill.)—Maps 912.773395
Mercer County (N.J.)—Maps 912.74965
Merchandise licensing 658.800687
Merchandising 381
Merchant marine 387.5
Merchant marine—Great Britain 387.50941
Merchant marine—United States 387.50973
Merchant marine—United States—History 387.50973
Merchant marine—Vocational guidance—United States
387.502373
Merchant mariners 387.5092
Merchant mariners—Great Britain 305.93875
Merchant mariners—Legal status, laws, etc. 341.75665
Merchant ships 387.2; 623.82
Merchants in literature 808.8035238; 809.9335238
Mercury 546.663
Mercury automobile 629.2222
Mercury cadmium tellurides 546.6632
Mercury—Environmental aspects 363.7384
Mercury (Planet) 523.41
Mercury—Toxicology 615.925663
Meredith, George, 1828–1909 823.8
Meredith, George, 1828–1909—Criticism and
interpretation 823.8
Merkel cell carcinoma 616.99488
Merkel cells 573.87536; 611.0181; 611.88
Merleau-Ponty, Maurice, 1908–1961 194
Merlin (Legendary character) in literature 398.45;
808.80351; 809.93351
Merlot (Wine) 641.2223; 663.223
Meroe (Extinct city) 939.78
Merrick County (Neb.) 978.2423
Merrick County (Neb.)—Maps 912.782423
Merrivale, Henry, Sir (Fictitious character) 813.52
Merrivale, Henry, Sir (Fictitious character)—Fiction
813.52
Merton, Thomas, 1915–1968 271.12502; 818.5409
Merton, Thomas, 1915–1968—Correspondence
271.12502; 818.5409
Merton, Thomas, 1915–1968—Diaries 271.12502
Mesa Verde National Park (Colo.) 978.827
Meson spectroscopy 539.72162
Mesons 539.72162
Mesoscopic phenomena (Physics) 530
Mesquite 583.748
Messenger RNA 572.88
Messerschmitt 109 (Fighter planes) 623.7464
Messiah 291.61
Messiah—Judaism 296.336
Messiah—Prophecies 232.12
Messianism 291.23
Messina (Italy) 945.811
Metabolism 572.4
Metabolism—Disorders 571.944; 616.39

Metabolism, Inborn errors of 616.39042
Metabolism, Inborn errors of—Diagnosis 616.3904275
Metabolism, Secondary 572.4
Metadata 025.3
METAFONT 686.22544
Metal castings 671.2
Metal cleaning 671.7
Metal coating 671.73
Metal crystals 548
Metal-cutting 671.53
Metal-cutting tools 671.53
Metal foams 620.16; 671.8
Metal houses 693.7; 728
Metal icons 739
Metal organic chemical vapor deposition 621.38152
Metal oxide semiconductors 537.6223; 621.38152
Metal oxide semiconductors, Complementary 537.6223; 621.395; 621.39732
Metal oxide semiconductors, Complementary—Computer-aided design 621.395
Metal polishes 667.72; 671.72
Metal-poor stars 523.86
Metal spraying 671.734
Metal stamping 671.334
Metal thread embroidery 746.44
Metal trade 338.47671
Metal vapor lasers 621.366
Metal-work 671; 684.09
Metal-work—Periodicals 672.05
Metal-work—United States—Periodicals 671.09/305
Metal-working machinery 681.7671
Metal-working machinery industry 338.476817671
Metalanguage 410.1
Metallic composites 620.16
Metalloenzymes 572.7
Metallography 669.95
Metalloproteins 572.6
Metallurgical analysis 669.0287
Metallurgical plants—Equipment and supplies 669.028
Metallurgy 669
Metallurgy—Periodicals 669.05
Metals 669
Metals—Analysis 669.92
Metals as an investment 332.64424
Metals at high temperatures 620.1617
Metals at low temperatures 620.1616
Metals—Cold working 671.3
Metals—Creep 620.16233
Metals—Effect of radiation on 620.16228
Metals—Environmental aspects 577.2753
Metals—Extrusion 671.34
Metals—Fatigue 620.166
Metals—Finishing 671.7
Metals—Fracture 620.166
Metals—Handbooks, manuals, etc. 620.16
Metals—Heat treatment 671.36
Metals—Mechanical properties 620.1623
Metals—Plastic properties 620.16233
Metals—Quenching 671.36
Metals—Rapid solidification processing 669.94
Metals—Testing 620.160287; 620.167
Metals—Therapeutic use 671
Metals—Toxicology 615.9253
Metamorphism (Geology) 552.4
Metamorphosis 571.876
Metapattern (Information modeling) 005.74
Metaphor—Therapeutic use 616.8914
Metaphysics 110
Metastasis 616.99407

Meteorites 523.51
Meteorites—Antarctica 523.5109989
Meteorological optics 551.565
Meteorological satellites 551.6354
Meteorological services 354.37
Meteorological stations 551.50723
Meteorology 551.5
Meteorology, Agricultural 630.25517
Meteorology in aeronautics 629.1324
Meteorology—Statistical methods 551.50727
Meteors 523.51
Methadone maintenance 616.8632061
Methamphetamine abuse 362.299; 616.864
Methane 665.776
Methanol as fuel 662.6692
Method (Acting) 792.028
Methodist Church 287
Methodist Church—Doctrines 230.7
Methodist Church—Missions 266.7
Methodist Church—Sermons 252.07
Methodist universities and colleges 378.0717
Métis 305.897071; 909.0497; 971.00497
Métis—Government relations 323.1197071
Métis—History 971.00497
Metric spaces 514.32
Metric system 389.152; 530.812
Metric system—Conversion tables 389.16
Metric system—Government policy 389.16
Metric system—Government policy—United States 389.160973
Metric time system 389.17
Metropolitan area networks (Computer networks) 004.67
Metropolitan areas 307.764
Metropolitan areas—United States 307.7640973
Metropolitan government 352.167
Metropolitan government—United States 352.1670973
Metropolitan Manila (Philippines)—Maps 912.59916
Metropolitan Museum of Art (New York, N.Y.) 708.1471
Metropolitan Opera (New York, N.Y.) 782.1097471
Mexican American art 700.896872073
Mexican-American Border Region 972.1
Mexican-American Border Region—Civilization 972.1
Mexican-American Border Region—History 972.1
Mexican American cookery 641.5926872073
Mexican American literature (Spanish) 860.809872073
Mexican American women 305.4886872073
Mexican Americans 305.86872073; 973.046872
Mexican Americans—Bibliography 016.30586872
Mexican Americans—Bibliography—Catalogs 016.30586872
Mexican Americans—Education 371.826872073
Mexican Americans—Ethnic identity 305.86872073
Mexican Americans—History 973.046872
Mexican Americans—Mental health services 362.208968073
Mexican Americans—Social conditions 305.86872073
Mexican Americans—Social life and customs 305.86872
Mexican Americans—Texas—Music 780.8968720764; 781.6268720764
Mexican fiction 863.0080972
Mexican fiction—20th century 863.00809720904
Mexican fiction—20th century—History and criticism 863.0099720904
Mexican literature—20th century 860.80972
Mexican states 320.472049
Mexican War, 1846–1848 973.62
Mexican War, 1846–1848—Campaigns 973.623
Mexican War, 1846–1848—Causes 973.621

Mexican War, 1846–1848—Personal narratives
973.62092
Mexican wit and humor, Pictorial 741.5972
Mexican wolf 599.77
Mexicans 305.86872
Mexicans—United States 305.86872073
Mexico 972
Mexico City (Mexico) 972.53
Mexico City (Mexico)—Description and travel
917.25304; 917.25304836
Mexico—Civilization 972
Mexico—Description and travel 917.204; 917.204836
Mexico—Economic conditions 330.972
Mexico—Economic conditions—1918– 330.972082
Mexico—Economic conditions—1982– —Periodicals
330.9720834
Mexico—Economic conditions—1982–1994 330.9720834
Mexico—Economic policy 338.972
Mexico—Economic policy—1970–1994 338.972
Mexico—Guidebooks 917.204; 917.204836
Mexico—History 972
Mexico—History—Conquest, 1519–1540 972.02
Mexico—History—Conquest, 1519–1540—Sources
972.02
Mexico—History—Spanish colony, 1540–1810 972.02
Mexico—History—1810– 972
Mexico—History—Revolution, 1910–1920 972.0816
Mexico—History—1910–1946 972.082
Mexico—Politics and government 972
Mexico—Politics and government—20th century
320.9720904; 972.082
Mexico—Politics and government—1910–1946
320.97209041; 972.0816; 972.082
Mexico—Politics and government—1970–1988
320.97209047; 972.083
Mexico—Social life and customs 972
Mey 788.52
MGA automobile 629.2222
MGB automobile 629.2222
Miami-Dade County (Fla.)—Maps 912.75938
Miami Dolphins (Football team) 796.3326409759381
Miami Dolphins (Football team)—History
796.3326409759381
Miami (Fla.) 975.9381
Miami (Fla.)—Guidebooks 917.5938104; 917.593810463;
917.593810464
Miami (Fla.)—History 975.9381
Miami (Fla.)—Pictorial works 975.938100222
Miami Metropolitan Area (Fla.) 975.938
Miami Metropolitan Area (Fla.)—Maps 912.759381
Micawber, Mr. (Fictitious character) 823.8
Mice 599.35; 599.353
Mice as laboratory animals 619.93
Mice—Genetics 599.353135
Michael (Archangel) 235.3
Michaels, Alex (Fictitious character) 813.54
Michelangelo Buonarroti, 1475–1564 709.2; 759.5;
851.4
Michelangelo Buonarroti, 1475–1564—Criticism and
interpretation 709.2; 759.5
Michelangelo Buonarroti, 1475–1564—Translations into
English 851.4
Michigan 977.4
Michigan—Economic policy 338.9774
Michigan—Genealogy 929.3774
Michigan—Guidebooks 917.74044; 917.740443;
917.740444
Michigan—History 977.4
Michigan, Lake 977.4

Michigan, Lake—Maps 912.774
Michigan—Maps 912.774
Michigan—Politics and government 320.9774; 977.4
Michigan—Politics and government—1951–
320.977409045
Micmac Indians—Folklore 398.2089973
Micmac mythology 299.72; 398.2089973
Microalgae 579.8
Microbial biotechnology 660.62
Microbial carcinogenesis 571.978; 616.99401
Microbial ecology 579.17
Microbial enhanced oil recovery 622.33827
Microbial genetics 579.135
Microbial metabolism 572.429
Microbiological laboratories 579.072
Microbiology 579
Microbiology—Cultures and culture media 579.0724
Microbiology—Laboratory manuals 579.078
Microbiology—Outlines, syllabi, etc. 579
Microbiology—Periodicals 579.05
Microbiology—Technique 579.072
Microbreweries 663.42
Microchemistry 543.0813
Microcirculation 612.135
Microcirculation disorders 616.14
Microclusters 539.6
Microcomputer workstations 004.16
Microcomputers 004.16
Microcomputers—Access control 005.8
Microcomputers—Buses 621.3981
Microcomputers—Design and construction 621.3916
Microcomputers—Dictionaries 004.1603
Microcomputers—Handbooks, manuals, etc. 004.16
Microcomputers—Maintenance and repair 621.39160288
Microcomputers—Periodicals 004.1605
Microcomputers—Programming 005.26
Microcomputers—Purchasing 004.160297
Microcomputers—Upgrading 621.3916
Microeconomics 338.5
Microelectromechanical systems 621.31042; 621.381
Microelectronic packaging 621.381046
Microelectronics 621.381
Microelectronics industry 338.47621381
Microelectronics—Materials 621.3810284
Microelectronics—Reliability 621.381
Microencapsulation 615.19
Microfabrication 621.3815; 670
Microfinance 332
Microfinance—Law and legislation 346.0822
Microforms 686.43
Microforms—Catalogs 011.36
Micrographics 686.43
Microirrigation 631.587; 635.0487
Microlaena 584.9
Microlithography 621.381531
Microlocal analysis 515.7
Micromachining 621.38152; 671.35
Microorganisms 579
Microorganisms—Physiology 571.29
Micropaleontology 560; 561.9
Microphone 621.38284
Microphotography 686.43
Microprocessors 004.16
Microprocessors—Design and construction 621.3916
Microprocessors—Programming 005.26
Microprogramming 005.6
Microreactors 660.2832
Microsatellites (Genetics) 572.8633
Microscope industry 338.47681413

Middle East—Periodicals 956.005
Middle East—Politics and government 956
Middle East—Politics and government—1945—
320.95609045; 956.04
Middle East—Politics and government—1945–1979
320.95609045
Middle East—Politics and government—1979—
320.95609048; 956.053
Middle East—Relations 303.48256
Middle East—Relations—Europe 303.4824056
Middle East—Social conditions 956
Middle East—Social life and customs 956
Middle East—Strategic aspects 355.033056
Middle East—Study and teaching 956.0071
Middle managers 305.554; 658.43
Middle managers—Salaries, etc. 331.28165843
Middle managers—Salaries, etc.—United States
331.281658430973
Middle managers—Salaries, etc.—United States—
Statistics 331.281658430973021
Middle managers—Salaries, etc.—United States—
Statistics—Periodicals 331.281658430973021
Middle managers—United States 658.43
Middle school education 373.236
Middle school education—United States 373.2360973
Middle school students 373.18
Middle school students—United States 373.18
Middle school teaching 373.1102
Middle school teaching—United States 373.1102
Middle schools 373.236
Middle schools—United States 373.2360973
Middle schools—United States—Curricula 373.19
Middle West 977
Middle West—Economic conditions 330.977
Middle West—Guidebooks 917.704; 917.70433;
917.70434
Middle West—Social life and customs 977
Middle West—Tours 917.704; 917.70433; 917.70434
Middlesex County (Va.)—Genealogy 929.375533
Middleware 005.713
Midheaven (Astrology) 133.53042
MIDI controllers 784.19028546
MIDI (Standard) 784.19028546
Midland County (Mich.) 977.448
Midland County (Mich.)—Maps 912.77448
Midlands (England) 942.4
Midlands (England)—History 942.4
Midlife crisis 305.244
Midnight Louie (Fictitious character) 813.54
Midnight Louie (Fictitious character)—Fiction 813.54
Midrash 296.14
Midrash—History and criticism 296.1406
Midrash—Translations into English 296.140521
Midway, Battle of, 1942 940.5426
Midwifery 618.2
Midwives 618.20092; 618.20233
Mies van der Rohe, Ludwig, 1886–1969 720.92
Mies van der Rohe, Ludwig, 1886–1969—Criticism and
interpretation 720.92
Migraine 616.857
Migrant agricultural laborers 331.544
Migrant agricultural laborers—Housing 331.544;
363.59624
Migrant agricultural laborers—United States
331.5440973
Migrant labor 331.544
Migration, Internal 304.8
Migration, Internal—Asia 304.8095
Migration, Internal—Developing countries 304.8091724

Migration, Internal—Law and legislation 342.08
Migration, Internal—United States 304.80973
Migrations of nations 304.8
Mikasuki Indians 975.9004973; 976.6004973
Mikveh 296.75
Militarism 355.0213
Military administration 355.6
Military art and science 355
Military art and science—Dictionaries 355.003
Military art and science—Encyclopedias 355.003
Military art and science—Europe—History 355.0094
Military art and science—Greece—History 355.00938
Military art and science—History 355.009
Military art and science—History—To 500 355.0093
Military art and science—History—Medieval, 500–1500
355.00902
Military art and science—History—20th century
355.00904
Military art and science in literature 808.80358;
809.93358
Military art and science—Periodicals 355.005
Military art and science—Terminology 355.0014
Military assistance, American 341.7280973; 355.0320973
Military assistance, American—Saudi Arabia
355.0325380973
Military base closures—United States 355.70973
Military bases 341.725; 355.7
Military bases, American 355.70973
Military bases, American—Directories 355.702573
Military bases, American—Law and legislation—
Philippines 341.7250266599073
Military bases, American—Philippines 355.709599
Military bases—United States 355.70973
Military biography 355.0092; 355.00922
Military biography—Dictionaries 355.00922
Military cinematography 778.538355
Military decorations 355.1342
Military decorations—United States 355.13420973
Military departments and divisions 355.3
Military education 355.0071
Military education—United States 355.0071073
Military engineering 623
Military engineers 623.092
Military ethics 174.9355
Military exchanges 355.341
Military exchanges—United States 355.341
Military fireworks 623.452
Military geography 355.47
Military geophysics 623.0155
Military helicopters 358.4183; 623.746047
Military history 355.009
Military history, Ancient 355.0093
Military history, Medieval 355.00902
Military history, Modern 355.0903
Military history, Modern—19th century 355.009033
Military history, Modern—20th century 355.0904
Military-industrial complex 355.0213
Military intelligence 355.3432
Military intelligence—United States 355.34320973
Military intelligence—United States—History
355.34320973
Military law 343.01
Military law—United States 343.7301
Military libraries 026.355
Military miniatures 745.59282
Military mountaineering 355.423; 356.164
Military museums 355.0074
Military music 781.599
Military nursing 355.345

Military occupation 341.66
Military occupation in literature 808.80358
Military offenses 355.1334
Military-owned business enterprises 338.62
Military parks 363.68
Military pensions 331.25291355
Military pensions—Law and legislation 343.0112
Military pensions—Law and legislation—United States 343.730112
Military pensions—United States 331.2529135500973
Military pensions—United States—Revolution, 1775–1783 331.252913550097309033
Military planning 355.684
Military planning—United States 355.684
Military police 355.13323
Military policy 355.0335
Military readiness 355.0332
Military readiness—Economic aspects 355.0332
Military research 355.07
Military research—United States 355.070973
Military research—United States—Periodicals 355.07097305
Military sealift 359.985
Military sealift—United States 359.9850973
Military service, Voluntary 335.22362
Military service, Voluntary—United States 355.223620973
Military sports 796.088355
Military supplies 355.8
Military surveillance 355.3433
Military telecommunication 355.85; 358.24; 623.73
Military uniforms 355.14
Military uniforms—History 355.1409
Military uniforms—History—18th century 355.1409033
Military uniforms—History—20th century 355.1409044
Military weapons 355.8
Militia 355.37
Militia movements 322.42
Militia movements—United States 322.420973
Milk 641.371
Milk—Composition 641.371
Milk-free diet 613.26
Milk-free diet—Recipes 641.563
Milk—Heat treatment 637.141
Milk trade 381.4171
Milken, Michael 364.168092
Milkfish 597.5
Milky Way 523.113
Mill, John Stuart, 1806–1873 192
Mill, John Stuart, 1806–1873—Contributions in political science 320.092
Mill, John Stuart, 1806–1873. On liberty 323.44
Millay, Edna St. Vincent, 1892–1950 811.52
Millay, Edna St. Vincent, 1892–1950—Criticism and interpretation 811.52
Millennialism 236.9
Millennialism in art 704.9482
Millennium 236.9
Millennium celebrations (Year 2000) 394.2
Millennium in art 704.9493942
Miller, Arthur, 1915– 812.52
Miller, Arthur, 1915– —Criticism and interpretation 812.52
Miller, Arthur, 1915– . Death of a salesman 812.52
Miller family 929.20973
Miller, Henry, 1891– 813.52; 818.5209
Miller, Henry, 1891– —Correspondence 818.5209
Miller, Henry, 1891– —Criticism and interpretation 818.5209

Miller, Reggie, 1965– 796.323092
Miller, Robin (Fictitious character) 813.54
Miller, Robin (Fictitious character)—Fiction 813.54
Miller, Shannon, 1977– 796.44092
Miller, William, 1782–1849 286.7092
Millhone, Kinsey (Fictitious character) 813.54
Millhone, Kinsey (Fictitious character)—Fiction 813.54
Millimeter astronomy 522.682
Millimeter wave devices 621.362; 621.3813
Millimeter waves 537.5344
Millinery 646.504
Millionaires 305.524
Millipedes 595.66
Mills and mill-work 622.79
Mills County (Iowa) 977.774
Mills County (Iowa)—Maps 912.77774
Mills family 929.20973
Mills, Todd (Fictitious character) 813.54
Milne, A. A. (Alan Alexander), 1882–1956 828.91209
Milne, A. A. (Alan Alexander), 1882–1956—Characters—Winnie-the-Pooh 823.912
Miłosz, Czesław 891.85173; 891.8587309
Miłosz, Czesław—Criticism and interpretation 891.8587309
Miłosz, Czesław—Translations into English 891.85173
Milton, John, 1608–1674 821.4
Milton, John, 1608–1674—Criticism and interpretation 821.4
Milton, John, 1608–1674—Criticism and interpretation—History 821.4
Milton, John, 1608–1674—Influence 821.4
Milton, John, 1608–1674—Knowledge—Literature 821.4
Milton, John, 1608–1674—Literary style 821.4
Milton, John, 1608–1674. Paradise lost 821.4
Milton, John, 1608–1674—Poetry 821.4
Milton, John, 1608–1674—Political and social views 821.4
Milton, John, 1608–1674—Prose 828.408
Milton, John, 1608–1674—Religion 821.4
Milton, John, 1608–1674. Samson Agonistes 821.4
Milton, John, 1608–1674—Technique 821.4
Mimamsa 181.42
Mimbres culture 978.901
Mimbres mythology 299.72
Mime 792.3
Mimicry (Biology) 578.47; 591.473
Mimicry (Chemistry) 571.964; 616.079
Mimosa 583.748
Minbars 726.2
Mind and body 128.2
Mind and body therapies 616.891
Mine drainage 622.5
Mine dusts 622.83
Mine explosions 622.82
Mine explosions—Prevention 622.82
Mine filling 622
Mine fires 622.82
Mine fires—Prevention and control 622.82
Mine haulage 622.66
Mine roof bolting 622.28
Mine roof control 622.28
Mine safety 622.8
Mine surveying 622.14
Mine ventilation 622.42
Mineral industries 338.2
Mineral industries—Australia 338.20994
Mineral industries—Data processing 622.0285
Mineral industries—Environmental aspects 333.85

Mineral industries—Environmental aspects—India 333.850954
Mineral industries—Periodicals 338.205
Mineral industries—United States 338.20973
Mineral industries—United States—Statistics 338.20973021
Mineral investment 332.6712; 338.23
Mineral lands 333.85
Mineral lands—Alaska 333.8509798
Mineralogical chemistry 552.06
Mineralogy 549
Mineralogy, Determinative 549.1
Minerals 333.85; 549
Minerals—Collection and preservation 549.075
Minerals in human nutrition 612.392
Miners 622.092
Mines and mineral resources 553; 622
Mines and mineral resources—Arizona 553.09791
Mines and mineral resources—Australia 553.0994
Mines and mineral resources—India 553.0954
Mines and mineral resources—United States 553.0973
Mines (Military explosives) 363.3498; 623.45115
Mingrelian literature 899.968
Miniature books 099
Miniature craft 745.5928
Miniature electronic equipment 542.84
Miniature furniture 749.0228
Miniature horses 636.1
Miniature makers 688.1092; 745.5928092
Miniature objects 745.5928
Miniature pinscher 636.76
Miniature quilts 746.460228
Miniature retail stores 381.1
Miniature roses 635.933734
Miniature schnauzer 636.755
Miniature wood-carving—Patterns 731.462; 736.4
Minicomputers 004.14
Minicomputers—Programming 005.24
Minimal architecture 724.6
Minimal brain dysfunction in children 618.928589
Minimal surfaces 516.362
Minimalist gardens 712.2
Minimalist theory (Linguistics) 415
Minimum wage 331.23
Minimum wage—Great Britain 331.23
Minimum wage—Law and legislation 344.0123
Minimum wage—Law and legislation—United States 344.730123
Minimum wage—United States 331.23
Mining corporations 338.7622
Mining engineering 622
Mining engineering—Data processing 622.0285
Mining engineering—Periodicals 622.05
Mining geology 622.0155
Mining law 343.0775
Mining law—United States 343.730775
Mining leases 333.339
Mining machinery 681.76
Mining machinery industry 338.4768176
Mining schools and education 622.0711
Minitab 519.502855369
Minkin, Miss (Fictitious character) 823.914
Minks 599.76627
Minneapolis Metropolitan Area (Minn.) 977.6579
Minneapolis Metropolitan Area (Minn.)—Maps 912.776579
Minneapolis (Minn.) 977.6579
Minneapolis (Minn.)—Guidebooks 917.7657904; 917.765790453; 917.765790454

Minnehaha County (S.D.) 978.3371
Minnehaha County (S.D.)—Maps 912.783371
Minnesota 977.6
Minnesota—Genealogy 929.3776
Minnesota—Guidebooks 917.7604; 917.760453; 917.760454
Minnesota—History 977.6
Minnesota—Maps 912.776
Minnesota Multiphasic Personality Inventory 155.283
Minnesota Multiphasic Personality Inventory for Adolescents 155.518283
Minnesota Twins (Baseball team) 796.3576409776579
Minnesota Twins (Baseball team)—History 796.3576409776579
Minnie Mouse (Fictitious character) 741.5979493
Minoans 939.1801
Minogue, Matt (Fictitious character) 823.914
Minogue, Matt (Fictitious character)—Fiction 823.914
Minolta camera 771.31
Minor league baseball 796.35764
Minor league baseball—United States 796.357640973
Minor league baseball—United States—History 796.357640973
Minorities 305.56; 305.8
Minorities and journalism 070.408
Minorities—Australia 305.800994
Minorities—Canada 305.800971
Minorities—Civil rights 323.1
Minorities—Education 371.82; 371.829
Minorities—Education (Elementary)—United States 372.1820973; 372.182900973
Minorities—Education (Higher)—United States 378.19820973; 378.1982900973
Minorities—Employment 658.30089
Minorities—Employment—United States 658.3008900973
Minorities—Great Britain 305.800941
Minorities in communication 384.08
Minorities in engineering 620.0088
Minorities in journalism 070.408
Minorities in mass media 305.56
Minorities in mathematics 510.8
Minorities in medicine 610.8
Minorities in science 500.8; 500.89
Minorities in technology 604.89
Minorities in the mass media industry 331.5
Minorities in the professions 331.71208693
Minorities—Legal status, laws, etc. 341.481; 342.0873; 346.013
Minorities—Legal status, laws, etc.—United States 342.730873; 346.73013
Minorities—Mental health services—United States 362.208693
Minorities—Soviet Union 323.147
Minorities—United States 305.560973; 305.800973
Minorities—United States—Biography 920.073
Minorities—United States—History 305.800973; 973.04
Minorities—United States—Study and teaching 305.80071073
Minority business enterprises 338.6422
Minority business enterprises—United States 338.64220973
Minority college students 378.1982; 378.19829
Minority college students—Recruiting—United States 378.161
Minority college students—United States 378.19820973; 378.1982900973
Minority gays 305.8
Minority lesbians 305.489664

Minority-owned architectural firms 720.68
Minority women 305.488
Minority women artists 700.8693
Minority women—United States 305.48800973
Minority youth 305.235
Minors 346.013
Minors—United States 346.730135
Minyan 296.45
Miombo 333.75; 577.3
Miombo ecology 577.3
Mīrābāī, fl. 1516–1546 891.4312
Mīrābāī, fl. 1516–1546—Translations into English 891.4312
Miracles 231.73; 291.2117
Miró, Joan, 1893– 709.2
Miró, Joan, 1893– —Exhibitions 709.2
Miscarriage 618.392
Miscarriage—Psychological aspects 618.392019
Miscommunication 153.6; 302.2
Mishnah 296.123
Mishnah. Avot 296.12347
Mishnah. Avot—Commentaries 296.1234707
Mishnah—Criticism, interpretation, etc. 296.12306
Miskito cosmology 299.73; 523.1089978
Missals 264.36
Missaukee County (Mich.) 977.466
Missaukee County (Mich.)—Maps 912.77466
Missing children 362.8297
Missing children United States 362.82970973
Missing persons 363.2336
Missing persons—Investigation—United States 363.23360973
Missing persons—Investigation—United States—Handbooks, manuals, etc. 363.23360973
Mission of the church 262.7
Missionaries 266.0092; 291.72092
Missionary stories 266
Missions 266; 291.72
Missions—Africa 266.0096
Missions—Anthropological aspects 306.69172
Missions—Asia 266.0095
Missions—Biblical teaching 266
Missions—India 266.00954
Missions—Sermons 266
Missions—South Africa 266.00968
Missions, Spanish 266.02346
Missions—Theory 266.001
Missions to Jews 266.0088296
Missions to Muslims 266.00882971
Mississippi 976.2
Mississippi—Genealogy 929.3762
Mississippi—Guidebooks 917.6204; 917.620463; 917.620464
Mississippi—History 976.2
Mississippi—History—Civil War, 1861–1865 973.7462
Mississippi—Race relations 305.8009762
Mississippi River 977
Mississippi River—Description and travel 917.704; 917.70433; 917.70434
Mississippi River—Maps 912.77
Mississippi River Valley 977
Mississippi River Valley—History 977
Mississippi River Valley—History—To 1803 977.01; 977.02
Mississippi—Social life and customs 976.2
Mississippian culture 977.01
Missouri 977.8
Missouri—Genealogy 929.3778

Missouri—Guidebooks 917.7804; 917.780443; 917.780444
Missouri—History 977.8
Missouri—Maps 912.778
Mistletoes 583.88
Mitchell, Benny (Fictitious character) 823.914
Mitchell County (Iowa) 977.7234
Mitchell County (Iowa)—Maps 912.777234
Mitchell family 929.20973
Mitchell, Margaret, 1900–1949 813.52
Mitchell, Margaret, 1900–1949. Gone with the wind 813.52
Mitchell, Maria, 1818–1889 520.92
Mitchell, Meredith (Fictitious character) 823.914
Mitchell, Meredith (Fictitious character)—Fiction 823.914
Miter boxes 621.992
Mites 595.42
Mithraism 299.15
Mitochondria 571.657
Mitsubishi trucks 629.2232
Mitsubishi trucks—Maintenance and repair 629.28732
Mitsubishi trucks—Maintenance and repair—Handbooks, manuals, etc. 629.28732
Mitterrand, François, 1916– 944.0838092
Mitterrand, François, 1916– —Influence 320.94409049
Mixed ability grouping in education 371.252
Mixed economy 330.126
Mixed media (Music) 780
Mixed media textiles 677
Mixed signal circuits 621.3815
Mixing 660.284292
Mizoram (India) 954.166
Mizoram (India)—History 954.166
Mizuhiki 745.54
ML (Computer program language) 005.133
MMX technology 006.7
Mnemonics 153.14
Mobile agents (Computer software) 006.3
Mobile (Ala.) 976.122
Mobile (Ala.)—History 976.122
Mobile communication systems 384.535; 621.3845
Mobile computing 004.165
Mobile cranes 621.873
Mobile dental clinics 362.1976
Mobile emergency mental health services 362.204251
Mobile home living 643.2
Mobile home living—United States 796.790973
Mobile home parks 643.2
Mobile homes 643.2
Mobile homes—United States—Periodicals 643.2
Mobile Metropolitan Area (Ala.)—Maps 912.76122
Mobile robots 629.892
Mochica goldwork 739.2208998
Modal analysis 624.171
Modality (Logic) 160
Model ordinances—United States 348.7302
Model theory 511.3
Modeling 745.5
Modeling agencies 746.92092
Modeling—Study and teaching (Elementary) 372.53
Models and modelmaking 688.1; 745.5928
Models and modelmaking—Collectors and collecting 688.1075
Models and modelmaking—Radio control systems 629.0460228; 796.15
Models (Persons) 746.92092
Models (Persons)—Vocational guidance 659.152; 746.92023

Modems 004.64
Modems—Handbooks, manuals, etc. 004.64
Modern dance 792.8
Modern movement (Architecture) 724.6
Modernism (Aesthetics) 111.85
Modernism (Art) 709.04
Modernism (Christian theology) 273.9
Modernism (Literature) 809.9112
Modigliani, Amedeo, 1884–1920 709.2
Modula-2 (Computer program language) 005.133
Modular construction 729.2
Modularity (Engineering) 620.0042
Modulation-doped field-effect transistors 621.3815284
Modules (Algebra) 512.4
Moduli theory 516.35
Mog (Fictitious character : Kerr) 823.914
Moguchaĩa kuchka (Group of composers) 780.92247
Mogul Empire 954.025
Mogul Empire—History 954.025
Mogul Empire—Politics and government 954.025
Mohave County (Ariz.) 979.159
Mohave County (Ariz.)—Road maps 912.79159
Mohawk Indians 305.89755; 971.30049755; 974.70049755
Mohawk language 497.55
Mohegan Indians 305.8973; 974.6004973
Mohs surgery 616.99477059
Moieties 306.83
Moldova 947.6
Molds (Fungi) 579.53
Mole (Fictitious character : Dunbar) 823.914
Molecular beam epitaxy 621.38152
Molecular biology 572.8
Molecular biology—Technique 572.8072
Molecular clouds 523.1125
Molecular computers 621.391
Molecular crystals 548
Molecular dynamics 541.394
Molecular ecology 577.14
Molecular electronics 621.381
Molecular endocrinology 573.448; 612.4
Molecular evolution 572.838
Molecular genetics 572.8
Molecular immunology 571.9648; 616.079
Molecular imprinting 668.92
Molecular microbiology 572.829
Molecular neurobiology 573.84
Molecular neurobiology—Periodicals 573.8405
Molecular pharmacology 615.1; 615.7
Molecular recognition 572.833
Molecular sieves 660.2842
Molecular spectroscopy 539.60287
Molecular structure 541.22
Molecular theory 541.22
Molecular toxicology 615.9
Molecular virology 572.8292
Molecules 539.6
Moles (Animals) 599.335
Moliceiros 623.8226
Molière, 1622–1673 842.4
Molière, 1622–1673—Criticism and interpretation 842.4
Molière, 1622–1673—Translations into English 842.4
Mollusks 594
Mollusks, Fossil 564
Mom (Fictitious character) 813.54
Mom (Fictitious character)—Fiction 813.54
Monacan Indians 975.4004973
Monaghan, Tess (Fictitious character) 813.54

Monarch butterfly 595.789
Monarchy 321.6
Monarchy—France 352.230944
Monarchy—Great Britain 352.230941
Monarchy—Great Britain—History 352.230941
Monarchy—Spain 352.230946
Monasteries 291.657
Monasteries—Remodeling for other use 726.70286
Monastic and religious life 248.894; 255
Monastic and religious life—History—Middle Ages, 600–1500 271.00902
Monastic and religious life of women 255.9
Monasticism and religious orders 255; 291.657
Monasticism and religious orders, Buddhist—Rules 294.3657
Monasticism and religious orders—England—History 271.00942
Monasticism and religious orders—England—History—Middle Ages, 600–1500 271.009420902
Monasticism and religious orders for women 271.9
Monasticism and religious orders—History 271
Monasticism and religious orders—History—Early church, ca. 30–600 271.009015
Monasticism and religious orders—History—Middle Ages, 600–1500 271.00902
Monasticism and religious orders—Rules 255; 271
Monet, Claude, 1840–1926 759.4
Monet, Claude, 1840–1926—Criticism and interpretation 759.4
Monet, Claude, 1840–1926—Exhibitions 759.4
Monetary policy 332.46
Monetary policy—Developing countries 332.491724
Monetary policy—Econometric models 332.46
Monetary policy—Europe 332.494
Monetary policy—Europe, Eastern 332.4947
Monetary policy—European Economic Community countries 332.494
Monetary policy—European Union countries 332.494
Monetary policy—Germany 332.4943
Monetary policy—Great Britain 332.4941
Monetary policy—India 332.4954
Monetary policy—Japan 332.4952
Monetary policy—United States 332.4973
Monetary policy—United States—History 332.4973
Monetary unions 332.4566
Monetary unions—European Economic Community countries 332.4566094
Monetary unions—European Union countries 332.4566094
Money 332.4
Money—European Economic Community countries 332.494
Money—European Union countries 332.494
Money—France 332.4944
Money—Germany 332.4943
Money—Great Britain 332.4941
Money—Great Britain—History 332.4941
Money—History 332.49
Money illusion 332.401
Money in literature 808.80355; 809.93355
Money laundering 345.0268; 364.168
Money laundering investigation 363.25968
Money laundering—United States 345.730268; 364.168
Money—Law and legislation 343.032
Money-making projects for children 650.12083
Money—Psychological aspects 332.4019
Money supply 332.414
Money—United States 332.4973
Money—United States—History 332.4973

Moral education—United States 370.1140973
Moral re-armament 248.25
Morale 355.123; 658.314
Moralities, English 822.0516
Moralities, English—History and criticism 822.051609
Moravian Church 284.6
More, Hannah, 1745–1833 828.609
More, Thomas, Sir, Saint, 1478–1535 942.052092
More, Thomas, Sir, Saint, 1478–1535. Utopia 321.07
Morgan County (Ill.) 977.3463
Morgan County (Ill.)—Maps 912.773463
Morgan County (Ohio) 977.194
Morgan County (Ohio)—Genealogy 929.377194
Morgan family 929.20973
Morgan, Rain, (Fictitious character) 823.914
Morgan, Rain, (Fictitious character)—Fiction 823.914
Morissette, Alanis 782.42166092
Morita psychotherapy 616.8914
Mormon Church 289.3
Mormon Church—Apologetic works 230.93; 289.3
Mormon Church—Controversial literature 289.3
Mormon Church—Doctrines 230.93
Mormon Church—Education 268.893
Mormon Church—History 289.309
Mormon handcart companies 978.02088283; 979.202
Mormon Pioneer National Historic Trail 978
Mormon press 070.482
Mormon temples 246.95893
Mormon women 305.41
Mormon women—Biography 289.30922
Mormon women—Religious life 248.843; 289.332082
Mormon youth 305.235
Mormon youth—Religious life 248.83
Mormons 289.3092
Mormons—Biography 289.30922
Morning customs 394
Moroccan-Spanish War, 1957–1958 964.051
Morocco 964
Morocco—Description and travel 916.404; 916.40453
Morocco—Economic conditions 330.964
Morocco—Guidebooks 916.404; 916.40453
Morocco—Social life and customs 964
Morphogenesis 571.833
Morphology 571.3
Morphology (Animals) 571.31
Morris County (N.J.)—Maps 912.74974
Morris family 929.20973
Morris, William, 1834–1896 709.2; 745.4492; 821.8
Morris, William, 1834–1896—Contributions in decorative arts 745.4492
Morris, William, 1834–1896—Criticism and interpretation 821.8
Morris, William, 1834–1896—Friends and associates 709.2; 821.8
Morris, William, 1834–1896—Knowledge—Printing 686.2092
Morris, William, 1834–1896—Poetic works 821.8
Morris, William, 1834–1896—Political and social views 320.5312092
Morris, Wright, 1910– 813.52
Morris, Wright, 1910– —Criticism and interpretation 813.52
Morrison family 929.20973
Morrison, Jim, 1943–1971 782.42166092
Morrison, Toni 813.54
Morrison, Toni. Beloved 813.54
Morrison, Toni—Criticism and interpretation 813.54
Morse code 621.3842

Morse, Inspector (Fictitious character) 791.4572; 823.914
Morse, Inspector (Fictitious character)—Fiction 823.914
Mortal Kombat (Game) 794.8225369
Mortality 304.64
Mortality—United States 304.64573
Mortgage-backed securities 332.6323
Mortgage-backed securities—United States 332.6323
Mortgage banks 332.32
Mortgage brokers 332.72
Mortgage consultants 332.72092
Mortgage guarantee insurance 368.852
Mortgage guarantee insurance—United States 368.85200973
Mortgage loans 332.72; 332.722
Mortgage loans—California 332.7209794
Mortgage loans—Law and legislation 346.04364
Mortgage loans—Law and legislation—United States 346.7304364
Mortgage loans—United States 332.720973; 332.7220973
Mortgage redemption fees 332.72
Mortgages 332.63244
Mortgages—United States 346.7304364
Mosaic (Computer file) 025.04
Mosaics 738.5
Mosaics—Technique 738.5
Moscow, Battle of, 1941–1942 940.5421731
Moscow (Russia) 947.31
Moscow (Russia)—Description and travel 914.73104; 914.7310486
Moscow (Russia)—Guidebooks 914.73104; 914.7310486
Moses (Biblical leader) 222.1092
Moses, Grandma, 1860–1961 759.13
Mosques 297.351; 297.65
Mosquitoes 595.772
Moss gardening 635.9382
Moss, Phil (Fictitious character) 823.914
Mössbauer effect 537.5352
Mössbauer spectroscopy 537.5352
Mosses 588.2
Motel management 647.94
Motels 647.94
Motels—United States 647.947302
Motels—United States—Directories 647.947302
Motets 782.26
Mother, 1878–1973 294.5092
Mother and child 306.8743
Mother goddesses 291.2114
Mother Goose 398.8
Motherboards (Microcomputers) 621.395
Motherhood 306.8743
Motherhood—Humor 306.87430207
Motherhood—Psychological aspects 155.6463
Motherhood—Religious aspects 291.44
Motherhood—Religious aspects—Christianity 248.8431
Motherhood—United States 306.87430973
Mothers 306.8743
Mothers and daughters 306.8743; 649.133
Mothers and daughters—Religious aspects 291.441
Mothers and daughters—United States 306.8743
Mothers and sons 306.8743
Mothers in motion pictures 791.436520431
Mothers in the Bible 220.83068743
Mothers—Literary collections 808.803520431
Mothers on television 791.456520431
Mothers—Prayer-books and devotions 242.6431; 242.8431
Mothers—Religious life 248.8431

Motion pictures—Semiotics 791.43014
Motion pictures—Setting and scenery 791.43025
Motion pictures—Social aspects 302.2343
Motion pictures—Social aspects—United States 302.23430973
Motion pictures—Soviet Union 791.430947
Motion pictures—Soviet Union—History 791.430947
Motion pictures—United States 791.430973
Motion pictures—United States—Catalogs 016.79143750973
Motion pictures—United States—History 791.430973
Motion pictures—Vocational guidance 791.430293
Motion pictures—Vocational guidance—United States 791.43029373
Motion study 658.5421
Motions (Law) 347.052
Motions (Law)—United States 347.7352
Motivation in animals 591.5
Motivation in education 370.154
Motivation in education—United States 370.1540973
Motivation (Psychology) 153.1534; 153.8
Motivation research (Marketing) 658.8342
Moto, Mr. (Fictitious character) 813.52
Moto, Mr. (Fictitious character)—Fiction 813.52
Motocross 796.756
Motor ability 152.3
Motor ability in children 155.4123
Motor fuels 629.2538
Motor fuels—Additives 629.2538; 665.53827
Motor learning 152.334; 370.155
Motor scooters 629.2275
Motor vehicles 388.34; 629.046; 629.2
Motor vehicles—Aerodynamics 629.046015336; 629.231
Motor vehicles—Crashworthiness 629.231
Motor vehicles—Design and construction 629.046; 629.231
Motor vehicles—Dynamics 629.046015313
Motor vehicles—Electronic equipment 629.046; 629.2549
Motor vehicles—Motors 629.046; 629.25; 629.2504
Motor vehicles—Motors—Exhaust gas—Environmental aspects 363.7387
Motor vehicles—Motors—Exhaust gas—Environmental aspects—United States 363.7387; 363.73926
Motor vehicles—Pollution control devices 625.2528
Motor vehicles—Registration and transfer 354.765284
Motorboat racing 797.14
Motorboats 387.231; 797.125
Motorboats—Models—Radio control 796.152
Motorcycle films 791.43655
Motorcycle jackets 391; 685.22
Motorcycle police 363.232
Motorcycle racing 796.75
Motorcycle racing fans 796.75092
Motorcycle supplies industry 338.476292275
Motorcycle workshops 629.286
Motorcycles 629.2275
Motorcycles—Customizing 629.2275
Motorcycles—History 629.227509
Motorcycles—Maintenance and repair 629.28775
Motorcycles, Racing 629.2275
Motorcycling 796.75
Motorcycling accident investigation 363.1259
Motorola 6800 series microprocessors 004.165
Motorola 68000 (Microprocessor) 004.165
Motorola 68000 series microprocessors 004.165
Motorsports 796.7
Mott, Lucretia, 1793–1880 305.42092
Moultry, Major (Fictitious character) 823.914

Mound-builders 977.01
Moundville Archaeological Park (Moundville, Ala.) 976.143
Mount Vernon (Va. : Estate) 973.41092; 975.5291
Mountain animals 591.753
Mountain ecology 577.53
Mountain ecology—United States 577.530973
Mountain resorts 647.94; 796.5
Mountain sheep 599.649
Mountaineering 796.522
Mountaineering accidents—Everest, Mount (China and Nepal) 796.522095496
Mountaineering—Alaska—McKinley, Mount 796.522097983
Mountaineering—Alaska—McKinley, Mount—History 796.522097983
Mountaineering—Colorado 796.52209788
Mountaineering—Colorado—Guidebooks 796.52209788
Mountaineering—Everest, Mount (China and Nepal) 796.522095496
Mountaineering—Everest, Mount (China and Nepal)—History 796.522095496
Mountaineering expeditions 796.522
Mountaineering—Himalaya Mountains 796.522095496
Mountaineering in motion pictures 791.43655
Mountaineering injuries 617.1027
Mountaineering injuries—Handbooks, manuals, etc. 617.1027
Mountaineering—Pakistan—K2 (Mountain) 796.522095491; 796.5220954913
Mountaineering—Scotland 796.52209411
Mountaineering—Scotland—Guidebooks 796.522; 796.52209411
Mountaineers 796.522092
Mountains 508.3143; 551.432; 910.02143
Mounted police 363.232
Mourning customs 393.9
Mouse (Fictitious character : Dunbar) 823.914
Mouse pads 004.76
Mouth 591.4; 612.31
Mouth bow 787.92
Mouth—Cancer 616.99431
Mouth—Diseases 617.522
Mouth—Histology 611.018931
Mouth—Microbiology 617.522
Mouth—Physiology 612.31
Mouth—Surgery 617.522059
Mouth—Surgery—Handbooks, manuals, etc. 617.522059
Movement (Acting) 792.028
Movement disorders 616.7; 616.83
Movement education 372.868
Movement education—Study and teaching (Elementary) 372.868
Movement notation 792.82
Movement, Psychology of 152.3
Movement therapy 615.82
Moving, Household 648.9
Moving, Household—Costs 338.436489
Mower County (Minn.) 977.617
Mower County (Minn.)—Maps 912.77617
Mowgli (Fictitious character) 823.8
Mowgli (Fictitious character)—Fiction 823.8
Mozambique 967.9
Mozambique—History 967.9
Mozambique—History—Independence and Civil War, 1975–1994 967.9051
Mozambique—Politics and government 967.9
Mozambique—Politics and government—1975–1994 320.967909047; 967.905

Mozart, Wolfgang Amadeus, 1756–1791 780.92
Mozart, Wolfgang Amadeus, 1756–1791—Childhood and youth 780.92
Mozart, Wolfgang Amadeus, 1756–1791. Concertos, piano, orchestra 784.262092
Mozart, Wolfgang Amadeus, 1756–1791—Criticism and interpretation 780.92
Mozart, Wolfgang Amadeus, 1756–1791. Operas 782.1092
Mozart, Wolfgang Amadeus, 1756–1791. Symphonies 784.2184092
Mozart, Wolfgang Amadeus, 1756–1791. Zauberflöte 782.1
Mozzarella cheese 637.356; 641.37356
MP3 (Audio coding standard) 006.5; 780.28565
MP3 players 006.5; 621.38933
MPLS standard 004.62; 621.38212
Mr. Croc (Fictitious character) 823.914
Mr. Men (Fictitious characters) 823.914
MS-DOS (Computer file) 005.4469
Mucous membrane—Immunology 616.079
Mueller family 929.20973
Muffin, Charlie (Fictitious character) 823.914
Muffin, Charlie (Fictitious character)—Fiction 823.914
Muffins 641.815
Muffler art 659.1342; 745.584
Muftis (Muslim officials) 297.14092
Muggeridge, Malcolm, 1903– 070.92
Mugging victims 362.88
Muhammad, Prophet 297.63
Muḥammad, Prophet, d. 632 297.63
Muḥammad, Prophet, d. 632—Biography 297.63
Muḥammad, Prophet, d. 632—Companions 297.648
Muḥammad, Prophet, d. 632—Companions—Biography 297.648
Muḥammad, Prophet, d. 632—Prophetic office 297.63
Muḥammad, Prophet, d. 632, in the Koran 297.63
Muhlenberg County (Ky.)—Genealogy 929.3769832
Muir, John, 1838–1914 333.72092; 508.794092
Mulberry (Fictitious character : Grindley) 823.914
Mulcahaney, Norah (Fictitious character) 813.54
Mulcahaney, Norah (Fictitious character)—Fiction 813.54
Mulcay, Kate (Fictitious character) 813.54
Mulcay, Kate (Fictitious character)—Fiction 813.54
Mulder, Fox (Fictitious character) 791.4575
Mulder, Fox (Fictitious character)—Fiction 813.54
Mule deer 599.653
Mule deer hunting 799.27653
Mulheisen, Detective Sergeant (Fictitious character) 813.54
Mulheisen, Detective Sergeant (Fictitious character)—Fiction 813.54
Muller, Kurt (Fictitious character) 813.54
Multi-user dungeons 793.932
Multicasting (Computer networks) 004.66
Multichip modules (Microelectronics) 621.381046
Multicultural education 370.117
Multicultural education—Australia 370.1170994
Multicultural education—Great Britain 370.1170941
Multicultural education—United States 370.1170973
Multicultural education—United States—Activity programs 371.3
Multicultural education—United States—Curricula 370.117
Multicultural education—United States—Handbooks, manuals, etc. 370.1170973
Multiculturalism 306.446
Multiculturalism—Canada 306.4460971

Multiculturalism—United States 305.800973
Multidimensional scaling 519.535
Multidisciplinary design optimization 620.0042
Multiengine flying 629.13252; 629.1325243
Multilevel marketing 658.84
Multilingual computing 005
Multilingual Web sites 025.04
Multilingualism 306.446
Multilingualism in children 306.446083; 404.2083
MultiMate 652.55369
MultiMate advantage 652.55369
Multimedia (Art) 702.81
Multimedia systems 006.7
Multimedia systems industry 338.470067
Multimedia systems—Law and legislation—United States 343.730999; 346.73048
Multimedia systems—Periodicals 006.705
Multiphase flow 620.1064
Multiphase flow—Mathematical models 620.1064
Multiple birth 618.25
Multiple chemical sensitivity 616.97
Multiple criteria decision making 658.403
Multiple integrals 515.43
Multiple intelligences 153.9
Multiple listing 333.33
Multiple organ failure 616.047
Multiple organ failure—Pathophysiology 616.047
Multiple personality 616.85236
Multiple personality—Treatment 616.8523606
Multiple pregnancy 618.25
Multiple pregnancy—Ultrasonic imaging 618.2507543
Multiple sclerosis 362.196834; 616.834
Multiple use management areas 333.7
Multiplex theaters 384.85; 725.823
Multiplication 513.213
Multiprocessors 004.35
Multiproduct firms 338.7
Multitasking (Computer science) 005.434
Multitrophic interactions (Ecology) 577.16
Multivariate analysis 519.535
Mummies 393.3
Mummies—Egypt 393.30932
Mummified animals 393.3; 590.752
Mummy films 791.43675
Munaẓẓamat al-Taḥrir al-Filasṭiniyah 322.42095694
Munch, Edvard, 1863–1944 760.092; 769.92
Munch, Edvard, 1863–1944—Exhibitions 760.092; 769.92
Munchausen syndrome by proxy 616.858223
Munich Four-Power Agreement (1938) 940.5312
Munich (Germany) 943.364
Munich (Germany)—Guidebooks 914.336404; 914.336404879; 914.33640488
Municipal archives 027.5
Municipal bond insurance 368.853
Municipal bonds 332.63233
Municipal bonds—Law and legislation 346.0922
Municipal bonds—Law and legislation—United States 346.730922
Municipal bonds—United States 332.632330973
Municipal corporations 342.09
Municipal corporations—Philippines 342.59909
Municipal emblems—Law and legislation 344.09
Municipal engineering 628
Municipal finance 336.014
Municipal finance—Accounting 657.835
Municipal finance—United States 336.01473; 352.42160973

Municipal finance—United States—Accounting
657.83500973
Municipal franchises 336.11
Municipal government 320.85; 352.16
Municipal government—United States 320.850973;
352.140973; 352.160973
Municipal officials and employees 352.63214
Municipal officials and employees—Ohio
352.6321409771
Municipal officials and employees—United States—
Directories 352.6321402573
Municipal services 352.14
Municipal services—United States 363.0973
Municipal solid waste incinerator residues 628.4457
Municipal universities and colleges 378.052
Municipal water supply 363.61
Municipal water supply—Law and legislation 343.0924
Municipal water supply—Management 363.61068
Munro, Alice 813.54
Munro, Alice—Criticism and interpretation 813.54
Muons 539.72114
Mural painting and decoration 751.73
Mural painting and decoration, Buddhist—India—Ajanta
751.730954792
Mural painting and decoration, Mexican 751.730972
Murasaki Shikibu, b. 978? 895.6314
Murasaki Shikibu, b. 978? Genji monogatari 895.6314
Murder 364.1523
Murder—California 364.15230979493
Murder—California—Los Angeles 364.15230979494
Murder—California—Pasadena 364.15230979493
Murder for hire 364.1523
Murder—Great Britain 364.15230941
Murder in literature 808.80355; 809.93355
Murder—New York (State)—New York 364.1523097471
Murder—Religious aspects 291.178331523
Murder—United States 364.15230973
Murder victims' families 362.88
Murderers 364.1523092
Murdoch, Iris 823.914
Murdoch, Iris—Criticism and interpretation 823.914
Murdoch, William (Fictitious character) 813.54
Murdock, Matt (Fictitious character) 813.54
Murdock, Matt (Fictitious character)—Fiction 813.54
Murdock, Page (Fictitious character) 813.54
Muridae 599.35
Murieta, Joaquín, d. 1853 949.404092; 979.404092
Murphy, Al (Fictitious character) 813.54
Murphy, Al (Fictitious character)—Fiction 813.54
Murphy family 929.20973
Murray County (Minn.) 977.627
Murray County (Minn.)—Maps 912.77627
Murray family 929.20973
Murray River Region (N.S.W.-S. Aust.) 994.4
Murray River Region (N.S.W.-S. Aust.)—Maps 912.944
Muscat (Wine) 641.2222; 663.222
Muscidae 595.774
Muscle cars 629.222
Muscle cars—United States—History 629.222;
629.2220973
Muscle contraction 573.75
Muscle strength 613.71
Muscles 612.74
Muscles—Diseases 616.74
Muscles—Physiology 612.74
Muscular dystrophy 616.748
Musculoskeletal emergencies 616.7025
Musculoskeletal system 611.7; 612.7
Musculoskeletal system—Diseases 616.7

Musculoskeletal system—Diseases—Diagnosis 616.7075
Musculoskeletal system—Magnetic resonance imaging
616.707548
Musée du Louvre 708.4361
Museum architecture 727.6
Museum conservation methods 069.53
Museum curators 069.092
Museum docents 069.15
Museum exhibits 069.5
Museum finance 069.0681
Museum libraries 027.68
Museum registration methods 069.52
Museum storage facilities 069.53; 727.6
Museum techniques 069.4
Museum visitors 069.1
Museums 069
Museums—Administration 069.068
Museums and the visually handicapped 069.17
Museums—Collection management 069.5
Museums—Data processing 069.0285
Museums—Educational aspects 069.15
Museums—Educational aspects—United States
069.0973
Museums—Management 069.068
Museums—New York (State)—New York 069.097471
Museums—New York (State)—New York—Guidebooks
069.097471
Museums—Philosophy 069.01
Museums—United States 069.0973
Museums—United States—Guidebooks 069.0973
Museums—United States—History 069.0973
Mushroom culture 635.8
Mushroom industry 338.1758
Mushrooms 579.6
Mushrooms, Edible 635.8
Mushrooms—Identification 579.6
Music 780
Music—500-1400 780.902
Music—500-1400—History and criticism 780.902
Music—500-1400—History and criticism—Bibliography
016.780902
Music—15th century 780.9024
Music—15th century—History and criticism 780.9024
Music—16th century 780.9031
Music—16th century—History and criticism 780.9031
Music—17th century 780.9032
Music—17th century—History and criticism 780.9032
Music—18th century 780.9033
Music—18th century—History and criticism 780.9033
Music—19th century 780.9034
Music—19th century—History and criticism 780.9034
Music—20th century 780.904
Music—20th century—Encyclopedias 780.90403
Music—20th century—History and criticism 780.904
Music—20th century—History and criticism—Periodicals
780.90405
Music—Acoustics and physics 781.23
Music—Addresses, essays, lectures 780
Music—Africa 780.96
Music—Africa—History and criticism 780.96
Music and folklore 780.0398
Music and literature 780.08
Music and youth 780.083
Music appreciation 781.17
Music—Asia 780.95
Music—Asia—History and criticism 780.95
Music—Bibliography 016.78
Music—Bibliography—Catalogs 016.78
Music—Bio-bibliography 780.92

Musicals—Stories, plots, etc. 782.140269
Musicals—United States 782.140973; 792.6097
Musicals—United States—Bibliography 016.782140973
Musicals—United States—History and criticism 782.140973; 792.60973
Musicals—Writing and publishing 782.1413
Musicians 780.92
Musicians—Biography 780.82
Musicians, Celtic 780.89916
Musico-callisthenics 780.77
Musicology 780.72
Muskegon County (Mich.) 977.457
Muskegon County (Mich.)—Maps 912.77457
Muskox 599.6478
Muslim pilgrims and pilgrimages 297.35
Muslim pilgrims and pilgrimages—Saudi Arabia—Mecca 297.352
Muslim women 305.486971
Muslim women—Conduct of life 297.57082
Muslim women—History 305.486971
Muslim women—India 305.486971054
Muslim women—India—Social conditions 305.486971054
Muslims 297.092
Muslims—Europe 305.697104; 940.0882971
Muslims—India 305.6971054
Muslims—Italy 305.6971045
Muslims—Philippines 305.69710599
Muslims—Spain 305.6971046
Muslims—Spain—History 946.02
Mussolini, Benito, 1883–1945 945.091092
Mustang 599.6655
Mustang automobile 629.2222
Mustang automobile—History 629.2222
Mustang automobile—Maintenance and repair 629.28722
Mustang automobile—Maintenance and repair—Handbooks, manuals, etc. 629.28722
Mustang (Fighter planes) 358.4383
Mustelidae 599.766
Mustian, Rosacoke (Fictitious character) 813.54
Mutagenesis 572.838
Mutagenicity testing 616.042
Mutagens 576.542
Muṭarrifiyah 297.824
Mutation (Biology) 576.549
Mutts (Dogs) 636.7
Mutual funds 332.6327
Mutual funds—Examinations, questions, etc. 332.6327
Mutual funds—Law and legislation 346.0922
Mutual funds—Law and legislation—United States 346.730922
Mutual funds—Taxation 336.24
Mutual funds—Taxation—Law and legislation 343.05246
Mutual funds—United States 332.6327
Mutual funds—United States—Directories 332.6327
Mutual funds—United States—Handbooks, manuals, etc. 332.6327
Mutual funds—United States—Periodicals 332.6327
Mutual funds—United States—Statistics 332.6327
Mutual funds—United States—Statistics—Periodicals 332.6327
Mutualism (Biology) 577.852
Muzzle-loading firearms 683.4
MX (Weapons system) 358.175482
My Lai Massacre, Vietnam, 1968 959.704342
Myalgic encephalomyelitis 616.744
Myasthenia gravis 616.7442
Mycobacterium 579.374

Mycology 579.5
Mycorrhizas 579.517852; 631.46
Mycoses 616.969
Mycotoxins 615.95295
Myers-Briggs Type Indicator 155.264
Myers family 929.20973
Mynahs 598.863
Myocardial infarction 616.1237
Myocardial infarction—Chemotherapy 616.1237061
Myocardial infarction—Diagnosis 616.1237075
Myocardial infarction—Nursing 610.73691
Myocardial infarction—Prevention 616.123705
Myocardial infarction—Treatment 616.123706
Myocardial revascularization 617.412
Myocardium 611.12; 612.17
Myocardium—Diseases 616.124
Myodocopida 595.33
Myofascial pain syndromes 616.74
Myofibroblasts 573.7536; 611.0181; 617.1
Myopia 617.755
Myriapoda 595.6
Myrtle Beach (S.C.)—Guidebooks 917.5787
Myst 793.932
Mysteries and miracle-plays, English 822.0516
Mysteries and miracle-plays, English—England—York 822.051608942843
Mystery in literature 808.801; 809.91
Mysticism 149.3; 248.22; 291.422
Mysticism—Catholic Church 248.22
Mysticism—Hinduism 294.5422
Mysticism—History 149.309
Mysticism—History—Middle Ages, 600–1500 248.220902
Mysticism—Judaism 296.712
Mysticism—Spain 248.220946
Myth 291.13
Myth—Psychological aspects 291.13019
Mythology 291.13; 398.2
Mythology, Celtic 299.16; 398.2089916
Mythology, Celtic—Dictionaries 299.16
Mythology, Chinese 299.51
Mythology, Classical 292.13
Mythology, Classical—Dictionaries 292.1303
Mythology—Dictionaries 291.1303
Mythology, Egyptian 299.31
Mythology, Germanic 293.13
Mythology, Greek 292.13; 398.20938
Mythology, Haitian 299.62097294; 398.2097294
Mythology, Hindu 294.513
Mythology, Indo-European 291.13
Mythology, Jewish 296.3
Mythology, Masai 299.62089965; 398.2089965
Mythology, Mingrelian 299.92968
Mythology, Norse 293.13
Mythology, Roman 292.13
Mythology, Tai 299.591
Myxomycetes 579.52
Nabis (Group of artists) 700.944; 759.4
Nabokov, Vladimir Vladimirovich, 1899–1977 813.54; 891.7142; 891.7342
Nabokov, Vladimir Vladimirovich, 1899–1977—Criticism and interpretation 813.54
Nabokov, Vladimir Vladimirovich, 1899–1977. Lolita 813.54
Nabokov, Vladimir Vladimirovich, 1899–1977—Translations into English 891.7142; 891.7342
Nahuatl language 497.452
Nahuatl poetry 897.4521; 897.4521008
Nahuatl poetry—Translations into English 897.4521008

Naidu, Sarojini, 1879–1949 821.912
Naidu, Sarojini, 1879–1949—Criticism and
  interpretation 821.912
Nails (Anatomy)—Diseases 616.547
Naipaul, V. S. (Vidiadhar Surajprasad), 1932– 823.914
Naipaul, V. S. (Vidiadhar Surajprasad), 1932– —
  Criticism and interpretation 823.914
Nameless Detective (Fictitious character) 813.54
Nameless Detective (Fictitious character)—Fiction
  813.54
Names 929.97
Names, Geographical 910.014; 910.3
Names, Geographical—England 914.20014; 914.2003
Names, Geographical—United States 917.30014;
  917.3003
Names, Indian 910.01408997
Names, Personal 929.4
Names, Personal—African 929.4096
Names, Personal—African—Dictionaries 929.409603
Names, Personal (Cataloging) 025.322
Names, Personal—Dictionaries 929.403
Names, Personal—Jewish 929.4089924
Names, Personal—United States 929.40973
Names, Personal—United States—Dictionaries
  929.4097303
Names, Scottish Gaelic 929.40899163
Namibia 968.81
Namibia—Economic conditions 330.96881
Namibia—Economic conditions—Periodicals
  330.96881005
Namibia—International status 341.29
Namibia—Politics and government 320.96881; 968.81
Namibia—Politics and government—1946–1990
  320.9688109045; 968.8103
Nānak, Guru, 1469–1538 294.663
Nance County (Neb.) 978.2425
Nance County (Neb.)—Maps 912.782425
Nanking Massacre, Nanjing, Jiangsu Sheng, China,
  1937 951.042
Nannies 649.1
Nannies—United States 649.1
Nannofossils 560; 561.9; 561.93
Nanofiltration 628.164; 660.284245
Nanoparticles 620.43
Nanostructure materials 620.11299; 620.5
Nanostructures 620.11299
Nanotechnology 620.5
Nanowires 621.3815
Nantucket Island (Mass.) 974.497
Nantucket Island (Mass.)—Guidebooks 917.449704;
  917.44970443; 917.44970444
Nantucket Island (Mass.)—History 974.497
Napa County (Calif.) 979.419
Napa County (Calif.)—Guidebooks 917.941904;
  917.94190453; 917.94190454
Napa Valley (Calif.) 979.419
Napa Valley (Calif.)—History 979.419
Napkin folding 642.7
Naples (Italy) 945.73
Naples (Italy)—Guidebooks 914.57304; 914.57304929;
  914.5730493
Napoleon I, Emperor of the French, 1769–1821
  944.046; 944.05092
Napoleon I, Emperor of the French, 1769–1821—
  Influence 940.27
Napoleon I, Emperor of the French, 1769–1821—
  Military leadership 355.0092
Napoleon III, Emperor of the French, 1808–1873
  944.07092

Napoleonic Wars, 1800–1815 940.27
Napoleonic Wars, 1800–1815—Campaigns 940.274
Napoleonic Wars, 1800–1815—Campaigns—Russia
  940.2742
Naps (Sleep) in the workplace 331.2576
Narayan, R. K., 1906– 823.912
Narayan, R. K., 1906– —Criticism and interpretation
  823.912
Narcissism 616.8585
Narcotic addicts 362.293092
Narcotic addicts—Psychology 616.86320019
Narcotic enforcement agents 363.45
Narcotic habit 362.293; 613.83; 616.8632
Narcotic laws 345.0277
Narcotic laws—United States 345.730277
Narcotics 362.293
Narcotics and crime 364.2
Narcotics and crime—United States 364.24
Narcotics, Control of 363.45
Narcotics, Control of—Andes Region 363.45098
Narcotics, Control of—Colombia 363.4509861
Narcotics, Control of—International cooperation 363.45
Narcotics, Control of—New York (State)—New York
  363.45097471
Narcotics, Control of—United States 363.450973;
  364.1770973
Narcotics, Control of—United States—Periodicals
  363.45097305
Narragansett Indians 305.8973; 974.5004973
Narration in the Bible 220.66
Narrative poetry, American 811.03
Narrative poetry, English 821.03; 821.0308
Narrative poetry, English—History and criticism
  821.0309
Narrative theology 230.046
Narrow gap semiconductors 537.6223
Narrow gauge railroads 385.5
Nasal dilator strips 616.212; 681.761
NASCAR (Association) 796.720973
Nashville (Tenn.) 976.855
Nashville (Tenn.)—Guidebooks 917.685504;
  917.68550453; 917.68550454
Nashville (Tenn.)—History 976.855
Nashville (Tenn.)—Maps 912.76855
Naskapi Indians 971.4004973
Nassau County (N.Y.)—Maps 912.747245
NASTRAN 624.17102855369
Natal astrology 133.5
Natchez (Miss.) 976.226
Natchez (Miss.)—History 976.226
National Aboriginal Day (Canada) 394.263
National Association for the Advancement of Colored
  People—Archives 026.3231196073
National banks (United States) 346.730821223
National Basketball Association 796.3230973;
  796.323640973
National Basketball Association—History 796.323640973
National Board of Medical Examiners—Examinations
  610.76
National Capital Region (Ont. and Québec)—Maps
  912.71383
National characteristics, American 305.813; 973
National characteristics, Argentine 305.86882; 982
National characteristics, Australian 305.824; 994
National characteristics, Austrian 305.836; 943.6
National characteristics, Brazilian 305.86881; 981
National characteristics, British 305.821; 941
National characteristics, Bulgarian 305.891811; 949.9
National characteristics, Canadian 305.811; 971

National characteristics, **Chinese** 305.8951; 951
National characteristics, **English** 305.821; 942
National characteristics, **French** 305.841; 944
National characteristics, **German** 305.831; 943
National characteristics, **Greek** 305.88; 949.5
National characteristics, **Irish** 305.89162; 941.5
National characteristics, **Israeli** 305.8924; 956.94
National characteristics, **Italian** 305.851; 945
National characteristics, **Japanese** 305.8956; 952
National characteristics, **Korean** 305.8957; 951.9
National characteristics, **Latin American** 305.868; 980
National characteristics, **Mexican** 305.86872; 972
National characteristics, **Philippine** 305.89921; 959.9
National characteristics, **Russian** 305.89171; 947
National characteristics, **Spanish** 305.861; 946
National characteristics, **Swiss** 305.835; 949.4
National Child Day (Canada) 394.264
National Collegiate Athletic Association—Handbooks, manuals, etc. 796.0430973
National Fire Protection Association. National Electrical Code (1993) 621.31924021873
National Football League 796.3326406
National Football League—History 796.3326406
National Gallery of Art (U.S.) 708.153
National Grange 630.6073
National Health and Nutrition Examination Survey (U.S.) 614.4273
National health insurance 368.42
National health insurance—Law and legislation 344.022
National health insurance—Law and legislation—United States 344.73022
National health insurance—United States 368.4200973
National Health Service (Great Britain) 362.10941
National Health Service (Great Britain)—Administration 362.10941
National Health Service (Great Britain)—History 362.10941
National Hockey League 796.96264
National Hockey League—History 796.96264
National income 339.32
National income—Accounting 339.32
National income—United States 339.373
National income—United States—Accounting 339.373
National Institute of Justice (U.S.)—Periodicals 364.97305
National Institutes of Health (U.S.) 610.72073
National liberation movements 322.42
National liberation movements—Namibia 322.42096881
National libraries 027.5
National Library of Australia 027.594
National Measurement System for Time and Frequency 681.11
National monuments 363.68
National music 781.599
National parks and reserves 363.68
National parks and reserves—California—Guidebooks 917.9404; 917.940453; 917.940454
National parks and reserves—East (U.S.)—Guidebooks 917.404; 917.40443; 917.40444
National parks and reserves—Law and legislation 346.046783
National parks and reserves—Law and legislation—United States 346.73046783
National parks and reserves—United States 333.7830973; 973
National parks and reserves—United States—History 973
National parks and reserves—United States—Management 333.7830973

National parks and reserves—West (U.S.)—Guidebooks 917.804; 917.80433; 917.80434
National Peace Garden Memorial (Washington, D.C.) 327.172
National protected areas systems 333.72
National Public Radio (U.S.) 384.54065
National romanticism (Architecture) 720.94309034
National school lunch program 371.7160973
National security 355.03
National security—Asia 355.03305
National security—Asia, Southeastern 355.033059
National security—Australia 355.033094
National security—Canada 355.033071
National security—Caribbean Area 355.0330729
National security—China 355.033051
National Security Council (U.S.) 353.12240973
National Security Council (U.S.)—Archives 026.35312240973
National Security Council (U.S.)—History 353.12240973
National security—Developing countries 355.03301724
National security—East Asia 355.03305
National security—Europe 355.03304
National security—Europe, Eastern 355.033047
National security—Europe, Northern 355.033048
National security—France 355.033044
National security—India 355.033054
National security—Israel 355.03305694
National security—Japan 355.033052
National security—Korea (South) 355.03305195
National security—Latin America 355.03308
National security—Law and legislation 343.01
National security—Law and legislation—United States 343.7301
National security—Mediterranean Region 355.03301822
National security—Middle East 355.033056
National security—Norway 355.0330481
National security—Pacific Area 355.03301823
National security—Pakistan 355.03305491
National security—Periodicals 355.0305
National security—Russia (Federation) 355.033047
National security—Scandinavia 355.033048
National security—South Africa 355.033068
National security—South Asia 355.033054
National security—Soviet Union 355.033047
National security—United States 355.033073
National security—United States—Decision making 353.12330973; 353.12340973
National security—United States—History 355.033073
National service 355.22363
National service—United States 355.2250973
National socialism 943.086
National socialism in literature 808.80358; 809.93358
National songs 781.599
National teacher examinations 371.120287
National Vocational Qualifications (Great Britain) 331.25920941; 370.1130941
Nationalism 320.54
Nationalism—Europe 320.54094
Nationalism—Europe—History 320.54094
Nationalism—France 320.540944
Nationalism—History 320.5409
Nationalism in literature 808.80358; 809.93358
Nationalism—India 320.540954
Nationalism—India—History 320.540954
Nationalism—Québec (Province) 971.404
Nationalism—Religious aspects 291.177
Nationalities, Principle of 320.15
Nationalsozialistische Deutsche Arbeiter-Partei 324.243038

Native plant gardening 635.9676
Nativism 149.7
Natural areas 333.78
Natural beef 641.362
Natural childbirth 618.45
Natural disaster warning systems 363.3472
Natural disasters 363.34
Natural family planning 613.9434
Natural foods 641.302
Natural foods industry 338.47641302
Natural gardens 635.95
Natural gardens—Design 712.6
Natural gas 553.285; 665.7
Natural gas—Alaska—Transportation 388.5609798
Natural gas—Analysis 665.73
Natural gas—Geology 553.285
Natural gas—Hydrates 665.7
Natural gas—Law and legislation 343.0926; 346.0468233
Natural gas—Law and legislation—United States 343.730926; 346.730468233
Natural gas pipelines 388.56; 665.744
Natural gas pipelines—Alaska 388.5609798
Natural gas pipelines—Alaska—Finance 388.560681
Natural gas pipelines—Canada 388.560971
Natural gas pipelines—Environmental aspects 333.8233
Natural gas pipelines—Environmental aspects—Northwest Territories 333.8233
Natural gas pipelines—Environmental aspects—Northwest Territories—Mackenzie River Valley 333.8233
Natural gas pipelines—Law and legislation 343.093
Natural gas pipelines—Law and legislation—United States 343.73093
Natural gas pipelines—Northwest Territories 388.5609719
Natural gas pipelines—Safety regulations 344.047
Natural gas pipelines—Safety regulations—United States 343.73093
Natural gas pipelines—United States—Maps 388.560973022
Natural gas—Prices 338.23285
Natural gas—Prices—United States 338.232850973
Natural gas—Prospecting 622.18285
Natural gas—Underground storage 665.742
Natural gas—United States 333.82330973; 338.272850973
Natural gas—United States—Analysis 665.73
Natural gas—United States—Rates 338.23285
Natural history 508; 578
Natural history—Alaska 508.798; 578.09798
Natural history—Antarctica 508.989; 578.09989
Natural history—Arctic regions 508.3113; 578.09113
Natural history—Arizona—Grand Canyon 508.79132; 578.0979132
Natural history—Australia 508.94; 578.0994
Natural history—Australia—Great Barrier Reef (Qld.) 508.943; 578.77890943
Natural history—Authorship 508
Natural history—Bibliography 016.508
Natural history—California 508.794; 578.09794
Natural history—Canada 508.71; 578.0971
Natural history—Colorado 508.788; 578.09788
Natural history—England 508.42; 578.0942
Natural history—England—Selborne 508.42274; 578.0942274
Natural history—Experiments 508.078
Natural history—Florida 508.759; 578.09759
Natural history—Florida—Everglades 508.75939; 578.0975939

Natural history—Galapagos Islands 508.8665; 578.098665
Natural history—Great Britain 508.41; 578.0941
Natural history—Hawaii 508.969; 578.09969
Natural history literature 508
Natural history—Massachusetts 508.744; 578.09744
Natural history—Massachusetts—Cape Cod 508.74492; 578.0974492
Natural history—Michigan 508.774; 578.09774
Natural history—Minnesota 508.776; 578.09776
Natural history museums 508.074
Natural history—New England 508.74; 578.0974
Natural history—New York (State)—Adirondack Mountains 508.7475; 578.097475
Natural history—New Zealand 508.93; 578.0993
Natural history—North America 508.7; 578.097
Natural history—Northwest, Pacific 508.795; 578.09795
Natural history—Outdoor books 508
Natural history—Periodicals 508.05
Natural history—Pictorial works 508.0222
Natural history—Religious aspects 291.175
Natural history—Rocky Mountains 508.78; 578.0978
Natural history—Sierra Nevada (Calif. and Nev.) 508.7944; 578.097944
Natural history—South Carolina 508.757; 578.09757
Natural history—Southwest, New 508.79; 578.0979
Natural history—Study and teaching 508.071
Natural history—Study and teaching (Elementary) 372.357
Natural history—United States 508.73; 578.0973
Natural history—West (U.S.) 508.78; 578.0978
Natural immunity 616.079
Natural landscaping 635.95
Natural language processing (Computer science) 006.35
Natural law 340.112
Natural law—History 340.1109
Natural monuments 719.32
Natural pesticides 632.95
Natural products 338.02
Natural resources 333.7
Natural resources—Accounting 333.714
Natural resources conservation areas 333.72
Natural resources conservation areas—Law and legislation 346.044
Natural resources—Law and legislation 346.044
Natural resources—Law and legislation—United States 346.73044
Natural resources—Management 333.7
Natural resources—United States 333.70973
Natural resources—United States—Information services 025.0633370973
Natural resources—United States—Management 333.70973
Natural selection 576.82
Natural theology 210
Natural theology—Early works to 1900 210
Naturalism 146
Naturalism in literature 808.8012; 809.912
Naturalists 578.092
Naturalization 323.623
Naturalization—United States 323.6230973; 342.73083
Nature 508; 578
Nature (Aesthetics) 750.117
Nature and nurture 155.7
Nature—Biblical teaching 261.8362
Nature conservation 333.9516
Nature conservation—Periodicals 333.951605
Nature conservation—United States 333.782160973

Nature craft 745.5
Nature—Effect of human beings on 304.2; 577.27
Nature—Effect of human beings on—Amazon River Region 304.209811
Nature—Effect of human beings on—History 304.2
Nature—Effect of human beings on—Maps 304.20223
Nature in literature 808.8036; 809.9336
Nature in music 781.56
Nature—Literary collections 808.8036
Nature—Miscellanea 508
Nature photography 778.93; 779.3
Nature photography—Handbooks, manuals, etc. 778.93
Nature—Psychic aspects 133.25
Nature—Psychological aspects 155.91
Nature—Religious aspects 291.178362
Nature—Religious aspects—Christianity 231.7
Nature—Religious aspects—Christianity—Meditations 242
Nature study 508
Nature study—Activity programs 508.078
Nature study—Study and teaching (Elementary) 372.357
Nature trails 634.93
Naturopathic schools 615.535071
Naturopathy 615.535
Nautical astronomy 527
Nautical charts 623.8922
Nautical charts—Atlantic coast (North America) 623.892234
Nautical charts—Atlantic coast (North America)—To 1800 623.8922340903
Nautical charts—Atlantic Coast (U.S.) 623.892234
Nautical charts—California, Southern 623.892297949
Nautical charts—Cumberland River (Ky. and Tenn.) 623.892297685
Nautical charts—Detroit River (Mich. and Ont.) 623.892977433
Nautical charts—Erie, Lake 623.8922977; 623.89297712
Nautical charts—Florida 623.8922348; 623.89229759
Nautical charts—Mississippi River 623.8922977
Nautical charts—New England 623.8922345; 623.8922974
Nautical charts—North America—Atlantic Coast 623.892234
Nautical charts—North America—Atlantic Coast—To 1800 623.8922340903
Nautical charts—Tennessee River 623.89229768
Nautical paraphernalia 623.863
Nautical training-schools 359.5
Nautilus shell cups 739.2284
Navajo art 704.03972
Navajo Indians 305.8972; 979.1004972
Navajo Indians—Folklore 398.2089972
Navajo Indians—Land tenure 346.730436089972
Navajo Indians—Pictorial works 305.8972; 979.004972
Navajo Indians—Religion 299.782
Navajo Indians—Relocation 979.1004972
Navajo Indians—Rites and ceremonies 299.74
Navajo Indians—Social life and customs 305.8972
Navajo Long Walk, 1863–1867 978.9004972
Navajo mythology 299.72
Navajo textile fabrics 746.14089972
Navajo textile fabrics—Catalogs 746.14089972; 746.72075
Navajo textile fabrics—Exhibitions 746.72074
Naval architecture 623.81
Naval architecture—Data processing 623.810285
Naval art and science 359
Naval art and science—Dictionaries 359.003; 623.803

Naval art and science—History 359.009
Naval art and science—History—20th century 359.00904
Naval battles 359.4
Naval education 359.00711
Naval history 359.009
Naval history, Modern 359.009
Naval libraries 026.359
Naval museums 387.0074
Naval research 359.07
Naval strategy 359.4
Naval tactics 359.42
Navarre (Spain) 946.52
Navarre (Spain)—Kings and rulers 946.520099
Navarre, Tres (Fictitious character) 813.54
Navier-Stokes equations 515.353
Navier-Stokes equations—Numerical solutions 515.353; 532.0501515353
Navies 359
Navigation 527; 623.89; 629.045
Navigation (Aeronautics) 629.13251
Navigation (Astronautics) 629.453
Navigation equipment industry 338.47623893
Navigation—Handbooks, manuals, etc. 623.89
Navigation—History 623.8909; 629.04509
Navigation—Polynesia 623.89099
Navigation—Safety measures 623.8884; 629.0450289
Navigation—Tables 623.89021; 629.045021
Navratilova, Martina, 1956– 796.342092
Naylor, Gloria 813.54
Naylor, Gloria—Criticism and interpretation 813.54
Nazca Lines Site (Peru) 985.27
Nâzım Hikmet, 1902–1963 894.3513
Nâzım Hikmet, 1902–1963—Translations into English 894.3513
Nazis 943.086
Nazis—Biography 943.0860922
NCAA Basketball Tournament 796.3230973
NCAA Basketball Tournament—History 796.3230973
Neal family 929.20973
Neanderthals 569.9
Neapolitan mastiff 636.73
Near-death experiences 133.9013
Near-death experiences—Psychological aspects 133.9013
Near-death experiences—Religious aspects 291.23
Near-death experiences—Religious aspects— Christianity 236.1
Near misses (Aeronautics) 363.12492
Near-rings 512.4
Nearing, Scott, 1883– 301.092; 335.0092
Nebraska 978.2
Nebraska—Guidebooks 917.8204; 917.820433; 917.820434
Nebraska—History 978.2
Nebraska—Maps 912.782
Nebraska—Social life and customs 978.2
Nebula Award 823.087607973
Nebulae 523.1135
Neck 611.93
Neck pain 617.53
Neck—Surgery 617.53059
Necrotizing fasciitis 616.92
Need (Psychology) in children 155.412
Needle biopsy 616.0758
Needlework 746.4
Needlework—Equipment and supplies—History 746.40284
Needlework industry and trade 746.4
Needlework—Patterns 746.4

Needlework—Periodicals 746.405
Negation (Logic) 160
Negative theology 211; 231
Negligence 346.032
Negligence, Comparative 346.032
Negligence, Comparative—United States 346.73032
Negotiable instruments 346.096
Negotiable instruments—Philippines 346.599096
Negotiable instruments—United States 346.73096
Negotiable instruments—United States—Cases
  346.730960264
Negotiable instruments—United States—States
  346.73096
Negotiation 158.5
Negotiation in business 658.4052
Negro leagues 796.357640973
Negro leagues—History 796.357640973
Nehru, Jawaharlal, 1889–1964 954.042092
Nehru, Jawaharlal, 1889–1964—Political and social
  views 954.042092
Neighborhood 307.3362
Neighborhood—United States 307.33620973
Nelson County (N.D.) 978.435
Nelson County (N.D.)—Maps 912.78435
Nelson family 929.20973
Nelson, Horatio Nelson, Viscount, 1758–1805 359.0092
Nemastomataceae 579.89
Nematoda 592.57
Nematode-plant relationships 571.999; 592.5717857
Nematologists 592.57092
Nemertea 592.32
Neo-Confucianism 181.112
Neo-Confucianism—Korea 181.112
Neo-impressionism (Music) 780.904
Neo-Kantianism 142.3
Neo-Nazis 320.533; 335.6
Neo-Nazism 320.533; 335.6
Neo-Scholasticism 149.91
Neoclassical school of economics 330.157
Neoclassicism (Architecture) 724.2
Neoclassicism (Art) 709.0341
Neogastropoda 594.32
Neoism 709.04
Neolithic period 930.14
Neolithic period—Europe 936
Neolithic period—Great Britain 936.101
Neon signs 621.3275
Neonatal intensive care 618.9201
Neonatal intensive care—Handbooks, manuals, etc.
  618.9201
Neonatology 618.9201
Neopaganism 299
Neoplatonism 186.4
Neoromanticism (Music) 780.904
Neotrypaea 595.384
Neovascularization 612.13
Nepal 954.96
Nepal—Civilization 954.96
Nepal—Description and travel 915.49604
Nepal—Economic conditions 330.95496
Nepal—Economic policy 338.95496
Nepal—Foreign relations 327.5496
Nepal—Guidebooks 915.49604
Nepal—History 954.96
Nepal—History—To 1768 954.96
Nepal—History—1768–1951 954.96
Nepal—Politics and government 320.95496
Nephrology 616.61
Nephrotic syndrome 616.61

Nephrotoxicology 616.61071
NEPSY (Neuropsychological test) 618.9280475
Neptune (Planet) 523.481
Neruda, Pablo, 1904–1973 861.62
Neruda, Pablo, 1904–1973—Translations into English
  861.62
Nerve gases 358.34; 623.4592
Nerve growth factor 573.8538
Nerves, Peripheral 573.85
Nerves, Peripheral—Diseases 616.87
Nervous system 573.8; 612.8
Nervous system—Aging 612.8
Nervous system—Cancer 616.9948
Nervous system—Degeneration 616.8047
Nervous system—Diseases 616.8
Nervous system—Diseases—Diagnosis 616.80475
Nervous system—Diseases—Genetic aspects 616.80442
Nervous system—Diseases—Handbooks, manuals, etc.
  616.8
Nervous system—Diseases—Immunological aspects
  616.80479
Nervous system—Diseases—Molecular aspects
  616.8047
Nervous system—Diseases—Patients 362.1968
Nervous system—Diseases—Patients—Rehabilitation
  616.8043
Nervous system—Imaging 616.804754
Nervous system—Infections 616.8
Nervous system—Laser surgery 617.48059
Nervous system—Pathophysiology 616.8047
Nervous system—Radiography 616.0047572
Nervous system—Surgery 617.48
Nestleton, Alice (Fictitious character) 813.54
Nestleton, Alice (Fictitious character)—Fiction 813.54
Netcentric computing 004.36
Netherlands 949.2
Netherlands—Civilization 949.2
Netherlands—Description and travel 914.9204;
  914.920473
Netherlands—Economic conditions 330.9492
Netherlands—Economic conditions—1945– 330.949207
Netherlands—Guidebooks 914.9204; 914.920473
Netherlands—History 949.2
Netherlands—History—Wars of Independence, 1556–
  1648 949.203
NetObjects Fusion 006.78769
Netscape 025.04
Netscape Communicator 005.713769
NetWare 005.71369
Network analysis (Planning) 658.4032
Network computers 004.36
Network File System (Computer network protocol)
  004.62
Network performance (Telecommunication) 384;
  621.382
Network publishing (Computer networks)
  070.50285467
Neural circuitry 573.85
Neural computers 006.32
Neural computers—Periodicals 006.3205
Neural conduction—Measurement 616.8047547
Neural networks (Computer science) 006.32;
  621.3822028563
Neural networks (Computer science)—Periodicals
  006.3205
Neural networks (Neurobiology) 573.85
Neural receptors 612.8042
Neural transmission 573.8
Neuralgia 616.87

Neuroanatomy 573.833; 611.8
Neuroanatomy—Atlases 611.80222
Neuroanatomy—Examinations, questions, etc. 611.8076
Neurobehavioral disorders 616.8
Neurobiology 573.8; 612.8
Neuroblastoma 616.9948
Neurochemistry 612.8042
Neuroendocrinology 612.8
Neurofibromatosis 616.99383
Neurogenetics 612.8
Neuroglia 611.0188
Neuroimmunology 616.80479
Neurolinguistic programming 158.1
Neurolinguistics 612.78
Neurologic examination 616.80475
Neurological emergencies 616.80425
Neurological intensive care 616.80428
Neurological nursing 610.7368
Neurologists 616.80092
Neurology 616.8
Neurology—Examinations, questions, etc. 616.80076
Neurology—Handbooks, manuals, etc. 616.8
Neuromuscular blocking agents 615.773
Neuromuscular diseases 616.744
Neuronal ceroid-lipofuscinosis 616.83
Neurons 611.0188
Neuroophthalmology 617.732
Neuropharmacology 615.78; 616.80461
Neurophysiology 573.8; 612.8
Neuropsychiatry 616.8
Neuropsychological tests 616.8; 616.80475
Neuropsychological tests—Handbooks, manuals, etc. 152; 616.80475
Neuropsychology 152
Neuropsychopharmacology 615.78
Neurosciences 612.8
Neurosciences—History 612.809
Neurosciences—Periodicals 573.805
Neuroses 616.852
Neurotoxicology 616.80471
Neurotransmitters 573.8
Neutrality 341.64
Neutrality—Europe 341.64094
Neutrality—United States 327.73; 341.640973
Neutrino astrophysics 523.0197215
Neutrinos 539.7215
Neutron radiography 620.11272; 621.4837
Neutron sources 539.7213
Neutron stars 523.8874
Neutrons 539.7213
Neutrons—Diffraction 539.75
Neutrons—Scattering 539.758
Neutrophils 612.112; 616.079
Nevada 979.3
Nevada—Guidebooks 917.9304; 917.930433; 917.930434
Nevada—History 979.3
Nevada—Maps 912.793
Nevada—Road maps 912.793
Nevelson, Louise, 1899–1988 709.2; 730.92
New Age movement 133; 239.93; 299.93
New Age movement—Dictionaries 299.93
New Age music 780.904
New Age musicians 780.92
New business enterprises 338.6
New business enterprises—Finance 658.15
New business enterprises—Handbooks, manuals, etc. 658.11
New business enterprises—Management 658.11
New business enterprises—Planning 658.4012

New business enterprises—Taxation 336.207
New business enterprises—United States 658.110973
New business enterprises—United States—Finance 658.15
New business enterprises—United States—Handbooks, manuals, etc. 658.110973
New business enterprises—United States—Management 658.110973
New Caledonian fiction (French) 843.008099597
New Caledonian poetry (French) 841.008099597
New Castle County (Del.) 975.11
New Castle County (Del.)—Antiquities 975.11
New Castle County (Del.)—Maps 912.7511
New Columbia 975.3
New Criticism—United States 801.95; 810.9973
New Deal, 1933–1939 973.917
New England 974
New England—Description and travel 917.404; 917.40443; 917.40444
New England—Description and travel—Early works to 1800 917.404
New England—Economic conditions 330.974
New England—Genealogy 929.1072074; 929.374
New England—Guidebooks 917.404; 917.40443; 917.40444
New England—History 974
New England—History—Colonial period, ca. 1600–1775 974.02
New England—Maps 912.74
New England—Pictorial works 779.9917400222; 974.00222
New England—Religious life and customs 277.4
New England—Road maps 912.74
New England—Social life and customs 974; 974.04
New England—Tours 917.404; 917.40443; 917.40444
New Forest (England : Forest) 942.275
New Hampshire 974.2
New Hampshire—Genealogy 929.3742
New Hampshire—Guidebooks 917.4204; 917.420443; 917.420444
New Hampshire—Maps 912.742
New Hanover County (N.C.)—Genealogy 929.375627
New Jersey 974.9
New Jersey—Census, 1990 304.60974909049
New Jersey—Economic policy 338.9749
New Jersey—Guidebooks 917.4904; 917.490443; 917.490444
New Jersey—History 974.9
New Jersey—History—Colonial period, ca. 1600–1775 974.902
New Jersey—History, Local 974.9
New Jersey—Maps 912.749
New Jersey—Officials and employees—Pensions 353.54909749
New Jersey—Pictorial works 917.4900222
New Jersey—Population 304.609749
New Jersey—Population—Statistics 304.609749021
New Jersey—Road maps 912.749
New Jersey—Tours 917.4904; 917.490443; 917.490444
New Jerusalem Church 289.4
New Jerusalem Church—Doctrines 230.94
New Jerusalem (Mormon theology) 236
New Kent County (Va.)—Genealogy 929.375543
New Market (Va.), Battle of, 1864 973.736
New Mexico 978.9; 978.96
New Mexico—Description and travel 779.99178900222; 917.8904; 917.890453; 917.890454
New Mexico—Guidebooks 917.8904; 917.890453; 917.890454

New Mexico—History 978.9
New Mexico—History—1848– 978.904
New Mexico—Maps 912.789
New Mexico—Social life and customs 978.9
New Mexico—Tours 917.8904; 917.890453; 917.890454
New Orleans (La.) 976.335
New Orleans (La.), Battle of, 1815 973.5239
New Orleans (La.)—Civilization 976.335
New Orleans (La.)—Guidebooks 917.633504;
   917.63350463; 917.63350464
New Orleans (La.)—History 976.335
New Orleans (La.)—Pictorial works 976.33500222
New Orleans (La.)—Social conditions 976.335
New Orleans (La.)—Social life and customs 976.335
New Orleans Saints (Football team) 796.332640976335
New Orleans Saints (Football team)—History
   796.332640976335
New products 658.575
New products—Environmental aspects 658.575
New products—Management 658.575
New products—Marketing 658.8
New South Wales 994.4
New South Wales—Description and travel 919.4404;
   919.440466; 919.44047
New South Wales—History 994.4
New South Wales—Maps 912.944
New South Wales—Road maps 912.944
New Thought 289.98; 299.93
New towns 307.768; 711.45
New wave films 791.43611
New wave films—France 791.436110944
New Year 394.2614
New York Central Railroad Company 385.09747
New York Giants (Football team) 796.33264097471
New York Giants (Football team)—History
   796.33264097471
New York Jets (Football team) 796.33264097471
New York Jets (Football team)—History
   796.33264097471
New York Knickerbockers (Basketball team)
   796.32364097471
New York Knickerbockers (Basketball team)—History
   796.32364097471
New York Metropolitan Area 974.71
New York Metropolitan Area—Guidebooks 917.47104
New York Mets (Baseball team)—History
   796.35764097471
New York (N.Y.) 974.71
New York (N.Y.)—Description and travel 917.47104;
   917.4710443; 917.4710444
New York (N.Y.)—Economic conditions 330.9747
New York (N.Y.)—Genealogy 929.37471
New York (N.Y.)—Guidebooks 917.47104; 917.4710443;
   917.4710444
New York (N.Y.)—History 974.71
New York (N.Y.)—History—1865–1898 974.71041
New York (N.Y.)—Maps 912.7471
New York (N.Y.)—Pictorial works 779.991747100222;
   917.47100222; 974.7100222
New York (N.Y.)—Politics and government 320.97471
New York (N.Y.)—Politics and government—1951–
   320.9747109045
New York (N.Y.)—Social life and customs 974.71
New York (N.Y.)—Social life and customs—Anecdotes
   974.71
New York (N.Y.)—Statistics, Vital 317.471
New York (N.Y.)—Tours 917.47104; 917.4710443;
   917.4710444

New York, New Haven, and Hartford Railroad Company
   385.09746
New York Region 974.71
New York Region—Guidebooks 917.47104; 917.4710443;
   917.4710444
New York (State) 974.7
New York (State)—Economic policy 338.9747
New York (State). Family Court (City of New York)
   346.7470150269
New York (State)—Genealogy 929.3747
New York (State)—Guidebooks 917.4704; 917.470443;
   917.470444
New York (State)—History 974.7
New York (State)—History—Colonial period, ca. 1600–
   1775 974.702
New York (State)—History—Colonial period, ca. 1600–
   1775—Sources 974.702072
New York (State)—History, Local 974.7
New York (State)—Maps 912.747
New York (State)—Pictorial works 974.700222
New York (State)—Politics and government 320.9747;
   974.7
New York (State)—Politics and government—To 1775
   320.97470933; 974.702
New York (State)—Politics and government—1775–
   1783 320.97470933; 974.703
New York (State)—Politics and government—1951–
   320.974709045
New York (State)—Tours 917.4704; 917.470443;
   917.470444
New York Stock Exchange 332.64273
New York Stock Exchange—History 332.64273
New York times 071.471
New York Yankees (Baseball team) 796.35764097471
New York Yankees (Baseball team)—History
   796.35764097471
New Zealand 993
New Zealand—Description and travel 919.304;
   919.30438; 919.3044
New Zealand—Economic conditions 330.993
New Zealand—Economic conditions—1945–1984
   330.993035
New Zealand—Economic policy 338.993
New Zealand fiction 823.0080993
New Zealand fiction—20th century 823.0080993
New Zealand—Foreign relations 327.93
New Zealand—Foreign relations—1945– 327.93
New Zealand—Guidebooks 919.304; 919.30438;
   919.3044
New Zealand—History 993
New Zealand—History—1840–1876 993.022
New Zealand literature 820.80993
New Zealand literature—History and criticism 820.9993
New Zealand—Maps 912.93
New Zealand—Pictorial works 919.300222
New Zealand poetry 821; 821.0080993
New Zealand poetry—20th century 821.91;
   821.910080993
New Zealand—Politics and government 320.493;
   320.993
New Zealand—Politics and government—1972–
   320.99309047
New Zealand—Race relations 305.800993
New Zealand—Road maps 912.93
New Zealand Sign Language 419.93
New Zealand—Social conditions 993
New Zealand—Social life and customs 993
New Zealand—Social life and customs—20th century
   993.04

Newaygo County (Mich.) 977.458
Newaygo County (Mich.)—Maps 912.77458
Newbery Medal 028.5079
Newbery Medal—Bibliography 011.62079; 028.162079
Newfoundland 971.8
Newfoundland dog 636.73
Newfoundland—History 971.8
Newhouse, Samuel I. 070.5092
Newman, John Henry, 1801–1890 282.092
News agencies 070.435
News audiences 302.23
News libraries 026.07
News radio stations 070.194
Newsletters 070.175
Newsletters—Publishing 070.175
Newspaper editors 070.41092
Newspaper layout and typography 686.2252
Newspaper publishing 070.5722
Newspapers 070.172
Newspapers—Headlines 070.172
Newspapers—Headlines—Humor 070.1720207
Newspapers in education 371.335
Newspapers—Sections, columns, etc. 070.44
Newsreaders (Computer software) 005.71376
Newton, Isaac, Sir, 1642–1727 530.092
Newton, Isaac, Sir, 1642–1727. Principia 531
Newton, John, 1725–1807 283.092
NeXT (Computer) 004.165
NeXT (Computer)—Programming 005.265
Nez Percé Indians 305.89741; 979.50049741
Nez Percé Indians—History 979.50049741
Ngũgĩ wa Thiong'o, 1938– 823.914
Ngũgĩ wa Thiong'o, 1938– —Criticism and interpretation
    823.914
Niagara Falls (N.Y. and Ont.) 971.339
Nibelungenlied 831.21
Nicaragua 972.85
Nicaragua—Description and travel 917.28504;
    917.2850454
Nicaragua—History 972.85
Nicaragua—History—1979–1990 972.85053
Nicaragua—Politics and government 320.97285; 972.85
Nicaragua—Politics and government—1979–1990
    320.9728509048; 972.85053
Nicaragua—Politics and government—1990–
    320.9728509049; 972.85054
Niceguy, Nev (Fictitious character) 823.914
Nicene Creed 238.142
Nicholas II, Emperor of Russia, 1868–1918 947.083092
Nicholas II, Emperor of Russia, 1868–1918—
    Assassination 947.083092
Nicholas County (Ky.)—Genealogy 929.3769417
Nicholas, of Cusa, Cardinal, 1401–1464 230.2092
Nichols, Beverley, 1899– 824.912
Nichols, Beverley, 1899– —Homes and haunts—
    England—Surrey 824.912
Nichols family 929.20973
Nicholson family 929.20973
Nicholson, Jack 791.43028092
Nickel—Metallurgy 669.7332
Nickel-plating 671.732
Nicollet County (Minn.) 977.632
Nicollet County (Minn.)—Maps 912.77632
Nicotine 615.952379
Nicotine—Physiological effect 615.78
Niebuhr, H. Richard (Helmut Richard), 1894–1962
    230.092
Niebuhr, Reinhold, 1892–1971 230.092

Nietzsche, Friedrich Wilhelm, 1844–1900 193
Nietzsche, Friedrich Wilhelm, 1844–1900—Aesthetics
    111.85092
Nietzsche, Friedrich Wilhelm, 1844–1900. Also sprach
    Zarathustra 193
Nietzsche, Friedrich Wilhelm, 1844–1900—
    Contributions in political science 320.092
Nietzsche, Friedrich Wilhelm, 1844–1900—Influence
    193
Nigella 583.34
Niger State (Nigeria) 966.965
Nigeria 966.9
Nigeria—Civilization 966.9
Nigeria—Civilization—20th century 966.903
Nigeria—Commerce 382.09669
Nigeria—Commerce—Periodicals 382.0966905
Nigeria—Constitutional law 342.669
Nigeria—Description and travel 916.6904; 916.690453
Nigeria, Eastern 966.94
Nigeria, Eastern—History 966.94
Nigeria—Economic conditions 330.9669
Nigeria—Economic conditions—1960– 330.966905
Nigeria—Economic conditions—1970– 330.9669053
Nigeria—Economic conditions—1970– —Periodicals
    330.9669053
Nigeria—Economic policy 338.9669
Nigeria—Economic policy—Periodicals 338.9669005
Nigeria—Foreign relations 327.669
Nigeria—Foreign relations—1960– 327.66909046
Nigeria—Foreign relations—1984–1993 327.66909048
Nigeria—Guidebooks 916.6904; 916.690453
Nigeria—History 966.9
Nigeria—History—Civil War, 1967–1970 966.9052
Nigeria—Maps 912.669
Nigeria—Periodicals 966.9005
Nigeria—Politics and government 320.9669; 966.9
Nigeria—Politics and government—1960–
    320.966909045; 320.966909046; 966.905
Nigeria—Politics and government—1960–1975
    320.966909046
Nigeria—Politics and government—1979–1983
    320.966909048; 966.9053
Nigeria—Politics and government—1984–1993
    320.966909048; 966.9053
Nigeria—Politics and government—1993–
    320.966909049; 966.9053
Nigeria—Social conditions 966.9
Nigeria—Social conditions—1960– 966.905
Nigeria—Social life and customs 966.9
Nigerian drama (English) 822; 822.00809669
Nigerian poetry (English) 821; 821.00809669
Night and all-weather operations (Military aeronautics)
    358.41423
Nightclubs 647.95; 792.7
Nightclubs—Law and legislation 343.07864795;
    343.0787927
Nighthawk, Jefferson (Fictitious character) 813.54
Nightingale, Florence, 1820–1910 610.73092
Nightmares 154.632
Nihilism 149.8
Nihilism in literature 808.80384; 809.93384
Nihilism (Philosophy) 149.8
Nike (Firm) 338.76870973
Nike (Firm)—History 338.76870973
Nikon camera 771.31
Nikon camera—Handbooks, manuals, etc. 771.31
Nikonos camera 778.730284
Nile River 962
Nilpotent Lie groups 512.55

Nimbus (Artificial satellite) 551.6354
Nin, Anaïs, 1903–1977 818.5209
Nin, Anaïs, 1903–1977—Criticism and interpretation
  818.5209
Nin, Anaïs, 1903–1977—Diaries 818.5203
Nineteen fifties 909.825
Nineteen nineties 909.829
Nineteen sixties 909.826
Nineteen thirties 909.823
Nineteen twenties 909.822
Ninjutsu 355.3432
Nintendo video games 794.8
Niobium 669.79
Niobium compounds 546.5242
Nipmuc Indians 305.8973; 974.4004973
Nirvana 294.3423; 294.523
Nirvana (Musical group) 782.421660922
Nissan trucks 629.2232
Nissan trucks—Maintenance and repair 629.28732
Nissan trucks—Maintenance and repair—Handbooks,
  manuals, etc. 629.28732
Nitrates 553.64; 661.65
Nitric oxide—Physiological effect 572.54
Nitrogen 546.711
Nitrogen compounds 547.04
Nitrogen cycle 577.145
Nitrogen fertilizers 631.84
Nitrogen—Fixation 572.545
Nitrogen-fixing microorganisms 579.3163
Nitrogen—Metabolism 572.511
Nitrogen oxides—Environmental aspects 628.532
Nitroso compounds 547.041
Nixon, Richard M. (Richard Milhous), 1913– 973.924092
Nixon, Walter L., 1928– —Impeachment 347.732234
Nkrumah, Kwame, 1909–1972 966.705092
Nō 792.0952
No-fault divorce 346.0166
No-fault divorce—United States 346.730166
No-load mutual funds 332.6327
Nō plays 895.62051
Nō plays—Translations into English 895.6205108
Noah (Biblical figure) 222.1109505
Noah family 929.20973
Noah's ark 222.1109505
Nobel Prizes 001.44
Nobility 929.7
Nobility—France 305.52230944
Nobility—Germany 305.52230943
Nobility—Great Britain 305.52230941
Nobility—Great Britain—Biography 929.72
Nobility—Russia 305.52230947
Nobles County (Minn.) 977.624
Nobles County (Minn.)—Maps 912.77624
Nocturnal animals 591.518
Noetherian rings 512.4
Noise 620.23
Noise control 620.23
Noise—Health aspects 363.74
Noise—Measurement 620.23
Noise pollution 363.74
Nolan family 929.20973
Nolan, Frank (Fictitious character) 813.54
Nomads 305.90691
Non-destructive testing 620.1127
Non-destructive testing—Periodicals 620.112705
Non-formal education 371.04; 374
Non-formal education—India 374.954
Non-governmental organizations 060

Non-governmental organizations—Developing countries
  068.1724
Non-governmental organizations—Law and legislation
  346.064
Non-insulin-dependent diabetes 616.462
Non-monogamous relationships 306.735; 306.8423
Non-Newtonian fluids 620.106
Non-timber forest products 634.98
Non-timber forest resources 333.75
Nonalignment 327.091716
Nonalignment—Developing countries 327.091716
Nonassociative algebras 512.24
Noncommutative differential geometry 512.55
Noncommutative rings 512.4
Nondurable goods 600
Nonequilibrium thermodynamics 536.7
Nonferrous metal industries 338.47669; 338.47669206;
  669.206
Nonferrous metals 669
Nonferrous metals—Metallurgy 669
Nongraded schools 371.255
Nongraded schools—United States 371.2550973
Nonlinear acoustics 534
Nonlinear assignment problems 519.76
Nonlinear boundary value problems 515.355
Nonlinear control theory 629.836
Nonlinear functional analysis 515.7
Nonlinear operators 515.7248
Nonlinear optics 535.2
Nonlinear oscillations 531.32
Nonlinear programming 519.76
Nonlinear theories 511.8
Nonlinear theories—Periodicals 511.8
Nonlinear waves 531.1133
Nonmonotonic reasoning 006.3; 160; 511.3
Nonparametric statistics 519.54
Nonpoint source pollution 363.7394
Nonprofit organizations 361.763
Nonprofit organizations—Accounting 657.98
Nonprofit organizations—Accounting—Standards
  657.980218
Nonprofit organizations—Accounting—Standards—
  United States 657.98021873
Nonprofit organizations—Finance 658.159
Nonprofit organizations—Law and legislation 346.064
Nonprofit organizations—Law and legislation—
  California 346.794064
Nonprofit organizations—Law and legislation—Canada
  346.71064
Nonprofit organizations—Law and legislation—
  Massachusetts 346.744064
Nonprofit organizations—Law and legislation—New
  York (State) 346.747064
Nonprofit organizations—Law and legislation—United
  States 346.73064
Nonprofit organizations—Management 658.048
Nonprofit organizations—Marketing 658.8
Nonprofit organizations—Political activity 322
Nonprofit organizations—Political activity—Law and
  legislation 342.05; 342.078
Nonprofit organizations—Taxation—Law and legislation
  343.066
Nonprofit organizations—Taxation—Law and
  legislation—United States 343.73066
Nonprofit organizations—United States 061.3;
  658.0480973
Nonprofit organizations—United States—Accounting
  657.98

Nonprofit organizations—United States—Management 658.0480973
Nonrelativistic quantum mechanics 530.12
Nonselfadjoint operators 515.7246
Nonsense literature, English 827.008
Nonsense verses, American 811.0708
Nonsense verses, English 821.0708
Nonsmooth optimization 519.3
Nonstandard mathematical analysis 515
Nontariff trade barriers 382.5
Nontraditional college students 378.1982
Nonverbal communication 302.222
Nonviolence 303.61
Nonviolence—Religious aspects 291.5697
Nonviolence—Religious aspects—Christianity 241.697
Nonwoven fabrics 677.6
Noodle soups 641.813
Norfolk County (Va.)—Genealogy 929.3755521
Norfolk (England) 942.61
Norfolk (England)—Antiquities 942.61
Norfolk (England)—Guidebooks 914.26104; 914.26104859; 914.2610486
Norfolk Island 994.82
Norfolk Island—History 994.82
Norfolk Metropolitan Area (Va.)—Maps 912.755521
Norgestrel 613.9432; 615.766
Normal basis theorem 512.3
Norman County (Minn.) 977.693
Norman County (Minn.)—Maps 912.77693
Normed linear spaces 515.732
Norris, Frank, 1870–1902 813.4
Norris, Frank, 1870–1902—Criticism and interpretation 813.4
North America 970
North America—Description and travel 917.04; 917.04539; 917.0454
North America—Discovery and exploration 970.01
North America—Geography 917
North America—History 970
North America—Maps 912.7
North America—Maps—To 1800 912.7
North America—Road maps 912.7
North American porcupine 599.35974
North Atlantic Treaty (1949) 341.720265
North Atlantic Treaty Organization 341.72; 355.031091821; 355.03301821
North Atlantic Treaty Organization—Armed Forces 355.0091821
North Atlantic Treaty Organization—Armed Forces—Procurement 355.6212091821
North Atlantic Treaty Organization—Armed Forces—Weapons systems 355.8091821
North Atlantic Treaty Organization—History 355.031091821
North Atlantic Treaty Organization—Membership 355.031091821
North Atlantic Treaty Organization—United States 355.0310973091821; 355.033573091821
North Carolina 975.6
North Carolina—Description and travel 917.5604
North Carolina—Genealogy 929.3756
North Carolina—Guidebooks 917.5604; 917.560443; 917.560444
North Carolina—History 975.6
North Carolina—Maps 912.756
North Carolina—Politics and government 320.9756; 975.6
North Carolina—Politics and government—1951– 320.975609045

North Carolina—Road maps 912.756
North Carolina—Social life and customs 975.6
North Carolina—Tours 917.5604; 917.560443; 917.560444
North Dakota 978.4
North Dakota—Maps 912.784
North Dakota—Road maps 912.784
North, Jerry (Fictitious character) 813.54
North, Jerry (Fictitious character)—Fiction 813.54
North Sea 551.46136
Northampton County (Va.)—Genealogy 929.375515
Northeastern States 974
Northeastern States—Guidebooks 917.404; 917.40443; 917.40444
Northern breed dogs 636.71
Northern fur seal 599.7973
Northern fur seal—Alaska—Pribilof Islands 599.7973097984
Northern Ireland 941.6
Northern Ireland—Civilization 941.6
Northern Ireland—Guidebooks 914.1604; 914.1604824; 914.1704
Northern Ireland—History 941.6
Northern Ireland—History—1969–1994 941.60824; 941.609
Northern Ireland—History—1969–1994—Pictorial works 941.608240222
Northern Ireland—Politics and government 320.9416; 941.6
Northern Ireland—Politics and government—1969–1994 320.9416; 320.941609047; 320.941609048; 320.941609049; 941.60824
Northern Ireland—Politics and government—1994– 320.941609049; 941.60824
Northern Ireland—Social life and customs 941.6
Northmen 948.022092
Northumberland County (Va.)—Genealogy 929.375521
Northumberland (England) 942.88
Northumberland (England)—Guidebooks 914.28804; 914.28804859; 914.2880486
Northwest, Canadian 971.2
Northwest, Canadian—Description and travel 917.19304; 917.193044
Northwest, Canadian—History 971.2
Northwest Coast of North America 979.5
Northwest Coast of North America—Description and travel 917.9504; 917.950443; 917.950444
Northwest, Old 977
Northwest, Old—History 977
Northwest, Old—History—1775–1865 977.02
Northwest, Pacific 979.5
Northwest, Pacific—Guidebooks 917.9504; 917.950443; 917.950444
Northwest, Pacific—History 979.5
Northwest, Pacific—Periodicals 979.5005
Northwest, Pacific—Social life and customs 979.5
Northwest, Pacific—Tours 917.9504; 917.950443; 917.950444
Northwest Passage 910.916327
Northwest Territories 971.92
Northwestern States 978
Northwestern States—Description and travel 917.8
Norton Utilities 005.43
Norway 948.1
Norway—Guidebooks 914.8104; 914.810449; 914.81045
Norway—History 948.1
Norwegian Americans 973.043982
Norwegian Americans—History 973.043982
Norwegian elkhound 636.753

Norwegian language—Technical Norwegian
439.82800246; 808.066
Norwegian literature 839.82
Nose 611.21
Nose—Diseases 616.212
Nosocomial infections 616.9
Nosocomial infections—Prevention 614.44
Nosology 616.0012
Nosology—Problems, exercises, etc. 616.0012
Nostradamus, 1503–1566 133.3092
Nostradamus, 1503–1566. Prophéties 133.3092
Notaries 347.016
Notaries—New York (State) 347.747016
Note pads 651.74; 676.2823
Note-taking 371.30281
Noturus 597.492
Nouwen, Henri J. M. 282.092
Nouwen, Henri J. M.—Diaries 282.092
Nova automobile 629.2222
Nova automobile—Maintenance and repair 629.28722
Nova automobile—Maintenance and repair—Handbooks,
manuals, etc. 629.28722
Nova Scotia 971.622
Nova Scotia—Genealogy 929.3716
Novachord 786.7
Novelists, American 813
Novell, Inc.—Examinations 005.71369
Novell IntranetWare 005.44769
Novell software 005.3
Novelties 688.726
Novelty balloons 688.726
Novelty films 791.4361
Novelty songs 782.42
Novenas 264.7
Novial (Artificial language) 499.99
Nowcasting (Meteorology) 551.6362
Noxious weeds 581.652; 632.5
Nuba (African people) 305.8965; 962.8
Nubia 939.78
Nubia—Antiquities 939.78
Nubia—Civilization 939.78
Nubia—History 939.78
Nuclear activation analysis 543.0882; 545.822
Nuclear arms control 327.1747
Nuclear arms control—Soviet Union 327.17470947
Nuclear arms control—United States 327.17470973
Nuclear arms control—Verification 327.1747
Nuclear astrophysics 523.0197
Nuclear chemistry 541.38
Nuclear counters 539.77
Nuclear disarmament 327.1747
Nuclear disarmament—United States 327.17470973;
341.7340973
Nuclear energy 333.7924
Nuclear energy—Law and legislation 341.755
Nuclear energy—Research—International cooperation
341.755
Nuclear engineering 621.48
Nuclear excitation 539.75
Nuclear facilities 621.483
Nuclear facilities—Decommissioning 621.483
Nuclear facilities—Safety measures 621.4835
Nuclear fission 539.762
Nuclear fuel claddings 621.48335
Nuclear fuel elements 621.48335
Nuclear fuels 621.48335
Nuclear fusion 539.764; 621.484
Nuclear industry 333.7924; 338.4762148
Nuclear industry—Government policy 333.7924

Nuclear industry—Government policy—United States
333.79240973
Nuclear industry—Great Britain 333.79240941
Nuclear industry—United States 333.79240973
Nuclear magnetic resonance 538.362
Nuclear magnetic resonance spectroscopy
538.3620287; 543.0877
Nuclear magnetic resonance spectroscopy—Diagnostic
use 616.07548; 616.8047548
Nuclear matter 539.7
Nuclear medicine 616.07575
Nuclear medicine—Periodicals 616.0757505
Nuclear nonproliferation 327.1747
Nuclear physics 539.7
Nuclear physics—History 539.709
Nuclear physics—Periodicals 539.705
Nuclear power plants 621.48; 621.483
Nuclear power plants—Accidents 363.1799
Nuclear power plants—California—Safety measures
363.179909794; 621.4835
Nuclear power plants—Design and construction
621.483
Nuclear power plants—Earthquake effects 621.4832
Nuclear power plants—Equipment and supplies
621.4830284; 621.4833
Nuclear power plants—Risk assessment 363.1799
Nuclear power plants—Safety measures 363.17995;
363.17996; 621.4835
Nuclear power plants—Waste disposal—Sweden
363.728909405
Nuclear pressure vessels 621.483
Nuclear pressure vessels—Testing 621.483
Nuclear reactions 539.75
Nuclear reactor accidents 621.4835
Nuclear reactors 621.483
Nuclear reactors—Fluid dynamics 621.4831
Nuclear reactors—Materials 621.4833
Nuclear reactors—Safety measures 621.4835
Nuclear receptors (Biochemistry) 572.8845
Nuclear shell theory 539.743
Nuclear spectroscopy 543.0877
Nuclear spin 539.725
Nuclear structure 539.74
Nuclear submarines 623.82574
Nuclear submarines—Decommissioning 359.93834
Nuclear warfare 355.0217
Nuclear warfare—Environmental aspects 577.274
Nuclear warfare—Moral and ethical aspects 172.422
Nuclear warfare—Religious aspects 291.178732
Nuclear warfare—Religious aspects—Catholic Church
261.8732
Nuclear warfare—Religious aspects—Christianity
261.8732
Nuclear warfare—Safety measures 363.349875
Nuclear-weapon-free zones 327.1747
Nuclear weapons 355.0217; 355.825119
Nuclear weapons—Great Britain 327.17470941
Nuclear weapons—History 355.021709
Nuclear weapons—India 327.17470954
Nuclear weapons (International law) 341.734
Nuclear weapons—Testing 621.451190287
Nuclear weapons—Testing—Law and legislation
341.734
Nuclear weapons—United States 327.17470973
Nuclear weapons—United States—Testing
621.451190287
Nuclear winter 577.274
Nucleic acid hybridization 572.84
Nucleic acids 547.79; 572.8

Nucleic acids—Structure 572.33
Nucleosides 572.85
Nucleosynthesis 523.02
Nucleotide sequence 572.8633
Nucleotide sequence—Data processing 572.86330285
Nuclides 539.74
Nude beaches 613.194; 796.53
Nude in art 704.9421
Nudger, Alo (Fictitious character) 813.54
Nudger, Alo (Fictitious character)—Fiction 813.54
Nudibranchia 594.36
Nudism 613.194
Nudist camps 613.194
Nudity 155.95; 177.4; 291.178
Nudity in motion pictures 791.43653
Null models (Ecology) 577.015195
Number concept in children 155.41323
Number theory 512.7
Number theory—Data processing 512.70285
Numbers in the Bible 220.68
Numbers, Prime 512.72
Numbers, Random 519.2
Numeracy 372.72
Numerals 513.5
Numeration 513.5
Numerical analysis 515; 519.4
Numerical analysis—Data processing 519.40285
Numerical analysis—Periodicals 519.405
Numerical grid generation (Numerical analysis) 519.4
Numerical integration 515.624
Numerical taxonomy 578.012
Numerical weather forecasting 551.634
Numerology 133.335
Numismatics 737
Numismatics—Collectors and collecting 737.075
Numismatics—India 737.4934; 737.4954
Numismatics, Roman 737.4937
Nunc dimittis (Music) 782.324
Nuns 255.9; 291.657
Nuremberg (Germany)—History—Bombardment, 1944 940.54213324
Nuremberg Trial of Major German War Criminals, Nuremberg, Germany, 1945–1946 341.690268
Nuremberg War Crime Trials, Nuremberg, Germany, 1946–1949 341.690268
Nureyev, Rudolf, 1938- 792.8028092
Nurse administrators 362.173068
Nurse and patient 610.730699
Nurse practitioners 610.730692; 610.73092
Nurse practitioners—Examinations, questions, etc. 610.73076
Nurseries (Horticulture) 631.52
Nursery growers 635.092
Nursery rhymes 398.8
Nursery rhymes, American 398.80973
Nursery rhymes, English 398.8
Nursery schools 372.216
Nursery schools—United States—Administration 372.1200973
Nurses 610.73
Nurses' aides 610.730698
Nurses—In-service training 610.7307155
Nurses—Job satisfaction 610.73019
Nurses—Malpractice 344.0414
Nurses—Malpractice—United States 344.730414
Nurses—Prescription privileges 610.73069
Nurses—Supply and demand 331.129161073
Nurses—Supply and demand—United States 331.1291610730973

Nursing 610.73
Nursing—Anecdotes 610.73
Nursing assessment 616.075
Nursing assessment—Handbooks, manuals, etc. 616.075
Nursing audit 610.73
Nursing—Authorship 808.06661
Nursing care plans 610.73
Nursing care plans—Handbooks, manuals, etc. 610.73
Nursing—Data processing 610.730285
Nursing diagnosis 616.075
Nursing diagnosis—Classification 616.075
Nursing diagnosis—Handbooks, manuals, etc. 616.075
Nursing—Effect of managed care on 362.173068
Nursing ethics 174.2
Nursing—Examinations, questions, etc. 610.73076
Nursing—Great Britain 610.730941
Nursing—Handbooks, manuals, etc. 610.73
Nursing—History 610.7309
Nursing home care 362.16
Nursing home patients 362.16
Nursing home patients—Mental health 362.16
Nursing homes 362.16
Nursing homes—Administration 362.16068
Nursing homes—Administration—Examinations, questions, etc. 362.16068
Nursing homes—Evaluation 362.160685
Nursing homes—Law and legislation 344.03216
Nursing homes—Law and legislation—United States 344.7303216
Nursing homes—Recreational activities 362.16
Nursing homes—United States 362.160973
Nursing homes—Utilization—United States—Statistics 362.160973021
Nursing informatics 610.730285
Nursing—Law and legislation 344.0414
Nursing—Law and legislation—United States 344.730414
Nursing libraries 026.61073
Nursing models 610.73011
Nursing—Outlines, syllabi, etc. 610.73
Nursing—Philosophy 610.7301
Nursing—Planning 610.73
Nursing—Practice 362.173068
Nursing—Psychological aspects 610.73019
Nursing—Quality control 362.1730685
Nursing records 651.504261
Nursing—Research 610.73072
Nursing—Research—Methodology 610.73072
Nursing school administrators 610.730711
Nursing schools 610.730711
Nursing schools—Accreditation—United States 610.73071173
Nursing schools—United States—Entrance examinations 610.73076
Nursing schools—United States—Statistics—Periodicals 610.73071173
Nursing services 362.173
Nursing services—Administration 362.173068
Nursing services—Business management 362.173068
Nursing services—Personnel management 362.1730683
Nursing—Standards 610.730218
Nursing—Study and teaching 610.730711
Nursing—Study and teaching—United States 610.73071173
Nursing—United States 610.730973
Nursing—United States—History 610.730973
Nursing—Vocational guidance 610.73069

Nursing—Vocational guidance—United States 610.730690973
Nutcracker (Choreographic work) 792.842
Nutrient cycles 577.14
Nutrition 572.4; 612.3; 613.2
Nutrition and dental health 617.601
Nutrition counseling 362.176
Nutrition—Developing countries 363.8091724
Nutrition—Dictionaries 613.203
Nutrition disorders 616.39
Nutrition disorders in children 618.9239
Nutrition—Encyclopedias 613.203
Nutrition—Evaluation 613.2
Nutrition—Handbooks, manuals, etc. 613.2
Nutrition—Periodicals 363.805; 613.205
Nutrition policy 363.8561
Nutrition policy—Developing countries 363.8561091724
Nutrition policy—United States 363.85610973
Nutrition—Psychological aspects 613.2019
Nutrition surveys—Developing countries 363.82091724
Nutrition surveys—United States 363.820973
Nutrition—Tables 613.2
Nutritionally induced diseases 616.39
Nutritionists 613.2092
Nuts 634.5
Nyaya 181.43
Nymphs (Greek deities) 292.2114; 398.21
Nymphs (Greek deities) in literature 808.80382922114; 809.93382922114
Nymphs (Insects) 595.7139
Oahu (Hawaii) 996.93
Oahu (Hawaii)—Guidebooks 919.69304; 919.6930441; 919.6930442
Oahu (Hawaii)—Maps 912.9693
Oahu (Hawaii)—Road maps 912.9693
Oak 583.46
Oakes, Blackford (Fictitious character) 813.54
Oakes, Blackford (Fictitious character)—Fiction 813.54
Oakland Athletics (Baseball team) 796.357640979466
Oakland Athletics (Baseball team)—History 796.357640979466
Oakland County (Mich.) 977.438
Oakland County (Mich.)—Maps 912.77438
Oakley, Annie, 1860–1926 799.31092
Oatcakes 641.815
Oates, Joyce Carol, 1938– 813.54
Oates, Joyce Carol, 1938– —Criticism and interpretation 813.54
Obedience (Law) 340.11
Obedience—Religious aspects 291.22
Obedience—Religious aspects—Christianity 234.6
Obesity 616.398
Obesity in adolescence 616.39800835
Obesity in children 618.92398
Obesity—Psychological aspects 616.3980019
Obesity—Treatment 616.39806
Obituaries 920
Object monitors (Computer software) 005.71376
Object-oriented databases 005.757
Object-oriented methods (Computer science) 005.117
Object-oriented programming (Computer science) 005.117
Object-teaching 268.6
Objections (Evidence) 347.062
Objections (Evidence)—California 347.794062
Objectivism (Philosophy) 121.4
Objectivity 121.4
Oboe and piano music 788.52
Oboe da caccia 788.52

Oboe d'amore 788.52
Oboe music 788.52
O'Brien County (Iowa) 977.714
O'Brien County (Iowa)—Maps 912.77714
O'Brien, Flann, 1911–1966 828.91209
O'Brien, Flann, 1911–1966—Criticism and interpretation 828.91209
O'Brien, Kali (Fictitious character) 813.54
Obscenity (Law) 344.0547; 345.0274
Obscenity (Law)—United States 344.730547; 345.730274
Observation (Educational method) 370.711
Observatories 522.1
Obsessive-compulsive disorder 616.85227
Obsessive-compulsive disorder—Treatment 616.8522706
Obstetrical emergencies 618.2025
Obstetrical endocrinology 612.63
Obstetricians—Malpractice 344.04121
Obstetricians—Malpractice—United States 344.7304121
Obstetrics 618.2
Obstetrics—Examinations, questions, etc. 618.20076
Obstetrics—Handbooks, manuals, etc. 618.2
Obstetrics—Outlines, syllabi, etc. 618.2
Obstetrics—Surgery 618.8
O'Casey, Sean, 1880–1964 822.912
O'Casey, Sean, 1880–1964—Criticism and interpretation 822.912
Occasional sermons 252.6
Occasional services 265.9
Occlusion (Dentistry) 617.643
Occult fiction 808.83937; 809.3937
Occultations 523.99
Occultism 133
Occultism—Dictionaries 133.03
Occultism—Early works to 1900 133
Occultism—Encyclopedias 133.03
Occultism—Europe—History 133.094
Occultism—History 133.09
Occultism—Religious aspects 291.175
Occultism—Religious aspects—Christianity 261.513
Occupational aptitude tests 153.94
Occupational dermatitis 616.5
Occupational diseases 613.62; 616.9803
Occupational health services 362.1; 658.382
Occupational mobility 305.9
Occupational retraining 362.0425
Occupational therapy 615.8515; 616.89165
Occupational therapy for children 615.8515083
Occupational therapy—Handbooks, manuals, etc. 615.8515
Occupational therapy services 362.178
Occupational therapy services—Administration 362.178; 615.8515068
Occupational therapy—Vocational guidance 615.8515023
Occupational training 331.2592; 370.113
Occupational training—European Economic Community countries 331.2592094
Occupational training—Government policy 331.2592
Occupational training—Government policy—United States 331.25920973
Occupational training—Great Britain 331.25920941
Occupational training, Military—United States 355.560973
Occupational training—United States 331.25920973
Occupations 331.7
Occupations—Canada 331.700971
Occupations—Classification 331.70012

Occupations in art 704.9493317
Occupations—Religious aspects 200.88
Occupations—United States 331.700973
Occupations—United States—Classification 331.70012
Occupations—United States—Dictionaries 331.70097303
Ocean 551.46
Ocean-atmosphere interaction 551.5246
Ocean bottom 551.46084
Ocean bottom—Law and legislation 341.448
Ocean circulation 551.47
Ocean color 551.4601
Ocean currents 551.4701
Ocean engineering 620.4162
Ocean—Folklore 398.232162
Ocean freight forwarders 388.044
Ocean liners 387.2432; 623.82432
Ocean—Maps 551.4600223
Ocean mining 622.295
Ocean mining—Law and legislation 341.762
Ocean—Songs and music 781.56
Ocean temperature 551.4601
Ocean tomography 551.4600287
Ocean travel 387.5; 910.45
Ocean travel—Periodicals 910.4505
Ocean wave power 333.914; 621.312134
Ocean waves 551.4702
Oceana County (Mich.) 977.459
Oceana County (Mich.)—Maps 912.77459
Oceania 995; 996
Oceania—Economic conditions 330.995
Oceania—Economic conditions—Periodicals 330.995005
Oceania—Geography 919.5
Oceania—Guidebooks 919.504
Oceania—History 995
Oceania—Periodicals 995.005
Oceania—Social life and customs 995; 996
Oceanic mixing 551.47
Oceanographic instruments 551.4600284
Oceanographic libraries 026.55146
Oceanographic research stations 551.460072
Oceanographic submersibles 623.8205; 623.8257;
  623.827
Oceanography 551.46
Oceanography—Antarctic Ocean 551.469
Oceanography—Arctic Ocean 551.468
Oceanography—Atlantic Ocean 551.461
Oceanography—Bibliography 016.55146
Oceanography—Charts, diagrams, etc. 5514600223
Oceanography—Mathematical models 551.460015118
Oceanography—North Atlantic Ocean 551.4611
Oceanography—Pacific Ocean 551.465
Oceanography—Pacific Ocean—Charts, diagrams, etc.
  551.4650223
Oceanography—Periodicals 551.46005
Oceanography—Remote sensing 551.4600287
Oceanography—Research 551.460072
Oceanography—Research—United States
  551.460072073
O'Connell, Daniel, 1775–1847 941.5081092
O'Connor family 929.209415; 929.20973
O'Connor, Flannery 813.54
O'Connor, Flannery—Criticism and interpretation
  813.54
O'Connor, Frank, 1903–1966 823.912
O'Connor, Sandra Day, 1930– 347.732634
Oconto County (Wis.) 977.537
Oconto County (Wis.)—Maps 912.77537
Octobriana (Fictitious character) 741.5947
Octopus 594.56

Ocular pharmacology 617.7061
Ocular toxicology 617.71
Odets, Clifford, 1906–1963 812.52
Odets, Clifford, 1906–1963—Criticism and
  interpretation 812.52
Odonata 595.733
O'Donnell, Rosie 792.7028092
Odysseus (Greek mythology) 883.01
Oedipus complex 150.1952
Off Off-Broadway theater 792.022
Off-road racing 796.72
Off-road vehicle trails 796.7
Off-road vehicles 629.22042
Offenses against the environment 363.7
Offertories (Music) 782.3235
Office buildings 725.23
Office buildings—Automation 725.23
Office buildings—New York (State)—New York
  725.23097471
Office buildings—New York (State)—New York—
  Directories 725.230257471
Office decoration—United States 747.79
Office equipment and supplies 651.2
Office equipment and supplies industry 338.476512
Office equipment leases 681.60687
Office furniture 651.23
Office furniture industry 338.4765123
Office information systems 651.8
Office layout 658.23
Office management 651.3
Office politics 650.13
Office practice 651
Office practice—Automation 651.8
Office practice—Automation—Periodicals 651.805
Office practice—Handbooks, manuals, etc. 651.3
Office practice—Problems, exercises, etc. 651.076
Office practice—Vocational guidance 651.023
Offset printing 686.2315; 686.2325
Offshore assembly industry 338.4767042
Offshore assembly industry—Mexico 338.476709721
Offshore gas well drilling 622.33819
Offshore oil industry 333.8232
Offshore oil industry—United States 333.8232
Offshore oil well drilling 622.33819
Offshore structures 627.98
Offshore structures—Design and construction 627.98
Offshore structures—Hydrodynamics 627.98015325
O'Flaherty, Liam, 1896– 823.912
O'Flaherty, Liam, 1896– —Criticism and interpretation
  823.912
Ogemaw County (Mich.) 977.475
Ogemaw County (Mich.)—Maps 912.77475
Ogham stones 491.6211
Ogilvie, James (Fictitious character) 823.914
Ogilvie, James (Fictitious character)—Fiction 823.914
Oglala Indians—Religion 299.7852
Ogle County (Ill.) 977.332
Ogle County (Ill.)—Maps 912.77332
Oglethorpe, James Edward, 1696–1785 975.802092
O'Hara, Frank 811.54
O'Hara, Frank—Criticism and interpretation 811.54
Ohayon, Michael (Fictitious character) 892.436
Ohayon, Michael (Fictitious character)—Fiction 892.436
Ohio 977.1
Ohio—Genealogy 929.3771
Ohio—Guidebooks 917.71044; 917.710443; 917.710444
Ohio—History 977.1
Ohio—Maps 912.771
Ohio River 977

On-demand printing 686.233
Onassis, Jacqueline Kennedy, 1929– 973.922092
Oncogenes 616.992042; 616.994042
Oncogenic viruses 616.9940194
Oncology 616.992; 616.994
Oncology—Terminology 616.9920014
One-act plays 808.8241
One-act plays, American 812.041; 812.04108
One-act plays, Australian 822.04108994
One-eyed Mack (Fictitious character) 813.54
One-eyed Mack (Fictitious character)—Fiction 813.54
One-person shows (Performing arts) 792.022
O'Neal, Shaquille 796.323092
Oneida County (Wis.) 977.525
Oneida County (Wis.)—Maps 912.77525
Oneida Indians 974.70049755
Oneida mythology 299.72
O'Neill, Eugene, 1888–1953 812.52
O'Neill, Eugene, 1888–1953—Criticism and
  interpretation 812.52
O'Neill, Tip 328.73092
Onion rings 641.6525
Onions 641.3525
Online algorithms 005.1
Online bibliographic searching 025.04
Online bibliographic searching—Handbooks, manuals,
  etc. 025.04
Online bibliographic searching—United States 025.04
Online chat groups 004.69; 005.71376; 025.04
Online data processing 004
Online data processing—Directories 025.04
Online databases 005.754
Online etiquette 395.5
Online information services 025.04
Online library catalogs 025.3132
Online library catalogs—Subject access 025.3132
Online stockbrokers 332.6420285
Onomastics 412
Onopordum 583.99
Ontario 971.3
Ontario—Description and travel 917.1304; 917.13044
Ontario—Genealogy 929.3713
Ontario—Guidebooks 917.1304; 917.13044
Ontario—History 971.3
Ontario—Maps 912.713
Ontario—Politics and government 971.3
Ontario—Social life and customs 971.3
Ontology 111
Onychophora 592.74
Opacity (Optics) 535.3
OPEC Fund for International Development 338.91177
Open adoption—United States 362.734
Open-air schools 371.384
Open-book management 658.3152
Open learning 374.4
Open plan schools 371.256; 371.3941
Open source software 005.3
Opening statements (Law) 347.075
Openings (Rhetoric) 808
Opera 782.1; 792.5
Opera—Anecdotes 782.1
Opéra comique 782.1
Opera companies 782.106; 792.506
Opera—Dictionaries 782.103
Opera—Humor 782.10207
Opera—New York (State)—New York 782.1097471;
  792.5097471
Opera—Production and direction 792.5
Opera programs 782.1078

Opera—United States 782.10973; 792.50973
Operant behavior 153.1526
Operant conditioning 153.1526
Operas 782.1
Operas—Analysis, appreciation 782.1117
Operas, Chinese—History and criticism 782.10951
Operas—Discography 016.78210266
Operas—Excerpts 782.1
Operas—Excerpts, Arranged 782.1
Operas—Excerpts—Scores 782.1
Operas—Excerpts—Vocal scores with piano 782.1
Operas—Librettos 782.10268
Operas—Scores 782.1
Operas—Stories, plots, etc. 782.10269
Operas—Vocal scores with piano 782.1
Operating room nursing 610.73677
Operating room technicians 617.917
Operating systems (Computers) 005.43
Operating systems (Computers)—Periodicals 005.4305
Operation Allied Force, 1999 949.7103
Operation Desert Shield, 1990–1991 956.704424
Operation Overlord 940.542142
Operation Restore Hope, 1992–1993 967.73053
Operational amplifiers 621.395
Operational amplifiers—Design and construction
  621.395
Operations research 003; 658.4034
Operator algebras 512.55
Operator theory 515.724
Operetta 782.12; 792.5
Ophiuroidea 593.94
Ophthalmic assistants 617.70233
Ophthalmic diagnostic equipment industry
  338.47681761
Ophthalmic plastic surgery 617.71
Ophthalmic zoster 617.7
Ophthalmologists 617.7092
Ophthalmology 617.7
Ophthalmology—Atlases 617.71
Ophthalmology—Dictionaries 617.7003
Ophthalmology—Examinations, questions, etc.
  617.70076
Ophthalmology—Handbooks, manuals, etc. 617.7
Ophthalmology—Practice 617.70068
Ophthalmology—Terminology 617.70014
Ophthalmoscopy 617.71545
Opossums 599.276
Oppenheimer, J. Robert, 1904–1967 530.092
Optical art 709.04072
Optical character recognition device industry
  338.7621399
Optical character recognition devices 006.424; 621.399
Optical coatings 621.36
Optical communications 621.3827
Optical communications—Equipment and supplies
  621.38270284
Optical communications—Law and legislation 343.0994
Optical data processing 006.42; 621.367
Optical detectors 681.25
Optical disks 004.565
Optical fiber detectors 681.25
Optical fibers 621.3692
Optical fibers in medicine 610.284
Optical glass 681.4
Optical illusions 152.148
Optical instruments 681.4
Optical instruments—Design and construction 681.4
Optical laboratories 681.4072
Optical materials 620.11295; 621.36

Optical materials—Effect of radiation on 621.366
Optical measurements 681.25
Optical mineralogy 549.125
Optical oceanography 551.4601
Optical pattern recognition 006.42
Optical publishing 070.5797
Optical radar 621.3848
Optical scanners 006.62
Optical spectrometers 535.84
Optical storage device industry 338.47004565
Optical storage devices 004.565; 621.39767
Optics 535
Optics, Adaptive 621.369
Optics—Periodicals 535.05
Optimality theory (Linguistics) 415
Optimism 149.5; 158.1
Options (Finance) 332.63228
Options (Finance)—Prices 332.63228
Options (Finance)—Prices—Mathematical models 332.63228
Options (Finance)—United States 332.63228
Optoacoustic spectroscopy 543.085
Optoelectronic devices 621.38152
Optoelectronics 621.381045
Optoelectronics industry 338.47621381045
Optoelectronics—Materials 621.3810450284
Optometrists 617.75092
Optometry 617.75
Optometry—Dictionaries 617.7503
Optometry—Practice 617.75068
Opus Dei (Society) 267.182
Oracle (Computer file) 005.7585
Oracles 133.3248
Oral communication 302.2242
Oral communication—Study and teaching (Elementary) 372.622
Oral contraceptives 613.9432
Oral contraceptives—Side effects 615.766
Oral history 900; 907.2
Oral hygiene products 617.601
Oral interpretation 808.54
Oral interpretation of poetry 808.54
Oral medicine 617.522
Oral reading 372.452
Orange County (Calif.) 979.496
Orange County (Calif.)—History 979.496
Orange County (Calif.)—Maps 912.79496
Orange County (Va.)—Genealogy 929.3755372
Oranges 641.3431
Orangutan 599.883
Oratorios 782.23
Orators 809.5
Oratory 808.51
Oratory—Early works to 1800 808.51
Orb weavers 595.44
Orbital mechanics 629.4113
Orbiting astronomical observatories 522.2919
Orbiting solar observatories 523.70723
Orbits 521.3
Orchestra 784.2
Orchestral music 784.2
Orchestral music—Analysis, appreciation 784.2117
Orchestral music, Arranged 784.2
Orchestral music—Bibliography 016.7842
Orchestral music—Bibliography—Catalogs 016.7842
Orchestral music—Scores 784.2
Orchestral music—Scores and parts 784.2
Orchestral musicians 784.2092
Orchid culture 635.9344

Orchids 584.4; 635.9344
Order (Grammar) 415
Order statistics 519.5
Ordered algebraic structures 511.33
Ordination of gays 262.1408664; 291.6108664
Ordination of lesbians 262.14086643; 291.61086643
Ordination of women 262.14
Ordination of women—Catholic Church 262.142082
Ordination of women—Christianity 262.14
Ordnance 355.8
Ore deposits 553
Ore-dressing 622.7
Ore handling 622.6
Ore handling—Equipment and supplies 622.6; 681.76
Oregon 979.5
Oregon—Description and travel 917.9504; 917.950443; 917.950444
Oregon—Genealogy 929.3795
Oregon—Guidebooks 917.9504; 917.950443; 917.950444
Oregon—History 979.5
Oregon—History—To 1859 979.5
Oregon—Maps 912.795
Oregon National Historic Trail 979.503
Oregon National Historic Trail—History 978.02
Oregon—Pictorial works 917.9500222; 979.500222
Oregon—Tours 917.9504; 917.950443; 917.950444
Organ donors 617.95
Organ masses 782.323
Organ music 786.5
Organ music, Arranged 786.5
Organ music—Bibliography 016.7865
Organ music—History and criticism 786.509
Organ (Musical instrument) 786.5; 786.519
Organ (Musical instrument)—History 786.51909
Organ (Musical instrument)—Instruction and study 786.7
Organ trafficking 364.15
Organic compounds 547; 572; 661.8
Organic compounds—Handbooks, manuals, etc. 547
Organic compounds—Synthesis 547.050459; 547.2; 660.2844
Organic conductors 620.19204295
Organic cyclic compounds 547.5
Organic electrochemistry 547.137
Organic farming 631.584
Organic gardening 635.0484; 635.987
Organic photochemistry 547.135
Organic reaction mechanisms 547.139
Organic reaction mechanisms—Problems, exercises, etc. 547.139076
Organic solvents 547.13482
Organic superconductors 537.623; 537.6233
Organic water pollutants 628.168
Organists 786.5092
Organization 658.1
Organization of African Unity 341.249
Organization of American States 341.245
Organization of Petroleum Exporting Countries 382.42282
Organizational behavior 158.26; 302.35; 658.0019
Organizational change 352.367; 658.406; 658.4063
Organizational change—Management 658.406
Organizational change—Periodicals 658.40605
Organizational change—United States 658.4060973
Organizational commitment 658.314
Organizational effectiveness—Evaluation 658.401
Organizational justice 331.011; 658.314
Organizational sociology 302.35
Organizational sociology—Research 302.35072

Organized crime 364.106
Organized crime—Italy 364.1060945
Organized crime—Russia (Federation) 364.1060947
Organized crime—United States 364.1060973
Organized crime—United States—History 364.1060973
Organized crime—United States—History—20th century 364.10609730904
Organochlorine compounds—Biodegradation 628.52
Organofluorine compounds 547.02
Organohalogen compounds 572.556
Organometallic chemistry 547.05; 572.51
Organometallic compounds 547.05; 572.51; 661.895
Organopalladium compounds 547.056362
Organophosphorus compounds 547.07
Organosilicon compounds 547.08
Organosodium compounds 572.52382
Organosulphur compounds 547.06; 572.554
Organotransition metal compounds 547.056
Orgasm 613.96
Oriental antiquities 930.0935
Oriental languages 490
Oriental literature 895
Orientalism 303.482182105; 950
Orientation and mobility instructors 362.4186
Orienteering 796.58
Origami 736.982
Origen 270.1092
Originality in literature 801; 809
Orissa (India) 954.13
Orissa (India)—Civilization 954.13
Orissa (India)—History 954.13
Orius 595.754
Orkney (Scotland) 941.132
Orkney (Scotland)—Social life and customs 941.132
Orlando (Fla.) 975.924
Orlando (Fla.)—Guidebooks 917.5924
Orlando Metropolitan Area (Fla.)—Maps 912.75924
Orlando Region (Fla.)—Guidebooks 917.5924
Ornamental climbing plants 635.974
Ornamental fishes 639.34
Ornamental grasses 635.9349
Ornamental shrubs 635.976
Ornamental trees 635.977; 715.2
Ornithological illustration—History 598.0221
Ornithologists 598.092
Ornithology 598
Ornithopters 629.13336
O'Rorke, Patrick (Fictitious character) 823.914
Orphan drugs 615.1
Orphan trains 362.7340973
Orphans 362.73
Orrell family 929.20973
Orthodontic appliances 617.64300284
Orthodontics 617.643
Orthodox Eastern Church 281.9
Orthodox Eastern church buildings 726.5819
Orthodox Eastern Church—Doctrines 230.19
Orthodox Eastern Church—Liturgy 264.019
Orthodox Eastern Church—Relations—Catholic Church 280.2
Orthodox Eastern preaching 251.088219
Orthodox Judaism 296.832
Orthodox Judaism—Israel 296.832095694
Orthodox Judaism—United States 296.8320973
Orthogonal polynomials 515.55
Orthogonalization methods 515.55
Orthopedic apparatus 617.9
Orthopedic apparatus industry 381.45681761
Orthopedic disability evaluation 616.7075

Orthopedic hospitals 362.19747
Orthopedic nursing 610.73677
Orthopedic surgery 617.47
Orthopedics 616.7
Orthopedics—Atlases 616.700222
Orthopedics—Diagnosis 616.7075
Orthopedics—Examinations, questions, etc. 616.70076
Orthopedics—Handbooks, manuals, etc. 616.7
Orthopedics—Terminology 616.70014
Orthopedists 617.47092
Orthoptera 595.726
Orthoptics 617.762
Orwell, George, 1903–1950 828.91209
Orwell, George, 1903–1950. Animal farm 823.912
Orwell, George, 1903–1950. Animal farm— Examinations 823.912
Orwell, George, 1903–1950—Criticism and interpretation 828.91209
Orwell, George, 1903–1950. Nineteen eighty-four 823.912
Orwell, George, 1903–1950—Political and social views 828.91209
OS/2 (Computer file) 005.4469
OS/2 warp 005.4469
Osage Indians 305.89752; 976.60049752; 978.0049752
Osage Indians—Rites and ceremonies 394.4089752
Osborne, John, 1929– 822.914
Osborne, John, 1929– —Criticism and interpretation 822.914
OSCAR (Artificial satellite) 621.3825
Osceola County (Iowa) 977.7116
Osceola County (Iowa)—Maps 912.777116
Osceola County (Mich.) 977.469
Osceola County (Mich.)—Maps 912.77469
Osceola, Seminole chief, 1804–1838 975.9004973
Oscillations 531.32
Oscillators, Crystal 621.38412
Oscillators, Electric 621.381533; 621.38412
Oscilloscopes 621.3747; 621.3815483
O'Shaughnessy, Kiernan (Fictitious character) 813.54
O'Shaughnessy, Kiernan (Fictitious character)—Fiction 813.54
O'Shea, Torie (Fictitious character) 813.54
OSI (Computer network standard) 004.62
Osiris (Egyptian deity) 299.31
Osler, William, Sir, 1849–1919 610.92
Osmosis 530.425; 541.3415
Osprey 598.93
Osseointegrated dental implants 617.692
Osseointegration 617.4710592
Osteichthyes 597
Ostenoselachidae 567.3
Osteoarthritis 616.7223
Osteopathic medicine 615.533
Osteopathic schools 615.5330711
Osteoporosis 616.716
Osteoporosis in women 616.716
Osteoporosis—Prevention 616.716
Ostomates 617.55059
Ostracoda 595.33
Ostracoda, Fossil 565.33
Ostreola 594.4
Ostrich farms 636.69401
Ostrich feather industry 338.176694
Ostrich feathers 636.694
Ostrich products industry 338.176694
Ostriches 598.524
Ostrovsky, Aleksandr Nikolaevich, 1823–1886 891.723

Ostrovsky, Aleksandr Nikolaevich, 1823–1886—
Translations into English 891.723
Oswald, Lee Harvey 364.1524092
Otani, Tetsuo, Supt. (Fictitious character) 823.914
Otani, Tetsuo, Supt. (Fictitious character)—Fiction
823.914
Othello (Fictitious character) 782.1; 822.33
Otitis 617.8
Otitis media in children 618.9209784
Otoe County (Neb.) 978.2273
Otoe County (Neb.)—Maps 912.782273
Otolaryngology 617.51
Otolaryngology—Atlases 617.5100222
Otolaryngology—Handbooks, manuals, etc. 617.51
Otolaryngology, Operative 617.51059
Otolith organs 612.858
Otsego County (Mich.) 977.484
Otsego County (Mich.)—Maps 912.77484
Ottawa County (Mich.) 977.415
Ottawa County (Mich.)—Maps 912.77415
Ottawa (Ont.) 971.384
Ottawa (Ont.)—Guidebooks 917.138404; 917.1384044
Otters 599.769
Otzi (Ice mummy) 937.3
Out-of-print books—Prices 017.8
Out-of-print books—Prices—United States 017.8
Outagamie County (Wis.) 977.539
Outagamie County (Wis.)—Maps 912.77539
Outboard motors 623.87234
Outboard motors—Maintenance and repair—Handbooks,
manuals, etc. 623.872340288
Outdoor cookery 641.578
Outdoor education 371.384
Outdoor furniture 684.18
Outdoor life 796.5
Outdoor living spaces 643.55
Outdoor medical emergencies 616.025; 616.0252
Outdoor photography 778.71
Outdoor recreation 796.5
Outdoor recreation—Colorado 796.509788
Outdoor recreation—Colorado—Guidebooks 796.509788
Outdoor recreation—Directories 796.5025
Outdoor recreation for women—Literary collections
810.80355
Outdoor recreation—Management 353.78; 796.5068
Outdoor recreation—Oregon—Guidebooks 796.509795
Outdoor recreation—United States 796.50973
Outdoor recreation—United States—Directories
796.502573
Outdoor recreation—United States—Periodicals
796.5097305
Outdoor recreation—Washington (State)—Guidebooks
796.509796
Outdoor sculpture 730
Outer Banks (N.C.) 975.61
Outer Banks (N.C.)—Guidebooks 917.56104;
917.5610443; 917.5610444
Outer space 999
Outer space—Civilian use 333.94
Outer space—Exploration 919.904
Outer space—Exploration—United States 333.940973;
919.904
Outlaws 364.3
Outlaws—West (U.S.)—Biography 978.020922
Outlet stores—Middle West—Directories 381.1502577
Outlet stores—New England—Directories 381.1502574
Outline maps 912
Outsider art 709.0407
Outtakes 778.5; 791.43; 791.45

Outward bound schools 371.384
Ovaries 612.62
Ovaries—Cancer 616.99465
Oven mitts 641.50284; 685.43
Over-the-counter markets 332.643
Over-the-counter markets—Law and legislation
346.0926
Overhead electric lines 621.31922
Overland journeys to the Pacific 978.02
Overpopulation 304.61; 363.91
Overtures 784.18926
Overuse injuries 617.1
Overweight women 305.48981
Overweight women in art 704.9424
Overweight women—Mental health 155.916
Ovid, 43 B.C.–17 or 18 A.D. 871.01
Ovid, 43 B.C.–17 or 18 A.D.—Criticism and
interpretation 871.01
Ovid, 43 B.C.–17 or 18 A.D. Fasti 871.01
Ovid, 43 B.C.–17 or 18 A.D. Metamorphoses 873.01
Ovid, 43 B.C.–17 or 18 A.D.—Translations into English
871.01
Oviraptor 567.912
Ovulation—Induction 618.17806
Ovum 571.845
Ovum implantation 612.63
Owen family 929.20973
Owen, Gareth Cadwallader (Fictitious character)
823.914
Owen, Gareth Cadwallader (Fictitious character)—
Fiction 823.914
Owen, Wilfred, 1893–1918 821.912
Owen, Wilfred, 1893–1918—Criticism and
interpretation 821.912
Owens, Jesse, 1913– 796.42092
Owens, Molly (Fictitious character) 813.54
Owls 598.97
Owls—North America 598.97097
Oxford (England) 942.574
Oxford (England)—Description and travel 914.257404;
914.257404859; 914.25740486
Oxford (England)—Guidebooks 914.257404;
914.257404859; 914.25740486
Oxford English dictionary 423
Oxford movement 283.4209034
Oxfordshire (England) 942.57
Oxidation 547.23; 660.2993
Oxidation, Physiological 572.53; 612.39
Oxidation-reduction reaction 541.393
Oxides 549.5
Oxyacetylene welding and cutting 671.522; 671.53
Oxygen 546.721
Oxygenated gasoline 665.53827
Ozark Mountains Region 976.71
Ozark Mountains Region—Social life and customs
976.71
Ozick, Cynthia 813.54
Ozick, Cynthia—Criticism and interpretation 813.54
Ozone 363.7384
Ozone—Environmental aspects 363.7384
Ozone layer 551.5142
Ozone layer depletion 363.73875
p-adic analysis 512.74
Pace family 929.20973
Pacharán 641.255; 663.55
Pachycephalidae 598.8
Pachycephalosaurus 567.914
Pacific Area 990
Pacific Area—Commerce 382.09182

Pacific Area—Description and travel 910.91823
Pacific Area—Economic conditions 330.99
Pacific Area—Economic policy 338.99
Pacific Area—Foreign economic relations 337.9
Pacific Area—Maps 912.9
Pacific Area—Social life and customs 990
Pacific Coast (Calif.) 979.4
Pacific Coast (Calif.)—Guidebooks 917.9404;
    917.940453; 917.940454
Pacific Coast (U.S.) 979
Pacific Coast (U.S.)—Guidebooks 917.9504; 917.950443;
    917.950444
Pacific Ocean 551.465
Pacific railroads 385.0979
Pacific salmon 597.56
Pacific settlement of international disputes 341.52
Pacific States 979
Pacific States—Description and travel 917.904;
    917.90433; 917.90434
Pacific States—Guidebooks 917.904; 917.90433;
    917.90434
Pacifism 327.172
Pacifists 327.172092
Pacifists—Biography 327.172092
Pack animals (Transportation) 636.0882
Package goods industry 338.476888
Package tours 910.2
Packaging 658.564; 688.8
Packaging—Design 688.8
Packaging—Law and legislation 343.082
Packaging—Law and legislation—United States
    343.7308
Packaging—Periodicals 688.805
Packaging waste—Environmental aspects 363.7288
Packet switching (Data transmission) 004.66
Packhorse librarians 027.473091734
Paclitaxel 616.994061
Padua (Italy) 945.32
Paganism 292
Page County (Iowa) 977.778
Page County (Iowa)—Maps 912.77778
Page County (Va.)—Genealogy 929.375594
Page family 929.20973
Page, Gideon (Fictitious character) 813.54
Page, Gideon (Fictitious character)—Fiction 813.54
Paging (Computer science) 005.435
Paige, Leroy, 1906– 796.357092
Pain 616.0472
Pain in children 618.92
Pain—Pathophysiology 616.0472
Pain—Psychological aspects 616.0472019
Pain—Religious aspects 291.442
Pain—Religious aspects—Christianity 248.86
Pain—Treatment 616.0472
Paine, Thomas, 1737–1809 320.51092
Paint 667.6
Paint-by-numbers 751.4
Paintbrushes 667.60284; 679.6
Painted country furniture 749
Painters 759
Painters—United States 759.13
Painting 745.723; 750
Painting, Abstract 759.0652
Painting, American 759.13
Painting, American—Exhibitions 759.13074
Painting—Appreciation 750.11
Painting, Australian 759.994
Painting, Brazilian 759.981
Painting, British 759.2

Painting, Canadian 759.11
Painting, Canadian—Exhibitions 759.11074
Painting—Catalogs 750.74
Painting, Chinese 759.951
Painting, Chinese—Song-Yuan dynasties, 960–1368
    759.9510902
Painting, Chinese—Ming-Qing dynasties, 1368–1912
    759.95109024; 759.9510903
Painting, Chinese—20th century 759.9510904
Painting, Chinese—Inscriptions 759.951
Painting—Conservation and restoration 751.62
Painting, Dutch 759.9492
Painting—England—London—Catalogs 709.421075
Painting, English 759.2
Painting, European 759.94
Painting, European—Exhibitions 759.94; 759.94074
Painting—Expertising 751.62
Painting, Flemish 759.94931
Painting, French 759.4
Painting, German 759.3
Painting, Indic 759.954
Painting, Indonesian 759.9598
Painting, Industrial 667.7
Painting, Italian 759.5
Painting, Italian—Italy—Venice 759.531
Painting, Japanese 759.952
Painting, Japanese—Kamakura-Momoyama periods,
    1185–1600 759.9520902; 759.95209031
Painting, Japanese—Edo period, 1600–1868
    759.9520903
Painting, Japanese—1868– 759.9520904
Painting, Japanese—20th century 759.9520904
Painting, Korean 759.9519
Painting, Korean—20th century 759.95190904
Painting, Mexican 759.972
Painting, Modern 759.06
Painting, Modern—17th century 759.04
Painting, Modern—17th–18th centuries—Netherlands
    759.949209032; 759.949209033
Painting, Modern—19th century 759.05
Painting, Modern—19th century—England 759.209034
Painting, Modern—19th century—France 759.409034
Painting, Modern—19th century—Germany 759.309034
Painting, Modern—19th century—Italy 759.509034
Painting, Modern—20th century 759.06
Painting, Modern—20th century—Spain 759.60904
Painting, Modern—20th century—United States
    759.130904
Painting—New York (State)—New York—Catalogs
    759.1471075
Painting—Philosophy 750.1
Painting, Polish 759.38
Painting—Russia (Federation)—Saint Petersburg—
    Catalogs 759.7075
Painting, Russian 759.7
Painting, Spanish 759.6
Painting—Study and teaching (Elementary) 372.52
Painting—Technique 751
Painting—Themes, motives 750
Paiute Indians 305.89745; 979.0049745
Pakistan 954.9; 954.91
Pakistan—Civilization 954.91
Pakistan—Description and travel 915.491045; 915.59104
Pakistan—Economic conditions 330.95491
Pakistan—Economic conditions—Periodicals
    330.95491005
Pakistan—Economic policy 338.95491
Pakistan—Foreign relations 327.5491
Pakistan—Guidebooks 915.49104; 915.491045

Pakistan—History 954.91
Pakistan—Officials and employees 352.6305491
Pakistan—Officials and employees—Pensions
  353.549095491
Pakistan—Periodicals 954.91005
Pakistan—Politics and government 320.95491; 954.904;
  954.91
Pakistan—Politics and government—1971–1988
  320.9549109047; 954.9105
Pakistan—Politics and government—1988–
  320.9549109049; 954.9105
Pakistan—Social conditions 954.91
Pakistan—Social life and customs 954.91
PAL (Computer program language) 005.7565
Palace of Knossos (Knossos) 939.18
Palaces 725.17
Palaces—Great Britain 728.820941
Palatine Americans—Genealogy 929.308931073
Palenque Site (Mexico) 972.75
Paleobiogeography 560.9
Paleobiology 560
Paleobotany 561
Paleobotany—Carboniferous 561.1
Paleobotany—Cenozoic 561.1
Paleobotany—Cretaceous 561.1
Paleobotany—Devonian 561.1
Paleobotany—Eocene 561.1
Paleobotany—Holocene 561.1
Paleobotany—Jurassic 561.1
Paleobotany—Mesozoic 561.1
Paleobotany—Miocene 561.1
Paleobotany—Oligocene 561.1
Paleobotany—Paleozoic 561.1
Paleobotany—Pennsylvanian 561.1
Paleobotany—Permian 561.1
Paleobotany—Pleistocene 561.1
Paleobotany—Quaternary 561.1
Paleobotany—Tertiary 561.1
Paleobotany—Triassic 561.1
Paleoceanography 551.46
Paleoclimatology 551.60909; 551.69
Paleoecology 560.45
Paleoecology—Quaternary 560.45
Paleogeography 551.7
Paleography 411.7
Paleolimnology 551.480901
Paleolithic period 569.9; 930.12
Paleolithic period—Europe 936
Paleomagnetism 538.727
Paleontological excavations 560
Paleontologists 560.92
Paleontology 560
Paleontology—Cambrian 560.1723
Paleontology—Carboniferous 560.175
Paleontology—Cenozoic 560.178
Paleontology—Cretaceous 560.177
Paleontology—Devonian 560.174
Paleontology—Eocene 560.1784
Paleontology—Holocene 560.1793
Paleontology—Jurassic 560.1766
Paleontology—Mesozoic 560.176
Paleontology—Miocene 560.1787
Paleontology—Mississippian 560.1751
Paleontology—Neogene 560.1786
Paleontology—Oligocene 560.1785
Paleontology—Ordovician 560.1731
Paleontology—Paleocene 560.1783
Paleontology—Paleogene 560.1782
Paleontology—Paleozoic 560.172

Paleontology—Pennsylvanian 560.1752
Paleontology—Permian 560.1756
Paleontology—Pleistocene 560.1792
Paleontology—Pliocene 560.1788
Paleontology—Precambrian 560.171
Paleontology—Proterozoic 560.1715
Paleontology—Quaternary 560.179
Paleontology—Silurian 560.1732
Paleontology, Stratigraphic 560.17
Paleontology—Tertiary 560.178
Paleontology—Triassic 560.1762
Paleopathology 616.070901
Palestine 956.94
Palestine—Antiquities 933
Palestine—Antiquities—Guidebooks 915.69404;
  915.6940454
Palestine—Description and travel 915.69404;
  915.6940454
Palestine—Economic conditions 330.95694
Palestine—Guidebooks 915.69404; 915.6940454
Palestine—Historical geography 911.5694
Palestine—History 956.94
Palestine—History—To 70 A.D. 933
Palestine—History—1799–1917 956.9403
Palestine—History—1917–1948 956.9404
Palestine in Judaism 296.31173
Palestine in the Bible 220.895694
Palestine—Politics and government 956.94
Palestine—Politics and government—1917–1948
  320.9569409041; 956.9404
Palestine—Politics and government—1917–1948—
  Sources 956.9404
Palestinian Arabs 305.89274
Palestinian Arabs—Israel 305.8927405694
Palestinian Arabs—Israel—Ethnic identity
  305.8927405694
Palestinian Arabs—Israel—Social conditions
  956.940049274
Palindromes 793.734
Palladium compounds 546.6362
Palliative treatment 362.175; 616.029
Pallopteridae 595.774
Palm Beach County (Fla.)—Maps 912.75932
Palm Connected Organizer (Computer) 004.16
Palmer, Arnold, 1929– 796.352092
Palmer family 929.20973
Palmistry 133.6
Palms 584.5; 635.97745
Palynology 561.13; 571.845
Pamphlets 002
Pamplemousse, Aristide (Fictitious character) 823.914
Pamplemousse, Aristide (Fictitious character)—Fiction
  823.914
Pan-Africanism 320.549096
Pan Am Flight 103 Bombing Incident, 1988
  363.124650941483
Pan American Health Organization 353.62117
Pan American Health Organization. Executive
  Committee 353.62242117; 362.1091812
Pan American World Airways, Inc.—History 387.706573
Pan-Americanism 327.17097
Pan-Pacific relations 327.091823
Panama 972.87
Panama Canal (Panama) 386.44
Panama Canal (Panama)—History 386.4409
Panama Canal Treaties (1977) 341.44602667307287
Panama hats 391.43; 687.4
Panama—History 972.87
Panama—History—American Invasion, 1989 972.87053

Parenting 649.1
Parenting—Handbooks, manuals, etc. 649.1
Parenting, Part-time 649.1
Parenting, Part-time—United States 306.874; 649.1
Parenting—Psychological aspects 649.1019
Parenting—Religious aspects 291.441
Parenting—Religious aspects—Catholic Church 248.845
Parenting—Religious aspects—Christianity 248.845
Parenting—Study and teaching 649.1071
Parenting—Study and teaching—United States
   649.1071073
Parenting—United States 649.10973
Parents 155.646
Parents' and teachers' associations 371.19206
Parents—Finance, Personal 332.0240431
Parents-in-law 306.87
Parents-in-law—United States 306.87
Parents of chronically ill children 306.874; 362.19892
Parents of deaf children 306.874
Parents of handicapped children 649.151
Parents of handicapped children—United States
   649.1510973
Parents—Prayer-books and devotions 242.645; 242.845
Parents—Religious life 248.845
Paridae 598.824
Paris, Bob 305.389664092
Paris, Charles (Fictitious character) 823.914
Paris, Charles (Fictitious character)—Fiction 823.914
Paris (France) 944.361
Paris (France)—Guidebooks 914.436104;
   914.436104839; 914.43610484
Paris (France)—History 944.361
Paris (France)—History—1789–1799 944.36104
Paris (France)—History—Commune, 1871 944.0812
Paris (France)—Pictorial works 779.991443610022
Paris (France)—Social life and customs 944.361
Paris (France)—Social life and customs—19th century
   944.36106
Paris (France)—Tours 914.436104; 914.436104839;
   914.43610484
Paris Peace Conference (1919-1920) 940.3141
Parish councils 254.02
Parishes 254
Park concessions 338.4791
Park family 929.20973
Park lodging facilities 338.4764794; 647.94
Park naturalists 333.783092; 508.092
Parker, Charlie, 1920–1955 788.73165092
Parker, Dorothy, 1893–1967 818.5209
Parker, Emmett (Fictitious character) 813.54
Parker family 929.20973
Parker (Fictitious character) 813.54
Parker (Fictitious character)—Fiction 813.54
Parkinson's disease 616.833
Parkinson's disease—Chemotherapy 616.833061
Parks 333.783
Parks—California—Guidebooks 917.9404; 917.940453;
   917.940454
Parks, Rosa, 1913– 323.092
Parliamentary practice 060.42
Parnell, Charles Stewart, 1846–1891 941.5081092
Parody 808.87
Parole 364.62
Parole—United States 364.620973
Parra, Nicanor, 1914– 861.62
Parra, Nicanor, 1914– —Translations into English
   861.62
Parricide 364.1523
Parrish, Maxfield, 1870–1966 759.13; 760.092

Parrish, Maxfield, 1870–1966—Criticism and
   interpretation 760.092
Parrish, Maxfield, 1870–1966—Themes, motives 759.13
Parrotlets 598.71; 636.6865
Parrots 598.71; 636.6865
Parrots—Behavior 636.6865
Parry, Amy (Fictitious character) 823.914
Parry, Will (Fictitious character) 823.914
Parsing (Computer grammar) 006.35
Parsnip (Fictitious character : Porter) 823.914
Parsons, Talcott, 1902– 301.092
Part-songs 783.1
Part-time employment 331.2572
Part-time employment—United States 331.2572
Part-time lawyers 331.2572
Part-time self-employment 658.041
Parthenon (Athens, Greece) 726.120809385
Partial differential operators 515.7242
Partially ordered sets 511.32
Participatory rural appraisal 307.1212
Particle acceleration 539.73
Particle accelerators 539.73
Particle beams 539.73
Particle image velocimetry 532.0532; 620.1064
Particle size determination 620.43
Particles 620.43
Particles (Nuclear physics) 539.72
Particles (Nuclear physics)—Experiments—Data
   processing 539.720724
Particles (Nuclear physics)—Instruments 539.720284
Particles (Nuclear physics)—Multiplicity 539.72; 539.75
Particles (Nuclear physics)—Technique 539.72
Partidul Comunist Român 324.2498075
Partition coefficient (Chemistry) 541.3413
Partitions (Mathematics) 512.73
Partnership 338.73
Partnership—Taxation 343.052662
Partnership—Taxation—United States 343.73052662;
   343.730662
Partnership—Taxation—United States—Cases
   343.730526620264; 343.7306620264
Partnership—United States 346.730682
Parton, Dolly 782.421642092
Pas de deux 792.8; 792.82
Pasadena (Calif.) 979.493
Pascal, Blaise, 1623–1662 194
Pascal, Blaise, 1623–1662. Pensées 230.2
Pascal (Computer program language) 005.133
Pascale, Lily (Fictitious character) 823.914
Paso doble (Dance) 793.33
Pasolini, Pier Paolo, 1922–1975 858.91409
Pasolini, Pier Paolo, 1922–1975—Criticism and
   interpretation 858.91409
Passacaglias (Organ) 786.51827
Passeriformes 598.8
Passion music 781.7255
Passive smoking 615.9523952
Passivity-based control 629.836
Passover 296.437
Passover—Christian observance 265.9
Passover cookery 641.5676437
Passover—Customs and practices 296.437
Passover food 296.437; 641.5676; 641.5676437
Passports 323.67
Pasta products 664.755
Pasta salads 641.83
Paste-up (Printing) 686.2252
Pastel drawing 741.235
Pastel drawing—Technique 741.235

Pasternak, Boris Leonidovich, 1890–1960 891.7142; 891.7342

Pasternak, Boris Leonidovich, 1890–1960. Doktor Zhivago 891.7143; 891.7342

Pasternak, Boris Leonidovich, 1890–1960—Translations into English 891.7142

Pasteur, Louis, 1822–1895 509.2

Pastis industry 338.4766355

Pastoral counseling 253.5; 291.61

Pastoral literature, English 820.80321734

Pastoral literature, English—History and criticism 820.9321734

Pastoral medicine 259.4

Pastoral poetry, English 821.0080321734

Pastoral poetry, Greek 881.0080321734; 881.01

Pastoral poetry, Greek—Translations into English 881.0080321734; 881.01080321734

Pastoral poetry, Latin 871.0080321734; 871.01

Pastoral poetry, Latin—Translations into English 871.0080321734; 871.01080321734

Pastoral prayers 264.13

Pastoral psychology 253.52

Pastoral theology 253

Pastoral theology—Catholic Church 253.08822

Pastoral theology—Handbooks, manuals, etc. 253

Pastoral theology—United States 253.0973

Pastry 641.865

Pastry War, 1838–1839 972.04

Pasture plants 581.755; 633.202

Pastures 633.202

Patañjali 181.452

Patañjali. Yogasūtra 181.452

Patchwork 746.46

Patchwork—Patterns 746.46041

Patchwork quilts 746.46

Patchwork quilts—Design 746.46

Patchwork—United States—Patterns 746.46041

Patent infringement 346.0486

Patent laws and legislation 346.0486

Patent laws and legislation—Europe 341.7586094; 346.40486

Patent laws and legislation—United States 346.730486

Patent laws and legislation—United States—Cases 346.7304860264

Patent laws and legislation—United States—Digests 346.73048602648

Patent lawyers 346.0486023

Patent licenses 346.0486

Patent literature 608

Patent practice 346.0486

Patent practice—United States 346.730486

Patent searching 025.06608

Patent suits 346.04860269

Patent suits—United States 346.7304860269

Patents 346.0486; 608

Patents and government-developed inventions 346.023

Patents (International law) 341.7586

Patents—United States 608.773

Pater, Walter, 1839–1894 824.8

Pater, Walter, 1839–1894—Criticism and interpretation 824.8

Paternal deprivation—Religious aspects 291.178358742

Paternity 346.0175

Path integrals 530.12

Pathogenic bacteria 579.3165; 616.014

Pathogenic fungi 616.015

Pathogenic fungi—Identification 616.015

Pathological laboratories 616.07

Pathological laboratories—Management 616.0756068

Pathologists 616.07092

Pathology 571.9; 616.07; 616.070246176

Pathology, Cellular 571.936; 611.01815

Pathology—Examinations, questions, etc. 616.07076

Pathology—Handbooks, manuals, etc. 616.07

Pathology, Molecular 571.948; 616.07

Pathology—Outlines, syllabi, etc. 616.07

Pathology, Surgical 617.07

Pathology—Terminology 616.07014

Patient advocacy 362.1068

Patient compliance 615.5

Patient education 615.5071

Patient education—Handbooks, manuals, etc. 615.5071

Patient education—Study and teaching 615.5071

Patient monitoring 616.028; 616.075

Patient participation 610.696

Patient satisfaction 362.1068

Patients' associations 362.106

Patients—Legal status, laws, etc. 344.041

Patients—Legal status, laws, etc.—United States 344.73041

Patio gardening 717

Patios 721.84

Patriarchs (Bible) 222.110922

Patriarchy 306.858

Patrick County (Va.)—Genealogy 929.3755695

Patrick, Saint, 373?–463? 270.2092

Patriotic music 781.599

Patriotism 323.65

Patriotism in literature 808.80358; 809.93358

Patriotism—United States 323.650973

Pattern bargaining 331.891

Pattern books 745.4

Pattern formation (Physical sciences) 500.201185

Pattern perception 152.1423

Pattern recognition systems 006.4

Patternmaking 671.23

Patterson family 929.20973

Patton family 929.20973

Paul, the Apostle, Saint 225.92

Paulding County (Ohio) 977.117

Paulding County (Ohio)—Genealogy 929.377117

Pauline churches 270.1

Pauling, Linus, 1901– 540.92

Pavarotti, Luciano 782.1092

Pavements 625.8

Pavements, Asphalt 625.85

Pavements, Bituminous 625.85

Pavements, Concrete 625.84

Pavements, Concrete—Maintenance and repair 625.840288

Pavements, Concrete—Testing 625.840287

Pavements—Design and construction 625.8; 629.13634

Pavements—Design and construction—Management 625.8068

Pavements—Maintenance and repair 625.76

Pavements—Maintenance and repair—Management 625.76

Pavements—Performance 625.8

Pavements—Testing 625.80287

Pavlova, Anna, 1881–1931 792.8028092

Pawnbroking 332.34

Pawnee Indians 305.8979; 976.6004979; 978.004979

Pawnee Indians—Rites and ceremonies 299.74

Pay equity 331.2153

Pay equity—United States 331.21530973

Payne family 929.20973

Payne, Robert (Fictitious character) 813.54

Payroll deductions—Law and legislation 343.05242

Payroll deductions—Law and legislation—United States 343.7305242
Payrolls 658.321
Payrolls—United States—Management 658.3210973
Paz, Octavio, 1914- 861.62
Paz, Octavio, 1914- —Translations into English 861.62
PC-DOS (Computer file) 005.4469
PC-write 652.55369
PDF (Computer file format) 005.72
Peabody, Amelia (Fictitious character) 813.54
Peabody, Amelia (Fictitious character)—Fiction 813.54
Peabody Awards 791.4407973
Peace 303.66; 327.172
Peace—Biblical teaching 220.8327172
Peace—Bibliography 016.327172
Peace Corps (U.S.) 361.6
Peace—History 327.17209
Peace in literature 808.80358; 809.93358
Peace movements 327.172
Peace movements—United States 327.1720973
Peace movements—United States—History 327.1720973
Peace of mind 158.1
Peace of mind—Religious aspects 291.44
Peace of mind—Religious aspects—Christianity 248.4
Peace officers 363.2
Peace—Periodicals 327.17205
Peace—Religious aspects 291.17873
Peace—Religious aspects—Buddhism 294.337873
Peace—Religious aspects—Catholic Church 261.873
Peace—Religious aspects—Christianity 261.873
Peace—Research 327.172072
Peace—Research—Directories 327.172072
Peace—Societies, etc. 327.17206
Peace—Societies, etc.—Directories 327.172025
Peace—Study and teaching 327.172071
Peace—Study and teaching—United States 327.172071073
Peace treaties 341.66
Peaceful change (International relations) 327.172
Peach, Percy (Fictitious character) 823.914
Peachtree complete accounting 657.02855369
Peachtree complete accounting for Windows 657.02855369
Peacock, Thomas Love, 1785–1866 823.7
Peafowl 598.6258
Pearl Harbor (Hawaii), Attack on, 1941 940.5426
Pearl (Middle English poem) 821.1
Pearse, Padraic, 1879–1916 941.50821092
Pearson family 929.20973
Peary, Robert E. (Robert Edwin), 1856–1920 919.804092
Peasantry 305.5633
Peasantry—Europe—History 305.5633094
Peasants in art 704.942
Peasants' War, 1524–1525 943.031
Pease family 929.20973
Peat 553.21
Peat bog ecology 577.687
Peatland conservation 333.918
Peatland ecology 577.687
Peccaries 599.634
Peckinpah, Sam, 1925–1984 791.430233092
Peckover, Henry (Fictitious character) 823.914
Peckover, Henry (Fictitious character)—Fiction 823.914
Pecos Bill (Legendary character)—Legends 398.2097302
Pedestrian facilities design 711.74
Pediatric anesthesia 617.96798
Pediatric anesthesia—Handbooks, manuals, etc. 617.96798

Pediatric cardiology 618.9212
Pediatric dermatology 618.925
Pediatric diagnostic imaging 618.9200754
Pediatric emergencies 618.920025
Pediatric emergencies—Handbooks, manuals, etc. 618.920025
Pediatric endocrinology 618.924
Pediatric gastroenterology 618.9233
Pediatric gynecology 618.92098
Pediatric hematology 618.9215
Pediatric intensive care 618.920028
Pediatric intensive care—Handbooks, manuals, etc. 618.920028
Pediatric nephrology 618.9261
Pediatric neurology 618.928
Pediatric neuropsychiatry 618.928
Pediatric neuropsychology 618.928
Pediatric nuclear medicine 618.92007575
Pediatric nursing 610.7362
Pediatric nursing—Handbooks, manuals, etc. 610.7362
Pediatric nursing—Outlines, syllabi, etc. 610.7362
Pediatric ophthalmology 618.920977
Pediatric orthopedics 618.927
Pediatric otolaryngology 618.9209751
Pediatric pathology 618.92007
Pediatric pharmacology 615.1083
Pediatric pharmacology—Handbooks, manuals, etc. 615.58083
Pediatric psychopharmacology 618.928918
Pediatric radiography 618.92007572
Pediatric radiology 618.9200757
Pediatric respiratory diseases 618.922
Pediatric toxicology 615.90083
Pediatric urology 618.926
Pediatricians 618.9200092
Pediatrics 618.92
Pediatrics—Examinations, questions, etc. 618.9200076
Pediatrics—Handbooks, manuals, etc. 618.92
Pediatrics—Moral and ethical aspects 174.2
Pediatrics—Outlines, syllabi, etc. 618.92
Pediatrics—Psychological aspects 618.9200019
Pediatrics—United States—Standards 618.9200021873
Pediculosis 616.57
Pedodontics 617.645
Pedophilia 306.77
Pedunculata 595.35
Peel, Emma (Fictitious character) 791.4372; 791.4572
Peel, Robert, Sir, 1788–1850 941.081092
Peer counseling 158.3
Peer counseling in the church 253.5
Peer counseling of students 371.4047
Peer-group tutoring of students 371.394
Peer pressure in adolescence 303.327
Peer pressure in adolescence—Religious aspects 291.178
Peer pressure in adolescence—United States 303.327
Peer pressure in children—Religious aspects 291.178
Peer review committees 362.1068
Peewit (Fictitious character : Peyo) 741.59493
Peirce, Charles S. (Charles Sanders), 1839–1914 191
Peirce, Charles S. (Charles Sanders), 1839–1914—Contributions in semiotics 191
Peking man 569.9
Pel, Evariste Clovis Desire (Fictitious character) 823.914
Pel, Evariste Clovis Desire (Fictitious character)—Fiction 823.914
Pelargoniums 635.93379
Pelicans 598.43

Pellam, John (Fictitious character) 813.54
Pellet fusion 621.484
Pelzer, David J. 362.76092
Pembina County (N.D.) 978.419
Pembina County (N.D.)—Maps 912.78419
Pembroke Welsh corgi 636.737
Pen drawing 741.26
Pen drawing—Technique 741.26
Pen pals 302.34
Penance 234.166
Pencil drawing 741.24
Pencil drawing—Technique 741.24
Pencils 674.88
Pendants (Jewelry) 739.278
Penguins 598.47
Penicillium 579.5654
Peninsular Campaign, 1862 973.732
Peninsular War, 1807–1814 940.27
Penis 573.656; 612.61
Penmanship 652.1
Penmanship—Study and teaching (Elementary) 372.634
Penn, William, 1644–1718 974.802092
Pennsylvania 974.8
Pennsylvania and Ohio Canal (Ohio and Pa.)
386.48097713
Pennsylvania—Description and travel 917.4804;
917.480443; 917.480444
Pennsylvania Dutch 974.80043931
Pennsylvania—Genealogy 929.3748
Pennsylvania—Guidebooks 917.4804; 917.480443;
917.480444
Pennsylvania—History 974.8
Pennsylvania—History—Colonial period, ca. 1600–1775
974.802
Pennsylvania—Maps 912.748
Pennsylvania—Politics and government 974.8
Pennsylvania—Politics and government—To 1775
320.974809033; 974.802
Pennsylvania Railroad 385.09748
Pennsylvania—Road maps 912.748
Pension trusts 332.67254
Pension trusts—Investments—Law and legislation
343.0524; 344.01252
Pension trusts—Investments—Law and legislation—
United States 343.730524; 344.7301252
Pension trusts—Law and legislation 343.064; 344.01252
Pension trusts—Law and legislation—United States
343.73064; 344.7301252
Pension trusts—Law and legislation—United States—
Forms 344.7301252
Pension trusts—Law and legislation—United States—
Periodicals 344.7301252
Pension trusts—Taxation—Law and legislation 343.0524
Pension trusts—Taxation—Law and legislation—United
States 343.730524
Pension trusts—Termination—Law and legislation
344.01252
Pension trusts—Termination—Law and legislation—
United States 344.7301252
Pension trusts—United States 332.67254
Pension trusts—United States—Directories 332.67254
Pension trusts—United States—Investments 332.67254
Pension trusts—United States—Management 332.67254
Pensions 331.252
Pensions—Law and legislation 344.01252
Pensions—Law and legislation—United States
344.7301252
Pensions—United States 331.2520973
Pentax cameras 771.31

Pentecost season 263.94
Pentecost season—Sermons 252.64
Pentecostal churches 289.94
Pentecostal churches—Sermons 252.0994
Pentecostalism 289.94
Pentium (Microprocessor) 004.165
Penzance (England) 942.375
Penzance (England)—History 942.37; 942.375
Peonies 635.93362
Pepper, Amanda (Fictitious character) 813.54
Pepper, Amanda (Fictitious character)—Fiction 813.54
Peppers 633.84
Peptic ulcer 616.343
Peptides 547.756; 572.65
Peptides—Synthesis 547.756
Pepys, Samuel, 1633–1703 941.066092
Pequot Indians 974.6004973
Pequot War, 1636–1638 973.22
Per saltum (Ordination) 262.14
Perception 153.7
Perception in animals 591.5
Perception (Philosophy) 121.34
Perceptual control theory 153.7; 591.5
Perceptual-motor learning 370.155
Perceptual-motor processes 152
Percolation (Statistical physics) 530.13
Percussion ensembles 785.68
Percussion instruments 786.8; 786.819
Percussion music 786.8
Percy, Walker, 1916– 813.54
Percy, Walker, 1916– —Criticism and interpretation
813.54
Peregrine falcon 598.96
Perennials 635.932
Peretz, Isaac Leib, 1851 or 2–1915 839.133; 839.18309
Peretz, Isaac Leib, 1851 or 2–1915—Translations into
English 839.133
Pérez Galdós, Benito, 1843–1920 863.5
Pérez Galdós, Benito, 1843–1920—Criticism and
interpretation 863.5
Perfection 179.9
Perfection—Religious aspects 291.22
Perfection—Religious aspects—Catholic Church 234.8
Perfection—Religious aspects—Christianity 234.8
Perfectionism (Personality trait) 155.232
Performance 700.1
Performance anxiety 152.46
Performance art 702.81
Performance art—United States 702.81
Performance contracts in education 371.15; 371.2;
371.393
Performance practice (Music) 781.46
Performance practice (Music)—17th century
781.4309032
Performance practice (Music)—18th century
781.4309033
Performance standards 658.3125
Performance technology 658.314
Performing arts 790.2; 791
Performing arts festivals 791.079
Performing arts—Finance 338.437902
Performing arts high schools 790.20712
Performing arts in literature 808.80357; 809.93357
Performing arts—India 790.20954
Performing arts—Law and legislation 343.0787902;
344.097
Performing arts—Law and legislation—United States
343.730787902; 344.73097
Performing arts libraries 026.7902

Personnel management—United States—Periodicals 658.30097305

Persons (Law) 346.012

Perspective 701.82; 742

Persuasion (Psychology) 153.852; 303.342

Persuasion (Rhetoric) 808

PERT (Network analysis) 658.4032

Perth Metropolitan Area (W.A.) 994.11

Perth Metropolitan Area (W.A.)—Maps 912.9411

Perthshire (Scotland) 941.28

Perthshire (Scotland)—History 941.28

Perturbation (Mathematics) 515.35

Peru 985

Peru—Description and travel 918.504; 918.50464

Peru—Economic conditions 330.985

Peru—Economic conditions—1968- 330.9850633

Peru—Economic conditions—1968- —Periodicals 330.9850633

Peru—Economic policy 338.985

Peru—Guidebooks 918.504; 918.50464

Peru—History 985

Peru—History—Conquest, 1522-1548 985.02

Peru—Politics and government 320.985; 985

Peru—Politics and government—20th century 320.9850904

Peru—Politics and government—1980- 320.98509048; 985.064

Peru—Social life and customs 985

Pessimism 149.6

Pessoa, Fernando, 1888-1935 869.141

Pessoa, Fernando, 1888-1935—Translations into English 869.141

Pesticide applicators (Persons) 632.95092

Pesticide buffer zones 363.7384; 632.95042

Pesticide residues in food 363.192

Pesticide waste 363.7288; 628.42

Pesticides 632.95; 668.65

Pesticides—Environmental aspects 577.279

Pesticides—Environmental aspects—United States 363.7384

Pesticides—Handbooks, manuals, etc. 632.95

Pesticides—Health aspects 363.1792

Pesticides—Law and legislation 344.046334

Pesticides—Law and legislation—United States 344.73046334

Pesticides—Toxicology 571.959

Pests 632.6

Pests—Biological control 632.96

Pests—Control 628.96; 632.6

Pet adoption 636.0887

Pet cleanup 363.7288

Pet food industry 338.4766466; 664.66

Pet loss 155.93

Pet medicine 636.089

Pet owners—Psychology 155.93

Pet supplies 636.08870284

Pet supplies industry 338.476360887

Peter I, Emperor of Russia, 1672-1725 947.05092

Peter, the Apostle, Saint 225.92

Peterloo Massacre, Manchester, England, 1819 942.073

Peters, Anna (Fictitious character) 813.54

Peters, Anna (Fictitious character)—Fiction 813.54

Peters family 929.20973

Peters, Toby (Fictitious character) 813.54

Peters, Toby (Fictitious character)—Fiction 813.54

Petersburg Region (Va.)—Maps 912.755581

Petersburg (Va.)—History—Siege, 1864-1865 973.737

Peterson family 929.20973

Peterson, Wesley (Fictitious character) 823.914

Petra (Extinct city) 939.48

Petrarch, 1304-1374 851.1

Petrarch, 1304-1374—Translations into English 851.1

Petri nets 511.3

Petroglyphs 709.0113

Petroleum 665.5

Petroleum—Analysis 665.5

Petroleum chemicals 661.804

Petroleum chemicals industry 338.2728

Petroleum—Dictionaries 665.503

Petroleum engineering 622.3382

Petroleum engineering—Dictionaries 665.503

Petroleum engineering—Periodicals 665.505

Petroleum engineers 665.5092

Petroleum geologists 553.28092

Petroleum—Geology 553.28; 553.282

Petroleum—Geology—Oklahoma 553.2809766

Petroleum—Geology—United States 553.280973

Petroleum in submerged lands 333.823209162

Petroleum in submerged lands—North Sea 333.82320916336

Petroleum industry and trade 338.2728; 338.27282; 380.142282; 380.1456655; 381.42282; 381.456655; 382.42282; 382.456655

Petroleum industry and trade—Alaska 338.2728209798

Petroleum industry and trade—Canada 338.27280971

Petroleum industry and trade—Environmental aspects 333.823214

Petroleum industry and trade—Environmental aspects— United States 333.823

Petroleum industry and trade—Finance 338.2328

Petroleum industry and trade—Government policy 333.8232

Petroleum industry and trade—Government policy— United States 333.82320973; 382.422820973

Petroleum industry and trade—Great Britain 338.272820941

Petroleum industry and trade—Iran 338.272820955

Petroleum industry and trade—Middle East 338.272820956

Petroleum industry and trade—Nigeria 338.2728209669

Petroleum industry and trade—Periodicals 338.2728205

Petroleum industry and trade—Political aspects 338.27282

Petroleum industry and trade—Soviet Union 338.27280947; 338.272820947

Petroleum industry and trade—Statistics 338.2728021

Petroleum industry and trade—Statistics—Periodicals 338.2728021; 338.27282021

Petroleum industry and trade—Texas 338.2728209764

Petroleum industry and trade—Texas—History 338.2728209764

Petroleum industry and trade—United States 338.272820973; 381.422820973; 381.4566550973

Petroleum industry and trade—United States— Mathematical models 338.27280973

Petroleum industry and trade—Venezuela 338.272820987

Petroleum law and legislation 343.0772

Petroleum law and legislation—Texas 343.7640772

Petroleum law and legislation—United States 343.730772; 346.730468232

Petroleum law and legislation—United States—Cases 343.730772

Petroleum pipeline failures 665.544

Petroleum pipelines 388.55; 665.544

Petroleum pipelines—Environmental aspects 388.55

Petroleum pipelines—Environmental aspects—Montana 388.5509786

Petroleum pipelines—Law and legislation 343.093
Petroleum pipelines—Law and legislation—Alaska 343.798093
Petroleum pipelines—Law and legislation—United States 343.73093
Petroleum pipelines—Louisiana—Maps 388.5509763022
Petroleum pipelines—Texas—Maps 388.5509764022
Petroleum pipelines—United States 388.550973
Petroleum products 665.53
Petroleum products—Prices 338.2328
Petroleum products—Prices—United States 338.23280973
Petroleum products—Underground storage 665.542
Petroleum—Prospecting 622.1828; 622.18282
Petroleum—Prospecting—Data processing 622.18280285
Petroleum refineries 665.53
Petroleum refineries—Safety measures 665.530289
Petroleum—Refining 665.53
Petroleum reserves 622.1828
Petroleum reserves—United States 333.8232110973; 553.280973
Petroleum—Storage 333.823211
Petroleum—Storage—United States 665.5420973
Petroleum—Taxation—Law and legislation 343.05582282
Petroleum—Taxation—Law and legislation—United States 343.7305582282
Petroleum—Transportation 665.543
Petroleum—United States 553.200973
Petroleum waste 665.538
Petrology 552
Petronius Arbiter 873.01
Petronius Arbiter. Satyricon 873.01
Petronius Arbiter—Translations into English 873.01
Pets 636.0887
Pets—Anecdotes 636.0887
Pets—Names 929.97
Pettis County (Mo.) 977.848
Pettis County (Mo.)—Maps 912.77848
Petunia (Fictitious character : Duvoisin) 813.54
Peyote songs 299.74; 782.25; 782.397
Peyotism 299.74
Pezizales 579.578
Pfaffian systems 515.36
Pfiesteriaceae 579.87
PFS:First choice (Computer file) 005.369
Phacoemulsification 617.742059
Phalangiidae 595.43
Phallicism 291.212
Phantom II (Jet fighter plane) 358.4383
Pharisees 296.812
Pharmaceutical arithmetic 615.1401513
Pharmaceutical arithmetic—Programmed instruction 615.1401513
Pharmaceutical biotechnology 615.19
Pharmaceutical biotechnology industry 338.476153
Pharmaceutical chemistry 615.19
Pharmaceutical ethics 174.2
Pharmaceutical industry 338.476151
Pharmaceutical industry—Quality control 615.190685
Pharmaceutical industry—United States 338.4761510973
Pharmaceutical industry—United States—Directories 381.45615102573
Pharmaceutical industry—United States—Periodicals 338.476151097305
Pharmaceutical policy 362.1782

Pharmaceutical policy—Developing countries 362.1782091724
Pharmaceutical policy—United States 362.17820973
Pharmaceutical services 362.1782
Pharmaceutical technology 615.19
Pharmacists 615.1092
Pharmacoepidemiology 363.194; 615.7042
Pharmacogenomics 615.7
Pharmacognosy 615.321
Pharmacokinetics 615.7
Pharmacology 615.1
Pharmacology—Examinations, questions, etc. 615.1076
Pharmacology—Handbooks, manuals, etc. 615.1
Pharmacology—History 615.109
Pharmacology—Outlines, syllabi, etc. 615.1
Pharmacology—Periodicals 615.105
Pharmacopoeias 615.11
Pharmacopoeias—India 615.1154
Pharmacy 615.1
Pharmacy colleges 615.10711
Pharmacy—Examinations, questions, etc. 615.1076
Pharmacy—Law and legislation 344.0416
Pharmacy—Law and legislation—Great Britain 344.410416
Pharmacy—Periodicals 615.105
Pharmacy—Practice 615.1068
Pharmacy school libraries 026.615
Pharmacy—Statistical methods 615.10727
Phase diagrams 089.94
Phase-locked loops 621.3815364
Phase rule and equilibrium 660.2963
Phase-transfer catalysis 547.1395
Phase transformations (Statistical physics) 530.414; 530.474
Pheasants 598.625
Phenogodidae 595.7644
Phenols 547.632
Phenomenological psychology 150.192
Phenomenology 142.7
Phenylacetates 547.632
Pheromones 573.929
Philadelphia Eagles (Football team) 796.332640974811
Philadelphia Eagles (Football team)—History 796.332640974811
Philadelphia Flyers (Hockey team) 796.962640974811
Philadelphia Flyers (Hockey team)—History 796.962640974811
Philadelphia Metropolitan Area (Pa.)—Maps 912.74811
Philadelphia (Pa.) 974.811
Philadelphia (Pa.)—Civilization 974.811
Philadelphia (Pa.)—Description and travel 917.481104
Philadelphia (Pa.)—Genealogy 929.374811
Philadelphia (Pa.)—Guidebooks 917.481104; 917.48110443; 917.48110444
Philadelphia (Pa.)—History 974.811
Philadelphia (Pa.)—History—Colonial period, ca. 1600–1775 974.81102
Philadelphia (Pa.)—Maps 912.74811
Philadelphia (Pa.)—Pictorial works 974.81100222
Philadelphia (Pa.)—Social life and customs 974.811
Philadelphia (Pa.)—Tours 917.481104; 917.48110443; 917.48110444
Philadelphia Phillies (Baseball team) 796.357640974811
Philadelphia Phillies (Baseball team)—History 796.357640974811
Philanthropinism 177.7
Philby, Kim, 1912– 327.12092
Philip II, King of Spain, 1527–1598 946.043092

Philip, Prince, consort of Elizabeth II, Queen of Great Britain, 1921- 941.085092
Philip, Sachem of the Wampanoags, d. 1676 973.24092
Philippine literature 809.89599
Philippine literature—History and criticism 809.89599
Philippines 959.9
Philippines—Civilization 959.9
Philippines—Constitutional law 342.599
Philippines—Description and travel 915.9904; 915.990448
Philippines—Economic conditions 330.9599
Philippines—Economic conditions—1946–1986 330.959804; 330.959904
Philippines—Economic conditions—1986- 330.9599047
Philippines—Economic conditions—1986- —Periodicals 330.9599047
Philippines—Economic policy 338.9599
Philippines—Foreign relations 327.599
Philippines—Foreign relations—1973- 327.599
Philippines—Guidebooks 915.9904; 915.990448
Philippines—History 959.9
Philippines—History—1898–1946 959.903
Philippines—History—Philippine American War, 1899–1902 959.9031
Philippines—History—Japanese occupation, 1942–1945 959.9035
Philippines—Maps 912.599
Philippines—Periodicals 959.9005
Philippines—Pictorial works 959.900222
Philippines—Politics and government 959.9
Philippines—Politics and government—1946- 320.959909045; 959.904
Philippines—Politics and government—1946–1973 320.959909045
Philippines—Politics and government—1973–1986 320.959909047; 959.904; 959.9046
Philippines—Politics and government—1986- 320.959909049; 959.9047
Philippines—Population 304.60599
Philippines—Social conditions 959.9
Philippines—Social life and customs 959.9
Phillips, Bino (Fictitious character) 813.54
Phillips, Bino (Fictitious character)—Fiction 813.54
Phillips family 929.20973
Philo, of Alexandria 181.06
Philology 400; 410
Philology, Modern 410
Philology, Modern—Periodicals 405; 410.5
Philology—Periodicals 410.5
Philosophers 109.2
Philosophers, Modern 190
Philosophical anthropology 128
Philosophical theology 230.01
Philosophy 100
Philosophy, African 199.6
Philosophy, American 191
Philosophy, American—20th century 191
Philosophy, Ancient 180
Philosophy, Ancient—History 180.9
Philosophy, Ancient, in literature 808.80384; 809.93384
Philosophy and civilization 306.01
Philosophy and cognitive science 153.01
Philosophy and religion 291.175
Philosophy and religion—History 261.51
Philosophy and science 501
Philosophy and social sciences 300.1
Philosophy, Asian 181
Philosophy—Authorship 808.0661
Philosophy—Bibliography 016.1

Philosophy, Buddhist 181.043
Philosophy, Chinese 181.11
Philosophy, Chinese—20th century 181.11
Philosophy, Comparative 100
Philosophy, Confucian 181.112
Philosophy—Dictionaries 103
Philosophy, English 192
Philosophy, English—20th century 192
Philosophy, French 194
Philosophy, French—20th century 194
Philosophy, German 193
Philosophy, German—20th century 193
Philosophy, Hindu 181.4
Philosophy—Historiography 107.22
Philosophy—History 109
Philosophy in literature 809.93384
Philosophy, Indic 181.4
Philosophy, Indic—20th century 181.4
Philosophy—Introductions 100
Philosophy, Islamic 181.07
Philosophy, Islamic—History 181.07
Philosophy, Jewish 181.06
Philosophy, Marxist 335.411
Philosophy, Medieval 189
Philosophy, Modern 190
Philosophy, Modern—17th century 190.9032
Philosophy, Modern—18th century 190.9033
Philosophy, Modern—19th century 190.9034
Philosophy, Modern—20th century 190.904
Philosophy of mind 128.2
Philosophy of mind—History 128.209
Philosophy of mind in children 128.2083
Philosophy of nature 113
Philosophy of nature—History 113.09
Philosophy—Periodicals 105
Philosophy, Russian 197
Philosophy, Scottish 192
Philosophy, Sikh 181.046
Philosophy—Study and teaching 107.1
Philosophy, Taoist 181.114
Phlebotomy 616.07561
Phlebotomy—Examinations, questions, etc. 616.07561
Phlebotomy—Handbooks, manuals, etc. 616.07561
Phlogiston 540.118
Phobias 616.85225
Phoenix Metropolitan Area (Ariz.) 979.173
Phoenix Metropolitan Area (Ariz.)—Maps 912.79173
Phonetics 414.8
Phonograph 621.38933
Phonons 530.416
Phoridae 595.774
Phosphatases 572.7553; 572.757
Phosphate industry 338.2764
Phosphate mines and mining 622.364
Phosphates 546.71224
Phosphatic fertilizers 631.85
Phosphatocopida 565.3
Phosphofructokinase 1 572.475
Phospholipids 572.57
Phosphors 535.353
Phosphorus 546.712; 661.0712
Photius I, Saint, Patriarch of Constantinople, ca. 820–ca. 891 270.3092
Photobiochemistry 572.435
Photobiology 571.455
Photocatalysis 541.395
Photochemistry 541.35
Photocopying 686.4
Photocopying—Fair use (Copyright) 346.0482

Physical education for handicapped persons
371.904486; 613.7087
Physical education for women 796.082
Physical education teachers—Training of 613.70711
Physical fitness 613.7
Physical fitness centers 796.068
Physical fitness for children 613.7042
Physical fitness for men 613.70449
Physical fitness for middle aged persons 613.7044
Physical fitness for the aged 613.70446
Physical fitness for women 613.7045
Physical fitness—Periodicals 613.705
Physical fitness—Testing 613.70287
Physical geography 910.02
Physical geography—Maps 912
Physical geography—United States 917.302
Physical geology 550
Physical instruments 530.0284
Physical laboratories 530.028
Physical measurements 530.8
Physical metallurgy 669.9
Physical optics 535.2
Physical sciences 500.2
Physical sciences—Philosophy 500.201
Physical therapists 615.82
Physical therapy 615.82
Physical therapy for children 615.82083
Physical therapy for the aged 615.820846
Physical therapy—Practice 615.82068
Physical therapy services 362.178
Physically handicapped 305.90816; 362.4
Physically handicapped athletes 305.90816
Physically handicapped children 305.90816; 362.43083;
371.916; 618.92
Physically handicapped children—Education 371.91
Physically handicapped—Education 371.91
Physician and patient 610.696
Physician practice acquisitions 338.8361362172
Physician practice patterns 362.172
Physician services utilization—United States—Statistics
362.1720973021
Physicians 610.6952; 610.92
Physicians' assistants 610.6953
Physicians' assistants—Examinations, questions, etc.
610.76
Physicians—Biography 610.92; 610.922
Physicians (General practice) 610.92
Physicians in art 704.942
Physicians—Malpractice 344.04121
Physicians—Malpractice—United States 344.730412;
344.7304121
Physicians—Malpractice—United States—Trial practice
344.73041210269
Physicians—Supply and demand—United States
331.129161069520973
Physicians—Supply and demand—United States—
Statistics 331.129161069520973
Physicians—United States—Biography 610.92273
Physicians—United States—Directories 610.2573
Physicists 530.092
Physicists—Biography 530.092
Physics 530
Physics—Data processing 530.0285
Physics—Dictionaries 530.03
Physics—Encyclopedias 530.03
Physics—Examinations, questions, etc. 530.076
Physics—Experiments 530.0724; 530.078
Physics—Handbooks, manuals, etc. 530
Physics—History 530.09

Physics—Laboratory manuals 530.078
Physics—Methodology 530.01
Physics—Periodicals 530.05
Physics—Philosophy 530.01
Physics—Problems, exercises, etc. 530.076
Physics—Religious aspects 291.175
Physics—Religious aspects—Christianity 261.55
Physics—Study and teaching 530.071
Physics—Study and teaching (Elementary) 372.35
Physics—Study and teaching (Higher) 530.0711
Physiognomy 138
Physiological optics 612.84
Physiology 571; 612
Physiology, Comparative 571.1
Physiology, Comparative—Periodicals 571.105
Physiology—Laboratory manuals 612.0078
Physiology, Pathological 616.07
Phytochemicals 572.2; 615.32
Phytoestrogens 575.6374; 615.32
Phytogeography 581.9
Phytopathogenic bacteria 632.32
Phytopathogenic fungi 632.4
Phytopathogenic microorganisms 632.3
Phytopathogenic microorganisms—Biological control
632.3
Phytopathogenic microorganisms—Control 632.3
Phytophthora 579.546
Phytoplankton 579.81776
Phytoremediation 628.4
Pi 512.73; 516.215
PI-algebras 512.24
Piaget, Jean, 1896– 155.413092
Pianists 786.2092
Piano 786.2; 786.219
Piano—Construction 786.21923
Piano—History 786.209; 786.21909
Piano—Instruction and study 786.2071
Piano—Maintenance and repair 786.21928
Piano—Methods 786.2143
Piano—Methods—Self-instruction 786.2143076
Piano music 786.2
Piano music (4 hands) 785.62192
Piano music (4 hands), Arranged 785.62192
Piano music—Analysis, appreciation 786.2117
Piano music, Arranged 786.2
Piano music—Bibliography 016.7862
Piano music (Blues) 786.21643
Piano music—History and criticism 786.209
Piano music—Interpretation (Phrasing, dynamics, etc.)
786.2146
Piano music (Jazz) 786.2165
Piano music (Pianos (2)) 785.62192
Piano music (Pianos (2)), Arranged 785.62192
Piano music (Ragtime) 786.21645
Piano—Performance 786.2143
Piano quartets 785.62194
Piano quintets 785.62195
Piano quintets—Scores 785.62195
Piano trios 785.62193
Piano trios—Scores 785.62193
Piano trios—Scores and parts 785.62193
Piano—Tuning 786.21928
Piano with orchestra 784.262
Piano with orchestra—Scores 784.262
Piatt County (Ill.) 977.3673
Piatt County (Ill.)—Genealogy 929.3773673
Piatt County (Ill.)—Maps 912.773673
Picaresque literature—History and criticism 809.3877
Picasso, Pablo, 1881–1973 709.2; 759.4

Pitching (Baseball) 796.35722
Piton (Computer program language) 005.265
Pitt, Charlotte (Fictitious character) 823.914
Pitt, Charlotte (Fictitious character)—Fiction 823.914
Pitt, Dirk (Fictitious character) 813.54
Pitt, Dirk (Fictitious character)—Fiction 813.54
Pittsburgh Metropolitan Area (Pa.)—Maps 912.74886
Pittsburgh (Pa.) 974.886
Pittsburgh (Pa.)—Genealogy 929.374886
Pittsburgh (Pa.)—History 974.886
Pittsburgh (Pa.)—Pictorial works 974.88600222
Pittsburgh Pirates (Baseball team) 796.357640974886
Pittsburgh Pirates (Baseball team)—History 796.357640974886
Pittsburgh Steelers (Football team) 796.332640974886
Pittsburgh Steelers (Football team)—History 796.332640974886
Pittsylvania County (Va.)—Genealogy 929.3755665
Pituitary gland—Diseases 616.47
Piyutim 296.452
Pizza 641.824
Pizza industry 338.47641824
PL/I (Computer program language) 005.133
Place marketing 910.688
Place (Philosophy) 114
Placenta 612.63
Placenta—Diseases 618.34
Plagiarism 808
Plague 616.9232
Plague—England 362.19692320942
Plague—England—London 362.196923209421
Plague—Europe 362.1969232094
Plague—Europe—History 362.1969232094
Plan of salvation (Mormon theology) 234.088283
Plane trigonometry 516.242
Planetariums 520.74
Planetary meteorology 551.50999
Planetary nebulae 523.1135
Planetary theory 523.401
Planetary volcanism 551.2109992
Planetology 523.4
Planets 523.4
Planets—Atmospheres 551.509992
Planets—Exploration 551.40723
Planets—Geology 559.92
Plankton 578.776
Planned communities 307.768
Planned communities—Law and legislation 346.045
Planning 658.4012
PlanPerfect 005.369
Plant biotechnology 630
Plant breeding 631.52; 631.523
Plant cell culture 571.6382
Plant cells and tissues 571.52
Plant cellular signal transduction 571.742
Plant chemical ecology 581.7
Plant clinics 632.3
Plant communities 581.782
Plant conservation 333.95316; 639.99
Plant conservation (International law) 341.7625
Plant cytogenetics 572.82
Plant diseases 571.92; 632.3
Plant diseases—Diagnosis 632.3
Plant diversity 333.953; 581.7
Plant diversity conservation 333.95316; 639.99
Plant ecology 581.7
Plant ecology—Australia 581.70994
Plant ecology—California 581.709794
Plant ecology—Methodology 581.701; 581.7072

Plant ecology—United States 581.70973
Plant ecophysiology 571.2
Plant engineering 660
Plant engineering—Handbooks, manuals, etc. 658.2
Plant extracts 615.321; 660.6
Plant gene silencing 572.8652; 631.5233
Plant genetic engineering 631.5233; 660.65
Plant genetics 581.35
Plant genome mapping 572.86332
Plant hormones 571.742
Plant layout 658.23
Plant lipids 572.572
Plant litter 577.57; 631.417
Plant maintenance 658.202
Plant maintenance—Management 658.202
Plant-microbe relationships 579.178
Plant-microbe relationships—Molecular aspects 632.3
Plant micropropagation 631.53
Plant microtubules 571.6542
Plant molecular biology 572.82
Plant molecular genetics 572.82
Plant molecular virology 572.82928
Plant morphogenesis 571.8332
Plant mutation breeding 631.5233
Plant names, Popular 580.14
Plant names, Popular—Dictionaries 580.3
Plant nematodes 632.6257
Plant-pathogen relationships 632.3
Plant-pathogen relationships—Molecular aspects 632.3
Plant pathologists 632.3092
Plant physiology 571.2
Plant poisoning in animals 571.957; 636.0895952
Plant populations 581.788
Plant propagation 631.53; 635.043
Plant quarantine facilities 363.19; 632.3
Plant regulators 571.72; 631.8
Plant remains (Archaeology) 930.1
Plant shutdowns 338.71
Plant shutdowns—United States 338.710973
Plant species 580.12
Plant species diversity 333.953; 581.7
Plant succession 581.7
Plant supports 631.54
Plant taxonomists 580.92
Plant tissue culture 571.5382
Plant viruses 579.28
Plantago 583.95
Plantation life—Southern States—History—19th century 975.03
Plantations 307.72
Plantations—Louisiana—Guidebooks 917.6304; 917.630463; 917.630464
Planting design 712.6; 715
Plants 580
Plants—Collection and preservation 5780.75
Plants, Cultivated 581.63; 630
Plants, Cultivated—Physiology 571.2
Plants—Development 571.82
Plants—Disease and pest resistance 571.962; 632.3
Plants—Disease and pest resistance—Genetic aspects 632.3
Plants, Edible 581.632
Plants, Effect of air pollution on 581.7
Plants, Effect of atmospheric carbon dioxide on 581.7
Plants, Effect of evaporation on 575.7
Plants, Effect of freezes on 571.4642; 632.11
Plants, Effect of global warming on 581.7
Plants, Effect of greenhouse gases on 571.956
Plants—Evolution 581.38

Political psychology 320.019
Political refugees 325.21
Political refugees—Legal status, laws, etc. 341.486
Political refugees—Legal status, laws, etc.—United States 342.73083
Political refugees—Vietnam 325.2109597
Political rights 323.5
Political science 320
Political science—Early works to 1800 320
Political science—Bibliography 016.32
Political science—Dictionaries 320.03
Political science—Europe 320.094
Political science—Europe—History 320.094
Political science—Great Britain—History 320.0941
Political science—Great Britain—History—17th century 320.0941
Political science—Greece—History 320.0938
Political science—History 320.09
Political science—History—20th century 320.0904
Political science literature 016.32
Political science—Mathematical models 320.0151
Political science—Methodology 320.01
Political science—Periodicals 320.05
Political science—Philosophy 320.01
Political science—Research 320.072
Political science—Study and teaching 320.071
Political science—United States 320.0973
Political science—United States—History 320.0973
Political socialization 306.2
Political sociology 306.2
Political stability 320.011
Political theology 261.7
Political violence 172.1
Political violence in literature 808.80358; 809.93358
Political violence in mass media 303.6
Politicians 324.2092
Politicians—United States 324.2092273
Politicians—United States—Biography 324.2092273
Politics and culture 306.2
Politics and education 379
Politics and education—United States 379.73
Politics and literature 809.93358
Politics in art 704.94932
Politics in literature 808.80358; 809.93358
Politics in the Bible 220.832
Politics, Practical 324
Polk County (Fla.)—Maps 912.75967
Polk County (Neb.)—Maps 912.782352
Polk County (Wis.)—Maps 912.77517
Polk, James K. (James Knox), 1795–1849 973.61092
Pollard, Tom (Fictitious character) 823.914
Pollen 571.8452
Pollen, Fossil 561.13
Pollen management 631.52
Pollifax, Emily (Fictitious character) 813.54
Pollifax, Emily (Fictitious character)—Fiction 813.54
Pollination 571.8642
Pollination by insects 571.8642; 576.875
Pollinators 571.8642; 591.5
Polling places 324.65
Pollock, Jackson, 1912–1956 759.13
Pollutants 363.738; 628.5
Pollutants—Analysis 628.5; 628.52
Pollution 363.73
Pollution control industry 338.476285
Pollution—Economic aspects 363.73
Pollution—Economic aspects—United States 363.730973
Pollution—Environmental aspects 363.732; 577.27

Pollution—Environmental aspects—Periodicals 363.73205; 577.2705
Pollution—India 363.730954
Pollution—Law and legislation 344.304632
Pollution—Law and legislation—United States 344.7304632
Pollution—Measurement 628.5; 628.50287
Pollution—Periodicals 363.7305; 604.7
Pollution prevention 354.335
Pollution—Religious aspects 291.1783628
Polo 796.353
Polo, Marco, 1254–1323? 915.042092
Polo, Marco, 1254–1323?—Journeys 915.042092
Polo, Nick (Fictitious character) 813.54
Polo, Nick (Fictitious character)—Fiction 813.54
Polycyclic aromatic hydrocarbons 547.61
Polyelectrolytes 541.372; 547.704572
Polyester thread 677.4743
Polyethylene 668.4234
Polygamy 306.8423
Polygamy—Religious aspects 291.441
Polyhedra 516.15
Polyimides 668.9
Polymer clay craft 731.2; 731.42; 738.12; 745.572
Polymer-impregnated concrete 620.136
Polymer liquid crystals 530.429
Polymer networks 547.7
Polymer solutions 547.70454
Polymerase chain reaction 572.43
Polymeric composites 620.192
Polymeric drugs 615.3; 615.7
Polymerization 547.28; 668.92
Polymers 547.7; 547.84; 620.192; 668.9
Polymers—Additives 668.9
Polymers—Analysis 547.7046; 547.84046
Polymers—Biodegradation 620.19204223
Polymers—Deterioration 620.1920422
Polymers—Dictionaries 668.903
Polymers—Effect of radiation on 620.19204228
Polymers—Electric properties 547.70457; 620.19204297
Polymers—Fracture 620.1920426
Polymers in medicine 610.284
Polymers—Mechanical properties 620.19204292
Polymers—Optical properties 620.19204295
Polymers—Periodicals 547.705
Polymers—Permeability 620.1920422; 668.9
Polymers—Spectra 547.84
Polymers—Surfaces—Analysis 668.9
Polymers—Testing 620.1920287
Polymers—Thermal properties 620.19204296
Polynesia 996
Polynesians 996
Polynomials 512.942
Polyorchidae 593.55
Polypropylene 668.4234
Polyradicion 584.4
Polysaccharides 572.566
Polysaccharides—Biotechnology 660.63
Polysomnography 616.8498
Polytopes 516.35
Polyurethanes 668.4239
Polyvinyl chloride 668.4236
Polyvinyl chloride industry 338.476684236
Pomo Indians 305.89757; 979.40049757
Pompeii (Extinct city) 937.7
Pond ecology 577.636
Ponds 551.482
Ponge, Francis 841.914
Ponge, Francis—Translations into English 841.914

Porsche automobiles—History 629.2222
Port William (Ky. : Imaginary place) 813.54
Port William (Ky. : Imaginary place)—Fiction 813.54
Portable computers 004.16
Portable computers—Periodicals 004.16
Portage County (Wis.) 977.553
Portage County (Wis.)—Maps 912.77553
Portal, Ellis (Fictitious character) 813.54
Portal hypertension 616.362
Porter family 929.20973
Porter, Katherine Anne, 1890–1980 813.52
Porter, Katherine Anne, 1890–1980—Bibliography
    016.81352
Porter, Katherine Anne, 1890–1980—Criticism and
    interpretation 813.52
Portfolio management 332.6
Portfolio management—Mathematical models
    332.6015118
Portland cement 666.94
Portland cement industry 338.4766694
Portland Metropolitan Area (Or.) 979.549
Portland Metropolitan Area (Or.)—Maps 912.79549
Portland (Or.) 979.549
Portland (Or.)—Guidebooks 917.954904; 917.95490443;
    917.95490444
Portland (Or.)—History 979.549
Portland (Or.)—Pictorial works 917.954900222
Portolá's Expedition, Calif., 1769–1770 979.402
Portrait drawing 743.42
Portrait drawing—Technique 743.42
Portrait painting 757
Portrait painting—Technique 751.4542
Portrait photographers 770.92
Portrait photography 778.92; 779.2
Portrait photography—United States 779.20973
Portrait sculpture, Roman 731.820937
Portraits 704.942; 757
Portsmouth (England) 942.2792
Portsmouth (England)—History 942.2792
Portugal 946.9
Portugal—Colonies 325.3469
Portugal—Colonies—Africa 325.3469096
Portugal—Guidebooks 914.6904; 914.690444
Portugal—History 946.9
Portugal—History—Period of discoveries, 1385–1580
    946.902
Portugal, Joe (Fictitious character) 813.54
Portugal—Politics and government 946.9
Portugal—Politics and government—1974–
    320.94609047; 946.9044
Portuguese language 469
Portuguese language—Conversation and phrase books
    469.834
Portuguese language—Conversation and phrase
    books—English 469.83421
Portuguese language—Dictionaries 469.3; 469.321
Portuguese language—Grammar 469.5; 469.82;
    469.82421
Portuguese language—Textbooks for foreign speakers—
    English 469.82421; 469.83421
Portuguese Sign Language 419.469
Posies 745.923
Positron annihilation 539.75
Posovac horse 636.1
Post anesthesia nursing 610.73677; 617.919
Post-communism—Russia (Federation) 306.094709049
Post-compulsory education 370
Post-compulsory education—Great Britain 370
Post-impressionism (Art) 709.0346; 759.056

Post-translational modification 572.645
Post-traumatic stress disorder 616.8521
Post-traumatic stress disorder—Diagnosis 616.8521
Post-traumatic stress disorder—Treatment 616.8521
Post-Zionism 320.54095694
Postage stamps 383.23; 769.56
Postage stamps as an investment 332.63
Postage stamps—Australia 769.56994
Postage stamps—Australia—Catalogs 769.56994075
Postage stamps—Canada 769.56971
Postage stamps—Catalogs 769.56075
Postage stamps—Dictionaries 769.5603
Postage stamps—Errors 769.56
Postage stamps—Forgeries 769.562
Postage stamps—Great Britain 769.56941
Postage stamps—Great Britain—Catalogs 769.56941075
Postage stamps—History 769.569
Postage stamps—Law and legislation 343.0992
Postage stamps—United States 769.56973
Postage stamps—United States—Catalogs 769.56973075
Postage stamps—United States—History 769.56973
Postage stamps—United States—History—19th century
    769.5697309034
Postage stamps—Varieties 769.56
Postal inspectors 383.46
Postal rates 383.23
Postal rates—United States 343.7309923; 383.230973
Postal service 383
Postal service—History 383.49
Postal service—Law and legislation 343.0992
Postal service—Law and legislation—United States
    343.730992
Postal service—United States 383.4973
Postal service—United States—Employees 383.49273
Postal service—United States—Examinations,
    questions, etc. 383.145076
Postal service—United States—History 383.4973
Postcards 741.683
Postcolonialism 320.909045
Postemployment benefits—United States—Accounting
    657.75
Postencephalitic Parkinson's disease 616.833
Poster presentations 060; 808.066
Posterior longitudinal ligament 611.72
Posterior longitudinal ligament—Diseases 616.77
Posters 741.674
Posters—19th century—Catalogs 741.67409034075
Postliberal theology 230.046
Postmasters general 354.7592293
Postmodernism 149.97
Postmodernism (Literature) 808.80113; 809.9113
Postmodernism—United States 700.41130973
Postnatal care 618.6
Postnatal care—Religious aspects 291.178321986
Postoperative care 617.919
Postoperative nausea and vomiting 617.01
Postpartum depression 618.76
Postpoliomyelitis syndrome 616.835
PostScript (Computer program language) 006.66
Postsecondary education 378
Poststructuralism 149.9
Posture 613.78
Potamonautidae 595.386
Potassium fertilizers 631.83
Potatoes 635.21; 641.3521
Potawatomi Indians 305.8973; 977.004973
Potbellied pig 636.485
Potbellied pigs as pets 636.485
Potential energy surfaces 541.28

Pre-Raphaelites 759.2
Pre-Raphaelitism 759.209034
Pre-Raphaelitism—England 709.4209034; 759.209034
Pre-Raphaelitism—Exhibitions 759.209034
Pre-Socratic philosophers 182
Pre-trial procedure 347.072
Pre-trial procedure—Massachusetts 347.744072
Pre-trial procedure—United States 347.73072
Preaching 251
Preaching to children 251.53; 252.53
Preaching to non church-affiliated people 251
Precancerous conditions 616.994071
Precast concrete construction 624.183414
Precious metals 669.2
Precious stones 553.8
Precious stones—Collection and preservation 553.8; 553.8075
Precious stones—Law and legislation 343.0787362; 346.046858
Precious stones—Psychic aspects 133
Precipitation (Chemistry) 541.3485
Precipitation (Meteorology) 551.577
Precision casting 671.255
Precision guided munitions—United States 358.171820973
Precognition 133.86
Predation (Biology) 591.53
Predatory animals 591.53
Predatory aquatic animals 591.530916
Predatory marine animals 591.5309162
Predestination 234.9
Prediction of scholastic success 371.264
Prediction theory 519.287; 519.54
Predictive astrology 133.5
Prefabricated houses 690.81
Prefect, Ford (Fictitious character) 791.4472; 791.4572; 823.914
Prefect, Ford (Fictitious character)—Fiction 823.914
Preferences (Philosophy) 128.3
Prefrontal cortex 573.86; 612.825
Pregnancy 612.63; 618.2; 649.10242
Pregnancy—Complications 618.3
Pregnancy—Complications—Diagnosis 618.3
Pregnancy—Complications—Handbooks, manuals, etc. 618.3
Pregnancy—Immunological aspects 618.2079
Pregnancy in middle age 618.200844
Pregnancy—Nutritional aspects 618.24
Pregnancy—Psychological aspects 618.20019
Pregnancy, Unwanted 306.8743
Pregnant schoolgirls 371.714
Pregnant women 618.2
Pregnant women—Prayer-books and devotions 242.6431
Prehistoric peoples 569.9
Prehistoric peoples—Africa 960.1
Prehistoric peoples—Australia 994.01
Prehistoric peoples—Europe 936
Prehistoric peoples—Great Britain 936.1; 936.101
Prehistoric peoples—India 934.01
Prehistoric peoples—Ireland 936.15
Prehistoric peoples—Oceania 990
Prehistoric peoples—Scotland 936.11
Prejudice in the Bible 220.8303385
Prejudices 303.385
Prejudices in children 303.385083; 649.7
Preliminary Scholastic Aptitude Test 378.1662
Preliminary Scholastic Assessment Test 378.1662
Premacanda, 1881–1936 891.4335

Premacanda, 1881–1936—Translations into English 891.4335
Premedical education 610.711
Premenstrual syndrome 618.172
Premises liability 346.036
Premises liability—United States 346.73036
Premonstratensian nuns 255.97; 271.97
Prenatal care 618.24
Prenatal diagnosis 618.32075
Prenatal influences 618.24
Preoperative care 617.919
Prepaid tuition plans 371.206; 378.106
Preparatory schools 373.222
Prepared piano music 786.28
Preprints 094
Presbycusis 362.420846; 618.9778
Presbyterian Church 285
Presbyterian Church—Doctrines 230.5
Presbyterian Church in the U.S.A. 285.132
Presbyterian Church—Sermons 252.05
Presbyterian theological seminaries 230.0735
Presbyterian universities and colleges 378.0715
Presbyterianism 285
Preschool children 649.123
Preschool children—Prayer-books and devotions 242.62; 242.82
Preschool enrollment 372.1219
Preschool teachers 372.11
Prescott family 929.20973
Presence of God 231.7
Preservation of materials 025.84
Preservation of organs, tissues, etc. 362.1783; 617.95
Preservation of organs, tissues, etc.—Law and legislation 344.04194
Preserved wood 674.386
Presidential candidates 324.092
Presidential libraries 026.321
Presidential press secretaries 352.232748
Presidents 352.23
Presidents—Assassination 364.1524
Presidents—Childhood and youth 352.23092
Presidents—Election 324.7
Presidents—France 352.230944
Presidents—Inauguration 394.4
Presidents—India 352.230954
Presidents' spouses 352.23092
Presidents' spouses—United States 973.099
Presidents' spouses—United States—Anecdotes 973.099
Presidents' spouses—United States—Biography 973.099
Presidents—Term of office—United States 352.23267
Presidents—United States 352.230973
Presidents—United States—Anecdotes 973.099
Presidents—United States—Biography 973.099
Presidents—United States—Election 324.973
Presidents—United States—Election—1948 324.9730918
Presidents—United States—Election—1952 324.9730918
Presidents—United States—Election—1980 324.9730926
Presidents—United States—Election—1984 324.9730927
Presidents—United States—Election—1988 324.9730927
Presidents—United States—Election—1992 324.9730928
Presidents—United States—Election—1996 324.9730929
Presidents—United States—Election—2000 324.9730929
Presidents—United States—Election—History 324.973
Presidents—United States—Election—History—20th century 324.973091
Presidents—United States—Genealogy 929.1072073; 929.20973
Presidents—United States—History 352.230973

Printing machinery and supplies—Catalogs 681.62029
Printing—Periodicals 686.209
Printing plants 725.21
Printing—Specimens 686.224
Printing—Style manuals 808.027
Printing supplies industry 338.476862
Printing—United States 686.20973
Printing—United States—History 686.20973
Prints 760; 769
Prints—20th century 769.90904
Prints, American 769.973
Prints, American—Catalogs 769.973075
Prints, American—Exhibitions 769.973074
Prints—Collectors and collecting 769.16
Prints, English 769.942
Prints—Exhibitions 769.074
Prints, French 769.944
Prints, German 769.943
Prints—Technique 760.28
Prion diseases 616.83
Prions 579.29
Prison administration 365.068
Prison administration—United States 365.068
Prison psychologists 155.962092
Prison psychology 365.6019
Prison reformers 365.7092
Prison sentences 364.65
Prisoner-of-war escapes 904.7
Prisoners 365.6
Prisoners—Civil rights 323.32927; 342.087
Prisoners—Drug use—United States 365.66
Prisoners—Education 365.66
Prisoners—Education—United States 365.66
Prisoners—Health and hygiene 365.66
Prisoners—Health and hygiene—United States 365.66
Prisoners—Legal status, laws, etc. 344.0356
Prisoners—Legal status, laws, etc.—United States 344.730356
Prisoners—Mental health services 365.66
Prisoners of war 355.113
Prisoners, Transportation of 364.6
Prisoners, Transportation of—Australia 994.02
Prisoners, Transportation of—Australia—History 994.02
Prisoners—United States 365.60973
Prisoners' writings, American 810.809206927
Prisoners' writings, American—History and criticism 810.99206927
Prisons 365
Prisons—Design and construction 725.6
Prisons—Government policy 365
Prisons—Government policy—United States 365.973
Prisons—Great Britain 365.941
Prisons—Law and legislation 344.035
Prisons—Law and legislation—United States 344.73035
Prisons—United States 365.60973; 365.973
Prisons—United States—History 365.973
Privacy 155.92; 323.448
Privacy, Right of 323.448
Privacy, Right of—Great Britain 323.4480941
Privacy, Right of—United States 323.4480973; 342.730858
Private art collections in art 704.949708
Private banks 332.123
Private companies 338.7
Private companies—Germany (West) 346.430668
Private companies—Great Britain 346.410668
Private companies—United States 346.730668
Private companies—United States—States 346.730668
Private flying 629.1325217; 797.5

Private investigators 363.289
Private investigators—United States 363.2890973
Private investigators—United States—Handbooks, manuals, etc. 363.2890973
Private libraries 027.1
Private planes 629.13330422
Private planes—Maintenance and repair 629.1346
Private revelations 248.29
Private schools 371.02
Private schools—United States 371.020973
Private security services 363.289
Private security services—United States 363.2890973
Private universities and colleges 378.04
Privatization 338.925
Privatization—Developing countries 338.925091724
Privatization—Europe, Central 338.9250943
Privatization—Europe, Eastern 338.9250947
Privatization—Great Britain 338.94105
Privatization in education 379.1
Privatization in education—United States 379.1
Privatization—Latin America 338.9805
Privatization—Poland 338.943805
Privatization—Russia (Federation) 338.94705
Privatization—United States 338.97305
Prizzi family (Fictitious characters) 813.54
Prizzi family (Fictitious characters)—Fiction 813.54
Pro-choice movement 363.46
Pro-choice movement—United States 363.460973
Pro/ENGINEER 620.0042028553042
Pro-life movement 363.46
Pro se representation 347.0504
Pro se representation—United States 347.73504
Probabilistic number theory 512.76
Probabilities 121.63; 519.2
Probabilities—Problems, exercises, etc. 519.2076
Probability forecasts (Meteorology) 551.633
Probability measures 519.2
Probate law and practice 346.052
Probate law and practice—California 346.794052
Probate law and practice—Connecticut 346.746052
Probate law and practice—Florida 346.759052
Probate law and practice—Massachusetts 346.744052
Probate law and practice—Michigan 346.774052
Probate law and practice—Minnesota 346.776052
Probate law and practice—New Jersey 346.749052
Probate law and practice—New York (State) 346.747052
Probate law and practice—Ohio 346.771052
Probate law and practice—Pennsylvania 346.748052
Probate law and practice—Texas 346.764052
Probate law and practice—United States 346.73052
Probate law and practice—United States—States 346.73052
Probate law and practice—Wisconsin 346.775052
Probation 364.63
Probation—England 364.630942
Probation—Great Britain 364.630941
Probation—United States 364.630973
Problem children 649.153
Problem children—Behavior modification 649.64
Problem children—Education 371.93
Problem children—Education—Great Britain 371.930941
Problem children—Education—United States 371.930973
Problem employees 658.3045
Problem families 362.82
Problem families in the Bible 220.830687
Problem solving 153.43
Problem solving—Study and teaching 370.1524
Problem-solving therapy 616.8914

Proverbs, Igbo 398.996332
Proverbs, Italian 398.951
Proverbs, Japanese 398.9956
Proverbs, Jewish 398.9924
Proverbs, Korean 398.9957
Proverbs, Romanian 398.9591
Proverbs, Russian 398.99171
Proverbs, Spanish 398.961
Proverbs, Turkish 398.99435
Proverbs, Yiddish 398.9391
Providence and government of God 231.5
Provincial birds 598
Provincial emblems 929.9
Provincial governments 320.83; 321.023
Provincial governments—Canada 320.471049
Provincial trees 582.16
Proxy 346.0666
Proxy—United States 346.730666
Prüfer rings 512.4
Pruning 631.542; 635.91542
Prussia (Germany) 943
Prussia (Germany)—History 943
Przewalski's horse 599.6655
Psalmody 264.2
Psalms (Music) 782.294
Pseudodifferential operators 515.7242
Pseudomonas aeruginosa infections 616.01432; 616.92
Psocoptera 595.732
Psoriasis 616.526
Psyllae 621.301502055360
Psyche (Greek deity) 299.2114
Psychiatric emergencies 616.89025
Psychiatric emergencies—Handbooks, manuals, etc. 616.89025
Psychiatric epidemiology 362.20422
Psychiatric ethics 174.2
Psychiatric hospital care 362.21
Psychiatric hospitals 362.21
Psychiatric nurses 610.7368
Psychiatric nursing 610.7368
Psychiatric nursing—Examinations, questions, etc. 610.7368
Psychiatric nursing—Handbooks, manuals, etc. 610.7368
Psychiatric records 651.504261
Psychiatric social work 362.20425
Psychiatric social work—United States 362.204250973
Psychiatrists 616.890092
Psychiatrists—Legal status, laws, etc. 344.0412
Psychiatrists—Legal status, laws, etc.—United States 344.730412; 344.7304121
Psychiatrists—Malpractice 344.04121
Psychiatrists—Malpractice—United States 344.7304121
Psychiatry 362.2; 616.89
Psychiatry—Case formulation 616.89
Psychiatry—Dictionaries 616.89003
Psychiatry—Differential therapeutics 616.8914
Psychiatry—Examinations, questions, etc. 616.890076
Psychiatry—Handbooks, manuals, etc. 616.89
Psychiatry—History 616.89009
Psychiatry—Outlines, syllabi, etc. 616.89
Psychiatry—Periodicals 616.89005
Psychiatry—Philosophy 616.89001
Psychiatry—Practice 616.890068
Psychiatry—Practice—United States 616.890068
Psychiatry—Terminology 616.890014
Psychiatry, Transcultural 616.89
Psychic ability 133.8
Psychic trauma 616.8521

Psychic trauma in children 618.928521
Psychics 133.8092
Psycho (Motion picture) 791.4372
Psychoacoustics 152.15
Psychoanalysis 150.195; 616.8917
Psychoanalysis and culture 150.195
Psychoanalysis and education 370.15
Psychoanalysis and feminism 150.195082
Psychoanalysis and history 150.195
Psychoanalysis and literature 801.92
Psychoanalysis and philosophy 150.19501
Psychoanalysis and the arts 700.105
Psychoanalysis—History 150.19509
Psychoanalysis—Periodicals 616.891705
Psychoanalysis—Philosophy 150.19501
Psychoanalysts 616.8917092
Psychoanalytic counseling 158.3
Psychoanalytic interpretation 616.8917
Psychobiology 152; 612.8
Psychodiagnostics 155.28; 616.89075
Psychodrama 616.891523
Psychodynamic psychotherapy 616.8914
Psychohistory 901.9
Psychokinesis 133.88
Psycholinguistics 401.9
Psychological abuse 616.8582
Psychological consultation 158.3; 158.3023
Psychological fiction, English 823.083
Psychological manifestations of general diseases 616.0019
Psychological mindedness 616.8914
Psychological tests 150.287
Psychological tests for children 155.41828
Psychological warfare 355.3434
Psychologists 150.92
Psychologists—Professional ethics 174.915
Psychology 150
Psychology and philosophy 150.1
Psychology and religion 291.175
Psychology, Applied 158
Psychology—Authorship 808.06615
Psychology—Authorship—Handbooks, manuals, etc. 808.06615
Psychology—Bibliography 016.15
Psychology, Comparative 156
Psychology—Dictionaries 150.3
Psychology—Early works to 1850 150
Psychology—Encyclopedias 150.3
Psychology—Examinations 150.76
Psychology—Examinations, questions, etc. 150.76
Psychology, Experimental 150.724
Psychology, Experimental—Methodology 150.724
Psychology, Forensic 347.067; 614.1
Psychology—History 150.9
Psychology—History—20th century 150.904
Psychology in literature 808.80353; 809.93353
Psychology, Industrial 158.7
Psychology—Mathematical models 150.151
Psychology—Methodology 150.1
Psychology, Military 355.0019
Psychology—Moral and ethical aspects 174.915
Psychology, Pathological 616.89
Psychology, Pathological—Philosophy 616.89001
Psychology—Periodicals 150.5
Psychology—Philosophy 150.1
Psychology—Philosophy—History 150.1
Psychology, Religious 200.19
Psychology—Research 150.72
Psychology—Research—Methodology 150.72

Public radio 384.54
Public records 353.387
Public records—Law and legislation 342.0662
Public records—Law and legislation—Florida 342.7590662
Public records—Law and legislation—Oregon 342.7950662
Public records—Law and legislation—Texas 342.7640662
Public records—Law and legislation—United States 342.730662
Public records—Law and legislation—United States—States 342.730662
Public relations 659.2
Public relations and politics 659.2932
Public relations consultants 659.2092
Public relations—Handbooks, manuals, etc. 659.2
Public relations—Management 659.2068
Public relations—United States 659.20973
Public schools 371.01
Public Schools of the District of Columbia 353.809753; 371.0109753
Public schools—United States 371.010973
Public schools—United States—Evaluation 379.1580973
Public schools—United States—Finance 379.110973
Public schools—United States—History 371.010973
Public service commissions 354.728
Public service employment 331.12042
Public service employment—United States 331.120420973
Public speaking 808.51
Public speaking—Handbooks, manuals, etc. 808.51
Public television 384.554
Public television—United States 384.5540973
Public universities and colleges 378.05
Public utilities 363.6
Public utilities—Accounting 657.838
Public utilities—Government policy 363.6
Public utilities—Government policy—United States 363.60973
Public utilities—Law and legislation 343.09
Public utilities—Law and legislation—United States 343.7309
Public utilities—Management 363.6068
Public utilities—Rates—Law and legislation 343.091
Public utilities—Rates—Law and legislation—United States 343.73091
Public utilities—United States 338.4736360973; 363.60973
Public utilities—United States—Rates 338.4336360973
Public utility holding companies 363.6
Public welfare 361.6
Public welfare administration 361.6
Public welfare—Canada 361.60971
Public welfare—Law and legislation 344.03
Public welfare—Law and legislation—Texas 344.76403
Public welfare—Law and legislation—United States 344.7303
Public welfare—New York (State)—New York 361.6097471
Public welfare—New York (State)—Periodicals 361.60974705
Public welfare—United States 361.60973
Public welfare—United States—History 361.60973
Public works 363
Public works—United States 352.770973
Public worship 264; 291.43
Public worship—Handbooks, manuals, etc. 264
Publicity 659; 659.2

Publishers and publishing 070.5
Publishers and publishing—Bibliography 016.0705
Publishers and publishing—Great Britain 070.50941
Publishers and publishing—India 070.50954
Publishers and publishing—Nigeria 070.509669
Publishers and publishing—United States 070.50973
Publishers and publishing—United States—Directories 070.502573
Publishers and publishing—United States—Management 070.5068
Puckett, Kirby 796.357092
Puddings 641.864
Pudus 599.65
Pueblo gods 299.73
Pueblo Incident, 1968 359.34320973
Pueblo Indians 305.8974; 978.9004974
Pueblo Indians—Antiquities 978.9004974
Pueblo Indians—Religion 299.784
Pueblo mythology 299.72
Pueblo pottery 738.3089974
Pueblo roads 388.10979; 979.01
Puerto Ricans 305.8687295
Puerto Ricans—New York (State)—New York 305.868729507471
Puerto Ricans—United States 305.8687295073; 973.04687295
Puerto Rico 972.95
Puerto Rico—Description and travel 917.29504; 917.2950453
Puerto Rico—Guidebooks 917.29504; 917.2950453
Puerto Rico—History 972.95
Puerto Rico—Politics and government 320.97295
Puerto Rico—Politics and government—1952– 320.9729509045
Puerto Rico—Social life and customs 972.95
Puffins 598.33
Pug 636.76
Puget Sound Region (Wash.) 979.77
Puget Sound Region (Wash.)—Guidebooks 917.977
Puget Sound Salish languages 497.9
Puget Sound (Wash.) 551.46632
Pulitzer Prizes 070.079
Pull toys 688.728; 745.592
Pulmonary circulation 612.2
Pulmonary function tests 616.240754
Pulmonary hypertension 616.24
Pulmonary surfactant 612.22
Pulmonary toxicology 616.200471
Pulmonata 594.38
Pulp literature 808.801
Pulping 676.1
Pulpwood industry 338.47634983
Pulsars 523.8874
Pulsating stars 523.84425
Pulse 616.0754
Pulse circuits 621.381534
Puma 599.7524
Pumping machinery 621.69
Pumping machinery—Handbooks, manuals, etc. 621.69
Pumpkin 635.62
Pumpkinseed oil 641.3385; 664.3
Punch and Judy 791.53
Punch (London, England) 052
Punchball 796.31
Punic War, 2nd, 218–201 B.C. 937.04
Punishment 303.36; 345.077; 364.6
Punishment—Philosophy 364.6019
Punjab (India) 954.5; 954.55; 954.552
Punjab (India)—History 954.5; 954.55; 954.552

Punjab (India)—History—Sources 954.50072; 954.550072; 954.5520072
Punjab (India)—Politics and government 320.9545; 320.954552; 954.5; 954.55; 954.552
Punk rock music 781.66
Punk rock music—History and criticism 781.66
Puns and punning 818.02
Puppet films 791.433
Puppet making 688.7224; 745.59224
Puppet plays, American 791.538; 812
Puppet theater 791.53
Puppet theater in Christian education 246.725
Puppet theater in education 371.399; 372.674
Puppeteers 791.53092
Puppets 791.53; 791.538
Puppies 636.707
Puppies—Training 636.70887
Puranas 294.5925
Puranas. Bhāgavatapurāṇa 294.5925
Puranas. Bhāgavatapurāṇa—Criticism, interpretation, etc. 294.5925
Puranas—Criticism, interpretation, etc. 294.5925
Purcell, Henry, 1659–1695 780.92
Purcell, Henry, 1659–1695—Criticism and interpretation 780.92
Purchasing 658.72
Purchasing agents 658.72
Purchasing—Handbooks, manuals, etc. 658.72
Purchasing—Periodicals 658.7205
Purim 296.436
Puritans 285.9
Puritans—England 285.90942
Puritans—England—History 285.90942
Puritans—England—History—16th century 285.9094209031
Puritans—New England 974.02
Puritans—New England—History 285.90974
Puritans—New England—History—17th century 285.9097409032; 974.02
Purity, Ritual 291.446
Purity, Ritual—Judaism 296.742
Push technology (Computer networks) 006.7876
Pushkin, Aleksandr Sergeevich, 1799–1837 891.713
Pushkin, Aleksandr Sergeevich, 1799–1837—Criticism and interpretation 891.713
Pushkin, Aleksandr Sergeevich, 1799–1837—Translations into English 891.713
Putnam family 929.20973
Putting (Golf) 796.35235
Puzzles 793.73
Pycnogonida 595.496
Pyle, Ernie, 1900–1945 070.4333092
Pym, Barbara 823.914
Pym, Barbara—Criticism and interpretation 823.914
Pynchon, Thomas 813.54
Pynchon, Thomas—Criticism and interpretation 813.54
Pyoderma in animals 636.089653
Pyramids 909
Pyramids—Egypt 932
Pyrometry 536.52
Pyruvate kinase 572.4751
Pysanky 745.5944
Pythons 597.9678
Pythons as pets 639.39678
Q&A (Computer file) 005.369
Q hypothesis (Synoptics criticism) 226.066
Qaddafi, Muammar 961.2042092
Qaddafi, Muammar. Kitāb al-akhḍar 320.531
QBasic (Computer program language) 005.133

Qi (Chinese philosophy) 181.11
Qi gong 613.71
QS-9000 (Standard) 338.476292220973
Quacks and quackery 615.856
Quakers 289.6
Qualia 121.3
Qualitative reasoning 006.333
Quality assurance 658.562; 658.568
Quality assurance—Management 658.562
Quality assurance—Standards 658.5620218
Quality circles 658.4036
Quality control 658.562
Quality control—Auditing 658.562
Quality control—Costs 658.562
Quality control—Handbooks, manuals, etc. 658.562
Quality control—Optical methods—Automation 670.425
Quality control—Periodicals 658.56205
Quality control—Standards 658.5620218
Quality control—Statistical methods 658.562015195; 658.5620727
Quality control—United States 658.5620973
Quality function deployment 658.562
Quality of life 306
Quality of life—United States 306.0973
Quality of life—United States—Statistics 306.0973
Quality of products 658.562
Quality of work life 306.36
Quantity cookery 641.57
Quantity surveying 692.5
Quantity surveying—Great Britain 692.50941
Quantity theory of money 332.401
Quantrill, Douglas (Fictitious character) 823.914
Quantrill, Douglas (Fictitious character)—Fiction 823.914
Quantum chaos 530.12
Quantum chemistry 541.28
Quantum chromodynamics 539.7548
Quantum computers 004.1; 621.391
Quantum dots 621.38152
Quantum electrodynamics 537.67
Quantum electronics 537.5
Quantum field theory 530.143
Quantum gravity 530.143
Quantum groups 530.143
Quantum Hall effect 537.6226
Quantum liquids 530.42
Quantum logic 530.12015113
Quantum optics 535.15
Quantum statistics 530.133
Quantum theory 530.12
Quantum theory—History 530.1209
Quantum theory—Mathematics 530.12
Quantum theory—Problems, exercises, etc. 530.12076
Quantum wells 537.6226
Quark-gluon plasma 539.721
Quarks 539.72167
QuarkXPress (Computer file) 686.225445369
Quarter horse 636.133
Quarter horse—Pedigrees 636.13322
Quarterback (Football) 796.3322; 796.33225
Quartets (Flute, violin, viola, violoncello) 785.44194
Quartets (Oboe, violin, viola, violoncello) 785.44194
Quartz crystals 133
Quartz mines and mining 622.36
Quasars 523.115
Quasiconformal mappings 515.93
Quasicrystals 530.41
Quasidifferential calculus 515.33
Quasimodo, Salvatore, 1901–1968 851.912

Quasimodo, Salvatore, 1901–1968—Translations into English 851.912
Quatermain, Allan (Fictitious character) 823.8
Quatermain, Allan (Fictitious character)—Fiction 823.8
Quaternions 512.5
Quattro 005.369
Quattro pro 005.369
Quayle, Dan, 1947– 973.928092
Quayle, Dan, 1947– —Humor 328.73092
Québec (Province) 971.4
Québec (Province)—Economic conditions 330.9714
Québec (Province)—Guidebooks 917.1404; 917.14044
Québec (Province)—History 971.4
Québec (Province)—History—Autonomy and independence movements 971.404
Québec (Province)—Politics and government 320.9714; 971.4
Québec (Province)—Politics and government—1960– 320.971409046; 971.404
Quechua Indians 305.898323; 980.00498323
Quechua language 498.323
Queen Anne's County (Md.)—Genealogy 929.375234
Queen Anne's County (Md.)—Maps 912.75234
Queen Charlotte Islands (B.C.) 971.112
Queen Charlotte Islands (B.C.)—Guidebooks 917.111204; 917.1112044
Queen Mary (Steamship) 387.2432; 623.82432
Queens 321; 352.23092
Queen's gambit (Chess) 794.122
Queens—Great Britain—Biography 941.0099
Queensland 994.3
Queensland—History 994.3
Queensland—Maps 912.943
Queensland—Pictorial works 919.4300222
Queensland—Road maps 912.943
Question-answering systems 006.3
Questioning 371.37
Questions and answers 030; 031.02
Quetzalcoatl (Aztec deity) 299.73
Queuing theory 519.82
Quiché Indians 305.897415; 972.8100497415
Quiché Indians—Religion 299.78415
Quick and easy cookery 641.512; 641.555
QuickBooks 657.904202855369
Quicken 332.024002855369
Quicken for Windows 332.024002855369
Quickstep (Dance) 793.33
Quiller (Fictitious character) 823.914
Quiller (Fictitious character)—Fiction 823.914
Quilting 746.46
Quilting—Patterns 746.46041
Quilting—United States—History 746.460973
Quilting—United States—Patterns 746.46041
Quilts 643.53; 746.46
Quilts, Amish 643.53
Quilts in interior decoration 747.9
Quilts, Mennonite 643.53
Quilts—United States 746.460973
Quilts—United States—History—20th century 746.4609730904
Quinault Indians 979.7004979
Quindecile (Astrology) 133.53044
Quinn family 929.20973
Quinn family (Fictitious characters) 813.54
Quinn, Garner (Fictitious character) 813.54
Quinn, Garner (Fictitious character)—Fiction 813.54
Quintana, Anthony (Fictitious character) 813.54
Quintets (Clarinet, violins (2), viola, violoncello) 785.44195

Quintets (Piano, violin, viola, violoncello, double bass) 785.28195
Quirts 685; 798.230284
Qumran community 296.815
Quotations 080
Quotations, American 081
Quotations, English 082
Qwilleran, Jim (Fictitious character) 813.54
Qwilleran, Jim (Fictitious character)—Fiction 813.54
R.E.M. (Musical group) 782.421660922
Rabbinical literature 296.1
Rabbinical literature—History and criticism 296.1
Rabbinical literature—History and criticism—Theory, etc. 296.1
Rabbinical literature—Translations into English 296.120521
Rabbinical seminaries 296.0711
Rabbis 296.092
Rabbis—Biography 296.0922
Rabbit automobile 629.2222
Rabbits 599.32; 636.9322
Rabbits—Physiology 571.1932
Rabelais, François, ca. 1490–1553? 843.3
Rabelais, François, ca. 1490–1553?—Criticism and interpretation 843.3
Rabelais, François, ca. 1490–1553?—Translations into English 843.3
Rabies 614.563; 616.953
Rabin, Yitzhak, 1922– 956.9405092
Raccoons 599.7632
Race 305.8; 599.97
Race awareness 155.82; 305.8
Race awareness in literature 808.80355; 809.93355
Race discrimination 305.8
Race discrimination—Law and legislation 341.481; 342.0873
Race discrimination—Law and legislation—United States 342.730873
Race discrimination—United States 305.800973
Race horses 636.12
Race—Origin 599.972
Race relations 305.8
Race relations in mass media 305.8
Race relations—Religious aspects 291.178348
Race relations—Religious aspects—Christianity 261.8348
Racetracks (Automobile racing) 796.72068
Racetracks (Automobile racing)—United States 796.7206873
Racetracks (Automobile racing)—United States—Directories 796.7206802573
Racetracks (Horse racing) 798.40068
Rachmaninoff, Sergei, 1873–1943 780.92
Racial profiling in law enforcement 363.23089
Racially mixed children 305.23
Racially mixed children—United States 305.23
Racially mixed people 305.804
Racially mixed people—United States 305.804073
Racine, Jean, 1639–1699 842.4
Racine, Jean, 1639–1699—Criticism and interpretation 842.4
Racine, Jean, 1639–1699—Translations into English 842.4
Racing greyhound 636.7534
Racing pigeons 636.5960888; 798
Racism 305.8; 320.56
Racism—Canada 305.800971
Racism—History 305.8009
Racism in anthropology 305.8; 599.9

Racism in language 306.44
Racism in literature 808.80355; 809.93355
Racism in mass media 305.8
Racism in social services 361
Racism—Religious aspects 291.178348
Racism—Religious aspects—Christianity 261.8348
Racism—United States 305.800973
Racism—United States—History 305.800973
Racketeering—United States 364.10670973
Racquetball 796.343
Radar 621.3848
Radar in navigation 623.8933
Radar in speed limit enforcement 388.3144
Radar in speed limit enforcement—Detection 388.3144
Radar meteorology 551.6353
Radar—Military applications 623.7348
Radcliffe, Ann Ward, 1764–1823 823.6
Radcliffe, Ann Ward, 1764–1823—Criticism and interpretation 823.6
Radhakrishnan, S. (Sarvepalli), 1888–1975 181.4; 954.04092
Radiant floor heating 697.72
Radiation 539.2
Radiation carcinogenesis 616.994071
Radiation chemistry 541.382
Radiation curing 660.298
Radiation dosimetry 612.01448
Radiation—Health aspects 363.1799; 612.01448
Radiation injuries 617.124
Radiation—Measurement 539.77
Radiation—Measurement—Instruments 539.770284
Radiation—Physiological effect 571.45; 612.01448
Radiation preservation of food 664.0288
Radiation—Safety measures 363.17996; 363.17997; 616.989705
Radiation sources 539.2
Radiation—Toxicology 571.9345; 616.9897
Radiation trapping 539.75
Radical economics 330.15
Radicalism 320.53
Radicalism—United States—History—20th century 303.484
Radicals (Chemistry) 541.224
Radiesthesia 133.323
Radio 384.5; 621.384
Radio acting 791.44028
Radio adaptations 791.446
Radio advertising 659.142
Radio announcing 791.443
Radio—Antennas 621.384135
Radio—Antennas—Design and construction 621.384135
Radio astronomy 522.682
Radio audiences 384.54092
Radio auroras 538.768
Radio broadcasters 384.54092
Radio broadcasting 384.54
Radio broadcasting—Great Britain 385.540941
Radio broadcasting—United States 384.540973
Radio broadcasting—United States—History 384.540973; 791.440973
Radio circuits 621.38412
Radio circuits—Design and construction 621.38412
Radio comedy writers 808.8222
Radio—Equipment and supplies 621.3840284
Radio—Examinations, questions, etc. 621.384076; 621.38416076
Radio frequency 621.384
Radio frequency allocation 384.54524

Radio frequency allocation—Law and legislation 343.09945
Radio frequency allocation—Law and legislation—United States 343.7309945
Radio frequency allocation—United States 384.545240973
Radio galaxies 523.112
Radio—History 384.509; 621.38409
Radio in aeronautics 629.135
Radio in education 371.3331
Radio in navigation 623.8932
Radio—Installation on ships 623.863
Radio—Interference 621.38411
Radio journalism 070.194
Radio—Law and legislation 341.7577; 343.09945
Radio—Law and legislation—United States 343.7309945
Radio meteorology 551.635
Radio music 781.544
Radio paging 621.3892
Radio plays 791.447; 792
Radio plays, African (English) 822.0220896
Radio plays, English 822.022
Radio—Production and direction 791.44023; 791.440232; 791.440233
Radio programs 384.5443
Radio programs for children 791.44083
Radio programs for gays 384.544308664; 791.44653
Radio programs, Musical 791.443
Radio programs, Public service 384.5443
Radio programs—United States 791.44750973
Radio programs—United States—Catalogs 016.79144750973
Radio—Receivers and reception 621.38418
Radio—Receivers and reception—Collectors and collecting 621.38418075
Radio relay systems 621.38782
Radio—Repairing 621.3840288; 621.384187
Radio scripts 791.447
Radio sources (Astronomy) 522.682
Radio stations 384.5453
Radio stations—Directories 384.5453025
Radio stations—United States—Directories 384.545302573
Radio stations—United States—Maps 384.54530973022
Radio—Study and teaching 621.384071; 621.38416071
Radio—Study and teaching—United States 621.384071073; 621.38416071073
Radio supplies industry 384.545
Radio telescopes 522.2; 522.682
Radio—Transmitters and transmission 621.384131
Radio wave propagation 621.38411
Radio wave propagation—Remote sensing 621.3678
Radio waves 621.38411
Radioactive dating 551.701
Radioactive pollution 363.1799
Radioactive pollution—Environmental aspects 577.277
Radioactive prospecting 622.159
Radioactive substances 539.752
Radioactive waste disposal 363.7289; 621.4838
Radioactive waste disposal in the ground 344.04626; 621.4838
Radioactive waste disposal in the ground—Environmental aspects 621.4838
Radioactive waste disposal in the ground—Risk assessment 363.1799
Radioactive waste disposal—Law and legislation 344.04622
Radioactive waste disposal—Law and legislation—United States 344.7304622

Radioactive waste disposal—North Carolina
363.728909756
Radioactive waste disposal—Risk assessment 621.4838
Radioactive waste disposal—United States—Periodicals
363.7289097305
Radioactive waste repositories 363.7289; 621.4838
Radioactive wastes 363.7289
Radioactive wastes—Characterization 363.728963
Radioactive wastes—Management 621.4838
Radioactive wastes—Transmutation 621.4838
Radioactivity 539.752
Radioactivity—Measurement 539.77
Radioactivity—Safety measures 363.1799
Radiobiology 571.45
Radiocarbon dating 551.701
Radiochemical laboratories 541.382072
Radiochemistry 541.38
Radioecology 577.277
Radiography 621.3673
Radiography in orthopedics 616.707572
Radiography, Medical 616.07572
Radiography, Medical—Examinations, questions, etc.
616.07572076
Radiography, Medical—Handbooks, manuals, etc.
616.07572
Radiography, Medical—Outlines, syllabi, etc. 616.07572
Radiography, Medical—Positioning 616.07572
Radiography, Medical—Positioning—Atlases
616.075720222
Radiography, Medical—Safety measures 616.075720289
Radioimmunoassay 616.0757
Radioimmunoimaging 616.07575
Radioisotope brachytherapy 615.8424; 616.99406424
Radioisotope scanning 616.07575
Radioisotope scanning—Atlases 616.075750222
Radioisotopes 539.752
Radioisotopes—Industrial applications 621.4837
Radiolaria 579.45
Radiologists 616.0757092
Radiology 616.0757
Radiology, Medical 616.0757
Radiometric ore sorters 622.7
Radiopharmaceuticals 616.07575
Radiosurgery 617.481059
Radiotelephone 621.3845
Radiotelephone—United States—Examinations
621.3845076
Radiotherapy 615.842
Radnóti, Miklós, 1909–1944 894.511132
Radnóti, Miklós, 1909–1944—Translations into English
894.511132
Radon 546.756
Radon—Environmental aspects 363.738; 628.535
Radon measures 515.42
Raffles (Fictitious character) 823.8
Raffles (Fictitious character)—Fiction 823.8
Rafting (Sports) 797.121
Rafting (Sports)—Washington (State) 797.12109797
Rafting (Sports)—Washington (State)—Guidebooks
797.12109797; 917.9704; 917.970443; 917.970444
Raga 781.264
Raga—Dictionaries 781.264
Ragas 781.264
Ragga (Music) 781.646
Ragsales 381.45687065
Ragtime music 781.64
Rahner, Karl, 1904– 230.2092
Rai (Music) 782.421630965
Railbiking 796.6

Railroad companies 385.065
Railroad engineering 625.1
Railroad law 343.095
Railroad law—United States 343.73095
Railroad museums 625.10074
Railroad stations—Great Britain 385.3140941
Railroad travel 385
Railroad travel—Europe—Guidebooks 914.04;
914.04559; 914.0456
Railroads 385; 625.1
Railroads and state 385
Railroads and state—United States 385.0973
Railroads—Australia 385.0994
Railroads—Australia—New South Wales—History
385.09944
Railroads—Australia—Victoria 385.09945
Railroads—British Isles—Maps 385.0941022
Railroads—Canada 385.0971
Railroads—Cars 625.2
Railroads—Cars—Dynamics 625.2015313
Railroads—China 385.0951
Railroads—Crossings 625.163
Railroads—Design and construction 625.1
Railroads—Employees—Legal status, laws, etc.
344.01761385
Railroads—Employees—Legal status, laws, etc.—United
States 344.7301761385
Railroads—England 385.0942
Railroads—France 385.0944
Railroads—Freight 385.24
Railroads—Freight cars 625.24
Railroads—Freight—Rates—Law and legislation
343.0958
Railroads—Freight—Rates—Law and legislation—United
States 343.730958
Railroads—Great Britain 385.0941
Railroads—History 385.09
Railroads—Illinois 385.09773
Railroads—India 385.0954
Railroads—Japan 385.0952
Railroads—Management 385.068
Railroads—Models 625.19; 625.19075
Railroads—Models—Electronic equipment 625.19
Railroads—Models—Periodicals 625.1905
Railroads—Models—Prices 625.19075
Railroads—Periodicals 625.1005
Railroads—Soviet Union 385.0947
Railroads—Timetables 385.2042
Railroads—Track 625.14
Railroads—Trains 385.37; 625.2
Railroads—United States 385.0973
Railroads—United States—Freight-cars 625.240973
Railroads—United States—History 385.0973
Railroads—United States—Mergers 385.1
Railroads—West (U.S.) 385.0978
Railroads—West (U.S.)—Periodicals 385.097805
Rain and rainfall 551.577
Rain forest animals 591.734
Rain forest conservation 333.7516
Rain forest conservation—Law and legislation
346.0467516
Rain forest ecology 577.34
Rain forest ecology—Study and teaching—Activity
programs 577.34071
Rain forest people 306.0809152
Rain forest plants 581.734
Rain forests 333.75
Rainbow 551.567
Rainbow trout 597.57

Raincoats 687.145
Raindrops 551.577
Raisin, Agatha (Fictitious character) 823.914
Raisin, Agatha (Fictitious character)—Fiction 823.914
Raja Rao 823.912
Raja Rao—Criticism and interpretation 823.912
Rajasthan (India) 954.4
Rajasthan (India)—History 954.4
Rajneesh, Bhagwan Shree, 1931- 299.93092
Rajneesh Foundation 299.93
Rajneesh Foundation—Doctrines 299.93
Raku pottery 738.37
Raleigh Metropolitan Area (N.C.) 975.655
Raleigh Metropolitan Area (N.C.)—Maps 912.75655
Raleigh, Walter, Sir, 1552?-1618 942.055092
Ralston, Deb (Fictitious character) 813.54
Ralston, Deb (Fictitious character)—Fiction 813.54
Rāma (Hindu deity) in literature 808.80382912113;
    809.93382912113
Ramadan 297.362
Ramakrishna, 1836-1886 294.555092
Raman effect 535.846
Raman spectroscopy 535.846; 543.08584
Ramanujan Aiyangar, Srinivasa, 1887-1920 510.92
Ramapithecus 569.88
Rammohun Roy, Raja, 1772?-1833 954.031092
Ramsay, Julian (Fictitious character) 823.914
Ramsay, Julian (Fictitious character)—Fiction 823.914
Ramses II, King of Egypt 932.014092
Ramsey County (N.D.) 978.436
Ramsey County (N.D.)—Maps 912.78436
Ramsey, Michael, 1904- 283.092
Ranch life—West (U.S.) 636.010978
Ranchers 636.092; 636.2092
Ranches 636.01; 636.201
Ranching 636.01; 636.201
Rand, Ayn 191
Randall family 929.20973
Randolph, A. Philip (Asa Philip), 1889- 323.092
Randolph County (Ill.) 977.392
Randolph County (Ill.)—Maps 912.77392
Randolph County (Mo.) 977.8283
Randolph County (Mo.)—Maps 912.778283
Randolph family 929.20973
Random fields 519.2
Random graphs 511.5
Random sets 519.2
Random walks (Mathematics) 519.282
Ranganathan, S. R. (Shiyali Ramamrita), 1892-1972
    020.92
Range management 636.0845
Ranger stations 634.93
Ranidae 597.89
Ranking and selection (Statistics) 519.5
Ransom, John Crowe, 1888-1974 811.52
Ransom, John Crowe, 1888-1974—Criticism and
    interpretation 811.52
Ranunculales 583.34
Rap (Music) 782.421649
Rap (Music)—History and criticism 782.42164909
Rap (Music)—History and criticism—Periodicals
    782.42164909005
Rap musicians 782.421649092
Rape 364.1532
Rape in the Bible 220.83641532
Rape—Prevention 362.883
Rape—Religious aspects 291.178331532
Rape—United States 362.8830973; 364.15320973
Rape victims 362.883

Raphael, 1483-1520 759.5
Raphael, 1483-1520—Criticism and interpretation
    759.5
Rapid chess 794.17
Rapid dominance (Military science) 355.422
Rapid eye movement sleep 612.821
Rappresentazioni sacre 782.1
Rapstone Valley (England : Imaginary place) 823.914
Rapstone Valley (England : Imaginary place)—Fiction
    823.914
Rapture (Christian eschatology) 236.9
Rare animals 591.68
Rare birds 598.168
Rare books 090
Rare books—Bibliography 011.44
Rare books—Bibliography—Catalogs 011.44
Rare books—Prices 016.09
Rare diseases 616
Rare earth metals 546.41; 661.041
Rare earths 546.41
Rare fishes 597.168
Rare fungi 579.516
Rare lichens 579.716
Rare plants 581.68
Rarefied gas dynamics 533.2
Rashi script 492.411
Rastafari movement 299.676
Rastafari movement—Jamaica 299.676097292
Rat attacks 599.352153
Ratio and proportion 513.24
Rational-emotive psychotherapy 616.8914
Rational expectations (Economic theory) 339.01
Rationalism 149.7; 211.4
Rationalism (Architecture) 724.6
Ratites 598.5
Rats 599.35; 599.352
Rats—Anatomy 571.319352
Rats as laboratory animals 619.93
Rats as pets 639.9352
Rats—Nervous system 573.819352
Rats—Nervous system—Atlases 573.819352
Rats—Physiology 571.19352
Rattan palms 584.5
Rattlesnakes 597.9638
Rattlesnakes as pets 639.39638
Rauschenberg, Robert, 1925- 709.2
Rauschenberg, Robert, 1925- —Exhibitions 709.2
Rave culture 306.1
Raven, John (Fictitious character) 813.54
Raven, John (Fictitious character)—Fiction 813.54
Raw materials 333.7
Rawlins, Easy (Fictitious character) 813.54
Rawlins, Easy (Fictitious character)—Fiction 813.54
Rawls, John, 1921- . Theory of justice 320.011; 340.11
Ray family 929.20973
Ray, Man, 1890-1976 709.2
Ray, Satyajit, 1921-1992 791.430233092
Ray, Satyajit, 1921-1992—Criticism and interpretation
    791.430233092
RDS (Radio) 384.54; 621.3841
Re-evaluation counseling 158.3
Reacher, Jack (Fictitious character) 813.54
Reaction-diffusion equations 515.353
Reaction mechanisms (Chemistry) 541.39
Reactive armor tiles 623.7475
Reactivity (Chemistry) 541.39
Reactor fuel reprocessing 621.48335
Reactor fuel reprocessing—Waste disposal 621.4838
Read, Herbert Edward, Sir, 1893-1968 828.91209

Reader-response criticism 801.95
Readers 428.6; 428.64
Readers' advisory services 028
Readers' advisory services—United States 025.560973
Readers—Biography 428.64
Readers—Business 428.6402465
Readers for new literates 428.62
Readers—Language and languages 400; 808.0427
Readers (Primary) 428.6
Readers—Science 428.640245
Readers (Secondary) 428.6
Readers—Social sciences 300
Readers—Technology 600
Readers' theater 808.545
Readers' theater—Study and teaching (Elementary) 372.676
Readers—United States 428.64
Readiness for school 372.21; 649.68
Readiness for school—Testing 372.126
Readiness for school—United States 649.68
Reading 028; 428.4; 428.4071
Reading—Ability testing 372.48; 428.4076
Reading (Adult education) 428.40715
Reading (Adult education)—United States 428.40715
Reading—Aids and devices 372.412; 428.4
Reading charts 372.412; 418.40284
Reading comprehension 372.47; 428.43
Reading disability 371.9144; 372.43; 616.855
Reading (Early childhood) 372.4
Reading (Early childhood)—United States 372.40973
Reading (Elementary) 372.4
Reading (Elementary)—Great Britain 372.40941
Reading (Elementary)—Language experience approach 372.475
Reading (Elementary)—Problems, exercises, etc. 372.4076
Reading (Elementary)—United States 372.40973
Reading (Elementary)—United States—Language experience approach 372.4750973
Reading (Elementary)—Whole word method 372.462
Reading games 372.4; 428.0071
Reading (Higher education) 428.40711; 428.430711
Reading (Higher education)—United States 428.4071173
Reading—Language experience approach 372.475
Reading—Parent participation 372.425; 649.58
Reading—Parent participation—United States 649.580973
Reading—Phonetic method 372.465
Reading—Phonetic method—United States 372.4650973
Reading (Preschool) 372.4
Reading (Primary) 372.4
Reading (Primary)—United States 372.40973
Reading, Psychology of 418.4019
Reading readiness 372.414
Reading—Remedial teaching 372.43; 428.42071
Reading—Remedial teaching—United States 428.42071073
Reading (Secondary) 428.40712
Reading (Secondary)—United States 428.4071273
Reading—United States 428.40973
Reading—United States—Ability testing 428.4076
Ready-reckoners 513.9
Reagan, Nancy, 1923– 973.927092
Reagan, Ronald 973.927092
Real estate agents 333.33092
Real estate agents—Licenses 346.0437
Real estate agents—Licenses—Texas 346.7640437

Real estate agents—Licenses—United States 333.330973
Real estate agents—Licenses—United States— Examinations, questions, etc. 333.33076
Real estate agents—United States 333.330973
Real estate appraisers 333.332092
Real estate business 333.33
Real estate business—Accounting 657.8335
Real estate business—California 333.3309794
Real estate business—Dictionaries 333.3303
Real estate business—Florida 333.3309759
Real estate business—Handbooks, manuals, etc. 333.33
Real estate business—Law and legislation 346.0437
Real estate business—Law and legislation—California 346.7940437
Real estate business—Law and legislation—Idaho 346.7960437
Real estate business—Law and legislation—Illinois 346.7730437
Real estate business—Law and legislation—Texas 346.7640437
Real estate business—Law and legislation—United States 346.730437
Real estate business—Law and legislation—Wisconsin 346.7750437
Real estate business—Mathematics 333.330151
Real estate business—New Jersey 333.3309749
Real estate business—New Jersey—Examinations, questions, etc. 333.3309749
Real estate business—Periodicals 333.3305
Real estate business—Software 333.33028553
Real estate business—Software—Catalogs 333.3028553
Real estate business—United States 333.330973
Real estate business—United States—Directories 333.3302573
Real estate business—United States—Examinations, questions, etc. 333.330973
Real estate business—United States—Finance 332.720973
Real estate business—United States—Management 333.33068
Real estate business—United States—States 333.330973
Real estate business—United States—States— Examinations, questions, etc. 333.33076
Real estate business—Vocational guidance 333.33023
Real estate development 333.7315
Real estate development—United States 333.73150973
Real estate development—United States—Forecasting— Tables—Periodicals 333.73150973
Real estate investment 332.6324
Real estate investment—Law and legislation 346.043
Real estate investment—Law and legislation—United States 346.73043; 346.730437
Real estate investment trusts 332.63247
Real estate investment trusts—United States 332.632470973; 346.73043
Real estate investment—United States 332.63240973
Real estate listings 333.33
Real estate management 333.33068; 333.5068
Real estate management—United States 333.5068
Real property 333.3
Real property and taxation 343.054
Real property and taxation—United States 343.73054
Real property—California 346.794043
Real property, Exchange of 333.33
Real property—Florida 346.759043
Real property—Great Britain 346.41043
Real property—Maryland—Baltimore County—Maps 333.30975271022

Real property—Maryland—Frederick County—Maps 333.30975287022

Real property—Maryland—Harford County—Maps 333.30975274022

Real property—Maryland—Howard County—Maps 333.30975281022

Real property—Michigan—Wayne County—Maps 333.30977433022

Real property—New York (State) 346.747043

Real property—North Carolina 346.756043

Real property—Pennsylvania—Philadelphia—Maps 333.30974811022

Real property tax 336.22

Real property tax—Law and legislation 343.054

Real property tax—Law and legislation—California 343.794054

Real property tax—Law and legislation—New Jersey 343.749054

Real property tax—Law and legislation—United States 343.73054

Real property tax—New York (State) 336.2209747

Real property tax—United States 336.220973

Real property—Texas 346.764043

Real property—United States 333.30973; 346.73043

Real property—United States—Digests 346.7304302648

Real property—United States—Foreign ownership 332.6324

Real property—United States—Outlines, syllabi, etc. 346.73043

Real property—Valuation 333.332

Real property—Valuation—Standards 333.3320218

Real property—Valuation—Standards—United States 333.332021873

Real property—Valuation—United States 333.3320973

Real-time data processing 004.33

Real-time programming 005.273

Realism 149.2

Realism in art 700.412; 709.0343

Realism in art—United States 700.4120973; 709.7309034

Realism in literature 808.8012; 809.912

Realism in motion pictures 791.43612

Realism in opera 782.1; 792.5

Reaney, James 818.5409

Reaney, James—Criticism and interpretation 818.5409

Reason 128.33

Reasoning 153.43; 160

Reasoning (Psychology) 153.43

Rebates 332.84

Rebecca (Fictitious character : De Rouffignac) 823.92

Rebus, Inspector (Fictitious character) 823.914

Rebus, Inspector (Fictitious character)—Fiction 823.914

Receivers 346.078

Receivers—Great Britain 346.41078

Recesses 371.242

Recipes 641.5

Recitation (Education) 371.37

Recitations 808.854

Reclamation of land 627.5; 631.64

Reclamation of land—Environmental aspects 577.273

Recluce (Imaginary place) 813.54

Recluce (Imaginary place)—Fiction 813.54

Recognition (International law) 341.26

Recognition (Psychology) 153.124

Recollection (Psychology) 153.123

Recombinant antibodies 615.37

Recombinant DNA 660.65

Recombinant human insulin 615.365

Recombinant human somatotropin 615.363

Reconciliation—Religious aspects 291.22

Reconciliation—Religious aspects—Christianity 234.5

Reconnaissance aircraft 358.4583

Reconstruction 973.8; 973.81

Reconstruction (1939-1951) 940.53144

Reconstruction (1939-1951)—Germany 940.531440943

Reconstruction—Georgia 975.8041

Reconstruction (Linguistics) 417.7

Record clubs 381.45780266

Recorder music 788.36

Recorder music (Jazz) 788.36165

Recorder (Musical instrument) 788.36; 788.3619

Recording and registration 346.0662

Recording instruments 621.38234

Records—Management 352.387; 651.5

Recovered memory 616.8914

Recovering addicts 362.29092

Recovering addicts—Prayer-books and devotions 291.43

Recovering alcoholics 616.861

Recreation 790

Recreation areas 790.068

Recreation areas—Access for the physically handicapped 711.558087; 796.068087

Recreation leaders 790.092

Recreation leadership 790.069

Recreation—Management 353.78; 790.069; 790.69

Recreation—Religious aspects 291.175

Recreation—United States 790.0973

Recreational dive industry 338.4779723

Recreational therapy 615.85153

Recreational vehicle living 796.79

Recreational vehicles 629.226; 796.79

Recruiting and enlistment 355.223

Recumbent bicycles 629.2272

Recursion theory 511.35

Recursive functions 511.35

Recursive partitioning 519.536

Recycled products 363.7282

Recycling industry 363.7282

Recycling (Waste, etc.) 363.7282; 602.86

Recycling (Waste, etc.)—United States 363.72820973

Red algae 579.89

Red Brigades 303.6250945

Red Cloud, 1822–1909 978.0049752

Red Cross 361.7634; 361.77

Red deer 599.6542

Red fox 599.775

Red River Rebellion, 1869–1870 971.051

Redemption 234.3

Redemption—Judaism 296.32

Redhorses 597.48

Reduced instruction set computers 004.3

Reducing diets 613.25

Reducing diets—Humor 613.250207

Reducing diets—Recipes 641.5635

Reducing exercises 613.71

Reduction (Chemistry) 547.23

Reductionism 150.194

Redwood (Wood) 585.5

Redwork 746.44

Reece, Caitlin (Fictitious character) 813.54

Reece, Caitlin (Fictitious character)—Fiction 813.54

Reed family 929.20973

Reed, Lou 782.42166092

Reef fishing 799.16

Reengineering (Management) 658.406; 658.4063

Reese, Ben (Fictitious character) 813.54

Reeve, Christopher, 1952– 791.43028092

Reeve family 929.20973
Reference books 011.02; 028.12; 028.7
Reference books—Bibliography 011.02
Reference books—English literature—Bibliography 016.8209
Reference (Linguistics) 401.43; 415
Reference (Philosophy) 121.68
Reference services (Libraries) 025.52
Reference services (Libraries)—Automation 025.520285
Reference services (Libraries)—United States 025.520973
Referendum 328.2
Referendum—California 328.2794
Referendum—United States 328.230973
Referral centers (Information services) 025.52
Reflecting telescopes 522.2; 681.412
Reflecting telescopes—Design and construction 522.2; 681.4123
Reflection groups 512.2
Reflex (Computer file) 005.75
Reflex sympathetic dystrophy 616.0472; 616.87; 616.88
Reflexes 152.322
Reflexology (Therapy) 615.822
Reflexotherapy 615.5
Reforestation 333.75153
Reform Judaism 296.8341
Reform Judaism—Customs and practices 296.4
Reformation 270.6; 940.23
Reformation—England 274.206
Reformation—Europe 274.06
Reformation—Germany 274.306
Reformed Church 284.2
Reformed Church—Doctrines 230.42
Reformed Church in America 285.7
Reformers 303.484092
Refractive keratoplasty 617.719059
Refractory coating 671.73
Refractory materials 620.143
Refrigerants 621.564
Refrigeration and refrigerating machinery 621.56
Refrigeration and refrigerating machinery—Handbooks, manuals, etc. 621.56
Refrigeration and refrigerating machinery—Maintenance and repair 621.560288
Refugees 325.21; 362.87
Refugees, Arab 362.87089927
Refugees—Education 371.82691
Refugees—Germany (West) 362.870943
Refugees—Government policy 325.21
Refugees—Government policy—United States 325.210973
Refugees—Housing 362.8783
Refugees—Indochina 362.870959
Refugees, Jewish 362.87089924
Refugees—Legal status, laws, etc. 341.486
Refugees—Legal status, laws, etc.—Europe 342.4083
Refugees—United States 362.870973
Refuse and refuse disposal 363.7285; 628.44
Refuse and refuse disposal—Biodegradation 628.445
Refuse and refuse disposal—Law and legislation 344.0462
Refuse and refuse disposal—Law and legislation—Great Britain 344.410462
Refuse and refuse disposal—Law and legislation—New Jersey 344.74904622
Refuse and refuse disposal—Law and legislation—United States 344.7304622
Refuse and refuse disposal—Management 353.93

Refuse and refuse disposal—New York (State) 363.728509747
Refuse and refuse disposal—Periodicals 363.72805
Refuse and refuse disposal—United States 363.72850973
Refuse as fuel 662.87
Regency—England 941.073
Regeneration (Biology) 571.889
Regeneration (Theology) 234.4
Regents 352.23
Reggae music 781.646
Reggae musicians 781.646092
Regional economics 330.9
Regional educational laboratories 370.724
Regional libraries 021.65
Regional planning 307.12
Regional planning—Canada 338.971
Regional planning—Developing countries 338.90091724
Regional planning—European Economic Community countries 307.12094; 338.94
Regional planning—Periodicals 338.9005
Regionalism 304.23; 352.288
Regionalism and education 370
Regionalism—Great Britain 320.80941
Registers of births, etc.—Australia 929.394
Registers of births, etc.—Australia—New South Wales 929.3944
Registers of births, etc.—England—London 929.3421
Registers of births, etc.—Great Britain 929.341
Registers of births, etc.—Great Britain—Manuscripts—Union lists 016.929341
Registers of births, etc.—Illinois—Boone County 929.377329
Registers of births, etc.—Louisiana—New Orleans 929.376335
Registers of births, etc.—Ontario 929.3713
Registers of births, etc.—Scotland—Aberdeen 929.34123
Registers of births, etc.—Scotland—Aberdeenshire 929.34124
Registers of births, etc.—United States 929.373
Regression analysis 519.536
Regression (Psychology) 616.8917
Regulators (Mathematics) 512.74
Rehabilitation 362.0425
Rehabilitation centers 362.1786
Rehabilitation counseling 361.06; 362.0425
Rehabilitation nursing 610.736
Rehabilitation technology 617.03
Reid, Thomas, 1710–1796 192
Reiki (Healing system) 615.851
Reilly, Cassandra (Fictitious character) 813.54
Reilly, Nina (Fictitious character) 813.54
Reilly, Nina (Fictitious character)—Fiction 813.54
Reilly, Regan (Fictitious character) 813.54
Reilly, Regan (Fictitious character)—Fiction 813.54
Reincarnation 133.90135; 291.237
Reincarnation—Christianity 236.2
Reincarnation therapy 616.8914
Reindeer 599.658
Reinforced concrete 620.137; 624.18341; 693.54
Reinforced concrete construction 624.18341; 693.54
Reinforced concrete, Fiber 620.137
Reinforced concrete—Specifications 693.540212
Reinforced concrete—Specifications—United States 693.540212
Reinforced masonry 624.183; 693.1
Reinforced plastics 620.1923; 668.416
Reinforcement (Psychology) 152.3224

Reinforcing bars—Corrosion 620.137
Reinsurance 368.0122
Reinsurance—Law and legislation 346.0860122
Reinsurance—Law and legislation—United States 346.730860122
Rejection (Psychology) in adolescence 155.5124
Rejuvenation 613
Relatedness (Psychology) 158.2
Relational databases 005.756
Relationship addiction 616.8584
Relationship banking 332.10688
Relationship marketing 658.812
Relativistic astrophysics 523.01
Relativistic quantum theory 530.12
Relativity 115
Relativity (Physics) 530.11
Relaxation 613.79
Relaxation (Nuclear physics) 530.416
Relexification (Linguistics) 401.4
Reliability (Engineering) 620.00452
Reliability (Engineering)—Mathematical models 620.004520151
Reliability (Engineering)—Periodicals 620.0045205
Reliability (Engineering)—Statistical methods 620.00452072
Religion 200; 291.042
Religion and culture 291.171
Religion and ethics 291.5
Religion and literature 809.93382; 809.9382
Religion and politics 291.177
Religion and politics—India 322.10954
Religion and politics—United States 322.10973
Religion and politics—United States—History 322.10973
Religion and politics—United States—History—20th century 322.109730904
Religion and science 215; 261.55; 291.175
Religion and science—Periodicals 215.05
Religion and sociology 306.6
Religion and state 291.177
Religion and state—United States 322.10973
Religion—Controversial literature 200
Religion—Dictionaries 200.3
Religion in literature 808.80382; 809.93382
Religion in the public schools 379.28
Religion in the public schools—Law and legislation 344.0796
Religion in the public schools—Law and legislation—United States 344.730796
Religion in the public schools—United States 379.280973
Religion—Methodology 210
Religion—Periodicals 200.5
Religion—Philosophy 210
Religion—Study and teaching 200.71
Religion—Study and teaching (Elementary) 372.84
Religions 200; 200.9; 291
Religions—Dictionaries 200.3; 291.03
Religions—Handbooks, manuals, etc. 291
Religions—Relations 291.172
Religious addiction 248.2
Religious biography 200.922
Religious broadcasting 253.78
Religious camps 796.5422
Religious communities 255
Religious dance, Modern 792.8
Religious education 291.75
Religious education of adults 268.434; 291.75
Religious ethics 291.5
Religious facilities 726

Religious films 791.43682
Religious fundamentalism 200.904
Religious institutions 306.6
Religious institutions—United States 291.650973
Religious institutions—United States—Directories 291.6502573
Religious libraries 026.2
Religious life 291.44
Religious life—Buddhism 294.3444
Religious life—Hinduism 294.544
Religious life—Islam 297.57
Religious life—Zen Buddhism 294.3444
Religious literature 808.80382
Religious pluralism 291.172
Religious pluralism—Christianity 261.2
Religious poetry 808.819382
Religious poetry, American 811.0080382
Religious poetry, Canadian 811.0080382
Religious poetry, English 821.0080382
Religious services industry 338.472
Religious tolerance 261.72
Relocation (Housing) 333.338
Remarriage 306.84
Remarriage—United States 306.84
Rembrandt Harmenszoon van Rijn, 1606–1669 759.9492
Rembrandt Harmenszoon van Rijn, 1606–1669—Catalogs 759.9492; 769.92
Rembrandt Harmenszoon van Rijn, 1606–1669—Criticism and interpretation 759.9492
Remedial teaching 371.102; 372.43
Remedies (Law) 347.077
Remedies (Law)—United States 347.7377
Remedies (Law)—United States—Cases 347.7377
Remedies (Law)—United States—Outlines, syllabi, etc. 347.7377
Remembrance Day (Canada) 394.264
Remington, Frederic, 1861–1909 709.2
Remington, Frederic, 1861–1909—Catalogs 709.2; 759.13
Remington, Frederic, 1861–1909—Criticism and interpretation 709.2
Reminiscing in old age 155.67; 305.26
Remnant vegetation 581.68
Remnant vegetation conservation 333.953216; 639.99
Remnant vegetation management 333.9532; 639.99
Remote control 620.46
Remote sensing 621.3678
Remote sensing—Data processing 621.36780285
Remote sensing—Equipment and supplies 621.36780284
Remote sensing equipment industry 338.476213678
Remote-sensing images 621.3678
Remote submersibles 623.827
Remote viewing (Parapsychology) 133.8
Renaissance 940.21
Renaissance—Italy 945.05
Renal circulation 612.463
Renal hypertension 616.132
Renault automobile 629.2222
Renewable energy sources 333.794; 621.042
Renewable energy sources—India 333.7940954
Renewable energy sources—Law and legislation 346.04679160262
Renewable energy sources—Law and legislation—United States 346.73046794
Renewable energy sources—Periodicals 621.04205
Renewable energy sources—United States 333.7940973
Renewable natural resources 333.794
Renko, Arkady (Fictitious character) 813.54

Restaurants—California—San Francisco 647.9579461
Restaurants—California—San Francisco Bay Area
647.957946
Restaurants—California—San Francisco Bay Area—
Guidebooks 647.957946
Restaurants—California—San Francisco—Guidebooks
647.9579461
Restaurants—Colorado 647.95788
Restaurants—Colorado—Guidebooks 647.95788
Restaurants—Decoration—United States 725.710973
Restaurants—England 647.9542
Restaurants—England—London 647.95421
Restaurants—England—London—Guidebooks 647.95421
Restaurants—Florida 647.95759
Restaurants—Florida—Guidebooks 647.95759
Restaurants—France 647.9544
Restaurants—France—Paris 647.9544361
Restaurants—France—Paris—Guidebooks 647.9544361
Restaurants—Georgia—Atlanta 647.95758231
Restaurants—Georgia—Atlanta—Guidebooks
647.95758231
Restaurants—Great Britain 647.9541
Restaurants—Great Britain—Guidebooks 647.9541
Restaurants—Guidebooks 647.95
Restaurants—Illinois—Chicago 647.9577311
Restaurants—Illinois—Chicago—Guidebooks
647.9577311
Restaurants—Ireland 647.95415
Restaurants—Ireland—Guidebooks 647.95415
Restaurants—Law and legislation 344.0464
Restaurants—Law and legislation—North Carolina
344.7560464
Restaurants—Louisiana—New Orleans 647.9576335
Restaurants—Louisiana—New Orleans—Guidebooks
647.9576335
Restaurants—Marketing 647.950688
Restaurants—Massachusetts—Boston 647.9574461
Restaurants—Massachusetts—Boston—Guidebooks
647.9574461
Restaurants—New England 647.9574
Restaurants—New England—Guidebooks 647.9574
Restaurants—New York (State)—New York 647.957471
Restaurants—New York (State)—New York—
Guidebooks 647.957471
Restaurants—Northwest, Pacific 647.95795
Restaurants—Northwest, Pacific—Guidebooks
647.95795
Restaurants—Prices 647.950681
Restaurants—Public relations 659.2964795
Restaurants—United States 338.476479573; 647.9573
Restaurants—United States—Directories 647.9573
Restaurants—United States—Guidebooks 647.9573
Restaurants—Washington (D.C.) 647.95753
Restaurants—Washington (D.C.)—Guidebooks
647.95753
Restaurants—Washington Region 647.95753
Restaurants—Washington Region—Guidebooks
647.95753
Restaurants—Washington (State)—Seattle 647.9579777
Restaurants—Washington (State)—Seattle—Guidebooks
647.9579777
Restitution 347.077
Restitution—Australia 347.94077
Restless legs syndrome 616.84
Restoration ecology 333.73153; 333.95153
Restoration movement (Christianity) 286.6
Restorative drying 660.28426
Restorative justice 345.001; 364.68
Restorative justice—Religious aspects 291.1783368

Restraining orders 347.077
Restraint of trade 343.0723
Restraint of trade—United States 343.730723
Résumés (Employment) 650.142
Résumés (Employment)—Handbooks, manuals, etc.
650.142
Resurrection 236.8
Resurrection (Jewish theology) 296.33
Resuscitation 615.8043
Retail trade 381.1; 658.87
Retail trade—Management 658.87
Retail trade—Mathematics 658.870151
Retail trade—Security measures 381.10684
Retail trade—United States 381.10973
Retail trade—United States—Statistics 381.10973021
Retail trade—United States—Statistics—Periodicals
381.10973021
Retaining walls 624.164
Retaining walls—Design and construction 624.164
Retief (Fictitious character) 813.54
Retief (Fictitious character)—Fiction 813.54
Retina 573.88; 612.843
Retina—Diseases 617.735
Retinal degeneration 617.735
Retinal detachment 617.735
Retinoids—Therapeutic use 616.5061; 616.994061
Retirees 305.90696
Retirees—Employment 331.5
Retirees—Employment—Law and legislation 344.015
Retirees—Finance, Personal 332.0240696
Retirees—Legal status, laws, etc. 346.013
Retirees—United States 306.380973
Retirees—United States—Finance, Personal
332.0240696
Retirees—United States—Life skills guides 646.790973
Retirement 306.38
Retirement communities—United States 646.790973
Retirement income 332.02401
Retirement income—Planning 332.02401
Retirement income—United States 331.2520973
Retirement income—United States—Planning 332.02401
Retirement, Places of 306.38
Retirement, Places of—United States 646.790973
Retirement—Planning 646.79
Retirement—Religious aspects 291.178
Retirement—United States 306.380973; 646.790973
Retirement—United States—Planning 646.790973
Retirement—United States—Planning—Handbooks,
manuals, etc. 646.790973
Retractable roofs 690.15; 721.5
Retreats 269.6
Retreats—Catholic Church 269.6
Retreats—Directories 647.94; 910.25
Retreats for youth 269.63
Retrievers 636.7527
Retrievers—Training 636.752735
Retrospective conversion (Cataloging) 025.3173
Retroviruses 579.2569
Rett syndrome 618.928588
Return migration 304.8
Reusable space vehicles 387.8; 629.441
Revegetation 631.64
Revelation 231.74
Revenue 336.02
Revenue stamps 769.572
Revenue stamps—United States 769.5720973
Revenue—United States 336.0273
Revenue—United States—States 336.201373
Revere, Paul, 1735–1818 973.3311092; 974.403092

Revisionism (Christian theology) 230.046
Revivals 269.24
Revolutionaries 322.42
Revolutions 303.64; 321.094
Revolutions in literature 808.80358; 809.93358
Revolutions—Latin America 303.64098
Revolutions—Religious aspects 261.7
Revolvers 623.4436; 683.436
Revues 782.140268; 792.6
Revues—Librettos 782.14; 782.140268
Rewriting systems (Computer science) 005.131; 511.3
Rex (Fictitious character : Rayner) 823.914
REXX (Computer program language) 005.133
Reye's syndrome 616.83
Reynolds, Alex (Fictitious character) 813.54
Reynolds family 929.20973
Rhea, Nicholas (Fictitious character) 823.914
Rheology 531.1134
Rhesus monkey 599.8643
Rhetoric 808
Rhetoric—Early works to 1800 808
Rhetoric—History 808.009
Rhetoric, Medieval 808.00902
Rhetoric—Philosophy 808.001
Rhetorical criticism 809.51
Rheumatism 616.723
Rheumatoid arthritis 616.7227
Rheumatology 616.723
Rheumatology—Examinations, questions, etc. 616.7230076
Rheumatology—Handbooks, manuals, etc. 616.723
Rhinoceroses 599.668
Rhinoplasty 617.5230592
Rhizobium 579.334
Rhizosphere 577.57
Rhode Island 974.5
Rhode Island—Genealogy 929.3745
Rhode Island—Guidebooks 917.4504; 917.450443; 917.450444
Rhode Island—History 974.5
Rhode Island—History—Colonial period, ca. 1600–1775 974.502
Rhode Island—Maps 912.745
Rhodenbarr, Bernie (Fictitious character) 813.54
Rhodenbarr, Bernie (Fictitious character)—Fiction 813.54
Rhodes, Dan (Fictitious character) 813.54
Rhodes, Dan (Fictitious character)—Fiction 813.54
Rhodes family 929.20973
Rhododendrons 583.66; 635.93366
Rhododendrons—Varieties 635.93366
Rhone-Rhine Canal (France) 386.48094439
Rhyme 808.1
Rhys, Jean 823.912
Rhys, Jean—Criticism and interpretation 823.912
Rhys, Madoc (Fictitious character) 813.54
Rhys, Madoc (Fictitious character)—Fiction 813.54
Rhythm and blues music 781.643
Rhythmic gymnastics 796.44
Ribbon work 745.44
Ribosomes 571.658
Ribs (Cookery) 641.66
Ricardo, David, 1772–1823 330.153092
Rice 338.17318; 633.18; 641.3318
Rice, Anne, 1941– 813.54
Rice, Anne, 1941– —Criticism and interpretation 813.54
Rice family 929.20973
Rice, Jerry 796.332092
Rice trade 338.17318; 380.141318

Rice—Varieties 633.187
Riceland animals 591.755
Rich, Adrienne Cecile 811.54
Rich, Adrienne Cecile—Criticism and interpretation 811.54
Rich people 305.5234
Richard I, King of England, 1157–1199 942.032092
Richard II, King of England, 1367–1400 942.038092
Richard III, King of England, 1452–1485 942.046092
Richards, Keith, 1943– 782.42166092
Richardson County (Neb.) 978.2282
Richardson County (Neb.)—Maps 912.782282
Richardson family 929.20973
Richardson, Henry Handel, pseud. 823.912
Richardson, Henry Handel, pseud.—Criticism and interpretation 823.912
Richardson, Samuel, 1689–1761 823.6
Richardson, Samuel, 1689–1761. Clarissa 823.6
Richardson, Samuel, 1689–1761—Criticism and interpretation 823.6
Richelieu, Armand Jean du Plessis, duc de, 1585–1642 944.032092
Richland County (N.D.) 978.412
Richland County (N.D.)—Maps 912.78412
Richland County (Wis.) 977.575
Richland County (Wis.)—Maps 912.77575
Richmond County (Va.) 975.523
Richmond County (Va.)—Genealogy 929.375523
Richmond Metropolitan Area (Va.) 975.5451
Richmond Metropolitan Area (Va.)—Maps 912.755451
Richmond (Va.) 975.5451
Richmond (Va.)—History 975.5451
Richmond (Va.)—History—Siege, 1864–1865 973.738
Richthofen, Manfred, Freiherr von, 1892–1918 940.44943092
Rickover, Hyman George 359.0092
Ricœur, Paul 194
Riddle family 929.20973
Riddles 398.6; 793.735; 808.882
Riddles, Chinese 398.6
Riddles, English (Old) 398.6
Ride films 791.436
Ride, Sally 629.450092
Riding habit 646.47
Riefenstahl, Leni 791.430233092
Riel, Louis, 1844–1885 971.051092
Riel Rebellion, 1885 971.054
Riemann surfaces 515.93
Riemannian manifolds 516.373
Rifles 355.82425; 623.4425; 683.422
Rifts (Geology) 551.872
Right and left (Political science) 320.5
Right and left (Political science) in literature 808.80358; 809.93358
Right of property 323.46
Right of property—United States 323.460973
Right of property—United States—History 323.460973
Right to die 174.24; 179.7
Right to die—Law and legislation 344.04197
Right to die—Law and legislation—United States 344.7304197
Right to die—Law and legislation—United States—States 344.7304197
Right to die—United States 362.175
Right to education 344.079
Right to health care 362.1
Right to health care—Religious aspects 291.178321
Right to health care—United States 362.10973
Right to housing 363.5

Right to labor 331.8892
Right to life 323.43
Right to refuse hazardous work 344.0465; 363.11
Righteous Gentiles in the Holocaust—Biography
  940.5318; 940.5318092
Riker, William T. (Fictitious character) 791.4375;
  791.4572
Riley, Dave (Fictitious character) 813.54
Riley, Dave (Fictitious character)—Fiction 813.54
Riley family 929.20973
Rilke, Rainer Maria, 1875–1926 831.912
Rilke, Rainer Maria, 1875–1926—Correspondence
  831.912
Rilke, Rainer Maria, 1875–1926—Translations into
  English 831.912
Rimbaud, Arthur, 1854–1891 841.8
Rimbaud, Arthur, 1854–1891—Translations into English
  841.8
Ringgold County (Iowa) 977.7873
Ringgold County (Iowa)—Maps 912.777873
Rings (Algebra) 512.4
Rio de Janeiro (Brazil) 981.53
Rio de Janeiro (Brazil)—Guidebooks 918.15304;
  918.1530464
Riot grrrl movement 305.42; 781.66
Riots 303.623
Riots—France—Paris 944; 944.0836
Riots—United States 364.143
Ripken, Cal, 1960– 796.357092
Ripley, Tom (Fictitious character) 813.54
Ripley, Tom (Fictitious character)—Fiction 813.54
Risk 338.5; 368
Risk assessment 363.102
Risk (Insurance) 368
Risk management 658.155
Risk managers 658.155092
Risk—Sociological aspects 302.12
Rissoles 641.812
Rites and ceremonies 291.38
Ritsos, Giannēs, 1909– 889.132
Ritsos, Giannēs, 1909– —Translations into English
  889.132
Ritual 291.38
Ritual abuse 133.422
Ritual abuse—United States 362.76; 364.155540973
Ritual abuse victims—Rehabilitation 616.8582
River boats 386.22436
River channels 551.442
River dolphins 599.538
Rivera, Diego, 1886–1957 759.972
Rivers 551.483
Rivers—China 551.4830951
Rivers, Larry, 1925– 709.2
Rivers—United States 551.4830973
Riverside County (Calif.) 979.497
Riverside County (Calif.)—Maps 912.79497
Riviera (France) 944.94
Riviera (France)—Guidebooks 914.49404; 914.49404839;
  914.4940484
Rizal, José, 1861–1896 959.902092
RLIN (Information retrieval system) 025.04
RLIN (Information retrieval system)—Handbooks,
  manuals, etc. 025.04
RMI (Computer architecture) 005.2762
RNA 572.88
RNA viruses 579.25
Rñiṅ-ma-pa (Sect) 294.3923
Ro (Artificial language) 499.99

Road construction contracts—United States 625.7
Road drainage 625.734
Road films 791.43655
Road materials 625.8
Road materials—Testing 625.80287
Road rage 363.1251
Road Runner (Fictitious character) 791.4375
Road scrapers 625.733
Roadrunner 598.74
Roads 388.1; 625.7
Roads—Design and construction 625.725; 713
Roads—Foundations 625.733
Roads—Guard fences 625.795
Roads—Interchanges and intersections 388.13
Roads—Lighting 628.95
Roads—Maintenance and repair 625.76
Roads—Maintenance and repair—Management
  625.76068
Roads—Maintenance and repair—Safety measures
  625.76
Roads—Safety measures 625.70289
Roads—Snow and ice control 625.763
Roads—Specifications—Maine 625.70212
Roads—Specifications—United States 625.70212
Roads—United States 388.10973; 625.70973
Roads—United States—History 388.10973
Roads—Virginia 388.109755
Roads—Widening 625.7
Roadside architecture 725.2
Roadside ecology 577.55
Roadside improvement 625.77
Roadside restaurants 647.95
Roanoke Colony 975.6175
Roasting (Cookery) 641.71
Robak, Don (Fictitious character) 813.54
Robak, Don (Fictitious character)—Fiction 813.54
Robber flies 595.773
Robbins family 929.20973
Robert I, King of Scots, 1274–1329 941.102092
Roberts County (S.D.) 978.312
Roberts County (S.D.)—Maps 912.78312
Roberts family 929.20973
Robertson family 929.20973
Robertson, Pat 269.2092; 973.927092
Robeson, Paul, 1898–1976 782.0092
Robespierre, Maximilien, 1758–1794 944.04092
Robicheaux, Dave (Fictitious character) 813.54
Robicheaux, Dave (Fictitious character)—Fiction 813.54
Robin Hood (Legendary character) in literature 398.352
Robin Hood (Legendary character)—Legends
  398.2094202
Robins 598.842
Robinson, David, 1965– 796.323092
Robinson, Edwin Arlington, 1869–1935 811.52
Robinson, Edwin Arlington, 1869–1935—Criticism and
  interpretation 811.52
Robinson family 929.20973
Robinson, Jackie, 1919–1972 796.357092
Robinson, Mary, 1944– 941.70824092
Robot industry 338.47629892; 380.145629892
Robotics 629.892
Robotics in sports 796.0284
Robotics laboratories 629.89072
Robotics—Periodicals 629.89205
Robotics—Research 629.89072
Robots 629.892
Robots—Control systems 629.892
Robots—Dynamics 629.892
Robots, Industrial 629.892; 670.4272

Robots—Kinematics 629.892
Robots—Motion 629.892
Rochdale (England) 942.7392
Rochdale (England)—Maps 912.427392
Rochester, John Wilmot, Earl of, 1647–1680 821.4
Rochester, John Wilmot, Earl of, 1647–1680—Criticism and interpretation 821.4
Rock bursts 622.28
Rock climbing 796.5223
Rock concerts 781.66078; 792.7
Rock concerts—Stage-setting and scenery 792.7
Rock County (Wis.) 977.587
Rock County (Wis.)—Genealogy 929.377587
Rock County (Wis.)—Maps 912.77587
Rock deformation 551.8
Rock excavation 624.152
Rock gardens 635.9672
Rock groups 781.66092
Rock mechanics 624.15132
Rock music 781.66
Rock music—To 1961 781.6609
Rock music—1961–1970 781.6609046
Rock music—1961–1970—Texts 782.421660268
Rock music—1971–1980 781.6609047
Rock music—1981–1990 781.6609048
Rock music—1991–2000 781.6609049
Rock music—Chronology 781.6609
Rock music—Discography 016.781660266; 016.782421660266
Rock music—History and criticism 781.6609
Rock music—History and criticism—Periodicals 781.6609005
Rock music—Periodicals 781.6605
Rock music—Religious aspects—Christianity 781.66
Rock music—Texts 782.421660268
Rock music—United States 781.660973
Rock music—United States—History and criticism 781.660973
Rock musicians 781.66092
Rock musicians—Biography 781.66092
Rock musicians—Interviews 781.66092
Rock musicians—United States—Biography 781.66092273
Rock musicians' writings 808.89927816
Rock paintings 709.0113; 759.0113
Rocketry 621.4356; 629.475
Rocketry—United States—History 621.43560973; 629.4750973
Rockets (Aeronautics) 621.4356
Rocks 552
Rocks—Analysis 552.06
Rocks, Carbonate 552.58
Rocks—Collection and preservation 552.0075
Rocks, Igneous 552.1
Rocks, Metamorphic 552.4
Rocks, Sedimentary 552.5
Rocks—Testing 552.06
Rockwell, Norman, 1894–1978 759.13
Rockwell, Norman, 1894–1978—Themes, motives 759.13
Rocky (Fictitious character : Ward) 791.4572
Rocky Mountain goat 599.6475
Rocky Mountain National Park (Colo.) 978.869
Rocky Mountain National Park (Colo.)—Guidebooks 917.8869
Rocky Mountain spotted fever 616.9223
Rocky Mountains 978
Rocky Mountains—Description and travel 917.804; 917.80433; 917.80434

Rocky Mountains—Guidebooks 917.804; 917.80433; 917.80434
Rocky Mountains Region 978
Rocky Mountains Region—Guidebooks 917.804; 917.80433; 917.80434
Rodents 599.35
Rodents as pets 636.935
Rodents, Fossil 569.35
Rodeos 791.84
Rodeos—United States 791.840973
Rodeos—United States—History 791.840973
Rodin, Auguste, 1840–1917 730.92
Rodin, Auguste, 1840–1917—Catalogs 730.92
Rodman, Dennis, 1961– 796.323092
Roe deer 599.659
Roethke, Theodore, 1908–1963 811.54
Roethke, Theodore, 1908–1963—Criticism and interpretation 811.54
Roger the Chapman (Fictitious character) 823.914
Roger the Chapman (Fictitious character)—Fiction 823.914
Rogers family 929.20973
Rogers, George (Fictitious character) 823.914
Rogers, George (Fictitious character)—Fiction 823.914
Rogers, Roy, 1911– 791.43028092
Rogers, Will, 1879–1935 792.7028092
Rogue Warrior (Fictitious character) 813.54
Rogue Warrior (Fictitious character)—Fiction 813.54
Rojas, Fernando de, d. 1541 868.6209
Rojas, Fernando de, d. 1541. Celestina 862.2
Role conflict 302.15
Role models 303.32
Role playing 616.891523
Role reversal 302.15
Rolette County (N.D.) 978.4592
Rolette County (N.D.)—Maps 912.784592
Rolfing 615.822
Roller bearings 621.822
Roller coasters 791.068
Roller hockey 796.21
Rolling (Metal-work) 671.32
Rolling Stones 782.421660922
Rollins family 929.20973
Rollover protective structures 620.86
Rolls-Royce automobile 629.2222
Rolls-Royce automobile—History 629.2222
Roman law 340.54; 349.37
Roman law—History 340.5409
Romance fiction 808.8385
Romance languages 440
Romance languages—Verb 440.045
Romance literature 808.8385
Romance philology 440
Romances 808.8133
Romances, English 821.03308
Romances, English—History and criticism 821.03309
Romances—History and criticism 809.133
Romances (Music) 784.18968
Romances—Translations into English 841.1
Romania 949.8
Romania—Description and travel 914.9804; 914.980432
Romania—Economic conditions 330.9498
Romania—Economic conditions—1945–1989 330.9498031
Romania—Economic policy 338.9498
Romania—Economic policy—1945–1989 338.9498
Romania—Foreign relations 327.498
Romania—Foreign relations—1944–1989 327.498
Romania—Geography 914.98

Romania—Guidebooks 914.9804; 914.980432
Romania—History 949.8
Romania—History—1944–1989 949.8031
Romania—Politics and government 320.9498
Romania—Politics and government—1944–1989
    320.949809045
Romanian language 459
Romanian language—Textbooks for foreign speakers—
    English 459.82421; 459.83421
Romanian poetry 859.1; 859.108
Romanian poetry—20th century 859.13; 859.1308;
    859.134; 859.13408
Romanian poetry—20th century—Translations into
    English 859.1308; 859.13408
Romanian poetry—Translations into English 859.108
Romans 937
Romans—England 936.204
Romans—France 936.402
Romans—Spain 936.603
Romanticism 808.80145; 809.9145
Romanticism—England 820.80145
Romanticism—France 840.80145
Romanticism—Germany 830.80145
Romanticism—Great Britain 820.80145
Romanticism in art 700.4145; 709.0342
Romanticism in music 780.9034
Rome 937
Rome—Antiquities 937
Rome—Army 355.00937
Rome—Biography 920.037
Rome—Civilization 937
Rome—History 937
Rome—History—To 510 B.C. 937; 937.01
Rome—History—Republic, 265–30 B.C. 937.02
Rome—History—Civil War, 49–45 B.C. 937.05
Rome—History—The five Julii, 30 B.C.–68 A.D. 937.07
Rome—History—Empire, 30 B.C.–284 A.D. 937.07
Rome—History—Empire, 30 B.C.–476 A.D. 937.06
Rome—History—Nero, 54–68 937.07
Rome—History—Germanic Invasions, 3rd–6th centuries
    937.09
Rome—History, Military 355.00937
Rome (Italy) 945.632
Rome (Italy)—Antiquities 937.6; 938.7
Rome (Italy)—Guidebooks 914.563204; 914.563204929;
    914.56320493
Rome (Italy)—History 945.632
Rome (Italy)—History—476–1420 945.632
Rome—Religion 292.07
Rome—Social life and customs 937
Rondels 808.814
Rondos (Piano) 786.21824
Ronsard, Pierre de, 1524–1585 841.3
Ronsard, Pierre de, 1524–1585—Criticism and
    interpretation 841.3
Roofing 695
Roofs 690.15
Roofs—Design and construction 690.15
Rookie football players 796.33264092
Room layout (Dwellings) 728
Roosevelt, Eleanor, 1884–1962 973.917092
Roosevelt, Franklin D. (Franklin Delano), 1882–1945
    973.917092
Roosevelt-Rondon Scientific Expedition (1913-1914)
    508.81
Roosevelt, Theodore, 1858–1919 973.911092
Root crops 633.4
Root crops—Tropics 635.10913
Roots (Botany) 575.54; 581.498

Roots (Botany)—Development 575.5438
Roots (Botany)—Formation 575.54386
Rope skipping 796.2
Roper, Douglas (Fictitious character) 823.914
Roper, Douglas (Fictitious character)—Fiction 823.914
Ropework 623.8882
Rorschach Test 155.2842
Rorty, Richard 191
Rosary 242.74
Roscommon County (Mich.) 977.476
Roscommon County (Mich.)—Maps 912.77476
Rose Bowl, Pasadena, Calif. (Football game) 791.33263
Rose Bowl, Pasadena, Calif. (Football game)—History
    791.33263
Rose culture 635.933734
Rose family 929.20973
Rose (Fictitious character : Munro) 813.54
Rose, Pete, 1941– 796.357092
Roseanne, 1952– 792.7028092
Roses 583.734; 635.933734
Roses in art 704.9434
Roses—Varieties 635.933734
Rosh ha-Shanah 296.4315; 394.267
Rosicrucians 135.43092
Ross, Barry (Fictitious character) 813.54
Ross, Betsy, 1752–1836 973.3092
Ross County (Ohio) 977.182
Ross County (Ohio)—Genealogy 929.377182
Ross, Danielle (Fictitious character) 813.54
Ross, Danielle (Fictitious character)—Fiction 813.54
Ross family 929.20973
Ross, Will (Fictitious character) 813.54
Rossetti, Christina Georgina, 1830–1894 821.8
Rossetti, Christina Georgina, 1830–1894—Criticism and
    interpretation 821.8
Rossetti, Dante Gabriel, 1828–1882 759.2; 821.8
Rossetti, Dante Gabriel, 1828–1882—Criticism and
    interpretation 759.2
Rossini, Gioacchino, 1792–1868 782.1092
Rostenberg, Leona 381.45002092
Rostnikov, Porfiry Petrovich (Fictitious character)
    813.54
Rostnikov, Porfiry Petrovich (Fictitious character)—
    Fiction 813.54
Roswell Incident, Roswell, N.M., 1947 001.9420978943
Roswell (N.M.) 978.943
Rotary combustion engines 621.434
Rotary tillers 631.51
Rotaviruses 579.254
Roth, Philip 813.54
Roth, Philip—Criticism and interpretation 813.54
Rothschild family 332.10922
Rotifera 592.52
Rotisserie League Baseball (Game)—Periodicals 793.93
Rotors—Dynamics 621.82
Rottentrolls (Fictitious characters) 823.914
Rottweiler dog 636.73
Roulette 795.23
Roundhouses (Railroads)—Great Britain 385.314
Rousseau, Jean-Jacques, 1712–1778 194
Rousseau, Jean-Jacques, 1712–1778. Nouvelle Héloïse
    843.5
Routers (Tools) 684.083
Roving vehicles (Astronautics) 629.44
Rowan County (N.C.)—Genealogy 929.375671
Rowan, Nick (Fictitious character) 791.4572
Rowe family 929.20973
Rowing 797.123
Rowing clubs 797.14

Rowlandson, Mary White, ca. 1635–ca. 1678
  974.4302092
Roy, M. N. (Manabendra Nath), 1887–1954 335.4092
Royal Canadian Mounted Police 363.20971
Royal Canadian Mounted Police—History 363.20971
Royal households—Great Britain 941
Royal Ulster Constabulary 363.209416
Royal weddings 392.508621
Różewicz, Tadeusz 891.85173; 891.85273; 891.8587309
Różewicz, Tadeusz—Translations into English
  891.85173; 891.85273
RPG IV (Computer program language) 005.133
Ruan 787.85
Rubber 620.194; 678.2
Rubber industry and trade 338.47678
Rubber stamp printing 761
Rubella 614.524; 616.916
Rubik's Cube 793.74
Rudolph, Wilma, 1940– 796.42092
Ruffed grouse 598.635
Rug and carpet industry 338.47677643
Rugby football 796.333
Rugosa 563.6
Rugrats (Fictitious characters) 791.4572
Rugs 746.7
Rugs, Hooked 746.74
Rugs, Hooked—United States 746.740973
Rugs, Oriental 746.75095
Rugs, Oriental—Exhibitions 746.75095074
Ruiz, Juan, fl. 1343 861.1
Ruiz, Juan, fl. 1343. Libro de buen amor 861.1
Rule of law 340.11
Rule of law—United States 340.11
Rule of the road at sea 623.8884
Rumpole, Horace (Fictitious character) 823.914
Rumpole, Horace (Fictitious character)—Fiction
  823.914
Runaway children 305.906923
Runaway husbands 306.88
Runaway teenagers 305.906923
Runaway teenagers in literature 808.8035206923;
  809.9335206923
Runaway teenagers—United States 362.74
Runes 133.33; 430
Runners (Sports) 796.42092
Running 796.42
Running backs (Football) 796.332092
Running backs (Football)—United States—Biography
  796.332092
Running—Physiological aspects 612.76
Running—Psychological aspects 796.42019
Running races 796.42
Running—Training 796.42071; 796.43071
Runoff 551.488
Runways (Aeronautics) 629.1363
Rural comedies 808.8252308321734
Rural credit—Law and legislation 346.073091734
Rural development 307.1412
Rural development—Africa 307.1412096
Rural development—Africa, Sub-Saharan 307.14120967
Rural development—Asia 307.1412095
Rural development—Bangladesh 307.1412095492
Rural development—China 307.14120951
Rural development—Developing countries
  307.1412091724
Rural development—Government policy 307.1412
Rural development—Government policy—United States
  307.14120973
Rural development—India 307.14120954

Rural development—Kenya 307.1412096762
Rural development—Malaysia 307.141209595
Rural development—Nigeria 307.141209669
Rural development—Pakistan 307.1412095491
Rural development—Philippines 307.141209599
Rural development projects 307.1412
Rural development—South Africa 307.14120968
Rural development—Thailand 307.141209593
Rural development—United States 307.14120973
Rural development—Zimbabwe 307.1412096891
Rural electrification 333.7932
Rural health services 362.104257
Rural health services—Texas 362.10425709764
Rural health services—United States 362.1042570973
Rural nursing 362.104257; 610.7343
Rural parents 306.874091734
Rural population 304.6091734
Rural population—United States 304.60973091734
Rural roads 625.5091734
Rural roads—Design and construction 625.5091734
Rural schools 371.0091734
Rural schools—United States 371.00973091734
Rural schools—United States—History 371.00973091734
Rural single parents 306.856091734
Rural telecommunication 384.091734
Rural-urban migration 307.24
Rushdie, Salman 823.914
Rushdie, Salman—Criticism and interpretation 823.914
Rushdie, Salman. Satanic verses 823.914
Rushes (Motion pictures) 778.53
Ruskin, John, 1819–1900 828.809
Ruskin, John, 1819–1900—Criticism and interpretation
  828.809
Ruskin, John, 1819–1900—Knowledge—Art 745.4492
Ruskin, John, 1819–1900—Political and social views
  828.809
Ruskin, John, 1819–1900—Religion 828.809
Russell, Bertrand, 1872–1970 192
Russell, Charles M. (Charles Marion), 1864–1926 709.2
Russell family 929.20973
Russia 947
Russia—Civilization 947
Russia—Civilization—1801–1917 947.08
Russia—Description and travel 914.704; 914.70486
Russia—Description and travel—Early works to 1800
  914.704
Russia—Economic conditions 330.947
Russia—Economic conditions—1861–1917 330.94708
Russia (Federation) 947.086
Russia (Federation)—Commerce 382.0947
Russia (Federation)—Commerce—Periodicals
  382.094705
Russia (Federation)—Description and travel 914.70486
Russia (Federation)—Economic conditions 330.947086
Russia (Federation)—Economic conditions—1991–
  330.947086
Russia (Federation)—Economic conditions—1991– —
  Periodicals 330.947086
Russia (Federation)—Economic policy 338.947
Russia (Federation)—Economic policy—1991– 338.947
Russia (Federation)—Foreign relations 327.47
Russia (Federation)—Guidebooks 914.70486
Russia (Federation)—History 947.086
Russia (Federation)—History—1991– 947.086
Russia (Federation)—Politics and government
  320.94709049; 947.086
Russia (Federation)—Politics and government—1991–
  320.94709049; 947.086
Russia (Federation)—Social conditions 947.086

Russia (Federation)—Social life and customs 947.086
Russia—History 947
Russia—History—To 1533 947
Russia—History—1237–1480 947.03
Russia—History—Time of Troubles, 1598–1613 947.044
Russia—History—1613–1689 947.04
Russia—History—Peter I, 1689–1725 947.05
Russia—History—1689–1801 947
Russia—History—Catherine II, 1729–1796 947.063
Russia—History—Alexander I, 1801–1825 947.072
Russia—History—1801–1917 947.08
Russia—History—Alexander II, 1855–1881 947.081
Russia—History—Alexander III, 1881–1894 947.082
Russia—History—Nicholas II, 1894–1917 947.083
Russia—History—1904–1914 947.083
Russia—History—Revolution, 1905–1907 947.083
Russia—History—February Revolution, 1917 947.0841
Russia—History—Sources 947.0072
Russia—Intellectual life 947
Russia—Intellectual life—1801–1917 947.07; 947.08
Russia—Politics and government 320.947; 947
Russia—Politics and government—1855–1881 320.94709034; 947.08
Russia—Politics and government—1894–1917 320.94709041; 947.08
Russia—Social life and customs 947
Russia—Social life and customs—1533–1917 947
Russian fiction 891.73; 891.73008
Russian fiction—19th century 891.73308
Russian fiction—19th century—History and criticism 891.73309
Russian fiction—20th century—History and criticism 891.734409
Russian language 491.7
Russian language—Business Russian 491.78002465
Russian language—Conversation and phrase books 491.7834
Russian language—Conversation and phrase books—English 491.783421
Russian language—Dictionaries 491.73
Russian language—Dictionaries—English 491.7321
Russian language—Grammar 491.75; 491.782; 491.782421
Russian language—Readers 491.786; 491.786421
Russian language—Textbooks for foreign speakers—English 491.782421; 491.783421
Russian language—Verb 491.75; 491.782; 491.782421
Russian literature 891.7; 891.708
Russian literature—To 1700 891.708001
Russian literature—To 1700—History and criticism 891.709001
Russian literature—19th century 891.708003
Russian literature—19th century—History and criticism 891.709003
Russian literature—20th century 891.708004; 891.7080042; 891.7080044
Russian literature—20th century—History and criticism 891.709004; 891.7090042; 891.7090044
Russian literature—20th century—Translations into English 891.708004; 891.7080042; 891.7080044
Russian literature—History and criticism 891.709
Russian literature—Translations into English 891.708
Russian philology 491.7
Russian poetry 891.71; 891.71008
Russian poetry—19th century 891.713; 891.71308
Russian poetry—19th century—Translations into English 891.71308
Russian poetry—20th century 891.714; 891.71408; 891.7142; 891.714208; 891.7144; 891.714408

Russian poetry—20th century—Translations into English 891.71408; 891.714408
Russian poetry—History and criticism 891.71009
Russian poetry—Translations into English 891.71008
Russian wit and humor 891.77008
Russians 305.89171
Russkaia pravoslavnaia tserkov' 281.947
Russkaia pravoslavnaia tserkov'—History 281.947
Russkaia pravoslavnaia tserkov'—History—20th century 281.947
Russo-Finnish War, 1939–1940 948.97032
Russo-Japanese War, 1904–1905 952.031
Russo-Turkish War, 1877–1878 947.081
Rut 591.562
Ruth, Babe, 1895–1948 796.357092
Ruth (Biblical figure) 222.3509505
Rutherford family 929.20941; 929.20973
Rutledge, Alex (Fictitious character) 813.54
Rutledge, Ian (Fictitious character) 813.54
Ruusbroec, Jan van, 1293–1381 248.22092
Rwanda 967.571
Rwanda—History 967.571
Rwanda—History—Civil War, 1994 967.57104
Ryan, Blackie (Fictitious character) 813.54
Ryan, Blackie (Fictitious character)—Fiction 813.54
Ryan, Jack (Fictitious character) 813.54
Ryan, Jack (Fictitious character)—Fiction 813.54
Ryan, Nolan, 1947– 796.357092
Rye flour 641.3314
Rye, John (Fictitious character) 813.54
Ryland, Garth (Fictitious character) 813.54
Ryland, Garth (Fictitious character)—Fiction 813.54
Saab 900 automobile 629.2222
Saab 900 automobile—Maintenance and repair 629.28722
Saab 900 automobile—Maintenance and repair—Handbooks, manuals, etc. 629.28722
Sabal 584.5
Sabbath 263.2; 296.41
Sabbath—Liturgy 296.45
Sabbath—Liturgy—Texts 296.45; 296.45047
Sabbath—Meditations 296.41
Sabbatical leave 371.104; 378.121
Sabbatical year (Judaism) 296.4391
SABRE (Computer system) 387.74220285
Sabrina the Teenage Witch (Fictitious character) 791.4572
Sac County (Iowa) 977.7424
Sac County (Iowa)—Maps 912.777424
Sacagawea, 1786–1884 978.0049745
Saccharides 572.56
Sacco-Vanzetti Trial, Dedham, Mass., 1921 345.7302523
Sackett family (Fictitious characters) 813.52
Sackett family (Fictitious characters)—Fiction 813.52
Sacramento (Calif.) 979.454
Sacramento (Calif.)—Antiquities 979.454
Sacramento County (Calif.) 979.453
Sacramento County (Calif.)—Maps 912.79453
Sacraments 234.16
Sacraments—Catholic Church 234.16; 264.0208
Sacred books 291.82
Sacred books—History and criticism 291.82
Sacred duets 783.122
Sacred songs 782.25
Sacred songs (High voice) 783.3125
Sacred songs (Medium voice) 783.4125
Sacred space 291.35
Sacred stones 291.212; 291.37

Saline water conversion 628.167
Saline water conversion plants 628.167
Saline water conversion—Reverse osmosis process 628.16744
Salinger, J. D. (Jerome David), 1919- 813.54
Salinger, J. D. (Jerome David), 1919- . Catcher in the rye 813.54
Salinger, J. D. (Jerome David), 1919- —Criticism and interpretation 813.54
Salmon 597.56; 639.3756
Salmon fishing 799.1756
Salmonidae 597.55
Salsa (Dance) 793.33
Salsa (Music) 781.64
Salsa (Music)—History and criticism 781.64
Salsas (Cookery) 641.814
Salt 553.632
Salt deposits 553.632
Salt-free diet 613.285
Salt-free diet—Recipes 641.5632
Salt industry and trade 338.476644; 664.4
Salt lake animals 591.7639
Salt marsh ecology 577.69
Salt mines and mining 338.27632
Salt springs 551.498
Salter, Charlie (Fictitious character) 813.54
Salter, Charlie (Fictitious character)—Fiction 813.54
Salts 546.34
Saltwater fishing 799.16
Saltwater fly fishing 799.16
Salvadorans 305.8687284
Salvage 343.0968
Salvage archaeology 930.1
Salvage (Waste, etc.) 363.7282
Salvation 234
Salvation—Biblical teaching 234
Salvation outside the church 234
Salve Regina (Music) 782.292
Salvinorin A 362.294; 615.7883
Sam (Fictitious character : Labatt) 813.54
Samanid dynasty, 9th–10th centuries 958.01
Samba (Dance) 793.33
Sambia (Papua New Guinea people)—Rites and ceremonies 392.14
Same-sex marriage 306.848
Same-sex marriage—Law and legislation 346.016
Same-sex marriage—Religious aspects 291.17835848
Sami (European people) 948.977
Samosas 641.812
Samoyed dog 636.73
Samplers 746.440433
Sampling (Statistics) 001.433; 519.52
Sampras, Pete 796.342092
Samson, Albert (Fictitious character) 813.54
Samson, Albert (Fictitious character)—Fiction 813.54
Samson, Bernard (Fictitious character) 823.914
Samson, Bernard (Fictitious character)—Fiction 823.914
Samson (Biblical judge) 222.32092
Samuel (Biblical judge) 222.43092
San Antonio Metropolitan Area (Tex.) 976.4351
San Antonio Metropolitan Area (Tex.)—Maps 912.764351
San Antonio (Tex.) 976.4351
San Antonio (Tex.)—Antiquities 976.4351
San Antonio (Tex.)—Guidebooks 917.6435104; 917.643510463; 917.643510464
San Antonio (Tex.)—History 976.4351
San Bernardino County (Calif.) 979.495

San Bernardino County (Calif.)—Maps 912.79495
San Diego (Calif.) 979.4985
San Diego (Calif.)—Description and travel 917.949804; 917.94980453; 917.94980454
San Diego (Calif.)—Guidebooks 917.9498504; 917.949850453; 917.949850454
San Diego County (Calif.) 979.498
San Diego County (Calif.)—Guidebooks 917.949804; 917.94980453; 917.94980454
San Diego County (Calif.)—Maps 912.79498
San Francisco 49ers (Football team) 796.332640979461
San Francisco 49ers (Football team)—History 796.332640979461
San Francisco Bay Area (Calif.) 979.46
San Francisco Bay Area (Calif.)—Guidebooks 917.94604; 917.9460453; 917.9460454
San Francisco Bay Area (Calif.)—Tours 917.94604; 917.9460453; 917.9460454
San Francisco (Calif.) 979.461
San Francisco (Calif.)—Guidebooks 917.946104; 917.94610453; 917.94610454
San Francisco (Calif.)—History 979.461
San Francisco (Calif.)—Maps 912.79461
San Francisco (Calif.)—Pictorial works 779.991794610022; 917.946100222; 979.46100222
San Francisco (Calif.)—Tours 917.946104; 917.94610453; 917.94610454
San Gabriel Mountains (Calif.) 979.493
San Gabriel Mountains (Calif.)—Guidebooks 917.9493
San Joaquin Valley (Calif.) 979.48
San Juan Islands (Wash.) 979.774
San Juan Islands (Wash.)—Guidebooks 917.977404; 917.97740443; 917.97740444
San Mateo County (Calif.) 979.469
San Mateo County (Calif.)—Maps 912.79469
Sanctification 234.8
Sanctions (International law) 341.582
Sanctuary gardens 635.9; 712
Sanctuary movement 261.832
Sand 553.622
Sand and gravel industry 338.2762
Sand and gravel industry—California 338.276209794
Sand and gravel industry—California—Los Angeles County—Maps 338.2762097493022
Sand Creek Massacre, Colo., 1864 973.737
Sand dollars 593.95
Sand dune ecology 577.583
Sand dunes 551.375
Sand, George, 1804–1876 843.8
Sand, George, 1804–1876—Criticism and interpretation 843.8
Sand toys 688.72
Sand traps 796.352068
Sandburg, Carl, 1878–1967 811.52
Sanders, Barry, 1968- 796.332092
Sanders, Deion 796.332092; 796.357092
Sanders, John, Inspector (Fictitious character) 813.54
Sanders, John, Inspector (Fictitious character)—Fiction 813.54
Sandhill crane 598.32
Sandino, Augusto César, 1895–1934 972.85051092
Sandpaintings 751.49
Sandplay—Therapeutic use 616.891653
Sandstone 553.53
Sandwich generation 306.87; 306.874
Sandwiches 641.84
Sandy soil gardening 635.955
Sanford, John B., 1904- 813.52
Sangamon County (Ill.) 977.356

Sangamon County (Ill.)—Genealogy 929.30977356; 929.377356
Sangamon County (Ill.)—Maps 912.77356
Sanilac County (Mich.) 977.443
Sanilac County (Mich.)—Maps 912.77443
Sanitary engineering 628
Sanitary landfills 628.44564
Sanitation 363.72
Śaṅkarācārya 181.482
Sankhya 181.41
Sanskrit drama 891.22; 891.22008
Sanskrit drama—History and criticism 891.22009
Sanskrit drama—Translations into English 891.22008
Sanskrit language 491.2
Sanskrit language—Grammar 491.25; 491.2824; 491.282421
Sanskrit literature 891.2; 891.208
Sanskrit literature—History and criticism 891.209
Sanskrit philology 491.2
Sanskrit poetry 891.21; 891.21008
Sanskrit poetry—History and criticism 891.21009
Sanskrit poetry—Translations into English 891.21008
Santa Barbara (Calif.) 979.491
Santa Barbara County (Calif.) 979.491
Santa Barbara County (Calif.)—Maps 912.79491
Santa Catalina Island (Calif.) 979.493
Santa Catalina Island (Calif.)—Guidebooks 917.9493
Santa Clara County (Calif.) 979.473
Santa Clara County (Calif.)—Maps 912.79473
Santa Claus 394.2663
Santa Fe (N.M.) 978.956
Santa Fe (N.M.)—Guidebooks 917.895604; 917.89560453; 917.89560454
Santa Fe (N.M.)—History 978.956
Santa Fe (N.M.)—Pictorial works 978.95600222
Santa Fe National Historic Trail 978; 978.02
Santa Fe National Historic Trail—History 978
Santayana, George, 1863–1952 191
Santeria 299.674
Santiago de Compostela (Spain) 946.11
Santo Daime (Cult) 299.93
SAP R/3 650.028553769
Sapindaceae 583.78
Sapir-Whorf hypothesis 401
Sappho 884.01
Sappho—Translations into English 884.01
Ṣaqqārah (Egypt) 932
Ṣaqqārah (Egypt)—Antiquities 932
Sarajevo (Bosnia and Hercegovina) 949.742
Sarajevo (Bosnia and Hercegovina)—History 949.742
Sarajevo (Bosnia and Hercegovina)—History—Siege, 1992– —Personal narratives, Bosnian 949.703
Sarasota County (Fla.) 975.961
Sarasota County (Fla.)—Maps 912.75961
Sarasota Metropolitan Area (Fla.) 975.961
Sarasota Metropolitan Area (Fla.)—Maps 912.75961
Saratoga Campaign, 1777 973.333
Sarawak 959.54
Sarawak—History 959.54
Sarawak—Politics and government 959.54
Sargassum 579.888
Sargat culture 957.3
Saroyan, William, 1908– 818.5209
Sarrasri, Daine (Fictitious character) 813.54
Sarraute, Nathalie 843.914
Sarraute, Nathalie—Criticism and interpretation 843.914
Sarton, May, 1912– 811.52

Sarton, May, 1912– —Diaries 818.5203
Sartre, Jean Paul, 1905– 194; 842.912; 842.914; 848.91409
Sartre, Jean Paul, 1905– —Criticism and interpretation 848.91409
Sartre, Jean Paul, 1905– —Translations into English 842.912; 842.914
SAS/ACCESS 005.3042
SAS/C 005.3042; 005.453
SAS (Computer file) 005.3042
SAS/GRAPH 005.3042
Saskatchewan 971.24
Sasquatch 001.944
Sassoon, Siegfried, 1886–1967 821.912
Sassoon, Siegfried, 1886–1967—Criticism and interpretation 821.912
Satanism 133.422
Satanism—Law and legislation 344.096; 345.0288
Satellite geodesy 526.1
Satellite meteorology 551.6354
Satellites 523.98
Sathya Sai Baba, 1926– 294.5092
Sati 393.9
Satire 808.87
Satire, English 827
Satire, English—History and criticism 827.009
Satire—History and criticism 809.7
Satire, Latin 877; 877.01
Satire, Latin—History and criticism 877.009; 877.0109
Satire, Latin—Translations into English 877.008; 877.0108
Saturated fatty acids 572.57
Saturated fatty acids in human nutrition 613.284
Saturday night live (Television program) 791.4572
Saturn launch vehicles 629.47
Saturn (Planet) 523.46
Sauce industry 338.47641814
Sauces 641.814
Saudi Arabia 953.8
Saudi Arabia—Economic policy 338.9538
Saudi Arabia—Guidebooks 915.3804; 915.380453
Saudi Arabia—History 953.8
Saudi Arabia—Social conditions 953.8
Saudi Arabian students 371.829927538
Sauk County (Wis.) 977.576
Sauk County (Wis.)—Maps 912.77576
Saunders County (Neb.) 978.2296
Saunders County (Neb.)—Maps 912.782296
Saunders family 929.20973
Sausage (Fictitious character) 823.914
Sausages 641.36
Saussure, Ferdinand de, 1857–1913 410.92
Savage family 929.20973
Savage family (Fictitious characters) 813.54
Savanna animals 591.748
Savanna ecology 577.48
Savannah (Ga.) 975.8724
Savannah (Ga.)—Guidebooks 917.5872404; 917.587240443; 917.587240444
Savannah (Ga.)—History 975.8724
Saving and investment 339.43
Saving and investment—Developing countries 339.43091724
Saving and investment—Japan 339.430952
Saving and investment—United States 339.430973
Savings and loan associations 332.32
Savings and loan associations—Corrupt practices 364.168

Savings and loan associations—Corrupt practices—
United States 332.320973; 364.168
Savings and loan associations—Illinois 332.3209773
Savings and loan associations—Illinois—Statistics—
Periodicals 332.3209773021
Savings and loan associations—Law and legislation
346.08232
Savings and loan associations—Law and legislation—
United States 346.7308232
Savings and loan associations—United States
332.320973
Savings and loan associations—United States—
Directories 332.3202573
Savings and loan associations—United States—
Management 332.32068
Savings and loan associations—United States—
Periodicals 332.320973
Savings and Loan Bailout, 1989–1995 332.320973
Savings banks 332.21
Savings banks—United States 332.210973
Savings banks—United States—Statistics—Periodicals
332.210973021
Savings bonds 332.6323
Savings bonds—United States 332.6323
Sawyer County (Wis.) 977.516
Sawyer County (Wis.)—Maps 912.77516
Sawyer, Tom (Fictitious character) 813.4
Sawyer, Tom (Fictitious character)—Fiction 813.4
Saxon (Fictitious character) 813.54
Saxon (Fictitious character)—Fiction 813.54
Saxophone and piano music 788.7
Saxophone music 788.7
Saxophone music (Jazz) 788.7165
Sayers, Dorothy L. (Dorothy Leigh), 1893–1957
823.912
Sayers, Dorothy L. (Dorothy Leigh), 1893–1957—
Criticism and interpretation 823.912
Sayler, Catherine (Fictitious character) 813.54
Sayler, Catherine (Fictitious character)—Fiction 813.54
Sāzmān-i Mujāhidīn-i Khalq (Iran) 955.054
Scagliola 666.89; 747.3
Scalare 597.74; 639.3774
Scalds and scaldic poetry 839.61
Scale insects 595.752
Scalia, Antonin 347.732634
Scaling (Social sciences) 300.72
Scallops 594.4
Scandals 302.24
Scandals in mass media 302.23
Scandinavia 948
Scandinavia—Civilization 948
Scandinavia—Description and travel 914.804;
914.80489; 914.8049
Scandinavia—Guidebooks 914.804; 914.80489; 914.8049
Scandinavia—History 948
Scandinavian languages 439.5
Scandinavian literature 839.5
Scanning electron microscopy 502.825
Scanning probe microscopy 502.85
Scanning systems 621.367
Scanning transmission electron microscopy 502.825;
570.2825
Scanning tunneling microscopy 502.825; 502.85
Scarabaeidae 595.7649
Scarecrow (Fictitious character : Baum) 791.4372;
813.4
Scarpetta, Kay (Fictitious character) 813.54
Scarpetta, Kay (Fictitious character)—Fiction 813.54
Scarves 646.48

Scattering (Physics) 539.758
Scepters 391.44; 739.2
Schartauanism 284.1
Schedules, School 371.242
Schedules, School—United States 371.2420973
Scheduling 658.53
Scheduling—Computer programs 005.369
Scheler, Max, 1874–1928 193
Scheme (Computer program language) 005.133
Schenkerian analysis 781
Schiller, Friedrich, 1759–1805 831.6
Schiller, Friedrich, 1759–1805—Criticism and
interpretation 831.6
Schism, The Great Western, 1378–1417 270.5;
282.09023
Schist sculpture 731.2
Schizophrenia 616.8982
Schizophrenia—Etiology 616.8982071
Schizophrenia—Pathophysiology 616.898207
Schizophrenia—Physiological aspects 616.8982
Schizophrenia—Treatment 616.898206; 616.89820651
Schizophrenics—Family relationships 616.8982
Schliemann, Heinrich, 1822–1890 930.1092
Schmidt family 929.20973
Schmidt, Inspector (Fictitious character) 813.52
Schmidt, Inspector (Fictitious character)—Fiction
813.52
Schmidt telescopes 522.2
Schnitzler, Arthur, 1862–1931 832.8; 833.8; 838.809
Schnitzler, Arthur, 1862–1931—Criticism and
interpretation 838.809
Schnitzler, Arthur, 1862–1931—Translations into
English 832.8; 833.8
Schoenberg, Arnold, 1874–1951 780.92
Schoenberg, Arnold, 1874–1951—Criticism and
interpretation 780.92
Scholarly periodicals 050
Scholarly periodicals—Editing 808.06605
Scholarly publishing 070.5
Scholarly Web sites 025.060012
Scholars 001.2092
Scholarships 371.223; 378.34
Scholarships—Directories 378.34025
Scholarships—United States 378.340973
Scholarships—United States—Directories 378.3402573
Scholastic Aptitude Test 378.1662
Scholastic Aptitude Test—Interpretation 378.1662
Scholastic Aptitude Test—Statistics 378.1662
Scholastic Assessment Test 378.1662
School administrators 371.20092; 371.2011
School administrators—Training of 371.20711
School administrators—Training of—United States
371.20711
School-age child care 362.712
School-age child care—United States 362.712
School attendance 371.294
School-based management 371.2
School-based management—United States 371.200973
School boards 379.1531
School boards—United States 379.15310973
School bookstores 381.4537132
School buildings 371.6
School buildings—United States 727.0973
School buildings—United States—Design and
construction 727.0973
School camps 371.384
School chaplains 371.2
School children—Food 371.716
School children—Mental health 371.713

School children—Psychology 371.8019
School children—Transportation 371.872
School children—Transportation—United States 371.8720973
School choice—United States 379.1110973
School contests 371.89
School contests—United States—Directories 371.89
School credits 371.218
School crossing guards 363.1257
School custodians 371.68
School day 371.244
School discipline 371.5
School discipline—Great Britain 371.50941
School discipline—Law and legislation 344.0793
School discipline—Law and legislation—United States 344.730793
School discipline—United States 371.50973
School districts 379.1535
School districts—Law and legislation 344.073
School districts—Law and legislation—New Jersey 344.749073
School employees 371.201
School enrollment 371.219
School environment 370.158
School facilities 371.6
School failure 371.285
School field trips 371.384
School grade placement 371.264
School grounds 371.61
School health services 371.71
School health services—United States 371.710973
School hygiene 371.71
School hygiene—United States 371.71
School improvement programs 371.207
School improvement programs—Great Britain 371.207
School improvement programs—United States 371.207
School integration 379.263
School integration—Arkansas 379.26309767
School integration—Arkansas—Little Rock—History—20th century 379.2630976773
School integration—United States 379.2630973
School librarians 027.8092
School libraries 027.8
School libraries—Activity programs 027.8
School libraries—Administration 025.1978
School libraries—Automation 027.80285
School libraries—United States 027.80973
School libraries—United States—Administration 025.19780973
School libraries—United States—Data processing 027.80285
School lunchrooms, cafeterias, etc. 371.716
School management and organization 371.2
School management and organization—Australia 371.200994
School management and organization—England 371.200942
School management and organization—Europe 371.20094
School management and organization—Great Britain 371.200941
School management and organization—Handbooks, manuals, etc. 371.2
School management and organization—Nigeria 371.2009669
School management and organization—United States 371.200973
School management and organization—United States—Data processing 371.200285

School management and organization—United States—Handbooks, manuals, etc. 371.200973
School management and organization—United States—Periodicals 371.20097305
School milk programs 371.716
School museums 069
School music—Instruction and study 372.87; 780.712
School music—Instruction and study—Activity programs 372.87044
School music—Instruction and study—Great Britain 372.870941
School natural areas 508.071
School nursing 371.712
School personnel management 371.201
School personnel management—United States 371.2010973
School plant management 371.6
School principals 371.20092; 371.2012
School principals—United States 371.20120973
School psychologists 371.713
School psychology 370.15; 371.713
School psychology—United States 370.150973; 371.7130973
School shootings 371.782
School sites 371.61
School social work 371.46; 371.7
School social work—United States 371.460973; 371.70973
School sports 796.069
School superintendents 371.20092; 371.2011
School superintendents—United States 371.2011
School supervision 371.203
School supervision—United States 371.2030973
School-to-work transition 371.227
School-to-work transition—United States 371.227
School vandalism 371.782
School violence 371.58; 371.782
School violence—United States 371.7820973
School violence—United States—Prevention 371.7820973
School violence—United States—Prevention—Handbooks, manuals, etc. 371.7820973
School week 371.242
School year 371.23
School yearbooks 371.805; 371.8976
Schools 371
Schools, American 371.00973
Schools—Decentralization—United States 379.1535
Schools—Furniture, equipment, etc. 371.63
Schools, German 371.00943
Schools of architecture 720.9
Schools of public health 362.1071
Schools—Public relations 659.2937; 659.29371
Schools—United States—Safety measures 363.1137100973; 363.11937100973
Schopenhauer, Arthur, 1788–1860 193
Schreiner, Olive, 1855–1920 823.8
Schreiner, Olive, 1855–1920—Criticism and interpretation 823.8
Schrödinger equation 530.124
Schrödinger operator 515.724
Schroeder family 929.20973
Schubert, Franz, 1797–1828 780.92
Schubert, Franz, 1797–1828. Songs 782.42168092
Schultz family 929.20973
Schumann, Robert, 1810–1856 780.92
Schumpeter, Joseph Alois, 1883–1950 330.092
Schutzhund (Dog sport) 791.8
Schuyler County (Ill.)—Maps 912.773475

Schuylkill County (Pa.)—**Genealogy** 929.374817
Schwarzenegger, Arnold 646.75092; 791.43028092
Schwarzkopf, H. Norman, 1934– 355.0092
Schweitzer, Albert, 1875–1965 610.92
Sciaenidae 597.725
Science 500
Science—Abstracts—Periodicals 505
Science, Ancient 509.3
Science and civilization 303.483
Science and state 338.926; 352.745
Science and state—Africa 338.9606
Science and state—Great Britain 338.94106
Science and state—United States 338.97306
Science and the arts 306.45; 700.105
Science—Bibliography 016.5
Science—Bibliography—Catalogs 016.5
Science—Bibliography—Periodicals 016.5
Science—Caricatures and cartoons 741.5973
Science—China 509.51
Science—China—History 509.51
Science clubs 506
Science—Computer programs 502.8553
Science—Computer simulation 501.13
Science consultants 506.84
Science—Data processing 502.85
Science—Dictionaries 503
Science—Encyclopedias 503
Science—Examinations 507.6
Science—Examinations, questions, etc. 507.6
Science—Experiments 507.8
Science—Experiments—History 507.24
Science fiction 808.838762
Science fiction, American 813.08762; 813.0876208
Science fiction, American—History and criticism 813.0876209
Science fiction, American—Periodicals 813.0876205; 813.0876208005
Science fiction, American—Women authors 813.08762089287
Science fiction, Australian 823.0876208994
Science fiction—Authorship 808.38762
Science fiction—Bibliography 016.808838762
Science fiction, Canadian 808.83876208971
Science fiction comic books, strips, etc. 741.5973
Science fiction—Dictionaries 809.3876203
Science fiction, English 823.08762
Science fiction, English—History and criticism 823.0876209
Science fiction, European 808.8387620894
Science fiction films 791.43615
Science fiction films—Catalogs 016.79143615
Science fiction films—History and criticism 791.43615
Science fiction—History and criticism 809.38762
Science fiction poetry, American 811.008014
Science fiction, Russian 891.7308762
Science fiction, Russian—Translations into English 891.730876208
Science fiction television programs 791.45615
Science—Great Britain 509.41
Science—Great Britain—History 509.41
Science—Great Britain—History—17th century 509.4109032
Science—Greece 509.495
Science—Greece—History 509.38; 509.495
Science—History 509
Science—History—19th century 509.034
Science—History—Bibliography 016.509
Science—Humor 502.07
Science in mass media 500

Science—India 509.54
Science—India—History 509.54
Science—Information services 026.5
Science—Japan 338.95206; 509.52
Science—Japan—History 509.52
Science—Japan—Information services 507.052
Science—Language 501.4
Science, Medieval 509.02
Science—Methodology 501
Science—Miscellanea 500
Science—Moral and ethical aspects 174.95
Science museums 507.4
Science news 500
Science—Periodicals 505
Science—Periodicals—Bibliography 016.505
Science—Periodicals—Bibliography—Union lists 016.505
Science—Philosophy 501
Science—Philosophy—History 501
Science projects 507.8
Science projects—Handbooks, manuals, etc. 507.8
Science publishing 070.57
Science, Renaissance 509.024
Science rooms and equipment 507.8
Science—Social aspects 303.483
Science—Social aspects—India 303.4830954
Science—Social aspects—Periodicals 303.48305
Science—Soviet Union 509.47
Science—Soviet Union—History 509.47
Science—Study and teaching 507.1
Science—Study and teaching—Activity programs 507.8
Science—Study and teaching (Elementary) 372.35; 372.35044
Science—Study and teaching (Elementary)—Activity programs 372.35044
Science—Study and teaching (Elementary)—Handbooks, manuals, etc. 372.35044
Science—Study and teaching (Elementary)—United States 372.350440973; 372.350973
Science—Study and teaching (Higher) 507.11
Science—Study and teaching (Higher)—United States 507.1173
Science—Study and teaching—Methodology 507.1
Science—Study and teaching—Periodicals 507.1
Science—Study and teaching (Primary) 372.35
Science—Study and teaching (Secondary) 507.12
Science—Study and teaching (Secondary)—Great Britain 507.1241
Science—Study and teaching (Secondary)—United States 507.1273
Science—Study and teaching—United States 507.1073
Science teachers 509.2
Science teachers—Training of 507.11
Science television programs 791.45656
Science—Terminology 501.4
Science—United States 509.73
Science—United States—History 509.73
Science—United States—Information services—Directories 026.502573
Science—Vocational guidance 502.3
Science writers 808.0665
Scientific apparatus and instruments 502.84
Scientific apparatus and instruments industry 338.475028
Scientific archives 026.5
Scientific expeditions 508
Scientific libraries 026.5
Scientific literature 500
Scientific recreations 793.8
Scientists 509.2

Sealing ships 387.248; 623.8248
Sealing (Technology) 621.885
Sealing (Technology)—Handbooks, manuals, etc. 621.885
Seals (Animals) 599.79
Seals (Closures) 621.885
Seals (Numismatics) 737.6
Seals (Numismatics)—China 737.60951
Seamanship 623.88
Seances 133.91
Search and rescue operations 363.3481
Search engines 005.758; 025.04
Search engines—Programming 005.758
Searches and seizures 345.0522
Searches and seizures—United States 345.730522
Searching, Bibliographical 025.524
Seashore animals 591.7699
Seashore biology 578.7699
Seashore ecology 577.699
Seaside resorts 647.94
Seasonal affective disorder 616.8527
Seasons 525.5; 578.43
Seasons in art 704.943
Seasons in literature 808.8033; 809.9333
Seattle Metropolitan Area (Wash.) 979.777
Seattle Region (Wash.) 979.7772
Seattle Region (Wash.)—Guidebooks 917.9777204; 917.977720443; 917.977720444
Seattle (Wash.) 979.7772
Seattle (Wash.)—Guidebooks 917.9777204; 917.977720443; 917.977720444
Seattle (Wash.)—History 979.7772
Seattle (Wash.)—Pictorial works 979.777200222
Seawater 551.4601
Seawater—Analysis 551.46010287
Seawater—Composition 551.4601
Seawater corrosion 620.11223
Secession 973.713
Secession—Southern States 973.713
Second Advent 236.9
Second Advent—Biblical teaching 236.9
Second language acquisition 418; 418.0071
Second person narrative 808.83923; 809.3923
Secondary recovery of oil 622.3382
Secondary School Admission Test 373.1262
Secret friends 177.62; 302.34
Secret societies 366
Secret societies—China 366.0951
Secret societies—History 366
Secretaries 651.3741; 651.3741092
Secretaries—Handbooks, manuals, etc. 651.3741
Secretaries of State (State governments) 352.3872130973
Secretaries—Vocational guidance 651.3741023
Secretion 571.79
Sects 291.9
Sects—United States 200.973
Secular humanism 211.6
Secularism 211.6
Secularism—India 211.60954; 322.10954
Secularism—United States 322.10973
Secularization (Theology) 230; 261
Securities 332.632
Securities—Canada 346.71092
Securities commissions 354.8828
Securities—European Economic Community countries 346.4092
Securities fraud 345.0268
Securities fraud—United States 345.730263

Securities—Great Britain 346.41092
Securities industry 332.632
Securities industry—Data processing 332.6320285
Securities industry—Law and legislation 341.75242; 346.092
Securities—Japan 346.52092
Securities, Privately placed 346.0666
Securities, Privately placed—United States 346.730666
Securities—Taxation—Law and legislation 343.05246
Securities—Taxation—Law and legislation—United States 343.7305246
Securities—United States 332.6320973; 346.73092
Securities—United States—Cases 346.7306660264; 346.730920264
Securities—United States—Digests 346.7309202648
Securities—United States—Examinations, questions, etc. 332.6320973; 346.73092076
Securities—United States—States 346.730666; 346.73092
Security Assistance Program 355.032; 355.0320973
Security classification (Government documents) 352.379
Security classification (Government documents)—United States 352.379
Security clearances 352.379
Security clearances—Law and legislation 342.0684
Security clearances—United States 352.379
Security consultants 658.47
Security, International 327.17; 341.72
Security (Law) 346.074
Security (Law)—British Columbia 346.711074
Security (Law)—United States 346.73074
Security (Law)—United States—Cases 346.730740264
Security (Law)—United States—Outlines, syllabi, etc. 346.73074
Security (Law)—United States—States 346.73074
Security systems 621.38928; 658.47
Security systems industry 338.4762138928
Seder 296.437
Sedimentary basins 551.44; 551.8
Sedimentation and deposition 551.303
Sedimentology 552.5
Sediments (Geology) 551.304
Sedum 583.72
Seed industry and trade 338.17
Seeds 575.68; 581.467
Seeds—Dispersal 581.467
Seeds—Growth 575.6838
Seeds in art 704.9434
Seeds—Size 581.467
Seeton, Miss (Fictitious character) 823.914
Seeton, Miss (Fictitious character)—Fiction 823.914
Seferis, George, 1900–1971 889.132
Seferis, George, 1900–1971—Translations into English 889.132
Sega Genesis video games 794.8
Seged 296.439
Segregated funds 332.6327
Segregation 344.0798
Seinfeld (Television program) 791.4572
Seismic event location 551.220287
Seismic prospecting 622.1592
Seismic reflection method 622.1592
Seismic refraction method 622.1592
Seismic tomography 551.10287; 551.220287
Seismic waves 551.22
Seismograms 551.22021
Seismological stations 551.22072
Seismology 551.22

Seneca Indians 305.89755; 974.70049755
Seneca Indians—Folklore 398.2089975
Seneca, Lucius Annaeus, ca. 4 B.C.–65 A.D. 872.01
Seneca, Lucius Annaeus, ca. 4 B.C.–65 A.D.—Influence 872.01
Seneca, Lucius Annaeus, ca. 4 B.C.–65 A.D.—Tragedies 872.01
Seneca, Lucius Annaeus, ca. 4 B.C.–65 A.D.— Translations into English 872.01
Senegal 966.3
Senegal—Economic conditions 330.9663
Senegal—Economic conditions—Periodicals 330.9663005
Senesh, Hannah, 1921–1944 940.5318092
Senghor, Léopold Sédar, 1906– 841.914
Senghor, Léopold Sédar, 1906– —Criticism and interpretation 841.914
Senile dementia 618.9768983
Seniority system of legislative committees 328.365
Sense organs 573.87
Senses and sensation 152.1; 573.87; 612.8
Senses and sensation—Testing 152.1
Sensory receptors 573.8728
Sentences (Criminal procedure) 345.0772
Sentences (Criminal procedure)—California 345.7940772
Sentences (Criminal procedure)—Florida 345.7590772
Sentences (Criminal procedure)—Great Britain 345.410772
Sentences (Criminal procedure)—Massachusetts 345.7440772
Sentences (Criminal procedure)—Minnesota 345.7760772
Sentences (Criminal procedure)—United States 345.730772
Sentences (Criminal procedure)—United States— Digests 345.73077202648
Sentences (Criminal procedure)—United States— Periodicals 345.73077205
Sentences (Criminal procedure)—Wisconsin 345.7750772
Sentra automobile 629.2222
Sentra automobile—Maintenance and repair 629.28722
Sentra automobile—Maintenance and repair— Handbooks, manuals, etc. 629.28722
Seoul (Korea) 951.95
Seoul (Korea)—Guidebooks 915.195
Seoul (Korea)—Pictorial works 951.95
Separated women 305.489653
Separation-individuation 155.41825
Separation of powers 320.404
Separation of powers—United States 320.473
Separation of powers—United States—Cases 342.73044
Separation of powers—United States—History 320.473
Separation (Technology) 660.2842
Separators (Machines) 660.2842
Sephardim 909.04924
Sephardim—History 909.04924
Septic tanks 628.742
Septicemia 616.944
Septoria diseases 632.45
Septuplets 306.875
Sepulchral monuments 731.549
Sequatchie County (Tenn.)—Genealogy 929.376877
Sequence stratigraphy 551.7
Sequences (Mathematics) 515.24
Sequential analysis 519.54
Sequential injection analysis 543.08
Sequential machine theory 511.3

Sequoia National Park (Calif.) 979.486
Sequoia National Park (Calif.)—Guidebooks 917.9486
Serbian language 491.82
Serbian language—Dictionaries 491.823
Serbian language—Dictionaries—English 491.82321
Serbian philology 491.82
Serbo-Croatian language 491.82
Serbo-Croatian language—Dictionaries 491.823
Serbo-Croatian language—Dictionaries—English 491.82321
Serendipity in science 501
Serer literature 896.321
Serge 677.6
Serging 646.2044
Serial murderers 364.1523
Serial murders 364.1523
Serial murders—United States 364.15230973
Serial publications 050
Serialized fiction 808.83
Serials control systems 025.3432
Serials librarianship 025.1732; 025.3432
Serials librarianship—United States 025.17320973
Serials subscription agencies 025.2832
Serials subscription agencies—Directories 070.572
Series authority records (Information retrieval) 025.3222
Series headings (Cataloging) 025.322
Series, Infinite 515.243
Series statements (Cataloging) 025.324
Serigraphy 764.8
Serigraphy, American 764.80973
Sermon on the mount 226.906
Sermon on the mount—Criticism, interpretation, etc. 226.906; 241.53
Sermons 291.43
Sermons, American 252.00973
Sermons, American—African American authors 252.008996073
Sermons, American—Women authors 252.0082
Sermons, English 252
Sermons, English—Scotland 252.009411
Sermons, Latin 252
Sermons, Latin—Translations into English 252
Sermons—Mormon authors 252.093
Sermons—Outlines, syllabi, etc. 251.02
Serotonin 612.8042; 615.78
Serotonin—Physiological effect 615.7; 615.71
Serotonin—Receptors 612.8042
Serra, Junípero, 1713–1784 979.402092
Servant of Jehovah 224.1
Service industries 338.4
Service industries—Canada 338.40971
Service industries—Canada—Statistics—Periodicals 338.40971021
Service industries—Management 658
Service industries—Marketing 658.8
Service industries—Marketing—Management 658.8
Service industries—Quality control 658.562
Service industries—United States 338.40973
Service industries—United States—Management 658.8
Service industries—United States—Marketing 658.8
Service industries—United States—Statistics 338.40973021
Service stations 629.286
Service stations—Collectibles—United States—Catalogs 629.2860973075
Service stations—Law and legislation 343.088566553827
Service stations—Law and legislation—United States 343.73088566553827

Service stations—United States—History 629.2860973
Servitudes 346.0435
Servitudes—United States 346.730435
Servlets 005.376
Servomechanisms 629.8323
Sesame Street (Television program) 791.4572
Session laws 348.022
Set theory 511.322
Setār (Iranian musical instrument) 787.82
Seton, Elizabeth Ann, Saint, 1774–1821 271.9102
Setting (Literature) 808.8022
Settlement costs 346.04373
Settlement costs—United States 346.7304373
Seven Wonders of the World 722; 930
Seven Years' War, 1756–1763 940.2534
Seventh-Day Adventists 286.732
Seventh-Day Adventists—Biography 286.7092
Seventh-Day Adventists—Doctrines 230.6732
Seventh-Day Adventists—Membership 286.732
Seventh-Day Adventists—Sermons 252.06732
Severance pay—Law and legislation 344.012596
Severance pay—Law and legislation—Great Britain 344.41012596
Seville (Spain) 946.86
Seville (Spain)—Guidebooks 914.68604; 914.6860483
Sewage 363.7284; 628.3
Sewage disposal 363.7284; 628.3
Sewage disposal in the ocean 363.7284
Sewage disposal plants 628.3
Sewage disposal plants—Management 620.3060
Sewage disposal, Rural 628.74
Sewage irrigation 628.3623
Sewage lagoons 628.351
Sewage—Microbiology 628.35
Sewage—Purification 363.7284; 628.3
Sewage—Purification—Activated sludge process 628.354
Sewage—Purification—Aeration 628.35
Sewage—Purification—Biological treatment 628.35
Sewage—Purification—Filtration 628.352
Sewage—Purification—Nitrogen removal 628.357
Sewage—Purification—Phosphate removal 628.358
Sewage sludge 628.364
Sewage sludge as fertilizer 631.869
Sewage sludge digestion 628.351
Sewage sludge—Drying 628.35; 628.354
Sewage sludge—Management 363.7284; 628.364068
Seward County (Neb.) 978.2324
Seward County (Neb.)—Maps 912.782324
Sewell, Hitchcock (Fictitious character) 813.54
Sewerage 628.2
Sewing 646.2
Sewing machines 646.2044; 681.7677
Sex 306.7
Sex addiction 616.8583
Sex addicts 362.27
Sex addicts—Religious life 291.566
Sex between psychotherapist and patient 616.8914
Sex—Biblical teaching 241.66
Sex (Biology) 571.8
Sex (Biology)—Evolution 576.855
Sex—Caricatures and cartoons 741.5973
Sex change 305.3
Sex crimes 364.153
Sex customs 306.7; 306.77
Sex customs—Europe 306.7094
Sex customs—Europe—History 306.7094
Sex customs—Great Britain 306.70941
Sex customs—Great Britain—History 306.70941

Sex customs—Great Britain—History—19th century 306.70941
Sex customs—History 306.709
Sex customs—United States 306.70973
Sex customs—United States—History 306.70973
Sex—Dictionaries 306.703
Sex differences 155.33; 612.6
Sex differences in education 370.151
Sex differences in education—United States 370.151
Sex differences (Psychology) 155.33
Sex differences (Psychology) in old age 155.67
Sex discrimination against women 305.42
Sex discrimination against women—Law and legislation 342.0878
Sex discrimination against women—Law and legislation—United States 342.730878
Sex discrimination against women—United States 305.420973
Sex discrimination in criminal justice administration—United States 364.973082
Sex discrimination in education 379.26
Sex discrimination in education—United States 379.26
Sex discrimination in employment 331.4133; 354.9082
Sex discrimination in employment—Great Britain 331.41330941
Sex discrimination in employment—Law and legislation 344.01133
Sex discrimination in employment—Law and legislation—Great Britain 344.4101133
Sex discrimination in employment—Law and legislation—United States 344.7301413J
Sex discrimination in employment—United States 331.41330973
Sex—Folklore 398.27
Sex—History 306.709
Sex—Humor 306.70207
Sex in art 700.4538; 704.9428
Sex in literature 808.803538; 809.933538
Sex in marriage—Religious aspects 291.441
Sex in motion pictures 791.436538
Sex in rabbinical literature 296.366
Sex instruction 613.9071; 613.96
Sex instruction for boys 613.953
Sex instruction for children 372.372; 612.60071; 613.9071; 649.65
Sex instruction for children—Religious aspects 291.566
Sex instruction for children—Religious aspects—Christianity 241.66
Sex instruction for gay men 613.96086642
Sex instruction for girls 613.955
Sex instruction for men 613.952; 613.96081
Sex instruction for teenagers 613.90712; 613.951071
Sex instruction for teenagers—Religious aspects 291.566
Sex instruction for women 613.954; 613.96082
Sex instruction for youth—United States 613.951071
Sex instruction literature 613.96
Sex instruction—United States—Curricula 613.9071273
Sex offenders—Rehabilitation 616.8583
Sex offenders—United States 364.153092273
Sex-oriented businesses 338.473067
Sex-oriented periodicals 306.705
Sex—Philosophy 306.701
Sex Pistols (Musical group) 782.421660922
Sex (Psychology) 155.3
Sex (Psychology) in literature 808.803538; 809.933538
Sex—Religious aspects 291.178357; 291.566
Sex—Religious aspects—Catholic Church 241.66
Sex—Religious aspects—Christianity 241.66; 261.8357

Sex—Religious aspects—Judaism 296.366
Sex role 155.3; 305.3
Sex role—History 305.309
Sex role in the work environment 306.3615
Sex role—Religious aspects 291.178343
Sex role—Religious aspects—Christianity 261.8343
Sex role—United States 305.30973
Sex therapy 616.858306
Sex tourism 306.74
Sexism 305.3
Sexism in higher education 378.008; 378.0082
Sexology 306.7
Sexology—History 306.709
Sexology—Research 306.7072
Sexton, Anne 811.54
Sexton, Anne—Criticism and interpretation 811.54
Sexual abuse victims 362.883
Sexual abuse victims—Rehabilitation 616.8583
Sexual behavior in animals 591.562
Sexual consent 176; 346.013
Sexual desire disorders 616.8583
Sexual deviation 306.77; 616.8583
Sexual dimorphism (Animals) 591.46
Sexual division of labor 306.3615
Sexual dominance and submission 306.775
Sexual ethics 176
Sexual ethics for teenagers 176.0835
Sexual ethics—United States 176.0973
Sexual excitement 155.31
Sexual exercises 613.96
Sexual fantasies in literature 808.803538; 809.933538
Sexual harassment 331.4133
Sexual harassment in education 371.58; 371.786; 379.26
Sexual harassment in education—United States 379.26
Sexual harassment in universities and colleges—United States 378.1958; 379.26
Sexual harassment—Law and legislation 344.014133
Sexual harassment—Law and legislation—United States 344.73014133
Sexual harassment of women 305.42
Sexual harassment of women—Law and legislation 344.014133
Sexual harassment of women—Law and legislation—United States 344.73014133
Sexual harassment of women—United States 305.420973
Sexual harassment—Prevention 658.3145
Sexual harassment—United States 305.30973
Sexual misconduct by clergy 253.2
Sexual selection in animals 591.562
Sexually abused children 362.76
Sexually abused children—Pastoral counseling of 261.83272; 291.1783272
Sexually abused children—United States 362.760973
Sexually transmitted diseases 616.951
Sexually transmitted diseases—Atlases 616.95100222
Seychelles 969.6
Seychelles—Guidebooks 916.9604
Seychelles literature (French Creole) 840
SGML (Document markup language) 005.72
Shackleton, Ernest Henry, Sir, 1874–1922 919.8904
Shackleton, Ernest Henry, Sir, 1874–1922—Journeys 919.8904
Shade-tolerant plants 635.9543
Shade trees 635.9771
Shades and shadows in art 701.8
Shadow (Fictitious character) 813.52
Shadow (Fictitious character)—Fiction 813.52

Shadow-pictures 791.53
Shadow shows 791.53
Shadowing (Differentiable dynamical systems) 515.352
Shaffer family 929.20973
Shaffer, Peter, 1926– 822.914
Shaffer, Peter, 1926– —Criticism and interpretation 822.914
Shaker decorative arts 745.088288
Shaker furniture 749.213088288
Shakers 289.8
Shakers—United States 289.8
Shakers—United States—History 289.8
Shakespeare, William, 1564–1616 822.33
Shakespeare, William, 1564–1616—Allusions 822.33
Shakespeare, William, 1564–1616. Antony and Cleopatra 822.33
Shakespeare, William, 1564–1616. As you like it 822.33
Shakespeare, William, 1564–1616—Authorship 822.33
Shakespeare, William, 1564–1616—Authorship—Baconian theory 822.33
Shakespeare, William, 1564–1616—Authorship—Marlowe theory 822.33
Shakespeare, William, 1564–1616—Authorship—Oxford theory 822.33
Shakespeare, William, 1564–1616—Bibliography 016.82233
Shakespeare, William, 1564–1616—Bibliography—Folios. 1623 822.33
Shakespeare, William, 1564–1616—Bibliography—Quartos 822.33
Shakespeare, William, 1564–1616—Biography 822.33
Shakespeare, William, 1564–1616—Characters 822.33
Shakespeare, William, 1564–1616—Characters—Dictionaries 822.33
Shakespeare, William, 1564–1616—Characters—Fools 822.33
Shakespeare, William, 1564–1616—Characters—Heroes 822.33
Shakespeare, William, 1564–1616—Characters—Mentally ill 822.33
Shakespeare, William, 1564–1616—Characters—Women 822.33
Shakespeare, William, 1564–1616—Childhood and youth 822.33
Shakespeare, William, 1564–1616—Comedies 822.33
Shakespeare, William, 1564–1616. Comedy of errors 822.33
Shakespeare, William, 1564–1616—Concordances 822.33
Shakespeare, William, 1564–1616—Contemporaries 822.309; 822.33
Shakespeare, William, 1564–1616. Coriolanus 822.33
Shakespeare, William, 1564–1616—Criticism and interpretation 822.33
Shakespeare, William, 1564–1616—Criticism and interpretation—Handbooks, manuals, etc. 822.33
Shakespeare, William, 1564–1616—Criticism and interpretation—History 822.33
Shakespeare, William, 1564–1616—Criticism and interpretation—History—18th century 822.33
Shakespeare, William, 1564–1616—Criticism and interpretation—History—20th century 822.33
Shakespeare, William, 1564–1616—Criticism, Textual 822.33
Shakespeare, William, 1564–1616. Cymbeline 822.33
Shakespeare, William, 1564–1616—Dictionaries 822.33
Shakespeare, William, 1564–1616—Dramatic production 822.33

Shakespeare, William, 1564–1616—Encyclopedias 822.33

Shakespeare, William, 1564–1616—Ethics 822.33

Shakespeare, William, 1564–1616—Examinations 822.33

Shakespeare, William, 1564–1616—Forgeries 822.33

Shakespeare, William, 1564–1616. Hamlet 822.33

Shakespeare, William, 1564–1616. Hamlet—Criticism, Textual 822.33

Shakespeare, William, 1564–1616. Hamlet—Examinations 822.33

Shakespeare, William, 1564–1616. Henry V 822.33

Shakespeare, William, 1564–1616. Henry V—Examinations 822.33

Shakespeare, William, 1564–1616—Histories 822.33

Shakespeare, William, 1564–1616—Illustrations 822.33

Shakespeare, William, 1564–1616. Julius Caesar 822.33

Shakespeare, William, 1564–1616. Julius Caesar—Examinations 822.33

Shakespeare, William, 1564–1616. King Henry IV 822.33

Shakespeare, William, 1564–1616. King Henry IV, Part 1 822.33

Shakespeare, William, 1564–1616. King Henry IV, Part 1—Examinations 822.33

Shakespeare, William, 1564–1616. King Henry VI 822.33

Shakespeare, William, 1564–1616. King Lear 822.33

Shakespeare, William, 1564–1616. King Lear—Criticism, Textual 822.33

Shakespeare, William, 1564–1616. King Lear—Examinations 822.33

Shakespeare, William, 1564–1616. King Richard II 822.33

Shakespeare, William, 1564–1616. King Richard III 822.33

Shakespeare, William, 1564–1616—Knowledge—Art 822.33

Shakespeare, William, 1564–1616—Knowledge—Botany 822.33

Shakespeare, William, 1564–1616—Knowledge—Folklore 822.33

Shakespeare, William, 1564–1616—Knowledge—History 822.33

Shakespeare, William, 1564–1616—Knowledge—Italy 822.33

Shakespeare, William, 1564–1616—Knowledge—Law 822.33

Shakespeare, William, 1564–1616—Knowledge—Literature 822.33

Shakespeare, William, 1564–1616—Knowledge—Manners and customs 822.33

Shakespeare, William, 1564–1616—Knowledge—Medicine 822.33

Shakespeare, William, 1564–1616—Knowledge—Music 822.33

Shakespeare, William, 1564–1616—Knowledge—Natural history 822.33

Shakespeare, William, 1564–1616—Knowledge—Occultism 822.33

Shakespeare, William, 1564–1616—Knowledge—Printing 822.33

Shakespeare, William, 1564–1616—Knowledge—Psychology 822.33

Shakespeare, William, 1564–1616—Knowledge—Rome 822.33

Shakespeare, William, 1564–1616—Knowledge—Sports 822.33

Shakespeare, William, 1564–1616—Language 822.33

Shakespeare, William, 1564–1616—Language—Glossaries, etc. 822.33

Shakespeare, William, 1564–1616—Literary style 822.33

Shakespeare, William, 1564–1616. Love's labour's lost 822.33

Shakespeare, William, 1564–1616. Macbeth 822.33

Shakespeare, William, 1564–1616. Macbeth—Examinations 822.33

Shakespeare, William, 1564–1616. Measure for measure 822.33

Shakespeare, William, 1564–1616. Merchant of Venice 822.33

Shakespeare, William, 1564–1616. Merchant of Venice—Examinations 822.33

Shakespeare, William, 1564–1616. Midsummer night's dream 822.33

Shakespeare, William, 1564–1616. Much ado about nothing 822.33

Shakespeare, William, 1564–1616. Othello 822.33

Shakespeare, William, 1564–1616. Othello—Examinations 822.33

Shakespeare, William, 1564–1616—Outlines, syllabi, etc. 822.33

Shakespeare, William, 1564–1616—Philosophy 822.33

Shakespeare, William, 1564–1616—Political and social views 822.33

Shakespeare, William, 1564–1616—Psychology 822.33

Shakespeare, William, 1564–1616—Religion 822.33

Shakespeare, William, 1564–1616. Romeo and Juliet 822.33

Shakespeare, William, 1564–1616. Romeo and Juliet—Examinations 822.33

Shakespeare, William, 1564–1616. Sonnets 821.3

Shakespeare, William, 1564–1616—Stage history 792.9

Shakespeare, William, 1564–1616—Stage history—To 1625 792.909031

Shakespeare, William, 1564–1616—Stage history—1800–1950 792.909034

Shakespeare, William, 1564–1616—Stage history—1950– 792.909045

Shakespeare, William, 1564–1616—Study and teaching 822.33

Shakespeare, William, 1564–1616—Technique 822.33

Shakespeare, William, 1564–1616—Themes, motives 822.33

Shakespeare, William, 1564–1616. Titus Andronicus 822.33

Shakespeare, William, 1564–1616—Tragedies 822.33

Shakespeare, William, 1564–1616—Tragicomedies 822.33

Shakespeare, William, 1564–1616. Troilus and Cressida 822.33

Shakespeare, William, 1564–1616. Twelfth night 822.33

Shakespeare, William, 1564–1616. Venus and Adonis 821.3

Shakespeare, William, 1564–1616—Versification 822.33

Shakespeare, William, 1564–1616. Winter's tale 822.33

Shaktism 294.5514

Shale shakers 622.3381

Shamanism 291.144; 291.61

Shame 152.4

Shame in adolescence 155.5124

Shanahan, Deets (Fictitious character) 813.54

Shanahan, Deets (Fictitious character)—Fiction 813.54

Shandy, Peter (Fictitious character) 813.54
Shandy, Peter (Fictitious character)—Fiction 813.54
Shanghai (China) 951.132
Shanghai (China)—Guidebooks 915.113204;
  915.11320459; 915.1132046
Shanghai (China)—History 951.132
Shannara (Imaginary place) 813.54
Shannara (Imaginary place)—Fiction 813.54
Shannon, Nick (Fictitious character) 823.914
Shape memory alloys 620.165
Shape theory (Topology) 514.24
Shapiro, Frank (Fictitious character) 823.914
Shapiro, Frank (Fictitious character)—Fiction 823.914
Shapiro, Nathan (Fictitious character) 813.52
Shapiro, Nathan (Fictitious character)—Fiction 813.52
Sharecropping (Islamic law) 346.167104344
Shared services (Management) 650; 658.402
Shared tenant services (Telecommunication) 384
Shareware (Computer software) 005.36
Sharing 177.7
Shark attacks 597.3153
Shark cartilage—Therapeutic use 616.994061
Shark industry 338.37273
Sharks 597.3
Sharks, Fossil 567.3
Sharp family 929.20973
Sharpe, Richard (Fictitious character) 823.914
Sharpe, Richard (Fictitious character)—Fiction 823.914
Shastasauridae 567.937
Shavuot 296.438
Shaw, Bernard, 1856–1950 822.912
Shaw, Bernard, 1856–1950—Appreciation 822.912
Shaw, Bernard, 1856–1950—Correspondence 822.912
Shaw, Bernard, 1856–1950—Criticism and
  interpretation 822.912
Shaw, Bernard, 1856–1950—Dictionaries 822.912
Shaw, Bernard, 1856–1950—Political and social views
  822.912
Shaw, Bernard, 1856–1950. Saint Joan 822.912
Shaw family 929.20973
Shawano County (Wis.) 977.536
Shawano County (Wis.)—Maps 912.77536
Shawm music 788.52
Shawnee Indians 305.8973; 974.004973; 976.6004973
Shawnee Indians—History 974.004973; 976.6004973
Sheaf theory 514.224
Shear walls 693.85
Sheboygan County (Wis.) 977.569
Sheboygan County (Wis.)—Maps 912.77569
Sheds 631.22; 690.892
Sheep 636.3
Sheep breeds 636.3
Sheep dogs 636.737
Sheep industry 338.1763
Sheet-metal work 671.823
Sheet-metal work—Patternmaking 671.821
Sheet-steel 672.823
Shelby County (Ill.) 977.3798
Shelby County (Ill.)—Genealogy 929.3773798
Shelby County (Ill.)—Maps 912.773798
Shelby County (Iowa) 977.7484
Shelby County (Iowa)—Maps 912.777484
Shelby County (Mo.) 977.8323
Shelby County (Mo.)—Maps 912.778323
Shelflisting 025.428
Shelley, Mary Wollstonecraft, 1797–1851 823.7
Shelley, Mary Wollstonecraft, 1797–1851—Criticism
  and interpretation 823.7

Shelley, Mary Wollstonecraft, 1797–1851. Frankenstein
  791.43651; 823.7
Shelley, Percy Bysshe, 1792–1822 821.7
Shelley, Percy Bysshe, 1792–1822—Criticism and
  interpretation 821.7
Shelley, Percy Bysshe, 1792–1822—Literary style 821.7
Shelley, Percy Bysshe, 1792–1822—Manuscripts 821.7
Shelley, Percy Bysshe, 1792–1822—Notebooks,
  sketchbooks, etc. 828.703
Shelley, Percy Bysshe, 1792–1822—Philosophy 821.7
Shelley, Percy Bysshe, 1792–1822—Poetry 821.7
Shelley, Percy Bysshe, 1792–1822—Political and social
  views 821.7
Shelley, Percy Bysshe, 1792–1822. Prometheus
  unbound 821.7
Shellfish culture 639.4
Shells 594.1477
Shells (Engineering) 624.17762
Shells—Pictorial works 595.14770222
Shelters for the homeless 361.05
Shelters for the homeless—United States 363.58
Shelving for books 684.16
Shelving (Furniture) 645.4; 684.16; 749.3
Shenandoah County (Va.)—Genealogy 929.375595
Shenandoah National Park (Va.) 975.59
Shenandoah National Park (Va.)—Guidebooks 917.559
Shepard family 929.20973
Shepard, Sam, 1943– 812.54
Shepard, Sam, 1943– —Criticism and interpretation
  812.54
Sheppard, Sam 345.7302523; 364.1523092
Sheridan, Charles (Fictitious character) 813.54
Sheridan County (N.D.) 978.476
Sheridan County (N.D.)—Maps 912.78476
Sheridan, Kate (Fictitious character) 813.54
Sheridan, Philip Henry, 1831–1888 973.73092
Sheridan, Richard Brinsley, 1751–1816 822.6
Sheriffs 363.282
Sherlock Holmes films 791.43651
Sherman family 929.20973
Sherman, William T. (William Tecumseh), 1820–1891
  973.7092
Sherman's March to the Sea 973.7378
Sherpa (Nepalese people) 954.96
Shetland pony 636.16
Shetland sheepdog 636.737
Shevchenko, Taras, 1814–1861 891.7912
Shī'ah 297.82
Shī'ah—Doctrines 297.2042
Shiawassee County (Mich.) 977.425
Shiawassee County (Mich.)—Genealogy 929.377425
Shiawassee County (Mich.)—Maps 912.77425
Shielding (Electricity) 621.38224
Shielding (Radiation) 621.48323
Shields family 929.20973
Shift systems 331.2572
Shigata, Mark (Fictitious character) 813.54
Shigata, Mark (Fictitious character)—Fiction 813.54
Shih tzu 636.76
Shiites 297.82
Shiloh (Ark. : Imaginary place) 813.54
Shiloh (Ark. : Imaginary place)—Fiction 813.54
Shiloh, Battle of, 1862 973.731
Shimura, Rei (Fictitious character) 813.54
Shin (Sect) 294.3926
Shin (Sect)—Doctrines 294.3420426
Shinto 299.561
Ship handling 623.88
Ship models 623.8201

Ship registers 387.2
Ship registers—Great Lakes 386.2240977
Ship simulators 623.81011
Shipbuilding 623.82
Shipbuilding contracts 623.82
Shipbuilding in literature 808.80356; 809.93356
Shipbuilding industry 338.4762382
Shipbuilding—United States 623.820973
Shipley family 929.20973
Shipment of goods 658.788
Shipping 387.5
Shipping—Great Lakes 386.5440977
Ships 387.2; 623.82
Ships—Automation 623.85
Ships—Cargo 387.544
Ships—Cargo—Safety regulations 341.75665
Ships—Electrical equipment 623.8503
Ships—Electronic equipment 623.8504
Ships—Hydrodynamics 623.81015325
Ships in art 704.94962382
Ships, Iron and steel 623.8207
Ships, Iron and steel—Standards—United States
    623.8207
Ships—Maintenance and repair 623.820288
Ships, Medieval 623.821
Ships—Passenger lists 387.542
Ships—Safety regulations 341.75665
Ships—Standards 623.82021
Ships—Standards—Soviet Union 623.8202147
Shipwreck victims 363.123
Shipwrecks 363.123; 910.452
Shipwrecks—England—Cornwall (County) 914.237
Shipwrecks—Great Lakes 977
Shock 616.047; 617.21
Shock waves 531.1133; 533.293
Shoe industry 338.4768531
Shoelaces 685.31
Shoemaker-Levy 9 comet 523.64
Shoemakers 685.310092
Shoes 391.413; 685.31
Sholem Aleichem, 1859–1916 839.133; 839.18309
Sholem Aleichem, 1859–1916—Translations into
    English 839.133
Shooting 799.31
Shoplifting 364.162
Shopping 381.1; 640.73
Shopping—California—Los Angeles—Guidebooks
    381.10979494
Shopping carts 688.6
Shopping centers 381.1; 658.87
Shopping centers—Law and legislation 343.0887
Shopping centers—Law and legislation—United States
    343.730887
Shopping centers—Management 658.87
Shopping centers—United States 381.10973
Shopping centers—United States—Directories
    381.102573
Shopping centers—United States—Statistics—
    Periodicals 381.10973021
Shopping—China—Hong Kong—Guidebooks
    381.10255125
Shopping—England—London—Guidebooks 381.1025421
Shopping—France—Guidebooks 381.102544
Shopping—Italy—Guidebooks 381.102545
Shopping malls 381.1
Shopping—New York (State)—New York—Guidebooks
    381.10257471
Shopping—United States—Directories 381.102573
Shopping—United States—Guidebooks 381.102573

Shore birds 598.33
Shore, Jemima (Fictitious character) 823.914
Shore, Jemima (Fictitious character)—Fiction 823.914
Shore protection 627.58
Shorelines—Monitoring 333.917; 551.458; 627.58
Short films 791.436
Short game (Chess) 794.17
Short game (Golf) 796.3523
Short people 305; 599.949
Short stories 808.831
Short stories, American 813.01; 813.0108
Short stories, American—African American authors
    813.0108896073
Short stories, American—Dictionaries 813.0103
Short stories, American—History and criticism 813.0109
Short stories, American—Jewish authors 813.01088924
Short stories, American—Periodicals 813.0105;
    813.0108005
Short stories, American—Southern States 813.0108975
Short stories, American—Texas 813.01089764
Short stories, American—Women authors 813.01089287
Short stories, Arabic 892.7301
Short stories, Arabic—Egypt 892.730108962
Short stories, Arabic—Egypt—Translations into English
    892.730108962
Short stories, Arabic—Translations into English
    892.730108
Short stories, Argentine 863.0108982
Short stories, Argentine—Translations into English
    863.0108982
Short stories, Australian 823.0108994
Short stories, Bengali 891.44301
Short stories, Bengali—Translations into English
    891.4430108
Short stories, Canadian 813.0108971
Short stories, Caribbean (English) 813.01089729
Short stories, Chinese 895.1301
Short stories, Chinese—Translations into English
    895.130108
Short stories, English 823.01; 823.0108
Short stories, English—20th century 823.0108091
Short stories, English—Irish authors 823.01089415
Short stories, English—Irish authors—20th century
    823.01089415
Short stories, Estonian 894.545301
Short stories, Estonian—Translations into English
    894.54530108
Short stories, French 843.01
Short stories, French—Translations into English
    843.0108
Short stories, German 833.01
Short stories, German—Translations into English
    833.0108
Short stories, Hindi 891.43301
Short stories, Hindi—Translations into English
    891.4330108
Short stories, Hungarian 894.511301
Short stories, Hungarian—Translations into English
    894.51130108
Short stories, Indic 891.4; 981.1
Short stories, Indic—Translations into English 891.1;
    891.4
Short stories, Italian 853.01
Short stories, Italian—Translations into English
    853.0108
Short stories, Japanese 895.6301
Short stories, Japanese—Translations into English
    895.630108
Short stories, Korean 895.7301

Short stories, Korean—Translations into English 895.730108
Short stories, Latin American 863.010898
Short stories, Latin American—Translations into English 863.010898
Short stories, New Zealand 823.0108993
Short stories, Puerto Rican 863.010897295
Short stories, Puerto Rican—Translations into English 863.010897295
Short stories, Russian 891.7301
Short stories, Russian—Translations into English 891.730108
Short stories, Scottish 823.01089411
Short stories, South African (English) 823.0108968
Short stories, Spanish 863.01
Short stories, Spanish—Translations into English 863.0108
Short stories—Translations into English 808.831
Short stories, Urdu 891.439301
Short stories, Urdu—Translations into English 891.43930108
Short stories, Vietnamese 895.92230108
Short stories, Vietnamese—Translations into English 895.922301; 895.92230108
Short stories—Women authors 808.831089287
Short stories, Yiddish 839.1301
Short stories, Yiddish—Translations into English 839.130108
Short story 808.831
Short take-off and landing aircraft 629.133340426
Short-term counseling 158.3
Short vacations 910
Shorthand 653.4; 653.42
Shorthand—Gregg 653.427
Shortwave radio 621.384151
Shortwave radio—Antennas 621.384135
Shortwave radio—Handbooks, manuals, etc. 621.384151
Shortwave radio—Receivers and reception 621.38418
Shortwave radio stations—Directories 621.38416
Shoshoni Indians 305.89745; 978.0049745
Shostakovich, Dmitrii Dmitrievich, 1906–1975 780.92
Shot (Pellets) 671.36
Shotguns 683.426
Shoulder 612.97
Shoulder—Diseases 617.572
Shoulder—Surgery 617.572059
Shoulder—Wounds and injuries 617.572044
Show jumping 798.25
Show riding 798.24
Show windows 659.157
Showers (Parties) 793.2
Shrews 599.336
Shrimp culture 639.58
Shrimps 595.388
Shropshire (England) 943.45
Shropshire (England)—Guidebooks 914.24504; 914.24504859; 914.2450486
Shrove Tuesday 394.25
Shrunken heads 399
Shudraga 787.82
Shugak, Kate (Fictitious character) 813.54
Shugak, Kate (Fictitious character)—Fiction 813.54
Siamese cat 636.825
Sibelius, Jean, 1865–1957 780.92
Siberia (Russia) 957
Siberia (Russia)—Description and travel 915.704; 915.70486
Siberia (Russia)—Economic conditions 330.957

Siberia (Russia)—History 957
Siberian husky 636.73
Sibley County (Minn.) 977.633
Sibley County (Minn.)—Maps 912.77633
Sicily (Italy) 945.8
Sicily (Italy)—Description and travel 914.5804; 914.5804929; 914.580493
Sicily (Italy)—Guidebooks 914.5804; 914.5804929; 914.580493
Sicily (Italy)—History 945.8
Sicily (Italy)—History—1016–1194 945.804
Sicily (Italy)—Kings and rulers 945.80099
Sicily (Italy)—Social life and customs 945.8
Sick 362.1
Sick building syndrome 613.5
Sick children 649.8
Sick—Dental care 617.600877
Sick (Jewish law) 296.7
Sick—Prayer-books and devotions 242.661
Sick—Psychology 616.0019
Sickle cell anemia 616.1527
Siddha yoga (Service mark) 294.5435
Siddur 296.45
Siddurim 296.45
Siddurim—Texts 296.45
Sidel, Isaac (Fictitious character) 813.54
Sidel, Isaac (Fictitious character)—Fiction 813.54
Sidescan sonar 551.460840284; 621.3895
Sidney, Philip, Sir, 1554–1586 821.3
Sidney, Philip, Sir, 1554–1586. Arcadia 821.3; 823.3
Sidney, Philip, Sir, 1554–1586. Arcadia—Criticism, Textual 821.3; 823.3
Sidney, Philip, Sir, 1554–1586—Criticism and interpretation 821.3
Siege warfare 355.44
Siege warfare—History 355.44
Sieges 904.7
Sierra Leone 966.4
Sierra Leone—Politics and government 966.4
Sierra Leone—Politics and government—1961– 320.966409046; 966.404
Sierra Nevada (Calif. and Nev.) 979.44
Sierra Nevada (Calif. and Nev.)—Description and travel 917.94404; 917.9440453; 917.9440454
Sierra Nevada (Calif. and Nev.)—Guidebooks 917.94404; 917.9440453; 917.9440454
Siganidae, Fossil 567.7
Sight-reading (Music) 781.423
Sight-reading (Music)—Study and teaching (Elementary) 372.873
Sight-singing 783.0423
Sigismondo (Fictitious character) 823.914
Sigismondo (Fictitious character)—Fiction 823.914
Sign language 419
Sign language—Dictionaries 419
Signal processing 621.3822; 621.3822028563
Signal processing—Data processing 621.38220285
Signal processing—Digital techniques 621.3822
Signal processing—Digital techniques—Data processing 621.3822
Signal processing—Digital techniques—Mathematics 621.3822
Signal processing—Mathematics 621.38220151; 621.3822015152433
Signal processing—Periodicals 621.382205
Signal processing—Statistical methods 621.3822015195
Signal theory (Telecommunication) 621.38223
Signal theory (Telecommunication)—Mathematics 621.382230151

Sino-Vietnamese Conflict, 1979 959.7044
Sintering 671.373
Sinuhe (Fictitious character) 823.92
Sinusitis 616.212
Sioux County (Iowa) 977.713
Sioux County (Iowa)—Maps 912.77713
Sipuncula 592.35
Sister cities 307.76
Sisters 306.875
Sisters in motion pictures 791.43652045
Site-specific art 700; 709.0407
Site-specific installations (Art) 702.81
Site-specific sculpture 731
Sitting Bull, 1834?–1890 978.00497452
Sitwell, Edith, Dame, 1887–1964 821.912
Sitwell, Edith, Dame, 1887–1964—Criticism and
    interpretation 821.912
Siva (Hindu deity) in literature 808.80382912113;
    809.93382912113
Sixteen Personality Factor Questionnaire 155.283
Size perception 153.752
Sjogren's syndrome 616.77
Ska (Music) 781.646
Skate sailing 796.9
Skateboarding 796.22
Skaters 796.912
Skating 796.91
Skating—History 796.9109
Skeleton 573.76; 611.71
Skepticism 121.2; 149.73; 186
Ski mountaineering 796.93
Ski racing 796.93
Ski resorts 796.93
Ski resorts—United States 796.930973
Ski resorts—United States—Directories 796.9302573
Ski runs 796.93
Skiffs 623.8202
Skiffs—Design and construction 623.8202
Skiing equipment industry 338.476887693
Skilled labor 331.794
Skin 573.5; 591.47; 612.79
Skin—Cancer 616.99477
Skin—Care and hygiene 646.726
Skin—Diseases 616.5
Skin—Diseases—Atlases 616.500222
Skin—Diseases—Diagnosis 616.5075
Skin—Diseases—Genetic aspects 616.5042
Skin—Diseases—Handbooks, manuals, etc. 616.5
Skin—Diseases—Immunological aspects 616.5079
Skin—Diseases—Treatment 616.506
Skin diving 797.23
Skin—Histopathology 616.507
Skin—Infections 616.5
Skin—Laser surgery 617.477059
Skin—Pathophysiology 616.507
Skin—Surgery 617.477
Skinner, B. F. (Burrhus Frederic), 1904– 150.19434092
Skis and skiing 796.93
Skis and skiing—Psychological aspects 796.93019
Skis and skiing—Training 613.711
Skis and skiing—West (U.S.) 796.930978
Skis and skiing—West (U.S.)—Guidebooks 796.930978
Skokie (Ill.) 977.31
Skull 599.948
Skull base—Surgery 617.514059
Skunks 599.768
Skunks as pets 636.9768
Sky 520
Sky art 709.04075

Skydiving 797.56
Skyscrapers 720.483
Skyscrapers—Design and construction 690
Skyscrapers—United States 720.4830973
Skysurfing 797.56
Skywalker, Luke (Fictitious character) 791.4375
Skywalker, Luke (Fictitious character)—Fiction 813.54
Slag glass 748
Slang 417.2
Slash-mulch systems 631.581
Slaughtering and slaughter-houses 338.476649029
Slaughtering and slaughter-houses—Canada
    338.4766490290971
Slaughtering and slaughter-houses—Canada—
    Statistics—Periodicals 338.4766490290971021
Slave insurrections 306.362; 326
Slave insurrections—United States 326.0973;
    975.00496073
Slave narratives 305.567092
Slave trade 306.362; 326; 382.44
Slave trade—Africa 326.096; 382.44096
Slave trade—Great Britain 382.440941
Slave trade—History 382.4409
Slavery 306.362; 326
Slavery—America 306.362097
Slavery—America—History 306.362097
Slavery and the church 261.834567
Slavery and the church—Methodist Episcopal Church
    261.834567
Slavery—Economic aspects—Southern States
    306.3620975
Slavery—Economic aspects—United States
    331.117340973
Slavery—History 306.36209
Slavery in literature 808.80355; 809.93355
Slavery in motion pictures 791.43655
Slavery—Law and legislation 342.087
Slavery—Law and legislation—United States 342.73087
Slavery—Law and legislation—United States—History
    342.73087
Slavery—Southern States—History 975.00496073
Slavery—United States 306.3620973
Slavery—United States—Historiography 306.3620973
Slavery—United States—Justification 306.3620973
Slaves 305.567
Slaves—Emancipation 342.087
Slaves—Emancipation—United States 973.714
Slavic languages 491.8
Slavic languages—Grammar 491.8045
Slavic periodicals 057
Slavic philology 491.8
Slavic philology—Periodicals 491.805
Sleds 388.341; 688.6
Sleep 154.6; 612.821
Sleep apnea syndromes 616.2
Sleep behavior in animals 591.519
Sleep disorders 616.8498
Sleep disorders—Diagnosis 616.8498
Sleep disorders in children 618.928498
Sleep—Physiological aspects 612.821
Sleep-wake cycle 154.6
Sleighs 388.341; 688.6
Slick, Sam (Fictitious character) 813.3
Slide-rule 510.284
Slider, Bill (Fictitious character) 823.914
Slider, Bill (Fictitious character)—Fiction 823.914
Slides (Photography) 371.33522; 778.2
Sligo (Ireland : County) 941.72
Sligo (Ireland : County)—History 941.72

Slip casting 738.142
Slip covers 646.21; 746.95
Slips (Clothing) 391.42; 646.42; 687.22
Slit drums 786.8845
Sloan, C. D. (Fictitious character) 823.914
Sloan, C. D. (Fictitious character)—Fiction 823.914
Sloan, Charley (Fictitious character) 813.54
Sloane, Sydney (Fictitious character) 813.54
Slocum, Joshua, b. 1844 910.92
Slopes (Physical geography) 551.43
Slopes (Soil mechanics) 624.151363
Sloshing (Hydrodynamics) 620.1064
Slot cars 629.2218
Slot clubs 795.27
Sloths 599.313
Slotting allowances 381.1; 658.82
Sloughi 636.7532
Slovak language 491.87
Slovakia 943.73
Slovenia 949.73
Slovenia—Description and travel 914.97304; 914.973043
Slovenian language 491.84
Slow learning children 371.926
Slow learning children—Education 371.926
Slugging (Ridesharing) 388.413212
Slugs (Mollusks) 594.3; 594.38
Slums 307.3364
Slums—United States 307.33640973
Small business 338.642
Small business—Accounting 657.9042
Small business—Data processing 658.05
Small business—Developing countries 338.642091724
Small business—Europe 338.642094
Small business—Finance 658.1592
Small business—Finance—Law and legislation 346.0652
Small business—Finance—Law and legislation—United States 346.730652
Small business—Government policy 338.642
Small business—Government policy—United States 338.6420973
Small business—Great Britain 338.6420941
Small business—Handbooks, manuals, etc. 658.022
Small business—India 338.6420954
Small business investment companies 332.6722
Small business—Law and legislation 346.0652
Small business—Law and legislation—United States 346.730652
Small business—Law and legislation—United States—Forms 346.7306520269
Small business—Management 658.022
Small business—Management—Handbooks, manuals, etc. 658.022
Small business—Personnel management 658.303
Small business—Philippines 338.64209599
Small business—Planning 658.4012
Small business—Public relations 659.28
Small business—Purchasing 658.72
Small business—Purchasing—Law and legislation 346.0652
Small business—Purchasing—Law and legislation—United States 346.730652
Small business—Taxation—Law and legislation 343.05268
Small business—Taxation—Law and legislation—United States 343.7305268; 343.73068
Small business—Technological innovations 338.642
Small business—Technological innovations—United States 338.642
Small business—United States 338.6420973

Small business—United States—Finance—Directories 658.15
Small business—United States—Information services 658.4038
Small business—United States—Management 658.0220973
Small business—United States—Periodicals 338.642097305
Small business—Valuation 658.1592
Small capitalization stocks 332.632044
Small capitalization stocks—United States 332.632044
Small churches 254
Small claims courts 347.04
Small claims courts—California 347.79404
Small claims courts—United States 347.7328; 347.734
Small claims courts—United States—States 347.7328; 347.734
Small colleges 378
Small colleges—United States 378.73
Small, David (Fictitious character) 813.54
Small, David (Fictitious character)—Fiction 813.54
Small gasoline engines 621.434
Small groups 302.34
Small libraries 027
Small libraries—Administration 025.1
Small presses 686.2
Small schools 371
Smallmouth bass 597.7388
Smallmouth bass fishing 799.17388
Smallpox 614.521; 616.912
Smallpox—Vaccination 614.521
Smalltalk (Computer program language) 005.133
Smart cards 004.56; 332.76
Smart, Christopher, 1722–1771 821.6
Smart, Christopher, 1722–1771—Criticism and interpretation 821.6
Smart (Computer file) 005.369
Smart materials 620.112
Smart structures 614.171
Smell 152.166; 573.877; 612.86
Smiley, George (Fictitious character) 823.914
Smiley, George (Fictitious character)—Fiction 823.914
Smith, Adam, 1723–1790 330.153092
Smith, Adam, 1723–1790. Inquiry into the nature and causes of the wealth of nations 330.153
Smith, Bill (Fictitious character) 813.54
Smith, Bill (Fictitious character)—Fiction 813.54
Smith, Brad (Fictitious character) 813.54
Smith, Brad (Fictitious character)—Fiction 813.54
Smith, Dean, 1931– 796.323092
Smith, Emmitt, 1969– 796.332092
Smith family 929.20973
Smith, Jill (Fictitious character) 813.54
Smith, Jill (Fictitious character)—Fiction 813.54
Smith, John, 1580–1631 973.21092
Smith, Joseph, 1805–1844 289.3092
Smith, Mac (Fictitious character) 813.54
Smith, Mac (Fictitious character)—Fiction 813.54
Smith, Margaret Chase, 1897– 328.73092
Smith, Truman (Fictitious character) 813.54
Smith, Truman (Fictitious character)—Fiction 813.54
Smith, Will, 1968– 791.43028092
Smithsonian Institution 069.09753
Smithsonian Institution—Guidebooks 069.09753
Smocking 746.44
Smoked fish 641.392
Smoked meat 641.49
Smoking 394.14
Smoking and fires 363.371

Smoking cessation programs 613.85
Smoking—Health aspects 613.85
Smoking in popular music 781.64159; 782.42164159
Smoking—United States 362.2960973
Smollett, Tobias George, 1721–1771 823.6
Smollett, Tobias George, 1721–1771—Criticism and interpretation 823.6
Smooth muscle—Diseases 616.74
Smoothing (Statistics) 511.42
Smuggling 364.133
Smuggling—Investigation 363.25933
SNA (Computer network architecture) 004.65
Snack food industry 338.476646
Snack foods 641.53; 664.6
Snags (Forestry) 577.3; 634.95
Snails 594.3; 594.38
Snakes 597.96
Snakes as pets 639.396
Snap net fishing 639.2756
Snaps (Fasteners) 621.88
Snipes 598.33
Sniping (Military science) 356.162
Snohomish County (Wash.) 979.771
Snohomish County (Wash.)—Maps 912.79771
Snow 551.5784
Snow and ice climbing 796.9
Snow, Ben (Fictitious character) 813.54
Snow, C. P. (Charles Percy), 1905– 823.912
Snow, C. P. (Charles Percy), 1905– —Criticism and interpretation 823.912
Snow camping 796.54
Snow ecology 577.586
Snow goose 598.4175
Snow leopard 599.7555
Snowballs 796.9
Snowboarding 796.939
Snowboards 796.939
Snowmen 736.94
Snowmobile trails 796.94
Snowshoes and snowshoeing 796.92
Snuff films 791.43655
Snyder family 929.20973
Snyder, Gary, 1930– 811.54
Snyder, Gary, 1930– —Criticism and interpretation 811.54
Soap 668.12
Soap operas 791.456
Soap operas—United States 791.456
Soap operas—United States—History and criticism 791.456
Sobibor (Poland : Concentration camp) 940.5318
Sobolev spaces 515.782
Soccer 796.334
Soccer—Coaching 796.334077
Soccer—Encyclopedias 796.33403
Soccer for children 796.334083
Soccer for children—Coaching 796.334083
Soccer—Goalkeeping 796.33426
Soccer—History 796.33409
Soccer—Rules 796.33402022
Soccer shoes 685.36
Soccer teams 796.33406
Soccer—Training 796.334071
Social action 361.2
Social adjustment 616.89
Social advocacy 362
Social archaeology 930.1
Social behavior in animals 591.56; 596.15
Social capital (Sociology) 302

Social case work 361.32
Social case work—Moral and ethical aspects 174.9362
Social case work—United States 361.320973
Social change 303.4
Social change in literature 808.80355; 809.93355
Social change—United States 303.40973
Social choice 302.13
Social choice—Mathematical models 302.13015118
Social classes 305.5
Social classes—Australia 305.50994
Social classes—Great Britain 305.50941
Social classes in literature 808.80355; 809.93355
Social classes—India 305.50954
Social classes—Soviet Union 305.50947
Social classes—United States 305.50973
Social conflict 303.6
Social conflict in literature 808.80355; 809.93355
Social conflict in mass media 303.6
Social contract 320.11
Social control 303.33
Social Democratic Party (Great Britain) 324.2410972
Social ecology 304.2
Social epistemology 300.1
Social ethics 170; 303.372
Social evolution 303.4
Social group work 361.4
Social group work—United States 361.40973
Social groups 305
Social hierarchy in animals 591.56
Social history 306.09
Social indicators—United States 301.0973
Social influence 303.34
Social institutions 306
Social institutions—United States 306.0973
Social interaction 302
Social isolation 302.545
Social justice 303.372
Social learning 303.32
Social legislation 344.01
Social marketing 658.8
Social medicine 306.461; 362.1
Social medicine—Australia 362.10994
Social medicine—Developing countries 362.1091724
Social medicine—United States 362.10973
Social mobility 305.513
Social mobility—United States 305.5130973
Social movements 303.484
Social movements—Europe 303.484094
Social movements—India 303.4840954
Social movements—Latin America 303.484098
Social networks 302; 302.4
Social norms 306
Social participation 302.14
Social perception 302.12
Social phobia 616.85225
Social planning 361.25
Social policy 361.25; 361.61
Social policy—Research 361.61072
Social prediction 303.49
Social problems 361.1; 362.042
Social problems—Moral and ethical aspects 170
Social problems—United States 361.10973
Social psychiatry 362.2
Social psychology 302
Social psychology in literature 808.80353; 809.93353
Social psychology—Methodology 302.01
Social psychology—Research 302.072
Social responsibility of business 658.408

Social responsibility of business—United States 658.4080973
Social role 302.15
Social science libraries 026.3
Social sciences 300
Social sciences and psychoanalysis 150.195
Social sciences—Authorship 808.0663
Social sciences—Bibliography 016.3
Social sciences—Data processing 300.285
Social sciences—Dictionaries 300.3
Social sciences—Examinations 300.76
Social sciences—Field work 300.72; 300.723
Social sciences—History 300.9
Social sciences—Mathematical models 300.15118
Social sciences—Methodology 300.1
Social sciences—Periodicals 300.5
Social sciences—Periodicals—Bibliography 016.3005
Social sciences—Periodicals—Bibliography—Union lists 016.3005
Social sciences—Philosophy 300.1
Social sciences—Research 300.72
Social sciences—Research—Methodology 300.72
Social sciences—Research—Moral and ethical aspects 174.93
Social sciences—Research—United States 300.72073
Social sciences—Simulation methods 300.11
Social sciences—Statistical methods 300.15195; 300.727
Social sciences—Statistical methods—Computer programs 300.285
Social sciences—Study and teaching 300.71
Social sciences—Study and teaching (Elementary) 372.83; 372.83044
Social sciences—Study and teaching (Elementary)— United States 372.83044097; 372.830440973; 372.830973
Social sciences—Study and teaching (Secondary) 300.712
Social sciences—Study and teaching (Secondary)— United States 300.71273
Social security 362; 368.4
Social security beneficiaries—United States 368.4300973
Social security—Canada 368.400971
Social security consultants 362.04
Social security—Cost-of-living adjustments—United States 368.4300973
Social security—Europe 368.40094
Social security—Great Britain 368.400941
Social security—Law and legislation 344.02
Social security—Law and legislation—European Economic Community countries 344.402
Social security—Law and legislation—Great Britain 344.4102
Social security—Law and legislation—United States 344.7302; 344.73023
Social security—Soviet Union 368.400947
Social security—United States 368.4300973
Social security—United States—Finance 368.43010973
Social security—United States—Handbooks, manuals, etc. 344.73023
Social security—United States—History 368.4300973
Social service 361
Social service and sex 362.8
Social service—Australia 361.994
Social service—Evaluation 361.0068
Social service—Field work 361.32
Social service—Great Britain 361.941
Social service—Moral and ethical aspects 174.9362
Social service—Philosophy 361.301

Social service—Public relations 659.29361
Social service—Research 361.0072
Social service—Research—Methodology 361.0072
Social service—United States 361.973
Social service—Vocational guidance—United States 361.002373; 361.3202373
Social skills 302.34
Social skills—Study and teaching (Elementary) 372.83
Social status 305
Social stratification 305
Social structure 301
Social surveys 300.723
Social systems 301
Social values 303.372
Social values—United States 303.3720973
Social work administration 361.0068; 361.3068
Social work administration—United States 361.0068; 361.3068
Social work education 361.0071; 361.3071
Social work education—United States 361.32071073
Social work with African American children 362.708996073
Social work with African Americans 362.8496073
Social work with children 362.7
Social work with children—Great Britain 362.70941
Social work with children—United States 362.70973
Social work with criminals 365.66
Social work with criminals—United States 365.66
Social work with gays 362.8
Social work with gays—United States 362.8
Social work with juvenile delinquents 364.6
Social work with juvenile delinquents—Great Britain 364.6
Social work with minorities 362.84
Social work with minorities—United States 362.8400973
Social work with teenagers 362.70835
Social work with teenagers—Great Britain 362.708350941
Social work with the aged 362.6
Social work with youth 362.7
Social workers 361.3092
Social workers—Legal status, laws, etc. 344.017613613
Social workers—Legal status, laws, etc.—United States 344.73017613613
Social workers—Supervision of 361.320683
Social workers—United States 361.32092273
Socialism 320.531; 335
Socialism—Africa 335.0096
Socialism and liberty 320.531
Socialism—Canada 335.00971
Socialism—Europe 335.0094
Socialism—Europe—History 335.0094
Socialism—Germany 335.00943
Socialism—Germany—History 335.00943
Socialism—Great Britain 320.5310941; 335.00941
Socialism—Great Britain—History 335.00941
Socialism—History 335.009
Socialism—India 335.00954
Socialism—Soviet Union 335.00947
Socialism—Soviet Union—History 335.4309
Socialism—Tanzania 335.009678
Socialism—United States 335.00973
Socialism—United States—History 335.00973
Socialist ethics 171.7
Socialist parties 324.2174
Socialists 335.0092
Socialization 303.32
Socially handicapped 305.56
Socially handicapped children—Education 371.82694

Socially handicapped children—Education (Elementary) 372.182694
Socially handicapped children—Education (Elementary)—United States 372.1826940973
Socially handicapped children—Education—United States 371.826840973
Socially handicapped—Education 371.82694
Socially handicapped—Education (Higher) 378.1982694
Socially handicapped—Education (Higher)—United States 378.19826940973
Socially handicapped—Education—India 371.826940954
Socially handicapped teenagers—United States 362.086940973; 362.7086940973
Socially handicapped youth 305.235; 371.82694
Socially handicapped youth—Education 371.82694
Socially handicapped youth—Education—United States 371.826940973
Socially handicapped youth—United States 362.086940973
Societies 060
Societies living in common without vows 307.774
Society for the Propagation of the Gospel in Foreign Parts (Great Britain) 266.3
Society of Friends 289.6
Society of Friends—Doctrines 230.96
Society of Friends—History 289.609; 289.673
Society of Rosicrucians 135.43
Society tales 891.73
Sociobiology 304.5; 577.8
Sociolinguistics 306.44
Sociolinguistics—India 306.440954
Sociological jurisprudence 340.115
Sociologists 301.092
Sociology 301
Sociology, Biblical 220.8301
Sociology, Christian 261.8
Sociology, Christian (Catholic) 261.808822
Sociology, Christian—History 261.809
Sociology, Christian—History—Early church, ca. 30–600 261.809015
Sociology, Christian—United States 261.80973
Sociology—Dictionaries 301.03
Sociology—Encyclopedias 301.03
Sociology—Examinations, questions, etc. 301.076
Sociology—History 301.09
Sociology in literature 808.80355; 809.93355
Sociology—India 301.0954
Sociology—Methodology 301.01
Sociology—Methodology—History 301.01
Sociology, Military 306.27
Sociology, Military—United States 306.270973
Sociology of disability 362.4
Sociology—Periodicals 301.05
Sociology—Philosophy 301.01
Sociology—Research 301.072
Sociology—Research—Data processing 301.0285
Sociology—Research—Methodology 301.072
Sociology, Rural 307.72
Sociology—United States 301.0973
Sociology—United States—History 301.0973
Sociology, Urban 307.76
Sociometry 302.015195
Socrates 183.2
Sodomy—Religious aspects 291.17835773; 291.566
Soft coated wheaten terrier 636.755
Soft computing 006.3
Soft contact lenses 617.7523
Soft drink industry 338.766362
Soft drinks 663.62

Soft tissue tumors 616.992; 616.994
Soft tissue tumors—Diagnosis 616.992075
Soft toy making 745.5924
Softball 796.3578
Softball for women 796.3578
Softball—Rules 796.3578
Softball teams 796.3578
Software compatibility 005.3
Software compatibility—Law and legislation 343.0999
Software configuration management 005.1
Software consultants 005.0684
Software documentation 005.15
Software engineering 005.1
Software engineering—Periodicals 005.105
Software engineering—Standards 005.10218
Software engineering—Study and teaching (Higher) 005.10711
Software failures 005
Software localization 005.1
Software maintenance 005.16
Software measurement 005.14
Software patterns 005.1
Software productivity 005
Software protection 005.8
Software protection—Law and legislation 346.0482
Software protection—Law and legislation—United States 346.730482
Software reengineering 005.1
Software refactoring 005.16
Software support 005.3
Soil absorption and adsorption 631.432
Soil animals 591.757
Soil biology 578.757
Soil bioventing 628.55
Soil chemistry 631.41
Soil compaction 624.151362; 631.433
Soil conservation 631.45
Soil conservation—United States 631.450973
Soil dynamics 624.15136
Soil ecology 577.57
Soil erosion 631.45
Soil fertility 631.422
Soil formation 551.305; 631.4
Soil geography 631.49
Soil infiltration rate 624.15136; 631.432
Soil management 631.4
Soil mechanics 624.15136
Soil microbiology 579.1757
Soil micromorphology 631.43
Soil moisture 631.432
Soil physics 631.43
Soil pollution 363.7396; 628.55
Soil pollution—Environmental aspects 628.55
Soil profiles 631.4
Soil remediation 628.55
Soil ripping 631.58
Soil science 631.4
Soil science in archaeology 930.1028
Soil stabilization 624.151363
Soil surveys 631.47
Soils 631.4
Soils—Analysis 631.41
Soils—Classification 631.44
Soils—Environmental aspects 577.57; 631.4
Soils—Fluorine content 631.416
Soils—Quality 631.4
Soils, Salts in 631.416
Soils—Tropics 631.4913
Sōka Gakkai 294.3928

Sophocles. Antigone 882.01
Sophocles—Criticism and interpretation 882.01
Sophocles. Oedipus Rex 882.01
Sophocles—Translations into English 882.01
Sordellina 788.49
Sorex 599.3362
Sosa, Sammy, 1968– 796.357092
Soties 842.05232
Sots art 709.4709045
Soukous (Music) 781.63
Soul 128.1
Soul music 781.644
Sound 534
Sound archives 025.1782
Sound—Equipment and supplies 621.3828;
    621.38930284
Sound—Equipment and supplies—Purchasing
    621.38970296
Sound—Experiments 534.078
Sound motion pictures 781.43
Sound motion pictures—History 791.4309
Sound production by animals 573.92
Sound—Recording and reproducing 621.3893; 778.5344;
    791.45024
Sound—Recording and reproducing—Digital techniques
    621.3893
Sound—Recording and reproducing—Equipment and
    supplies 621.38930284
Sound recording industry 338.47384
Sound recording industry—United States 781.49068
Sound recording libraries 026.384
Sound recordings 011.38; 621.38932; 780.266
Sound recordings—Catalogs 011.38
Sound recordings in education 371.3332
Sound recordings in ethnomusicology 780.89
Sound recordings—Pirated editions 346.0482
Sound recordings—Pirated editions—United States
    346.730482
Sound—Transmission 534.2
Sound-waves 534
Sounding and soundings 551.4600287
Soundproofing 693.834
Sounds 534
Soups 641.813
Source code (Computer science) 005.3
Source separation (Recycling) 363.7282; 628.4458
South Africa 968
South Africa—Bibliography 016.968
South Africa—Bibliography of bibliographies
    016.016968
South Africa—Description and travel 916.804;
    916.80465
South Africa—Economic conditions 330.968
South Africa—Economic conditions—1991– 330.968064
South Africa—Economic policy 338.968
South Africa—Foreign relations 327.68
South Africa—Foreign relations—1961–1978 327.68
South Africa—Foreign relations—1978–1989 327.68
South Africa—Guidebooks 916.804; 916.80465
South Africa—History 968
South Africa—Maps 912.68
South Africa—Maps, Tourist 912.68
South Africa—Pictorial works 968.00222
South Africa—Politics and government 320.968; 968
South Africa—Politics and government—1909–1948
    320.96809041
South Africa—Politics and government—1948–1994
    320.96809045; 968.06

South Africa—Politics and government—1978– —
    Periodicals 320.96809048
South Africa—Politics and government—1978–1989
    320.968
South Africa—Politics and government—1989–1994
    320.96809049; 968.064
South Africa—Politics and government—1994–
    320.96809049
South Africa—Politics and government—1994– —
    Periodicals 320.96809049
South Africa—Race relations 305.800968
South Africa—Road maps 912.68
South Africa—Social conditions 968
South Africa—Social conditions—1961–1994 968.06
South Africa—Social life and customs 968
South African drama (English) 822; 822.0080968
South African fiction (English)—History and criticism
    823.009968
South African literature (English) 820; 820.80968
South African literature (English)—History and criticism
    820.9968
South African periodicals 050.968
South African poetry (English) 821; 821.0080968
South African War, 1899–1902 968.048
South America 980
South America—Geography 918
South America—Guidebooks 918.04; 918.0439; 918.044
South Asia 954
South Asia—Antiquities 934
South Asia—Civilization 954
South Asia—Economic policy 338.954
South Asia—Foreign relations 327.0954
South Asia—History 954
South Asia—Periodicals 954.005
South Asia—Politics and government 320.954
South Asia—Religion 200.954
South Asia—Social conditions 954
South Asian libraries 026.954
South Asian type 686.21911
South Australia 994.23
South Australia—History 994.23
South Carolina 975.7
South Carolina—Genealogy 929.3757
South Carolina—Guidebooks 917.5704; 917.570443;
    917.570444
South Carolina—History 975.7
South Carolina—History—Colonial period, ca. 1600–
    1775 975.702
South Carolina—History—Revolution, 1775–1783
    975.703
South Carolina—History—Civil War, 1861–1865 975.703
South Carolina—Politics and government 975.7
South Carolina—Politics and government—To 1775
    320.975709032
South Carolina—Politics and government—1775–1865
    320.975709034; 975.703
South Dakota 978.3
South Dakota—Maps 912.783
South Pole 998.9
Southampton (England) 942.276
Southampton (England)—History 942.276
Southern African Development Coordination Conference
    337.168
Southern Baptist Convention 286.132
Southern Baptist Convention—History 286.13209
Southern Baptist Convention—History—20th century
    286.1320904
Southern Pacific Railroad Company 385.0978
Southern Region (Sudan) 962.9

Southern Region (Sudan)—Politics and government 962.9

Southern States 975

Southern States—Church history 277.5

Southern States—Civilization 975

Southern States—Civilization—20th century 975.04; 975.043

Southern States—Civilization—Periodicals 975.005

Southern States—Description and travel 917.504; 917.50443; 917.50444

Southern States—Description and travel—Early works to 1800 917.504

Southern States—Economic conditions 330.975

Southern States—Genealogy 929.375

Southern States—Guidebooks 917.504; 917.50443; 917.50444

Southern States—History 975

Southern States—History—Colonial period, ca. 1600–1775 975.02

Southern States—History—1865–1951 975.04

Southern States—Politics and government 320.975; 975

Southern States—Politics and government—1865–1950 320.97509034; 975.04

Southern States—Politics and government—1951– 320.97509045

Southern States—Race relations 305.800975

Southern States—Social conditions 975

Southern States—Social life and customs 975

Southern States—Social life and customs—1775–1865 975.03

Southern States—Social life and customs—1865– 975.04

Southern States—Social life and customs—1865– — Humor 975.040207

Southwell, Robert, Saint, 1561?–1595 821.3

Southwest, New 979

Southwest, New—Description and travel 917.904; 917.90434

Southwest, New—Guidebooks 917.904; 917.90433; 917.90434

Southwest, New—History 979

Southwest, New—History—To 1848 979

Southwest, Old 976

Southwest, Old—History 976

Southwestern States 979

Souvenir china 666.5; 738.2

Souvenirs (Keepsakes) 745

Sovereignty 320.15

Soviet literature 891.708004

Soviet literature—History and criticism 891.709004

Soviet Union 947.084

Soviet Union—Armed Forces 355.00947

Soviet Union—Armed Forces—Appropriations and expenditures 355.622460947

Soviet Union—Armed Forces—History 355.00947

Soviet Union—Bibliography 016.947

Soviet Union—Church history 274.7

Soviet Union—Civilization 947.084

Soviet Union—Civilization—Western influences 947.084

Soviet Union—Commerce 380.10947; 381.0947; 382.0947

Soviet Union—Defenses 355.033047

Soviet Union—Description and travel 914.70484

Soviet Union—Economic conditions 330.947084

Soviet Union—Economic conditions—1955–1965 330.9470852

Soviet Union—Economic conditions—1965–1975 330.9470853

Soviet Union—Economic conditions—1975–1985 330.9470853

Soviet Union—Economic policy 338.947

Soviet Union—Economic policy—1917–1928 338.947

Soviet Union—Economic policy—1959–1965 338.947

Soviet Union—Economic policy—1966–1970 338.947

Soviet Union—Economic policy—1971–1975 338.947

Soviet Union—Economic policy—1976–1980 338.947

Soviet Union—Economic policy—1981–1985 338.947

Soviet Union—Economic policy—1986–1991 338.947

Soviet Union—Ethnic relations 305.800947

Soviet Union—Foreign economic relations 337.47

Soviet Union—Foreign relations 327.47

Soviet Union—Foreign relations—1917–1945 327.47

Soviet Union—Foreign relations—1945–1991 327.47

Soviet Union—Foreign relations—1953–1975 327.47

Soviet Union—Foreign relations—1975–1985 327.47

Soviet Union—Foreign relations—1985–1991 327.47

Soviet Union—Foreign relations—Afghanistan 327.470581

Soviet Union—Foreign relations—China 327.47051

Soviet Union—Foreign relations—Germany 327.47043

Soviet Union—Foreign relations—India 327.47054

Soviet Union—Foreign relations—Japan 327.47052

Soviet Union—Foreign relations—Middle East 327.47056

Soviet Union—Geography 914.7

Soviet Union—Guidebooks 914.70484

Soviet Union—Historiography 947.084072

Soviet Union—History 947.084

Soviet Union—History—20th century 947.084

Soviet Union—History—Revolution, 1917–1921 947.0841

Soviet Union—History—Revolution, 1917–1921—Anniversaries, etc. 947.0841

Soviet Union—History—Revolution, 1917–1921—Influence 947.0841

Soviet Union—History—Revolution, 1917–1921—Personal narratives 947.0841

Soviet Union—History—Revolution, 1917–1921—Sources 947.0841

Soviet Union—History—1917–1936 947.0841

Soviet Union—History—Allied intervention, 1918–1920 947.0841

Soviet Union—History—1925–1953 947.0842

Soviet Union—History—German occupation, 1941–1944 947.0842

Soviet Union—History—1953–1985 947.085

Soviet Union—History—1985–1991 947.0854

Soviet Union—History, Military 355.00947

Soviet Union—Intellectual life 947.084

Soviet Union. Komitet gosudarstvennoĭ bezopasnosti—History 363.2830947

Soviet Union—Military policy 355.033547

Soviet Union—Periodicals 947.08405

Soviet Union—Politics and government 320.947

Soviet Union—Politics and government—1917–1936 320.94709042

Soviet Union—Politics and government—1936–1953 320.9470904; 947.084; 947.0842

Soviet Union—Politics and government—1945–1991 320.94709045; 947.085

Soviet Union—Politics and government—1953–1985 320.94709045; 947.0852

Soviet Union—Politics and government—1985–1991 320.94709048; 947.0854

Soviet Union—Relations 303.48247

Soviet Union—Relations—Foreign countries 303.48247

Soviet Union—Religion 200.947

Soviet Union—Social conditions 947.084

Soviet Union—Social conditions—1945–1991 947.085

Soviet Union—Social conditions—1970–1991 947.0853

Soviet Union—Social life and customs 947.085
Soviet Union—Social life and customs—1917–1970 947.084
Soviet Union. Sovetskaĭa Armiĭa 355.00947
Soviet Union. Voenno-Morskoĭ Flot 359.00947
Soybean 641.35655; 664.805655
Soybean—Bibliography 016.63334
Soybean industry 338.47664805655
Soybean products 641.35655
Soybean products—Bibliography 016.664726
Soyinka, Wole 822.914
Soyinka, Wole—Criticism and interpretation 822.914
Space and time 114; 530.11
Space and time in mass media 115; 530.11
Space (Art) 701.8
Space astronomy 520; 522
Space biology 571.0919
Space colonies 620.419; 629.442
Space colonies in literature 808.80356; 808.838762; 809.38762; 809.93356
Space debris 363.7280919; 629.416
Space environment 629.416
Space flight 629.4; 629.41
Space flight in art 704.94962941
Space flight to Mars 629.4553
Space flight to the moon 629.454
Space flight to Venus 629.4552
Space flights 910.919
Space in economics 338.6042
Space industrialization 338.0919
Space industrialization—United States 338.0919
Space interferometry 523.7
Space law 341.47; 341.75679
Space medicine 616.980214
Space mining 622.0999
Space mining—Law and legislation 341.762
Space photography 910.9190222
Space plasmas 523.01; 530.44
Space probes 629.435
Space robotics 629.892
Space sciences 500.5
Space sciences—Experiments 620.419
Space ships 629.47
Space shuttles 629.441
Space stations 629.442
Space stations—Automation 629.47
Space surveillance 623.71
Space toys 688.72; 745.592
Space trajectories 629.41
Space travelers 910.919092; 919.904092
Space vehicles 629.47
Space vehicles—Auxiliary power supply 629.4744
Space vehicles—Design and construction 629.471
Space vehicles—Dynamics 629.411; 629.471
Space vehicles—Guidance systems 629.4742
Space vehicles in art 704.94962947
Space vehicles—Materials 629.472
Space vehicles—Nuclear power plants 629.4753
Space vehicles—Optical equipment 629.474
Space vehicles—Propulsion systems 629.475
Space warfare 358.8
Spades (Game) 795.41
Spain 946
Spain—Civilization 946
Spain—Civilization—711–1516 946.02
Spain—Description and travel 914.604; 914.60483
Spain—Economic conditions 330.946
Spain—Economic conditions—1918–1975 330.94608
Spain—Economic conditions—1975- 330.946083

Spain—Economic conditions—1975- —Periodicals 330.946083
Spain—Guidebooks 914.604; 914.60483
Spain—History 946
Spain—History—Gothic period, 414–711 946.01
Spain—History—711–1516 946.02; 946.82
Spain—History—Ferdinand and Isabella, 1479–1516 946.03
Spain—History—Civil War, 1936–1939 946.081
Spain—History—Civil War, 1936–1939—Participation, American 946.081373
Spain—History—Civil War, 1936–1939—Participation, British 946.081341
Spain—History—Civil War, 1936–1939—Personal narratives 946.081092
Spain—Pictorial works 946.00222
Spain—Politics and government 946
Spain—Politics and government—20th century 320.9460904; 946.08
Spain—Politics and government—1931–1939 320.94609043; 946.081
Spain—Politics and government—1975- 320.94609048
Spain—Social conditions 946
Spain—Social conditions—To 1800 946
Spain—Social life and customs 946
Spalding family 929.20973
Spalliera painting 751.73
Spam (Trademark) 664.92
Spanish American fiction 863.008098
Spanish American fiction—20th century 863.0080980904
Spanish American fiction—20th century—History and criticism 863.009980904
Spanish American literature 860.8098
Spanish American literature—To 1800 860.80980903
Spanish American literature—To 1800—History and criticism 860.9980903
Spanish American literature—20th century 860.80980904
Spanish American literature—20th century—History and criticism 860.9980904
Spanish American literature—History and criticism 860.998
Spanish American poetry 861.008098
Spanish-American War, 1898 973.89
Spanish-American War, 1898—Regimental histories 973.894
Spanish drama 862.008
Spanish drama—Classical period, 1500–1700 862.3; 862.308
Spanish drama—Classical period, 1500–1700—History and criticism 862.309
Spanish language 460
Spanish language—Conversation and phrase books 468.34
Spanish language—Conversation and phrase books—English 468.3421
Spanish language—Conversation and phrase books (for medical personnel) 468.342102461
Spanish language—Dictionaries 463
Spanish language—Dictionaries—English 463.21
Spanish language—Examinations 468.0076
Spanish language—Examinations, questions, etc. 468.0076
Spanish language—Glossaries, vocabularies, etc. 468.2421
Spanish language—Grammar 465; 468.2; 468.2421
Spanish language—Grammar—Handbooks, manuals, etc. 468.2421

Spanish language—Readers 468.6; 468.6421
Spanish language—Readers—Civilization, Hispanic
   468.6421
Spanish language—Readers—Legends 468.6421
Spanish language—Self-instruction 468.2421
Spanish language—Slang 467.09
Spanish language—Technical Spanish 468.00246;
   808.066; 808.0666
Spanish language—Textbooks for foreign speakers—
   English 468.2421; 468.3421
Spanish language—Verb 465; 468.2; 468.2421
Spanish language—Verb—Tables 468.2421
Spanish language—Vocabulary 468.1; 468.2421
Spanish literature 860; 860.8
Spanish literature—To 1500 860.8001; 860.8002
Spanish literature—To 1500—History and criticism
   860.9001; 860.9002
Spanish literature—Classical period, 1500–1700
   860.8003
Spanish literature—Classical period, 1500–1700—
   History and criticism 860.9003
Spanish literature—19th century 860.8006
Spanish literature—19th century—History and criticism
   860.9006
Spanish literature—History and criticism 860.9
Spanish mission buildings—California 979.4
Spanish moss industry 338.4758485
Spanish opening (Chess) 794.122
Spanish poetry 861; 861.008
Spanish poetry—Classical period, 1500 1700 861.3;
   861.308
Spanish poetry—Classical period, 1500–1700—History
   and criticism 861.309
Spanish poetry—20th century 861.62; 861.6208
Spanish poetry—20th century—Translations into
   English 861.6208
Spanish poetry—Translations into English 861.008
Spanish Sign Language 419.46
Spanish Succession, War of, 1701–1714 940.2526
Spanish wit and humor 867.008; 868.02
Spanish wit and humor, Pictorial 741.5946
Spark, Muriel 823.914
Spark, Muriel—Criticism and interpretation 823.914
Sparta (Extinct city) 938.9
Sparta (Extinct city)—History 938.9
Spatial ability 153.752
Spatial analysis (Statistics) 001.422
Spatial behavior in animals 591.566
Spatial systems 003.7
Spearman, Henry (Fictitious character) 813.54
Spearman, Henry (Fictitious character)—Fiction 813.54
Spearmint 583.96; 633.82; 641.3382
Special days 394.2
Special districts 352.19
Special districts—United States 352.190973
Special education 371.9
Special education—Great Britain 371.90941
Special education—Handbooks, manuals, etc. 371.9
Special education—Law and legislation 344.0791
Special education—Law and legislation—United States
   344.730791
Special education—Massachusetts 371.909744
Special education—Social aspects—United States
   306.43
Special education—Study and teaching 371.9043
Special education teachers 371.9043
Special education—United States 371.90973
Special education—United States—Computer-assisted
   instruction 371.904334

Special education—United States—Periodicals
   371.9097305
Special events 394.2
Special events—Marketing 659
Special forces (Military science)—United States
   356.160973
Special librarians 026.00092
Special libraries 026
Special libraries—Administration 025.196
Special libraries—Great Britain 026.000941
Special libraries—Great Britain—Handbooks, manuals,
   etc. 026.000941
Special libraries—United States 026.000973
Special months 394.26
Special needs adoption—United States 362.734
Special operations (Military science) 356.16
Special prosecutors 345.01
Special relativity (Physics) 530.11
Special weeks 394.26
Special years 394.4
Specialists 001
Specialized journalism 070.449
Specialty stores 381.1
Species 576.86; 578.012
Species diversity 577
Species pools 578.7
Speciesism 179.3
Speciesism—Religious aspects 201.5693
Specific language impairment in children 618.92855
Specification writing 692.3
Specifications 658.562
Spectacled bear 599.78
Spectral theory (Mathematics) 515.7222
Spectrograph 621.367
Spectrometer 621.361
Spectroscopic imaging 543.0858
Spectrum analysis 535.84; 547.30858
Spectrum analysis—Periodicals 543.085805
Speech 302.2242; 612.78
Speech disorders 371.9142; 616.855
Speech disorders—Diagnosis 616.855075
Speech disorders in children 371.9142; 618.92855
Speech disorders—Patients 362.196855
Speech disorders—Patients—Rehabilitation 616.85503
Speech disorders—Research—Methodology 616.8550072
Speech perception 401.9
Speech perception in infants 401.9
Speech—Physiological aspects 612.78
Speech processing systems 006.454; 006.54
Speech processing systems industry 338.47006454
Speech—Study and teaching (Elementary) 372.622
Speech synthesis 006.54
Speech therapists 616.85506092
Speech therapy 371.9142; 616.85506
Speech therapy for children 371.9142; 618.9285506
Speech therapy—Handbooks, manuals, etc. 616.85506
Speech therapy—Periodicals 616.8550605
Speeches, addresses, etc. 808.85
Speeches, addresses, etc., American 815; 815.008
Speeches, addresses, etc., American—Indian authors
   973.0497
Speechwriting 808.5
Speed bumps 625.794
Speed humps 625.794
Speed limits 388.3144
Speed reading 372.455; 428.432
Speed traps 343.0946
Speer, Albert, 1905– 943.086092
Speleology 796.525

Speller, Kerstin (Fictitious character) 813.54
Spellers 428.1
Spelling bees 372.632079; 418
Spelling errors 428.1
Spelling reform 428.1
Spelt 633.11
Spencer family 929.20973
Spenser, Edmund, 1552?-1599 821.3
Spenser, Edmund, 1552?-1599—Criticism and
  interpretation 821.3
Spenser, Edmund, 1552?-1599. Faerie queene 821.3
Spenser, Edmund, 1552?-1599—Homes and haunts—
  Ireland 821.3
Spenser, Edmund, 1552?-1599—Philosophy 821.3
Spenser, Edmund, 1552?-1599. Shepheardes calender
  821.3
Spenser (Fictitious character) 813.54
Spenser (Fictitious character)—Fiction 813.54
Spent reactor fuels 363.7289; 621.4838
Spent reactor fuels—Storage 621.4838
Sperm competition 571.845
Sperm whale 599.547
Spermatozoa 571.845
Spermatozoa—Motility 571.845
Spermatozoa—Motility—Disorders 571.93845
Spherical astronomy 522.7
Sphynx cat 636.8
Spice shakers 641.33830284; 683.82; 688.8
Spice trade in literature 808.80355; 809.93355
Spices 641.3383
Spider-Man (Fictitious character) 741.5973
Spider-Man (Fictitious character)—Fiction 813.54
Spiders 595.44
Spiders as pets 639.7
Spielberg, Steven, 1947- 791.430233092
Spies 327.12092
Spin doctors 659.2
Spin fishing 799.12
Spin glasses 530.413
Spina bifida 616.73; 616.83
Spinal adjustment 615.82
Spinal cord 573.869; 612.83
Spinal cord—Surgery 617.482
Spinal cord—Wounds and injuries 617.482044
Spinal cord—Wounds and injuries—Complications
  617.482044
Spinal cord—Wounds and injuries—Treatment
  617.4820446
Spine 611.711
Spine—Abnormalities 616.73; 617.56
Spine—Diseases 616.73
Spine—Magnetic resonance imaging 616.7307548
Spine—Surgery 617.471; 617.56059
Spinor analysis 515.63
Spinoza, Benedictus de, 1632-1677 199.492
Spinoza, Benedictus de, 1632-1677. Ethica 170.92
Spiral computed tomography 616.07572
Spirit writings 133.93
Spiritual biography 291.4
Spiritual direction 253.53
Spiritual exercises 248.3
Spiritual formation 248.4
Spiritual formation—Catholic Church 248.482
Spiritual healing 234.131; 291.31
Spiritual healing—Biblical teaching 234.13
Spiritual journals 248.46
Spiritual journals—Authorship 248.46
Spiritual life 291.44
Spiritual life—Anglican Communion 248.483

Spiritual life—Buddhism 294.3444
Spiritual life—Catholic Church 248.482
Spiritual life—Christianity 248.4
Spiritual life—Christianity—History of doctrines 248.09;
  248.409
Spiritual life—Christianity—Meditations 242
Spiritual life—Church of Jesus Christ of Latter-day
  Saints 248.489332
Spiritual life—Hinduism 294.544
Spiritual life—Judaism 296.7
Spiritual life—Mormon Church 248.48933
Spiritual life—Orthodox Eastern Church 248.4819
Spiritual life—Seventh-Day Adventists 248.486732
Spiritual life—Society of Friends 248.4896
Spiritual life—Tantric Buddhism 294.3444
Spiritual life—Taoism 299.51444
Spiritual life—Zen Buddhism 294.3444
Spiritual retreats for women 269.643; 291.4
Spiritual warfare 235.4
Spiritual warfare—Biblical teaching 235.4
Spiritualism 133.9; 291.21
Spiritualism—United States 133.90973
Spirituality 291.4
Spirituality—Catholic Church 248.482
Spirituals (Songs) 782.253
Spirituals (Songs)—History and criticism 782.25309
Spiro Site (Okla.) 976.679
Spitfire (Fighter planes) 358.4383; 623.7464
Splake 639.37554
Spline theory 511.42
Spline theory—Data processing 511.42
Split annuities 332.02401; 368.37
Spokane County (Wash.) 979.737
Spokane County (Wash.)—Maps 912.79737
Spokane (Wash.) 979.737
Spokane (Wash.)—History 979.737
Sponge divers 639.7
Sponge painting 751.49
Sponges 593.4
Spooning (Hugging) 306.7
Spores (Botany), Fossil 561.13
Sport clothes 646.47
Sporting goods 688.76
Sporting goods industry 338.476887; 380.14568876
Sporting goods industry—Canada 338.4768870971
Sporting goods industry—Canada—Statistics—
  Periodicals 338.4768870971021
Sporting guns 799.213
Sports 796
Sports accidents 617.1027
Sports addiction 616.8584
Sports administration 796.069
Sports administration—United States 796.069
Sports and state 353.78; 796; 796.069
Sports and tourism 338.4791
Sports—Anecdotes 796
Sports betting 796
Sports betting—Law and legislation 344.099
Sports betting—United States 796
Sports—Bibliography 016.796
Sports cards 769.49796
Sports cards—Collectors and collecting 769.49796075
Sports cards—Collectors and collecting—United States
  769.497960973075
Sports—Caricatures and cartoons 741.5973
Sports cars 629.2221
Sports cars—Periodicals 629.222105
Sports—Demographic aspects 306.483
Sports—Encyclopedias 796.03

Sports facilities 725.8043
Sports for children 796.083
Sports for girls 796.083
Sports for physically handicapped children 796.087
Sports for the handicapped 796.087
Sports for the physically handicapped 796.087
Sports for women 796.082
Sports for women—United States 796.0820973
Sports for women—United States—History 796.0820973
Sports—Great Britain 796.0941
Sports—Great Britain—History 796.0941
Sports gynecology 618.10088796
Sports—History 796.09
Sports—Humor 796.0207
Sports in art 704.949796
Sports injuries 617.1027
Sports injuries—Diagnosis 617.1027
Sports injuries—Handbooks, manuals, etc. 617.1027
Sports injuries—Patients 617.1027
Sports injuries—Patients—Rehabilitation 617.1027
Sports injuries—Prevention 617.1027
Sports injuries—Treatment 617.1027
Sports journalism 070.449796
Sports—Law and legislation 344.099
Sports—Law and legislation—United States 344.73099
Sports—Law and legislation—United States—Periodicals 344.73099
Sports—Management 796.069
Sports massage 615.822088796
Sports medicine 617.1027
Sports medicine—Handbooks, manuals, etc. 617.1027
Sports—Miscellanea 796
Sports—Moral and ethical aspects 175
Sports museums 796.074
Sports—Philosophy 796.01
Sports physical therapists 615.82092
Sports physical therapy 617.1027
Sports physicians 617.1027092
Sports—Physiological aspects 612.044
Sports—Psychological aspects 796.01
Sports records 796.021
Sports records—Periodicals 796.021
Sports—Rules 796
Sports sciences 613.71; 796.015
Sports—Social aspects 306.483
Sports—Social aspects—United States 306.4830973
Sports—Sociological aspects 306.483
Sports teams 796.06
Sports tournaments 790.134
Sports uniforms 796.0284
Sports—United States 796.0973
Sports—United States—History 796.0973
Sports—United States—Marketing 796.0698
Sports upsets 796
Sports videos 778.598796
Sports—Vocational guidance 796.023
Sports—Vocational guidance—United States 796.02373
Sportscasters 796.092
Sportsmanship 175
Spotsylvania County (Va.) 975.5365
Spotsylvania County (Va.)—Maps 912.755365
Spotted owl 598.97
Spotting (Cleaning) 648.1
Spouses 306.872
Spouses of clergy 253.22
Spouses of clergy—Religious life 248.844
Spouses—Prayer-books and devotions 242.644; 242.844
Spouses—Religious life 248.844
Spraying 660.294515

Spread spectrum communications 384; 621.382
Spring 508.2; 578.43
Spring animals 591.76
Spring, Penny (Fictitious character) 813.54
Spring, Penny (Fictitious character)—Fiction 813.54
Springsteen, Bruce 782.42166092
Sprint (Computer file) 652.55369
Spruce 585.2
SPSS (Computer file) 005.3042
SPSS for Windows 300.2855369; 519.402855369
SPSS/PC+ (Computer file) 005.369; 300.2855369
SPSS X 005.329
Spy stories, English 823.0872; 823.087208
Spy stories, English—History and criticism 823.087209
Spy television programs 791.45658
SQL (Computer program language) 005.7565
SQL server 005.7585
Square dancing 793.34
Square-riggers 623.822
Squares (Instruments) 681.2
Squash rackets (Game) 796.343
Squeak toys 688.72
Squirrels 599.36
Sraffa, Piero 330.15
Sri Lanka 954.93
Sri Lanka—Civilization 954.93
Sri Lanka—Description and travel 915.49304; 915.4930432
Sri Lanka—Economic conditions 330.95493
Sri Lanka—Economic conditions—Periodicals 330.95493005
Sri Lanka—Economic policy 338.95493
Sri Lanka—Ethnic relations 305.80095493
Sri Lanka—Foreign relations 327.5493
Sri Lanka—Guidebooks 915.49304; 915.4930432
Sri Lanka—History 954.93
Sri Lanka—History—To 1505 954.93; 954.9301
Sri Lanka—History—1505–1948 954.9301; 954.9302
Sri Lanka—Maps 912.5493
Sri Lanka—Politics and government 320.95493; 954.93
Sri Lanka—Politics and government—1978– 320.9549309048; 954.9303
Sri Lanka—Social life and customs 954.93
St. John, Jeremiah (Fictitious character) 813.54
St. Louis Cardinals (Baseball team) 796.357640977866
St. Louis Cardinals (Baseball team)—History 796.357640977866
Stability 531.3
Stability of ships 623.8171
Stacking chairs 645.4; 684.13
Stadiums 796.068
Stafford County (Va.) 975.526
Stafford County (Va.)—Maps 912.75526
Stafford family 929.20973
Stafford, Jean, 1915– 813.54
Staffordshire (England) 942.46
Staffordshire (England)—Guidebooks 914.24604; 914.24604859; 914.2460486
Staffordshire pottery 738.37
Stage lighting 792.025
Stage management 792.023; 792.025
Stagonospora diseases 632.45
Stains and staining (Microscopy) 570.2827
Stair building 694.6
Stakes (Mormon Church) 262.4
Stalag Luft III 940.547243094381
Stalin, Joseph, 1879–1953 947.0842092
Stalingrad, Battle of, 1942–1943 940.5421747
Stalkers 364.15

Stalking 364.15
Stalking victims 362.88
Stamford (Conn.) 974.69
Stamford (Conn.)—History 974.69
Stamp collecting 737.6075; 769.56; 769.56075
Stamp collecting—Handbooks, manuals, etc. 769.56075
Stamp collecting—United States 769.56973
Stamp duties 336.272
Stamp duties—Great Britain 343.41057
Stamp duties—Pakistan 343.5491057
Stamp pads 681.6
Stand-up comedy 792.23
Standard language 418
Standard poodle 636.728
Standardization 389.6
Standardization—United States 389.60973
Standards, Engineering 620.00218
Standards of length 530.81
Stanhope, Hester Lucy, Lady, 1776–1839 915.6041092
Stanley Cup (Hockey) 796.962648
Stanley Cup (Hockey)—History 796.962648
Stanley, Henry M. (Henry Morton), 1841–1904
 916.70423092
Stanze di Raffaello (Vatican Palace, Vatican City)
 945.634
Staphylinidae 595.7642
Staphylococcal infections 616.92
Staphylococcus 579.353
Staple removers 651.2; 681.6
Star Hill Farm (Imaginary place) 823.914
Star quilts 746.46
Star trek, Deep Space Nine (Television program)
 791.4572
Star Trek films 791.4375
Star Trek films—Religious aspects 791.4375
Star trek (Television program) 791.4572
Star Trek television programs 791.4575
Star Trek television programs—Religious aspects
 791.4575
Star trek, the next generation (Television program)
 791.4572
Star Wars figures 688.7221; 791.4375
Star Wars films 791.4375
Star Wars films—Dictionaries 791.4375
Star Wars films—History and criticism 791.4375
Starbuck, Shawn (Fictitious character) 813.54
Starch 664.2
Starfishes 593.93
Stark, David (Fictitious character) 813.54
Stars 523.8
Stars—Atlases 523.80223
Stars—Atmospheres 523.86
Stars—Catalogs 523.80216
Stars—Clusters 523.85
Stars—Evolution 523.88
Stars—Formation 523.88
Stars—Globular clusters 523.855
Stars in art 704.943
Stars—Observers' manuals 523.80223
Stars—Spectra 523.87
Stars—Structure 523.86
State action (Civil rights) 342.085
State action (Civil rights)—United States 342.73085
State boards of education 379.152
State courts 347.733
State departments of education 353.8213
State governments 352.13
State governments—United States 320.473; 352.130973
State libraries 027.5

State library agencies 027.5
State-local relations 352.143
State-sponsored terrorism 327.117; 363.32
State succession 341.26
State universities and colleges 378.053
Statecharts (Computer science) 005.12
Statehood (American politics) 320.473049
States, Small 327.101
Statesmen 321.00922
Statics 620.103; 620.1053
Statins (Cardiovascular agents) 615.718
Stationary bicycles 613.710284
Stationery 676.2823
Stations of the Cross 232.963
Stations of the Cross—Meditations 232.963
Statistical consultants 310.92
Statistical decision 519.542
Statistical hypothesis testing 519.56
Statistical mechanics 530.13; 530.133
Statistical physics 530.13; 530.1595
Statistical services 310.6
Statistical thermodynamics 536.7
Statisticians 310.92
Statistics 001.4; 001.422; 310; 519.5
Statistics—Dictionaries 519.503
Statistics—Graphic methods 001.4226
Statistics—Periodicals 310.5; 519.505
Statistics—Problems, exercises, etc. 519.5076
Statius, P. Papinius (Publius Papinius). Silvae 871.01
Statue of Liberty (New York, N.Y.) 974.71
Status of forces agreements 341.728
Statutes 348.02
Stay of proceedings (Criminal procedure) 345.07
Stead, Christina, 1902– 823.912
Stead, Christina, 1902– —Criticism and interpretation
 823.912
Steam-boilers 621.183
Steam-boilers—Efficiency 621.183
Steam engineering 621.1
Steam-engines 621.1
Steam locomotives 625.261
Steam locomotives—Great Britain 625.2610941
Steam locomotives—Great Britain—History 625.2610941
Steam locomotives—History 625.26109
Steam locomotives—United States 625.2610973
Steam power plants 621.1; 621.312132
Steam-turbines 621.165; 621.24
Steamboats 623.82436
Steaming (Cookery) 641.587
Stearns County (Minn.) 977.647
Stearns County (Minn.)—Maps 912.77647
Steed, John (Fictitious character) 791.4372; 791.4572
Steel 669.1
Steel alloys 620.17; 669.142
Steel bands (Music) 786.843
Steel castings 672.2
Steel—Corrosion 620.1723
Steel—Electrometallurgy 669.142
Steel founding 669.142
Steel—Heat treatment 672.36
Steel industry and trade 338.47669142
Steel industry and trade—Statistics 338.47669142021
Steel industry and trade—Statistics—Periodicals
 338.47669142021
Steel industry and trade—United States
 338.476691420973
Steel industry and trade—United States—History
 338.476691420973

Steel industry and trade—United States—Statistics 338.476691420973021

Steel industry and trade—United States—Statistics—Periodicals 338.476691420973021

Steel—Metallurgy 669.142; 669.1424

Steel, Stainless 620.17

Steel, Stainless—Corrosion 620.1723

Steel, Structural 624.1821

Steel tube industry 338.47672832

Steel—Welding 672.52

Steele family 929.20973

Steele, Rayford (Fictitious character) 813.54

Steelhead fishing 799.1757

Steer roping 791.84

Steer wrestling 791.84

Stefanos, Nick (Fictitious character) 813.54

Stefanos, Nick (Fictitious character)—Fiction 813.54

Stegosaurus 567.9153

Stein, Edith, Saint, 1891–1942 271.97102

Stein, Gertrude, 1874–1946 818.5209

Stein, Gertrude, 1874–1946—Bibliography 016.8185209

Stein, Gertrude, 1874–1946—Criticism and interpretation 818.5209

Stein, Gertrude, 1874–1946—Friends and associates 818.5209

Steinbeck, John, 1902–1968 813.52

Steinbeck, John, 1902–1968—Bibliography 016.81352

Steinbeck, John, 1902–1968—Criticism and interpretation 813.52

Steinbeck, John, 1902–1968. Grapes of wrath 813.52

Steinbeck, John, 1902–1968. Grapes of wrath—Examinations 813.52

Steiner, Rudolf, 1861–1925 299.935092

Steiner systems 516.13

Stellar associations 523.8

Stem vegetables 635.3; 641.353

Stems (Botany) 575.4; 581.495

Stencil work 745.73

Stendhal, 1783–1842 843.7

Stendhal, 1783–1842—Criticism and interpretation 843.7

Stendhal, 1783–1842. Red and the black 843.7

Stengel, Casey 796.357092

Stentz family 929.20973

Step dancing 793.3

Stepfamilies 306.874

Stepfamilies—United States 306.874

Stephen, Leslie, Sir, 1832–1904 828.809

Stephens, James, 1882–1950 821.912

Stephens, James, 1882–1950—Criticism and interpretation 821.912

Stephenson County (Ill.) 977.333

Stephenson County (Ill.)—Maps 912.77333

Stephenson family 929.20973

Stepmothers 306.8743

Stepmothers—United States 306.8743

Stepparents 306.874

Stepparents—United States 306.874

Steppe animals 591.744

Stepping motor industry 338.476298323

Stereochemistry 541.223; 572.33

Stereoencephalotomy 617.481

Stereophonic sound systems 621.389334

Stereoscopic views 778.4

Stereotype (Psychology) 303.385

Stereotype (Psychology) in literature 808.80353; 809.93353

Sterilization 614.48

Sterilization (Birth control) 363.97; 613.942

Sterilization of women 613.942

Sterilization of women—Law and legislation 344.048

Stern, Howard, 1954– 791.44028092

Sterne, Laurence, 1713–1768 823.6

Sterne, Laurence, 1713–1768—Criticism and interpretation 823.6

Sterne, Laurence, 1713–1768. Life and opinions of Tristram Shandy, gentleman 823.6

Steroid hormones 573.44579; 612.405

Steroid hormones—Physiological effect 612.405

Steroid hormones—Receptors 573.44579

Steroid saponins 572.579

Steroids 547.73; 572.579

Steuben Glass, Inc. 748.2914783

Stevens County (Minn.) 977.642

Stevens County (Minn.)—Maps 912.77642

Stevens family 929.20973

Stevens, Wallace, 1879–1955 811.52

Stevens, Wallace, 1879–1955—Criticism and interpretation 811.52

Stevenson, Adlai E. (Adlai Ewing), 1900–1965 973.921092

Stevenson, James, 1929– 741.642092

Stevenson, James, 1929– —Childhood and youth 741.642092

Stevenson, Robert Louis, 1850–1894 828.809

Stevenson, Robert Louis, 1850–1894—Correspondence 828.809

Stevenson, Robert Louis, 1850–1894—Criticism and interpretation 828.809

Stewardship, Christian 248.6

Stewart, James, 1908– 791.43028092

Stewart, Martha 640.92

Stews 641.823

Stick fighting 796.8

Sticklebacks 597.672

Stickler syndrome 616.77

Sticky notes 651.74; 676.2823

Stieglitz, Alfred, 1864–1946 770.92

Stiles 631.27

Still-life painting—Technique 751.45435

Stillbirth 618.32

Stillbirth—Proof and certification 614.1

Stilton cheese 637.354; 641.37354

Stir frying 641.77

Stochastic analysis 519.2

Stochastic approximation 519.2

Stochastic control theory 629.8312

Stochastic differential equations 519.2

Stochastic geometry 519.2

Stochastic integrals 519.2

Stochastic music 781.3

Stochastic partial differential equations 519.2

Stochastic processes 519.23; 530.1923

Stochastic processes in music 781.32

Stochastic programming 519.7

Stochastic systems 519.23

Stock car racing 796.72

Stock car racing—United States 796.720973

Stock car racing—United States—History 796.720973

Stock cars (Automobiles) 629.228

Stock certificates 332.6322

Stock exchanges 332.642

Stock exchanges—Dictionaries 332.64203

Stock exchanges—Law and legislation 346.0926

Stock exchanges—Law and legislation—United States 346.730926

Stock exchanges—United States 332.6420973

Stock footage 791.4302; 791.4502

Stream conservation 333.916216
Stream ecology 577.64
Stream measurements 551.4830287
Streaming technology (Telecommunications) 006.7876
Street addresses 383.145
Street films 791.43655
Street life 307.76; 909.09732
Street luge racing 796.6
Street newspapers 070.5722; 305.569
Street photography 778.94
Street poetry 808.81
Street-railroad stations—Remodeling for other use 725.310286
Street-railroads 388.46
Street-railroads—England—London 388.4609421
Street vendors 381.18
Streeter (Fictitious character) 813.54
Streisand, Barbra 782.42164092
Strength of materials 620.112
Streptococcus 579.355
Streptomyces 579.378
Stress echocardiography 616.1207543
Stress in adolescence 155.518
Stress in children 155.418
Stress management 155.9042
Stress (Psychology) 155.9042
Stress (Psychology)—Religious aspects 291.442
Stress (Psychology)—Religious aspects—Christianity 248.86
Stress relieving (Materials) 620.1124
Stretching exercises 613.71
Strikes and lockouts 331.892
Strikes and lockouts—Public utilities—Law and legislation 344.01892813636
Strikes and lockouts, Sympathetic 331.8923
Strikes and lockouts, Sympathetic—Law and legislation 344.018923
Strindberg, August, 1849–1912 839.726
Strindberg, August, 1849–1912—Drama 839.7274
Strindberg, August, 1849–1912—Translations into English 839.726
String bands 784.7
String ensembles 785.7
String figures 793.96
String orchestra music 784.7
String quartets 785.7194
String quartets—Parts 785.7194
String quartets—Scores 785.7194
String quartets—Scores and parts 785.7194
String quintets (Violins (2), violas (2), violoncello) 785.7195
String sextets (Violins (2), violas (2), violoncellos (2)) 785.7196
String trios 785.7193
String trios—Scores 785.7193
Stringed instruments 787; 787.19
Stringed instruments, Bowed 787; 787.19
Stringed instruments, Bowed—Instruction and study 787.071
Stringed instruments in art 704.949787
Stringed instruments—Tuning 787.1928
Strip mining 622.292
Strip quilting—Patterns 746.46041
Striped bass fishing 799.1732
Striptease—Law and legislation 344.099; 345.027
Stromatoporoidea 563.58
Structural adjustment (Economic policy) 338.9
Structural adjustment (Economic policy)—Africa 338.96

Structural adjustment (Economic policy)—Africa, Sub-Saharan 338.967
Structural adjustment (Economic policy)—Europe, Eastern 338.947
Structural adjustment (Economic policy)—Latin America 338.98
Structural adjustment (Economic policy)—Nigeria 338.9669
Structural analysis (Engineering) 624.171
Structural analysis (Engineering)—Data processing 624.1710285
Structural analysis (Engineering)—Matrix methods 624.171015129434
Structural anthropology 301
Structural control (Engineering) 624.171
Structural design 624.1771
Structural drawing 692.1
Structural dynamics 624.171
Structural dynamics—Mathematical models 624.171
Structural engineering 624.1
Structural failures 624.171
Structural linguistics 410.18
Structural optimization 624.17713
Structural optimization—Data processing 624.177130285
Structural stability 624.171
Structuralism 149.96
Structuralism (Literary analysis) 801.95
Structure-activity relationships (Biochemistry) 572.4
Structured notes (Securities) 332.632
Structured programming 005.113
Strudel 641.865
Stuart family 929.20973
Stuart, House of 929.72
Stuart, Jeb, 1833–1864 973.73092
Stuart, Jesse, 1906–1984 818.5209
Stuart, Jesse, 1906–1984—Criticism and interpretation 818.5209
Stubbs family 929.20973
Student activities 371.8
Student adjustment 370.158
Student affairs services 371.4; 371.7; 378.194; 378.197
Student affairs services—United States 378.1940973
Student affairs services—United States—Administration 378.197068
Student aid 371.22; 378.3
Student aid—Law and legislation—United States 344.730795
Student aid—United States 378.30973
Student aid—United States—Directories 378.302573
Student aid—United States—Handbooks, manuals, etc. 378.30973
Student aid—United States—Periodicals 378.3097305
Student aid—United States—Statistics 378.30973021
Student aspirations 371.4; 371.8
Student assistance programs 371.7
Student cooperatives 334.088375; 371.83
Student counselors 371.4
Student counselors—Legal status, laws, etc. 344.0794
Student counselors—Legal status, laws, etc.—United States 344.730794
Student counselors—Training of 371.40711
Student counselors—Training of—United States 371.4071173
Student discounts 338.52; 658.82
Student ethics 174.9375
Student evaluation of teachers 371.144
Student exchange programs 370.1162

Student exchange programs—United States 370.11620973
Student expulsion 371.543
Student financial aid administration 371.22; 371.22068; 378.3068
Student financial aid administrators 371.22092; 378.3092
Student government 371.59; 373.159; 378.1959
Student government—Elections 371.59
Student housing 371.871; 378.19871
Student-led parent conferences 371.192
Student loan funds 371.224; 378.362
Student loan funds—United States 378.3620973
Student mobility 371.291
Student movements 371.81; 378.1981
Student movements—United States 378.19810973
Student newspapers and periodicals 371.805; 371.897
Student Nonviolent Coordinating Committee (U.S.) 323.06073
Student participation in curriculum planning 375.001
Student protesters 371.81
Student publications 371.897
Student records 371.2; 371.21; 371.8
Student Self-Concept Scale 371.8019
Student service—United States 361.370973
Student strikes 371.81; 378.1981
Student suspension 371.543
Student teachers 370.711
Student teachers—Supervision of 370.711
Student teachers—Supervision of—United States 370.71173
Student teaching 370.71; 370.711; 371.102
Student teaching—Great Britain 370.71141; 371.102
Student teaching—Handbooks, manuals, etc. 371.102
Student teaching—United States 370.71173
Student television stations 384.55453
Student unions 371.8
Student volunteers in medical care 610.730698
Student volunteers in social service 361.7
Students 371.8
Students—Civil rights 323.3
Students—Drug use 371.784
Students, Foreign 371.82691; 378.1982691
Students, Foreign—Great Britain 378.19826910941
Students, Foreign—United States 371.826910973; 378.19826910973
Students, Foreign—United States—Handbooks, manuals, etc. 371.826910973; 378.19826910973
Students—Health and hygiene 371.71
Students—Legal status, laws, etc. 344.0793
Students—Legal status, laws, etc.—United States 344.730793
Students—Mental health 371.713
Students—Psychology 371.8019
Students—Social conditions 371.8
Students—Substance abuse 371.784
Students, Transfer of 371.2914; 378.16914
Study skills 371.30281; 372.130281; 378.170281
Study skills—Handbooks, manuals, etc. 371.30281; 373.130281
Study skills—Programmed instruction 371.30281
Study skills—United States 378.170281
Stuffed foods (Cookery) 641.8
Stuffing (Cookery) 641.81
Stunt flying 797.54
Stunt kites 629.13332; 796.158
Stunt performers 791.43028; 791.43028092
Stutsman County (N.D.) 978.452
Stutsman County (N.D.)—Maps 912.78452

Stuttering 371.9142; 616.8554
Stuttering in children 371.9142; 618.928554
Stuttering—Treatment 616.855406
Style, Literary 808
Styron, William, 1925- 813.54
Styron, William, 1925- —Criticism and interpretation 813.54
Subacute care 362.1
Subaru automobile 629.2222
Subaru automobile—Maintenance and repair 629.28722
Subaru automobile—Maintenance and repair—Handbooks, manuals, etc. 629.28722
Subcellular fractionation 571.65072
Subchapter S corporations 346.730668
Subchapter S corporations—Taxation 343.73067
Subchapter S corporations—Taxation—Problems, exercises, etc. 343.73067
Subconsciousness 154.2
Subcontracting 346.022
Subcontracting—United States 346.73022
Subculture 306.1
Subduction zones 551.136
Subject cataloging 025.47
Subject headings 025.49
Subject headings—Art 025.497
Subject headings—Canada 025.49971
Subject headings—Children's literature 025.49808899282
Subject headings—Education 025.4937
Subject headings—Engineering 025.4962
Subject headings—Law 025.4934
Subject headings, Library of Congress 025.49
Subject headings—Music 025.4978
Subject headings—Nuclear energy 025.493337924
Subject headings—Social sciences 025.493
Subject (Philosophy) 126
Subjectivity 126
Sublanguage 418
Sublime, The 111.85
Subliminal perception 153.736
Subliminal projection 153.736
Submanifolds 516.362
Submarine geology 551.4608
Submarine medicine 616.98022
Submarine warfare 359.93; 940.451
Submarines (Ships) 359.933; 359.9383; 623.8257
Submarines (Ships)—History 359.938309
Submarines (Ships)—United States 359.93830973
Subnational governments 320.8; 321.023
Subnational governments—Foreign relations 327.1
Subscription television 384.5554
Subsidiary corporations 346.0668
Subsidiary corporations—United States 346.730668
Substance abuse 362.29; 616.86
Substance abuse—Etiology 616.86071
Substance abuse in pregnancy 618.3; 618.3268
Substance abuse—Nursing 610.7368
Substance abuse—Psychological aspects 616.860019
Substance abuse—Relapse—Prevention 616.8606
Substance abuse—Treatment 616.8606
Substance abuse—Treatment—Social aspects 362.29
Substance (Philosophy) 111.1
Substitute teachers 371.14122
Subtraction 513.212
Subud 299.933
Suburban life 307.74
Suburban life in literature 808.80321733; 809.93321733
Suburbs 307.74
Suburbs—United States 307.740973

Superconducting Super Collider 539.736
Superconducting Super Collider—Location 539.736
Superconductivity 537.623
Superconductivity—Periodicals 537.62305
Superconductors 537.623; 621.35
Supercritical fluid chromatography 543.-896
Supercritical fluids 660.042
Supercross 796.756
Superfluidity 530.42
Superior, Lake 977.49
Superior, Lake, Watershed 977.49
Superlattices as materials 537.622
Superman (Comic strip) 741.5973
Supermarkets 381.148
Supernatural in literature 808.8037
Supernovae 523.84465
Supersonic planes 629.13230509
Superstition 001.96
Superstring theories 539.7258
Supersymmetry 539.725
Supervenience (Philosophy) 110
Supervision of employees 658.302
Supervision of employees—Handbooks, manuals, etc.
 658.302
Supervisors 658.302
Supervisors, Industrial 658.302
Supervisory control systems 620.46; 629.8
Suppers 641.53
Supply and demand 338.521
Supply-side economics 330.15
Support services (Management) 650
Supramolecular chemistry 547.1226
Supramolecular electrochemistry 547.137
Supranationalism 321.04; 327.17; 341
Suquamish Indians 979.7004979
Suretyship and guaranty 368.84
Suretyship and guaranty—United States 346.73074
Surf lifesaving (Aquatic sports) 363.14; 797.3
Surface active agents 668.1
Surface active agents—Analysis 668.1
Surface brightness (Astronomy) 523.01522
Surface chemistry 541.33
Surface mount technology 621.381531
Surface plates 681.2
Surface preparation 671.7
Surfaces 516.352
Surfaces, Algebraic 516.352
Surfaces (Physics) 530.417; 530.427
Surfaces (Physics)—Optical properties 530.427
Surfaces (Technology) 620.44
Surfaces (Technology)—Analysis 620.440287
Surfaces (Technology)—Testing 620.440287
Surfers 797.32092241
Surfing 797.32
Surgeons 617.092
Surgeons general (Military personnel) 355.345
Surgery 617
Surgery—Complications 617.01
Surgery—Examinations, questions, etc. 617.0076
Surgery—Handbooks, manuals, etc. 617
Surgery—History 617.09
Surgery, Military 617.99
Surgery—Nutritional aspects 617.919
Surgery, Operative 617.91
Surgery, Operative—Atlases 617.9100222
Surgery, Operative—Handbooks, manuals, etc. 617.91
Surgery—Outlines, syllabi, etc. 617
Surgery, Plastic 617.95
Surgery, Plastic—Complications 617.95

Surgical diseases 617
Surgical emergencies 617.026
Surgical instruments and apparatus 617.9178
Surgical instruments and apparatus—Atlases 617.9178
Surgical intensive care 617.919
Surgical nursing 610.73677
Surgical wound infections 617.01
Suriname 988.3
Surplus agricultural commodities, American—India
 341.7592
Surplus agricultural commodities, American—Indonesia
 341.7592
Surplus agricultural commodities, American—Pakistan
 341.7592
Surplus agricultural commodities, American—Vietnam
 341.7592
Surplus commodities 338.47
Surplus government property—United States—
 Purchasing 352.54
Surplus industrial property 658.78
Surplus military property 355.62137
Surrealism 709.04063
Surrealism (Literature) 809.91163
Surrey (England) 942.21
Surrey (England)—Maps 912.4221
Surry County (Va.)—Genealogy 929.3755562
Surveying 526.9
Surveying—Handbooks, manuals, etc. 526.9
Surveying—Instruments 526.90284
Surveying—Law and legislation 346.0432
Surveying—Law and legislation—United States
 346.730432
Surveying—Periodicals 526.905
Surveyor Program (U.S.) 629.4353
Surveyors 526.9092
Surveys 001.433
Survival after airplane accidents, shipwrecks, etc.
 613.69
Survival analysis (Biometry) 610.727
Survival skills 613.69
Sus 599.6332
Sushi 641.392
Suspense fiction 808.83872
Suspension bridges 624.5
Suspicion 152.4
Suspicion in literature 808.80353; 809.93353
Sussex County (Del.)—Genealogy 929.37517
Sustainable agriculture 333.7616; 631.58
Sustainable architecture 720.47
Sustainable development 338.927
Sustainable development—Africa 338.96
Sustainable development—United States 338.973
Sustainable forestry 634.92
Sutcliffe, Evelyn (Fictitious character) 813.54
Sutcliffe, Peter 364.1523092
Sutherland, Joan, 1926– 782.1092
Sutpen family (Fictitious characters) 813.52
Sutpen family (Fictitious characters)—Fiction 813.52
Sutton Valley Pony Club (Imaginary organization)
 823.914
Suzuki motorcycle 629.2275
Suzuki motorcycle—Maintenance and repair 629.28775
Suzuki motorcycle—Maintenance and repair—
 Handbooks, manuals, etc. 629.28775
SV40 (Virus) 579.2445
Swahili language 496.392
Swallows 598.826
Swamp ecology 577.68
Swann family 929.20973

Swans 598.418
Swansea (Wales) 942.982
Swansea (Wales)—History 942.982
Swap shops 381.19
Swaps (Finance) 332.5
Swaps (Finance)—Taxation 336.2783325
Swaps (Finance)—Taxation—Law and legislation 343.05246
Swarm intelligence 006.3
Swarming (Military science) 355.422
Swashbuckler films 791.43658
Swearingen family 929.20973
Sweat suits 646.47; 687.16
Sweaters 746.92
Sweatshirts 391
Sweatshops 331.25
Sweden 948.5
Sweden—Description and travel 914.8504; 914.850459; 914.85046
Sweden—Economic policy 338.9485
Sweden—Guidebooks 914.8504; 914.850459; 914.85046
Sweden—History 948.5
Sweden—Pictorial works 948.500222
Swedenborg, Emanuel, 1688–1772 289.4092
Swedish Americans 973.04397
Swedish Americans—History 973.04397
Swedish language 439.7
Swedish language—Dictionaries 439.73
Swedish language—Dictionaries—English 439.7321
Swedish language—Grammar 439.75; 439.782; 439.782421
Swedish Sign Language 419.485
Swedish students 371.82397; 378.1982397
Swedish wit and humor, Pictorial 741.59485
Sweeteners 664.5
Swift County (Minn.) 977.641
Swift County (Minn.)—Maps 912.77641
Swift, Jonathan, 1667–1745 828.509
Swift, Jonathan, 1667–1745—Criticism and interpretation 828.509
Swift, Jonathan, 1667–1745. Gulliver's travels 823.5
Swift, Jonathan, 1667–1745—Poetic works 821.5
Swift, Jonathan, 1667–1745—Political and social views 828.509
Swift, Jonathan, 1667–1745. Tale of a tub 823.5
Swift, Jonathan, 1667–1745—Technique 828.509
Swim clubs 797.2106
Swimming 797.21
Swimming coaches 797.21092
Swimming for children 797.21083
Swimming for handicapped persons 797.21087
Swimming—Physiological aspects 612.044
Swimming pools 643.55; 797.2
Swimming pools—Design and construction 690.896
Swimming pools—Maintenance and repair 643.55; 690.8960288
Swimming—Study and teaching 797.21071
Swimming—Training 797.2107
Swinburne, Algernon Charles, 1837–1909 821.8
Swinburne, Algernon Charles, 1837–1909—Criticism and interpretation 821.8
Swine 636.4
Swine—Diseases 636.40896
Swine—Feeding and feeds 636.40855
Swine—Fetuses—Anatomy—Laboratory manuals 571.863319633078
Swine influenza—Vaccination—United States 614.518
Swing (Dance) 793.33
Swing (Golf) 796.3523

Swinnerton, Frank, 1884– 823.912
Swiss literature 830; 830.809494
Swiss wit and humor, Pictorial 741.59494
Switched multi-megabit data service 004.66
Switching circuits 621.3815372
Switching theory 621.3815372
Switzerland 949.4
Switzerland—Description and travel 914.9404; 914.940473; 914.940474
Switzerland—Guidebooks 914.9404; 914.940473; 914.940474
Switzerland—History 949.4
Switzerland—Pictorial works 949.400222
Swordfish fisheries 338.372778; 639.2778
Swordplay 796.86
Swords 623.441; 739.722
Swords—Japan 623.441; 739.7220952
Swordsmen in literature 808.80352355
Sydney Basin (N.S.W.) 994.4
Sydney Metropolitan Area (N.S.W.) 994.41
Sydney Metropolitan Area (N.S.W.)—Maps 912.9441
Sydney (N.S.W.) 994.41
Sydney (N.S.W.)—Guidebooks 919.44104; 919.4410466; 919.441047
Sydney (N.S.W.)—Pictorial works 919.44100222
Sylvester, Ben (Fictitious character) 813.54
Symbiosis 577.85; 591.785
Symbolic anthropology 306.4
Symbolic interactionism 302
Symbolism 302.2223
Symbolism (Art movement) 709.0347
Symbolism in architecture 720.1
Symbolism in art 700.415; 704.946
Symbolism in literature 808.8015; 809.915
Symbolism in the Bible 220.64
Symbolism of colors in art 704.946
Symbolism of numbers 133.335
Symmetric spaces 516.362
Symmetry 701.8
Symmetry groups 512.2
Symmetry (Music) 781.2
Symmetry (Physics) 539.725
Symmorphosis 571.3; 571.833
Sympathetic nervous system 573.85
Symphonic poems 784.21843
Symphonies 784.2184
Symphonies—Analysis, appreciation 784.2184117
Symphonies (Chamber orchestra) 784.3184
Symphonies—Excerpts 784.2184
Symphonies (Organ) 786.5184
Symphonies—Scores 784.2184
Symphonies (String orchestra) 784.7184
Symphony 784.2184
Symphony orchestras 784.2
Symplectic manifolds 516.362
Symptoms 616.047
Synagogue archives 027.67
Synagogue officers 296.61
Synagogue trustees 296.61
Synagogues 296.65
Synanthropic plants 581.6
Synchrotron radiation 539.735
Synchrotron radiation sources 539.735
Synchrotrons 539.735
Syndicalism 335.82
Synesthesia 152.189
Synge, J. M. (John Millington), 1871–1909 822.912
Synge, J. M. (John Millington), 1871–1909—Criticism and interpretation 822.912

Synge, J. M. (John Millington), 1871–1909—Journeys—Ireland—Aran Islands 828.91203
Synoptic problem 226.066
Synthesizer music 786.74
Synthesizer (Musical instrument) 786.74; 786.7419
Synthetic aperture radar 621.38485
Synthetic fuels 662.66
Synthetic lubricants 621.89
Synthetic vaccines 615.372
Syphilis 616.9513
Syria 956.91
Syria—Antiquities 939.43
Syria—Description and travel 915.69104; 915.6910442
Syria—Guidebooks 915.69104; 915.6910442
Syria—History 956.91
Syria—History—20th century 956.9104
Syrphidae 595.774
System 7 005.4469
System analysis 003
System design 004.21; 621.392
System failures (Engineering) 620.00452
System identification 003.1
System safety 620.86
System theory 003
Systematic reviews (Medical research) 616.0072
Systematic Screening for Behavior Disorders 362.20422; 618.9289075
Systemic grammar 415
Systemic lupus erythematosus 616.77
Systemic memory hypothesis 113; 153.12
Systems engineering 620.001171
Systems engineering—Periodicals 620.001171
Systems librarians 025.00285
Systems migration 620.001171
Systems programming (Computer science) 005.42
Systems software 005.43
T cells 616.0797
T-shirts 391
Taarab (Music) 782.42163
Tabasaran literature 899.964
Tablature (Musical notation) 780.148
Table etiquette 395.54
Table service 642.6
Table setting and decoration 642.8
Table tennis 796.346
Tables 684.13
Tabletop hockey (Game) 794.7
Tablets (Medicine) 615.43
Tabulata 563.6
Tachyglossidae 599.29
Tacitus, Cornelius 878.0109; 937.07092
Tacitus, Cornelius—Translations into English 878.0109
Tacos 641.84
Tactics 355.42
Tae kwon do 796.8153
Taeniodonta 569.31
Taffeta 677.6
Taft, William H. (William Howard), 1857–1930 973.912092
Tag games 796.14
Taggants 363.33; 662.2
Tagore, Rabindranath, 1861–1941 891.4414
Tagore, Rabindranath, 1861–1941—Criticism and interpretation 891.4414
Tagore, Rabindranath, 1861–1941—Translations into English 891.4414
Taguchi methods (Quality control) 658.562
Tahiti 996.211
Tahiti—Discovery and exploration 996.211

Tahiti—Guidebooks 919.621104
Tahoe, Lake, Region (Calif. and Nev.) 979.438
Tahoe, Lake, Region (Calif. and Nev.)—Guidebooks 917.943804; 917.94380453; 917.94380454
Tai chi 613.7148
Taiga ecology 577.37
Taiga plants 581.737
Tailgate parties 642.3
Tailoring 646.4
Tailoring (Women's) 646.404
Tailwater ecology 577.64
Taiwan 951.249
Taiwan—Economic conditions 330.951249
Taiwan—Economic conditions—1975– 330.95124905
Taiwan—Economic policy 338.951249
Taiwan—Economic policy—1945– 338.951249
Taiwan—Foreign relations 327.51249
Taiwan—Foreign relations—1945– 327.51249
Taiwan—Guidebooks 915.124904; 915.1249045
Taiwan—Pictorial works 915.124900222; 951.24900222
Taiwan—Politics and government 951.249
Taiwan—Politics and government—1945– 320.95124909045; 951.24905
Taj Mahal (Agra, India) 954.2
Talbot County (Md.) 975.232
Talbot County (Md.)—Maps 912.75232
Talented students 371.95; 378.198279
Tales 398.2
Tales—Africa 398.2096
Tales—Africa, West 398.20966
Tales—Arab countries 398.209174927
Tales—Asia 398.2095
Tales—Australia 398.20994
Tales—China 398.20951
Tales—China—Tibet 398.209515
Tales—France 398.20944
Tales—Germany 398.20943
Tales—Ghana 398.209667
Tales—Great Britain 398.20941
Tales—India 398.20954
Tales—Iran 398.20955
Tales—Ireland 398.209415
Tales—Ireland—History and criticism 398.209415
Tales—Italy 398.20945
Tales—Japan 398.20952
Tales—Korea 398.209519
Tales, Medieval 891.6631
Tales—Mexico 398.20972
Tales—Nepal 398.2095496
Tales—Nigeria 398.209669
Tales—Philippines 398.209599
Tales—Poland 398.209438
Tales—Russia 398.20947
Tales—Scotland 398.209411
Tales—Southern States 398.20975
Tales—Soviet Union 398.20947
Tales—Texas 398.209764
Tales—Thailand 398.209593
Tales—Turkey 398.209561
Tales—United States 398.20973
Talismans 133.44
Talk shows 791.456
Talk shows—United States 791.456
Talking books 002; 011.38
Tall buildings 720.483
Tall buildings—Design and construction 690; 720.483
Tall buildings—Fires and fire prevention 628.922
Tall women 305.9081

Tallahassee (Fla.)—Genealogy—Periodicals 929.1072075988
Tallchief, Maria 792.8028092
Tallinn (Estonia) 947.98
Tallinn (Estonia)—Guidebooks 914.798
Talmud 296.12
Talmud—Criticism, Redaction 296.125066
Talmud—Introductions 296.125061
Tama County (Iowa) 977.756
Tama County (Iowa)—Maps 912.77756
Tamar, Hilary (Fictitious character) 823.914
Tamboril 786.94
Tambour work 746.44
Tamerlane, 1336–1405 950.2092
Tamil (Indic people) 305.894811; 909.0494811
Tamil (Indic people)—Sri Lanka—Politics and government 323.1194811; 954.93
Tamil language 494.811
Tamil language—Grammar 494.8115; 494.81182; 494.81182421
Tamil literature 894.811; 894.81108
Tamil literature—History and criticism 894.81109
Tamil philology 494.811
Tamil poetry 894.8111; 894.8111008
Tamil poetry—To 1500 894.81111; 894.8111108
Tamil poetry—To 1500—Translations into English 894.8111108
Tampons 613.4; 677.8
Tan singing 782.42162914072983
Tanagers 598.075
Tanbur 787.82
Tangerine industry 338.17431
Tango (Dance) 793.33
Tangos 784.18885
Tanikawa, Shuntarō, 1931– 895.615
Tanikawa, Shuntarō, 1931– —Translations into English 895.615
Tank warfare 358.18
Tanks (Military science) 358.1883; 623.74752
Tanks (Military science)—Germany—History 623.747520943
Tanner, Evan (Fictitious character) 813.54
Tanner, Evan (Fictitious character)—Fiction 813.54
Tanner, John Marshall (Fictitious character) 813.54
Tanner, John Marshall (Fictitious character)—Fiction 813.54
Tanning 675.23
Tantric Buddhism 294.3925
Tantrism 294.5514
Tanzania 967.8
Tanzania—Description and travel 916.7804; 916.780442
Tanzania—Economic conditions 330.9678
Tanzania—Economic conditions—1964– 330.967804
Tanzania—Economic conditions—1964– —Periodicals 330.967804
Tanzania—Economic policy 338.9678
Tanzania—History 967.8
Tanzanite 553.87
Taoism 299.514
Taoism—Sacred books 299.51482
Taoist astrology 133.5949514
Tap dance teachers 792.78
Tap dancers 792.78
Tap dancing 792.78
Tapestry 746.3
Taphonomy 560
Taran (Fictitious character : Alexander) 813.54
Tarantulas 595.44
Tarantulas as pets 639.7

Tarawa, Battle of, 1943 940.5426
Tardive dyskinesia 616.83
Target acquisition 658.16
Target costing 658.1552
Target practice 799.3
Tariff 382.7
Tariff—Canada 382.70971
Tariff—Great Britain 382.70941
Tariff—Law and legislation 343.056
Tariff—Law and legislation—Canada 343.71056
Tariff—Law and legislation—European Economic Community countries 343.4056
Tariff—Law and legislation—North America 343.7056
Tariff—Law and legislation—United States 343.73056
Tariff—Law and legislation—United States—Periodicals 343.73056
Tariff on farm produce 382.41
Tariff on information technology products 336.266004
Tariff preferences—United States 382.753
Tariff—United States 382.70973
Tariff—United States—History 382.70973
Tarka 788.35
Taro leaf blight 633.68
Tarot 133.32424
Tartans 929.6
Tartans—Scotland 929.609411
Tarzan (Fictitious character) 813.52
Tarzan (Fictitious character)—Fiction 813.52
Tasmania 994.6
Tasmania—History 994.6
Tasmania—Maps 912.946; 912.96
Tasmanian devil 599.27
Taste 573.878; 612.87
Tatting 746.436
Tatting—Patterns 746.436041
Tattooing 391.65
Tatum, Bert (Fictitious character) 813.54
Tatum, Nan (Fictitious character) 813.54
Taurine—Physiological effect 612.0157
Taurus automobile 629.2222
Taurus automobile—Maintenance and repair 629.28722
Taurus automobile—Maintenance and repair—Handbooks, manuals, etc. 629.28722
Taverns (Inns) in literature 808.80355; 809.93355
Tax accounting 657.46
Tax accounting—Law and legislation 343.042
Tax accounting—Law and legislation—United States 343.73042
Tax administration and procedure 343.04
Tax administration and procedure—United States 343.7304
Tax administration and procedure—United States—Periodicals 343.730405
Tax assessment 336.222
Tax assessment—Law and legislation 343.042
Tax assessment—Law and legislation—Great Britain 343.41042
Tax auditing 343.04
Tax auditing—United States 343.7304
Tax collection 343.042
Tax collection—United States 343.73042
Tax consultants 343.052044
Tax credits 336.206
Tax credits—Law and legislation 343.05237
Tax credits—Law and legislation—United States 343.7305237
Tax evasion 345.0233
Tax evasion—India 364.133
Tax evasion—United States 345.730233

Tax exemption—Law and legislation 343.0523
Tax exemption—Law and legislation—United States 343.730523
Tax havens 343.0523
Tax incidence 336.294
Tax penalties 343.052
Tax penalties—United States 343.73052
Tax planning 336.2
Tax planning—United States 336.200973; 343.7304
Tax protests and appeals 343.042
Tax protests and appeals—United States 343.73040269
Tax refunds 336.2
Tax return preparation industry 338.4765746
Tax returns 343.052044
Tax returns—United States—Data processing 343.7305204402854
Tax shelters—Law and legislation 343.05238
Tax shelters—Law and legislation—United States 343.7305238
Tax sparing 341.4844
Taxation 336.2
Taxation—Canada 336.200971
Taxation—Developing countries 336.20091724
Taxation—European Economic Community countries 336.20094
Taxation—Great Britain 336.200941
Taxation—Law and legislation 343.04
Taxation—Law and legislation—Australia 343.9404
Taxation—Law and legislation—California 343.79404
Taxation—Law and legislation—Canada 343.7104
Taxation—Law and legislation—Florida 343.75904
Taxation—Law and legislation—Great Britain 343.4104
Taxation—Law and legislation—India 343.5404
Taxation—Law and legislation—North Carolina 343.75604
Taxation—Law and legislation—Philippines 343.59904
Taxation—Law and legislation—Philippines—Cases 343.599040264
Taxation—Law and legislation—South Africa 343.6804
Taxation—Law and legislation—United States 343.7304
Taxation—Law and legislation—United States—Dictionaries 343.7304; 343.730403
Taxation—Law and legislation—United States—Legal research 343.7304072
Taxation—Law and legislation—United States—Outlines, syllabi, etc. 343.7304
Taxation—Law and legislation—United States—Periodicals 343.730405
Taxation—Law and legislation—United States—States 343.73043
Taxation, State 336.2013
Taxation—United States 336.200973
Taxation—United States—History 336.200973
Taxation—United States—States 336.201373
Taxation—United States—States—Law and legislation—Cases 343.730430264
Taxicabs 388.34232
Taxicabs—Fares—New York (State)—New York 388.413214
Taxidermy 590.752; 596.0752
Taxpayer compliance 336.291
Tay-Sachs disease 616.858845
Taylor County (Iowa) 977.779
Taylor County (Iowa)—Maps 912.77779
Taylor, Edward, 1642–1729 811.1
Taylor, Edward, 1642–1729—Criticism and interpretation 811.1
Taylor, Elizabeth, 1932– 791.43028092
Taylor family 929.20973

Taylor, James Hudson, 1832–1905 266.0092
Taylor, Peter Hillsman, 1917– 813.54
Taylor, Peter Hillsman, 1917– —Criticism and interpretation 813.54
Tazewell County (Ill.) 977.354
Tazewell County (Ill.)—Maps 912.77354
Tazewell County (Va.)—Genealogy 929.3755763
Tchaikovsky, Peter Ilich, 1840–1893 780.92
Tcl (Computer program language) 005.133
TCP/IP (Computer network protocol) 004.62
Te Deum laudamus (Music) 782.292
Tea 633.72; 641.3372; 641.877
Tea cakes 641.865
Teacher-administrator relationships 371.106
Teacher-counselor relationships 371.106
Teacher effectiveness 371.102
Teacher exchange programs 370.1163
Teacher morale 371.10019
Teacher orientation 371.1; 371.14
Teacher participation in administration 371.106
Teacher participation in administration—United States 371.1060973
Teacher participation in educational counseling 371.4046
Teacher-principal relationships 371.106
Teacher-student relationships 371.1023
Teacher-student relationships—United States 371.10230973
Teachers 371.1; 371.10092
Teachers and community 306.432; 371.19
Teachers' assistants 371.14124
Teachers—Certification 371.12
Teachers—Certification—Minnesota 371.1209776
Teachers—Certification—United States 371.120973
Teachers—Certification—United States—Periodicals 371.12097305
Teachers colleges 370.711
Teachers—Dismissal of 371.100683
Teachers—Dismissal of—Law and legislation 344.078
Teachers—Great Britain 371.100941
Teachers—In-service training 370.7155
Teachers—In-service training—Great Britain 370.7155
Teachers—In-service training—United States 370.7155
Teachers—Job stress 371.10019
Teachers—Legal status, laws, etc. 344.078
Teachers—Legal status, laws, etc.—Great Britain 344.41078
Teachers—Legal status, laws, etc.—Indiana 344.772078
Teachers—Legal status, laws, etc.—United States 344.73078
Teachers—Legal status, laws, etc.—Wisconsin 344.775078
Teachers' lounges 371.625
Teachers of socially handicapped children 371.1
Teachers of the deaf 371.912
Teachers—Pensions 331.252913711
Teachers—Pensions—California 331.252913711009794
Teachers—Pensions—California—Statistics—Periodicals 331.252913711009794021
Teachers—Pensions—United States 331.25291371100973
Teachers—Prayer-books and devotions 242.68
Teachers, Probationary 371.144
Teachers—Professional ethics 174.9372
Teachers—Professional ethics—United States 174.9372
Teachers—Psychology 371.10019
Teachers—Rating of 371.144
Teachers—Rating of—Great Britain 371.1440941
Teachers—Rating of—United States 371.1440973

Teachers—Rating of—United States—Handbooks, manuals, etc. 371.1440973
Teachers—Salaries, etc. 331.2813711
Teachers—Salaries, etc.—California 331.2813711009794
Teachers—Salaries, etc.—Great Britain 331.281371100941
Teachers—Salaries, etc.—Maryland 331.2813711009752
Teachers—Salaries, etc.—Maryland—Statistics—Periodicals 331.2813711009752021
Teachers—Salaries, etc.—United States 331.281371100973
Teachers—Supply and demand 331.12313711
Teachers—Supply and demand—United States 331.1231371100973
Teachers—Tenure 371.104
Teachers—Tenure—New Jersey 371.104
Teachers—Tenure—United States 371.104
Teachers—Time management 371.1024
Teachers—Training of 370.711
Teachers—Training of—Great Britain 370.71141
Teachers—Training of—India 370.71154
Teachers—Training of—United States 370.71173
Teachers—Training of—United States—Evaluation 370.71173
Teachers' unions 331.88113711
Teachers' unions—United States 331.8811371100973
Teachers—United States 371.100973
Teachers—United States—Attitudes 371.10019
Teachers—United States—Biography 371.0092
Teachers—United States—Handbooks, manuals, etc. 371.100973
Teachers—United States—Job stress 371.10019
Teachers—United States—Statistics 371.100973021
Teachers—Workload 371.1412
Teachers' workshops 370.715
Teaching 371.102
Teaching—Aids and devices 371.33
Teaching—Computer network resources 025.06371102
Teaching—Evaluation 371.144
Teaching, Freedom of 371.104
Teaching—Handbooks, manuals, etc. 371.102
Teaching hospitals 610.7155
Teaching—Humor 371.1020207
Teaching—Philosophy 371.10201
Teaching—Psychological aspects 370.15
Teaching teams 371.148
Teaching teams—United States 371.1480973
Teaching—United States 371.1020973
Teaching—United States—Examinations 370.76
Teaching—Vocational guidance 371.10023
Teaching—Vocational guidance—United States 371.1002373
Teagarden, Aurora Roe (Fictitious character) 813.54
Team boats 386.22; 623.82
Team learning approach in education 371.36
Teams in the workplace 658.402; 658.4036
Teams in the workplace—Data processing 658.40360285
Teams in the workplace—Handbooks, manuals, etc. 658.402
Teams in the workplace—Management 658.402; 658.4036
Teams in the workplace—Training of 658.31243
Teamwork (Sports) 796
Tearooms 647.95
Teasing 158.2; 302.3
Technetium compounds 546.5432
Technical assistance 338.91
Technical assistance, American—Afghanistan 341.759
Technical college libraries 027.7

Technical editing 808.0666
Technical education 607.1
Technical education—Great Britain 607.1142
Technical education—United States 607.1073
Technical institutes 607.11
Technical libraries 026.6
Technical literature 620
Technical manuals 600
Technical publishing 070.57
Technical reports 025.1736
Technical services (Libraries) 025.02
Technical writing 808.066; 808.0666
Technical writing—Handbooks, manuals, etc. 808.066; 808.0666
Technics organ 786.59
Techno music 781.64
Technological forecasting 601.12
Technological innovations 338.064
Technological innovations—Economic aspects 338.064
Technological innovations—Economic aspects—Great Britain 338.0640941
Technological innovations—Economic aspects—Japan 338.0640952
Technological innovations—Economic aspects—United States 338.0640973
Technological innovations—Management 658.514
Technological innovations—Social aspects 303.483
Technological literacy 600
Technological literacy—Law and legislation 344.095
Technological unemployment 331.137042
Technology 600
Technology and civilization 303.483
Technology and law 344.095
Technology and state 338.926; 338.927; 352.745
Technology and state—United States 338.97306
Technology and state—United States—States 338.97306
Technology and the arts 700.105
Technology assessment 303.483
Technology—Dictionaries 603
Technology—History 609
Technology—India 609.54
Technology—India—Periodicals 609.5405
Technology—Information services—Directories 607.2
Technology—Miscellanea 600
Technology—Periodicals 605
Technology—Philosophy 601
Technology—Religious aspects 291.175
Technology—Religious aspects—Christianity 261.56
Technology—Risk assessment 363.102; 620.004
Technology—Social aspects 303.483
Technology—Social aspects—United States—History 303.4830973
Technology—Study and teaching 607.1
Technology—Study and teaching (Elementary) 372.358
Technology transfer 338.926
Technology transfer—Developing countries 338.926091724
Technology transfer—Economic aspects 338.926
Technology transfer—Government policy 338.926
Technology transfer—Government policy—United States 338.97306
Technology transfer—United States 338.97306
Technology—United States 609.73
Technology—United States—History 609.73
Technology—United States—Information services 607.273
Technology—Vocational guidance 602.3
Tectonite 552.4
Tecumseh, Shawnee Chief, 1768–1813 974.004973

Teddy bears 688.7243
Teddy bears—Collectors and collecting 688.7243075
Teddy (Fictitious character : Stevenson) 813.54
Teenage boys 305.235
Teenage boys in literature 808.80352055; 809.93352055
Teenage boys—Prayer-books and devotions 242.632
Teenage girls 305.235
Teenage girls—Health and hygiene 613.04243
Teenage girls in motion pictures 791.43652055
Teenage girls—Prayer-books and devotions 242.633
Teenage girls—Psychology 305.235
Teenage girls—Religious life 248.833
Teenage girls—United States—Psychology 305.235
Teenage parents 362.829
Teenage pregnancy 306.8743
Teenage pregnancy—United States 306.8743
Teenage travel programs 910.835
Teenagers 305.235; 649.125
Teenagers—Alcohol use 362.2920835
Teenagers—Alcohol use—United States
362.29208350973
Teenagers—Conduct of life 170.835
Teenagers—Drug use 362.290835
Teenagers—Drug use—United States 362.2908350973
Teenagers—Drug use—United States—Prevention 649.4
Teenagers—Health and hygiene 613.0433
Teenagers—Life skills guides 646.700835
Teenagers—Medical care 362.10835
Teenagers—Medical care—United States 362.108350973
Teenagers—Prayer-books and devotions 242.63; 242.83
Teenagers—Religious life 248.83
Teenagers—Sexual behavior 306.70835
Teenagers—Substance use 616.8600835
Teenagers—Suicidal behavior 362.280835
Teenagers—Suicidal behavior—United States
362.2808350973
Teenagers—United States 305.2350973
Teenagers—United States—Attitudes 305.2350973
Teenagers—United States—Life skills guides
646.7008350973
Teenagers—United States—Sexual behavior 306.70835
Teenagers—United States—Social conditions
305.2350973
Teenagers' writings 808.899283
Teeth 573.356; 591.4; 611.314; 612.311
Teeth—Anatomy 611.314
Teeth—Care and hygiene 617.601
Teeth—Radiography 617.607572
Teethers 649.1220284; 688
Tefillin 296.4612
Tegus as pets 639.39582
Teichmüller spaces 515.94
Teilhard de Chardin, Pierre 194
Tekakwitha, Kateri, 1656–1680 282.092
Telecommunication 384; 621.382
Telecommunication—Deregulation—United States
384.041
Telecommunication—Dictionaries 384.03; 621.38203
Telecommunication—Equipment and supplies
621.3820284
Telecommunication equipment industry 338.47621382
Telecommunication—Europe 384.094
Telecommunication—European Economic Community
countries 384.094
Telecommunication—Handbooks, manuals, etc. 384;
621.382
Telecommunication—History 384.09
Telecommunication in education 371.358
Telecommunication in literature 808.80355; 809.93355

Telecommunication in medicine 362.1028; 610.28
Telecommunication—Law and legislation 341.7577;
343.0994
Telecommunication—Law and legislation—United States
343.730994
Telecommunication—Law and legislation—United
States—Cases 343.7309940264
Telecommunication—Law and legislation—United
States—Periodicals 343.73099405
Telecommunication—Management 384.068
Telecommunication—Message processing 384.043
Telecommunication—Periodicals 384.05; 621.38205
Telecommunication policy 343.0994; 384.068
Telecommunication policy—Developing countries
384.068
Telecommunication policy—Europe 384.068
Telecommunication policy—United States 384.068
Telecommunication—Switching systems 621.382;
621.3821
Telecommunication systems 621.382
Telecommunication systems—Design and construction
384; 621.382
Telecommunication systems—Periodicals 621.38205
Telecommunication—Technological innovations 621.382
Telecommunication—Traffic 621.382
Telecommunication—United States 384.0973
Telecommunication—United States—Periodicals
384.097305
Telecommunication wiring 621.382; 621.3823
Telecommunications devices for the deaf 384.0420872
Telecommuting 331.25
Teleconferencing 384.64; 621.382; 621.385
Teleconferencing equipment industry 338.47621382;
338.47621385
Teleconferencing in education 371.358
Telemarketing 658.84
Telematics 384.3
Telemeter 621.38419
Teleology 124
Telepathy 133.82
Telephone 384.6; 621.385; 621.386
Telephone—Area codes 384.6
Telephone cards 384.63
Telephone companies 384.6065
Telephone conferencing 384.64
Telephone cramming 364.163
Telephone credit cards 384.63
Telephone—Deregulation—United States 384.63
Telephone—Directories—Yellow pages 910.25
Telephone—Emergency reporting systems 384.64
Telephone etiquette 395.59
Telephone in business 651.73
Telephone—Law and legislation 343.09943
Telephone—Law and legislation—United States
343.7309943
Telephone selling 658.84; 658.85
Telephone sex 363.47
Telephone slamming 345.0268; 364.168
Telephone slamming—Law and legislation 345.0268
Telephone supplies industry 380.145621385
Telephone surveys 658.83
Telephone switching systems, Electronic 621.387
Telephone systems 621.385
Telephone—United States 384.60973
Telephone—United States—Rates 384.630973
Teleportation 133.88
Telescope makers 681.4123092
Telescopes 522.2
Telescopes—Design and construction 522.2

Tender offers (Securities)—Law and legislation 346.0662
Tender offers (Securities)—Law and legislation—United States 346.730662
Tenebrionidae 595.769
Tenement houses 363.5
Tennessee 976.8
Tennessee—Genealogy 929.3768
Tennessee—Guidebooks 917.6804; 917.680453; 917.680454
Tennessee—History 976.8
Tennessee—Maps 912.768
Tennessee River 976.8
Tennis 796.342
Tennis—Coaching 796.342077
Tennis for children 796.342083
Tennis—History 796.34209
Tennis players 796.342092
Tennis—Psychological aspects 796.342019
Tennis—Training 796.342071
Tennyson, Alfred Tennyson, Baron, 1809–1892 821.8
Tennyson, Alfred Tennyson, Baron, 1809–1892—Criticism and interpretation 821.8
Tennyson, Alfred Tennyson, Baron, 1809–1892. Idylls of the king 821.8
Tennyson, Alfred Tennyson, Baron, 1809–1892. In memoriam 821.8
Tennyson, Alfred Tennyson, Baron, 1809–1892—Knowledge—Literature 821.8
Tennyson, Alfred Tennyson, Baron, 1809–1892—Literary style 821.8
Tennyson, Alfred Tennyson, Baron, 1809–1892—Manuscripts 821.8
Tennyson, Alfred Tennyson, Baron, 1809–1892—Religion 821.8
Tent caterpillars 595.78
Tenzin Gyatso, Dalai Lama XIV, 1935– 294.3923092
Teotihuacán Site (San Juan Teotihuacán, Mexico) 972.52
Tephritidae 595.774
Teratology 571.976
Terence 872.01
Terence—Criticism and interpretation 872.01
Teresa, Mother, 1910– 271.97
Teresa, of Avila, Saint, 1515–1582 271.97102
Teresa, of Avila, Saint, 1515–1582. Moradas 248.482
Terminal care 362.175; 616.029
Terminal care—Moral and ethical aspects 174.24
Terminal care—Psychological aspects 362.175019
Terminally ill 305.90814; 362.175
Terminally ill children 362.198920029
Terminally ill children—Psychology 155.937083
Terminally ill parents 362.175
Terminators (Astronomy) 523.4
Terminologists 409.2
Termites 595.736
Terns 598.338
Terpenes 547.71
Terqa (Extinct city) 939.43
Terra-cotta industry 338.4766673; 338.47738
Terrell family 929.20973
Terrestrial heat flow 551.14
Territorial waters 341.448
Territoriality (Zoology) 591.566
Terrorism 303.625; 341.773; 363.32
Terrorism—Bibliography 016.303625
Terrorism—Great Britain 345.4102
Terrorism—Handbooks, manuals, etc. 303.625
Terrorism—History 303.62509; 341.77309

Terrorism—History—Chronology 303.62509
Terrorism in mass media 303.625
Terrorism—India 345.5402
Terrorism—Middle East 363.320956
Terrorism—Periodicals 303.62505; 363.3205
Terrorism—Prevention 363.32
Terrorism—United States 303.6250973; 363.320973
Tesla, Nikola, 1856–1943 621.3092
Tess (Fictitious character : Wiebe) 813.6
Test anxiety 371.26019
Test bias 371.26013
Test of English as a Foreign Language 428.0076
Test of English as a Foreign Language—Validity 428.0076
Test of English for International Communication 428.0076
Test pressings (Sound recordings) 621.38932; 781.49
Test-taking skills 371.26
Testing 389
Testing laboratories 001.4
Testis 573.655; 612.61
Testis—Physiology 612.61
Testosterone—Therapeutic use 615.366
Testudinidae 597.924
Tet Offensive, 1968 959.704342
Teton Indians 305.89752; 978.0049752
Tetragnathidae 595.44
Tetrahydrobiopterin 572.7
Tetratomidae 595.769
TeX (Computer file) 686.22544
Texas 976.4
Texas—Civilization 976.4
Texas—Economic conditions 330.9764
Texas—Encyclopedias 976.4003
Texas—Genealogy 929.3764
Texas—Guidebooks 917.6404; 917.640463; 917.640464
Texas—History 976.4
Texas—History—To 1846 976.4; 976.402
Texas—History—Revolution, 1835–1836 976.403
Texas—History—Revolution, 1835–1836—Personal narratives, Mexican 976.403
Texas—History—Republic, 1836–1846 976.404
Texas—History—Civil War, 1861–1865 973.7464
Texas—History—Anecdotes 976.4
Texas—History, Local 976.4
Texas Longhorns (Football team) 796.332630976431
Texas Longhorns (Football team)—History 796.332630976431
Texas—Maps 912.764
Texas—Politics and government 320.9764
Texas—Politics and government—1951– 320.976409045
Texas Rangers (Baseball team) 796.3576409764531
Texas Rangers (Baseball team)—History 796.3576409764531
Texas Rangers—History 363.209764
Texas—Road maps 912.764
Texas—Social life and customs 976.4
Texas—Tours 917.6404; 917.640463; 917.640464
Text editors (Computer programs) 652.5
Text files 005.72
Text processing (Computer science) 005
Text-sound compositions 786.76
Textbook bias 371.32
Textbooks 371.32
Textbooks—Authorship 808.066371
Textbooks—United States 371.320973
Textile crafts 746
Textile design 677.022
Textile fabrics 646.11; 677.02864

Textile fabrics—Conservation and restoration 746.0288
Textile fabrics—Electrostatic charging 620.197; 677
Textile fabrics in interior decoration 747.9
Textile fabrics—Testing 677.0287
Textile fibers 677.02832
Textile fibers, Synthetic 677.4
Textile industry 338.47677; 677
Textile industry—Dictionaries 677.003
Textile industry—England 338.4767700942
Textile industry—England—Yorkshire 338.476770094281
Textile industry—India 338.4767700954
Textile industry—Periodicals 338.47677005
Textile industry—United States 338.4767700973
Textile museums 746.074
Textile painting 746.6
Textile printing 667.38; 746.62
Textile research 677.0072
Textile schools 677.0071
Texture (Art) 702.8
Textured books 096.2
Th1 cells 571.966
Th2 cells 571.966
Thacker family 929.20973
Thackeray, William Makepeace, 1811–1863 823.8
Thackeray, William Makepeace, 1811–1863—Criticism and interpretation 823.8
Thackeray, William Makepeace, 1811–1863—Technique 823.8
Thai language 495.91
Thai language—Conversation and phrase books 495.91831
Thai language—Conversation and phrase books—English 495.9183421
Thailand 959.3
Thailand—Civilization 959.3
Thailand—Economic conditions 330.9593
Thailand—Economic conditions—Periodicals 330.9593005
Thailand—Economic policy 338.9593
Thailand—Guidebooks 915.9304; 915.930444
Thailand—History 959.3
Thailand—Social life and customs 959.3
Thalassemia 616.152
Thalia (Tex. : Imaginary place) 813.54
Thalia (Tex. : Imaginary place)—Fiction 813.54
Thames River (England) 942.2
Thames River (England)—History 942.2
Thames Valley (England) 942.2
Thames Valley (England)—Guidebooks 914.2204; 914.2204859; 914.220486
Thanatology 306.9
Thanet, Luke (Fictitious character) 823.914
Thanet, Luke (Fictitious character)—Fiction 823.914
Thanksgiving cookery 641.568
Thanksgiving Day 394.2649
Thanksgiving decorations 745.5941
Thatcher, John Putnam (Fictitious character) 813.54
Thatcher, John Putnam (Fictitious character)—Fiction 813.54
Thatcher, Margaret 941.0858092
Theater 792; 792.015
Theater and youth 792.0226
Theater architecture 725.822
Theater architecture—Bibliography 016.725822
Theater architecture—England 725.8220942
Theater architecture—United States 725.8220973
Theater—Bibliography 016.792
Theater—China 792.0951
Theater—Dictionaries 792.03

Theater—England 792.0942
Theater—England—History 792.0942
Theater—England—History—16th century 792.094209031
Theater—England—History—17th century 792.094209032
Theater—England—History—19th century 792.094109034; 792.094209034
Theater—England—London 792.09421
Theater—England—London—History 792.09421
Theater—England—London—History—16th century 792.0942109031
Theater—France 792.0944
Theater—France—Paris 792.0944361
Theater—France—Paris—History 792.0944361
Theater—France—Paris—History—18th century 792.094436109033
Theater—Great Britain 792.0941
Theater—Great Britain—History 792.0941
Theater—Great Britain—History—19th century 792.094109034
Theater—Great Britain—History—20th century 792.09410904
Theater—Greece 792.0938
Theater—Greece—History 792.0938
Theater—History 792.09
Theater—History—Medieval, 500–1500 792.0902
Theater—History—20th century 792.0904
Theater in art 704.949792
Theater—India 792.0954
Theater—Japan 792.0952
Theater—Moral and ethical aspects 175
Theater—New York (State)—New York 792.097471
Theater—New York (State)—New York—History 792.097471
Theater—New York (State)—New York—History—20th century 792.0974710904
Theater—Periodicals 792.05
Theater—Philosophy 792.01
Theater—Political aspects 792
Theater—Production and direction 792.023; 792.0232; 792.0233
Theater—Semiotics 792.014
Theater—United States 792.0973
Theater—United States—History 792.0973
Theater—United States—History—20th century 792.09730904
Theaters 725.822
Theaters—Electronic sound control 621.3893
Theaters—England—London 725.82209421
Theaters—England—London—History—16th century 725.8220942109031
Theaters—New York (State)—New York 725.822097471
Theaters—New York (State)—New York—History 725.822097471
Theaters—Stage-setting and scenery 792.025
Theaters—Stage-setting and scenery—Exhibitions 792.025074
Theatrical agents 792.092
Theatrical companies 792.06
Theatrical makeup 792.027
Theatrical publishing 070.57
Thebes (Egypt : Extinct city) 932
Theft 364.162
Theism 211.3
Thematic Apperception Test 155.2844
Thematic maps 912
Theodicy 214; 231.8
Theodicy—History of doctrines 214; 231.8

Theologians 291.2092
Theologians, Muslim 297.2092
Theological libraries 026.2
Theological seminaries 200.711
Theology 230
Theology—Bibliography 016.2912
Theology—Bibliography—Catalogs 016.23; 016.2912
Theology—Dictionaries 230.03
Theology, Doctrinal 230
Theology, Doctrinal—Asia 230.095
Theology, Doctrinal—History 230.09
Theology, Doctrinal—History—Early church, ca. 30–600 230.09015
Theology, Doctrinal—History—16th century 230.09031; 270.6
Theology, Doctrinal—History—19th century 230.09034
Theology, Doctrinal—History—20th century 230.0904
Theology, Doctrinal—India 230.0954
Theology, Doctrinal—Introductions 230
Theology, Doctrinal—South Africa 230.0968
Theology—History 230.09
Theology—History—Early church, ca. 30–600 230.09015
Theology—Methodology 230.01
Theology of religions (Christian theology) 261.2
Theology—Periodicals 230.05; 291.205
Theology, Practical 230; 253
Theology—Study and teaching 230.071
Theology—Study and teaching—United States 291.2071073
Theomachy 291.211
Theory of constraints (Management) 658.4; 658.5
Theory of distributions (Functional analysis) 515.782
Theosophy 299.934
Thera Island (Greece) 949.585
Thera Island (Greece)—Antiquities 939.15
Therapeutic alliance 616.8914; 616.8917
Therapeutic embolization 617.05
Therapeutics 615.5
Therapeutics—Handbooks, manuals, etc. 615.5
Therapeutics—Periodicals 615.505
Therapeutics, Physiological 615.5
Therapeutics, Surgical 617.91; 617.919
Therapeutics, Surgical—Handbooks, manuals, etc. 617.91; 617.919
Therapsida 567.93
Thérèse, de Lisieux, Saint, 1873–1897 271.97102
Theresienstadt (Concentration camp) 940.5318
Therevidae 595.773
Thermal analysis 543.086
Thermal pollution of rivers, lakes, etc. 628.16831
Thermal pollution of rivers, lakes, etc.—Environmental aspects 577.62726
Thermal stresses 620.1121
Thermochemistry 541.36
Thermochemistry—Tables 541.36021
Thermoclines (Oceanography) 551.4601
Thermodynamics 536.7; 541.369; 621.4021; 660.2969
Thermoelectric apparatus and appliances 621.31243
Thermography 621.362
Thermometers 681.2
Thermoplastic composites 620.1923
Thermoplastics 668.423
Thermosetting plastics 668.422
Thermostat 697.07; 697.9322
Thermotherapy 615.832
Thesauri 413.1
Thin film devices 621.38152
Thin film devices—Design and construction 621.38152
Thin films 530.4175; 530.4275; 621.38152

Thin films—Magnetic properties 530.4175
Thin films, Multilayered 530.4275; 621.38152
Thin films, Multilayered—Magnetic properties 530.4175; 530.4275
Thin films—Optical properties 530.4175
Thin layer chromatography 543.08956
Thin people 305.9081
Thin-walled structures 624.171
Thinnes, John (Fictitious character) 813.54
Thirty Years' War, 1618–1648 940.24
Thomas, à Becket, Saint, 1118?–1170 942.031092
Thomas, Aquinas, Saint, 1225?–1274 189.4
Thomas, Aquinas, Saint, 1225?–1274—Ethics 171.2092
Thomas, Clarence, 1948- 347.732634
Thomas, Dylan, 1914–1953 821.912
Thomas, Dylan, 1914–1953—Childhood and youth 821.912
Thomas, Dylan, 1914–1953—Criticism and interpretation 821.912
Thomas, Edward, 1878–1917 821.912
Thomas, Edward, 1878–1917—Correspondence 821.912
Thomas, Edward, 1878–1917—Criticism and interpretation 821.912
Thomas family 929.20973
Thomas, Frank, 1968- 796.357092
Thomas, R. S. (Ronald Stuart), 1913- 821.914
Thomas, R. S. (Ronald Stuart), 1913- —Criticism and interpretation 821.914
Thompson family 929.20973
Thompson, Hunter S. 070.92
Thomson, James, 1700–1748 821.5
Thoreau, Henry David, 1817–1862 818.309
Thoreau, Henry David, 1817–1862—Criticism and interpretation 818.309
Thoreau, Henry David, 1817–1862—Diaries 818.303
Thoreau, Henry David, 1817–1862—Homes and haunts—Massachusetts—Walden Woods 818.303
Thoreau, Henry David, 1817–1862—Knowledge—Natural history 818.309
Thoreau, Henry David, 1817–1862. Walden 818.303
Thorn (Fictitious character) 813.54
Thorn (Fictitious character)—Fiction 813.54
Thorndyke, Doctor (Fictitious character) 823.912
Thorndyke, Doctor (Fictitious character)—Fiction 823.912
Thoroughbred horse 636.132
Thoroughbred horse—Pedigrees 636.13222
Thorpe, Jim, 1887–1953 796.092
Thorssen, Alix (Fictitious character) 813.54
Thought and thinking 153.42
Thought and thinking—Problems, exercises, etc. 153.42
Thought and thinking—Study and teaching 153.42071; 370.152
Thought and thinking—Study and teaching (Elementary) 372.019
Thought and thinking—Study and teaching (Primary) 372.241019
Thought and thinking—Study and teaching—United States 370.1520973
Thought experiments 100
Thought insertion 616.89
Thraxas (Fictitious character : Scott) 823.914
Threads (Computer programs) 005.27; 005.434
Three-body problem 521
Three-day event (Horsemanship) 798.24
Three-dimensional display systems 006.693; 621.367
Three-dimensional imaging in medicine 616.0754
Three-manifolds (Topology) 514.3

Three Mile Island Nuclear Power Plant (Pa.)
363.1799097818
Threshold limit values (Industrial toxicology) 363.179;
615.902
Thresholds (Doorsills) 690.1822; 721.822
Thrift institutions 332.32
Thrift institutions—Law and legislation 346.08221;
346.08232
Thrift institutions—Law and legislation—United States
346.7308221; 346.7308232
Thrift institutions—United States 332.320973
Throat singing 783.04
Thrombolytic therapy 616.135061
Thrombopoietin 573.159; 612.115
Thrombosis 616.135
Thrush Green (Imaginary place) 823.914
Thrush Green (Imaginary place)—Fiction 823.914
Thucydides 938.007202
Thucydides. History of the Peloponnesian War 938.05
Thunder Bay (Ont. : District) 971.312
Thunderbird automobile 629.2222
Thunderbird automobile—History 629.2222
Thunderbird automobile—Maintenance and repair
629.28722
Thunderbird automobile—Maintenance and repair—
Handbooks, manuals, etc. 629.28722
Thunderstorm forecasting 551.6454
Thunderstorms 551.554
Thurber, James, 1894–1961 818.5209
Thyroid gland 573.47; 612.44
Thyroid gland—Cancer 616.99444
Thyroid gland—Diseases 616.44
Tiaras 391.7; 739.278
Tibbett, Henry (Fictitious character) 823.914
Tibbett, Henry (Fictitious character)—Fiction 823.914
Tibet (China) 951.5
Tibet (China)—Civilization 951.5
Tibet (China)—Description and travel 915.1504;
915.150459; 915.15046
Tibet (China)—Guidebooks 915.1504; 915.150459;
915.15046
Tibet (China)—History 951.5
Tibet (China)—History—1951– 951.505
Tibet (China)—Politics and government 951.5
Tibet (China)—Politics and government—1951–
320.951509045; 951.505
Tibetan language 495.4
Tibetan language—Grammar 495.45; 495.482;
495.482421
Tibia—Fractures 617.158
Tick-borne diseases 616.968
Ticker symbols 332.6320148
Ticket brokerage 381.4579
Ticks 595.429
Tide pool ecology 577.699
Tides 551.4708
Tie-dyeing 746.664
Tied aid 338.91
Tiepolo, Giovanni Battista, 1696–1770 741.945
Tiger shark 597.34
Tigers 599.756
Tikal Site (Guatemala) 972.812
Tile industry 338.476914
Tile laying 698
Tiles 691.4
Tiles in interior decoration 747.9
Tillage 631.51
Tilley, Clare (Fictitious character) 823.914
Tillich, Paul, 1886–1965 230.092

Timber 338.17498
Timber circles 725.9; 930.1
Time 115; 529
Time delay systems 629.83
Time division multiple access 621.38456
Time management 640.43; 650.1; 658.4093
Time management—Computer programs 005.369
Time management—Religious aspects 291.44
Time management—Religious aspects—Christianity
248.4
Time management—United States 640.430973
Time measurements 529.7
Time perception 153.753
Time—Psychological aspects 153.753
Time-series analysis 519.55
Time-sharing computer systems 004.3
Time—Sociological aspects 304.23
Time—Systems and standards 389.17
Time travel 530.11
Timelost (Game) 794.82
Times Square (New York, N.Y.) 974.71
Times Square (New York, N.Y.)—History 974.71
Timor Timur (Indonesia) 959.87
Timor Timur (Indonesia)—Politics and government
320.95987; 959.86
Timura, Safar (Fictitious character) 813.54
Tin Woodman (Fictitious character) 791.4372; 813.4
TINA (Telecommunication system) 004.65; 384.3
Tinnitus 617.8
Tintoretto, 1518–1594 759.5
Tippecanoe County (Ind.) 977.295
Tippecanoe County (Ind.)—Genealogy 929.30977295
Tipperary (Ireland : County) 941.92
Tipperary (Ireland : County)—History 941.92
Tippets (Fishing) 688.79124
Tire industry 678.32
Tires 678.32
Tissue banks 571.5074
Tissue culture 571.538
Tissue expansion 617.95
Tissues 571.5
Titanic (Steamship) 363.123091631; 910.91634
Titanic (Steamship) in motion pictures 791.43658
Titanium 669.7322
Titanium alloys 620.189322
Tithes 248.6
Tithes—Biblical teaching 248.6
Title pages 686.2252
Tito, Josip Broz, 1892–1980 949.7023092
Tiv literature 896.36
TJ (Fictitious character : Impey) 823.914
TK!Solver 005.369
Tlingit Indians—Folklore 398.2089972
Toads 597.87
Toasts 808.51
Tobacco 583.952
Tobacco habit 616.865
Tobacco habit—Treatment 616.86506
Tobacco habit—United States 362.2960973
Tobacco industry 338.17371
Tobacco pipes 688.42
Tobias, Andrew P. Managing your money
332.024002855369
Toccatas 784.18947
Tocqueville, Alexis de, 1805–1859 306.2092;
944.007202
Tocqueville, Alexis de, 1805–1859. De la démocratie en
Amérique 306.2092
Todd County (Ky.)—Genealogy 929.376977

Toddlers 649.122
Toddlers—Development 155.422; 305.232; 612.654
Toeplitz operators 515.7246
Toff (Fictitious character) 823.912
Toff (Fictitious character)—Fiction 823.912
Tohono O'Odham Indians 305.89745; 979.10049745
Toilet preparations 646.7
Toilet training 649.62
Toilets 696.182
Toilets—History 392.36
Tokens—United States—Catalogs 737.30973
Tokyo (Japan) 952.135
Tokyo (Japan)—Description and travel 915.213504;
    915.21350449; 915.2135045
Tokyo (Japan)—Guidebooks 915.213504; 915.21350449;
    915.2135045
Tokyo (Japan)—History 952.135
Tole painting 745.723
Tolerance (Engineering) 620.0045
Toleration 179.9; 302.14
Tolkien, J. R. R. (John Ronald Reuel), 1892–1973
    828.91209
Tolkien, J. R. R. (John Ronald Reuel), 1892–1973—
    Bibliography 016.82891209
Tolkien, J. R. R. (John Ronald Reuel), 1892–1973—
    Criticism and interpretation 828.91209
Tolkien, J. R. R. (John Ronald Reuel), 1892–1973—
    Dictionaries 828.91209
Tolkien, J. R. R. (John Ronald Reuel), 1892–1973. Lord
    of the rings 823.912
Tolkien, J. R. R. (John Ronald Reuel), 1892–1973. Lord
    of the rings—Criticism, Textual 823.912
Toll-free telephone calls 384.64
Toll-free telephone calls—United States—Directories
    384.64
Toll roads 388.122
Toll roads—Law and legislation 343.0942
Toll roads—Law and legislation—New Jersey
    343.7490942
Tolstoy, Leo, graf, 1828–1910 891.733
Tolstoy, Leo, graf, 1828–1910. Anna Karenina 891.733
Tolstoy, Leo, graf, 1828–1910—Criticism and
    interpretation 891.733
Tolstoy, Leo, graf, 1828–1910—Religion 270.092;
    891.733
Tolstoy, Leo, graf, 1828–1910—Translations into
    English 891.733
Tolstoy, Leo, graf, 1828–1910. War and peace 891.733
Tom (Fictitious character : Granada Media) 791.4572
Tom Kitten (Fictitious character) 823.912
Tomato sauces 641.814; 664.58
Tomatoes 635.642
Tombs 363.75
Tombs—Egypt 932
Tombstone (Ariz.) 979.153
Tombstone (Ariz.)—History 979.153
Tomcat (Jet fighter plane) 358.4383
Tomography 616.0757
Tomography—Atlases 616.07570222
Tomography, Emission 616.07575
Tonality 781.258
Tonga 996.12
Tonga—Politics and government 320.99612
Tonga—Politics and government—Periodicals 320.99612
Tonghak Incident, 1894 951.902
Tongue twisters 818.02
Tony Awards 792.0797471
Tools 621.9
Tools—Collectors and collecting 621.90075

Tools—Collectors and collecting—United States
    621.90075
Tools, Prehistoric 930.12
Toolsheds—Design and construction 690.89
Toothed whales, Fossil 569.5
Topiary work 715.1
Topiramate 615.784
Topographic maps 912
Topological algebras 512.55
Topological degree 514.2
Topological dynamics 514.74
Topological groups 512.55
Topological spaces 514.3
Topological transformation groups 514
Topology 514
Toponymy 910.014
Tops 796.2
Torah cases 296.461
Torah scrolls 296.4615
Torka (Fictitious character : Sarabande) 813.54
Tornadoes 551.553
Toronto Maple Leafs (Hockey team) 796.9626409713541
Toronto Maple Leafs (Hockey team)—History
    796.9626409713541
Toronto Metropolitan Area (Ont.) 971.3541
Toronto Metropolitan Area (Ont.)—Maps 912.713541
Toronto (Ont.) 971.3541
Toronto (Ont.)—Description and travel 917.1354104;
    917.13541044
Toronto (Ont.)—Guidebooks 917.1354104; 917.13541044
Toronto (Ont.)—History 971.3541
Tort liability of Indian tribal governments 342.088
Tort liability of police 344.052
Tort liability of police—United States 344.73052
Tortillas 641.82
Torts 346.03
Torts—Australia 346.9403
Torts—Great Britain 346.4103
Torts—Great Britain—Cases 346.41030264
Torts—Massachusetts 346.74403
Torts—North Carolina 346.75603
Torts—Pennsylvania 346.74803
Torts—Philippines 346.59903
Torts—United States 346.7303
Torts—United States—Cases 346.73030264
Torts—United States—Outlines, syllabi, etc. 346.7303
Total hip replacement 617.580592; 617.5810592
Total hip replacement—Reoperation 617.5810592
Total knee replacement 617.5820592
Total productive maintenance 658.202
Total quality control 658.4013; 658.562
Total quality management 658.4013; 658.562
Total quality management—Handbooks, manuals, etc.
    658.562
Total quality management in government 352.357
Total quality management—Periodicals 658.56205
Total quality management—United States
    658.40130973; 658.5620973
Totalitarianism 320.53
Totem poles 730.8997; 736.4
Totem poles in art 704.9497317
Totemism 291.211
Toucans 598.72
Touch 152.182; 612.88
Touch—Psychological aspects 152.182
Toulouse-Lautrec, Henri de, 1864–1901 760.092
Toulouse-Lautrec, Henri de, 1864–1901—Criticism and
    interpretation 759.4; 760.092

Traditional medicine—Africa 615.882096
Traditional veterinary medicine 636.089; 636.0895882
Trafalgar, Battle of, 1805 940.2745
Traffic accident investigation 363.12565
Traffic accidents 363.125
Traffic accidents—Florida—Statistics—Periodicals 363.125209759021
Traffic congestion 388.3142
Traffic flow 388.314
Traffic flow—Mathematical models 388.31
Traffic noise 363.741; 625.79
Traffic regulations 343.0946
Traffic safety 363.125
Traffic safety—Religious aspects 291.1783
Traffic safety—United States 363.1250973
Traffic signs and signals 625.794
Traffic surveys—New Mexico—Maps 388.4131409789022
Traffic surveys—Tennessee—Maps 388.31409768022
Traffic violations 345.0247
Traffic violations—California 345.7940247
Tragedy 808.82512
Tragedy—History and criticism 809.9162
Traherne, Thomas, d. 1674 821.4
Traherne, Thomas, d. 1674—Criticism and interpretation 821.4
Trail of Tears, 1838 973.04975
Trail riding 798.23
Traill County (N.D.) 978.414
Traill County (N.D.)—Maps 912.78414
Trails 796.51
Trainspotting 625.2
Trampling 591.5
Tranquilizing drugs 615.7882
Trans-Alaska Pipeline (Alaska) 333.8231409798
Transaction costs 338.5142; 658.1552
Transaction systems (Computer systems) 005.758
Transactional analysis 616.89145
Transboundary animal diseases 636.08969
Transcendence (Philosophy) 111.6
Transcendental Meditation 158.125
Transcendental numbers 512.73
Transcription 653.14
Transcultural medical care 362.1
Transcultural nursing 362.173; 610.73
Transdermal medication 615.6
Transdetermination (Cytology) 571.8636
Transducers 681.2
Transesophageal echocardiography 616.1207543
Transfer RNA 572.886
Transfer students 371.2914; 378.16912
Transference (Psychology) 154.24; 616.8917
Transfinite numbers 511.322
Transformations (Mathematics) 511.33
Transgenes 660.65
Transgenes—Expression 660.65
Transgenic animals 636.0821
Transgenic plants 631.5233
Transients (Electricity) 621.31921
Transistor circuits 621.381528
Transistor radios 621.38418
Transistor radios—Collectors and collecting 621.38418075
Transistors 621.381528
Transit police 363.287
Transition metal complexes 546.6
Transition metal compounds 546.6
Transition metal oxides 546.6
Transition metals 546.6
Translating and interpreting 418.02

Translating and interpreting—Data processing 418.020285
Translating and interpreting—Handbooks, manuals, etc. 418.02
Translating and interpreting—History 418.0209
Translating and interpreting—Periodicals 418.0205
Translating and interpreting—Social aspects 306.44; 418.02
Translating services 418.02
Translations 418.02
Translators 418.02092
Translators (Computer programs) 005.45
Transleations (Spirits) 133.9
Transluminal angioplasty 617.413
Transmission electron microscopy 502.825; 570.2825
Transmission of texts 801.959
Transmyocardial laser revascularization 617.412059
Transnational crime 364.135
Transnational voting 324.65
Transnationalism 305.8
Transparency 535.3
Transparent watercolor painting 751.422
Transparent watercolor painting—Technique 751.422
Transpersonal psychology 150.198
Transpersonal psychotherapy 616.8914
Transplant surgeons 617.95
Transplantation immunology 617.95
Transplantation of organs, tissues, etc. 617.95
Transplantation of organs, tissues, etc.—Complications 617.95
Transplantation of organs, tissues, etc.—Moral and ethical aspects 174.25
Transplantation of organs, tissues, etc.—Nursing 610.73677
Transplantation of organs, tissues, etc.—Periodicals 617.95
Transport of sick and wounded 362.188; 610.73; 616.0252
Transport planes 387.73340423; 623.7465; 629.133340423
Transport planes—History 629.133340423
Transport theory 530.138
Transport workers 388.092
Transportation 388
Transportation and state—European Economic Community countries 388.094
Transportation and state—New Jersey 388.09749
Transportation, Automotive 388.3
Transportation, Automotive—United States 388.30973
Transportation—Bibliography 016.388
Transportation buildings 690.53
Transportation consultants 388.092
Transportation engineering 629.04
Transportation—Europe 388.094
Transportation—History 388.09
Transportation—Law and legislation 343.093
Transportation—Law and legislation—United States 343.73093
Transportation—Mathematical models 388.015118
Transportation, Military 358.25
Transportation—Planning 388.068
Transportation—Planning—Mathematical models 388.068
Transportation problems (Programming) 519.72
Transportation—United States 388.0973
Transportation—United States—History 388.0973
Transportation—United States—Planning 388.068
Transportation—United States—Statistics 388.0973021
Transputers 004.357; 621.3916

Transsexual students 371.8266
Transsexual youth 305.235
Transsexualism 306.77
Transsexualism—Religious aspects 291.1783576
Transsexuals 305.9066
Transsexuals—Identity 155.3; 305.9066
Transsexuals in literature 808.80352066; 809.93352066
Tranströmer, Tomas, 1931– 839.7174
Tranströmer, Tomas, 1931– —Translations into English 839.7174
Transubstantiation 234.163
Transvaginal ultrasonography 618.047543
Transvestism 306.77
Transvestites 306.77
Transylvania (Romania) 949.84
Transylvania (Romania)—History 949.84
Trapp Family Singers 782.50922
Trapping 639.1
Traps (Petroleum geology) 553.28
Trapshooting 799.313
Trash art 745.584
Traumatology 617.1
Travel 910.202; 910.4
Travel agents 338.4791
Travel agents—Handbooks, manuals, etc. 338.4791
Travel agents—Vocational guidance 338.4791023
Travel—Anecdotes 910.4
Travel costs 338.4391
Travel—Guidebooks 910.202
Travel—Guidebooks—Bibliography 016.010202
Travel—Handbooks, manuals, etc. 910.202
Travel—Health aspects 613.68
Travel—Health aspects—Developing countries—Handbooks, manuals, etc. 613.68091724
Travel—Health aspects—Handbooks, manuals, etc. 613.68
Travel in literature 808.80355; 809.93355
Travel paraphernalia 910.284
Travel—Periodicals 910.5
Travel photography 778.9991
Travel restrictions 910
Travel with dogs 636.70887; 910.4
Travel writing 808.06691
Traveler, Moroni (Fictitious character) 813.54
Traveler, Moroni (Fictitious character)—Fiction 813.54
Travelers' writings 808.80355
Travelers' writings, American—History and criticism 810.9355
Travelers' writings, English—History and criticism 820.9355
Traveling theater 792.022
Travelogues (Motion pictures) 910.4
Travis, Melanie (Fictitious character) 813.54
Travis, Melanie (Fictitious character)—Fiction 813.54
Travis, Sheila (Fictitious character) 813.54
Travis, Sheila (Fictitious character)—Fiction 813.54
Treasure hunt (Game) 796.14
Treasure hunts 622.19
Treasure, Mark (Fictitious character) 823.914
Treasure, Mark (Fictitious character)—Fiction 823.914
Treasure-trove 622.19
Treaties 341.37
Treaties—Collections 341.026
Treaty-making power 328.346
Treaty-making power—United States 328.730746
Treaty on European Union (1992) 341.2422
Treblinka (Concentration camp) 940.5318
Tree crops 634
Tree planting 634.9565; 635.977

Trees 582.16
Trees—Australia 582.160994
Trees—Diseases and pests 634.963
Trees—Folklore 398.242
Trees, Fossil 561.16
Trees (Graph theory) 511.52
Trees (Graph theory)—Data processing 511.520285
Trees—Identification 582.16
Trees in art 704.9434
Trees in cities 635.977091732
Trees in cities—New York (State)—New York—Handbooks, manuals, etc. 635.977097471
Trees—Symbolic aspects 302.2223
Trees—United States 582.160973
Trees—United States—Identification 582.160973
Trees—West (U.S.)—Identification 582.160978
Trellises 717
Treloar, Gabe (Fictitious character) 813.54
Trempealeau County (Wis.) 977.549
Trempealeau County (Wis.)—Maps 912.77549
Tres (Musical instrument) 787.87
Trethowan, Perry (Fictitious character) 823.914
Trevor, Hannah (Fictitious character) 813.54
Trial practice 347.07
Trial practice—California 347.79407
Trial practice—Massachusetts 345.744075; 347.74407
Trial practice—New Jersey 347.74907
Trial practice—New York (State) 347.74707
Trial practice—Philippines 347.59907
Trial practice—United States 347.737; 347.7375
Trial practice—United States—Periodicals 347.73705
Trials 345.07; 347.07
Trials (Murder) 345.02523
Trials (Sex crimes) 345.0253
Trials—United States 345.7307; 347.737
Trials (Witchcraft)—Massachusetts—Salem 345.74450288
Triangle 516.15
Triangles (Interpersonal relations) 158.2
Triangles (Interpersonal relations) in literature 808.80353; 809.93353
Triangular norms 514.3; 515.724
Triangular stamps 769.56
Triangularization (Mathematics) 512.9434
Triangulation 526.33
Triathlon 796.4257
Tribology 621.89
Tribology—Handbooks, manuals, etc. 621.89
Triceratops 567.9158
Trick films 791.4361
Trick photography 778.8
Tricks 793.8
Trifonov, ĪUriĭ Valentinovich, 1925– 891.7344
Trifonov, ĪUriĭ Valentinovich, 1925– —Criticism and interpretation 891.7344
Trigg County (Ky.)—Genealogy 929.376979
Trigonometry 516.24
Trilliaceae 584.32
Trilobites 565.39
Trinidad 972.983
Trinidad and Tobago 972.983
Trinidad and Tobago—Economic conditions 330.97298
Trinidad and Tobago—Economic conditions—Periodicals 330.97298005
Trinidad and Tobago—History 972.983
Trinidad and Tobago—Politics and government 972.983
Trinidad and Tobago—Social life and customs 972.983
Trinidad—History 972.983

Trinity 231.044
Trinity Church (New York, N.Y.) 283.7471
Trinity—History of doctrines 231.04409
Trinity—History of doctrines—Early church, ca. 30–600 231.04409015
Trinity—History of doctrines—Middle Ages, 600–1500 231.0440902
Trio sonatas (Violins (2), continuo) 785.28193183
Trios (Piano, clarinet, violin) 785.24193
Trios (Piano, clarinet, violoncello) 785.24193
Trios (Piano, flute, violoncello) 785.24193
Tritium 546.213
Triumph automobile 629.2222
Triumph motorcycle—History 629.2275
Triuridaceae 584.37
Troi, Deanna (Fictitious character) 791.4375; 791.4575; 813.54
Trojan War 939.21
Trolling (Fishing) 799.128
Trollope, Anthony, 1815–1882 823.8
Trollope, Anthony, 1815–1882—Criticism and interpretation 823.8
Tropical crops 630.913; 631.0913
Tropical fish 597.0913; 639.34
Tropical fruit 634.6
Tropical medicine 616.9883
Tropical medicine—Handbooks, manuals, etc. 616.9883
Tropical meteorology 551.50913; 551.6913
Tropical nuts 634.50913; 641.3450913
Tropical nuts—Diseases and pests 634.50913
Tropical plants 580.913; 581.70913
Tropics 909.093
Tropics—Climate 551.6913
Troposphere 551.513
Trotter, Tilly (Fictitious character) 823.914
Trotter, Tilly (Fictitious character)—Fiction 823.914
Trout 597.57
Trout fishing 799.1757
Trout fishing—Pennsylvania 799.175709748
Trout fishing—Pennsylvania—Guidebooks 799.175709748
Trout fishing—United States 799.17570973
Troy, (Extinct city) 939.21
Troy (Extinct city)—Legends 398.2323921
TRS-80 computers 004.165
TRS-80 computers—Programming 005.265
Truck accidents 363.1259
Truck campers 629.226
Truck farming 635
Truck industry 338.47629224
Trucking 388.324
Trucking—Deregulation—United States 388.3240973
Trucking—Law and legislation 343.09483
Trucking—Law and legislation—United States 343.7309483
Trucking—United States 388.3240973
Trucking—United States—Directories 388.32402573
Trucks 388.34; 629.2232; 629.224
Trucks—History 629.223209; 629.22409
Trucks—Maintenance and repair 629.28732; 629.2874
Trucks—Maintenance and repair—Handbooks, manuals, etc. 629.28732
Trucks—Motors—Maintenance and repair 629.250288; 629.25040288
Trucks—Motors—Maintenance and repair—Handbooks, manuals, etc. 629.250288
Trucks—Parts 629.224
Trucks—Pictorial works 629.22320222; 629.2240222
Trucks—Purchasing 629.22320298

Trucks—Purchasing—Periodicals 629.22320298
Trucks, Rental 388.32404
Trucks—Routes—United States—Maps 388.32420973022
Trudeau, Pierre Elliott 971.0644092; 971.0646092
Truffaut, François 791.430233092
Truffaut, François—Criticism and interpretation 791.430233092
Truffières 635.8
Truffle culture 635.8
Truman, Harry S., 1884–1972 973.918092
Truman, Harry S., 1884–1972—Correspondence 973.918092
Trump, Donald, 1946– 333.33092
Trumpet music (Jazz) 788.92165
Trunked radio 621.384
Trust 158.2
Trusts and trustees 346.059
Trusts and trustees—Great Britain 346.41059
Trusts and trustees—Taxation—United States 343.7305264; 343.73053
Trusts and trustees—United States 346.73059
Trusts, Industrial 338.85
Trusts, Industrial—Government policy 338.85
Trusts, Industrial—Government policy—United States 338.850973
Trusts, Industrial—United States 338.850973
Truth 111.8; 121
Truth commissions 323.49; 353.462743
Truth—Deflationary theory 121
Truth—Religious aspects 210; 291.2
Truth, Sojourner, d. 1883 305.567092
Truthfulness and falsehood 177.3
Tryon, Glynis (Fictitious character) 813.54
Tryon, Glynis (Fictitious character)—Fiction 813.54
Tsunamis 551.47024
TSvetaeva, Marina, 1892–1941 891.7142
TSvetaeva, Marina, 1892–1941—Translations into English 891.7142
Tuatara 597.945
Tuba 788.98; 788.9819
Tuberculosis 614.542; 616.995
Tubes, Steel 672.83
Tubman, Harriet, 1820?–1913 305.567092; 326.092
Tubular bells 786.845
Tucker family 929.20973
Tucson (Ariz.) 979.1776
Tucson (Ariz.)—Guidebooks 917.9177604; 917.917760453; 917.917760454
Tucson (Ariz.)—Maps 912.791776
Tucson Metropolitan Area (Ariz.) 979.1776
Tucson Metropolitan Area (Ariz.)—Maps 912.791776
Tugboats 623.8232
Tulips 584.32; 635.93432
Tumor markers 616.994075
Tumor markers—Diagnostic use 616.994075
Tumor necrosis factor 616.079
Tumors 616.992
Tumors—Classification 616.9920012; 616.992075; 616.9940012; 616.994075
Tumors—Immunological aspects 616.992079
Tumors in children 362.19892994; 618.92992; 618.92994
Tuna 597.783
Tunable lasers 621.366
Tundra animals 591.7586
Tundra ecology 577.586
Tundra swan 598.418
Tungsten 669.734
Tungsten—Metallurgy 669.734

Tunicata 596.2
Tunisia 961.1
Tunisia—Guidebooks 916.1104; 916.110452
Tunneling 624.193
Tunneling (Physics) 530.416
Turbellaria 592.42
Turboexpanders 621.406
Turbomachines 621.406
Turbomachines—Fluid dynamics 621.406
Turbulence 532.0527; 620.1064
Turbulence—Mathematical models 620.1064
Turbulence—Measurement 620.1064
Turf management 635.9642
Turgenev, Ivan Sergeevich, 1818–1883 891.733
Turgenev, Ivan Sergeevich, 1818–1883—Criticism and
    interpretation 891.733
Turgenev, Ivan Sergeevich, 1818–1883—Translations
    into English 891.733
Turkey 956.1
Turkey—Antiquities 939.2
Turkey—Economic conditions 330.9561
Turkey—Economic conditions—1960– 330.956103
Turkey—Economic conditions—1960– —Periodicals
    330.956103
Turkey—Economic policy 338.9561
Turkey—Foreign relations 327.561
Turkey—Foreign relations—1980– 327.561009048
Turkey—Guidebooks 915.6104; 915.610439; 915.61044
Turkey—History 956.1
Turkey—History—1288–1453 956.1015
Turkey—History—Ottoman Empire, 1288–1918
    956.015; 956.1015
Turkey—History—1453–1683 956.1015
Turkey—History—19th century 956.1015
Turkey—History—20th century 956.102
Turkey hunting 799.248645
Turkey—Politics and government 956.1
Turkey—Politics and government—1909– 956.102
Turkey—Politics and government—1960–1980
    320.956109046; 956.103
Turkey—Politics and government—1980–
    320.956109048; 956.1038
Turkey—Social conditions 956.1
Turkey—Social life and customs 956.1
Turkeys 598.645; 636.592
Turkic languages 494.3
Turkish language 494.35
Turkish language—Conversation and phrase books
    494.35834
Turkish language—Conversation and phrase books—
    English 494.3583421
Turkish wit and humor 894.357008
Turner family 929.20973
Turner, Frederick Jackson, 1861–1932. Frontier in
    American history 973.01
Turner, J. M. W. (Joseph Mallord William), 1775–1851
    759.2
Turner, J. M. W. (Joseph Mallord William), 1775–1851—
    Catalogs 759.2
Turner, J. M. W. (Joseph Mallord William), 1775–1851—
    Criticism and interpretation 759.2
Turner, J. M. W. (Joseph Mallord William), 1775–1851—
    Exhibitions 759.2
Turner, Paul (Fictitious character) 813.54
Turner, Paul (Fictitious character)—Fiction 813.54
Turner, Ted 384.555092
Turning 621.94; 674.88; 684.083
Turnipseed, Anna (Fictitious character) 813.54
Turnkey computer systems 004.1

Turtles 597.92
Turtles as pets 639.392
Turtles, Fossil 567.92
Tuscany (Italy) 945.5
Tuscany (Italy)—Description and travel 914.5504;
    914.5504929; 914.550493
Tuscany (Italy)—Guidebooks 914.5504; 914.5504929;
    914.550493
Tuscarawas County (Ohio) 977.166
Tuscarawas County (Ohio)—Genealogy 929.377166
Tuscola County (Mich.) 977.445
Tuscola County (Mich.)—Maps 912.77445
Tutankhamen, King of Egypt—Tomb 932.014
Tutors and tutoring 371.394
Tuttle family 929.20973
Tutu, Desmond 283.092
TV lamps 621.322; 738.8
Twain, Mark, 1835–1910 813.4; 818.409
Twain, Mark, 1835–1910. Adventures of Huckleberry
    Finn 813.4
Twain, Mark, 1835–1910. Adventures of Huckleberry
    Finn—Examinations 813.4
Twain, Mark, 1835–1910. Adventures of Tom Sawyer
    813.4
Twain, Mark, 1835–1910—Childhood and youth 818.409
Twain, Mark, 1835–1910—Correspondence 818.409
Twain, Mark, 1835–1910—Criticism and interpretation
    818.409
Twain, Mark, 1835–1910—Friends and associates
    818.409
Twain, Mark, 1835–1910—Journeys 818.403; 818.409
Twain, Mark, 1835–1910—Journeys—Europe 818.403
Twain, Mark, 1835–1910—Journeys—West (U.S.)
    818.403
Twain, Mark, 1835–1910—Knowledge—Literature
    818.409
Twain, Mark, 1835–1910—Political and social views
    818.409
Twain, Shania 782.421642092
Tweenies (Fictitious characters) 791.4575
Twelve-step programs 362.29186; 616.8606
Twelve-step programs—Religious aspects 291.442
Twelve-step programs—Religious aspects—Christianity
    248.8629
Twelve-step programs—Religious aspects—
    Christianity—Meditations 242.4
Twelve-tone system 781.268
Twentieth century 909.82
Twenty-first century 909.83
Twenty-first century—Forecasts 303.490905
Twig (Fictitious character : Stewart) 823.914
Twig furniture 684.104; 749
Twilight zone (Television program) 791.4572
Twins 306.875; 649.144
Twins—Psychology 155.444
Twisted pair cables 621.31934
Two-phase flow 620.1064
Two-story houses 643.2; 728.372
Tyler, Anne 813.54
Tyler, Anne—Criticism and interpretation 813.54
Tyler, John, 1790–1862 973.58092
Tyler's Insurrection, 1381 942.038
Type and type-founding 686.221; 686.224
Type and type-founding—Digital techniques 686.221
Type and type-founding—History 686.22109; 686.22409
Type ornaments 686.224
Typesetting 686.225
Typewriting 652.3; 652.3024; 652.3026
Typewriting—Problems, exercises, etc. 652.307

Typhoon protection 363.34922; 693.8
Typographers 686.22092
Typology (Linguistics) 410.1; 415.01
Typology (Psychology) 155.26
Typology (Theology) 220.64
Tyrannosaurus rex 567.9129
Tyrrell County (N.C.)—Genealogy 929.3756172
Tyson, Mike, 1966- 796.83092
Tzotzil literature 897.415
Tzutuhil literature 897.415
U.S. Customs Service—Appropriations and expenditures 352.4482460973
U.S. Customs Service—Periodicals 352.448097305
U.S. Global Change Research Program 363.73874072073
U.S. Nuclear Regulatory Commission—Appropriations and expenditures 353.9992460973
U.S. Nuclear Regulatory Commission. Office for Analysis and Evaluation of Operational Data—Periodicals 353.999235097305; 363.179960973
U2 (Musical group) 782.421660922
Uganda 967.61
Uganda—Constitutional law 342.6761
Uganda—Economic conditions 330.96761
Uganda—Economic conditions—1979- 330.96761043
Uganda—Economic conditions—1979- —Periodicals 330.96761043
Uganda—Economic policy 338.96761
Uganda—Guidebooks 916.76104; 916.761044
Uganda—Politics and government 320.96761
Uganda—Politics and government—1979- 320.9676109048
Ugarit (Extinct city) 939.44
Ukraine 947.7
Ukraine—Economic conditions 330.9477
Ukraine—Economic conditions—1991- 330.9477086
Ukraine—Economic conditions—1991- —Periodicals 330.9477086
Ukraine—History 947.7
Ukraine—History—Revolution, 1917-1921 947.70841
Ukraine—History—Autonomy and independence movements 947.7085
Ukraine—Politics and government 947.7
Ukraine—Politics and government—1917-1945 320.947709041; 947.70841
Ukraine—Politics and government—1945-1991 320.947709045; 947.7085
Ukraine. Verkhovna Rada 328.477
Ukraine. Verkhovna Rada—Elections, 1994 324.9477086
Ukrainian language 491.79
Ukrainian language—Grammar 491.795; 491.7982; 491.7982421
Ukrainians—Canada—History 971.00491791
Ukrainians in literature 808.803520391791
Ulcerative colitis 616.3447
Ulster County (N.Y.)—Genealogy 929.374734
Ulster (Northern Ireland and Ireland) 941.6
Ulster (Northern Ireland and Ireland)—History 941.6
Ulster (Northern Ireland and Ireland)—Social life and customs 941.6
Ultima (Game) 793.932
Ultra-Orthodox Jews 296.832
Ultraproducts 511.3
Ultrasonic imaging 616.07543
Ultrasonic testing 620.11274
Ultrasonic waves—Industrial applications 620.28
Ultrasonics in obstetrics 618.207543
Ultrasonics in ophthalmology 617.71543
Ultrastructure (Biology) 571.633
Ultraviolet astronomy 522.68

Ultraviolet radiation 535.014
Ultraviolet radiation—Physiological effect 571.456
Umatilla Indians 979.5004979
Umbrellas and parasols 685
Ummah (Islam) 297.272; 320.55; 322.1
Unamuno, Miguel de, 1864-1936 868.6209
Unamuno, Miguel de, 1864-1936—Translations into English 868.6209
Uncertainty (Information theory) 003.54
Underachievers 371.28; 371.9
Underachievers—Education 371.9
Underachievers—Education—United States 371.90973
Undercover operations—United States 363.232
Underground areas 551.447
Underground construction 624.19
Underground dance music 781.554
Underground ecology 577.584
Underground electric lines 621.31923
Underground newspapers 070.172
Underground parking facilities 388.474; 725.38
Underground press 070.593
Underground press publications 070.593
Underground railroad 973.7115
Underground storage tanks 681.76
Underground storage tanks—Law and legislation 343.07868176
Undertakers and undertaking 363.75
Undertakers and undertaking—United States 363.750973
Underwater acoustic telemetry 621.389
Underwater acoustics 534.23; 620.25
Underwater archaeology 930.102804
Underwater cameras 778.730284
Underwater exploration 551.4607
Underwater photography 778.73
Underwater physiology 612.014415
Underwood family 929.20973
Unemployed 331.137
Unemployed—Great Britain 331.137941
Unemployed youth 305.235; 331.34137
Unemployment 331.137
Unemployment—Europe 331.13794
Unemployment—European Economic Community countries 331.13794
Unemployment—Great Britain 331.137941
Unemployment—Mathematical models 331.137015118
Unemployment—Psychological aspects 331.137019
Unemployment—United States 331.137973
Unesco 001.0601; 341.767
UNESCO Prize for the Promotion of the Arts 707.9
Unesco. Programme on Man and the Biosphere 304.2
Unesco—United States 341.767
Unetice culture 943.71021
Unfinished motion pictures 791.43
Ungulates 599.6
Unicode (Computer character set) 005.72
Unicorns 398.2454
Unidentified flying objects 001.942
Unidentified flying objects—Encyclopedias 001.94203
Unidentified flying objects—Periodicals 001.94205
Unidentified flying objects—Sightings and encounters 001.942
Unidentified flying objects—Sightings and encounters— New Mexico—Roswell 001.9420978943
Unidentified flying objects—Sightings and encounters— Psychological aspects 001.942
Unidentified flying objects—Sightings and encounters— United States 001.9420973
Unification Church 289.96

United States—Bibliography 016.973
United States—Bibliography—Catalogs 016.973
United States—Biography 920.073
United States—Biography—Dictionaries 920.07303
United States—Boundaries—Mexico 976.44
United States. Bureau of Land Management 352.570973
United States. Bureau of Land Management—
Appropriations and expenditures 352.572460973
United States Capitol (Washington, D.C.) 725.1109753;
975.3
United States—Census 317.3
United States—Census, 19th, 1970 304.6097309047;
317.3
United States—Census, 21st, 1990 304.6097309049
United States—Census—Bibliography 016.3173
United States. Central Intelligence Agency 327.1206073
United States. Central Intelligence Agency—History
327.1206073
United States—Church history 277.3
United States—Civilization 973
United States—Civilization—To 1783 973.2
United States—Civilization—19th century 973.5
United States—Civilization—1865–1918 973.8
United States—Civilization—20th century 973.9
United States—Civilization—1918–1945 973.91
United States—Civilization—1945– 973.92
United States—Civilization—1970– 973.92
United States—Civilization—Periodicals 973.05
United States—Climate 551.6973
United States. Coast Guard 359.970973; 363.2860973
United States. Coast Guard—Appropriations and
expenditures 353.36
United States—Commerce 380.10973; 381.0973;
382.0973
United States—Commerce—European Economic
Community countries 382.097304
United States—Commerce—History 382.0973
United States—Commerce—Japan 382.0973052
United States—Commerce—Mexico 382.0972073
United States—Commerce—Periodicals 380.102573
United States—Commerce—Soviet Union 382.0973047
United States—Commercial policy 382.30973
United States—Commercial policy—History 382.30973
United States—Commercial treaties 337.73
United States. Congress 328.73
United States. Congress—Committees 328.730765
United States. Congress—Dictionaries 328.73003
United States. Congress—Directories 328.730025
United States. Congress—Elections 324.973
United States. Congress—Elections, 1996 324.9730929
United States. Congress—Ethics 328.730766
United States. Congress—History 328.7309
United States. Congress. House 328.73072
United States. Congress. House—Election districts
328.7307345
United States. Congress. House—Ethics 328.730766
United States. Congress. House—Rules and practice
328.7305
United States. Congress. House—Speaker 328.730762
United States. Congress. House—Speaker—History
328.730762
United States. Congress. House—Voting 328.730775
United States. Congress—Leadership 328.730762
United States. Congress—Management 328.730068
United States. Congress—Officials and employees
328.730762
United States. Congress—Reform 328.730704
United States. Congress—Rules and practice 328.7305
United States. Congress. Senate 328.73071

United States. Congress. Senate—Committees
328.730765
United States. Congress. Senate—Ethics 172.0973
United States. Congress. Senate—History 328.7307109
United States. Congress. Senate—Majority leader
328.730762
United States. Congress. Senate—Majority leader—
History 328.730762
United States. Congress. Senate—Rules and practice
328.7305
United States. Congress—Term of office 328.73073
United States. Congress—Voting 328.730775
United States. Constitution 342.73023
United States. Constitution. 1st–10th Amendments
342.7303
United States. Constitution. 1st–10th Amendments—
History 342.73039
United States. Constitution. 1st Amendment 342.73085
United States. Constitution. 1st Amendment—Cases
342.73085
United States. Constitution. 4th Amendment
345.730522
United States. Constitution. 14th Amendment
342.73085
United States Constitution Bicentennial, 1987–1991
342.73029
United States. Constitution—Signers—Biography
973.30922
United States. Constitutional Convention. (1787)
342.730242; 342.730292
United States. Continental Army 973.344
United States. Continental Congress 973.312
United States. Declaration of Independence 973.313
United States—Defenses 355.033073
United States—Defenses—Economic aspects 355.033073
United States—Defenses—Periodicals 355.03307305
United States. Dept. of Agriculture 354.50973
United States. Dept. of Agriculture—Appropriations and
expenditures 354.52460973
United States. Dept. of Agriculture—Reorganization
353.52280973
United States. Dept. of Commerce 354.730973
United States. Dept. of Defense 355.60973
United States. Dept. of Defense—Appropriations and
expenditures 355.62260973
United States. Dept. of Defense—Management
355.60973
United States. Dept. of Defense—Procurement
355.62120973
United States. Dept. of Defense—Procurement—Corrupt
practices 355.62120973
United States. Dept. of Energy 354.40973
United States. Dept. of Energy—Appropriations and
expenditures 354.42460973
United States. Dept. of Housing and Urban
Development 353.550973
United States. Dept. of Housing and Urban
Development—Appropriations and expenditures
353.552460973
United States. Dept. of Justice 353.40973
United States. Dept. of Justice—Appropriations and
expenditures 353.42460973
United States. Dept. of Labor 354.90973
United States. Dept. of Labor—Appropriations and
expenditures 354.92460973
United States. Dept. of State 353.130973
United States. Dept. of State—Appropriations and
expenditures 353.132460973
United States. Dept. of the Army 355.60973

United—United

United States. Dept. of the Army—Appropriations and
expenditures—Periodicals 355.62260973
United States. Dept. of the Interior 355.30973
United States. Dept. of the Interior—Appropriations and
expenditures 353.32460973
United States. Dept. of the Treasury 352.40973
United States. Dept. of the Treasury—Appropriations
and expenditures 352.42460973
United States. Dept. of Transportation 354.760973
United States. Dept. of Transportation—Appropriations
and expenditures 354.762460973
United States. Dept. of Veterans Affairs 353.5380973
United States. Dept. of Veterans Affairs—
Appropriations and expenditures 353.5382460973
United States—Description and travel 917.304;
917.304929; 917.304931
United States—Description and travel—Anecdotes
917.304
United States—Description and travel—Early works to
1800 917.304
United States—Directories 917.30025; 973.025
United States—Distances, etc. 912.73
United States. District Court (Massachusetts)—Rules
and practice 347.7322
United States—Economic conditions 330.973
United States—Economic conditions—1865–1918
330.97308
United States—Economic conditions—1918–1945
330.973091
United States—Economic conditions—1971–1981
330.9730924; 330.9730925
United States—Economic conditions—1981-
330.9730927
United States—Economic conditions—1981- —
Periodicals 330.9730927
United States—Economic conditions—Periodicals
330.973005
United States—Economic policy 338.973
United States—Economic policy—To 1933 338.973
United States—Economic policy—1933–1945 338.973
United States—Economic policy—1945–1960 338.973
United States—Economic policy—1961–1971 338.973
United States—Economic policy—1971–1981 338.973
United States—Economic policy—1981–1993 338.973
United States—Economic policy—1993- 338.973
United States—Emigration and immigration 304.80973;
325.73
United States—Emigration and immigration—
Bibliography 016.32573
United States—Emigration and immigration—
Government policy 325.73
United States—Emigration and immigration—
Government policy—History 325.73
United States—Emigration and immigration—History
325.73
United States. Environmental Protection Agency
354.3280973
United States—Ethnic relations 305.800973
United States. Federal Aviation Administration
354.790973
United States. Federal Aviation Administration—
Appropriations and expenditures 354.792460973
United States. Federal Bureau of Investigation
363.250973
United States. Federal Communications Commission
343.730994; 353.75280973
United States. Federal Communications Commission—
Appropriations and expenditures 354.75282460973

United States. Federal Energy Regulatory Commission
354.4280973
United States. Federal Trade Commission 354.730973
United States. Food and Drug Administration
353.9970973
United States—Foreign economic relations 337.73
United States—Foreign economic relations—China
337.73051
United States—Foreign economic relations—Europe
337.7304
United States—Foreign economic relations—European
Economic Community countries 337.7304
United States—Foreign economic relations—European
Union countries 337.4073; 337.7304
United States—Foreign economic relations—Japan
337.52073; 337.73052
United States—Foreign economic relations—Korea
(South) 337.5195073
United States—Foreign economic relations—Latin
America 337.7308
United States—Foreign economic relations—Mexico
337.73072
United States—Foreign economic relations—Soviet
Union 337.47073; 337.73047
United States—Foreign public opinion, European 973
United States—Foreign public opinion, German 973
United States—Foreign public opinion, Soviet
303.387917; 973
United States—Foreign relations 327.73
United States—Foreign relations—1775–1783
327.73009033
United States—Foreign relations—1783–1815
327.73009033
United States—Foreign relations—1861–1865
327.73009034; 973.72
United States—Foreign relations—1865–1921
327.73009034
United States—Foreign relations—1897–1901
327.73009034
United States—Foreign relations—20th century
327.7300904
United States—Foreign relations—1913–1921
327.73009041
United States—Foreign relations—1933–1945
327.73009043
United States—Foreign relations—1945–1953
327.73009044; 327.73009045
United States—Foreign relations—1945–1989
327.73009045
United States—Foreign relations—1945–1989—
Philosophy 327.73009045
United States—Foreign relations—1945–1989—Public
opinion 327.73009045
United States—Foreign relations—1953–1961
327.73009045
United States—Foreign relations—1961–1963
327.73009046
United States—Foreign relations—1963–1969
327.73009046
United States—Foreign relations—1969–1974
327.73009047
United States—Foreign relations—1977–1981
327.73009047
United States—Foreign relations—1981–1989
327.73009048
United States—Foreign relations—1981–1989—Public
opinion 327.73009048
United States—Foreign relations—1989- 327.73009049

392

United States—Foreign relations—1989–1993
327.73009049
United States—Foreign relations—1993–2001
327.73009049
United States—Foreign relations—2001– 327.73009051
United States—Foreign relations administration
353.130973
United States—Foreign relations—Afghanistan
327.730581
United States—Foreign relations—Asia 327.7305
United States—Foreign relations—Australia 327.73094;
327.94073
United States—Foreign relations—Canada 327.71073;
327.73071
United States—Foreign relations—China 327.51073;
327.73051
United States—Foreign relations—Cuba 327.7291073;
327.7307291
United States—Foreign relations—Dominican Republic
327.7307293
United States—Foreign relations—El Salvador
327.7307284
United States—Foreign relations—Europe 327.7304
United States—Foreign relations—Germany 327.73043
United States—Foreign relations—Germany (West)
327.73043
United States—Foreign relations—Great Britain
327.41073; 327.73041
United States—Foreign relations—India 327.73054
United States—Foreign relations—Indonesia
327.730598
United States—Foreign relations—Iran 327.73055
United States—Foreign relations—Iraq 327.730567
United States—Foreign relations—Israel 327.7305694
United States—Foreign relations—Japan 327.52073;
327.73052
United States—Foreign relations—Korea 327.730519
United States—Foreign relations—Korea (South)
327.7305195
United States—Foreign relations—Law and legislation
342.730412
United States—Foreign relations—Mexico 327.72073;
327.73072
United States—Foreign relations—Middle East
327.73056
United States—Foreign relations—Moral and ethical
aspects 172.4
United States—Foreign relations—Nicaragua
327.7307285
United States—Foreign relations—Pakistan 327.7305491
United States—Foreign relations—Panama 327.7307287
United States—Foreign relations—Persian Gulf Region
327.730536
United States—Foreign relations—Philippines
327.730599
United States—Foreign relations—Philosophy 327.73
United States—Foreign relations—Russia 327.73047
United States—Foreign relations—Russia (Federation)
327.73047
United States—Foreign relations—South Africa
327.73068
United States—Foreign relations—Soviet Union
327.47073; 327.73047
United States—Foreign relations—Taiwan 327.73051249
United States—Foreign relations—Treaties 341.026473
United States—Foreign relations—Turkey 327.730561
United States—Foreign relations—Vietnam 327.597073
United States. Forest Service 354.550973

United States. Forest Service—Appropriations and
expenditures 354.552460973
United States—Gazetteers 917.3003
United States—Genealogy 929.1072073
United States—Genealogy—Bibliography
016.9291072073
United States—Genealogy—Bibliography—Catalogs
016.9291072073; 016.929373
United States—Genealogy—Bibliography—Microform
catalogs 016.9291072073; 016.929373
United States—Genealogy—Directories 016.929373;
929.102573
United States—Genealogy—Handbooks, manuals, etc.
929.1072073
United States—Genealogy—Periodicals 929.1072073;
929.37305
United States—Genealogy—Societies, etc.—Directories
929.102573
United States. General Accounting Office 352.430973
United States. General Services Administration
352.50973
United States—Geography 917.3
United States. Government Printing Office 070.509753
United States—Guidebooks 917.304; 917.304929;
917.304931
United States—Historical geography 911.73
United States—Historical geography—Maps 911.73
United States—Historiography 973.072
United States—History 973
United States—History—Colonial period, ca. 1600–1775
973.2
United States—History—Colonial period, ca. 1600–
1775—Sources 973.2072
United States—History—French and Indian War, 1755–
1763 973.26
United States—History—Revolution, 1775–1783 973.3
United States—History—Revolution, 1775–1783—
Biography 973.30922
United States—History—Revolution, 1775–1783—
Campaigns 973.33
United States—History—Revolution, 1775–1783—
Causes 973.311
United States—History—Revolution, 1775–1783—
Encyclopedias 973.303
United States—History—Revolution, 1775–1783—
Influence 973.3
United States—History—Revolution, 1775–1783—Naval
operations 973.35
United States—History—Revolution, 1775–1783—
Participation, German 973.342
United States—History—Revolution, 1775–1783—
Personal narratives 973.3092
United States—History—Revolution, 1775–1783—Social
aspects 973.31
United States—History—Revolution, 1775–1783—
Sources 973.3072
United States—History—1783–1865 973.5
United States—History—War of 1812 973.52
United States—History—War of 1812—Campaigns
973.523
United States—History—War of 1812—Naval operations
973.525
United States—History—1815–1861 973.5
United States—History—1849–1877 973.5
United States—History—Civil War, 1861–1865 973.7
United States—History—Civil War, 1861–1865—
Anecdotes 973.7
United States—History—Civil War, 1861–1865—
Bibliography 016.9737

United States—History—Civil War, 1861–1865—
  Biography 973.70922; 973.730922
United States—History—Civil War, 1861–1865—
  Campaigns 973.73
United States—History—Civil War, 1861–1865—Causes
  973.711
United States—History—Civil War, 1861–1865—
  Dictionaries 973.703
United States—History—Civil War, 1861–1865—
  Influence 973.7
United States—History—Civil War, 1861–1865—Medical
  care 973.775
United States—History—Civil War, 1861–1865—Naval
  operations 973.75
United States—History—Civil War, 1861–1865—
  Participation, Afro-American 973.7415
United States—History—Civil War, 1861–1865—
  Periodicals 973.705
United States—History—Civil War, 1861–1865—
  Personal narratives 973.781
United States—History—Civil War, 1861–1865—
  Personal narratives, Confederate 973.782
United States—History—Civil War, 1861–1865—Pictorial
  works 973.70222
United States—History—Civil War, 1861–1865—
  Registers of dead 973.76
United States—History—Civil War, 1861–1865—Secret
  service 973.785; 973.786
United States—History—Civil War, 1861–1865—Social
  aspects 973.71
United States—History—Civil War, 1861–1865—Sources
  973.7072
United States—History—Civil War, 1861–1865—Women
  973.7082; 973.73082
United States—History—1865– 973.8; 973.9
United States—History—1865–1898 973.8
United States—History—1865–1921 973.8
United States—History—20th century 973.9
United States—History—1901–1909 973.911
United States—History—1901–1953 973.91
United States—History—1913–1921 973.913
United States—History—1919–1933 973.91
United States—History—1933–1945 973.917
United States—History—1945– 973.92
United States—History—1945–1953 973.918
United States—History—1961–1969 973.922; 973.923
United States—History—1961–1969—Sources
  973.922072
United States—History—1969– 973.92
United States—History—Anecdotes 973
United States—History—Bibliography 016.973
United States—History—Bibliography of bibliographies
  016.016973
United States—History—Chronology 973.0202
United States—History—Dictionaries 973.03
United States—History—Encyclopedias 973.03
United States—History—Errors, inventions, etc. 973
United States—History—Examinations 973.076
United States—History—Examinations, questions, etc.
  973.076
United States—History, Local 973
United States—History, Local—Anecdotes 973
United States—History, Military 355.00973
United States—History, Military—To 1900 355.00973
United States—History, Military—20th century
  355.009730904
United States—History, Naval 359.00973
United States—History—Outlines, syllabi, etc. 973.0202
United States—History—Philosophy 973.01

United States—History—Pictorial works 973.0222
United States—History—Religious aspects—Christianity
  277.3
United States—History—Sources 973.072
United States—History—Sources—Bibliography 016.973
United States—History—Sources—Bibliography—
  Catalogs 016.973
United States—History—Study and teaching (Higher)
  973.0711
United States—History—Study and teaching
  (Secondary) 973.0712
United States—History—Textbooks 973
United States. Immigration and Naturalization Service
  353.4840973
United States. Immigration and Naturalization
  Service—Appropriations and expenditures
  353.4842460973
United States—Imprints 015.73
United States—Intellectual life 973
United States—Intellectual life—1865–1918 973.8
United States—Literary collections 810.803273
United States—Maps 912.73
United States—Maps—Bibliography 016.91273
United States—Maps—Bibliography—Catalogs
  016.91273
United States—Maps for children 912.73
United States—Maps, Outline and base 912.73
United States. Marine Corps 359.960973
United States. Marine Corps—History 359.960973
United States Marine Memorial (Arlington, Va.)
  359.961; 359.961609755295; 731.76
United States. Maritime Administration 354.78270973
United States. Maritime Administration—Appropriations
  and expenditures 354.78272460973
United States marshals 347.016
United States Military Academy 355.0071173
United States Military Academy—History 355.0071173
United States—Military policy 355.033573
United States—Moral conditions 306.0973
United States. National Aeronautics and Space
  Administration 354.79
United States. National Aeronautics and Space
  Administration—Appropriations and expenditures
  354.79
United States. National Labor Relations Board
  344.7301; 354.970973
United States. National Oceanic and Atmospheric
  Administration 354.3690973
United States. National Oceanic and Atmospheric
  Administration—Appropriations and expenditures
  354.3692460973
United States. National Park Service—Vocational
  guidance—Handbooks, manuals, etc. 363.6802373
United States Naval Academy 359.0071173
United States Naval Expedition to Japan, 1852–1854
  952.048
United States. Navy 359.00973
United States. Navy—Aviation boatswain's mates—
  Handbooks, manuals, etc. 623.746049
United States. Navy—Aviation—History 359.940973
United States. Navy—Gays 359.0086642
United States. Navy—History 359.00973; 359.30973
United States. Navy—Hospital corpsmen 359.345
United States. Navy—Procurement 359.62120973
United States. Navy. SEALs 359.9840973
United States. Navy. SEALs—History 359.9840973
United States. Navy—Watch duty—Handbooks,
  manuals, etc. 359.4

United States. Navy—Women 359.00820973; 359.3480820973

United States—Officials and employees 352.630973

United States—Officials and employees—Foreign countries 352.630973

United States—Officials and employees—Pensions 353.5490973

United States—Officials and employees—Political activity 342.73068; 342.730684

United States—Officials and employees—Retirement 342.730686

United States—Officials and employees—Salaries, etc. 331.28135173; 352.670973

United States—Officials and employees—Selection and appointment 352.650973

United States. Panama Canal Commission 354.78

United States. Panama Canal Commission—Appropriations and expenditures 354.78

United States—Pictorial works 779.9917300222; 917.300222; 973.0222

United States—Politics and government 320.473; 320.973; 973

United States—Politics and government—To 1775 320.9730903; 973.2

United States—Politics and government—1775–1783 320.97309033; 973.31

United States—Politics and government—1775–1783—Sources 973.31

United States—Politics and government—1783–1789 320.97309033; 973.318

United States—Politics and government—1783–1809 320.97309033; 973.4

United States—Politics and government—1783–1865 320.97309033; 973.5

United States—Politics and government—1789–1809 320.97309033; 973.4

United States—Politics and government—1829–1837 320.97309034; 973.56

United States—Politics and government—1845–1861 320.97309034; 973.6

United States—Politics and government—1849–1861 320.97309034; 973.6

United States—Politics and government—1861–1865 320.97309034; 973.7

United States—Politics and government—1865–1900 320.97309033; 973.8

United States—Politics and government—1901–1909 320.97309041; 973.911

United States—Politics and government—1901–1953 320.97309041; 973.91

United States—Politics and government—1913–1921 320.97309041; 973.913

United States—Politics and government—1919–1933 320.97309041; 973.91

United States—Politics and government—1933–1945 320.97309043; 973.917

United States—Politics and government—1945–1953 320.97309045; 973.918

United States—Politics and government—1945–1989 320.97309045; 973.92

United States—Politics and government—1961–1963 320.97309046; 973.922

United States—Politics and government—1961–1963—Sources 320.97309046; 973.922; 973.922072

United States—Politics and government—1969–1974 320.97309047; 973.924

United States—Politics and government—1974–1977 320.97309047; 973.925

United States—Politics and government—1977–1981 320.97309047; 973.926

United States—Politics and government—1977–1981—Caricatures and cartoons 320.97309047

United States—Politics and government—1981–1989 320.97309048; 973.927

United States—Politics and government—1981–1989—Caricatures and cartoons 320.97309048; 973.9270207

United States—Politics and government—1989–1993 320.97309049; 973.928

United States—Politics and government—1989–1993—Caricatures and cartoons 973.9280207

United States—Politics and government—1993–2001 320.97309049; 973.929

United States—Politics and government—1993–2001—Caricatures and cartoons 973.9290207

United States—Politics and government—1993–2001—Humor 973.9290207

United States—Politics and government—2001- 320.97309051; 973.93; 973.931

United States—Politics and government—Humor 320.9730207

United States—Population 304.60973

United States—Population—History 304.60973

United States—Population—Maps 304.60973022

United States—Population policy 363.90973

United States Postal Service 354.7590973

United States—Race relations 305.800973

United States—Race relations—Political aspects 305.800973

United States. Real Estate Settlement Procedures Act of 1974 346.7304373

United States—Relations 327.73

United States—Relations—Australia 327.73094

United States—Relations—Canada 303.48271073

United States—Relations—China 303.48251073

United States—Relations—Foreign countries 327.73

United States—Relations—Great Britain 303.48251073

United States—Relations—Japan 303.48252073

United States—Relations—Korea (South) 303.4825195073

United States—Relations—Mexico 303.48272073

United States—Relations—Russia 303.48247073

United States—Relations—South Africa 327.68073

United States—Religion 200.973

United States—Religion—1945–1960 200.973

United States—Religious life and customs 200.973; 277.3

United States—Road maps 912.73

United States—Rural conditions 307.720973

United States. Securities and Exchange Commission 354.880973

United States. Small Business Administration 354.2990973

United States. Small Business Administration—Appropriations and expenditures 354.2992460973

United States—Social conditions 973

United States—Social conditions—To 1865 973

United States—Social conditions—1865–1918 973.8

United States—Social conditions—1933–1945 973.917

United States—Social conditions—1945- 973.92

United States—Social conditions—1960–1980 973.92

United States—Social conditions—1980- 973.92

United States—Social conditions—Encyclopedias 973.03

United States—Social life and customs 973

United States—Social life and customs—To 1775 973.2

United States—Social life and customs—1775–1783 973.3

United States—Social life and customs—19th century 973.5

United States—Social life and customs—1865–1918 973.8

United States—Social life and customs—20th century 973.91

United States—Social life and customs—1918–1945 973.91

United States—Social life and customs—1945–1970 973.92

United States—Social life and customs—1971- 973.92

United States—Social policy 361.610973

United States—Social policy—1980–1993 361.61097309048

United States—Social policy—1993- 361.61097309049

United States. Social Security Administration 353.540973

United States—Statistical services 317.3

United States—Statistics 317.3

United States—Statistics—Periodicals 317.305

United States—Study and teaching 973.072

United States. Supreme Court 347.7326

United States. Supreme Court—Biography 347.732634

United States. Supreme Court—Decision making 347.7326

United States. Supreme Court—Encyclopedias 347.732603

United States. Supreme Court—History 347.732609

United States. Supreme Court—Officials and employees—Selection and appointment 347.732634

United States. Tax Court 343.73040269

United States. Taxpayer Relief Act of 1997 343.7304

United States—Territorial expansion 973

United States—Tours 917.304; 917.304929

United States. Veterans Administration 353.5380973

United States. Veterans Administration—Appropriations and expenditures 353.5382460973

United States. Veterans Administration. Dept. of Medicine and Surgery 353.6086970973

United States. Veterans Administration. Dept. of Medicine and Surgery—Officials and employees 353.6263086970973

United Way of America 361.8

United Way of America—Finance—Statistics 361.8

Unity School of Christianity 289.97

Unity School of Christianity—Doctrines 230.997

Universal design 745.4

Universalism 289.134

Universals (Linguistics) 410.1; 415.01

Universals (Philosophy) 111.2

Universities and colleges 378

Universities and colleges—Accreditation—United States 379.158

Universities and colleges—Administration 378.101

Universities and colleges—Africa 378.6

Universities and colleges—Australia 378.94

Universities and colleges—California 378.794

Universities and colleges—California—Directories 378.794025

Universities and colleges—Complaints against 378

Universities and colleges—Europe—History 378.4

Universities and colleges—Examinations 378.166

Universities and colleges—Graduate work 378.155

Universities and colleges—Great Britain 378.41

Universities and colleges—India 378.54

Universities and colleges—India—Administration 378.1010954

Universities and colleges—Latin America 378.8

Universities and colleges—Law and legislation 344.074

Universities and colleges—Law and legislation—United States 344.73074

Universities and colleges—Ontario 378.713

Universities and colleges—Public relations 659.29378

Universities and colleges—Public relations—United States 659.2937873

Universities and colleges—United States 378.73

Universities and colleges—United States—Administration 378.1010973

Universities and colleges—United States—Admission 378.16160973

Universities and colleges—United States—Admission—Handbooks, manuals, etc. 378.16160973

Universities and colleges—United States—Alumni and alumnae 378.198

Universities and colleges—United States—Curricula 378.1990973

Universities and colleges—United States—Curricula—Directories 378.19902573

Universities and colleges—United States—Data processing 378.730285

Universities and colleges—United States—Directories 378.73025

Universities and colleges—United States—Entrance examinations 378.1662

Universities and colleges—United States—Entrance requirements 378.16170973

Universities and colleges—United States—Evaluation 379.1580973

Universities and colleges—United States—Examinations 378.1660973

Universities and colleges—United States—Faculty 378.120973

Universities and colleges—United States—Graduate work 378.1550973

Universities and colleges—United States—Graduate work—Directories 378.15502573

Universities and colleges—United States—Graduate work—Handbooks, manuals, etc. 378.1550973

Universities and colleges—United States—Planning 378.1070973

University autonomy—United States 378.101

University cooperation 378.104

University extension 378.175

University hospitals 362.11

University of Cambridge—History 378.42659

University of Georgia—Football—History 796.332630975818

University of Nebraska (Lincoln campus)—Football 796.3326309782293

University of Notre Dame—Football 796.332630977289

University of Notre Dame—Football—History 796.332630977289

University of Oxford—History 378.42574

University of Wisconsin System 378.77583

University of Wisconsin System—Employees—Statistics—Periodicals 378.1109775021

University press publications 070.594

University presses 070.594

University System of Georgia—Periodicals 378.75805

University towns 307.76

UNIX (Computer file) 005.432

UNIX (Computer file)—Periodicals 005.43205

UNIX device drivers (Computer programs) 005.713

UNIX System V (Computer file) 005.432

Unlicensed motor vehicle drivers 364.147

Unmarried couples 306.735

Unmarried couples—Legal status, laws, etc. 346.015; 346.016

Unmarried couples—Legal status, laws, etc.—Great Britain 346.41015; 346.41016
Unmarried couples—Legal status, laws, etc.—United States 346.73016
Unmarried mothers 306.8743
Unmarried mothers—Services for 362.8392
Unmarried mothers—United States 306.8743
Unparliamentary language 060.42014; 328.014
Unsolicited electronic mail messages 005.713; 384.34
Unsolicited electronic mail messages—Law and legislation 343.09944
Unsteady flow (Fluid dynamics) 620.1064
Upanishads 294.59218
Upanishads—Criticism, interpretation, etc. 294.59218
Updike, John 813.54
Updike, John—Criticism and interpretation 813.54
Upholstered furniture 645.4
Upholstery 645.4; 684.12
Upholstery—Fire testing 628.9222
Upland ecology 577
Uplands 551.43
Upper class 305.52
Upper class—United States 305.520973
Upper class women 305.48
Upper Peninsula (Mich.) 977.49
Upper Peninsula (Mich.)—Social life and customs 977.49
Uranium 553.4932
Uranium ores 553.4932
Urantia book 299
Urantia book—Concordances 299
Uranus (Planet) 523.47
Urban animals 591.756
Urban anthropology 307.76
Urban ecology 304.2091732; 307.76
Urban ecology (Biology) 577.56
Urban economics 330.91732
Urban folklore 398.2091732
Urban folklore—Religious aspects 291.175
Urban folklore—United States 398.20973091732
Urban forestry 635.977091732
Urban geography 307.76; 910.U6891732
Urban health 362.1042
Urban hydrology 628.21
Urban parks 363.68; 712.5
Urban policy 307.76; 320.85
Urban policy—Great Britain 307.760941
Urban policy—United States 307.760973
Urban pollution 363.73091732
Urban poor 362.5091732
Urban poor—United States 362.50973091732
Urban renewal 307.3416
Urban renewal—Europe 307.3416094
Urban renewal—New York (State)—New York 307.3416097471
Urban renewal—United States 307.34160973
Urban runoff 628.21
Urban runoff—Management 628.21068
Urban schools 371.0091732
Urban schools—United States 371.00973091732
Urban transportation 388.4
Urban transportation—Planning 388.4068
Urban transportation—United States 388.40973
Urban universities and colleges 378.0091732
Urban youth 305.235091732
Urban youth—United States 305.2350973091732
Urbanization 307.76
Urbanization—China 307.760951
Urbanization—Developing countries 307.76091724

Urbanization—India 307.760954
Urbanization—United States 307.760973
Urdu language 491.439
Urdu poetry 891.4391; 891.4391008
Urdu poetry—Translations into English 891.4391008
Urdu wit and humor 891.4397008
Urinary incontinence 616.62
Urinary organs 612.463
Urinary organs—Calculi 616.622
Urinary organs—Calculi—Treatment 616.62206
Urinary organs—Diseases 616.6
Urinary tract infections 616.6
Urine—Analysis 616.07566
Urogynecology 616.6
Urology 616.6
Uropodidae 595.429
Uru mythology 299.82
Uruguay round (1987-1994) 382.92
Used aircraft—Purchasing 629.133340297
Used car trade 381.45629222
Used cars 629.222
Used cars—Purchasing 629.2220296; 629.2220297
Used computers 621.39
Used machinery 621.8
Used telecommunication equipment industry 338.47621382
Usenet (Computer network) 004.69; 005.713; 384.33
User interfaces (Computer systems) 005.437
Ut pictura poesis (Aesthetics) 700.1
Utah 979.2
Utah—Guidebooks 917.9204; 917.920433; 917.920434
Utah—History 979.2
Utah Jazz (Basketball team) 796.3236409792258
Utah Jazz (Basketball team)—History 796.3236409792258
Ute Indians 305.89745; 979.0049745
Ute Indians—Wars, 1879 973.83
Uther Pendragon (Legendary character) 820.80351
Utilitarianism 171.5
Utilities (Computer programs) 005.43
Utility theory 330.137
Utopian socialism 335.02
Utopias 321.07; 335.02
Utopias—History 335.0209
Utopias in literature 808.80372; 809.93372
Uttar Pradesh (India) 954.2
V-chips 363.31
Vacation homes 643.2; 728.72
Vacation rentals 333.338; 643.2; 647.94
Vacation schools 371.232; 373.1232; 374.8
Vacation schools—United States 371.2320973; 373.12320973
Vacation schools—United States—Directories 371.23202573; 373.123202573
Vacations 910.2
Vaccination 614.47
Vaccination—Complications 614.47
Vaccination of children 614.47083
Vaccines 615.372
Vacuum 533.5
Vacuum cleaners 643.6
Vacuum metallurgy 669.0284
Vacuum technology 621.55
Vacuum-tubes 621.384132
Vagrancy in literature 808.80355; 809.93355
Vail, Martin (Fictitious character) 813.54
Vaishnava temples 294.535; 726.145512
Vaishnavism 294.5512
Val Baker, Denys, 1917- 828.91209

Valdemar (Imaginary place) 813.54
Valence (Theoretical chemistry) 541.224
Valentine, Dan (Fictitious character) 813.54
Valentine decorations 745.5941
Valentines 741.684
Valéry, Paul, 1871–1945 841.912
Valéry, Paul, 1871–1945—Philosophy 841.912
Valéry, Paul, 1871–1945—Translations into English 841.912
Valhalla 293.23
Vallejo, César, 1892–1938 861.62
Vallejo, César, 1892–1938—Translations into English 861.62
Valley of the Kings (Egypt) 932
Vālmīki. Rāmāyaṇa 294.5922046
Valuation 332.63221
Value 338.521
Value-added tax 336.2714; 352.44
Value-added tax—Great Britain 336.27140941
Value-added tax—Law and legislation 343.055
Value-added tax—Law and legislation—Great Britain 343.41055
Value analysis (Cost control) 658.1552
Value distribution theory 515.982
Values 121.8; 303.372
Values clarification 170
Values—Psychological aspects 153.45
Valves 621.84
Valves—Handbooks, manuals, etc. 621.84
Vampire films 791.43675
Vampire films—History and criticism 791.43675
Vampires 133.423; 398.45
Vampires in literature 808.80375; 809.93375
Van Buren County (Mich.) 977.413
Van Buren County (Mich.)—Maps 912.77413
Van de Kamp, Binky (Fictitious character) 813.54
Van industry 338.476292234
Van Pelt, Lucy (Fictitious character) 741.5973
Van Vliet, Claire 811.54
Vance family 929.20973
Vance, Philo (Fictitious character) 813.52
Vance, Philo (Fictitious character)—Fiction 813.52
Vancouver (B.C.) 971.133
Vancouver (B.C.)—Description and travel 917.113304; 917.1133044
Vancouver (B.C.)—Guidebooks 917.113304; 917.1133044
Vancouver Island (B.C.) 971.12
Vancouver Island (B.C.)—Guidebooks 917.11204; 917.112044
Vander Poele, Nicholas (Fictitious character) 823.914
Vander Poele, Nicholas (Fictitious character)—Fiction 823.914
Vanderbilt family 929.20973
Vans 629.2234
Vans—Purchasing 629.22340297
Vans—Purchasing—Periodicals 629.22340297
Vanuatu 995.95
Vanuatu—Politics and government 320.99595
Vanuatu—Politics and government—Periodicals 320.99595
Vapor barriers 693.893
Vapor-plating 671.735
Vargas Llosa, Mario, 1936– 863.64
Vargas Llosa, Mario, 1936– —Criticism and interpretation 863.64
Variable stars 523.844
Variation (Biology) 576.54
Variational inequalities (Mathematics) 515.64
Variations (Guitar) 787.871825

Variations (Harpsichord) 786.41825
Variations (Orchestra) 784.21825
Variations (Organ) 786.51825
Variations (Piano) 786.21825
Variations (Piano, 4 hands) 785.621921825
Variations (Piano with orchestra) 784.2621825
Variations (Violoncello and piano) 787.41825
Varicose veins 616.143
Vasari, Giorgio, 1511–1574 709.2
Vasari, Giorgio, 1511–1574—Criticism and interpretation 709.2
Vascular endothelium 612.13
Vascular endothelium—Pathophysiology 616.13
Vascular system of plants 575.7
Vase-painting, Greek 738.3820938
Vases, Greek 738.3820938
Vāstu 133.333
Vasugupta. Śivasūtra 294.595
Vatican Council (2nd : 1962–1965) 262.52
Vatican Palace (Vatican City) 945.634
Vaudeville 792.7
Vaudeville—United States 792.70973
Vaughan, Henry, 1622–1695 821.4
Vaughan, Henry, 1622–1695—Criticism and interpretation 821.4
Vaulting 796.44
VAX-11 (Computer) 004.145
VAX-11 (Computer)—Programming 005.245
VAX computers 004.145
VAX computers—Programming 005.245
VAX/VMS 005.4449
VBScript (Computer program language) 005.2762
Veblen, Thorstein, 1857–1929 330.092
Vector analysis 515.63
Vector bundles 514.224; 516.362
Vector control 614.43
Vector processing (Computer science) 005.35
Vector spaces 512.52
Vedanta 181.48
Vedas 294.5921
Vedas—Criticism, interpretation, etc. 294.5921046
Vedas. Ṛgveda 294.59212
Vedas. Ṛgveda—Criticism, interpretation, etc. 294.59212046
Vedic literature 294.5921
Vedic literature—History and criticism 294.5921046
Vega, Lope de, 1562–1635 862.3
Vega, Lope de, 1562–1635—Criticism and interpretation 862.3
Vegan cookery 641.5636
Veganism 179.3; 613.262
Vegetable amaranths 635.4
Vegetable gardening 635
Vegetable gardening—Great Britain 635.0941
Vegetable gardening—United States 635.0973
Vegetable peeling machines 641.650284; 683.82
Vegetable trade 338.175
Vegetable trade—United States 338.1750973
Vegetable trade—United States—Statistics—Periodicals 338.1750973021
Vegetables 635; 641.35; 664.8
Vegetables—Heirloom varieties 635
Vegetables—Preservation 641.4
Vegetables—Seeds 635.0421
Vegetarian children 613.262083
Vegetarian convenience foods 641.5636; 664.6
Vegetarian cookery 641.5636
Vegetarian foods 641.3; 641.5636

Vegetarianism 613.262
Vegetarians 613.262
Vegetation and climate 581.42; 581.7
Vegetation dynamics 581.7
Vegetation mapping 580.723
Vegetative propagation 631.53
Vehicles 629.046
Vehicles, Military 355.83
Vehicles, Remotely piloted 629.046
Veins—Diseases 616.14
Velociraptor 567.912
Venango County (Pa.)—Genealogy 929.374896
Vendetta 364.256
Vending machines 629.82
Vendors and purchasers 346.04363
Vendors and purchasers—California 346.79404363
Vendors and purchasers—Massachusetts 346.74404363
Vendors and purchasers—New Jersey 346.74904363
Vendors and purchasers—New York (State) 346.74704363
Vendors and purchasers—Ohio 346.77104363
Vendors and purchasers—Texas 346.76404363
Vendors and purchasers—United States 346.7304363
Vendors and purchasers—United States—Cases 346.73043630264
Veneer industry 338.4767483
Veneers and veneering 674.83
Venezuela 987
Venezuela—Guidebooks 918.704; 918.704642
Venezuela—Politics and government 320.987; 987
Venezuela—Politics and government—1974– 320.98709047; 987.0633; 987.064
Venezuelan Sign language 419.87
Venice (Italy) 945.31
Venice (Italy)—Description and travel 914.53104; 914.53104929; 914.5310493
Venice (Italy)—Guidebooks 914.53104; 914.53104929; 914.5310493
Venice (Italy)—Social life and customs 945.31
Venice (Italy)—Tours 914.53104; 914.53104929; 914.5310493
Venison industry 338.4766492
Ventilation 697.92
Ventriloquism 793.89
Ventriloquists 793.89092
Ventura County (Calif.) 979.492
Ventura County (Calif.)—Maps 912.79492
Ventura publisher (Computer file) 686.22544536
Venture capital 332.04154; 658.15224
Venture capital—Law and legislation 346.065
Venture capital—Law and legislation—United States 346.73065
Venture capital—United States 332.04150973
Venture capital—United States—Directories 332.04154
Venus (Planet) 523.42
Verbal behavior 153.6
Verbal self-defense 153.6
Verdi, Giuseppe, 1813–1901 782.1092
Verdi, Giuseppe, 1813–1901. Operas 782.1092
Verilog (Computer hardware description language) 621.392
Verismo (Opera) 782.1; 792.5
Verity, William Clarence (Fictitious character) 823.914
Vermeer, Johannes, 1632–1675 759.9492
Vermeer, Johannes, 1632–1675—Criticism and interpretation 759.9492
Vermicomposting 631.875; 639.75
Vermiculturists 639.75092
Vermilion County (Ill.) 977.365

Vermilion County (Ill.)—Maps 912.77365
Vermont 974.3
Vermont—Genealogy 929.3743
Vermont—Guidebooks 917.4304; 917.430443; 917.430444
Vermont—History 974.3
Vermont—History, Local 974.3
Vermont—Maps 912.743
Vermont—Social life and customs 974.3
Vermont—Tours 917.4304; 917.430443; 917.430444
Vernacular architecture 720; 728; 779.4
Vernal pool ecology 577.636
Vernon County (Wis.) 977.573
Vernon County (Wis.)—Maps 912.77573
Verona (Italy) 945.34
Verse satire, English 821.07; 821.0708
Verse satire, Latin 871; 871.01
Verse satire, Latin—Translations into English 871.008; 871.0108
Versification 808.1
Vertebrae 573.76
Vertebrates 596
Vertebrates—Anatomy 571.316
Vertebrates—Evolution 596.138
Vertebrates, Fossil 566
Vertex operator algebras 512.55
Vertigo 616.841
Very high speed integrated circuits 621.3815
Very large array telescopes 522.2
Very long baseline interferometry 543.0853
Vespertilionidae 599.47
Vespidae 595.798
Vestibular apparatus—Diseases 617.882
Vests 646.45
Veterans 362.86
Veterans, Disabled 362.408697
Veterans, Disabled—Legal status, laws, etc. 343.0116
Veterans, Disabled—Legal status, laws, etc.—United States 343.730116
Veterans, Disabled—United States 362.4086970973
Veterans—Education 371.223
Veterans—Education—United States 343.730114
Veterans—Employment—United States 362.86840973
Veterans' hospitals 362.11
Veterans—Legal status, laws, etc. 343.011
Veterans—Legal status, laws, etc.—United States 343.73011
Veterans—Legal status, laws, etc.—United States— States 343.73011
Veterans—Loans 343.011
Veterans—Loans—United States 343.73011
Veterans—Medical care—Law and legislation 343.0115
Veterans—Medical care—Law and legislation—United States 343.730115
Veterans—Scholarships, fellowships, etc. 371.223
Veterans—Services for 362.86
Veterans—Services for—United States—Handbooks, manuals, etc. 362.860973
Veterinarians 636.089092
Veterinary anatomy 636.0891
Veterinary biologicals 636.0896
Veterinary chiropractic 636.0895534
Veterinary colleges 636.0890711
Veterinary dentistry 636.08976
Veterinary dermatology 636.08965
Veterinary drug industry 338.4763608951
Veterinary drug residues 615.954
Veterinary drug residues—Toxicology 615.954
Veterinary drugs 636.08951

Vietnam—Social life and customs 959.7
Vietnam Veterans Memorial (Washington, D.C.)
959.70436
Vietnamese 362.849592
Vietnamese Americans 973.0495; 973.049592
Vietnamese Conflict, 1961–1975 959.7043
Vietnamese Conflict, 1961–1975—Aerial operations,
American 959.704348
Vietnamese Conflict, 1961–1975—Atrocities 959.70438
Vietnamese Conflict, 1961–1975—Australia
959.7043394
Vietnamese Conflict, 1961–1975—Campaigns
959.70434
Vietnamese Conflict, 1961–1975—Campaigns—Laos
959.70434; 959.704342
Vietnamese Conflict, 1961–1975—Commando
operations—United States 959.704342; 959.704345
Vietnamese Conflict, 1961–1975—Conscientious
objectors—United States 959.70431
Vietnamese Conflict, 1961–1975—Laos 959.70434
Vietnamese Conflict, 1961–1975—Literature and the
conflict 813.5409
Vietnamese Conflict, 1961–1975—Missing in action—
United States 959.70437
Vietnamese Conflict, 1961–1975—Motion pictures and
the conflict 791.43658
Vietnamese Conflict, 1961–1975—Naval operations,
American 959.704345
Vietnamese Conflict, 1961–1975—Peace 959.70431
Vietnamese Conflict, 1961–1975—Personal narratives
959.7043092
Vietnamese Conflict, 1961–1975—Personal narratives,
American 959.7043092
Vietnamese Conflict, 1961–1975—Personal narratives,
Australian 959.7043092
Vietnamese Conflict, 1961–1975—Personal narratives,
Vietnamese 959.7043092
Vietnamese Conflict, 1961–1975—Pictorial works
959.70430222
Vietnamese Conflict, 1961–1975—Press coverage
959.70438
Vietnamese Conflict, 1961–1975—Prisoners and
prisons 959.70437
Vietnamese Conflict, 1961–1975—Prisoners and
prisons, North Vietnamese 959.70437
Vietnamese Conflict, 1961–1975—Protest movements—
United States 959.70431
Vietnamese Conflict, 1961–1975—Reconnaissance
operations, American 959.704342
Vietnamese Conflict, 1961–1975—Regimental
histories—United States 959.70434
Vietnamese Conflict, 1961–1975—Riverine operations,
American 959.704345
Vietnamese Conflict, 1961–1975—Search and rescue
operations 959.70434; 959.704348
Vietnamese Conflict, 1961–1975—Sources 959.7043072
Vietnamese Conflict, 1961–1975—Underground
movements 959.70431
Vietnamese Conflict, 1961–1975—United States
959.7043373
Vietnamese Conflict, 1961–1975—Veterans—United
States 959.7043373
Vietnamese poetry 895.9221; 895.9221008
Vietnamese poetry—Translations into English
895.9221008
Vietnamese wit and humor 895.9227008
View cameras 771.32
Viking Mars Program (U.S.) 629.43543
Viking ships 623.8210948

Vikings 948.022
Vikings—Social life and customs 948.022
Vilas County (Wis.) 977.523
Vilas County (Wis.)—Maps 912.77523
Villa, Pancho, 1878–1923 972.081092
Villages 307.762
Villages—England—History 942.009734
Villon, François, b. 1431 841.2
Villon, François, b. 1431—Translations into English
841.2
Vimes, Samuel (Fictitious character) 823.914
Vincent family 929.20973
Vineyards 663.2
Vintners 663.20092
Viola and piano music 787.3
Viola music 787.3
Violence 303.6
Violence—Forecasting 616.8582
Violence in art 700.103
Violence in children 362.27
Violence in mass media 303.6
Violence in motion pictures 791.43655
Violence in popular culture 303.6
Violence in sports 796
Violence in the workplace 658.473
Violence in the workplace—Prevention 658.473
Violence in women 305.489692; 364.374
Violence on television—Law and legislation
343.7309946
Violence on television—Law and legislation—United
States 343.7309946
Violence—Physiological aspects 616.858207
Violence—Psychological aspects 616.8582
Violence—Religious aspects 291.5697
Violence—Religious aspects—Christianity 241.697;
261.8
Violence—South Africa 303.60968
Violence—United States 303.60973
Violence—United States—History 303.60973
Violence—United States—Prevention 303.60973
Violent crimes 364.15
Violent crimes—United States 364.150973
Violent offenders 364.3
Violets 583.625
Violin 787.2; 787.219
Violin and piano music 787.2
Violin and piano music, Arranged 787.2
Violin and viola with orchestra 784.24
Violin and violoncello music 785.7192
Violin—Construction 787.21923
Violin—Instruction and study 787.2071
Violin music 787.2
Violin music (Violins (2)) 785.72192
Violin—Studies and exercises 787.2076
Violin with orchestra 784.272
Violin with orchestra, Arranged 784.272
Violoncello and piano music 787.4
Violoncello and piano music, Arranged 787.4
Violoncello music 787.4
Violoncello with orchestra 784.274
Vipaśyanā (Buddhism) 294.34435
Viral carcinogenesis 616.9940194
Viral genetics 579.2135
Viral vaccines 615.372
Virgil 871.01; 873.01
Virgil. Aeneid 873.01
Virgil—Bibliography 016.87101
Virgil. Bucolica 871.01
Virgil—Criticism and interpretation 871.01

Virgil. Georgica 871.01; 873.01
Virgil—Translations into English 873.01
Virgin Islands of the United States 972.9722
Virgin Islands of the United States—History 972.9722
Virginia 975.5
Virginia City (Nev.) 979.356
Virginia City (Nev.)—History 979.356
Virginia—Description and travel 917.5504; 917.550443; 917.550444
Virginia—Genealogy 929.3755
Virginia—Guidebooks 917.5504; 917.550443; 917.550444
Virginia—History 975.5
Virginia—History—Colonial period, ca. 1600–1775 975.502
Virginia—History—Colonial period, ca. 1600–1775—Sources 975.502072
Virginia—History—Civil War, 1861–1865 975.503
Virginia—History—Civil War, 1861–1865—Artillery operations 973.73
Virginia—History—Civil War, 1861–1865—Campaigns 973.73
Virginia—Maps 912.755
Virginia—Politics and government 320.9755
Virginia—Politics and government—1951– 320.975509045
Virginia—Road maps 912.755
Virginia—Social life and customs 975.5
Virginia—Social life and customs—To 1775 975.502
Virginia—Tours 917.5504; 917.550443; 917.550444
Virola (Genus) 583.22
Virology 579.2; 616.0194
Virtual computer systems 005.43
Virtual corporations 338.7; 658.04
Virtual pets 688.726; 793.9
Virtual reality 006
Virtual reality in education 371.3346
Virtual reality in management 658.056
Virtual storage (Computer science) 004.5
Virtue 179.9
Virtue epistemology 121
Virtues 241.4
Virulence (Microbiology) 616.01
Virus diseases 614.575; 616.925
Virus diseases—Epidemiology 614.575
Virus diseases—Immunological aspects 616.925079
Virus diseases of plants 632.8
Virus-resistant transgenic plants 632.8
Viruses 579.2
Visas 323.67
Visas—United States 342.73082
Viscosity 531.1134
Viscous flow 532.0533
VisiCalc 005.369
Vision 573.88; 612.84
Vision disorders 617.7; 617.712; 617.75
Vision disorders in children 618.920977
Vision—Testing 617.715
Visionary architecture 720.1
Viśiṣṭādvaita 181.483
Visitation rights (Domestic relations) 346.017
Visitors' centers 338.4791
Visitors' centers—Law and legislation 344.09
Visitors, Foreign 910.92
Visual aids 371.335
Visual anthropology 301
Visual anthropology—Periodicals 301.05
Visual communication 302.23; 384
Visual education 371.335
Visual FoxPro for Windows 005.7565

Visual learning 370.1523; 371.335
Visual literacy 371.335
Visual pathways 612.84
Visual perception 152.14
Visual programming (Computer science) 006.66
Visual programming languages (Computer science) 006.663
Visual training 617.7; 617.75
Visualization 153.32
Visually handicapped 362.41
Visually handicapped children—Education 371.911
Visually handicapped—Education 371.911
Visually handicapped teachers 371.100871
Vitaceae 583.86
Vital statistics 310
Vitamin D 612.399
Vitamin industry 380.145615328; 381.45615328
Vitamin therapy 615.328
Vitamins 572.58; 612.399; 613.286
Vitamins in human nutrition 612.399; 613.286
Viticulture 634.8
Viticulture in literature 808.80364; 809.93364
Viticulture in the Bible 220.86348
Vivaldi, Antonio, 1678–1741 780.92
Vivekananda, Swami, 1863–1902 294.555092
Viverridae 599.742
Vivisection 179.4
Viziers 352.2930917671
Vlad III, Prince of Wallachia, 1430 or 31–1476 or 7 949.8201092
VM/CMS 005.4429
Vocabulary 418; 428.1
Vocabulary—Problems, exercises, etc. 428.1
Vocabulary tests 428.1076
Vocal duets 783.12
Vocal ensembles 782.506
Vocal music 782
Vocal music—History and criticism 782.009
Vocal quartets 783.14
Vocal trios 783.13
Vocation 158.6
Vocation—Christianity 253.2
Vocational education 370.113; 373.246; 374.013
Vocational education—Europe 370.113094
Vocational education—European Economic Community countries 370.113094
Vocational education facilities 371.621
Vocational education—Great Britain 370.1130941; 374.0130941
Vocational education—Parent participation 370.113085
Vocational education—United States 370.1130973; 373.2460973
Vocational education—United States—Evaluation 379.158
Vocational evaluation 371.425
Vocational guidance 158.6; 331.702; 371.425
Vocational guidance—Bibliography 016.331702
Vocational guidance for the handicapped 331.702087; 371.904
Vocational guidance for the handicapped—United States 650.140870973
Vocational guidance for women 650.14082
Vocational guidance for women—United States 331.702082
Vocational guidance—Handbooks, manuals, etc. 650.14
Vocational guidance—United States 650.140973
Vocational guidance—United States—Directories 331.70202573

Vocational guidance—United States—Handbooks, manuals, etc. 331.7020973
Vocational interests 158.6
Vocational interests—Testing 153.94
Vocational interests—United States 158.60973
Vocational rehabilitation 362.0425
Vocational rehabilitation—United States 362.0425
Vocational training centers 370.113; 374.8
Voegelin, Eric, 1901– 193
Voice 612.78
Voice culture 808.5
Voice culture—Exercises 808.5
Voice disorders 616.855
Voice disorders—Treatment 616.85506
Voice mail systems 651.73
Voice types (Singing) 783.2
Volcanic activity prediction 551.210112
Volcanic fields 551.21
Volcanic hazard analysis 363.3495
Volcanic plumes 551.23
Volcanism 551.21
Volcanism—Effect of environment on 551.21
Volcanoes 551.21
Volcanological research 551.21072
Voles 599.354
Volkswagen automobiles 388.342; 629.2222
Volkswagen automobiles—Maintenance and repair 629.28722
Volkswagen automobiles—Maintenance and repair—Handbooks, manuals, etc. 629.28722
Volkswagen Beetle automobile 629.2222
Volkswagen Beetle automobile—History 629.2222
Volleyball 796.325
Volleyball—Coaching 796.325
Volleyball—Training 796.325
Voltage-frequency converters 621.3815322
Voltage regulators 621.371
Voltaire, 1694–1778 843.5; 848.509
Voltaire, 1694–1778. Candide 843.5
Voltaire, 1694–1778—Translations into English 843.5
Volterra equations 515.45
Voltohmmeters 621.374
Volumetric analysis 545.2
Voluntarism 361.37
Voluntarism (Church finance) 262.00681
Voluntarism—Directories 302.14
Voluntarism—Great Britain 361.370941
Voluntarism—India 361.370954
Voluntarism—Management 361.37068
Voluntarism—United States 302.14; 361.370973
Voluntarism—United States—Handbooks, manuals, etc. 302.14; 361.370973
Voluntarism—United States—Management 361.37068
Volunteer libraries 027
Volunteer workers in community development 361.37
Volunteer workers in education 371.14124
Volunteer workers in medical care 362.1
Volunteers 361.37092
Volunteers' liability 346.031
Volvo automobile 629.2222
Volvo automobile—Maintenance and repair 629.28722
Volvo automobile—Maintenance and repair—Handbooks, manuals, etc. 629.28722
Von Braun, Wernher, 1912–1977 621.4356092
Von Neumann algebras 512.55
Vonnegut, Kurt 813.54
Vonnegut, Kurt—Criticism and interpretation 813.54
Voodooism 299.675
Voodooism—Haiti 299.675097294

Voodooism in motion pictures 791.4367; 791.4368299675
Vorkosigan, Miles (Fictitious character) 813.54
Vorkosigan, Miles (Fictitious character)—Fiction 813.54
Voronoi polygons 516.22
Vortex-motion 532.0595
Vote-by-mail elections 324.65
Voter registration 324.64
Voting 324.9
Voting—Religious aspects 291.177
Voting—United States 324.973
Votive offerings in art 704.9482
Voyager (Airplane) 629.1309; 910.41
Voyager Project 919.9204
Voyages and travels 910.4
Voyages and travels—1951–1980 910.409045
Voyages around the world 910.41
VP-planner 005.369
VP-planner plus 005.369
VSATs (Telecommunication) 384.51
Vultures 598.92; 598.94
Vulva—Diseases 618.16
Vygotskiĭ, L. S. (Lev Semenovich), 1896–1934 150.92
Wabasha County (Minn.) 977.613
Wabasha County (Minn.)—Maps 912.77613
Waco Branch Davidian Disaster, Tex., 1993 363.230973; 364.13; 976.4284063
Waferboard 674.83
Waffen-SS—History 940.541343
Wage bargaining 331.89
Wage-price policy 331.21
Wage-price policy—Great Britain 331.2941
Wage-price policy—United States 331.2973
Wager, Gabriel (Fictitious character) 813.54
Wager, Gabriel (Fictitious character)—Fiction 813.54
Wages 331.21
Wages—Accounting 657.74
Wages—Effect of international trade on 331.215
Wages—Great Britain 331.2941
Wages—Hotels 331.28164794
Wages—Hotels—Law and legislation 344.0128164794
Wages—Hotels—Law and legislation—United States 344.730128164794
Wages-in-kind 331.2166
Wages—Japan 331.2952
Wages—Law and legislation 344.0121
Wages—Law and legislation—Oregon 344.7950121
Wages—Law and legislation—United States 344.730121
Wages—Montana 331.29786
Wages—Montana—Statistics 331.29786021
Wages—New Hampshire 331.29742
Wages—New Hampshire—Statistics—Periodicals 331.29742021
Wages—United States 331.2973
Wages—United States—Statistics 331.2973021
Wages—United States—Statistics—Periodicals 331.2973021
Wages—Washington (State) 331.29797
Wages—Washington (State)—Seattle Metropolitan Area 331.2979777
Wages—Washington (State)—Seattle Metropolitan Area—Statistics 331.2979777
Wages—Washington (State)—Seattle Metropolitan Area—Statistics—Periodicals 331.2979777021
Wages—Wisconsin 331.29775
Wages—Wisconsin—Statistics 331.29775021
Wagner family 929.20973
Wagner, Honus, 1874–1955 796.357092
Wagner, Richard, 1813–1883 782.1092

Wagner, Richard, 1813–1883—Criticism and interpretation 782.1092
Wagner, Richard, 1813–1883. Operas 782.1092
Wagner, Richard, 1813–1883. Ring des Nibelungen 782.1
Waka 895.6104
Waka—Translations into English 895.6104
Wakeboarding 797.3
Walcott, Derek 811.54
Walcott, Derek—Criticism and interpretation 811.54
Walden Woods (Mass.) 974.44
Walden Woods (Mass.)—Social life and customs 974.44
Waldheim, Kurt 943.6053092
Waldorf method of education 371.39
Wales 942.9
Wales—Civilization 942.9
Wales—Guidebooks 914.2904; 914.2904859; 914.290486
Wales—History 942.9
Wales—History—To 1536 942.9
Wales—History—1063–1536 942.9
Wales—History—1284–1536 942.9
Wales, North 942.91
Wales, North—Guidebooks 914.29104; 914.29104859; 914.2910486
Wales—Social life and customs 942.9
Wales, South 942.94
Wales, South—Guidebooks 914.29404; 914.29404859; 914.2940486
Wałęsa, Lech, 1943– 943.8056092; 943.8057092
Walk-a-thons 361.70681
Walk-in coolers and freezers 641.450284; 664.02850284
Walker, Alice, 1944– 813.54
Walker, Alice, 1944– —Criticism and interpretation 813.54
Walker, Amos (Fictitious character) 813.54
Walker, Amos (Fictitious character)—Fiction 813.54
Walker, C. J., Madam, 1867–1919 338.766855092
Walker County (Tex.)—Genealogy 929.3764169
Walker family 929.20973
Walker, John Anthony, 1937– 327.12092
Walking 796.51
Walking—California—San Francisco—Guidebooks 917.946104; 917.94610453; 917.94610454
Walking—England—Guidebooks 914.204; 914.204859; 914.20486
Walking—England—London—Guidebooks 914.2104; 914.2104859; 914.210486
Walking—Ireland—Guidebooks 914.1704
Walking (Sports) 613.7176; 796.51
Wallace family 929.20973
Wallenberg, Raoul, 1912–1947 940.5477943912092
Walleye (Fish) 597.758
Walls 721.2
Walpole, Hugh, Sir, 1884–1941 823.912
Walpole, Hugh, Sir, 1884–1941—Criticism and interpretation 823.912
Walras, Léon, 1834–1910 330.157092
Walrus 599.799
Walsh County (N.D.) 978.418
Walsh County (N.D.)—Maps 912.78418
Walsh functions 515.2433
Walt Disney Company 741.50979493
Walt Disney Company—History 384.806579494
Walt Disney Productions—Collectibles—Catalogs 741.50979493
Walt Disney World (Fla.) 791.06875924
Walt Disney World (Fla.)—Guidebooks 791.06875924
Walter family 929.20973
Walton, Sam, 1918– 381.149092

Walworth County (Wis.) 977.589
Walworth County (Wis.)—Maps 912.77589
Wapello County (Iowa) 977.793
Wapello County (Iowa)—Maps 912.77793
Waqf 346.064
Waqf—India 346.54064
Waqf—Pakistan 346.5491064
War 355.02
War and civilization 303.66
War and emergency powers 342.062
War and emergency powers—United States 342.730412
War and emergency powers—United States—History 342.73062
War and society 303.66
War casualties 305.906949; 355.02; 363.3498
War crime trials 341.69
War crime trials—Press coverage 070.44934169
War crimes 341.69; 364.138
War criminals 341.69092
War—Economic aspects 330.9
War films 791.43658
War films—History and criticism 791.43658
War games 793.92
War games, Naval 793.92
War—History 355.0209
War in art 707.94935502
War in literature 808.80358; 809.93358
War (International law) 341.6
War—Literary collections 808.80358
War, Maritime (International law) 341.63
War memorials 355.16
War—Moral and ethical aspects 172.42
War neuroses 616.85212
War of Attrition, Middle East, 1969–1970 956.04
War (Philosophy) 172.42
War poetry 808.819358
War poetry, American 811.0080358
War poetry, English 821.0080358
War posters 769.5
War—Press coverage 070.44935502
War—Psychological aspects 355.02019
War—Religious aspects 291.17873
War—Religious aspects—Christianity 261.873
War stories 808.839358
War tax resistance 336.2
War tax resistance—United States 336.2; 345.730233
War victims 363.3498
War victims—Legal status, laws, etc. 341.67
Ward County (N.D.) 978.463
Ward County (N.D.)—Maps 912.78463
Ward, Eric (Fictitious character) 823.914
Ward, Eric (Fictitious character)—Fiction 823.914
Ward family 929.20973
Wards (Mormon Church) 262.22088283
Warehouses—Management 658.785
Warhol, Andy, 1928– 700.92
Warhol, Andy, 1928– —Criticism and interpretation 700.92
Warhol, Andy, 1928– —Exhibitions 700.92
Warhol, Andy, 1928– —Themes, motives 700.92
Warlordism 321.9
Warlordism and international relations 321.9
Warner family 929.20973
Warning labels 363.19
Warranty 343.08
Warranty of title 346.072
Warranty—United States 343.7308
Warren County (Ill.) 977.3415
Warren County (Ill.)—Genealogy 929.3773415

Warren County (Ill.)—Maps 912.773415
Warren County (Iowa) 977.782
Warren County (Iowa)—Maps 912.77782
Warren family 929.20973
Warren, Robert Penn, 1905- 813.52
Warren, Robert Penn, 1905- . All the king's men 813.52
Warren, Robert Penn, 1905- —Criticism and interpretation 813.52
Warren, Robert Penn, 1905- —Fictional works 813.52
Warren, Robert Penn, 1905- —Poetic works 811.52
Warsaw (Ind.) 977.282
Warsaw (Ind.)—Genealogy 929.377282
Warsaw (Poland) 943.84
Warsaw (Poland)—History 943.84
Warsaw (Poland)—History—Warsaw Ghetto Uprising, 1943 940.5318094384
Warsaw (Poland)—Pictorial works 914.384; 943.84
Warsaw Treaty Organization 341.72; 355.0310947
Warshawski, V. I. (Fictitious character) 813.54
Warshawski, V. I. (Fictitious character)—Fiction 813.54
Warships 359.835
Warships—Recognition 623.825
Warwickshire (England) 942.48
Warwickshire (England)—Guidebooks 914.24804; 914.24804859; 914.2480486
Washboard bands 784.4
Washbowls 643.52; 696.182
Washington, Booker T., 1856–1915 370.92
Washington County (Ill.)—Maps 912.77388
Washington County (Ky.)—Genealogy 929.3769493
Washington County (Md.)—Genealogy 929.375291
Washington County (Md.)—Maps 912.75291
Washington County (Tenn.)—Genealogy 929.376897
Washington County (Wis.)—Maps 912.77591
Washington (D.C.) 975.3
Washington (D.C.)—Description and travel 917.5304; 917.530441; 917.530442
Washington (D.C.)—Genealogy 929.309753; 929.3753
Washington (D.C.)—Guidebooks 917.5304; 917.530441; 917.530442
Washington (D.C.)—History 975.3
Washington (D.C.)—Maps 912.753
Washington (D.C.)—Pictorial works 779.99175300222; 917.5300222; 975.300222
Washington (D.C.)—Politics and government 320.9753
Washington (D.C.)—Politics and government—1967–1995 320.975309045
Washington (D.C.)—Tours 917.5304; 917.530441; 917.530442
Washington—Genealogy 929.3797
Washington, George, 1732–1799 973.41092
Washington, Martha, 1731–1802 973.41092
Washington Metropolitan Area 975.3
Washington Metropolitan Area—Guidebooks 917.53
Washington Metropolitan Area—Maps 912.753
Washington Redskins (Football team) 796.3326409753
Washington Redskins (Football team)—History 796.3326409753
Washington Region 975.3
Washington Region—Guidebooks 917.5304; 917.530441; 917.530442
Washington Region—Tours 917.5304
Washington (State) 979.7
Washington (State)—Guidebooks 917.9704; 917.970443; 917.970444
Washington (State)—Maps 912.797
Washtenaw County (Mich.) 977.435
Washtenaw County (Mich.)—Maps 912.77435
Wasps 595.79; 595.798

Waste disposal in the ground 628.4456
Waste disposal in the ocean 363.728
Waste in government spending 336.39
Waste in government spending—United States 336.73
Waste minimization 363.728
Waste paper—Recycling 676.142
Waste products 628.4458
Waste products as fuel 662.87
Waste products as road materials 625.8
Waste spills 628.1683
Wastebaskets 645.4; 684.1
Watchtowers 725.97
Water 546.22; 553.7
Water—Analysis 628.161
Water—Analysis—Laboratory manuals 628.161
Water birds 598.176
Water chemistry 551.48
Water conservation 333.9116
Water consumption 628.144
Water—Distribution 628.144
Water dragons (Reptiles) 597.955
Water-electrolyte imbalances 616.3992
Water gardens 635.9674; 714
Water in landscape architecture 714
Water in the body 571.75
Water jet cutting 621.93
Water—Law and legislation 346.04691
Water—Law and legislation—California 346.79404691
Water—Law and legislation—United States 346.7304691
Water—Law and legislation—West (U.S.) 346.7804691
Water levels 333.9111
Water levels—Great Lakes 333.91630977
Water lilies 583.29
Water—Microbiology 579.176
Water-pipes 628.15
Water-pipes—Corrosion 628.15
Water—Pollution 363.7394
Water—Pollution—Environmental aspects 577.627
Water—Pollution—Law and legislation 344.3046343
Water—Pollution—Law and legislation—United States 344.73046343
Water—Pollution—Mathematical models 628.168015118
Water—Pollution—Superior, Lake, Watershed 628.168097749
Water polo 797.25
Water-power 333.914
Water puppetry 791.53
Water—Purification 628.162
Water—Purification—Adsorption 628.164
Water—Purification—Arsenic removal 628.1666
Water—Purification—Chlorination 628.1662
Water—Purification—Coagulation 628.1622
Water—Purification—Disinfection 628.1662
Water—Purification—Disinfection—By-products 628.1662
Water—Purification—Filtration 628.164
Water—Purification—Membrane filtration 628.164
Water—Purification—Organic compounds removal 628.164
Water—Purification—Ozonization 628.1662
Water—Purification—Slow sand filtration 628.164
Water quality 363.73942
Water quality bioassay 628.161
Water quality biological assessment 628.161
Water quality—Illinois 363.7394209773
Water quality management 363.61
Water quality management—Colorado River Watershed (Colo.-Mexico) 363.7394560978
Water quality management—Periodicals 628.16805

Web servers 004.678
Web site development 005.276; 070.5797
Web site development industry 338.47005276
Web sites 005.276; 005.72; 025.04
Web sites—Authoring programs 005.276; 005.72
Web sites—Design 005.72
Web sites—Directories 025.04
Web sites—Registration with search engines 025.04
Web typography 686.22; 760
Web usage mining 006.3
Webb, Beatrice Potter, 1858–1943 335.14092
Webb, Beatrice Potter, 1858–1943—Diaries 335.14092
Webb family 929.20973
Webcasting 006.7876; 070.5797
Weber, Max, 1864–1920 301.092
Weber, Max, 1864–1920—Contributions in political science 320.092
Weber, Max, 1864–1920. Protestantische Ethik und der Geist des Kapitalismus 261.85; 306.6
Webmasters 005.276
Webster County (Iowa) 977.751
Webster County (Iowa)—Maps 912.77751
Webster County (Mo.) 977.8823
Webster County (Mo.)—Maps 912.778823
Webster, John, 1580?–1625? 822.3
Webster, John, 1580?–1625?—Criticism and interpretation 822.3
Webster, John, 1580?–1625? White devil 822.3
Webster, Noah, 1758–1843 423.092
Wechsler Intelligence Scale for Children 155.41393
Weddell seal 599.796
Wedding decorations 745.926
Wedding etiquette 395.22
Wedding music 781.587
Wedding photography 778.993925
Wedding sermons 252.1
Wedding stationery 395.4
Wedding supplies and services industry 338.473925
Weddings 395.22
Weddings in popular culture 392.5
Weddings—Literary collections 808.803543
Weddings—Planning 395.22
Weddings—United States—Planning 395.220973
Weddings—United States—Planning—Handbooks, manuals, etc. 395.220973
Wedgwood ware 738.37
Weed scientists 632.5092
Weedless gardening 635.0481
Weeds 581.652; 632.5
Weeds—Biological control 632.5
Weeds—Control 632.5
Weeds—Physiology 632.5
Weight gain 613.24; 613.25
Weight lifting 796.41
Weight loss 613.2; 613.25
Weight loss preparations 616.398061
Weight loss—Psychological aspects 613.25019
Weight loss—Religious aspects 613.25
Weight training 613.713
Weights and measures 389.1; 530.81
Weights and measures, Ancient 389.10901; 530.810901
Weights and measures—Tables 530.81
Weights and measures—United States 389.10973; 530.810973
Weil, Simone, 1909–1943 194
Weimaraner (Dog breed) 636.752
Weizmann, Chaim, 1874–1952 956.9404092
Welded joints 671.52042
Welding 671.52

Welding—Health aspects 616.9803
Welding—Periodicals 671.5205
Welfare economics 330.1556
Welfare state 361.65
Welles, Orson, 1915– 791.430233092
Welles, Orson, 1915– —Criticism and interpretation 791.430233092
Wellhead protection 363.739472; 628.114
Wellington, Arthur Wellesley, Duke of, 1769–1852 941.07092
Wellington, Arthur Wellesley, Duke of, 1769–1852—Military leadership 355.0092
Wellington (N.Z.) 993.63
Wellington (N.Z.)—Description and travel 993.604; 993.60438; 993.6044
Wells 628.114
Wells-Barnett, Ida B., 1862–1931 323.092
Wells County (N.D.) 978.458
Wells County (N.D.)—Maps 912.78458
Wells—Design and construction 628.114
Wells family 929.20973
Wells, H. G. (Herbert George), 1866–1946 823.912
Wells, H. G. (Herbert George), 1866–1946—Criticism and interpretation 823.912
Welsh language 491.66
Welsh language—Textbooks for foreign speakers—English 491.6682421; 491.6683421
Welsh literature 891.66; 891.6608
Welsh literature—History and criticism 891.6609
Welsh poetry 891.661; 891.661008
Welsh poetry—To 1550 891.6611; 891.661108
Welsh poetry—To 1550—History and criticism 891.661109
Welsh poetry—Translations into English 891.661008
Welty, Eudora, 1909– 813.52
Welty, Eudora, 1909– —Criticism and interpretation 813.52
Wendar (Imaginary place) 813.54
Wentworth, Bea (Fictitious character) 813.54
Wentworth, Lyon (Fictitious character) 813.54
Werewolves 398.2454
Werner family 929.20973
Wescott, Sam (Fictitious character) 813.54
Wesker, Arnold, 1932– 822.914
Wesker, Arnold, 1932– —Criticism and interpretation 822.914
Wesley, Charles, 1707–1788 287.092
Wesley, John, 1703–1791 287.092
West Bank 956.953
West Bank—Economic conditions 330.95695
West Bank—Politics and government 956.953
West Bengal (India) 954.14
West Bengal (India)—Politics and government 954.14
West Country (England) 942.3
West Country (England)—Guidebooks 914.2304; 914.2304859; 914.230486
West, Delilah (Fictitious character) 813.54
West, Delilah (Fictitious character)—Fiction 813.54
West family 929.20973
West Highland white terrier 636.755
West Indian literature (English)—History and criticism 810.99729
West Indies 972.9
West Indies—Guidebooks 917.2904; 917.290452
West Indies—History 972.9
West Indies—Maps 912.729
West Indies—Maps—Early works to 1800 912.729
West Indies—Social life and customs 972.9
West, Mae 791.43028092

West, Nathanael, 1903–1940 813.52
West, Nathanael, 1903–1940—Criticism and
   interpretation 813.52
West Nile fever 616.925
West, Rebecca, Dame, 1892– 828.91209
West, Rebecca, Dame, 1892– —Criticism and
   interpretation 828.91209
West, Roger (Fictitious character) 823.912
West, Roger (Fictitious character)—Fiction 823.912
West (U.S.) 978
West (U.S.)—Civilization 978
West (U.S.)—Description and travel 917.804;
   917.80433; 917.80434
West (U.S.)—Discovery and exploration 978.02
West (U.S.)—Guidebooks 917.804; 917.80433; 917.80434
West (U.S.)—Historiography 978.0072
West (U.S.)—History 978
West (U.S.)—History—To 1848 978.01; 978.02
West (U.S.)—History—1860–1890 978.02
West (U.S.)—History—1890–1945 978.03
West (U.S.)—History—Sources 978.0072
West (U.S.)—In art 704.949978
West (U.S.)—In art—Exhibitions 704.949978074
West (U.S.)—Pictorial works 917.800222
West (U.S.)—Social life and customs 978
West Virginia 975.4
West Virginia—Genealogy 929.3754
West Virginia—Maps 912.754
West Virginia—Road maps 912.754
Westchester County (N.Y.) 974.7277
Westchester County (N.Y.)—Maps 912.747277
Western Australia 994.1
Western Australia—Description and travel 919.4104;
   919.410466; 919.41047
Western Australia—History 994.1
Western European Union 341.242
Western films 791.436278
Western films—Catalogs 016.791436278
Western films—History and criticism 791.43627809
Western films—United States—History and criticism
   791.4362780973
Western horses 636.1
Western horses—Training 636.1
Western Mande languages 496.34
Western Pacific Railroad Company 385.0979
Western riding 798.23
Western stories 813.0874; 813.087408
Western stories—History and criticism 813.087409
Western Wall (Jerusalem) 296.482
Westminster Confession of Faith 238.5
Westminster Palace (London, England) 942.132
Westmoreland County (Pa.)—Genealogy 929.374881
Westmoreland County (Va.)—Genealogy 929.375524
Westmoreland, William C. (William Childs), 1914– —
   Trials, litigation, etc. 345.730256
Wetland agriculture 630.914
Wetland animals 591.768
Wetland conservation 333.91816
Wetland conservation—Law and legislation
   346.04691816
Wetland conservation—Law and legislation—United
   States 346.7304691816
Wetland conservation—United States 333.918160973
Wetland ecology 577.68
Wetland forestry 634.9
Wetland management 333.918
Wetland mitigation 333.918153
Wetland mitigation banking 333.91816
Wetland mitigation sites 333.918153

Wetland plants 581.768
Wetlands 333.918; 578.768
Wetlands—Law and legislation 346.046918
Wetlands—Law and legislation—Massachusetts
   346.744046918
Wetlands—Law and legislation—United States
   346.73046918
Wetlands—United States 333.9180973
Wetshoe, Hugh (Fictitious character) 741.5973
Wetzel County (W. Va.)—Genealogy 929.375418
Wetzon, Leslie (Fictitious character) 813.54
Wetzon, Leslie (Fictitious character)—Fiction 813.54
Wexford County (Mich.) 977.467
Wexford County (Mich.)—Maps 912.77467
Wexford, Inspector (Fictitious character) 823.914
Wexford, Inspector (Fictitious character)—Fiction
   823.914
Wexford (Ireland : County) 941.885
Wexford (Ireland : County)—History 941.885
Whale watching 599.50723
Whale watching industry 338.475995
Whales 599.5; 639.9795
Whales, Fossil 569.5
Whaling 639.28
Whaling—History 639.2809
Wharton, Edith, 1862–1937 813.52
Wharton, Edith, 1862–1937—Bibliography 016.81352
Wharton, Edith, 1862–1937—Criticism and
   interpretation 813.52
Wheat 633.11; 664.722
Wheat-free diet—Recipes 641.563
Wheatley, Phillis, 1753–1784 811.1
Wheelchair sports 796.0456
Wheelchair track-athletics 796.42
Wheelchairs 617.03
Wheeler family 929.20973
Wheels 621.8
Whelan, Murray (Fictitious character) 823.914
Whipped cream 641.37148
Whippet 636.7532
Whiskers 573.58; 599.147
Whiskey 641.252; 663.5
Whiskey—Scotland 641.25209411
Whistle blowing 342.068
Whistler, James McNeill, 1834–1903 759.13; 760.092
Whistler, James McNeill, 1834–1903—Catalogs 759.13;
   760.092
Whistling music 782.98
Whitbread Round the World Race 797.14
White, Blanche (Fictitious character) 813.54
White collar crime investigation—United States
   363.259680973
White collar crimes 364.168
White collar crimes—United States 364.1680973
White collar crimes—United States—Cases
   345.7302680264
White collar workers 331.792
White County (Ill.) 977.396
White County (Ill.)—Maps 912.77396
White dwarfs 523.887
White, E. B. (Elwyn Brooks), 1899– 818.5209
White, Ellen Gould Harmon, 1827–1915 286.7092
White family 929.20973
White House (Washington, D.C.) 725.1709753; 975.3
White House (Washington, D.C.)—Guidebooks 917.53
White matsutake 579.6; 641.358
White Mountains (N.H. and Me.) 974.22
White Mountains (N.H. and Me.)—Guidebooks 917.422
White, Patrick, 1912– 823.912

White, Patrick, 1912– —Criticism and interpretation 823.912
White shark 597.33
White supremacy movements—United States 305.8034073
White-tailed deer 599.652
White-tailed deer hunting 799.27652
White-water canoeing 797.122
White whale 599.542
White, William Allen, 1868–1944 818.5209
Whitefield, George, 1714–1770 269.2092
Whitefield, Jane (Fictitious character) 813.54
Whitefield, Jane (Fictitious character)—Fiction 813.54
Whitehall boats 623.829
Whitehead, Alfred North, 1861–1947 192
Whites 305.8034
Whites on television 791.4565203034
Whites—Race identity 305.8034
Whites—United States—Race identity 305.8034073
Whiteside County (Ill.) 977.335
Whiteside County (Ill.)—Maps 912.77335
Whitestone-McCallum, Heather 791.62
Whitman, Walt, 1819–1892 811.3
Whitman, Walt, 1819–1892—Criticism and interpretation 811.3
Whitman, Walt, 1819–1892—Friends and associates 811.3
Whitman, Walt, 1819–1892. Leaves of grass 811.3
Whitman, Walt, 1819–1892—Manuscripts 811.3
Whitman, Walt, 1819–1892—Poetry 811.3
Whitman, Walt, 1819–1892—Political and social views 811.3
Whitney family 929.20973
Whittier, John Greenleaf, 1807–1892 811.3
Whitworth family 929.20973
Who (Musical group) 781.660922
Whole and parts (Philosophy) 111.82
Wholesale price indexes 338.528
Wholesale trade 658.86
Wholesale trade—United States—Statistics 381.20973021
Wholesale trade—United States—Statistics—Periodicals 381.20973021
Whooping crane 598.32; 639.97832
Wickiups 392.36008997
Wicomico County (Md.) 975.225
Wicomico County (Md.)—Maps 912.75225
Wide area networks (Computer networks) 004.67
Wide area networks industry 381.4500467
Wide gap semiconductors 621.38152
Widowers 305.389654
Widows 305.489654
Widows—Finance, Personal 332.0240654
Widows—United States—Life skills guides 646.008654
Widows—United States—Psychology 155.64430973
Wiesel, Elie, 1928– 813.54
Wiesel, Elie, 1928– —Criticism and interpretation 813.54
Wiesenthal, Simon 940.5318092
Wife abuse 362.8292
Wife abuse—Great Britain 362.82920941
Wife abuse—United States 362.82920973
Wife abuse—United States—Periodicals 362.8292097305
Wikis (Computer science) 004.693; 005.72
Wilberforce, William, 1759–1833 326.092
Wilcox, Carl (Fictitious character) 813.54
Wilcox, Carl (Fictitious character)—Fiction 813.54
Wilcox family 929.20973
Wild animal trade—Law and legislation 343.0853

Wild animals as pets 636.0887
Wild boar 599.6332
Wild flower gardening 635.9676
Wild flower industry 338.1759
Wild flowers 582.13
Wild flowers—California 582.1309794
Wild flowers—North America 582.13097
Wild flowers—Northwest, Pacific—Identification 582.1309795
Wild flowers—Rocky Mountains—Identification 582.130978
Wild flowers—Southwest, New—Identification 582.130979
Wild flowers—Texas—Identification 582.1309764
Wild horses 599.6655
Wild horses—Law and legislation 346.0469596655
Wild horses—Law and legislation—United States 346.730469596655
Wild plant trade—Law and legislation 343.0853
Wild plants, Edible 581.632
Wild ponies 333.9596655; 599.6655
Wild rice 584.9
Wild turkey 598.645
Wilde, Cat (Fictitious character) 813.54
Wilde, Oscar, 1854–1900 828.809
Wilde, Oscar, 1854–1900—Criticism and interpretation 828.809
Wilde, Oscar, 1854–1900—Dramatic works 822.8
Wilde, Oscar, 1854–1900. Picture of Dorian Gray 823.8
Wilder, Laura Ingalls, 1867–1957 813.52
Wilder, Thornton, 1897–1975 818.5209
Wilder, Thornton, 1897–1975—Criticism and interpretation 818.5209
Wilderness area users 333.782092
Wilderness areas 333.782
Wilderness areas—United States 333.7820973
Wilderness, Battle of the, Va., 1864 973.736
Wilderness lodges 647.94; 728.7
Wilderness survival 613.69
Wilderness survival—Handbooks, manuals, etc. 613.69
Wildlife attracting 639.9
Wildlife conservation 333.9516; 639.9
Wildlife conservation (International law) 341.7625
Wildlife conservation—Law and legislation 346.04695
Wildlife conservation—Law and legislation—United States 346.730469516
Wildlife crimes 364.18
Wildlife habitat improvement 639.92
Wildlife management 639.9
Wildlife monitoring 333.954
Wildlife painting 758.3
Wildlife photography 778.932; 779.32
Wildlife products 338.372
Wildlife products industry 338.372
Wildlife refuges 639.95
Wildlife rehabilitation 639.9
Wildlife smuggling 364.18
Wildlife watching 639.9
Wildlife watching industry 338.4759
Wildlife wood-carving 736.4
Wile E. Coyote (Fictitious character) 791.4375
Wilkes County (Ga.)—Genealogy 929.3758172
Wilkes County (N.C.)—Genealogy 929.375682
Wilkin County (Minn.) 977.691
Wilkin County (Minn.)—Maps 912.77691
Wilkinson family 929.20973
Will 153.8
Will County (Ill.) 977.325
Will County (Ill.)—Maps 912.77325

William I, King of England, 1027 or 8-1087 942.021092
William, of Ockham, ca. 1285-ca. 1349 189.4
William, Prince, grandson of Elizabeth II, Queen of Great Britain, 1982- 941.085092
Williams, Charles, 1886-1945 828.91209
Williams, Charles, 1886-1945—Criticism and interpretation 828.91209
Williams family 929.20973
Williams, Race (Fictitious character) 813.52
Williams, Race (Fictitious character)—Fiction 813.52
Williams, Raymond 828.91409
Williams, Raymond—Knowledge and learning 828.91409
Williams, Raymond—Political and social views 828.91409
Williams, Roger, 1604?-1683 286.1092
Williams, Ted, 1918- 796.357092
Williams, Tennessee, 1911-1983 812.54
Williams, Tennessee, 1911-1983—Criticism and interpretation 812.54
Williams, Tennessee, 1911-1983. Streetcar named Desire 812.54
Williams, William Carlos, 1883-1963 811.52
Williams, William Carlos, 1883-1963—Correspondence 811.52
Williams, William Carlos, 1883-1963—Criticism and interpretation 811.52
Williamsburg County (S.C.)—Genealogy 929.375783
Williamsburg (Va.) 975.54252
Williamson County (Ill.)—Maps 912.773993
Williamson County (Tenn.)—Genealogy 929.376856
Williamson, Henry, 1895-1977 823.912
Wills 346.054
Wills—Georgia 346.758054
Wills—Great Britain 346.41054
Wills—Ontario 346.713054
Wills—United States 346.73054
Wills—United States—Cases 346.730540264
Wills—United States—Outlines, syllabi, etc. 346.73054
Wills—United States—States 346.73054
Willum, Persis (Fictitious character) 813.54
Wilmington (N.C.) 975.627
Wilmington (N.C.)—Genealogy 929.375627
Wilson, August 812.54
Wilson, August—Criticism and interpretation 812.54
Wilson County (N.C.)—Genealogy 929.375643
Wilson family 929.20973
Wilson, Harold, Sir, 1916- 941.0856092
Wilson, Woodrow, 1856-1924 973.913092
Wimsey, Peter, Lord (Fictitious character) 823.912
Wimsey, Peter, Lord (Fictitious character)—Fiction 823.912
Winchester rifle 683.422
Winchester shotguns 683.426
Winchester (Va.) 975.5991
Winchester (Va.)—Genealogy 929.3755991
Wind chill index 551.525
Wind energy conversion systems 333.92; 621.312136; 621.45
Wind ensembles 785.43
Wind forecasting 551.6418
Wind instruments 788; 788.19
Wind power 333.92; 621.45
Wind power plants 621.312136
Wind-pressure 621.45; 624.175
Wind quintets (Bassoon, clarinet, flute, horn, oboe) 784.43195
Wind tunnels 629.13452
Wind turbines 621.45

Windmills 621.453
Window dressers 659.157
Window gardening 635.9678
Windows 690.1823; 721.823
Windows (Computer programs) 005.437
Windows (Computer programs)—Periodicals 005.437
Windows in interior decoration 747.3
Windows—Maintenance and repair 690.18230288
Winds 551.518
Windsocks 551.5180284; 681.75
Windsor Castle 942.296
Windsor, Edward, Duke of, 1894-1972 941.084092
Windsor, Wallis Warfield, Duchess of, 1896- 941.084092
Windsurfers (Sailboats) 797.33
Windsurfing 797.33
Wine and wine making 641.22; 641.872; 663.2
Wine and wine making—Australia 641.220994
Wine and wine making—California 641.2209794
Wine and wine making—California—Guidebooks 641.2209794
Wine and wine making—California—Napa Valley 641.220979419
Wine and wine making—Encyclopedias 641.2203
Wine and wine making—France 641.220944
Wine and wine making—France—Bordelais 641.220944714
Wine and wine making—France—Burgundy 641.220944141
Wine and wine making—France—Guidebooks 641.220944
Wine and wine making—Germany 641.220943
Wine and wine making—Germany (West) 641.220943
Wine and wine making—Italy 641.220945
Wine and wine making—New Zealand 641.220993
Wine and wine making—Periodicals 641.2205
Wine and wine making—South Africa 641.220968
Wine and wine making—Spain 641.220946
Wine and wine making—United States 641.220973
Wine as an investment 332.63
Wine districts 634.8; 641.22
Wine glasses 642.7; 748.83
Wine industry 338.476632
Wine labels—Law and legislation 343.08556632
Wine lists 641.22
Wine tasting 641.22
Wineries 663.2
Winfrey, Oprah 791.45028092; 791.45092
Wings (Insignia) 358.4114; 387.74044027
Winnebago County (Ill.) 977.331
Winnebago County (Ill.)—Maps 912.77331
Winnebago County (Wis.) 977.564
Winnebago County (Wis.)—Maps 912.77564
Winneshiek County (Iowa) 977.732
Winneshiek County (Iowa)—Maps 912.77732
Winnicott, D. W. (Donald Woods), 1896-1971 150.195092
Winnie the Witch (Fictitious character) 823.914
Winslow family (Fictitious characters) 813.54
Winslow family (Fictitious characters)—Fiction 813.54
Winslow, Steve (Fictitious character) 813.54
Winslow, Steve (Fictitious character)—Fiction 813.54
Winter 398.33; 578.43
Winter garden plants 635.953
Winter gardening 712.2
Winter, Holly (Fictitious character) 813.54
Winter, Holly (Fictitious character)—Fiction 813.54
Winter Olympics 796.98
Winter Olympics—History 796.9809

Winter sports 796.9
Winton automobiles 629.2222
Wire bonding (Electronic packaging) 621.381046
Wire products industry 380.145671842
Wireless communication systems 384.5
Wiretapping 345.052
Wiretapping—United States 345.73052
Wirt, Mildred A. (Mildred Augustine), 1905- 813.52
Wirt, Mildred A. (Mildred Augustine), 1905- —
Characters—Nancy Drew 813.52
Wirt, Mildred A. (Mildred Augustine), 1905- —
Characters—Nancy Drew—Bibliography 016.81352
Wisconsin 977.5
Wisconsin—Genealogy 929.3775
Wisconsin—Guidebooks 917.75044; 917.750443;
917.750444
Wisconsin—History 977.5
Wisconsin—Maps 912.775
Wisconsin—Population 304.609775
Wisdom (Biblical personification) 220.68
Wisdom (Gnosticism) 299.932
Wisdom literature 223
Wisdom literature—Criticism, interpretation, etc.
223.06
Wise family 929.20973
Wishes—Religious aspects 291.4
Wit and humor 808.7; 808.882
Wit and humor—History and criticism 809.7
Wit and humor, Pictorial 741.5; 741.5973
Wit and humor—Psychological aspects 808.701
Wit and humor—Religious aspects 200.207
Wit and humor—Religious aspects—Christianity
230.0207
Wit and humor—Therapeutic use 616.8914
Witch World (Imaginary place) 813.52
Witch World (Imaginary place)—Fiction 813.52
Witchcraft 133.43
Witchcraft—Europe 133.43094
Witchcraft—Europe—History 133.43094
Witchcraft—History 133.4309
Witchcraft in the Bible 220.813343
Witchcraft—Massachusetts—Salem 133.43097445
Witchcraft—Massachusetts—Salem—History
133.43097445
Witches 398.45
Withholding tax—Law and legislation 343.05242
Withholding tax—Law and legislation—United States
343.73052424
Witkiewicz, Stanisław Ignacy, 1885–1939 891.85272
Witkiewicz, Stanisław Ignacy, 1885–1939—
Translations into English 891.85272
Witness bearing (Christianity) 248.5
Witnesses 347.066
Witnesses—Protection 363.23
Witnesses—United States 347.7366
Wittgenstein, Ludwig, 1889–1951 192
Wittgenstein, Ludwig, 1889–1951. Philosophische
Untersuchungen 192
Wittgenstein, Ludwig, 1889–1951. Tractatus
logico-philosophicus 192
Witwatersrand (South Africa) 968.22
Witwatersrand (South Africa)—Road maps 912.6822
Wives 306.872
Wives—Religious life 248.8435
Wiyot Indians 305.8973; 979.412004973
Wiyot Indians—Wars, 1860 973.68
Wizard of Oz (Fictitious character) 791.4372; 813.4
Wizard of Oz (Motion picture) 791.4372

Wodehouse, P. G. (Pelham Grenville), 1881–1975
823.912
Wodehouse, P. G. (Pelham Grenville), 1881–1975—
Criticism and interpretation 823.912
Wok cookery 641.77
Wolfe, Nero (Fictitious character) 813.52
Wolfe, Nero (Fictitious character)—Fiction 813.52
Wolfe, Thomas, 1900–1938 813.52
Wolfe, Thomas, 1900–1938—Bibliography 016.81352
Wolfe, Thomas, 1900–1938—Criticism and
interpretation 813.52
Wolfram, von Eschenbach, 12th cent. 831.21
Wolfram, von Eschenbach, 12th cent. Parzival 831.21
Wollongong Metropolitan Area (N.S.W.) 994.46
Wollongong Metropolitan Area (N.S.W.)—Maps
912.9446
Wollstonecraft, Mary, 1759–1797 828.609
Wollstonecraft, Mary, 1759–1797—Criticism and
interpretation 828.609
Wolsey, Thomas, 1475?–1530 942.052092
Wolves 599.773
Wolves—North America 599.773097
Wolves—Yellowstone National Park
333.9597730978752; 599.7730978752
Womanist theology 230.082
Wombats 599.24
Women 305.4
Women accountants 657.092
Women—Africa 305.4096
Women—Africa—Social conditions 305.42096
Women—Africa, Sub-Saharan 305.40967
Women—Africa, Sub-Saharan—Social conditions
305.420967
Women Airforce Service Pilots (U.S.) 940.544973
Women—Alcohol use 362.292082
Women and communism 335.4082
Women and peace 327.172082
Women and peace—History 327.172082
Women and psychoanalysis 616.8917082
Women and religion 200.82; 291.178344
Women and socialism 335.0082
Women—Arab countries 305.409174927
Women—Arab countries—Social conditions
305.4209174927
Women architects 720.82
Women artists 700.82; 704.042
Women artists—Biography 704.042
Women artists—Psychology 704.042
Women—Asia 305.4095
Women—Asia—Social conditions 305.42095
Women athletes 796.082
Women athletes—Biography 796.082
Women—Australia 305.40994
Women—Australia—History 305.40994
Women—Australia—Social conditions 305.420994
Women authors 809.89287
Women authors, American 810.99287
Women authors, American—20th century—Biography
810.992870904
Women authors, American—20th century—Interviews
810.992870904
Women authors, English 820.99287
Women—Bangladesh 305.4095492
Women—Bangladesh—Social conditions 305.42095492
Women—Biblical teaching 220.83054
Women—Bibliography 016.3054
Women—Biography 920.72
Women—Biography—Dictionaries 920.72
Women—Canada 305.40971

Women in public life—United States 305.420973; 320.082

Women in rural development—India 307.1412082

Women in science 305.435; 500.82

Women in science—United States 305.4350973

Women in technology 305.436; 604.82

Women in the Bible 220.83054; 220.92082

Women in the Bible—Biography 220.92082

Women in the Bible—Meditations 220.83054

Women in the Catholic Church 282.082

Women in the Catholic Church—United States 282.082

Women in the civil service 352.63082

Women in the Koran 297.12283054

Women in the Mormon Church 289.3082

Women in the theater 792.082

Women—India 305.40954

Women—India—History 305.40954

Women—India—Social conditions 305.420954

Women inventors 604.82

Women inventors—United States—Biography 604.820973

Women—Iran 305.40955

Women—Ireland 305.409415

Women—Ireland—History 305.409415

Women—Ireland—Social conditions 305.4209415; 305.4209417

Women—Japan 305.40952

Women—Japan—Social conditions 305.420952

Women—Latin America 305.4098

Women—Latin America—History 305.4098

Women—Latin America—Social conditions 305.42098

Women lawyers 340.082

Women lawyers—United States 340.0820973; 349.73082

Women—Legal status, laws, etc. 346.0134

Women—Legal status, laws, etc.—India 346.540134

Women—Legal status, laws, etc.—United States 346.730134

Women—Legal status, laws, etc.—United States—Cases 346.7301340264

Women—Legal status, laws, etc.—United States—History 346.73013409

Women legislators 328.082

Women legislators—United States 328.730082

Women legislators—United States—Biography 328.730082; 328.730922

Women—Life skills guides 646.70082

Women—Literary collections 808.80352042

Women—Louisiana 305.409763

Women—Louisiana—New Orleans 305.40976335

Women mathematicians 305.4351

Women—Mental health 362.2082; 616.890082

Women—Mental health—Sociological aspects 362.2082

Women—Middle East 305.40956

Women—Middle East—Social conditions 305.420956

Women military cadets 355.00711; 378

Women murderers 364.1523082

Women museum curators 305.43096

Women musicians 780.82

Women musicians—Periodicals 780.8205

Women—New Zealand 305.40993

Women—New Zealand—History 305.40993

Women—Nigeria 305.409669

Women—Nigeria—Social conditions 305.4209669

Women—Nutrition 613.2082

Women-owned business enterprises 338.6422082

Women-owned business enterprises—United States 338.70820973

Women—Pastoral counseling of 259.082

Women—Periodicals 305.405

Women—Philippines 305.409599

Women—Philippines—Social conditions 305.4209599

Women philosophers 108.2; 190.82

Women photographers 770.82

Women pioneers—West (U.S.)—Biography 920.720978

Women pioneers—West (U.S.)—History 978.0082

Women poets, American 811.0099287

Women poets, English 821.0099287

Women—Prayer-books and devotions 242.643; 242.843

Women—Psychology 155.333; 155.633

Women publishers 070.5092

Women railroad employees 385.082

Women—Religious aspects 291.178344

Women—Religious aspects—Buddhism 294.3378344

Women—Religious aspects—Christianity 261.8344

Women—Religious life 200.82; 248.843; 291.44082

Women—Russia (Federation) 305.40947

Women—Russia (Federation)—Social conditions 305.420947

Women—Saudi Arabia 305.409538

Women—Saudi Arabia—Social conditions 305.4209538

Women school administrators—United States 371.200820973

Women scientists—Biography 509.22

Women—Sexual behavior 306.7082

Women singers 782.0082

Women—Social conditions 305.42

Women—Social life and customs 305.42

Women social reformers—United States—Biography 303.4840922

Women—South Africa 305.40968

Women—South Africa—Social conditions 305.420968

Women—South Asia 305.40954

Women—South Asia—Social conditions 305.420954

Women—Southern States 305.40975

Women—Southern States—History 305.40975

Women—Southern States—History—19th century 305.4097509034

Women—Southern States—Social conditions 305.420975

Women—Southern States—Social life and customs 305.420975

Women—Soviet Union 305.40947

Women—Soviet Union—Social conditions 305.420947

Women—Substance use 362.29082; 616.860082

Women—Suffrage 324.623

Women—Suffrage—Great Britain 324.6230941

Women—Suffrage—Great Britain—History 324.6230941

Women—Suffrage—United States 324.6230973

Women—Suffrage—United States—History 324.6230973

Women tennis players—Biography 796.342082

Women—Texas—Biography 920.7209764

Women transmitters of the Hadith 297.1240082

Women travelers—Biography 910.82

Women—Turkey 305.409561

Women—Turkey—Social conditions 305.4209561

Women—United States 305.40973

Women—United States—Biography 305.4092273; 920.720973

Women—United States—Biography—Dictionaries 920.72097303

Women—United States—Economic conditions 305.420973

Women—United States—History 305.40973

Women—United States—History—19th century 305.4097309034

Women—United States—History—20th century 305.409730904

Wordsworth, William, 1770–1850 821.7
Wordsworth, William, 1770–1850—Aesthetics 821.7
Wordsworth, William, 1770–1850—Correspondence 821.7
Wordsworth, William, 1770–1850—Criticism and interpretation 821.7
Wordsworth, William, 1770–1850—Criticism and interpretation—History 821.7
Wordsworth, William, 1770–1850—Knowledge—Art 821.7
Wordsworth, William, 1770–1850—Knowledge—Literature 821.7
Wordsworth, William, 1770–1850. Lyrical ballads 821.7
Wordsworth, William, 1770–1850—Philosophy 821.7
Wordsworth, William, 1770–1850—Political and social views 821.7
Wordsworth, William, 1770–1850. Prelude 821.7
Wordsworth, William, 1770–1850—Religion 821.7
Wordsworth, William, 1770–1850—Technique 821.7
Work 306.36
Work and family 306.36
Work and family—United States 306.360973
Work design 620.8; 658.54
Work environment 331.25
Work ethic 306.3613
Work—History 331.09
Work—Physiological aspects 612.042
Work—Psychological aspects 158.7
Work—Religious aspects 291.1785
Work—Religious aspects—Christianity 261.85
Work—Social aspects 306.36
Workaholism 155.232; 616.8584
Workers' compensation 368.41
Workers' compensation—Law and legislation 344.021
Workers' compensation—Law and legislation—Alabama 344.761021
Workers' compensation—Law and legislation—California 344.794021
Workers' compensation—Law and legislation—Florida 344.759021
Workers' compensation—Law and legislation—Georgia 344.758021
Workers' compensation—Law and legislation—Kentucky 344.769021
Workers' compensation—Law and legislation—Maine 344.741021
Workers' compensation—Law and legislation—Massachusetts 344.744021
Workers' compensation—Law and legislation—Nebraska 344.782021
Workers' compensation—Law and legislation—New Jersey 344.749021
Workers' compensation—Law and legislation—North Carolina 344.756021
Workers' compensation—Law and legislation—North Dakota 344.784021
Workers' compensation—Law and legislation—Ohio 344.771021
Workers' compensation—Law and legislation—Oregon 344.795021
Workers' compensation—Law and legislation—Pennsylvania 344.748021
Workers' compensation—Law and legislation—Texas 344.764021
Workers' compensation—Law and legislation—United States 344.73021
Workers' compensation—Law and legislation—United States—States 344.73021

Workers' compensation—Law and legislation—Virginia 344.755021
Workers' compensation—Texas 368.41009764
Workers' compensation—United States 368.4100973
Workers' compensation—United States—Cost control 658.3254
Workers' compensation—United States—Periodicals 368.410097305
Workers' compensation—United States—States 368.4100973
Workflow 658.51; 658.53
Working capital 658.15244
Working class 305.562
Working class—Dwellings 307.33608623
Working class—Education 371.82623
Working class families 306.8508623
Working class families—England 306.85086230941
Working class families—United States 306.85086230973
Working class—France 305.5620944
Working class—Great Britain 305.5620941
Working class—Great Britain—History 305.5620941
Working class—Great Britain—History—19th century 305.562094109034
Working class—India 305.5620954
Working class—Japan 305.5620952
Working class—Political activity 323.3223
Working class—Soviet Union 305.5620947
Working class—United States 305.5620973
Working class—United States—History 305.5620973
Working dogs 636.73
Working mothers 306.8743
Working mothers—United States 306.8743
Working poor 305.569
Workshops 684.08
Workshops—Equipment and supplies—Design and construction 684.08
Workweek 658.3121
World AIDS day 362.1969792
World Bank 332.1532
World Bank—Developing countries 332.1532091724
World Bank—Periodicals 332.153205
World beat (Music) 781.63162
World citizenship 323.6
World Council of Churches 270.820601
World Cup (Rugby football) 796.33365
World Cup (Soccer) 796.334668
World Cup (Soccer)—History 796.33466809
World Habitat Day 307.76; 363.5
World health 362.1
World Heritage areas 363.69
World history 909
World history—Early works to 1800 909
World history—Sources 909
World maps 912
World maps—Early works to 1800 912
World maps, Outline and base 912
World maps, Physical 912
World Meteorological Organization 551.50601
World politics 909
World politics—To 1900 320.9
World politics—19th century 909/81
World politics—1900–1918 320.9041
World politics—1900–1945 320.9041
World politics—20th century 320.904
World politics—1919–1932 320.9042
World politics—1933–1945 320.9043
World politics—1945- 320.9045
World politics—1945- —Maps 909.8250223
World politics—1945- —Periodicals 320.9045; 909.8205

World War, 1939–1945—Campaigns—Western Front
940.5421

World War, 1939–1945—Campaigns—Yugoslavia
940.542197

World War, 1939–1945—Canada 940.5371

World War, 1939–1945—Caricatures and cartoons
940.530207

World War, 1939–1945—Causes 940.5311

World War, 1939–1945—Children 940.53083

World War, 1939–1945—Children—Great Britain
940.530830941

World War, 1939–1945—Chronology 940.530202

World War, 1939–1945—Concentration camps 940.5317

World War, 1939–1945—Concentration camps—
Germany 940.531743

World War, 1939–1945—Conscientious objectors—
United States 940.53086

World War, 1939–1945—Cryptography 940.5485

World War, 1939–1945—Dictionaries 940.5303

World War, 1939–1945—Diplomatic history 940.532

World War, 1939–1945—Economic aspects 940.53113

World War, 1939–1945—England 940.5342

World War, 1939–1945—Europe 940.53

World War, 1939–1945—France 940.5344

World War, 1939–1945—Germany 940.5343

World War, 1939–1945—Great Britain 940.5341

World War, 1939–1945—Greece 940.53495

World War, 1939–1945—Historiography 940.53072

World War, 1939–1945—Influence 940.5314

World War, 1939–1945—Japan 940.5352

World War, 1939–1945—Japanese Americans 940.5404

World War, 1939–1945—Jewish resistance 940.5318

World War, 1939–1945—Jews 940.53089924

World War, 1939–1945—Jews—Rescue 940.5318

World War, 1939–1945—Maps 940.30223; 940.530222

World War, 1939–1945—Medical care 940.5475

World War, 1939–1945—Medical care—United States
940.547573

World War, 1939–1945—Motion pictures and the war
791.43658

World War, 1939–1945—Naval operations 940.545

World War, 1939–1945—Naval operations, American
940.545973

World War, 1939–1945—Naval operations, British
940.545941

World War, 1939–1945—Naval operations, Canadian
940.545971

World War, 1939–1945—Naval operations, French
940.545944

World War, 1939–1945—Naval operations, German
940.545943

World War, 1939–1945—Naval operations, Italian
940.545945

World War, 1939–1945—Naval operations, Japanese
940.545952

World War, 1939–1945—Naval operations, Soviet
940.545947

World War, 1939–1945—Naval operations—Submarine
940.5451

World War, 1939–1945—Pacific Ocean 940.5426

World War, 1939–1945—Participation, Jewish 940.5404

World War, 1939–1945—Peace 940.5312

World War, 1939–1945—Personal narratives 940.548

World War, 1939–1945—Personal narratives, Albanian
940.54814965

World War, 1939–1945—Personal narratives, American
940.548173

World War, 1939–1945—Personal narratives,
Australian 940.548194

World War, 1939–1945—Personal narratives, Austrian
940.5482336

World War, 1939–1945—Personal narratives,
Belarusian 940.5481478

World War, 1939–1945—Personal narratives, Belgian
940.5481493

World War, 1939–1945—Personal narratives, Brazilian
940.548181

World War, 1939–1945—Personal narratives, British
940.548141

World War, 1939–1945—Personal narratives, Bulgarian
940.5482499

World War, 1939–1945—Personal narratives, Canadian
940.548171

World War, 1939–1945—Personal narratives, Croatian
940.54824972

World War, 1939–1945—Personal narratives, Czech
940.54814371

World War, 1939–1945—Personal narratives, Danish
940.5481489

World War, 1939–1945—Personal narratives, Dutch
940.530893931

World War, 1939–1945—Personal narratives, Finnish
940.54814897

World War, 1939–1945—Personal narratives, French
940.548144

World War, 1939–1945—Personal narratives, German
940.548243

World War, 1939–1945—Personal narratives, Greek
940.5481495

World War, 1939–1945—Personal narratives,
Hungarian 940.5482439

World War, 1939–1945—Personal narratives, Italian
940.548245

World War, 1939–1945—Personal narratives, Japanese
940.548252

World War, 1939–1945—Personal narratives, Jewish
940.53089924

World War, 1939–1945—Personal narratives, Korean
940.5482519

World War, 1939–1945—Personal narratives, Latvian
940.54814796

World War, 1939–1945—Personal narratives,
Lithuanian 940.54814793

World War, 1939–1945—Personal narratives, New
Zealand 940.548193

World War, 1939–1945—Personal narratives,
Norwegian 940.5481481

World War, 1939–1945—Personal narratives, Philippine
940.5481599

World War, 1939–1945—Personal narratives, Polish
940.5481438

World War, 1939–1945—Personal narratives, Romanian
940.5482498

World War, 1939–1945—Personal narratives, Russian
940.548147

World War, 1939–1945—Personal narratives, Serbian
940.54814971

World War, 1939–1945—Personal narratives, Slovenian
940.54814973

World War, 1939–1945—Personal narratives, Soviet
940.548147

World War, 1939–1945—Personal narratives, Spanish
940.548246

World War, 1939–1945—Personal narratives, Ukrainian
940.5481477

World War, 1939–1945—Personal narratives, Yugoslav
940.5481497

World War, 1939–1945—Pictorial works 940.530222

World War, 1939–1945—Poland 940.53438
World War, 1939–1945—Prisoners and prisons 940.5472
World War, 1939–1945—Prisoners and prisons, American 940.547273
World War, 1939–1945—Prisoners and prisons, British 940.547241
World War, 1939–1945—Prisoners and prisons, French 940.547244
World War, 1939–1945—Prisoners and prisons, German 940.547243
World War, 1939–1945—Prisoners and prisons, Italian 940.547245
World War, 1939–1945—Prisoners and prisons, Japanese 940.547252
World War, 1939–1945—Prisoners and prisons, Russian 940.547247
World War, 1939–1945—Prisoners and prisons, Soviet 940.547247
World War, 1939–1945—Propaganda 940.5488
World War, 1939–1945—Radar 940.544
World War, 1939–1945—Refugees 940.5308691
World War, 1939–1945—Regimental histories—Germany 940.541343
World War, 1939–1945—Regimental histories—Great Britain 940.541241
World War, 1939–1945—Regimental histories—United States 940.541273
World War, 1939–1945—Religious aspects 940.5478
World War, 1939–1945—Religious aspects—Catholic Church 940.5478
World War, 1939–1945—Reparations 940.531422
World War, 1939–1945—Science 940.53; 940.548
World War, 1939–1945—Secret service 940.5485
World War, 1939–1945—Secret service—Germany 940.548743
World War, 1939–1945—Secret service—Great Britain 940.548641
World War, 1939–1945—Secret service—United States 940.548673
World War, 1939–1945—Sources 940.53
World War, 1939–1945—Soviet Union 940.5347
World War, 1939–1945—Tank warfare 940.541
World War, 1939–1945—Underground movements 940.5337
World War, 1939–1945—Underground movements—Europe 940.5336
World War, 1939–1945—Underground movements—France 940.53360944
World War, 1939–1945—United States 940.5373
World War, 1939–1945—War work—Red Cross 940.54771
World War, 1939–1945—Women 940.53082
World War, 1939–1945—Women—United States 940.530820973
World Wide Web 025.04
World Wide Web—Business services 025.04
World Wide Web—Periodicals 004.678
World Wide Web—Personal home pages 025.04
World Wide Web—Services 025.04
World Wide Web—Subject access 025.04
Worms 592.3
Worms as pets 639.75
Worry 152.46
Worry in children 155.41246
Worship 264
Worship in the Bible 264
Worship programs 264; 291.43
Worship (Religious education) 264.00834

Worth County (Iowa) 977.7232
Worth County (Iowa)—Maps 912.777232
Wound healing 617.1; 617.14
Wounded Knee Massacre, S.D., 1890 973.86
Wounds and injuries 617.1
Wounds and injuries—Surgery 617.1
Wounds and injuries—Treatment 617.106
Wreaths 745.926
Wreckers (Vehicles) 629.225
Wrestlers 796.812092
Wrestling 796.812
Wrestling in literature 808.80355; 809.93355
Wright County (Minn.) 977.651
Wright County (Minn.)—Maps 912.77651
Wright family 929.20973
Wright, Frank Lloyd, 1867–1959 720.92
Wright, Frank Lloyd, 1867–1959—Criticism and interpretation 720.92
Wright, Frank Lloyd, 1867–1959—Exhibitions 720.92
Wright, Frank Lloyd, 1867–1959—Themes, motives 720.92; 748.5913
Wright, Judith 821.914
Wright, Judith—Criticism and interpretation 821.914
Wright, Orville, 1871–1948 629.130092
Wright, Richard, 1908–1960 813.52
Wright, Richard, 1908–1960—Criticism and interpretation 813.52
Wright, Richard, 1908–1960. Native son 813.52
Wright, Wilbur, 1867–1912 629.130092
Writer's block 808.0019
Writing 411
Writing centers 808.0071
Writing, Copperplate 745.6197
Writing—History 411.09; 652.109
Writing—Identification 363.2565
Writing, Italic 745.61977
Writing—Materials and instruments 681.6
Written communication 302.2244; 411
Written communication—Study and teaching (Elementary) 372.623
Wrongful death 346.0323
Wrongful death—United States 346.730323
Wyandot Indians 305.89755; 971.40049755; 973.0049755
Wyandot Indians—History 971.40049755; 973.0049755
Wycliffe, Charlie (Fictitious character) 823.914
Wycliffe, Charlie (Fictitious character)—Fiction 823.914
Wycliffe, John, d. 1384 270.5092
Wynn family 929.209429
Wyoming 978.7
Wyoming—Guidebooks 917.8704; 917.870433; 917.870434
Wyoming—History 978.7
X-files (Television program) 791.4572
X, Malcolm, 1925–1965 320.54092
X-ray astronomy 522.6863
X-ray binaries 523.841
X-ray crystallography 548
X-ray lasers 621.366
X-ray microscopy 502.82
X-ray optics 621.36
X-ray spectroscopy 543.08586
X-ray telescopes 522.2
X-rays 539.7222
X-rays—Diffraction 539.7222
X-rays—Scattering 539.7222
X Window System (Computer system) 005.432
Xanth (Imaginary place) 813.54
Xanth (Imaginary place)—Fiction 813.54
Xena, Warrior Princess (Fictitious character) 791.4572

XENIX 005.4469
Xenobiotics—Metabolism 615.9
Xenografts 617.95
Xenophobia in language 306.44
Xeriscaping 635.9525
Xerogels 541.34513
Xinjiang Uygur Zizhiqu (China) 951.6
Xinjiang Uygur Zizhiqu (China)—Description and travel
915.1604; 915.160459; 915.16046
XML (Document markup language) 005.72
XyWrite 652.55369
Yacht building 623.8223; 797.1246
Yacht clubs 797.124606
Yacht racing 797.1246; 797.14
Yacht racing—Rules 797.14
Yachting 797.1246
Yachting—Caribbean Area—Guidebooks 623.8922365;
623.8929729
Yachting—New England—Guidebooks 623.892245;
623.892974; 797.12460974
Yachts 623.8223; 797.1246
Yachts—Design and construction 623.81223; 623.8223
Yachts in art 704.94962382023
Yachts—Maintenance and repair 623.82230288
Yahoo! games 794.8
Yaka literature (Congo and Angola) 896.393
Yakama Indians 305.89741; 979.70049741
Yalta Conference (1945) 940.53141
Yama (Fictitious character) 823.914
Yamagochi (Game) 794.18
Yamaguchi, Kristi 796.912092
Yamaha all terrain vehicles 629.22042
Yamaha all terrain vehicles—Maintenance and repair
629.287042
Yamaha all terrain vehicles—Maintenance and repair—
Handbooks, manuals, etc. 629.287042
Yamaha motorcycle 629.2275
Yamaha motorcycle—Maintenance and repair 629.28775
Yamaha motorcycle—Maintenance and repair—
Handbooks, manuals, etc. 629.28775
Yang-Baxter equation 530.143
Yanomamo Indians 305.898; 981.00498
Yantras 294.537
Yavapai County (Ariz.) 979.157
Yavapai County (Ariz.)—Road maps 912.79157
Yeadings, Mike (Fictitious character) 823.914
Yeadings, Mike (Fictitious character)—Fiction 823.914
Year 2000 date conversion (Computer systems) 005.16
Year 2000 date conversion (Computer systems)—
United States 005.16
Year-round schools 371.236
Year-round schools—United States 371.2360973
Yearbooks 050
Yeast 664.68
Yeast fungi 579.562; 579.563
Yeast fungi—Biotechnology 660.62
Yeats, Jane (Fictitious character) 813.54
Yeats, W. B. (William Butler), 1865–1939 821.8
Yeats, W. B. (William Butler), 1865–1939—Aesthetics
821.8
Yeats, W. B. (William Butler), 1865–1939—Bibliography
016.8218
Yeats, W. B. (William Butler), 1865–1939—Criticism
and interpretation 821.8
Yeats, W. B. (William Butler), 1865–1939—Criticism,
Textual 821.8
Yeats, W. B. (William Butler), 1865–1939—Dramatic
works 822.8

Yeats, W. B. (William Butler), 1865–1939—Friends and
associates 821.8
Yeats, W. B. (William Butler), 1865–1939—
Knowledge—Folklore 821.8
Yeats, W. B. (William Butler), 1865–1939—
Knowledge—Literature 821.8
Yeats, W. B. (William Butler), 1865–1939—
Knowledge—Occultism 821.8
Yeats, W. B. (William Butler), 1865–1939—
Knowledge—Performing arts 822.8
Yeats, W. B. (William Butler), 1865–1939—Poetic
works 821.8
Yeats, W. B. (William Butler), 1865–1939—Political and
social views 821.8
Yeats, W. B. (William Butler), 1865–1939—Technique
821.8
Yellow fever 616.928
Yellow jackets (Insects) 595.798
Yellowstone National Park 978.752
Yellowstone National Park—Description and travel
917.875204; 917.87520433; 917.87520434
Yellowstone National Park—Guidebooks 917.875204;
917.87520433; 917.87520434
Yeltsin, Boris Nikolayevich, 1931– 947.0854092
Yemba language 496.36
Yen, Japanese 332.4952
Yeshivas 296.0711
Yeti 001.944
Yevtushenko, Yevgeny Aleksandrovich, 1933– 891.7144
Yevtushenko, Yevgeny Aleksandrovich, 1933– —
Translations into English 891.7144
Yi (Chinese people) 951.3004
Yi jing 299.51282
Yiddish language 439.1
Yiddish literature 839.108
Yiddish poetry 839.11; 839.1108
Yiddish poetry—Translations into English 839.1108
Yiddish wit and humor 839.17008
Yin-yang 181.11
Yoga 181.45; 291.436
Yoga, Haṭha 613.7046
Yoga, Rāja 181.45; 294.5436
Yoga (Tantric Buddhism) 294.34436
Yogācāra (Buddhism) 294.385
Yogbo (Legendary character) 398.208996337
Yoknapatawpha County (Imaginary place) 813.52
Yoknapatawpha County (Imaginary place)—Fiction
813.52
Yom Kippur 296.432
Yom Kippur—Liturgy 296.4532
Yom Kippur—Liturgy—Texts 296.4532
Yom Kippur sermons 296.4732
York County (Neb.) 978.2345
York County (Neb.)—Maps 912.782345
York County (Pa.) 974.841
York County (Pa.)—Genealogy 929.374841
York County (Pa.)—History 974.841
York County (Pa.)—Maps 912.74841
York County (Va.) 975.5423
York County (Va.)—Genealogy 929.3755423
York (England) 942.843
York (England)—Antiquities 936.2843
York (England)—Description and travel 914.284304;
914.284304859; 914.28430486
York (England)—Guidebooks 914.284304;
914.284304859; 914.28430486
York (England)—History 942.843
York plays 822.051608942843

York, Sarah Mountbatten-Windsor, Duchess of, 1959– 941.085092
Yorkshire (England) 942.81
Yorkshire (England)—Guidebooks 914.28104; 914.28104859; 914.2810486
Yorkshire terrier 636.76
Yorktown (Va.) 975.5423
Yorktown (Va.)—History 975.5423
Yorktown (Va.)—History—Siege, 1781 973.337
Yoruba (African people) 305.896333
Yoruba (African people)—Folklore 398.208996333
Yoruba (African people)—Religion 299.68333
Yoruba language 496.333
Yoruba language—Textbooks for foreign speakers— English 496.33382421; 496.33383421
Yosemite National Park (Calif.) 979.447
Yosemite National Park (Calif.)—Guidebooks 917.944704; 917.94470453; 917.94470454
Yosemite National Park (Calif.)—History 979.447
Yosemite National Park (Calif.)—Pictorial works 979.44700222
Yosemite Valley (Calif.) 979.447
Yosemite Valley (Calif.)—History 979.447
Young adult consumers 305.242; 658.8340842
Young adult drama 808.8299283
Young adult drama, American 812.0809283
Young adult drama, English 822.00809283
Young adult fiction, American—History and criticism 813.0099283; 813.54099283
Young adult literature 808.899283
Young adult literature—Bibliography 011.625
Young adult poetry, American 811.00809283
Young adult services librarians 027.626092
Young adults 305.242
Young adults—Books and reading 028.55
Young adults' libraries 027.626
Young adults' libraries—Administration 025.197626
Young adults' libraries—United States 027.6260973
Young adults—Religious life 248.83
Young adults—United States 305.2420973
Young adults—United States—Life skills guides 646.7008420973
Young adults—United States—Psychology 305.2420973
Young, Brigham, 1801–1877 289.3092
Young businesspeople 338.00842
Young England movement 324.24102; 941.081
Young families 306.85
Young family 929.20973
Young Germany 830.9007
Young men 305.242
Young men—Conduct of life 170.8421
Young men—England 305.242
Young men—England—Midlands 305.242
Young men—France 305.242
Young men—Ireland 305.242
Young men—Ireland—Dublin 305.242
Young men—New York (State) 305.242
Young men—New York (State)—New York 305.242
Young men—United States 305.242
Young, Steve, 1961– 796.332092
Young women 305.242
Young women—Australia 305.242
Young women—Crimes against 362.88
Young women—Crimes against—Prevention 362.88
Young women—England 305.242
Young women—England—History 305.242
Young women—England—History—19th century 305.242
Young women—England—London 305.242

Young women—France 305.242
Young women—France—Paris 305.242
Young women—Ireland 305.242
Young women—Massachusetts 305.242
Young women—Massachusetts—Boston 305.242
Young women—Mississippi 305.242
Young women—New York (State) 305.242
Young women—New York (State)—New York 305.242
Young women—Religious life 248.833
Young women—Scotland 305.242
Young women—Travel 910.8422
Young women—Travel—South America 918.008422
Young women—United States 305.242
Youngstown (Ohio) 977.139
Youngstown (Ohio)—Maps 912.77139
Youth 305.235
Youth—Alcohol use 362.2920835
Youth—Alcohol use—United States 362.29208350973
Youth and violence 303.60835
Youth—Books and reading 028.55
Youth centers 362.7083
Youth—Conduct of life 170.835
Youth—Drug use 362.290835; 613.83
Youth—Drug use—New York (State) 362.29083509747
Youth—Drug use—New York (State)—New York 362.290835097471
Youth—Drug use—United States 362.2908350973
Youth—Employment 331.34
Youth—Employment—Great Britain 331.340941
Youth—Employment—United States 331.340973
Youth—Government policy 305.235; 362.7
Youth—Great Britain 305.2350941
Youth—Great Britain—Social conditions 305.2350941
Youth hostels 647.94
Youth in literature 808.80352055; 809.93352055
Youth in motion pictures 791.43652055
Youth in public worship 264.0083
Youth league football 796.33262
Youth league football—Coaching 796.33262
Youth—Political activity 323.352
Youth—Prayer-books and devotions 242.63; 242.83
Youth—Psychology 155.5
Youth—Religious life 248.83
Youth—Services for 362.7083
Youth—Services for—United States 362.70830973
Youth—Sexual behavior 306.70835
Youth shelters 362.71; 362.74
Youth—Social conditions 305.235
Youth—Substance use 362.290835
Youth—Substance use—United States 362.2908350973
Youth—Suicidal behavior 362.280835
Youth—Suicidal behavior—United States 362.2808350973
Youth—Tobacco use 362.2960835
Youth—Tobacco use—United States 362.29608350973
Youth—Travel 910.835; 910.842
Youth—Travel—Europe 914.00835; 914.00842
Youth—Travel—Europe—Guidebooks 914.040835
Youth—United States 305.2350973
Youth—United States—Books and reading 028.5350973; 028.55
Youth—United States—Life skills guides 646.7008350973
Youth—United States—Sexual behavior 306.70835
Youth—United States—Social conditions 305.2350973
Youth workers 362.7
Youthfulness 305.235
Youths' writings, American 810.809283
Ypres, 3rd Battle of, Ieper, Belgium, 1917 940.431

Yucatán Peninsula 972.6
Yucatán Peninsula—Guidebooks 917.2604; 917.2604836
Yugoslav War, 1991–1995 949.703
Yugoslav War, 1991–1995—Atrocities 949.703
Yugoslav War, 1991–1995—Bosnia and Hercegovina
949.703
Yugoslav War, 1991–1995—Campaigns 949.703
Yugoslav War, 1991–1995—Diplomatic history 949.703
Yugoslav War, 1991–1995—Peace 949.703
Yugoslav War Crime Trials, Hague, Netherlands, 1994–
341.690268
Yugoslavia 949.7
Yugoslavia—Description and travel 914.9704;
914.970424; 914.97104; 914.971043
Yugoslavia—Economic conditions 330.9497
Yugoslavia—Economic conditions—1945–1992
330.9497023
Yugoslavia—Economic policy 338.9497
Yugoslavia—Economic policy—1945–1992 338.9497
Yugoslavia—Foreign relations 327.497
Yugoslavia—Foreign relations—1945–1980 327.497
Yugoslavia—Guidebooks 914.9704; 914.970424;
914.97104; 914.971043
Yugoslavia—History 949.7
Yugoslavia—History—1980–1992 949.7024
Yugoslavia—Politics and government 320.9497; 949.7
Yugoslavia—Politics and government—1945–1980
320.9497; 320.949709045; 949.7023
Yugoslavia—Politics and government—1980–1992
320.949709048; 949.7024
Yukon Territory 971.91
Yupik Eskimo law 340.520899714
Yupik Eskimos 305.89714; 979.80049714
Yupik Eskimos—Folklore 398.2089971
Z (Computer program language) 005.133
Zacchaeus (Biblical character) 226.4092
Zaharias, Babe Didrikson, 1911–1956 796.352092
Zail Singh, Giani 954.052092
Zakarpats'ka oblast' (Ukraine) 947.79
Zakarpats'ka oblast' (Ukraine)—History 947.79
Zamba (Music) 784.1888
Zambia 968.94
Zambia—Economic conditions 330.96894
Zambia—Economic conditions—1964– 330.9689404
Zambia—Economic policy 338.96894
Zambia—Guidebooks 916.89404; 916.8940442
Zambia—History 968.94
Zambia—Politics and government 320.96894; 968.94
Zambia—Politics and government—1964–1991
320.9689409046; 968.9404
Zambonis (Trademark) 796.910284
Zanzibar 967.81
Zanzibar—History 967.81
Zapata, Emiliano, 1879–1919 972.081092
Zapping (Television) 302.2345
Zarzuelas 782.12; 792.5
Zebra mussel 594.4
Zebras 599.6657
Zelda (Fictitious character : Kvasnosky) 813.54
Zen, Aurelio (Fictitious character) 823.914
Zen, Aurelio (Fictitious character)—Fiction 823.914
Zen Buddhism 294.3927
Zen Buddhism—Doctrines 294.3420427
Zen Buddhism—Psychology 294.3927019
Zen meditations 294.34432
Zen poetry 808.819382943927
Zeolites 549.68; 666.86
Zero-base budgeting 352.48; 658.154
Zhongguo gong chan dang 324.251075

Zhuangzi. Nan-hua ching 299.51482
Ziggy (Fictitious character) 741.5973
Zilog Z-80 (Microprocessor) 621.3916
Zimbabwe 968.91
Zimbabwe—Antiquities 968.9101
Zimbabwe—Description and travel 916.89104;
916.8910451
Zimbabwe—Economic conditions 330.9689105
Zimbabwe—Economic conditions—1980– 330.9689105
Zimbabwe—Economic conditions—1980– —Periodicals
330.9689105
Zimbabwe—Economic policy 338.96891
Zimbabwe—Guidebooks 916.89104; 916.8910451
Zimbabwe—History 968.91
Zimbabwe—History—1890–1965 968.9102
Zimbabwe—History—Chimurenga War, 1966–1980
968.9104
Zimbabwe—Periodicals 968.91005
Zimbabwe—Politics and government 320.96891; 968.91
Zimbabwe—Politics and government—1965–1979
320.96891
Zimbabwe—Politics and government—1980–
320.9689109048; 968.9105
Zimbabwe—Social life and customs 968.91
Zimmerman family 929.20973
Zinc 669.52
Zinc industry and trade 338.4766952
Zionism 320.54095694
Zionism and Judaism 296.382
Zionism—History 320.54095694
Zionism—History—Sources 320.54095694
Zionism—Philosophy 320.54095694
Zionism—United States 320.540956940973
Zionism—United States—History 320.540956940973
Zionists—Biography 320.54092
Zip codes 383.1455
Zip codes—California—Los Angeles County—Maps
912.79493
Zip codes—California—Orange County—Maps 912.79496
Zip codes—California—San Bernardino County—Maps
912.79495
Zip codes—California—San Diego County—Maps
912.79498
Zip codes—California—Santa Barbara County—Maps
912.79491
Zip codes—California—Santa Clara County—Maps
912.79473
Zip codes—Oregon—Portland Metropolitan Area—Maps
912.79549
Zip codes—United States—Directories 383.145502573
Zip codes—United States—Maps 383.14550973022
Zip codes—Washington (State)—King County—Maps
912.79777
Zipping (Video recordings) 302.2345
Zizith 296.461
Zoarcidae 597.63
Zodiac 133.52
Zola, Emile, 1840–1902 843.8
Zola, Emile, 1840–1902—Criticism and interpretation
843.8
Zombie films 791.43675
Zombies 398.21
Zombiism 299.675
Zone plates 681.4
Zone system (Photography) 771.49
Zoning law 346.045
Zoning law—Massachusetts 346.744045
Zoning law—New Jersey 346.749045
Zoning law—United States 346.73045

Zoo animals 590.73; 636.0889
Zoo animals—Diseases 636.0896
Zoo animals—Infancy 591.39073
Zoo exhibits 590.73
Zoo keepers 636.0889092
Zooflagellates 579.42
Zoogeography 590.9; 591.9
Zoological illustration 743.6
Zoological libraries 026.59
Zoological models 590.228
Zoological museums 590.74
Zoologists 590.92
Zoology 590
Zoology—Africa 590.96; 591.96
Zoology—Arctic regions 590.9113
Zoology—Australia 590.994; 591.994
Zoology—Australia—Periodicals 591.99405
Zoology—Classification 590.12
Zoology—Dictionaries 590.3
Zoology, Economic 591.6
Zoology—Galapagos Islands 590.98665; 591.98665
Zoology—Miscellanea 590
Zoology—North America 590.97; 591.97
Zoology—Periodicals 590.5
Zoology—Pictorial works 758.3
Zoology—Polar regions 590.911
Zoology—Pre-Linnean works 590
Zoology—Variation 576.54
Zoom lens photography 778.32
Zoonoses 571.98; 616.959
Zooplankton 592.1776
Zoos 590.73
Zoot Suit Riots, Los Angeles, Calif., 1943 979.494052
Zoroaster 295.63
Zoroastrian astrology 133.5945
Zoroastrianism 295
Zorro films 791.43651
Zorro television programs 791.45651
Zuckerman, Nathan (Fictitious character) 813.54
Zuckerman, Nathan (Fictitious character)—Fiction
  813.54
Zulu (African people) 305.8963986
Zulu (African people)—History 968.4
Zulu language 496.3986
Zulu language—Textbooks for foreign speakers—
  English 496.398682421; 496.398683421
Zulu War, 1879 968.4045
Zuni Indians 305.8979; 978.9004979
Zuni literature 897.9